The Conduct
of Soviet
Foreign Policy

The Conduct
of Soviet
Foreign Policy

edited by

Erik P. Hoffmann
State University of New York at Albany

Frederic J. Fleron, Jr.
State University of New York at Buffalo

Aldine Publishing Company / New York

ABOUT THE EDITORS

ERIK P. HOFFMANN is Associate Professor of Political Science, Graduate School of Public Affairs, State University of New York at Albany. He is co-author of *In Quest of Progress: Soviet Perspectives on Advanced Society* and *The Modernization of the Soviet Union and East-West Relations* (both forthcoming), and he has contributed essays to *World Politics, Problems of Communism, Soviet Union,* and other journals and books. He is also an Associate of the Research Institute on International Change, Columbia University, and Managing Editor for Politics and Government of *Soviet Union.*

FREDERIC J. FLERON, JR. is Professor of Political Science, State University of New York at Buffalo. He is editor of *Communist Studies and the Social Sciences: Essays on Methodology and Empirical Theory,* co-author of *Comparative Communist Political Leadership,* editor of *Technology and Communist Culture: The Socio-Cultural Impact of Technology Transfer under Socialism,* and has contributed numerous articles to scholarly journals and books.

First published 1971
Second edition 1980
Aldine Publishing Company
200 Saw Mill River Road
Hawthorne, N.Y. 10532

ISBN Cloth: 0-202-24155-6
      Paper: 0-202-24156-4
Library of Congress Catalog Card Number 80-68483
Printed in the United States of America
10 9 8 7 6 5 4 3

To Our Students

Contents

Introduction

More and more American college students are studying Soviet foreign policy. Courses in this field are plentiful, and student interest is high. But teachers of these courses must cope with several problems: (1) primary source materials are relatively scarce; (2) accessible documents are not easily interpreted by either expert or novice; (3) Western scholars have produced relatively few monographs and analytical essays in the field; (4) the best of these essays are widely scattered throughout many scholarly journals; and (5) almost none of this literature is closely linked to the broader field of international relations.

The first of these problems is particularly difficult to cope with. Some very basic facts about Soviet intentions and activities are not known. Memoir literature is virtually nonexistent, and candid interviews with Soviet foreign affairs officials are not common. New information about Soviet behavior is sometimes gleaned from Western archives, from the statements and actions of foreign officials (Communist and non-Communist) who have dealt with their Russian counterparts, and from the observable activities of Soviet representatives abroad. But the college student, even if he reads Russian, does not have access to the key sources of information that might facilitate the study of Soviet domestic politics. Central Committee decrees, for example, almost never deal with the USSR's international affairs. Not surprisingly, there is much more public communication between Communist Party leaders and domestic audiences than between Party leaders and Soviet personnel abroad.

The second problem is more serious than commonly recognized. Through the *World Marxist Review, International Affairs,* or the *Current Digest of the Soviet Press*, the college student may gain access to selected "primary"

1

source materials. Many of these are purposeful attempts to influence individuals and groups in other Communist and non-Communist countries.
But what do these documents reveal: Official Soviet policy? Policy alternatives under consideration? Actual Soviet behavior? Desired events?
Moreover, how does one distinguish among these and other possibilities?
How does one determine the purposes, or "propaganda goals," of
statements in the Soviet press? How does one ascertain "to *what extent*, and
in *what manner, which* statements emanating from *which* sources are
credibly representative of the international relations perspectives of *which*
persons or identifiable groups"?[1] These are just a few of the
methodological questions confronting the student of Soviet foreign policy.
Valuable Soviet documents have been compiled, but problems of interpretation persist.

The small number of detailed studies of Soviet foreign policy is more
understandable in this light. Fortunately, Western and Soviet scholars are
devoting more attention to this subject, and several major textbooks and
monographs have appeared in recent years. But many excellent interpretive
essays have not reached the wide audience they deserve. In fact three
distinguished anthologies on Soviet foreign policy are now out of print:
Alexander Dallin (ed.), *Soviet Conduct in World Affairs* (New York: Columbia University Press, 1960); Ivo Lederer (ed.), *Russian Foreign Policy:
Essays in Historical Perspective* (New Haven: Yale University Press, 1962);
and Vernon V. Aspaturian (ed.), *Process and Power in Soviet Foreign
Policy* (Boston: Little, Brown and Co., 1971).

The essays in the present collection focus on contemporary Soviet foreign
policy. As were the Dallin, Lederer, and Aspaturian anthologies, this collection is intended primarily for classroom and scholarly use. Our main purpose is to stimulate discussion and thought, not to defend a particular position or point of view. Indeed, we have carefully selected studies that present
alternative viewpoints and that have stimulated lively, often heated, discussion in our own classes. In the past, we have had to rely on the unsatisfactory arrangement of using library reserve shelves to make these valuable articles available to our students. (A few relevant articles are readily accessible
in the Bobbs-Merrill Reprint Series and hence have been omitted from our
collection.)[2] By reprinting what we feel to be some of the most thought-
provoking and informative essays on Soviet foreign policy to have appeared
in recent years in a single volume, we hope to disseminate more widely some
key literature on Soviet international behavior.

The structure of this anthology and the introductions to each section are a
modest effort to link the study of Soviet foreign policy with the broader

1. William Zimmerman, *Soviet Perspectives on International Relations, 1956-1967*
(Princeton: Princeton University Press, 1969), p. 12 (italics in original).
2. For example, Daniel Bell, "Ten Theories in Search of Reality," *World Politics*, X, 3
(April, 1958), pp. 327-365; Historicus (George Morgan), "Stalin on Revolution," *Foreign Af-*

field of international relations. Our main purpose is to examine the internal and external factors that shape Soviet foreign policy and behavior. After a brief section on methodology, each section focuses on the effect of a single factor (or set of similar factors) on Soviet actions. Soviet policy and behavior are the dependent variables—that which we seek to understand or explain—in every section. The independent variables—domestic Soviet politics, ideology, Western diplomacy, the global economy, the strategic balance, international communism, developments in the Third World—vary from section to section. In other words, each section examines the influence of a different set of factors on Soviet decisions and actions. Above all, we are interested in analyzing the forces that shape Soviet international behavior; we are not directly concerned with the effects of Soviet foreign policy on Soviet domestic politics or on the behavior of other Communist and non-Communist countries.

We should also point out that our set of factors is by no means complete. We could easily have included chapters on the impact of geography or changing weapons technology on Soviet policy. But our primary purpose is to assess the impact of some very important factors on Soviet policy and behavior, especially the relations of the Soviet Union with the West.

In assembling this anthology, we have attempted to produce a volume that would complement other works in the field that are suitable for both graduate and undergraduate courses in Soviet foreign policy. Many teachers of these courses have found that a useful combination of texts for such courses is *Expansion and Coexistence: The History of Soviet Foreign Policy, 1917-1973* by Adam Ulam for a general history of Soviet foreign policy; *The Foreign Policy of the Soviet Union* edited by Alvin Rubinstein for analyses and interpretations; and the present anthology for Western interpretive essays. Hence, we took into account the nature of the other texts that this anthology was designed to supplement in reaching our own decisions concerning which elements of Soviet foreign policy to emphasize and which to ignore.

We present various Western interpretations of issues for which Rubinstein presents Soviet interpretations: the origins of the Cold War, competitive coexistence, the strategic balance, Soviet policy toward the Third World, and international communism. We present alternative Western interpretations to Ulam's views on such questions as the origins of the Cold War and the impact of ideology, international communism, Western diplomacy, and the Third World on Soviet foreign policy. In addition, we have presented alternative Western interpretations of factors minimized or ignored by Ulam and Rubinstein: the global economy, the impact of scien-

---

fairs, XXVII, 2 (January, 1949), pp. 175-213; X (George F. Kennan), "The Sources of Soviet Conduct," *Foreign Affairs*, XXV, 4 (July, 1947), pp. 566-582.

tific and technological changes on international relations, linkages between domestic politics and foreign policy, and the evolving nature and use of Soviet power. We have also included analyses of recent developments in China, the Middle East, Afghanistan, and elsewhere.

We continue to find the diagram on page 8 useful and wish to call it to the attention of all readers. The relationships outlined in this diagram were the foundation of Michael Brecher's later work.[3] However, some of the terms in the diagram are not self-evident and require further definition than we gave them in the first edition of this book. The *global system,* for Brecher, is "the total web of relationships among all actors within the international system (states, blocs, organizations)."[4] On the other hand, "a *subordinate system* represents an intermediate level of interaction between the global system and the relationships between any two states. Theoretically there may be as many subordinate systems as there are foreign policy issues, but logically they can be grouped into four categories: (1) geographic, with contiguous membership; (2) geographic, with noncontiguous members; (3) organizational, with contiguous membership; and (4) organizational, with noncontiguous members."[5] Following Brecher's usage, the term *subordinate system* "refers mainly to the first type, that is, a regional system of which the state under analysis is a member," whereas the term *subordinate other* "encompasses the second, third, and fourth types."[6] The remainder of the terms in the diagram are more or less self-explanatory, although the reader may wish to consult Brecher's original article or later work for a fuller discussion of these factors.

In keeping with each author's original manner, we have retained the original orthographies and styles in the reprinted articles which follow. It must be emphasized that articles in the same section present several different viewpoints. In Part III, "Communist Ideology, Belief Systems, and Soviet Foreign Policy," for example, some writers argue that Soviet ideology has a great impact on foreign policy behavior, while others contend that this factor has little influence under most conditions. By juxtaposing different arguments on the same subject, many of them classic statements of their respective positions, one can more easily compare and evaluate the logical and empirical evidence presented and the conclusions reached. It is precisely this kind of critical analysis we hope to encourage.

3. Michael Brecher, *The Foreign Policy System of Israel: Setting, Images, Process* (New Haven: Yale University Press, 1972), Chapter 1; Michael Brecher, *Decisions in Israel's Foreign Policy* (London: Oxford University Press, 1974), Introduction; and Michael Brecher, *Israel, the Korean War and China: Images, Decisions and Consequences* (Jerusalem: Jerusalem Academic Press, 1974).

4. Michael Brecher, Blema Steinberg, and Janice Stein, "A Framework for Research on Foreign Policy Behavior," *The Journal of Conflict Resolution*, XIII, 1 (March, 1969), p. 82.

5. *Ibid.,* p. 83.

6. *Ibid.,* p. 83.

PART I

The Study of
Soviet Foreign Policy

Soviet foreign policy is a field in which "theories" abound. A survey of the literature in 1956 identified at least eight prevalent theories, each purporting to have found the main factor that influences and "explains" Soviet foreign policy behavior (for example, Marxist political philosophy, Great Russian imperialism, bureaucratic tyranny, Byzantine traditions, national defense, Eurasian environmental characteristics, the urge to the sea, Russian national character).[1] A recent review of the literature again reveals many diverse theories that focus on four major themes: the impact of ideology, "Soviet nationhood," history, and geography on the foreign policy of the USSR.[2]

Most of these theories contend that one or more factors are especially important determinants of Soviet behavior in all or most situations. Implicit are generalizations to the effect that certain factors consistently influence Russian actions more than others. Reference to these factors, it is claimed, will always or usually provide the best possible explanation of Soviet policies and performance. Critics reply that there is little empirical evidence to support the

1. William Glaser, "Theories of Soviet Foreign Policy: A Classification of the Literature," *World Affairs Quarterly,* XXVII, 2 (July, 1956), pp. 128-152. See also Daniel Bell, "Ten Theories in Search of Reality," *World Politics,* X, 3 (April, 1958), pp. 327-365.

2. Richard Brody and John Vesecky, "Soviet Openness to Changing Situations: A Critical Evaluation of Certain Hypotheses About Soviet Foreign Policy Behavior," in Jan Triska (ed.), *Communist Party-States: Comparative and International Studies* (Indianapolis: Bobbs-Merrill, 1969), pp. 353 – 385. See also William Welch, *American Images of Soviet Foreign Policy* (New Haven: Yale University Press, 1970). This important analysis of numerous American theories of

sweeping generalizations contained in most existing theories, that certain Russian political, economic, and environmental characteristics may or may not influence Soviet behavior generally or in specific cases, and that factors may vary in relative importance in different situations. Yet broad generalizations — verified, unverified, and unverifiable — are integral parts of past and present theories of Soviet foreign policy.

Different theories affect not only one's perception of the *facts,* but also one's assumptions about which *facts* are *factors* (i. e., relevant variables). One's theoretical orientation, whether consciously or unconsciously held, significantly affects the form, nature, and quality of one's explanations. Indeed, some philosophers argue that "One theory cannot be understood literally as fitting *the facts* better than another because each, in a significant sense, carries with it its own facts and observation reports. . . . To adopt a theory is ultimately to change one's observational framework, and this means more than one's perspective on a basically unchanging reality; it means, in one degree or another, to accept a new reality."[3]

A recent discussion of conceptual models and the study of foreign policy illuminates these ideas. A "rational policy" model, an "organizational process" model, and a "bureaucratic politics" model are outlined.[4] Each has its own basic unit of analysis, organizing concepts, dominant inference patterns, and general and specific propositions.

The "rational policy" model is the most widely used by students of international relations and Soviet foreign policy.[5] It assumes that national governments act purposefully and respond in a calculating manner to perceived problems. However, if one accepts the view that conceptual models do not order "reality" but create it, one must seriously consider alternative paradigms. Students of Soviet foreign policy may find the "organizational process" and "bureaucratic politics" models particularly appealing, because they directly challenge the view that the USSR is a "totalitarian" or "monolithic" state.[6] They also focus attention on the implementation of policy, not merely

Soviet foreign policy came to hand after the present work went to press, and hence the views presented therein unfortunately could not be incorporated into our discussion.

3. John G. Gunnell, "The Idea of the Conceptual Framework: A Philosophical Critique," *Journal of Comparative Administration,* I, 2 (August, 1969), p. 165. On the controversial subject of the nature and functions of theories and models, see, for example, Abraham Kaplan, *The Conduct of Inquiry* (San Francisco: Chandler, 1964).

4. Graham Allison, "Conceptual Models and the Cuban Missile Crisis," *American Political Science Review,* LXIII, 3 (September, 1969), pp. 689-718. See also James Rosenau, "Foreign Policy as Adaptive Behavior: Some Preliminary Notes for a Theoretical Model," *Comparative Politics,* II, 3 (April, 1970), pp. 365-387; and K. J. Holsti, "National Role Conceptions in the Study of Foreign Policy," *International Studies Quarterly,* XIV, 3 (September, 1970), pp. 233-309.

5. For example, see Hans Morgenthau, *Politics Among Nations* (4th ed.; New York: Knopf, 1967); Joseph Frankel, *The Making of Foreign Policy* (London: Oxford University Press, 1963); and Arnold Horelick and Myron Rush, *Strategic Power and Soviet Foreign Policy* (Chicago: University of Chicago Press, 1966).

6. See Carl Linden, *Khrushchev and the Soviet Leadership, 1957–1964* (Baltimore: The Johns Hopkins Press, 1966); and Michel Tatu, *Power in the Kremlin from Khrushchev to Kosygin*

on the decisions made by Soviet leaders. In short, alternative modes of analysis contain different assumptions and often produce very different explanations (for example, of the Cuban missile crisis).

An important question to ask is, "Which theories and models best help one to explain and understand what one wants to know about Soviet foreign policy behavior?" One's approach to the subject will shape both the questions one asks and the answers one finds. The "rational policy" model, for example, relies heavily on the "motive-belief" pattern of explanation. Explanation of this kind "consists of showing what goal the government was pursuing in committing the act and how this action was a reasonable choice, given the nation's objectives."[7] However, it is very difficult to ascertain the motives and beliefs of Soviet decision-makers in general and in specific instances. Perhaps the easiest task is to document the views of an individual Party leader on a single issue at a given moment in time. But even this may require considerable "Kremlinological" insight and skillful use of content analysis.[8] Furthermore, the relationships between beliefs and behavior pose formidable research problems in all of the social sciences. They present especially great problems in the study of international relations, where much available data are contained in highly manipulative communications and reliable and significant information are often lacking.

Knowledge of many factors that *may* influence Soviet behavior is important to the student of Soviet foreign policy. The conceptual framework depicted in Figure 1 suggests numerous possible influences. "All foreign policy systems," it is argued, "comprise a set of components which can be classified in three general categories, inputs, process, and outputs. The notion of flow and dynamic movement in a system which is constantly absorbing demands and channelling them into a policy machine which transforms these inputs into decisions and outputs is portrayed [below]."[9]

The creators of this framework emphasize that foreign policy decision-makers act in accordance with their perceptions of reality. "Underlying this research design is the view that the operational environment affects the results or outcomes of decisions directly but influences the choice among policy

(New York: Viking Press, 1969).

7. Allison, *op. cit.,* p. 693.

8. See Frederic J. Fleron, Jr., "Introduction," and Erik P. Hoffmann, "Methodological Problems of Kremlinology," in Frederic J. Fleron, Jr. (ed.), *Communist Studies and the Social Sciences: Essays on Methodology and Empirical Theory* (Chicago: Rand McNally, 1969), pp. 1 – 33, 129 – 149. Also see Alexander George, *Propaganda Analysis* (Evanston, Illinois: Row, Peterson & Company, 1959).

9. For elaboration of this research design and statement with some preliminary findings supported by quantitative data, see Michael Brecher, Blema Steinberg, and Janice Stein, "A Framework for Research on Foreign Policy Behavior," *The Journal of Conflict Resolution,* XIII, 1 (March, 1969), p. 80. On the nature of "issue areas," see James Rosenau, "Foreign Policy as an Issue-Area," in James Rosenau (ed.), *Domestic Sources of Foreign Policy* (New York: Free Press, 1967), pp. 11 – 50; and James Rosenau, "Pre-theories and Theories of Foreign Policy," in R. Barry Farrell (ed.), *Approaches to Comparative and International Politics* (Evanston, Illinois: Northwestern University Press, 1966), pp. 27 – 92.

INPUTS

OPERATIONAL ENVIRONMENT

External:	Global	(G)
	Subordinate	(S)
	Subordinate Other	(SO)
	Bilateral	(B)
	Dominant Bilateral	(DB)
Internal:	Military Capability	(M)
	Economic Capability	(E)
	Political Structure	(PS)
	Interest Groups	(IG)
	Competing Elites	(CE)

COMMUNICATION—The transmission of
data about the operational environment
by mass media and face-to-face contacts

PSYCHOLOGICAL ENVIRONMENT

Attitudinal Prism: Ideology, historical
legacy, personality predispositions

Elite Images: of the operational
environment, including competing
elites' advocacy and pressure potential

PROCESS

FORMULATION of strategic and tactical
decisions in four <u>issue areas</u>:

	Military-Security	(M-S)
	Political-Diplomatic	(P-D)
	Economic-Developm'l	(E-D)
	Cultural-Status	(C-S)

IMPLEMENTATION of decisions by
various structures: head of state, head of
government, foreign office, etc.

OUTPUTS—the substance of acts or
decisions

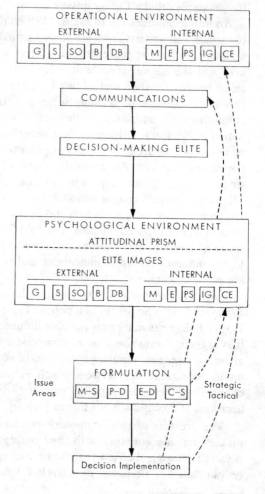

Figure 1. Conceptual Framework for a Foreign Policy System

Reprinted from Michael Brecher, Blema Steinberg, and Janice Stein, "A Framework for
Research on Foreign Policy Behavior," *The Journal of Conflict Resolution*, XIII, 1 (March,
1969), p. 80. Copyright 1969 by The University of Michigan, reprinted by permission.

options, that is, the decisions themselves, only as it is filtered through the images of decision-makers."[10] An important but difficult task of the analyst is to identify and suggest relationships among factors that may link elite images with decisions, policies, and behavior. Whether certain factors do indeed influence Soviet actions in general or in specific cases are, of course, empirical questions.

It must be emphasized that this "systems" model is not the only or necessarily the best method of studying foreign policy behavior.[11] Like any theory, model, or conceptual framework, it contains numerous explicit and implicit assumptions and is not "value-free." Recalling our earlier discussion, one might reject out of hand the authors' assertions that "All data regarding foreign policy can be classified in one of these categories," and that "All foreign policy issues may be allocated to four issue areas."[12] To be sure, other conceptual frameworks may generate different data and produce better explanations. But this framework does identify numerous potentially relevant sets of factors that may influence the external behavior of the Soviet Union, and it also suggests some possible general relationships among these factors. For both these reasons the framework merits careful study.

Considering the difficulties involved in using the "motive-belief" pattern of explanation and in studying the "psychological environment" of foreign policy-makers, it is perhaps unfortunate that many analysts assume that certain factors significantly influence Soviet behavior in all or most situations. It is probably more fruitful simply to look at specific situations and ask, "Why were these decisions reached and why were these actions taken?" (Why did the USSR sign the Nazi-Soviet pact? Why were satellite regimes created in Eastern Europe after World War II? Why does the Soviet Union pursue its present policies in Eastern Europe, the Middle East, Southeast Asia, Latin America, Africa? Why do Soviet leaders compete and cooperate with the United States in various fields?) Careful study of individual events, policies, and policy changes has made it possible and will continue to make it possible to evaluate the relative importance of factors — external and internal — that influence individual Soviet decisions and types of activities. From this less shaky empirical base, with its emphasis on discovering and describing the actual behavior of Soviet officials at home and abroad, one can gradually verify, refine, or reformulate one's generalizations so that, employed with caution, they may help to explain Soviet behavior in other contexts.

Professors Zimmerman and Gati, in their essays below, examine the state of contemporary research on Soviet foreign policy. Zimmerman notes that some theorists emphasize the importance of external factors ("macro-anal-

10. Brecher, Steinberg, and Stein, *op. cit.,* p. 81.

11. For an analysis of many of these same questions that does not utilitze systems theory, see Harold and Margaret Sprout, *The Ecological Perspective on Human Affairs with Special Reference to International Politics* (Princeton: Princeton University Press, 1965).

12. Brecher, Steinberg, and Stein, *op. cit.,* pp. 80, 87.

ysis") on Soviet international behavior, while others stress the impact of domestic factors ("micro-analysis"). He contends that both are essential components of adequate explanations, and that both derive their importance from their effect on elite attitudes, which in turn shape the purposes and policies of Soviet leaders. (Compare these views with the conceptual framework above.)

Zimmerman maintains that changes in the international environment have significantly altered the attitudes and perspectives of many leading Soviet officials, and that this has increased their propensity and capacity to respond to external influences in a flexible manner. He concludes that the increasing "reactive" or responsive capabilities of Soviet leaders greatly enchance the potential influence of external factors (for example, the actions of other important nations) on Soviet international behavior.

But to describe changes in elite perspectives is merely the first step toward understanding the effects these changes have on Soviet performance under various circumstances. And to observe divergences in the perspectives of Soviet officials is not to explain their impact on or their relationship to other factors that influence behavior. Fully aware of these problems, Zimmerman bemoans the paucity of tested and testable hypotheses in the theory of international relations and its subfield, Soviet foreign policy.

Zimmerman urges greater analysis of external influences and the ways in which Soviet policy-makers, individually and collectively, react to these influences. Stressing the complexity of the entire field, he identifies many key questions and relationships that must be examined. But crucial questions remain. What kinds of explanation should be sought? What kinds of data should be collected? How can these data be acquired? For what purposes should they be used?

Some of these questions are discussed in the essay by Professor Gati. His analysis focuses on two major textbooks in the field of Soviet foreign policy and their strikingly different methodological approaches. Ulam's *Expansion and Coexistence* is a "traditional history"; Triska and Finley's *Soviet Foreign Policy* is primarily "social science" research. Each seeks to provide different kinds of insights into Soviet international behavior. The reader must decide for himself which is more successful and why. Perhaps he will conclude that both books and the two following essays raise more questions than they resolve.[13]

---

13. The Ulam and Triska and Finley books "reflect the present state of flux in Soviet studies. Both are important efforts to explain Soviet foreign policy behavior. But they are based on fundamentally different concepts of explanation. Ulam's analysis is essentially eliminative — that is, he seeks to demonstrate that other possible explanations of events do not logically and empirically 'fit' as well as his. Triska and Finley, employing various deductive and inductive research strategies, seek to generate and verify probabilistic generalizations to be used in explaining different aspects of Soviet behavior. The strength of the former approach is that it helps us to understand complex nonrecurring events about which information is difficult to obtain; the strength of the latter is that it helps to uncover trends and behavioral patterns through more rigorous analysis of available data." Erik P. Hoffmann, a book review, *The Journal of Politics*, XXXI, 3 (August, 1969), pp. 828 – 829.

History, Social Science, and
the Study of Soviet Foreign Policy*

1.

The nearly simultaneous appearance of two significant works on Soviet behavior in world politics provides an opportunity to consider and contrast divergent approaches to the study of Soviet foreign policy. *Expansion and Coexistence and Soviet Foreign Policy* make a methodological inquiry particularly interesting and apposite because of the authors' fundamentally different modes of analysis.

A professor of government, Ulam has nevertheless written an interpretive history, one in which the emphasis is on specific events, trends, external and internal circumstances, and the leaders who have made policy. Largely chronological in its basic organization, the book exhibits the hallmarks of historical scholarship in its thoroughness and judicious presentation of available information. Avoiding jargon, Ulam attempts to explain the past and present significance of historical events and influences. His book is a comprehensive and often brilliant *tour de force* that surpasses any other previous effort in making the history of Soviet foreign policy intelligible.

*Reprinted from *Slavic Review: American Quarterly of Soviet and East European Studies,* XXIX, 4 (December, 1970), pp. 682–687 (slightly revised), by permission of the author and the publisher. This chapter was originally prepared as a review article. The studies analyzed herein are Jan F. Triska and David D. Finley, *Soviet Foreign Policy* (New York: Macmillan Company, 1968) and Adam B. Ulam, *Expansion and Coexistence: The History of Soviet Foreign Policy, 1917 –67* (New York: Praeger, 1968), two widely adopted texts on Soviet foreign behavior.

In sharp contrast to Ulam's traditional-historical approach, Triska and Finley concern themselves with the systematic study of recurring patterns in Soviet policies and especially with the dissection of the decision-making process in the Soviet system. Disaffected by contradictory interpretations, they strive to overcome the primary limitation of historical and intuitive knowledge, that of "perceptive relativity" — the fact that different observers perceive the same phenomenon differently. Therefore, they look for causal relationships by means of statistical inference and experimentation, assuming that the facts, relationships, and conclusions thus established will compel agreement by all observers. To accomplish their objective, they employ a wide variety of empirical methods and approaches such as content analysis, decision theory, role theory, bargaining and game theories, a "multiple-symmetry" model, as well as elaborate statistical and mathematical techniques. To the social scientist they demonstrate the attraction and usefulness of systematic empirical research in the study of Soviet politics. To the historian and the humanist who is unaccustomed to the language, symbols, typologies, and techniques of modern social science, *Soviet Foreign Policy* may well seem overwhelming at first, surprising later, but probably provocative and stimulating in the end; at the very least, the authors will have imparted a concern for precision and refinement in Soviet studies.

2.

Broadly speaking, there are two types of data used in all political and historical research: "words" and "deeds." Of the two, scholars generally rely on words since they seldom have the opportunity to observe deeds. In the study of Soviet foreign policy, our sources therefore inevitably include the Soviet political elite's communications about the goals, instruments, and implementation of foreign policy. The crucial methodological question — one that is explicitly raised by Triska and Finley — is *how* to use the voluminous Soviet literature on foreign policy.

The importance of this question lies in our preoccupation with, and perhaps somewhat uncritical acceptance of, what the Soviet leadership professes to be doing or would do in the future. What Samuel L. Sharp once called the "doubtful art of quotation" has long characterized not only the Kremlinological literature but a good many other scholarly works on Soviet foreign policy as well. In varying degrees, the impression is created that Soviet communications more or less accurately reflect Soviet behavior. This assumption, taken literally, is questionable. Suppose that a Soviet leader says to an American audience, "We will bury you!" Do we interpret his statement to mean that *(a)* he will definitely do it; *(b)* he would like to do it and do it now; *(c)* he would like to do it in the future; *(d)* he would do it now or in the future but only if and when the opportunity arose and he had the resources to do it? And can we even assume that he is using the word "bury" in the same way as his audience and his country's decision-makers? Surely there can be no correct or valid answer to these questions, insofar as the Soviet leader could also have intended to make the statement for many purposes — for example, to communicate with his own bureaucrats, to pacify the Chinese, or to warn the American military establishment.

The public statements of foreign policy-makers, then, represent a hazardous source of information about foreign policy *behavior*. But they represent a particularly hazardous source for understanding foreign policy *intentions*. For there is a seemingly perpetual discrepancy between what any man or group would like to do and what he or the group may actually decide to do or be capable of doing. To the extent that Soviet leaders appear particularly committed to the perfection of man and his environment and hence promote high hopes about the future, such discrepancy may be especially acute. Accordingly, textual analysis of the Soviet elite's descriptive or prescriptive communications presents a major methodological challenge to students of the Soviet political system.

How, then, can the printed word emanating from the Soviet Union be used? What do these statements mean generally and in different contexts? How does one know that what he is observing is what he thinks he is observing, and that what he is measuring is what he thinks he is measuring? In the language of the social scientist, these are questions of validity.

Significantly, these are questions on which the historian and the social scientist begin to part. The former seeks to be primarily "discriminating and judicious," the latter "methodical and systematic." There is a difference. For example, in his chapter on Khrushchev's foreign policy from 1956 to 1965, Ulam discusses the 22nd Congress of the CPSU. He observes, *inter alia*, that "Khrushchev's language was still opprobrious (the West, previously referred to as 'the capitalist nations,' was now almost invariably described as the 'imperialist' ones), his tone threatening (as in his relating of the latest and biggest Soviet atomic tests). But there was a hint of moderation in the language about Germany. . ." (p. 656). Ulam then conveys the conclusion that the Soviet leadership experienced a period of hesitation and perhaps confusion in regard to foreign policy at this time. While his argument seems sound and the reconstruction of the background of the Congress is well rounded, another analyst may well take issue with Ulam's selection of what constituted the important parts of the various speeches dealing with foreign policy and ask for "hard" or more conclusive evidence to support his conclusions.

In contrast, Triska and Finley examined the printed record of the 22nd Party Congress with a view of seeking *verifiable generalizations* about a specific question: that of the role of doctrine in the formulation of Soviet foreign policy. They were interested in the frequency of doctrinal stereotypes in the various speeches on foreign policy. For this reason, they prepared fourteen specific "propositions" (pp. 119 – 122) to find out, for example, if the impact of doctrine was generally greater in the Soviet public analysis of long-range policies than in the analysis of short-term policies (Proposition #8; p. 120). Or, they asked if the older members of the foreign policy elite speaking at the Congress used doctrinal stereotypes more frequently than did the younger members of the elite (Proposition #14; p. 122). Their data, derived from elaborate content analysis of the documents, "clearly confirmed" both propositions. How?

> Quantitative content analysis of public statements is one imperfect but promising method by which modern social scientists seek to overcome the obstacles to investigating motivation in human behavior. Basically, quantitative content analysis discovers the frequency of use of selected verbal symbols and semantic formulations and uses this information as one ground for concluding some of the attitudes or beliefs of the speaker [p. 116]. . . . [I]nstances of words or phrases prejudged to have a high doctrinal loading [were counted]. . . . A word/phrase list for this purpose was developed and amended during the analysis. Terminology was included or rejected according to our prior judgment as to whether or not it constituted a short-hand symbol for a concept or relationship or characteristic property clearly derived from Marxist-Leninist theoretical formulation. The results of this analysis were then expressed by a fraction representing the number of doctrinally stereotyped words or phrases in proportion to the total number of words in the statement analyzed. We called this fraction a *Doctrinal Stereotype Quotient* (DSQ) [pp. 118 – 119].

What did the DSQ reveal about the role of Marxist-Leninist ideology as an "active ingredient" in foreign policy decisions? The substantive conclusions which emerged indicated that the older members of the elite and those whose lives had been devoted mainly to Party work tended to use doctrinal formulations more frequently than others. Those with a primary preoccupation with domestic politics also adopted Marxist-Leninist terminology more often than those primarily concerned with foreign affairs. Moreover, the authors report that broad generalizations about the international situation and about Soviet foreign policy intentions seem to have led to the inclusion of more ideological referents than specific conclusions about a particular policy situation. (In fact, analysis of additional data about Khrushchev's communications during the 1962 Cuban missile crisis offers the optimistic conclusion that the possibility of recourse to ideology in time of international crisis is not very great at all.)

Such generalizations are based on three assumptions: first, that there exists a properly identified foreign policy elite in the Soviet Union, an assumption whose validity Triska and Finley convincingly demonstrate in a chapter on "The Men Who Make Soviet Foreign Policy" (pp. 75 – 106).

The second, infinitely more complex, assumption is that political communications in the Soviet Union (or, for that matter, elsewhere) actually reflect the leaders' *thought*. Linguists and psychologists have confirmed the existence of a positive relationship between communications and thought patterns; indeed, if such relationships could not be postulated, there would be little or no substance to scholarly research in the social sciences and humanities, which are based, as such research must be, on the printed word.

But the relationship confirmed is that between language and thought and *not* necessarily between language and *action*. In other words, we know that what one communicates has an impact on others and is an expression of his thought patterns; we do not know whether one's political communication discloses that which he is *doing* or intends to do. Given this uncertainty, the strictly policy-oriented student of Soviet foreign behavior may well be somewhat disappointed by, and skeptical about, the ultimate practical or applied value of textual analysis of any sort. For at best it can reveal what the Soviet leaders think and not necessarily what they do. Thus, even systematic textual analysis raises a number of perplexing questions about language, thought, policy, and their relationships — questions which become particularly troublesome in the study of any country's foreign policy.

Third, the generalizations offered by Triska and Finley not only raise the question of validity, but also of reliability. The reliability of all generalizations must be ascertained by further testing with different observers utilizing the same instruments. If such tests produce similar results, we shall have gained partial confirmation of important propositions about the functions and place of doctrine in the thought processes of the Soviet foreign policy elite.

Soviet communications about foreign policy, then, lend themselves to different modes of analysis. The historical-traditional approach provides the reader with commentary about the *inputs* and the *outputs* of Soviet foreign policy, stressing the probable causes and consequences of the most dramatic developments of each period. Given the emphasis on that which is unique, there is no attempt to reach such generalized conclusions which would hold true in the future as well. As utilized by Triska and Finley, social science approaches offer, or seek to offer, verifiable propositions, primarily about the decision-making process (even if some of these propositions are gained from nonrecurring data), that provide insights mostly about the *inputs* of Soviet foreign policy: how incoming information is selected and interpreted, goals formulated, and decisions reached. Substantively, both books point to the presence of divergent opinions and contending forces within the Soviet foreign policy-making apparatus.

3.

The mode of analyzing Soviet foreign policy actions or deeds also separates the historian and the social scientist. Understandably enough, Ulam is interested in, and is fascinated by, the great events and conflicts of the past fifty years: the conclusion of World War I, relations with Germany and with the Allies before World War II, the origins and development of the Cold War, the significance of Stalin's death, the emerging Sino-Soviet conflict, the confrontation over Cuba — events whose uniqueness he explicitly recognizes. While he does offer occasional generalizations about Soviet policy, Ulam prefers to concentrate on the concrete event and the leading personality. His method is in good part intuitive. While he seeks objectivity and fairness in the treatment of Soviet actions or deeds, Ulam's handling of the data suggests he finds impartiality beyond reach if not actually repugnant.

On the whole, Ulam's judgments are based on an appreciation of the relationships between Soviet domestic and foreign policies; on the impact of the Russian tradition; on the role of leading personalities (rather than the larger foreign policy elite); and on the conviction that Soviet behavior abroad can best be understood in terms of power politics. His treatment of the Cold War, for example, is thus "conventional" in the sense that he accepts Soviet policies as essentially inevitable — as if, given Soviet goals and perceptions and Western policies, the Soviet leaders had no real options other than those they actually chose. *To suggest inevitability in retrospect but at the same time deny the possibility of generalizations of the "if . . . then" variety concerning future Soviet actions is the historian's self-imposed, and perhaps unnecessary, limitation.*

In contrast, Triska and Finley seek to ascertain the relative importance of factors or the impact of major events in the international system on the formulation of Soviet foreign policy. In order to arrive at generalizations, they examine fifteen recent international events, ranging from the civil war in Laos to the COMECON integration problems of 1961 – 1963 (pp. 127 – 148). They classify the Soviet leadership's perception of these events as indications of success, failure, threat, or opportunity, and conclude — on the basis of subsequent Soviet reactions — that perceptions of failure and threat are "more likely to induce abrupt changes" in Soviet policy than perceptions of success and opportunity. In other words, "failures" and "threats" abroad constitute an important factor to which Soviet leaders respond and adapt policies accordingly. Significantly, relatively few such events perceived as failures or threats are thought to have led to lasting change in Soviet policy (p. 145). Thus Triska and Finley emphasize continuity and stability, stipulating that radical change can be expected only with a change of elite personalities. "If an 'ideological purist' were to attain 'dictator' status in the USSR," they observe, "we might expect an abrupt rise in the application of doctrinal propositions, especially in the crisis context." However, since only the older members of the elite are said to be doctrine-oriented, Triska and Finley consider the prospect of such change unlikely (p. 147).

Thus, Triska and Finley focus on the permanent and repetitive elements in Soviet behavior. They are far more concerned with verifying empirical generalizations than with analyzing the causes and consequences of unique historical events. Although the evidence they have so diligently collected is restricted in both time and place, their qualifications are not always sufficient to dispel an unfortunate impression of finality. Paradoxically, the qualifications they do introduce significantly weaken the scope and degree of confirmation of their generalizations, in part because of the great number of complex variables on which they depend.

What we have, then, are two impressive and stimulating studies of Soviet foreign policy. Their substantive conclusions are certainly compatible, although their views on what constitutes understanding, what questions should be studied, and what kinds of information should be gathered are profoundly different. One is conventional and highly readable, the other experimental. Primarily, Ulam seeks understanding of *what, when,* and *who*; Triska and Finley of *what, who,* and *how.* Both books address themselves to questions of *why* — Ulam by informed and sophisticated speculation, Triska and Finley by systematic and controlled investigation of propositions about presumed relationships. Together, the two books underline the increasing gap in Soviet studies between the methodologies of history and social science.

Elite Perspectives and the
Explanation of Soviet Foreign Policy*

1.

Analysts have vacillated between two major orientations in explaining foreign policy behavior. Theorists of international politics have generally adopted a macro-analytic approach in which the internal dynamics of a state's behavior — including such factors as the particular political structure of the polity, the perspectives and personalities of the decision-makers, and the articulated attitudes and demands of the citizenry — are "black-boxed" in the name of analytic parsimony. They anthropomorphize the state, treating it as a unitary rational decision-maker whose behavior is explained largely as a response *(a)* to the anarchic quality of politics in an international arena devoid of international government, *(b)* to changes in the structure of the international system (e.g., changes in the number of major actors — the great powers, in the distribution of power among the major actors, or in the relative power differential separating the major actors from the "bit" players on the international scene), or *(c)* to calculated moves by rival states.

In contrast, those whose interest in international politics has developed out of an initial comparative politics or area studies concern have shown themselves more prone to adopt micro-analytic approaches to foreign policy analyses. These men view the attributes of foreign policy as resultants of internal political processes or as resultants of the interplay of phenomena particular to

*Copyright by the Board of Editors of the *Journal of International Affairs,* reprinted from volume XXIV, Number 1, pages 84–98, 1970. Permission to reprint is gratefully acknowledged to the Editors of the *Journal* and the author.

the state in question. According to these analysts, policy attributes may grow out of entirely *nonhuman factors* such as a state's geopolitical position or its natural resource endowment. Or they may stem from *domestic societal forces* such as a state's national character, "modal personality," political culture, belief system or ideology, or social structure. Or they may have their origins in factors which shape the *effective structure of a state,* factors ranging from the state's formal constitutional framework on the one hand to structural impacts on information flows within the state on the other, or finally according to our *micro-analysts,* foreign policy attributes may be thought to originate in the *idiosyncrasies of particular decision-makers* — their anxieties, their aspirations, and their perceptions. In short, the *micro-analysts* have tended to regard the nature of the individual *components* of a polity, such as those we have just enumerated, and not situationally induced general propensities of a state as providing the most important clues to a proper understanding of any state's foreign policy. This has been particularly true in western analysis of Soviet foreign policy.

There has, of course, always been a willingness on the part of western observers to recognize Moscow's sensitivity to the global distribution of power (macro-analysis). Arnold Horelick and Myron Rush in *Strategic Power and Soviet Foreign Policy* (1966), for instance, argued that the strategic superiority of the United States provided an external environment in which the Soviet Union was not prone to resort to "the dangerous employment of . . . strategic power for political ends."[1] Indeed, as early as 1951, Raymond Garthoff had affirmed this centrality of the balance of power concept in Soviet foreign policy calculus. At times Soviet decision-makers have been thought by western observers to retreat or otherwise adapt their tactics when confronted by an asymmetrical and unfavorable power configuration, and then to return to the fray under more propitious circumstances. Only recently, though, has the consistently *reactive nature* of Soviet foreign policy been stressed, first by Marshall Shulman in *Stalin's Foreign Policy Reappraised* (1963), and then more elaborately by Jan Triska and David Finley in their stimulus-response model of Soviet-American interaction.[2]

The prevailing orientation to the explanation of Soviet foreign policy in the West, however, has been micro-analytic. There have been several reasons for the western emphasis on the internal origins of Soviet international behavior. The cold war created an atmosphere conducive to stressing the extent to which the foreign policy of the Soviet Union differed from that of other states, while

---

1. Arnold Horelick and Myron Rush, *Strategic Power and Soviet Foreign Policy* (Chicago: University of Chicago Press, 1966), p. 218.
2. Marshall D. Shulman, *Stalin's Foreign Policy Reappraised* (Cambridge, Mass.: Harvard University Press, 1963); and Jan Triska and David Finley, "Soviet-American Relations: A Multiple Symmetry Model," *The Journal of Conflict Resolution,* IX, No. 1 (March, 1965), pp. 37 – 53.

Soviet studies remained somewhat divorced, conceptually and methodologically, from the mainstream of comparative politics and international relations inquiry. But more importantly, there was compelling evidence to suggest that Soviet foreign policy did differ from that of other states and that the explanation for the unique in Soviet policies, goals, and instrumentalities was to be found in the radical transformation of the Russian polity and Russian society brought about by or after the Bolshevik seizure of power in 1917.

That this was the conclusion of Soviet specialists may be seen by identifying the themes and preoccupations which have been at the core of the scholarly dialogue on Soviet foreign policy. One central theme has been that of historical comparison or "continuity and change." There has been a major preoccupation with the Soviet Union's international performance capability, with the general tendency being to stress the Soviet Union's ability to act efficaciously in international politics. A third central theme has pertained to the role of ideology in shaping Soviet foreign policy.[3] Implicit in these themes were several assumptions about the nature of the Soviet political system. The focus on continuity and change obviously reflected an assumption that Soviet foreign policy differed substantially from the foreign policy of the antecedent Tsarist regime. Beyond that, it revealed an assumption that the major variable warranting attention in foreign policy analysis was the Soviet political system — perhaps as shaped by a particular leader. (There was of course a wide range of opinion within the broad consensus. Interpretations varied from the emphasis of Robert Tucker on the idiosyncratic psychodynamics of the leader to the structural focus of Marshall Shulman.)[4] Similarly, the significance attached to the Soviet political system in explaining Soviet foreign policy underlay the attention paid to the international performance capability of the Soviet Union, for central to western calculations of this capability was the notion that the Soviet Union was an archetypical totalitarian mobilization system. It was assumed that the Soviet Union was impermeable to extra-national influences and insulated from the constraints of an open, pluralist society whose decision-makers are obliged to take the opinions of domestic critics into account. Furthermore, many experts argued that the Soviet Union, as a totalitarian system, was favored in its competition with an "instrumental" system like that of the United States because the Soviet elite could secure greater social mobilization of society.

It was the attention of ideology, however, which most revealed the assumptions about the Soviet Union which disposed scholars to a micro-analytic

3. Definitions of ideology abound. Usage here follows that of Zbigniew Brzezinski and Samuel Huntington in *Political Power USA/USSR* (New York: Viking Press, 1964), in which they distinguish between Soviet *ideology* and more traditional *belief systems*. Ideology is a revolutionary belief system which is explicit and simplified and which conveys fairly general but direct perspectives about the future good society, the antecedent reality, and the means whereby the present reality might be transformed into a better future society.

4. See Robert C. Tucker, *The Soviet Political Mind* (New York: Praeger, 1963); and Marshall D. Shulman, *op. cit.,* Chapter 2.

interpretation of Soviet foreign policy. This attention partly stemmed from a sense that the peculiar quality of Soviet beliefs gave the USSR an advantage in its global competition with the United States. Scholars noted the preoccupation of Soviet ideology with violence, conflict, and qualitative change, and also the lesser role attributed to nation-state interaction in the overall world historical process. They contrasted this to the allegedly legalistic and ahistorical belief system of American decision-makers disposed to assume a natural international harmony of interests, to view stability rather than conflict as a norm (both in the sense of the expected and the desired), and to believe in the efficacy of incremental and intra-systemic change. More specifically, western analysts focused on Soviet ideology because it was thought that the all-encompassing character of Soviet beliefs — embracing a critique of the existing order, notions about a better future society, and policy prescriptions for transforming the real into the desired — provided the key to the seemingly uniquely purposive character of Soviet behavior.

Indeed, the belief was widespread that ideology would retain its significance in explaining Soviet foreign policy long after it had ceased to play a significant role domestically in a Soviet Union developed beyond the era of collectivization and mass purges. One reason for this belief was, as Adam Ulam argued, that "while the Soviet citizen, including the indoctrinated party member, has numerous occasions to discover the contradictions or irrelevances of Marxism in his daily life, he enjoys no such tangible experience insofar as the world outside the USSR is concerned."[5] For an ordinary citizen as well as for a party ideologue, international relations lacked the salience of domestic affairs; therefore beliefs about the structure of the international system, the nature and identity of the Soviet Union's major antagonists, and the future transformations of international politics were less likely to be called into question. A second argument also buttressed the assumption of the continued significance of ideology and its implication for the continued preeminent role of the Soviet political system in explaining foreign policy behavior. It was acknowledged that, at least in the long run, ideological erosion domestically was to be anticipated in the complex large-scale Soviet industrial society. In order to maintain the institutionalized revolutionary zeal integral to the nature of the Soviet regime, foreign policy would become a surrogate for rapid industrialization. In the post-industrialization phase of Soviet society the barricades to be stormed would be found in the international arena.

2.

Compelling as all the arguments for continued attention to the unique impact of ideology on Soviet foreign policy are, the dominant cast to Soviet perspectives on international relations during the 1960's provides little support for

5. Adam Ulam, *The New Face of Soviet Totalitarianism* (New York: Praeger, 1965), p. 74.

such a conclusion and much evidence which points in the opposite direction. Not only do the main trends in Soviet perspectives on the international system bear a marked similarity to western conventional wisdom, but the evidence indicates that Moscow's reading of the contemporary international scene has led the Soviet leadership to propositions and steps inconsonant with any determination to maintain the institutionalized revolutionary zeal which many have thought the most characteristic feature of the Soviet system.

Conventional Bolshevik assumptions about international relations constituted a logical adaptation of Marxism to early twentieth-century reality and to the fact that, contrary to expectation, the communist revolution occurred in Russia alone. As a result, the imagery of fundamental conflict was altered from that of a struggle waged within a state between the dominant but moribund capitalists and the emerging proletariat to one taking place in the horizontally structured environment of international politics. Vertical, class, and economic concepts were transposed and adjusted to account for the basically horizontal, international, and political arena in which the Soviet leaders were to engage their class enemies. Once the Bolsheviks were in power, capitalism became equated with a system of states as well as with a global socio-economic system. Marxism as modified by Leninist and Stalinist experience was projected onto the international arena. Soviet notions about the actors in international politics became inextricably linked with Soviet assumptions concerning the major agents in the historical process. Given the assumption that classes are the movers of history, it was only natural that, as Zbigniew Brzezinski has noted, "the interplay of nation-states" was considered "merely one, and often only a formal aspect of international affairs."[6]

Traditional Soviet ideas about the hierarchical structure of the international order were strongly conditioned by Bolshevik conceptions of power. Since the key question of politics is *kto-kogo* (who [eliminates] whom), the very notion of non-hierarchical power relations was anathema. States, classes, and individuals, except for historically brief moments in which one actor supplanted another, were either on top or not, and values were allocated accordingly. Similarly, traditional Soviet appraisals of the motives and behavior of the major imperialist powers illustrated the extent to which, to paraphrase Alfred G. Meyer, Soviet commentators on the international scene let Lenin do their thinking for them. The bourgeoisie, it was assumed, made the key political decisions; the state was little more than a front organization for Wall Street. As the major imperialist power, the United States' motives were easily understood: the capitalist ruling circles, animated by considerations of power and profit, were seeking to dominate the world and destroy socialism. And finally, Soviet assumptions about the transformation of the international system were

    6. Zbigniew Brzezinski, *Ideology and Power in Soviet Politics* (New York: Praeger, 1962), p. 105.

also reflective of doctrinal projections. Whereas western analysis has tended to assume that the natural condition of a multi-sovereign system is equilibrium, both doctrinal predispositions and experiences encouraged Soviet observers to expect violence, revolution, qualitative change, and disequilibrium. Because the revolution was inevitable, there was but a single outcome to the international "equation." Ultimately, the contemporary international system would be displaced by "international relations of a new type."

In the late 1950's and the 1960's, however, a significant transformation in Soviet perspectives on international relations took place.[7] By the end of Khrushchev's tenure, *states* had taken precedence over the *world systems* of capitalism and socialism as the main actors in the international arena. In part, the change reflected Soviet adjustment to the passing of rigid bipolarity and to fissiparous tendencies evident within the two camps. In addition, Soviet observers in the 1960's seemed to attach somewhat greater significance than previously to the role of institutions in the determination of actor capability.

Perhaps the most striking aspect of the transformation in Soviet perspectives pertained to the new depiction of the hierarchical structure of the modern international system, one which diverged fundamentally from conventional Bolshevik expectations about power relations. According to Soviet commentary, in the "new, third stage of capitalism's general crisis," it was no longer the case that the international system was a rigidly hierarchical order headed by a single dominant power. Now there were two leading states, the two superpowers, the United States and the Soviet Union. Their competition provided the framework within which, in the views of some Soviet observers, even small, formally independent states, although economically tied to imperialism and politically linked to the United States, need not always be considered dependent countries. In the last years of Khrushchev's rule, moreover, Soviet observers, responding to their accurate perception of the increased assertiveness of the second-level great powers in the two camps, began to evidence increasing concern over the danger of catalytic war, and thus to recognize that the question of war and peace was no longer solely a matter of relations between the leaders of the imperialist and socialist camps.

The main contradiction in the world, nevertheless, continued to consist of the relationship between the imperialist and socialist camps, and it was to this relationship that Soviet observers looked in analyzing the global distribution of power. Here an interesting progression occurred. Prior to 1959, the term of reference utilized in describing the balance of power was "distribution of power" (usually *sootnoshenie sil,* occasionally *rasstanovka sil*). In 1959, although formulations involving the generic phrase "distribution of power"

7. The summary of the evolution of Soviet perspectives in the Khrushchev and post-Khrushchev periods was drawn heavily from my *Soviet Perspectives on International Relations, 1956–1967* (Princeton: Princeton University Press, 1969), especially pp. 276–280.

prevailed quantitatively, formulations containing *pereves sil* (favorable balance or preponderance of power) also made their appearance. After late 1961, the focal term of reference became *ravnovesie sil* (equilibrium). This progression corresponded to changing Soviet appraisals of existing as well as ontological reality; that is, to changes in the Soviet perception of the distribution of power and in Soviet expectations of the imminence of revolutionary advance. These shifts in formulation had distinct limits. At the height of revolutionary optimism in 1958 – 60, Soviet observers continued to accord the United States world power status. In 1962 – 64, while acknowledging implicitly that a reversal in socialist fortunes had occurred, these same observers continued to insist on the Soviet Union's position as a world power, at the same time integrating this temporary reversal into their perception of the world historical process by elongating their time perspective.

The evolution of Soviet views about American foreign policy behavior was equally profound during the last years of Khrushchev's rule. The analysis of American capabilities was increasingly explicit and detailed. The depiction of the American decision-making process reflected a shift in focus from Wall Street to Washington and implied a belated recognition that the Keynesian revolution had indeed transformed the relationship between the political and economic systems in the capitalist world. It also revealed an awareness that the enhanced role of international relations in world events had greatly augmented the position of the state and especially the institution of the Presidency. The most dramatic change in Soviet perceptions was with respect to the characterization of the motives of the majority of the American ruling elite ("the realists"). Khrushchev himself professed to detect a "reappraisal of values" within the American ruling group and thus, in effect, asserted that the motives of American imperialism had changed. In the atomic age under conditions of mutual deterrence, security was considered the primary value of the dominant element within the American leadership. The United States, while doubtless the major adversary, was no longer to be regarded as the main enemy, largely because the realistic elements of her leadership could be expected to prevent the outbreak of general war.

Khrushchev's "prettification" of American imperialism — as the Chinese Communists described his reappraisal — was tied directly to his efforts to sustain a belief in the inevitability of revolution under atomic age conditions; to sustain, in other words, the expectation that the contemporary international system would in fact be transformed into a socialist "international relations of a new type." The dilemma posed by the constraints Soviet decision-makers considered operative in the atomic age — tersely summarized in July, 1963, by the observation that "the atomic bomb does not observe the class principle" — was as simple as it was intractable. In doctrinal terms, the dilemma constituted a challenge to the unity of theory and practice. How could the triumph of socialism be secured without general war? How could the creation of an "international relations of a new type" be accomplished while avoiding the violent destruction of the existing international system? Khrushchev's answer contemplated that Soviet missiles would deter the outbreak of general war and deprive imperialism of its capacity to impede artificially (through the "export of counter-revolution") processes taking place within states as a result of the disequilibrating tendencies inherent in a revolutionary epoch. The plausibility of such a vision, however, relied on the behavior of the decision-makers in the leading capitalist power, the United States, that is, on a contingency neither "objectively" determined by the "world historical process" nor sufficiently subject to the influence of *right-thinking* communists. Under nuclear age conditions, the unity of theory and practice was ruptured. Even accepting Soviet postulates, international relations could no longer be considered a closed system, a general theory with a predictable solution at a single point.

To proceed one step further, it was not only the inevitability of the desirable which was called into question by international developments in the 1960's. The Sino-Soviet conflict even produced open misgivings about the very desirability of a communist international system. In the words of one Soviet spokesman:

> The new world system of Socialist states is now in the making. Entirely new, previously unknown relations are being established between them, and these relations are a prototype of the relations soon to be established all over the world.... Will this be a truly fraternal alliance of the nations, completely free of hostility and mistrust, or a system of states still tainted with mistrust between peoples, without real fraternal mutual assistance and help for each other, a system with trends to isolation and autarchy?[8]

And with these misgivings, Soviet leaders began to regard the contemporary international system more favorably, as was most vividly evident in the aftermath of the Cuban missile crisis when Moscow declared:

> gone are the days when the working men rising in struggle against capitalism had indeed nothing to lose but their chains. Through selfless, heroic struggle, the masses have won immense material, political and cultural gains, gains that are embodied in the socialist world system. Tomorrow the whole world and the civilization created by their labor will belong to the working people.[9]

Developments in the years following Khrushchev's ouster were generally not as dramatic as those of the early 1960's. After 1965, Khrushchev's successors showed little enthusiasm for affirming the clearly revisionist statements to which Khrushchev and the specialists in the Academy of Sciences' Institute of World Economy and International Relations had given voice. Khrushchev's successors, for multiple reasons, did not repudiate the slogan, "workers of the world unite, you have nothing to lose but your chains." While in 1963 – 64 the

8. V. G. Korionov, "Proletarian Internationalism — Our Victorious Weapon," *International Affairs* (Moscow), No. 8 (August, 1963), p. 13
9. See "The Policy of Peaceful Coexistence Proves Its Worth," *World Marxist Review*, No. 12 (December, 1962), p. 6.

Clausewitzian dictum that war is the continuation of politics by other means was increasingly subject to criticism in the Soviet Union, it was generally rendered token obeisance in the years immediately following Khrushchev's ouster. Indeed, Khrushchevian doctrine that peaceful coexistence was the general line of Soviet foreign policy was abandoned.

Nevertheless, despite the fact that Khrushchev's successors were markedly less prone than he to engage in explicit doctrinal innovation, the trend of Soviet analysis of the structure of the international system, their projections for the future development of the international system, and even of American foreign policy, followed the pattern of the last years of the Khrushchev era. That direction had been toward a closer approximation of reality — or to western perceptions of reality — and to an evident cynicism with respect to a future communist international order. The emphasis in post-Khrushchevian commentary has been on the state and the state system. Increasingly, there has been a tendency to dissociate the world historical process from analyses of world politics. It has recently been asserted that "Ultimate victory on a world scale belongs to Socialism as the most progressive social system. . . . The operative word is *ultimate*. Meanwhile it is the ups and downs of the struggle that in the main constitute the content of international affairs."[10]

In analogous fashion, the changes in the Soviet depiction of the global hierarchy are largely explained by the capacity of Soviet observers to react to changes in the international order. In Soviet commentary the gap between the superpowers and other great powers narrowed, and the border separating the lesser-ranked great powers and the "major independents" became more ill-defined. Khrushchevian claims about the global distribution of power were consciously reduced while his calculation of the situational aspects of power was retained. Even post-Khrushchevian commentary on American foreign policy, which after the American bombing of North Vietnam moved away from Khrushchev's benign assumption that the "realists" constituted a majority within the American ruling group, could be said to constitute a step toward a more realistic appraisal of American actions. Certainly, post-Khrushchevian utterances about the rate of historical development were more realistic. Khrushchev had spoken of the full-scale building of communism and in 1960 – 61 had held high expectations for major revolutionary advances in the 1960's and 1970's. His successors, in contrast, consoled themselves that "Marxist-Leninists" had no "grounds for regretting the tempo of the development of the revolutionary processes in the world" by pointing to the time required to displace feudalism with capitalism:

The replacement of feudalism by capitalism occupied an epoch which embraced several centuries. . . . *In comparison with this replacement* [italics added], the replace-

10. S. L. Sanakogev, "The World Socialist System and the Future of Mankind," *International Affairs* (Moscow), No. 10 (October, 1960), p. 62.

ment of capitalism is taking place at a significantly more rapid tempo, spreading simultaneously over an immeasurably larger zone.[11]

In a sense, post-Khrushchevian commentary has retained the belief that ours is a revolutionary epoch while simultaneously postponing the time when the "international relations of a new type" would be created so far into the future as to be of little operative significance for Soviet foreign policy at the onset of the 1970's.

All things considered, there has been a marked tendency for Soviet perspectives to converge with western analysis. Western analysis traditionally has tended to underplay the internal elements affecting the foreign policy of the main actors in the international system; the early Soviet view gave inadequate weight to national interests *per se* and obfuscated the existential realm of international relations and the allegedly ontological realm of the world historical process. Both traditional appraisals postulated a single solution to the international relations equation: generalizing from one historically limited vantage point, the western solution postulated equilibrium; operating from an entirely different vantage point, the Bolsheviks expected disequilibrium. At the onset of the 1970's, neither western nor Soviet observers consider international relations a closed system. Instead, both maintain open-ended perspectives on the process of world politics — even though one might be more disposed to view equilibrium, and the other disequilibrium, as the norm. Western and Soviet perspectives on the basic structure of the modern international system are essentially similar. Soviet analysis of the internal politics of American foreign policy seems to accept basic western assumptions pertaining to the locus of decision-making within a capitalist state. Soviet commentary reveals, moreover, the same preoccupation with the political significance of technology — especially weapons technology — generally found among western analysts and an analogous attention to the constraints imposed on the behavior of states in the atomic age.

3.

It seems evident that much of the importance attached to ideology in explaining Soviet foreign policy has been misplaced. Ideology continues to serve as the language of politics — "proletarian internationalism" masks and legitimates Soviet imperial politics as surely as "law and order" masks and legitimates the repression of American blacks. To a considerable extent it remains the language of analysis, although there was a growing tendency in the 1960's for specialists to adopt the vocabulary and tools of their western counter-

---

11. M. Marinin, "Sotsialisticheskii internationalizm; politika voinstvuiushchego imperializma," *Mirovaia ekonomika i mezhdunarodnye otnosheniia,* No. 6 (June, 1966), p. 16.

parts.[12] Significantly, however, ideology has neither hindered nor enhanced the general Soviet appraisal of international relations. Aside from the Soviet assessment of relations among communist states, the maintenance of *elan* domestically through the retention of doctrinal purity internationally has been consistently sacrificed to the aspiration to pursue foreign policy goals rationally and efficiently. In the atomic age international relations have had a salience for Soviet "high priests" which has confounded the predictions of those who assumed that international relations would be the last doctrinal redoubt.

Consequently, it seems equally clear that the traditional rationale for the attention accorded to the internal origins of Soviet foreign policy can no longer be considered tenable. Indeed, one can go further and assert that in principle one ought to accord as much weight to international system-level explanations of Soviet foreign policy as one would in the case of any other state. A model of Soviet foreign policy which takes into account the impact of the international system only in the sense that it pays attention to Moscow's likely tactical policy changes in response to alterations in the global power configuration is analytically incomplete. It ignores the extent to which changes in the international environment alter elite attitudes and affect the goals and purposes for which decision-makers exercise power. The Soviet Union has proved more penetrable than conventional wisdom supposed. Changes in the international environment and in the USSR's role and status in the international system, by producing changes in Soviet perspectives, have altered Soviet foreign policy behavior. A reactive approach will presumably provide a better framework for understanding Soviet behavior in the 1970's precisely because of international system-generated changes in Soviet perspectives, with their attendant changes in Soviet goals. Attention to the international system has the distinct advantage that it calls attention to an important if obvious point, namely, that what other actors do (especially the United States) affects Soviet foreign policy, both directly and indirectly. Moscow *qua* unitary rational decision-maker does react; more than this, the context of policy debates in the conflict-ridden, oligarchic Kremlin is altered by American actions.

The difficulty with all this is that an international system-level explanation, while essential for an understanding of the major reorientation in Soviet thinking in the post-Stalin period, provides little in the way of guidance for the prediction of day-to-day state behavior. While calling attention to the interactive nature of nation-state behavior, it provides no criteria for anticipating *what kind* of reaction will be forthcoming from *which persons* in Moscow under *what circumstances*, and no standards for estimating which responses within

---

12. The emergence of international relations as a discipline in the Soviet Union is treated in Zimmerman, *op. cit.,* pp. 27–74. For an extensive discussion of problems of theory in international relations, see "Problemy teorii mezhdunarodnykh otnoshenii," in *Mirovaia ekonomika i mezhdunarodnye otnosheniia,* No. 9 (September, 1969), pp. 88–106.

a broad range of options are most and least probable under specified conditions. Nor does it take into account the fact that organizational behavior everywhere is frequently such that policies are continued in blithe disregard of a changing milieu.

Hence we have come full circle, back *inter alia* to the cognitive and affective maps of particular decision-makers — but at a greater level of specificity than in the summary of Soviet assessments presented in this essay, and within a general framework which stresses the impact of external factors on Soviet behavior. Rather than describe what in the 1960's has been the dominant strand in Soviet commentary, one is directed *(a)* to an analysis of differences in Soviet perspectives, and *(b)* to a search for propositions which relate external and internal variables to the perspectives and perceptions of the decision-makers. Here one is no longer concerned with how communists or even Soviet communists think, but with how which Soviet policy-maker with what career background occupying which political role assesses the international system and the actors in that system.

The evidence of the past decade amply demonstrates that, the general re-orientation in Soviet perspectives notwithstanding, there are divergent assessments of considerable policy relevance. Such divergences often seem only to concern nuances in interpretation. Yet even a dispute over what seems a nuance, for example, the difference between those who affirm that the global distribution of power *has shifted* and those who assert that it is shifting in favor of socialism, may portend crucially divergent policy choices. At other times there is no question that divergent assessments have immense policy consequences. Witness the consequences of asserting that: *(a)* there can be "no more dangerous illusion" than to believe that nuclear war can be an instrument of foreign policy (General Nikolai Talenskii, May, 1965), as opposed to *(b)* it is "mistaken and even harmful" to assert there can be no victors in a "world nuclear-rocket conflict" (Colonel I. Grudinin, July, 1966).

Unfortunately, while students of Soviet foreign policy have become reasonably aware of ongoing divergences in perspective within the Politburo and among various sub-elites, we are only in the initial stages of developing propositions which account for the differences detected. A few points have become clear. In international affairs as elsewhere, the reacquisition of old attitudes requires appreciably less information inflow than does the reinforcement of new insights. Thus there is a strong propensity among Soviet policy-makers to grasp at the belief that it is somehow possible (perhaps by general and complete disarmament, perhaps by an effective anti-ballistic missile) to eliminate the mutual vulnerability characteristic of the atomic age. Those persons directly involved professionally with international affairs seem to be among those who sense most keenly the imperatives of the atomic age, while among the least inclined to accept these imperatives are those whose status and influence are threatened by new and less doctrinaire modes of thought.

These few points of enlightenment show that much remains to be done. Only the slightest beginnings have been made with respect to several basic issues. With regard to Soviet perceptions of western signals, it is now presumably accepted that some western actions will be "read" in Moscow as evidence of an accommodating temper rather than as a sign of political weakness or as a Machiavellian maneuver. When this "proper reading" is most likely to occur is far less well established. No considerable literature exists which attempts to clarify the impact of recruitment patterns on Soviet foreign policy. How do past career experiences color the perspectives of Politburo members? In particular, does the Komsomol-secret police route to the Politburo encourage a more hostile assessment of the outside world than that adopted by persons with other career progressions?[13] Does it matter, for instance, whether the Central Committee and Politburo are made up predominantly of persons whose first major political appointment came during the years 1936 – 1940 as a direct result of the Great Purge rather than in the period 1941 – 45, when to identify with the Party was to identify with the nation?

It is to questions such as these that Soviet specialists will have to address themselves if we are to anticipate Soviet behavior with reasonable accuracy. The Soviet Union is no longer a purposeful political system ruled by leaders sharing an outlook on international events which the label "Bolshevik" aptly describes. It is precisely because it is now so difficult to anticipate Soviet leaders' thinking without an examination of the specific international context, the roles of particular individuals and institutions in the Soviet system, and the recruitment patterns which particular occupants of leadership positions may have experienced, that the empirical investigation of contemporary Soviet assessments of the international scene matters so much in our efforts to explain Soviet foreign policy.

13. For a provocative essay suggesting that this may not be the case, see Jerry F. Hough, "Ideology and Ideological Secretaries as a Source of Change in the Soviet Union," a paper delivered at the Mid-West Association for the Advancement of Slavic Studies, April 11, 1969, at Lincoln, Nebraska.

PART II

Domestic Politics and the Formation of Soviet Foreign Policy

This is the first of two sections on domestic or internal influences on Soviet foreign policy. The present section is devoted to internal influences from "the operational environment"; the next section analyzes domestic inputs from "the psychological environment" (see the conceptual framework page 8 above). At the outset, it must be emphasized that one cannot discuss the impact of "domestic politics" on "Soviet foreign policy" without first stipulating which internal factors and which aspects of Soviet international behavior one is talking about. Some domestic influences have greatly affected major Soviet foreign policy decisions, while other domestic factors have had little or no discernible effect on the same decisions. *Which* factors have *what kind of* influence under *what* conditions during *which* time periods are empirical questions, albeit difficult ones. Informed observers, in efforts to identify and confirm these relationships, can and do differ. But one cannot meaningfully analyze "the" influence of domestic politics on international behavior.

In an important anthology, *Domestic Sources of Foreign Policy,* a central premise and basic dilemma are clearly stated. "The premise is that domestic sources of foreign policy are no less crucial to its content and conduct than are the international situations toward which it is directed. The dilemma is that the links between the domestic sources and the resulting behavior — foreign policy — are not easily observed and are thus especially resistant to coherent analysis."[1] In the Soviet context, this dilemma is particularly acute. One has no a priori reason to reject the central premise, but verification of the presumed relationships has relied heavily on informed speculation and generalization from one or two cases. The conceptualization and measurement of "influence" are particularly intractable problems. For example, it is exceedingly difficult to ascertain the calculations of Soviet leaders and the information they have at their disposal when they make their decisions. And it is equally difficult to determine which factors are decisive in their final selections (or compromises) among perceived alternatives. The analyst's sources of information are almost always limited to a handful of written documents, from which inferences must be made with utmost care and sophistication.

Professor Dallin, in his essay below, suggests five sets of domestic factors that may influence Soviet foreign policy behavior. Particularly important is his emphasis on the changing nature of the Soviet political system. In the course of the past fifty years, the structure and functions of the Communist Party have undergone significant transitions. This suggests that domestic sources of foreign policy — and their relative importance in different situations — have also undergone major changes.[2] For example, since 1956 there has been a dramatic increase in the quantity and quality of Soviet research on international affairs. This is perhaps especially true of research on the United States and on the developing countries, which "are being increasingly studied within the context of their own specific requirements and possibilities rather than according to preconceived dogmatic theories."[3] Whether this fresh information is being used in the formulation and implementation of policy is a very difficult empirical question. But the fact remains that large quantities of accurate information are now available to Soviet decision-makers — information of the kind that was simply not available prior to 1956. Good scientific and social science research institutes are not automatically major "domestic" influences on Soviet foreign policy, but they are surely very important potential factors in most policy areas.

The identification of potentially significant influences on Soviet foreign policy does not constitute verification of their actual impact under different conditions. Nor does identification of variables that may be related to one another warrant undocumented assertions about the nature of these relation-

1. James Rosenau, "Introduction," in James Rosenau (ed.), *Domestic Sources of Foreign Policy* (New York: Free Press, 1967), p. 2. See also Henry Kissinger, "Domestic Structure and Foreign Policy," in James Rosenau (ed.), *International Politics and Foreign Policy* (New York: Free Press, 1969), pp. 261 – 275.
2. See Edward Morse, "The Transformation of Foreign Policies: Modernization, Interdependence, and Externalization," *World Politics,* XXII, 3 (April, 1970), pp. 371 – 392.
3. Elizabeth Valkenier, "Recent Trends in Soviet Research on the Developing Countries," *World Politics*, XX, 4 (July, 1968), p. 659. See also William Zimmerman, *Soviet Perspectives on International Relations, 1956 – 1967* (Princeton: Princeton University Press, 1969), especially pp.

ships. The formulation and testing of unconfirmed empirical generalizations (hypotheses) are highly desirable, but one must very carefully distinguish among generalizations that are well confirmed, partially confirmed, or not at all confirmed by the data available.

The article by Professor Ploss focuses on the relationships between domestic and foreign policy in the post-Stalin era. His central hypothesis is that Soviet international behavior is significantly influenced by "domestic politics in the form of bureaucratic group struggle over functions and funds." In another context, a respected student of American politics concludes that "interest group influence on foreign policy is slight."[4] Professors Armstrong and Pipes[5] would perhaps agree that this is also true in the Soviet Union. Professors Dallin and Linden,[6] on the other hand, would probably argue that certain institutional and nonassociational groups in Soviet society have vested interests in different foreign policies, and that some of these groups significantly influence the formulation of policy alternatives and actual decisions. Professor Aspaturian emphasizes that Soviet behavior in this respect is very similar to that of all nations. "Foreign policy, including external defense, is more a function of preserving the social order and the interests of its dominant groups than of the state or the national interests in the abstract . . . [and] functions more to serve tangible internal interests than intangible or abstract ideological interests abroad."[7] For example, the Russian military heavy-industrial "complex" in fact and/or in rhetoric favors an aggressive foreign policy. Other coalitions of interests clearly favor a less militant posture and less defense spending.[8]

The analysis of "Interest Group" and "Political Structure" influences (see the conceptual model above) on Soviet foreign policy is hazardous for both empirical and conceptual reasons. Not only is "influence" exceedingly difficult to measure, but Soviet specialists simply do not agree on what constitutes an "interest group."[9] Therefore, one must very carefully examine the way that this concept is used before evaluating the descriptive accuracy or explanatory power of propositions employing the concept.

Professor Armstrong suggests that one aspect of domestic politics — the

4. Lester Milbrath, "Interest Groups and Foreign Policy," in Rosenau (ed.), *Domestic Sources of Foreign Policy,* p. 251.

5. See the chapter by John Armstrong below. Also Richard Pipes, "Domestic Politics and Foreign Affairs," in Ivo Lederer (ed.), *Russian Foreign Policy: Essays in Historical Perspective* (New Haven: Yale University Press, 1962), pp.145 – 169.

6. See the chapter by Alexander Dallin below. Also Carl Linden, *Khrushchev and the Soviet Leadership, 1957 – 1964* (Baltimore: The Johns Hopkins Press, 1966).

7. Vernon Aspaturian, "Internal Politics and Foreign Policy in the Soviet System," in R. Barry Farrell (ed.), *Approaches to Comparative and International Politics* (Evanston, Ill.: Northwestern University Press, 1966), p. 230. Also see Linden, *op. cit.*

8. See Linden, *op. cit.*; and Aspaturian, *op. cit.*, especially pp. 256 – 287.

9. See Philip Stewart, "Soviet Interest Groups and the Policy Process," *World Politics,* XXII, 1 (October, 1969), pp. 29 – 50.

competition for power among political leaders — is generally the most important factor influencing Soviet international behavior, and that foreign policy issues tend to be manipulated not in the interests of the USSR as a whole, or even of congeries of interests, but primarily to the personal benefit of individual Politburo members and cliques. Professor Pendill, in his article below, challenges this view. On at least one major issue (Soviet policy toward the Third World) resolved during an intense power struggle (1953 – 1956), he finds far-reaching decisions that may have been "truly collective" or "bipartisan." Careful investigation reveals little evidence that this issue was used as a "pawn" in personal rivalry for power and position.

There is probably more agreement among scholars that group influence on foreign policy varies with the *issue*.[10] Ploss and Linden emphasize that genuine policy choices are always present, and that since Stalin's death the power and prestige of Soviet leaders are dependent on the success of their policies, domestic and foreign. Perhaps this was more true of Khrushchev than of the present leadership. However, high Party officials, individually and collectively, often appeal to bureaucratic institutions and groups for political support and technical expertise in the constant competition over policy alternatives and resource allocation. Thus, institutional and nonassociational interests can and do exert considerable influence on *some* policy issues — generally and in single instances.

Furthermore, political leaders who hold certain views on foreign policy often hold distinct sets of views on domestic policy. There may not be any apparent logical connection between the two (for example, Barry Goldwater's simultaneous call for a weak Federal Government and an aggressive foreign policy), but political attitudes do cluster. As Linden persuasively argues, competing Soviet views on domestic and foreign policy also tend to cluster:

> The antagonism in the post-Stalin period between those leaning toward orthodoxy
> and conservatism, on the one hand, and those disposed to reform and innovation,
> on the other, can be roughly defined in terms of an internal versus an external
> orientation in policy. The more orthodox emphasize the necessities of the world
> struggle and the dangers from the outside enemy. Those inclined toward reform
> stress internal problems, the prospects for a relatively stable international environ
> ment, and the possibilities of developing less dangerous forms of struggle with the
> adversary abroad. In domestic policy the orthodox stress the ideological function of
> the party, doctrinal continuity, the need for limits on de-Stalinization, maintenance
> of centralized control of the economy, close supervision of the intelligentsia, and a
> heavy industry-defense weighted resource allocation policy. The reformers, by com
> parison, lean toward innovation in theory and practice, pragmatic solutions to
> economic problems, greater reliance on material rewards than on ideological stimuli,
> more local initiative and less centralization, and concessions to the consumer.[11]

10. See Milbrath in Rosenau (ed.), *Domestic Sources of Foreign Policy,* p. 248.
11. Linden, *op. cit.,* pp. 18 – 19.

How these attitudes and interests affect Soviet policy in different "issue areas" is the key question. Professor Rosenau hypothesizes that "The more an issue encompasses a society's resources and relationships, the more will it be drawn into the society's domestic political system and the less will it be processed through the society's foreign political system."[12] But this hypothesis and others have not been and perhaps cannot be rigorously tested in the Soviet context. For the time being, at least, conceptual confusion and inadequate evidence place a premium on insightful, informed speculation and on cautious inferences from available data. There is little general theory about the relationships between domestic and foreign policies, and even data on American politics are sometimes difficult to muster.[13] In the study of Soviet foreign policy, these problems are compounded.

12. James Rosenau, "Foreign Policy as an Issue-Area," in Rosenau (ed.), *Domestic Sources of Foreign Policy,* p. 49.
13. For an important study of pressure groups, public opinion, and foreign policy-making in the United States, see Raymond Bauer, Ithiel Pool, and Lewis Dexter, *American Business ana Public Policy: The Politics of Foreign Trade* (New York: Atherton, 1963).

Soviet Foreign Policy
and Domestic Politics:
A Framework for Analysis*

Soviet foreign policy has usually been analyzed in terms of the leaders' objectives, their perceptions and initiatives in the outer environment of world politics, and their responses to developments abroad. Far less attention has been paid to another complex of variables which shapes Soviet policy — those internal to the USSR. These include not only resources and strategic capabilities but also intangible elements such as national style and tradition, elite conflicts, and a variety of domestic pressures exerted, directly or indirectly, on Soviet decision-makers. While it would be an oversimplification to think of Soviet foreign policy as purely and simply a dependent variable of domestic inputs, such an approach might well be a lesser error than to assume (as was generally done in the Stalin era and is often still an operative assumption) that Soviet leaders are immune to various constraints, diverse opinions, and political pressures arising out of their own polity and society.[1]

*Copyright by the Board of Editors of the *Journal of International Affairs,* reprinted from Volume XXIII, Number 2, pages 250–265, 1969. Permission to reprint is gratefully acknowledged to the Editors of the *Journal* and the author.

1. Of those who have dealt explicitly with this problem, John Armstrong has tended to write off domestic social and political constraints on Soviet foreign policy (e.g., in his "The Domestic Roots of Soviet Foreign Policy," *International Affairs* (London), January 1965, pp. 37–47), as has Richard Pipes (e.g., in his contribution to Ivo Lederer, ed., *Russian Foreign Policy* [Yale University Press, 1962]). Robert M. Slusser (e.g., in his paper in Peter Juviler and Henry Morton, eds., *Soviet Policy-Making* [Praeger, 1966] concentrates heavily on "Kremlinological" aspects, of

This essay explores some aspects of the interaction between Soviet domestic political processes and foreign policy. It is not concerned with the impact of "objective" factors such as geography and natural resources, nor does it seek to probe the reverse phenomenon — the effect of external forces (real, imagined, or contrived) — on Soviet internal development. This process has been more satisfactorily identified and illustrated, as in the Soviet manipulation of the image of the "enemy," and in the assumptions underlying Western thinking about the Soviet Union that fomented the "containment" policy.

1.

American scholarship has in recent years seen various attempts to bring foreign policy studies into the ambit of contemporary political science. Some studies have focused on decision-making; others have probed the "linkages" of domestic and foreign policies by means of original and imaginative constructs. However, little effort has been made thus far to test the applicability of such concepts to Soviet politics.[2] Similarly, attempts have only just begun to look upon general hypotheses about modernization as providing relevant categories and insights for an understanding of communist systems as well as those of the "underdeveloped" states. It is from the literature of development that we adapt the following hypothetical trends for our point of departure.

(1) All developing systems tend to bring an increasing part of the population into (passive or active) political participation.

(2) Such systems eventually tend to produce integration at the level of the nation-state, at the expense of both parochial and internationalist preoccupations.

(3) Over time, developing systems tend to focus priority of attention, resources, and operationally relevant objectives on the domestic, rather than foreign, arena.[3]

While we would assert that all three of these dynamic tendencies can be identified in the Soviet case, too, there are also countervailing forces at work due to the inherent structure or systemic characteristics of totalitarianism. Among these, two are particularly noteworthy:

---

varying or uncertain degrees of verifiability. Two approaches closer to the assumptions implicit in the present essay are Sidney Ploss, "Studying the Domestic Determinants of Soviet Foreign Policy," *Canadian Slavic Studies,* I, no. 1 (spring, 1967); and, at greater length, Vernon V. Aspaturian, "Internal Politics and Foreign Policy in the Soviet System," in R. Barry Farrell, ed., *Approaches to Comparative and International Politics* [Northwestern University Press, 1966], pp. 212 – 87.

2. Two exceptions are Jon D. Glassman, "Soviet Foreign Policy Decision-Making," *Columbia Essays in International Affairs,* III (Columbia University Press, 1968); and David Finley, unpublished doctoral dissertation, Stanford University (1966).

3. See, for instance, Karl W. Deutsch, "Social Mobilization and Political Development," *American Political Science Review,* September 1961, pp. 497 – 500.

(4) Of all sectors of public policy, foreign affairs are least susceptible to direct involvement by broader strata of the population and to verification of official pronouncements. They inevitably require, in Communist as in other polities, greater reliance on authoritative institutions.[4]

(5) Of all political systems, the totalitarian is best able to override, delay, or distort the typical tendencies of modernizing systems to bring about certain changes in political development. It does so, for instance, by reducing participation to ritualistic ratification and explication, and by seeking to limit pluralism and the delegation of decision-making to functional-instrumental, rather than to political problem-areas.

We face in the Soviet experience, therefore, contradictory trends. It is our contention here that the specific weight of these and other relevant elements has tended to change over time, and that the dynamics of change tend to follow a plausible and intelligible pattern. This does not imply a deterministic perspective: we merely contend that Soviet development can be usefully examined in relation to an ideal type and that deviations from it are susceptible to rational explanation by identifying intervening variables responsible for such departures from it.

At the risk of oversimplification, these relevant political variables may be categorized according to the following schema.

(1) "Unwitting" elements, such as continuities in political cultures and projections of domestic experience and categories of perception onto the international arena.

An example of the former (as E. H. Carr has pointed out) is the Russian tradition of strong central authority in the state. The latter is illustrated by the prevalence of hierarchical relations between superiors and subordinates within the Party and state bureaucracy, making Soviet officials relatively unprepared to deal as coequals with representatives of other sovereign units in international intercourse. On the other hand, such features are of varying persistence: the assumption of the unilinear parallelism of revolutions, axiomatic in the early years of the Soviet regime (and still pronounced in Chinese analyses) appears to have lost much of its erstwhile policy relevance.[5]

(2) Perceptions and assumptions of the policy-makers regarding popular attitudes and, in particular, the existence or absence of either diffuse or specific support at home.

This aspect of the leadership's decision-making calculus has generally been

4. See, e.g., Leonard Schapiro, "Has Russia Changed?" *Foreign Affairs*, April 1960, p. 399.

5. A striking example in a related area is the projection by the Chinese communist leadership of its guerilla warfare strategy of having "the countryside surround the cities" to the international scene in formulating the general strategy for the struggle of the underdeveloped against the industrial countries. Western observers (Tang Tsou and Morton Halperin) detected and predicted such an approach even before Lin Piao expressed it as explicit policy. *American Political Science Review*, Volume LIX (March 1965), pp. 80-99.

ignored, perhaps because we have no certain knowledge of the assessments made by Soviet authorities. Still, there are some indirect indicators that may be resorted to: other estimates may be inferred or, frankly, guessed. Relevant dimensions include (a) the expected stress to which loyalty and compliance would be subjected under crisis conditions — what might be called the assumed support/alienation quotient of various social groups — such as behavior in case of war; and (b) reaction to particular foreign policy moves — what V. O. Key referred to as the decision-makers' anticipation of "contingent opinion"[6] — such as the probable response to an armed conflict with China.

(3) Elite cleavages and policy conflicts relevant to foreign affairs. This element includes *(a)* policy disputes and differences directly related to foreign policy and typically expressed either in bureaucractic politics or in esoteric debate; *(b)* policy conflicts focusing primarily on other areas but with inevitable implications for foreign relations; and *(c)* cleavages in the elite due primarily to power struggles, factionalism, and personality conflicts.

The Soviet record suggests that — at least until quite recently — policy and power conflicts have tended to overlap quite extensively. Thus the Stalin-Trotsky duel in the 1920's, the Malenkov-Zhdanov struggle in 1946 – 48, and the Khrushchev-Molotov fight in 1955, each involved all these facets: conflicts over domestic and foreign policies, differences in ideological formulations, and the struggle for power. Indeed, communist labels, such as "revisionism," "dogmatism," and the "general line," typically refer to syndromes comprising all these dimensions, though their relative prominence may vary from case to case. An unpublicized foreign policy debate, for example, preceded the shift from the "anti-Versailles" orientation which prevailed in the 1920's to the anti-Nazi alignment sought in 1934; another example is the split over the inevitability of a new "two-camp" polarization between the communist and capitalist systems in 1945 – 46 (as reported by Maxim Litvinov); a third, the debate over the desirability (and possibility) of a relaxation of tensions with the West, in the post-Stalin years. Among the many political conflicts with significant implications for foreign policy but dealing first of all with other matters, the most continuous and contested is the fight over resource allocation, the national budget, and investment policy. Under conditions of resource scarcity in a centralized command economy, decisions regarding procurement of weapons systems, foreign economic assistance, space programs, massive investment in chemical fertilizer production, or significant expansion of housing construction or consumer goods are all bound to have reciprocal consequences for foreign affairs.

Another useful way of distinguishing among policy conflicts is suggested by the labels employed by Robert Levine[7] and others, separating "systemic"

---

6. V. O. Key, *Public Opinion and American Democracy* (Knopf, 1961), p. 13.
7. Robert Levine, *The Arms Race* (Harvard University Press, 1963), pp. 28 – 29, 46ff.

from "marginalist" differences. While the former relate to fundamental differences over policy objectives, the latter describe conflicts over alternative ways of achieving shared goals. Methodologically, this distinction raises special difficulties in the Soviet case. Not only is overt dissent over foreign policy even less permissible than public differences on internal affairs, but even when couched in indirect, esoteric argument, systemic differences — to be voiced at all — must be cloaked in "marginalist" terms. It follows that technical differences in judgment regarding the relative cost, desirability, or effectiveness of particular tactics may (or may not) conceal more profound differences over policy objectives. This is also true of Soviet debates over strategic posture, in which (much as in the United States) differences over technical matters often conceal fundamentally divergent assumptions regarding the prospects of international war and peace.

(4) Attempts by individuals and groups outside the circle of policy-makers to make themselves heard or to be consulted before basic decisions are made. There was virtually none of this in the Stalin era, but the proliferation of such efforts in recent years constitutes one of the most intriguing developments in Soviet foreign as well as domestic affairs. Here one should differentiate between those officially consulted as experts — such as military men, academic specialists on foreign areas, and scientists — and those who volunteer their advice and opinion.

This element includes, in particular, the Soviet equivalent of interest groups as well as the initiative of personalities of high public visibility (such as prominent scientists, novelists, and poets) to make known their views. The most significant among the groups involved, for our purposes, are the military and the creative intelligentsia; but it should be borne in mind that such groups are themselves by no means homogeneous in political orientation. Possibly others have similarly begun to exert influence on foreign policy decisions, largely through personal and informal access to policy-makers and their staff. Finally, in the most recent period there have been instances of incipient opinion groups, cutting across occupational and generational lines, taking the initiative to submit petitions or protests on a wide range of issues, from miscarriages of justice to the Soviet intervention in Czechoslovakia.

(5) The broadening base of participation may, in theory, extend to public opinion — at least to the general mass of the "politically relevant" (or, to use Gabriel Almond's phrase, the "attentive public"), who constitute a growing share of the population. If the crystallization of interest groups is still at an early and informal stage, the vocal articulation of independent public opinion has never been and still is not sufficient to inhibit Soviet decision-makers.

The impact of these five categories has been quite uneven and unequal. Among the significant trends has been not only a slow widening of the circle of those consulted, but also increasing intercommunication and interaction among diverse elements, both within the same category and among different categories. This tendency was perhaps most visible in the Khrushchev days, illustrated by the informal alliances of certain civilian and military leaders against other civilian and military leaders over divergent approaches to both domestic and foreign affairs;[8] and in the occasional efforts of authority figures to secure the tacit support of particular interest groups.

To point to these tendencies — some of them, still quite fragile — is not to deny that the power to make final decisions remains normally in the hands of a very few nor that, for instance, during crises abroad (such as the Cuban Missile Crisis of October 1962) the leadership can in effect ignore "outside" opinion and function with only a minimum of concern for its subsequent accountability to formally responsible institutions such as the Party Central Committee and the less influential Supreme Soviet of the USSR.

2.

One perspective on the interactions of these influences on the elite's decision-making evolves from considering the changing focus of Soviet foreign policy during the "modernizing" phase of Soviet domestic development. Throughout this period and until the fifties, Soviet foreign policy required far-reaching adaptation, repeated postponement of goals, and painful compromises with reality. During the early years the Soviet leaders — after wars and revolutions, famines and revolts — were compelled to operate from a perception of their domestic "front" as imposing severe constraints in their pursuit of desired objectives. If some leaders were inclined to dismiss these constraints, the virtually simultaneous shift in early 1921 from the militancy of War Communism to the New Economic Policy at home and to its equivalent of "coexistence" abroad signaled the recognition of such weakness. Along with economic and military factors the sociopolitical fabric of Soviet society was a major source of this perceived inferiority to the outside world.

Indeed, throughout the interwar period Soviet policy generally avoided foreign adventures and involvement in violent conflict abroad. More than once the response of the Soviet regime to potential foreign threats was one of reluctant accommodation, retrenchment, and even appeasement — from the Treaties of Brest-Litovsk (1918) and Riga (1920) to the Litvinov Protocol and the effort to propitiate Japan in 1931 – 32. This policy was especially evident during the phases of intense socio-economic transformations "from above," such as the First Five-Year Plan, collectivization of agriculture, and the Great Purge. The reluctant alliance with France and Czechoslovakia in 1934 – 35 responded to a similar defensiveness born of a quest for time in which to improve the relative power position of the Soviet state.[9] In every instance the

8. See Thomas W. Wolfe, *Soviet Strategy at the Crossroads* (Harvard University Press, 1964); Roman Kolkowicz, *The Soviet Military and the Communist Party* (Princeton University Press, 1967); Carl Linden, *Khrushchev and the Soviet Leadership* (Johns Hopkins Press, 1966).
9. It is well to note, however, that perceived weakness need not always produce a conciliatory

desire to gain time was both pragmatically rational and ideologically rooted in the belief that the "correlation of forces" would necessarily change in the Soviet Union's favor as its enemies were bound to encounter greater "contradictions" while its own power and cohesion were bound to grow.

This policy of relative caution and diplomatic and military restraint reflected among other things a fear of dubious or divided loyalties at home, especially on the part of certain social and ethnic strata. Among these were the "bourgeois" specialists — such as engineers, officers, and intellectuals needed by the regime; the millions of kulaks; later, during World War II, entire nationalities, such as the Volga Germans, Crimean Tatars, Kalmyks, Balkars, and Ingush; and, after 1948, Soviet Jews. These — and others — were deemed politically suspect, whether these assumptions on the part of the leadership were in fact justified or not.[10]

Actually Soviet policy toward such groups tended to undermine the accommodation of their members to the status quo. In effect, "integration from above" (or the forcible removal of such groups) at least temporarily weakened the system still more by generating social and individual destabilization — most dramatically illustrated by the effects of the Great Purge.

Gradually, however, these sources of inherited and man-made weakness of the system vanished. Some of the old "hostile" classes died out; others were effectively absorbed and assimilated; and a general changeover of generations tended to lessen the strains of diffuse hostility. Some of the groups involved (for example, the kulaks) and some of the disruption occasioned by their removal or liquidation (for example, the purge of the Old Bolsheviks) were by definition nonrepetitive. True, alienating effects reverberated for some time after the victimization of the different groups themselves (as became apparent in 1939–41), but it remains an open question to what extent Stalin was cognizant of these sources of socio-political stress among his subjects or perceived them as constraints on the making of policy.

Moreover, with the passage of time the Soviet system began to acquire greater popular legitimacy and support as a result of many different processes. One was its very survival and the concomitant accommodation of a citizenry impressed by the absence of viable alternatives to it and the gradual effects of sustained political socialization. Another was the support given the regime by those who found personal success, recognition, or fulfillment within the system. The partial solidarity between state and society born of the shared challenge of foreign invasion and brutality bred legitimacy and a sense of national identification nurtured by the common experience of a victorious war which also saw a revival of national patriotic symbols. The seeming validation of

mood in Moscow; nor does a willingness to seek a detente or compromise need to stem from weakness alone.

10. These perceptions are the obverse of Soviet efforts to exploit irredentist sentiments in neighboring areas, e.g., in Moldavia, Karelia, Azerbaidzhan, or Sinkiang ("Eastern Turkestan").

ideological tenets by the course of history, highlighted by communist victories in and after World War II, and including the establishment of a communist "world system" in Eastern Europe and the Far East were significant elements.

Thus, by the 1950's, the earlier sources of widespread popular disloyalty — objectively as well as those perceived by the Soviet leadership — had vanished, particularly after Stalin's death. Yet, ironically, the Soviet system itself, by the logic of its development, had simultaneously begun to manufacture new constraints and sources of dissent as essentially unintended consequences of successful modernization. Creeping pluralism invades totalitarian life as it must invade all developing politics. The growing complexity of society and economy are bound to produce greater functional specialization, greater multiplicity of role conflicts, a greater awareness of divergent group interests, and at least their incipient aggregation. At the same time, political articulation and participation tend to increase while the pressures of forcible social, political, and economic mobilization are somewhat relaxed; while the system has more material resources to spare from its all-out mobilization and survival needs; and as important choices among alternative strategies need to be made. Different elite elements tend to opt for different priorities in resource allocation, reflecting different values with different political implications (even if the options are not, on the face of it, "political"). As terror tends to recede at this stage, dissenting voices may be heard with greater impunity, precisely at a time when the regime must make greater efforts to manufacture a genuine consensus. The more modernized society must rely more heavily on "experts," who in turn tend to press for better information and greater rationality and often seek access to policy-makers, thus introducing notes which clash with the repetitive refrains of the ideologues and the timid, conservative bureaucrats.

In addition, the fear of a return to one-man rule (among those who remember the Stalin era and also among some who deplore the improvisations of the Khrushchev days) supports "collective" decision-making at the highest level, which requires the adjustment of conflicting opinions and preferences — or else stalemate and inaction. Collective leadership invariably creates a situation in which outside influences can more effectively be brought to bear on the narrow circle of decision-makers. And if, by comparison with the Khrushchev era, there has in recent years been a distinct de-emphasis on simple ideological formulae, there is by the same token greater confusion about the shape of things to come and uncertainty about the "proper" priorities and policies to be pursued. There is simply a greater range of choice among possible courses of action. Such open-endedness is heightened still further by the failure of events to conform to prior expectations — neither in what used to be the communist "Bloc," nor in the Third World, nor in the capitalist West. Thus, one unintended consequence of the Sino-Soviet dispute is a further disorientation regarding the international environment: to many Soviet observers it is no longer so axiomatic what the rank order of friends and enemies is, or which strategies and tactics are legitimate and which are taboo.

Thus, as the stage of all-out mobilization and terror is completed, a number of mutually reinforcing processes tend to destroy the earlier "simplicity" of relatively uncontested totalitarian policy-making. But if at the same time Soviet foreign policy is no longer significantly constrained by the leadership's earlier uncertainty regarding the loyalty of its own population, it has tended to become increasingly contested by various elements — more powerful, more autonomous, and more articulate — *within* the system. As the Soviet Union moves into the 1970's, it is hardly an exaggeration to say that there are within the Soviet elite conflicting perceptions and images of the outside world; conflicting priorities and values regarding foreign objectives; and advocates of conflicting foreign policy strategies and tactics — either explicitly voiced or else implied in their stated goals.[11]

3.

It is significant, while we chart the increasing range of choice and the commensurate freedom of alternative of the Soviet elite, to pause momentarily over the salient continuities as well as the marked changes in Soviet foreign policy formation. One tendency which, though persistent, has often been underestimated abroad, is to give priority to domestic over foreign objectives unless a manifest threat or crisis looms abroad — a low-risk strategy that has satisfied both the present-minded pragmatists and the ideologically committed who expect greater things in the future. A related practice — rarely spelled out — has been to give clear priority to the interests of the Soviet state over those of revolutionary movements abroad. Despite charges of "selling out" its comrades and of "betraying" its verbal commitment to "internationalism," Soviet policy has been typically guided by a *sacro egoismo* not unfamiliar to other states.

There has also been a significant continuity in the terms and categories in which foreign policy alternatives have been perceived and discussed. While the traditional dichotomy into "Left" and "Right" is an inadequate diagnostic tool, it is descriptive of profoundly divergent attitudes which, in their extreme manifestations, reflect conflicting values and orientations. Communists themselves have, of course, continued to use these terms and, while they frequently serve as pejorative labels, it is important to realize how often there has been a congruence of cleavages over foreign policy approaches with those over other issues. More recently (and most obviously, in the Sino-Soviet dispute) such differences have been replicated among communist states as well.

11. See, e.g., William Zimmerman, *Soviet Perspectives on International Relations* (Princeton University Press, 1969).

These divergencies should not suggest that the spectrum of expressed opinions always extends from one polarity to the other, nor that there are not various intermediate positions. Nor *must* there be such congruence at all times: in American politics not all "doves" are liberals; not all politicians assume ideologically coherent or consistent postures on all issues that arise. Under Soviet conditions, when the range of alternatives is never publicly ventilated and when information and sophistication are far more unevenly distributed within the elite, it would be naive to expect such consistency, even if there are in the ideological set strong compulsions in the direction of such totalism. All the more striking, then, is the extent to which (just as in China and Yugoslavia) shifts in Soviet domestic, foreign, and ideological positions have tended to go hand in hand: this was as true of the turn to the "Right" in 1921, as it was of the turn to the "Left" in 1946–48, and of the turn to the "Right" in 1955–56.[12]

Some significant elements of this cleavage may be presented schematically in dichotomic form.[13]

PRIORITIES AND COMMITMENTS

Left	Right
Goal-orientedness (utopianism)	Pragmatism
Optimism	Pessimism
"Red" (partisanship)	"Expert" (rationality)
Transformation	Stability
Monolithism	Pluralism
Politics	Economics
Mobilization	Normalcy
Heavy industry	Consumer goods
Uneven ("breakthrough") development	Even development
Central command economy	Market economy
Cultural revolution	Tradition persistence
Tension-management	Consensus-building
Dialectic ("The worse, the better")	Linear ("The better, the better")
Centralization	Decentralization
Violence	Gradualism
Three-class alliance strategy	Four-class alliance
Inevitability of international conflict	Avoidability of conflict
Voluntarism	Determinism

12. Such parallel "fever curves" also extend, in the interwar period, to the "general line" dictated to the Communist International. The one significant exception — which confirms the rule — relates to the 1928–33 period when Soviet foreign policy remained "rightist" while at a time of drastic domestic transformation foreign communist parties pursued an "ultra-leftist" course intended to paralyze the potential enemy's rear in case of a showdown.

13. It is, of course, not being suggested that this is an exhaustive enumeration of divisive

Against this background one can see both the predisposition to make different assessments of the "correlation of forces" in world politics (or in individual foreign countries) and the tendency to link certain "readings" of reality to other, seemingly unrelated policy positions. Thus, the "Left" has invariably perceived opportunities to be exploited where the "Right" has seen none (and has charged the former with adventurism): this was the case with Zinoviev's associates in the Communist International until at least 1923; with the militant line symbolized by Andrei Zhdanov and Josip Tito in 1947 – 48; and with the Maoists seeking to convince the Khrushchevites after 1957.

A subsidiary aspect of this divergence has been the debate over Soviet strategy toward the non-communist world, with positions at different times ranging from advocacy of communist equivalents of "rollback," liberation, and deterrence, to détente, bluff, and compromise. These differences have given rise to specific disagreements over the intentions of other powers, such as the war scare of 1927, Stalin's views of Hitler's intentions in 1939 – 41, and the vigorous disagreement in the 1960's over U.S. intentions (with the polar positions represented, on the one hand, by the advocates of *ad hoc* agreements with the U. S. — since "men of reason" were in charge both "here" and "there" — and by those, on the other hand, who, like Marshal Malinovsky, insisted on the intrinsic, unchanging aggressiveness of American imperialism).

The question of whether one can do business with capitalism (literally or figuratively) is also of old vintage. It arose in Lenin's lifetime in connection with disagreements in the Soviet leadership over the foreign trade monopoly and foreign economic concessions. It was intensely disputed at the time the Kellogg-Briand Pact was concluded. It reemerged in the Khrushchev era in the arguments over the desirability of maximizing scientific and cultural relations abroad, the reliability of other powers as treaty partners (for instance, in regard to disarmament), and the risks of inviting foreign enterprises (like French, Italian, or Japanese) to help develop the Soviet economy.

Similarly related to basic ideological orientations has been the disagreement over the very nature of international tensions, involving a difficult search for satisfactory answers to whether tension is functional or dysfunctional:[14] a dilemma reminiscent of the ultra-left phase starting in 1928 as well as of the Maoist commitment to the dialectical belief in "the worse, the better."

Still another complex of policy disagreements has concerned the search for the wisest alliance strategy — both for the Soviet state and for communist parties abroad with the pivotal element (wooed as an ally in "Rightist" phases, and spurned as alien in "Leftist" ones) as the uncommitted, unpolarized

---

variables. Moreover, in addition to pseudo-rational elements, a variety of other factors — from personality elements to great-power compulsions — need to be considered in a fuller catalog.

14. See, for instance, Roman Kolkowicz, "The Dilemma of Superpower: Soviet Policy and Strategy in Transition" (IDA Research Paper P-383, October 1967).

middle: the nationalist movements, the peasantry, Social-Democracy, and the neutralist powers.

The tendency to link policy positions in regard to seemingly unrelated fields was most pronounced in the final years of the Khrushchev era. A more detailed study could show the interlocking nature of alignments over such varied issues as de-Stalinization, the new CPSU Program of 1961, the doctrine of peaceful transition to power, the debate between consumer-goods advocates and those whom Khrushchev derisively called "metal-eaters," the Albanian heresy, the role of non-party experts in advising the Chairman, reconciliation with Tito, the "spirit of Camp David," the shift from reliance on Soviet ground forces to stress on the rocket command, the proper response to Maoist charges against the Soviet leadership, the release of manpower from the armed forces to the civilian economy, freedom of artistic expression in the Soviet Union, and the nuclear test-ban treaty. To be sure, not all advocates of policies on any one of these took explicit positions on all other issues; and on many of the issues the alternatives were not even discussed esoterically in any detail. For this reason the military have been in a somewhat privileged position. Since strategic debates have been quasi-legitimate since 1954, the range of opinions voiced in them has tended to skew arguments somewhat toward the "hawkish" end of the political spectrum.

If policy disagreements within the Soviet elite since 1965 have been harder to identify, we should not conclude that their scope or intensity has lessened. Time and again we have learned in retrospect that what seemed to be policy consensus actually concealed bitter debates and that what appeared to be "marginalist" differences easily escalated into more fundamental cleavages.[15] While a fuller analysis would identify the limits of dissent as well, it is surely a safer course to assume the existence at all times of significant disagreements in the Soviet elite over objectives and policies than to accept at face value the professed commitment to common orthodoxy and the ritual appeal to concord and continuity.

Of course, not all differences over foreign policy can be explained in terms of a Left/Right spectrum. Many are typical of great-power dilemmas and frustrations.[16] Others are characteristic of divergencies between practitioners in the field and policy-makers at home.[17] Some stem from different functional orientations and jurisdictional biases of the actors.[18] And, of course, some are

15. It would be rewarding to re-examine the foreign-policy positions of men like Leonid Krasin, Nikolai Bukharin, and Maxim Litvinov.

16. It is suggestive of the shared problems of superpowers that some Soviet debates, especially over strategic problems, have virtually paralleled American discussions, on such questions as, "Is nuclear war unthinkable?" or "The political uses of military power," or the possibility of effective arms control and arms limitation, or the parity vs. superiority debate.

17. As the differences between Soviet negotiators in the ENDC negotiations in Geneva and decisions made, in apparent contradiction, by the authorities in Moscow.

18. Soviet experience provides a long list of such cases, ranging from "marginalist" differences

apparently rooted in honest differences in individual perceptions, judgments, and priorities.

4.

Soviet society becomes increasingly permeated by an awareness of multiple truths, multiple interests, and multiple forces at work both at home and abroad. In foreign affairs there is as yet lacking any institutionalized mechanism by which "outsiders" can affect policy formation legitimately and overtly: major influence thus continues to be exerted informally and indirectly. Resource allocation serves, however, as a quasi-institutionalized arena in which interest groups feel relatively free to do battle from time to time — with obvious implications for foreign affairs, but also with inherent limits on the specificity of policy articulation and with unequal opportunities for various groups. Military-industrial elements, for instance, have easier access to the budgetary trough than members of the creative intelligentsia, not to say spokesman for the kolkhoz peasantry.

The Party bureaucracy, which, until recently, appeared fairly indifferent to foreign-policy problems, now seems to be taking a more active part in silencing rivals and in promoting an essentially conservative line toward the Soviet-oriented parts of the communist camp — a line perhaps congruent with the orientation of traditionalist-military elements as well. Still, the efforts of the bureaucracy cannot be expected to stem the general tendency toward broader participation in the discussion of alternatives in foreign affairs. Indeed, in future domestic crises in the Soviet Union success may well go to him who is able to articulate the policy preferences of a greater range of elite groupings.

Such an increase in participation — even if it does not extend to policy-making proper — must be considered generally a healthy development, for reasons that scarcely require elaboration. But it is well to bear in mind some possibly counterproductive consequences. Since broader participation carries no assurance of moderation, the regime may find it harder to execute retreats in foreign relations — and an intense nationalist streak might prove more congenial to a large sector of the influential elite than would a liberal, cosmopolitan position. While the resultant multiplicity of perspectives may assure the avoidance of dangerously biased inputs, it also tends to circumscribe rationality in policy-making. Herbert Dinerstein has suggested that *both* ideology and factional politics have tended to limit or undermine rationality

---

between different desks of the Soviet Foreign Ministry (e.g., over Korea and Cyprus) to fundamental rivalry dating back to the 1920's. More than once the diplomats were disturbed and felt undercut by the efforts of the Comintern; while the foreign trade officials generally tended to have an even more pronounced conservative bias than political negotiators. A unique role, worthy of closer study, was of course occupied by the Beria machine and its representatives in the diplomatic and intelligence services — often at variance with that of the Foreign Ministry.

in Soviet foreign policy.[19] If the impact of "ideology" continues to weaken as elements of pluralism multiply, the simultaneous growth in the pressures exerted by elite factions and interest groups sets the stage for bargains and compromises which are apt to produce policy decisions well shy of clear and rational behavior. (To give but one recent example: it seems probable that the partial ABM system erected around Moscow was precisely the result of a compromise between the advocates of a larger system and its opponents.)

It would be foolish, however, to assume that present trends are bound to continue unchanged. As the economy develops, for instance, the reciprocal linkage between military and investment decisions and foreign policy may no longer be so simple or direct. Already the earlier assumption of the Soviet option as "guns versus butter" has proved to be vastly oversimplified — as indicated by Western surpise at Soviet ability, in the 1960's, to increase strategic capabilities while also raising the standard of living.

As the Soviet system matures, it may also happen that the compulsion toward totalism in policy orientation will yield to a more relaxed and sophisticated tolerance of ambiguity. But it would be premature to see the kernel of such a development in the recent attempt to pursue a repressive policy at home and in the "Bloc" while striving for limited accommodation and agreements with the United States. Nor should one as yet detect such a trend in the changed response to Peking: the proclivity of the Khrushchev era to move toward greater domestic "liberalization" as Sino-Soviet positions polarized seems to have been supplanted by an attitude which permits a confrontation with the Maoists without requiring any adjustment in Soviet domestic policy.

In the short run there may, of course, be all manner of reversals and zigzags. In the long run, however, "monolithic" policy-making is bound to remain — indeed, to become even more of — a myth. The increased influence of wider elements of Soviet society is likely to be exerted in support of a national policy of reasonable security, but it is also likely to express priority for welfare and prosperity objectives at home over expensive, risky, and decreasingly compelling goals of a "forward" foreign policy, whatever the ideological rationale.

No less importantly, while the circle of effective actors may remain restricted for some time to come, in the long run the professional and personal contacts of scientists and scholars, of novelists and poets, of tourists and technicians who become conversant with the outside world, and the growing familiarity of Soviet youth with foreign heroes and achievements, as well as cultural and academic exchanges, may well have as great a cumulative impact in fundamentally restructuring the image of the outside world in the minds of Soviet citizens. This is especially true for the younger generation who some day will be making the crucial decisions over life and death.

19. Herbert S. Dinerstein, *Fifty Years of Soviet Foreign Policy* (Johns Hopkins Press, 1968).

The Domestic Roots
of Soviet Foreign Policy*

In any country the nature of the relationship between internal and external affairs, if it can be determined, provides a significant clue to the future development of foreign policy. Aside from this general consideration, several special circumstances have recently heightened interest in the relation between Soviet domestic politics and foreign policy. The upheavals in Soviet ruling circles in the mid-1950's raised the question of whether equally drastic changes in foreign policy might follow. The open friction between the USSR and other Communist countries — particularly China — induces one to speculate about the nature of internecine rivalry in the Communist world. The sudden removal of Nikita Khrushchev from his positions as head of the Soviet Communist Party and Government has made the relationship between internal and external affairs in the USSR one of the most urgent questions confronting political observers everywhere.

Is it feasible, though, to analyze, to generalize, about the relationship between Soviet domestic and external policies? Certainly it is hard to study this relationship even in democratic, "open" societies. The problem is greatly complicated by the obscurity in which policy formation in the USSR is deliberately hidden. Not only is current policy consideration concealed, but there is

*Reprinted from *International Affairs,* XLI, 1 (January, 1965), pp. 37 – 47, by permission of the author and the publisher.

no systematic disclosure, through legislative investigation, publication of official records, or writing of personal accounts, of the factors behind policy decisions even in the distant past. Nevertheless, the exigencies of the Soviet struggle for power lead contestants to reveal more than their normally secretive tendencies would lead one to expect, especially in periods of upheaval like the last 12 years.

Another obstacle is almost as hard to overcome as the veil of official secrecy. Soviet society is rapidly changing. Many generalizations which held good even in the early 1950s are now subject to question, and one can anticipate even more rapid change in the future. Most observers would probably agree, however, that the essential nature of the Communist power structure has not basically changed. This power system now has a history of almost half a century — a far longer experience than that of any other modern totalitarianism. Much of this history remains obscure, but important aspects are now reasonably determinable. While one cannot hope to base fully confident predictions upon analysis of the Soviet experience in the relation of internal to foreign affairs, attentive examination of this experience is an indispensable step in the process of reasonably probable inferences about the future.

The question at issue is the relation between domestic politics, in the sense of internal competition for power, and foreign policy, not the relation between the interests of the USSR (or the Russian nation) and world Communism. An example may help make the distinction clearer. Lenin's decision to make peace with Germany at Brest-Litovsk basically represented a choice between the immediate security of the Soviet state and the immediate, all-out promotion of world revolution. Lenin evidently decided in favor of the former on the basis of a rational calculation that the best chance for eventual triumph of Communism throughout the world was its secure establishment in Russia — a calculation which eventually led to Stalin's doctrine of "socialism in one country." It is true that Lenin had to engage in a short, sharp struggle with his colleagues to secure acceptance of the Brest-Litovsk concessions. Lenin's personal position of leadership was never, however, in danger because of this policy difference.[1] Consequently, the dispute must be regarded entirely as one concerning choice of alternative policies, not as an issue of domestic politics in the sense of conflict between competitors for power.

Probably such competition for personal power did not seriously affect the conduct of foreign policy as long as Lenin dominated the Soviet regime. The situation changed rapidly when Stalin began his protracted conflict with "opposition" groups in the twenties. Stalin could not rest his claim to power upon the charisma, the intense personal devotion which had been Lenin's

1. See especially Louis Fischer, *The Soviets in World Affairs* (New York: Jonathan Cape, 1930), I, Chapter 1.

major instrument in dominating the party leadership. Instead, Stalin was obliged to resort to manipulation and trickery; and it seems clear that he personally enjoyed these tactics. At the same time, because his hegemony was not based on the respect of his followers, Stalin never felt secure. Hence, his insistence, approaching paranoia, on eliminating all opposition or potential opposition to his authority, regardless of the cost.

Three instances of Stalin's subordination of Soviet foreign policy objectives to his personal interests stand out. One of the best known is the sharp reversal of policy in China in 1927. Stalin had insisted that the Chinese Communist Party collaborate with non-Communist nationalists, first with Chiang Kai-shek and then (after Chiang attacked the Communists) with the "left" group of the Kuomintang in Wuhan. Eventually even the latter group turned upon its Communist allies. The whole prospect of Communist association in a victorious anti-Western nationalist front vanished. Stalin's critics at home — particularly Trotsky — seized on the manifest failure in China to demonstrate Stalin's incompetence. Although his personal power was not really endangered, Stalin wanted to recoup his prestige prior to the opening of the 15th Congress of the Soviet Communist Party. Blaming the Chinese failure upon the local Communist leadership was not enough; he needed the appearance of spectacular success. Consequently, he sharply reversed the earlier cautious line by ordering violent uprisings against the Chinese nationalist leadership, especially in Canton.[2] These rebellions were bloodily suppressed, and Chinese Communism remained in eclipse for almost a decade.

Stalin's sacrifice of Soviet objectives during the Spanish Civil War in order to destroy those he distrusted was a considerably more complicated affair. Many of Stalin's critics have contended that the destruction of the Anarchist and semi-Trotskyite forces in Catalonia in the spring of 1937 was designed merely to serve Stalin's personal interests. There is some merit in this argument, but it is quite possible that the defeat of the extreme left-wing forces was desirable from the standpoint of Soviet efforts to secure Western support for a policy of collective security to restrain Germany and Italy. Stalin's subsequent liquidation of the Communist control apparatus in Spain had no such rational justification. Old Bolshevik political leaders like Antonov-Ovseenko were purged because Stalin feared they might retain their earlier association with Trotsky. Skilled NKVD control agents were purged (unless, like Alexander Orlov, they successfully fled) as collaborators of Stalin's disgraced police chiefs.[3] Outstanding military officers, who (as Khrushchev later noted) had

2. Robert C. North, *Moscow and Chinese Communists* (Stanford: Stanford University Press, 1953), Chapter 7; Conrad Brandt, *Stalin's Failure in China* (Cambridge, Mass.: Harvard University Press, 1958), Chapters 4, 5.

3. David C. Cattell, *Communism and the Spanish Civil War* (Berkeley: University of California Press, 1955), pp. 102 *et seq.*, 208 *et seq.*; John A. Armstrong, *The Politics of Totalitarianism* (New York: Random House, 1961), pp. 42–43; and Il'ia Ehrenburg, "Liudi, gody, zhizn," in

acquired invaluable experience in combat in Spain, were executed.[4] As a result, the remnants of the Communist control apparatus were unable to dominate the Spanish Republic during its last months. Even more important, from the standpoint of Soviet interests, was the loss of painfully acquired military experience.

The most spectacular and, in the long run, the most important example of Stalin's sacrifice of foreign policy interests to his mania for undisputed control was the break with Josip Tito in 1948. It is true that one cannot be sure that Stalin's motive in this instance was "domestic" politics, though there are good reasons for thinking that he believed Tito's defiance was related to the covert deviation of certain high Soviet officials. Given the complete dependence of the European satellites upon the USSR at that time, however, the quarrel with Tito was scarcely distinguishable from a domestic controversy. The damaging repercussions for Soviet foreign policy scarcely need recounting here. Aside from the considerable injury to the Soviet strategic position in southeast Europe, the complete split with Yugoslavia was a very severe blow to the prestige of the USSR and Communism in general. It is, of course, possible that Stalin calculated that these liabilities were offset by monolithic control of the remaining European satellites. That this was not a wise calculation is fairly well demonstrated by the frantic efforts which his successors made to repair the breach.

As was just suggested, it is possible that Stalin consciously thought that he was promoting the interests of the Soviet Union and of world Communism by his ruthless pursuit of personal power. It is conceivable that he may have reasoned that only absolute, rigid control by the "indispensable" leader would preserve the unity and strength of the Communist world.[5] After the revelations which Khrushchev and other Soviet spokesmen have made about Stalin, it is hardly possible to argue that his more extreme actions, such as those outlined above, can be rationally regarded as in accord with Soviet interests.[6] Of course, it is possible that Stalin's mind was so warped that he could not distinguish his personal position from the interests of the regime as a whole. Whether or not this was the case, his objective sacrifice of Soviet foreign policy interests seems indisputable. One should not, however, carry this interpretation too far; certainly many of Stalin's errors — including, probably, the Nazi-Soviet pact

---

Novyi Mir, June 1962, p. 124. Ehrenburg's "Kotov" was really Orlov's successor, the NKVD officer Eitingon.

4. The "secret speech" at the 20th Party Congress, in *Current Soviet Policies II* (New York: Praeger, 1957), p. 181.

5. "He may be given the dubious credit of the sincere conviction that what he did served the interest of the revolution and that he alone interpreted those interests aright." Isaac Deutscher, *Stalin: A Political Biography* (New York: Oxford University Press, 1949), p. 378.

6. In other words (to use the convenient terminology advanced by Herbert Simon in *Administrative Behavior* [New York: Macmillan, 1957], p. 76), Stalin's behavior may have been "personally rational," but it was not "organizationally rational."

of 1939 — were the result of genuine miscalculation of Soviet and Communist interests, rather than the result of personal obsession.

But Stalin's ruthlessness in subordinating all policy considerations to his personal aims was sufficiently frequent and evident (at least to his major lieutenants) to leave a deep impress on the mentality of the Soviet elite. Today it is easy to forget that two-thirds of the life span of the Soviet system was passed under the shadow of Stalin. Every major figure (and nearly all of the minor ones) in the present elite spent most of his active career in Stalin's service. The effect of Stalin's teaching and, more significantly, his example will not be erased as long as this group remains in power.

The harshest lesson which the elite has learned is that the consequence of defeat in the struggle for power is personal destruction. This grim lesson was reinforced soon after Stalin's death by the execution of Beria and his followers. It is instructive to note that Beria apparently anticipated what his fate would be if he became powerless, and drew the "Stalinist" conclusion that his own survival was the paramount consideration. The steps he took in internal Soviet affairs are too complicated to relate in detail here, but some, at least, might have been very injurious to the system. Apparently Beria, working through the police apparatus, tried to gain effective control of a broad belt of territory on the periphery of the USSR, including, in addition to his Transcaucasian stronghold, Latvia, Lithuania, the Ukraine, and the Central Asian republics. If he had been successful in doing this he could have assured his own safety, but only at the cost of disrupting the monolithic pattern of the Soviet system. In foreign affairs, Beria's policies are not so clear, but there is reason to believe that he contemplated major concessions to the Western powers and the European satellite populations in order to secure personal support.[7]

It is harder to be certain that any of the contestants for power in the USSR since 1953 has jeopardized Soviet foreign policy interests in order to attain personal objectives. The coincidence of the sudden war scare, which Khrushchev initiated by threatening Turkey in the autumn of 1957, and his disgracing the popular Marshal Georgi K. Zhukov, is suspicious, but there is no direct evidence to indicate that Khrushchev was trying to divert the Soviet public from his domestic political move. It appears certain that Khrushchev remained relatively free from Stalin's obsessive fear of potential opposition. Aside from the Beria group, Khrushchev's opponents were allowed their lives. If rumors are accurate, however, at least some of Khrushchev's defeated rivals suffered great personal hardship as well as humiliation.[8] In any case, their careers were ruined, at least as long as Khrushchev remained master of the country, for in a totalitarian state there is no alternative position for a man whom the

7. Armstrong, *op. cit.,* pp. 244 – 247.
8. "Les Droits de l'Homme selon les Communistes (Le Sort de D. T. Chêpilov)," in *Est et Ouest,* May 16 – 31, 1962, pp. 17 – 18.

regime rejects. Under these circumstances, it seems reasonable to predict that ambitious and determined future contestants for power will not hesitate to juggle foreign interests to secure domestic political victory.

In a very important sense the subordination of Soviet interests abroad to the demands of the domestic power struggle is only a special case of the more general practice of Soviet leaders of making policy a pawn in personal contests. In order to illustrate this general tendency, it is scarcely necessary to go further back than the period following Stalin's death. It will be recalled that a major criticism directed against Georgi M. Malenkov before his forced resignation as premier in early 1955 was his emphasis on the development of consumer-goods industries at the same rate as heavy industry. Scarcely was Malenkov's defeat sealed, however, before Khrushchev and his associates muted this criticism; at the 20th Party Congress only a year later practically nothing was heard of it. On the contrary, within a very short time Khrushchev was stressing the production of consumer goods in terms which were virtually identical to those Malenkov had used.[9] One is bound to conclude that Khrushchev and his faction recognized the pressing need for diversion of industrial facilities to relieve the more urgent needs of the Soviet consumer, though they had earlier found the shibboleth of priority for heavy industry a convenient lever to dislodge Malenkov.

The issue of industrial reorganization in 1956–57 developed in a very similar fashion, though here Khrushchev and his group were the innovators. The functional need for reorganization of the cumbersome ministerial system was fairly obvious, but the *manner* of reorganization carried major political implications. The central ministerial bureaucracies were the stronghold of supporters of Malenkov and Lazar M. Kaganovich. If the ministries were only partially broken up, or replaced by broad regional economic directorates, the economic bureaucracies might retain much of their power. If, on the other hand, the reorganization involved transfer of industrial direction to the provincial level, Khrushchev's supporters in the territorial party machine would assume dominant positions. Consequently, Khrushchev's decision (after some hesitation) to demand the latter type of reorganization was a sharp thrust at Malenkov, Kaganovich, and their associates. As speakers at the 22nd Party Congress later complained, this incident was a major factor impelling the "anti-Party" group to make its disastrous attempt in June 1957 to depose Khrushchev.[10] Only a few months had elapsed after Khrushchev's spectacular

9. In 1953, Malenkov advocated developing heavy and light industry "at the same rate," while Khrushchev emphasized heavy industry as the basis of further development; in 1962 Khrushchev declared that "in the future light and heavy industry will develop at the same pace."
10. See the speeches by E. A. Furtseva and A. I. Mikoyan in *XX S'ezd Kommunisticheskoi Partii Sovetskogo Soiuza, Stenograficheskii Otchet* (Moscow: Gosudarstvennoi Izdatel'stvo Politicheskoi Literatury, 1962), pp. 396, 449.

victory, however, before it became apparent that transfer of industrial direction to the provincial level — where more than 100 control units were established — had led to fragmentation of economic activity and the danger of provincial autarky. After 1958 Khrushchev, having attained his political objectives, moved steadily in the direction of constituting larger economic control units. In a word, the functionally efficient solution lay about midway between those which the contending factions sought, for political reasons, to impose in 1957.

In the field of foreign policy, the reversals of policy were not so sharp, but the tendency of a competitor to adopt his defeated rivals' policies has nevertheless been apparent. One of the secret charges (corroborated by considerable circumstantial evidence) brought against Beria was that he tried to send a clandestine personal emissary to effect a reconciliation with Tito.[11] But Beria's elimination did not mean that these conciliatory efforts were abandoned; on the contrary, throughout Malenkov's direction of state affairs there was a notable *rapprochement* between Yugoslavia and the Soviet Union. It must have been apparent to the great majority of the Soviet leaders (Molotov, hopelessly compromised by his involvement in Stalin's vicious attacks on Tito, was the exception) that closer ties between the two countries would be useful to Soviet foreign policy. Moreover, Tito's prestigious position in the world Communist movement meant that the Soviet leader who restored *Party* relations between Yugoslavia and the USSR would gain a notable advantage in the contest for power in the Soviet Communist Party.

As soon as Malenkov was deposed as head of government, Khrushchev devoted extraordinary effort to attaining this objective; his partial success in the summer of 1955 received almost unprecedented stress in local Party meetings throughout the Soviet Union. During the next two years (despite some friction over the Hungarian revolution) Tito and Khrushchev exchanged visits and Tito gave Khrushchev moral support in his struggle with his rivals. After the defeat of the "anti-Party" group, the *Party* aspect of Yugoslav-Soviet relations rapidly cooled. At the state level (with some exceptions) cordiality has continued. It would appear that Khrushchev as a contestant for Soviet power no longer needed to draw on Tito's prestige as a Communist leader; but Khrushchev as leader of Soviet Communism continued to foster Yugoslav-Soviet cooperation in the interests of Soviet foreign policy, particularly in relation to China.

Finally, one may note the attitudes of Soviet leaders toward the effects of nuclear weapons. Early in 1954 Malenkov said that nuclear war would mean the "destruction of civilization." This was a novel thesis for a Leninist, for it clearly implied that the march of history toward Communism could be terminated by an "accidental" factor. Khrushchev, by implication, sharply

11. Armstrong, *op. cit.,* p. 248.

refuted Malenkov's assertion, maintaining that nuclear war would destroy capitalism, but not "socialism." Leading military figures like Marshal Zhukov took the same position. After the rout of the "anti-Party" group (followed a few months later by the dismissal of Marshal Zhukov) Khrushchev moved to adopt a position closer to Malenkov's, though not precisely identical with it: that, though "socialism" would prevail, nuclear war would mean destruction of "major centers of civilization."

It seems clear that any Soviet leadership is now compelled by the logic of facts to accept the catastrophic implications of general nuclear war. Indeed, Khrushchev stressed repeatedly the need for avoiding such a war, even going so far as to revise explicitly Leninist teachings on the inevitability of war while capitalist states exist. Certainly it would have been just as logical for Khrushchev to have taken this position in 1954 when the USSR's weakness in nuclear weapons made it even more important for the country to avoid nuclear war. But then Khrushchev stood to gain by picturing Malenkov as "weak" in his foreign policy stand. Khrushchev, having eliminated all rival power alignments at home, had sufficient leeway to take a position which is more rational from the standpoint of Soviet interests.

On the basis of these examples, one can generalize — with at least a fair measure of probability — that *in the short run* contestants for leadership in the Soviet Union will manipulate policy issues to strengthen their domestic power positions. This manipulation (which sometimes involves at least marginal sacrifice of Soviet interests) will, however, last only as long as the power struggle is in doubt. Thus the "short run" is a matter, at most, of a very few years. In the *longer run*, any victorious contestant tends to take the position which is consonant with a rational calculation of Soviet interests. This is not the place to discuss at length what those interests may be, but one may summarize them very generally as the maximization of the power of the Communist system in the USSR and abroad. From the tactical standpoint, the pursuit of these interests is characterized by a delicate mixture of dynamic expansionism and caution. Taken as a whole this policy is functionally rational from the standpoint of the Communist ideology (though in any given instance it may be based on an error in judgment), however little one may think it serves the true interests of the Soviet peoples and others whom it affects.

One can, of course, speculate that a leader with quite different objectives and personality might arise in the USSR. Such a man might, conceivably, be genuinely devoted to liberalism and peace as they are understood in Western democratic countries. Conversely, he might be a fanatic like Hitler, eager to gamble on quick victory. Such types do not, however, appear to be produced by the selection process which has brought forth the contestants for supreme power in the Soviet Union. There are those who argue that broad, secular changes in Soviet society will alter the personality types who attain leadership positions. Possibly this is true — but in this instance it would seem most prudent to interpret "secular" in its most literal sense. For the foreseeable future, neither the liberal statesman nor the *fanatic* adventurer appears likely to assume direction of Soviet affairs.

One possibility does, however, deserve serious consideration. An individual contestant in the power struggle may see his only hope for victory in taking a desperate step which would jeopardize the existence of the Soviet system, or even the peace of the world. As was briefly discussed above, Lavrenti Beria seems to have been in this position in 1953; but his moves jeopardized Soviet stability rather than world peace. It is possible that a future contestant for power might calculate that his only hope for personal safety lay in a dramatic diversion in the foreign field. Between 1953 and 1957 there was a tendency for widening circles of officials to play a role on the periphery of the power struggle. These broader groups have had no direct voice in the selection of leaders, except in crises like the June 1957 plenary session of the Party Central Committee, and (though the evidence is not yet clear) in the Central Committee session which ousted Khrushchev on October 14, 1964. Nevertheless, the contestants for power have evidently paid close attention to attitudes among such circles of higher- and medium-level officials. Consequently, these attitudes may be regarded as a sort of oligarchic public opinion which may influence the development of policy and especially the manner in which it is expressed. Given the permanent elimination of the terror which cowed officials under Stalin, the increase in their sense of self-importance and assertiveness seems to be an irreversible trend. Now that Khrushchev has passed from the Soviet scene, this "public opinion" is even more significant; a future contestant for power may find it crucially important to impress these officials with his ability to achieve rapid and striking successes. For a contestant who is in an insecure position at home, the temptation to seek such a dramatic success in foreign policy may be very great — given the high personal cost of failure in the power struggle. Obviously, the cost of such an adventure to the Soviet Union and to the world could be appalling.

It would be interesting to extend the discussion of the relation between internal strife and foreign policy to the controversies which are prevalent today in the Communist bloc as a whole. As the example of Tito's relations to Stalin and Khrushchev suggests, there is no clear line of demarcation between the domestic politics of a single Communist country and intra-bloc politics. One is tempted to generalize that, insofar as the personal positions of rival leaders may be threatened by intra-bloc disputes, the same rules would apply to such controversies as to internal Soviet power struggles. Differences in national charactertistics — which affect even Communist regimes — and the widely varying stages of development of the Communist systems, should make one very cautious in reaching conclusions based on evidence drawn from the Soviet system alone. For example, the more recent the seizure of power by a Communist regime, the stronger seems its tendency to seek radical solutions in foreign affairs. Consequently, policy disputes between Communist bloc regimes on the timing of expansionist moves and the degree of risk to be taken quite possibly reflect differing perceptions of what are the appropriate tactics for the Communist movement as a whole, rather than manipulation of policy for the sake of enhancing either personal or national power.

A special case, however, is worth noting. Most observers of the current controversy between the Soviet and the Chinese Communist regimes have concluded that both have too many interests in common (particularly in opposition to the Western democratic powers) to permit their cleavage to go to the extreme of armed conflict. From the standpoint of world Communist interests, and very probably even the interests of the individual Communist regimes, this is true. If one can apply the generalizations elaborated earlier in this article, however, what is rational for the Communist system is not necessarily determinative for individual Communist leaders. Recent Chinese attacks on Khrushchev's leadership and retaliatory Soviet denunciations of the ruling group in Peking indicate that both sides have been playing the dangerous game of intervention in the internal affairs of the rival regime. If a Soviet or Chinese Communist leader in a key position were seriously threatened by the influence which the other country's regime could exercise among his own elite, he might feel obliged to take drastic action against the other Communist regime, including even the use of force. While such action would almost certainly be highly dysfunctional from the standpoint of his own regime as a whole, it would be a wholly rational personal response to extreme danger. Khrushchev's removal may temporarily diminish the force of the Chinese denunciation of Soviet leadership. It is conceivable that the new Soviet leadership may make far-reaching concessions to the Chinese position, but resumed hostility between the two Communist powers appears more probable. In the near future, however, any Soviet leader is likely to be less secure than Khrushchev was when his quarrel with Peking began. Consequently, the scope for Chinese Communist intrigue among the Soviet elite will broaden. Apparently the reverse is not true, for the Chinese ruling group has been able to maintain a much more "monolithic" front than the Soviet equivalent. Under these circumstances, it is possible, though hardly probable, that a Soviet leader might decide on forcible action against the Chinese Communist regime.

If the above analysis of the effects of the current instability in Soviet politics is correct, what are the implications for Western policy? There is probably little that the Western statesmen can do to avert the extreme contingency — the precipitation of a catastrophic world war by a desperate contender in the Soviet power struggle. This possibility (fortunately, it does not seem more than a possibility) is a chastening reminder that even the best Western policy cannot avoid catastrophe in extreme contingencies. The best that can be done — and it is extremely important that it be done — is to study the development of the Soviet power struggle closely and continuously.

The more likely contingency is a repetition of the short-run manipulation of Soviet foreign policy in the course of an internal power struggle. Here, too, direct intervention by Western policy-makers is scarcely feasible. It is possible that such a situation would permit the West to make small gains; it is also possible that the Western powers might rationally calculate that small concessions were desirable. If it is true that in the long run (and not such a *very long run* at that) any Soviet leader victorious in the power struggle will return to the basic interests of Soviet policy, the West cannot gain by making important concessions to "help" a contestant in this struggle. Careful observation of Soviet internal political developments, but steadfast adherence to major Western interests, is far safer than an attempt to adjust our policies to the changing of the guard in the Kremlin.

FIVE

C. GRANT PENDILL, JR.

"Bipartisanship" in Soviet
Foreign Policy-Making

What influence, if any, do factional differences within the Kremlin leadership have on Soviet foreign policy? Are foreign policy issues used as political footballs in the succession game of *kto-kovo* (who gets whom) in the USSR? How "collective" is Soviet collective leadership when decisions are being made which result in an about-face in Soviet economic, political, military, propaganda, and ideological policies toward the outside world? Can we find evidence that Soviet decision-makers are motivated more by considerations of their own careers and power position? Or do they look primarily at matters of the overall "national" interest? These are the types of questions which have aroused the curiosities of Sovietologists particularly since the death of Stalin ended the "cult of the personality" and Khrushchev's "subjectivism" culminated in his ouster over five years ago.

In an attempt to gain an empirical handle on this important yet elusive aspect of Kremlinology, one period has been isolated for study.[1] Between the 19th and 20th Congresses of the CPSU, factionalism within the Soviet leadership was pronounced — Stalin died, Beriya was eliminated, Malenkov and Molotov were effectively reduced in power, and Khrushchev emerged trium-

1. This paper is based upon the author's doctoral dissertation, *Foreign Policy and Political Factions in the USSR, 1952–1956: The Post-Stalin Power Struggle and the Developing Nations* (Ann Arbor, Michigan: University Microfilms, 69–21, 415), supervised by Alvin Z. Rubinstein.

phant. Simultaneously there was a pronounced long-term shift of emphasis in Soviet policy toward expanding the influence of the USSR in the under-developed areas of the world.[2] This aspect of changing foreign policy was chosen because Soviet moves were true initiatives in the sense that the rulers were not obliged to act in order to preserve the national security of the USSR. There was wide latitude. Decisions involved taking advantage of opportunities which presented themselves rather than reacting to threats on Soviet territory, established interests, or even prestige. Therefore, one could suppose that con-tenders for power within the CPSU leadership might be more willing to use policy-making in this area of foreign policy as a means for weakening the authority of their opponents and strengthening their own positions than in more crucial Cold War areas.

For research purposes, we postulated that early post-Stalin foreign policy decisions about the underdeveloped world were strongly influenced by differ-ences among those Soviet leaders aspiring to ruling primacy. There are a number of ways in which foreign policy decisions could be used by leadership factions for internal purposes as suggested by this hypothesis. In order to prove (or disprove) the hypothesis, however, two steps need to be taken. First, links must be found which join factions with specific foreign policies. Once such links are established then covariance can be looked for. Yet some types of covariance would substantiate the hypothesis while others would refute it or leave it in limbo, dealt with only inconclusively. What criteria can we use to evaluate the validity of the hypothesis?

In order to assert that foreign policy decisions concerning the under-developed world were "strongly" influenced by factional rivalries, we ought to find a faction of the Soviet leadership closely associating itself with a particular approach toward the underdeveloped world while opposed in this approach by a contending faction. Then, if the policy approach were pursued in such a way as to give one or the other of the factions an advantage in the power struggle, we could conclude that this facet of foreign policy was being "strongly" influenced by factional differences.

There are variations on this theme. A faction could initiate a certain policy in an attempt to weaken an opponent or it might oppose an innovation by the opponent for the same purpose. Credit for the success of a policy might be taken by a faction or, conversely, blame for a failure could be shifted onto a factional contender. In a more indirect manner, a foreign policy approach, for example, a vociferous propaganda campaign, may be used as a diversion to draw attention away from the final *coup de grace* in a battle for primacy.[3]

---

2. This term has been used as a catch-all for all the economically developing countries of Asia, Africa, and Latin America — former colonies and independent aligned and nonaligned nations.

3. Vernon V. Aspaturian, "Internal Politics and Foreign Policy in the Soviet System," in R. Barry Farrell (ed.), *Approaches to Comparative and International Politics* (Evanston, Ill.:

There are a number of circumstances under which we would have to conclude that this working hypothesis had not been supported, that Soviet policies toward the underdeveloped world were not subject to factional influences. One would be if there appeared to be no differences among the Soviet leaders over foreign policy matters, that is, that they agreed on approaches to be taken toward the developing nations. Similarly, it might be possible to detect differences over policies yet determine that these disagreements were not used by any faction to enhance its own position or detract from that of a rival faction. This would be the epitome of Leninist "democratic centralism," which postulates that only rational, selfless considerations motivate Communist policy-makers. Such conditions would be observable if differences of opinion were expressed and changes in policy came about but the balance of power did not change. Again, we could find that, while some foreign policy issues are used as weapons between warring factions, policies bearing on the underdeveloped world are not involved. In such a case the assumption that Soviet policies toward the Third World might be more susceptible to factional usage than intra- or inter-bloc policies would have to be questioned. Finally, lack of information or absence of links between power and policy could leave us unable to draw any meaningful conclusions.

Having spelled out the circumstances under which one could judge whether or not the working hypothesis had been substantiated, let us consider the approach taken in this study. One of the major methodological problems has been to establish links between the two variables — factions and foreign policies. A number of the links are quite straightforward. Soviet leaders who are members of a faction, or closely identified with one, may, through their words or actions, take a position in favor of or opposed to a particular policy alternative. This could take the form of announcing a new policy, attacking an old policy, accepting credit for success, or admitting guilt for past faults. Similar action may be taken, in a more indirect manner, not by the factional leader himself but by a cohort or in a publication which is identified with a faction.

However, because power struggles within the Soviet leadership generally became known *post factum,* and then in all-too-sketchy partisan terms, and because Soviet foreign policy decisions are arrived at under conditions of secrecy, circumstantial evidence has to be used extensively. Ties may be inferred from a congruency of Soviet policies and events within the power struggle. Changes in a policy may come about as a result of changes in the personnel responsible for its implementation. The coincidence of the time factor may be the only lead we can find to relate the two variables. Though fragile links, if many such ties of coincidence are found to support each other, they can open doors to understanding.

In order to obtain as full a picture as possible of both policies and factions

Northwestern University Press, 1966), pp. 247–248.

and then relate them, we adopted an interdisciplinary approach utilizing a variety of methods in the full study. These included a computer program designed to facilitate the analysis of over 9,000 press items devoted to the underdeveloped areas in *Pravda* and *Izvestiya,* a graphic presentation of changes in diplomatic representations and ambassadorial assignments, a statistical summary of foreign trade, and historical descriptions of changing attitudes in international groupings and of doctrinal revisions.

Since some investigation of these separate topics, by themselves, has been published by reputable experts, and since the purpose of this study has been to discover relationships rather than to unearth new primary data, we relied heavily on secondary sources.[4] The tasks have been to choose from the secondary (and primary) materials those data and findings which are relevant for our present purposes and then to summarize and combine them into integrated data banks which we could then draw on for purposes of synthesis. The remainder of this paper will be drawn from the synthesis of the detailed study.

Stalinist Background

During Stalin's last years factionalism was at a minimum. Rather, the autocrat was manipulating his lieutenants. Soviet relations with the underdeveloped areas were at a low ebb yet not stagnant. Trade was down and declining from a postwar high in 1948.[5] The USSR was feeling the effect of the Western embargo imposed during the Korean War. In order to obtain required raw materials, the sale of Soviet goods was promoted beginning in late 1951. However, Stalin took a strictly businesslike view of this trade — a tactical necessity — for, as he made clear in his "two parallel world markets" thesis of October 1952, these underdeveloped areas were still part of the capitalist world market and any aid to them was a form of aid to the enemy.

Through the Cominform Stalin shifted the tactics of international Communism during 1951 – 52 away from violent revolution and toward the establishing of a broad anti-imperialist front in India, Burma, Pakistan, Ceylon, and Indonesia.[6] In spite of certain successes, such as Communist gains in Indian elections in late 1951 and 1952, Stalin was not ready to follow through and permit a full parliamentary strategy. During the 19th CPSU Congress he gave Soviet support to the "fraternal" parties of the dependent countries and called for a strengthening of a "democratic antiwar front of supporters of peace," yet

4. We have selected the footnotes in this paper from the original manuscript with the hope of giving the reader a sampling of the major works utilized as well as offering support for the argumentation.

5. Joseph S. Berliner, *Soviet Economic Aid* (New York: Praeger, 1958), p. 84.

6. John H. Kautsky, *Moscow and the Communist Party of India* (New York: Wiley, 1956), pp. 140, 147.

the national parties were not to go so far as actively to seek alliances with the leaders of the "bourgeois" parties.[7]

Stalin's lack of interest in the underdeveloped areas was reflected in the relatively limited amount of press coverage devoted to these areas by *Pravda* and *Izvestiya* during 1952 and its predominantly "anti-" character, according to our computer categories.[8] The 19th Congress had introduced some "pro-" bias into the press, but in November this reverted to a very strong "anti-" content which continued through that winter until after Stalin's death.

Beriya's Bid for Power

Stalin's heirs wanted to extricate themselves from the the rigid, dangerous situation which the dictator left when he died in March 1953. A number of conciliatory moves were made toward the West in the spring of 1953, culminating in the settlement of the Korean War. There were differing emphases within the party Presidium, however, with Molotov in a strong position and not inclined to move away from Stalin's policies and Beriya apparently ready to make concessions in relations with the satellites, the West, and to some extent the underdeveloped world.[9]

The basis for this latter contention may be found in Soviet policies toward Iran during the spring of 1953 after Premier Mossadegh had broken diplomatic relations with Great Britain and legalized the Communist Tudeh party. Stalin had supported Mossadegh's defiance of the West and was extremely critical of the Shah. Then in March and April 1953, right after Stalin's death, the Soviet press shifted its coverage dramatically, dropping criticism of the Shah while praising both Mossadegh and the Tudeh. This constituted a significant new approach stressing local nationalists.

This policy change may be linked to Beriya in two ways. First, the only person to be brought into the reduced Soviet governing bodies after Stalin's death was a Presidium candidate, Jafar Bagirov, who was a close associate of Beriya, had been first secretary of the Azerbaydzhan party since 1933,[10] and

7. Marshall D. Shulman, *Stalin's Foreign Policy Reappraised* (Cambridge, Mass.: Harvard University Press, 1963), pp. 247, 253.

8. The computer analysis was a quantitative measure, consisting of a month-by-month count of press items and words in *Pravda* and *Izvestiya*, with a printout presentation both in figures and in histograms with the 50 months along the horizontal axis. A qualitative element was introduced by dividing the press coverage into three broad types of contents, reflecting different Soviet attitudes toward events or personalities: (1) "anti-," including "anti-U.S.," "anti-West," "anti-local authorities," and "anti-local conditions"; (2) "pro-," including "pro-Soviet," "pro-Communism," "pro-local Communist party," and "pro-local progressive events"; and (3) "neutral," which applies to objective reporting without value judgments.

9. Zbigniew K. Brzezinski, *The Permanent Purge* (Cambridge, Mass.: Harvard University Press, 1956), p. 161; Robert Conquest, *Power and Policy in the U.S.S.R.* (New York: St. Martin's Press, 1962), p. 215.

10. John A. Armstrong, *The Politics of Totalitarianism* (New York: Random House, 1961),

was reported to have had great influence on the Tudeh party over a considerable time, including the early postwar period when the USSR attempted to annex Azerbaydzhani Iran. It is not unreasonable to expect that Bagirov, with Beriya's support, was playing an important if not decisive role in Soviet policy toward Iran. A second link, again of an indirect nature, was the recall of Ambassador Sadchikov in late June 1953 — at the same time Beriya was arrested and just before both Beriya and Bagirov were denounced at the July party plenum. Sadchikov was replaced by a career diplomat who had served under the new Soviet Foreign Minister, Molotov.[11]

In spite of this evidence, Beriya's downfall was due to much more important factors related to internal affairs and policies toward the Communist bloc.[12] Therefore, we are not able to assert that there was a strong relationship between Beriya's power struggle and policies toward the underdeveloped nations.

Initial Malenkov-Molotov Policy Formulation

The expansion of Soviet economic ties with the underdeveloped world, initiated by Stalin, continued through 1953 on a broader, more organized basis, unaffected by Beriya's downfall. The USSR ceased its criticism of the UN's Expanded Program of Technical Assistance in July 1953[13] and during the latter half of the year concluded trade negotiations with many countries, including Egypt, Argentina (first credit extended to an underdeveloped nation), India, and Israel.[14] Malenkov's report of August 8, 1953 placed these economic moves into the context of his "new course," the first stage of which concentrated on importation of necessary foodstuffs and raw materials. Malenkov also made favorable remarks toward many of the non-Communist governments of developing countries, omitting the usual criticism of the national bourgeoisie.[15]

The volatile course of events in Iran during the summer of 1953 forced the Soviet leadership to face a crucial decision. While the Soviet government was making a series of cooperative gestures toward Premier Mossadegh, the Shah and General Zahedi lost out in an attempt to replace the Premier and were

p. 247.

11. William B. Ballis, "Soviet-Iranian Relations during the Decade 1953 – 64," *Bulletin of the Institute for the Study of the USSR,* XII (November, 1965), pp. 9 – 10.

12. Edward Crankshaw, *Russia without Stalin* (New York: Viking Press, 1956), p. 90; Boris Nicolaevsky, *Power and the Soviet Elite* (New York: Praeger, 1965), pp. 118, 134; Myron Rush, *Political Succession in the USSR* (New York: Columbia University Press, 1965), pp. 58 – 59.

13. Alvin Z. Rubinstein, *The Soviets in International Organizations* (Princeton, N. J.: Princeton University Press, 1964), p. 32.

14. Robert L. Allen, *Soviet Economic Warfare* (Washington, D. C.: Public Affairs Press, 1961), p. 129.

15. J. M. Mackintosh, *Strategy and Tactics of Soviet Foreign Policy* (London: Oxford University Press, 1962), pp. 77, 119 – 120, 130.

forced to flee. The Tudeh obtained freedom of action and Communist demonstrations broke out across the country. The "bourgeois nationalist" Mossadegh and the Communist Tudeh were ready to take over. Soviet support of both might have led to victory. However, the Tudeh was not satisfied with the prospects of sharing power and the Soviets may have gained confidence from the world reaction of awe at the first Soviet hydrogen bomb test, announced August 12. The Soviets chose a "dogmatic" course, putting their support behind the Tudeh and urging the bypassing of Mossadegh. With the division of these two anti-Western forces, the takeover failed.[16]

It would be reasonable to assume that those Soviet leaders most closely concerned with relations with foreign Communist parties, Secretaries Khrushchev and Suslov, and also Foreign Minister Molotov, favored support for this revolution, yet there is no evidence that this was an issue of factional difference. Soviet interest in these events was high (greater press coverage on Iran than in any other period from 1952 to 1956). Yet there was probably considerable wavering on the entire Iranian situation, as the high proportion of "neutral" press content would indicate. The failure of this coup must certainly have cooled down those "dogmatic" Soviet leaders who favored quick results in the form of Soviet takeovers and victories for Communist parties in the underdeveloped countries, and tended to give more credence to the practical advisability of cooperating with the liberation movements even though they were bourgeois.

During 1953 there was a significant discrepancy between the types of content emphasized by the two Soviet newspapers. The computer program indicated only one other such period, the winter of 1954–55. From May through November 1953 *Pravda* averaged 16.6 percentage points more "anti-" content than *Izvestiya,* although *Pravda* had been more "pro-" the preceding year. *Izvestiya,* on the other hand, averaged 14.0 percentage points more "neutral" than *Pravda* between June and November. If we assume that *Pravda* represented the party apparat and *Izvestiya* was the organ of the government at this time, then these differences mean that there were rather different approaches being advocated toward the underdeveloped world by the Khrushchev (party) and Malenkov (government) factions. *Pravda* was sticking to the "dogmatic" hard line of criticizing Western imperialism while *Izvestiya* was initiating a "revisionist" approach by introducing more objective reporting and editorializing less. Malenkov and his supporters were apparently more willing to revise the Stalinist approach to the "dependent" areas than were Khrushchev and those party *apparatchiki* aligned with him. This hypothesis is further supported by the finding that, in October 1953, the month after

16. David J. Dallin, *Soviet Foreign Policy after Stalin* (Philadelphia: Lippincott, 1961), pp. 213, 220, 294.

Khrushchev was recognized as the first secretary by the party Central Committee plenum, *Izvestiya* fell back into an "anti-" line.

These different emphases were apparently worked out within the collective leadership and resolved by "democratic centralism."

A Coordinated Policy Drive — 1954

Once differences between the newspapers had been resolved, analysis of the press indicates that after several months of caution and uncertainty a carefully organized, controlled, broad propaganda campaign was undertaken to lay a basis for an expansion of Soviet relations with the underdeveloped world through diplomacy and trade and in international organizations. Afghanistan was the object of an extensive drive through relief, assistance, conferences, and exchanges. Turkey was subjected to both weaning and cajoling in an attempt to turn her away from Western ties. Conciliation with Iran had little favorable results, as did vacillation toward Nasser, who was hard on Egyptian Communists. Arms were furnished to Colonel Arbenz in Guatemala but that revolution failed.

There were difficulties in implementing this new policy of expanding governmental relations when applied to countries which had influential national Communist parties. In India the Soviets had trouble in influencing the Communist party of India to cooperate somewhat with the Nehru government and to focus on American imperialism rather than on British colonialism. However, developments in Syria supported those Soviet leaders who favored a positive attitude toward the "national bourgeoisie." The secretary of the Syrian Communist party was elected to the parliament in September 1954 with the backing of petty bourgeois, nationalist elements whose cooperation he had encouraged.[17]

The most significant gain for the Communist movement during 1954 was the conclusion of the Geneva Indochina accord, which brought the first territorial gain to the Communist bloc since Czechoslovakia and mainland China. It came about as a result of an amalgamation of both the "dogmatic" approach through armed struggle and a "revisionist" willingness to come to terms with the capitalist enemy. The hard-line approach of Molotov appeared dominant at first, as the French were losing militarily.[18] Khrushchev took a very aggressive position, probably to align himself with Molotov, and Malenkov was forced in early 1954 to shift to a less conciliatory attitude toward the West. As the possibility of U.S. "massive retaliation" became more real and the

17. Walter Z. Laqueur, *The Soviet Union and the Middle East* (London: Routledge & Kegan Paul, 1959), pp. 198–199, 250–251.
18. Herbert S. Dinerstein, *War and the Soviet Union* (New York: Praeger, 1959), pp. 100, 115.

French deadline approached, Soviet concern rose and they began to encourage their Communist allies to find a diplomatic solution.[19] The computer analysis indicates that in May 1954 Soviet press coverage shifted from an "anti-U.S." emphasis to an "anti-West" one, suggesting that criticism was to be concentrated on the immediate French colonizers rather than on the overall threat of U.S. "imperialism." This success may have encouraged Soviet leaders to combine different approaches into a flexible policy toward the underdeveloped world that could lead to more than just obtaining raw materials or reducing Western influence.

The 1954 policy of expansion was a quantitative, not qualitative, change and does not appear to have been subject to factional differences. Malenkov was leading the way and Molotov was cooperating, with Khrushchev's support. The motivations may have differed — Molotov more concerned with blocking the West out of these areas or supporting Communist takeovers, Malenkov more interested in first obtaining raw materials needed by the USSR and then pursuing long-term gains for Communism — but they could agree on the overall desirability of extending Soviet influence into the underdeveloped world.

Factional Strife and Policy Reevaluation, 1954 – 1955

The period of October 1954 to March 1955 was one in which differences between Malenkov and Khrushchev came out into the open and during which there were foreign policy controversies also. An intense anti-American campaign was undertaken by the Communists in late 1954 over issues such as West German rearmament within NATO, the formation of SEATO, the Chinese "offshore islands," and the Turkish-Iraqi defense treaty which was followed by the Baghdad Pact. The Khrushchev-oriented Soviet delegation which went to Peking in September 1954 probably gained Chinese Communist support for a coordinated hard line against the United States and opposition to Malenkov's concepts of mutual deterrence, conciliation with the capitalist world, and consumer production.[20] By insisting that international tensions were mounting and undertaking these moves, Khrushchev was implementing a plan to win support against Malenkov from Molotov, Mikoyan and Shepilov (who were included on the China trip), and from the military-heavy industrial complex.

Patterns of press coverage of the developing nations offer some interesting sidelights on these overall developments. In October 1954 a cautious shift away from the previous "pro-" content appeared and then developed during the next two months into a definite shift away from this "pro-" to an "anti-U.S."

19. Boris Nicolaevsky, "Battle in the Kremlin," *The New Leader* (August 12, 1957), p. 7.
20. Donald S. Zagoria, *The Sino-Soviet Conflict, 1956 – 61* (Princeton, N. J.: Princeton University Press, 1962), pp. 405 – 406.

content, a reversion to the Stalinist hard line. At the same time, during November and December there was the second significant divergency between *Pravda* and *Izvestiya*, *Pravda* being considerably more "anti-" than *Izvestiya*. This occurred congruently with the heavy-industry – consumer-goods debate, supporting our thesis that once again the Malenkov *(Izvestiya)* faction favored a positive approach toward the underdeveloped world, stressing Soviet achievements and potentials, while Khrushchev *(Pravda)* and his allies were at this time putting greater emphasis on the negative goal of opposing the West.

Throughout the heightened international tensions propaganda campaign of late 1954 to early 1955, Soviet policy toward the underdeveloped nations appeared to become polarized. The Soviet leaders began to recognize that they could profitably cooperate with some of these nations and not with others if they ceased to lump them together. Those countries firmly tied to the West were included as targets for vilification.

On the other hand, the scope and depth of Soviet conciliatory moves were impressive and indicate a coordinated program. A decree was issued against crude anti-Islamic propaganda, signaling a change in attitude toward the Arab world. Criticism of Nasser was dropped and Soviet-Egyptian trade and aid relationships were established. Soviet concessions toward Iran and Turkey were made in an attempt to dissuade them from joining the Baghdad Pact. For the first time Nehru was given clearly favorable written praise, and India was granted the most significant foreign aid yet offered to a non-Communist country by the USSR for the Bhilai steel plant. In January 1955 an article appeared in the Cominform publication which laid the basis for doctrinal innovation in regard to the "national bourgeoisie." Foreign Minister Molotov summarized the combined "hard-soft" policy in his February report to the Supreme Soviet and it was applied the next month to the Pushtunistan issue when, for the first time, Moscow overtly supported Afghan claims against Pakistan.

These events can be related to factionalism within the Soviet leadership. After the divergency between *Pravda* and *Izvestiya* was reconciled in January 1955, *Pravda* assumed a leading role. Apparently Shepilov, editor-in-chief of *Pravda*, received policy-making authority in foreign propaganda matters and Pospelov, the party Secretariat head of *Agitprop*, switched from his somewhat neutral, pro-Malenkov inclination to Khrushchev's side. This shift in the press also supports the contention that the decision to reduce Malenkov from the premiership was not made at the Central Committee plenum in late January but rather early in the month. Molotov undoubtedly favored the "hard," anti-West aspect of the new "hard-soft" line while Mikoyan would have preferred the "soft" position toward local nationalists.

The overall contradiction between word and deed in this period leads one to suspect that the belligerent propaganda campaign was manipulated to hold the West at bay and divert attention from internal difficulties as Khrushchev weakened Malenkov's prestige.

Khrushchev's New Offensive Unfolds
during the Pre-summit Thaw

Not long after Khrushchev and Bulganin had taken over from Malenkov in February 1955, an all-out peace campaign was launched toward the West. The rapidity of this switch supports the hypothesis that the war scare had been trumped up to facilitate factional interests. In April the press coverage of the underdeveloped world shifted most significantly from its previously strongly "anti-" content to a predominantly "pro-" orientation, most of which was "pro-Soviet." The preparation for a new campaign was seen in the Soviet Foreign Ministry "Statement on Security in the Near and Middle East" of April that encouraged Arab opposition to Western alliances and, more significantly, expressed a willingness to cooperate with Arab nationalists. Coming right after the Baghdad Pact and just before the Afro-Asian Bandung Conference, it indicated to the underdeveloped countries that those which cooperated could count on the USSR for assistance. An important conference of Soviet Orientologists was held and their journal came out again for the first time in eighteen years. Finally, the Bandung Conference, which the USSR supported even though not invited, had a special influence upon Soviet policy.[21] Its impact upon world opinion must have given support to those Soviet policy-makers who were opting for greater latitude in dealing with national governments of underdeveloped countries.

Beginning after the Bandung Conference, a new energy, flexibility, and sometimes reckless willingness to experiment were introduced into Soviet policies toward the developing areas. A highly authoritative editorial appeared in *Kommunist* on May 25th criticizing previous evaluations of the role of the "national bourgeoisie" in colonial and semi-colonial areas. Shortly thereafter Khrushchev and Bulganin agreed with Tito's implicit rejection of the "two-camp" thesis when they recognized his neutral, unaligned position which was similar to that of many of the underdeveloped nations.[22] A number of traditional diplomatic and economic exchanges were undertaken, including Nehru's unprecedented visit to the USSR.

Of a much more radical nature was the encouragement the USSR gave to Egypt's interest in purchasing arms from the Communist bloc. Nasser had long wanted to achieve a truly independent position, which implied adequate military armament. Inquiries had received no encouragement from either East or West. After the agreement with the British in the fall of 1954 Nasser expected — in vain — Western help. The formation of the Baghdad Pact and Israel's attack on the Gaza Strip added an urgency to Nasser's perceived military needs. Soviet Ambassador Solod responded to Nasser's approaches in late

---

21. George M. Kahin, *The Asian-African Conference* (Ithaca, N. Y.: Cornell University Press, 1956), pp. 129–130.
22. Richard Lowenthal, *World Communism* (New York: Oxford University Press, 1964), p. 16.

May. It appears, however, that no final decision was made until after the July 1955 Central Committee plenum, indicating that the Soviet leaders realized the gravity of this extension of previous gradualistic expansion and wanted to have a firm position at home before taking this risky step.

The temporary coalition between Khrushchev and Molotov, formed during late 1954 as Malenkov was demoted, broke down very shortly after the immediate factional aim was achieved and fell completely apart at the July 1955 plenum. There had been differences within this coalition over several issues, including personal precedence, the appointment of party officials as diplomats, and particularly Yugoslav Communism. A gradual rapprochement had been undertaken with Tito after Stalin's death. Then in February 1955 Molotov critcized Tito and the latter's rebuttal was unexpectedly published in Shepilov's *Pravda* along with a mild editorial implying that Molotov's "dogmatic" position was no longer acceptable. In May, Shepilov — not Molotov — was included in the high-level Soviet delegation which visited Yugoslavia, indicating that Molotov's opposition to establishing party ties with Tito had been overruled. At the July plenum Molotov was isolated and forced to acknowledge his shortcomings.[23] It appears that he was relieved of many important functions and Shepilov, newly elected party secretary, took on greater responsibility in foreign affairs, particularly as concerned the underdeveloped world.

Khrushchev-Shepilov Underdeveloped Nations Policy in Full Bloom

Khrushchev used the July 1955 plenum to obtain support for his new campaign aimed at taking full advantage of opportunities in the underdeveloped world. Khrushchev is said to have described the very favorable situation on the "periphery of capitalism" as containing the possibility of sealing the fate of capitalism if India followed China in joining the socialist camp. Khrushchev's aim was to draw these underdeveloped areas away from the capitalist camp into that of socialism. The first explicit indication of a break with the Stalinist "two-camp" thesis was carried by *Kommunist* in an article which listed four categories of countries in Asia.[24]

Shortly thereafter Molotov made a second confession, this time of errors in theory. This allowed Khrushchev to reconcile the concept of "different roads to socialism," important for the underdeveloped world, with that of the leading role of the USSR. Molotov, an old Bolshevik, was reduced as an expert in ideological matters and the way was opened for further doctrinal changes. Molotov's humiliation gave Khrushchev and Shepilov more authority over foreign affairs. Khrushchev, together with Bulganin, took over high-level

23. George D. Embree, *The Soviet Union between the 19th and 20th Party Congresses, 1952 – 1956* (The Hague, The Netherlands: Martinus Nijhoff, 1959), p. 263.
24. V. Mikheev, "Novaya Aziya" [New Asia], *Kommunist*, August 25, 1955, pp. 85 – 88.

negotiations almost completely after the July plenum, and Molotov was apparently not among those Soviet leaders who met in October to plan the Geneva Foreign Ministers' Conference and its implications for the Twentieth Party Congress. Changes in diplomatic assignments to underdeveloped countries during the winter of 1955 – 56[25] indicate that Khrushchev and Shepilov were strengthening their authority to implement policy through the Ministry of Foreign Affairs at the expense of Molotov. Finally, it was Shepilov, not Molotov, who delivered the report on foreign affairs to the Twentieth Congress.

The spirit of Geneva characterized Soviet relations with the West in late 1955 and early 1956. The rather mild Western position may have encouraged Khrushchev to pursue a forceful, active campaign in the underdeveloped world. In addition to a series of moves which fit into the Malenkov pattern of cautious expansion of contacts through international groupings and meetings as well as diplomatic and economic relations, Shepilov brought the Egyptian arms deal to completion. Through this military aid coup the new Soviet leadership succeeded in hurdling the Baghdad Pact, creating a military counterforce within the Arab world, and encouraging "positive neutralism," a policy for the underdeveloped world which was not only anti-imperialist, but also leaning toward or indebted to the Communist bloc.[26]

The Khrushchev-Bulganin trip through India, Burma, and Afghanistan in November-December 1955 was the most publicized activity undertaken by the USSR throughout the entire four years under consideration and the prototype of Khrushchev's new style. In preparation for the Indian tour the "Shepilov letter" was allegedly sent to the Indian Communist party, with instructions not to interfere in Soviet diplomatic efforts aimed at courting the Indian government while advising the Indian comrades not to take all the public professions at face value. In spite of these machinations of international Communism, Khrushchev and Bulganin made a joint political statement with Premier Nehru and concluded a trade agreement which resulted in India's ranking first among the underdeveloped nations as a trading partner with the USSR, both in imports and exports. There appears to have been some criticism of this trip within the Soviet leadership, but the glowing reports of success overcame all objections and made the trip an impressive victory for Khrushchev's offensive.

Just as the Egyptian arms deal and the trip to the Far East may be regarded as the culmination of the implementation of Khrushchev's policy, so may the Twentieth Party Congress be looked upon as the high point of doctrinal readjustment. Many of the Stalinist concepts had been changed in practice over the three years since the dictator's death, yet not until the Twentieth

25. Andrey I. Lebed (ed.), *Key Officials of the Government of the USSR and Union Republics,* Series II, No. 81 (Munich: Institute for the Study of the USSR, Research Section, 1962), *passim;* Boris Meissner, "Der Auswärtige Dienst der UdSSR" [The Foreign Service of the USSR], *Osteuropa,* III (February, 1953), 49 – 54; IV (April, 1954), 112 – 118; V (February, 1955), 42 – 44.
26. Keith Wheelock, *Nasser's New Egypt* (New York: Praeger, 1960), p. 231.

Congress were the necessary changes in theory made and integrated into the doctrinal generalization of "peaceful coexistence." War was not a "fatalistic inevitability" because of the deterrent effect of socialist forces. Encirclement of the USSR had ended and a "peace zone" had emerged from the "two-camp" thesis. "Different roads to socialism" were recognized, as was the important role of the "national bourgeoisie" in achieving independence.

Although Khrushchev and his colleagues had only begun to apply their innovative policies toward the underdeveloped world by the time of the Twentieth Congress, they did have some results to show for their efforts. In this way, policies toward the underdeveloped world did assist them in establishing themselves as successful victors in the factional struggle within the Soviet leadership.

Conclusions

Our purpose has been to summarize the relationship between political factions and foreign policy in the USSR from 1952 to early 1956. We postulated that early post-Stalin policies toward the underdeveloped world were strongly influenced by factional differences between the Soviet leaders.

I must conclude that the hypothesis was substantiated only in part and that much of the evidence until 1955 negated it. Although there were very significant changes in Soviet policies toward the developing nations between the Nineteenth and Twentieth Party Congresses and intense struggles for power during the same period, policies toward the underdeveloped world were not "strongly" influenced by factional differences. Rather, they were generally developed collectively.

On occasion, however, some of the issues involved in the changing policies vis-à-vis the developing areas were used for factional advantages. Once Khrushchev had achieved his initial victories over Malenkov and Molotov in his struggles during early 1955, then the evidence clearly supports our hypothesis as policies toward the underdeveloped world were specifically used to broaden his power. Khrushchev took over Malenkov's careful extension of Stalin's trade expansion and added his own energetic, sometimes reckless style. He tried to make such a success of this "new" campaign — one of economic and military aid, political and propaganda captation, and doctrinal revisions — that his leadership position would be unassailable.

Khrushchev was strongly aided in this program by Shepilov, who had seen the potentialities for Soviet incursions into the underdeveloped world and used these issues as a means for reducing the prestige of Molotov and raising his own. Starting in late 1954, Shepilov had hitched his horse to the Khrushchev wagon and pulled especially hard in the direction of revising the Molotov approach toward the former colonies. The Twentieth Party Congress gave evidence of the success of the Khrushchev-Shepilov campaign as Khrushchev's broad doctrinal revisions were accepted and Shepilov's authority in foreign affairs rose over Molotov's.

Thus during the final year of our study, policies toward the underdeveloped world were used by one faction not so much to gain power over another faction as to retain an advantage previously won.

If policies toward the underdeveloped areas were not "strongly" influenced by factional differences, then one must deduce that these issues were decided by the Presidium in a "collective" or "bipartisan" manner, based on the merits as seen by the oligarchy. Policy alternatives would have been formulated through the various levels of the party and state hierarchies. Soviet leaders were able to disagree with one another on approaches in this area of foreign policy primarily on the basis of advantages which could accrue to the USSR and only secondarily in terms of their own power positions.

The conclusion that factional differences did not have a very pronounced effect upon foreign policies toward the underdeveloped world can have some important implications for Western evaluation of Soviet foreign policy-making in general. Those "bipartisan" policies arrived at and pursued under a truly "collective" leadership could be expected to be more deliberate, cautious, and open to rational influences, from within the decision-making body as well as from without. During such periods the organizational framework of foreign policy-making takes on added importance, indicating the advisability of keeping abreast of changes in such formal structures and their staffing.

In times when foreign policies are being used as weapons in a struggle for power, however, different guidelines prevail. A propaganda campaign may not be a substantial policy expression, but rather a front to keep the West at bay while the Soviet leadership is weakened by internal rivalry and strife. At other times a faction may choose to take a risky course which could have dangerous consequences yet promises brilliant successes in order to project itself ahead of opposing factions. If Western policy-makers are alert to the varying relationships which exist between Soviet foreign policies and leadership factions they will be in a better position to deal effectively with critical situations of various kinds.

Studying the Domestic Determinants
of Soviet Foreign Policy*

Some 15 to 20 years have passed since George F. Kennan and Barrington Moore, Jr., expressed the basic viewpoints of American students of Soviet affairs on the subject of the forces which shape Soviet foreign policy. In the meantime, important political and social changes have occurred on the Soviet scene. The autocratic form of government which Stalin personified has been replaced by an oligarchic regime headed by less omnipotent figures. A population which is more loosely controlled resorts to work slow-ups and petitions to demand a better and freer life. More information has become available about the sections of opinion and configuration of interests in bureaucratic quarters. The aim of these preliminary notes is accordingly to reexamine the viewpoints of Kennan and Moore in the light of contemporary history, and to suggest a possibly useful mode of inquiry into a slightly explored but perhaps important area of scholarship.

In his "Sources of Soviet Conduct," which first appeared in 1947, Kennan argued that the process of political consolidation of the Soviet regime was never completed and that the men in the Kremlin were always preoccupied with the struggle to secure and make absolute their power over Russian

*Reprinted with permission from *Canadian Slavic Studies,* I, 1 (Spring, 1967), pp. 44 – 59. This article was originally prepared for discussion at the Inter-university Research Colloquium on the Soviet Union and Eastern Europe, held at the Institute for Sino-Soviet Studies of George Washington University.

society. The Soviet leaders endeavored to secure their power primarily against forces at home, but also against the outside world, since ideology taught them that the outside world was hostile and that it was their duty eventually to overthrow the political forces beyond their borders. Kennan felt that as the remnants of capitalism were liquidated in Russia, one of the most basic of the compulsions which came to act upon the Soviet leaders was the necessity to justify the retention of dictatorial authority at home by stressing the menace of capitalism abroad. Moreover, Kennan held that many of the phenomena which Americans found disturbing in the conduct of Soviet foreign policy — secretiveness, lack of frankness, and duplicity — were essential to "the internal nature of Soviet power," by which he apparently meant the moral climate of the regime, and would endure until "the internal nature of Soviet power" had changed.[1]

Moore in 1950 found acceptable the argument that the authoritarian nature of the Soviet regime is a source of an aggressive and expansionist foreign policy insofar as the real or imagined threat of potential attack made it easier to drive the Russian masses through one set of Five-Year Plans after another. In this sense, the Soviet rulers were more desirous of creating an illusion of the threat of general war rather than fomenting general war itself as a means of maximizing their power. But these were afterthoughts, overshadowed by Moore's central thesis that the main outlines of Soviet foreign policy were reactions to alterations in the distribution of political power in the world at large. As far as internal factors like specific historical background, cultural tradition, and ideology(gies) were concerned, Moore emphasized the conditioning influence which they might have in molding the Soviet's response to an international situation. It should be added that in his outstanding book, Moore did suggest that Soviet foreign policy was made not only by the impersonal interplay of social forces but also by the personal ambitions of individual leaders. For example, he attributed a lag in Soviet recognition of the danger of Nazism to factional struggles within the Russian Communist party, centering around differing evaluations of the political situation abroad as well as personal rivalries, and suspected that at all times during the 1930's there was a group of Soviet leaders who believed in the possibility of good relations with the Hitler regime.[2]

Since Kennan and Moore wrote their essays a division of opinion has persisted over the relative weight to be given to internal and external happenings and stimulants of the Kremlin's international policy. Robert C. Tucker has adhered to the general concept of Kennan, focusing upon domestic political development and the impact of the personality of Soviet leaders, mainly

1. George F. Kennan, *American Diplomacy*, 1900–1950 (Chicago, 1952), pp. 107–128. See also Kennan's remarks in Carl J. Friedrich, ed., *Totalitarianism* (New York, 1964), p. 35.

2. Barrington Moore, Jr., *Soviet Politics — The Dilemma of Power: The Role of Ideas in Social Change* (New York, 1963), pp. 350–383.

Stalin.[3] Marshall D. Shulman, like Moore a decade earlier, has interpreted Soviet foreign policy largely in terms of responsiveness to changes in world power relationships. Doubtlessly alluding to Tucker, Shulman claims that his own analysis has merit because "it departs from familiar interpretations of Soviet policy which emphasize enigmatic and occult characteristics or the psychology of particular Soviet leaders" and "reveals patterns of behavior which bear some relationship to what we know of human behavior elsewhere in the world." Unlike Moore, however, Shulman deplores and avoids any attempt to investigate the mainsprings of Soviet policy from the angle of internal power politics, which he terms "the shenanigans in the Kremlin."[4]

While acknowledging the contribution which each of the aforementioned scholars has made to our understanding, it seems to me that the speculative model of Kennan and Tucker has more heuristic and predictive value than that of Moore and Shulman. Its underlying assumptions encourage us to search for information which helps to clarify matters of importance like influential trends of thought and the process of decision-making in the USSR, as well as the interaction of domestic and foreign policy considerations. Specifically, the analyst is challenged to find answers to questions of evidence along the following lines: What do Soviet sources have to say about the relationship of the internal and foreign policies of a Communist government? Are there different appraisals among Soviet policy-makers and subtleties regarding the consolidation of interior rule and, if so, of corresponding shades of opinion on foreign affairs? And is there a repeated coincidence of movement towards both the reform of domestic institutions and a variety of limited accommodation with the U.S.? Having derived partial answers to such questions, we may be in a better position to evaluate Soviet conduct and frame policy proposals which are sensible and statesmanlike.

A general discussion of the problem in recent Soviet literature[5] states that the internal and foreign policies of all governments are interconnected and puts emphasis on internal factors as the determinants of a government's transactions in the international field. The following elements are seen at work in the Soviet case, as in any other: (1) economics; (2) politics; (3) ideology; (4) personality of leaders; and (5) chance. Lenin is cited to the effect that "the very deepest roots of both the internal and foreign policy of our state are shaped

---

3. Robert C. Tucker, *The Soviet Political Mind: Studies in Stalinism and Post-Stalin Change* (New York, 1963), *passim.*

4. Marshall D. Shulman, "Some Implications of Changes in Soviet Policy toward the West: 1949–1952," *Slavic Review,* XX, No. 4 (December, 1961), 630–640 and *Stalin's Foreign Policy Reappraised* (Cambridge, Mass., 1963). See also the disdainful reference to "the mental exercise of analyzing obscure signposts indicating behavior and thinking within the Kremlin," in Bernhard J. Bechhoefer, "The Soviet Attitude toward Disarmament," *Current History,* No. 266 (October, 1963), 193–199.

5. "Nauchnye osnovy vneshnei politiki," in A. A. Arzumanyan *et al., Stroitel'stvo Kommunizma i mirovoi revoliutsionnyi protsess* (Moscow, 1966), pp. 409–415.

by economic interests," and the original adds: "by the economic situation of the dominant classes of our state." This apparently signifies that the holders of power who rule in the name of the so-called dominant classes of workers and peasants give priority to tasks of internal construction, the fulfillment of which will sooner or later improve the material lot of Soviet citizens, over schemes to aggrandize the Soviet Union abroad. That much can be inferred from the 1961 party program, which declares that "The CPSU considers that the chief aim of its foreign policy activity is to provide peaceful conditions for *the building of a Communist society in the USSR* and developing the world socialist system, and together with the other peace-loving peoples to deliver mankind from a world war of extermination" (italics added).[6] More recently, the idea of the preeminence of domestic policy in the USSR was conveyed as follows: "The central problem of the internal policy of the Communist party is systematic improvement of the material and cultural conditions of the life of all the toilers of our country and creation of the essential economic preconditions for this. . . . Of course, for the successful fulfillment of the tasks which are set by internal policy it is essential to assure a favorable international atmosphere for the peaceful labor of the people building communism."[7]

The element of domestic politics, which admittedly enters into the calculations of Soviet policy-makers, is not spelled out in the discussion of Arzumanyan *et al.,* and the reader is led to believe that such phenomena as palace intrigue and parliamentary deals are completely alien to the Soviet milieu. Other Soviet propagandists have alleged that only capitalist states are concerned mostly about the political function of maintaining internal control of their population and subordinate the expansion of borders or defense of territory to this main, domestic function of the state.[8] Still others have claimed apropos of politics that the absence in the USSR of a privately owned munitions industry which is operated for private profit and the existence of party controls over the armed forces, prohibits the advent of a military-industrial lobby and its unwarranted influence in governmental chambers.[9] What Arzumanyan *et al.* may have in mind in their reference to the politics of Soviet foreign policy is how Soviet leaders handle the political question of "nonantagonistic contradictions of socialism" like the discrepancy between limited production of consumer goods and rising popular demand, something related to the perennial issue of guns or butter (about which, more below). By "ideology," the authors plainly allude to the theories of social development which fall under the rubric of "Marxism-Leninism," and they imply that old habits of thought may sometimes be operative. The haphazard impact of

6. *Pravda,* November 1, 1961.
7. V. Stepanov, *ibid.,* August 10, 1966.
8. Iu. M. Borodai, ed., *Marksizm-leninizm — teoreticheskaia osnova stroitel'stva Kommunizma* (Moscow, 1965), p. 101.
9. Iu. Zhukov, *Pravda,* March 29, 1964.

personalities and chance is pointed up through the use of a Marxian letter of 1871 to the effect that "accidents" and "the character of people who at first stand at the head of the movement" might seriously accelerate or retard the inevitable course of history.

At the same time, the authors take into account the possibility of exterior initiatives, calling the tune and therefore reject the view of some that foreign policy is nothing more than a function of internal events. An unprovoked act of aggression committed against a state may impose upon its ruling circles a number of tasks which are not inherent in their philosophy or method of government. There is reciprocity between internal and foreign policy, since class relations are not limited to the national level, but have expanded into a worldwide system of economic and political entanglements. The capitalist system of states indeed exerts an "enormous" — but not "decisive" — influence on the internal and foreign policy of every state on the globe. Summarizing, the authors instruct that, "It follows from the Marxist-Leninist proposition about the system of states that internal policy is determined not only by the class relations inside a given country, but also by international class relations on the scale of the entire system of states; that the foreign policy of a given country is an integral part of the entire existing system of international relations; and that internal and foreign policy are inseparable from one another, both on the national scale and on the scale of the entire system of states."

There is merit to the Soviet disquisition, as far as it goes. The Soviet leaders' preoccupation with internal affairs is suggested by a number of materials which are designed for the orientation of CPSU officials. It is approvingly recalled that in the Leninist golden age of 1923 – 24 the Politburo examined almost 4,000 questions and only about one-fifth were related to the activities of the commissariat of foreign affairs, Comintern, and trade union International.[10] The curriculum of the Higher Party School in 1963 featured 1,500 hours of study, only 80 of which were devoted to the international Communist, labor, and national-liberation movements.[11] A survey of the lead articles in *Pravda* has disclosed that on an average there are seven a month on general domestic policy, five on industry, five on agriculture, five on political indoctrination and party organization, one on cultural policy, and seven on foreign policy.[12]

The effect of Stalin's warfare mentality on the conduct of Soviet foreign relations has been reasonably if not elaborately pointed out in party literature. Diplomatic contacts, especially at the highest level, were sharply reduced in view of Stalin's prophecy that the U.S. and USSR would ultimately engage in armed conflict.[13] Stalin aroused the displeasure of Communist China, Ru-

10. *Trinadtsatyi s'ezd RKP (b), Mai 1924 goda, stenograficheskii otchet* (Moscow, 1963), p. 73.

11. *Spravochnik partiinogo rabotnika, Vypusk piatyi* (Moscow, 1964), p. 258.

12. Wolfgang Leonhard, *The Kremlin Since Stalin* (New York, 1962), p. 22.

13. N. M. Druzhinin *et al., Sovetskaia istoricheskaia nauka of xx k xxii s'ezdu KPSS*

mania, Bulgaria, and Hungary by creating joint-stock companies, and instead of patiently discussing points of difference with Yugoslavia, he caused a rift.[14] In conformity with his mistrust of national reformers and line of self-isolation, Stalin kept the Soviet Union aloof from the newly emancipated nations in the underdeveloped regions.[15] Khrushchev's "subjectivist" errors in foreign policy have been hinted, but never pinpointed, in Soviet media. Western correspondents reported at the time of the premier's fall that his successors reproached him for personal initiatives which resulted in the serious loss of national prestige *vis-à-vis* Washington (the Cuban missile crisis) and good will inside the Eastern bloc (the Rumanian oil issue), as well as aggravation of the dispute with Peking.[16]

The record as viewed from Moscow and corroborated by independent sources also lends some support to the contention that the Kremlin must adjust its internal policy to modifications in the structure of world politics. The 17th CPSU(B) Congress in 1934 endorsed a five-year plan which called for higher rates of growth of light rather than heavy industry, but for a number of reasons, including German rearmament and hostility, these directives to ensure economic balance were altered.[17] (True, Hitler's rise to power was facilitated by the tactics of Stalin's Comintern with respect to the German social-democrats, but those tactics presumably were not decisive.) Soviet investment policy in 1949 underwent another drastic shift away from the renewed direction of balancing heavy and light industry.[18] The postwar forcing of military production which may be traced to 1949 can be related to the formation of NATO, which to be sure was a U.S. response, or maybe over-response, to the Communist political militancy in Central Europe. The argument of Soviet defensiveness appears to become more strained, however, once Moscow in the 1960's justified increases of its military budget in terms of American policy in Berlin and Southeast Asia. In those instances, the U.S. moderately answered Communist challenges to its overseas commitments and made no gesture which could be classified as detrimental to Soviet security concerns, no matter how liberally those concerns might be interpreted.

The fact that Soviet publicists deem it necessary to dispute "the simplified formula that 'foreign policy is a function of internal' events" suggests that certain members of the home audience raise the question of why a "peace-loving" state like the Soviet Union must habitually deny to its rank and file citizens a wide assortment of consumer durables and nourishing foodstuffs for

(Moscow, 1962), p. 494.

14. V. A. Zorin, ed., *Vneshniaia politika SSSR na novom etape* (Moscow, 1964), pp. 42–43.

15. *Ibid.,* p. 8.

16. Cf. *Le Monde,* October 30, 1964, *Neue Zuercher Zeitung,* October 30, 1964, and the *New York Times*, October 31, 1964.

17. Druzhinin, *op. cit.,* p. 412.

18. *Narodnoe Khoziaistvo SSSR v 1958 godu* (Moscow, 1959), p. 139.

the sake of building industrial-military power. *It cannot be stressed too heavily that the traditional patterns of investment and resource allocation which greatly favor the interest of industrial-military power over the interest of popular consumption are essentially legitimized in terms of international imperatives.* The 1961 party program held out the prospect of eliminating the national shortage of housing in ten years and providing an abundance of material benefits for the whole population in twenty years. But the qualification was made that, "The set program can be fulfilled with success under conditions of peace. Complications in the international situation and the resultant necessity to increase defense expenditures may hold up the fulfillment of the plans for raising the living standard of the people. An enduring normalization of international relations, reduction of military expenditures, and, in particular, the realization of general and complete disarmament under an appropriate agreement between countries, would make it possible greatly to surpass the plans for raising the people's living standard."

Once the preeminence of internal affairs and the dependence of investment policy upon an estimate of the international situation are accepted, the commanding influence of domestic politics in the form of bureaucratic group struggle over functions and funds may be hypothesized. Such a hypothesis rests on our knowledge of simultaneous and obviously interrelated conflict over economic and foreign policy within the Soviet hierarchy. This knowledge is derived to some extent by cross-checking the statements of topmost leaders on relevant issues and official decisions with accusations made against these leaders after they have fallen from power and the policies in force at the time of the denunciations. This inductive procedure will enable the analyst to discern only the contours of the dual struggle over power and policy, but that seems better than relying on deductive or intuitive processes.

The Malenkov-Khrushchev dispute of 1953 – 54 is one example of how bureaucratic infighting over issues of personal power and resource allocation can be a strong undercurrent of the formulation of foreign policy. Malenkov uniquely disputed the validity of the practice of giving preferential treatment to heavy industry, telling the USSR Supreme Soviet in August 1953 that "Heretofore we have not had the opportunity to develop light industry and the food industry *at the same rate* as heavy industry. Now we can and, consequently, must speed up the development of light industry in every way in order to secure a faster rise in the living standards and cultural level of the people" (italics added).[19] Malenkov gained the upper hand for a time, and in 1953 the rate of growth of the output of light industry not only matched but exceeded that for heavy industry.[20] Malenkov's determination to enforce his

----

19. *Pravda,* August 9, 1953.
20. See the official data cited in Leonard Schapiro, *The Communist Party of the Soviet Union* (New York, 1960), p. 553, note 1.

will on the issue of economic priorities apparently moved him to indicate that external risks had to be avoided lest East-West tension increase and require the Soviet to raise its military expenditure, which would be detrimental to the cause of bolstering light industry. The indicator was provided in Malenkov's unilateral and controversial statement of March 12, 1954 that nuclear war would result in "the destruction of world civilization."[21] On the practical level, the party Presidium headed by Malenkov stabilized defense spending and conducted vigorous diplomatic activity to settle the war in Indochina and redefine security arrangements in Europe so as to prevent the adherence of West Germany to NATO.

Khrushchev, a personal rival of Malenkov's since at least 1951, had a different set of objectives which interlaced ambitions of power and policy. First, the majority of the members of the party Presidium had to be persuaded to transfer from Malenkov to the party first secretary the right to steer the work of the Presidium. Second, the presidial majority had to be convinced that the interests of agriculture and defense required the expansion of heavy industry. Third, the U.S. had to be represented as an implacable antagonist which had to be restrained by a consistent military buildup in the Soviet Union and strengthening of the industrial base in Communist China. Khrushchev's opposition was expressed at the time by distinctive nuance in public speeches which acquired political meaning after his ascendancy in the Presidium was attended by appropriate changes of state policy.

Only a few weeks after Malenkov approved of developing light and heavy industry at equal rates, Khrushchev in his report on agriculture to the Central Committee plenum refused to endorse this viewpoint. Khrushchev instead accented the role of heavy industry in equipping agriculture, the sharp upswing of which was the most vital and important task in economic life.[22] Khrushchev, and especially his allies Bulganin and Voroshilov, spared no black paint in imaginatively depicting the U.S. as a plotter of surprise attack on the USSR, and they insisted upon a further strengthening of Soviet defenses.[23] Moreover, Khrushchev, Bulganin, and Mikoyan visited China in September 1954 and made agreements for technical assistance which put a further drain on the resources of Soviet heavy engineering.

The position of Khrushchev's group could only be reinforced by the U.S. determination to rearm West Germany and bring it into NATO. Shortly afterward, in January or February 1955, decisions were reached to oust Malenkov from the premiership and under the stewardship of Khrushchev to resume the policy of forcing the heavy and defense industries. The "theoreticians" who were denounced for having favored light industry were identified a few years later, when one of Khrushchev's lieutenants directly attacked Malenkov on

21. *Pravda,* March 13, 1954.
22. *Ibid.,* September 15, 1953.
23. See the citations in the Soviet press as noted in Arnold L. Horelick and Myron Rush, *Strategic Power and Soviet Foreign Policy* (Santa Monica, 1965), pp. 31ff.

this score.[24] In foreign policy, Malenkov in 1955 was obliquely discredited as "weak-nerved" and Khrushchev combined flexibility on the Austrian peace treaty with the launching of a risk-fraught course of politico-military adventure in the Middle East.[25]

Shortly after Malenkov was deposed, a philosophical argument over the stages of Communist development which had implications for Soviet domestic and foreign policy raged between Khrushchev and Molotov. Molotov, true to his reputation as a devoted follower of Stalin and insular Great Russian, urged a circumspect policy at home and abroad. He did so publicly in esoteric fashion by denying in a speech to the Supreme Soviet on February 8, 1955 that socialism had been built in the USSR and that the Communist regimes of Europe and Asia had taken more than the first steps toward socialism. It followed from these premises that bolder measures could not be adopted to increase free ("Communist") services to the Soviet people, deny the inevitability of world war, and self-assuredly bargain with the West, or hope for expanding the zone of Sovietization without the assistance of the Red Army. Khrushchev's counter-thesis that socialism had irrevocably triumphed in the Soviet Union was a doctrinal sign that conditions were ripe for a more equal distribution of wealth in the country, that Soviet power could prevent world war, and that under the Soviet nuclear shield, Communist regimes might emerge anywhere without fear of Western intervention to throttle them.[26]

Molotov's apprehension about the Kremlin's base of strength would probably have never created a political uproar unless it had been shared by various representatives of the elite and in the context of oligarchic politics had to be discredited so as to neutralize the influence of these representatives. One such leader of conservative opinion was the writer Kochetov, whose novel *Brothers Yershov* (1957) deplored the lack of ideological clarity after the attack on Stalin at the 20th Congress and insinuated that a popular revolution in the Soviet Union could not be excluded. In Kochetov's novel, a Soviet party member tells another in October 1956: "Is Hungary really cut off from us by an impenetrable wall? Do not the enemies of Communism harass us all they can? Of course they do, it's an all-out offensive, and a fierce one. And what are we going to do? Are we going to sit and wait till they start hanging us by the feet on the very same trees that we have planted?" Kochetov's adherence to circles which are especially hostile towards the U.S. was later suggested by the fact that shortly after the aborted summit conference in May, 1960, he condemned those interested in East-West dialogue as "some simpletons" who had become "too ecstatic over the murky and devious utterances of the

24. L. F. Ilyichev, *Pravda*, October 26, 1961.

25. See the instructive articles of Boris I. Nicolaevsky, "Malenkov's Heyday and Deposition," *The New Leader*, August 12, 1957, pp. 6 – 8, and "The Meaning of Khrushchev's Victory," *ibid.*, September 2, 1957, pp. 5 – 8.

26. See the speech of A. I. Mikoyan to the 22nd CPSU Congress in *Pravda*, October 22, 1961.

[American] President."[27] It may be hazarded that the Molotovs and Kochetovs would not be adverse to using cold war stereotypes for the purpose of maintaining time-honored institutions and ideological clarity in the USSR.

The interconnection of domestic and foreign policy may also be surmised from Khrushchev's repeated advocacy of internal reform and *détente* with the U.S. at one and the same time. In January 1958, Khrushchev publicly advised the sale of state-owned agricultural machinery to the collective farms, thus embarking on a course of raising collective farm income. Khrushchev in the same speech proposed a heads-of-government meeting, evidently to induce the kind of external atmosphere needed to liberate investment funds earmarked for conventional military projects.[28] After high-level talks in July 1963 to conclude an agreement to limit nuclear testing, Khrushchev implied the linkage of effort to pull up weak sectors of the economy and curtail military procurement by telling a delegation of American farm experts: "Now we shall reduce expenditure on defense, and this money as well we shall direct to the production of chemical fertilizers."[29] Once more, in August 1964, the premier fought for new approaches to the chronic peasant question, including a scheme for the decentralization of marketing practices in the socialized sector, and he told the British publisher Lord Roy Thomson that he was ready for a summit meeting to ease the burden of military spending.[30]

Significantly, Khrushchev's willingness to parley with the American president in 1964 was expressed after U.S. planes had bombed shore installations in North Vietnam (the Tonkin Gulf incident) which suggested that the premier was bent on furthering domestic experimentation even at the cost of impairing the Soviet's renown as a bulwark of "anti-imperialism." Khrushchev furthermore was drumming up support for a new international conference of the pro-Moscow parties in order to read out of the movement the Chinese Communists, who noisily held that the CPSU was betraying the cause of world revolution for the sake of domestic reconstruction. True, the Sino-Soviet dispute went on after the fall of Khrushchev, albeit in subdued tones until Peking's massive anti-Soviet campaign in the summer of 1966. Moscow, however, adopted a more forward tactic in its foreign policy and, as if in criticism of Khrushchev's final demarches, it was argumentatively stated that, "It would be an error to assume that at some stage the foreign policy of the USSR is guided exclusively or predominantly by the principle of proletarian internationalism and at some other stage by the principle of peaceful coexistence. . . . The paramount role in the foreign-policy activity of socialist states belongs, in our view, to proletarian internationalism."[31] The observer might be war-

27. *Pravda*, May 23, 1960.
28. *Pravda*, January 25, 1958.
29. N. S. Khrushchev, *Stroitel'stvo Kommunizma v SSSR i razvitie sel'skogo khoziaistva* (Moscow, 1964), VIII, 51.
30. *Pravda,* August 11 and 17, 1964.
31. V. Trukhanovskii, *Mezhdunarodnaia zhizn'*, no. 8, 1966, pp. 76 and 82.

ranted in suspecting that the events surrounding the ouster of Khrushchev confirmed the opinion and prediction which David J. Dallin ventured in 1955: "In a way the nearly four decades of Soviet history may be viewed as a very slow process of divorce of the Russia which is a part of World Communism and the Russia which is a new post-revolutionary national formation. The painful evolution still in its beginnings will not be completed without a re-sounding fight at the top of the Soviet regime."[32]

The sway of group and personal ambitions and manipulation of images of the outer world in the making of a Communist government's foreign policy is further suggested by the nature of Moscow's criticism of Peking in the 1960's. Whether the specific charges are truthful cannot be ascertained and is not actually relevant; what counts is the plausibility of the indictment in the circle of Soviet officials. According to the report of CPSU Central Committee Secretary Suslov to the Committee in February 1964, "the adventurous course of the Chinese leaders in the international arena is connected with their errors in domestic policy." The Great Leap campaign was allegedly motivated by nationalistic ambition to catch up rapidly with other socialist countries and occupy a dominant position in the world socialist system. The same nationalistic tendency was seen in Peking's agitation of passions over border questions, use of inflammatory propaganda during the Cuban missile crisis, and desire to build a nuclear arsenal. More personally, Suslov averred that Chinese Communist domestic and foreign policy could not be understood without realization that Mao Tse-tung craved recognition as the chief of the world Communist movement and a classicist of Marxism-Leninism.[33] A speaker in the discussion of Suslov's report added that Peking blamed outsiders for its internal difficulties: "instead of seriously analyzing the reasons for their own failures and finding correct means to overcome the effects of miscalculations, the Chinese splitters, concealing from their people the real state of affairs, try to shift the responsibility for their errors on to the Communist parties and leadership of other socialist countries."[34] Similarly, Academician B. G. Gafurov told a conference of ideological functionaries in June 1964: "I should like only to emphasize that the chauvinistic and adventurous course of Chinese foreign policy was especially activated after a series of reversals in the economy. This foreign-policy course was to distract the popular masses from internal reversals, hunger, and poverty. The CPC leadership sees a panacea for all its ills in the kindling of nationalism and chauvinism."[35]

To sum up, the Soviet viewpoint is that a Communist government ordinarily seeks to apply most of its energies to the solution of its domestic

32. David J. Dallin, *The Changing World of Soviet Russia* (New Haven, 1956), pp. 349–350.
33. *Plenum TsK KPSS, 14–15 fevralia 1964 goda, stenograficheskii otchet* (Moscow, 1964), pp. 543–544.
34. A. D. Skaba, *ibid.*, p. 593.
35. *Za chistotu marksizma–leninizma* (Moscow, 1964), p. 232.

problems and for that reason will not assume a belligerent posture toward other states unless it feels threatened by them. However, Soviet sources attest that the spirit of domestic leadership and politics in a Communist state may introduce serious complications into the international environment. The Communist leader of policy may be fatalistic and underrate diplomacy, thereby contributing to the rise of world tensions. He may intimidate and take unfair advantage of alliance partners, which can generate resentment and suspicion between nations. The leader is also capable of inspiring militaristic enterprises with a view towards channeling popular discontent into a direction which he thinks beneficial for the structure of internal power. While CPSU literature explicitly denies that there are professional groups in the Eastern bloc which have a vested interest in the manufacture of armaments and the endurance of international frictions, it provides circumstantial evidence of factional conflict inside the Soviet party over germane matters like estimates of the world situation, levels of military expenditures, and the stability of interior rule.

All this suggests that the dynamics of Soviet foreign policy that Kennan attributed to the inner workings of the Stalin regime almost twenty years ago have since provided the stuff of controversy in the closed system of committee politics which replaced the narrowly court politics of the Stalin era. Under Malenkov and Khrushchev, a unified viewpoint was lacking on the extent to which the Kremlin commands the allegiance of its subjects and needs to harp on the theme of vigilance in the face of outside perils as an instrument to promote mass dicipline. Cohesion was less than total on the doctrinally stipulated hostility of the West and the urgency of subverting its worldwide positions. Some notable collisions also occurred over the extent to which Stalin should be criticized, and this issue has involved questions of social morality and publicity of governmental business — questions bearing on what Kennan termed "the internal nature of Soviet power."

The Kremlin's deliberations and controversies over foreign policy in the 1950's and 60's hardly transpired in isolation from the outer world, and in updating our constructs we might do well to combine the one-dimensional insights of Kennan and Moore, simultaneously keeping in mind the primacy of domestic power considerations. Some practitioners have outdistanced many theorists in reaching this assumption. During the Cuban missile crisis in 1962, for example, an awareness of multi-sided interaction guided the counsel which U.S. roving ambassador Averell Harriman proffered to the White House. Arthur M. Schlesinger, Jr., who was then a presidential assistant, recalls that at the peak of the crisis he received a telephone call from Harriman at the U.S. mission in New York to the effect that Khrushchev "was desperately signaling a desire to cooperate in moving toward a peaceful solution." Harriman further said of Khrushchev: "We must give him an out. If we do this shrewdly, we can downgrade the tough group in the Soviet Union which persuaded him to do this. But if we deny him an out, then we will escalate this business into a nuclear war." Schlesinger adds that, "These words from the most experienced of all American diplomats seemed utterly convincing to me."[36]

One wonders what might have happened if President Eisenhower's speechwriters had not filtered out of the draft text of a public message of April 16, 1953 "a presidential offer to travel abroad to meet Malenkov" and exchange of American and Soviet airtime to allow the leaders of each nation to address the people of the other."[37] Or if West Germany was not rearmed and brought into NATO? Or if concern for his image as an alert chief executive had not prompted Mr. Eisenhower to declare that he was responsible for the decision to make the U-2 overflight of Soviet territory on the eve of the Paris Conference in May 1960? Or if in June 1961, President Kennedy had not refused to accept the Soviet proposal that the communique of the Vienna summit meeting indicate that he and Khrushchev had made some progress towards peace settlements? Or if the circumstance of the U.S. presidential campaign of 1964 had not made it impolitic for the American leader to respond to Khrushchev's latest bid for a summit conference? This is not to say that the U.S. Government acted wrongly in all of these complex situations, but that in some of them a display of flexibility may have had as important an effect on the collective mind of the Kremlin as did the adaptability shown with respect toward the Cuban missile affair and limited nuclear test-ban treaty.

If these impressions have any virtue, it follows that the student of Soviet foreign relations who wishes to go beyond mere description might find it profitable to look for causation in the intermeshing of various systems of national politics and policies. He may investigate foremost the conflicts of bureaucratic and philosophic interest within the Soviet political community and the effect of diplomatic and military decisions taken in world capitals like Washington, Peking, and Bonn on the resolution of those conflicts of rival interests. Of course, this is a matter of the skillful utilization of those methodological techniques which were originally devised by Boris I. Nicolaevsky and Franz Borkenau to shed a measure of light on the secret intrigues of the Kremlin and subsequently enabled analysts such as Donald S. Zagoria and Victor Zorza to track the vicissitudes of the Sino-Soviet conflict before it rose to the surface. The failure of most commentators to utilize those techniques in studying the struggle for power in the Soviet Union may be regarded as one of the foremost reasons why the demise of Khrushchev came as so rude a shock to many "experts," not to speak of interested laymen. It is to be hoped that in the future we shall not see a repetition of the error of 1957 – 64, when it was usually said that "Khrushchev is no Stalin," but the party leader was nonetheless viewed by many as unchallengeable.

36. Arthur M. Schlesinger, Jr., *A Thousand Days: John F. Kennedy in the White House* (Cambridge, Mass., 1965), pp. 821 – 822.

37. Emmet John Hughes, *The Ordeal of Power: A Political Memoir of the Eisenhower Years* (New York, 1963), pp. 108 – 109.

The following pointers on methodology are by no means exhaustive, but will give the student who has a command of the Russian language and the factional history of Communism a few working tools, and he can later make all kinds of refinements. To begin, an official reappraisal of investment, defense, and foreign policies may be reasoned from a combination of factors. One is the publication in the Soviet press of a direct statement that the heavy financial burden of producing nuclear weapons has had an adverse effect on proper development of the Soviet economy. Such a statement takes on added meaning if accompanied by agitation of the question of economic imbalance in the professional journals such as *Voprosy Ekonomiki* and the appearance of various doctrinal formulas on the subject of purchasing power and production in party political magazines such as *Kommunist.* The acrimonious nature of policy reappraisal may be inferred if such a statement about nuclear weapons and economic health is reported in a press organ which slants the foreign news in a way that conveys an impression of U.S. reasonableness and if the statement is ignored by another which selectively emphasizes U.S. firmness. This slanting of the news, a common feature of the press in authoritarian states such as Spain under Franco, also extends to coverage of how economic priorities are handled in other lands of the Eastern bloc. Policy debate may furthermore be signalled by the presentation of conflicting lists of diplomatic priorities in the articles and speeches of Central Committee members and diverse patterns of verbal approval or reservation by Committee members, with special reference to such items as disarmament and arms control.

At this point, Borkenau would probably add his maxim that "Spricht man von Kämpfen, muss man auch die Kämpfenden identifizieren" (If we talk about struggles, we must also identify the antagonists). A pitfall to be avoided is the foregone conclusion that a topmost leader's adherence to any one of the major apparatuses of Soviet rule presupposes his orientation as a "world revolutionist" or "coexistence man." There are certainly grounds for believing that the party apparatus harbors many officials who are of the opinion that world war is inevitable or that it can be prevented only by developing the industrial and military power of the USSR and expanding the zone of Sovietization. It would follow that any leader whose "constituency," or base of power, was in the party apparatus would unhesitatingly urge a line of doctrinaire intransigence toward the U.S. This apparently was true of party secretary Zhdanov in the postwar period and perhaps is true of Brezhnev today, but hardly seems applicable to Khrushchev, at least by the time his official career was ended. Which, of course, is to suggest that the party apparatus is subject to divisions of opinion and may be led in directions which may not conform to its "objective" interest. Similarly, diverse pressures of a functional and ideological nature are intrinsic to the state apparatus by virtue of its organization into civilian and industrial-military departments. One has only to inspect the record of the ups and downs in the political fortunes of business executives such as Voznesenskii and Saburov in the 1940's and later Mikoyan and Kosygin to suppose that Russia's technocratic class — distinguished as it is by general class interests — is no more cohesive than any other. In view of these circumstances, which give rise to temporary alignments of party and state leaders on various issues, the analyst may best ground his pertinent speculations on a detailed comparison of the differential verbal behavior and prominence of Soviet political personalities.

PART III

Communist Ideology,

Belief Systems,

and Soviet Foreign Policy

Observers of Soviet behavior have long been vexed by the question of the motivational role of Communist ideology. Many writers on this subject can be located on a spectrum running between two extreme positions based on certain assumptions about the motives of Soviet leaders: (1) that Communist ideology is a post facto rationalization of actions motivated by other considerations (personal power, national interest, imperialism, etc.); or (2) that ideology motivates Soviet leaders to take particular kinds of actions, or at least serves as "a guide to action."[1] Several of the chapters in this section represent positions which approach one or the other extreme, while others implicitly or explicitly reject this dichotomy and approach the question of the motivational role of Communist ideology from quite different perspectives.

Professor Sharp (see Chapter 7 below) comes down clearly on the side of national interest as the key to Soviet politics, including foreign policy. Sharp rejects the view that "the *ultimate* aims of the Communist creed are operative

---

1. Several articles have appeared in the last decade or so that classify the literature on Soviet ideology and foreign policy, and the student should consult them for a more detailed categorization. For example: William Glaser, "Theories of Soviet Foreign Policy: A Classification of the Literature," *World Affairs Quarterly*, XXVII, 2 (July, 1956), pp. 128–152; Daniel Bell, "Ten Theories in Search of Reality," *World Politics*, X, 3 (April, 1958), pp. 327–365; Adam Bromke, "Ideology and National Interest in Soviet Foreign Policy," *International Journal*, XXII, 4 (Autumn, 1967), pp. 547–562.

in policy determinations" and function as "a guide to action." He would probably concur with the findings of two major recent studies which conclude that "At no point does it appear that Leninist theory excludes a significant range of policy choices from being considered by the Soviet leadership,"[2] and that Soviet political leaders and analysts "rather than let Lenin do their thinking for them, found they could utilize Lenin to legitimate their thinking no matter how un-Leninist those thoughts might be. . . . [For] the ideological high priests under Khrushchev created the doctrinal legitimation for regarding *Leninism* as irrelevant to atomic age international politics by declaring that the period when the nature of imperialism determined the style of international politics had been historically transcended."[3]

While admitting that Communist ideology may be significant for the internal working of the regime, Professor Daniels (see Chapter 9) concludes that "foreign policy is one of the least ideological aspects of Soviet politics, in reality if not in words. Rather than foreign policy being governed in any substantial way by ideological requirements, the chief connection of the two lies in the decisions and situations which foreign policy considerations bring about and require the ideology to justify or explain away." For both Sharp and Daniels, ideology serves mainly as a post facto rationalization for policy.

However, R. N. Carew Hunt (in Chapter 7) contends that both ideology and "power politics" have a significant impact on Soviet foreign policy. He emphasizes that Soviet ideology affects the thinking and perceptions of Soviet leaders, whose actions are often influenced by the concepts and principles "to which all Communists subscribe." Indeed, Hunt maintains that certain Marxist beliefs have "led the Soviet rulers to take so distorted a view of the world as to make it harder to deal with them than with any government in the annals of diplomacy; and this . . . is just what may be expected from an 'ideology' in the sense in which Marx originally used the term." Hunt concludes that "There is no yardstick that permits a measure of the exact relation between power politics and ideology in the policies that result; but surely neither factor can be ignored."

David Forte also believes that "Soviet ideology bears an intimate relationship to Soviet foreign policy . . . and is not a mere philosophical rationalization for basically nationalist designs."[4] In support of these views, Forte presents a

    2. Michael Gehlen, *The Politics of Coexistence* (Bloomington, Ind.: Indiana University Press, 1967), p. 294.
    3. William Zimmerman, *Soviet Perspectives on International Relations, 1956–1967* (Princeton: Princeton University Press, 1969), pp. 287, 290.
    4. David Forte, "The Response of Soviet Foreign Policy to the Common Market, 1957–63," *Soviet Studies,* XIX, 3 (January, 1968), p. 373. Cf. Barrington Moore, Jr., "The Relations of Ideology and Foreign Policy," in Barrington Moore, Jr., *Soviet Politics — The Dilemma of Power* (Cambridge, Mass.: Harvard University Press, 1951), pp. 384–401 (reprinted in Alexander Dallin [ed.], *Soviet Conduct in World Affairs* [New York: Columbia University Press, 1960], pp. 75–91); and Bertram D. Wolfe, "Communist Ideology and Soviet Foreign Policy," *Foreign*

detailed study of the Soviet response to the early development of the European Economic Community (the Common Market). Significantly, he found that shifts in ideological premises nearly always *preceded* changes in policy; ideological change thus "set the stage for new practical policies."[5] Far from rationalizing or legitimizing policies already initiated, Soviet leaders and ideologists — at least on this crucial issue and during this period — played important parts in assessing the situation, planning new courses of action, and reformulating ideological principles in anticipation of policy changes.

In his contribution to the debate with Sharp and Hunt, Richard Lowenthal emphasizes three exceedingly important ideas: first, that some parts of an ideology have a much greater influence on elite perceptions, beliefs, and behavior than others; second, that a crucial question to ask about any ideological statement or belief is, "What *functions* does it perform?"; and, third, that the "operative" parts of Soviet ideology are those that maintain and justify the predominant role of the Communist Party in the Soviet political system.

Lowenthal is by no means the only scholar to distinguish among the component elements of Soviet ideology and to suggest that certain parts perform different functions under various circumstances.[6] Zbigniew Brzezinski, in his monumental study *The Soviet Bloc: Unity and Conflict,* carefully distinguishes among the "philosophical component," the "doctrinal component," and the "action program" of Soviet ideology. Brzezinski notes that these three elements "cannot always be neatly compartmentalized and will often overlap," but he stresses that their susceptibility to change and their impact on policy vary considerably.[7] J.M. Bochenski also identifies three basic aspects of Marxism-Leninism: "the basic dogma," "the systematic superstructure," and "the declassified doctrines."[8] Other scholars distinguish among "ideology," "dogma," and "doctrine"; "operational ideology" (the way Soviet leaders think), "official ideology" (what the people are told), and "national ideology"

Affairs, XLI, 1 (October, 1962), pp. 152 – 170.

5. Forte, *op. cit,* pp. 373, 386ff.

6. For example, Alfred G. Meyer, "The Functions of Ideology in the Soviet Political System," *Soviet Studies,* XVII, 3 (January, 1966), pp. 273 – 285. For general discussions of the functions performed by attitudes, opinions, values, and beliefs, see M. Brewster Smith, Jerome Bruner, and Robert White, *Opinions and Personality* (New York: John Wiley, 1964); and Daniel Katz, "The Functional Approach to the Study of Attitudes," *Public Opinion Quarterly,* XXIV, 2 (Summer, 1960), pp. 163 – 204.

7. Zbigniew K. Brzezinski, *The Soviet Bloc: Unity and Conflict* (Cambridge, Mass.: Harvard University Press, 1967), p. 489: from the important chapter "Ideology and Power in Relations among Communist States," pp. 485 – 512. See also Brzezinski's *Ideology and Power in Soviet Politics* (New York: Praeger, 1967), especially Chapter 5. On the important subject of *change* in the content and functions of Marxist theory and ideology, see Robert C. Tucker, *The Marxian Revolutionary Idea* (New York: Norton, 1969), especially "The Deradicalization of Marxist Movements," pp. 172 – 214.

8. J. M. Bochenski, "The Three Components of Communist Ideology," *Studies in Soviet Thought,* II, 1 (March, 1962), pp. 7 – 11.

(what the people believe); and even "popular ideology," "cadre ideology," and "ideologists' ideology."[9]

Assessing the impact of Soviet ideology on foreign policy, Professor Ulam (see Chapter 8 below) identifies three potential *uses* of Marxism: (1) "implied prescriptions (implied, because Marx and Engels never devoted much attention to the problem of the foreign policy of a socialist state)"; (2) "an analytical discipline for viewing international as well as domestic politics"; and (3) "a symbol and quasi-religion giving its practitioners the sense that they are moving forward with the forces of history and that the success of their state is predicated upon the truth of the doctrine." The first of these, he argues, no longer plays a significant part in the conduct of Soviet foreign policy, "while the analytical and symbolical uses of Marxism remain important and necessary to the understanding of Soviet policy." Ulam would perhaps agree that even the *"Realpolitik"* pursuit of "national interest" is "totally conditioned by the way in which the policy-makers apprehend reality."[10]

Ulam also anticipates Alfred G. Meyer's important arguments on the "legitimizing" and "self-legitimizing" functions of Soviet ideology — that is, the use of ideological statements "to convince the citizenry that the party and its leaders have a legitimate claim to rule them," and as "a continual attempt on the part of the rulers to convince *themselves* of their legitimacy."[11] Ulam's essay, published over a decade ago, retains a special significance in that it is written by the author of *Expansion and Coexistence*, by far the most comprehensive and influential interpretive history of Soviet foreign policy by any Western scholar.

Careful readers have undoubtedly noted that we have yet to present a precise, lucid, and succinct definition of the concept "ideology." David Joravsky, in a stimulating and insightful paper, offers just such a definition: "When we call a belief ideological, we are saying at least three things about it: although it is unverified or unverifiable, it is accepted as verified by a particular group, because it performs social functions for that group." Joravsky explains that "'Group' is used loosely to indicate such aggregations as parties, professions, classes, or nations," and "'Because' is also used loosely, to indicate a functional correlation rather than a strictly causal connection between acceptance of a belief and other social processes."[12]

Joravsky's distinction between unverifiable beliefs ("grand ideology") and verifiable but unverified beliefs ("petty ideology") is important. Beliefs of the former kind include powerful emotional appeals such as "All men are created equal," whereas more specific and perhaps verifiable derivatives of this precept

9. For example, Kurt Marko, "Soviet Ideology and Sovietology," *Soviet Studies*, XIX, 4 (April, 1968), pp. 465–481.

10. Forte, *op. cit.*, p. 373.

11. Meyer, *op. cit.*, especially pp. 279–281.

12. David Joravsky, "Soviet Ideology," *Soviet Studies*, XVIII, 1 (July, 1966), p. 3.

include propositions such as, "Universal suffrage would allow the poor to control or even take the property of the rich."[13] Fundamental Soviet beliefs at the level of grand ideology include: "matter is all that exists, reality is essentially dialectical, the triumph of communism is inevitable, the aims of communism coincide with the aims of working mankind, the Party is the vanguard of mankind and will lead it to communism."[14] Beliefs at the level of petty ideology include many of Khrushchev's major doctrinal innovations: "Wars are not inevitable," "violent revolutions are not inevitable," "peaceful coexistence with the West is possible and desirable," "different roads to socialism are possible and desirable," "countries of the Third World 'peace zone' are unaligned and uncommitted to either the socialist or capitalist 'camps.'" In short, petty ideology consists of the more "specific, verifiable beliefs that cluster about the grand ideologies," and both the content and the social functions of petty ideology are more susceptible to change than those of grand ideology.

Theoretical ideology, in both its grand and petty forms, must be sharply distinguished from "political realism," which Joravsky defines as "a constantly shifting jumble of commitments to particular judgements and persons."

> Perhaps the most basic, the golden rule of the "realistic" politician, is his practical way of recognizing that politics is the business of arranging people in hierarchies of power. . . . His basic principle, though rarely stated, is evident in his behaviour: If a belief reduces one's influence in one's group, it is wrong; if it increases one's influence, it is right. This is an ideological principle.[15]

Joravsky goes on to observe that "it is clear to most Western students of Soviet affairs that grand and petty ideology have been giving way to political 'realism' in the thinking of the Soviet elite. This is the process that Meyer calls 'the routinization of indoctrination'; others have called it the erosion, exhaustion, or even the end of ideology."[16] The latter phrases are very misleading, Joravsky argues, because they suggest that "political realism" is devoid of ideology merely because it does not contain serious philosophical or theoretical statements.

This gradual transformation has created difficult problems for analysts of Soviet ideology and political behavior. In essence, "political realism" consists of the "basic rules of thought" that shape the motives, beliefs, judgments, and actions of Soviet leaders. But the lack of data on the belief systems of Soviet officials, the nature of the Soviet policy-making process, and the organizational, social, and psychological constraints on Party leaders, make it exceedingly difficult to study the "operative" political beliefs of Soviet elites, individually or collectively.

---

13. *Ibid.*, pp. 3 – 8.
14. Richard DeGeorge, *Patterns of Soviet Thought* (Ann Arbor, Mich.: University of Michigan Press, 1966), pp. 234ff.
15. Joravsky, *op. cit.*, p. 9.
16. *Ibid.*, p. 10.

In view of these problems, the contribution by Alexander George (see Chapter 10 below) is particularly important. For George attempts to reconstruct both the philosophical and the instrumental beliefs that comprise "the operational code" of Soviet leaders, especially in the Lenin and Stalin eras. In far greater detail than Lowenthal and others, George describes the maxims or "approaches to political calculation" that seem to have shaped Soviet decisions and behavior. "Knowledge of the actor's beliefs helps the investigator to clarify the general criteria, requirements, and norms the subject attempts to meet in assessing opportunities that arise to make desirable gains, in estimating the costs and risks associated with them, and in making utility calculations." These considerations greatly influence foreign policy decisions, and are almost certainly what Joravsky had in mind when he referred to "political realism," as distinct from theoretical ideology.

George's reformulation of Soviet "optimizing strategy" is particularly interesting in light of past and present Soviet performance, for example, the "dual policy" of the 1920's and "peaceful coexistence" of the 1950's and 1960's. George argues that knowledge of belief systems and the ways in which they change provides "one of the important inputs needed for behavioural analyses of political decision-making and leadership styles. The 'operational code' construct does this insofar as it encompasses that aspect of the political actor's perception and structuring of the political world to which he relates, and within which he attempts to operate to advance the interests with which he is identified. This approach should be useful for studying an actor's decision-making 'style,' and its application in specific situations."

The chapter by Kelly and Fleron examines some of the important research questions explicitly and implicitly raised by George; it is a sort of lament for what is not known about the motivational linkage between Communist ideology and behavior. The authors point to the tradition among "experts" on Communist affairs to treat their subject as a more or less unique phenomenon. This has had the adverse effect, they argue, of isolating the study of Communist ideology from the conceptual, empirical, and theoretical advances in psychology and social psychology in recent decades.

Analysis of the psychological dimension of individual political leaders was *au courant* in the study of Soviet foreign policy two decades ago, but fell into disrepute after the appearance of Nathan Leites' *The Operational Code* and *A Study of Bolshevism,* which some felt were at least premature and not firmly data-based, and others viewed as utterly bizarre. Recently, however, George and others have shown renewed interest in this aspect of inquiry, not only in the study of Soviet foreign policy, but also in the study of foreign policy more generally.[17] Both the general theorist and the area specialist will benefit if this renewed interest is pursued jointly, rather than separately as in the past.

Kelly and Fleron present some hypotheses drawn from psychological theories which may describe the relationship of Communist ideology to the political behavior of Soviet leaders. So little has been done in the area of applying that literature to the study of Communist ideological beliefs that it is easy to dip into various theories and extract small parts for purposes of illustration. Extreme eclecticism characterizes the Kelly-Fleron chapter, some parts of which may be contradictory, empirically if not logically (for example, the conclusions of Davies and those of the positivist learning theorists). Each theory would have to be analyzed separately and in greater depth to have significant utility for the study of the relationship between Communist beliefs and behavior. In essence, Kelly and Fleron identify some possibilities for the application of psychological theory to the study of Communist ideology and behavior.

When the question of the motivational role of Communist ideology for Communist behavior is placed in the broader context of the relationship between belief systems and behavior, one finds a huge set of potentially relevant variables and important questions which have not been applied in the Soviet context. And although psychological theories are not the only source of such variables and questions (the same could be said of Marxist theory, Christian theology, and many others), it does seem that there is more systematic evidence for psychological theory than there is for any of the others. It may be that our insistence on such "evidence" is epistemologically unsound, but that evidence is nevertheless the main standard of usefulness and proof currently employed in science and philosophy.

In the study of international relations, then, the key issue "is not *whether* psychological processes are relevant, but *how* they are relevant."[18] Fundamen-

17. Cf. William Zimmerman, "Elite Perspectives and the Explanation of Soviet Foreign Policy," Chapter 2 above; Jan F. Triska and David D. Finley, *Soviet Foreign Policy* (New York: Macmillan, 1968), especially Chapters 4 and 9; Robert C. Angell and J. David Singer, "Social Values and Foreign Policy Attitudes of Soviet and American Elites," *Journal of Conflict Resolution,* VII, 4 (December, 1964), pp. 329 – 491; Ralph K. White, "Images in the Context of International Conflict: Soviet Perceptions of the U.S. and the U.S.S.R.," in Herbert C. Kelman (ed.), *International Behavior: A Social-Psychological Analysis* (New York: Holt, Rinehart & Winston, 1965), pp. 236 – 276; J. David Singer (ed.), *Human Behavior and International Politics* (Chicago: Rand McNally, 1965); David Finlay, Ole Holsti, Richard Fagan, *Enemies in Politics* (Chicago: Rand McNally, 1967); Joseph De Rivera, *The Psychological Dimension of Foreign Policy* (Columbus, Ohio: Merrill, 1968); "Leadership: The Psychology of Political Men," *Journal of International Affairs,* XXIV, 1 (1970), "Image and Reality in World Politics," *Journal of International Affairs,* XXI, 1 (1967); Michael Brecher, Blema Steinberg, and Janice Stein, "A Framework for Research on Foreign Policy Behavior," *Journal of Conflict Resolution*, XIII, 1 (March, 1969), pp. 75 – 101.

18. Herbert C. Kelman, "The Role of the Individual in International Relations: Some Conceptual and Methodological Considerations," *Journal of International Affairs*, XXIV, 1 (1970), p. 4. See also John G. Gunnell, "The Idea of the Conceptual Framework: A Philosophical

tal questions concerning the psychological environment of Soviet foreign policy-makers (see the conceptual framework, page 8 above) include: How do Soviet leaders perceive their "national interests"? How do they perceive the interests, capabilities, and intentions of other nations? To what extent does Soviet ideology shape these perceptions? Which parts of the ideology shape attitudes, images, and beliefs more than others? What effects do these attitudes, images, and beliefs have on Soviet behavior? Why do they have these effects? When do they do so? In short, "whose images count, under what conditions, and at what points in the international policy-making process"?[19]

Thus, if ideology is "a broad system of concepts with educational and integrative functions,"[20] and if "the chief function of ideology — whether theoretical, 'realistic', or a mixture of the two — is to rationalize a group's readiness to act, or to refuse to act,"[21] some parts of Soviet ideology may significantly influence the social-psychological processes of Soviet leaders (e.g., "those relating to motivation, perception, trust and suspicion, definition of the situation, stress, communication, leadership, influence, norm formation, role prescription, group cohesiveness, loyalty").[22] For foreign policy-makers, particularly important general processes include defining the nature of a situation, formulating possible initiatives and responses, assessing threats, risks, and likely consequences of different policies, and developing criteria for choosing among alternative courses of action. Hence Zimmerman concludes (see his essay above) that the serious researcher finds himself returning to the study of "the cognitive and affective maps of particular decision-makers — but at a greater level of specificity . . . and within a general framework which stresses the impact of external factors on Soviet behavior."

Herbert C. Kelman, a distinguished social psychologist, adds an important caveat. He warns that the study of foreign policy-making should not be based entirely on psychological variables. Such an analysis would be inadequate because "it ignores the role of situational constraints (i.e., constraints deriving from the specific context in which national decision-makers arrive at their decision and in which they interact with their counterparts in other nations) and/or structural constraints (i.e., constraints deriving from the structure of national and international political systems)."[23] But Kelman also argues that certain social-psychological processes can and should "enter importantly into

Critique," *Journal of Comparative Administration,* I, 2 (August, 1969), pp. 140 – 176.

19. Herbert C. Kelman, "Social-Psychological Approaches: The Question of Relevance," in Kelman (ed.), *International Behavior,* p. 456.

20. Rudolf Schlesinger, "More Observations on Ideology," *Soviet Studies*, XIX, 1 (July, 1968), p. 87.

21. Joravsky, *op. cit.*, p. 15.

22. Herbert C. Kelman, "Social-Psychological Approaches to the Study of International Relations: Definition of Scope," in Kelman (ed.), *International Behavior*, p. 17.

23. Kelman, "The Role of the Individual in International Relations: Some Conceptual and Methodological Considerations," *op. cit.,* p. 9.

various general conceptualizations of the interaction between nations and foreign policy-making" — particularly those internal constraints and personality dispositions of important decision-makers. Situational and psychological constraints both

> may operate to varying degrees, depending on the occasion for the decision and on numerous other factors, and they may interact with one another in various ways. Structural factors may create dispositional constraints, and dispositional factors, in turn, may create structural constraints. We are dealing here with societal and inter-societal processes and with the complex functioning of national and international systems. These processes, however, can be in part illuminated by a microanalysis of the cognitive and social processes that occur at the locus of decision-making, as long as we recognize that these merely represent the culmination of a large array of prior events and interactions. Most important, by studying the perceptions and action tendencies of the decision-maker and the interactions within the decision-making unit, we can learn a great deal about the nature of the constraints that operate in different situations and the way in which they affect each other and the final decision outcome.[24]

For the researcher, then, it is very difficult to ascertain what Soviet leaders believe and which perceived factors and beliefs actually shape policies and behavior under different circumstances. Joravsky notes that after the first five or ten years of Soviet rule, Party leaders ceased to make serious efforts to state their operative political beliefs in explicit theoretical form, and, as a result, a significant portion of the political process ceased to be publicly documented. "After that brief period, the increasing replacement of theoretical ideology by closemouthed 'realism', and the growing passion for closed politics, limited the Western student to very gross inferences about the interaction of political beliefs and political processes."[25]

As a result of this situation, Joravsky argues, "The Western student of Soviet ideology faces a choice. He can limit himself to areas of thought where Soviet ideology can be identified from the vantage point of genuine knowledge and its social functions discovered by rigorous empirical scholarship. Or he can turn boldly to the political process, where ideology is most important — and nearly impossible to study in a rigorously empirical scholarly fashion. He can aspire to a scientific analysis of Soviet ideology or to an ideological critique of it. The choice can hardly be thoroughly rational; it is unavoidably influenced by one's ideological hopes and fears concerning the relationship between politics and scholarship."[26]

For the most part, students of Soviet ideology have chosen the latter approach — they have engaged in ideological critiques of Communist ideology rather than in scientific analysis. In some cases these ideological critiques (or "counter-ideologies") have masqueraded as "scientific" analysis, especially by

24. *Ibid.,* pp. 9 – 10.
25. Joravsky, *op. cit.,* pp. 12 – 13.
26. *Ibid.,* p. 15.

some American academics who wish to market their "services" to American policy-makers. As Kelly and Fleron point out, every "expert" on Communist affairs is expected to have some answer to the question of the motivational link between Communist ideology and Communist behavior. However, the locked door of the archive and the paucity of candid interviews have made impossible rigorous scientific analysis of the social functions performed by Soviet ideology. Hence it is impossible for the more objective scholar to refute the theories (and rantings and ravings) of anti-Communist counter-ideologists.[27] Yet concerted efforts in these directions must be made. For, as a respected social psychologist reminds us, "situations defined as real are real in their consequences."[28]

27. Not surprisingly, this latter form of ideology may also perform important social functions. See the chapter by Spiro and Barber below.

28. W. I. Thomas, quoted in Urie Bronfenbrenner, "Allowing for Soviet Perceptions," in Roger Fisher (ed.), *International Conflict and Behavioral Science* (New York: Basic Books, 1964), p. 166. For evidence that Soviet international perceptions are becoming increasingly similar to Western perceptions, see Zimmerman, *Soviet Perspectives on International Relations, 1956–1967.* For another example, consider the following comments of the distinguished Soviet Academician, N. N. Inozemtsev, from an article justifying the importance of American area studies programs in the USSR: "One of the important tasks of our American area studies is the concrete analysis of the complex and in many ways contradictory process of the elaboration and formulation of the course of U. S. foreign policy. This process is influenced by external and internal factors; it reflects changes in the international situation and in the domestic situation within the United States. It is affected by the internal struggle among various groupings in the ruling elite of the U. S. A. and by the nature of foreign-policy doctrines and concepts." From "The U. S. A. Today and Soviet American Area Studies," *Ekonomika, politika, ideologia,* I, 1 (January, 1970), pp. 6–14, translated in *The Current Digest of the Soviet Press,* XXII, 11 (April 14, 1970), p. 5.

SEVEN

Ideology and Power Politics:

A Symposium *

The Importance of Doctrine
R. N. CAREW HUNT

The term "ideology" is one which is more often used than defined. As the present study will be concerned with what the Russian Communists, and Communists in general, mean by it, a definition taken from a Soviet source is in order. The *Filosoficheskii Slovar* (Philosophical Dictionary, 1954 ed.), calls ideology "a system of definite views, ideas, conceptions, and notions adhered to by some class or political party," and goes on to say that it is always "a reflection of the economic system predominant at any given time." In a class-divided society the ideology will be that of one or another of the struggling classes, but under socialism, when there is no longer any class division, it will be that of society as a whole. A quotation from Lenin is added to the effect that there can be no "middle way" between the ideology of the bourgeoisie and that of the proletariat. The one is false and the other true.

Such a summation, albeit neat, is not altogether satisfactory. Broadly speaking, Marx was right in contending that the ideology of a society — the complex of ideas which determine its "way of life" — will be that of its dominant class, that is, of those whose abilities (whether used rightly or wrongly is irrelevant in this context) have raised them above the common herd. But this sociological fact applies equally to the Soviet Union, where the party certainly

*Reprinted from *Problems of Communism,* VII, 2 (March-April, 1958), pp. 10–30, and VII, 3 (May-June, 1958), pp. 50–52, by permission of the authors and the publisher.

constitutes such a class and indeed is assigned the duty of fertilizing the masses with its ideas. Undoubtedly the current Soviet ideology is intended to strengthen the party and reinforce its claim to rule. But one must probe further to explain why the party should have adopted the particular body of doctrine that it has. The fact is that the ideology has been largely determined by the type of collective society which has been established in the Soviet Union.

The authors of the October Revolution were Marxists, and were thus committed to abolishing the capitalist system and replacing it by a nationwide planned economy. For a brief period the experiment of allowing the workers to take charge was tried out, but, when this led to chaos, the party assumed control and has ever since retained it.

If a Communist regime is to be set up in a backward country, the first prerequisite, as Lenin saw, is industrialization; this is likely to be carried out as rapidly as possible, since the quicker the country is developed, and particularly its war potential, the stronger will be the position of its rulers. The execution of such a program of necessity demands the centralization of power in the hands of a small group of leaders, along with the adoption of such unpopular measures as the fixing of wages, the direction of labor, and the prohibition of strikes. And as large-scale planning geared to an expanding economy is impracticable if the plan is liable to be upset at any moment by a vote in a popular assembly, it is not to be expected that the planners will long tolerate any opposition. Furthermore, they will be tempted to interfere in one branch of human activity after another, seeing that all can be so manipulated as to assist the execution of their grand design.

All this has happened in the Soviet Union, and the outcome has been an ideology which derives from the logic of collectivism. Its basic principles are to be found in Marx's revolutionary doctrine, the implications of which were spelled out by Lenin and Stalin when confronted with the practical problem of setting up the type of social order Marx had advocated. Communist literature and propaganda have made us familiar with the doctrine, and there is no need to analyze it here even if space permitted. The issue to be decided is what role ideology plays today, and how far it influences Soviet policy.

Myths and the Masses

Virtually all analysts would agree that in the years of struggle before the October Revolution the Bolsheviks took the theory which lay behind their movement in deadly earnest; there is also general agreement that in the 1920's the doctrine acted as a stimulus to the workers, who took pride in building up their country. In the 1930's, however, the situation changed. Stalin assumed absolute power. The machinery of the state and of the secret police was greatly strengthened, and all prospect of establishing a genuine classless society disappeared. With the Stalin-Hitler Pact, if not before, the Soviet Union entered an era which can plausibly be represented as one of naked power politics, perpetuated after World War II in the aggressive and obstructive policies pursued by the regime. Hence it is sometimes argued that Communist ideology has now ceased to possess any importance; that it is simply a top-dressing of sophistries designed to rationalize measures inspired solely by Soviet interests; and that apart from a few fanatics, such as may be found in any society, no one believes in the doctrine any longer, least of all the leaders themselves.

Yet such unqualified assertions are erroneous. Consider, first, the outlook of the ordinary Soviet citizen *vis-à-vis* the ideology. Day in, day out, he is subjected to intensive and skillfully devised propaganda through every known medium, designed to demonstrate that the ideology on which the Soviet Union is based makes it the best of all possible worlds, and that on this account it is encircled with jealous enemies bent on its destruction. The Soviet leadership has always considered it essential that every citizen possess as deep an understanding of Communist principles as his mind is capable of assimilating, and those holding positions of consequence are obliged recurrently to pass through carefully graded schools of political instruction.

It is significant that whenever the leaders feel themselves in a tight corner — as in the recent aftermath of de-Stalinization and the intervention in Hungary — their invariable reaction is to intensify indoctrination in an attempt to refocus public attention on "first principles." As hard-headed men they would certainly not attach such importance to indoctrination if they did not know that it paid dividends — and experience has proved that the persistent repetition of a body of ideas which are never challenged is bound to influence the minds of their recipients. Of course, the present generation does not react to the formal ideology with the same fervor as did its forebears who made the revolution, and there are doubtless those who view official apologetics with a large degree of cynicism. But between total commitment and total disillusionment there are many intermediate positions; it is quite possible for a man to regard much of what he is told as nonsense while still believing that there is something of value behind it, especially if he identifies that "something" with the greatness of his country as "the first socialist state" and believes in its historic mission.

Leadership Credence — A Hope or a Habit?

More significant, in the present context, than the attitude of the ordinary citizen is that of the ruling elite which is responsible for policy. What its top-ranking members believe is a question which no one, of course, can answer positively. But before surmising, as do some analysts, that the Soviet leadership cannot possibly believe in the myths it propounds, we should remind ourselves that no class or party ever finds it difficult to persuade itself of the soundness of the principles on which it bases its claim to rule.

The Soviet leaders are fortified in this conviction by the very nature of their creed. They have been nurtured in it from birth, and it would be strange indeed if they had remained unaffected. It has become second nature to these men to regard history as a dialectical process — one of incessant conflict between progressive and reactionary forces which can only be resolved by the victory of the former. The division of the world into antagonistic camps, which is an article of faith, is simply the projection onto the international stage of the struggle within capitalistic society between the bourgeoisie, which history has condemned, and the proletariat, whose ultimate triumph it has decreed. The leaders seem to be confident that history is on their side, that all roads lead to communism, and that the contradictions of capitalism must create the type of situation which they can turn to their advantage.

Democratic governments desirous of recommending a certain policy normally dwell upon its practical advantages. But in the Soviet Union this is not so. Any important change of line will be heralded by an article in *Pravda* often of many columns, purporting to show that the new policy is ideologically correct because it accords with some recent decision of a party congress, or with Lenin's teaching, or with whatever other criterion may be adopted. How far the policy in question will have been inspired by considerations of ideology as opposed to others of a more mundane nature can never be precisely determined. This, however, is not an exclusive feature of the Communist system; in politics, as for that matter in personal relations, it is seldom possible to disentangle all the motives which determine conduct. The policies of any party or government are likely to reflect its political principles even if they are so framed as to strengthen its position, and there is no reason why the policies adopted by the Soviet leaders should constitute an exception.

Analysts of the "power politics" school of thought hold that the Kremlin leaders are concerned solely with Soviet national interest, and merely use the Communist movement to promote it. Yet here again the difficulty is to disengage factors which are closely associated. The future of the Communist movement cannot be disassociated from the fortunes of the Soviet Union. If the Soviet regime were to collapse, that movement would count for little, and whether it would long survive even in China is doubtful. Recognizing this, non-Russian Communist parties generally have remained subservient to Moscow even when threatened with large-scale defections of rank-and-file members in the face of particularly odious shifts in the Moscow line.

The "Separate Paths" Issue

The quarrel between the Soviet and the Yugoslav Communist parties — which an intergovernmental agreement of June 1956 has failed to resolve — is a good example of the interpenetration of ideological and non-ideological factors in policy determinations. The immediate occasion of the quarrel was Tito's unwillingness to allow the spread of Soviet influence through the presence of

Soviet military officers and technological experts on Yugoslav soil. As a result Stalin determined to crush Tito, and resorted to various political and economic measures in an unsuccessful attempt to do so. It was at least a year before the struggle was extended to the ideological plane. But that it should have been was inevitable. One may well sympathize with Tito's desire for independence and hope that other national leaders will follow his example. Yet from the Communist point of view, if the movement is to be an international one, it must have an international center, and upon historical grounds alone Moscow has a strong claim to the mantle. Ever since Communist parties were formed, it was in fact to Moscow that their internal disputes were referred for settlement, just as it was Moscow which directed their general policy. Whether this role was performed well or ill is beside the point.

Hence the principle of "separate paths to socialism," approved by the Twentieth CPSU Congress for tactical reasons, is one which Moscow can accept only with reservations. If it merely means that in establishing communism in a given country consideration must be given to local conditions, and that every country's experience adds to the common store, then it is not only unobjectionable but is a salutary corrective to the earlier dogmatism which insisted on the universal applicability of the Russian experience. Such is the attitude nowadays expressed by Soviet theoreticians, though they insistently stress the dangers of exaggerating the importance of national characteristics, denying "the common laws of socialist development," or playing down the October Revolution. The official Soviet position is best expressed in an article in *New Times,* March 1956, which states that "while *serving as an example* to other working-class parties, the CPSU *draws upon their experience and formulates it in general theoretical principles* for the benefit of all working-class parties."

Clearly the Soviet leaders are on the defensive in this matter. They recognize that concessions must be made, but will make no more than they can help. The desire to perpetuate their own power doubtless influences their stand, but considering the fact that communism professes to be a world movement, it would be unreasonable to conclude that either national or personal interests are the sole factors motivating them.

Inefficiency — An Index of Ideology

Indeed, if the analysis given earlier in this article of the genesis of the Communist ideology is correct, the attitude of the Soviet leaders *must* be attributed at least in part, to the theoretical principles which distinguish Communist regimes from other forms of dictatorship. Certainly the leaders shape and phrase their domestic and foreign policies to fit the general framework established by these principles, and the latter often do not allow much room for maneuver. In fact, their application may sometimes weaken rather than strengthen the country.

To take a simple example, much waste would be avoided if small traders were permitted to operate on a profit basis; the fishmonger, for instance, would have an incentive to put his fish on ice, which he frequently fails to do to the discomfort of the public. Allowance of profits, however, would constitute a return to private enterprise, which cannot be tolerated.

Similarly, in the Communist view it has long been regarded as indefensible to subordinate a higher to a lower form of socialized enterprise. Thus, while it has been apparent for years that Soviet agriculture would be more efficient if the Machine Tractor Stations were handed over to the collective farms, the issue has been consistently dodged, because the MTS are fully state-owned organs and therefore "higher" than the farms, which still belong in part to the peasants. When the economist Venzher advocated this measure some years ago, he was slapped down at once by Stalin, the fact that it had already been adopted in Yugoslavia only making his suggestion the more objectionable. Just two years ago Khrushchev launched an extensive program to strengthen the organization and power of the MTS. Very recently, however, he indicated that the regime was — at long last — prepared to yield to practical necessity on this point; in a speech on farm policy, he advocated the transfer of farm machinery to the collectives, and although his proposals are not yet legalized, it would appear that a number of MTS have already been dissolved.

The principle of hierarchy has not been repudiated, however, and still governs other aspects of agricultural organization — for example, the relative status of the two forms of agricultural enterprise. From the standpoint of productive efficiency the collective farms are bad, but the state farms are worse. Nonetheless, the latter represent a "higher type" of organization, and thus the present virgin lands campaign has been based upon them.

Dogmatism in Foreign Policy

The same point can be scored by examining the Soviet Union's treatment of its satellites. Poland affords a good example. With the country at its mercy after World War II, the Soviet regime decided, among other measures, to integrate the Polish economy with its own. Now had Poland been regarded merely as a colony to be exploited, the operation would have been viewed primarily as a business proposition, and due attention would have been paid to such questions as the nature of the country's resources and the aptitudes of its people. The need to proceed with caution was very evident. The traditional hostility of the Poles to everything Russian should have been taken into account, as well as the fact that the Polish Communist Party had no public support (due in part to the liquidation of its established leaders during the Great Purges). Yet it was decided that the country must pass through, in shorter time intervals, precisely those stages of development which the Soviet Union had traversed. The result was a serious disruption of the economy through the erection of a top-heavy industrial structure on the basis of a depressed agriculture. This policy cannot be attributed to Stalin alone as it was continued after his death. It proved disastrous, and is only intelligible on the assumption that it was primarily motivated by ideological considerations.

The argument can be carried further. By its behavior throughout its history, the Soviet Union has incurred the hostility, or at least the suspicion, of the entire free world. Yet there was no practical reason why it should have done so. After the October Revolution the Bolshevik regime was faced with appalling domestic problems, and it had nothing to gain by courting the animosity of the West. The Soviet leaders might well have built up their country in accordance with the principles to which they were committed without exciting such widespread hostility. What governments do at home is commonly regarded as their own affair. Fundamentally, the regime in Yugoslavia is as Communist as that of the Soviet Union, and was established with an equal ruthlessness. But Tito, having asserted his independence from Moscow, has muffled his attacks on the West, and in turn the Western governments have demonstrated their desire — albeit tempered with caution — to believe in his good faith.

What no country will tolerate is the attempt, deliberately engineered by a foreign power, to overthrow its form of government; this has been the persistent aim and effort of the Soviet regime in defiance of its express diplomatic guarantees of noninterference. It is hard to see how this strategy has assisted the development of Soviet Russia, and that it has never been abandoned cannot be dissociated from those messianic and catastrophic elements in the Communist creed which influence, perhaps impel, the Soviet drive for world power.

In conclusion, it is frequently stated that communism has created an ideological cleavage between the West and the Soviet bloc. Yet this statement would be meaningless if the issue today were, as some believe, simply one of power politics. An ideology is significant only if it makes those who profess it act in a way they would not otherwise do. The fact that large numbers of persons accept communism would not constitute a danger if it did not lead them to support policies which threaten the existence of those who do not accept it. It is true that many people, especially in backward countries, call themselves Communists without having any clear idea of what it means. Yet the movement would not be the force it has become were there not in every country men and women who sincerely believe in the ideas behind it which form collectively what we call its ideology.

To represent this ideology as a species of opium with which the Soviet leaders contrive to lull the people while taking care never to indulge in it themselves is to attribute to them an ability to dissociate themselves from the logic of their system — an ability which it is unlikely they possess. For the concepts which make up that system, fantastic as many of them appear to be, will be found on examination to be interrelated, and to be logical extensions of the basic principles to which all Communists subscribe.

To turn it the other way around, Communists claim a theoretical justification for the basic principles in which they believe. But these principles must be translated into appropriate action; and action, if directed by the rulers of a powerful country like the Soviet Union, will take the form of *Realpolitik*. There is no yardstick which permits a measure of the exact relationship between power politics and ideology in the policies which result; but surely neither factor can be ignored.

National Interest: Key to Soviet Politics
SAMUEL L. SHARP

An enormous body of Western research and analysis focuses on Marxist-Leninist ideology as a clue to understanding Kremlin policy. This extensive and intensive preoccupation with matters doctrinal is, at least in part, the result of a rather widely circulated belief that the democratic world was guilty of neglect when it refused to take seriously the "theoretical" writings and pronouncements of Adolf Hitler. It has been alleged that these writings later guided Hitler's actions and that a ready key to his conduct was thus overlooked.

When, at the end of World War II, the Soviet Union appeared on the international scene as a power — and a menace — of the first order, led by a group consistently claiming its adherence to a body of doctrine as a guide to action, legions of experts began to dissect that body in a search for a key to Soviet behavior, current and future. The material at hand was certainly more promising than the intellectually scrawny homunculus of Nazi or Fascist "ideology." After all, Marxism has its not entirely disreputable roots in legitimate Western thought. Even in terms of sheer bulk there was more to operate on, what with Lenin's and Stalin's additions and modifications of the original scriptures and the voluminous exegetic output of a generation of Soviet propagandists.

The massive study of Communist ideology has had one happy result in that some serious scholarly output has been provided to counterbalance party-line apologias, thereby destroying a number of primitive notions concerning the Soviet system and what makes it tick. At the same time, in this writer's view, preoccupation with the search for a formula of interpretative and predictive value has produced its own distortions. These distortions seem to be the composite result of cold-war anxieties, faulty logic, and disregard of some of the elementary principles and practices of international relations. To these causes must be added the human tendency to look beyond the simple and obvious for the complicated and mysterious in attempting to explain any condition which is exasperating and which is therefore perceived as strange and unique. Baffled by the Soviet phenomenon, millions in the Western world have found a negative consolation of sorts in the famous statement by Winston Churchill that Russian policy is "a riddle wrapped in a mystery inside an enigma." But how many have bothered to read the qualifying words which followed? Having disclaimed ability to forecast Soviet actions, Churchill added: *But perhaps there is a key. That key is Russian national interest.* [1]

Clearly implied in this observation was the logical supposition that the policy-makers of the Soviet Union act in what they believe to be the best interest of the state over whose destinies they are presiding. In this sense the Soviet Union is to be looked upon as an actor, a protagonist, on the stage of international politics; and in this writer's view, its actions can be interpreted most fruitfully in terms of behavior *germane* to the practice of international politics. Without denying the possible pitfalls of this approach, the writer proposes to argue its usefulness as a key to understanding a phenomenon which the non-Communist world can ill afford to envelop in a fog of self-generated misinterpretation.

The Doubtful Art of Quotation

Whenever the suggestion is made that the concept of national interest be applied as an explanation of Soviet behavior on the international scene, objections are raised in many quarters. The most vigorous protests come, of course, from Soviet sources. It is a standard claim of Soviet spokesmen that their state is by definition something "different" (or "higher") and that the foreign policy of this entity is different in principle *(printsipialno otlichna)* from that of other states because the latter are capitalist and the former is socialist.[2] It would seem that only uncritical adherents of communism could take such statements seriously. Yet non-Communists very often cite them as a convenient *ipse dixit* in support of their own claim that the Soviet Union is indeed "different," though not in the way Soviet propaganda wants one to believe. The claim is that the Soviet Union is, at best, "a conspiracy disguised as a state" and cannot be viewed as a "normal" member of the world community of nations. There is no attempt to explain on what basis some Soviet statements are to be taken as reliable indices of regime motivations, while other statements, no less abundantly scattered throughout the Marxist-Leninist scriptures, are rejected as lie and deception.

1. Radio broadcast of October 1, 1939, reprinted in W. Churchill, *The Gathering Storm* (Boston: Houghton-Mifflin, 1948), p. 449. Author's italics.

2. To quote just one recent source, cf. V. I. Lissovskii, *Mezhdunarodnoe Pravo* [International Law], (Kiev, 1955), p. 397.

It is surely dubious scholarship to collect quotations (sometimes reduced to half a sentence) from Lenin and Stalin without regard to the time, place, circumstances, composition of the audience, and, whenever ascertainable, immediate purposes of such utterances. What results from such compilations, no matter how laboriously and ingeniously put together, is, as a thoughtful critic has pointed out, "a collection of such loose generalizations and so many exceptions and contradictions that few readers can find much guidance in it."[3] Stalin, for example, can be quoted as once having said that "with a diplomat words must diverge from facts" and that "a sincere diplomat would equal dry water, wooden iron"; yet this not too astute observation was made in 1913 in an article dealing with bourgeois diplomacy written by an obscure Georgian revolutionary who probably had never met a diplomat. His view in this instance is identifiable as a variant of the classic image of the diplomat as "an honorable gentleman sent abroad to lie for his country." This image may very well have stayed with the congenitally suspicious and pessimistic Stalin in later life, and thus might indeed afford us a clue to his "real" nature. However, sound scholarship would seek to reconstruct the attitudes of the Kremlin ruler out of words and deeds of a more relevant period of his life rather than from this loose piece of Djugashvili prose torn out of context.

The Vital Factor of Feasibility

Some objections to the interpretation of Soviet policies in terms of national interest are rooted in the aforementioned line of analysis which conjures up the ghost of Adolf Hitler. The democracies erred, did they not, in initially looking upon Hitler's aims as an expression of "legitimate" (we will return to this phrase in a moment) — however distasteful — national aspirations, only to discover later that they were dealing with a maniac whose appetites were unlimited. Since it is generally agreed that Soviet policy, like Hitler's, belongs to the totalitarian species, would it not be impardonable to repeat the same mistake by looking upon the aims of the Soviet leaders as the expression of the aspirations of a "normal" nation-state?

Two points should be made here. First, Hitler bears comparison with no

---

3. Marshall Knappen, *An Introduction to American Foreign Policy* (New York: Harper & Bros., 1956). The quote is from the chapter entitled "Capabilities, appeal and intentions of the Soviet Union" and refers specifically to the well-known effort by Nathan Leites in *A Study of Bolshevism* (Glencoe, Ill.: Free Press, 1953) to construct out of thousands of quotes from Lenin and Stalin bolstered with excerpts from nineteenth-century Russian literature, an "image of Bolshevism" and an "operational code" of the Politburo. See also the remarks on "Difficulties of content analysis" and "The problem of context" in John S. Reshetar, Jr., *Problems of Analyzing and Predicting Soviet Behavior* (New York: Doubleday & Co., 1955). In all fairness to Leites and his prodigious undertaking it must be pointed out that he was aware of a "spurious air of certainty" in his formulations, which were intended to be only "guesses about the mind of the Soviet Politburo" (*op. cit.,* p. 27).

one; there is no other leader in history who has combined his precise mental makeup with his enormous concentration of power. He was, as his biographer Allan Bullock pointed out, a man "without aims," that is, without *limited* and therefore tractable aims.[4] At one point in his career Hitler began to disregard the cardinal rule of politics — the necessity of aligning ambitions with capacity to translate them into reality. He broke the barrier of the *feasible*, motivated by what could most likely be diagnosed as the death-wish. Whatever else may be said about the Soviet leaders, no one, including people who suspect them of ideological self-deception, has denied them the quality of caution. Far from seeking self-destruction, they are lustily bent on survival. This in itself, even in the complete absence of scruples, makes their aims *limited*.

Mr. Carew Hunt argues elsewhere in these pages that there are "messianic and catastrophic elements in the Communist creed which influence . . . the Soviet drive for world power." While there may indeed be a degree of messianism in the Soviet leadership's view of its mission, the "catastrophic" tendency seems to be held carefully in check. Hitler was propelled by the absurd notion that he had to accomplish certain aims before he reached the age of sixty — an arrogant and, from the point of view of German national interest, totally irrelevant assumption. Granted that the Soviet leaders aim at "world power" (a concept which in itself should be defined more explicitly than it usually is), they have long since decided not to fix any specific time limit for the achievement of this ultimate aim. Certainly the present generation of leaders has acted to modify (perhaps "refine" is a better word) the aggressive drive for power abroad at least to an extent which will allow some enjoyment at home of the tangible fruits of the revolution this side of the Communist heaven. Even back in the early days of Bolshevik rule, Lenin, though at times carried away by expectations of spreading revolution, never sacrificed practical caution to missionary zeal; repeatedly he warned his followers to look after the "bouncing baby" (the Soviet state), since Europe was only "pregnant with revolution" (which it wasn't).

An Applicable Concept of Interest

The second point to be made is a crucial one. Reluctance to analyze Soviet aims in terms of national interest is due, in part, to the aura of legitimacy which surrounds the "normal" run of claims of nation-states, giving rise to the notion that the term itself infers something legitimate. However, suggesting that Kremlin moves can best be understood in terms of what the leaders consider advantageous to the Soviet state by no means implies subscribing to their aims or sympathizing with them. In international relations the maxim *tout comprendre c'est tout pardonner* does not apply. The concept of national interest, by

4. Allan Bullock, *Hitler – A Study in Tyranny* (New York: Harper & Bros., 1953).

focusing attention on the *objective sources of conflict* — that is, those which *can* be explained rationally as issues between nations — permits us to view the international scene in terms of a global problem of power relations rather than a cops-and-robbers melodrama. We can then perceive which are the *tractable* elements in the total equation of conflict, and devote our energies to reducing or altering these factors.

This approach seems to the writer to be indispensable both to the scholar and to the statesman. The scholar who accepts the "natural" (in terms of the nature of international politics) explanation for Kremlin behavior is not likely to violate the "law of parsimony" by unnecessarily piling up hypotheses which are unprovable and which in any case simply confuse the issue, insofar as dealing practically with the Soviet Union is concerned. The statesman finds that he is coping with a phenomenon which he knows how to approach both in accommodation and in opposition, rather than with some occult and other-worldly force.

Those who object to the framework of analysis here proposed would say, as does Mr. Hunt, that there are many cases on record when the Soviet leaders have acted in a way clearly inconsistent with the Russian national interest and intelligible only in terms of ideological dogmatism. The answer to this argument is simple: it does not matter what Mr. Hunt — or anybody else — considers to be the Russian national interest; as the term is defined here, the only view which matters is that held by the Soviet leaders. By the same token it is a rather fruitless thing to speak of "legitimate" vs. "illegitimate" Soviet interests. One of the essential attributes of sovereignty (and the Soviet leaders are certainly jealous where their own is involved!) is that it is up to the sovereign to determine what serves him best.

Yet doesn't this reasoning render pointless the entire conceptual approach proposed? If Soviet national interest is what the Soviet leaders take it to be, and if one agrees — as one must — that their view of the world is derived largely from their adherence to Marxism-Leninism, isn't this another way of saying that Soviet behavior is the result of ideological conditioning? Not quite. The point at issue is whether the "pure" Soviet view of the world is important *as a guide to action,* whether the *ultimate* aims of the Communist creed are operative in policy determinations. In the present writer's view they are not; the fault of the opposing line of analysis is that in dwelling on the supposed impact of ideology on the leadership, it tends to ignore the degree to which the pursuit of ultimate goals has been circumscribed in time and scope by considerations of *the feasible*. In simple arithmetic, doctrine minus those aspects which are not empirically operative equals empirically determined policy. If a policy action is called "revolutionary expediency," it is still expediency. Why then introduce into the equation an element which does not affect the result?

A supporting view in this respect is W. W. Rostow's characterization of Soviet foreign policy as a series of responses to the outside world which, especially before 1939, "took the form of such actions as were judged most likely, *on a short-range basis,* to maintain or expand the national power of the Soviet regime." Despite the Soviet Union's vastly greater ability to influence the world environment in the postwar era, says Rostow, "there is no evidence that the foreign policy criteria of the regime have changed."[5] If some instances of Soviet behavior appear to have produced results actually detrimental to the Soviet interest, we must not only refrain from applying our view of Soviet interest but also — as Rostow's viewpoint suggests — judge the policy decisions involved in terms of their validity at the time they were made and not in the light of what happened later (remembering, too, that mistakes and miscalculations are common to all policy-makers, not just those who wear "ideological blinders").

The words "on a short-range basis" have been underscored above to stress that the term "policy," if properly applied, excludes aims, ambitions, or dreams not accompanied by action visibly and within a reasonable time capable of producing the results aimed at or dreamed of. In the case of the Soviet leaders, concentration on short-range objectives and adjustment to political realities has, in the brilliant phrase suggested by Barrington Moore, Jr., *caused the means to eat up the ends.*[6]

The objection will still be raised that the Soviet leaders mouth every policy decision in terms of ideological aims. Enough should have been said on this score to obviate a discussion here; as able students of the problem have pointed out, the Soviet leaders' claim to rule rests on their perpetuation of the ideology and their insistence on orthodoxy; they have no choice but to continue paying lip-service to the doctrine, even if it is no longer operative. The liberal mind somehow balks at this image of total manipulation, of an exoteric doctrine for public consumption which has no connection with its esoteric counterpart — that is, the principles or considerations which really govern Kremlin behavior. Yet allowance must be made for this possibility.

Moscow and International Communism

One serious argument of those who reject the image of the Soviet Union as a "legitimate" participant in the balance-of-power game played in the arena of international politics is that the Soviet leaders consistently violate the rules of the game by enlisting out-of-bounds help from foreign Communist parties.

5. W. W. Rostow *et al., The Dynamics of Soviet Society* (New York: W. W. Norton & Co., 1952), p. 136. Author's italics.
6. Barrington Moore, Jr., *Soviet Politics – The Dilemma of Power* (Cambridge: Harvard University Press, 1950).

This point invites the following brief observations:

1) Early in its history the Communist International was transformed into a tool of Soviet foreign policy, at a time when few other tools were available to Moscow.

2) As soon as the Soviet state felt at all sure of its survival (after the period of civil war, foreign intervention, and economic chaos), it reactivated the apparatus of foreign policy along more traditional lines.

3) Under Stalin, the Third International was reduced to a minor auxiliary operation. An index of his attitude toward it is the fact that he never once addressed a Comintern congress. Probably the International was kept up in the interwar period because it seemed to produce marginal dividends in terms of nuisance value. Moreover, Stalin could hardly have divorced himself from it officially at a time when he was jockeying for total power inside Russia, since this would have helped to confirm his opponents' accusations that he was "betraying the revolution." But he certainly did everything to show his belief in the ineffectiveness of the organization and its foreign components as against the growing power of the Soviet state.

4) When the entire record of Soviet success and failure is summed up, the achievements are clearly attributable to Soviet power and diplomacy with no credit due to the international Communist movement. Furthermore, the ties between the Soviet Union and foreign parties have never deterred Moscow from useful alliances or cooperation with other governments — including, from one time to another, the astutely anti-Communist Turkish government of Ataturk; the more brutally anti-Communist regime of Adolf Hitler; and, during World War II, the Western powers. That the Soviet leaders, by virtue of their doctrine, entertained mental reservations about the durability of friendly relations with these governments can hardly be doubted. But it is equally clear that the cessation of cooperation was due in each case to the workings of power politics rather than Soviet ideological dictate — that is, to the historical tendency of alliances to disintegrate when what binds them (usually a common enemy) disappears.

5) Finally, it might be argued that the Soviet appeal to foreign Communist parties is not dissimilar to the practice of various governments of different periods and persuasions to appeal for support abroad on the basis of some sort of affinity — be it Hispanidad, Slav solidarity, Deutschtum, or Pan-Arabism. The Soviet appeal is admittedly broader and the "organizational weapon" seems formidable, but their importance should not be exaggerated. Actually, there is no way at all to measure the effectiveness of the appeal *per se* since Communist "success" or "failure" in any situation always involves a host of other variables — including military, geographical, social, political, or economic factors. In the last analysis, virtually every instance where Moscow has claimed a victory for communism has depended on Soviet manipulation of traditional levers of national influence.

An Exception to Prove the Rule

There remains one area of Soviet "foreign policy" where the Soviet leaders have supplemented power politics — or more accurately in this instance naked force — with an attempt to derive special advantage, a sort of "surplus value," from claiming ideological obeisance to the Soviet Union as the seat of the secular church of communism. This area is the so-called Soviet orbit in Eastern Europe.

The term "foreign policy" is enclosed in quotation marks here because Stalin obviously did not consider areas under the physical control of Soviet power as nations or governments to be dealt with in their own right. He was clearly impatient with the claim of at least some Communist parties that their advent to power had changed the nature of their relationship to Moscow, and that the party-to-party level of relations must be separated from the government-to-government level (as Gomulka argued in 1948). In Stalin's thinking, especially after 1947, the East European regimes were not eligible for more real sovereignty than the "sovereign" republics of the Soviet Union. He attempted to extend the principle of *democratic centralism* (a euphemism for Kremlin control) to these countries, allowing them only as much of a façade of sovereignty as was useful for show toward the outside world.

One need not necessarily dig into doctrine to explain this attitude; in fact, doctrine until recently said nothing at all about relations between sovereign Communist states. The explanation lies to a large extent in Stalin's personal predilection for total control, plus the need to tighten Moscow's bonds to the limit, by whatever means or arguments possible, in the face of the bipolarization of global power after World War II.

Stalin's successors began by pressing the same claims of ideological obeisance from the satellites. But rather striking — in the same period that their foreign policy has scored substantial successes in other areas in traditional terms of diplomatic advances and manipulation of the economic weapon[7] — they have failed in the one area where they attempted to substitute the ties of ideology for the give-and-take of politics. Communist parties in power, it turned out (first in the case of Yugoslavia, while Stalin still reigned, and later in Poland, not to mention the very special case of China), claimed the right to be sovereign — or at least semi-sovereign — actors on the international scene. Whether or not this makes sense ideologically to the Soviet leaders is unimportant; they have recognized the claim.

It is not necessary to review here the post-Stalin history of fluctuating Soviet relations with Eastern Europe which began with the B. & K. pilgrimage to Belgrade. Let us take only the most recent attempt to reformulate the nature of relations between the USSR and other Communist countries — the interparty declaration issued on the occasion of the fortieth anniversary of the

7. Samuel L. Sharp, "The Soviet Position in the Middle East," *Social Science,* National Academy of Economics and Political Sciences, Vol. 32, No. 4, October, 1957.

Bolshevik revolution. On the surface, the declaration, published in the name of twelve ruling Communist parties, seems to reimpose a pattern of ideological uniformity as well as to recognize the special leadership position of the Soviet Union.[8] However, the circumstances of the gathering and the internal evidence of the declaration, together with the reports of some of the participants, show a far more complex situation.

The following aspects of the conference deserve attention: First, the very fact that the parties representing governments of sovereign countries were singled out for a special meeting and declaration instead of being lumped together with the mass of parties (many of them illegal, some leading no more than a paper existence) is a significant departure from past practice. Second, the Yugoslav party, though represented at the festivities, refused to sign the declaration, apparently after long negotiations. Third, attempts to revive in any form an international, Moscow-based organization resembling the Comintern were unsuccessful. Gomulka's report on the meeting made it clear that the Polish party opposed both a new Comintern (for which it nevertheless had a few good words) and a new Cominform (for which it had nothing but scorn.)[9]

A point of particular significance was the revelation that future international gatherings of Communist parties, especially those in power, are to be based on previous agreements concerning the agenda. According to Gomulka, problems which each party thinks it can best solve *for itself and its country* will not be decided by interparty conferences.[10]

Perhaps most significant for the purposes of the present discussion was a statement by Mao Tse-tung, who next to Khrushchev and Suslov was the main speaker at the meeting of the "ruling" parties and was billed as co-sponsor of the declaration. Mao bolstered his argument for the recognition of the leading position of the Soviet Union in the "socialist camp" with the remark that "China has not even one-fourth of a sputnik while the Soviet Union has two."[11] Now, the possession of a sputnik is a symbol of achievement and a source of prestige for the Soviet Union, but certainly not in terms of ideology. It was Soviet national power to which Mao paid deference.

In sum, the entire circumstances of the gathering indicate a disposition on the part of the Soviet Union to substitute — wherever it has to — the give-and-take of politics for its former relationship with the orbit countries, which relied on naked power to enforce demands of ideological subservience.

8. The text of the declaration, adopted at a meeting held on November 14–16, 1957, was published in *Pravda* on November 22. A separate "peace manifesto" issued in the name of all of the Communist parties present at the congregation appeared in *Pravda* a day later.

9. Gomulka's report was published in *Trybuna Ludu,* Warsaw, November 29, 1957.

10. Gomulka, *ibid.* See also an analysis of the conference entitled, "Gescheiterte Komintern-Renaissance" [Failure of Comintern Revival], *Ost-Probleme,* Bad Godesberg, X, No. 1 (January 3, 1958).

11. Cited in Friedrich Ebert's report to the East German party (SED), published in *Neues Deutschland,* East Berlin, November 30, 1957, p. 4.

From all the foregoing, it should be clear that the task of the non-Communist world is not to worry itself sick over the ultimate goals of the Soviet leadership or the degree of its sincerity, but to concentrate on multiplying situations in which the Soviet Union either will be forced or will choose to play the game of international politics in an essentially traditional setting. How the Kremlin leaders will square this with their Marxist conscience is not really our problem.

The Logic Of One-Party Rule
RICHARD LOWENTHAL

To what extent are the political decisions of the Soviet leadership influenced by its belief in an official ideology — and to what extent are they empirical responses to specific conflicts of interest, expressed in ideological terms merely for purposes of justification? The phrasing of the question at issue suggests the two extreme answers which are *prima facie* conceivable — on the one hand, that ideology provides the Kremlin with a ready-made book of rules to be looked up in any situation; on the other, that its response to reality takes place without any reference to ideology. Yet any clear formulation of this vital issue will show that both extremes are meaningless nonsense.

A ready-made book of rules for any and every situation — an unvarying roadmap to the goal of communism which the Soviet leaders must predictably follow — cannot possibly exist, both because the situations to be met by them are not sufficiently predictable, and because no government which behaved in so calculable a manner could conceivably retain power. On the other hand, empirical *Realpolitik* without ideological preconceptions can exist as little as can "empirical science" without categories and hypotheses based on theoretical speculation. Confronted with the same constellation of interests and pressures, the liberal statesman will in many cases choose a different course of action from the conservative — and the totalitarian Communist's choice will often be different from that of either.

It seems surprising, therefore, that at this late stage of discussion Professor Sharp is apparently in earnest in defending the extreme of the *Realpolitik* interpretation and in denying completely the relevance of Communist ideology for the formation, and hence the understanding, of Soviet foreign policy. The latter, he assures us, can be adequately understood in terms of national interest, just as with any other state. When reminded by Mr. Carew Hunt of certain irrational features of Soviet foreign policy, he replies that what matters is not any outsider's concept of Soviet interests, but the Soviet leaders' own. Yet this reduces his thesis to a tautology: he "proves" that national interest motivates Soviet foreign policy by the simple device of labeling whatever motivates it "national interest."

Surely Professor Sharp cannot have it both ways. Either there are objective criteria of national interest, recognizable by the scholar — and then the view that these interests explain Soviet actions is capable of proof or refutation; or else it is admitted that different statesmen may interpret national interest in different but equally "legitimate" ways — and then the concept of a self-contained study of international relations collapses, because a consideration of the internal structures of different national communities and of the "ideologies" reflecting them becomes indispensable for an understanding of their foreign policies.

The latter observation does not, of course, apply to Communist states alone, although it is only reasonable to expect the influence of the monopolistic ideology of a single-party state to be specially pervasive. Mr. George Kennan, in his 1950 lectures on American diplomacy, has convincingly shown the relevance of ideological factors to an understanding of modern United States foreign policy as well. To deny this influence *a priori* and to admit, as Professor Sharp apparently would, only the *Ding an sich* of national interest on one side, and the accidental element of human error or pathology (such as Hitler's "death-wish") on the other, seems to this writer to be an unjustifiable renunciation of one of the limited roads to understanding which are available to present-day political science.

The Function of Doctrine

Assuming, then, that the Soviet leaders' ideology is relevant to their conduct, the real problem remains to discover which are the actual operative elements in it, and in what way they affect policy decisions. Clearly it would be folly to expect that Soviet policy could be predicted solely from an exegetic study of the Marxist-Leninist canon. Not only is it impossible for any group of practical politicians to base their decisions on an unvarying book of rules; there is any amount of historical evidence to show that the rules have been altered again and again to fit the practical decisions *ex post facto.* Moreover, there are vast parts of the Communist ideological structure, such as the scholastic refinements of "dialectical materialism" or the labor theory of value, which in their nature are so remote from the practical matters to be decided that their interpretation cannot possibly affect policy decisions. They may be used in inner-party arguments to *justify* what has been decided on other grounds, but that is all.

How, then, are we to distinguish those elements of Soviet ideology which are truly operative politically from those which are merely traditional scholastic ballast, linked to the operative elements by the historical accident of the founding fathers' authorship? The answer is to be found by going back to the original Marxian meaning of the term "ideology" — conceived as a distorted reflection of social reality in the consciousness of men, used as an instrument of struggle. The fundamental, distinctive social reality in the Soviet Union is the rule of the bureaucracy of a single, centralized, and disciplined party, which wields a monopoly of political, economic, and spiritual power and permits no independent groupings of any kind. The writer proposes as a hypothesis that the operative parts of the ideology are those which are indispensable for maintaining and justifying this state of affairs: "Marxism-Leninism" matters inasmuch as it expresses, in an ideologically distorted form, the logic of one-party rule.[1]

Totalitarian Parallels

There are a few interconnected ideological features which are common to all the totalitarian regimes of our century — whether of the nationalist-fascist or of the Communist variety. We may designate them as the elements of chiliasm, of collective paranoia, and of the representative fiction. Each totalitarian regime justifies its power and its crimes by the avowed conviction, first, that its final victory will bring about the Millennium — whether defined as the final triumph of communism or of the master race — and second, that this state of grace can only be achieved by an irreconcilable struggle against a single, omnipresent, and multiform enemy — whether Monopoly Capitalism or World Jewry — whose forms include every particular opponent of the totalitarian power. Each also claims to represent the true will of the people — the *volonté générale* — independent of whether the people actually support it, and argues that any sacrifice may be demanded from the individual and the group for the good of the people and the defeat of its devilish enemies.

The Communist version of these basic beliefs is superior to the Nazi version in one vital respect. Because the appeal of racialism is in its nature restricted to a small minority of mankind, the Nazis' goal of world domination could not possibly have been attained without a series of wars, preferably surprise attacks

---

1. While this comes close to the position outlined in Mr. Carew Hunt's paper, I cannot follow him in his assumption that the totalitarian party monopoly is a by-product of the attempt to establish collectivist economic planning or to achieve the speedy industrialization of a backward country. This neo-Marxist view, held by such otherwise divergent authors as Professor Hayek and Milovan Djilas, is contradicted by the fact that the Bolshevik party monopoly, including the ban on inner-party factions, was fully established by Lenin at the time of the transition to the "New Economic Policy" (1921), when economic planning was reduced to a minimum and forced industrialization not yet envisaged. Independent of the concrete economic program, totalitarianism was implicit in the centralized, undemocratic structure of a party consciously created as an instrument for the conquest of power, and in the ideological characteristics resulting (to be discussed further in this article). Of course, totalitarian power, once established, favors total economic planning and the undertaking of revolutionary economic tasks by the state; but this is a consequence, not a cause. Marx never developed a concept of total planning, and even Lenin never imagined anything of the kind before 1918. But Marx in his youth at least equated the "dictatorship of the proletariat" with the Jacobin model, and Lenin followed this model throughout.

launched against isolated opponents. Because the appeal of communism is directed to all mankind, it can be linked with the further doctrine of the inevitable victory of the rising forces of socialism over the imperialist enemy, which is disintegrating under the impact of its own internal contradictions. This central ideological difference, and not merely the psychological difference between Hitler and the Soviet leaders, explains why the latter are convinced that history is on their side and that they need not risk the survival of their own regime in any attempt to hasten its final triumph: they believe in violence, revolutionary and military, as one of the weapons of policy, but they do not believe in the inevitability of world war.

Awkward Aims and Claims

Yet the Communist version of totalitarian ideology also suffers from some weaknesses and contradictions from which the Nazi and Fascist versions are free. In the first place, its vision of the Millennium has more markedly utopian features — the classless society, the end of exploitation of man by man, the withering away of the state — which make awkward yardsticks for the real achievements of Communist states. Second, in a world where nationalism remains a force of tremendous strength, an internationalist doctrine is bound to come into conflict with the interests of any major Communist power, or with the desire of smaller Communist states for autonomy.

Third, by rejecting the "Fuehrer principle" and claiming to be "democratic," Communist ideology makes the realities of party dictatorship and centralistic discipline more difficult to justify; yet because appeal to blind faith is not officially permitted, justification is needed in "rational" terms. It is precisely this continuous need for the pretense of rational argument — the awkward heritage of communism's origin from revolutionary Western democracy — which has led to the far greater elaboration of its ideology compared to that of "irrationalist" right-wing totalitarianism, and which gives its constant interpretation so much greater importance in preserving the cohesion of the party regime. Due to the fictions of democracy and rationality, the morale of party cadres has been made dependent on the appearance of ideological consistency.

The result of these inherent weaknesses of Communist ideology is that the component doctrines — dealing with the "dictatorship of the proletariat," the party's role as a "vanguard" embodying the "true" class consciousness, "democratic centralism," "proletarian internationalism," and the "leading role of the Soviet Union" — become focal points of ideological crises and targets of "revisionist" attacks whenever events reveal the underlying contradictions in a particularly striking way. Yet these are the very doctrines which the regime cannot renounce because they are the basic rationalizations of its own desire for self-preservation.

We can expect, then, that Communist ideology will have an effective influence on the policy decisions of Soviet leaders when, and only when, it expresses the needs of self-preservation of the party regime. We can further expect that ideological changes and disputes within the Communist "camp" will offer clues to the conflicts and crises — the "contradictions" — which are inseparable from the evolution of this, as of any other, type of society. The fruitful approach, in this writer's view, consists neither in ignoring Communist ideology as an irrelevant disguise, nor in accepting it at its face value and treating it as a subject for exegesis, but in using it as an indicator of those specific drives and problems which spring from the specific structure of Soviet society — in regarding it as an enciphered, continuous self-disclosure, whose cipher can be broken by sociological analysis.

Two Camps — One Enemy

Let us now apply this approach to the doctrine of the "two camps" in world affairs. The "two-camp" concept was not, of course, a Stalinist invention, although this is sometimes supposed. The postwar situation with its alignment of the Communist and Western powers in two openly hostile politico-military blocs merely gave plausibility to a world image which was inherent in Leninism from the beginning, but which attracted little attention in the period when the Communist "camp" was just an isolated fortress with several outposts. Nor has the doctrine disappeared with the post-Stalin recognition of the importance of the uncommitted, ex-colonial nations and of the tactical value of incorporating them in a "peace zone;" it remains one of the basic ideas of the Moscow twelve-party declaration of last November and one of the fundamental subjects of ideological disagreement between the Soviets and the Yugoslav Communists.

The Yugoslavs can reject the "two-camp" doctrine because they admit the possibility of "roads to socialism" other than Communist party dictatorship — "reformist" roads for advanced industrial countries with parliamentary traditions, "national revolutionary" roads for ex-colonial countries. It follows from this view that Communist states have no monopoly on progress, and that alliances have no ultimate ideological meaning.

The Soviets still assert that while there can be different roads to Communist power, and minor differences in the use of power once gained, there is no way of achieving socialism except by the "dictatorship of the proletariat exercised by its vanguard." It follows that tactical agreements with semi-socialist neutrals are not different in kind from the wartime alliance with the Western "imperialists," or the prewar pact with Hitler — maneuvers which are useful in dividing the forces of the "class enemy" but which remain subordinate to the fundamental division of the world into the Communists versus the Rest.

In other words, the "two-camp" doctrine is the Communist version of what we have called the element of "collective paranoia" in totalitarian ideology — its need for a single, all-embracing enemy which is assumed to pull the wires of every resistance to the party's power. The term "paranoia" is used here not to infer that the phenomenon in question is due to psychotic processes in either the leaders or the mass following of totalitarian parties, but merely to describe, through a convenient psychological analogy, the ideological mechanism of projection which ascribes the regime's drive for unlimited power to an imagined all-enemy. The essential point is that in the nature of totalitarianism, any independent force — either inside or outside the state — is regarded as ultimately hostile; the concept of "two camps" and that of "unlimited aims" are two sides of the same phenomenon.

Moscow's Double-Indemnity Tactics

Now Professor Sharp is, of course, entirely right in asking where this doctrine impinges on actual Soviet foreign policy — given the undoubted facts that actual Soviet aims, and the risks incurred in their pursuit, are limited at any given moment; that the Soviets are perfectly capable of concluding "temporary" alliances with "bourgeois," "imperialist," or even "fascist" states; and that most other alliances in this impermanent world are proving to be "temporary" as well, for quite nonideological reasons. The present writer would suggest to him that the difference has manifested itself in the peculiar suspicion with which the Soviets treated their "imperialist" allies even at the height of the war, seeking in particular to isolate their own population from contact; in the manner in which they sought to create additional "guarantees" for the reliability of those allies by the use of local Communist parties wherever this was possible; and above all, in the difference between the traditional and the Communist concepts of "spheres of influence" as illuminated by the different interpretations of the Yalta agreements.

The peculiar forms taken by Moscow's suspicion of its wartime allies are too well known to need elaboration here; but it is less generally realized that such behavior was merely the reverse side of Soviet efforts to "strengthen" such temporary alliances where possible, by the use of party ties. Existence of the party channel has not, of course, been a *sine qua non* for Moscow's intragovernmental deals, as is shown by the examples of Russo-Turkish cooperation after World War I, the Stalin-Hitler pact, and perhaps also present Soviet cooperation with Egypt. But wherever Communist parties were tolerated by the partner, Soviet foreign policy has assigned to them a vital role. Indeed, the implication that Stalin never used the foreign Communists for any important purposes is perhaps the most astonishing aspect of Professor Sharp's article.

In the 1920's, Stalin's Chinese policy was openly run in double harness; diplomatic support for the Nationalist advance to the North was supplemented by an agreement of affiliation between the Chinese Communist Party and the Kuomintang, enabling the Communist to occupy influential political and military positions — an attempt no less serious for its ultimate total failure in 1927.

In the 1930's, a variant of the same "dual policy" was evident when Moscow supported the League and "collective security," while Communist parties in France and Spain pursued "popular front" policies which soft-pedalled economic and social demands for the sake of influencing governmental foreign policy. In the Spanish case the Communists, aided by the Republicans' dependence on Soviet supplies, ended up in virtual control of the republic on the eve of its final collapse.

Again during World War II, Communists in the resistance movements and in the free Western countries were ordered to pursue the same tactics of social moderation and occupation of key positions as were practiced in China in the 1920's and Spain in the 1930's. Wartime military and political cooperation between "Soviet China" and Chiang Kai-shek was urged in the same spirit, with considerable success. All these are the foreign policy methods of a state *sui generis* — a one-party state enabled by its ideology to make use of a disciplined international movement organized for the struggle for power. To compare them — and the secondary opportunities for infiltration and espionage which they offer in addition to their main political objectives — to the use of vague cultural influences like "Hispanidad" is to show a notable degree of innocence.

Yalta — A Historic "Misunderstanding"

The crucial example to illustrate the role of ideology in Soviet foreign policy, however, remains the history of the postwar division of Europe. The writer is not concerned here with the political controversy over whether this division, as first laid down in the wartime agreements at Teheran and Yalta, was inevitable in the light of the military situation as seen at the time, or whether the Western statesmen committed an avoidable mistake of disastrous dimensions. What matters in the present context is the different meaning attached by the Western and Communist leaders, in concluding these agreements, to the concept of "spheres of influence," and the consequences of this "misunderstanding."

That Great Powers are in a position to exert a measure of influence over their smaller neighbors, and that they use this influence in one way or another to increase as far as possible their security against attack by other Great Powers, is an experience general in the politics of sovereign states and unlikely to be superseded by any amount of declamation about "equality of rights"; hence, the fact that the wartime allies, in drawing a military line of demarcation from north to south across the center of Europe, should have tried to agree about their postwar spheres of influence is, by itself, proof of realistic foresight rather than of morally reprehensible cynicism.

To Mr. Roosevelt and Mr. Churchill, however, these spheres of influence meant what they had traditionally meant in the relations of sovereign states — a gradual shading over from the influence of one power or group of powers to that of the other, a shifting relationship which might be loosely described in terms of "percentages of influence," ranging from 50/50 to 90/10. To the Soviets, "spheres of influence" meant something completely different in the framework of their ideology — the ideology of the single-party state. To them there could be no securely "friendly" government except a government run by a Communist party under their discipline; no sphere of influence but a sphere of Communist rule; no satisfactory percentage short of 100. Hence the consistent Soviet efforts, which began even before the end of the European war, to impose total control by Communist parties in every country on their side of the demarcation line — an effort that was finally successful everywhere but in Finland and Eastern Austria; hence also the indignant protests of the Western powers that the Soviets had broken the agreements on free elections and democratic development, and the equally indignant Soviet retort that they were only installing "friendly governments" as agreed, that theirs was the truly "democratic" system, and that they had kept scrupulously to the essential agreement on the military demarcation line.

A large section of Western opinion has concluded from this experience that agreements with the Soviets are useless in principle, because "you cannot trust them"; and Professor Sharp's insistence on national interest as the sole key to Soviet policy is probably at least in part a reaction against this emotional and moralizing approach. In fact, any interpretation of the postwar experience overlooking the fact that the Soviets have for reasons of national self-interest, kept to the "self-enforcing" agreement on the demarcation line, would be as seriously one-sided as one overlooking the fact that they have, for reasons of ideology or party interest, broken every agreement on "percentages" and free elections.

There is no need, however, to base future policy on either of two one-sided views equally refuted by experience. Nobody in the Western world has argued more powerfully against the "moralizing" approach to foreign policy, and for a return to the give-and-take of diplomacy based on real interests, than George Kennan; yet in his recent Reith lectures as before, he insists that the specific ideological distortion in the Soviet leaders' image of the world, far from being magically cured by a return to diplomacy, has to be taken into account continuously in judging which kind of agreements are possible and which are not. After all, the peoples of Eastern Europe are still paying for the illusion of the West that the Soviet Union was a state like any other, pursuing its power interests without regard to ideology.

The Soviet Dilemma in Eastern Europe

If we now turn to interstate and interparty relations within the Communist camp, we seem at first sight to have entered an area where ideology is adapted quite unceremoniously to the changing requirements of practical politics. Lenin, having barely seized power in Russia and looking forward to an early spreading of Communist revolution, could talk airily enough about the sovereign equality and fraternal solidarity of sovereign "socialist" states. Stalin, having determined after the failure of short-term revolutionary hope to concentrate on "socialism in a single country," came to regard international communism as a mere tool of Soviet power, and to believe that revolutionary victories without the backing of Soviet arms were neither possible nor desirable; he wanted no sovereign Communist allies, only satellites, and he got them in postwar Eastern Europe.

The independent victories of the Yugoslav Communists at the end of the war and of the Chinese Communists in 1949 nevertheless posed the problem he had sought to avoid, and thus required a revision of policy and ideology. But, so one argument goes, the stubborn old man had lost the flexibility to accept the situation; he precipitated a needless quarrel with the Yugoslavs and generally prevented the necessary adjustment while he lived. His heirs, however, hastened to correct his mistakes and to put inter-Communist relations back on a basis of sovereign equality and diplomatic give-and-take, not only with China and Yugoslavia but, after some trial and error, with all Communist states. Or did they?

In the above "common-sense" account, not only the facts of the final phase are wrong; by deliberately neglecting the ideological aspect, it loses sight of all the real difficulties and contradictions which remain inherent in the situation. Because the Soviet Union is both a great power and a single-party state tied to an international ideology, it cannot be content either to oppress and exploit other Communist states or to come to terms with them on a basis of expediency; it must act in a way that will ensure the ideological unity of the Communist "camp" and its own authority at the center.

Stalin's insistence on making the "leading role of the Soviet Union" an article of the international creed expressed not just the idiosyncrasies of a power-mad tyrant, but his perception of one side of the dilemma — the risk that a recognition of the sovereign equality of other Communist states might loosen the solidarity of the "camp" in its dealings with the non-Communist world, and weaken the ideological authority of the Soviet party leaders, with ultimate repercussions on their position in the Soviet Union itself. His successors disavowed him because his Yugoslav policy had failed, and because they perceived the other side of the dilemma — that rigid insistence on Soviet hegemony might break up the unity of the "camp" even more quickly, and might in particular lead to open conflict with China. But by going to Peiping and Belgrade and admitting the "mistakes" of Stalin's "Great Russian chauvinism" (as well as the "mistakes" of his internal terrorist regime), they precipitated the very crisis of authority which he had feared.

The Reassertion of Soviet Primacy

Even Khrushchev and his associates, however, never intended to grant effective sovereign equality to the other Communist satellite regimes of Eastern Europe, which in contrast to Yugoslavia and China had come into being exclusively through the pressure of Soviet power; they merely had planned to make the satellite regimes more viable by reducing Soviet economic exploitation and administrative interference, while maintaining full policy control. In the one case in which not full sovereignty, but at least effective internal autonomy, was in fact granted — the case of Poland — the Soviet leaders were forced to act against their will as a result of open local defiance in a critical international situation. To say that the other East European participants in the Moscow twelve-party meeting of last November, or for that matter the participants from Outer Mongolia and North Korea, represented "governments of sovereign countries" is to mistake the fancies of Communist propaganda for political facts. Nor do the facts bear out Professor Sharp's interpretation that the outcome of the conference showed the Soviet leaders' willingness to rely in their future relations with these "sovereign governments" on the give-and-take of diplomacy. Rather, they confirm Mr. Carew Hunt's view that the need for a single center of international authority is inherent in the Soviet Communist Party's conception of its own role and in its ideology.

The real purpose of that conference was to exploit the recent successes of the Soviet Union as a military and economic power in order to restore the indispensable but lately damaged ideological authority of its leaders in the international Communist movement. The principle of "proletarian internationalism" — that is, unity in foreign policy — had been recognized by all participants, including for the first time in many years the Yugoslavs, before the conference started. Now Moscow was aiming at the further recognition both of its own leadership role and of the need for doctrinal unity, a joint struggle against "revisionism" on the basis of common principles, abolishing once and for all the heresy of "polycentrism" (that is, the concept of a plurality of truly autonomous Communist movements).

As it turned out, the Yugoslavs refused both propositions, while the Polish Communists and the non-ruling but important Italian Communist Party accepted them only with mental reservations, insisting in practice on their right to decide for themselves how the "common principles" would be applied in their own countries. As opposed to this partial failure, however, Moscow was successful in winning full acceptance of the new dispensations by the Chinese Communists and the satellites, as well as in getting agreement on a new, elaborate international liaison machinery within the secretariat of the Soviet Communist Central Committee, in implementation of its renewed claim to international authority.

Moscow's partial failure, therefore, does not indicate that the Soviets will be content with less than they demanded, but that conflict continues. The Soviet press has already reactivated its campaign against Polish "revisionist" ideologies, insisting to Mr. Gomulka that revisionism is the chief internal danger in *all* Communist movements, including that of Poland. Moreover, the proposition defending a Communist party's autonomy in deciding its policy — conceded in principle at the time of Khrushchev's Belgrade visit and at the Twentieth CPSU Congress — is now singled out as a "revisionist" heresy; increasingly the example of Imre Nagy is invoked to show how a demand for autonomy led him down a "road" of "betrayal" and finally "counterrevolution." While the methods of Khrushchev remain conspicuously different from those of Stalin, the logic of the one-party regime, which requires insistence on Soviet authority as a precondition for unity both in foreign policy and in ideological principles, has forced the present first secretary to reassert some of the very doctrines he rashly threw overboard in 1955 – 56.

Ideology on the Home Front

Ultimately, the need to fight "revisionism" in Eastern Europe, even at the price of renewed difficulties with both Yugoslavia and Poland, arises from the need to strengthen the ideological defenses of the party regime in Russia itself. To admit that in Hungary the workers rose against a Communist government would call into question the basic identification of the ruling party with the working class — the fiction of the "dictatorship of the proletariat." To let Yugoslav propaganda for "workers' management" pass unchallenged would confirm the implication that Soviet factories, having no workers' councils with similar rights, are managed in the interest not of the workers but of the privileged bureaucracy. To keep silent when the Poles proudly report the improvement of their agricultural yields since the dissolution of most of their collective farms would encourage Soviet peasants to dream of similar reforms. To condone the increased, if still limited, freedom of artistic, literary, and philosophical discussion now permitted in Poland and Yugoslavia would strengthen the demands of Soviet writers and scholars for similar freedom.

The obvious and intended implication here is that Soviet reconciliation with Yugoslavia and the near-revolutionary changes in Poland merely aggravated pressures for change which *already* existed in Russia itself. Thus the present account would be incomplete without some attempt to indicate, however sketchily, how ideological changes can be used as aids in interpreting the Soviet domestic scene as well as Kremlin foreign policy and bloc relations.

Earlier in the paper, reference was made to some of the basic tenets which seem inseparably bound up with the preservation and justification of a Communist one-party regime. But within this unchanging framework, considerable variations in detail have taken place in the history of the Soviet Union. The appearance or disappearance of one of these "ideological variables" may be a valuable indicator of the kind of pressures which are exerted on the regime by the growing society and of the manner in which the leaders try to maintain control, sometimes by partly ceding to such pressures and seeking to canalize them, other times by a sharp frontal counterattack.

The "Permanent" Revolution

Among the most revealing of these variables are Soviet doctrines dealing with the economic role of the state and with the "class struggle" within Soviet society. The underlying reality is that a revolutionary party dictatorship, once it has carried out its original program and by this contributed to the emergence of a new privileged class, is bound to disappear sooner or later — to fall victim to a "Thermidor" — unless it prevents the new upper class from consolidating its position by periodically shaking up the social structure in a "permanent revolution from above." The ideological expression of this problem is the classical doctrine that the dictatorship of the proletariat should gradually "wither away" after it has succeeded in destroying the old ruling classes; thus, if continued dictatorship is to be justified, new goals of social transformation must be set and new "enemies" discovered.

In the early period of Stalin's rule, the new "goal" was the forced collectivization of the Russian countryside; the prosperous peasants — the *kulaks* — took the place of the former landowners and capitalists as the "enemy class" which had to be liquidated. Summing up the achievement in 1937, Stalin wrote in his "Short Course" on party history that collectivization had been a second revolution, but a revolution carried out from above, by state power "with the help of the masses," not just by the masses from below. The ideological groundwork was thus laid for assigning the state a function of continuous economic transformation from above, in addition to its terminable revolutionary task.

The second step, also taken by Stalin in 1937, at the height of the Great Blood Purge, consisted in proclaiming the doctrine that the "class struggle" in the Soviet Union was getting more acute as the "construction of socialism" advanced, because the "enemies" were getting more desperate. This was the ideological justification of the purge itself; at the same time, it was a veiled indication that another revolution from above was in effect taking place, though Stalin refrained this time from trying to define the "enemies" in social terms. In fact, what Stalin accomplished was a mass liquidation of both the bearers of the party's older revolutionary tradition — considered unsuited to the tasks of a bureaucratic state party — and of the most confident and independent-minded elements of the new privileged bureaucracy; the end result was a transformation of the party's social and ideological composition through the mass incorporation of the surviving frightened bureaucrats.

Stalin's final ideological pronouncement was contained in his political testament, "Economic Problems of Socialism," published in 1952. In this work he mapped out a program for the further revolutionary transformation of Soviet society, with the taking over of *kolkhoz* property by the state as its central element.

Khrushchev's Formula for Perpetual Rule

The first major renunciation of these Stalinist ideological innovations was made by Khrushchev in his "secret speech" at the Twentieth Congress. Apart from his factual disclosures concerning Stalin's crimes, he denounced Stalin's doctrine of the sharpening class struggle with societal progress as dangerous nonsense, calculated to lead to the mutual slaughter of loyal Communists after the real class enemy had long been liquidated. This statement affords the master clue to the puzzle of why Khrushchev made the speech: it was a "peace offering" to the leading strata of the regime in the party machine, army, and managerial bureaucracy alike — a response to their pressure for greater personal security. But by his concession, Khrushchev reopened the problem which Stalin's doctrine and practice had been intended to solve — that of preserving and justifying the party dictatorship by periodic major shakeups of society.

By the spring and summer of 1957, Khrushchev showed his awareness of the practical side of the problem: his dismantling of the economic ministries, breaking up the central economic bureaucracy, and strengthening the power of the regional party secretaries, was another such revolutionary shakeup. By November, he responded to the ideological side of the problem. First he repeated, in his solemn speech on the fortieth anniversary of the Bolshevik seizure of power, his rejection of Stalin's doctrine of ever-sharpening class struggle and ever-present enemies, thus indicating his wish to avoid a return to Stalin's terroristic methods even while following his social recipe of permanent revolution. Then he proceeded to develop his own alternative justification for maintaining the party dictatorship — a unique argument which identified the strengthening of party control with the "withering away of the state" predicted by Lenin.

Reviving this formula for the first time since it was buried by Stalin, Khrushchev explained that the military and police apparatus of the state would have to be maintained as long as a hostile capitalist world existed outside; but he added that the economic and administrative functions of the state bureaucracy would henceforth be steadily reduced by decentralization and devolution, thus strengthening the organs of regional self-government and of national autonomy within the various republics. At the same time, he quietly took steps to strengthen the control of the central party secretariat — his own seat of power — over the republican and regional party organs, thus following the old Leninist principle that the fiction of national autonomy must be balanced by the fact of centralized discipline within the ruling party.

In short, the same aim of maintaining the social dynamism of the party dictatorship and justifying its necessity, which Stalin achieved by exalting the economic role of the state, is pursued by Khrushchev by means of the reverse device of claiming that the state's economic functions have begun to "wither away." On the face of it, this doctrinal manipulation seems to reduce the role of ideology to that of ingenious trickery, obscuring rather than reflecting the underlying social realities. Yet in fact, the very need for a change in the ideological argument reflects the change that is taking place in the underlying social situation — the resistance against a return to naked terrorism, the growing desire for a lessening of state pressure and a greater scope for local activity. Whether in industry or agriculture, in the control of literature, or in relations with the satellite states, the basic conditions which the regime needs for its self-perpetuation have remained the same — but they can no longer be assured in the same way. That, too, is reflected in the variables of the official ideology.

Form and Function
R. N. CAREW HUNT

It seems to me important to distinguish between the *function* of the Soviet ideology and the peculiar *form* it has assumed. In the last analysis, its *function* is to provide a rationalization of the one-party system of government and of the policies to which the Soviet rulers are committed. The doctrine of the party is thus its central theme, and to this are related all its other elements, "proletarian democracy," "proletarian internationalism," "capitalist encirclement," "socialist realism," *etc.* On the other hand, the *form* it has taken derives primarily from Marxism with its insistence upon conflict as the mainspring of history and the force behind all progress within society — a conflict which is teleological and can only end in one way. The division of the world into two antagonistic camps, the one "progressive" and the other "reactionary," and the belief that the victory of the former, as represented by the Soviet Union, is predestined by the logic of history, is simply the Marxist class struggle between the bourgeoisie and the proletariat projected onto the international plane, and it constitutes the basis of all Soviet political thinking. It has led the Soviet rulers to take so distorted a view of the world as to make it harder to deal with them than with any government in the annals of diplomacy; and this, as Mr. Lowenthal says, is just what may be expected from an "ideology" in the sense in which Marx originally used the term.

Professor Sharp argues that Soviet national interests alone count, though his definition of these interests is tautological, as Mr. Lowenthal rightly points out. Yet to take a single example: if the Soviet rulers had consulted their national interests only, how are we to explain their strenuous efforts to promote revolution in China during the 1920's, that is, at a time when their country was weak, and was seeking to strengthen its position by entering into trade agreements and diplomatic relations with the Western powers? Such zeal for the welfare of the Chinese masses is intelligible only on the assumption that the rulers believed that they had a mission to spread the revolution wherever there was a chance of doing so effectively. Lenin had repeatedly declared this to be a primary obligation before he seized power — that is, before there was any question of promoting national interests — while after the revolution he never said a word to suggest that there was any connection between the two.

Naturally, the concepts of an ideology have to be translated into action, and when this action is undertaken by a powerful country such as Russia has now become, it can be plausibly represented as *Realpolitik*. Yet it does not follow that it belongs solely, or even primarily, to this category, or that we can afford to ignore the principles of which it claims to be the expression. The objection to such agreements as that of Yalta is precisely that they failed to take this into account, and assumed that any conflicts which might later arise with the Russians would be of a political nature only.

Further, it is not easy to see what process of logic entitles us to assume that, while the leaders of the West believe in their standard of values and seek to formulate their policies in accordance with them, the Soviet rulers neither believe in theirs nor seek to apply them. Doubtless Professor Sharp is right in saying that they proceed with caution. But this has no bearing upon the matter, as there is nothing in their ideology which requires them to act otherwise.

Finally, I would join issue with Mr. Lowenthal on one point where we disagree. Certainly Marx, who had no interest in social technology, did not develop a concept of total planning. Yet he and Engels consistently advocated the replacement of "the anarchy of social production" under capitalism by production to be carried out upon a "common plan," though who was to do the planning was not explained. Yet this was sufficient to excite the suspicion of his Anarchist opponents. Both the Anarchists and the Marxists agreed that the state must be abolished; but whereas the Anarchists held that the whole object of the revolution was to destroy it, Marx held that its object was to set up a new form of society in which the means of production would be developed in the interests of all, though once it was established, the state would "wither away." The Anarchists reasoned, however, that in any such society it would be necessary to retain some form of coercive authority, and whether it was called the state or something else was immaterial. Subsequent events were to prove how right they were.

From the early days of the revolution Lenin made clear that his objective was a nationwide planned economy, though it was left to his successor to introduce it. My contention is that if such an economy is to be introduced and made effective, the state (or the party) will have to do many unpopular things. The reason why the Soviet Union has become so powerful in so short a time is precisely because its rulers were able to enforce measures which would never have been tolerated under a democracy, and one of the functions of the ideology is to justify their right to act in this manner. Naturally, such a policy has led to the emergence of a bureaucracy which is the virtual owner of the means of production. My criticism of Djilas is that he approves the economic objectives of communism, but objects to the state of affairs to which the attempt to realize them inevitably gives rise. He wants a "democratic communism." It is a contradiction in terms.

The Policy Pie
SAMUEL L. SHARP

The differences of opinion expressed by the participants in the symposium on the roles of ideology and of power politics in Soviet policy decisions bring to mind the story about a product labeled "rabbit pie" which, on closer scrutiny, turns out to be not quite pure rabbit but a mixture of rabbit and horse meat, in the proportion of one horse to one rabbit. Although Mr. Lowenthal insists that I deny "completely" the relevance of Communist ideology to the formation of Soviet policies, or that I overlook "completely" the use made of foreign Communist parties by the Soviet Union, this is not so. The controversy is actually one about the proportions in which the ingredients of ideology and power politics appear in the final product, Soviet policy (especially within the area to which my original arguments were directed, namely foreign policy).

I find it difficult to pick a quarrel with Mr. Hunt since, while seeming to argue that the product is pure rabbit (ideology), he is careful at all times to leave open a gate wide enough for the horse (power politics) to be brought in. At his most specific, Mr. Hunt argues that the significance of ideology lies in that "it makes those who profess it act in a way that they would not otherwise do," presumably with a frequent sacrifice of efficiency for the sake of principle. The burden of proof, of course, rests on him, and in his comments appearing in the current issue he refers to Soviet support of the nationalist revolution in China in the 1920's as obviously the result of "zeal for the welfare of the Chinese masses" (Mr. Hunt is ironical, I hope) or of a sense of "mission" to spread revolution *whenever there was a chance of doing so effectively.* This, he maintains, was a mistake from the standpoint of Soviet state interests because Russia was then seeking trade agreements and diplomatic recognition from the West. His argument, however, is debatable. The establishment of Communist regimes outside Russia, if it could be "effectively" achieved, would have been definitely to the advantage of the weak Soviet state under the circumstances of the time. The case of Soviet "support" for the Chinese revolution ("encouragement" would be more accurate) is, of course, notorious because there was nothing "effective" about it: it was a case of miscalculation to be sure, but not necessarily a miscalculation caused by ideological zeal or a sense of mission. As to the effect of the policy on relations with the West, Stalin apparently was following in the footsteps of nineteenth-century Tsarist foreign ministers who attempted to "bring in the East in order to redress an unfavorable balance in the West" (as suggested, with respect to Lenin's policies, by E. H. Carr).

Since Mr. Lowenthal agrees that ideology will effectively influence policy decisions of the Soviet leaders "when, and only when, it expresses the needs of self-preservation of the party regime" (and I need not remind him that those in charge of a going concern tend to identify the interests of the concern with their own continued tenure), there would be little for me to object to were it not for his previously mentioned distortions of my views, his introduction of the gratuitous compliment of "innocence" (hereby acknowledged as an undeserved but charming relief from the much stronger epithets collected by this writer on other occasions), and for his own excursion into the theory of international relations and recent diplomatic history which — to return the compliment — is not only innocent but presumptuous.

Mr. Lowenthal states that the doctrine of "two camps" was not invented by Stalin, but was "inherent in Leninism." This is unhistorical. The temptation to present the world as divided into "good" and "bad" camps is as old as international conflict itself. And certainly in recent times the "two-camps" image has been used on both sides of the dividing line; it fits admirably into a bipolarized world situation. "At the present moment in world history nearly every nation must choose between alternative ways of life," declared President Truman in his message to Congress in March 1947, several months before the late Andrei Zhdanov came out with the first vigorous postwar reformulation of the old cliche on the Soviet side. Politics operates this side of the ultimate. The persistence of the enemy image and the drive for "unlimited power" may well be present in the minds of the Soviet leaders, but the history of future years will be shaped, not by this admittedly unfriendly view of the outside world, but by what the Soviet leaders are *persuaded or compelled* to do; not by their "collective paranoia" (a term given a completely arbitrary definition by Mr. Lowenthal), but rather by their desire for survival and appraisal of the limits of the feasible. I do not doubt that they will grasp every opportunity to press any advantages to the utmost. This makes them unpleasant and tough opponents, but not totally intractable ones. To posit a world that would be animated by general harmony were it not for a single disturber of the peace is to sacrifice all history on the altar of deceptive imagery.

Mr. Lowenthal points out the difference between the "traditional" and Soviet concepts of spheres of influence, ascribing the controversy over the Yalta agreements to this difference. However, there is a built-in and often deliberate vagueness in the concept of spheres of influence, and differences of interpretation are not necessarily rooted in differences of *Weltanschauung*. Examining the historical record, one will find that conflicts of interpretation have usually occurred between those who acquired a sphere of influence and those who conceded one. This is not the time and, Mr. Lowenthal will admit, not exactly the place to enter into a debate over what Yalta meant and whether the representatives of the West were on that occasion laboring under an illusion about the real nature of the Soviet Union, or rather were trying to

military theaters. Nor is it correct to say that complete Communist control was immediately imposed throughout the Soviet sphere of influence. In at least some countries (especially Czechoslovakia, but also, to some extent, Poland and Hungary until 1947) there was the kind of fuzzy situation characteristic of an in-between area. The Soviet Union, for a variety of practical considerations, on some occasions actually seems to have curbed the enthusiasm of local Communists for a speedy transition to full control. The present writer certainly did not err on the side of optimism about the lasting nature of this halfway arrangement. It was obvious that the fuzziness could not survive the onset of the cold war; yet it is wrong to mistake one of the symptoms of the cold war for its cause.

There is no serious controversy between Mr. Lowenthal and myself with regard to recent developments in Eastern Europe, except that I offer a guess while he professes to know for certain what the meaning of these developments is. Of course, the Soviet Union would like to derive advantages in its dealings with "ruling" Communist parties from the magic of ideological control. However, in this case as in others, the intentions of the Soviet leaders, or their views about what would be the optimum situation, do not exclusively determine the outcome. When they saw the need to shift relations with at least some of the countries in the Soviet sphere to a more "traditional" basis, this was done whether graciously or not. If the Soviet Union appears currently to be reassuring its ideological domination over Eastern Europe, this reflects an acknowledgment by the leaders of these countries of Russia's strengthened international power position. Obviously, the Soviet Union, like any big power in a position of leadership, will try to hold together by various means the grouping over which it presides. To the extent that its leaders disregard the general rules of international relations from which no one is exempt, they will be inviting trouble and failure. There are no cut-rate worlds to be had.

A Difference in Kind
RICHARD LOWENTHAL

I am sorry that Professor Sharp should feel that I have distorted his position. He, in turn, has certainly mistaken my meaning if he attributes to me the view that our world would be animated by general harmony were it not for a single disturber of the peace. That view is nothing but a reflection of the Leninist dogma of the two camps, which consists precisely in the delusion of seeing all conflicts, and ultimately all independent forces, as manifestations of a single enemy. It is not unhistorical to regard this outlook as characteristic of the totalitarian movements of our time; on the contrary, it is unhistorical to confuse it with the age-old tendency to regard one's own side in a given conflict as good and the enemy as bad.

I agree with Professor Sharp on one point of great practical importance — that the Soviets are not intractable in his sense, that is, that they are tough politicians liable to be influenced by the hard facts of power and the processes for negotiation, rather than madmen pursuing a preordained plan of world conquest regardless of risk. But while Soviet policy differs from Hitler's in this vital respect, I hold that it is also different in kind from that of nontotalitarian great powers. Professor Sharp persists in seeking to blur this difference, while I wish to show that it is not confined to motives and ultimate aims, but constantly affects the Soviets' *modus operandi.*

For instance, Professor Sharp accepts my formula that Soviet ideology influences policy decisions only when it expresses the needs of self-preservation of the party regime, but adds that it is normal for any government to identify the interests of its country with its own. But my point is that the interests of a one-party government which uses an international movement as a weapon are highly peculiar, and I gave examples to show just how they affect its foreign relations. Since we wrote, the new Soviet quarrel with Yugoslavia — a quarrel which both Khrushchev and Tito would have liked to avoid for realistic reasons, but which was forced on them by Tito's need to justify ideologically his position outside the Warsaw pact, and Khrushchev's need to restore ideological unity and discipline within the bloc — has further illustrated my thesis.

Again, Professor Sharp claimed in his article that taking the entire Soviet record to date, the achievements are clearly attributable to Soviet power and diplomacy with no credit due to the international Communist movement. I find it impossible to fit into this formula the victory of communism in China, which has been to an overwhelming extent the outcome of the struggle of indigenous forces under indigenous leadership, but has resulted in a major shift in the balance of world power in favor of the Soviets. Some rabbit!

But we remain farthest apart on the Soviet conquest of Eastern Europe. In referring to Yalta, I explicitly disclaimed any intention to pass judgment on whether the Western statesmen committed an avoidable mistake of disastrous dimensions. I was concerned to show that, whether the concessions were avoidable or not, the later fate of the Soviet sphere of influence was implicit in the nature of Soviet power. Professor Sharp denies this on the ground that the "peoples' democracies" were somewhat fuzzy coalition regimes until 1947, and concludes that their later total sovietization was a symptom and not a cause of the cold war. Yet readers of this journal are familiar with the overwhelming evidence that preparations for total sovietization, such as the occupation of all key positions of power (armed forces, police, press, *etc.),* by Communists and the systematic undermining of the independence of the other parties were begun throughout the area almost from the moment of the first entry of Soviet forces. I can find no evidence to back the hypothesis that these preparations would not have been pursued to their logical conclusions if the West had acquiesced in the first steps instead of reacting to the challenge of the forcible expansion of the Soviet system, nor can I accept the implication that the cold war began only when the West took up the challenge.

Soviet Ideology and
Soviet Foreign Policy*

1.

None of the perplexing problems of contemporary international affairs has
given rise to more confusing discussion than the relationship of Soviet ideology
to the foreign policy of the USSR. The very vagueness of the term "Soviet
ideology" or "Communist ideology" (and are they synonymous?), the uncertainty to what extent this uncertain force motivates the makers of Soviet
policies, have compounded our difficulties in understanding the behavior of
one of the world's two superpowers. Are Russia's rulers motivated by cynical
power politics? Are they ideological fanatics? Is the content of their ideology
the gospel of Marx, Engels, and Lenin, or something else? Questions can be
compounded ad infinitum.

And this is no academic problem, for the West has sought some way of
understanding the basis of Soviet policies, some means of both peaceful accommodation with the USSR and preservation of the confines of the free world.
The means hinge on the character of Soviet policy. Mr. John Foster Dulles has
formulated one approach to the problem, viewing Soviet ideology as exerting
an influence on the foreign policy of the USSR. Proclaiming the peaceful

*Reprinted by permission of Princeton University Press and the author from *World Poli-
tics,* XI, 2 (January, 1959), pp. 153–172. Copyright 1959 by Princeton University Press. The
author wishes to acknowledge his debt to the Russian Research Center, Harvard University.

content of democratic ideology, Mr. Dulles wrote: "unhappily, it is otherwise with the creed of Communism, or at least that variety of Communism which is espoused by the Soviet Communist Party." Marx, Lenin, and Stalin have all consistently taught the use of force and violence and Mr. Dulles sees the relationship between ideology and action as a fairly direct one, for he goes on to say, "these teachings of Marx, Lenin and Stalin have never been disavowed by the Soviet Communist Party of which Mr. Khrushchev is now the First Secretary. . . . Therefore, I believe that it is necessary that at least that part of the Soviet Communist creed should be abandoned."[1] And the dependence of the international behavior of the USSR on its alleged philosophy is also maintained by those who, unlike Mr. Dulles, believe that the ideology does not necessarily encourage the use of force or violence. A British political scientist sees the content of the Bolsheviks' ideology as a reassuring rather than a depressing portent for world peace. "They will, while they retain their present philosophy, understand neither our society nor their own. . . . We cannot rely on their good will, but we can, if we act wisely, rely on their patience. Their false philosophy teaches them that time is their ally; and the more they can be persuaded to let time pass quietly the better for us and for them. Let us at least thank God that Hitler is dead and that the dictators we have to deal with are sane."[2]

The crucial problem is the meaning of the term "ideology." Most of us, if asked about the meaning and content of our own ideology, would begin by recognizing that while in many cases it is the product of certain ethical, religious, and political teachings, the relationship is never simple, but modified by a large number of factors, like the conditions of our material and social life, our experience, etc. We do not usually assume that the motives and aims of the policies of the United States or Great Britain can be fully explained by the ideas of John Locke, Thomas Jefferson, or John Stuart Mill. "Freedom," said a famous English jurist, "has been secreted in the interstices of procedure." And, to paraphrase, the Western notions of freedom, of the proper aims of politics, foreign policy included, have been formulated through the experience of life, the experience of trying to realize the precepts of democracy and liberalism. The more sophisticated writers on the Soviet Union and communism have realized that one cannot explain the behavior of the rulers of Russia, or certain aspects of the mentality of Soviet society, by pointing to a passage in the Communist Manifesto or a phrase from Stalin or Lenin. But in our search for the meaning of Soviet ideology, we have not fully recognized that that ideology has been secreted in the interstices of the totalitarian system, which has now existed for over forty years, and that the early millenarian

1. John Foster Dulles in a letter to *The New Statesman*, February 8, 1958.
2. John Plamenatz, *German Marxism and Russian Communism* (London, 1954), pp. 350.

Communist faith has been modified by the experience of almost two generations' application of the original theories to the stubborn facts of life.

We should not, however, go to the other extreme and assume that the rulers
of Russia have remained totally unaffected by the doctrines in which they have
been brought up and which they have been proclaiming. The relationship
between ideology and action eludes a straightforward definition, but it is naive
to assume that a group of men, even when endowed with totalitarian powers
and with what to an outsider appears an infinite possibility of political manipulation, can remain unaffected by their habits of thought and speech, and can
indulge in unrestrained Machiavellian politics. At times, tired of explaining
Soviet politics by quoting from the scriptures of Marxism-Leninism, we assign
the role of ideology to the realm of "propaganda" with which the leaders of
the Communist Party of the USSR beguile their subjects while they themselves
enjoy cynical freedom from ideological scruples. But again, the picture is not
so simple. Stalin, or Khrushchev and his colleagues, may think primarily of
expanding their power and increasing that of the USSR, but their choice of
means to that end is inextricably intertwined with their philosophy of power,
in which again ideology plays a crucial part.

The content of what must be called the working creed of the Soviet leaders
is not easy to define. It is not wise to seek a definition which ignores the
changing character of Soviet society and the changing generations and personalities of the leaders. But it is possible to make certain generalizations and
then to see how they apply in the Soviet evaluation of the outside world.

The original doctrine of Marx-Engels still remains the official creed of the
Soviet Union, but somewhat in the manner in which a modern secularized
society acknowledges being based on religion. Gone in Soviet Russia today is
the sense of the practical immediacy of the socialist doctrine which characterized the ten or fifteen years after the November Revolution. The reasons are
manifold. One of them may be that Marxian socialism, as interpreted first by
Lenin and then by Stalin (and we shall not enter here into the question of
whether this is the "correct" interpretation of Marxism), has as its two main
historical functions, first, the channeling of the revolutionary impulses of a
society undergoing industrialization, and then the guidance of this society
toward the achievement of a modern industrial state.[3] If this be essentially
correct, then Marxian phrases and prescriptions simply have very little immediate relevance to the problems of the Soviet state and society of today.
Paradoxically, the success of Marxism in Russia has meant its decline in
importance, insofar as the original doctrine of Marx-Engels is concerned. If
this statement appears extravagant, let us look at some concrete examples. Is
the average citizen of Russia, or a Soviet leader when not giving an official

---

3. This interpretation is presented in my article, "The Historical Role of Marxism and the
Soviet System," *World Politics,* VIII, No. 1 (October 1955), pp. 20–45.

speech, really concerned with the problem of creating an egalitarian society? Is the world revolution viewed with the same intensity of feeling or related to the internal problems of the Soviet Union as it was in the first few years after the Revolution? It is unlikely that a member of the Presidium loses any sleep over the meaning of Marxian "negation of negation" or over any other subtleties of the dialectic which once constituted the intellectual fare of the Communists and, what is more important, which were bound up with the actual problems of the internal and external politics of the USSR. Phrases from Marx and Engels will still take their place in official speeches, and in the philosophical journals obscure Party hacks will adorn with scriptural invocations the latest economic or political decisions of the government. And the doctrine will be stretched to justify any practical needs of policy. Collaboration with the West was not only the logical outcome of the dire need in which the Soviet Union found itself after the German attack, but also a theoretically correct application of the Marxian injunction to collaborate with the progressive part of the capitalist camp against its reactionary component. The possibility of peaceful coexistence and the unavoidability of a clash "sometime" between the camps of socialism and capitalism are interchangeable ideological interpretations given out with equal facility according to the turn of international events.

What then remains of original Marxism which is pertinent to the actual conduct of Soviet policy as distinguished from the language in which this policy is proclaimed or rationalized? First of all, there is no doubt that the tone of Soviet policies, domestic as well as foreign, is still greatly affected by the original *Weltanschauung* of Marx. The father of modern socialism proclaimed his theory at a time when the tendency of liberalism was to proclaim the eventual solution of international difficulties and the harmonious coexistence of nations. *Without necessarily assimilating all governments to the same pattern,* free trade, the liberals believed (and the term at its broadest meant a free interchange of people and ideas as well as goods), would bring about a degree of international harmony, with such irrational phenomena as war and imperialism gradually withering away. The general tenor of Marx's philosophy was to discount the notion of an automatic harmony of interests within an industrial society and, by the same token, in international relations. He held that in the world at large, just as within an individual society, growth, development, and clashes of interests and struggles were unavoidable and would continue until socialism became the predominant, if not the only, form of social and political organization.

This legacy of Marxism has become an important part of the Soviet habitual view of international relations. It has expressed itself in two general characteristics of Soviet foreign policy. The first has been an unusual sensitivity to economic and social developments in states playing a major role in international relations. The United States or France, for instance, does not appear in Soviet eyes primarily as a state having certain historical and power interests *qua* state, but as a conglomeration of class interests and certain social and economic pressures which determine the policy of the capitalist state, regardless of the dressing-up of these postulates in terms of national interests or honor. This instinct of Soviet international policy has contributed both to its strength and to its weakness. It has endowed the Russian policy-makers with a degree of sophistication about international relations surpassing the old platitudes of the diplomatic art; it has also, at times, made them the dupes of the rigid dogmatisms which they have erected to account for the international situation. Thus the belated recognition of the threat of Hitlerism which, according to a dogmatic oversimplification, should have proved but a prelude to a Communist revolution in Germany. Thus the initial underestimate of the strength of national and democratic impulses which made the West stand up to Hitler, an underestimate which almost proved fatal to the Soviet Union. In a subsequent passage, we shall discuss what has happened in recent years to this Marxian technique of viewing the world outside the Soviet Union.

The second aspect of the legacy of Marxism to the policy-makers of the Soviet Union is subtler and more paradoxical in its effect. While the technique of viewing the world through the prism of Marxian categories of economic development and class conflict may be narrow and lead to serious miscalculations, it is still a rationalist technique. The other Marxian element is quasi-religious in its manifestations. It consists in an attachment to the symbols and phrases of the doctrine rather than to its analytical content. Just as in internal Soviet politics the official doctrine has been considered infallible and any errors or shortcomings in Soviet politics, economy, or culture have been attributed to mistakes or malevolence on the part of an individual, so in external relations the Soviet state has pursued the injunctions of Marxism-Leninism and any departure from them (read a reversal in the foreign policy of the USSR) has been attributed to an individual's inability to apply Marxism-Leninism correctly to the given situation, or to his malice and treason. The terror of the Stalin era has been ascribed by his successors not to certain organic features of a totalitarian system but solely to the pathological tendencies of the aging despot. When trying to reestablish a *modus vivendi* with Yugoslavia in the spring of 1955, Khrushchev felt constrained after arriving in Belgrade to blame the whole tangled story of the difficulties between the two states on the sinister malevolence of one man, Lavrenti Beria. To a Western commentator, grounded in the iconoclastic liberal tradition, the tendency of the Soviet leaders to invoke the magic formula of their doctrine as an explanation and guide to everything, *at the same time that they increasingly ignore and reject certain specific prescriptions of Marxism-Leninism,* smacks either of calculated hypocrisy or of a facile propaganda device. Yet such judgments are often oversimplified. The practitioners of the world's most totalitarian system must feel the need to believe in the infallibility of their doctrine; that the doctrine itself has become blurred or irrelevant to current situations does not change their tendency to use the magic incantation of Marxism. In both 1948 and 1958, in trying to account for their difficulties with Yugoslavia, the Soviets fell back upon the same ideological device: in 1948 the Yugoslav Communist Party was accused of the betrayal of Marxism-Leninism; in 1958, of revisionism. The whole complex of grievances against Tito and his regime has been reduced to an infraction of orthodoxy, of which the Communist Party of the Soviet Union is the only and infallible exponent. Three years of efforts by the Khrushchev regime to alter through diplomacy and compromise what they themselves had branded as Stalin's erroneous and paranoiac condemnation of the Yugoslavs have ended for the time being in a milder version of the Stalinist fiat: since Yugoslavia is a source of trouble for the Soviet Union, since her anomalous position is in itself an open encouragement of independent-minded Communist satellites, the Yugoslavs obviously cannot be bona fide Communists. Once again the Soviets have demonstrated that they cannot regard an international situation as essentially a series of concrete issues between states, but rather as an ideological conflict or betrayal.

If we think of the potential uses of Marxism for actual politics, we might separate three main strains: first, as a body of implied prescriptions (implied, because Marx and Engels never devoted much attention to the problem of the foreign policy of a socialist state); second, as an analytical discipline for viewing international as well as domestic politics; and, finally, as a symbol and quasi-religion giving its practitioners the sense that they are moving forward with the forces of history and that the success of their state is predicated upon the truth of the doctrine. It is asserted here that the first strain no longer plays any significant part in Soviet foreign policies, while the analytical and symbolical uses of Marxism remain important and necessary to the understanding of Soviet policy. In pondering the interconnection of the three elements of the ideological inheritance of the Soviet system, we are immediately struck by certain parallels to a society undergoing the process of secularization: when specific points of a religious creed lose their veracity or relevance for people, can they for long retain a general religious outlook and belief in the doctrine as a whole? Similarly, if the Marxian doctrine loses its specific relevance, can the frame of mind engendered by it and the belief itself endure? It is tempting for a Western observer to answer this question in the negative and to envisage a time when the realities of the world will bring about a reorientation of Soviet values. Mr. Kennan in his famous essay postulated the possibility of a change in the Soviet outlook consequent upon the failure of their assumptions about capitalism: "the palsied decrepitude of the capitalist world is the keystone of Communist philosophy. Even the failure of the United States to experience the early economic depression which the ravens of the Red Square have been predicting with such complacent confidence since hostilities ceased would have deep and important repercussions throughout the Communist world."[4] And further: "For no mystical Messianic movement — and particularly not that of the Kremlin — can face frustration indefinitely without eventually adjusting itself in one way or another to the logic of that state of affairs."[5]

Mr. Kennan overlooked, perhaps, the natural intransigence of religious millenarian movements to purely rational objective facts. *Credo quia absurdum* is not entirely atypical of the attitude of religious or political fanaticism. But the most fundamental objection to the postulating of an erosion of the ideology by contact with reality is that this ideology is propagated within a totalitarian system. If the rulers of this system see in the ideology, as we have seen, not only the rationale of their absolute power but a source of their inner security and effectiveness, then the doctrine will not be soon or easily repudiated just because the West increases its material welfare. Furthermore, while the Soviet citizen, including the indoctrinated Party member, has numerous occasions to discover the contradictions or irrelevancies of Marxism in his daily life, he enjoys no such tangible experiences insofar as the world outside the USSR is concerned. And to the Soviet leaders, the field of foreign relations offers the best opportunity to attempt to demonstrate the viability of Marxism, conscious as they are of the necessity of preserving and developing the ideological *élan* of the Communist Party and of the regime. Marxism may be irrelevant to the problems of the Soviet Union now that its industrialization is accomplished and the state has shown no signs of withering away or becoming, in essence, less authoritarian. If some meaning is to be attached to the ideology, if it is not to fade out completely in the minds of the Soviet people, then it must show its effectiveness in propelling Soviet society into economic and scientific development at a *faster pace* than that achieved by societies inspired by the rival creed. And most important of all, the Soviet brand of Marxism must be shown to be advancing in the world at large, proving alluring to societies emerging from backwardness and colonial rule. The battle to preserve Soviet ideology in the USSR and with it the rationale of the totalitarian system is thus being fought in a world context, and the spread of Soviet ideology, influence, and prestige throughout the world becomes increasingly crucial to the preservation of the Soviet system as we know it.

The latter statement sounds like a truism. But we may best put it in perspective by contrasting the present situation with that which prevailed in the first decade after the Revolution. The Russian Communists, a group devoted much more literally to their ideology than the current rulers of Russia, were confronted with the seeming failure of the ideological premises on which the Revolution had been undertaken. It was only their own weak and backward country which remained under the rule of their version of socialism. Elsewhere in the world the wave of revolutionary feeling had subsided and

4. "The Sources of Soviet Conduct," reprinted in *American Diplomacy, 1900–1950* (Chicago, 1951), p. 123.
5. *Ibid.,* p. 124.

capitalism appeared to be stabilized. The logical response to the situation was to build the prerequisites of socialism in Russia; and the ideology was vindicated by the industrialization of the Soviet state. The terrible cost of the transformation and the increasingly ruthless totalitarian methods employed cannot obscure the fact that Marxism, and the ideological fervor generated by it, were crucial factors in the achievement. And conversely, the achievement appeared to vindicate the ideology, and the totalitarian system of the USSR. Today, it may be flatly asserted that the growth of the USSR can proceed on its own momentum. If the ideology is to become increasingly decorative and meaningless, in terms of concrete problems of Soviet life, where, in the last resort, will be the rationale for the totalitarian system, for the assumed omnipotence and omniscience of the highest councils of the Communist Party of the USSR? The focus of "proving" Marxism-Leninism, and by the same token of preserving something of the old ideological *élan* and sense of mission without which the most efficient totalitarian regime runs the danger of internal disintegration, has shifted once again beyond the geographical confines of the USSR.

2.

To the outsider, the shifting trends of Soviet policy appear almost incomprehensible. The Khrushchev who in 1955 and 1956 proclaimed the legitimacy of seeking various roads to socialism is the same person who in the spring of 1958 led the attack upon the "revisionism" of the Yugoslav Communists.[6] In 1956, in his "secret" report on Stalin and Stalinism, Khrushchev bluntly blamed the Yugoslav situation on the pathological characteristics of the late despot.[7] And yet in 1958 the charge advanced against the Yugoslav Communist Party repeated many points of the Stalinist indictment of 1948–1949. The Yugoslavs indulged in revisionism by stressing the possibility of separate roads to socialism; they implied that the Soviet Union could also be guilty of increasing international tension, etc. As a matter of record, the Yugoslav Party program for its 7th Congress in 1958 did not say anything that Tito and his

---

6. From Khrushchev's report to the 20th Party Congress: "As far back as on the eve of the great October revolution, V. I. Lenin wrote 'All nations will arrive at socialism — this is inevitable — but not all will do so in exactly the same way.' . . . Historical experience has fully confirmed this brilliant precept of Lenin's. . . . In the Federal People's Republic of Yugoslavia, where power belongs to the working people and society is founded on public ownership of the means of production, unique specific forms of economic management and organization of the state apparatus are arising in the process of socialist construction." *Current Soviet Policies, II,* ed. by Leo Gruliow (New York, 1957), pp. 37–38.

7. "The July plenary session of the Central Committee studied in detail the reasons for the development of conflict with Yugoslavia. It was a shameful role that Stalin played there. The 'Yugoslav affair' contained no problems that could not have been solved through Party discussions among comrades. . . . No matter how much or how little Stalin shook not only his little finger but everything else that he could shake, Tito did not fall. Why? The reason was that in this case of disagreement with the Yugoslav comrades, Tito had behind him a state and a people who had gone through a severe school of fighting for liberty and independence, a people who gave support to their leaders." Quoted in *ibid.,* p. 183.

group had not been saying before, and most of which had been acquiesced in by Khrushchev and his colleagues in 1955 and 1956. Even the charge that the Soviet Union was contributing to world tension had been acknowledged by Khrushchev, though blamed on Stalin, and the indictment against Molotov, Kaganovich, and Malenkov upon their expulsion from the Central Committee of the CPSU in July 1957 accused them of attempting, as high officials of the Soviet Union, to perpetuate international tensions. There is no phrase in the Yugoslav program the truth of which had not been conceded by the present leadership of the Soviet Union during the past three years.

Explanations of this *volte-face* by the Soviet leadership have ranged from the alleged pressure exerted by the Chinese Communists on behalf of Communist orthodoxy, to the existence of a Stalinist group in the Central Committee which out of nostalgia for the late dictator and his policies continues to embarrass Khrushchev and compels him to resort to former policies and tactics. Yet there is no tangible evidence in support of either thesis. True, attacks upon the Yugoslavs began to appear in the Chinese Communist press before the Soviets made a full-fledged attack. But it is perfectly natural that this should have occurred, if a joint attack upon Tito had been determined sometime before. Ever since the rise of Communist China, the satellites have looked upon it hopefully as the best means of eventually obtaining a modicum of independence from the Russians. Long after Yugoslavia's breach with the Russians in 1948, the Yugoslav press continued to extol Communist China. If once again the Yugoslav experiment had to be branded as unsocialist, and the satellites again be called to task, it was sound strategy and psychology that the initiative should appear to come from China rather than from the USSR.

The notion of a Stalinist faction in the Presidium and the Central Committee also requires a qualification. As in any political and particularly any totalitarian situation, there is no doubt that the inside group at the summit of power in Russia is split up into, if not open, then latent factions. Every faction will exploit its opponents' failures, whether these failures are grounded in alleged "liberalism" or in alleged "Stalinism." But there is no iota of evidence to indicate the existence of a specific "Stalinist" faction. The complex of methods of governing associated with Stalin is so abhorrent, even in the eyes of high Party officials in the USSR, that it has been part of a sound psychological campaign by Khrushchev to brand his opponents as would-be renovators of Stalinism. It is clear, for example, that Malenkov, Molotov, and Kaganovich plotted against Khrushchev, and that during the winter of 1956–1957 they probably came close to replacing him by Shepilov or Pervukhin. But that they did so in the name of abstract Stalinism is as little probable and worthy of belief as the charge in their indictment that they opposed the USSR's attempting to catch up with and overtake the United States in the production of butter, milk, and meat.

The reasons for Russia's reversal of attitude toward Yugoslavia are to be sought in the reappraisal of policies toward the satellites which the Soviet leadership as a whole seems to have undertaken during recent years. The history of this reappraisal provides the best illustration of the interweaving of ideology, power motives, and internal politics in the making of Soviet foreign policy.

At the time of Stalin's death, Russian domination of the satellites was absolute and extended to the smallest details of their internal policies. Whatever changes the rulers were forced to make in the Stalinist pattern insofar as internal Soviet politics was concerned, there appeared no logical reason, granting their totalitarian premises, to change substantially the system of terror and close control which held Eastern Europe in subjugation to the USSR. Yet parallel with so-called liberalization in Soviet Russia, a new course was set in the satellites. Terror was relaxed and some semblance of internal autonomy was granted to the local Communists, who, at first incredulously, listened to their Russian masters urging them to do certain things on their own. Many satellite Communist leaders most closely associated with the Stalinist era of repression were either pushed to the second rank (e.g., Chervenkov in Bulgaria, Cepicka in Czechoslovakia, Berman in Poland, and others) or obligingly died (this being the case with Gottwald and Bierut). The highest Party and state offices in the satellites were separated and the local Stalins were either fired or told to share their power with a wider circle of Party colleagues.[8] Soviet pressure for show trials of "deviationists" and other morbid paraphernalia of Communist statecraft of the Stalin era disappeared. For the first time since 1948 the satellite regimes enjoyed some power of decision on such issues as the pace of collectivization, cultural policies, etc.

Now, it is easy to see in the new course of 1953–1956, which was not consistent and uniform insofar as all the European satellites of the USSR were concerned, the reflection of internal dissension and uncertainty within the Kremlin circle itself. But it is reasonably clear that the new policies represented a measure of consensus among the successors of Stalin. Just as in internal politics they decided to eliminate the most oppressive measures and techniques of Stalin, so in their relations with the satellites they tended to substitute the ties of mutual interest and ideology for the most stringent aspects of foreign control. In both cases, one of the main reasons was ideological. Stalin's tech-

8. The satellite Parties were told in 1953–1954 that the office of Secretary-General could no longer be combined with that of President or Prime Minister. In Imre Nagy's statement, which appears well authenticated, he mentions the discussion of Malenkov, Molotov, and Khrushchev with the Hungarian leaders in May 1953, which was designed among other things to end Rakosi's absolute domination of Hungarian communism: "Comrade Khrushchev noted 'the matter involved was that the leadership of the Party and the state should not be concentrated in the hands of one man or a few men, this is not desirable.'" Imre Nagy, *On Communism, in Defense of the New Course* (New York, 1957), p. 250.

niques, his successors held, were partly pathological, partly obsolete in their severity. The maximum of control which they obtained did not compensate for the sapping of the vital forces of the Communist parties at home and abroad, for the impairing and tarnishing of the attraction of revolutionary socialism in the uncommitted parts of the world.

This ideological element was twofold in character. One side of the decision was the feeling that the Communist parties in the Soviet Union and the Soviet bloc could not be allowed to ossify and to become nothing but bodies of bureaucrats and spies driven by compulsion and ritualistic obeisances without, in the long run, creating a basic danger to the regime. The phrase "contact with the masses" is not used by the Communists entirely hypocritically. To give up some degree of control in exchange for popularity was deemed to be a reasonable gamble. The other side of the ideological element in the new course was the apparent conviction of the masters of the Kremlin that, when stripped of its worst excesses, communism possessed enough historical truth and popular attraction to secure the devotion of even those who had suffered for years under its "errors." In the immemorial manner of politicians, the Soviet leaders assumed that they could have their cake and eat it, too; that the fundamental features of internal totalitarianism and essential control over the satellites could be preserved, and yet the removal of the worst abuses would procure them genuine loyalty, would release new creative impulses and ideological fervor among the Communists at home and abroad.[9] In an ideological revival, Stalin's successors wanted to anticipate and forestall two great dangers. The first was that the gradual erosion of ideology through the continuance of methods of the Stalin era would strip the Party entirely of its meaning and its *esprit de corps.* If that happened, the Party, while nominally in existence and in power, could in fact be supplanted by another organization, the security apparatus or the army. In foreign affairs the prevalence of the 1948 – 1952 pattern of relations could lead to the second danger — the complete attenuation of ideological ties between the Communist Party of the USSR and the foreign Communists, whether in the satellites or in other countries. If that were to happen, what of the future relations of the USSR with the Communists in China, what of the loyalty of other Communists in the eventuality of a clash with the West? Thus what are, from the perspective of the West, rather intangible theoretical categories had for the Soviet leaders concrete ideological meaning readily translatable into considerations of power.

9. While there was general agreement on the overall character of domestic reforms and the shift in foreign tactics, the pace and methods of the modification of Stalinism were the subject of considerable maneuvering within the Soviet elite. Thus the fall of Beria in the summer of 1953 was not unconnected, it is safe to say, with his attempt to claim the main credit for the alleged return to "socialist legality" and more liberal nationality policies. Malenkov's fall from the premiership was expedited by the other leaders' alarm over his identification with the policy of increased consumers' goods. In addition to administrative and inner-Party intrigues, the struggle for power in the USSR has consisted during the last five years in each faction's trying to claim credit for the more liberal policies — policies on which all of them in principle were agreed.

The new course in inter-Communist relations was thus to parallel the de-Stalinization at home. But on this count Stalin's successors, as they must have ruefully realized by the fall of 1956, fell into the very error of their dreaded predecessor. It was Stalin who applied without any inhibitions the methods he found workable in the USSR in dealing with non-Soviet Communists. And the post-Stalin regime, which by relaxation of terror reaped the dividends of a certain popularity and increased *esprit de corps* among the Communists and the population at large in the USSR, blithely expected the same results from similar policies in other Communist states. Stalin could be denounced and his regime, in which the present rulers had been important figures, could be revealed as having indulged in wholesale murder and atrocities, and yet the totalitarian structure could be preserved and Soviet communism appear stronger for having acknowledged its errors. It appeared equally simple to proclaim Tito as having been unjustly denounced, Gomulka mistakenly imprisoned, and Rajk judicially murdered, and to expect a growth in the popularity of communism and affection toward the USSR in Yugoslavia, Poland, and Hungary. Being intelligent men, the Soviet leaders must have expected some form of shock to result from the revelations and the institution of the new course, but having been imprisoned within the Soviet system and within their own ideological premises for forty years, they evidently did not expect that the shock would take the form of revulsion toward communism, demoralization of local Communist parties, and even open hostility toward the Soviet Union.

Having decided upon the modification of Stalinist practices, the Soviet leaders proceeded boldly. The visit of Khrushchev and Bulganin to Belgrade in the spring of 1955 was a stroke of diplomacy as startling in terms of what had gone before as would be a visit of Eisenhower and Dulles to Peking or of Macmillan and Selwyn Lloyd to Cairo! But quite apart from the assumed humility of the Soviets toward the man and regime they had tried for years to overthrow, and against which they had hurled the most fantastic accusations and insults, the visit dramatized the importance attached by the Soviet Union to the principle of the ideological unity of the Communist world. Again, being realists, the Soviet leaders must have realized that the Communists in the satellites would draw their own conclusions from the Soviets bowing in effect to the defier of Stalin. A premium would be put upon a certain amount of nationalist intransigence, and the Communists of Poland or Rumania would no longer be terrified of standing up to their Soviet colleagues. But if the Yugoslav gamble worked, what was lost in absoluteness of control would be counterbalanced by the growth of genuine ideological unity. Soviet Russia could resume the ideological and diplomatic offensive in Asia and Africa without a Communist state standing as visible proof that the USSR was dominated by imperialist rather than ideological motives. To liquidate the Yugoslav defection, this time through diplomacy, became one of the main Soviet objectives, and the reasons for it are to be found not only in the "propaganda" aspects of Soviet foreign policy but in the need for ideological self-assurance. An outside observer may have from the beginning foreseen the gross psychological error inherent in the method of rapprochement with Tito. He may have argued, as undoubtedly some have argued in the Politburo, that a more gradual and cautious reestablishment of friendly relations with Yugoslavia would have produced less of a shock on the satellites (and the same observation applies to the unmasking of Stalin by Khrushchev). Yet one is left with some appreciation of the boldness of the move and of the new demonstration of the flexibility of Soviet policy. The policy initiated by the post-Stalin Presidium had, however, this distinguishing characteristic: it freely envisaged the abandonment of a certain amount of control — something the old despot had been unwilling to do — in the expectation of considerable ideological gains.

Khrushchev and Co., then, took a fairly long-run point of view: the Communist bloc would be reconstructed, this time with Yugoslavia as a valued member. Day-to-day control of the satellites' affairs would be abandoned by the Russians, but their foreign and defense policies would be more effectively synchronized with those of the USSR. Their internal sovietization would proceed ever so much more intensely and healthily, now that it was not being accomplished under extreme duress. The new policies would obviate, or at least postpone, a clash with the Chinese Communists which would have been unavoidable had the old Stalinist policies been rigidly adhered to. The united Communist bloc would be much more attractive to the new uncommitted nations, and Asian and African leftists would not have the dismaying example of the Soviet-Yugoslav dispute to dampen their pro-Communist inclinations. Finally, within the Soviet Union the fact that the Communist states were united and more freely associated on the international scene would help in the ideological reactivation of communism in Russia.

Within two years the main premise of the new Soviet policies was exposed as hollow. The tie of ideology did not prove strong enough to hold the Communist bloc together and subservient to Russia in the absence of more tangible means of control. The return of Yugoslavia to the Soviet bloc could not simply obliterate the seven years during which the Yugoslav leaders had learned to be independent. For ideological and power reasons of his own, Tito was only too glad to arrive at a *modus vivendi* with the Russians. The continued isolation from the Communist bloc was slowly undermining the morale of the CPY, the main support of his totalitarian regime, as witnessed by the Djilas affair. But the Yugoslav Communists could not now settle for what they would gladly have taken from Stalin in 1948: internal autonomy, but in other respects unquestioning adherence to the USSR. This time the Yugoslavs were ready to reenter the Soviet bloc only as representatives and propagators of the idea of equality of socialist states. The Soviet Union as the leading socialist state would still enjoy primacy, but each member of the bloc should be granted external and internal independence. What was implicit in the Soviet *theory* of the new course the Yugoslavs were eager to make explicit in *practice.*

The imperfect reconciliation became an additional disruptive influence within the Soviet sphere. The events of October 1956 represented a serious blow to Soviet policies. Again the policy habit acquired within the Soviet context proved almost disarmingly naive when applied to another country. It was easy for the Russians to imagine that with the worst repression abolished in Poland and the deviant Communists rehabilitated, Soviet influence would be made more secure and Polish communism would become even more loyal to the USSR. But Gomulka was not only readmitted to the Communist Party but was carried to power, and the Polish army passed from the control of Soviet officers. And finally the events of Hungary demonstrated vividly that not only Soviet influence but communism in Eastern Europe rest mainly upon force, and that any weakening in the network of Soviet controls and terror would not readily be compensated by an enhanced ideological solidarity with the Soviet Union. It is not too much to assume that the events in Eastern Europe had a certain unsettling effect upon the Russian Communists, and that their intellectual and artistic side effects, which spilled over the borders of the Soviet Union, went in the opinion of the leaders beyond the legitimate and safe limits of liberalization.

The balance sheet of the new policy was therefore largely negative. But it is instructive to see that the Soviets did not panic at the failure of their design. We have no means of knowing what discussions went on in Moscow after the Polish and Hungarian events. But it is unlikely that the Soviets would have or could have implemented the policy of complete return to Stalinism either in their internal affairs or in dealing with Eastern Europe. The pendulum had swung too far, and the decision was taken in the winter of 1956–1957 to restore a form of balance between the old and the new policies. It was hoped that the fortieth anniversary of the October Revolution in 1957 would see the beginning of a new Communist International to replace the Cominform, dissolved in 1956 as a relic of the Stalinist era and discredited in its only major undertaking: the attempt to undermine and overthrow Tito. The Cominform had been organized in the summer of 1947 mainly to give an international appearance to the Soviet control of the Communist parties in power, and thus to obviate the trouble which the Soviets already discerned in the Yugoslav situation.[10] Now, in a different atmosphere, the new Communist organization, in which various ruling and perhaps other Communist parties would associate in apparent equality, would again give an international appearance to Soviet guidance. But, as we know, the Yugoslav Communists for obvious reasons refused to participate in a new Cominform. Their refusal, it seems, was supported by the Poles, and thus for the time being no international Communist

10. Adam B. Ulam, *Titoism and the Cominform* (Cambridge, Mass.), 1952, p. 68.

agency would be created to "internationalize" Soviet control of the satellites' policies. The new method of "domesticating" Tito proved no more successful than the previous ones. Furthermore, the carrier of the Titoist virus had again been taken into the Communist camp as a bona fide member, visiting the satellite capitals and entertaining in Yugoslavia delegations of the Polish, Hungarian, and Rumanian Communists.

It is in the light of these developments that the Soviet decision to denounce the Yugoslav Communists, in terms considerably milder than those of 1948, becomes understandable. If in 1948 Tito and his group were denounced as followers of Bukharin and Vollmar, and then as agents of Western imperialism, they are in 1958 "revisionists" and fence-sitters. Again obscure doctrinal excommunications are pronounced by the Soviet Communists to account for the failure to solve their own ideological dilemma: how can an international political movement be genuinely international and yet be run and controlled by a single state? And that problem is but the other side of the internal dilemma: how can you have ideological fervor and socialist *élan* in a totalitarian and bureaucratic state? These seemingly intangible theoretical questions appear to the Soviet leaders with the increasing urgency of problems of power. It is almost pathetic to observe the Soviets' attempting to develop within the last few years some of the paraphernalia of popular government. Stalin never went abroad, with the exception of the wartime trip to Teheran. The current leaders travel assiduously, especially in the satellite areas. They do not confine themselves, as was the pre-1953 pattern, to conferences with high state and Party officials. They address themselves to crowds. The visit of Voroshilov to Poland in the spring of 1958 was an exhibition of the new technique. The aged titular head of the USSR visited factories, farms, and Party gatherings. He was accompanied by a retinue of dignitaries, including — most significantly — high officials of the Byelorussian, Ukrainian, and Lithuanian parties, who shared in the frantic visiting and speech-making. It is unlikely that this search for popularity will lead the Soviets to put it to test by removing the more tangible forms of insurance of their satellites' loyalty. Veiled threats accompany professions of ideological brotherhood, as during Khrushchev's tour of Hungary. But in the speeches and activities connected with the satellites there has definitely been a new tone since 1955: an attempt by the Soviet leaders to convince not only others but, one might almost say, themselves that the Communist commonwealth of states is based upon ideological ties rather than upon force or threats of force. Even the reversal of the new course, the stiffened Soviet attitude toward manifestations of satellite "nationalism," does not change that tendency basically.

The problem of working out a feasible pattern of relations between the states in the "camp of socialism" is increasingly becoming one of the main problems of Soviet policy, and not only of *foreign* policy. The earlier attempted solution — strict subordination by force — has proved impractical, and no matter how much is said about the return to Stalinism, the situation prior to 1953 simply cannot be reproduced. Enough of Marxist historical sophistication remains to the rulers of the Kremlin to prevent them from attempting to turn back history. Not because of any increased humanitarianism, but because of changed conditions, they will try to supplement force with diplomacy and with an increased community of interests between themselves and their satellites. Much has been said about the "erosion" of Soviet ideology, but ideologies and social movements are not eroded by the mere passage of time or the impact of statistics. Nineteenth-century liberalism was eroded, and with it much of the influence of the West in other parts of the world, largely by the abrasive force of nationalism. Communism has up to now managed to turn this abrasive force to its own uses, but it has begun to experience its unsettling effect within its own system.

3.

The example of Soviet policy within the Communist bloc is perhaps sufficient to point out the involved nature of the ideological element in the policy as a whole. The contribution of the ideology is not simply to endow the Soviet rulers with a propensity for violence and conquest. Nor is Marxism-Leninism an unsubstantial line of fortifications separating the Soviet Union from the rest of the world, quite ready to collapse at repeated trumpetings of the facts of the West's material and political stability and peaceful intentions toward the USSR. Soviet ideology in the sense discussed here is neither a detailed guide to action nor a superficial creed vulnerable to exposure. Quite apart from its textual content, belief in this ideology represents the most cohesive force in the Soviet system, one which has enabled Communist Party rule and the dynamics of industrialization to persist through decades of oppression, misrule, and economic suffering. It has been observed that Communist ideology now has but little relevance insofar as domestic problems of the Soviet Union are concerned. Were the USSR to cease being a one-party state equipped with totalitarian paraphernalia, the process of industrialization and modernization would go on under the aegis of another ideology and another political system. There has been no change or reform in the social or economic field in the last six years which might not have been effected in the USSR for purely pragmatic reasons. If the ideology is to remain demonstrably important to the Soviet citizen, and demonstrably correct to the Party members, and the perpetuation of the Communist Party rule rests in the long run upon these assumptions, then there must be another dimension than the domestic one in which Communist ideology does make a difference. Successful proselytizing becomes an important factor in the preservation of the faith. Foreign successes, the preservation and expansion of collaboration within the Communist bloc, become important insofar as the preservation of the present pattern of communism in the USSR is concerned.

If this hypothesis is correct, then there is little foundation in the hope often expressed in the West that the growth and maturity of the USSR as a modern and industrial state will necessarily be reflected in more peaceful and less expansive policies. As we have seen, the growing power and prosperity of the USSR *as a state,* even the increased material well-being of its citizens, accentuate rather than diminish the ideological crisis. This ideological crisis is not, as is often imagined, simply the matter of everyday reality of Soviet life not conforming to the precepts of Marx and Lenin, but of the existence and growth of social and economic forces which impinge upon the foundations of the totalitarian system in Russia. At the height of the collectivization struggle, Stalin propounded his famous formula, then the rationalization for the ruthless suppression of the peasants, that the closer the goal of socialism the sharper becomes the character of the class struggle. This terrible formula, pronouncing in effect that increased success will necessitate more terror, was declared un-Marxist by Stalin's successors.[11] But it unwittingly contained an important insight; in the measure that the Communist movement achieves its objectives, it becomes increasingly difficult to preserve the totalitarian system, to continue to exact sacrifices and deny basic freedoms and amenities of life. The program of ideological revival devised by the despot's successors has aimed at preventing communism from "withering away," and thus at preserving the rationale of Soviet totalitarianism. An increasingly great part in this revival has been played by the renewed missionary character of communism. Thus the success of communism as a self-proclaimed worldwide liberation and peace movement, and as a tenable basis for the association of Communist states, becomes increasingly important to the continuance of the present form of the Communist regime in the USSR.

Most studies of Soviet foreign policy imply or state the question: What can the West do about it? And in the process of asking this question, we very often and unavoidably distort the problem according to our hopes or fears, or indulge in a natural irritation because the drift of world affairs has not gone according to our plans and expectations. We have attempted here to sketch the connection between Soviet ideology, so different now and yet descended in many ways from the prototypes of Marxism and Leninism, and actual Soviet policies. All that a study of this kind can do is to suggest a certain range of problems and characteristics of Russian policies. It cannot, nor can the most detailed scheme of the politics of the USSR, predict or outline the eventuality of either a peaceful resolution of the East-West conflict or of its catastrophic settlement. Nor is it possible to sketch an "unavoidable" pattern of development of Soviet policies either toward a repetition of the Stalinist pattern, or

11. See Khrushchev's speech quoted in *Current Soviet Policies, II,* p. 177.

toward an erosion of totalitarianism. Very often in our analyses we tend to be more deterministic than our antagonists.

Yet, within a shorter range of time and without attempting to answer the really unanswerable and, alas, most important questions, it is possible to outline some basic difficulties of the Soviet international position. It has been suggested here that the ideological crisis created, paradoxically, by the successes of the Communist system impels it to seek a justification of the ideology in the international sphere. Thus, and not only because of the natural tendency of a totalitarian system, the USSR is bent upon ideological and power expansion. Here we encounter one of those "inherent contradictions" with which the Marxists upbraid the capitalist system, but of which their own offers glittering examples. Just as within the Soviet Union the reality of a modernized and industrialized society clashes with the ideological premises, and the contradiction is encompassed only by the chains of totalitarianism, so within the Communist bloc the reality of Soviet domination clashes with the ideological premise of the equality of socialist states, and the contradiction is concealed (imperfectly, as Yugoslavia, Hungary, and Poland have demonstrated) only by an enormous preponderance of power, which is for the time being on the side of the USSR. Here, then, are the Algerias and Cypruses of the Soviet camp, and the proverbial forces of history which appear to be working for the Soviets in disrupting the liberal world are impinging upon the combination of socialism and totalitarianism which is Soviet ideology.

Doctrine and Foreign Policy*

Soviet Russia under Khrushchev and since his fall has not ceased to bear out the paradoxical reality of a dogmatic movement that is hardly ever doctrinaire. Particularly in the realm of official utterances about foreign policy, the Soviet authorities continue to exemplify both terms of this seeming contradiction: they cling to the rigid self-righteousness of Marxist-Leninist orthodoxy, and they bend or twist the orthodoxy in innumerable practical applications to make it yield the interpretation that squares with prudence, challenge, or opportunity. In specific statements about the West as well as in general pronouncements about the communist movement, but above all in the context of the Sino-Soviet schism, the leadership has hewed to the old Stalinist use of doctrine as an instrument of policy rationalization and justification, however much it tries to sustain the illusion of unyielding doctrinal rigor in the eyes of the world communist movement, the Soviet masses, and itself as well.

Communist ideology, particularly in its foreign policy aspect, is often discussed but seldom defined. "Ideology," "doctrine," and "theory" are commonly used as synonyms, with little effort to distinguish them. Theory, in the ordinary usage, denotes a hypothesis or guess that might be true or might not.

*Reprinted from *Survey: A Journal of Soviet and East European Studies,* 57 (October, 1965), pp. 3–13, by permission of the author and the publisher. Copyright 1965, *Survey*, London, England.

Communist Ideology
Belief Systems + Soviet F. Policy.

Soviet perspectives on 3°W.

- Nat'l Interest
    Key to Soviet Politics.

- Paranoia in F.P. of Soviet
                            Union.

VISITORS TO CAMPUS TOURS ·1983

NNAIRE

t of _____

tive U of T Student ? _____

ng U of T ? _____

of U of T ? _____

ated with other educational institution ? _____

ation _____

did you find out about Campus Tours ? _____

you see the announcement on "TELIDON" ?   Yes _____ No _____

ease comment on your impression of the Tour:

_____

_____

_____

Would you recommend the tours to your friends ?   Yes _____ No _____

Doctrine suggests a hard-and-fast teaching or policy on any particular subject. Ideology designates a general system of doctrine and belief that is professed by a particular political movement or regime. All three terms are used by the Russians — *teoriya, uchenie,* and *ideologiya* — but in their usage the meanings of the first two are virtually identical with the definition of ideology. There is certainly nothing tentative or partial in the official communist commitment to Marxism-Leninism.

According to official communist spokesmen ever since Lenin's time, Marxism-Leninism offers both a scientific prediction of the course of history and a guide to successful revolutionary action. In particular, it is supposed to give the analytic key to understanding the weaknesses of capitalist society and the forces that can overthrow it. It is also supposed to be the vital factor in clarifying the class consciousness of the proletariat and galvanizing its will to seize power.

Contained in this official view of the ideology are several different conceptions of its actual political role. These different conceptions are inherent, in turn, in the unacknowledged contradiction within the original corpus of Marxism, between the scientific-analytic-predictive-deterministic side of the ideology, and its revolutionary-moralistic-hortatory-activist side.[1] From the analytic standpoint, Marxism may have the force of prophecy, or, more modestly, it may serve to interpret political and social situations around the world and suggest to the policy-maker whether a given move will work or not. From the moralistic standpoint, Marxism may be the categorical imperative to fight and risk death for revolution and the worldwide victory of the proletariat, or it may be simply an instrument of propaganda to get the workers or anybody else to do what the communists want.

All four of these functions of ideology have figured in Soviet foreign policy at one time or another, though with different weights. The trend has been clearly and heavily toward the propaganda function, with some residual role for the interpretive function. The most important function of all, however, is not inherent in the origins of the ideology but developed historically during the early years of the Soviet regime. This is the function of legitimizing the regime and its authority in the eyes of the communist rulers themselves, however much the specific acts of the regime may appear to deviate from the original spirit of Marxism-Leninism. Ideology thus becomes a self-justifying dogma of a quasi-religious nature, totally dependent for its day-to-day meaning on the interpretations which the political authorities decide to lay down.

Lenin himself began the practice of dogmatic ideological restatement, beginning with his propositions about the role of the conspiratorial party in

1. Cf. Alfred G. Meyer, *Marxism: The Unity of Theory and Practice* (Cambridge, Mass., 1954), and R. V. Daniels, "Fate and Will in the Marxian Philosophy of History," *Journal of the History of Ideas,* October 1960.

bringing about revolution, and culminating in his retraction of the revolution-ary war commitment in 1918 in favor of the Russia-first "citadel of revolution" doctrine. Stalin merely spelled out the implications of Lenin's policy with his own doctrine of "socialism in one country," according to which Russia could overcome its own relative backwardness and progress through "socialism" to "communism" independently of any proletarian success elsewhere.

The legacy of ideological manipulation during the period of Lenin's leader-ship and Stalin's rise was to tie both the meaning and the function of Marxist-Leninist theory to the authority of the communist party-state. The leader has had the power since Stalin's time to establish the meaning of ideology in an absolutely binding way. Criticism of his interpretation is heresy or treason, literally a crime against the state. There is no force to keep his interpretations honestly in conformity with the original meaning of the ideology; on the other hand there is every temptation to modify the meaning of the ideology, through reinterpretation, to make each new practical policy or expedient appear con-sistent with the original ideology. Thus, as the analysis of some recent Soviet policy shifts will show, ideology cannot determine or limit action except for some short-run rigidities; it is action, rather, that eventually supplies the up-to-date meaning of ideology.

While ideology is consequently very flexible over the years, it is rigid and dogmatic at any given moment. The authorities cannot admit that their rein-terpretations are novelties, since this would defeat the whole purpose of doctri-nal rationalization of new policies as the supposedly imperative application of Marxism-Leninism. To sustain their self-justification, they are compelled to enforce their interpretation of ideology with all the power at the disposal of the state. In no realm of thought can they tolerate the autonomy that might allow the party's ideological authority to be questioned — hence the principle of party decision in art and science that has stood for thirty-five years.

Despite the administrative burden and intellectual stifling that this entails, it nevertheless constitutes an element of major strength for the regime. The imposed ideology serves as a vehicle of mental discipline, to enforce the tests and demands of political conformity on every citizen in the land. It matters not so much what particular idea or ideology or verbal formula is proclaimed, but that some official thought is available to answer every public question and that the regime constantly exacts conformity. The exercise of doctrinal au-thority therefore becomes a necessary element in sustaining the general au-thority of the regime, a permanent fixture in the communist system of totalitarian rule.[2]

It follows from the foregoing that communist ideology is primarily signifi-

---

2. For a fuller development of this point, see my studies, *The Conscience of the Revolution: Communist Opposition in Soviet Russia* (Cambridge, Mass., 1960), pp. 248–52, and "What the Russians Mean," *Commentary,* October 1962.

cant for the internal working of the regime. Foreign policy is one of the least ideological aspects of Soviet politics, in reality if not in words. Rather than foreign policy's being governed in any substantial way by ideological requirements, the chief connection of the two lies in the decisions and situations which foreign policy considerations bring about and require the ideology to justify or explain away.

There is one respect in which foreign developments have struck more deeply at the system of ideological authority in the USSR. This is the factual emergence of new power centers in the communist world, in the now well-recognized phenomenon of polycentrism, above all as represented by China. The establishment of a communist regime in China strong enough to rival the Soviet Union for influence in the world communist movement has had a serious effect not only on the unity of the movement from country to country, but also on the intrinsic character of the movement. China, by challenging the single ideological authority of the leaders of Soviet Russia, threatened the entire system of mental discipline formerly imposed by the single authoritative interpretation of doctrine. Such a challenge may not have been intended by the Chinese or foreseen by the Russians, but it was inherent in the emergence of a second power center within the single ideological movement.

Far from ideology's serving as a bond between Russia and China, inhibiting their conflict, it was bound by its nature to force the conflict to the open cleavage the world has witnessed since 1961. The communist system, with its peculiar imposition of a constantly revised ideology, depends on a single authority that will hand down authoritative interpretations of doctrine to fit the practical needs of each new development on the world scene. Given two centers of power, each strong enough to issue its own interpretations of doctrine, and each seeing the practical requirements of policy in a different light, each is led to make theoretical pronouncements inconsistent with the view of the other. By its nature the movement cannot tolerate such differences, though neither center is willing to make the symbolic surrender of authority implicit in a recognition of the rival's theoretical correctness. Therefore every hairsplitting theoretical issue becomes the potential source of a major political clash, no less than the theological subtleties that led up to the Great Schism between the churches of Rome and of Constantinople in the eleventh century. The problem cannot logically be resolved until each center has anathematized the other and read it out of the movement — so splitting the movement into two, each with its own authoritative center issuing its own binding interpretations of a once common ideology. The dogmatic ideology of revolution may be compatible in practice with peaceful coexistence with the anti-revolutionaries, but it is a direct cause of rupture with all co-revolutionaries who are able and willing to proclaim their independence.

Khrushchev's career bears eloquent witness to the function of Soviet ideology as the instrument of political authority and justification after the fact.

For all his railing at the perversions of Stalinism, Khrushchev did little to alter the basic workings of the Stalinist state, and in the manipulation of doctrine as the Marxist high priest he all but outdid his former boss. In one central area of theory after another, Khrushchev laid down new pronouncements to accommodate his foreign policy or to embarrass his communist challengers, and when his startling overthrow ended his tenure of power in 1964, the principles of the Marxist philosophy of politics were in a shambles. No one in Russia could criticize the mess while he was in power, nor have they so far done so since his fall, but in the name of battling "revisionism," the Peking wing of the movement has done us the service of calling attention to most of Khrushchev's arbitrary modifications of theory.

Khrushchev was involved in ideological manipulations in the very first phase of his maneuvering for the succession, between 1953 and 1956. The area of theory he moved into was, significantly, international; the particular issue he raised was the Marxist assessment of the capitalist powers and the prospects for war and victory. Khrushchev chose his stand as a maneuvering point against his rival Malenkov, and proceeded to stress the possibility of war, the assurance that communism could emerge even from a nuclear conflict, and the necessity of continuing Russia's heavy industry stress and military buildup.

How contrived Khrushchev's interpretations were became obvious when, as soon as he had humbled Malenkov in 1955, he reversed his field and adopted most of his rival's views in order to force the hand of his next victim, the hard-liner Molotov. The whole maneuver was strongly reminiscent of Stalin's manipulation of the issue of economic development in the 1920's, first to defeat Trotsky with a moderate line and then to break Bukharin by pressing an exaggerated version of Trotsky's program.

The maneuvers of 1955 were only the prelude to Khrushchev's grand slam of theoretical innovation, the twentieth congress of the CPSU in February 1956. The congress is justly famous for his not-so-secret "secret speech" denouncing the excesses of Stalinism. For the theoretical guidelines of the Soviet Union and the world communist movement, however, the most significant new interpretations were contained in Khrushchev's open report to the congress. Regarding the international relations of the communist movement, Khrushchev proclaimed three sweeping innovations, couched of course in the language of undeviating Leninist orthodoxy: the doctrine of peaceful coexistence and non-inevitability of war; the doctrine of separate national roads to socialism; and the doctrine of non-violent communist revolution. All these propositions were radical breaks with Leninism; all were prompted by pragmatic temptations of foreign policy or domestic politics; and all were instrumental in precipitating the schism and polycentrism that subsequently sapped the strength and resolve of the communist movement.

"Peaceful coexistence" was Khrushchev's doctrinal sanction for policies to reduce tension with the West and lessen the threat of nuclear war. He tried to make it look like an old idea:

The Leninist principle of peaceful coexistence of states with different social systems has always been and remains the general line of our country's foreign policy. It has been alleged that the Soviet Union puts forward the principle of peaceful coexistence merely out of tactical considerations, considerations of expediency. Yet it is common knowledge that we have always, from the very first years of Soviet power, stood with equal firmness for peaceful coexistence. Hence it is not a tactical move, but a fundamental principle of Soviet foreign policy. . . . Indeed, there are only two ways: either peaceful coexistence or the most destructive war in history. There is no third way.

Interestingly, Khrushchev gave the Chinese a credit line for peaceful coexistence as it had been enunciated in their 1955 "five principles" agreement with India. He was sufficiently aware of the novelty of his line to try to dispose of doctrinaire doubts: "There is, of course, a Marxist-Leninist proposition that wars are inevitable as long as imperialism exists." But now, Khrushchev contended, the "degree of organization and the awareness and determination of the people" could offset the "economic basis of wars under imperialism." This was hardly consistent with Marxist teaching about the influence of economic base on political superstructure, but for Khrushchev it was enough to observe,

Now there is a world camp of socialism, which has become a mighty force. In this camp the peace forces find not only the moral, but also the material means to prevent aggression.

The notion of separate roads to socialism, meaning the possibility of independent decisions and policies on the part of various communist governments, was anathema in Stalin's time. Tito's line in Yugoslavia after 1948 was the first attempt at such a separate road, and even this came only after Stalin had read Tito out of the communist movement. A greater problem for the integrity of Stalin's unilinear conception of communism came with the accession of the Chinese communists in 1949, though they were content for the time being to confine their separate roads to the realm of practice and not to challenge Soviet doctrinal supremacy. Khrushchev's embrace of the separate-roads doctrine followed as the obvious corollary of his rapprochement with Tito in 1955 (and as an effective move in his maneuvering against Molotov). "Alongside the Soviet form of reconstructing society on socialist lines," Khrushchev told the twentieth congress, "we now have the form of people's democracy." ("People's democracy" had hitherto been regarded by the Russians as a preliminary to socialist construction, not an alternative route.) Khrushchev's gestures to both Peking and Belgrade were explicit:

Much that is unique in socialist construction is being contributed by the People's Republic of China. . . . Having taken over the decisive commanding positions, the people's democratic state is using them in the social revolution to implement a policy of peaceful reorganization of private industry and trade, and their gradual transformation into a component of socialist economy.

The leadership of the great cause of socialist reconstruction by the Communist Party of China and the communist and workers' parties of the other people's democracies, exercised in keeping with the peculiarities and specific features of each country, is creative Marxism in action.

In the Federal People's Republic of Yugoslavia . . . specific concrete forms of economic management and organization of the state apparatus are arising in the process of socialist construction.

Khrushchev's third line of departure from Lenin followed closely on the separate-roads idea:

It is probable that more forms of transition to socialism will appear. Moreover, the implementation of these forms need not be associated with civil war under all circumstances. Our enemies like to depict us Leninists as advocates of violence always and everywhere. True, we recognize the need for the revolutionary transformation of capitalist society into socialist society. It is this that distinguishes the revolutionary Marxists from the reformists, the opportunists. There is no doubt that in a number of capitalist countries the violent overthrow of the dictatorship of the bourgeoisie and the sharp aggravation of class struggle connected with this are inevitable. But the forms of social revolution vary. It is not true that we regard violence and civil war as the only way to remake society.

Though the practical import of all this was restricted — Khrushchev had in mind as the "non-violent" model the communist takeover in Czechoslovakia in 1948 — it was nonetheless a far cry from Lenin's insistence that the "bourgeois" state must everywhere be "smashed" with revolutionary force.

Altogether, Khrushchev's modifications of the international theory of communism constituted a long step towards the revisionism that the Chinese were soon to charge him with. His purpose was pragmatic — a restatement of theory so that it would not impede his realistic or opportunistic foreign policy in the two directions he proposed to push: accommodation with different communist states which he could not control; and the reduction of the danger of nuclear war with the United States.

The international doctrines of 1956 served Khrushchev sufficiently well for the rest of his career, though they did not prevent his great diplomatic setback, the loss of China. The Chinese communists, for their part, seized upon Khrushchev's interpretations as an object of power contest, so that they might assert their independence of Soviet doctrinal authority by taking issue with the new Moscow line.

The Chinese revolt built up gradually between 1956 and 1960. Its particular foci were the appraisal of Stalin and (of more relevance to foreign policy) the question of unity or autonomy within the communist movement — i.e., the issue of separate roads to socialism. Preferring not to attack Khrushchev head-on the Chinese made Yugoslavia the butt of their critique of tendencies that weakened "international proletarian solidarity." In the spring of 1958, in the face of a projected state visit to Yugoslavia by Soviet Chief of State Voroshilov, the Chinese opened their blistering attack on the new program of the League of Communists of Yugoslavia — a document of surrender to capitalism, in Peking's view.

By this point the Chinese clearly had the ideological initiative. Khrushchev endorsed Mao's attack on revisionism, and could only add (in his Sofia speech of June 1958) that "attempts to find different shades in the criticism of present-day revisionism on the part of the fraternal parties are in vain." Mao, his appetite for authority in the movement whetted by Khrushchev's gestures of appeasement, immediately struck out in another direction — the transition to communism. The actual move, in the fall of 1958, was the program to reorganize the loosely-collectivized Chinese peasants into tightly knit communes, and with this the strong theoretical suggestion that China was leaping ahead of Russia on the path of transition from the socialist to the communist form of society.

This time the Russians rebelled, and dismissed the Chinese commune experiment as an aberration entirely irrelevant to the transition to communism. Khrushchev then threw himself into a glowing exposition of the Soviet transition to communism, in his report to the twenty-first congress of the CPSU in January 1959. This was the first Soviet treatment of the subject since Stalin's speeches of the 1930's, and Khrushchev's motive of countering the Chinese commune claims came clearly through the lines:

> The Marxist-Leninist party considers the setting up of a communist society its final aim. But society cannot switch over to communism from capitalism without passing through the socialist phase of development. From capitalism, Lenin said, mankind can switch over directly only to socialism, that is, to communal ownership of production means and distribution of products to individuals in accordance with their work. Our party looks farther ahead. Socialism must inevitably develop gradually into communism, on the banner of which is written: From each according to his abilities, to each according to his needs.

As to the concrete details of the stateless society of communism, Khrushchev took pains to rule out any expectations that might interfere with the practical operations of the Soviet state. For him, as for Stalin, there would be no equalizing of rewards for the foreseeable future of the transition period: "One cannot fail to see that equalization would lead to unjust distribution. Both the good and bad workers would receive the same. . . . Equalization would mean not a transition to communism but the discrediting of communism."

From the old promise of the "withering away of the state," Khrushchev escaped by defining the future regime "dialectically" as "communist public self-government," with "certain public functions . . . analogous to present state functions." He thus anticipated the doctrine, spelled out in the party program of 1961, of the permanence of the communist state in everything but name, and of the Communist Party in name as well as in fact.

During the following year Khrushchev vigorously pursued the line of peaceful coexistence, capped in September 1959 by his visit to the United States and his guarded censure of the Chinese in their first clash with India. In Peking following his American tour, he spoke forcefully against the use of war to expand communism:

> We must think realistically and understand the contemporary situation correctly. This, of course, does not by any means signify that if we are so strong, then we must test by force the stability of the capitalist system. This would be wrong: the peoples would not understand and would never support those who would think of acting in this way. We have always been against wars of conquest. Marxists have recognized, and recognize, only liberating, just wars; they have always condemned, and condemn, wars of conquest, imperialist wars.

After some mutterings of disquiet about revisionism and the exclusion of China from international agreements, Peking finally drew up its lines of ideological battle against Moscow in April 1960. On the occasion of the ninetieth anniversary of the birth of Lenin, the Chinese theoretical journal *Red Flag* published, under the title "Long Live Leninism," an extended attack on the errors of "modern revisionism":

> Are the teachings of Marxism-Leninism now "outmoded"? Does the whole, integrated teaching of Lenin on imperialism, on proletarian revolution and proletarian dictatorship, on war and peace, and on the building of socialism and communism still retain its vigorous vitality? . . . Is it that there can be no question of war even if imperialism and the system of exploitation are allowed to survive for ever?
>
> As long as the peoples of all countries enhance their awareness and are fully prepared, with the socialist camp also mastering modern weapons, it is certain that if the US or other imperialists refuse to reach an agreement on the banning of atomic and nuclear weapons and should dare to fly in the face of the will of all humanity by launching a war using atomic and nuclear weapons, the result will be the very speedy destruction of these monsters encircled by the peoples of the world, and the result will certainly not be the annihilation of mankind. We consistently oppose the launching of criminal wars by imperialism. . . . But should the imperialists impose such sacrifices on the peoples of various countries, we believe that, as the experience of the Russian revolution and the Chinese revolution shows, those sacrifices would be repaid. On the debris of a dead imperialism, the victorious people would create very swiftly a civilization thousands of times higher than the capitalist system and a truly beautiful future for themselves. . . .
>
> We believe in the absolute correctness of Lenin's thinking: War is an inevitable outcome of systems of exploitation and the source of modern wars is the imperialist system. Until the imperialist system and the exploiting classes come to an end, wars of one kind or another will always occur.

In their efforts to discredit Khrushchev, the Chinese had (perhaps deliberately) confused the Lenin and Stalin doctrine of inevitable war among capitalist countries, with the question of likely war between capitalist and communist states. (On this the Soviet leaders had never been dogmatic. Stalin himself had maintained in his valedictory article of 1952 that the rivalries among the capitalists were stronger than the contradictions between the capitalist camp and the socialist camp.) The purpose of the Chinese communists, again, was to raise a theoretical point which the Russians could not accept without acknowledging Chinese initiative, but could not reject without risking the appearance of softness and revisionism.

The now familiar political clash between the Russians and the Chinese began soon after this ideological challenge, with the confrontation at the Rumanian Communist Party congress in June 1960, and the acrimony surrounding the Albanian problem. There followed the decisive conference of 81 communist parties in November 1960, with its bitter behind-the-scenes exchanges and its expression of superficial unity in the statement published in December.

In 1961, to offset the Chinese pretensions to Marxist superiority and keep his foreign policy free of strictures about inevitable war, Khrushchev gave renewed attention to the updating of ideology. This time he put emphasis on the theory of the internal development of the communist society, with the occasion for discussion provided by the proposal and adoption of the new program of the Soviet Communist Party.

In his presentation of the program (notably in his address to the twenty-second congress in October 1961), Khrushchev made it official that Soviet Russia had entered on the stage of the all-out building of communist society. Like Stalin before him, he was at pains to square the revised vision of the communist utopia with his practical intentions regarding Soviet internal development and leadership in the communist camp. As he spelled out the expected provisions of communism, it was evident that he envisaged only more of the same Soviet reality, ameliorated by an American living standard.

Khrushchev complicated the problem of accommodating the utopian theory of communism by enunciating a new political doctrine, devoid in fact of any textual roots in Marxism. As this was stated in the program, "The dictatorship of the proletariat has fulfilled its historic mission and has ceased to be indispensable in the USSR. . . . The state . . . has . . . become a state of the entire people. . . . The state as an organization of the entire people will survive until the complete victory of communism." Such a non-class notion of the state had been explicitly rejected by Marx in his criticism of the German social-democrats. At an opportune moment Peking picked up the cry of orthodoxy:

> In the view of Marxist-Leninists, there is no such thing as a non-class or supra-class state. So long as the state remains a state, it must bear a class character; so long as the state exists, it cannot be a state of the "whole people." As soon as society becomes classless, there will no longer be a state. . . . In calling a socialist state the "state of the whole people" is one trying to replace the Marxist-Leninist theory of the state by the bourgeois theory of the state? Is one trying to replace the state of dictatorship of the proletariat by a state of a different character? If that is the case, it is nothing but a great historical retrogression.[3]

Finally, Khrushchev's international application of the transition-to-commu-

3. Letter of the CC of the CCP to the CC of the CPSU, 14 June 1963.

nism vision showed an interesting twist. As earlier understood, all socialist states were to accomplish the transition to communism at the same time, which implied that Russia, with its head start, would have to lend a substantial hand to countries such as China. The final draft of the 1961 program got around this: The transition by the various bloc countries could occur merely "in the same historical epoch," no definition being given of the length of an epoch. Separate roads to socialism were thus to carry separate arrival dates, and presumably separate national responsibilities for completing the journey at all. Thus did polycentrism show its mark on what had originated as a movement of international revolution.

The history of official Soviet thinking during the Khrushchev era repeatedly confirms the instrumental character of contemporary communist ideology. Ideology serves foreign policy as justification after the fact, while the principal concern of Soviet policy-makers in the realm of doctrine — since the fall of Khrushchev no less than before — is to retain a free hand for any opportune move, unrestricted by possible theoretical inhibitions.

As an instrument of policy, communist ideology has figured more prominently in the internal politics of the movement than in the more pragmatic area of relations with the non-communist world. Ideology has notably been employed as a device both to provoke and to discredit opposition factions and dissident communist governments. Within the Soviet Union, the ideological statement of foreign policy was adroitly employed by Khrushchev in his political contest with Malenkov and Molotov in the mid-1950's. Within the communist bloc, ideology has provided the most visible arena of political contest between the Soviet Union and the Chinese People's Republic, with a series of ideological initiatives taken by both sides to force the rival either to follow abjectly or to stand and fight.

As in the earlier history of the Soviet Union, the use of ideology as a political instrument in the Khrushchev era had a substantial impact on the meaning of the doctrine itself. Nevertheless, as was the characteristic under Stalin, there was no official acknowledgment that the doctrine was being modified. Every reinterpretation was represented as a mere restating and application of the original orthodoxy.

With the schism between Moscow and Peking, however, this reinterpretation was carried on in different directions, independently. The consequence was, as it could only have been, the crystallization of two distinct and mutually exclusive versions of the Marxist-Leninist orthodoxy. Neither Communist power, after the parting of their ideological ways in 1960, could acknowledge the virtue of the other without undermining its own authority at home as well as abroad. The ideological habits of communism thus had, in a peculiar way, a profound impact on the course of foreign policy, not in uniting the bloc, not in guiding the campaign against the West, but in driving home an unbridgeable wedge into what had once passed as a monolithic revolutionary whole.

The "Operational Code": A Neglected Approach to the Study of Political Leaders and Decision-Making*

In the past two decades the field of international relations studies has become increasingly diversified and is now marked by sharp differences over questions of scope, method, and theory. This heterogeneity, however, should not be allowed to obscure broad agreement on some fundamental propositions of overriding importance. One of these is the feeling shared by traditionalists and scientifically-oriented investigators alike, and by many academic scholars as well as sophisticated policy-makers, that the way in which the leaders of nation-states view each other and the nature of world political conflict is of fundamental importance in determining what happens in relations among states.

Reflecting the perspective of the policy maker, for example, Louis Halle, a former State Department planner, writes that the foreign policy of a nation addresses itself not to the external world, as is commonly stated, but rather to "the image of the external world" that is in the minds of those who make foreign policy. Halle concludes his book on American foreign policy with a sober warning: "In the degree that the image is false, actually and philosophically false, no technicians, however proficient, can make the policy that is

*Reprinted from *International Studies Quarterly*, XIII, 2 (June, 1969), pp. 190–222, by permission of the author and the Wayne State University Press. Copyright 1969 by Wayne State University Press. This article is a slightly modified version of a publication with the same title issued by The RAND Corporation as RM-5427 in August, 1967. The author wishes to express appreciation for permission to reprint.

based on it sound."[1] Essentially the same point has emerged from the work of many scientifically-oriented scholars who, influenced by psychological theories of cognition, have been struck by the role that the subjective perceptions and beliefs of leaders play in their decision-making in conflict situations.

Convergence on this fundamental point provides an opportunity, therefore, for establishing a more fruitful dialogue among academic scholars of various persuasions and policy-oriented researchers. To call attention to this opportunity and to help structure some of the central research questions, I decided a few years ago to reexamine an older study that had pioneered in the analysis of elite belief systems. I refer to Nathan Leites' concept of "operational code." It must be said immediately that this term is a misnomer insofar as it implies, incorrectly, a set of recipes or repertoires for political action that an elite applies mechanically in its decision-making.

A closer examination of what Leites had in mind indicates that he was referring to a set of general beliefs about fundamental issues of history and central questions of politics as these bear, in turn, on the problem of action. The actor's beliefs and premises that Leites singled out have a relationship to decision-making that is looser and more subtle than the term "operational code" implies. They serve, as it were, as a prism that influences the actor's perceptions and diagnoses of the flow of political events, his definitions and estimates of particular situations. These beliefs also provide norms, standards, and guidelines that influence the actor's choice of strategy and tactics, his structuring and weighing of alternative courses of action. Such a belief system influences, but does not unilaterally determine, decision-making; it is an important, but not the only, variable that shapes decision-making behavior. With this caveat in mind, let me recall briefly the origins, nature, and impact of Leites' study before proceeding to indicate how his approach can be codified into a more explicit and usable research model.

I. Background

It is now over fifteen years since Nathan Leites published *A Study of Bolshevism,*[2] which broke important ground in the newly emerging behavioral approach to the study of political elites. During and after World War II, many students of world politics turned their attention to the ways in which different elites approached problems of international conflict and cooperation. They posed questions for research that could not be satisfactorily answered by traditional approaches, such as systematic biographical analysis of a ruling group according to the social origins, education, training, and other background characteristics of its members. Biographical profiles of this kind often

---

1. *American Foreign Policy* (London: G. Allen, 1960), pp. 316, 318.
2. (Glencoe, Ill.: Free Press, 1953), hereafter cited as *Study.*

suggested factors that helped account for the emergence and formation of leadership groups, but they did not illuminate adequately the political orientations, styles of calculation, and behavior of the ruling groups in question.[3]

Leites' book was by no means universally acclaimed. But there were those who welcomed it not merely for its insights into Bolshevik mentality; some thought it introduced a new genre of elite study that might fill some of the needs for a behavioral approach to studies of political leadership.

Thus the eminent anthropologist, Clyde Kluckhohn, praised *A Study of Bolshevism* as being "a work of gigantic stature that is likely to *faire école* in politics and the other behavioral sciences for many years to come."[4] This expectation has not materialized. *A Study of Bolshevism* inspired few efforts at similar research on other leadership groups.[5]

Among the reasons for this, I believe, is the unusually complex nature of Leites' work, which is not one but several interrelated studies that are subtly interwoven. While the complexity of the work adds to its richness and intellectual appeal, it has also made it unusually difficult for readers to grasp its structure or to describe its research mode.[6]

I wish to call particular attention in this paper to that portion of *A Study of Bolshevism* known as the "operational code." Leites employed this phrase to refer to the precepts or maxims of political tactics and strategy that characterized the classical Bolshevik approach to politics. Leites initially published this portion of his larger treatise separately, and in abbreviated form as *The Operational Code of the Politburo.*[7] Two years later his more detailed statement of the "operational code" appeared in the full-scale *A Study of Bolshevism* (1953), but now several new dimensions were added and interwoven with it. Hence, the "operational code" became embedded in a much more ambitious

---

3. For a useful critique of the systematic multi-biographical study of elite groups, see Morris Janowitz, "The Systematic Aspects of Political Biography," *World Politics,* VI (April, 1954). A comprehensive critical appraisal of elite theories and related empirical researches is provided in Dankwart A. Rustow, "The Study of Elites," *World Politics,* XVIII (July, 1966).

4. In his review article, "Politics, History, and Psychology," *World Politics,* VIII (October, 1955), p. 117

5. An early attempt was made by Theodore Chen to apply the "operational code" approach to Communist Chinese leaders. More recently, in December 1966, Robert North organized a conference of Chinese area specialists at Stanford University to consider again the utility and feasibility of doing a study of the Chinese Communist operational code. Other studies pursue similar research objectives, though not modeled on the operational code: see, for example, Davis B. Bobrow, "The Chinese Communist Conflict System," *Orbis,* IX (Winter, 1966); Howard L. Boorman and Scott A. Boorman, "Strategy and National Psychology in China," *The Annals,* 370 (March, 1967); Tang Tsou and Morton H. Halperin, "Mao Tse-tung's Revolutionary Strategy and Peking's International Behavior," *American Political Science Review,* LIX (March, 1965).

6. A helpful effort to identify the several components of *A Study of Bolshevism* is provided by Daniel Bell, "Bolshevik Man, His Motivations: A Psychoanalytic Key to Communist Behavior," *Commentary,* XIX (1955), pp. 179–87; much of this essay was reproduced in the same author's "Ten Theories in Search of Reality: The Prediction of Soviet Behavior in the Social Sciences," *World Politics,* X (April, 1958).

7. New York: McGraw-Hill, 1951.

socio-psychological account of the historical origins and meanings of Bolshevism. The reader was provided not only with the "operational code" but, as Daniel Bell noted, also with a special kind of history of the changing moral temper of an important element of the radical reform-minded Russian intelligentsia. A third component of the study, in some ways the most ambitious, was Leites' delineation of the "Bolshevik character" which, he suggested, constituted in some respects a distinct type in social history in the sense that any individual is unique though resembling others in important respects.[8]

Hence *A Study of Bolshevism* emerges as far more than a list of maxims of political strategy. Rather, the "operational code" blends and merges at many points with the discussion of "Bolshevik character." The maxims of political strategy that comprise the "operational code" take on the character of *rules of conduct* held out for good Bolsheviks and *norms of behavior* that, ideally, are internalized by the individual who thereby acquires a new and different character structure — that of the reliable, "hard-core" Bolshevik. In the terminology of modern ego psychology, the individual who succeeds in internalizing this preferred character structure thereby accomplishes an "identity transformation."

Leites dealt briefly, and necessarily speculatively, with the origins of the "Bolshevik character." He saw it as being, in part, a *reaction* to those qualities of the reform-minded Russian intelligentsia of the nineteenth century that had, in Lenin's judgment, proven to be quite unsuitable for the task of making a successful revolution.

In dealing with the origins of the Bolshevik character and, in particular, with its "reactive" aspects, Leites employed a method that drew in part, but only in part, on psychoanalytic theory. This has further complicated the task of understanding the research model on which his complex study is based. Since the question is germane to the task of "disentangling" the operational code portion of the work, some clarification of the role psychoanalytic theory played in Leites' study is necessary before proceeding.

It is true that Leites felt that the full significance of important elements of the emergent Bolshevik character could be better understood by regarding them as "reaction formations" (and other ego defense mechanisms) to powerful unconscious wishes that had helped to shape the older character structure of Russian reform-minded intellectuals.[9] But, according to Leites, the Bolshevik character also represented a *conscious* effort by Lenin and his associates

---

8. In this connection see, for example, Michael Walzer's study of the origins of modern radical politics in the sixteenth century and his effort to construct a general model of radical politics that encompasses Bolshevism as well as Puritanism. *The Revolution of Saints* (Cambridge, Mass.: Harvard University Press, 1965).

9. The psychoanalytic hypotheses employed by Leites were touched upon at various points in *A Study of Bolshevism* and discussed more fully in his article, "Panic and Defenses Against Panic in the Bolshevik View of Politics," in *Psychoanalysis and the Social Sciences,* IV (New York: International Universities Press, 1955), pp. 135–44.

to reverse certain traditional aspects of Russian character. Leites therefore employed psychoanalytic theory to illuminate the unconscious significance of Bolshevik beliefs; but he noted explicitly that his "delineation of the preconscious and conscious content" of Bolshevik doctrine and the operational code did not require the reader either to accept the theory of psychoanalysis or to agree with the particular use Leites made of it in his admittedly speculative attempt to illuminate the possible unconscious significance of some of these Bolshevik beliefs.[10]

What emerges from this is that the set of beliefs about politics associated with the concept, "operational code," can be investigated without reference to psychoanalytic hypotheses. These beliefs, implicitly or explicitly held by the political actor, can be inferred or postulated by the investigator on the basis of the kinds of data, observational opportunities, and methods generally available to political scientists. In this respect, the "operational code" approach does not differ from research efforts to identify many other beliefs, opinions, and attitudes of political actors. Leites' use of psychoanalytic theory, therefore, offers no impediment to "factoring out" the operational code part of his study.

At the same time, it is one of the attractive features of the operational code construct for behaviorally-inclined political scientists that it can serve as a useful "bridge" or "link" to psychodynamic interpretations of unconscious dimensions of belief systems and their role in behavior under different conditions.[11] Thus, once an actor's approach to political calculation has been formulated by the researcher, he can proceed — if he so wishes and is able to do so — to relate some of the beliefs in question to other motivational variables of a psychodynamic character. With the belief system of the political actor in hand, the investigator can move more easily than would otherwise be possible into the sphere of unconscious motives and defenses against them that affect the strength and operation of these beliefs in the actor's political behavior in different circumstances, and to an assessment of the extent to which these beliefs are subject to reality-tests of various kinds. An elite's fundamental beliefs about politics are probably resistant to change for various reasons, of which unconscious motivations are but one factor.[12]

10. *Study,* p. 22. Daniel Bell, *op. cit.,* also called attention to the fact that Leites regards Bolshevik character as both a conscious and unconscious reaction to features of the earlier pre-Bolshevik character.

11. I have suggested elsewhere ("Power as a Compensatory Value for Political Leaders," *Journal of Social Issues,* XXIV [July, 1968]) that political scientists interested in applying personality theories to the study of political leaders need to build a number of conceptual "bridges" that reflect the problems, theoretical interests, and available data of their discipline in order to make more effective use of personality theories rooted in psychoanalysis. The "operational code" construct is one such "bridge." The belief system about politics is part of the cognitive and affective portion of the ego structure of personality; as such it serves an adaptive function for coping with reality. But at the same time the emergence of a belief system may be affected by developmental problems encountered in personality formation; if so, beliefs may then also serve ego defensive functions *vis-à-vis* unconscious wishes and anxieties.

12. In this connection, Leites argued that the fact that beliefs comprising the operational code

Another shortcoming of the *Study* should be mentioned. Leites did not structure and synthesize the various beliefs, rules, and maxims about politics associated with his concept of "operational code." The relationship of the different elements of the Bolshevik view of politics to each other and to the problem of making specific choices of action remained somewhat obscure.[13] That is, he did not clarify sufficiently the order, hierarchy, and interrelationships among the various elements of the "code." I will attempt to redress this by reinterpreting various components of the so-called code and restructuring it into a more tightly knit set of beliefs about fundamental issues and questions associated with the classical problem of political action. To repeat, it is in this sense — as a set of premises and beliefs about politics and not as a set of rules and recipes to be applied mechanically to the choice of action — that the "operational code" construct is properly understood.

II. The "Operational Code" and Cognitive Limits on Rational Decision-Making

A political leader's beliefs about the nature of politics and political conflict, his views regarding the extent to which historical developments can be shaped, and his notions of correct strategy and tactics — whether these beliefs be referred to as "operational code," "Weltanschauung," "cognitive map," or an "elite's political culture" — are among the factors influencing that actor's decisions. The "operational code" is a particularly significant portion of the actor's entire set of beliefs about political life.[14] Not all the beliefs and attitudes that influence a political actor's behavior, then, will be considered here. A comprehensive model of decision-making behavior, for example, would also consider the actor's ethical and normative beliefs.[15]

It is widely recognized that there are important cognitive limits on the

---

appeared to be held with unusual stubbornness, exaggeration, and intensity raised the presumption that adherence to them was reinforced by defenses against strong unconscious wishes or fears and, hence, that they were relatively impervious to many kinds of rational tests. (We shall return to this point below.)

13. This point was well made recently by John Weakland in a perceptive and balanced appraisal of *A Study of Bolshevism.* Weakland notes that Leites' work is "remarkably simple in overall organization, and for a work aiming to present a code, it gives little attention to synthesis and systematization. . . . We are presented with a list of themes, but these parts of the code are not interrelated. . . . And there is even less attention given to questions of more complex structure, such as possible relationships between themes or principles of different levels . . ." John H. Weakland, "Investigating the Operational Code of the Chinese Communist Leadership," an unpublished paper written for the Politburo Feasibility Study Conference, Stanford University, 16–18 December, 1966.

14. For a more general discussion of political belief systems, see Lucian W. Pye and Sidney Verba (eds.), *Political Culture and Political Development* (Princeton, N.J.: Princeton University Press, 1965), particularly the "Introduction" by L. Pye and "Conclusion: Comparative Political Culture" by S. Verba.

15. These were considered by Leites in *Study,* especially pp. 99–144.

possibility of rational decision-making in politics as in other sectors of life.[16] In contrast to models of "pure" rationality in statistical decision theory and formal economics, efforts at rational decision-making in political life are subject to constraints of the following kind: (1) The political actor's information about situations with which he must deal is usually incomplete; (2) his knowledge of ends-means relationships is generally inadequate to predict reliably the consequences of choosing one or another course of action; and (3) it is often difficult for him to formulate a single criterion by means of which to choose which alternative course of action is "best."[17]

Political actors have to adapt to and try to cope with these cognitive limits or "boundaries" to rational decision-making. There are, no doubt, a variety of ways in which different political leaders deal with this problem in similar or different political settings. This is, indeed, an aspect of comparative political research that has received little systematic attention.[18] How do political leaders in varying political cultures and institutional structures approach the task of making calculations, of deciding what objectives to select, and how to deal with uncertainty and risk — that is, more generally, how to relate means and ends, etc.? What styles of political calculation and strategies are developed for this purpose by different leaders? This has to do, of course, with the familiar problem of the relation of knowledge to action on which many observers and practitioners of politics have reflected. What is proposed here is that this classical problem be conceptualized more rigorously and studied more systematically than in the past.[19]

16. In recent years a number of social scientists have attempted to draw upon the field of cognitive psychology in order to elaborate better decision-making models for studies of world politics. While cognitive theory is relevant and suggestive, it does not lend itself readily to the task. Considerable adaption and development are needed. In particular, investigators will have to articulate the substantive beliefs and cognitive problems that are relevant in decision-making in political settings, and they will also have to define more specifically the special contexts in which these political beliefs originate, operate in decision-making, and change. For a useful discussion and statement of a still quite general model, see Richard A. Brody, "Cognition and Behavior: A Model of International Relations," in O. G. Harvey (ed.), *Experience, Structure, and Adaptability* (New York: Springer, 1966).

17. For useful discussions of these cognitive limits and some of their implications in the area of political decision-making, see James G. March and Herbert A. Simon, *Organizations* (New York: John Wiley, 1958); and Charles E. Lindblom, "The Science of Muddling Through," *Public Administration Quarterly*, XXIX (Spring, 1959), pp. 79 – 88. Lindblom's views have been elaborated in subsequent publications.

18. For interesting developments in this direction, however, see Albert Hirschman's effort to identify some characteristic features of the problem-solving and decision-making styles of Latin American reform leaders, in his *Journeys Toward Progress* (New York: Twentieth Century Fund, 1963); and the research by Wendell Bell and James Mau on "images of the future," as a key variable in social change in developing countries.

19. For insightful essays on some of these questions, see, for example, David S. McLelland, "The Role of Political Style: A Study of Dean Acheson," in Roger Hilsman and Robert C. Good (eds.), *Foreign Policy in the Sixties* (Baltimore: Johns Hopkins University Press, 1965); Peter Gourevitch, "Political Skill: A Case Study," in John D. Montgomery and Arthur Smithies (eds.), *Public Policy* (Cambridge, Mass.: Harvard University Press, 1965), especially pp. 266 – 68; Erwin C. Hargrove, *Presidential Leadership: Personality and Political Style* (New York: Macmillan,

The issues and questions referred to in the preceding paragraph comprise one part of the "operational code" construct. We shall refer to the "answers" given by a political actor to these questions as his "instrumental beliefs," that is, his beliefs about ends-means relationships in the context of political action.

There is another set of more general issues and questions that are part of an operational code. These are what may be called the political actor's "philosophical" beliefs, since they refer to assumptions and premises he makes regarding the fundamental nature of politics, the nature of political conflict, the role of the individual in history, etc.[20]

It is in terms of these two sets of beliefs — the specific contents of which will be discussed shortly — that I have redefined and restructured the concept of "operational code." What emerges is a research construct for empirical work on decision-making that focuses more clearly than did *A Study of Bolshevism* on the interrelated set of beliefs about the nature of political conflict and an effective approach to calculation of political strategy and tactics.

A Study of Bolshevism emphasized the "answers" that, in Leites' judgment, the old Bolsheviks gave to these central questions about politics and the relation of knowledge to action. However, he did not explicitly state all the issues and questions themselves. This I shall attempt to do here in order to facilitate similar studies of other leaders and other leadership groups, and thereby lead to systematic comparative studies.

There are, of course, difficult problems in employing knowledge of a leader's "operational code," or belief system about politics, for purposes of explaining or predicting his behavior in specific instances.[21] The investigator's knowledge of the actor's general belief system can assist, but not substitute for, analysis of specific situations and assessment of institutional and other pressures on the political actor's decisions. Knowledge of the actor's approach to calculating choice of action does *not* provide a simple key to explanation and prediction; but it can help the researcher and the policy planner to "bound" the alternative ways in which the subject may perceive different types of situations and approach the task of making a rational assessment of alternative courses of

---

1966); Michael Brecher, "Elite Images and Foreign Policy Choices: Krishna Menon's View of the World," *Pacific Affairs,* XL (Spring and Summer, 1967). Systematic research on presidential leadership styles is currently being undertaken by Professor James David Barber, Department of Political Science, Yale University.

20. I have borrowed here and adapted the general distinction between "epistemological" and "instrumental" beliefs made by O. G. Brim, D. C. Glass, D. E. Lavin, and N. Goodman, *Personality and Decision Processes: Studies in the Social Psychology of Thinking* (Stanford: Stanford University Press, 1962). In attempting to apply their useful distinction to the subject matter of the "operational code" I have found it necessary to formulate differently the specific issues and questions related to the problem of political action.

21. Leites himself did not overlook these problems or oversimplify the task of utilizing the operational code, with its ambiguous and inconsistent prescriptions, for explaining or predicting Soviet behavior. See *Study,* pp. 16–18.

action. Knowledge of the actor's beliefs helps the investigator to clarify the general criteria, requirements, and norms the subject attempts to meet in assessing opportunities that arise to make desirable gains, in estimating the costs and risks associated with them, and in making utility calculations.

Whether it be from the standpoint of philosophy, history, psychology, sociology, economics, or political science, students of human behavior have long agreed that any individual must necessarily simplify and structure the complexity of his world in order to cope with it. In everyday life as in the laboratory, problem-solving often requires deliberate or unwitting simplification of a more complex reality. This applies also to the political actor, for he too must somehow comprehend complex situations in order to decide how best to deal with them.[22] In doing so, the actor typically engages in a "definition of the situation," that is, a cognitive structuring of the situation that will clarify for him the nature of the problem, relate it to his previous experience, and make it amenable to appropriate problem-solving activities. The political actor perceives and simplifies reality partly through the prism of his "cognitive map" of politics. This includes the belief system that has been referred to in the past as the "operational code" of a political actor.

We turn now to the content of an operational code. I have identified a number of questions about politics that, together, hopefully cover most of the central issues connected with the problem of knowledge and action. The "answers" a political actor gives to these questions serve to define his fundamental orientation towards the problem of leadership and action. Before proceeding, we take note of the possibility that in some non-Western cultures the problem of knowledge and its relation to the calculation of political action may be approached differently and, hence, the list of fundamental questions identified here may not be entirely applicable.

Most of the observations Leites made about the classical Bolshevik approach to political calculation can be subsumed under one or another of these questions. We will not take up here whether Leites' construction of the classical Bolshevik belief system was valid in all respects. But we shall consider later the question of the extent to which some of the old Bolshevik beliefs have since changed. And we shall suggest some of the ways in which knowledge of this belief system relates to the task of explaining or predicting Soviet behavior.

The immediate objective of this paper — to explicate in detail the nature of the belief system associated with the concept of operational code — does not require us to delve deeply into these additional questions. Of more immediate concern is the adequacy of our explication and restructuring of the code. One useful way of assessing this is to see whether the Bolshevik beliefs described in the *Study* can be subsumed under the various philosophical and instrumen-

22. This point has been emphasized particularly in the writings of Charles E. Lindblom. See also March and Simon, *op. cit.,* pp. 139, 151.

tal questions we have formulated. We need deal only summarily with Leites' study for this purpose; we shall ignore those dimensions of his multifaceted study that do not constitute the operational code *per se* but comprise related questions concerning the "Bolshevik character," the social-psychological origins of the Bolshevik belief system, and the underlying psychodynamic processes about which Leites speculated.

III. The Philosophical Content of an Operational Code

1. *What is the "essential" nature of political life? Is the political universe essentially one of harmony or conflict? What is the fundamental character of one's political opponents?*[23]

A political actor's belief system about the nature of politics is shaped particularly by his orientation to other political actors. Most important of these are one's opponents. The way in which they are perceived — the characteristics the political actor attributes to his opponents — exercises a subtle influence on many other philosophical and instrumental beliefs in his operational code.[24] In the classical Bolshevik belief system the "image of the opponent" was perhaps the cornerstone on which much of the rest of their approach to politics was based. The old Bolsheviks perceived the capitalist opponent as thoroughly hostile at bottom, whatever facade he might display, and possessed of great shrewdness and determination to annihilate his class opponent.

Accordingly, for the old Bolsheviks the political universe was one of acute conflict. The fundamental question of politics and history, as formulated by the Bolsheviks, was "who [will destroy] whom?" This conflict between Communists and their class enemies was viewed as fundamental and irreconcilable. It was not attributable to particular historical personages but sprang from the "objective" historical conditions described by Marxist dialectics.

Consistent with these views was another Bolshevik belief regarding the instability of any "intermediate" historical position between being annihilated or achieving world hegemony. So long as the Bolsheviks had not yet achieved world hegemony, the danger of being annihilated by the enemy would remain an ever-present one.

Other answers to the first question posed here are possible and have been given by different elites. For example, the traditional "idealist" conception of international affairs postulates a fundamental harmony of interests among peoples and nations that is only temporarily disrupted because of the wickedness or weakness of certain individuals and the lack of adequate institutions, a view with which "realists" have increasingly taken issue.[25]

23. The summary presented here is drawn from *Study,* pp. 27 – 30 ("Politics Is a War") and pp. 429 – 41 ("Who-Whom?").

24. For this reason, it is of particular interest that in his more recent work Leites has found indications of an amelioration in the Soviet leaders' image of their opponent. (See below.)

25. On this point see, for example, Robert E. Osgood, *Ideals and Self-Interest in America's*

It is important to recognize that on this issue as on other elements of the belief system, not all members of a ruling group will necessarily agree; moreover, beliefs can change significantly over a period of time. Thus, in research since the publication of *A Study of Bolshevism* Nathan Leites noted various indications of an important modification in this basic Bolshevik belief which, in turn, has potentially far-reaching implications for the Soviet style of political behavior.

2. *What are the prospects for the eventual realization of one's fundamental political values and aspirations? Can one be optimistic, or must one be pessimistic on this score; and in what respects the one and/or the other?*[26]

The conventional Bolshevik position was optimistic, drawing as it did upon ideological-doctrinal premises regarding the eventual triumph of Communism on a worldwide scale. Yet, it was an optimism tinged with conditional pessimism, that is, an underlying belief that catastrophe could not be excluded and was an ever-present danger. One had to be constantly aware of the possibility of catastrophe and avoid contributing to its actualization by defective calculations and inept political behavior.

3. *Is the political future predictable? In what sense and to what extent?*[27]

The classical Bolshevik position on this issue reflected the strong "determinist" streak in the Marxist view of history; but this view was balanced by strong "indeterminist" conceptions. Thus, the Bolsheviks believed that while the direction and final outcome of the major historical development from capitalism to Communism are predictable, nonetheless the rate of this development and its particular paths are not. At many junctures or branch points of historical development, therefore, more than one outcome is "objectively possible."

This general belief has had important implications for the way in which Bolsheviks approached the problem of "action." The passive orientation to action that was logically and psychologically implicit in the "determinist" view of history was counterbalanced by the "indeterminist" conception of the many zig-zags that historical developments could take prior to reaching their predictable final outcome. From an operational standpoint the latter, "indeterminist," component of the belief dominated in that it emphasized the importance of intelligent, well-calculated action as a means of expediting the historical

---

Foreign Relations (Chicago: University of Chicago Press, 1953); and Kenneth Waltz, *Man, the State and War* (New York: Columbia University Press, 1959).

26. The summary which follows draws from *Study,* pp. 404 – 16 ("The Incessant Danger of Attack," and "The Uncertainty of Survival Before Victory").

27. The summary presented here draws from *Study,* pp. 32, 77 – 85 ("Unpredictable Aspects of the Future").

process. As a result, the Bolshevik answer to this question encouraged and, when reinforced by the other beliefs already referred to, even drove its adherents towards "voluntarism" and initiative rather than fatalism and passivity.

Elaborating on this philosophical theme, the Bolsheviks believed that "objective conditions" from time to time create certain "opportunities" for the Party to advance its interests at the expense of its opponents. However, it was regarded as not predictable and by no means certain that the Party would succeed in "utilizing" these opportunities for advance and in transforming them into realities.

> 4. *How much "control" or "mastery" can one have over historical development? What is one's role in "moving" and "shaping" history in the desired direction?* [28]

The classical Bolshevik answer to this question follows from beliefs held with respect to the preceding issues. Thus, in the Bolshevik view, the Party is obliged to seize and utilize any "opportunity" for advance, for men can determine within fairly wide limits the cost and duration of an "inevitable" social change. The answer to this question, therefore, emphasizes the role that dedicated, disciplined, and intelligent political actors can play in "moving" history in the desired direction.

> 5. *What is the role of "chance" in human affairs and in historical development?* [29]

The classical Bolshevik answer was that all politically important events are explainable by the laws of Marxism-Leninism; therefore, that history can be importantly shaped by "accidental" events is rejected.

Consistent with this general belief was the Politburo's tendency, often noted by Western observers, to perceive connections between events where we see none; to regard unrelated details as symptomatic of major political trends; and to believe there is complicated planning behind events which we know to be fortuitous. Bolshevik thought minimized the role of chance — with all its unsettling implications for their belief system — by distorting the image of the opponent and perceiving him as preternaturally calculating and powerful, which, in turn, had other unsettling implications.

Related to this was the emphatic negative the Bolsheviks gave to the question: Can one "muddle through"? [30] It is not only not possible to "muddle through," they believed, but extremely dangerous to try to do so. Accompanying this was the related belief that there is in every situation just one "correct" line or policy. All other policies or choices of action may result in, or tend to

28. See *Study,* pp. 85 – 92 ("Transforming Opportunities into Realities").
29. See *Study,* pp. 67 – 73 ("The Denial of Accidents").
30. See *Study,* pp. 49, 264 – 68.

lead to, ruin — that is, the "catastrophe" held to be an ever-present possibility, as noted above. In the Bolshevik belief system, moreover, political mistakes were rarely harmless or anything less than acutely dangerous. ("Every small step has to be carefully weighed.")

As the preceding discussion has suggested, these beliefs about the major philosophical issues concerning politics are related to each other. This set of beliefs, in turn, is logically and psychologically related to a set of "instrumental" beliefs that refer more specifically to key aspects of the problem of knowledge and action. What should be stressed before proceeding is that the answers different political leaders or elite groups give to the basic questions implicit in the traditional problem of knowledge and action are affected by their philosophical beliefs about the nature of politics.

IV. The Instrumental Beliefs in an Operational Code

1. *What is the best approach for selecting goals or objectives for political action?*[31]

The classical Bolshevik answer to the question of how best to set one's goals in embarking upon action was influenced by two of the general philosophical beliefs already alluded to: the mixture of determinist and indeterminist conceptions regarding future historical developments and the view of one's role in "moving" history in the right direction. Recall in this connection, too, the general injunction implicit in the Bolshevik answer to the third and fourth of the philosophical beliefs noted earlier, namely that the Party is obliged to seize all "opportunities" that arise for making advances. How, then, did the Bolsheviks orient themselves more specifically to the critical question of determining what one should strive for, and what the goals and objectives of action should be when an "opportunity" to make gains arises?

The classical Bolshevik "answer" (perhaps partly at the preconscious level) was along the following lines:

(a) One should *not* approach the task of setting the objective or goal of political action by trying first to calculate precisely the probability of achieving each of the alternative objectives that might be pursued in a given situation.

(b) Further, one should not limit the objective one strives for in a particular situation to that which, on the basis of such calculations, appears to be quite likely or rather certain of being achieved by the means at one's disposal. (Note here the Bolshevik admonition against the tend-

---

31. The discussion of this question draws from and freely interprets materials in *Study,* pp. 32, 77–92, 47–49, 514–24.

ency to allow assessments of available means and their presumed limited efficacy unduly to circumscribe and limit the magnitude of the objective or goal to be pursued.)

(c) In setting one's goals, therefore, one must counter tendencies towards an overly conservative approach to political action: a reluctance to push for useful gains against seemingly difficult odds, and the related tendency to "pare down" the goals of action to those that seem highly feasible and likely to be achieved.

(d) Against this conservative approach to calculation of ends-means relationships to politics, the Bolsheviks argued on behalf of a strategy of attempting to optimize or maximize the gains that might be derived in a given situation. (Note here the Bolshevik tendency to reject what has been called the "satisficing" strategy that many other decision-makers often prefer to an "optimizing" one.)[32]

Let us consider now how some of the familiar cognitive limits on rational decision-making are dealt with in support of the preference for an optimizing strategy rather than a more conservative approach. In Bolshevik thinking on this central issue, the problem of uncertain or incomplete knowledge relevant to choice of action is "bounded" in a special way. In behalf of the preferred optimizing approach, the Bolshevik code argues — not unrealistically, it may be said — in the following vein:

(a) Political action often has to begin with incomplete knowledge about possible outcomes; it is action itself and only action that will increase knowledge.

(b) What can be achieved in a particular situation cannot be predicted in advance — it can only become known in the process of "struggle" in which one attempts to get the most out of a situation.

(c) In choosing the goals or objectives of a particular course of action, therefore, one should limit them only by assessing what is "objectively possible" in that situation — that is, not impossible to achieve by intelligent use of resources at one's disposal.

The operative belief, restated, is that in initiating an action the Party must be concerned only with ascertaining that the goals it sets are "objectively possible" (in the general and somewhat vague sense already indicated) — not that they can be achieved with high probability. For what can be achieved cannot be predicted in advance; it depends on the "relationship of forces" which can be known only in the process of "struggle" carried out "to the end."

---

32. On this point see, for example, March and Simon, *op. cit.,* pp. 140–41, 169.

What is important, therefore, is that the limited knowledge available to assess the likely consequences of alternative courses of action should not lead the political actor who engages in ends-means calculations to make an overly conservative choice of what to strive for.

Applying these beliefs to the problem of action, the Bolsheviks developed *a special kind of optimizing strategy.* In undertaking an initiative to advance their interests, they often set for themselves not a single objective but a set of graduated objectives. The standard task faced by all decision-makers — namely, that of attempting to reconcile what is desirable with what is thought to be feasible — is not over-determined in this optimizing strategy. Rather, action is oriented in a specific situation to a series of objectives embracing payoffs that are graduated (but perhaps inversely related) in degree of utility and feasibility. The optimizing strategy calls for striving simultaneously for a maximum payoff — even though the probability of achieving it appears to be low — and the more modest payoffs which appear to be less difficult and more probable. There seems to be an implicit assumption that such a strategy not only provides an opportunity to achieve the maximum payoff in a given situation but, should that prove infeasible or emerge as too costly or risky, it will enable one to settle, if necessary, for one of the lesser of the graduated objectives that will constitute the largest payoff that could have been squeezed out of the "opportunity" the situation afforded. The contrast here is with "adventures" where there are no lesser objectives, but only a maximum payoff or a severe loss. (See below.)

Such an optimizing strategy, therefore, is consonant with the general philosophical belief alluded to earlier: namely, that what can be achieved in a particular situation cannot be predicted in advance, that action must begin with incomplete knowledge and a measure of uncertainty regarding possible outcomes, and that it is only through "struggle" that one can find out how much a given "opportunity" to advance will yield.[33]

It should not be assumed that resort to an optimizing strategy of this kind necessarily implies neglect of risk and cost calculations. On the other hand, adherents of this strategy may not give due recognition to the possibility that striving for the maximum possible payoff in a given situation may well entail special costs and risks. Thus, if the optimizing strategy is not correctly perceived as such by the opponent, it may well unduly arouse his sense of danger and mobilize his potential for resistance and counteraction in a way that pursuit of more modest objectives might avoid doing.[34]

33. During the course of efforts to assess Soviet intentions in placing missiles in Cuba, Charles Bohlen, a leading U. S. specialist on the Soviet Union, cited one of Lenin's adages which compared national expansion to a bayonet drive: "If you strike steel, pull back; if you strike mush, keep going." Theodore C. Sorensen, *Kennedy* (New York: Harper & Row, 1965), p. 677.

34. For a discussion of the possibility that the Bolshevik tendency to push to the limit led

We shall shortly discuss Bolshevik beliefs about calculation, control, and acceptance of risks. Here we note that the general Bolshevik answer to the question under discussion proclaimed the need for important limits to this preferred optimizing strategy. Thus, the injunction to optimize was "bounded" by the somewhat contradictory maxim: "Avoid adventures." This maxim, or rule of action, conveys several different imperatives:

(a) A generalized injunction not to embark on forward operations against an opponent that are not carefully calculated in advance to exclude complacent overestimates of one's own strength and underestimates of his strength. Complacent miscalculations of this kind reflect a failure to assess properly whether the "objective conditions" permit a responsible effort to make gains of any kind, and, if so, what the range of objectives should be that one can safely pursue in the given situation.

(b) A generalized injunction against undertaking action that has an uncertain chance of yielding any payoff but is coupled, at the same time, with a large risk of severe loss if it fails. Actions to advance one's interests should be avoided when they cannot utilize the optimizing strategy noted above in which graduated objectives and payoffs are pursued. An action is "adventuristic" if it has no lesser objectives and no possibility of lesser payoffs — that is, one for which the expected outcomes are limited to a maximum payoff or a severe loss.

(c) A generalized injunction against permitting one's calculations and choice of action to be dominated by prospects of immediate or short-term gains while ignoring the possibility of the longer-range costs and risks attached to the same action.

We may summarize our discussion of the first instrumental belief in the Bolshevik code as follows: Choose an optimizing strategy that pursues graduated objectives, but "avoid adventures."

The fact that not one but several graduated objectives may serve to orient Soviet action in conflict situations is particularly important in the sphere of world politics. The optimizing strategy that lies behind Soviet initiatives in foreign policy from time to time has evidently complicated the task of Western governments in trying to assess Soviet intentions and to devise appropriate countermeasures. On various occasions in the past, unfamiliarity with this aspect of the Soviet operational code seems to have resulted in unnecessary perplexity, confusion, and alarm in attempts to assess Soviet intentions. Western observers have responded to Soviet initiatives (such as the Berlin blockade

---

to an underestimation of the undesired consequences of such conduct, see Leites, *Study*, pp. 33 – 34, 36 – 37, 39.

of 1948) on the assumption that Soviet leaders were pursuing a single objective. Equivocal indications of what the Soviets were after were variously interpreted in terms of what "the" Soviet intention really was, as if the Soviets were pursuing only a single objective rather than a set of graduated objectives. Some Western interpretations focused on indications that the Soviets were pursuing an extremely ambitious objective, thus heightening apprehensions regarding the aggressive bent of Soviet policy, the "risks" Soviet leaders were willing to take, and the "danger" of war. Other interpretations focused on indications that the Soviets were pursuing only a quite modest, even "defensive" objective, thus encouraging the belief that the crisis could be quickly and easily terminated if only the Western policies that had "provoked" the Soviets were altered and concessions made to satisfy them.[35]

It is not possible to discuss in detail here the consequences of Western responses based upon misperception of the nature of Soviet optimizing strategy. One might assume that Western responses in such situations would be more effective if based on awareness that the opponent is pursuing a set of graduated objectives ranging from relatively modest to quite ambitious goals, and that he relies heavily on feedback in deciding how far to go. But we must also consider the possibility that Western responses to Soviet initiatives have occasionally been more effective precisely because they focused on the most ambitious gains the Soviets may have had in mind in pursuing this kind of optimizing strategy.

2. How are the goals of action pursued most effectively?

The classical Bolshevik answer to this question can be summarized in three maxims: "push to the limit," "engage in pursuit" of an opponent who begins to retreat or make concessions, *but* "know when to stop."[36]

The first part of the answer, "push to the limit," enjoins that maximum energy be exerted to attain the objectives of action. The "struggle" to attain them should not be curtailed prematurely; pressure should be maintained against the opponent even though he doesn't give signs of buckling and even though it seems to stiffen his resistance at first.

The second part of the answer invokes the principle of "pursuit." Once some progress, some weakening of the opponent's position has been achieved, it is imperative not to yield to the temptation of relaxing pressure. When an opponent begins to talk of making some concessions or offers them, it should be recognized that this is a sign of weakness on his part. Additional and

---

35. In the Cuban missile crisis, U.S. policy-makers at first entertained various theories, partly overlapping and partly divergent, as to Soviet intentions. They seem to have settled on an interpretation that avoided attributing to the Soviet leaders a single motive in favor of a theory that the Soviets expected that the deployment of missiles would give them prospects for a variety of specific gains in foreign policy. See particularly Roger Hilsman, *To Move a Nation* (New York: Doubleday, 1967), pp. 161–65, 201–02; and Sorensen, *op. cit.*, pp. 676–78.

36. See *Study*, pp. 30–34, 505–12, 442–49, 52–53, 514–24.

perhaps major gains can be made by continuing to press the opponent under these circumstances.

Once again, however, the Bolshevik operational code set important limits, though of a generalized character, to the preceding two maxims. These limits are, characteristically, embodied in a general injunction, "know when to stop," which is directed against the psychological danger of being carried away by one's success to the point of failing to calculate soberly and rationally the costs and risks of continuing efforts to press forward. Once again, a general injunction of this type lacks operational content; it does not suggest how the maxim is to be applied meaningfully in specific situations; but it is presumably a valuable part of the cognitive and affective makeup of a good Bolshevik.

It has been of considerable value on occasion to Western leaders to understand that their Soviet counterparts structure the problem of action with a set of beliefs and maxims that seem to contradict or, rather, oppose one another. There is, as a result, what might be called a "tension of opposites" in their cognitive structuring of the problem of action. We saw this already in the beliefs held with respect to the first of the instrumental issues: attempt to optimize gains, but don't engage in "adventures." And we see it again here with reference to the second instrumental issue: "push to the limit" and "pursue" a retreating opponent, but "know when to stop."[37]

Another "tension of opposites" may be discussed at this point that applies to situations in which a Bolshevik leader feels himself put on the defensive by some action of the opponent. The maxims which "bound" this problem of action and create a tension are "resist from the start" any encroachment by the opponent, no matter how slight it appears to be; *but* "don't yield to enemy provocations" and "retreat before superior force."[38]

"Yielding" to an opponent is so worrisome a danger in the classical Bolshevik code (and, presumably, so anxiety-arousing a fantasy in the old Bolshevik psyche) that it gave rise to a strong injunction to be ultra-sensitive to encroachments of any kind. No matter how trivial they seem, the opponent's encroachments are to be opposed because failure to "resist from the start" may encourage him to step up his attack. (This is related to fears associated with the second of the philosophical beliefs in which ideological/doctrinal optimism regarding the final triumph of Communism is mixed with a certain pessimism, that is, an underlying belief that nonetheless catastrophe and major setbacks cannot be excluded.)

3. *How are the risks of political action calculated, controlled, and accepted?*

The Bolsheviks' answer to this question was importantly influenced by their experience in struggling against vastly stronger, dangerous opponents — first

---

37. A similar "tension of opposites" has been noted in the Chinese Communist approach to the problem of strategy and action. See Tang Tsou and Morton H. Halperin, *op. cit.*, p. 89.

38. For a discussion of these maxims, see *Study*, pp. 55 – 57, 449 – 61, 46 – 47, 57 – 60, 475 – 503. See also N. Leites, *Kremlin Thoughts: Yielding, Rebuffing, Provoking, Retreating*, The RAND Corporation, RM-3618-ISA (May, 1963).

the Tsarist government and then, after the revolution, the leading capitalist powers. If we recall the Bolshevik answer to the earlier question on choosing one's objectives in embarking in political action, the present question can be reformulated as follows: *How does one pursue an optimizing strategy while at the same time knowing how to calculate and control its risks?*

(a) The Bolsheviks recognized that it was of course possible, in principle, to "provoke" a strong opponent into a major attack designed to crush the Bolshevik party (or, later, the Soviet Union). Behavior that might have this effect upon the opponent, therefore, was to be avoided. Nonetheless, it was believed that considerable scope was left short of this for lesser, well-calculated efforts to advance at the stronger opponent's expense. The opponent, it was believed, would be deterred by various constraints from lashing back in an effort to crush the Bolsheviks. The opponent's evaluation of his overall self-interest would keep him from translating his basic hostility — always present — into an operational plan for liquidating the Bolshevik party (and, later, the Soviet Union).

(b) It is often safe to pursue even quite major objectives at the expense of a stronger opponent (as in the Berlin blockade of 1948 – 1949 and in the Cuban missile crisis). In the Soviet view, the risks of offensive actions of this kind can often be controlled by *limiting the means* they employ on behalf of their ambitious objectives. In the Soviet view, it is possible to pursue quite large gains at an enemy's expense in this fashion without triggering a strong, undesired reaction.

We digress briefly at this point to take note of an important difference that often characterized Soviet and U.S. approaches to the calculation and acceptance of risks during the period of the Cold War. The question of how to keep conflicts between them safely limited was answered somewhat differently in the "limitations" theories of the two sides. The U.S. theory, strongly reinforced by our reading of the lessons of the Korean War, has been that a limitation on one's objectives is essential to keep limited conflicts from expanding dangerously.[39] This seemed to be borne out by the consequences — that is, Chinese Communist intervention — of our failure to keep the U.S. objective limited in the Korean War. After defeating the North Koreans we enlarged our war aims to include unification of North Korea and South Korea by force of arms, which triggered the Chinese Communist intervention.

The Soviet theory of limitations, on the other hand, holds that it is often

---

39. See, for example, R. E. Osgood, *Limited War* (Chicago: University of Chicago Press, 1957); W. W. Kaufmann, "Limited Warfare," in Kaufmann (ed.), *Military Policy and National Security* (Princeton: Princeton University Press, 1956); Morton H. Halperin, *Limited War in the Nuclear Age* (New York: John Wiley, 1963).

safe to pursue even large, far-reaching objectives in limited conflicts without immediate danger or undue risk of their expanding. What is critical in the Soviet view is not so much the limitation of one's objectives but rather limitation of the means one employs on their behalf. (Examples of this theory of limitations are Soviet behavior in the Berlin blockade and Chinese behavior in the Quemoy crisis of 1958. In both cases far-reaching objectives were evidently among those being pursued, but the risks of doing so were controlled by limiting the means employed against the two Western outposts.)

(c) It is a Soviet belief that the fact that risks of high magnitude are in some sense present in a conflict situation — e.g., the danger of war between the Soviet Union and the United States — is less important than (1) whether that undesired consequence is immediately at hand or at some remove in time, and (2) whether the Soviet leaders believe themselves able to control the intermediate events of the sequence that could result in war. Soviet leaders have displayed considerable confidence in their ability to control and avoid quite unacceptable, more distant risks in this way. Their approach to risk calculation is often more sophisticated than that of Western leaders in that Soviet leaders distinguish not only the magnitude of risks but also between risks that are immediate and those which are more remote.

Hence Soviet leaders believe, and often act on the premise, that in a struggle to make important gains one can accept seemingly high risks so long as the undesired event is several steps removed in a possible temporal sequence and so long as, in addition, they believe they can control the sequence of events leading to it. In a number of cases (the North Korean attack on South Korea, some of the Berlin crises, the Cuban missile crisis) the Soviets acted in ways that seemed to indicate to Western leaders and publics that Soviet leaders were prepared to risk and indeed were risking general war. The risk of general war, however, was in fact several steps removed; and Soviet leaders could well believe that they retained the possibility of calling off the crisis or redirecting it into safer channels, if necessary.

In other words, Soviet leaders do not settle for a single probability estimate of unwanted risks that may develop in the future; rather, they attempt to subject such estimates of probability to sequential analysis. We may contrast this style of risk calculation with the tendency of Western leaders and publics to blur the time component of the different risks created by a Soviet initiative, or by their own actions, a tendency which disposes Westerners in some situations to magnify their estimates of the prevailing risks and to greater conservatism in risk acceptance.

In this respect, therefore, as in others previously noted, Soviet and U.S. approaches to risk calculation and risk acceptance have often differed. Soviet understanding of the ways in which undesired risks could be calculated and controlled often constituted an advantage. As for Western leaders and publics, their tendency to perceive and interpret Soviet risk acceptance behavior erroneously from the standpoint of their own approach to risk calculation inclined them to make distorted judgments regarding Soviet intentions and the riskiness and significance of Soviet Cold War initiatives. (One may note briefly that, over time, Western leaders have perhaps come to understand better the Soviet approach to risk calculation and risk acceptance.)

4. *What is the best "timing" of action to advance one's interest?*[40]

Once again the Bolshevik answer displays a tendency to state the matter in terms of opposites (excluding middle positions). Thus, the Bolshevik code says, somewhat enigmatically or tritely: "There must be neither procrastination nor precipitate action." The Party must be able to bide its time indefinitely, if need be. But it is forbidden to defer an advance that is feasible now (even though difficult) in the necessarily uncertain expectation that advance would be easier at some later date. Action, therefore, tends to be either required or impermissible; there is nothing in between.

5. *What is the utility and role of different means for advancing one's interests?*

Of a number of Bolshevik views about the utility of different means, mention will be made here of one that has been rather unfamiliar to Westerners and is perhaps more idiosyncratic than other Bolshevik beliefs about means. This is the belief that in order to deter a powerful enemy "it often pays to be rude."[41] Rude and even violent language, which may or may not be accompanied by small damaging actions, is expected to serve this purpose by heightening the opponent's estimates of one's strength and determination and/or by weakening the mass support for his policies. The tactic of rudeness was believed to be not overly risky because, in Bolshevik thought, a "serious" powerful opponent is expected not to allow himself to become emotionally aroused by such tactics.

V. Changes in the Belief System

Even a belief system that reflects well-considered evaluations of past political experience is subject to change under certain conditions. Resistance to chang-

40. See *Study,* p. 34.
41. See *Study,* pp. 34–42.

ing beliefs may be accentuated by personality rigidities, which may be greater in some members of a ruling group than in others; but a variety of other factors may be operative.

Some political elites have a pronounced tendency to perceive and to deal with present problems in the light of authoritative diagnoses they have made of past experiences. They attach considerable importance to making correct diagnoses of past events which, they feel, provide usable "lessons" of history in the form of models and precedents. The tendency to approach calculation of present policy in this manner is particularly pronounced in radically oriented elites, such as the Marxists, who claim to have a special understanding of history and historical development. As a result, a body of general beliefs develops about the nature of political conflict and basically correct or incorrect approaches to dealing with opponents that takes on a doctrinal character. Special precautions may be taken to safeguard the content of such beliefs from arbitrary, unauthorized changes. Beliefs about politics, then, become part of the sacred political culture of the elite that is systematically transmitted to new leaders. Change in such an elite's belief system, then, does not follow simply from the fact that the composition of the top leadership changes.

As noted earlier, indications are available that some changes in important elements of the classical Bolshevik operational code took place or became noticeable in the Khrushchev era. I believe that the restructuring and synthesis in this paper of the major elements of this kind of belief system facilitates inquiry into the possibility of changes in its content and of their implications. Thus, as was suggested earlier, the first philosophical belief in our list appears to be of critical importance in shaping the character of the belief system as a whole and in regulating its impact on the actor's political behavior. Particularly close attention should be given, therefore, to possible shifts in the political actor's image of his opponent and, related to this, his view of the fundamental nature of political conflict.[42]

Let us look briefly now at Leites' more recent research on the Soviet elite from this standpoint. Leites studied statements by Khrushchev and other contemporary Soviet leaders in order to establish whether they held the same set of beliefs regarding the nature of political conflict and the same image of the opponent as Lenin and Stalin had earlier held. He noted various indications that a somewhat more moderate view had emerged of the basic "who-whom" problem that Lenin had so starkly formulated (see p. 174 above), and that the

---

42. This would appear to apply also to the Chinese Communist leadership. (See the forthcoming report by Robert C. North on the Stanford University conference which considered the feasibility of research on the Chinese politburo.) Among those scholars who have examined the problem of evaluating and changing beliefs about the opponent are Morton Deutsch, William Gamson, Andréa Modigliani, John Kautsky, Charles E. Osgood, Amitai Etzioni, Ralph K. White, Milton Rokeach, and Joseph deRivera.

related fear of annihilation had softened. The hypothesis of a change in these beliefs was stated cautiously by Leites.

> When one strikes a balance . . . it would seem that Bolshevik fears of annihilation have declined, which presumably decreases the urgency of total victory as an antidote against extinction.[43]

Such change would be of considerable significance since, as Leites noted, the aggressiveness and expansionist drive in the older variant of Bolshevism had probably been motivated to a significant extent by this basic view of the nature of political conflict and the related fear of annihilation.[44]

If this fundamental belief was attenuated over time, one would expect that such a change would influence other components of the belief system as well. Leites found indications that this was the case. Examining evidence bearing on the question: "Are They Relaxing?" Leites concluded, again cautiously: "Despite the Cuban affair, it cannot be excluded that they are relaxing, to some limited extent."[45] Posing another question: "Are They Mellowing?" and reviewing relevant statements by Khrushchev and other leaders, Leites concluded:

> Thus it would seem that the Bolshevik fear of yielding has, after all, declined, and the insistence on "utilizing possibilities" weakened. . . . contemporary Soviet leaders probably feel less constrained to push forward into any possible accessible space without regard for delayed and indirect consequences. They may even have gained for themselves some slight liberty to concede without an immediate concession in return.[46]

We turn briefly now to the task of accounting for an amelioration in elements of the older Bolshevik belief system. This task is admittedly formidable; the following remarks are by no means intended as an authoritative explanation. Any effort to explain such a change should probably consider several factors and the interactions among them. Changes in top Soviet leadership following Stalin's death in 1953 were undoubtedly of great importance. As Leites noted, Stalin had bent some of the Bolshevik beliefs of Lenin's time in a harsher direction. Even before the accentuation of Stalin's paranoid tendencies in his later years, idiosyncratic elements of his personality had probably rendered his adherence to the Bolshevik belief system relatively impervious to reality-testing.[47] Khrushchev's mind was apparently less "closed" in this respect than Stalin's; he was more receptive to recognizing relevant experi-

---

43. *Kremlin Moods,* The RAND Corporation, RM-3535-ISA (January, 1964), p. 126.
44. *Ibid.,* p. 91.
45. *Ibid.,* pp. 164–66.
46. *Ibid.,* p. 211.
47. The importance of Stalin's personality for his political behavior has been emphasized particularly by Robert Tucker. See his "The Dictator and Totalitarianism," *World Politics* (July, 1965), and his earlier analysis, "Stalinism and the World Conflict," *Journal of International Affairs,* VIII, No. 1 (1954).

ences and historical changes as being in some sense "critical tests" of basic components of the belief system, and also more capable of cautiously modifying some of these beliefs.

While the difference between Stalin's and Khrushchev's personalities was perhaps critical in this respect, other factors also must be taken into account. The growth of Soviet power may have contributed to Khrushchev's reassessment of the "danger of annihilation." Perhaps of greater importance was the fact that historical experience demonstrated, more during Khrushchev's rule than in Stalin's, that perhaps after all the United States would not engage in an unprovoked war with the Soviet Union. U.S. leaders had not only failed to wage preventive war while the Soviet Union was weak in the immediate post-World War II period, they also seemed prepared to allow it to approach parity with the United States. Well might these historic developments encourage post-Stalin leaders to alter somewhat the earlier image of the U.S. elite as an overwhelmingly hostile, shrewd, determined opponent and to permit themselves to feel a somewhat greater sense of security.[48]

In accounting for changes in the Soviet belief system, therefore, it appears necessary to give weight not only to changes in personality variables but also to the impact of significant historical developments. In addition to those already mentioned, reference should be made to events such as the emergence of greater independence and conflict within the international Communist movement after Stalin's death. It is probably the case that changes in top leadership made it easier to reconsider older beliefs in the light of new developments.

Changes in the belief system that manifested themselves during Khrushchev's period are indeed of considerable significance for world politics. But it is necessary to note that they evidently constituted modifications of the classical Bolshevik belief system, not its abandonment or radical transformation. There remained substantial elements of continuity with the past in the belief system and political culture of post-Stalin Soviet leadership.[49]

VI. Conclusion

This paper has formulated and illustrated the set of beliefs about basic issues concerning the nature of politics and political action that have been heretofore

48. Interestingly, Khrushchev's period also saw the emergence of a less favorable image of the United States as an opponent. There was both less idealization of, and less respect for, the U.S. elite than in the old Bolshevik view. This historic class enemy was not perceived as an "aging," "declining" elite, one which was weaker, less intelligent, less determined than in the past. The changed characteristics imputed to the United States leadership, however, were seen as making it in some respects possibly more dangerous. (See *Kremlin Moods*, pp. 91 – 126, 1 – 13.)

49. This point was emphasized in Leites' *Kremlin Moods*. There is, in the writer's knowledge, no similar study of further changes in the belief system that may have emerged in the post-Khrushchev era. However, Vernon V. Aspaturian is studying Soviet images of the Kennedy Administration.

implied by the term "operational code." This term is a misnomer in important respects; it should probably be replaced by some other way of referring to these beliefs, such as "approaches to political calculation." I have tried in this paper to codify the general issues and questions around which such a belief system is structured in the hope that it will encourage and facilitate systematic efforts to apply this research approach to a variety of other ruling groups and individual political leaders as well. The possibility emerges of a useful new dimension for comparative studies of different leaders and elite groups.

I have argued in this paper that knowledge of this belief system provides one of the important inputs needed for behavioral analyses of political decision-making and leadership styles. The "operational code" construct does this insofar as it encompasses that aspect of the political actor's perception and structuring of the political world to which he relates, and within which he attempts to operate to advance the interests with which he is identified. This approach should be useful for studying an actor's decision-making "style," and its application in specific situations.

As noted earlier, this paper focuses on the political actor's orientation towards opponents (domestic and international) rather than towards other types of political actors. I believe this focus is justified; a belief system about politics is influenced particularly by the actor's assumptions about the nature of political conflict and by his image of opponents.

Of course, the image of the opponent may play a less central and a somewhat different role in the belief systems of elites who do not attribute (as did the Bolsheviks) an irreconcilable hostility to their political enemies. When political opponents are perceived as limited (and perhaps temporary) adversaries, important consequences may be expected to follow for other elements in the belief system. Particularly in such cases is it desirable to supplement attention to the actor's image of the opponent with observations about his orientation towards political friends and followers.

There remain, of course, important questions concerning data and methods to be employed for research directed towards constructing a political actor's belief system about politics. These problems are not considered here; I would suggest here merely that questions of data and methods be approached in an eclectic and pragmatic spirit. Even provisional answers to the research questions encompassed by the operational code are likely to be useful. Opportunities for research of this kind vary considerably, depending on the particular leaders or elite groups that happen to be of interest. Different research methods may be employed for using materials that are already available and, when opportunities permit, for acquiring new data more systematically. Data relevant to the operational code may be obtained from various kinds of content analysis — both via qualitative analysis of texts (as in Leites' study) or more rigorous quantitative analysis (as by Professor Ole Holsti in his study of John

Foster Dulles' image of the Soviet opponent).[50] Similarly, when interviewing is possible, several variants of open-ended, in-depth, or structured interview techniques might be employed. Useful data and inferences on these matters are likely to be obtained also by those who have opportunities to engage in "participant observation," whether as researchers, political journalists, or political participants. Finally, inferences about various aspects of an actor's operational code are possible from case studies of his behavior in particular situations.[51]

50. Ole Holsti, "Cognitive Dynamics and Images of the Enemy," in D. J. Finlay, O. R. Holsti, and R. R. Fagen, *Enemies in Politics* (Chicago: Rand McNally, 1967).

51. For example, Arnold Horelick, "The Cuban Missile Crisis: Analysis of Soviet Calculations and Behavior" (see Chapter 21 below).

ELEVEN

RITA M. KELLY AND
FREDERIC J. FLERON, JR.

Personality, Behavior,
and Communist Ideology*

Ever since Western scholars have been trying to analyze the political behavior
of Communist leaders, they have felt compelled to present some answer to the
question: in what ways does the official ideological system affect the actions
and decisions of these leaders? After fifty years of Communist rule in the Soviet
Union, however, there is no one consistent answer. Confusion and contradiction still reign.[1] In the literature on the subject one finds that the position a
scholar takes is very often related to his particular field of specialization. For
example, if one has an anthropological or psychoanalytic bent, then one tends
to follow the point of view advocated by Dicks and Leites. The ideology fulfills
important functions for the maintenance of the leader's ego and, hence, the
official ideology is a strong, dominant motivating force, not easily subject to

*This chapter is an expanded version of an article which appeared under the same title
in *Soviet Studies,* XXI, 3 (January, 1970), pp. 297 – 313. Reprinted by permission of the authors
and the publisher. Copyright © 1970 by Rita M. Kelly and Frederic J. Fleron, Jr.
    1. The best summary of the many different theories which attempt to interpret and explain
what determines Soviet political behavior is still Daniel Bell's "Ten Theories in Search of Reality:
The Prediction of Soviet Behavior," *World Politics,* X, 3 (April, 1958), pp. 327 – 365. Cf. William
Glaser, "Theories of Soviet Foreign Policy: A Classification of the Literature," *World Affairs
Quarterly,* XXVII, 2 (July, 1956). A collection of articles which quickly illustrates that the debate
has ranged from a complete denial of any motivational impact of ideology to views verging toward
ideological determinism is the Hunt-Sharp-Lowenthal symposium reprinted above from *Problems
of Communism.*

change.[2] Political scientists, although they vary considerably, tend to take a more pragmatic and cynical point of view. Avid Kremlinologists generally discount the official ideology as a major motivating force and concentrate on "who is doing-in whom." To many of them ideology is almost entirely a polemical and political weapon or a useful opium for the masses.[3] A geopolitical theorist tends to claim that traditional national and strategic interests constitute the main motivating force for behavior. Ideology is only added verbiage justifying what the leaders would do in any case.[4] Historians emphasize the similarity between contemporary behavior and the traditional Slavic character and institutions, saying the latter determine most of Soviet behavioral patterns.[5] The social psychologists and sociologists seem to take a more intermediate position, i.e., ideology is sometimes only a polemical tool and at other times a major determinant of how the Soviets think and act.[6]

Rigid compartmentalization of inquiry, whether by academic discipline or geographic area, greatly hampers the construction of empirical theory. Without such theory, we are unable either to explain or to predict phenomena.

2. See Henry V. Dicks, "Observations on Contemporary Russian Behavior," *Human Relations*, V, 2 (1952), pp. 111 – 175, and Nathan Leites, *A Study of Bolshevism* (Glencoe, Ill.: Free Press, 1953). Jan Triska, Zbigniew Brzezinski, and others have held similar positions, even though they are not anthropologists or psychoanalysts by training. See Triska's article, "A Model for Study of Soviet Foreign Policy," in *The American Political Science Review*, LII, 2 (March, 1958), pp. 64 – 83, and just about any of Brzezinski's articles and books.

3. Examples of Kremlinologists who seem to incline toward this view are Myron Rush, *The Rise of Khrushchev* (Washington, D. C.: Public Affairs Press, 1958), and R. Conquest, *Power and Policy in the USSR: The Study of Soviet Dynasties* (New York: St. Martin's Press, 1961). Cf. also Conquest, *The Politics of Ideas in the USSR* (New York: Praeger, 1967).

4. The clearest spokesman for the position has been Samuel Sharp. See "National Interest: Key to Soviet Politics," Chapter 7 above. Barrington Moore, Jr., in "The Relations of Ideology and Foreign Policy," *Soviet Politics: The Dilemma of Power* (Cambridge: Harvard University Press, 1950), takes a similar but more qualified position. While the ideology did not force the Soviet Union to join or abandon any alliance that it would not have joined or abandoned simply on the basis of national interest, in some cases it slowed or speeded up the process.

5. Scholars who have represented this group include Nicholas Berdyaev, Sir Bernard Pares, Sir John Maynard, Edward Crankshaw, Ernest Simmons, and Cyril E. Black. A good but brief illustration of how present-day historians tend to view the problem is found in Black, "The Modernization of Russian Society," *The Transformation of Russian Society* (Cambridge: Harvard University Press, 1960), pp. 661 – 680.

6. See Raymond A. Bauer, Alex Inkeles, and Clyde Kluckhohn, *How the Soviet System Works* (Cambridge: Harvard University Press, 1956), pp. 29 – 35. Though sociologists tend to be more moderate in the positions they hold with regard to how ideology influences political behavior, a great deal of diversity exists about the question of how ideology influences scientists. For a view which asserts that science and ideology are bound to oppose each other, see Bell's "The End of Ideology in the Soviet Union?" in Milorad M. Drachkovitch (ed.), *Marxist Ideology in the Contemporary World* (New York: Praeger, 1966), pp. 76 – 112. For the opposite position see George Fischer's article "Sociology," in George Fischer (ed.), *Science and Ideology in Soviet Society* (New York: Atherton Press, 1967). Those interested in this issue of how science and ideology are related should also consult David Joravsky, "Soviet Ideology," *Soviet Studies*, XVIII, 1 (July, 1966), pp. 2 – 19; "Ideology, Science and the Party," *Problems of Communism*, XVI, 1 (January-February, 1967), pp. 67 – 75; *The Lysenko Affair* (Cambridge: Harvard University Press, 1970).

Previous discussions of the motivational role of ideology in Communist systems illustrate some of the factors contributing to such an outcome. The question of the relationship between Communist ideology and Communist behavior has been discussed in isolation from more general empirical theory. Most students of Communist ideology and behavior have tended to view the relationship between *Communist* thought and action as a unique problem.[7] However, any discussion of the motivational role of *Communist* ideology is merely part of the more general question of the motivational role of ideology in determining or at least influencing behavior in any political system. Therefore, research done on the more general question must be relevant to the specific question.

But there has been felt, in the United States in particular, a special urgency about answering the question of what behavioral consequences the Communist ideology has. This demand for immediate answers has contributed to a tendency to proceed to generalizations about Communist ideology after examining only the available empirical data on Communist systems, and without undertaking the more arduous (but certainly more fruitful) task of studying the motivational role of Communist ideology in the context of general empirical theory. The pronounced policy science orientation of Communist studies in the United States has had serious effects on both the questions asked about ideology in Communist systems and the answers given to those questions. The position taken seems to be: "If we are to be relevant as Soviet or Communist 'experts,' we have to be able to give some immediate answer concerning the motivational role of ideology in Communist systems because, whatever the answer, it has critical implications for U.S. policy decisions." For one reason or another, Communist ideology is viewed as a relevant variable in this context and must be taken into account by American policy-makers. So every Communist "specialist" has an answer to this vital question of the motivational role of Communist ideology and seeks to justify it usually by pointing to certain actions in the past which conformed to his interpretation of the motivational role of Communist ideology. Most frequently these interpretations have been based on very scanty, impressionistic data. Relatively few attempts have been made to apply our rich variety of reliable contemporary research techniques to systematically collected data. The frequently heard argument is that the research methods and techniques of modern social and behavioral science cannot be systematically applied to the study of Communist systems because we do not have open access to those systems. Although this is often true, there are many areas which have been left unexplored despite the availability of techniques which would permit us to analyze available data relevant to the

---

7. . For example, see P. B. Reddaway, "Aspects of Ideological Belief in the Soviet Union," *Soviet Studies,* XVII, 4 (April, 1966), p. 472.

testing of basic propositions from empirical theory. The recent study by Triska and Finley is an excellent example of innovation in this regard.[8]

What follows is based on our conviction that scarcity of data concerning relevant variables does not justify sloppy methodology or exclusion of relevant variables. Inaccessibility of data is a frustrating problem, but it is a pragmatic, technical one. It is not a legitimate excuse for lowering standards for the evaluation of empirical research. Further, the absence of available data on relevant variables does not make those variables any less relevant; it merely means that we ought to be more cautious in our conclusions and more re-strained in our prognostications to policy-makers. The purpose of this chapter is to discuss some variables which psychological theory suggests are relevant to the relationship between ideology and behavior, but which have been gener-ally absent in previous discussions of the motivational impact of Communist ideology on Communist behavior.

Problems of Conceptualization

Unfortunately, as Nathan Glazer has observed, one of the pressing conceptual problems of social psychology is that "no study of the relation between atti-tudes and personality has yet . . . solved the problem of distinguishing ideology — the views one picks up — from character — the orientations that are basic to a person.[9] This statement refers to the fact that very few individuals in a society will have a belief and value system that coincides exactly with that of the official ideological system, and that many of the variables relating to why such a divergence exists involve the specific personality traits and personality processes of each individual. Although the conceptual problem is still not satisfactorily resolved in the eyes of most psychologists, progress has been made in establishing a framework for what variables and distinctions must be considered in attempts to relate a formal ideology to an individual's or a group's ideology.

In an attempt to clarify the relationship of an ideological system to an individual, Milton Rokeach introduced the concept of "belief-disbelief sys-tem." In his discussion of this concept he points out that as the term "belief-disbelief system" is applied to individuals and to groups, it necessarily must include "*all* of a person's beliefs and therefore is meant to be more inclusive than what is normally meant by ideology. Ideology refers to a more or less institutionalized set of beliefs — 'The beliefs someone picks up.' Belief-disbelief systems contain these too but, in addition, they contain highly personalized pre-ideological beliefs."[10]

8. Jan F. Triska and David D. Finley, *Soviet Foreign Policy* (New York: Macmillan, 1968).
9. Nathan Glazer, "New Light on the Authoritarian Personality," *Commentary*, XVII (March, 1954), p. 293.
10. Milton Rokeach, *The Open and Closed Mind* (New York: Basic Books, 1960), p. 35. For

Since ideological beliefs constitute much less than the total belief-disbelief system of an individual or a group, it obviously is grossly insufficient to study only the content and structure of the ideological system when one is looking for determinants of human behavior. One must first and foremost look at the content and structure of the individual's entire belief system.

When looking at the belief system of an individual or group, one must be as concerned about the various content levels within that belief system. One way the former distinctions can be made is by presenting a broad definition of beliefs that allows the notion of hierarchy to be built into it. One group of scholars has proposed that beliefs be generally defined as follows: beliefs "are existential propositions held by individual human beings regarding the structure and operation of the social and physical universe and one's place in it. . ." They are "vectors which bear upon an individual as he confronts a choice of conduct." Within the context of this broad definition, they suggest that four distinctions be made:

1. *Cognitive Standards:* the existential propositions which serve as criteria to establish the validity and/or the applicability of information and are not themselves subject to ultimate verification.

2. *Appreciative Standards:* existential propositions which serve as criteria to evaluate the potential results of an act particularly in reference to its gratificatory significance.

3. *Knowledge:* an existential proposition than an individual accepts as established fact which is subject to further empirical verification.

4. *Power:* an existential proposition regarding man's perception of his relative capacity to influence and/or control the structure and operation of the social and physical world.[11]

These four subdefinitions of beliefs are given because they provide not only useful distinctions for the study of belief-disbelief systems in general (and of Communist ideologies in particular) but also because they introduce the notion of content hierarchy within belief systems. An examination of the four subdefinitions should suggest, for example, that those elements of a belief system or ideology that fall in the categories of (4) *Power* and (3) *Knowledge* would be much more susceptible to change through scientific discovery and changing circumstances over time than (1) *Cognitive Standards* and (2) *Appreciative Standards.* It is also a feasible and testable hypothesis that Appreciative

a more recent discussion of the relationship between ideology and belief systems, see Samuel H. Barnes, "Ideology and the Organization of Conflict: On the Relationship between Political Thought and Behavior," *Journal of Politics,* XXVIII, 3 (August, 1966), pp. 513–530.

11. Philip E. Jacob and James J. Flink, "Values and Their Function in Decision-Making," *The American Behavioral Scientist,* V, Supplement No. 9 (May, 1962), p. 23.

Standards will change before Cognitive Standards will change. Hence, if one could identify in either an individual's or a group's belief system (or in the Marxian ideological system) those aspects which would fall in which of the above categories, then one could proceed to the formulation and testing of hypotheses regarding them. In addition, one could hypothesize which elements of the belief system in Marxian ideology are set for individuals and groups by *(a)* the socialization process during childhood, *(b)* educational and higher vocational training, *(c)* indoctrination of Party doctrine, *(d)* the role individuals perform in society, or *(e)* any other variable considered relevant. As will be shown below, all these variables plus many others help to determine what an individual's, or a group's, or a nation's operative ideology will be.

Once the distinctions in terms of content are understood, one can further try to determine the consistency with which an individual holds specific beliefs at each structural level of the belief-disbelief system. This endeavor can be accomplished by evaluating whether that belief fits into the structure of the individual's belief system at (1) the specific opinionation level, (2) the habitual opinionation level, (3) the attitudinal level, or (4) the ideological level. If beliefs are held at the specific opinionation level, it means that they "are not related in any way to other opinions, . . . are not in any way characteristic of a person who makes them, . . . and are not reproducible in the sense that if the same or a similar question were asked again under different circumstances, the answer might be different."[12] In other words, such opinions would not be very likely to influence behavior. If they did, they would do so in a random, inconsistent fashion.

The chief characteristic of habitual opinions is that they are reproducible and "form a relatively constant part of an individual's make-up. In other words these are opinions which are voiced in the same or a similar manner on different occasions, and which are not subject to sudden arbitrary changes, such as are opinions at the lowest level."[13] At the more general attitudinal level, "we find not only that an individual holds a particular opinion with regard to a particular issue with a certain degree of stability; we also find that he holds concurrently a large number of other opinions on the same issue which in combination define his attitude towards that issue."[14]

Finally, at the most general level are found "ideologies" which Eysenck defines as clusterings of attitudes. Beliefs held at these latter three levels are quite likely to influence behavior, with those at the "ideological" level being the most likely to do so. The higher the level the greater value the individual places on the belief and the larger is his vested interest in the belief.

    12. H. J. Eysenck, *The Psychology of Politics* (London: Routledge & Kegan Paul, 1954), p. 111.
    13. *Ibid.,* pp. 111–112.
    14. *Ibid.,* p. 112.

Although Eysenck's use of the ubiquitous and ambiguous word "ideologies" is unfortunate in the above context, it should not blur the rather obvious point that is being made, which is: no individual can or does hold all beliefs with equal strengths and no person can simultaneously and consistently act on all his beliefs. Specific circumstances, his own physical and mental limitations and those of the system in which he operates, simply make this impossible. Moreover, some beliefs become more internalized and habitual than others, and some are held more dogmatically than others. In terms of trying to answer questions regarding which beliefs are operative and which are most susceptible to change, attention must be directed to this problem of how beliefs are held and structured.

Sources of Personal Ideology

The map on the following pages, created by M. Brewster Smith,[15] provides a paradigm for viewing the many different general classes of variables which can influence personal behavior in general and political behavior in particular. As this map shows, three out of the five broad classes of variables involve variables from the social environment, most of which cannot be controlled by the individual. The least controllable class of variables by far is that involving the distal social antecedents such as the prior history of one's country before one was born and while one was growing up, its existing economic and political system, and other broad social determinants such as the existence of a formal, established ideological system like Marxism-Leninism-Stalinism. All of these "givens" can affect the motivating forces of an individual, but the extent to which they either can or will do so is largely determined by the variables listed under II, i.e., the more immediate social environment as it affects an individual as he is reared, educated, and socialized into the society and its culture.

It is obvious from the vast literature on socialization that the socio-economic status of an individual's family will, in part, determine how a child or even an adult will perceive objective reality.[16] It more often than not will partly determine his opportunities for educational and occupational training which,

15. A discussion of the main sections of this map and their connections can be found in M. Brewster Smith, "A Map for the Analysis of Personality and Politics," *Journal of Social Issues,* XXIV, 3 (July, 1968), pp. 15 – 28. An expanded version of this article appears as "Personality in Politics: A Conceptual Map with Application to the Problem of Political Rationality," in Oliver Garceau (ed.), *Political Research and Political Theory: Essays in Honor of V. O. Key, Jr.* (Cambridge: Harvard University Press, 1968), pp. 77 – 101, reprinted in M. Brewster Smith, *Social Psychology and Human Values* (Chicago: Aldine Publishing Co., 1969). The other essays in the above issue of *The Journal of Social Issues* are relevant to the present discussion, especially the introductory essay by Fred I. Greenstein, "The Need for Systematic Inquiry into Personality and Politics: Introduction and Overview," pp. 1 – 14. Cf. also Fred I. Greenstein, *Personality and Politics: Problems of Evidence, Inference, and Conceptualization* (Chicago: Markham Publishing Co., 1969), esp. chapter 2.
16. Two good studies of political socialization are: Herbert H. Hyman, *Political Socialization:*

in turn, will also help to determine how much, and what forms of, the official, formal ideology he (or she) will be exposed to. Obviously, exposure to the formal ideology is a prerequisite to its becoming any sort of a motivational force in behavior. It is true, of course, that most Soviet children are exposed to at least the essential elements of the formal ideology through the school system, the Octobrists, the Pioneers, and the Komsomol organization, but even this exposure does not guarantee that the belief and value systems of the formal ideology will be internalized by the individuals receiving that exposure. It is always possible, and quite likely, that the other socialization experiences and interactions with one's fellow human beings will lead one to internalize and, as an adult, act upon a belief quite different from the one formally taught. For example, while the national or Party ideology may assume that human beings are basically good and perfectable, an individual's early childhood and adult experiences may lead him to believe otherwise. As an adult, he may find it politically necessary and expedient to affirm the official ideological position, but in his decision-making and behavior he will be motivated by his belief based on experience rather than by the stated ideological position.[17]

Figure 1. General Schematic Map*

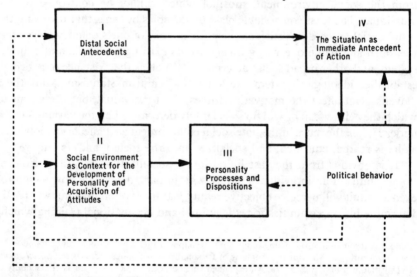

*Adapted from M. Brewster Smith, "A Map for the Analysis of Personality and Politics," *The Journal of Social Issues,* XXIV, 3 (July, 1968), 17. Reprinted by permission of the author and publisher.

A Study in the Psychology of Political Behavior (New York: The Free Press, 1959), and Fred I. Greenstein, *Children and Politics* (New Haven: Yale University Press, 1965).

17. Philip Worchel in "Social Ideology and Reactions to International Events," *Journal of Conflict Resolution,* XI, 4 (December, 1967), pp. 414–431, found, for example, that the ideological orientation toward others that a person develops through the socialization process is definitely related to the way one reacts toward alternative resolutions of international conflict situations.

Figure 2. Detailed Schematic Map*

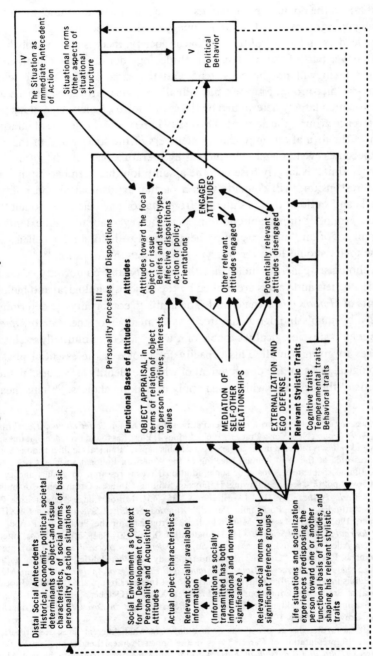

*Adapted from M. Brewster Smith, "A Map for the Analysis of Personality and Politics," *The Journal of Social Issues*, XXIV, 3 (July 1968), p. 25. Reprinted by permission of the author and publisher.

When one considers not only the socio-economic diversity of families and individuals in the Soviet Union, but also its vast numbers of ethnic, linguistic, and religious groups and traditions, one sees that, even among those who become leaders and a part of the elite in the society, there is a high probability that whatever part of the written, formal ideology does become a motivating force for them will not be consistent, and the same applies to the whole decision-making group. Since an individual's personal attitudes, beliefs, and values are often largely determined by the social norms, beliefs, etc., of his peer and reference groups, the amount of diversity in terms of the degree of internalization of the formal ideology among members of the society and of the elite group becomes even greater. The increasing literature on "interest groups" in the Soviet Union is largely based on the assumption that membership in such an "interest group" will coincide with a particular ideological and political emphasis and outlook that is different from that of one belonging to another "interest group."[18] Important questions here, however, are to what extent can the members of an "interest group" be expected to hold similar beliefs, and what scholars should look for in trying to answer this question.[19]

Psychologists generally hold that the diversity and conformity of an individual's beliefs and values are limited by the basic psychological and biological limits of *Homo sapiens* in general. The limits to conformity are determined basically by man's biological nature. "As a member of the *Homo sapiens* species man is physiologically capable of a wide variety of mutually exclusive responses to given stimuli. This capacity for choice is the essential physio-psychological basis for the development of what we identify as 'values,' namely standards of the desirable which men apply in making choices."[20] This means

---

18. See, for example, the work of Roger Pethybridge, *A Key to Soviet Politics: The Crisis of the Anti-Party Group* (New York: Praeger, 1962). Sidney I. Ploss has found evidence that this split in beliefs and values is reflected in the Soviet press. See his paper, "Political Conflict and the Soviet Press," presented at the 1964 Annual Meeting of the American Political Science Association, Chicago, Illinois, September 1964. For some additional recent research on groups and group values in Soviet politics, see the following: H. Gordon Skilling, "Interest Groups and Communist Politics," *World Politics,* XVIII, 3 (April, 1966), 435–451; Milton Lodge, "Soviet Elite Participatory Attitudes in the Post-Stalin Period," *American Political Science Review,* LXII, 3 (September, 1968), pp. 827–839; Milton Lodge, "'Groupism' in the Post-Stalin Period," in *Midwest Journal of Political Science,* XII, 3 (August, 1968), pp. 330–351; Sidney I. Ploss,"Interest Groups," in Allen Kassof (ed.) *Prospects for Soviet Society* (New York: Praeger, 1968), pp. 76–103; Michael P. Gehlen, "Group Theory and the Study of Soviet Politics," in Sidney I. Ploss (ed.), *The Soviet Political Process: Aims, Techniques, and Examples of Analysis* (Waltham, Mass.: Blaisdell Publishing Co., 1970); Philip D. Stewart, "Soviet Interest Groups and the Policy Process: The Repeal of Production Education," *World Politics,* XXII, 1 (October, 1969), pp. 29–50; H. Gordon Skilling and Franklyn Griffiths (eds.), *Interest Groups in Soviet Politics* (Princeton: Princeton University Press, 1971).

19. For a further discussion of this point along somewhat different lines, see Frederic J. Fleron, Jr., "Representation of Career Types in the Soviet Political Leadership," in R. Barry Farrell (ed.), *Political Leadership in Eastern Europe and the Soviet Union* (Chicago: Aldine Publishing Co., 1970), pp. 108–139.

20. Jacob and Flink, *op. cit.,* p. 13.

that the norms governing the responses of individuals or groups to given stimuli vary widely. Values and beliefs are not, in fact, universally shared phenomena. Individuals deviate from the norm. Moreover, since beliefs and values are learned and, hence, transmitted by one generation to another by socially agreed upon symbols, they are more likely to change than biological phenomena. Communicating an official, ideological system such as Marxism-Leninism-Stalinism can seldom be uniform and precise whether it be from one age group to another, from one occupational or elite group to another, or, as polycentrism has revealed, from one nation to another. In addition, whatever is internalized by the individual or the group is interpreted in terms of his or their own past experiences and is continually reevaluated and changed as a result of new experiences. Consequently, even within "interest groups," a good deal of diversity can and should be expected.

It is, nonetheless, generally true that a great many of the beliefs and values that influence decision-making are determined for an individual by the groups to which he belongs, for the limits of diversity in beliefs and values are of a psychological and sociological nature. Yet, simple membership in a group (including "an interest group") does not seem to be so significant a determination of an individual's beliefs and values as the specific roles he plays in the society. There are a great number of specialized roles in human societies which make individuals dependent and less than self-sufficient and autonomous.

Each of these specialized roles involves specific rights and obligations on the part of the person to whom they are assigned. These rights and obligations are expectancies held by the person playing the role which, if they are to be adequately filled, must be inculcated in the individual role player as moral imperatives in his socialization into the role. . . . Ultimately, most human norms, especially those which apply to public policy decisions, can be conceived as role expectancies and variations in "value" profiles can be understood as differences in role expectancies.[21]

What this means for students of Communist political systems is that less emphasis should probably be put on studies of "interest groups," defined as broad occupational groupings, and more emphasis should be placed on the types of roles individuals play within such groupings.[22] It also seems to indicate that if one really wants to know what importance ideology has in decision-making in the Soviet Union, one must identify and specify the role expectancies of individuals in various decision-making positions in the Soviet Union.[23] If existential propositions from the ideological belief system and normative

21. *Ibid,* p. 14. Cf. Seymour Lieberman, "The Effects of Changes in Roles on the Attitudes of Role Occupants," and Robert K. Merton, "Occupational Roles: Bureaucratic Structure and Personality," in Neil J. and William T. Smelser (eds.), *Personality and Social Systems* (New York: John Wiley & Sons, 1963), pp. 264–279 and 255–263, respectively.

22. For an excellent discussion related to this point, see John Wilson Lewis, "Chinese Communist Party Leadership and the Succession to Mao Tse-tung: An Appraisal of Tensions" (Washington, D.C.: U.S. Department of State, Bureau of Intelligence and Research, Policy Research Study, January 1964), esp. p. 2.

23. Cf. Erik P. Hoffmann, "Role Conflict and Ambiguity in the Communist Party of the

propositions from the ideology constitute an important and integral part of these role expectancies, then the chances are high that these role expectancies are those parts of the ideology that will influence political decision-making.

Ideology and Behavior

In political science, as well as in the field of Communist studies in particular, there is a great tendency to equate values and ideology with supposed purposes of actions or with different outcomes. Following in the tradition of Lasswell and Kaplan in *Power and Society,* [24] many scholars of Communist systems use what can be called a "motive-belief" type of explanation to link ideology, values, or belief systems to political behavior and decision-making. The logic of this type of explanation is something as follows: A desired event — or a goal event — often thought to be set by an ideology is said to be the motive or the cause for a certain action or series of actions. This is very often done when it can be found in a written statement that this or that is part of an action program or this or that is a stated goal and over a period of time this or that actually is fulfilled. In other words it is assumed that "if X values Y, it means that X acts so as to bring about the consumption of Y."[25] At worst, such types of explanation mean: "Y happened, therefore, X must have valued Y."

Unfortunately, the demonstration of such a causal relationship is not so easily accomplished. Psychologists have known for a long time that neither words nor actions are invariably accurate reflections of underlying beliefs, attitudes, or goals. A person's beliefs and attitudes prejudice an issue by determining his *set,* that is, his way of reacting to new facts and experiences. They become *mental habits* which, *if aroused,* determine actions. But since attitudes are intervening variables and must be measured indirectly, to assert that a particular attitude regarding a goal, object, or belief motivated a person, one must be able to link that attitude with his antecedent conditions and

---

Soviet Union," in Roger E. Kanet (ed.), *The Behavioral Revolution and Communist Studies: Applications of Behaviorally-Oriented Political Research on the Soviet Union and Eastern Europe* (New York: Free Press, 1971).

24. Harold Lasswell and Abraham Kaplan, *Power and Society* (New Haven: Yale University Press, 1950).

25. An example of the use of the motive-belief type of explanation in Soviet studies can be found in Myron Rush, *Political Succession in the USSR* (New York: Columbia University Press, 1965), p. 67, where he tries to explain why Khrushchev became the leader of the anti-Malenkov group in 1954-55. For an analysis and criticism of Rush's use of motive-belief explanation, see Frederic J. Fleron, Jr., "Soviet Area Studies and the Social Sciences: Some Methodological Problems in Communist Studies," *Soviet Studies,* XIX, 3 (January, 1968), pp. 336 – 337. (This article is reprinted in Frederic J. Fleron, Jr. [ed.], *Communist Studies and the Social Sciences: Essays on Methodology and Empirical Theory* [Chicago: Rand McNally,, 1969], pp. 1 – 33.) For a more detailed general discussion of motive-belief explanation, see Quentin Gibson, *The Logic of Social Enquiry* (London: Routledge & Kegan Paul, 1960), chapter 4.

consequent behavior. It is not sufficient to study just the verbal statements of attitudes or just the consequent behavior. One must analyze all of the above plus the need level and drives of the individual or of the individuals that compose a group.[26] It is known, for example, that two people can hold the same belief with the same degree of strength and intensity and still behave differently. Obviously, something besides "ideology" is involved even when an individual ostensibly acts as though "ideology is motivating" his behavior.

The use of this motive-belief type of explanation causes other problems as well. At the group level of analysis there is the very real problem of determining empirically whether or not a group actually believes that a stated or written goal, such as the withering away of the state, is an operative one, that is, that it is a goal actually desired and thought possible. If there is such a thing as a group goal, it can only be a composite of the goals of the individuals that constitute the group. It is true that one can speak of a goal as a property of the group without worrying in detail about its origins. However, before one can go further and assert that a particular stated goal is operative, one must determine the extent to which the group members do in fact accept the group goals.

This question of whether or not groups can have properties separate and distinct from the individuals who compose them is one to which scholars of Communist systems should pay more attention. When the issue involves evaluation of an official statement to the effect that the Communist Party represents the "will of the people," even though only one person is generally allowed to run for an office, Western scholars generally follow the principle of Methodological Individualism, that is, they assert the statement is false because there can be no such group characteristic as "will of the people" unless it can be demonstrated that each and every member of the electorate (the people) has had the opportunity to express this individual will in a truly democratic, secret election. In this context, the group property, "will of the people," is said to be dependent upon counting the different "wills" of each person and coming up with a majority. When the issue involves ideology, on the other hand, scholars often disregard the scientific principle of Methodological Individualism. In this context statements such as "the Party believes," or "the army took the position," or the "economic managers acted on the basis of," etc., are often made. Yet here the basic methodological issue is the same. The "will of the people" refers to the beliefs and values of individuals within a group. The operative beliefs and values of the Party, of the army, etc., also refer to the beliefs and values of individuals within these groups. Since all groups are composed of aggregates of individuals, the characteristics or properties of all groups must be dependent upon the characteristics and properties of the individuals who compose them. Hence, group concepts of the behavior

26. Eysenck, *op. cit.,* pp. 238 – 39.

of groups must refer to the complex patterns of descriptive, empirical relations among individuals.[27]

Whether or not the group as such actually has a particular goal or part of the belief system as an operative basis of reference or action will be a function of a number of things. To go back to Smith's map, it depends, first of all, upon how the individual mediates the "self-other" relationships within his own particular group and his perception of society, as well as his objective position, role, and function in society.

A second circumstance affecting whether or not a goal or belief will become operative for a group is the position of the group itself, its habitual pattern of behavior, and its roles and functions in society.[28] A good illustration of how these variables can mediate the possible impact upon a stated belief or goal is the decision-making situation of an economic manager in the Soviet Union. It has been often asserted that the main reason that the profit motive was not introduced into the Soviet economic system was the ideological belief in the superior value of the Marxian theory of surplus value. While historically this may well be true, it is largely irrelevant to a contemporary discussion of decision-making for most Soviet political and economic leaders. The decisions and responses of an economic manager, for example, would more likely be determined by the habit of conforming to "success indicators" and group norms for managers than they would be by any ideological belief or goal considerations. Even for the planning officials in Gosplan this ideological problem is not an immediate criterion for their decisions. Their goals have already been set for them. Until recently, the vast majority accepted these goals and the supposed rationale behind them without question.[29] The same was probably true even for the Politburo members. The ideological belief only became important for decision-making when economists such as Liberman demonstrated that it had to be questioned in order to enable the economy to perform efficiently, and provided an alternative to it. Once they had demonstrated that the Marxian theory of surplus value was not supported by facts at the knowledge level in the belief system, then the political question arose: do we or do we not accept these findings even though they disprove and reject some of our most basic ideological tenets? An important point must be noted here. Even at this point no part of the written content of the ideology per se becomes the criterion for decision-making! What happens is that some other criteria are used to accept or reject this element of Marxian ideology.

Other circumstances which help to determine whether or not a stated goal or belief will become operative for a group are: (1) the motives of each in-

27. May Brodbeck, "Methodological Individualism: Definition and Reduction," *Philosophy of Science*, XXV, 1 (January, 1958), pp. 1 – 22.

28. C. N. Cofer and M. H. Appley, *Motivation: Theory and Research* (New York: Wiley, 1963), pp. 779 – 780.

29. For important discussions of the variables related to density of doctrinal stereotypes, see Triska and Finley, *op. cit.,* pp. 119 – 127.

dividual for behavior in general; (2) each individual's judgment of the relative positive and negative weights for him of engaging in the activities necessary to achieve the group goal; (3) each individual's subjective estimate of the probability that a group goal can and will be achieved; (4) the clarity of the group goal; and (5) the amount of interdependency and cohesiveness of the group members.[30] Unmentioned still is perhaps the most important consideration — what motivated the individual to accept the goal (or belief) to begin with. An individual's motive for accepting the goal or belief will generally be as influential in determining whether or not it affects his political behavior as the actual goal or belief itself.[31]

Motivation

Psychologists generally assert that motivation for human behavior can be broken down into the following categories: (1) within the human organism itself there exist a variety of internal urges, whims, wishes, feelings, emotions, drives, instincts, wants, desires, demands, purposes, interests, aspirations, needs, and/or "motives"; (2) on the basis of interaction between the organism and its environment there develop incentives, goals, or object values which attract or repel the organism; and (3) there are strictly environmental determinants, e.g., the application of some irresistible force which of necessity leads to a particular response. Categorizing these types of motivation somewhat differently, one finds that some (emotion, force, drive, instinct, need) are at a biological level; others (urge, wish, feeling, impulse, want, striving, desire, demand) have significant "mental" import; and still others (purpose, interest, intention, attitude, aspiration, plan, motive, incentive, goal, value) require interaction with objects or states in the environment.[32] To satisfy any one of these items is, in a sense, to behave in a manner to fulfill a goal or, better, a "need." All are an inherent part of an individual's total personality; and all will at some time or another become the motivation or a part of the motivation for behavior, including political behavior. The question is: when?

One theory of motivation that has recently gained prominence in the discipline of political science is Abraham Maslow's theory of five main categories of human needs.[33] This theory of motivation, more than any other, makes a clear distinction among the different goals (or needs) of human beings and tackles directly the problem of when various needs are capable of motivating behavior. Hence, although the theory is not empirically proven, it does provide

---

30. Cofer and Appley, *op. cit.*, pp. 779–780.

31. Cf. Fred I. Greenstein, *Personality and Politics.*

32. For a good discussion of the different theories of motivation and the extent to which evidence exists to support them, see Cofer and Appley, *op. cit.*,

33. Abraham Maslow, "A Theory of Motivation," *Psychological Review,* L (1943), pp. 370 –396. The theory was applied to political behavior by James C. Davies in *Human Nature in Politics: The Dynamics of Political Behavior* (New York: Wiley, 1963).

a very useful model and aid for illustrating some of the basic issues involved in the study of motivation.

According to Maslow, all human beings have the following levels of needs: (1) individuals have basic *physical needs,* such as the need for food, water, and sex; (2) they also have *safety needs,* that is, a need for order, predictability, and dependability of their environment; (3) they have a *need for belonging,* which includes the need to be loved, to have affection, and friends; (4) they have a *need for self-esteem,* such as feeling equal to others; and (5) they have a *need for self-actualization,* i.e., a need to fulfill themselves. In Maslow's opinion, individuals pursue these five needs for their own sake throughout their lives. The needs are universal to the human organism regardless of the culture in which it lives or the ideology it is said to have embraced. In addition, these needs, which establish "goals" for an individual (consciously or unconsciously), are in a hierarchical arrangement. This notion of hierarchy means the following: until there is a substantial and relatively durable satisfaction of the physical needs, it will not be possible for the second level of needs, the safety needs, to emerge fully. Before the third level of needs, the need for belonging, can manifest itself as a strong force of motivation, the safety needs must be reasonably well met; and before the need for self-esteem can blossom forth, the need for belonging must be fairly well satisfied; and finally, before an individual can attain the highest level of motivation, which falls under the broad category of the need for self-actualization, all of the other four types of needs must be adequately fulfilled.

Maslow's hierarchical theory has many implications for the study of politics and the study of ideology. It helps one realize, for example, that neither politics nor any written, official ideological system necessarily performs any directly significant function in the fulfillment of the more basic needs. To satisfy their physical needs, the needs of belonging, and even basic safety needs, individuals usually turn to the local grocery store and to their family and friends. It is true that the political and economic system and the stage of development of a country will determine how well these needs can be met, but, nonetheless, whether one is a peasant in the Soviet Union or a member of the Politburo, the sources for fulfillment of these needs tend to be one's immediate family, circle of friends, and professional colleagues. In the words of Davies, "It is only when the achievement of these needs is threatened by individuals or groups too powerful to be dealt with privately that people turn to politics to secure their ends. Politics is generally only an indirect and instrumental means to the attainment of these ends. In other words, from a psychological point of view, politics is a form of exceptional, non-routine human behavior.[34] It might be added that in most political systems it would be even more exceptional and non-routine to find that a person's manner and motivation for fulfilling these lower needs were directly influenced by the official ideological system, for

34. Davies, *op. cit.,* p. 10.

when individuals do not have these basic needs met, they tend to withdraw not only from any concern from politics, but also from a formal system of ideology.

Maslow's theory implies (and research on various revolutions tends to support this implication) that extreme deprivation of either the physical or safety needs can and often will lead to depoliticization.[35] There are numerous examples in the history of the Soviet Union to support this contention. Bauer, for example, found that in the 1930's and 1940's the physical and safety needs of the Soviet populace were so severely unfulfilled that most of the people simply withdrew from politics, creating the illusion and, in fact, the reality that the Soviet political system was very stable. It was stable, to a very large extent, simply because the people withdrew from either supporting or opposing it. Marxian ideology and/or any correspondence or discrepancy between that ideology and the practices of the Party were, for all practical purposes, irrelevant to their actual political behavior.[36]

The same can be said for what happened in the Ukraine during Hitler's invasion. Initially the population's hostility to the Soviet system (at perhaps an ideological level) led them to greet the Nazi army joyously. When, however, they found that the Nazis were quite willing to starve and kill them, the Ukrainians chose to support the Soviet military and to fight Hitler. It does not appear that this was an ideological decision. It was a very basic human necessity of survival.

At the decision-making level these same hierarchical needs may apply. It is thought that most individuals who engage in politics have successfully attained the self-actualization level.[37] This means that the most common level of motivation for intense political participation is one in which the other needs have already been well met. In other words, as Davies argues, most political actors may enjoy intense political participation for its own sake and "not primarily because [they] thereby feed or protect [themselves] or because [they] can give socially acceptable vent to [their] aggressions, gain great deference, or bend people to [their] will."[38] While there are certainly exceptions to this generalization (and these will be discussed below), it seems reasonable to assume that many aspects of an ideological belief system can become operative only when the key decision-makers have attained this level. It is highly unlikely, for example, that any political leader will worry about implementing

---

35. The more empirical studies on revolution consistently show that revolutions based on the masses occurred only after a significant increase in economic development had prevailed for a number of years. The sudden drop in prosperity immediately prior to the revolutions, while perhaps a necessary condition for the occurrence of a revolution, did not constitute severe deprivation. Cf. Crane Brinton, *The Anatomy of Revolution* (New York: Vintage Books, 1952), and Raymond Tanter and Manus Midlarsky, "A Theory of Revolution," *Journal of Conflict Resolution,* XI, 3 (September, 1967), pp. 264 – 280.

36. Bauer, Inkeles, and Kluckhohn, *op. cit.*

37. Davies, *op. cit.*, p. 59.

38. *Ibid.*

immediately a stated ideological goal or tenet if he thinks his life, livelihood, or professional position is in danger (as seems often to have been the case in the Soviet Union, particularly during the various succession crises). It is also highly unlikely that a preference for one version of an ideological position will receive high consideration if a political actor feels his sense of belonging to the in-group and personal self-esteem are being threatened. Under these circumstances ideology is likely to become not a goal or criterion for behavior, but rather a tool, polemical or otherwise, to achieve a more basic human need.

What all this means is that before one can successfully analyze the function of ideology in decision-making, one probably must know not only the content of the ideology and the existing rules and norms of the political process in a system but also at what level of the human need hierarchy the political actors can act and are acting, because the criteria for making decisions and acting will vary according to these need levels. And to repeat, ideological goal considerations are highly unlikely to become criteria for decision-making until and unless political actors have most of their lower-level needs fairly well met and do not fear that they will suddenly no longer be so.

One very good illustration of how severe deprivation or the fear of such deprivation can lead even the most political members of a society to abandon considerations of principle and ideology in order to satisfy lower-level needs is found in the behavior of some of the victims of the Great Purge Trials in the 1930's in the Soviet Union. The individuals who were forced to confess to sins against Marxism, the Party, the government, and the state were severely deprived of the food, sleep, and any order or predictability regarding when they would be fed or allowed to rest, or how they would be treated. They were additionally deprived of any clear sense of belonging, even to a group of persecuted prisoners. Having been cut off from their families and persuasively told they were traitors to the system and to the society, they were further isolated from their fellow victims and allowed to learn of their welfare only from periodical screams and reports that the others had confessed to the alleged crimes. This severe deprivation along with a simultaneous severe lowering of their own feelings of self-esteem and dignity as human beings certainly reduced their physical and mental capability of being strongly motivated by any "orthodox" ideological considerations and, indeed, perhaps even higher-level ethical values. As Davies, in somewhat stronger terms, put it:

> At no time did they in any usual sense actually become social or political. They confessed their sins against society not so much because of a sense of social responsibility as to get sleep and bread. . . . In short, they had a stark, naked, physical need to survive, however hopeless, and to gain some sense of identity and worth, however contemptible.[39]

When these basic needs are not met, a human being ceases to be "political." If they are not ever adequately met, human beings will never become "poli-

39. *Ibid.*, p. 19.

tical." Although it is true that some of the lower-level human needs, such as the need for self-preservation, can become the main motivating force for political behavior and can obstruct the potential motivating force of an individual's basic beliefs and values, these needs usually are satisfied and play little or no motivating role in often mundane day-to-day political situations.

PERSONALITY PROCESSES AND MOTIVATION

At the lower left corner of III in Smith's map (Figure 2), under the heading "Externalization and Ego Defense," one finds, in a somewhat different form, an illustration of how the basic human needs elaborated by Maslow fit into a total motivational framework. Individuals have these needs. However, the manner in which specific individuals will try to cope with threats to the meeting of these needs will depend upon their previous life and personality development. Individuals who are more prone to be anxiety-ridden and to have more internal conflicts than others will probably have their belief and value systems as well as their political decisions determined, to a higher degree than other individuals, by their need to defend their ego rather than by the objective facts.[40] Beliefs and values for them would be more likely to fulfill the function of ego defense than the function of object appraisal. Such individuals may latch onto and subscribe to an ideological system because of these needs. They may also reject the formal ideology for the same reason. (It would be interesting to compare and analyze in these terms the members of *Agitprop* and the dissident writers and intellectuals in the Soviet Union. Basic personality needs and processes certainly must account for much of the divergence in beliefs, values, and behaviors. While it may be that members of these two groups differ substantially in their basic personality traits and the functions which their beliefs and values fulfill for their personality maintenance, it is equally possible that a similar proportion within each group are using, in different ways, the official ideological system as a means of justifying a particular manner of satisfying and defending needs and egos.)

The heading "Mediation of Self-Other Relationships" refers not only to the nature and type of interaction one has with others, but also to the need an individual has for identifying with and being similar to or different from one's peers and reference groups. The role this personality process can have in motivating political behavior should be fairly obvious. Individuals who have a need to conform or who have habituated themselves to conforming will be more likely to adopt as their own large segments of a formal and official ideological system than those who do not. Also, an intense dislike for a person or the converse, a strong liking for a person, could lead to either the rejection or the acceptance of a particular ideological point of view in a given situation.

Certainly one of the needs human beings have is the need to know and to

---

40. Nathan Leites' work, *A Study of Bolshevism*, is a detailed and elaborate application of this generalization to the Soviet leadership group.

feel that the beliefs they hold are based on the "truth." The personality process related to "Object Appraisal" refers to this need. Most individuals, including "Communist" ones, like to assert that they hold this or that belief or opinion because they have objectively analyzed a problem and on the basis of existing knowledge and experience have reached an objective conclusion regarding what means will lead to what ends. If an individual does hold a belief because of this motivation, however, it means only that that particular belief is not a function of his other needs, but rather the end product of what the individual perceives to be the objective situation based upon his previous experience and present knowledge. It does not necessarily mean that the belief held will be any more "operative," i.e., acted upon more consistently, than other beliefs which are held because they fulfill some other function for the maintenance and operation of the personality of the individual concerned.[41]

This point is important to note because when most scholars of Communist systems talk about ideology as a motivating force in decision-making, they do so largely in terms of what seems to them to be a means-end relationship among beliefs, values, and goals. To most scholars an aspect of the ideological system is considered to be "operative" when, ostensibly at least, the actors involved have made something of an objective appraisal of the situation and then take concrete political actions in terms of goal attainment or instrumental action which can be related to some element in the written ideological system. If such a relationship is observed often, it is argued that the political actors actually "believe" in the ideology. It is also sometimes argued that if the leaders act irrationally or inefficiently and a correspondence between this behavior and some element in the ideological system can be seen, then they also must "believe" in that ideological tenet. Hence, the question of objective appraisal is very important.

Apparently, it is thought that if and only if significant elements of the official ideology are held as either objective truths or attainable goals and values, the ideology or elements of it will be "operative" for an individual, group, or society. One of the crucial questions here is what is meant and perhaps what should be meant by the term "operative." If that term refers to the functions an official ideological system fulfills, then it should be obvious by now that an official ideology can and probably does fulfill quite different functions for individuals, groups, and indeed nations. While a specific decision-making body may act as though all or most of its members believe in a particular tenet or goal in one circumstance, it may well be that all or sections of the group are acting that way for quite different reasons. In another, ostensibly similar, situation, the majority of these individuals may take quite a different stand, giving the impression that this aspect of the ideology is not "operative." The reason for taking the different stand could have nothing to do with belief or lack of it in a particular ideological tenet or goal. It could simply mean, and probably often does mean, that in the new situation different motivating forces were at work and the strength of one force simply overrode another.

From this brief discussion of motivation it seems clear that one of the most important reasons for the existing controversy over the motivational role of the Communist official ideological system in political behavior is, indeed, the fact that the positions advocated by different scholars are based on limited methodologies and on limited views of what variables need to be considered. The anthropological and psychoanalytic schools tend to concentrate on character and ego development, which in turn leads them to emphasize temperamental and stylistic traits and ego defenses in the personality. In terms of Smith's map these variables concern primarily only small sections of I, II, and III. Kremlinologists tend to concentrate most on the variables relating to IV, the immediate situational context, and on intense conflict situations. In the past at least, intense conflict in the Soviet Union has often posed severe dangers to individuals and forced them to be concerned about protecting what Maslow would call their lower-level needs. Given this framework, it is not surprising that Kremlinologists are inclined to believe that ideology is primarily a polemical tool. Much the same can be said for the geopolitical theorists, only they tend to pay more attention to the distal social determinants (I) than the Kremlinologists do. The historians obviously study the distal social determinants most intensely. Since the ideological system is only one of numerous variables in this class of variables and historians do not, unless they are doing a study involving biographical data, usually concern themselves with personality dispositions and processes, it would be expected that they would stress the importance of non-ideological determinants of behavior. The social psychologists and sociologists, whose theoretical and methodological orientations encourage them to look to empirical theories of motivation, naturally take a more intermediate position, for as it has been demonstrated, motivation is extremely complex. What will be a strong motivating force in one context will not be in another. Until and unless scholars of Communist ideologies recognize this fact and also develop a methodological and theoretical orientation which will take into consideration all of the different aspects of the problem, progress will not be made. It is hoped that this paper will stimulate thought in the direction of developing such an orientation.

PART IV

Western Diplomacy, International Communism, and Soviet Foreign Policy: The Origins of the Cold War

This is the first of three sections on the influence of international politics on Soviet foreign policy. There is much disagreement about *whether* external factors significantly shape Soviet behavior, *which* factors exert influence under various circumstances, and *in what manner* they do so. "Traditional" historians contend that external factors had little effect on Soviet policies and actions during and immediately after World War II. "Revisionist" historians assert that external influences — especially American diplomacy — had a significant impact on Soviet behavior. The former emphasize the aggressive, inflexible, inexorable, inevitable nature of Soviet policies, especially in Eastern Europe; the latter stress the adaptive, responsive, reactive, flexible nature of Soviet policy, particularly Stalin's willingness to consider alternative courses of action and to negotiate certain crucial issues with his American and British allies. The chief implication of the former interpretation is that Soviet "expansionism" was the primary cause of the breakdown of Allied cooperation and the onset of the Cold War; the latter view concludes that unrealistic and sometimes truculent Western diplomacy (especially between 1945 and 1947) was a major cause of the Cold War in that it reduced policy alternatives open to Stalin and thus induced him to choose "hard-line" policies (for example, the satellization of *all* of Eastern Europe) he might not have chosen otherwise.

Thanks to Professor Graebner's review of the literature on the origins of the Cold War, these introductory notes can be brief. One of his major points is that there are various "orthodox" and "revisionist" interpretations; few analysts of either persuasion fully agree on the relative importance of key factors. A second significant observation is that a definitive analysis of Cold War origins is impossible without more information from *Russian* sources.

Evidence concerning Western intentions and behavior is more accessible, although subject to varying interpretations. In his famous "X" article, George F. Kennan unwittingly provided the rationale for more than two decades of American foreign policy. His language suggested that military "containment" of Russian "expansive tendencies" should be the cornerstone of American policy.[1] But Kennan and fellow members of the State Department's Policy Planning Staff did not in 1947 see any danger of Soviet military expansion into Western Europe. What they did consider a serious threat was that large Western European countries and major industrial centers might come under Soviet control by internal political changes — that is, by local Communist parties seizing power.

The military implications of the "containment" doctrine had a vastly greater impact on American foreign policy than did its political or ideological implications. As Kennan ruefully observed in his memoirs, a "serious deficiency of the X-Article — perhaps the most serious of all — was the failure to make clear that what I was talking about when I mentioned the containment of Soviet power was not the containment by military means of a military threat, but the political containment of a political threat."[2]

Professor Schlesinger, in his article below, presents a classic "traditional" or "orthodox" interpretation of the origins of the Cold War. He stresses three factors often de-emphasized or omitted in other assessments — "the intransigence of Leninist ideology, the sinister dynamics of a totalitarian society, and the madness of Stalin" — and concludes that "The Cold War could have been avoided only if the Soviet Union had not been possessed by convictions both of the infallibility of the communist word and of the inevitability of a communist world."

Professors Williams and Lasch, in contrast, present "revisionist" viewpoints. Directly addressing himself to Schlesinger, Williams sharply criticizes the view that Stalin's paranoia was "a primary operational factor" in the genesis of the Cold War. Even if Stalin had been paranoid, Williams contends, other factors would be equally crucial to an accurate historical explanation of the Cold War's origins. For example, he observes that no major American policy-maker in the mid-1940's seems to have perceived Stalin's paranoia and acted on this belief — in other words, United States' policies and counterresponses were not adapted accordingly. Had flexible American initiatives failed

1. X (George F. Kennan), "The Sources of Soviet Conduct," *Foreign Affairs,* XXV, 4 (July, 1947), pp. 566 – 582.
2. George F. Kennan, *Memoirs: 1925 – 1950* (Boston: Atlantic-Little, Brown, 1967), p. 358.

because of Stalin's intransigence, this might well constitute indirect evidence of Stalin's "madness." But Williams concludes that Stalin was not intransigent and, considering American policies, Soviet actions cannot be accurately described as paranoid.

Lasch is particularly critical of the view that misunderstandings, misperceptions, and "communication problems" were major factors contributing to the inception and escalation of the Cold War. Russian leaders probably understood Western policies very well and had good reason to consider them hostile, Lasch implies. Indeed, revisionists argue that the primary goal of American policy in 1945 was "to force the Soviet Union out of Eastern Europe," and Lasch would very likely contend that this view gains considerable credence in light of Allied decisions at Teheran (November–December, 1943), the Moscow "percentages" agreement (October, 1944), the Allied armistice agreements with Rumania, Bulgaria, and Hungary (September, 1944–January, 1945), and the decisions, "nondecisions," and unresolved issues at Yalta (February, 1945) and Potsdam (July-August, 1945).

To the "orthodox" observer, the famous Yalta "Declaration on Liberated Europe" was a major Allied policy agreement that the Soviet Union repeatedly violated in subsequent months and years; to the "revisionist," this document was merely rhetoric intended for domestic consumption in the democracies, a statement whose real purpose was to mask previous explicit and implicit agreements regarding separate Allied "spheres of influence" in Western and Eastern Europe. Revisionist historians dare suggest that the American decisions to drop atomic bombs on Japan may have been a show of force primarily intended to dislodge the Red Army from Eastern Europe and to renege on previous Allied agreements. Orthodox historians retort that this argument stands or falls on the crucial assumption that there *was* in fact "atomic diplomacy," and that no convincing evidence has been produced to confirm this because no such bargaining or threats took place.[3]

Professor Starobin's article is an important contribution because it emphasizes one factor — international Communism — virtually ignored in previous explanations of Cold War origins. Starobin describes the real and "incipient" diversity in the nonruling Communist parties, "among whom the changes produced by the war had outmoded earlier ideological and political premises," and he notes the apparent indecisiveness of Soviet policy toward this "nascent polycentrism" as late as 1947. Starobin argues that probably the most important single factor shaping Soviet foreign policy was Stalin's wish to unify and

3. Adam Ulam, "Re-reading the Cold War," *Interplay,* II, 8 (March, 1969), pp. 51–53. Cf. Gabriel Kolko, *The Politics of War: The World and United States Foreign Policy, 1943–1945* (New York: Random House, 1968); Barton Bernstein and Allen Matusow (eds.), *The Truman Administration: A Documentary History* (New York: Harper & Row, 1966); and the references listed by Graebner at the end of his article (especially Gar Alperovitz, *Atomic Diplomacy,* and Herbert Feis, *The Atomic Bomb and the End of World War II*).

control the international Communist movement. To do this, the Soviet leader could hardly create close economic and political ties with the major "imperialist" and "colonial" states, or accept greater ideological and institutional diversity within the USSR. All of these considerations were interrelated, and in many ways the policies chosen were logically consistent with one another. Each of these factors may well have contributed to Stalin's eventual decision to reconstruct the shattered Soviet economy in the time-tested autarkic manner, with assistance from the new satellite regimes in Eastern Europe, rather than await possible (but improbable) large-scale American assistance or German reparations.

In short, the implications of the Starobin argument are that American "hard-line" policies under President Truman may have made Stalin's basic decisions somewhat easier, but that Western diplomacy and actions were probably not the decisive factor in shaping Soviet policy. Cooperation with the United States, "different roads to socialism" in the world Communist movement and in Eastern Europe, greater internal diversity at home — all were new and untried paths. In time of war, these paths were worth exploring, and some had to be explored. In time of peace, old policies were less risky and probably more in line with Stalin's personal goals and those of other Soviet leaders. Above all, the Red Army remained in Eastern Europe, which it had occupied before the end of the war by virtue of its military victories over Nazi Germany and by explicit agreements with the other Allied powers. James F. Byrnes touched on a crucial issue when he said of Yalta, "It was not a question of what we would *let* the Russians do, but what we could *get* the Russians to do."[4]

What is the Cold War? How did it originate? What were its consequences? Was it avoidable? Why condemn it? Has it ended? These are among the important questions analyzed from various points of view in the next two sections.

---

4. Quoted in John Bagguly, "The World War and the Cold War," in David Horowitz (ed.) *Containment and Revolution* (Boston: Beacon Press, 1967), p. 110. For an important new study of Yalta, see Diane S. Clemens, *Yalta* (New York: Oxford University Press, 1970).

Cold War Origins and the Continuing
Debate: A Review of the Literature*

More than twenty years have passed since scholars and journalists began their examination of the Cold War to explain its existence. Despite the ensuing flood of literature, much of it excellent by any standards, the Cold War remains the most enigmatic and elusive international conflict of modern times. Writers differ in their judgments of causation and responsibility in 1968 as greatly as they did when the examination began; twenty years of scholarship have produced no consensus. Nor are those who have committed themselves along the way inclined to alter their assumptions and conclusions. The record of national behavior has been clear enough. But beyond the recognition of day-to-day events the quest for meaning leads to a realm of secrecy and confusion where national purposes and individual motivations are reduced to conjecture. This absence of certainty encourages many who are attracted to the Cold War, as actors and students, to hold fast to established intellectual preferences. It is not strange that scholars, editors, politicians, and statesmen choose to disagree. And the resolution of the quarrel is nowhere in sight.

Since 1945 the great confrontation between the United States and the USSR has been the central fact of international life, perhaps no less so than the Brit-

*Reprinted from *The Journal of Conflict Resolution,* XIII, 1 (March, 1969), pp. 123 – 132, by permission of the author and the publisher. Copyright © 1969 by The University of Michigan.

ish – French struggle for world leadership in the Second Hundred Years' War. But any historic conflict between two giants, always diplomatically unsettling and potentially disastrous, would of necessity separate those who view such struggles as fundamental, even inevitable, from those who prefer to dwell on the immediate issues and the possibilities of their avoidance or solution. Those who accept the Cold War as an historic confrontation which always pits any two nations, recently elevated to prominence, in a struggle for power can find respectability for their view in the prophecies of Alexis de Tocqueville. This French traveler wrote over a century ago that one day the United States and Russia would each sway the destinies of half the globe; and it is doubtful that the two nations could have reached such positions of primacy except as rivals. If the struggle for power and prestige between the United States and the USSR is the logical product of modern history, its significance far transcends what is known as the Cold War. Those who interpret the Cold War as an imperial struggle might, as does Desmond Donnelly (1965), find its inception in the British – Russian conflict across Central Asia in the nineteenth century. Or, according to Walter LaFeber (1967), the historian might find the origins in the Russo – American rivalry over Manchuria at the turn of the century.

Those who attribute the Cold War to ideology — be it the Soviet-based doctrines of Communist expansion and revolution or the anti-Soviet attitudes which such doctrines produced — discover the origins of the Cold War in the Second Russian Revolution of 1917. John F. O'Conor (1961), who attributes the Cold War to Soviet expansionism, began his study of origins with the murder of the Romanov family in July, 1918. Similarly André Fontaine, in his more recent *History of the Cold War, 1917–1950* (1967), attributes Soviet aggressiveness to Communist ideology which, he believes might have been uprooted by a more concerted military effort against the Red Army in 1918 and 1919. For Frederick L. Schuman (1962) and D. F. Fleming (1961), two critics of American policies, the Cold War indeed began in 1918, not in any Bolshevik declaration of ideological warfare against the West, but in the Western invasion of Russia and the international ostracism of the Bolshevik regime which followed.

Still, most students of the Cold War find its origins in the events of the Second World War. If to some degree the Great War of 1914 was the cause of the Second, many historians would consider it even truer that the Second World War produced the Cold War. On April 25, 1945, Russian and American forces met along the Elbe in the middle of Europe. "This symbolic event," John Lukacs has written (1962, p. 3), "marks the supreme condition of contemporary history. . . . That supreme condition is not the Atomic Bomb and not Communism; it is the division of Germany and of most of Europe into American and Russian spheres of influence. The so-called cold war grew out of this division." Even those writers who find the Soviet – American confrontation more thoroughly grounded in history agree that the struggle entered a new stage of intensity with the rise of Russia to predominance on the European continent after the battle of Stalingrad.

Russia's penetration of Europe to the Elbe in April 1945 upset Western calculations on two fronts. Germany's total destruction, the high purpose of Allied wartime policy, had permitted the Red Army to challenge the traditional European balance of power. Second, Russia's military dominance of Slavic Europe, the result not of aggression but of victory, gave the Soviets the power, if not the intention, to impose their will on the states of eastern Europe. What is more, Stalin had made clear throughout the war years that Russia would interfere in the postwar politics of Slavic Europe to the extent of insuring pro-Soviet governments along Russia's western periphery. Thus the Kremlin gave the United States and Britain the ultimate choice of recognizing Soviet political and strategic interests in eastern Europe or accepting the postwar disintegration of the Grand Alliance as the price of clinging to their principles of self-determination. It is in these Soviet demands and their fundamental rejection by the Western world that such writers as Herbert Feis (1957), William H. McNeill (1953), Martin F. Herz (1966), Norman A. Graebner (1962), and even Frederick L. Schuman (1962) find the origins of the Cold War.

Was this giant political and military confrontation across Europe in 1945 avoidable? Did it result from unacceptable Soviet behavior or from the West's refusal to recognize the results of its neglect of eastern and central Europe during the months following Munich? Were military strategies available to the Western allies which might have disposed of Nazi power without placing Slavic Europe under direct Soviet control? Or was the division of Europe the necessary price of victory? Judgments on such questions are crucial to any interpretation of the Cold War. Despite their complexities, those judgments are basically three. Those who are concerned less with Soviet power than with Soviet behavior quite logically place the burden of wartime and postwar disagreement on the Soviet Union. Schuman, on the other hand, recalls that Munich gave Hitler a free hand in eastern Europe and permitted him to invade Russia in June 1941 with ample preparation and on his own terms. The West, in abdicating its responsibilities in 1938, concludes Schuman, had no right, after 20,000,000 Russian deaths, to demand equal rights in liberated Europe seven years later. Placing his emphasis on the realities of a divided Europe, Louis B. Halle, in *The Cold War as History* (1967), eschews moral judgment and views the Soviet – American confrontation in 1945 as a tragic and unavoidable condition created by the war itself, not unlike that which faces a scorpion and a tarantula in a bottle, each compelled to protect itself by seeking to kill the other. "This," writes Halle (1967, p. xiii), "is not fundamentally a case of the wicked against the virtuous . . . and we may properly feel sorry for both parties, caught, as they are, in a situation of irreducible dilemma."

Those charged with the formulation of American policy toward Europe from 1945 until 1947 created the intellectual foundations of orthodoxy. They rejected as immoral, and thus diplomatically unjustifiable, Soviet actions in eastern Europe, the Soviet refusal to permit free elections or accept the principle of four-power agreement on German reconstruction, the Soviet failure to disarm or withdraw forces to the old Russian border, the Soviet rejection of any agreement on the control of atomic energy, and eventually the Soviet resort to the veto to prevent action in the United Nations. What was the significance of this Russian behavior beyond a rejection of the Western blueprint for the postwar world? In defending their policies the Soviets claimed no more than the right to manage the political evolution of liberated Europe in terms of their own security interests. From the beginning, however, American officials interpreted Soviet defiance as evidence of a more sinister design, aimed not alone at the protection of Soviet commitments in eastern Europe, but also at the extension of Soviet power and influence beyond the regions of direct Soviet control. George F. Kennan warned from Moscow in May 1945 that Russia was an imperialistic nation, now in possession of great power and time, already determined "to segregate from the world economy almost all the areas in which it has been established" (quoted in Kennan, 1967, p. 537). The Soviets, wrote Kennan, were determined to gain Western recognition of their security interests in eastern Europe. By standing firm in rejecting the Soviet position the West would exert pressure on Soviet control and prevent any further Russian advances toward the west.

During April 1945, Ambassador Averell Harriman returned from Moscow and reported to President Harry Truman that the Soviets, having broken the Yalta agreements, would proceed to create additional pressures on world diplomacy. Harriman feared, moreover, that Stalin was prepared to exploit the devastation and economic dislocation of western Europe to extend Soviet influence into that region. Several weeks later Harriman complained that Hitler had opened "the gates of Eastern Europe to Asia." Similarly State Department offical Joseph M. Jones declared that the USSR "had demonstrated beyond any doubt that it was aggressive and expanding, and that its immediate design for dominion included as much of Europe and Asia and North Africa as it could get away with short of war with its Western allies" (Jones, 1955, p. 41). By 1947 many United States spokesmen no longer limited the Soviet challenge to an imperialistic design but rather to a Moscow-centered ideological crusade aimed at the total destruction of the Western traditions of government and society. They viewed Stalin's ruthless transformation of the eastern European nations into Russian satellites, following the Truman Doctrine and the Marshall Plan, as proof less of Soviet insecurity than of the unlimited ambitions of Soviet Communism, demanding after 1948 a Western policy of military containment in Europe.

What policy choices were available to Western leaders in the formulation of an allegedly *defensive* policy designed to blunt Soviet expansionism? The simplest decision, one overwhelmingly acceptable to concerned Americans and confirmed at Potsdam in July – August, 1945, was the refusal to recognize the Soviet sphere of influence. Western leaders, secondly, made it clear that Soviet expansion would not extend beyond the region of Soviet control in Europe; nor would it remain in Iran or reach Japan. Beyond setting the limits of Soviet expansion in a divided world, American spokesmen recognized the need to create some new international equilibrium that would offset Russia's military preponderance on the European continent. This would demand a new balancing role, one formerly conducted by Britain, for the United States. Such cabinet spokesmen as Secretary of the Navy James V. Forrestal and Secretary of War Henry L. Stimson had no interest in ideological policies. For Stimson the issue in Soviet-American relations was not self-determination as much as the established limits of power and change. Finally, Western leaders recognized in past Soviet actions no threats to Western security which required any specific settlements of major issues or any resort to force. These decisions established the character of the Cold War. On the one hand the positions taken and the interests at stake eliminated any concessions to Soviet demands through diplomatic negotiation. To gain objectives not achievable through the normal devices of diplomacy, the contestants would exert pressure on the will of their opponents by every means available short of war. In practice such behavior would comprise a tacit admission by Western leaders that both the political price of recognizing the status quo and the military price of undoing it exceeded by far the cost of sustaining the diplomatic, economic, and military policies of the Cold War.

Historians of the fifties tended to accept the Cold War orthodoxy laid down by United States and British officials in speeches, writings, memoirs, communications, and recorded conversations between 1945 and 1950. Such writers accepted the notion of Soviet aggressiveness as valid and of Western firmness as necessary. They accepted the logic of U. S. containment policy and regarded it generally as the most successful of the nation's postwar decisions, both in concept and in execution. Feis, in his judicious volume *Between War and Peace,* recognized the failures of Western purpose at Potsdam, but he accepted the orthodox position that the Soviets must bear the responsibility for the breakdown of Allied unity. "The western allies," ran his conclusion, "were standing out against both Soviet expansionism and Communist social ideals" (Feis, 1960, p. 322). From the challenge of Soviet aggressiveness there could be no retreat. "The survival of freedom was dependent solely upon the United States," wrote John W. Spanier in 1960 (p. 33). More recently such students of postwar United States foreign policy as Charles Burton Marshall (1965), Dexter Perkins (1967), and David Rees (1967) have continued in the sixties to view the Soviet Union as an expansive force and have regarded Stalin as the exponent, not of Russian security, but of the Communist program. This is not to say that any of these writers laud every American decision or accept the rationale of every official utterance. They do, however, agree that the nation's general reaction to a divided Europe in 1945 and thereafter — both in rejecting any agreement on spheres of influence and in creating a countering strategy — was the proper one.

Those who have rejected one or more aspects of the official, or orthodox, interpretation of the Cold War are not of one mind. Their disagreement with official doctrine is not over the nature, or even the morality, of Soviet behavior, but over its meaning. Soviet policies in eastern Europe following Yalta had been anticipated by both British and American leaders as early as 1943 with the knowledge that they would not be prevented. Then why were they not accepted? E. H. Carr, the British historian, raised the question of Soviet behavior in *The Times* of London on November 6, 1944. Denying that Russia had any greater expansionist designs toward Europe than England, he warned not only that the Soviets would seek security guarantees in eastern Europe but also that "it would be foolish, as well as somewhat hypocritical, to construe insistence on this right as the symptom of an aggressive policy." This theme — that a postwar Russian sphere of influence was a logical expression of the times and no danger to Western security — Walter Lippmann developed fully in *The Cold War* (1947). Lippmann recognized the existence of a Russian problem but rejected the official concept. Permitting the record to speak for itself, assigning no blame or assigning it equally, a number of writers have accepted both a more limited view of the Soviet challenge and the need for policies which reflect the limited choices which have confronted the West since 1944. For it was quite clear from the outset that the mere rejection of Soviet behavior in eastern Europe would in no way influence the course of events in the regions under Russian control.

In varying degrees such writers as Hans J. Morgenthau (1951), John Lukacs (1962), Isaac Deutscher (1966), Louis B. Halle (1967), Paul Seabury (1967), Charles O. Lerche (1965), Marshall Shulman (1966), and Wilfrid Knapp (1967) have questioned the fears and the ideological assumptions which guided the evolution of United States policy in the postwar years.[1] Seabury, for example, in *The Rise and Decline of the Cold War,* traces the development of many American Cold War attitudes and questions their usefulness as the bases of policy. From writings such as these Stalin emerges less an expansionist than a realist, determined to pursue a spheres of influence policy as the surest guarantee of Russian security. Most would agree with Deutscher that the Western dread of Soviet expansionism was mistaken. Employing a different analysis, Morgenthau, in *The Defense of the National Interest,* separated the issue of imperialism from that of world revolution and insisted that the USSR represented the former and not the latter threat. George F. Kennan's official

---

1. In this connection see Luard (1964), another valuable study of the Cold War. The essays in this volume were prepared by British scholars.

communications of 1945 – 1947 warned official Washington of Soviet belligerence toward the outside world and suggested the countering policy of containment. His *Memoirs, 1925 – 1950,* published in 1967, restated his underlying assumptions of the postwar years. But he made it clear that he did not, either in 1947 or afterward, approve of the intensity, the militarization, or the crusading zeal which came to characterize the American response to the Soviet challenge. This criticism of containment — that it embodied no clear, precise objectives and thus eliminated any genuine effort at negotiation — characterized the views of many writers who nevertheless have insisted that the power and the ambitions of the USSR, even if limited, necessitated some Western response.

Kennan's dissatisfaction with United States policy increased with the passage of time. Indeed, many whose writings have praised the Truman Doctrine and the Marshall Plan, as prudent and necessary reactions to the Soviet presence in central and eastern Europe, believe that the United States soon lost its balance and restraint. After 1950, and especially after the Korean war, a new globalism encouraged the national executive to extend United States commitments into Asia and the Pacific under the doubtful assumption that the West faced, not a limited if powerful antagonist in Europe, but rather an international conspiracy emanating from the Kremlin and designed to establish Soviet influence over the entire world.

During the sixties another group of scholars has rejected the precepts of orthodoxy completely. Beginning with the assumption that a war-battered Soviet Union had the right to demand friendly buffer states as a defense against Western encirclement, these revisionists have charged U.S. policy with provoking and sustaining the Cold War. They argue that the USSR emerged from the war weak and insecure, that it desired an accommodation with the West based on the minimum acceptance of a Soviet sphere of influence. It was the repeated British and American protests against the imposition of a Soviet hegemony in eastern Europe that inaugurated the successive responses which led to the Cold War. The United States, charge the revisionists, was not powerless to prevent the Cold War. Lippmann had argued the revisionist case in *The Cold War* (1947). The British physicist, P. M. S. Blackett, stated it differently a year later in his *Military and Political Consequences of Atomic Energy.* The USSR, declared Blackett, had a right not only to defend her western frontiers but also to extend her frontiers as far as possible in response to the Baruch Plan for the control of atomic energy. That plan, the Russians believed, would have rendered them vulnerable to Western military power. K. Zilliacus, a British official and writer, carried the revisionist cause forward another step with the publication of his book, *I Choose Peace* (1949). Zilliacus argued that British wartime and postwar policy, from Munich to Churchill's Fulton speech of March 1946, had been as much anti-Soviet as anti-German.

It was the anti-Communist bias of Churchill and Bevin in 1945 that made agreement with the Kremlin impossible.

In large measure the American revisionism of the sixties found its inception in D. F. Fleming's *The Cold War and Its Origins, 1917–1950* (1961). Critics have termed Fleming's book as little more than a collection of contemporary comments. In large measure the charge is true. But Fleming's massive Cold War studies illustrate, as have no other published volumes, the extent to which every fundamental American decision after 1944 created doubts in the nation's intellectual community, especially among leading members of the press. Much of that early criticism followed a pattern, suggesting conceptual weaknesses in policy that would become more obvious, embarrassing, and costly with the passage of time. Employing a succession of unilateral (purely American) explanations for the origins of the Cold War, Fleming consistently attributes Soviet suspicion and misbehavior to Western aggressiveness. "From the first," he writes (1961, p. 31), "it was the West which was on the offensive, not the Soviets." If Fleming's detailed and often disturbing catalogue of American editorial, official, and semi-official opinion offers some explanation of United States policy, it avoids any analysis of Soviet purpose and ignores the anti-American polemics of Soviet officials. Fleming traces forty years of American opposition to Soviet ideas and actions, but he makes no effort to account for it except in the general terms of anti-Communism.

But David Horowitz, in his *Free World Colossus* (1965), explains the unity of American policy in the Cold War by characterizing it as "counterrevolutionary" rather than "counterexpansionary." The purpose of American policy since 1945, writes Horowitz (p. 423), is to crush any movement anywhere in the world that threatens radical change against the will of the United States government. To prevent change, the nation has employed the concept of containment and has built up vast excesses of power in order to force a showdown with the USSR and thereby terminate the processes of revolution elsewhere in the world. It was this purpose that led to the extension of American power and American commitments into Asia and Latin America after 1950. Thus Horowitz, no less than Fleming, sees the United States in the role of the aggressor and demonstrates, as do others, that Stalin's disturbing policies of 1947 and 1948 — the rejection of the Marshall Plan, the establishment of the Cominform, the Czech coup, and the Berlin blockade — were the result rather than the cause of U.S. containment policy.

William A. Williams, in *The Tragedy of American Diplomacy* (1959, revised edition 1962), likewise finds a single and persistent motive in American Cold War policy — the determination to compel the Kremlin to accept this nation's concept of itself and the world. This purpose, writes Williams, comprises especially the expansion of the open door principle of trade and investment into areas under Soviet control. The Marshall Plan as originally conceived, he believes, would have given the United States considerable influence over the internal and external affairs of the USSR. Soviet rejection, therefore, should have been anticipated. When the Marshall Plan failed to open eastern Europe, the Truman administration adopted both the concept of negotiating from strength and the buildup of American power to achieve the dismantling of the Iron Curtain. In their ultimate failure, Washington officials underestimated the strength and determination of the Soviet opposition (Williams, 1962, pp. 205–209).

More recently Walter LaFeber has adopted the concept of the open door to explain United States aggressiveness *vis-à-vis* the Soviet Union in 1945 and the years that followed. Opposed to the formation of political blocs, writes LaFeber, the United States government, led by Secretary of State James F. Byrnes, attempted to use its predominant economic power to penetrate Europe. Whereas that policy, culminating in the Marshall Plan, triumphed in western Europe, it failed to penetrate the Iron Curtain. Meanwhile the United States, with its vast economic power, might have extended credit to the Soviet Union in 1945 to relieve its economic plight. Instead the Truman administration cancelled Lend-Lease abruptly and without explanation; in March 1946 Stalin announced another five-year plan to rebuild Russian industry and assure the technological and financial independence of the Soviet Union. Again the quest for the open door failed to achieve anything except the breakdown of diplomacy (LaFeber, 1967, pp. 6–20).

If American economic power could not penetrate the Soviet sphere, perhaps another force was available in 1945 to turn the Russians out of eastern Europe. Gar Alperovitz, in his *Atomic Diplomacy: Hiroshima and Potsdam* (1965), has discovered the origins of the Cold War in the atomic diplomacy which led to Potsdam and the decision to use the bomb against Japanese targets. Alperovitz develops three specific themes. First, he argues along with Fleming, Horowitz, and Williams that U.S. policy toward Russia changed precipitously under Truman in April, 1945, when the new administration sought to impose an immediate settlement on Russia over eastern Europe. Second, he believes that this change to a tough policy occurred because of Truman's assumption that the atomic bomb, then being developed, would strengthen his diplomacy with the Kremlin, making the desired settlement possible without war. Third, Alperovitz attempts to explain why Truman delayed the Potsdam Conference, attending ultimately only with reluctance, and then used the atomic bomb against Japan long after he knew of the Japanese premier's willingness to surrender provided its emperor were retained. While admitting that such questions cannot be answered with complete confidence for lack of evidence, he suggests that Truman delayed his trip to Potsdam until the bomb had been fully developed and then used it, not to end the war in the Pacific, but to demonstrate this new power to the Soviet Union. As one American official explained in May 1945, "Mr. Byrnes did not argue that it was necessary to use the bomb against the cities of Japan in order to win the war. . . . [His] view

[was] that our possessing and demonstrating the bomb would make Russia more manageable in Europe."[2] Still, if the President hoped to exert diplomatic pressure on Stalin he failed to exploit the bomb either at Potsdam or thereafter. Indeed, the bomb had no appreciable effect on Soviet policy whatever. The showdown over eastern Europe never came.

Late in 1966 Arthur M. Schlesinger, Jr., wrote a letter to the *New York Review of Books:* "Surely the time has come to blow the whistle before the current outburst of revisionism regarding the origins of the Cold War goes much further." Then in the autumn of 1967 Schlesinger published a full article in *Foreign Affairs* in which he argued for greater orthodoxy and insisted that Stalin's paranoia and rigidity were sufficient to explain the failure of postwar accommodation. Still the revisionist attack on U.S. Cold War policy has tended to become increasingly pronounced with the passage of time.[3] As long as much of the American and most of the Russian evidence remains hidden from view the final judgment on Cold War origins will remain elusive. But the publication of British and American memoirs and documents over the past decade reveals both an inflexible opposition to Soviet behavior and an illusion that somehow the postwar Soviet dominance in Europe could be undermined without the price of war. Revisionist studies, moreover, have traced the descent into the Cold War through a series of cause-and-effect relationships in which key Soviet decisions throughout the postwar era appear to be reactions to, not the causes of, Western demonstrations of power and determination. After more than twenty years of Cold War, the quest for understanding raises one fundamental and still unanswered question: Why did the United States after 1939 permit the conquest of eastern Europe by Nazi forces, presumably forever, with scarcely a stir, but refused after 1944 to acknowledge any primary Russian interest or right of hegemony in the same region on the heels of a closely won Russian victory against the German invader? When scholars have answered that question fully the historical debate over Cold War origins will be largely resolved.

References

Alperovitz, Gar. *Atomic Diplomacy: Hiroshima and Potsdam.* New York: Simon & Schuster, 1965.
Deutscher, Isaac. "Twenty Years of Cold War." In *Ironies of History,* London, 1966.
Donnelly, Desmond. *Struggle for the World: The Cold War and Its Causes.* London: St. Martin's Press, 1965.

2. Alperovitz, 1967, p. 242. Feis (1961) has challenged this interpretation of the use of the atomic bomb against Japan. He believes that Truman ordered its employment against Hiroshima as another weapon, however destructive, to terminate the war promptly and thus save American and Japanese lives.
   3. For a popular defense of revisionism, see Lasch (1968).

Feis, Herbert. *Churchill, Roosevelt, Stalin: The War They Waged and the Peace They Sought.* Princeton, N.J.: Princeton University Press, 1957.
——. *Between War and Peace: The Potsdam Conference.* Princeton, N.J.: Princeton University Press, 1960.
——. *Japan Subdued.* Princeton, N.J.: Princeton University Press, 1961. [Revised edition appeared as *The Atomic Bomb and the End of World War II.* Princeton, N.J.: Princeton University Press, 1966. Eds.]
Fleming, D.F. *The Cold War and Its Origins, 1917–1950.* Garden City, N.Y.: Doubleday, 1961.
Graebner, Norman A. *Cold War Diplomacy, 1945–1960.* Princeton, N.J.: Princeton University Press, 1962.
Halle, Louis B. *The Cold War as History.* New York: Harper & Row, 1967.
Herz, Martin F. *Beginnings of the Cold War.* Bloomington: Indiana University Press, 1966.
Horowitz, David. *The Free World Colossus: A Critique of American Foreign Policy in the Cold War.* New York: Hill & Wang, 1965.
Jones, Joseph Marion. *The Fifteen Weeks.* New York: Viking Press, 1955.
Kennan, George F. *Memoirs, 1925–1950.* Boston: Little, Brown, 1967.
Knapp, Wilfrid. *A History of War and Peace, 1939–1965.* London: Oxford University Press, 1967.
LaFeber, Walter. *America, Russia, and the Cold War, 1945–1966.* New York: Wiley, 1967.
Lasch, Christopher. "The Cold War, Revisited and Re-Visioned," *New York Times Magazine,* January 14, 1968.
Lerche, Charles O., Jr. *The Cold War and After.* Englewood Cliffs, N.J.: Prentice-Hall, 1965.
Luard, Evan (ed.). *The Cold War: A Reappraisal.* New York: Praeger, 1964.
Lukacs, John. *A History of the Cold War.* Rev. edn. Garden City, N.Y.: Doubleday, 1962.
Marshall, Charles Burton. *The Cold War: A Concise History.* New York: Franklin Watts, 1965.
McNeill, William H. *America, Britain, and Russia: Their Cooperation and Conflict, 1941–1946.* London: Oxford University Press, 1953.
Morgenthau, Hans J. *In Defense of the National Interest.* New York: Knopf, 1951.
O'Conor, John F. *The Cold War and Liberation.* New York: Vantage Press, 1961.
Perkins, Dexter. *The Diplomacy of a New Age.* Bloomington: Indiana University Press, 1967.
Rees, David. *The Age of Containment: The Cold War, 1945–1965.* London: St. Martin's Press, 1967.
Schuman, Frederick L. *The Cold War: Retrospect and Prospect.* Baton Rouge: Louisiana State University Press, 1962.
Seabury, Paul. *The Rise and Decline of the Cold War.* New York: Basic Books, 1967.
Shulman, Marshall D. *Beyond the Cold War.* New Haven: Yale University Press, 1966.
Spanier, John W. *American Foreign Policy Since World War II.* New York: Praeger, 1960.
Williams, William A. *The Tragedy of American Diplomacy.* Rev. edn. New York: World Publishing, 1962.

THIRTEEN   ARTHUR M. SCHLESINGER, JR.

Origins of the Cold War*

I

The Cold War in its original form was a presumably mortal antagonism,
arising in the wake of the Second World War, between two rigidly hostile
blocs, one led by the Soviet Union, the other by the United States. For nearly
two somber and dangerous decades this antagonism dominated the fears of
mankind; it may even, on occasion, have come close to blowing up the planet.
In recent years, however, the once implacable struggle has lost its familiar
clarity of outline. With the passing of old issues and the emergence of new
conflicts and contestants, there is a natural tendency, especially on the part of
the generation which grew up during the Cold War, to take a fresh look at the
causes of the great contention between Russia and America.

Some exercises in reappraisal have merely elaborated the orthodoxies promulgated in Washington or Moscow during the boom years of the Cold War.
But others, especially in the United States (there are no signs, alas, of this in
the Soviet Union), represent what American historians call "revisionism" —
that is, a readiness to challenge official explanations. No one should be
surprised by this phenomenon. Every war in American history has been fol-

*Reprinted from *Foreign Affairs,* XLVI, 1 (October, 1967), pp. 22–52, by permission of
the author and the publisher. Copyright 1967 by the Council on Foreign Relations, Inc., New
York.

lowed in due course by skeptical reassessments of supposedly sacred assumptions. So the War of 1812, fought at the time for the freedom of the seas, was in later years ascribed to the expansionist ambitions of Congressional war hawks; so the Mexican War became a slaveholders' conspiracy. So the Civil War has been pronounced a "needless war," and Lincoln has even been accused of maneuvering the rebel attack on Fort Sumter. So too the Spanish-American War and First and Second World Wars have, each in its turn, undergone revisionist critiques. It is not to be supposed that the Cold War would remain exempt.

In the case of the Cold War, special factors reinforce the predictable historiographical rhythm. The outburst of polycentrism in the communist empire has made people wonder whether communism was ever so monolithic as official theories of the Cold War supposed. A generation with no vivid memories of Stalinism may see the Russia of the forties in the image of the relatively mild, seedy, and irresolute Russia of the sixties. And for this same generation the American course of widening the war in Vietnam — which even non-revisionists can easily regard as folly — has unquestionably stirred doubts about the wisdom of American foreign policy in the sixties which younger historians may have begun to read back into the forties.

It is useful to remember that, on the whole, past exercises in revisionism have failed to stick. Few historians today believe that the war hawks caused the War of 1812 or the slaveholders the Mexican War, or that the Civil War was needless, or that the House of Morgan brought America into the First World War or that Franklin Roosevelt schemed to produce the attack on Pearl Harbor. But this does not mean that one should deplore the rise of Cold War revisionism.[1] For revisionism is an essential part of the process by which history, through the posing of new problems and the investigation of new possibilities, enlarges its perspectives and enriches its insights.

More than this, in the present context, revisionism expresses a deep, legitimate, and tragic apprehension. As the Cold War has begun to lose its purity of definition, as the moral absolutes of the fifties become the moralistic clichés of the sixties, some have begun to ask whether the appalling risks which humanity ran during the Cold War were, after all, necessary and inevitable; whether more restrained and rational policies might not have guided the energies of man from the perils of conflict into the potentialities of collaboration. The fact that such questions are in their nature unanswerable does not mean that it is not right and useful to raise them. Nor does it mean that our sons and daughters are not entitled to an accounting from the generation of Russians and Americans who produced the Cold War.

1. As this writer somewhat intemperately did in a letter to *The New York Review of Books,* October 20, 1966.

II

The orthodox American view, as originally set forth by the American government and as reaffirmed until recently by most American scholars, has been that
the Cold War was the brave and essential response of free men to Communist
aggression. Some have gone back well before the Second World War to lay
open the sources of Russian expansionism. Geopoliticians traced the Cold War
to imperial Russian strategic ambitions which in the nineteenth century led to
the Crimean War, to Russian penetration of the Balkans and the Middle East,
and to Russian pressure on Britain's "lifeline" to India. Ideologists traced it
to the Communist Manifesto of 1848 ("the violent overthrow of the bourgeoisie lays the foundation for the sway of the proletariat"). Thoughtful observers
(a phrase meant to exclude those who speak in Dullese about the unlimited
evil of godless, atheistic, militant communism) concluded that classical Russian imperialism and Pan-Slavism, compounded after 1917 by Leninist messianism, confronted the West at the end of the Second World War with an
inexorable drive for domination.[2]

The revisionist thesis is very different.[3] In its extreme form, it is that, after

---

2. Every student of the Cold War must acknowledge his debt to W. H. McNeill's remarkable
account, *America, Britain and Russia: Their Cooperation and Conflict, 1941–1946* (New York,
1953) and to the brilliant and indispensable series by Herbert Feis: *Churchill, Roosevelt, Stalin:
The War They Waged and the Peace They Sought* (Princeton, 1957); *Between War and Peace: The
Potsdam Conference* (Princeton, 1960); and *The Atomic Bomb and the End of World War II*
(Princeton, 1966). Useful recent analyses include André Fontaine, *Histoire de la Guerre Froide*
(2 v., Paris, 1965, 1967); N. A. Graebner, *Cold War Diplomacy, 1945–1960* (Princeton, 1962);
L. J. Halle, *The Cold War as History* (London, 1967); M. F. Herz, *Beginnings of the Cold War*
(Bloomington, 1966); and W. L. Neumann, *After Victory: Churchill, Roosevelt, Stalin and the
Making of the Peace* (New York, 1967).

3. The fullest statement of this case is to be found in D. F. Fleming's voluminous *The Cold
War and Its Origins* (New York, 1961). For a shorter version of this argument, see David
Horowitz, *The Free World Colossus* (New York, 1965); the most subtle and ingenious statements
come in W. A. Williams' *The Tragedy of American Diplomacy* (rev. ed., New York, 1962), and
in Gar Alperovitz's *Atomic Diplomacy: Hiroshima and Potsdam* (New York, 1965), and in
subsequent articles and reviews by Mr. Alperovitz in *The New York Review of Books.* The fact
that in some aspects the revisionist thesis parallels the official Soviet argument must not, of course,
prevent consideration of the case on its merits, nor raise questions about the motives of the writers,
all of whom, so far as I know, are independent-minded scholars.

I might further add that all these books, in spite of their ostentatious display of scholarly
apparatus, must be used with caution. Professor Fleming, for example, relies heavily on newspaper
articles and even columnists. While Mr. Alperovitz bases his case on official documents or
authoritative reminiscences, he sometimes twists his material in a most unscholarly way. For
example, in describing Ambassador Harriman's talk with President Truman on April 20, 1945,
Mr. Alperovitz writes, "He argued that a reconsideration of Roosevelt's policy was necessary"
(p. 22, repeated on p. 24). The citation is to pp. 70–72 in President Truman's *Years of Decision.*
What President Truman reported Harriman as saying was the exact opposite: "Before leaving,
Harriman took me aside and said, 'Frankly, one of the reasons that made me rush back to
Washington was the fear that you did not understand, as I had seen Roosevelt understand, that
Stalin is breaking his agreements.'" Similarly, in an appendix (p. 271) Mr. Alperovitz writes that
the Hopkins and Davies missions of May 1945 "were opposed by the 'firm' advisers." Actually
the Hopkins mission was proposed by Harriman and Charles E. Bohlen, who Mr. Alperovitz

the death of Franklin Roosevelt and the end of the Second World War, the United States deliberately abandoned the wartime policy of collaboration and, exhilarated by the possession of the atomic bomb, undertook a course of aggression of its own designed to expel all Russian influence from Eastern Europe and to establish democratic-capitalist states on the very border of the Soviet Union. As the revisionists see it, this radically new American policy — or rather this resumption by Truman of the pre-Roosevelt policy of insensate anti-communism — left Moscow no alternative but to take measures in defense of its own borders. The result was the Cold War.

These two views, of course, could not be more starkly contrasting. It is therefore not unreasonable to look again at the half-dozen critical years between June 22, 1941, when Hitler attacked Russia, and July 2, 1947, when the Russians walked out of the Marshall Plan meeting in Paris. Several things should be borne in mind as this reexamination is made. For one thing, we have thought a great deal more in recent years, in part because of writers like Roberta Wohlstetter and T. C. Schelling, about the problems of communication in diplomacy — the signals which one nation, by word or by deed, gives, inadvertently or intentionally, to another. Any honest reappraisal of the origins of the Cold War requires the imaginative leap — which should in any case be as instinctive for the historian as it is prudent for the statesman — into the adversary's viewpoint. We must strive to see how, given Soviet perspectives, the Russians might conceivably have misread our signals, as we must reconsider how intelligently we read theirs.

For another, the historian must not overindulge the man of power in the illusion cherished by those in office that high position carries with it the easy ability to shape history. Violating the statesman's creed, Lincoln once blurted out the truth in his letter of 1864 to A. G. Hodges: "I claim not to have controlled events, but confess plainly that events have controlled me." He was not asserting Tolstoyan fatalism but rather suggesting how greatly events limit the capacity of the statesman to bend history to his will. The physical course of the Second World War — the military operations undertaken, the position of the respective armies at the war's end, the momentum generated by victory, and the vacuums created by defeat — all these determined the future as much as the character of individual leaders and the substance of national ideology and purpose.

Nor can the historian forget the conditions under which decisions are made,

---

elsewhere suggests were the firmest of the firm — and was proposed by them precisely to impress on Stalin the continuity of American policy from Roosevelt to Truman. While the idea that Truman reversed Roosevelt's policy is tempting dramatically, it is a myth. See, for example, the testimony of Anna Rosenberg Hoffman, who lunched with Roosevelt on March 24, 1945, the last day he spent in Washington. After luncheon, Roosevelt was handed a cable. "He read it and became quite angry. He banged his fists on the arms of his wheelchair and said, 'Averell is right; we can't do business with Stalin. He has broken every one of the promises he made at Yalta.' He was very upset and continued in the same vein on the subject."

especially in a time like the Second World War. These were tired, overworked, aging men: in 1945, Churchill was 71 years old, Stalin had governed his country for 17 exacting years, Roosevelt his for 12 years nearly as exacting. During the war, moreover, the importunities of military operations had shoved postwar questions to the margins of their minds. All — even Stalin, behind his screen of ideology — had became addicts of improvisation, relying on authority and virtuosity to conceal the fact that they were constantly surprised by developments. Like Eliza, they leaped from one cake of ice to the next in the effort to reach the other side of the river. None showed great tactical consistency, or cared much about it; all employed a certain ambiguity to preserve their power to decide big issues; and it is hard to know how to interpret anything any one of them said on any specific occasion. This was partly because, like all princes, they designed their expressions to have particular effects on particular audiences; partly because the entirely genuine intellectual difficulty of the questions they faced made a degree of vacillation and mind-changing eminently reasonable. If historians cannot solve their problems in retrospect, who are they to blame Roosevelt, Stalin, and Churchill for not having solved them at the time?

III

Peacemaking after the Second World War was not so much a tapestry as it was a hopelessly raveled and knotted mess of yarn. Yet, for purposes of clarity, it is essential to follow certain threads. One theme indispensable to an understanding of the Cold War is the contrast between two clashing views of world order: the "universalist" view, by which all nations shared a common interest in all the affairs of the world; and the "sphere-of-influence" view, by which each great power would be assured by the other great powers of an acknowledged predominance in its own area of special interest. The universalist view assumed that national security would be guaranteed by an international organization. The sphere-of-interest view assumed that national security would be guaranteed by the balance of power. While in practice these views have by no means been incompatible (indeed, our shaky peace has been based on a combination of the two), in the abstract they involved sharp contradictions.

The tradition of American thought in these matters was universalist — that is, Wilsonian. Roosevelt had been a member of Wilson's subcabinet; in 1920, as candidate for Vice President, he had campaigned for the League of Nations. It is true that, within Roosevelt's infinitely complex mind, Wilsonianism warred with the perception of vital strategic interests he had imbibed from Mahan. Morever, his temperamental inclination to settle things with fellow princes around the conference table led him to regard the Big Three — or Four — as trustees for the rest of the world. On occasion, as this narrative will show, he was beguiled into flirtation with the sphere-of-influence heresy. But in principle he believed in joint action and remained a Wilsonian. His hope for Yalta, as he told the Congress on his return, was that it would "spell the end of the system of unilateral action, the exclusive alliances, the spheres of influence, the balances of power, and all the other expedients that have been tried for centuries — and have always failed."

Whenever Roosevelt backslid, he had at his side that Wilsonian fundamentalist, Secretary of State Cordell Hull, to recall him to the pure faith. After his visit to Moscow in 1943, Hull characteristically said that, with the Declaration of Four Nations on General Security (in which America, Russia, Britain and China pledged "united action . . . for the organization and maintenance of peace and security"), "there will no longer be need for spheres of influence, for alliances, for balance of power, or any other of the special arrangements through which, in the unhappy past, the nations strove to safeguard their security or to promote their interests."

Remembering the corruption of the Wilsonian vision by the secret treaties of the First World War, Hull was determined to prevent any sphere-of-influence nonsense after the Second World War. He therefore fought all proposals to settle border questions while the war was still on and, excluded as he largely was from wartime diplomacy, poured his not inconsiderable moral energy and frustration into the promulgation of virtuous and spacious general principles.

In adopting the universalist view, Roosevelt and Hull were not indulging personal hobbies. Sumner Welles, Adolf Berle, Averell Harriman, Charles Bohlen — all, if with a variety of nuances, opposed the sphere-of-influence approach. And here the State Department was expressing what seems clearly to have been the predominant mood of the American people, so long mistrustful of European power politics. The Republicans shared the true faith. John Foster Dulles argued that the great threat to peace after the war would lie in the revival of sphere-of-influence thinking. The United States, he said, must not permit Britain and Russia to revert to these bad old ways; it must therefore insist on American participation in all policy decisions for all territories in the world. Dulles wrote pessimistically in January 1945, "The three great powers which at Moscow agreed upon the 'closest cooperation' about European questions have shifted to a practice of separate, regional responsibility."

It is true that critics, and even friends, of the United States sometimes noted a discrepancy between the American passion for universalism when it applied to territory far from American shores and the preeminence the United States accorded its own interests nearer home. Churchill, seeking Washington's blessing for a sphere-of-influence initiative in eastern Europe, could not forbear reminding the Americans, "We follow the lead of the United States in South America"; nor did any universalist of record propose the abolition of the Monroe Doctrine. But a convenient myopia prevented such inconsistencies from qualifying the ardency of the universalist faith.

There seem only to have been three officials in the United States Government who dissented. One was the Secretary of War, Henry L. Stimson, a classical balance-of-power man, who in 1944 opposed the creation of a vacuum in Central Europe by the pastoralization of Germany and in 1945 urged "the settlement of all territorial acquisitions in the shape of defense posts which each of these four powers may deem to be necessary for their own safety" in advance of any effort to establish a peacetime United Nations. Stimson considered the claim of Russia to a preferred position in Eastern Europe as not unreasonable: as he told President Truman, "he thought the Russians perhaps were being more realistic than we were in regard to their own security." Such a position for Russia seemed to him comparable to the preferred American position in Latin America; he even spoke of "our respective orbits." Stimson was therefore skeptical of what he regarded as the prevailing tendency "to hang on to exaggerated views of the Monroe Doctrine and at the same time butt into every question that comes up in Central Europe." Acceptance of spheres of influence seemed to him the way to avoid "a head-on collision."

A second official opponent of universalism was George Kennan, an eloquent advocate from the American Embassy in Moscow of "a prompt and clear recognition of the division of Europe into spheres of influence and of a policy based on the fact of such division." Kennan argued that nothing we could do would possibly alter the course of events in Eastern Europe; that we were deceiving ourselves by supposing that these countries had any future but Russian domination; that we should therefore relinquish Eastern Europe to the Soviet Union and avoid anything which would make things easier for the Russians by giving them economic assistance or by sharing moral responsibility for their actions.

A third voice within the government against universalism was (at least after the war) Henry A. Wallace. As Secretary of Commerce, he stated the sphere-of-influence case with trenchancy in the famous Madison Square Garden speech of September 1946 which led to his dismissal by President Truman:

> On our part, we should recognize that we have no more business in the *political* affairs of Eastern Europe than Russia has in the *political* affairs of Latin America, Western Europe, and the United States. . . . Whether we like it or not, the Russians will try to socialize their sphere of influence just as we try to democratize our sphere of influence. . . . The Russians have no more business stirring up native Communists to political activity in Western Europe, Latin America, and the United States than we have in interfering with the politics of Eastern Europe and Russia.

Stimson, Kennan, and Wallace seem to have been alone in the government, however, in taking these views. They were very much minority voices. Meanwhile universalism, rooted in the American legal and moral tradition, overwhelmingly backed by contemporary opinion, received successive enshrinements in the Atlantic Charter of 1941, in the Declaration of the United Nations in 1942, and in the Moscow Declaration of 1943.

IV

The Kremlin, on the other hand, thought *only* of spheres of interest; above all, the Russians were determined to protect their frontiers, and especially their border to the west, crossed so often and so bloodily in the dark course of their history. These western frontiers lacked natural means of defense — no great oceans, rugged mountains, steaming swamps, or impenetrable jungles. The history of Russia had been the history of invasion, the last of which was by now horribly killing up to twenty million of its people. The protocol of Russia therefore meant the enlargement of the area of Russian influence. Kennan himself wrote (in May, 1944), "Behind Russia's stubborn expansion lies only the age-old sense of insecurity of a sedentary people reared on an exposed plain in the neighborhood of fierce nomadic peoples," and he called this "urge" a "permanent feature of Russian psychology."

In earlier times, the "urge" had produced the tsarist search for buffer states and maritime outlets. In 1939 the Soviet-Nazi pact and its secret protocol had enabled Russia to begin to satisfy in the Baltic states, Karelian Finland and Poland, part of what it conceived as its security requirements in Eastern Europe. But the "urge" persisted, causing the friction between Russia and Germany in 1940 as each jostled for position in the area which separated them. Later it led to Molotov's new demands on Hitler in November 1940 — a free hand in Finland, Soviet predominance in Rumania and Bulgaria, bases in the Dardanelles — the demands which convinced Hitler that he had no choice but to attack Russia. Now Stalin hoped to gain from the West what Hitler, a closer neighbor, had not dared yield him.

It is true that, so long as Russian survival appeared to require a second front to relieve the Nazi pressure, Moscow's demand for Eastern Europe was a little muffled. Thus the Soviet government adhered to the Atlantic Charter (though with a significant if obscure reservation about adapting its principles to "the circumstances, needs, and historic peculiarities of particular countries"). Thus it also adhered to the Moscow Declaration of 1943, and Molotov then, with his easy mendacity, even denied that Russia had any desire to divide Europe into spheres of influence. But this was guff, which the Russians were perfectly willing to ladle out if it would keep the Americans, and especially Secretary Hull (who made a strong personal impression at the Moscow conference), happy. "A declaration," as Stalin once observed to Eden, "I regard as algebra, but an agreement as practical arithmetic. I do not wish to decry algebra, but I prefer practical arithmetic."

The more consistent Russian purpose was revealed when Stalin offered the British a straight sphere-of-influence deal at the end of 1941. Britain, he suggested, should recognize the Russian absorption of the Baltic states, part of Finland, eastern Poland, and Bessarabia; in return, Russia would support any special British need for bases or security arrangements in Western Europe. There was nothing specifically communist about these ambitions. If Stalin achieved them, he would be fulfilling an age-old dream of the tsars. The British reaction was mixed. "Soviet policy is amoral," as Anthony Eden noted at the time; "United States policy is exaggeratedly moral, at least where non-American interests are concerned." If Roosevelt was a universalist with occasional leanings toward spheres of influence and Stalin was a sphere-of-influence man with occasional gestures toward universalism, Churchill seemed evenly poised between the familiar realism of the balance of power, which he had so long recorded as an historian and manipulated as a statesman, and the hope that there must be some better way of doing things. His 1943 proposal of a world organization divided into regional councils represented an effort to blend universalist and sphere-of-interest conceptions. His initial rejection of Stalin's proposal in December 1941 as "directly contrary to the first, second and third articles of the Atlantic Charter" thus did not spring entirely from a desire to propitiate the United States. On the other hand, he had himself already reinterpreted the Atlantic Charter as applying only to Europe (and thus not to the British Empire), and he was, above all, an empiricist who never believed in sacrificing reality on the altar of doctrine.

So in April 1942, he wrote Roosevelt that "the increasing gravity of the war" had led him to feel that the Charter "ought not to be construed so as to deny Russia the frontiers she occupied when Germany attacked her." Hull, however, remained fiercely hostile to the inclusion of territorial provisions in the Anglo-Russian treaty; the American position, Eden noted, "chilled me with Wilsonian memories." Though Stalin complained that it looked "as if the Atlantic Charter was directed against the USSR," it was the Russian season of military adversity in the spring of 1942, and he dropped his demands.

He did not, however, change his intentions. A year later Ambassador Standley could cable Washington from Moscow: "In 1918 Western Europe attempted to set up a *cordon sanitaire* to protect it from the influence of bolshevism. Might not now the Kremlin envisage the formation of a belt of pro-Soviet states to protect it from the influences of the West?" It well might; and that purpose became increasingly clear as the war approached its end. Indeed, it derived sustenance from Western policy in the first area of liberation.

The unconditional surrender of Italy in July 1943 created the first major test of the Western devotion to universalism. America and Britain, having won the Italian war, handled the capitulation, keeping Moscow informed at a distance. Stalin complained:

> The United States and Great Britain made agreements but the Soviet Union received information about the results . . . just as a passive third observer. I have to tell you that it is impossible to tolerate the situation any longer. I propose that the [tripartite military-political commission] be established and that Sicily be assigned . . . as its place of residence.

Roosevelt, who had no intention of sharing the control of Italy with the

Russians, suavely replied with the suggestion that Stalin send an officer "to General Eisenhower's headquarters in connection with the commission." Unimpressed, Stalin continued to press for a tripartite body; but his Western Allies were adamant in keeping the Soviet Union off the Control Commission for Italy, and the Russians in the end had to be satisfied with a seat, along with minor Allied states, on a meaningless Inter-Allied Advisory Council. Their acquiescence in this was doubtless not unconnected with a desire to establish precedents for Eastern Europe.

Teheran in December 1943 marked the high point of three-power collaboration. Still, when Churchill asked about Russian territorial interests, Stalin replied a little ominously, "There is no need to speak at the present time about any Soviet desires, but when the time comes we will speak." In the next weeks, there were increasing indications of a Soviet determinatión to deal unilaterally with Eastern Europe — so much so that in early February 1944 Hull cabled Harriman in Moscow:

> Matters are rapidly approaching the point where the Soviet Government will have to choose between the development and extension of the foundation of international cooperation as the guiding principle of the postwar world as against the continuance of a unilateral and arbitrary method of dealing with its special problems even though these problems are admittedly of more direct interest to the Soviet Union than to other great powers.

As against this approach, however, Churchill, more tolerant of sphere-of-influence deviations, soon proposed that, with the impending liberation of the Balkans, Russia should run things in Rumania and Britain in Greece. Hull strongly opposed this suggestion but made the mistake of leaving Washington for a few days; and Roosevelt, momentarily free from his Wilsonian conscience, yielded to Churchill's plea for a three-months' trial. Hull resumed the fight on his return, and Churchill postponed the matter.

The Red Army continued its advance into Eastern Europe. In August the Polish Home Army, urged on by Polish-language broadcasts from Moscow, rose up against the Nazis in Warsaw. For 63 terrible days, the Poles fought valiantly on, while the Red Army halted on the banks of the Vistula a few miles away, and in Moscow Stalin for more than half this time declined to cooperate with the Western effort to drop supplies to the Warsaw Resistance. It appeared a calculated Soviet decision to let the Nazis slaughter the anti-Soviet Polish underground; and, indeed, the result was to destroy any substantial alternative to a Soviet solution in Poland. The agony of Warsaw caused the most deep and genuine moral shock in Britain and America and provoked dark forebodings about Soviet postwar purposes.

Again history enjoins the imaginative leap in order to see things for a moment from Moscow's viewpoint. The Polish question, Churchill would say at Yalta, was for Britain a question of honor. "It is not only a question of honor for Russia," Stalin replied, "but one of life and death. . . . Throughout history Poland had been the corridor for attack on Russia." A top postwar priority for any Russian regime must be to close that corridor. The Home Army was led by anti-communists. It clearly hoped by its action to forestall the Soviet occupation of Warsaw and, in Russian eyes, to prepare the way for an anti-Russian Poland. In addition, the uprising from a strictly operational viewpoint was premature. The Russians, it is evident in retrospect, had real military problems at the Vistula. The Soviet attempt in September to send Polish units from the Red Army across the river to join forces with the Home Army was a disaster. Heavy German shelling thereafter prevented the ferrying of tanks necessary for an assault on the German position. The Red Army itself did not take Warsaw for another three months. Nonetheless, Stalin's indifference to the human tragedy, his effort to blackmail the London Poles during the ordeal, his sanctimonious opposition during five precious weeks to aerial resupply, the invariable coldness of his explanations ("the Soviet command has come to the conclusion that it must dissociate itself from the Warsaw adventure"), and the obvious political benefit to the Soviet Union from the destruction of the Home Army — all these had the effect of suddenly dropping the mask of wartime comradeship and displaying to the West the hard face of Soviet policy. In now pursuing what he grimly regarded as the minimal requirements for the postwar security of his country, Stalin was inadvertently showing the irreconcilability of both his means and his ends with the Anglo-American conception of the peace.

Meanwhile Eastern Europe presented the Alliance with still another crisis that same September. Bulgaria, which was not at war with Russia, decided to surrender to the Western Allies while it still could; and the English and Americans at Cairo began to discuss armistice terms with Bulgarian envoys. Moscow, challenged by what it plainly saw as a Western intrusion into its own zone of vital interest, promptly declared war on Bulgaria, took over the surrender negotiations and, invoking the Italian precedent, denied its Western Allies any role in the Bulgarian Control Commission. In a long and thoughtful cable, Ambassador Harriman meditated on the problems of communication with the Soviet Union. "Words," he reflected, "have a different connotation to the Soviets than they have to us. When they speak of insisting on 'friendly governments' in their neighboring countries, they have in mind something quite different from what we would mean." The Russians, he surmised, really believed that Washington accepted "their position that although they would keep us informed they had the right to settle their problems with their western neighbors unilaterally." But the Soviet position was still in flux: "the Soviet Government is not one mind." The problem, as Harriman had earlier told Harry Hopkins, was "to strengthen the hands of those around Stalin who want to play the game along our lines." The way to do this, he now told Hull, was to be understanding of their sensitivity, meet them much more than half way, encourage them and support them wherever we can, and yet oppose them promptly with the greatest of firmness where we see them going wrong. . . . The only way we can eventually come to an understanding with the Soviet Union on the question of non-interference in the internal affairs of other countries is for us to take a definite interest in the solution of the problems of each individual country as they arise.

As against Harriman's sophisticated universalist strategy, however, Churchill, increasingly fearful of the consequences of unrestrained competition in Eastern Europe, decided in early October to carry his sphere-of-influence proposal directly to Moscow. Roosevelt was at first content to have Churchill speak for him too and even prepared a cable to that effect. But Hopkins, a more rigorous universalist, took it upon himself to stop the cable and warn Roosevelt of its possible implications. Eventually Roosevelt sent a message to Harriman in Moscow emphasizing that he expected to "retain complete freedom of action after this conference is over." It was now that Churchill quickly proposed — and Stalin as quickly accepted — the celebrated division of southeastern Europe: ending (after further haggling between Eden and Molotov) with 90 percent Soviet predominance in Rumania, 80 percent in Bulgaria and Hungary, fifty-fifty in Yugoslavia, and 90 percent British predominance in Greece.

Churchill in discussing this with Harriman used the phrase "spheres of influence." But he insisted that these were only "immediate wartime arrangements" and received a highly general blessing from Roosevelt. Yet, whatever Churchill intended, there is reason to believe that Stalin construed the percentages as an agreement, not a declaration; as practical arithmetic, not algebra. For Stalin, it should be understood, the sphere-of-influence idea did not mean that he would abandon all efforts to spread communism in some other nation's sphere; it did mean that, if he tried this and the other side cracked down, he could not feel he had serious cause for complaint. As Kennan wrote to Harriman at the end of 1944:

> As far as border states are concerned the Soviet government has never ceased to think in terms of spheres of interest. They expect us to support them in whatever action they wish to take in those regions, regardless of whether that action seems to us or to the rest of the world to be right or wrong. . . . I have no doubt that this position is honestly maintained on their part, and that they would be equally prepared to reserve moral judgment on any actions which we might wish to carry out, i.e., in the Caribbean area.

In any case, the matter was already under test a good deal closer to Moscow than the Caribbean. The communist-dominated resistance movement in Greece was in open revolt against the effort of the Papandreou government to disarm and disband the guerrillas (the same Papandreou whom the Greek colonels have recently arrested on the claim that he is a tool of the communists). Churchill now called in British Army units to crush the insurrection.

This action produced a storm of criticism in his own country and in the United States; the American government even publicly dissociated itself from the intervention, thereby emphasizing its detachment from the sphere-of-influence deal. But Stalin, Churchill later claimed, "adhered strictly and faithfully to our agreement of October, and during all the long weeks of fighting the Communists in the streets of Athens not one word of reproach came from *Pravda* or *Izvestia,*" though there is no evidence that he tried to call off the Greek communists. Still, when the communist rebellion later broke out again in Greece, Stalin told Kardelj and Djilas of Yugoslavia in 1948, "The uprising in Greece must be stopped, and as quickly as possible."

No one, of course, can know what really was in the minds of the Russian leaders. The Kremlin archives are locked; of the primary actors, only Molotov survives, and he has not yet indicated any desire to collaborate with the Columbia Oral History Project. We do know that Stalin did not wholly surrender to sentimental illusion about his new friends. In June 1944, on the night before the landings in Normandy, he told Djilas that the English "find nothing sweeter than to trick their allies. . . . And Churchill? Churchill is the kind who, if you don't watch him, will slip a kopeck out of your pocket. Yes, a kopeck out of your pocket!. . . Roosevelt is not like that. He dips in his hand only for bigger coins." But whatever his views of his colleagues it is not unreasonable to suppose that Stalin would have been satisfied at the end of the war to secure what Kennan has called "a protective glacis along Russia's western border," and that, in exchange for a free hand in Eastern Europe, he was prepared to give the British and the Americans equally free hands in their zones of vital interest, including in nations as close to Russia as Greece (for the British) and, very probably — or at least so the Yugoslavs believe — China (for the United States). In other words, his initial objectives were very probably not world conquest but Russian security.

V

It is now pertinent to inquire why the United States rejected the idea of stabilizing the world by division into spheres of influence and insisted on an East European strategy. One should warn against rushing to the conclusion that it was all a row between hard-nosed, balance-of-power realists and starry-eyed Wilsonians. Roosevelt, Hopkins, Welles, Harriman, Bohlen, Berle, Dulles, and other universalists were tough and serious men. Why then did they rebuff the sphere-of-influence solution?

The first reason is that they regarded this solution as containing within itself the seeds of a third world war. The balance-of-power idea seemed inherently unstable. It had always broken down in the past. It held out to each power the permanent temptation to try to alter the balance in its own favor, and it built this temptation into the international order. It would turn the great powers of 1945 away from the objective of concerting common policies toward competition for postwar advantage. As Hopkins told Molotov at Teheran, "The President feels it essential to world peace that Russia, Great Britain, and the United States work out this control question in a manner which will not start each of the three powers arming against the others." "The greatest likelihood of eventual conflict," said the Joint Chiefs of Staff in 1944 (the only conflict which the J.C.S., in its wisdom, could then glimpse "in the foreseeable future" was between Britain and Russia), " . . . would seem to grow out of either nation initiating attempts to build up its strength, by seeking to attach to herself parts of Europe to the disadvantage and possible danger of her potential adversary." The Americans were perfectly ready to acknowledge that Russia was entitled to convincing assurance of her national security — but not this way. "I could sympathize fully with Stalin's desire to protect his western borders from future attack," as Hull put it. "But I felt that this security could best be obtained through a strong postwar peace organization."

Hull's remark suggests the second objection: that the sphere-of-influence approach would, in the words of the State Department in 1945, "militate against the establishment and effective functioning of a broader system of general security in which all countries will have their part." The United Nations, in short, was seen as the alternative to the balance of power. Nor did the universalists see any necessary incompatibility between the Russian desire for "friendly governments" on its frontier and the American desire for self-determination in Eastern Europe. Before Yalta the State Department judged the general mood of Europe as "to the left and strongly in favor of far-reaching economic and social reforms, but not, however, in favor of a left-wing totalitarian regime to achieve these reforms." Governments in Eastern Europe could be sufficiently to the left "to allay Soviet suspicions" but sufficiently representative "of the center and *petit bourgeois* elements" not to seem a prelude to communist dictatorship. The American criteria were therefore that the government "should be dedicated to the preservation of civil liberties" and "should favor social and economic reforms." A string of New Deal states — of Finlands and Czechoslovakias — seemed a reasonable compromise solution.

Third, the universalists feared that the sphere-of-interest approach would be what Hull termed "a haven for the isolationists," who would advocate America's participation in Western Hemisphere affairs on condition that it did not participate in European or Asian affairs. Hull also feared that spheres of interest would lead to "closed trade areas or discriminatory systems" and thus defeat his cherished dream of a low-tariff, freely trading world.

Fourth, the sphere-of-interest solution meant the betrayal of the principles for which the Second World War was being fought — the Atlantic Charter, the Four Freedoms, the Declaration of the United Nations. Poland summed up the problem. Britain, having gone to war to defend the independence of Poland from the Germans, could not easily conclude the war by surrendering the independence of Poland to the Russians. Thus, as Hopkins told Stalin after Roosevelt's death in 1945, Poland had "become the symbol of our ability to work out problems with the Soviet Union." Nor could American liberals in general watch with equanimity while the police state spread into countries which, if they had mostly not been real democracies, had mostly not been tyrannies either. The execution in 1943 of Ehrlich and Alter, the Polish social-ist trade union leaders, excited deep concern. "I have particularly in mind," Harriman cabled in 1944, "objection to the institution of secret police who may become involved in the persecution of persons of truly democratic convictions who may not be willing to conform to Soviet methods."

Fifth, the sphere-of-influence solution would create difficult domestic prob-lems in American politics. Roosevelt was aware of the six million or more Polish votes in the 1944 election; even more acutely, he was aware of the broader and deeper attack which would follow if, after going to war to stop the Nazi conquest of Europe, he permitted the war to end with the communist conquest of Eastern Europe. As Archibald MacLeish, then Assistant Secretary of State for Public Affairs, warned in January 1945, "The wave of disillusion-ment which has distressed us in the last several weeks will be increased if the impression is permitted to get abroad that potentially totalitarian provisional governments are to be set up without adequate safeguards as to the holding of free elections and the realization of the principles of the Atlantic Charter." Roosevelt believed that no administration could survive which did not try everything short of war to save Eastern Europe, and he was the supreme American politician of the century.

Sixth, if the Russians were allowed to overrun Eastern Europe without argument, would that satisfy them? Even Kennan, in a dispatch of May 1944, admitted that the "urge" had dreadful potentialities: "If initially successful, will it know where to stop? Will it not be inexorably carried forward, by its very nature, in a struggle to reach the whole — to attain complete mastery of the shores of the Atlantic and the Pacific?" His own answer was that there were inherent limits to the Russian capacity to expand — "that Russia will not have an easy time in maintaining the power which it has seized over other people in Eastern and Central Europe unless it receives both moral and material assistance from the West." Subsequent developments have vindicated Ken-nan's argument. By the late forties, Yugoslavia and Albania, the two East European states farthest from the Soviet Union and the two in which commu-nism was imposed from within rather than from without, had declared their independence of Moscow. But, given Russia's success in maintaining centralized control over the international communist movement for a quarter of a century, who in 1944 could have had much confidence in the idea of communist revolts against Moscow?

Most of those involved therefore rejected Kennan's answer and stayed with his question. If the West turned its back on Eastern Europe, the higher probability, in their view, was that the Russians would use their security zone, not just for defensive purposes but as a springboard from which to mount an attack on Western Europe, now shattered by war, a vacuum of power awaiting its master. "If the policy is accepted that the Soviet Union has a right to penetrate her immediate neighbors for security," Harriman said in 1944, "penetration of the next immediate neighbors becomes at a certain time equally logical." If a row with Russia were inevitable, every consideration of prudence dictated that it should take place in Eastern rather than Western Europe.

Thus idealism and realism joined in opposition to the sphere-of-influence solution. The consequence was a determination to assert an American interest in the postwar destiny of all nations, including those of Eastern Europe. In the message which Roosevelt and Hopkins drafted after Hopkins had stopped Roosevelt's initial cable authorizing Churchill to speak for the United States at the Moscow meeting of October 1944, Roosevelt now said, "There is in this global war literally no question, either military or political, in which the United States is not interested." After Roosevelt's death Hopkins repeated the point to Stalin: "The cardinal basis of President Roosevelt's policy which the American people had fully supported had been the concept that the interests of the U.S. were worldwide and not confined to North and South America and the Pacific Ocean."

VI

For better or worse, this was the American position. It is now necessary to attempt the imaginative leap and consider the impact of this position on the leaders of the Soviet Union who, also for better or for worse, had reached the bitter conclusion that the survival of their country depended on their unchallenged control of the corridors through which enemies had so often invaded their homeland. They could claim to have been keeping their own side of the sphere-of-influence bargain. Of course, they were working to capture the resistance movements of Western Europe; indeed, with the appointment of Oumansky as Ambassador to Mexico they were even beginning to enlarge underground operations in the Western Hemisphere. But, from their viewpoint, if the West permitted this, the more fools they; and, if the West stopped it, it was within their right to do so. In overt political matters the Russians were scrupulously playing the game. They had watched in silence while the British shot down Communists in Greece. In Yugoslavia Stalin was urging Tito (as Djilas later revealed) to keep King Peter. They had not only acknowledged Western preeminence in Italy but had recognized the Badoglio regime; the Italian communists had even voted (against the Socialists and the Liberals) for the renewal of the Lateran Pacts.

They would not regard anti-communist action in a Western zone as a *casus belli,* and they expected reciprocal license to assert their own authority in the East. But the principle of self-determination was carrying the United States into a deeper entanglement in Eastern Europe than the Soviet Union claimed as a right (whatever it was doing underground) in the affairs of Italy, Greece, or China. When the Russians now exercised in Eastern Europe the same brutal control they were prepared to have Washington exercise in the American sphere of influence, the American protests, given the paranoia produced alike by Russian history and Leninist ideology, no doubt seemed not only an act of hypocrisy but a threat to security. To the Russians, a stroll into the neighborhood easily became a plot to burn down the house: when, for example, damaged American planes made emergency landings in Poland and Hungary, Moscow took this as attempts to organize the local resistance. It is not unusual to suspect one's adversary of doing what one is already doing oneself. At the same time, the cruelty with which the Russians executed their idea of spheres of influence — in a sense, perhaps, an unwitting cruelty, since Stalin treated the East Europeans no worse than he had treated the Russians in the thirties — discouraged the West from accepting the equation (for example, Italy= Rumania) which seemed so self-evident to the Kremlin.

So Moscow very probably, and not unnaturally, perceived the emphasis on self-determination as a systematic and deliberate pressure on Russia's western frontiers. Moreover, the restoration of capitalism to countries freed at frightful cost by the Red Army no doubt struck the Russians as the betrayal of the principles for which *they* were fighting. "That they, the victors," Isaac Deutscher has suggested, "should now preserve an order from which they had experienced nothing but hostility, and could expect nothing but hostility . . . would have been the most miserable anti-climax to their great 'war of liberation.' " By 1944 Poland was the critical issue; Harriman later said that "under instructions from President Roosevelt, I talked about Poland with Stalin more frequently than any other subject." While the West saw the point of Stalin's demand for a "friendly government" in Warsaw, the American insistence on the sovereign virtues of free elections (ironically in the spirit of the 1917 Bolshevik decree of peace, which affirmed "the right" of a nation "to decide the forms of its state existence by a free vote, taken after the complete evacuation of the incorporating or, generally, of the stronger nation") created an insoluble problem in those countries, like Poland (and Rumania) where free elections would almost certainly produce anti-Soviet governments.

The Russians thus may well have estimated the Western pressures as calculated to encourage their enemies in Eastern Europe and to defeat their own minimum objective of a protective glacis. Everything still hung, however, on the course of military operations. The wartime collaboration had been created by one thing, and one thing alone: the threat of Nazi victory. So long as this threat was real, so was the collaboration. In late December 1944, von Rundstedt launched his counteroffensive in the Ardennes. A few weeks later, when Roosevelt, Churchill, and Stalin gathered in the Crimea, it was in the shadow of this last considerable explosion of German power. The meeting at Yalta was still dominated by the mood of war.

Yalta remains something of an historical perplexity — less, from the perspective of 1967, because of a mythical American deference to the sphere-of-influence thesis than because of the documentable Russian deference to the universalist thesis. Why should Stalin in 1945 have accepted the Declaration on Liberated Europe and an agreement on Poland pledging that "the three governments will jointly" act to assure "free elections of governments responsive to the will of the people"? There are several probable answers: that the war was not over and the Russians still wanted the Americans to intensify their military effort in the West; that one clause in the Declaration premised action on "the opinion of the three governments" and thus implied a Soviet veto, though the Polish agreement was more definite; most of all that the universalist algebra of the Declaration was plainly in Stalin's mind to be construed in terms of the practical arithmetic of his sphere-of-influence agreement with Churchill the previous October. Stalin's assurance to Churchill at Yalta that a proposed Russian amendment to the Declaration would not apply to Greece makes it clear that Roosevelt's pieties did not, in Stalin's mind, nullify Churchill's percentages. He could well have been strengthened in this supposition by the fact that *after* Yalta, Churchill himself repeatedly reasserted the terms of the October agreement as if he regarded it, despite Yalta, as controlling.

Harriman still had the feeling before Yalta that the Kremlin had "two approaches to their postwar policies" and that Stalin himself was "of two minds." One approach emphasized the internal reconstruction and development of Russia; the other its external expansion. But in the meantime the fact which dominated all political decisions — that is, the war against Germany — was moving into its final phase. In the weeks after Yalta, the military situation changed with great rapidity. As the Nazi threat declined, so too did the need for cooperation. The Soviet Union, feeling itself menaced by the American idea of self-determination and the borderlands diplomacy to which it was leading, skeptical whether the United Nations would protect its frontiers as reliably as its own domination in Eastern Europe, began to fulfill its security requirements unilaterally.

In March Stalin expressed his evaluation of the United Nations by rejecting Roosevelt's plea that Molotov come to the San Francisco conference, if only for the opening sessions. In the next weeks the Russians emphatically and crudely worked their will in Eastern Europe, above all in the test country of Poland. They were ignoring the Declaration on Liberated Europe, ignoring the

Atlantic Charter, self-determination, human freedom, and everything else the Americans considered essential for a stable peace. "We must clearly recognize," Harriman wired Washington a few days before Roosevelt's death, "that the Soviet program is the establishment of totalitarianism, ending personal liberty and democracy as we know and respect it."

At the same time, the Russians also began to mobilize communist resources in the United States itself to block American universalism. In April 1945 Jacques Duclos, who had been the Comintern official responsible for the Western communist parties, launched in *Cahiers du Communisme* an uncompromising attack on the policy of the American Communist Party. Duclos sharply condemned the revisionism of Earl Browder, the American Communist leader, as "expressed in the concept of a long-term class peace in the United States, of the possibility of the suppression of the class struggle in the postwar period and of establishment of harmony between labor and capital." Browder was specifically rebuked for favoring the "self-determination" of Europe "west of the Soviet Union" on a bourgeois-democratic basis. The excommunication of Browderism was plainly the Politburo's considered reaction to the impending defeat of Germany; it was a signal to the communist parties of the West that they should recover their identity; it was Moscow's alert to communists everywhere that they should prepare for new policies in the postwar world.

The Duclos piece obviously could not have been planned and written much later than the Yalta conference — that is, well before a number of events which revisionists now cite in order to demonstrate American responsibility for the Cold War: before Allen Dulles, for example, began to negotiate the surrender of the German armies in Italy (the episode which provoked Stalin to charge Roosevelt with seeking a separate peace and provoked Roosevelt to denounce the "vile misrepresentations" of Stalin's informants); well before Roosevelt died; many months before the testing of the atomic bomb; even more months before Truman ordered that the bomb be dropped on Japan. William Z. Foster, who soon replaced Browder as the leader of the American Communist Party and embodied the new Moscow line, later boasted of having said in January 1944, "A postwar Roosevelt administration would continue to be, as it is now, an imperialist government." With ancient suspicions revived by the American insistence on universalism, this was no doubt the conclusion which the Russians were reaching at the same time. The Soviet canonization of Roosevelt (like their present-day canonization of Kennedy) took place after the American President's death.

The atmosphere of mutual suspicion was beginning to rise. In January 1945 Molotov formally proposed that the United States grant Russia a $6 billion credit for postwar reconstruction. With characteristic tact he explained that he was doing this as a favor to save America from a postwar depression. The proposal seems to have been diffidently made and diffidently received. Roosevelt requested that the matter "not be pressed further" on the American side until he had a chance to talk with Stalin; but the Russians did not follow it up either at Yalta in February (save for a single glancing reference) or during the Stalin-Hopkins talks in May or at Potsdam. Finally the proposal was renewed in the very different political atmosphere of August. This time Washington inexplicably mislaid the request during the transfer of the records of the Foreign Economic Administration to the State Department. It did not turn up again until March 1946. Of course this was impossible for the Russians to believe; it is hard enough even for those acquainted with the capacity of the American government for incompetence to believe; and it only strengthened Soviet suspicions of American purposes.

The American credit was one conceivable form of Western contribution to Russian reconstruction. Another was lend-lease, and the possibility of reconstruction aid under the lend-lease protocol had already been discussed in 1944. But in May 1945 Russia, like Britain, suffered from Truman's abrupt termination of lend-lease shipments — "unfortunate and even brutal," Stalin told Hopkins, adding that, if it was "designed as pressure on the Russians in order to soften them up, then it was a fundamental mistake." A third form was German reparations. Here Stalin, in demanding $10 billion in reparations for the Soviet Union, made his strongest fight at Yalta. Roosevelt, while agreeing essentially with Churchill's opposition, tried to postpone the matter by accepting the Soviet figure as a "basis for discussion — a formula which led to future misunderstanding. In short, the Russian hope for major Western assistance in postwar reconstruction foundered on three events which the Kremlin could well have interpreted respectively as deliberate sabotage (the loan request), blackmail (lend-lease cancellation), and pro-Germanism (reparations).

Actually the American attempt to settle the fourth lend-lease protocol was generous and the Russians for their own reasons declined to come to an agreement. It is not clear, though, that satisfying Moscow on any of these financial scores would have made much essential difference. It might have persuaded some doves in the Kremlin that the U.S. government was genuinely friendly; it might have persuaded some hawks that the American anxiety for Soviet friendship was such that Moscow could do as it wished without inviting challenge from the United States. It would, in short, merely have reinforced both sides of the Kremlin debate; it would hardly have reversed deeper tendencies toward the deterioration of political relationships. Economic deals were surely subordinate to the quality of mutual political confidence; and here, in the months after Yalta, the decay was steady.

The Cold War had now begun. It was the product not of a decision but of a dilemma. Each side felt compelled to adopt policies which the other could not but regard as a threat to the principles of the peace. Each then felt compelled to undertake defensive measures. Thus the Russians saw no choice but to consolidate their security in Eastern Europe. The Americans, regarding

Eastern Europe as the first step toward Western Europe, responded by asserting their interest in the zone the Russians deemed vital to their security. The
Russians concluded that the West was resuming its old course of capitalist
encirclement; that it was purposefully laying the foundation for anti-Soviet
regimes in the area defined by the blood of centuries as crucial to Russian
survival. Each side believed with passion that future international stability
depended on the success of its own conception of world order. Each side, in
pursuing its own clearly indicated and deeply cherished principles, was only
confirming the fear of the other that it was bent on aggression.

Very soon the process began to acquire a cumulative momentum. The
impending collapse of Germany thus provoked new troubles: the Russians, for
example, sincerely feared that the West was planning a separate surrender of
the German armies in Italy in a way which would release troops for Hitler's
eastern front, as they subsequently feared that the Nazis might succeed in
surrendering Berlin to the West. This was the context in which the atomic
bomb now appeared. Though the revisionist argument that Truman dropped
the bomb less to defeat Japan than to intimidate Russia is not convincing, this
thought unquestionably appealed to some in Washington as at least an advantageous side-effect of Hiroshima.

So the machinery of suspicion and counter-suspicion, action and coun-
ter-action, was set in motion. But, given relations among traditional national
states, there was still no reason, even with all the postwar jostling, why this
should not have remained a manageable situation. What made it unmanage-
able, what caused the rapid escalation of the Cold War and in another two
years completed the division of Europe, was a set of considerations which this
account has thus far excluded.

VII

Up to this point, the discussion has considered the schism within the wartime
coalition as if it were entirely the result of disagreements among national states.
Assuming this framework, there was unquestionably a failure of communication between America and Russia, a misperception of signals and, as time went
on, a mounting tendency to ascribe ominous motives to the other side. It seems
hard, for example, to deny that American postwar policy created genuine
difficulties for the Russians and even assumed a threatening aspect for them.
All this the revisionists have rightly and usefully emphasized.

But the great omission of the revisionists — and also the fundamental
explanation of the speed with which the Cold War escalated — lies precisely
in the fact that the Soviet Union was *not* a traditional national state.[4] This is

4. This is the classical revisionist fallacy — the assumption of the rationality, or at least
of the traditionalism, of states where ideology and social organization have created a different

where the "mirror image," invoked by some psychologists, falls down. For the Soviet Union was a phenomenon very different from America or Britain: it was a totalitarian state, endowed with an all-explanatory, all-consuming ideology, committed to the infallibility of government and party, still in a somewhat messianic mood, equating dissent with treason, and ruled by a dictator who, for all his quite extraordinary abilities, had his paranoid moments.

Marxism-Leninism gave the Russian leaders a view of the world according to which all societies were inexorably destined to proceed along appointed roads by appointed stages until they achieved the classless nirvana. Moreover, given the resistance of the capitalists to this development, the existence of any non-communist state was *by definition* a threat to the Soviet Union. "As long as capitalism and socialism exist," Lenin wrote, "we cannot live in peace: in the end, one or the other will triumph — a funeral dirge will be sung either over the Soviet Republic or over world capitalism."

Stalin and his associates, whatever Roosevelt or Truman did or failed to do, were bound to regard the United States as the enemy, not because of this deed or that, but because of the primordial fact that America was the leading capitalist power and thus, by Leninist syllogism, unappeasably hostile, driven by the logic of its system to oppose, encircle, and destroy Soviet Russia. Nothing the United States could have done in 1944 – 45 would have abolished this mistrust, required and sanctified as it was by Marxist gospel — nothing short of the conversion of the United States into a Stalinist despotism; and even this would not have sufficed, as the experience of Yugoslavia and China soon showed, unless it were accompanied by total subservience to Moscow. So long as the United States remained a capitalist democracy, no American policy, given Moscow's theology, could hope to win basic Soviet confidence, and every American action was poisoned from the source. So long as the Soviet Union remained a messianic state, ideology compelled a steady expansion of communist power.

It is easy, of course, to exaggerate the capacity of ideology to control events. The tension of acting according to revolutionary abstractions is too much for most nations to sustain over a long period: that is why Mao Tse-tung has launched his Cultural Revolution, hoping thereby to create a permanent revolutionary mood and save Chinese communism from the degeneration which, in his view, has overtaken Russian communism. Still, as any revolution grows older, normal human and social motives will increasingly reassert themselves. In due course, we can be sure, Leninism will be about as effective in governing

---

range of motives. So the Second World War revisionists omit the totalitarian dynamism of Nazism and the fanaticism of Hitler, as the Civil War revisionists omit the fact that the slavery system was producing a doctrinaire closed society in the American South. For a consideration of some of these issues, see "The Causes of the Civil War: A Note on Historical Sentimentalism" in my *The Politics of Hope* (Boston, 1963).

the daily lives of Russians as Christianity is in governing the daily lives of Americans. Like the Ten Commandments and the Sermon on the Mount, the Leninist verities will increasingly become platitudes for ritual observance, not guides to secular decision. There can be no worse fallacy (even if respectable people practiced it diligently for a season in the United States) than that of drawing from a nation's ideology permanent conclusions about its behavior.

A temporary recession of ideology was already taking place during the Second World War when Stalin, to rally his people against the invader, had to replace the appeal of Marxism by that of nationalism. ("We are under no illusions that they are fighting for us," Stalin once said to Harriman. "They are fighting for Mother Russia.") But this was still taking place within the strictest limitations. The Soviet Union remained as much a police state as ever; the regime was as infallible as ever; foreigners and their ideas were as suspect as ever. "Never, except possibly during my later experience as ambassador in Moscow," Kennan has written, "did the insistence of the Soviet authorities on isolation of the diplomatic corps weigh more heavily on me . . . than in these first weeks following my return to Russia in the final months of the war. . . . [We were] treated as though we were the bearers of some species of the plague" — which, of course, from the Soviet viewpoint, they were: the plague of skepticism.

Paradoxically, of the forces capable of bringing about a modification of ideology, the most practical and effective was the Soviet dictatorship itself. If Stalin was an ideologist, he was also a pragmatist. If he saw everything through the lenses of Marxism-Leninism, he also, as the infallible expositor of the faith, could reinterpret Marxism-Leninism to justify anything he wanted to do at any given moment. No doubt Roosevelt's ignorance of Marxism-Leninism was inexcusable and led to grievous miscalculations. But Roosevelt's efforts to work on and through Stalin were not so hopelessly naïve as it used to be fashionable to think. With the extraordinary instinct of a great political leader, Roosevelt intuitively understood that Stalin was the *only* lever available to the West against the Leninist ideology and the Soviet system. If Stalin could be reached, then alone was there a chance of getting the Russians to act contrary to the prescriptions of their faith. The best evidence is that Roosevelt retained a certain capacity to influence Stalin to the end; the nominal Soviet acquiescence in American universalism as late as Yalta was perhaps an indication of that. It is in this way that the death of Roosevelt was crucial — not in the vulgar sense that his policy was then reversed by his successor, which did not happen, but in the sense that no other American could hope to have the restraining impact on Stalin which Roosevelt might for a while have had.

Stalin alone could have made any difference. Yet Stalin, in spite of the impression of sobriety and realism he made on Westerners who saw him during the Second World War, was plainly a man of deep and morbid obsessions and compulsions. When he was still a young man, Lenin had criticized his rude and arbitrary ways. A reasonably authoritative observer (N. S. Khrushchev) later commented, "These negative characteristics of his developed steadily and during the last years acquired an absolutely insufferable character." His para-noia, probably set off by the suicide of his wife in 1932, led to the terrible purges of the mid-thirties and the wanton murder of thousands of his Bolshevik comrades. "Everywhere and in everything," Khrushchev says of this period, "he saw 'enemies,' 'double-dealers' and 'spies.' " The crisis of war evidently steadied him in some way, though Khrushchev speaks of his "nervousness and hysteria . . . even after the war began." The madness, so rigidly controlled for a time, burst out with new and shocking intensity in the postwar years. "After the war," Khrushchev testifies,

> the situation became even more complicated. Stalin became even more capricious, irritable and brutal; in particular, his suspicion grew. His persecution mania reached unbelievable dimensions. . . . He decided everything, without any consideration for anyone or anything.
>
> Stalin's wilfulness showed itself . . . also in the international relations of the Soviet Union. . . . He had completely lost a sense of reality; he demonstrated his suspicion and haughtiness not only in relation to individuals in the USSR, but in relation to whole parties and nations.

A revisionist fallacy has been to treat Stalin as just another *Realpolitik* states-man, as Second World War revisionists see Hitler as just another Stresemann or Bismarck. But the record makes it clear that in the end nothing could satisfy Stalin's paranoia. His own associates failed. Why does anyone suppose that any conceivable American policy would have succeeded?

An analysis of the origins of the Cold War which leaves out these factors — the intransigence of Leninist ideology, the sinister dynamics of a totalitarian society, and the madness of Stalin — is obviously incomplete. It was these factors which made it hard for the West to accept the thesis that Russia was moved only by a desire to protect its security and would be satisfied by the control of Eastern Europe; it was these factors which charged the debate between universalism and spheres of influence with apocalyptic potentiality.

Leninism and totalitarianism created a structure of thought and behavior which made postwar collaboration between Russia and America — in any normal sense of civilized intercourse between national states — inherently im-possible. The Soviet dictatorship of 1945 simply could not have survived such a collaboration. Indeed, nearly a quarter-century later, the Soviet regime, though it has meanwhile moved a good distance, could still hardly survive it without risking the release inside Russia of energies profoundly opposed to communist despotism. As for Stalin, he may have represented the only force in 1945 capable of overcoming Stalinism, but the very traits which enabled him to win absolute power expressed terrifying instabilities of mind and tempera-ment and hardly offered a solid foundation for a peaceful world.

VIII

The difference between America and Russia in 1945 was that some Americans fundamentally believed that, over a long run, a *modus vivendi* with Russia was possible; while the Russians, so far as one can tell, believed in no more than a short-run *modus vivendi* with the United States.

Harriman and Kennan, this narrative has made clear, took the lead in warning Washington about the difficulties of short-run dealings with the Soviet Union. But both argued that, if the United States developed a rational policy and stuck to it, there would be, after long and rough passages, the prospect of eventual clearing. "I am, as you know," Harriman cabled Washington in early April, "a most earnest advocate of the closest possible understanding with the Soviet Union so that what I am saying relates only to how best to attain such understanding." Kennan has similarly made it clear that the function of his containment policy was "to tide us over a difficult time and bring us to the point where we could discuss effectively with the Russians the dangers and drawbacks this status quo involved, and to arrange with them for its peaceful replacement by a better and sounder one." The subsequent careers of both men attest to the honesty of these statements.

There is no corresponding evidence on the Russian side that anyone seriously sought a *modus vivendi* in these terms. Stalin's choice was whether his long-term ideological and national interests would be better served by a short-run truce with the West or by an immediate resumption of pressure. In October 1945 Stalin indicated to Harriman at Sochi that he planned to adopt the second course — that the Soviet Union was going isolationist. No doubt the succession of problems with the United States contributed to this decision, but the basic causes most probably lay elsewhere: in the developing situations in Eastern Europe, in Western Europe, and in the United States.

In Eastern Europe, Stalin was still for a moment experimenting with techniques of control. But he must by now have begun to conclude that he had underestimated the hostility of the people to Russian dominion. The Hungarian elections in November would finally convince him that the Yalta formula was a road to anti-Soviet governments. At the same time, he was feeling more strongly than ever a sense of his opportunities in Western Europe. The other half of the Continent lay unexpectedly before him, politically demoralized, economically prostrate, militarily defenseless. The hunting would be better and safer than he had anticipated. As for the United States, the alacrity of postwar demobilization must have recalled Roosevelt's offhand remark at Yalta that "two years would be the limit" for keeping American troops in Europe. And, despite Dr. Eugene Varga's doubts about the imminence of American economic breakdown, Marxist theology assured Stalin that the United States was heading into a bitter postwar depression and would be consumed with its own problems. If the condition of Eastern Europe made unilateral action seem essential in the interests of Russian security, the condition of Western Europe and the United States offered new temptations for communist expansion. The Cold War was now in full swing.

It still had its year of modulations and accommodations. Secretary Byrnes conducted his long and fruitless campaign to persuade the Russians that America only sought governments in Eastern Europe "both friendly to the Soviet Union and representative of all the democratic elements of the country." Crises were surmounted in Trieste and Iran. Secretary Marshall evidently did not give up hope of a *modus vivendi* until the Moscow conference of foreign secretaries of March 1947. Even then, the Soviet Union was invited to participate in the Marshall Plan.

The point of no return came on July 2, 1947, when Molotov, after bringing 89 technical specialists with him to Paris and evincing initial interest in the project for European reconstruction, received the hot flash from the Kremlin, denounced the whole idea, and walked out of the conference. For the next fifteen years the Cold War raged unabated, passing out of historical ambiguity into the realm of good versus evil and breeding on both sides simplifications, stereotypes, and self-serving absolutes, often couched in interchangeable phrases. Under the pressure even America, for a deplorable decade, forsook its pragmatic and pluralist traditions, posed as God's appointed messenger to ignorant and sinful man, and followed the Soviet example in looking to a world remade in its own image.

In retrospect, if it is impossible to see the Cold War as a case of American aggression and Russian response, it is also hard to see it as a pure case of Russian aggression and American response. "In what is truly tragic," wrote Hegel, "there must be valid moral powers on both the sides which come into collision. . . . Both suffer loss and yet both are mutually justified." In this sense, the Cold War had its tragic elements. The question remains whether it was an instance of Greek tragedy — as Auden has called it, "the tragedy of necessity," where the feeling aroused in the spectator is "What a pity it had to be this way" — or of Christian tragedy, "the tragedy of possibility," where the feeling aroused is "What a pity it was this way when it might have been otherwise."

Once something has happened, the historian is tempted to assume that it had to happen; but this may often be a highly unphilosophical assumption. The Cold War could have been avoided only if the Soviet Union had not been possessed by convictions both of the infallibility of the communist word and of the inevitability of a communist world. These convictions transformed an impasse between national states into a religious war, a tragedy of possibility into one of necessity. One might wish that America had preserved the poise and proportion of the first years of the Cold War and had not in time succumbed to its own forms of self-righteousness. But the most rational of American policies could hardly have averted the Cold War. Only today, as Russia begins to recede from its messianic mission and to accept, in practice if not yet in principle, the permanence of the world of diversity, only now can the hope flicker that this long, dreary, costly contest may at last be taking on forms less dramatic, less obsessive, and less dangerous to the future of mankind.

The Cold War Revisionists*

It becomes increasingly clear that many of the policies and actions of the New and Fair Deals, and of the upper-class Daniel Boones of the New Frontier, are producing something less than happiness and security. One of the reactions of liberals within the Establishment is to blame that Nasty Old Populist Lyndon, and to regroup with their own kind. That course has its intellectual and moral difficulties, however, as well as its pragmatic risks, and no one has pointed them out more directly than Daniel P. Moynihan.

One has to respect the integrity and the historical accuracy of his remarks to the A.D.A. on September 24. "The war in Vietnam," he candidly announced, "was thought up and is being managed by the men John F. Kennedy brought to Washington." Then, addressing his audience directly, he remarked that there were few present "who did not contribute something considerable to persuade the American people that we were entirely right to be setting out on the course that has led us to the present point of being waist-deep in the big muddy. It is this knowledge, this complicity if you will, that requires of many of us a restraint. . . . Who are we to say we would have done better?"

Brave words — and largely true.

But also terribly and dangerously misleading. For there is neither logical nor moral discrepancy between acknowledging responsibility and admitting

*Reprinted from *The Nation*, CCV, 16 (November 13, 1967), pp. 492 – 495, by permission of the author and the publisher.

error. It is neither the act of a trimmer or coward, nor an abstract proposition advanced by an academic. Senator Fulbright and others have done it.

There is no transcendent reason to persist in rationalizing a mistake, or in hanging on to see it through. Explanations can no doubt be found for such action, but they do not speak to the central point. Those who realize that have clearly become increasingly nervous in the service of the Establishment. They know that the primary objective is to discover the where and the why of the mistake, and then rectify it as rapidly and effectively as possible.

A good deal of evidence suggests that Arthur M. Schlesinger, Jr., would like to rectify while at the same time prove that no mistakes were made of major dimensions. His little essays on the war in Vietnam, for example, are interesting exercises in trying to achieve that magical success. He does not succeed because no one can succeed in that enterprise: there are momentum, drift and chance in human affairs, but the initial course determines the effect of the momentum, drift and chance.

The difficulties of Schlesinger's approach are even more evident in his essay on "The Origins of the Cold War," printed in the October issue of *Foreign Affairs* (that *House Beautiful* of the Department of State). The article subtly admits some minor degree of American responsibility for the onset of the cold war as part of a central and overt attempt to modify the attitudes and policies of that era in the knowledge of their clearly dangerous consequences. But he maintains that there were no major American mistakes, and no major American responsibility, because nothing else could have been done. The trouble, he insists, was that "Stalin alone could have made any difference," and Stalin was paranoid.

There is a great book to be written some day explaining how Schlesinger and a good many other historians of his generation came by the power to render such flat-out psychiatric judgments without professional training and without direct access to their subjects. My own candidates for that undertaking are Robert Coles, Abraham H. Maslow, or Rollo May, men who somehow acquired a sense of the limits of their approach even as they mastered its discipline.

Meanwhile, the first point to be made about Schlesinger's attempt to fix the origins of the cold war in Stalin's paranoia is that *no major American policymaker between 1943 and 1948 defined and dealt with the Soviet Union in those terms.* Schlesinger offers not the slightest shred of evidence that such was the case. The reason is simple: there is no such evidence.

Even if Schlesinger's characterization of Stalin as a paranoid were granted, the argument would still be unable to account either for the nature or the adoption of American policy. There is only one circumstance in which his proposition would become directly relevant: If a different American policy had been carefully formulated and then seriously tried over a significant period of time, only to fail because of Russian intransigence, then Schlesinger's argument that Stalin's paranoia caused the cold war would bear on the case.

It is particularly important to grasp that point because Schlesinger does not introduce paranoia until after he has demonstrated that Stalin was acting on a rational and conservative basis. Long before he mentions paranoia, Schlesinger notes the ambivalence of Soviet leaders toward an accommodation with the United States, and makes it clear that American leaders were operating on that estimate of the situation — not on the proposition that the Russians were paranoid. While entering the caveat that "no one, of course, can know what was really in the minds of the Russian leaders," he nevertheless concludes that "it is not unreasonable to suppose that Stalin would have been satisfied at the end of the war to secure . . . 'a protective glacis along Russia's western border' . . . . His initial objective was very probably not world conquest but Russian security." And he makes it clear that Stalin kept his word about giving the British the initiative in Greece.

Schlesinger does not resort to explaining Soviet action in terms of paranoia until he has to deal with American efforts to exert direct influence on affairs in Eastern Europe. Then he casually asserts that it was a factor: "given the paranoia produced alike by Russian history and Leninist ideology, [American action] no doubt seemed not only an act of hypocrisy but a threat to security."

That offhand introduction of paranoia as a primary operational factor in historical explanation staggers the mind. It is simply not convincing to hold that a man (in this instance, Stalin) who believes he has negotiated a clear security perimeter is paranoid because he reacts negatively when one of the parties to the understanding (in this case the United States) unilaterally asserts and acts on a self-proclaimed right to intervene within that perimeter. When examined closely in connection with foreign affairs, the most that can be made of Schlesinger's argument is that Stalin may have had strong paranoid tendencies, and that the American thrust into Eastern Europe (and elsewhere throughout the world) could very well have pushed him gradually into, and perhaps through, the psychic zone separating neurosis from psychosis.

The most significant aspect of Schlesinger's argument that emerges at this point is his admission that America's assertion of its right to intervene anywhere in the world, and its action in doing so in Eastern Europe, had a primary effect on Soviet behavior. For in saying that, however he qualifies it later, Schlesinger has granted the validity of one of the major points made by the critics of the official line on the cold war. Many criticisms could be made of his description of the nature and dynamism of American global interventionism, which he labels "universalism," but the most important weakness in his analysis is the failure to discuss the explicit and implicit anti-communism that was a strong element in the American outlook from the moment the Bolsheviks seized power in 1917. That omission gravely undercuts the attempt he makes later to substantiate a vital part of his argument.

For, having admitted the reality and the consequences of American interventionism, Schlesinger faces the difficult problem of demonstrating the truth
of three propositions if he is to establish Soviet responsibility for the cold war.
First, he must show that a different American policy could not have produced
other results. Second, he must sustain the thesis that the Soviet response to
American universalism was indeed paranoid. Third, he must prove that the
American counterresponse was relevant and appropriate.

Schlesinger's argument that an alternate American policy would not have
made any difference has two themes. He says that a serious effort to negotiate
around the Soviet bid for a $6 billion loan would "merely have reinforced both
sides of the Kremlin debate" because "economic deals were merely subordinate to the quality of mutual political confidence." That judgment completely
overlooks the impact which a serious American economic proposal would have
made on the "quality of political confidence."

In the end, however, Schlesinger falls back on Soviet paranoia as the reason
that a different approach would have made no difference. Here, however, he
introduces a new factor in his explanation. In the early part of the argument,
he holds that the Soviets "thought *only* of spheres of influence; above all, the
Russians were determined to protect their frontiers, and especially their border
to the west, crossed so often and so bloodily in the dark course of their
history." But later Schlesinger suggests that the paranoia was partially caused,
and significantly reinforced, by the Marxist ideology of capitalist antagonism
and opposition.

However, Soviet leaders did not detect capitalist hostility merely because
they were viewing the world through a Marxist prism. Such enmity had
existed, and had been acted upon, since November, 1917, and anti-communism
was an integral part of the universalism that guided American leaders at the
end of World War II. As Schlesinger demonstrates, willy-nilly if not intentionally, American leaders were prepared to work with Russian leaders if they
would accept key features of the American creed. It is possible, given that
truth, to construct a syllogism proving that Stalin was paranoid because he did
not accept the terms. But that kind of proof has nothing to do with serious
historical inquiry, analysis and interpretation.

The real issue at this juncture, however, is not how Schlesinger attempts
to establish Stalin's paranoia. The central question is whether or not Soviet
actions are accurately described as paranoid. The evidence does not support
that interpretation. Consider the nature of Soviet behavior in three crucial
areas.

First, the Russians reacted to American intervention in Eastern Europe by
consolidating their existing position in that region. Many Soviet actions implementing that decision were overpowering, cruel and ruthless, but the methods
do not bear on the nature of the policy itself. The Soviet choice served to verify

an important point that Schlesinger acknowledges: Stalin told Harriman in October, 1945, that the Soviets were "going isolationist" in pursuit of their national interests. Russian policy at that time in Eastern Europe was neither paranoid nor messianic Marxism.

Second, the Soviets pulled back in other areas to avoid escalating a direct national or governmental confrontation with the United States. They did so in the clash over rival claims for oil rights in Iran; and that policy was even more strikingly apparent in Stalin's attempt to postpone Mao's triumph in China. In the first instance, prudence belies paranoia. In the second, any messianic urges were suppressed in the national interest.

Third, the Soviets acquiesced in the activities of non-Russian Communist movements. While the term *acquiesced* is not perfect for describing the complex process that was involved, it is nevertheless used advisedly as the best single term to describe the *effect* of Soviet action. Stalin and his colleagues no doubt sought results other than those that occurred in many places — China and Yugoslavia come particularly to mind — and clearly tried to realize their preferences. Nevertheless, they did acquiesce in results that fell far short of their desires.

Schlesinger makes a great deal, as do all official interpreters of the cold war, of the April, 1945, article by Jacques Duclos of the French Communist Party. Let us assume that Duclos wrote the article on orders from Moscow, even though the process that produced the action was probably far more complex than indicated by that simple statement. The crucial point about Duclos' article is that it can be read in two ways. It can be interpreted as a messianic cry for non-Soviet Communist parties to strike for power as part of a general push to expand Russian boundaries or the Soviet sphere of influence. But it can as persuasively be read as primarily a call for non-Soviet Communists to reassert their own identity and become militant and disruptive as part of the Russian strategy of consolidation in the face of American universalism.

Official explanations of the cold war generally imply that American leaders heard the Duclos piece as a bugle call for Communist aid in behalf of Soviet expansion. In truth, no significant number of American leaders feared a Russian military offensive at any time during the evolution of the cold war. When the Duclos article appeared, and for a long period thereafter, they were far more concerned with devising ways to use the great preponderance of American power to further the universalism and interventionism of the United States in Eastern Europe and elsewhere.

But the most astonishing use of the Duclos article by any defender of the official line on the cold war is made by Schlesinger when he employs it to avoid any serious discussion of the impact of the dropping of two atomic bombs in August, 1945. In truth, astonishing is a very mild word for Schlesinger's performance on this point. He says merely that the Duclos article came many months before the bombs were dropped, and then proceeds to ignore the *effect* of the bomb on Soviet leaders. All he adds is a flat assertion that the critics are "not convincing" in their argument that "the bomb was dropped less to defeat Japan than to intimidate Russia" (which is a strained interpretation of what they have said). That is not even to the point, for one could agree that the bomb was dropped only to finish the Japanese and still insist that it had a powerful effect on Soviet thought and action in connection with its future relations with the United States.

The argument could be made, of course, that only a Russia gone paranoid would have been upset by the American act. The issue of psychotic behavior might better be raised about the Americans. It could also be maintained that the United States had no responsibility for the effects of the bomb on Soviet leaders because the motive in using it was not anti-Soviet. That is about like saying that a man who constantly interferes in the affairs of his neighbors, and who suddenly starts using a 40-millimeter cannon to kill cats in his back yard, bears no responsibility for the neighbor's skepticism about his good intentions. Schlesinger is fully warranted in making a careful examination of the period before the bomb, but he has no justification for so nearly ignoring the role of the bomb in the origins of the cold war.

Finally, there is the question of the relevance and appropriateness of the American response to the Soviet policy of consolidation in Eastern Europe, and the related call for non-Russian Communists to reassert their identity and policies. The answer, put simply and directly, is that the increasingly militarized holy war mounted by American leaders was grossly irrelevant to the situation and highly conducive to producing problems that were more dangerous than those the policy was supposed to resolve.

The fashion of the moment among those who are nervous in the service of the Establishment is to wring one's hands and explain that George F. Kennan did not mean what he wrote in his famous "Long Letter," first filed as a dispatch to the State Department and then printed as the X-article in *Foreign Affairs.* Poor Kennan, the argument seems to be, the one time he left his style in the inkwell was unfortunately the time he needed it most.

It is a ludicrous argument. In the first place, Kennan had ample opportunity to revise the document before it was declassified and published. Furthermore, style is an expression of thought and the intransigent and quasi-military metaphors of the article do accurately express Kennan's deep, abiding and militant anti-communism. In addition, nothing prevented him from immediately revising and clarifying the article if people were getting an erroneous impression of his ideas from an accurate reading of his language; and nothing prevented him from resigning in urgent protest against the rapid emotional militarization of his strategy. Finally, those liberals who enlisted in the cold war had as much to do with that implementation of his policy as did the conservatives. The truth is that Senator Robert A. Taft made a far more courageous and public fight to prevent that from happening than did either Kennan or those liberals who now wring their hands about the state of the nation and the dangers of the Vietnamese War. And so did the radicals who are now far stronger than they were in 1945, 1946 and 1947 — or even 1948.

It is nevertheless true that the contemporary trauma of Establishment liberals is very real. They have come to recognize, or at least sense, the dangerous consequences of American universalism and the global interventionism that it produces. But they cannot wrench themselves free of the false syllogism by which they equate universal interventionism with internationalism, and they cannot tune out the siren call to save the world. They are still practicing the nonintellectualism (and worse) of pinning the label "isolationist" on anyone who has the temerity to point out that universalism is an extremely dangerous *reductio ad absurdum* of internationalism.

Richard H. Rovere spoke to these points in *The New Yorker* of October 28, where he supplied further documentation of the nervousness within the Establishment. In some respects, at any rate, he speaks more directly and candidly about the issues than does Schlesinger. Thus he says that the war in Vietnam is "an application of established policy that has miscarried so dreadfully that we must begin examining not just the case at hand but the whole works."

He also acknowledges the relationship between foreign aid given within that framework and the rise of anti-Americanism and wars. And he bluntly admits that American democracy "is in many ways a fraud." Most important, Rovere speaks directly to the necessity of acting now to change American attitudes and policies before the mistakes of the past lead to very serious disruption and disaffection.

Unless the liberals abandon universalism, they face the serious possibility of being overpowered by the conservatives inside the Establishment at the same time that they are being shunted aside by the radicals in the society at large. One is reluctant to conclude, once and for all, that Schlesinger has allowed his archaic interpretation of American history to blind him to the essential truth that his beloved Vital Center retains its vitality only as it moves left.

That estimate is difficult to accept because of his great intelligence, but it is even more painful to accept because it means that the liberals are becoming mere role players in a Greek tragedy rather than sustaining their activities as protagonists in the Christian tragedy. If that is the case, it could very well mean that America can renounce universalist interventionism only as it is forced to do so.

The Cold War, Revisited and Re-Visioned*

More than a year has passed since Arthur Schlesinger, Jr., announced that the time had come "to blow the whistle before the current outburst of revisionism regarding the origins of the cold war goes much further." Yet the outburst of revisionism shows no signs of subsiding. On the contrary, a growing number of historians and political critics, judging from such recent books as Ronald Steel's *Pax Americana* and Carl Oglesby's and Richard Shaull's *Containment and Change,* are challenging the view, once so widely accepted, that the cold war was an American response to Soviet expansionism, a distasteful burden reluctantly shouldered in the face of a ruthless enemy bent on our destruction, and that Russia, not the United States, must therefore bear the blame for shattering the world's hope that two world wars in the 20th century would finally give way to an era of peace.

"Revisionist" historians are arguing instead that the United States did as much as the Soviet Union to bring about the collapse of the wartime coalition. Without attempting to shift the blame exclusively to the United States, they are trying to show, as Gar Alperovitz puts it, that "the cold war cannot be understood simply as an American response to a Soviet challenge, but rather as the insidious interaction of mutual suspicions, blame for which must be shared by all."

*©1968 by The New York Times Company. Reprinted by permission of the author and publisher from *The New York Times Magazine,* January 14, 1968.

Not only have historians continued to reexamine the immediate origins of the cold war — in spite of attempts to "blow the whistle" on their efforts — but the scope of revisionism has been steadily widening. Some scholars are beginning to argue that the whole course of American diplomacy since 1898 shows that the United States has become a counterrevolutionary power committed to the defense of a global status quo. Arno Mayer's monumental study of the Conference of Versailles, *Politics and Diplomacy of Peacemaking,* which has recently been published by Knopf and which promises to become the definitive work on the subject, announces in its subtitle what a growing number of historians have come to see as the main theme of American diplomacy: "Containment and Counterrevolution."

Even Schlesinger has now admitted, in a recent article in *Foreign Affairs,* that he was "somewhat intemperate," a year ago, in deploring the rise of cold war revisionism. Even though revisionist interpretations of earlier wars "have failed to stick," he says, "revisionism is an essential part of the process by which history . . . enlarges its perspectives and enriches its insights." Since he goes on to argue that "postwar collaboration between Russia and America [was] . . . inherently impossible" and that "the most rational of American policies could hardly have averted the cold war," it is not clear what Schlesinger thinks revisionism has done to enlarge our perspective and enrich our insights; but it is good to know, nevertheless, that revisionists may now presumably continue their work (inconsequential as it may eventually prove to be) without fear of being whistled to a stop by the referee.

The orthodox interpretation of the cold war, as it has come to be regarded, grew up in the late forties and early fifties — years of acute international tension, during which the rivalry between the United States and the Soviet Union repeatedly threatened to erupt in a renewal of global war. Soviet-American relations had deteriorated with alarming speed following the defeat of Hitler. At Yalta, in February, 1945, Winston Churchill had expressed the hope that world peace was nearer the grasp of the assembled statesmen of the great powers "than at any time in history." It would be "a great tragedy," he said, "if they, through inertia or carelessness, let it slip from their grasp. History would never forgive them if they did."

Yet the Yalta agreements themselves, which seemed at the time to lay the basis of postwar cooperation, shortly provided the focus of bitter dissension, in which each side accused the other of having broken its solemn promises. In Western eyes, Yalta meant free elections and parliamentary democracies in Eastern Europe, while the Russians construed the agreements as recognition of their demand for governments friendly to the Soviet Union.

The resulting dispute led to mutual mistrust and to a hardening of positions on both sides. By the spring of 1946 Churchill himself, declaring that "an iron curtain has descended" across Europe, admitted, in effect, that the "tragedy" he had feared had come to pass: Europe split into hostile fragments, the eastern half dominated by the Soviet Union, the western part sheltering nervously under the protection of American arms. NATO, founded in 1949 and countered by the Russian sponsored Warsaw Pact, merely ratified the existing division of Europe.

From 1946 on, every threat to the stability of this uneasy balance produced an immediate political crisis — Greece in 1947, Czechoslovakia and the Berlin blockade in 1948 — each of which, added to existing tensions, deepened hostility on both sides and increased the chance of war. When Bernard Baruch announced in April, 1947, that "we are in the midst of a cold war," no one felt inclined to contradict him. The phrase stuck, as an accurate description of postwar political realities.

Many Americans concluded, moreover, that the United States was losing the cold war. Two events in particular contributed to this sense of alarm — the collapse of Nationalist China in 1949, followed by Chiang Kai-shek's flight to Taiwan, and the explosion of an atomic bomb by the Russians in the same year. These events led to the charge that American leaders had deliberately or unwittingly betrayed the country's interests. The Alger Hiss case was taken by some people as proof that the Roosevelt Administration had been riddled by subversion.

Looking back to the wartime alliance with the Soviet Union, the American Right began to argue that Roosevelt, by trusting the Russians, had sold out the cause of freedom. Thus Nixon and McCarthy, aided by historians like Stefan J. Possony, C. C. Tansill, and others, accused Roosevelt of handing Eastern Europe to the Russians and of giving them a preponderant interest in China which later enabled the Communists to absorb the entire country.

The liberal interpretation of the cold war — what I have called the orthodox interpretation — developed partly as a response to these charges. In liberal eyes, the right-wingers made the crucial mistake of assuming that American actions had been decisive in shaping the postwar world. Attempting to rebut this devil theory of postwar politics, liberals relied heavily on the argument that the shape of postwar politics had already been dictated by the war itself, in which the Western democracies had been obliged to call on Soviet help in defeating Hitler. These events, they maintained, had left the Soviet Union militarily dominant in Eastern Europe and generally occupying a position of much greater power, relative to the West, than the position she had enjoyed before the war.

In the face of these facts, the United States had very little leeway to influence events in what were destined to become Soviet spheres of influence, particularly since Stalin was apparently determined to expand even if it meant ruthlessly breaking his agreements — and after all it was Stalin, the liberals emphasized, and not Roosevelt or Truman, who broke the Yalta agreement on Poland, thereby precipitating the cold war.

These were the arguments presented with enormous charm, wit, logic, and power in George F. Kennan's *American Diplomacy* (1951), which more than any other book set the tone of cold war historiography. For innumerable historians, but especially for those who were beginning their studies in the fifties, Kennan served as the model of what a scholar should be — committed yet detached — and it was through the perspective of his works that a whole generation of scholars came to see not only the origins of the cold war, but the entire history of 20th century diplomacy.

It is important to recognize that Kennan's was by no means an uncritical perspective — indeed, for those unacquainted with Marxism it seemed the only critical perspective that was available in the fifties. While Kennan insisted that the Russians were primarily to blame for the cold war, he seldom missed an opportunity to criticize the excessive moralism, the messianic vision of a world made safe for democracy, which he argued ran "like a red skein" through American diplomacy.

As late as 1960, a radical like Staughton Lynd could still accept the general framework of Kennan's critique of American idealism while noting merely that Kennan had failed to apply it to the specific events of the cold war and to the policy of containment which he had helped to articulate. "Whereas in general he counseled America to 'admit the validity and legitimacy of power realities and aspirations . . . and to seek their point of maximum equilibrium rather than their reform or their repression' — 'reform or repression' of the Soviet system were the very goals which Kennan's influential writings of those years urged."

Even in 1960, however, a few writers had begun to attack not the specific applications of the principles of *Realpolitik* but the principles themselves, on the grounds that on many occasions they served simply as rationalizations for American (not Soviet) expansionism. And whereas Lynd in 1960 could still write that the American demand for freedom in Eastern Europe, however misguided, "expressed a sincere and idealistic concern," some historians had already begun to take a decidedly more sinister view of the matter — asking, for instance, whether a country which demanded concessions in Eastern Europe that it was not prepared to grant to the Russians in Western Europe could really be accused as the "realist" writers had maintained, of an excess of good-natured but occasionally incompetent altruism.

Meanwhile the "realist" interpretation of the cold war inspired a whole series of books — most notably, Herbert Feis's series (*Churchill-Roosevelt-Stalin; Between War and Peace; The Atomic Bomb and the End of World War II*); William McNeill's *America, Britain and Russia: Their Cooperation and Conflict;* Norman Graebner's *Cold War Diplomacy;* Louis J. Halle's *Dream and Reality* and *The Cold War as History;* and M. F. Herz's *Beginnings of the Cold War.*

Like Kennan, all of these writers saw containment as a necessary response to Soviet expansionism and to the deterioration of Western power in Eastern

Europe. At the same time, they were critical, in varying degrees, of the legalis-
tic-moralistic tradition which kept American statesmen from looking at foreign relations in the light of balance-of-power considerations.

Some of them tended to play off Churchillian realism against the idealism
of Roosevelt and Cordell Hull, arguing for instance, that the Americans should
have accepted the bargain made between Churchill and Stalin in 1944,
whereby Greece was assigned to the Western sphere of influence and Rumania,
Bulgaria, and Hungary to the Soviet sphere, with both liberal and Communist
parties sharing in the control of Yugoslavia.

These criticisms of American policy, however, did not challenge the basic
premise of American policy, that the Soviet Union was a ruthlessly aggressive
power bent on world domination. They assumed, moreover, that the Russians
were in a position to realize large parts of this program, and that only counter-
pressure exerted by the West, in the form of containment and the Marshall
Plan, prevented the Communists from absorbing all of Europe and much of
the rest of the world as well.

It is their criticism of these assumptions that defines the revisionist historians and distinguishes them from the "realist." What impresses revisionists is
not Russia's strength but her military weakness following the devastating war
with Hitler, in which the Russians suffered much heavier losses than any other
member of the alliance.

Beginning with Carl Marzani's *We Can Be Friends: Origins of the Cold War*
(1952), revisionists have argued that Russia's weakness dictated, for the moment at least, a policy of postwar cooperation with the West. Western leaders'
implacable hostility to Communism, they contend, prevented them from seeing this fact, a proper understanding of which might have prevented the cold
war.

This argument is spelled out in D. F. Fleming's two-volume study, *The Cold
War and Its Origins* (1961); in David Horowitz's *The Free World Colossus*
(1965), which summarizes and synthesizes a great deal of revisionist writing;
in Gar Alperovitz's *Atomic Diplomacy: Hiroshima and Potsdam* (1965); and
in the previously mentioned *Containment and Change.*

But the historian who has done most to promote a revisionist interpretation
of the cold war, and of American diplomacy in general, is William Appleman
Williams of the University of Wisconsin, to whom most of the writers just
mentioned owe a considerable debt. Williams's works, particularly *The
Tragedy of American Diplomacy* (1959), not only challenge the orthodox
interpretation of the cold war, they set against it an elaborate counterinterpre-
tation which, if valid, forces one to see American policy in the early years of
the cold war as part of a larger pattern of American globalism reaching as far
back as 1898.

According to Williams, American diplomacy has consistently adhered to the policy of the "open door" — that is, to a policy of commercial, political, and cultural expansion which seeks to extend American influence into every corner of the earth. This policy was consciously and deliberately embarked upon, Williams argues, because American statesmen believed that American capitalism needed ever-expanding foreign markets in order to survive, the closing of the frontier having put an end to its expansion on the continent of North America. Throughout the 20th century, the makers of American foreign policy, he says, have interpreted the national interest in this light.

The cold war, in Williams's view, therefore has to be seen as the latest phase of a continuing effort to make the world safe for democracy — read liberal capitalism, American-style — in which the United States finds itself increasingly cast as the leader of a worldwide counterrevolution.

After World War II, Williams maintains, the United States had "a vast proportion of actual as well as potential power vis-à-vis the Soviet Union." The United States "cannot with any real warrant or meaning claim that it has been *forced* to follow a certain approach or policy." (Compare this with a statement by Arthur Schlesinger: "The cold war could have been avoided only if the Soviet Union had not been possessed by convictions both of the infallibility of the communist word and of the inevitability of a communist world.")

The Russians, by contrast, Williams writes, "viewed their position in the nineteen-forties as one of weakness, not offensive strength." One measure of Stalin's sense of weakness, as he faced the enormous task of rebuilding the shattered Soviet economy, was his eagerness to get a large loan from the United States. Failing to get such a loan — instead, the United States drastically cut back lend-lease payments to Russia in May, 1945 — Stalin was faced with three choices, according to Williams:

He could give way and accept the American peace program at every point — which meant, among other things, accepting governments in Eastern Europe hostile to the Soviet Union.

He could follow the advice of the doctrinaire revolutionaries in his own country who argued that Russia's best hope lay in fomenting worldwide revolution.

Or he could exact large-scale economic reparations from Germany while attempting to reach an understanding with Churchill and Roosevelt on the need for governments in Eastern Europe not necessarily Communist but friendly to the Soviet Union.

His negotiations with Churchill in 1944, according to Williams, showed that Stalin had already committed himself, by the end of the war, to the third of these policies — a policy, incidentally, which required him to withdraw support from Communist revolutions in Greece and in other countries which under the terms of the Churchill-Stalin agreement had been conceded to the Western sphere of influence.

But American statesmen, the argument continues, unlike the British, were in no mood to compromise. They were confident of America's strength and Russia's weakness (although later they and their apologists found it convenient to argue that the contrary had been the case). Furthermore, they believed that "we cannot have full employment and prosperity in the United States without the foreign markets," as Dean Acheson told a special Congressional committee on postwar economic policy and planning in November, 1944. These considerations led to the conclusion, as President Truman put it in April, 1945, that the United States should "take the lead in running the world in the way that the world ought to be run"; or more specifically, in the words of Foreign Economic Administrator Leo Crowley, that "if you create good governments in foreign countries, automatically you will have better markets for yourselves." Accordingly, the United States pressed for the "open door" in Eastern Europe and elsewhere.

In addition to these considerations, there was the further matter of the atomic bomb, which first became a calculation in American diplomacy in July, 1945. The successful explosion of an atomic bomb in the New Mexican desert, Williams argues, added to the American sense of omnipotence and led the United States "to overplay its hand" — for in spite of American efforts to keep the Russians out of Eastern Europe, the Russians refused to back down.

Nor did American pressure have the effect, as George Kennan hoped, of promoting tendencies in the Soviet Union "which must eventually find their outlet in either the break-up or the gradual mellowing of Soviet power." Far from causing Soviet policy to mellow, American actions, according to Williams, stiffened the Russians in their resistance to Western pressure and strengthened the hand of those groups in the Soviet Union which had been arguing all along that capitalist powers could not be trusted.

Not only did the Russians successfully resist American demands in Eastern Europe, they launched a vigorous counterattack in the form of the Czechoslovakian coup of 1948 and the Berlin blockade. Both East and West thus found themselves committed to the policy of cold war, and for the next 15 years, until the Cuban missile crisis led to a partial détente, Soviet-American hostility was the determining fact of international politics.

Quite apart from his obvious influence on other revisionist historians of the cold war and on his own students in other areas of diplomatic history, Williams has had a measurable influence on the political radicals of the sixties, most of whom now consider it axiomatic that American diplomacy has been counterrevolutionary and that this fact reflects, not a series of blunders and mistakes as some critics have argued, but the basically reactionary character of American capitalism.

Some radicals now construe these facts to mean that American foreign policy therefore cannot be changed unless American society itself undergoes a revolutionary change. Carl Oglesby, for instance, argues along these lines in *Containment and Change*. From Oglesby's point of view, appeals to conscience or even to enlightened self-interest are useless; the cold war cannot end until the "system" is destroyed.

Williams thought otherwise. At the end of the 1962 edition of *The Tragedy of American Diplomacy,* he noted that "there is at the present time no radicalism in the United States strong enough to win power, or even a very significant influence, through the processes of representative government" — and he took it for granted that genuinely democratic change could come about only through representative processes. This meant, he thought, that "the well-being of the United States depends — *in the short-run but only in the short-run* — upon the extent to which calm and confident and enlightened conservatives can see and bring themselves to act upon the validity of a radical analysis."

In an essay in *Ramparts* last March, he makes substantially the same point in commenting on the new radicals' impatience with conservative critics of American diplomacy like Senator Fulbright. Fulbright, Williams says, attracted more support for the position of more radical critics than these critics had attracted through their own efforts. "He hangs tough over the long haul, and that is precisely what American radicalism has never done in the 20th century."

As the New Left becomes more and more beguiled by the illusion of its own revolutionary potential, and more and more intolerant of radicals who refuse to postulate a revolution as the only feasible means of social change, men like Williams will probably become increasingly uncomfortable in the presence of a movement they helped to create. At the same time, Williams's radicalism, articulated in the fifties before radicalism came back into fashion, has alienated the academic establishment and prevented his works from winning the widespread recognition and respect they deserve. In scholarly journals, many reviews of Williams's work — notably a review by Oscar Handlin of *The Contours of American History* in the *Mississippi Valley Historical Review* a few years ago — have been contemptuous and abusive in the extreme. The result is that Williams's books on diplomatic history are only beginning to pass into the mainstream of scholarly discourse, years after their initial publications.

Next to Williams's *Tragedy of American Diplomacy,* the most important attack on the orthodox interpretation of the cold war is Alperovitz's *Atomic Diplomacy*. A young historian trained at Wisconsin, Berkeley, and King's College, Cambridge, and currently a research fellow at Harvard, Alperovitz adds very little to the interpretation formulated by Williams, but he provides William's insights with a mass of additional documentation. By doing so, he has made it difficult for conscientious scholars any longer to avoid the challenge of revisionist interpretations. Unconventional in its conclusions, *Atomic Diplomacy* is thoroughly conventional in its methods. That adds to the book's persuasiveness. Using the traditional sources of diplomatic history — official records, memoirs of participants, and all the unpublished material to which scholars have access — Alperovitz painstakingly reconstructs the evolution of

American policy during the six-month period from March to August, 1945. He proceeds with a thoroughness and caution which, in the case of a less controversial work, would command the unanimous respect of the scholarly profession. His book is no polemic. It is a work in the best — and most conservative — traditions of historical scholarship. Yet the evidence which Alperovitz has gathered together challenges the official explanation of the beginnings of the cold war at every point.

What the evidence seems to show is that as early as April, 1945, American officials from President Truman on down had decided to force a "symbolic showdown" with the Soviet Union over the future of Eastern Europe. Truman believed that a unified Europe was the key to European recovery and economic stability, since the agricultural southeast and the industrial northwest depended on each other. Soviet designs on Eastern Europe, Truman reasoned, threatened to disrupt the economic unity of Europe and therefore had to be resisted. The only question was whether the showdown should take place immediately or whether it should be delayed until the bargaining position of the United States had improved.

At first it appeared to practically everybody that delay would only weaken the position of the United States. Both of its major bargaining counters, its armies in Europe and its lend-lease credits to Russia, could be more effectively employed at once, it seemed, than at any future time. Accordingly, Truman tried to "lay it on the line" with the Russians. He demanded that they "carry out their [Yalta] agreements" by giving the pro-Western elements in Poland an equal voice in the Polish Government (although Roosevelt, who made the Yalta agreements, believed that "we placed, as clearly shown in the agreement, somewhat more emphasis" on the Warsaw [pro-Communist] Government than on the pro-Western leaders). When Stalin objected that Poland was "a country in which the USSR is interested first of all and most of all," the United States tried to force him to give in by cutting back lend-lease payments to Russia.

At this point, however — in April, 1945 — Secretary of War Henry L. Stimson convinced Truman that "we shall probably hold more cards in our hands later than now." He referred to the atomic bomb, and if Truman decided to postpone the showdown with Russia, it was because Stimson and other advisers persuaded him that the new weapon would "put us in a position," as Secretary of State James F. Byrnes argued, "to dictate our own terms at the end of the war."

To the amazement of those not privy to the secret, Truman proceeded to take a more conciliatory attitude toward Russia, an attitude symbolized by Harry Hopkins's mission to Moscow in June, 1945. Meanwhile, Truman twice postponed the meeting with Churchill and Stalin at Potsdam. Churchill complained, "Anyone can see that in a very short space of time our armed power on the Continent will have vanished."

But when Truman told Churchill that an atomic bomb had been successfully exploded at Alamogordo, exceeding all expectations, Churchill immediately understood and endorsed the strategy of delay. "We were in the presence of a new factor in human affairs," he said, "and possessed of powers which were irresistible." Not only Germany but even the Balkans, which Churchill and Roosevelt had formerly conceded to the Russian sphere, now seemed amenable to Western influence. That assumption, of course, had guided American policy (though not British policy) since April, but it could not be acted upon until the bombing of Japan provided the world with an unmistakable demonstration of American military supremacy.

Early in September, the foreign ministers of the Big Three met in London. Byrnes — armed, as Stimson noted, with "the presence of the bomb in his pocket, so to speak, as a great weapon to get through" the conference — tried to press the American advantage. He demanded that the governments of Bulgaria and Rumania reorganize themselves along lines favorable to the West. In Bulgaria, firmness won a few concessions; in Rumania, the Russians stood firm. The American strategy had achieved no noteworthy success. Instead — as Stimson, one of the architects of that strategy, rather belatedly observed — it had "irretrievably embittered" Soviet-American relations.

The revisionist view of the origins of the cold war, as it emerges from the works of Williams, Alperovitz, Marzani, Fleming, Horowitz, and others, can be summarized as follows. The object of American policy at the end of World War II was not to defend Western or even Central Europe but to force the Soviet Union out of Eastern Europe. The Soviet menace to the "free world," so often cited as the justification of the containment policy, simply did not exist in the minds of American planners. They believed themselves to be negotiating not from weakness but from almost unassailable superiority.

Nor can it be said that the cold war began because the Russians "broke their agreements." The general sense of the Yalta agreements — which were in any case very vague — was to assign to the Soviet Union a controlling influence in Eastern Europe. Armed with the atomic bomb, American diplomats tried to take back what they had implicitly conceded at Yalta.

The assumption of American moral superiority, in short, does not stand up under analysis.

The opponents of this view have yet to make a very convincing reply. Schlesinger's recent article in *Foreign Affairs,* referred to at the outset of this article, can serve as an example of the kind of arguments which historians are likely to develop in opposition to the revisionist interpretation. Schlesinger argues that the cold war came about through a combination of Soviet intransigence and misunderstanding. There were certain "problems of communication" with the Soviet Union, as a result of which "the Russians might conceivably have misread our signals." Thus the American demand for self-determination in Poland and other East European countries "very probably" appeared to the Russians "as a systematic and deliberate pressure on Russia's western frontiers."

Similarly, the Russians "could well have interpreted" the American refusal of a loan to the Soviet Union, combined with cancellation of lend-lease, "as deliberate sabotage" of Russia's postwar reconstruction or as "blackmail." In both cases, of course, there would have been no basis for these suspicions; but "we have thought a great deal more in recent years," Schlesinger says, ". . . about the problems of communication in diplomacy," and we know how easy it is for one side to misinterpret what the other is saying.

This argument about difficulties of "communications" at no point engages the evidence uncovered by Alperovitz and others — evidence which seems to show that Soviet officials had good reason to interpret American actions exactly as they did: as attempts to dictate American terms.

In reply to the assertion that the refusal of a reconstruction loan was part of such an attempt, Schlesinger can only argue weakly that the Soviet request for a loan was "inexplicably mislaid" by Washington during the transfer of records from the Foreign Economic Administration to the State Department! "Of course," he adds, "this was impossible for the Russians to believe." It is impossible for some Americans to believe. As William Appleman Williams notes, Schlesinger's explanation of the "inexplicable" loss of the Soviet request "does not speak to the point of how the leaders could forget the request even if they lost the document."

When pressed on the matter of "communications," Schlesinger retreats to a second line of argument, namely that none of these misunderstandings "made much essential difference," because Stalin suffered from "paranoia" and was "possessed by convictions both of the infallibility of the communist word and of the inevitability of a communist world."

The trouble is that there is very little evidence which connects either Stalin's paranoia or Marxist-Leninist ideology or what Schlesinger calls "the sinister dynamics of a totalitarian society" with the actual course of Soviet diplomacy during the formative months of the cold war. The only piece of evidence that Schlesinger has been able to find is an article by the Communist theoretician Jacques Duclos in the April, 1945, issue of *Cahiers du communisme,* the journal of the French Communist Party, which proves, he argues, that Stalin had already abandoned the wartime policy of collaboration with the West and had returned to the traditional Communist policy of world revolution.

Even this evidence, however, can be turned to the advantage of the revisionists. Alperovitz points out that Duclos did not attack electoral politics or even collaboration with bourgeois governments. What he denounced was precisely the American Communists' decision, in 1944, to withdraw from electoral politics. Thus the article, far from being a call to world revolution, "was one of many confirmations that European Communists had decided to abandon violent revolutionary struggle in favor of the more modest aim of electoral success." And while this decision did not guarantee world peace, neither did it guarantee 20 years of cold war.

Schlesinger first used the Duclos article as a trump card in a letter to *The New York Review of Books,* Oct. 20, 1966, which called forth Alperovitz's rejoinder. It is symptomatic of the general failure of orthodox historiography to engage the revisionist argument that Duclos's article crops up again in Schlesinger's more recent essay in *Foreign Affairs,* where it is once again cited as evidence of a "new Moscow line," without any reference to the intervening objections raised by Alperovitz.

Sooner or later, however, historians will have to come to grips with the revisionist interpretation of the cold war. They cannot ignore it indefinitely. When serious debate begins, many historians, hitherto disposed to accept without much question the conventional account of the cold war, will find themselves compelled to admit its many inadequacies. On the other hand, some of the ambiguities of the revisionist view, presently submerged in the revisionists' common quarrel with official explanations, will begin to force themselves to the surface. Is the revisionist history of the cold war essentially an attack on "the doctrine of historical inevitability," as Alperovitz contends? Or does it contain an implicit determinism of its own?

Two quite different conclusions can be drawn from the body of revisionist scholarship. One is that American policy-makers had it in their power to choose different policies from the ones they chose. That is, they could have adopted a more conciliatory attitude toward the Soviet Union, just as they now have the choice of adopting a more conciliatory attitude toward Communist China and toward nationalist revolutions elsewhere in the Third World.

The other is that they have no such choice, because the inner requirements of American capitalism *force* them to pursue a consistent policy of economic and political expansion. "For matters to stand otherwise," writes Carl Oglesby, "the Yankee free-enterpriser would . . . have to . . . take sides against himself. . . . He would have to change entirely his style of thought and action. In a word, he would have to become a revolutionary Socialist whose aim was the destruction of the present American hegemony."

Pushed to what some writers clearly regard as its logical conclusion, the revisionist critique of American foreign policy thus becomes the obverse of the cold war liberals' defense of that policy, which assumes that nothing could have modified the character of Soviet policy short of the transformation of the Soviet Union into a liberal democracy — which is exactly the goal the containment policy sought to promote. According to a certain type of revisionism, American policy has all the rigidity the orthodox historians attribute to the USSR, and this inflexibility made the cold war inevitable.

Moreover, Communism really did threaten American interests, in this view. Oglesby argues that, in spite of its obvious excesses, the "theory of the International Communist Conspiracy is not the hysterical old maid that many leftists seem to think it is." If there is no conspiracy, there is a world revolution and it *"does* aim itself at America" — the America of expansive corporate capitalism.

Revisionism, carried to these conclusions, curiously restores cold war anti-Communism to a kind of intellectual respectability, even while insisting on its immorality. After all, it concludes, the cold warriors were following the American national interest. The national interest may have been itself corrupt, but the policy-makers were more rational than their critics may have supposed.

In my view, this concedes far too much good sense to Truman, Dulles, and the rest. Even Oglesby concedes that the war in Vietnam has now become irrational in its own terms. I submit that much of the cold war has been irrational in its own terms — as witness the failure, the enormously costly failure, of American efforts to dominate Eastern Europe at the end of World War II. This is not to deny the fact of American imperialism, only to suggest that imperialism itself, as J. A. Hobson and Joseph Schumpeter argued in another context long ago, is irrational — that even in its liberal form it may represent an archaic social phenomenon having little relation to the realities of the modern world.

At the present stage of historical scholarship, it is, of course, impossible to speak with certainty about such matters. That very lack of certainty serves to indicate the direction which future study of American foreign policy might profitably take.

The question to which historians must now address themselves is whether American capitalism really depends, for its continuing growth and survival, on the foreign policy its leaders have been following throughout most of the 20th century. To what extent are its interests really threatened by Communist revolutions in the Third World? To what extent can it accommodate itself to those revolutions, reconciling itself to a greatly diminished role in the rest of the world, without undergoing a fundamental reformation — that is, without giving away (after a tremendous upheaval) to some form of Socialism?

Needless to say, these are not questions for scholars alone. The political positions one takes depend on the way one answers them. It is terribly important, therefore, that we begin to answer them with greater care and precision than we can answer them today.

SIXTEEN

Origins of the Cold War*

I

It is surely a suggestive irony that just at the point when younger American historians had made serious intellectual headway with their reinterpretation of the cold war, fixing historical responsibility in terms of the mistakes, delusions, and imperatives of United States policy, the Soviet Union astonished friends and foes by overwhelming Czechoslovakia and turning its clock of history backwards. If the cold war has not revived, small thanks are due the Soviet leaders. Their extraordinary nervousness, their maneuvers to propitiate both the outgoing and incoming American Administrations, indicate very plainly how much they have feared political retaliation; this in itself is a comment on where responsibility for the cold war today should rest. That Prague should have been the vortex in 1968 as it was in 1948 of critical problems within communism is uncanny, but on deeper examination it may not be fortuitous.

After all, the least credible explanation of Moscow's desperate attempt to resolve the crisis within its own system of states and parties is the one which pictures Czechoslovakia as the helpless Pauline at the crossroads of Europe,

---

*Reprinted from *Foreign Affairs,* XLVII, 4 (July, 1969), pp. 681–696, by permission of the author and the publisher. Copyright 1969 by the Council on Foreign Relations, Inc., New York.

about to be dishonored by West German *revanchards,* with agents of the CIA grinning in the background, suddenly saved by the stalwart defenders of socialist honor and morality. Today this type of argument is reserved within the communist world for its most backward members — that is, for the Soviet public and the fringes of the most insignificant and expendable communist parties. Yet arguments of this kind had wide currency a generation ago. New Left historians would have us believe that Stalin was simply reacting to external challenge. In their view, the cold war might not have set in if small-minded American politicians had not been determined to reverse bad bargains, if congenital imperialists had not been mesmerized by the monopoly of atomic weapons that statesmen and scientists knew to be temporary. Since all this is so plainly a half-truth when juxtaposed to events of today, then clearly the half-truth of yesteryear will hardly explain the whole of the cold war.

Sophisticated communists, both East and West, are asking why Czechoslovakia, which escaped the upheavals in Poland and Hungary of 1956 after a decade of Stalinist pressure, then experienced such a mounting crisis in the subsequent decade of relative détente and peaceful competition. How is it that twenty years after communist rule had been secured in February 1948 basic verities are now placed in question — whether centralized planning may not be counterproductive, whether a one-party regime can really articulate the needs of a politically evolved people, whether the inner relations of such an unequal alliance as that administered by the Soviet Union are not so inherently antagonistic as to become explosive? Indeed, why did the rebirth of Czechoslovak political life in the first half of 1968 — viewed with hope and excitement by Western communists — raise such menacing ghosts from the past and such fearful question marks for the future that supposedly sober-minded men in Moscow took fright?

Twice within a dozen years the unmanageability of the communist world has been revealed. The crisis which shattered the Sino-Soviet alliance after manifesting itself first in Eastern Europe now rebounds at the supposed strongpoint of Czechoslovakia. And it has done so both in conditions of intense external pressure and times of relatively peaceful engagement. Perhaps it is here, in the dimension of communism as a contradictory and intractable system, that one may find the missing element in the discussions thus far on the origins of the cold war.

II

That world history would someday polarize around two great nations, America and Russia, was a de Tocquevillean insight with which communists were familiar a long time ago. Stalin gave it what seemed like a very clear definition back in 1927 during a talk with an American labor delegation. He envisaged that a socialist center would arise "binding to itself the countries gravitating toward socialism" and would engage the surviving capitalist center in "a struggle between them for the possession of the world economy." The fate of both would be decided by the outcome of this struggle. What appeared at first glance as a sweeping projection was, however, profoundly ambiguous on close examination. Stalin did not spell out how the countries "gravitating to socialism" would get there. Good communists believed this could come about only by the formulas of the October Revolution; yet even Lenin, in 1922, had lamented that perhaps a "big mistake" was being made in imposing Russian precepts on foreign communists. Nor did Stalin elucidate how new nations recruited to socialism would order their relations with Russia as the hub of the socialist center. Presumably "proletarian internationalism" would replace the domination of the weak by the strong which was, in their view, the hallmark of capitalism. Yet even by 1927 the Russification of the international movement had brought catastrophic results — in Germany and China.

Stalin did not, moreover, meet the fundamental intellectual challenge of whether "the struggle for the possession of the world economy" necessarily had to be military in character. On this crucial point, everything could be found in the Leninist grabbag. "Peaceful coexistence" is there, but so is the expectation of "frightful collisions" between the first workers' state and its opponents; the caution that socialism had to be secured in one country first is to be found along with pledges that once socialism was strong enough in Russia, it would raise up revolts in the strongholds of capitalism.

The one possibility which Leninism did not anticipate was a stalemate between rival systems, precluding a "final conflict." The notion was not even entertained that an equilibrium between contending forces might set in, that the subsequent evolution of both contenders under the impact of this equilibrium could alter their distinguishing characteristics and therefore outmode the original Leninist theorems.

Out of such doctrinal ambiguities the Second World War created policy choices affecting most of humanity. The Soviet Union and the international communist movement found themselves allied with democratic-capitalist states among whom public power had grown drastically in an effort to overcome the great depression; the welfare state was expanded by the very demands of warfare while democracy was in fact enhanced. Keynes had made a serious rebuttal to Marx. Would capitalism in the West collapse in a repetition of the crisis of the 1930's after withstanding the test of war? Or had the war itself changed something vital within the workings of capitalism? Moreover, the first global war in history led to the end of colonialism and hence a new relation of metropolitan states to subject peoples. Would the former necessarily collapse because, in Lenin's analysis, they had depended so heavily on colonies? Or might they undergo transformations — short of socialism — to make them viable? Would the countries of the underdeveloped world make socialism the indispensable form of their modernization or might they, dialectically enough, find a new relation with capitalism?

Thus, the war brought on to the world stage a powerful Russia on whose survival a rival system's survival also depended. Simultaneously America came to center stage with a greatly expanded economy no longer limited by laissez-faire economics and inwardly altered by technological change created by the war. America was indispensable to Russia as an ally but formidable as a rival in a sense far deeper than its outward power. This wartime relationship was unexpected, and it challenged ideology and practice on all sides.

Something very particular happened within communism, considered as a most uneven system of a single state and a variety of parties. The fortunes of war, thanks perhaps to Churchill's postponement of the second front, brought the Soviet armies beyond their own borders where they had to be welcomed by the West if only because their help was also being solicited on the plains of Manchuria once Hitler was defeated. Yet at the moment of Russia's greatest need and harshest difficulties, the communist movements *least* helpful to her were those of Eastern Europe; in the one country outside of Russia where a decade before the communists had been a real power — namely, in Germany — the party lay shattered. No anti-Hitler force of any practical significance emerged. On the East European landscape there were only two exceptions. In Yugoslavia a handful of veterans of Comintern intrigue and the hard school of the International Brigades in Spain had succeeded in establishing their power — prior to the arrival of Soviet forces in the Danubian basin. In Czechoslovakia, a communist movement of a very different sort — that is, with a legal and parliamentary tradition — was joined by Slovak guerrillas. Both came to terms with the leadership of the government-in-exile, which both Moscow and the West recognized. A long-term cooperation of diverse social forces was implied.

On the other hand, the communist movements underwent a spectacular resurrection in a wide arc from Greece through Italy, France, the Low Countries, and Scandinavia, while in widely separated corners of Asia they also flourished — in Northwest China, in the peninsula of Indochina, in the Philippines and Malaya. All of them were successful to the degree that they identified with the defense of their nationhood and either subordinated social issues or subsumed them in national ones; where this proved too complicated, as in India, long-term disabilities resulted. But all of these movements grew at a distance from the Soviet armies; their postwar fate could not depend on physical contact. Even parties at the periphery of world politics showed striking changes. They entered cabinets in Cuba and Chile, emerged from prewar disasters with great dynamism in Brazil, became legal in Canada, and stood chance of legitimizing their considerable influence in Britain and the United States. In these latter countries, they could hope to achieve "citizenship" only by ceasing to be propagandist groups reflecting Soviet prestige, and only as they grappled with the specific peculiarities of their societies in rapid change.

Yet for all this success, and perhaps because of it, communism faced the gravest problems. The peculiarity of the moment lay in the fact that some definition of Russia's relation with the West was essential to assure the most rapid conclusion of the war in Europe, and this had to precede a common strategy in Asia. Hence Moscow was obliged to define relations with the communist parties. Simultaneously these movements — of such unequal potential and geographical relation to Russia — had to make a fresh judgment of their strategies in view of those changes within capitalism which challenged their own doctrine. Perhaps the most ambitious attempt to do this came in May 1943 with the dissolution of the Communist International.

Stalin, who had sworn at Lenin's bier to guard this "general staff of the world revolution" like the apple of his eye, was now abandoning it; and in so doing he signaled to Churchill and Roosevelt that he would project the postwar Soviet interest in essentially Russian terms. This decision was consistent with the fact that the Russian Communists had not been able to rely on ideology or internationalism in mobilizing their own peoples for the enormous sacrifices of the war. They had been forced to appeal to the Russian love of soil and the solace of the Orthodox faith. "They are not fighting for us," Stalin had once mused to Ambassador Harriman. "They are fighting for Mother Russia."

All of this would not, of course, make Russia easier to deal with. And in studying the details in the monumental accounts of Herbert Feis or W. H. McNeill, one is struck by Stalin's political opportunism and the enormous part which is played in his calculations by the need to exact material resources from friend and foe. Throughout 1944, Stalin dealt with anyone who would cease fighting, or mobilize men and matériel for the Soviet armies, safeguard their lines, and pledge reparations; and everyone was suitable to Moscow in terms of these objectives — agrarians and monarchists in the Axis satellites, veteran communist-haters in Finland, a Social Democratic old-timer in Austria, Dr. Beneš in Prague, or Comrade Tito in the Yugoslav mountains. Had the putsch against Hitler succeeded in July 1944, Stalin was prepared, by his committee of Nazi generals rounded up at Stalingrad, to bargain.

His only real complication arose over Poland. Here the Soviets had the tactical advantage that a generation earlier the victors at Versailles had been willing to establish the Curzon Line as Russia's western frontier. Churchill and Roosevelt were now obliged not only to ratify this line but to impose it on the intractable London Poles. Moscow's own dilemma lay in the fact that the pro-Soviet Poles, exiled in the USSR, had little political substance; they had one thing in common with their counterparts in London — lack of standing inside Poland. The Polish Communists had been decimated in the great purges and the Polish officer corps had been wiped out in the Katyn murders. Perhaps it was the need to shift the balance in his favor that led Stalin to such extraordinary measures as letting the "Home Army" be wiped out at the banks of the Vistula or continuing to murder Polish Socialists as they came to Moscow as guests. The earlier hope of some prestigious figure who would bridge the gap between Poles and yet be satisfactory to all the great powers had faded with the death in an airplane accident of General Wladislaw Sikorski.

But it is questionable whether this Soviet use of vestigial figures of Comintern experience should be viewed, as of 1944, in terms of "communization." Everything we know of the Kremlin at that time denies this. In the remarkable account by Milovan Djilas in his "Conversations with Stalin," the Kremlin was far from being a citadel of revolution, as this young Montenegrin idealist expected (like so many in Moscow for the first time, before and after him). The Kremlin was really a sort of Muscovite camping-ground such as the great Russian painter, Repin, might have portrayed. Crafty and boorish men, suspicious of all foreigners and of each other, contemptuous of communists who were non-Russian but expecting their obedience, were crowded around the maps of Europe as around some Cossack campfire, calculating how much they could extract from Churchill and Roosevelt, to whom they felt profoundly inferior.

Thus, when Ulbricht and Rakosi, Anna Pauker, and even Dimitroff were being prepared to return to the homelands where they had previously failed, Stalin advised them not to spoil their second chance by their chronic leftism and adventurism.[1] They did not go back as revolutionaries. For all of Moscow's hopes that they root themselves in native soil, they were intended to be the guarantors of control, to stabilize this backyard of Europe and mobilize its resources on Russia's behalf. The troubles with the Yugoslavs began for the very reason that as revolutionaries they would not let themselves be used.

Was Stalin already building a bloc? To be sure he was. But he also knew that the onetime *cordon sanitaire* was a veritable swamp of historic and intractable rivalries and economic backwardness, even though wealthier in immediate resources than the USSR itself. Hoping to transform this bloc, Stalin also entertained most seriously the idea of a long-term relationship with America and Britain based on some common policy toward Germany that would make its much greater resources available to Russia. Thus, when Churchill came to Moscow in September 1944 to work out a spheres-of-influence agreement, demanding 50–50 and 75–25 ratios in the political control of areas already liberated by the Soviet armies, Stalin agreed by the

---

1. Herbert Feis is the source for the famous and revealing anecdote that when Stalin said farewell to Dr. Beneš, after signing a mutual assistance pact, he urged Beneš to help make Klement Gottwald, the Communist leader now become Premier, "more worldly and less provincial" — an amazing piece of arrogance. Having themselves helped emasculate their foreign friends, the Russians now taunted them and hoped that perhaps the bourgeois world might make men of them (*Churchill, Roosevelt and Stalin,* Princeton: Princeton University Press, 1957, p. 569).

stroke of a pen. He did so without comment. He contemptuously left it to Churchill to decide whether the piece of paper should be retained by him or destroyed. The cobbler's son from Gori, the onetime seminary student, was giving a descendant of the Marlboroughs a lesson in *Realpolitik*.

But as he disposed of Greeks and interposed with Yugoslavs (without asking their consent), the Soviet dictator demanded no quid pro quo in Western Europe where the ultimate world balance could be determined, and where communist movements had powerfully revived, guided by intimates of Stalin — Togliatti and Thorez — whose work he respected. Molotov is on record as inquiring about the disposition of Italian colonies, but not about the operations of the American Military Government in Italy in which Russian participation was passive. At the moment when the French Communists were debating whether to turn in their arms, Moscow recognized the Gaullist regime and invited it to sign a treaty with what de Gaulle was to call "chère et puissante Russie." Churchill's assault on Belgian and Greek Communists was reproved, in private. But no Soviet leverage was employed to help them, and the Greek Communists were advised to strike the best bargain they could to avert civil war. Only much later, when assistance was useless to them, did the Soviets reluctantly help the Greeks, though their hapless plight was useful for cold-war propaganda. Even as late as February 1945, at Yalta, Stalin pledged to renew his pact with Chiang Kai-shek in return for special treaty control of Dairen and the Manchurian railways. Half a year later, the Soviet armies ransacked the industrial installations that were by right Chinese. In central Asia they dickered with warlords, advising them against joining the Chinese Communists. Stalin shied away from the governance of Japan, asking and getting its northern islands instead. All this was accompanied by rather snide references by Molotov to Mao Tse-tung's "margarine communists." American liberals and roving ambassadors may have been more naïve .but they were also less offensive in believing the Chinese Communists to be "agrarian reformers."

III

How then did the communist parties respond to the Comintern's dissolution? Its final document had some curious and pregnant phrases, alluding to "the fundamental differences in the historical development of the separate countries of the world" — differences, it was now discovered, which had "become apparent even before the war"; communists were now told most authoritatively that they were "never advocates of the outmoded organizational forms." This suggests that a great watershed had been reached. The implicit self-criticism was bound to encourage those Western communists for whom the "popular front" of the 1930's and the experience of the Spanish Republic were not defensive deceptions but major experiments in skirting the limits of Leninism. The Chinese Communists, as the specialized literature shows, saw in the disappearance of the Communist International a ratification of their own "New Democracy," in which the peasantry and the "national bourgeoisie" had been credited with revolutionary potentials for which no precedent existed in the Russian experience.

The most interesting instance of how new systems of ideas and new organizational forms were bursting the Leninist integument came in the minor party of a major country — among the American Communists. Their leader, Earl Browder, concluded that peaceful coexistence had become obligatory; he saw such coexistence as a whole historical stage in which the contradictions between antagonistic social systems would have to work themselves out — short of war; it is curious that he ruled out war as too dangerous to both sides *before* the advent of the atomic bomb. To give this very novel view some inner logic, Browder postulated a new type of state power, intermediate between capitalism and socialism, which, he thought, would prevail between the Atlantic and the Oder-Neisse Line. Thus he anticipated the "people's democracy" concept which was to have wide currency in the next few years only to be brusquely rejected by the end of 1948, when the cold war demanded rationales of another kind.

To what extent Browder had sanction in Moscow, or only *thought* he had, or whether this sanction was ever intended to be more than temporary, are all fascinating matters; but for our discussion what seems more important is the fact that Browder revealed the incoherence of communism and tried to overcome it. Perhaps America was not so backward as European communists traditionally assumed. The more advanced country was simply showing a mirror to the less advanced of the problems of their own future, to borrow an image from Marx.

One may put this dilemma in very specific terms. In 1944 – 45, a quasi-revolutionary situation prevailed in key areas of Western Europe and East Asia. The communist parties had become mass movements. They were no longer Leninist vanguards but had significant military experience. The old order had been discredited and few charismatic rivals existed. One of two options could be taken, each of them having its own logic. If the communists seized power they might be able to hold it, as in Yugoslavia, with great good luck. But as the Greek experience was to show, the success of a prolonged civil war would involve the rupture of the Anglo-Soviet-American coalition; and the war with Hitler was by no means over, while the Pacific war appeared only begun. To pursue this option meant to oblige the Soviet Union to assist revolutions at a distance from its own armies at a moment of its own greatest weakness and when it seriously entertained the possibility of a long-range postwar relationship with the West. Alternatively, the USSR would be obliged to disavow its own ideological and political allies in an even more explicit way than the dissolution of the Comintern suggested. Stalin's entire diplomacy warned against revolution now. So did his opinion, in a speech of November

6, 1944, that whatever disagreements existed among the great powers could be overcome; he had said flatly that "no accidental, transitory motive but vitally important long-term interests lie at the basis of the alliance of our country, Great Britain, and the United States."

On the other hand, to reject the revolutionary path meant for the Western parties (if not for the Chinese and Vietnamese) forgoing an opportunity that might not return; for a generation this choice caused intense misgivings and internal battles within these parties. To take part in the whole-hearted reconstruction of their societies on a less-than-socialist basis would have involved a revision of fundamental Leninist postulates, a fresh look at capitalism, and presumably a redefinition of their relations with the Soviet Union. Having taken such a sharply Russocentric course, could Stalin give his imprimatur to the embryonic polycentrism of that time? The USSR was in the paradoxical position of trying to be a great power with a shattered economic base, and of trying to lead a world movement whose interests were quite distinct from those of Russia, both in practice and in ideas. The ambiguities inherent in communism, in Stalin's projections of 1927, had come home to roost.

IV

If one tries, then, to make intellectual sense and order out of the bewildering events between early 1945 and mid-1947, the least satisfactory themes are the ones which have been so popular and have dominated the discussion of the origins of the cold war. The revisionist historians are so hung up on the notion that a meticulous rediscovery of America will reveal the clues to the cold war that they ignore the dimension of communism altogether. They have little experience with communism (and perhaps they are better off for it) but they have yet to show the scholarship required to explore it. To say this is not to deny the value of reappraising American policy, especially since so many of today's follies have roots in the past. Communists, anti-communists, and ex-communists have all had troubles with the imperatives of coexistence. But this is quite different from explaining the cold war on one-sided grounds and succumbing to the elementary fallacy of *post hoc, propter hoc.*

On the other hand, the most sophisticated and persuasive rebuttal to the younger historians — that by Arthur Schlesinger, Jr., in these pages[2] — suffered from the limitations of his own major premise: the assumption that communism was a monolithic movement which disintegrated only as the cold war was vigorously prosecuted. Certainly the monolith functioned in a pellmell fashion after 1948 but one wonders whether its explosive decomposition in the late fifties, continuing to the events in Czechoslovakia, can be comprehended without realizing that all the elements of crisis within it were already present

2. *Foreign Affairs,* October, 1967. [See Chapter 13. Ed.]

in its immediate postwar years. It was the futile attempts by Stalin and the communists who everywhere followed him (even if hesitantly and in bewilderment) to stifle the nascent polycentrism and to curtail the inchoate attempts to adjust to new realities which constitute communism's own responsibility for the cold war. Herein also is the key to communism's own disasters.

Thus, the events of 1946 and 1947 were in fact incoherent and contradictory, and for that very reason offer an important clue to the origins of cold war. For example, Earl Browder was roundly denounced by the French Communist leader, Jacques Duclos, in an article written early in 1945 (with data that were available only in Moscow), on the grounds that the very concept of peaceful coexistence and Europe's reconstruction on a bourgeois-democratic basis was heresy; yet the curious thing is that most of the communist parties continued to operate on Browder's assumptions — including the party led by Duclos. Such a state of affairs suggests that the Duclos article was not the tocsin of the cold war but one of the elements of communism's incoherence. By the close of 1946, only the Yugoslavs — and William Z. Foster, who had ousted Browder in the United States — were convinced that even the "temporary stabilization" of capitalism was unlikely. This concept was, of course, an echo from the 1920's. "Relative and temporary stabilization" was Stalin's own justification in the late 1920's for "turning inward" and seeking a truce in external affairs. Ruling out this concept in the 1940's, Foster went even further than Tito in raising the alarum over an ever-more-imminent danger of an American attack on the Soviet Union. It is not generally known that when Browder's successor visited Europe in March 1947 he was amazed to find that few Communist leaders agreed with his views, and one of those who disagreed most sharply was Jacques Duclos.

In studying the French Communists of that period one finds unusual emphasis on the need for a policy of "confident collaboration" with "all of the Allied nations, without exception," and a declaration by Duclos that "we are not among those who confuse the necessity and fertility of struggle with the spirit of adventurism. That is why — mark me well — we ask of a specific historic period what it can give and only what it can give . . . but we do not ask more, for we want to push ahead and not end up in abortive and disappointing failures."

In this same year of 1946, it is sometimes forgotten that the Chinese Communists negotiated seriously for a long-term coalition with Chiang Kaishek. They did so under the aegis of General George Marshall, which suggests that their own antagonism to "American imperialism" had its limits; their view that the United States was necessarily hostile to a unified China with a large communist component was a later development. During the recent Great Proletarian Cultural Revolution, Chinese historians blamed this coalition strategy on the now-disgraced Liu Shao Chi, alleging that he was under the influence of "Browder, Togliatti, Thorez, and other renegades to the proletariat." But the official Chinese Communist documents show that at the time Mao Tse-tung took credit for it and was himself viewed as a "revisionist" — by the Indian Communists, for example. In those same months, Ho Chi Minh led a coalition delegation to Paris, trying to work out the terms for remaining within the French Union; it is a curious but revealing detail that Ho had the previous winter dissolved his own creation, the Communist Party of Indochina, in favor of an Association of Marxist Studies, without, however, receiving a rebuke from Jacques Duclos.

Throughout 1946, almost every communist leader in the West voiced the view that peaceful roads to socialism were not only desirable but were — because of objective changes in the world — now theoretically admissible. If in Eastern Europe this popularity of the "people's democracy" can be explained in terms of Stalin's attempt to stabilize a chaotic region of direct interest to Russia, in Western Europe it was part of a serious effort to implement the non-revolutionary option which the communists had chosen, and for which they needed a consistent justification.

Nor were the Soviet leaders immune to what was happening within communism. Stalin himself can be cited in contradictory assertions which also stimulated the diversity within the communist world as well as baffling some of its members. Early in February 1946 Stalin declared that wars could not be abolished so long as imperialism prevailed; this came in his election campaign speech which is viewed by Sovietologists as another tocsin of the cold war. Yet throughout 1946 Stalin gave interviews to British and American newsmen, and held a long discussion with Harold Stassen that spring, in which the key theme was the viability of peaceful coexistence. In September 1946 Stalin declared that the ruling circles of both Britain and the United States were *not* in fact oriented toward war — a view which communists from China to Italy hailed, although it baffled Tito and William Z. Foster. Stalin also told a British Labor delegation headed by Harold Laski that socialism might well come to Britain by parliamentary means, with the monarchy remaining as a genuine institution. Earlier in the year, in a polemic with a certain Professor Razin on the significance of the doctrines of Clausewitz, Stalin is quoted as believing "it is impossible to move forward and advance science without subjecting outdated propositions and the judgments of well-known authorities to critical analysis. This applies . . . also to the classics of Marxism." Significantly, this exchange was published a full year later — in February 1947 — on the eve of cold-war decisions which made such thinking heretical throughout the communist movement.

Yet in 1946 Soviet diplomacy was in fact moving "with all deliberate speed" toward settlements of a partial kind with the West — as regards the peace treaties, the evacuation of northern Persia, and other matters. Browder was cordially received in Moscow in May after his expulsion from the American party — a rather unprecedented detail in the annals of communism. The deposed communist leader was heard out by Molotov, at the latter's request, and was given a post which enabled him to work energetically for the next two years in behalf of the proposition that Stalin wanted an American-Soviet settlement.

All students of this period have paused on the famous Varga controversy. The title of the book which the foremost Soviet economist, Eugene Varga, published in November 1946 (it was completed the year before) in itself suggests what was bothering Russian leaders, namely: *Changes in the Economy of Capitalism Resulting from the Second World War.* Within six months, Varga was under severe attack, which he resisted for the following two years. Major issues lay at the heart of the controversy. When might a crisis of over-production be expected in the United States? How severe would it be? And to what extent would rearmament or a program for rebuilding Western Europe affect capitalism's inherent propensity for crisis, which was, of course, taken for granted? Another question was whether the new role of governmental power, so greatly enhanced by the war, might not have a bearing on both the onset of the crisis and the terrain of communist activities. Varga did forecast an early crisis, after a brief postwar boom. In so doing, he surely misled Stalin into one of his most fundamental cold-war miscalculations. But Varga also clung to the view that something important had changed within classical capitalism; he insisted that "the question of greater or smaller participation in the management of the state will be the main content" of the political struggle in the West, and he deduced that people's democracy was in fact a transitional form between the two systems, replacing the "either-or" notions of classical Leninism. There was a plaintive protest in Varga's answer to his critics (one of whom was Vosnessensky, who would shortly disappear because of mysterious heresies of his own). "It is not a matter of enumerating all the facts so that they inevitably lead to the former conclusions of Marxism-Leninism," Varga argued, "but to use the Marxist-Leninist method in studying these facts. The world changes and the content of our work must change also."

V

In what sense, then, did all these crosscurrents determine Stalin's decision for cold war? It would seem that the matter turned on the incompatibility between immediate Soviet objectives and the real interests of the communist parties — or more exactly, in the particularly Stalinist answer to these incompatibilities. The Russians, it will be remembered, had set out to achieve rapid and ambitious reconstruction including, of course, the acquisition of nuclear weapons. They were most concerned with reparations. When it became plain that little help would come by loans or trade with the West (they had used up what was still in the pipelines after the abrupt cessation of lend-lease in mid-1945 and were not getting a response to their $6 billion request to Washington), they needed either the resources of Germany beyond what they could extract from their own Eastern Zone, or a desperate milking of their friends and former foes in Eastern Europe. At home, moreover, they could not rely on the ultrachauvinist themes which had served them during the war; rejecting liberalization of Soviet society, they tightened the screws and fell back on the doctrine of the primacy of the Soviet party, the purity of its doctrine, and the universal validity of that doctrine. Consistent with these objectives, the Soviet leaders wanted to erase all sympathy for America which until then was widespread in the Soviet Union.[3]

These objectives, taken together, ran counter to all the tendencies among the foreign communist parties. Both the revolutionary ambitions of the Yugoslavs, their jealous quest for autonomy as well as the emphasis on peaceful non-Soviet roads to socialism — that is, the "revisionist" themes so urgently needed by the parties in the West — could be countenanced by Moscow only if it were prepared to accept diversity within international communism. This very diversity (which they had themselves half entertained) now became an obstacle. The Stalinist premise that what was good for Russia was good for all other communists (a notion which he himself considered abandoning) was now reaffirmed.

The origins of the cold war lie deeper, however, than any analysis of Russia's own interest. Nor can they be understood only in terms of an attempt to prevent economic recovery and political stability in Western Europe. The cold war's origins must be found in a dimension larger than the requirements of Soviet internal mobilization or the thrust of its foreign policy; they lie in the attempt to overcome the incipient diversity within a system of states and parties, among whom the changes produced by the war had outmoded earlier ideological and political premises. The conditions for the transformation of a monolithic movement had matured and ripened. The sources of the cold war lie in communism's unsuccessful attempt to adjust to this reality, followed by its own abortion of this attempt. For Stalin the cold war was a vast tug-of-war with the West, whereby not only internal objectives could be realized but the international movement subordinated; its constituent parts went along — bewildered but believing — on the assumption that, in doing so, they would survive and prosper. The price of the Stalinist course was to be fearsome indeed; and by 1956 the Soviet leaders were to admit that the cold war had damaged the USSR more than the West, that a stalemate of systems had to

---

3. This task was assigned to the late Ilya Ehrenburg following his 1947 visit to the States, when he deliberately oversimplified everything American with the crudest methods. The pattern for this had been set late in 1946 by Andrei Zhdanov.

be acknowledged, and ineluctable conclusions had to be drawn. Thus, the cold war arose from the failure of a movement to master its inner difficulties and choose its alternatives.

The analysis could be continued to the turning-point of mid-1947 — the Marshall Plan decision and Stalin's riposte, for example, in humiliating his Czechoslovak and Polish partners, who thought in terms of what might be good for them, and indirectly for the Soviet Union. Such an analysis would take us through the near-insurrections of late 1947 in France and Italy, adventurist upheavals in Asia, the Berlin blockade, and the coup in Prague in 1948. But this involves another subject — how the cold war was fought. It was indeed fought by both sides. But to say this cannot obscure the crisis within communism, where its origins lie. The record would show how recklessly entire communist movements were expended and to what a dangerous brink the Soviet Union itself was brought. In 1956, Khrushchev was to lament these miscalculations but he did so with such a *désinvolture* as to leave a memory-bank of disasters and skeletons that still rattle in communism's closets. Was the cold war but a test of strength between systems? Or has it not also been the process whereby communism disclosed such an intellectual and political bankruptcy that a dozen years after Khrushchev's revelations, the issues still agonize — as in Czechoslovakia — all the states and parties involved? A world movement claiming to comprehend history and accepting the responsibility for "making history" still grapples with the alternatives opened by the Second World War. It has yet to face what it has tried to avoid at such a heavy cost to coexistence — namely, understanding itself.

PART V

From Cold War to Competitive Coexistence:
Western Diplomacy, the Strategic Balance,
The Global Economy, the Third World,
International Communism, and
Soviet Foreign Policy

From the Soviet perspective the basic goal of socialist foreign policy is "to secure the most favorable external conditions for the building of socialism and communism."[1] Yet this basic goal must be adapted to the objective conditions of a given epoch. "Each epoch has its own specifics, which depend on what social system plays the leading role and facilitates progress...."[2]

Soviet analysts identify two epochs in the history of the USSR's foreign policy. In the first period, from 1917 to 1945, the USSR struggled alone to build a socialist society. Capitalist systems were dominant, Soviet Russia weak and vulnerable. In the second period, beginning with the defeat of German and Japanese fascism in World War II and the establishment of "people's democracies" in Eastern Europe, socialism became a regional and then a global system. "The cardinal feature of the second stage is that the world socialist community has firmly grasped the historical initiative."[3]

The essence of the second period, according to Soviet theorists, is "the shift of the correlation of forces in favor of socialism." A chief factor producing this shift is the disintegration of the capitalist colonial system. The

The editors wish to thank Robbin F. Laird for his substantive contributions to this introductory essay.

1. *A Study of Soviet Foreign Policy* (Moscow: Progress, 1975), p. 12.
2. *Ibid.*, p. 17.
3. *Ibid.*, p. 18.

weakening of direct Western political control over Asian and African countries means that the Third World no longer plays the role of a reserve and
supply base for imperialism. Soviet writers conclude: "The formation of
the socialist community and the appeareance of new countries on the international political scene have fundamentally changed the balance of strength
in the world. The possibilities of imperialists for pursuing an aggressive
policy have narrowed substantially."[4]

Soviet authors attribute the ascendancy of socialism in part to what they
term "the third phase of the general crisis of capitalism." The "first phase"
was the decline of capitalist economies and societies after World War I. The
successful Bolshevik revolution of 1917, the repulsion of Western and
Japanese military intervention in the Russian civil war of 1917 to 1920, and
the creation of the first socialist state "objectively" demonstrated the
possibility of a noncapitalist path to development.

Moreover, increasing divisiveness within the capitalist world spawned the
rise of German, Japanese, and Italian fascism. Before and after the Nazi-
Soviet nonaggression pact of 1939 to 1941, the fascist coalition threatened—
and eventually engaged the Red Army in—a two-front war in European
Russia and in the Soviet Far East. Hence, a "second phase" was ushered in
by the Allied defeat of fascism in World War II and by the emergence of
new socialist regimes in Eastern Europe and revolutionary movements in
the Third World. The formation and consolidation of an international
socialist system was the major force shaping this second stage.

According to Soviet analysts, the current "third phase" of capitalism's
decline, which began in the mid 1950's, is characterized by the mounting
"antagonistic" and "interimperialist contradictions" within and among the
major Western nations. The problems of the capitalist states are becoming
more acute, it is argued, because of the increased influence of socialism
upon world historical development. Soviet writers contend: "In the
economic sphere capitalism's crisis is manifested by the fact that the leading
imperialist powers are losing their supremacy."[5] Furthermore, "the sharply
accentuated uneven development of the capitalist countries is leading to a
further aggravation of imperialist contradictions and to an intensification
of the competitive struggle, in which the USA's chief rivals are the Common
Market and Japan."[6]

"Peaceful coexistence" with the West is perceived to have passed through
two phases which parallel the rise of the power of socialism. The first phase
(1917-1953) was a *defensive* form of coexistence. Socialism had to be built
and consolidated in the face of extreme hostility from the capitalist world.
Soviet Russia, the first socialist state, was militarily and economically

4. *Ibid.,* p. 24.
5. *Ibid.,* p. 25.
6. *Ibid.,* p. 25-26.

vulnerable and had to make the most of its very limited political and diplomatic resources. By contrast, the second phase is an *active* form of peaceful coexistence in which socialism is allegedly becoming the ascendent historical force. Under Stalin's successor, Nikita Khrushchev, peaceful coexistence became the cornerstone or "general line" of Soviet foreign policy. Under Leonid Brezhnev peaceful coexistence was temporarily reduced to equal status with other goals and principles, as it had been under Stalin and Lenin before him.

However, throughout the 1970's, peaceful coexistence—now more often referred to as "detente"—was returned to a central place in the theory and practice of Soviet foreign policy. With the winding down of the Vietnam War, Soviet leaders again viewed the expansion of East-West cooperation as possible and desirable, for the USSR's military power had protected—and would continue to protect—the socialist world from capitalist aggression. "Soviet foreign policy paralyzes the aggressive actions of the imperialists. The Soviet Union's immense military and economic potential serves the cause of peace."[7] In short, the new active phase of peaceful coexistence is characterized by a growing Soviet capability (real and perceived) to influence the course of historical development in favor of socialism. However, Soviet domestic and foreign policy initiatives, which are taking place in an increasingly complex international system, are becoming, by choice or circumstance, increasingly sensitive and responsive to external trends and conditions.

The international behavior of the USSR is more and more shaped by an important objective force which Soviet political leaders and social theorists term "the scientific-technological revolution" (STR). Remarkable scientific, technical, and socioeconomic changes have indeed transformed capitalist and socialist societies and the relations between them since World War II. These changes have had both positive and negative consequences. On the one hand, the STR creates pressures for a more efficient division of labor in the global economy and for international cooperation in a broad range of scientific and technological fields. On the other hand, the STR has produced the danger of thermonuclear warfare, not only among the superpowers but among lesser powers as well. For the first time in world history, nations have the power to annihilate one another and permanently to damage the earth and its environment. But the very destructiveness of modern weapons technology reduces the possible benefits of initiating an all-out war and thereby restrains potential aggressors. Civil defense programs notwithstanding, there are not likely to be "winners" after a nuclear exchange.

It is to Khrushchev's credit that he not only recognized this fact, but adjusted the Soviet concept and policy of peaceful coexistence accordingly.

7. *Ibid.,* p. 30.

The downing of an American U-2 spy plane in the Soviet Union in 1960 dramatically discredited Khrushchev's initiatives to improve political and economic relations with the United States, and it also exacerbated the Sino-Soviet split. Khrushchev and Mao Tse-tung already had sharp disagreements about the military assertiveness of the United States, and about the appropriate uses of the Soviet Union's newly developed strategic weapons capability. The U-2 incident belied Khrushchev's contention that the United States now sought to extend its power only by peaceful means. Criticism from the Chinese and from conservative Soviet leaders no doubt contributed to Khrushchev's rash and extremely dangerous attempt to redress the East-West strategic balance by implanting nuclear weapons in Cuba in 1962. However, the signing of the U.S.-Soviet nuclear test-ban treaty less than a year later exemplified Khrushchev's efforts to reduce the international tensions and dangers produced by the awesome new weapons technologies. As a Soviet writer stated a decade afterward: "In the nuclear age, peaceful coexistence of the socialist and capitalist countries is dictated by the objective necessity of social development. Wars of plunder and conquest cannot be a method of settling international disputes. History poses the problem thusly: either peaceful coexistence or a catastrophic thermonuclear world war."[8]

Soviet analysts do not maintain that the avoidance of nuclear war through a policy of peaceful coexistence signifies the reconciliation of capitalism and socialism. Peaceful coexistence and detente, in Soviet theory and practice, consist of both competition (conflict) *and* cooperation with major Western nations. "The contradiction between socialism and capitalism has been and remains the principal contradiction of our epoch. A political, economic, and ideological struggle has been and will continue to be waged between them."[9]

What does change, however, are the forms of competition between the two systems. "The main thing is to divert the historically inevitable class struggle between socialism and capitalism into a channel that is not fraught with wars, dangerous conflicts, or an arms race."[10]

This last goal has proved to be particularly elusive. Throughout the 1970's, while the United States was trimming its existing and projected military capabilities, the USSR launched a major build-up of strategic and conventional weapons and significantly expanded and upgraded the Soviet navy. Moreover, Soviet leaders, unlike their American counterparts, have repeatedly insisted that detente does not preclude intense competition between the USSR and the West in the developing world, including the use of Cuban proxy forces to promote selected "wars of national liberation," as in

8. Vitalii Korionov, *The Policy of Peaceful Coexistence in Action* (Moscow: Progress, 1975), p. 28.
9. *A Study of Soviet Foreign Policy*, p. 29.
10. *The Policy of Peaceful Coexistence in Action*, p. 33.

Angola, Ethiopia, and South Yemen. Furthermore, the harassment and incarceration of Soviet dissidents intensified during the 1970's, symbolized by the forced internal exile of Nobel Peace Prize laureate Andrei Sakharov. This third trend clashed sharply with President Carter's particular concern about the suppression of "human rights" in the USSR.

Yet, in the early 1970's, the Brezhnev administration initiated a serious attempt to increase economic, military, and political cooperation with the United States and Western Europe, thereby to reduce East-West conflict for the long rather than the short term and for the mutual benefit of developed socialist and advanced capitalist countries. The SALT negotiations, the settling of the postwar boundary disputes between Western and Eastern Europe, and the Soviet efforts to enhance East-West trade—especially the flow of advanced technology to the Soviet Union to develop the natural resources of Siberia and to help meet the energy and mineral needs of the West—are prime examples.

Differing views of detente in the East and West, and differing views of detente within and among the major Western powers, have seriously undermined Soviet-American ties. Relations between the U.S. and USSR have deteriorated to the point where two American Presidents have rejected the very term "detente," and Soviet leaders felt they had little to lose by U.S. displeasure over the forceful occupation of Afghanistan in 1979, the first overt use of Soviet military power outside the Soviet bloc since World War II. One important consequence of this Soviet action was an immediate stepping-up of the Soviet-American arms race. Both sides have now placed renewed emphasis on developing new military technologies that would offset the other's offensive and defensive capabilities. And both sides are more vigorously pursuing geopolitical advantages (e.g., in the Persian Gulf and the Horn of Africa) to preserve or enhance their perceived security and economic interests.

But the Brezhnev collective leadership has not abandoned peaceful coexistence. In the Soviet view, active coexistence may consist of various combinations of competition and cooperation. Depending on the circumstances, Soviet policymakers place greater or lesser emphasis on *expanding* the areas of East-West cooperation, and on the *extent* of cooperation with *various* Western partners, especially the U.S., Western Europe, and Japan. As a Soviet analyst, buttressing his authoritative interpretation with quotes from Brezhnev, asserted shortly after the Soviet occupation of Afghanistan:

> Detente...has demonstrated its viability and stability. It advances thanks to its profoundly objective, historical basis, thanks to the political forces of our time, *including the policies of certain Western countries*, which realistically see the mainstream of history and work for the triumph of detente, for peace and security....*There is no reasonable alternative to detente in present-day international relations.* It is noteworthy that in the complex situation of the beginning of 1980

the Soviet Union found it necessary to reaffirm its confidence in the vitality of detente....Detente is an absolutely necessary and indispensable prerequisite for any constructive approach to the solution of crucial world issues."[11]

Briefly stated, Soviet writers usually emphasize the following three basic principles of peaceful coexistence and detente: 1) the repudiation of nuclear war as a means of resolving political disputes between industrialized capitalist and socialist countries; 2) the expansion of mutually advantageous cooperation between capitalism and socialism; and 3) the recognition of national sovereignty and noninterference in the internal affairs of other nations.[12] Unlike most Westerners, Soviet officials do not find this third principle incompatible with Soviet military and economic support for promising "national liberation movements" in Third World countries.

* * *

Does the current active phase of Soviet foreign policy revolve primarily around the inevitability of confrontation between capitalism and socialism, while avoiding nuclear war, or does it give considerable emphasis to the expansion and deepening of cooperation with the West?

Serious dispute exists in the United States and Western Europe concerning which element—competition or cooperation—is and should be predominant in the current phase of East-West relations.

One school of thought emphasizes that the present-day Soviet concepts of detente and peaceful coexistence are merely tactical in nature. The Soviet Union, it is argued, wants to cooperate with Western nations only in areas to its advantage and to the disadvantage of capitalism. The inevitability of military competition, Soviet territorial expansion, and violent conflict between East and West—occasionally direct, but more often by proxy forces—are underscored.

Another Western school of thought emphasizes that the current stage of detente represents a strategic shift in Soviet thinking. These U.S. and West European analysts contend that the USSR seriously wishes to avoid direct nuclear warfare, has accepted the need to channel historical conflict into nonmilitary forms of competition, and is striving to broaden and deepen East-West cooperation in various fields. American receptivity to these initiatives, it is argued, will in due course mitigate the "siege mentality" of Soviet leaders and restrain the USSR from using its newly developed military might throughout the world. U.S.-Soviet collaboration on global and bilateral issues, together with regularized competition in economic, military, and political spheres, can increasingly supersede confrontation and defuse international tensions.

---

11. Vladimir Gantman, "Detente and the System of International Relations," *Social Sciences* (Moscow), 2 (1980), pp. 177, 180-181 (emphases added). See also Georgii Arbatov, "Vneshniaia politika SShA na poroge 80-kh godov," *SShA*, 4 (1980), especially pp. 51-52.
12. *The Policy of Peaceful Coexistence in Action*, pp. 28-29.

Influential advocates of the first position are Zbigniew Brzezinski, President Jimmy Carter's national security advisor, and Harvard University professor Richard Pipes. In their contributions to this volume and elsewhere, Brzezinski and especially Pipes stress the historical continuity in the Soviet policy of peaceful coexistence. Whereas in earlier periods peaceful coexistence was a tactic to protect the Soviet Union from outside invasion, peaceful coexistence is now a tactic to promote Soviet ascendancy in the international arena.

The current Soviet policy of detente, in this view, has several dimensions. Economically, detente is designed to compensate for Soviet weaknesses in technology, organization, manpower, and labor incentives, without risking potentially destabilizing reforms of existing Party and state institutions and institutional relationships. While modernizing the USSR's economic system and increasing industrial and agricultural productivity, the Brezhnev collective leadership allegedly seeks to maximize the dependence of the West on Soviet raw materials, especially in the energy area.

Politically, the goals of detente are to gain international recognition of the USSR's superpower status, to extend Soviet influence throughout the world, and to consolidate the domestic political order. Militarily, detente is accompanied by a weapons and troop build-up in the USSR. In addition to efforts to upset the balance of strategic and conventional forces in Western Europe, the highest Party officials are thought to place a premium on the capacity to mount flexible military interventions in Third World countries. Finally, detente is designed to enable the Soviet Union to become directly involved in influencing Western policy. This influence is to be achieved by promoting the image of the USSR as a peace-loving power and a responsible business partner, thereby validating the arguments of Western (e.g., Eurocommunist) opponents of capitalist military-industrial complexes, and reducing the West European nations' political, economic, and military dependence upon the United States.

In contrast, Marshall Shulman, chief advisor on Soviet affairs to former Secretary of State Cyrus Vance, and Princeton University professor Robert C. Tucker are major proponents of a second orientation. In their essays in this section and elsewhere, Shulman and especially Tucker argue that the current phase of peaceful coexistence represents a historic shift in the foreign policy of the Soviet Union toward cooperation with the West. While recognizing the continued presence of the competitive elements of East-West relations, Shulman and Tucker stress considerably more than Brzezinski and Pipes the possibility and desirability of broadening and deepening the cooperative aspects of detente.

Shulman, in particular, is sensitive to the ongoing political conflict within the Soviet elite regarding the present phase of coexistence. The right tendency fears the abandonment of autarky; the center recognizes the necessity to link modernization with involvement in the global economy; and the left places greater emphasis on limited decentralization to promote a broad range of interdependent relations with the capitalist and developing nations. For Shulman, the expansion of East-West ties can help both the Soviet and American economies. The ability to compete economically in the developed world and to penetrate global markets is an important dimension of power which the USSR and the U.S. can no longer minimize. Also, better trade relations provide incentives for improved political relations, including the possibility of Soviet restraint, and even of cooperative efforts to reduce tensions, in selected Third World trouble spots.

Militarily, the strategic competition provides an important source of conflict and cooperation. Brzezinski and Shulman, as members of the Carter administration, both supported the Strategic Arms Limitation Treaty (SALT). Arms control negotiations, and SALT in particular, are founded on the recognition of the increasing interdependence of U.S. and Soviet security interests. For example, the U.S. and USSR have a common interest in preventing nuclear war and the proliferation of nuclear weapons among middle-sized and Third World countries. But Shulman, more than Brzezinski, stresses the complementarity of U.S. and Soviet security needs, and the mutual benefits of diverting scarce resources to the nonmilitary sectors of their respective economies. Finally, the broadening of scientific and technical cooperation, such as in the environmental, energy-related, and medical areas, provides other channels for the expression of some degree of commonality of interests between the Soviet Union and the West. In short, while competition remains central to East-West relations, pressures for cooperation are becoming a significant reality as well. Agreed-upon modes of competition and active collaboration in certain fields may even be a necessity, if wars are to be avoided and peaceful change is to be ensured.

The strength of Pipes's position rests upon three basic aspects of Soviet behavior during the period of detente launched in the early 1970's. First, the Soviet Union has engaged in a broad-scale arms build-up, not a reduction. Second, Soviet leaders have excluded from the detente relationship conflict between the USSR and the West in the developing world. Third, the repression of Soviet dissidents has accompanied detente, not the toleration of dissent or "loyal opposition" of various kinds.

But the weakness of Pipes's position and the concomitant strength of Shulman's is that, the vestiges of cold war conflict notwithstanding, Soviet officials and theorists are well aware that the relationship between domestic and foreign policies and the very nature of international politics are undergoing major transformations. That is, Soviet analysts understand that socioeconomic conditions within the USSR and the national interests of capitalist and communist nations are dramatically changing under the impact of the forces of advanced modernization—a process the Soviets refer to as "the scientific-technological revolution." Hence, the current phase of detente is characterized by evolving Soviet perspectives on the STR, "developed socialism," and the changing international system—and on the interrelationships among these complex and dynamic clusters of variables. Significantly, the new Soviet orientations link domestic modernization—especially economic growth and productivity—with improved East-West and North-South relations in the era of the STR (see the two chapters by Robbin Laird and Erik Hoffmann below).

In short, there has been a strategic shift in Soviet thinking about detente, but it may be even deeper than Shulman himself suggests. A new Soviet approach to international politics is emerging which is rooted in a better understanding of advanced modernization, and which is oriented toward much broader and deeper interaction with the West (the United States *and/or* Western Europe and Japan) than was legitimate in earlier periods of Soviet history. Soviet analysts are arguing that a new era has just begun in which the USSR must significantly increase cooperation with the highly industrialized capitalist nations, in order to develop the capabilities of the Soviet economy and polity in rapidly changing conditions, and to compete more effectively for economic and political advantage over those very same nations.

Although this gradual reorientation is portentous, the current Soviet approach to international politics still emphasizes competition as much as it does cooperation. The aging Brezhnev administration made the highly significant decision to prop up a faltering Marxist regime in Afghanistan by sending in the Red Army, thereby abandoning detente with the United States for the immediate future, risking the deterioration of political and commercial relations with Western Europe and Japan, and eliciting the condemnation of the entire Islamic world. And future Soviet leaders are unlikely to forswear assistance to selected "national liberation movements."

However, what Soviet analysts perceive to be changing are the sources, ground-rules, and geographical and substantive areas of competition and cooperation needed to promote the modernization of the USSR and its allies in Eastern Europe and elsewhere. As Georgii Shakhnazarov, head of the Soviet Political Sciences Association, asserts: "It is a distinctive feature of the present historical moment that the interests of survival, the scientific and technological revolution, and all the other objective trends of social development operate in such a way as to draw peoples and countries closer together and prompt them to solve the problems of mankind through common efforts, while at the same time the struggle between the two social systems continues to unfold."[13]

These competing pressures and trends are the subject of the remaining

---

13. Georgii Shakhnazarov, "New Factors in Politics at the Present Stage," *Social Sciences* (Moscow), 1 (1977), p. 49.

essays in this section. Thomas Wolfe, Franklyn Holzman, and Robert Legvold assess the military, economic, and political elements of East-West relations in the 1970's and their broader implications. Donald Zagoria, Kenneth Maxwell, and John Campbell offer different interpretations of Soviet aims and accomplishments throughout the Third World and in Africa and the Mediterranean (including the Middle East) respectively. All of the authors are sensitive to the influence of external events on Soviet international behavior. Maxwell, in particular, urges us to view developments in Africa in light of their impact on East-West competition.

Soviet relations with other communist states have also influenced East-West conflict and cooperation. The USSR's armed intervention in Hungary in 1956 and in Czechoslovakia in 1968 (discussed in the chapter by Christopher Jones below) had far-reaching effects on the ruling and nonruling parties of the international communist movement. Nonetheless, peaceful coexistence or detente with the West followed shortly thereafter in both cases, suggesting that the reassertion of Soviet hegemony in Eastern Europe had relatively little, or perhaps a curiously indirect, influence on East-West relations.

The same cannot be said of the intense Sino-Soviet rivalry, which broke out into armed conflict between the two major communist powers in 1969 and which has profoundly altered the structure and functioning of the present-day international system (see this section's concluding essays by Thomas Robinson and Harry Gelman). The substance, style, and timing of the recent American-Chinese rapprochement have clearly upset, even angered, the Soviet leadership. Whereas some top United States officials probably felt uneasy about the anti-Soviet pronouncements of Teng Hsiao-ping during his visit here in 1979, Soviet leaders have been understandably prone to see a unity of purpose and strategy in Chinese and American actions. After all, we provided an extraordinary forum for the Chinese Deputy Premier to voice his hostility toward the USSR, we did nothing to rebut his statements, and we even signed a joint communique condemning "hegemony" (read: the expansion of Soviet influence) in Asia. China was shortly thereafter granted "most-favored-nation" trading status with the U.S. and invited to join the International Monetary Fund and the World Bank—foreign trade opportunities which have never been proffered to the Soviet Union, despite its repeated requests throughout the 1970's. Accurately or not, Soviet officials have concluded that the American courting of China is part of a deliberate effort to undermine East-West detente.

Our future ties with the Soviet Union will depend on many factors indirectly related or unrelated to the normalization of U.S.-Chinese relations and are particularly difficult to predict in light of rapidly changing international developments. But Soviet officials' and citizens' unhappiness with American policy toward China will probably not alter most Soviet leaders' perceptions of their nation's self-interest vis-a-vis the West in the 1980's. The Brezhnev administration persistently sought to sign SALT I and II and to expand East-West industrial and agricultural trade and technology exchange throughout the 1970's. Moreover, U.S. actions toward China have not increased the political, economic, and strategic "costs" to the USSR of making progress on these fronts. If anything, the improvement of American-Chinese relations, and the prospect of long-term economic and even military ties between China and Western nations, may increase the costs to the Soviet Union of *not* concluding Salt II and III agreements, of *not* enhancing East-West trade, and of *not* utilizing advanced Western technology and management techniques.

Strategic arms limitation treaties are based on mutual surveillance, not on trust, as President Carter has bluntly stressed, and trade is likewise founded on the perception of mutual benefit and self-interest. The opening up of Chinese markets to Western capital and technology would seem likely to spur Soviet efforts to expand economic ties with the United States and/or Western Europe and Japan, quite possibly on terms more favorable to capitalist multinational corporations. This could well induce Western businessmen and legislators to pursue economic detente more actively—and evenhandedly—with both major communist powers.

In short, the emergence of China as a world power is now forcing both the United States and the Soviet Union to reassess their overall goals and strategies and their relations with one another in a world that is no longer bipolar. The old question of how best to influence Soviet international behavior is now being raised under quite new conditions—the interjection of dramatic American-Chinese cooperation and dramatic U.S.-Soviet conflict prior to the signing of the painstakingly negotiated SALT II agreement; the Russian occupation of Afghanistan; the turmoil in Iran that followed the ouster of the Shah; the imminent departure of the present generation of elderly Soviet leaders and of key Chinese officials (to say nothing of the ongoing uncertainties of the American electoral process); and the rapid development of the worldwide STR, especially in the military and industrial spheres.

The political implications of our overplaying the China "card" would be to support those present and future Soviet leaders who would emphasize confrontation rather than cooperation with the West, and autarkic or relatively independent development of the Soviet economy. Two probable results of a pro-Chinese American policy would be to strengthen Soviet economic ties with Western Europe and to exacerbate political strains within the Western alliance.

Another American policy would be to provide Brezhnev and his successors with positive and negative incentives to participate actively in an international division of economic and scientific labor, and to take an increasingly comprehensive view of detente, especially the broadening and deepening of Soviet-American cooperation.[14]

To further this second course of development, and as a goal with equal merit in its own right, the United States must also strengthen American-Chinese cooperation and strongly support the present Chinese drive to create a more technologically advanced society based on substantially increased interdependence with the West. By so doing, the United States may help to give both the Soviet Union and China a greater stake in participating responsibly and effectively in the global economy, in developing the non-military sectors of their own economies, and in contributing to the peaceful resolution of international conflict.

14. For a thorough discussion of these themes, see Erik P. Hoffmann and Robbin F. Laird, *The Modernization of the Soviet Union and East-West Relations* (forthcoming).

United States – Soviet Cooperation:
Incentives and Obstacles*

One of the most significant realignments of the recent past, East and West, is a *rapprochement* between the United States and Soviet Russia, an uncertain move by the two military superpowers and erstwhile cold-war adversaries into limited collaborative relations for purposes of maintaining international peace and security.

This realignment was made possible, on the Soviet side, by the death of Stalin and ensuing reorientation of Soviet policy in both internal and external affairs. It emerged slowly in the course of a post-Stalin dialogue between leaders of the two countries. The Geneva summit meeting of 1955 and the Camp David talks in 1959 between President Eisenhower and Premier Khrushchev were landmarks in the growth of this dialogue. The late 1950's and early 1960's witnessed a series of concrete steps that gave substance to the new trend in the relations between the two countries.

These steps included the limited nuclear test-ban agreement of 1963, the previous year's agreement on neutralization of Laos, the creation of the permanent direct communication channel between Moscow and Washington (called the "hot line"), the agreement on peaceful uses of the Antarctic, the agreement not to place bombs in orbit, the recently concluded multilateral treaty on

*Reprinted from *The Annals of the American Academy of Political and Social Science,* 372 (July, 1967), pp. 2 – 13, by permission of the author and the publisher.

principles for the use by all states of outer space, the growth of cultural and scientific exchange, the regularizing of contacts and discussion between the political leaders and diplomatic officials of the two countries, the continuing negotiations on arms control and disarmament, the talks on measures to prevent proliferation of nuclear weapons, the United States-Soviet agreement on direct air connections, and the conclusion of the consular convention. At the same time, there have also been a number of setbacks to the new trend in United States-Soviet relations. The U-2 episode of 1960 and the Cuban missile crisis of 1962 are both noteworthy examples. In the middle 1960's, moreover, the growth of Soviet-American political cooperation has been seriously retarded and complicated by war in Vietnam, and especially by the United States policy, initiated in early 1965, of bombing raids on North Vietnam, a Soviet ally. At this time of writing (May 1967), the future of Soviet-American cooperation is deeply clouded.

Even without these serious setbacks, the *rapprochement* between the two great powers would by no means have been describable as a "condominium," not to mention the conspiratorial "collusion" for joint Soviet-American world rule which has been conjured up in various statements emanating from Peking. On the other hand, we should not minimize the potential importance of the emergence in the post-Stalin era of a new Soviet-American relationship, the replacement of the old cold-war antagonism with a more complex and constructive interaction in which competition and cooperation are conjoined. What I wish to do in what follows is to explore the possible meaning of this realignment, and to consider some requisites of stable cooperative relations between the two countries.

The Historical Background

Although ideologically at opposite poles, the United States and Soviet Russia were not wholly unprepared in a psychological sense for the new trend in their relations which developed after Stalin. There was no tradition of enmity between their peoples. America has always enjoyed great popularity in the minds of many Russians, and even the Soviet Communist regime, speaking through Stalin, once defined the Bolshevik "style" in work as a combination of "Russian revolutionary sweep" with "American efficiency."[1] Americans, for their part, were perhaps less inclined to positive feelings toward Russia. But during the Second World War, they generally admired the Russian war effort, and ordinary Russians were more aware than their government ever acknowledged of the contribution of American Lend-Lease assistance to that effort. A large fund of mutual good will resulted.

1. J. Stalin, *Works* (Moscow, 1953), p. 194. The statement was made in Stalin's lectures of 1924 on "The Foundations of Leninism."

Not surprisingly, the idea and, to some extent, the fact of Soviet-American political collaboration have a history going back to that period. For in 1941 the two countries suddenly became involved in a "cooperative relationship" of the most elementary kind — a coalition war for survival against a common enemy. It was only natural under those conditions that some should conceive of a continuing cooperative relationship in the postwar period. Such a concept entered into the architecture of the United Nations as an organization, the Security Council in particular. Optimistic expectations were not borne out, however, and the wartime alliance gave way to the cold-war hostilities of 1946 – 1953. Not until after Stalin's death did a change in the Soviet leadership and political outlook begin to make possible the more hopeful and constructive pattern of United States-Soviet relations that some had envisaged during World War II. The prerequisites for this development had been present in the Soviet internal situation ever since the end of the war. But Stalin, the most absolute of twentieth-century dictators, was for psychological reasons unable to recognize and accept them, and continued to the end of his days to press the Cold War against the manifold "enemies" with which his paranoid personality and hostile actions peopled the world.[2]

The men who came to power in the Soviet system after Stalin's death represented a generation of somewhat younger leaders who, unlike Stalin himself, had never been revolutionaries. Rather, they had come up in political life as executives and managers. They were typified by Malenkov and Khrushchev and, more recently, by Brezhnev and Kosygin. Communist in ideology, the post-Stalin leaders give little evidence of being radical in their outlook; they are an essentially *postrevolutionary* leadership presiding over a relatively deradicalized Soviet Marxist movement, one that has gone very far toward accommodating itself to the world that it remains ideologically committed to transform.

The deradicalization of Soviet communism has certain obviously important foreign-policy implications. They could be summed up by saying that fifty years after the Bolshevik Revolution, the Soviet Union can no longer accurately be described as a "revolutionary power." Its leadership remains ideologically committed to the goal of a world-wide Communist revolution, but the pattern of Soviet conduct in world affairs has increasingly become that of a status-quo power rather than a revolutionary one.[3] Of course, "status-quo power" is itself a concept with a range of possible meanings. In the Soviet case, we do not have a power so rigidly wedded to the international status quo that

2. This thesis has been elaborated with supporting evidence in this writer's *The Soviet Political Mind* (New York: Frederick A. Praeger, 1963), Chapters 2 and 8.

3. This refers, of course, to the pattern of action in the non-Communist part of the world. Soviet policy toward the *Communist* part has long been protective of the status quo, as was best shown by the Soviet intervention in Hungary in 1956 to keep communism intact in a country where its fortunes were uncertain owing to popular revolution.

it would actively resist revolutionary change in the non-Communist part of the world. As its response to the Cuban revolution makes clear, for example, Soviet Russia, even in this era of deradicalization, is still willing to welcome and give assistance to a regime moving on its own into the Communist orbit. The thesis here being advanced is simply that the commitment to world Communist revolution, while still intact ideologically, has become very weak as a political motivation and has ceased to be a mainspring of Soviet initiative in world affairs. Soviet ideological behavior has registered the trend in question through emphatic pronouncements against "export of revolution" and through affirmation of the idea that Communist revolution should occur, if at all, as an indigenous development in the country concerned and, if possible, as a nonviolent one.

If the contemporary Soviet Union is no longer to any significant extent a revolution-making power but rather one which finds the international status quo not hard to live with, the explanation is to be sought not solely in the change of leadership and outlook attendant upon the death of Stalin and the passing from the political scene of the remnants of the Bolshevik old guard (such as Molotov) who had survived in power with Stalin. Among other factors reinforcing the status-quo tendency is the growing polycentrism of the Communist world in our time. The fourteen Communist-ruled states and the eighty or so Communist parties elsewhere in the world are no longer under Soviet control as in Stalin's time. Moreover, Soviet political and ideological ascendancy in the polycentric world of Communist states and parties has been powerfully challenged by Communist China under Mao. Further enlargement of the sphere of Communist political power could, in these conditions, complicate the Soviet effort to retain an ascendant position. Indeed, Moscow's position as capital of world communism could be further undermined rather than bolstered by Communist revolutions that brought to power parties looking to China for leadership. The otherwise curious spectacle of Soviet support for a non-Communist India in its latter-day hostilities with Communist China finds part of its explanation here.

Still another force behind the evolution of the Soviet state from the role of a revolutionary power to that of a status-quo power is the need for international stability as a setting for internal Soviet development and reform. The post-Stalin leadership inherited from Stalin a country in internal crisis caused by the long regime of terror, bureaucratic stultification, gross mismanagement, neglect of crying welfare needs of the people, and resulting catastrophically low morale. In Stalin's final years, all these problems had gone largely unrecognized in an atmosphere of relentless pursuit of the Cold War abroad. Indeed, it may have been in part Stalin's unwillingness to face the necessity for change and reform inside the Soviet Union which spurred him to keep the nation's attention constantly fixed upon the machinations of foreign "enemies." With his death, there was an underlying change in the relationship of internal and external politics of the Soviet regime.

Instead of predicating the internal policy upon the needs of the Cold War abroad, the post-Stalin leadership, under Malenkov and Beria at first and subsequently under Khrushchev and others, tended to give the position of priority to internal needs and problems and to seek a cold war *détente*. Not only would such a *détente* relieve external dangers to Soviet security (for example, by ending the Korean War); it might also make it possible to reallocate scarce Soviet funds to internal developmental needs, and especially to the long neglected consumer-goods industries. Thus, the commitment to internal development and reform was a factor favoring international stabilization.

Nor is this, as might be supposed, a strictly short-term proposition. A Soviet regime attempting, as part of its reform policy, to rule Russia without the terror that was the hallmark of Stalinism must necessarily seek substantial and continuing improvement in the living standards of the Soviet population, and the pressure to do this rises as public opinion emerges as a force in the no-longer-totalitarian single-party system. But with a gross national product far lower than America's, Soviet Russia can divert large resources to welfare needs only if it can substantially reduce or control defense expenditures. These considerations point to *détente* and international stabilization as a long-range Soviet interest, to arms control and negotiated disarmament measures as a way of enabling Russia to control arms outlays without falling behind in relative military power vis-à-vis the United States, and to a new political relationship with the United States as a precondition of achieving such ends.

Competitive Coexistence

The new foreign orientation of the post-Stalin Soviet leadership reflected these underlying realities. Ideologically, it expressed itself in the doctrine of "competitive coexistence," which was advanced in the time of Khrushchev and incorporated into the Program of the Soviet Communist party in 1961. That doctrine portrays the United States and the Soviet Union as, respectively, the leaders of two ideologically opposed "systems" competing by peaceful means — economic, political, cultural — for dominant world influence, the chief stake in the contest being the future development of the underdeveloped countries of the Third World toward either Soviet communism or American capitalism. Internal economic development is a principal arena of this external competition, for it is a question of which developmental model, the Soviet or the American, will prove more compellingly attractive in the long run.

But competitive coexistence was presented in the post-Stalin Soviet doctrine as involving a measure of cooperation between the competitors. Rather in the manner in which our economists have described "oligopolistic competition," in which two or more dominant firms cooperate to prevent price wars and maintain general market stability while competing (for example, through advertising) to improve their relative shares of the market, Soviet theorists of competitive coexistence have envisaged the Soviet Union and the United States as engaging in political cooperation to prevent war and maintain overall international stability while they carry on long-range nonmilitary competition (for example, through propaganda and ideology) to enhance their relative influence in the world. Being Marxist, they have presented this notion of a dual competitive-cum-cooperative relationship with America as a "dialectical" approach to coexistence. The basis of the cooperation, according to the Soviet view, as formulated by both political leaders and theoretical specialists, is the shared vital interest of the two great powers in reducing the chances of war. Cooperation for this purpose would involve the development of close and regular contact on all problems of mutual concern, the attempt to negotiate solutions of issues concealing threats to peace, the defusing of trouble spots in various parts of the world (Laos, for example), and the stopping of local conflicts before they grow into great conflagrations threatening to involve the major powers. In effect, the new Soviet doctrine has seen in United States-Soviet political cooperation a way of keeping competitive coexistence peaceful, of maintaining a relatively stable international environment within which the nonmilitary competition for influence can proceed.

The United States government has, since President Eisenhower's time, tended to respond favorably to the concept of a changed relationship involving some cooperation as well as continued political rivalry with Soviet Russia. It, too, has shown awareness that such cooperation could prove a requisite for cosurvival in the nuclear age. It, too, has an interest in curbing the astronomical costs of modern military technology, the spiral of the arms race. Without some success along that line, it can no more get to what is now called the "Great Society" than Soviet Russia can get to what it calls "Full Communism" (two visions of the social goal which have, by the way, more than a little in common). So, the new Soviet foreign orientation of the post-Stalin period found a receptive audience in Washington. President Kennedy's speech at American University, "Toward a Strategy of Peace," was one of the significant markers of this trend in United States official thinking. President Johnson, too, has strongly endorsed the concept of a cooperative relationship with Russia. "We've got to get into the habit of peaceful cooperation," he said, for example, in a public pronouncement of September 1966 to the Soviet people, emphasizing the common interest of the two countries in the avoidance of war, the historical record of friendliness between the two peoples, and the desirability of extending cooperative relations beyond what had so far been accomplished.[4]

4. *The New York Times,* September 28, 1966, p. 14.

Obstacles to Cooperation

Taking stock of the outcome so far, we must admit that the experiment in Soviet-American collaboration has not yet borne great fruit in deeds or brought about a stable *entente* between the two governments. Although by no means insignificant in their cumulative entirety, the cooperative acts and agreements noted earlier are little more than a series of tentative and cautious beginnings. Let us consider, for example, some of what has *not* yet been done. So far, progress on arms control and disarmament has been small. The treaty on nonproliferation of nuclear weapons would, it is true, be a very great step forward in this field. But at present it still remains under negotiation, and the outcome is uncertain. Part of the responsibility for that rests with the failure of the United States and Soviet Union to match the renunciation being asked of others with some renouncing on their own parts — such as the renouncing of the right of *first use* of nuclear weapons — and to give guarantees to the nonnuclear states against nuclear blackmail or nuclear attack by governments which might try to violate the system.

What is more, the United States and Soviet Union may be on the threshold of another fateful round of the arms race, involving the deployment of anti-ballistic missiles systems and resulting further development of offensive weapons by both sides, all of which may represent a serious setback for the cause of arms control (for example, by necessitating a resumption of nuclear tests above ground). They have not so far been willing to transform the costly competitive race to the moon into a cooperative venture. They have done next to nothing to place economic assistance to underdeveloped countries on a cooperative and multilateral basis, although the emerging crisis of economic growth and overpopulation makes the need for a cooperative approach to the problem painfully obvious.

There is no single or simple explanation for the tentativeness of United States-Soviet cooperation and for the modest character of the positive results so far. One of the explanations, however, lies in the strength of the resistances and obstacles on both sides to a working accord between the United States and Soviet governments on important international problems. Realism not only compels us to acknowledge the existence of these obstacles, but also to admit that they make themselves felt on both sides. Thus, both great powers encounter resistances within their respective alliance systems to a Soviet-American *entente*. They emanate in particular from certain governments whose leaders fear that United States-Soviet cooperation could be injurious to their own national interests. The importance that both the United States and Soviet Union attach to the preservation of their alliance structures forces them to take account of these counter-pressures. Soviet policy-makers have had to contend in particular with Communist Chinese objections to the relationship with the United States; and the United States government has had especially to contend with concern in West Germany over the possible impact of Soviet-American cooperation upon German reunification and other interests.

A further obstacle to collaborative relations between the two great powers is the persistence on both sides of old habits of mind born in the era of the Cold War, habits of ingrained hostility and distrust, habits of seeing the struggle against the other side as the supreme proper concern of national policy, and cooperation between Russia and America as unnecessary for security purposes, or undesirable, or both. To make matters still more complicated, these habits of mind are unevenly distributed on both sides. Some American and Soviet political leaders are more flexible and conciliation-minded, more able and willing to conceive of collaborating with adversaries and to experiment along those lines, whereas others are more rigid and doctrinaire, more inclined to rely on military might in relations with the other side, more convinced that the only effective way to talk to them is in the language of cold power. In the jargon of recent times, we have the "soft-liners" and the "hard-liners," the "doves" and the "hawks." These terms are obvious oversimplifications, but the divisions to which they point are real and enormously important facts of political life in *both* of the capitals. The recent United States Senate debate over ratification of the consular convention with the Soviet Union made the division on the American side more dramatically apparent than before. Because of the single-party system and official control of the press on the other side, the division is less apparent in the Soviet leadership. Yet those of us who regularly study the Soviet press have found abundant evidence that it exists.

And so, on both sides, there are influential elements who *oppose* a Soviet-American working relationship and who resist efforts in that direction to the extent that they can. In a curious way, moreover, they reinforce each other. For insofar as the Soviet hard-liners gain the ascendancy inside the Soviet Union's regime, the policy orientation that they pursue tends to support the arguments of their opposite numbers in Washington about the difficulty of working cooperatively with the Russians. The same process also works in reverse: ascendancy of those who favor a hard-line policy in Washington plays into the hands of the Moscow opponents of Soviet-American cooperation, for it leads to actions by the United States government which make the latter's argument in the internal policy debate on the Soviet side more plausible. Thus, the tough policy that the United States government has pursued in Vietnam during the last two years has resulted, among other things, in a growth of influence of hard-line elements inside the Soviet government and a worsening of the position of the proponents of better relations with Washington.

Still a further serious obstacle to a stable and self-sustained United States-Soviet working relationship is the continuance of political rivalry between them at the level of intensity that has marked it during the past decade. Both great powers have vigorously engaged in a political influence contest, particularly in the Third World, employing diplomacy, economic assistance, arms exports, technical aid, propaganda, and so on. Experience makes it quite clear that this influence contest can create situations that, in turn, impose great strain upon the fabric of Soviet-American relations. Thus, for example, Moscow, pursuing political influence, has in recent months created an arms imbalance in North Africa by shipping much military equipment to Algeria, which has led to a plea from Morocco to the United States for matching arms assistance. The dynamics of situations of this kind contain within themselves the potentiality of armed conflicts which, in turn, create more international tension and threaten to involve the superpowers. The earlier history of present events in Indochina bears witness in its way to the relevance of this proposition.

So, the whole concept of a "nonmilitary" Soviet-American competition for influence in the uncommitted countries has a certain unreality. For competitive coexistence tends to remain peaceful only so long as neither side is conspicuously or irretrievably *losing*. The game shows a dangerous tendency to cease being peaceful when: (1) a change of regime seriously adverse to one or the other side occurs or threatens to occur within a given country that has been an object of competition, and (2) circumstances permit the application of force to prevent or reverse this adverse outcome. An intense competitive struggle to draw uncommitted countries into one orbit of influence or another is, therefore, a serious bar to the development of stable cooperative relations between the United States and Soviet Union.

All of these obstacles to Soviet-American cooperation have made themselves felt in recent years and help to explain why more has not been achieved. In this connection, special mention must be made of the war in Vietnam. On the surface, this war has not completely put a stop to United States-Soviet political collaboration. Yet, in a deeper way, the war, and especially the bombing of North Vietnam which began in early 1965, has had a very depressing effect upon the whole post-Stalin growth of working relations between Moscow and Washington. Changes that slowly were taking place in the official Soviet image of the American political leadership have been set back or reversed, and an image of the American leadership that resembles the old cold-war stereotypes has reemerged in the Soviet official press. A relapse into old suspicions, old animosities, and old anti-American Soviet reflexes may be reflected in this. In part, it may reflect increased influence of the hard-line element in the Soviet leadership under the impact of Vietnam, and in part it may express a general tendency of the Soviet political mind to reconsider its earlier more hopeful view of American leaders. Furthermore, in the general atmosphere of West European apathy or opposition to America's Vietnamese action, the Soviet leadership has been presented with fresh opportunities to cultivate political relationships in Europe that might not otherwise have existed or have been so beckoning, and consequently we have seen in the past two years a tendency for Moscow to exploit centrifugal forces in the Western alliance structure, to give the emphasis not to closer relations with Washington but rather to closer relations with West European capitals, Paris included. Finally, the dialogue between Soviet and American leaders, a dialogue which lies at the core of the cooperative relationship, has suffered and greatly been diminished as a result of Vietnam. On the whole, the injury done to the emergent *entente* with the Soviet Union may be far from the least of the tragedies of the Vietnamese war from the American point of view.

Yet I do not believe that the new Soviet-American relationship is or need be permanently impaired. Given in the near future a negotiated peace in Vietnam, the underlying forces in the world situation which impel the two superpowers to collaborative action should reassert themselves. Fundamental security interests of both powers, and indeed of all peoples, are involved. Hence it seems premature to assume a permanent shift of Soviet diplomatic emphasis to the Western European scene or to treat the whole venture of cooperative relations between the United States and the Soviet Union as a matter of historical interest only. What may be useful, then, is to reflect on the experience of the past decade in this field, and try to draw some lessons from it.

Requisites of Soviet – American Cooperation

(1) It appears that, notwithstanding all the obstacles explored above, the incentives to cooperative action by the two superpowers are quite strong, sufficiently so to provide a basis for greater success in this field than has been achieved so far. The fundamental incentive is the common interest in reducing the danger of a thermonuclear holocaust. This primary common interest, reinforced by a further common interest in curtailing the cost of military preparations and establishments, dictates United States-Soviet cooperation in all feasible measures of arms control and disarmament. Further, the primary common interest in preventing a general war gives rise to a set of secondary common interests in stabilizing or settling crisis situations in which the threat of armed violence is latently present.

Beyond these shared interests in avoiding war, in bringing the arms race under control, and in the defusing of world trouble-spots, the United States and the Soviet Union have an underlying, although as yet imperfectly cognized, common interest in working together to meet certain other problems and dangers. The population explosion, the growing disparity between the wealthy nations and the poor nations and the associated problem of economic development, and the problem of air and water pollution are high on the list of situations that contain a mounting threat of disorder on a world scale, situations of unprecedented urgency and seriousness. Only through international cooperation can these dangers be contained, much less allayed, and without cooperation between the two most powerful and wealthy of industrialized nations, no efforts by the United Nations or regional associations of states can bear great fruit. In effect, international cooperation is becoming a vital necessity in the face of the rise of a plethora of problems that, by their very nature, cannot be satisfactorily resolved within the confines of the nation-state. In the continuing absence of an effective system of world order, the United States and Soviet Russia can alone provide by their cooperative action an interim response to the need for a cooperative international approach to these problems. It is not only, then, the danger of war which provides the underlying motivation for their cooperation, but also the political, demographic, economic, and technological challenges to prolonged meaningful human living on this planet.

(2) A cooperative arrangement between the United States and the Soviet Union cannot easily be enduring and stable unless it becomes more close and extensive than political leaders on either side have apparently envisaged, and unless it takes precedence over such important competing concerns as the integrity of their regional alliance structures. Up to now, the tendency on both sides has been to think in terms of a modicum of cooperation combined with a high level of continued political rivalry throughout the world. The experience of the past decade suggests, however, that unless the cooperative working relationship transcends this, unless it goes beyond a *détente* and becomes an *entente,* it may not be viable at all.

This view is admittedly at variance with the thinking of some respected American specialists in foreign-policy problems. They take a continued intense process of Soviet-American competition for influence as a constant and feel, in part because of pressures from within the Western alliance system, that cooperative relations with Moscow neither need be nor ought to be extended beyond a minimum of mutually advantageous action, chiefly in the sphere of arms control, to reduce the hazards of nuclear war.[5] However, such a scenario for American-Soviet relations may be more of a utopia than the just-mentioned *entente.* For it overlooks the essential indivisibility of these relations, the virtual impossibility of maintaining stable cooperative arrangements in one field — the delicate and difficult area of arms control — while pursuing as vigorously as ever a worldwide political competition for influence which keeps the competitors mutually estranged and periodically generates high tension between them. The cooperative links between Washington and Moscow cannot be expected to prosper if frequently subjected to extreme political turbulence in a world of intense Soviet-American political rivalry.

This is not to argue that some sort of global bargain between the two powers is the precondition of their successful cooperation in world affairs. An antecedent general settlement of outstanding international issues, however desirable in the abstract, does not appear realistically attainable in the near future.

5. See, for example, the argument of Marshall D. Shulman in "'Europe' versus *Détente?,*" *Foreign Affairs* (April, 1967).

Undoubtedly, there are various issues — and German reunification is almost certainly one of them — which will have to be lived with until the slow passage of time and efforts of diplomacy can bring possibilities of resolution that do not now exist. The point being made here is simply that the competitive process, although it clearly cannot altogether be stopped, need not on the other hand be taken as a simple given, an unalterable fact of international life, something over which the two governments have no control. Rather, it has an interactive dynamic of its own which can be curbed and brought under control, given the settled will on both sides to do so. It is something to which limits can be set. And difficult as this might be to achieve, it would probably be less difficult than to achieve progress on the terribly complex technical problems of arms control and disarmament *without* curtailment of the power rivalry between the two principals. On the other hand, progress on arms-control measures should become increasingly feasible in a setting of lessened political competition between the chief governments concerned.

The theory of competitive coexistence, as elaborated on the Soviet side and more or less accepted with much ideological rationalization on the American side, envisages an indefinitely prolonged process of political competition tempered by cooperative steps to keep this competition peaceful. But that is a formula for an inherently unstable and deeply troubled United States-Soviet relationship. To stabilize it, the cooperative aspect will have to be given primacy over the competitive aspect. The two governments will have to show a settled disposition to reach settlements where possible. They will have to neutralize or otherwise defuse various danger points in world politics, such as Southeast Asia; to forestall the eruption of crisis situations that place great strain upon their relations; to avoid getting into conflicts which give rise to domestic pressures against cooperative relations; and, in general, to adopt a conflict-resolving posture in their interrelations and their approach to world problems. Clearly, this would imply certain significant modifications in the habitual modes of thought and conduct of both main powers on the international scene. Above all, instead of regarding the promotion of a particular form of society as their highest mission in history, the leaders would have to conceive it as their supreme goal to serve the cause of order in human affairs, pending the slow creation in time of order-maintaining institutions on a world scale.

(3) This raises the whole question of the form that a United States-Soviet *entente* might take. Manifestly, close relationships between great powers can take a multitude of forms, depending upon the purposes that animate them and other factors. A United States-Soviet working relationship could conceivably fall into the pattern of imperialistic great-power alliances of the past, with a division of Soviet and American spheres of influence in the world. In effect, the interests of the two powers, narrowly conceived, would become the touchstone of their cooperative action. Although the United States and Russia have

the combined physical power to enforce such a condominium, an attempt to cooperate along those lines would not, for a great many reasons, be likely to succeed for long. Not only would it be beset by manifold resistances from smaller states whose interests were being overridden by the great powers; it would conflict with the aspirations of the two peoples themselves, and would encounter resistances, both internal and external.

An alternative form of *entente,* although historically unprecedented, would be more in accord with the needs of the situation and the spirit of the two peoples. Instead of cooperating politically in their own national interests, narrowly conceived, the governments of the United States and Soviet Union would seek to exert their influence separately and jointly on behalf of the growth of order, which is in the interest not simply of these two major nations but of all. They would work not only in their bilateral relations but in the United Nations and its working bodies, in their regional alliances, and in every aspect of foreign policy, to promote constructive change and peaceful solutions of world problems. In effect, the United States-Soviet cooperative relationship would become a kind of trusteeship under which the two governments would jointly act as sponsors of international order pending the creation of a workable formal system of world order in the future. They would form, as it were, an informal interim system of order, a holding operation to help man survive long enough to move into the new form of international life that is needed but does not yet exist.

Such an undertaking would tap the deeper sources of idealism present in both the American and Russian peoples. Among contemporary nations, these two are notable for the stubborn streak of idealistic aspiration that marks them both in very different ways. Both have a universalism and a commitment to world order. They conceive it differently, it is true. Americans tend to think in terms of a world order under law, whereas Russians, insofar as they are Communists, tend rather to think in terms of a world order under ideology. No easy reconciliation of these disparate approaches to world order will be possible. But the younger generations, those who come to positions of power and influence in ten or fifteen years time, may find it easier than their elders did to make the necessary mutual adjustment. What their elders can do is to give them a chance to try.

(4) Finally, it is, in my opinion, an essential requisite for stable cooperation between the United States and Soviet Union that an element of mutual trust be built over time into their mutual relations. The foundation of this trust might be the recognition by leading persons on both sides that the two countries have acquired, by virtue of modern military technology, not only certain common security interests but a *mutual* security interest. That is to say, given the unheard-of possibilities of destruction inherent in total thermonuclear war in our time, each of the two superpowers has, whether it recognizes this or not, acquired a certain interest in the *other's* security, or (what amounts to the same

thing) its sense of security. For nervousness, tension, insecurity on either side have become dangerous to both. It is in this context that the growth of mutual trust becomes a factor of great potential importance.

Considering the heritage of mutual mistrust and suspicion born of the Cold War and the whole past history of our relations, the idea of building trust into Soviet-American relations may seem wildly unrealistic. Moreover, there is a certain tendency to suppose that the sole proper basis for Soviet-American relations, including cooperative action in arms control, is the rationally calculated self-interest of both parties, their common desire to survive. This may be so, but it is not self-evidently so. For it may be that in certain situations now emerging on the horizon of Soviet-American relations, the dictates of calculated self-interest will depend on what image of the other side goes into the calculation: the picture of a malevolent force operating only on the basis of calculated self-interest, or, alternatively, that of a force moved by certain human feelings and not foreign to benevolence. If this is so, then the growth of trust — the kind of trust that may have been emerging, for example, in the relations between Kennedy and Khrushchev — could prove of decisive significance.

To build mutual trust into United States-Soviet relations will at best be a long slow process, and probably never complete, at least in the present generation. But without it, there can be no genuine *entente,* and many problems will be far harder to resolve. In particular, the arms race will probably not be brought under control.

U.S.-Soviet Relations*

The American-Soviet relationship during the coming years will be shaped by the interaction of three dynamic forces.

The first is the thrust of domestic developments within the two political systems and societies, which will necessarily affect such matters as national will, allocation of resources, and overall political orientation, as well as the internal political-social stability and international appeal of the two entities.

The second is the nature of the power balance—strategic and conventional—between the two states which, depending on how it is weighed, will have its psychological spillover, conditioning the national sense of security and the self-assurance of leaders of the two states, and which in any case will either widen or limit the opportunities confronting the two powers.

The third force is the pattern of autonomous global and regional developments which—irrespective of actual policies pursued by either Washington or Moscow—may create pressures for international involvement, reaction, or withdrawal, thereby directly or indirectly structuring the American-Soviet relationship to the advantage or disadvantage of one or the other, even though it occasionally compels both parties into a more cooperative relationship.

*Zbigniew K. Brzezinski, "U.S.-Soviet Relations," in Henry Owen, ed., *The Next Phase in Foreign Policy.* Copyright ©1973 by the Brookings Institution, Washington, D.C. Reprinted by permission of the author and the publisher.

The interaction of these factors may cumulatively, and very gradually, induce subtle but important changes in the way in which the two major powers (or more correctly, their "political elite") perceive each other. Moreover, to the extent that the second and third sets of factors involve considerations of global magnitude, the U.S.-Soviet relationship, because of its very complexity and scale, is not likely to lend itself to simple, clear-cut formulas but instead will prompt a web of crosscutting policies, some cooperative, some competitive, and some directly antagonistic.

Domestic Developments

Both the United States and the Soviet Union face major domestic problems, and these will probably become more, rather than less, acute during the seventies. However, these internal difficulties differ in kind, and their ebb and flow is unlikely to be synchronous. Even more conjectural is their eventual outcome.

Two broad generalizations about these internal difficulties serve as a starting point. America is openly experiencing a broad social turbulence, which has long-range constitutional and political implications; the Soviet Union is suffering from a less visible—indeed, a deliberately obscured—political paralysis, which could at some point erupt into the open and which is in any case pregnant with social implications. Second, change in the American political and social system is dynamic, with the system continuously adjusting and changing as new claims, new outlooks, new groups, and new leaders assert themselves in a competitive free-for-all; in contrast, the Soviet system, dominated by an extremely conservative leadership, is in a metastable state, a term used in the natural sciences to denote a precariously rigid condition of stability in which even a slight turbulence can start a highly destabilizing chain reaction.[1]

The problems of America can best be understood as involving the uneasy interaction between several historical levels of American society in a setting of accelerating velocity of social change. A preindustrial America, an industrial America, and a postindustrial America are clashing; with the American inclination to favor change and innovation, the first two tend to suffer from acute neglect, and American cities and more traditional industries are becoming monuments to obsolescence while the country plunges into the technetronic age. This condition accentuates social alienation, racial hostility, and generation gaps.

If man's history can be seen as a continuous struggle to assert himself against nature, the industrial age can be interpreted as the phase of the con-

---

1. Metastable state: "A peculiar state of pseudo equilibrium, in which the system has acquired energy beyond that for its most stable state, yet has not been rendered unstable." *International Encyclopedia of Chemical Science* (Van Nostrand, 1964), p. 733.

flict in which man began to gain supremacy. Today, parts of America are the battlefields on which he won his struggle: pollution, ecological devastation, and aesthetic neglect are the carnage of man's victory over nature. Because of that victory, a new phenomenon is taking shape in America and is likely to dominate the seventies: a realization that man, having asserted himself over his environment, must seriously pose and answer—on a social scale—more basic questions about the purposes of social existence. This emphasizes the mounting national debate about the nature of society and the role of science, a debate both philosophical and political.

These developments are inimical to stability, to established values, and to accepted perspectives. They have already contributed to a fragmentation of national will, to a widespread mood of pessimism among American intellectuals, and to uncertainty about historical directions within that part of the American community which has traditionally provided national leadership. This condition, in turn, is likely to precipitate sharp swings in political orientation, probably prompting in the more immediate future a national inclination to take refuge from the anxieties of a change that is too rapid in a combination of social conservatism and technological-managerial innovation.

Soviet internal dilemmas can be best understood as containing a growing contradiction between the political system that performed the historical function of modernizing and pushing forward the large-scale industrialization of Russia (while simultaneously restructuring Russian society along ideological lines) and the further requirements of the scientific, intellectual, and social growth of Soviet society. That society no longer needs a highly centralized and ideologically dogmatic political system to continue growing; indeed, the system has become an impediment to growth, as the more thoughtful Soviet citizens (Peter Kapitza, Andrei Sakharov) recognize. The problem is made worse by the domination of the political system by an aging bureaucratic oligarchy, evidently unwilling or unable to recognize the need for wide-ranging systemic reforms.

This condition in turn aggravates other problems confronting the Soviet political system: the lack of regular procedures for changing the political leadership, the reliance on complex and Byzantine bureaucratic infighting as a means of formulating policy, the severe restrictions on creative policy-oriented debates, the stifling of independent thought through narrow-minded censorship. The fact of the matter is that change in the Soviet political system has not kept up with the changes that the system itself has produced in Soviet society.

As a result, a form of political paralysis at the top makes the political system unresponsive to the more basic social problems confronting the Soviet Union: the unrest of the young, likely to become quite strong in the second half of the seventies; widespread social poverty (estimated by Academician Sakharov as afflicting approximately 40 percent of the Soviet people); growing national aspirations of the non-Russians who represent more than 50 percent of the Soviet population and who, while not directly secessionist, are beginning to demand a greater share in national decision making and in resource allocation.

Given the closed character of and the highly bureaucratized process of selection within the Soviet elite, significant changes in the nature of the Soviet political rulers are not likely until toward the end of the decade, when the first truly post-Stalinist generation will begin to reach the apex of the political pyramid. Accordingly, during the seventies the present Soviet elite will probably concentrate its efforts on preserving the political system, while importing and adapting the latest technology to encourage Soviet economic growth. Soviet leaders see that growth as essential to their domestic and foreign goals, believing that domestic problems can be contained and controlled if respectable economic growth can be maintained. To be expected, for example, is a massive effort in the computer field, emulating the East German fusion of the Leninist-Stalinist political system of controls with the adoption of the latest techniques of economic management.[2]

A return to one-man rule is also to be expected. Collective leadership has not been the norm in the Soviet system, but rather a reaction to the excesses of Stalin and the unpredictabilities of Khrushchev. Increasingly, the necessities for effective decision making are being weighed against the fear of personal dictatorship, and as this fear recedes into the past, the need for greater efficiency is generating mounting pressures against the ineffective mode of collective leadership. Ways will undoubtedly be sought to institutionalize one-man rule so as to limit the accumulation of arbitrary power while rendering decision making more effective. Moreover, Soviet officials by and large prefer the presence of a strong man to the uncertainties of collective rule; this preference is already reflected in the inclination to rehabilitate Stalin himself.

The discussion of tendencies and trends is all very well, but more extreme and dramatic, though inherently unpredictable, developments in both the Soviet Union and the United States cannot be excluded. What about a major crisis, a breakdown? What if the American turbulence gets out of hand or the Soviet metastability is shaken? These are unanswerable questions; guesses and hunches operate on a different level than prognoses. Suffice it

2. The gravity of Soviet backwardness is illustrated by the fact that in 1970 the United States had approximately 70,000 computers in operation, and was expecting to install 18,000 more before the end of the year; the number operating in the Soviet economy was approximately 3,500. Based on data obtained from *Technology Review*, Vol 72 (February 1970); R.V. Burks, "Technological Innovation and Political Change in Communist Europe" (RAND Corp., August 1969; processed); and Richard W. Judy, "The Case of Computer Technology," in Stanislaw Wasowski (ed.), *East-West Trade and the Technology Gap: A Political and Economic Appraisal* (Praeger Publishers, 1970).

to say that inherent in the American turbulence is the possibility of spreading social anarchy made more bitter by intensified racial conflict, involving the gradual dissolution of effective government, especially if national leadership—both political and social—becomes fragmented and demoralized. In the Soviet case, a breakdown would probably precipitate bitter, even murderous, institutional conflict at the top, involving the secret police, the army, and the central bureaucrats, aggravated perhaps by eruptions from below, especially from the non-Russians.

But short of these apocalyptic—and not very probable—contingencies, what are the initial foreign policy implications of this analysis of the domestic scene? More specifically, is the United States likely to become more isolationist? Is the Soviet Union likely to become less ideological? Will both turn inward?

These tendencies are already manifest in the two countries, but only to a highly qualified degree. Although isolationism has gained strength in America, particularly as a reaction to the Vietnam war, and has become the reigning orthodoxy of the dogmatic liberal circles, practical reality makes isolationism no longer feasible. The metropolitan global order simply leaves no room for it. American global involvement, through communications, investments, travel, and so forth, is so much a part of the fabric of global society that it cannot be undone. More likely is an active and occasionally bitter debate about new forms of international participation, especially about problems that America has been the first society to confront, and a somewhat more selective security engagement in the affairs of other states.

Thus, paradoxically, American domestic difficulties may continue to dictate that the United States play a creative role in the global drama, though one different in its emphases from the politically interventionist policies of the fifties and sixties. The balance of emphasis may gradually shift from the political-security field to a vaguer but no less important function as the globe's principal source of social, technological, and cultural innovations. Such a shift, provided it is gradual, could enhance America's international role.

That there has been a waning of ideological fervor in the Soviet Union is evident. This has been balanced, however, by a marked growth, especially within the ruling elite, of a nationalist big power sentiment and of an intense desire to see the Soviet Union recognized as the preeminent global power. There are ideological overtones to this outlook, but the concept of world revolution has been overshadowed by the more tangible and immediate identification with state nationalism. Precisely because the Soviet system appears to be losing its innovative quality, there may develop within it an even greater reliance on military power as a compensatory mechanism. Unable to project outward an appealing cultural and ideological image, the Soviet elite may find increasing gratification in "big power chauvinism." Protracted rivalry with the United States is inherent in this orientation. However, such a rivalry could eventually have the effect of compelling the Soviet elite (particularly when the younger generation comes to the top) to confront more directly the need for systematic domestic reform, especially as it begins to be clear that it is the very character of the Soviet system that inhibits it from becoming a successful and attractive rival to the American system.[3]

The Power Relationship

The central reality of this relationship—a reality unlikely to be changed during the 1970s—is mutual nonsurvivability in the event of a comprehensive war. This basic condition—in effect a reciprocal hostage relationship between the two societies—will continue. Agreements through the Strategic Arms Limitation Talks (SALT) such as the one reached by President Nixon in Moscow in 1972 may regularize it and hence give it a measure of psychological compatibility; failure to reach follow-on agreements at SALT could intensify mutual anxieties, complicate the calculabilities of the strategic relationship, prompt even some technological assymmetries (probably to our advantage), but—short of a truly massive U.S. effort on a scale not likely to be forthcoming—still not alter the fundamental reciprocity of nonsurvivability.

This is a very basic change in the relationship between the two states, a change that is yet to be psychologically and politically assimilated. Its international effects are only beginning to be felt. It is safe to assume, however, that these effects will become more and more pronounced as the decade moves on. Of the two sides, the Soviet Union appears to be more aware of this change and hence more inclined to extract political advantages from it.

Such heightened Soviet awareness is understandable, because for more than two decades American-Soviet hostility has been conducted against a background of overwhelming American strategic superiority—a superiority so real that American policy makers often took it for granted to a degree that made them unaware that they were politically exploiting it. The classic example is provided by the Cuban missile crisis. The author has had the opportunity to discuss that crisis with several of the top American policy makers of the time; they are convinced that American strategic superiority was not decisive—that the outcome was essentially a function of conventional American superiority in the Caribbean, plus a combination of will

3. The Soviet elite has been concerned about the declining international standing of the Soviet Union, particularly as the leading scientific nation. In 1959, a twelve-nation poll put the Soviet Union ahead of the United States as the leading scientific power 42 percent to 23 percent; in 1969, the American advantage over the Soviet Union was 54 percent to 10 percent (Gallup Poll, as cited by the *New York Times* [Jan. 22, 1970], p. 6). For a discussion of the attractiveness of the Soviet model, particularly in regard to the scientific-technological revolution, see Part 3 of Zbigniew Brzezinski, *Between Two Ages* (Viking Press, 1971).

and diplomatic skill in bargaining with Moscow. In other words, they have explicitly stated that the result would have been the same had strategic symmetry prevailed.

This viewpoint reveals the subjective state of mind of the American policy makers but is deficient as an objective analysis of the actual conflict relationship. It takes into account neither the subjective state of mind of the Soviet leaders, who may have been analyzing the power relation differently, nor the alternatives that might have been available to them if strategic symmetry had existed.[4]

Had such symmetry prevailed, it might have been much more difficult for the United States to achieve its principle objective in Cuba (the removal of hostile missiles) through the exercise of its conventional superiority (naval blockade), while simultaneously offsetting its own conventional inferiority in a politically sensitive and vital area (West Berlin) by the inhibiting threat of American strategic superiority. That potential American losses in a nuclear war may have been subjectively "unacceptable" to the American policy makers was no reassurance to the leaders in the Kremlin who *knew* that such a war would mean almost complete devastation of the Soviet Union. It was this asymmetry that inhibited the Soviet Union from responding to the American blockade of Cuba with a blockade of Berlin.

Cuba was a turning point in the American-Soviet power relationship. That the Soviet leaders did take their relative weakness more seriously than American policy makers of the time admit is indicated by the determined Soviet effort to undo the strategic asymmetry that prevailed in the fall of 1962, and to undo it undramatically, that is, without precipitating massive American countermeasures. Apparently the Soviet leaders did not wish to resign themselves to permanent strategic inferiority—a position to which, in the wake of the Cuban crisis, they were publicly consigned by some American spokesmen. One can only surmise how, following the Cuban debacle, the internal Kremlin postmortems went: the military demanding assurances that never again would Soviet armed forces be so humiliated, the ideologues pointing to the damage done to Soviet revolutionary prestige, the top leaders blaming Khrushchev for allowing the Soviet Union to risk war at a time of great American superiority,[5] all in the context of hurt na-

4. At the time of the Cuban crisis, America had approximately 200 ICBMs, 150 Polaris missiles, and 700 long-range bombers; Soviet strategic forces included 75 soft ICBMs, 30 missile-firing submarines (largely diesel-powered), and 190 long-range bombers. It has been very roughly estimated that in the event of a war American losses would have been in the vicinity of 30 million lives; Soviet losses approximately four times higher.

5. One of the important Soviet intentions in Cuba was to offset American strategic superiority by making the United States vulnerable to Soviet IRBMs. This was explained to Soviet-bloc ambassadors by Anastas Mikoyan during his visit to the United States immediately after the Cuban crisis. "The missile deployment in the Caribbean," he said, "was aimed on the one hand to defend Castro and on the other to achieve a definite change in the power relation between the socialist and the capitalist worlds" (from an unpublished paper by the former Hungarian chargé to Washington, Janos Radvanyi: "An Untold Chapter of the Cuban Missile Crisis").

tional pride and mounting determination to undo what had made the injury possible.[6]

A further consideration is worth noting here. The Soviet leaders are professional power practitioners. Their ideology, as well as their life-long training, makes them place a heavy premium on power relationships. With the notable exception of Khrushchev, they are not risk takers; but they are not above using power when power is available.[7] Thus, if it is correct to assume that from the Soviet point of view the Cuban confrontation brought to the surface the political intolerability of strategic and conventional inferiority, it follows that the elimination of such asymmetry may open up opportunities and options previously closed to the Soviet leaders, despite the subjective estimates of American policy makers to the contrary. The Soviet Politburo, moreover, to a far greater extent than its American equivalent, combines in one group men who have extensive backgrounds in defense industries and in the military, and this is likely to predispose them to place a greater value on maximizing power; indeed some of them may even be tempted by a vision of a Soviet Union strategically superior to the United States.[8]

To seek strategic superiority in a setting of reciprocal nonsurvivability might be tantamount to pursuing a mirage. However, Soviet discussions of strategic relationships place much less emphasis on what might happen if a war breaks out and much more on the general international and political

---

6. To assume that the spectacle of Soviet ships submitting to armed American inspection did not rankle is to be guilty of a profound misunderstanding of the Russian psyche—to ignore the element of personal and national humiliation involved in the crisis. Shortly after the crisis I wrote, "It is most unlikely that Khrushchev will either forget or forgive the events of the week of October 22, no matter how much he is now flattered by his 'imperialist' enemies.... Khrushchev knows what made him exercise self-restraint, and he is unlikely to forget his recent 'small injury.' That is why this is no time for rejoicing; it is time to think ahead" ("Surprise a Key to Our Cuba Success," *Washington Post*, Nov. 4, 1962).

7. I agree here with the testimony of Cyril Black of Princeton University, who stated to the U.S. Senate that "my impression is that if our positions would have been reversed in the 1945-55 period, which is what you are suggesting, I think, they would have used their superior power a great deal more than we did to extract concessions through threats." Hearings before the Subcommittee on Strategic Arms Limitation Talks of the Senate Committee on Armed Services, 91 Cong. 2 sess. (March 18, 1970), p. 28.

8. The Soviet military are explicit on this point. For a plea for Soviet "superiority in military equipment," see Major General A. Lagovsky, *Krasnaya Zvezda*, Sept. 25, 1969. While such statements are occasionally made in the United States by American military figures, they are balanced by just as assertive voices to the contrary. Soviet mass media are not equally available to Soviet critics of military spending. See also the revealing testimony of Thomas W. Wolfe before the Subcommittee on Strategic Arms Limitation Talks of the Senate Committee on Armed Services (May 20, 1970), especially his citation of sources indicating that approximately 40 percent of the Soviet economy "is either controlled by military agencies or harnessed in one way or another to the defense industry sector." Dr. Wolfe goes on to suggest that there is a possibility that "any professed Soviet interest in a parity agreement via the SALT talks might best be interpreted as a holding strategem, designed to inhibit new U.S. programs

implications of the new balance of power than do American discussions.[9] In contrast, much of the American discussion can be characterized as reflecting either *statistical determinism* ("we have enough if we can inflict so many million casualties") or a *megadeath complex* ("since we will both be dead, more or less power makes no difference"), without sufficient emphasis on the political process of stable bargaining, and even bluffing, during a crisis situation.

The real question for the seventies is not what might happen if war breaks out (we know the answer to that), but what might happen before the fighting or, more correctly, before the nonfighting. "We have enough" is usually calculated in terms of what is needed to fight; what is forgotten is the more important political fact that one may need more to bargain than to fight.

It is at this stage that such elements as the psychological self-confidence of leaders and, just as important, the self-assurance of a nation may come into play. This is not to suggest that "brinkmanship" or a massive effort to attain U.S. "superiority" would be rewarding, but rather that insecurity among leaders or within a nation can prompt either excessive reaction or underreaction, with highly destabilizing consequences. This is more dangerous to the side that in the past benefited, often unknowingly, from the advantages of considerable superiority.

There are two further implications for the seventies. Asymmetry of power made credibility important. The more powerful party had a real stake in making its deterrent power and its will "credible" to the weaker party it wished to restrain from some particular action. Otherwise, its power would have been futile unless actually used—a situation costly to both the stronger side and the weaker one. In a setting of parity, whether formalized by SALT or dynamically competitive, credibility becomes largely a matter of will alone; this is dangerous because it could tempt one or both sides to bluff in order to make its determination "credible."

As a consequence, a measure of imprecision, of ambiguity, may become a greater source of stability and restraint than credibility. In asymmetry, it was important to the stronger side that the weaker side know precisely what might happen to it if certain bounds were exceeded; in parity, some ambiguity as to what each can do to the other may prove a greater source of restraint, if the ambiguity is not so great as to undermine the relationship of mutual nonsurvivability. It may be assumed that, even with agreement in SALT, ongoing weapons research will continue to introduce some cau-

---

while buying the Soviet Union time for a further technological effort intended to produce conditions for a breakthrough to superiority" (p. 58).

9. An excellent statement of this sort is an article by General S. Ivanov, "V.I. Lenin and Military Strategy," *Kommunist Vooruzhennykh Sil,* April 1970.

tionary ambiguity—as well as some unsettling anxiety—into an otherwise relatively symmetrical relationship.

The other consideration pertains to conventional forces, and it is an ominous one. The seventies will see a further reduction in the enormous gap between U.S. and Soviet long-range general purpose (air and sea) capability. The Soviet Union will achieve a respectable reach in its naval and airborne forces; it is to be expected that Moscow will be tempted to use such forces occasionally in pursuit of political objectives, as the United States has done for almost two decades. This growth in Soviet conventional power, especially since it will take place in a strategic context in which the United States will no longer enjoy a clear advantage, will provide Moscow with options hitherto unavailable to it. What has already happened in the Middle East may be only a foretaste of confrontations to come in other areas. The effect of this will be to create a novel situation of overlapping imperial power,[10] perhaps even with Fashoda-like incidents, complicating future U.S.-Soviet relations and leaving them clouded with uncertainty.

In this case, internal domestic unity, including a broad consensus on foreign policy goals, may become the crucial variable. Indecision, division, and polarization within the United States, not to speak of declining relative American military might, would be likely (in spite of a technological gap between the more advanced American economy and the Soviet one) to increasingly tempt the Soviet Union to exploit its power—first in reasonably contiguous areas, then beyond.

The International Scene

From the standpoint of U.S.-Soviet relations, the international setting during the 1970s is unlikely to be more stable than it has been for the last two decades. If anything, it will probably be even more turbulent. Such turbulence is likely to have twin—and somewhat contradictory—effects on both Washington and Moscow: on the one hand, it may create temptations to become more involved, with Moscow probably somewhat more susceptible than Washington, given the more recent vintage of its globalism; on the other hand, global turbulence may increase the respective stakes of the two major powers in avoiding a complete breakdown of world order into anarchy and thus generate some countervailing incentive for cooperation.

Global instability will probably neither have a uniform pattern nor pose a common ideological threat. Rather, such instability may vary significantly from region to region, reflecting altogether different political malaises.

In Europe, the Western countries have already begun to experience some of the pains of transition to the postindustrial age that have been afflicting

---

10. See Zbigniew Brzezinski, "Peace and Power," *Encounter,* Vol. 31 (November 1968).

the United States; social turmoil in several of these Western European states is to be expected. In some of them, notably Italy, the future political orientation of the country may be at stake. Communist parties will try to exploit all this—but generally without much success.

In Eastern Europe, sources of instability are more political and nationalist in character. Explosive events cannot be ruled out, especially should there be division and weakness in the Kremlin. The death of Tito may prompt a highly divisive political conflict in Yugoslavia, generating acute nationality tensions and tempting the Soviet leaders to apply their influence to neutralize the Yugoslav attraction for Eastern Europe. Elsewhere in Eastern European countries, nationalism will not only retain its intensity, but also, even in such traditionally pro-Russian areas as Czechoslovakia, acquire an intensely anti-Russian character. Any major conflict in the Kremlin, or on the Amur River, will be echoed in Warsaw or Prague or Budapest. Eastern Europe is thus likely to remain a major complication in the American-Soviet relationship, since Soviet determination to maintain imperial hegemony over the region will not only be contested by local resentment, but will also inhibit all-European reconciliation and U.S.-Soviet cooperation. The issue of Eastern Europe will not be resolved until the Soviet Union learns the same lesson that the United States has learned in Latin America: spheres of imperial hegemony can be maintained only at very high cost, both in effort expended and in international goodwill.

The Middle East and Africa—whatever the short-term prospects for a peaceful settlement—are likely to remain dominated by passionate ethnic-racial conflicts. Arab-Israeli hostility and South African-black African conflicts are not likely to abate. Moreover, the social revolution in Arab countries may increasingly pit the radicalized urban masses against the currently dominant nationalist anti-Western but Western-educated middle classes. For the Soviet Union, these conflicts will present an almost irresistible temptation not only to support black Africa in its disputes with the remaining white ruling groups in Africa, but also to aid in eliminating the remnants of Western influence in the oil-producing regions and to try to establish the Soviet presence even more effectively on the approaches to the Indian Ocean and the Arabian Gulf. This would breed greater conflicts and tensions with the West.

Social fragmentation may well be the prospect for parts of South Asia, given the magnitude of its social problems, the declining scale of external aid, and the gradual fading of the established postcolonial elite. Even short of that, continued Indian-Chinese rivalry will probably create additional openings for Soviet influence in India, although Indian rulers will hold it within limits dictated by their independence and neutrality. Despite that rivalry, it is unlikely that Soviet leaders will wish to become more actively involved in the problems of adjoining Southeast Asia; they will almost certainly rely on supporting North Vietnam and other states, rather than on cooperation with the United States, to contain Chinese influence in the region.

More generally, the Far East is likely to confront both Moscow and Washington—especially Moscow—with difficult problems. The Sino-Soviet conflict is not likely to end; at best, there may be periodic abatements and atmospheric improvements. In the longer run, the national and ideological estrangement between the Soviet Union and China, accompanied by a gradually growing Chinese nuclear arsenal, is apt to intensify Soviet anxieties. War between the two powers will remain a real possibility; even if (as seems likely) it does not occur, geographical contiguity will continue to create types of psychological stress that are not part of the American-Soviet relationship. Accordingly, Moscow will probably seek to improve its relations with Tokyo, and Washington will continue the efforts launched by President Nixon during his trip to China to normalize its relations with Peking. These efforts, in turn, will impinge on the American-Soviet relationship: the United States will fear an attempt by the Soviet Union to undermine the Washington-Tokyo relationship; Moscow will fear American-Chinese collusion or encirclement.

In the Western Hemisphere, Latin America is likely to undergo intense political-ideological conflicts, dominated by anti-American passions. These conflicts will probably not assume the form of classic communist revolutionary activity led by a formal Communist party, but will be both nationalist and radical in orientation—a combination of Peronism, Castroism, Fanonism, and Marxism. The fact that their sharp edge will be directed against the United States will tempt Moscow to give some of these revolutionary activities its tacit or indirect support. More demonstrative encouragement may be forthcoming from Moscow for established anti-American governments in Latin America, with Soviet naval visits to Latin American ports becoming routine during the seventies.

These geographical or regional developments, which may stimulate strains in the American-Soviet relationship, will be countervailed by the emergence of functional global concerns that will, as evidenced in agreements reached at the 1972 Moscow summit meeting, work to expand American-Soviet ties and increase cooperative undertakings. Such ventures will range from cooperation in outer space, through joint ecological projects, to mutual understandings designed to develop a common response to the challenge of the scientific-technological revolution. Preoccupation with these functional concerns—a preoccupation that is already linking more and more American and Soviet collaborators—will help to remove ideological blinders and stimulate a wider sense of joint responsibility in a global city otherwise threatened by spreading anarchy.

Moreover, the more immediate political dangers facing both Washington and Moscow—though complicating relations between them—may have the effect of diluting the preoccupation of the two capitals with each other. The anti-American political revolution in Latin America, though welcomed and probably abetted by Moscow, will not lend itself to simple categorization as a Soviet plot; the Sino-Soviet conflict, though seen in Moscow as exploited by Washington, similarly cannot easily be construed as having been engineered by Washington.

The resulting dilution or dispersal of hostility may make cooperation in other areas more feasible, although a realistic assessment compels the conclusion that the global scene will not be generally conducive to a termination of the American-Soviet rivalry. It will take enormous restraint on both sides to avoid becoming entangled in situations that could become a dangerous test of will in a setting of increasingly complicated power relationships.

Reciprocal U.S.-Soviet Perceptions

This complicated web of relations will affect, over time, the manner in which the two major entities perceive each other. There has already been significant change from the unmitigated hostility of the fifties.

In the United States, the cold war has become unfashionable, and the Soviet Union is viewed with mixed feelings (although the Soviet Union's occupation of Czechoslovakia and the Soviet anti-Semitism have reawakened some of the declining hostility). The change is slow, to be sure—although it was given impetus by the Moscow summit meeting. Some elements of American opinion still hold firmly to positions formulated during the more acute phase of the cold war; others go further in advocating wider U.S.-Soviet collaboration. The American image of the Soviet Union is thus pluralistic; change in it takes place through each domestic debate, with sharply conflicting estimates often clashing openly.

Change in the Soviet attitude is less visible and can be perceived only after the fact. As yet, there is no evidence that the current political elite wants a broad and enduring accommodation with the United States to resolve conflicts in third areas. On the contrary, the present Soviet leadership—capitalizing on the domestic effects of the American involvement in Vietnam and exploiting any tendency toward U.S. foreign policy passivity—is attempting to undermine the U.S. political position in countries important to the post-World War II American international system. This objective is being pursued with a degree of energy and initiative exceeding any comparable U.S. effort to weaken or complicate the Soviet position in areas of political import to Moscow. Thus the Soviet Union has been more active politically and economically in Western Europe than the United States has been in Eastern Europe, and Soviet efforts to cultivate Turkey and Iran have been more extensive than the sporadic American efforts to preserve or expand its links with such Arab states as Algeria and Egypt.

A broadly gauged American-Soviet accommodation, going far beyond agreements reached at the 1972 summit meeting, would require a more basic shift in values and aspirations, both ideological and nationalist, on the Soviet side than on the American.[11] Changes of this sort occur very slowly in any case. There may be key persons in the Soviet establishment who would seek such an accommodation, but they lack the kind of open facilities for promoting their views available to members of the American establishment who advocate a wide-ranging Soviet-American rapprochement.

Moreover, the official interpretation of the ruling party places special emphasis on the ideological front, with the Central Committee asserting, ex cathedra, that "the contemporary stage in historical development is distinguished by intense sharpening of the ideological struggle between capitalism and socialism" (plenary meeting of the CPSU Central Committee, April 1968). The effect of such authoritative declarations is to inhibit the appearance of less orthodox views of the world scene.[12] Inherent in this ideological rigidity is the risk that Soviet policy makers may misinterpret the nature of contemporary American developments. Reading available Soviet analyses of contemporary America, Soviet leaders may reach the same conclusion about American society that Khrushchev reportedly reached about Kennedy after their Vienna meeting. This could prompt dangerous miscalculations.

One can only hope that recent Soviet efforts to promote broad and systematic studies of the United States will eventually yield a more sophisticated, less black-and-white picture of American developments than have heretofore been available to Soviet officialdom. Although the late sixties and early seventies have seen a striking intensification in anti-American propaganda in Soviet mass media, Soviet officials and the Soviet establishment appear to have acquired a somewhat more balanced view of the United States, less dominated by doctrinal prejudices. In this connection, it appears that studies currently being promoted by the new Soviet Institute on the United States are reasonably informative on the more narrowly tech-

---

11. For a perceptive comparative analysis, see Richard Pipes, "Russia's Mission, America's Destiny," *Encounter*, Vol. 35 (October 1970).

12. Domestic official and semiofficial Soviet analyses of the American-Soviet relationship are still strikingly characterized by self-righteousness. The intellectual crudeness of the following passage is quite revealing because its author is obviously a member of the Soviet establishment (his father is, as of this writing, the Soviet foreign minister) and the medium is the authoritative Soviet journal on the United States: "The foreign political activity of the imperialists, and primarily of the United States, is spearheaded against the world socialist system. Direct military adventures, an aspiration to hinder the economic growth of the socialist countries, and the ideological intrigues of bourgeois propaganda are counterposed to the Soviet Union's foreign policy, which is built on the principle of a profound love of peace, consistent internationalism, and defense of the revolutionary gains of peoples in the USSR and the fraternal socialist countries" (Anatoliy A. Gromyko, "The Dilemmas of American Diplomacy," *USA: Economics, Politics, and Ideology*, No. 6 [Moscow; June 1970], p. 14).

nical front and, although more ideological on the political plane, not without some insight.[13] In time, information of this sort may undermine perceptions based primarily on ideological postulates, but this will be a lengthy process.

Ideological hostility may also be reduced by the expansion and institutionalization of American-Soviet negotiations. SALT has already become, in fact, the equivalent of a standing American-Soviet commission on security matters. The continuing mutual education and cross-feeding of information means that officials of each side are now indirectly involved in the policy-making process of the other. Future American strategic decisions are bound to be influenced not only by the initial agreement reached at Moscow in 1972, but also by the continuing American-Soviet dialogue in SALT; eventually this will probably be true of the Soviet side. Protracted negotiations on the European security problem or on the Middle East are also likely to create, in effect, standing American-Soviet commissions on major regional issues. In addition, there will be gradually developing functional cooperation in space, exploitation of the ocean floor, and the like.

In the meantime, considerations more immediate than gradual changes in perception may help to deter Soviet leaders from aggressively exploiting real or imagined opportunities, perceived by them as inherent in the current American domestic travails. Among these considerations the Sino-Soviet conflict is crucial. During the last few years a fundamentally important change in the Soviet view of world affairs has matured in Moscow: for a great many Soviet officials—and certainly citizens—the United States is no longer the number one enemy of the Soviet Union, having been replaced in that position by China. The United States still remains the number one rival, but imperceptibly it is being replaced by China as the principal and enduring hostile threat.[14]

This is a basic shift—one that has not yet been fully reflected in official dogma—and it matches the parallel, gradual American redefinition of the Soviet Union from America's principal enemy to American's principal rival. Such change introduces some subtle qualifications into the otherwise highly competitive and often intensely conflicting relationship; it thus spells some dilution of unmitigated hostility, and emphasizes the increasingly complex relations that will prevail between Moscow and Washington.

13. In this connection, it is revealing to compare two major articles on the contemporary United States published in the first issue of the new institute's magazine, *USA: Economics, Politics, and Ideology*. The first is by Academician N. Inozemtsev, "Modern United States and Soviet American Studies," and the second by the institute's director, Yuri Arbatov, "American Foreign Policy at the Threshold of the 1970's." While one is still quite doctrinaire in its analysis, the other recognizes the pluralistic character of the American political process.

14. The large-scale and costly deployment of Soviet forces, strategic and conventional, along the Chinese frontier reflects this new perception, irrespective of whether this deployment is defensive or offensive in character.

Future U.S. Policy

In view of these mixed relations, the American-Soviet competition will be multifaceted. It could continue to involve violence by proxy (as in the Middle East and perhaps in such areas as southern Africa), with each major power assisting and sponsoring its "agent"; it will certainly involve intense political competition in such militarily stable areas as Europe (both Western and Eastern) and Japan; it will involve rivalry for influence in regions that are socially unstable, such as Latin America; it will involve (within limits set by SALT) an increasingly complex race in military technology, as well as in the more conventional forms of military power; finally, it will include protracted scientific-technological competition—with, in all probability, greater attention to the two systems' respective capacities to form a more fulfilling and creative society. This competition will be paralleled by limited cooperation in certain regions, such as Europe, and certain functional areas, such as strategic arms and technology.

Several implications for the conduct of foreign policy in the seventies are suggested by this analysis.

1. The American-Soviet relationship will continue to shape a tense, unstable, and competitive peace, which will have major philosophical implications for the future, for at stake are different concepts of social organization and personal freedom represented by the two systems. A waning in the vitality of one or the other power would thus represent a shift of historic magnitude.

2. The Washington-Moscow relationship will include some cooperation, but this will not be so marked or dramatic as to resolve conflict in third areas or lead to a global settlement in the seventies. Rivalry between the two powers will continue throughout the decade; in some respects, the rivalry will be more tense, complex, and far-reaching than in the past. At the same time, it will not be dominated by the one-sided hostility that characterized the asymmetrical conflicts of the earlier cold war, and it is likely to have less significance for other states previously affected by the cold war. In effect, the relationship will be an uneasy balance between the simultaneous efforts of each side to compete effectively and to avoid a direct confrontation.

3. At various specific junctures in the American-Soviet rivalry, the elements of national will and direction will be more important than heretofore. Accordingly, the United States will have to undertake a major intellectual effort to define socially acceptable international goals as the foundation for a consistent foreign policy, one capable of commanding the popular support it enjoyed in most of the fifties and early sixties. This is true even though, in the longer run, the ability of one or the other society to maintain its social creativity is likely to be of more consequence; in this, despite its domestic tensions, the United States has a clear advantage.

4. Despite continuing progress in arms control, deterring occasional

clashes with the Soviet Union is likely to require a continuing and substantial defense effort. Forseeable arms control arrangements are not likely—until they are accompanied by wider-ranging political accommodation—to obviate the need for continuing development and modernization of strategic and of conventional U.S. defense forces.

5. At the same time, it will be desirable to expand ongoing American-Soviet discussions about Southeast Asia, the Middle East, and Europe and to extend them to other zones of probable contention, seeking both to anticipate possible clashes and to explore the feasibility of accommodation. Such multiple dialogues could create a framework that might eventually be infused with cooperative substance. Some progress has already been achieved in Europe; it will be harder to repeat elsewhere. Prospects for success will be enhanced if the United States can match increased Soviet diplomatic activity with initiatives of its own designed to expand U.S. links with areas of more direct concern to the Soviet Union, such as Eastern Europe and China. Otherwise, the incentive for Soviet cooperation will be lacking.

6. In addition, the expansion of narrower, more functional cooperative ventures with the Soviet Union in such fields as science, education, and ecology should remain an active U.S. preoccupation. Such ties—building on agreements reached at the Moscow summit—will act as countervailing influences to the escalation of otherwise unavoidable tensions and conflicts. At the same an expansion of these ventures might induce in the Soviet elite a less doctrinal perspective on the American-Soviet relationship, a perspective that would be more responsive to the increasingly interdependent character of global politics.

7. Most important, the nature of the American-Soviet relationship will be such that a bilateral U.S.-Soviet focus will not suffice to promote a metropolitan global order that is stable and capable of absorbing inevitable local tensions. The United States will thus have to rely primarily on the cooperation of like-minded states such as Western Europe and Japan to create a community of the developed nations in which the Soviet Union could eventually play some role.[15] The creative phase of the fifties, which saw the forging of a new Atlantic relationship, will have to be matched in the seventies with just such a broad concept, more commensurate to the emerging condition of global interdependence.

This suggests a final thought. The American-Soviet relationship in the seventies will operate in an international system that is becoming increasingly will like a metropolitan political process. It is messy, unclear, with ill-

15. I have tried elsewhere to develop more fully my concept of such a community of the developed nations: "Toward a Community of the Developed Nations," *Department of State Bulletin* (March 13, 1967; written while I was serving in the State Department); *Between Two Ages*, pp. 293-309; and "America and Europe," *Foreign Affairs*, Vol. 49 (October 1970).

defined sovereignties and jurisdictions, with only partially effective restraints on misconduct; and yet—because of the impact of science and particularly because of the dread of nuclear weapons—it is confined by an awareness of mutual interdependence, international and ideological animosities notwithstanding. The postwar era has witnessed the gradual growth of this new metropolitan global process, and the growth has been accelerated by the entrance of some parts of the world community into the new postindustrial technetronic age, which is inherently intolerant of the nation-state compartmentalization prevalent during the recent stage of mankind's political evolution.

In that context, the United States needs to be realistic and patient in the management of its relations with Moscow; excessive hopes and excessive hostility can be equally damaging. The United States also needs to see the competitive relationship in a wider perspective and to look beyond it to a time when both competition and cooperation between the two powers can be subsumed into a larger community of the developed nations.

Toward a Western Philosophy of Coexistence*

The barometer of tension has risen and fallen many times during the last 26 years or so of our relationship with the Soviet Union. While some fear the present abatement is no more than a lull or a truce, it seems probable that we are on our way to some new stage. What the nature of this stage may be, however, has not yet become clear in our public discourse, nor have we begun to clarify for ourselves the direction in which we would like to shape events, to the extent that it lies within our power to do so. Despite the distractions of our time, there is an urgency to the task, for decisions have to be made and they should be governed by a perspective that is larger than our immediate national preoccupations.

Let us begin with three questions: How should the present stage of our relations with the Soviet Union be characterized? Are we witnessing a historic shift in the foreign policy of the Soviet Union? What should be our philosophy toward our relations with the Communist world, our objectives, our criteria for weighing alternative policies?

II

For those who live by words or phrases that sum up the entire situation at a glance, there is no simple substitute for the term "cold war." That term was

---

*Reprinted from *Foreign Affairs* (October, 1973) by permission of the author and the publisher. Copyright 1973 by Council on Foreign Relations, Inc.

once defined by the late George Lichtheim as "competitive attempts to alter the balance of power (between the Soviet Union and the United States) without overt resort to force." By this definition, the term still has a certain validity, although it does not convey the elements of collaborative action which have lately become evident; moreover, the term has acquired such emotional baggage, such connotations of absolute and intractable hostility, that it deserves to be retired. The ambiguities of the word "détente," which has come into wide usage, have led to much confusion. In its simplest meaning, "détente" suggests a relaxation of tension, but some have taken this to mean a "rapprochement," while others see it as signifying only a subjective easing in the symptoms of tension without any real change in its causes; they sometimes use the term "true détente" to distinguish a more fundamental moderation in the adversary relationship.

The Soviet preference is for the term "peaceful coexistence," which they have generally defined as a form of struggle between states with different social systems without resort to war, but specifically emphasizing the continuing ideological conflict. In earlier periods, the term suggested a temporary and tactical turn of events, but in recent Soviet usage "peaceful coexistence" has come to imply a long-term political strategy. The acceptance by the United States of the determination that in a nuclear age there is no alternative to "peaceful coexistence"—in the statement of Basic Principles of Relations between the two countries signed at the Moscow Summit in 1972—is regarded by the U.S.S.R. as the fundamental contractual basis for the "normalization" of the relationship. In the context of this statement of Basic Principles, the term implies a mixture of competition, restraint and cooperation—which may be as good a working definition as any.

Leaving aside questions of nomenclature, the important point about the nature of the association is that it has become a multi-level relationship, and the movements on the various planes on which the two nations now interact are not always in the same direction. It is therefore necessary to bring to bear a more differentiated analysis of the relationship, in order to distinguish our interests in its various aspects.

Briefly, we can distinguish the following seven planes in the relationship between the Soviet Union and the United States:

(1) The plane of *strategic-military competition*. Clearly this deserves to be considered first, for both sides have come to a sober recognition that their most urgent requirement is to avoid a general nuclear war. The Strategic Arms Limitation Talks (SALT) have begun an important educational process, in which the Soviet Union and the United States are moving toward a more enlightened understanding of their real security interests, of the limited political advantages of their strategic arsenals, of the increased dangers and high costs of an unrestrained strategic-military competition, and of the desirability and complexity of finding an equilibrium at moderate levels. Despite SALT, however, the strategic-military competition

is not yet stabilized, for both countries continue to raise the quantitative or qualitative levels of their nuclear arsenals.

(2) The plane of *conventional military competition*. During the past decade, both countries have greatly increased their capabilities for conventional war, and for reaching distant conflicts with modernized forces. Although each shows signs of moving toward restraint in avoiding direct involvement with the other, this remains a potential source of danger in the coming decade, for there has not yet evolved a codification of the rules of the game for the establishment of bases and the use of conventional forces in areas of strategic importance and political instability. What is more imminently dangerous is the large, competitive and unregulated traffic in arms to the developing countries, which is likely to exacerbate local conflicts and increase the risk of involvement of the great powers.

(3) The plane of *political competition*. In the present fluid environment, the two great powers are engaged in the competitive politics of maneuver for relative political influence in Europe, the Middle East, Asia, Africa and Latin America. The easing of the German problem, which had appeared to be the most intractable and decisive territorial issue between the United States and the Soviet Union until less than five years ago, has been a key factor in opening the way to an improvement in relations generally, and also to a period of flexible maneuvering for influence in Western Europe. The Soviet Union is not a status quo power, except in Eastern Europe, and it is in a historical phase of development in which it is seeking a global presence and influence commensurate with its status as a great power. It is encouraged in its effort by its perception of the United States as having passed the zenith of its influence as a world power. Urgent aspects of the political competition from the Soviet point of view are its effort to limit the developing American relationship with the People's Republic of China and to contain the widening diplomatic activities of China on the world stage, particularly in East and West Europe. But also to be noted on the political plane of the relationship are some elements of coöperation. In the Middle East, which both sides have recognized as an area of imminent danger, the political competition is accompanied by consultation and a substantial degree of restraint to reduce the danger of their direct involvement with each other. There have also been consultations and tacit coöperation in regard to Southeast Asia and Berlin, in which the Soviet Union balanced relations with its allies against larger considerations.

(4) The plane of *economic competition and coöperation*. The competitive side of economic relations concerns the use of trade and economic assistance as a source of political influence, particularly in areas rich in energy resources. In Europe and Japan, where the United States is involved in trade, monetary and investment problems, the Soviet Union is more than an interested spectator. The coöperative side of the economic relationship is reflected in the massive Soviet effort to expand its imports of grain,

technology and consumer goods, and to develop Western markets for Soviet goods to pay for these imports in the future. U.S.-Soviet trade has increased from a little over $200 million in 1971 to $642 million in 1972; for 1973, trade is running at an annual rate of $1.4 billion, of which almost $800 million is in agricultural products. Currently, Soviet imports from the United States exceed its exports by more than five times. Of greater significance is the determined Soviet effort to seek long-term, large-scale Western investment in the development of Soviet natural resources in Siberia and other areas.

(5) The plane of *ideological conflict.* Although Soviet policy is characterized by increasing pragmatism, the Soviet leadership insists upon the continuation and the intensification of the ideological struggle, at home and abroad, against an enemy identified as "American imperialism." This insistence clearly has its roots in organizational politics within the Soviet system, but it presents operational problems in foreign policy, for the continued reliance of the Soviet Union upon an external ideological adversary, as a device necessary to its system of political control, sets limits in practice on the realization of its policy of "peaceful coexistence." In the United States, once-virulent expressions of anti-Communist ideology have been defused by the fact that a conservative American President, formerly of that persuasion, now serves as the instrument of conciliation. The pragmatic American temper is inclined to allow this plane of the relationship to be expressed in terms of the relative performance of the two systems, without benefit of an accompanying verbal barrage.

(6) The plane of *cultural relations.* In a period in which the technology of transport and communications has advanced rapidly, international life has been inescapably characterized by increasing interpenetration of each other's societies. This presents serious operational difficulties for the Soviet system of political control, at home and in Eastern Europe. Moreover, the widening of human contacts is understood in the West as a necessary ingredient of "peaceful coexistence," as a solvent of hostile stereotypes and a means of moderating residual adversary sentiments. This problem was dramatically illustrated at the Helsinki meeting of the Conference on Security and Cooperation in Europe, where the Western commitment to freedom of information and travel was countered by Soviet efforts to contain cultural exchanges in controllable channels. Nowhere are the asymmetries of the Soviet and Western systems more in evidence than in the inequalities to be observed in the implementation of cultural relations, less in the performing arts than in the exchange of scholars, students and journalists.

(7) The plane of *functional cooperation.* In the course of two summit meetings, the Soviet Union and the United States have signed more than ten bilateral agreements covering such areas of functional cooperation as environmental protection, medical science and public health, outer space,

science and technology, agriculture, oceanography, transportation, commerce and the peaceful uses of atomic energy. Many of these provide for Joint Commissions to implement the agreements. Although these agreements are of limited scope and are in fields of peripheral significance, they perform a symbolic function as a token that the two political leaderships recognize some degree of commonality of interests, and they may be of increasing practical importance as awareness grows of the urgency of environmental problems. Taken together with the agreements related to security, commerce, taxation, maritime affairs and cultural relations, these forms of cooperation constitute the "web of interdependency" which the two countries are consciously weaving.

Several general observations are needed to make this contrapuntal analysis more complete. Although the level of "atmospherics" is properly suspect as fickle and subject to manipulation, it is worth recording that the tone of the relationship has been businesslike, frank in its acknowledgement of differences, but free of the emotional inflammation of those differences which marked earlier periods.

It is also important to remind ourselves that the background against which this relationship has been developing is one of rapid transformation in international politics. Partly as a consequence of the reduction in tension between the Soviet Union and the United States, international politics is marked less by intense polarization than by fluidity and a blurring of alignments. Non-military forms of power, particularly economic and technological, have become increasingly important as sources of political influence. The return of Japan and Western Europe as significant factors in world politics and the emergence of China from her diplomatic isolation have transformed the play of international politics. Against this background, it is clear that the Soviet-American relationship is less the dominant axis of international politics than heretofore, and, further, that the major transforming forces of the world are less subject to the control of the two superpowers than each had taken for granted in an earlier period. The widening gap between the industrialized and the developing nations is among the most ominous of the trends pointing to the possibility of anarchic and violent ruptures in the international system.

Finally, we have become more conscious of how deeply the internal politics of each country is involved in the relations between the Soviet Union and the United States. At one level, we watch the fascinating drama of the summits between a General Secretary of the Communist Party and a President who have much in common—both conservative, pragmatic realists, former hard-liners. Behind the President is a distracted society, and a shifting balance in which entrenched pro-military pressures contend with a growing impulse toward anti-militarism and a reduction in America's involvements abroad, while the staunchest champions of "peaceful coexistence" are to be found among the private interests of the business community. Behind the General Secretary is a society of paradoxes: militarily strong but economically weak, tightly controlled but nervously insecure, in which the support for "peaceful coexistence" from the champions of economic modernization is ranged against military interests and the orthodox Party apparatus whose vested interest in an "imperialist enemy" is combined with a fear of the effect of modernization upon the system.

Clearly the future course of events depends only in part upon the chieftains, however committed they may be; it is to the inner politics and the underlying forces operating in the two societies that we must look in order to judge the prospects for continuity of the present stage of their relationship. The American side of this equation is presumably familiar to our readers; in the following section, we turn to an analysis of the Soviet view of the relationship and the factors that influence its behavior.

III

Are we witnessing a historic shift in Soviet foreign policy? According to Leonid Brezhnev, the answer is an emphatic yes. At Bonn in May, the General Secretary told the people of West Germany that the 24th Soviet Party Congress in 1971 set, and the April 1973 plenum of the Party's Central Committee reaffirmed, the foreign policy goal of implementing a "radical turn toward détente and peace on the European continent." To achieve a better life for the Soviet people, he said, the Soviet leadership had turned resolutely away from isolation and autarky, and was bending its energies toward peaceful construction at home and comprehensive cooperation with the outside world.

Then, on June 22, 1973, in a talk to American businessmen in Washington, Brezhnev went further. Looking back over 42 years of Party and government experience, he said, "we have certainly been prisoners of those old tendencies, those old trends, and to this day we have not been able fully to break those fetters...." The cold war, he said, "put the brake on the development of human relations, of normal human relations between nations, and it slowed down the progress and advance of economic and scientific times. And I ask you gentlemen, as I ask myself, was that a good period? Did it serve the interests of the peoples? And my answer to that is no, no, no and again no." Summing up, he said: "it has been and is my very firm belief that human reason and common sense and the human intellect will always be victorious over obscurantism."

And again in Washington: "I wish especially to emphasize that we are convinced that on the basis of growing, mutual confidence, we can steadily move ahead. We want the further development of our relations to become a maximally stable process, and what is more, an irreversible one."

That this is the ascendant sentiment of the Soviet leadership was underscored by the award, on May Day of this year, of the Lenin Peace Prize to the General Secretary, and an orchestrated wave of praise of

Brezhnev in the Soviet press for his "personal contribution" to the Party's "peace program."

In the rest of the world, which has seen other "peace campaigns" come and go, Brezhnev's affirmations have been welcomed with a certain reserve. Do they represent more than a tactical turn toward a low-tension policy to gain economic help and political advances? Will the new policy last?

Undoubtedly, the present course offers tactical advantages to the Soviet Union, but there is reason to believe that something more fundamental may be involved, that the Soviet leadership is responding to "objective factors" in the situation which require a long-term commitment to a policy of low tension abroad and consolidation in the Soviet sphere. It is essential to view the present Soviet policy in the perspective of 20 years of halting, inconsistent, incomplete, resisted efforts to shake off the Stalinist legacy in Soviet foreign policy. In a significant sense, Brezhnev's foreign policy represents the culmination of a process which Khrushchev began but was unable to carry through.

From the Geneva summit of 1955 and the landmark 20th Party Congress of 1956, Khrushchev sought to break away from the Leninist doctrine of the "fatal inevitability of war" and the Stalinist spirit of isolation and unmitigated hostility, and to establish the basis for "businesslike" relations with the West. A combination of factors prevented the consistent realization of his purpose: his own flamboyant and impulsive temperament, the strength of the political opposition, which he inflamed with a series of Party reorganizations, and the fatal effects of a series of misfortunes—the U-2 affair, the failures in agriculture, the Cuban missile episode, and the open conflict with the Chinese Communists. By his injudicious efforts to exploit the first Soviet Sputnik and intercontinental missile as symbols of a "shift in the balance of power," he galvanized the U.S. missile program and further deepened the Soviet strategic inferiority. By his polemical rhetoric about "wars of national liberation," he evoked American preparations for "counterinsurgency" and the apprehensions that contributed to the American involvement in Vietnam. Nevertheless, it was Khrushchev who dared to start the process of de-Stalinization, who faced the implications of the nuclear age, and foresaw the advantageous possibilities of a long-term political strategy of "peaceful coexistence."

For its first five years, from 1964 to 1969, the Brezhnev-Kosygin group was occupied with the consolidation of a consensual leadership at home; the effects of the Vietnam War and a perceived American propensity for intervention; and the accelerated effort to build strategic forces, a large modern navy and modernized and mobile ground forces. During the 16 months between the first U.S. proposal of SALT and the first Soviet response, a debate raged over the desirability and the possibility of an agreement with the Americans to stabilize the strategic military competition. Then came Czechoslovakia, and another year went by, while new weapons were introduced into the strategic competition.

Three events in 1969 helped open possibilities for a further development in Soviet policy: in the Federal Republic, the election of Willy Brandt as Chancellor, whose Ostpolitik overture offered the possibility for clearing away the obstacle of German issue; in the United States, Richard Nixon becoming President, with a declaration that the "era of negotiation" was a possible option; and in November, the start of the SALT process. Perhaps it was the working of the dialectic, but the following year found Soviet relations with the United States in a downward spiral as a result of events in the Middle East and the Caribbean, while SALT became bogged down in the issue of whether offensive or defensive weapons were to be limited first.

The decisive turn in Soviet policy and in Soviet-American relations came in the early months of 1971. It was then that Brezhnev took personal charge of relations with the United States and the Federal Republic of Germany, and of the Soviet position in the SALT negotiations. A channel of confidential communications was opened between Brezhnev and Nixon, which was to lead to the May 1971 agreement that broke the impasse in SALT. Vietnam was, in its own dialectical way, beginning to wind down. By February, internal debate in the Soviet Union on the policy to be promulgated at the 24th Party Congress in March and on the Ninth Five-Year Plan was brought to an abrupt close by the decisive commitment of Brezhnev's personal prestige to the line of "normalization" of relations with the United States. The move in this direction, which was to culminate in the Moscow summit of May 1972, was reënforced by the change in Chinese policy toward a more flexible diplomacy and the opening of contacts with the United States, which made improved Soviet relations with the United States both possible and necessary.

Among the factors responsible for this sequence of evolution in Soviet policy, the following six appear to have been of major importance:

(1) The condition of the *Soviet economy* is clearly the primary determinant of present Soviet foreign policy. The current Five-Year Plan, begun in 1971, projected widespread modernization of technology, improvements in productivity, and large increases in consumer goods, but the performance of the Soviet economy has fallen far short of expectations. Poor harvests have created substantial shortages of both food and feed grains, compounding the effects of low agricultural and industrial productivity and a shortage of industrial manpower. Rather than face the politically painful choice of instituting substantial economic reforms, the Soviet leadership has opted for a massive effort to overcome its shortcomings by increasing the flow of trade, advanced technology and capital from abroad. To overcome its shortage of hard currency, the Soviet Union seeks help in developing its manufactures for Western markets, and invites Western capital and technology to help exploit Soviet natural resources, such as its large Siberian reserves of natural gas, to be paid for out of the export of these resources. In his meetings with

West German and American businessmen, Brezhnev has projected opportunities for vast joint production ventures over periods of 20 to 30 years. The realization of these expectations manifestly requires an international climate of reduced tension.

(2) The *achievement of strategic parity* with the United States has made it possible for the Soviet leadership to consider a stabilization of the strategic competition on the basis of the principle of "equal security," which it understands to mean the end of the U.S. policy of negotiating from "positions of strength." The Soviet leadership has expressed its awareness that the stark alternative to this stabilization would be a further upward spiral into increasingly complex and costly weapons systems, and that this would further impede the development of Soviet industrial technology.

(3) *Soviet perceptions of the United States* encourage it to believe that the President's proffered "era of negotiation" represents a serious and durable option because, according to Soviet analysts, it is a realistic and necessary response to such "objective factors" as the rise of economic and social problems in the United States and the decline of U.S. power and influence in the world. These in turn create opportunities for relative increases in Soviet political influence in a climate of reduced tension.

(4) *Soviet perceptions of Europe as an emerging economic power center* present both a potential problem and an opportunity. It has responded with a determined effort to encourage Europe to develop in the direction of a neutral "independence" rather than toward a closer Atlantic association with the United States. It anticipates that in a climate of reduced tension, symbolized by the European security conference, Europe will not develop its military capabilities and will diminish its support for NATO. On the economic side, the Soviet Union no longer mounts a rearguard action against West European integration. Having accepted the reality of the European Economic Community, it now bends its efforts to keep open and further develop trading relations between it and COMECON, the East European economic organization. Similarly, Soviet perceptions of the growing economic strength of Japan lead it to anticipate and to encourage a competitive struggle between the "triangle" of Western industrial powers: the United States, Western Europe and Japan. This, too, is more likely to flourish in a climate of "peaceful coexistence."

(5) *Soviet apprehensions of China* are difficult to weigh as a factor in Soviet foreign policy, but it is clear that this is a matter of visceral intensity to the Russians, and that it has both immediate and long-term dimensions. One aspect of the change in Chinese policy toward a policy of enlarged contacts with the West was that it relieved the Soviet Union of the inhibiting charge by the Chinese of "collusion with imperialism" against the policy of "peaceful coexistence." Moreover, the fear of a Chinese-American alliance, or of American aid to China, has increased the Soviet incentive to accelerate the "normalization" of its relations with the United States. On at

least three occasions, beginning in 1970, the Soviet Union has sought to
enlist the United States in an agreement to take joint action with the Soviet
Union in the event of "provocative action" by a third nuclear power—
presumably China—but the proposal was converted at American insistence
into Article IV of the Agreement on the Prevention of Nuclear War, signed
in Washington on June 22, 1973.

This article commits the two countries to enter into urgent consultations
in the event of a risk of nuclear war between them, or involving other countries. According to Henry Kissinger, it was felt that this article, and the
commitment in Article II of the agreement to refrain from the threat or use
of force against each other or against other countries, would instead serve
to reduce the danger of war between Russia and China. Meanwhile,
Moscow is concerned with Chinese diplomatic efforts in Western Europe
warning against the dangers of a détente with the Soviet Union, and even
more, with Chinese efforts to stimulate a greater degree of independence on
the part of the countries of Eastern Europe. The 4,500-mile border between
the Soviet Union and China is a further source of conflict, which four years
of negotiations have been unable to resolve, and the Soviets maintain a
massive army on this front. It seems plausible that Soviet interest in quiescent relations in the West is strengthened by the necessity of avoiding a two-
front engagement in the event of active hostilities with China. In July,
Brezhnev's declaration to a North Vietnamese delegation in Moscow of
Soviet interest in "the establishment of equal and good-neighborly coöperation among all Asian states without exception" has been regarded as an invitation to China to work toward a modus vivendi, particularly in a post-
Mao situation.

(6) The Soviet *desire to consolidate its position in Eastern Europe* may be
dealt with more briefly, but it is by no means a negligible factor impelling
the Soviet leadership to a policy of "peaceful coexistence." The persistence
of nationalism and the social and political effects of advancing industrialization combine to make this area one of unrest and potential distur-
bances, and the Soviet problem of control is likely to be made more difficult
by the increasing contacts of the West with the states of Eastern Europe.
The Soviet Union seeks assurance that there will be no exacerbation of these
difficulties from the West, and no interference in the event of trouble. It
clearly would like to avoid the embarrassment of another Czechoslovakia,
although there can be no doubt that the Soviet leadership is determined to
maintain the position to which it feels it is entitled in Eastern Europe as a
result of World War II, and which it believes it requires for reasons of
security and as a symbol of its historical and ideological advance. Although
the climate of détente creates complications for the Soviet Union in Eastern
Europe, as at home, it is also a necessary condition, the Soviets believe, for
Western acceptance of the status quo in what they regard as the Soviet
sphere. The progress that has been made toward the Western acceptance of

the German Democratic Republic as a separate state is regarded as an encouraging mark of the success of this policy.

These six factors, however, do not tell the whole story, for foreign policy in the Soviet Union, as elsewhere, is not purely an exercise in rational choices, but also involves the interplay of domestic politics. As Brezhnev has indicated, his movement toward the fuller implementation of a policy of "peaceful coexistence" has not been without opposition, and occasional rumbles of dire forebodings may still be observed as reminders that some interests in the Soviet Union are watching for signs that their skepticism is justified.

As might be expected, some of the skepticism is to be found among the professional military services, which, like their opposite numbers in the United States, identify their claims upon the national budget with national security, with mistrust of the SALT process and the assumed deviousness of their adversary. The main source of opposition, however, comes from the orthodox wing of the Party and its large ideological apparatus, and from the even larger apparatus of the political police. For them, "peaceful coexistence" means trouble—a weakening of the ideological élan which is their stock-in-trade, an opening of the country to influences which they can only regard as "subversive," increased trouble with intellectuals and nationality groups, and an erosion of the image of the "imperialist threat" which legitimizes their power and on which their careers depend.

The burden of their argument, as it is illuminated by an occasional tracer shot fired from *Red Star*, the military newspaper, *Kommunist*, the Party's theoretical organ, or even *Pravda*, is that the abandonment of autarky opens the way to a fatal dependence upon the capitalist countries, that the bid for foreign trade and investment is unlikely to be productive, that the operational effects of a détente policy will weaken the Soviet system at home and in Eastern Europe, and that behind the facade of SALT, the American "imperialists" are improving their lead in new weapons technology. Some remain unenthusiastic about the reconciliation with West Germany, against which residual mistrust is still strong, and whose Social-Democratic leadership represents a traditional ideological enemy.

The debate is joined by spokesmen of the "peaceful coexisteence" policy from different lines of defense. Some, like Georgy Arbatov, the head of the Institute of the U.S.A., in *Kommunist* last February, seek to persuade the hard-liners that under present circumstances, "peaceful coexistence" represents the most effective form of struggle against American imperialism. Others, like Dmitry Tomashevsky, of the Institute of World Economics and International Relations, in *Red Star* this past July, argue forcefully and openly the need for Western capital and technology as the paramount considerations of the moment. An unusually broad perspective was represented in an article in *Izvestia* last February, entitled, "The Logic of Coexistence," by Vladimir Osipov, an observer on the staff of the newspaper. Osipov wrote of "a whole new series of new factors in the life of the international community of states which now speak for all-around coöperation," and concluded that "the global nature of the interdependence of states makes anachronistic foreign policy concepts of former centuries based on the opposition of some countries to others and the knocking together of military alliances."

The net result of these conflicting domestic pressures has been that Brezhnev has won a free hand to implement his policy of "peaceful coexistence" abroad, while the apparatus of orthodoxy and control has been given a free hand to tighten the lines of ideological vigilance at home, and to prosecute the "ideological struggle" between capitalism and Soviet socialism with renewed vigor. Perhaps this too represents the dialectic at work.

At the plenum of the Central Committee in April of this year, Brezhnev was strengthened by the removal from the Politburo of Pyotr Y. Shelest, an apparent hard-liner, but at the same time the prime spokesmen for military and secret police interests respectively, Marshal Andrei A. Grechko and Yuri V. Andropov, were added.

Although some skeptics in the West believe that Brezhnev speaks publicly of his domestic opposition to encourage Western responsiveness, it seems probable that he does feel the need of some early and tangible signs that the policy with which he has identified himself is successful. Hence, the Soviet impatience for the symbolism of an East-West summit meeting before the end of this year to cap the proceedings of the Conference on Security and Coöperation in Europe, and the urgency of his presentations to West German and American businessmen. The ratification of the Moscow-Bonn Treaty and the commitment of the United States to "peaceful coexistence" in the statement of Basic Principles have been widely hailed in the Soviet press as early evidence of Brezhnev's success.

In the light of Soviet domestic politics and the "objective factors" listed above, what can we conclude about the prospects for continuity in Soviet foreign policy? It is surely conceivable that if Soviet expectations of a substantial expansion of trade and foreign investment are unrealized, if the arms competition mounts, if another Czechoslovakia should occur in Eastern Europe, or if a conflict in the Middle East or elsewhere should threaten a Soviet-American confrontation, there would be pressures upon Brezhnev for a policy change, or even the possibility of his replacement by a coalition of disaffected interests. Even without these events, given the age of the present Soviet leadership, it is always possible that younger men may come to power in the Soviet Union, and by no means is it clear what their propensities would be—at least, it cannot be taken for granted that they would automatically subscribe to the pragmatic inclination because they belong to another generation.

A reasonable conclusion would seem to be that in the absence of extreme irrationality the margins within which the present policy would change would be relatively limited in the event any of the contingencies described above should come to pass. Although it is possible, and may even be probable, that we will go through periods in which the policy of "peaceful coexistence" may be inflected to a somewhat more militant degree, the underlying conditions determining Soviet foreign policy would constrain a return to the more extreme forms of militancy and hostility of the past. It seems apparent that even to the extent such changes may stem from the workings of Soviet domestic politics, the amplitude of their effects would be substantially influenced by our own actions.

IV

This brings us to the question of our philosophy. To the extent that we can be said to have had a philosophy about this in the past, it was a negative one—"containment" or "anticommunism." They were the challengers to the status quo, and we were its defenders. For the most part, we reacted to crises as we saw them coming, sometimes reasonably, sometimes with clouded judgment.

Now we have the possibility of thinking more clearly and less reactively about our relations with the Soviet Union, and about the place of this relationship in the whole of our foreign policy. In a time of turbulent and swift change, the central purpose of our foreign policy is to do what we can to help shape a world environment in which the values we hold to be the essence of our society—when we are true to ourselves—can endure and grow in realization. The main task of our foreign policy therefore is to work closely with those nation, which share these values to strengthen the international system, in the sense of a codification of civilized practices among nations, and the further development of its institutionalization in the United Nations. This does not mean defending the status quo, which would in any case be an impossible task. Against the inexorable pressures for change which mark this period in international life, imperialism and hegemonial control over territory cannot provide a lasting stability. The alternative to international violence and anarchy is the development of an international system which can accommodate change without violence, and in which security does not depend upon the control of territory. What follows from this is that the guiding purpose of our policy toward the Soviet Union should be to draw it, over time, into constructive participation in this kind of an international system.

This means working toward some fundamental transformations. It does not mean trying to convert the Soviet Union to capitalism; the difference in social systems need not be a source of conflict, and in any case, both societies are likely to evolve considerably in the coming decades, each in its own way. What it does mean is that we declare quite frankly our interest in encouraging the Soviets to work constructively and responsibly within an international system which is neither their nor our hegemonial domain. That we will continue to be rivals for a considerable time seems dictated by our situations. But that rivalry can be less dangerous to the world and less overcast with hostility if it operates within commonly accepted rules of the game, and in time it may be diminished by a recognition of our growing common needs.

What general principle should guide our policies toward the internal situation in the Soviet Union? As individuals, we find repellent the extent of the police control over the creative life and the human rights of the people of the Soviet Union, and we hope that a period of prolonged low tension on the international plane, despite its immediate regressive effects, will in the long run contribute to an easing of this repugnant aspect of the Soviet system. As individuals and private groups, we can and should express our humanitarian concern over the violation of human rights in the Soviet Union, as we should do in our own country and elsewhere, including countries that are allied to us. The prospect of a modernized Soviet Union, in which the people are well-fed and well-housed and clothed, and in which there is room for the free expression of the human spirit, would be cause for rejoicing, for they are our fellow men. But as a government, our concerns are properly limited to those aspects of the Soviet system that bear directly upon its foreign policy; for example, the extent of military influence in Soviet politics.

If these represent our long-term purposes, what principles should guide our present responses to the Soviet Union? Granted that the Soviet leadership sees present tactical advantages in moving toward a political strategy of "peaceful coexistence." But if we are correct in believing that this course also reflects a longer-term movement toward a moderated and codified mixture of competition, restraint and cooperation, what follows?

There can be no doubt that we should welcome this development, and do all we can to encourage it and to translate it into concrete measures. In doing so, we should be under no illusions. The relationship has its dangers and its difficulties. The Soviet Union is still committed to fundamentally different objectives than we are; it will take advantage of opportunities that present themselves to increase its influence, and to work toward an expanded hegemonial sphere. Under conditions of a relaxation of tension, we shall be obliged to call upon deeper, steadier and more positive motivations from our people and our allies than we have been accustomed to doing during the simpler years of the cold war. We shall have to clarify our understanding of the kind of military balance that is needed, and the role of other forms of power. We shall have to look freshly and thoughtfully at the profound changes taking place within and among the nations of the world. For all that, we should encourage the present turn of Soviet policy, above all because it offers the possibility of reducing the risk of nuclear war and of bringing some sanity and a sense of proportion to bear upon the management of the weapons of mass destruction we have learned to make. We should welcome it because we can compete effectively on its terms, and because it offers the possibility of long-term transformations in a constructive direction.

V

To reduce these general principles to specifics, let us return to the multi-level analysis introduced at the outset, and see what criteria should guide us in the decisions we have to make about each of the aspects of our relationship.

(1) On the plane of strategic-military competition, a number of basic issues of strategic doctrine and policy remain unresolved: whether we can accept parity or should try to regain superiority; whether parity means equality or an asymmetrical balance; whether we should place our reliance on mutual deterrence or require the additional forces capable of fighting a nuclear war and capable of striking Soviet military targets. We tend to resolve these issues not by rational discussion and decision, but by the interplay of political and economic pressures and the behind-the-scenes struggles of bureaucratic groups. We clearly need to subordinate this process to an overarching judgment of our real security interests in a nuclear age. The determination of our military requirements on the basis of rational principles, clearly articulated and enforced upon lower-order parochial interests, would orient and mobilize an enlightened public opinion to balance private pressures, and would affect the interplay of pressures in the adversary system. Two criteria for a clearer concept of security which flow from our preceding discussion are: first, that a military equilibrium with the Soviet Union is a necessary condition for international stability, in Europe and centrally; and second, that our optimum security interests would be best served by having that equilibrium as stable and at as moderate a level as can be managed by negotiation. Illustratively, these criteria would suggest that the pursuit of superiority, in the belief that it offers putative political if not military advantages, is an anachronistic mode of thought which leads inescapably to a higher level of competition. Further, if we interpret parity as meaning equality in respect to numbers of each kind of weapons system, both sides will be building up to higher levels. Given the large and still growing weapons arsenals on both sides and the real possibilities for the spread of nuclear weapons to more countries and even to groups of people, we are too complacent about the possibility of nuclear war. We should seek a radical acceleration of the SALT process to reduce overall numbers of weapons on both sides, and to bring under control qualitative developments in multiple warheads and accuracy, which will otherwise create great instability. We should ponder the lesson that short-sighted "bargaining" tactics have had the effect of undermining the essential purpose of SALT. The complexities of working out equitable arms-limitation arrangements require

more effective staff support for arms control as an integral aspect of our security policy than we now have in the much weakened Arms Control and Disarmament Agency, and a more effective and better informed public constituency.

(2) The competition in conventional weapons may represent a more imminent hazard in the next few years. The probabilities of conflict arising out of competing efforts to use armed forces to influence the outcome in unstable areas appear to be increasing. The criteria to bring to bear in this field are: first, that a military equilibrium in the conventional field is needed to perform the negative function of assuring that neither side will intervene with force to encourage or prevent political change; second, that the equilibrium should be as low as negotiation and mutual example can make it; and third, that a codification of rules of engagement in unstable areas is urgently needed. This would suggest that the competition in conventional weapons and their employment should be made a matter for highest-level negotiation, analogous to SALT. This may be no less complex a problem than SALT, as the talks on force reductions in Europe are demonstrating, because it is more directly related to conflicting political objectives. One aspect of the problem that may be amenable to agreement would be the competition in arms sales, which is exacerbating the problems of the Middle East and the subcontinent, and is encouraging the rise of military dictatorships throughout the developing world. The convening of an international conference on the arms trade, as proposed by Senator Mondale, might at least serve to open to public attention the shadowy world of the traffic in conventional weapons.

(3) In respect to the political competition, we need to define the principles to guide our responses to Soviet efforts to expand their influence in the developing world and in Western Europe and Japan, and also to guide our conduct in relation to Eastern Europe and China. As we have seen, the Soviet Union is becoming a global presence and seeks to expand its political influence wherever it can. In the past, we have tended to feel that any expansion of Soviet influence is dangerous and should be resisted. What criteria can guide our present responses to this expansion? We can affirm, first, that a responsible and constructive participation by the Soviet Union in assisting the developing countries with such problems as economic development, population and environment is desirable and should be encouraged—through the United Nations where possible; and second, that in those instances in which Soviet influence becomes so preponderant as to threaten the independence of the country involved, efforts should be made to balance that influence by political and economic means. Two additional considerations tend to make the issue less acute: the demonstrated capacity of the developing countries to resist threats to their independence, and the limitations of Soviet resources, which have had the effect of concentrating Soviet efforts upon a limited number of countries. In Europe, the Soviet

Union seeks, through bilateral contacts and the Conference on Security and Cooperation in Europe, to influence the nations of Western Europe toward a more neutralist orientation and to gain acceptance from the West of a Soviet sphere of influence in Eastern Europe. The criterion discussed earlier, of the central importance to the United States of a close association with the nations of Western Europe in strengthening the international system in accordance with their shared values, would suggest that active competition against this Soviet effort is required, and similar considerations would apply in relation to Japan. In Eastern Europe, the principles of the right of free access and of noninterference by force in processes of internal change should argue against the acceptance by the West of hegemonial control by the Soviet Union over Eastern Europe, which is in any case an anachronistic and unstable relationship. At present, Soviet senstivities are delicate on this issue, but over time the Soviets may come to appreciate their own interests in a more resilient relationship which permits the states of Eastern Europe to participate actively in the functional forms of association which are developing across Europe.

A few brief points need to be added about the political competition as it affects our relations with the People's Republic of China. Although it has clearly been desirable to have developed contacts with China and although these contacts have had a useful effect upon our relations with the Soviet Union, it should not be part of our objective to exacerbate the Sino-Soviet conflict, and we should exercise care to see that our actions cannot be interpreted as having that intent. Our objective should be to encourage both countries to move in the direction of moderation and coöperation; in particular, we look forward to the time when China will feel sufficiently secure to participate in international arms-limitations arrangements.

(4) The economic aspect of the Soviet-American relationship involves some of the most interesting and difficult decisions of all. We have seen that the hope of the Soviet leadership for increased trade and investment from the West, and particularly from the United States, is a major factor in its present policy. Of course, much of the response of American firms is based upon their private interests and is governed by coördinated government policy only to the extent that it depends upon large-scale credits, government guarantees, or legislative action on the Most Favored Nation provision. Even to this extent it is a useful exercise to weigh the considerations involved from a national point of view. If purely economic considerations are weighed, it is apparent that the advantages are heavily in favor of the Soviet Union, although the prospect of selling in Soviet markets has a strong appeal for particular sectors of the business community, and Soviet sources could help to fill America's future energy needs. Among the non-economic arguments in favor of a positive response, it is said that the growth of economic interdependence will encourage restraint in Soviet behavior, contribute to a relationship of confidence, and may lead to long-term transfor-

mations in the Soviet system. On the other side, the fear is expressed that U.S. trade and investment may help to strengthen the Soviet Union for later economic or military challenges to the United States, that large-scale credits will give the Soviet Union leverage as a debtor state, and that this influx of trade and technology helps to postpone needed economic reforms in the Soviet system.

What criteria should the United States apply in deciding at what level, with what types of trade and investment, and in what time scale it should respond? On balance, it would seem that a positive response would be useful, mainly for noneconomic reasons. If we judge the present Soviet course a desirable one from our point of view, it is obviously necessary to sustain the economic motivation at some level. A modest affirmative response, largely in grain, consumer goods and machinery, with the prospect of a gradually upward-sloping increase over the years, involving an increasing mix of long-term investments in jointly financed resource-development projects, would represent a conservative course, and would hold out a continuing incentive to the Soviet leadership to conduct itself with restraint. If we were to withhold trade and investment in the expectation that it would oblige the Soviet Union to institute fundamental economic reforms, this would be a risky course, and the consequences would be unpredictable, whereas the influx of American technology and businessmen is more likely over a period of time to encourage internal pressures for modernized administration, some decentralization in planning, and a greater reliance upon market mechanisms.

Questions have been raised whether the increase of trade and investment should be made subject to more explicit conditions. For example, the Senate has passed an amendment proposed by Senator Humphrey requesting the President to seek an agreement with the Soviet Union for the mutual reduction of armaments and military expenditures in conjunction with the granting of credits and guarantees by the United States government. Whether such an agreement proves feasible or not, the amendment serves to register the point that future levels of military expenditure in the Soviet Union will be taken into account as part of the context in which future credits will be discussed. Senator Jackson's amendment, tying the Most Favored Nation clause to the question of unrestricted emigration, with particular reference to the emigration of Soviet Jews, has resulted in an unprecedented effort on the part of the Soviet Union to satisfy the Congress on a matter regarded in Moscow as a sensitive internal affair. As a general principle, the effective combination of private and group pressure with a formal government position of noninterference in Soviet internal affairs might have long-run advantages over an explicit and frontal government-sponsored challenge.

(5) The ideological aspect of the relationship could be conducted anywhere on the decibel scale from a quiet competition of ideas to a noisy brouhaha between ideologues. There is a fundamental contradiction in the

Soviet position that "peaceful coexistence between states with different social systems is possible," but that it is consistent with, and even intensifies, the "ideological struggle." Although the Soviet press has recently been unaccustomedly moderate in its tone of reporting on life in America, it continues to use "imperialism" as a synonym for U.S. policy and regularly calls for a "systematic struggle against reactionary ideology and propaganda." It is evident that this campaign represents an organizational concession to domestic cold warriors, but the effect is of more than domestic consequence. From the point of view of the United States, a campaign of "ideological struggle" against the "imperialist enemy" perpetuates attitudes of implacable hostility and sets narrow limits on the relaxation of tension, and there is a strange inconsistency between this Soviet stance and its attacks on foreign radio broadcasts as contravening the spirit of "peaceful coexistence."

(6) The cultural-relations aspect of Soviet-American relations presents a number of dilemmas. In principle, the two sides are agreed that cultural relations should be expanded. In the Basic Principles of Relations, the President and the General Secretary reaffirmed "their intention to deepen cultural ties with one another and to encourage fuller familiarization with each other's cultural values." Another agreement on the subject was signed in Washington this June. In his television speech to the American people, Secretary Brezhnev said: "To live at peace, we must trust each other, we must know each other better. We, for our part, want Americans to visualize our way of life and our way of thinking as completely and correctly as possible." The sentiments are unexceptional, but the implementation presents difficulties. The American side, in meshing itself with Soviet institutions and practices, becomes centralized, involved in government channels, quotas, tit-for-tat games of reciprocity over various restrictions and other degrading exercises, which demonstrate the truth of the French saying: "each one takes on the visage of his adversary." In the Soviet system, cultural relations are regarded as a highly sensitive matter, subject to an elaborate and pervasive control apparatus which limits exchanges to officially selected delegations and representatives in approved fields. In all Soviet institutions, the "Foreign Departments" that have the responsibility for monitoring and approving all contacts with foreigners have their own standards for judging the utility of cultural relations. Undoubtedly there is some mutual benefit even in the constricted and asymmetrical exchanges now possible, but it is much less useful than it could be if it conformed to the standard expressed by Secretary Brezhnev. Our guiding criterion is to be found in the belief that unrestricted human contacts are integral to the "normalization" of relations between nations, and while adapting to the unhappy limitations of the present, we should not lose sight of the aspiration to bring cultural relations with the Soviet Union into conformity with prevailing standards elsewhere.

(7) There is a potential future importance in the bilateral agreements on functional cooperation in various fields, and the various Joint Commissions provided for under these agreements, which may be greater than is now appreciated. Even today, American-Soviet relations are at their best when they bring together specialists with common professional interests, and the reports of close and successful collaboration in, for example, oceanography and environmental problems are most encouraging. In the longer run, it seems likely that increasing awareness of the urgency of problems relating to pollution, the environment and resources needed to sustain life on the planet will affect ways of thinking about national sovereignty, and that collaboration in these fields will have a broadening effect on the context in which security problems will be faced. When the time comes that this aspect of the Soviet-American relationship becomes central rather than peripheral, the essential character of that relationship cannot but change in its fundamental perspectives.

Whether it will take years or decades for the sense of living on the same small planet to loom larger in the consciousness of men than the rivalry of nations, no one of course can say. Change sometimes moves like a glacier, sometimes like an avalanche. We have negotiated the passage from the simplified enmities of the past to that patchwork-quilt mixture of striving with and against each other which has no simple designation. To move now from the ambiguities of coexistence to a more constructive and less dangerous stage will take patience and faith in our sense of direction in the world, while we sustain an effectively functioning society at home.

Détente: Moscow's View*

Today, there is no question of any signficance which can be decided without the Soviet Union or in opposition to it....Moreover, it is precisely our proposals...that are at the center of political discussions.—*A.A. Gromyko at the XXIVth Party Congress (1971)*[1]

Soviet Historical Background

In the accounts they left behind, travelers who had visited Russia between the seventeenth and nineteenth centuries liked to stress the unusually low business ethics of the native population. What struck them was not only that Russian merchants, shopkeepers, peddlers, and ordinary *muzhiks* engaged in the most impudent cheating, but that once they were found out they showed no remorse. Rather than apologize, they shrugged the matter off by quoting a proverb which from frequent repetition became very familiar to resident Westerners: "It is the pike's job to keep the carps awake." This version of *caveat emptor*—"let the buyer beware"—not only enjoins the customer to look out for his interests but it also implies that if

*Reprinted from Richard Pipes, *Soviet Strategy in Europe* (New York: Crane, Ruzzak & Co., 1976), pp. 3-42, by permission of the author and the publisher.
  1. *XXIV S" ezd KPSS—Stenograficheskii Otchet,* vol. 1 (Moscow, 1971), p. 482.

he is hoodwinked, the fault is entirely his, insofar as the pike (in this case the seller) has a nature-given right to gobble up unwary fish. It is a distillation of centuries of experience, a kind of folkish anticipation of Social Darwinism, to which a large majority of the Russian population (with the notable exception of the intelligentsia) had learned to adhere, whether placed by fortune in the role of pike or of its potential victim.

All people tend to some extent to base their understanding of foreign civilizations on personal experience and self-image and to assume that underneath the cloak of even the most exotic exterior there thinks the same mind and beats the same heart. But no one is more prone to work on this assumption than a person whose occupation is commerce and whose political creed is liberalism. The idea of human equality, the noblest achievement of "bourgeois" culture, is also the source of great political weakness because it denies a priori any meaningful distinctions among human beings, whether genetic, ethnic, racial, or other, and therefore blinds those who espouse it to a great deal of human motivation. Those differences that cannot be ignored, the commercial-liberal mind likes to ascribe to uneven economic opportunity and the resulting cultural lag. The most probable cause of this outlook, and the reason for its prevalence, lies in the contradiction between the "bourgeois" ideal of equality and the undeniable fact of widespread inequality. Such an outlook enables the "bourgeois" to enjoy his advantages without guilt, because as long as all men are presumed to be the same, those who happen to be better off may be said to owe their superior status to personal merit. In the United States, a country whose underlying culture is permeated with the commercial ethos and liberal ideology, this way of thinking is very common. Among the mass of the people it expresses itself in a spontaneous and rather endearing goodwill toward foreigners, accompanied by an unconscious and (to foreigners) irritating assumption that the American way is *the* way. Among the more learned, it conceals itself behind theoretical façades that appear to be supremely sophisticated but on closer inspection turn out to be not all that different from the ideas held by the man on the street. The various theories of "modernization" that have acquired vogue among American sociologists and political scientists since World War II, once they are stripped of their academic vocabulary, say little more than when all the people of the globe have attained the same level of industrial development as in the United States, they will become like Americans.

This outlook is so deeply ingrained in the American psyche and is so instinctively and tenaciously held that it produces among U.S. legislators, diplomats, and other politicians a strong distaste for any sustained analysis of foreign civilizations, because such analysis might (indeed, almost certainly would) demand recognition of permanent cultural pluralities and thus call for an effort at learning and imagination not required by its more comforting alternative. It is probably true that only those theories of international relations that postulate a fundamental convergence of all human aspirations with the American ideal have any chance of acceptance in the United States. It is probably equally true that no major power can conduct a successful foreign policy if such policy refuses to recognize that there exist in the world the most fundamental differences in the psychology and aspirations of its diverse inhabitants.

The current policy of "détente," as practiced in Washington, is no exception to these rules. To me at least, it appears to be without theoretical underpinnings and to repose on nothing more substantial than a vaguely felt and poorly articulated faith that the march of human events follws the script written by the Founding Fathers, and that if one can only avoid general war long enough all will be well. We are told that détente is vital because the only alternative to it is a nuclear holocaust. This, however, is an appeal to fear, not to reason. When pressed further, the proponents of détente justify it with offhand allusions to the "web of interests" that allegedly enmeshes the Soviet Union with the rest of the world and gradually forces it to behave like any other responsible member of the international community—as if a metaphor were a substitute for evidence or analysis. A convincing argument in favor of the present détente policy would require a close investigation of the internal situation in the Soviet Union, as it was, is, and becomes, insofar as a basic postulate of this policy holds that its pursuit will exert a lasting influence on the mind and behavior of the men whó rule the USSR. It would demand, at the very least, an inquiry into the social structure of the USSR, its various "interest groups," the Communist party apparatus, the internal agitation and propaganda as they relate to détente, Soviet public opinion, and the Soviet government's ability to maintain its internal controls. It would seek to explain the apparent contradictions between the Soviet government's professions of détente and certain contrary actions such as incitement of its population to the "ideological struggle" against the West, the pursuit of an unabated pace of armaments, and the appeals made to the Arabs in 1973 to persevere with their oil embargo. Furthermore, it would analyze the probable effects of détente on the Western alliance system, on the morale of the dissidents and the non-Russian inhabitants of the Soviet Union, and on U.S.-Chinese relations. It would try to do this and much more that is clearly relevant. But in fact little analysis of this type has been attempted, and virtually none of it has been made public.

What makes such failure inexcusable is that the other party to détente certainly has done its homework. Whatever the limitations of their understanding of the United States (and they are considerable), the leaders of the Soviet Union at least have made the mental effort to place themselves in the position of the U.S. government and public. With the help of the expertise available at such of their international research institutes as IMEMO (The Institute of World Economy and International Relations) and IShA (Institute of the U.S.A.), they have devised a policy of détente which serves their immediate interests without jeopardizing their long-term aspirations. *They* at least know what it is they want and how to try to go about getting it, by objectively analyzing Western strengths and weaknesses. And although the results of détente to date probably have not justified the Politburo's most sanguine expectations, thanks to an effort to understand the rival power it at least has managed to extract more than it has had to concede.

The purpose of this paper is to try to show how détente is viewed by Moscow. Much attention is given to internal factors, it being my conviction that in Russia, as elsewhere, political thinking and behavior are shaped largely by the experience gained in the arena of domestic politics. The argument in favor of this postulate is that politicians make their careers within a domestic power apparatus and, as a rule, gain the right to conduct their country's international affairs only after having successfully fought their way to the top of an internal power structure. (At any rate, the contrary almost never happens.) Foreign policy is thus an extension of domestic politics: It involves the application to other countries of habits acquired at home, in dealing with one's own subjects. The approach is also historical. Experience indicates that a country's internal politics evolve more gradually and prove more resistant to change than its foreign politics. It should be apparent that this approach differs fundamentally from that underlying the present administration's approach to the Soviet Union. The administration appears to assume the primacy of international politics (that is, the decisive impact of international relations on a country's domestic politics) and to ignore historical experience in favor of a "behavioral" response to the immediately given situation.

* * *

The first historical fact to be taken into account when dealing with the political life of Russia is that country's peculiar governmental tradition. For economic and geopolitical reasons that cannot be gone into here, during the nearly seven centuries that have elapsed since the founding of the Moscow monarchy the Russian state has claimed and, to the extent permitted by its limited means, actually exercised a kind of "proprietary" or "patrimonial" authority over the land and its inhabitants.[2] In a regime of this type, the government and its bureaucratic-military service elite feel that the country literally belongs to them and that in their capacity as its administrators and defenders they have the right to live at its expense without owing an accounting to anyone. Although Russian history has known several "liberal" interludes—notably the reigns of Catherine II and Alexander II—when attempts were undertaken to depart from this patrimonial tradition, these proved short-lived and without lasting effects. By expropriating all the

---

2. The historical evolution of this type of state authority is the theme of my book *Russia Under the Old Regime* (New York: Scribner's, 1975).

"productive wealth" and much private property besides, the Soviet regime has dramatically reverted to this tradition (even though this had not been its founders' intention). In Communist Russia, as in Muscovit *Rus'*, the government as reprsented by the bureaucratic and military elites owns the country. No comforts or privileges in the USSR can be acquired save by favor of the state; and none are likely to be retained ψnless the state remains internally frozen and externally isolated.

This basic fact of Russian history has had many consequences for the *modus operandi* of Russian politicians, whatever the regime and its formal ideology. One of them of special relevance to détente is the intrinsically illiberal, antidemocratic spirit of Russian ruling elites. In "capitalist" countries it is in the interest of the elite composed of property owners to restrain the powers of the state, because the state is an adversary who, by means of taxes, regulations, and the threat of nationalization, prevents it from freely enjoying its property. By contrast, in the USSR or any other state where "property" is merely conditional possession dispensed by, and held at the grace of, the state, the elite has an interest in preventing the diminution of the state's power because this would inevitably result in the mass of the population demanding its rightful share of goods. The Soviet elite instinctively dislikes democratic processes, social initiative, and private property at home as well as abroad. In its relations with foreign powers it prefers to deal on a state-to-state basis, preferably on a "summit" level, bypassing as much as possible unpredictable legislatures that represent the citizenry. Because it fears emboldening its own population, it rejects people-to-people contacts, unless suitably chaperoned. Nor is the Soviet elite averse to corrupting democratic processes in foreign countries. In its relations with the Nixon Administration, the Soviet government placed its authority squarely behind the president during his various contests with Congress. Thus, in violation of accepted international practices, during President Nixon's June 1974 visit to Moscow, Brezhnev publicly sided with him against congressional critics of his foreign policy. The Soviet government has also openly encouraged private lobbies (for example, the National Association of Manufacturers) to apply pressure on Congress on its behalf and has urged the administration in various unsubtle ways to bypass Congress in concluding various agreements with it. Entering into business arrangements with the European governments and private enterprises, the Soviet government has been known to insist cn secrecy, which, in the long run, also tends to subvert democratic procedures.[3] In countries of the so-called Third

---

3. It is reported, for instance, that the Finnish government, which owing to Soviet pressures must pay nearly double the prevailing world price for the oil it imports from the USSR, is pressured not to reveal this unpalatable act to its citizenry (*Neue Zürcher Zeitung*, 19 June 1974). Similarly, in their dealings with private West European banks, Russia and the "Peoples' Democracies" are insisting, with apparent success, on a high degree of secrecy. See Christopher Wilkins in *The Times* (London), 17 December 1973.

World, representatives of the USSR openly exhort local governments to strengthen the "public" sector of the economy at the expense of the private.[4] Just as the capitalist entrepreneur feels most comfortable in an environment where everybody pursues his private profit, so the Soviet elite prefers to be surrounded by regimes of the "patrimonial" type, run by elites like itself.

Second, attention must be called to the persistent tradition of Russian expansion. Its causes are to be sought not in racial or cultural propensities (as a matter of fact, Russians are not noted for imperialist fantasies and dislike leaving their homeland), but rather in the same economic and geopolitical factors that account for Russia's peculiar tradition of government. Climate and topography conspire to make Russia a poor country, unable to support a population of high density: Among such causes are an exceedingly short agricultural season, abundant rainfall where the soil is of low quality and unreliable rainfall where it happens to be fertile, and great difficulties of transport (long distances, severe winters, and so on). The result has been unusually high population mobility, a steady outflow of the inhabitants in all directions, away from the historic center of Great Russia in the taiga, a process that, to judge by the censuses of 1959 and 1970, continues unabated to this very day. The movement is partly spontaneous, partly government sponsored. It is probably true that no country in recorded history has expanded so persistently and held on so tenaciously to every inch of conquered land. It is estimated, for example, that between the middle of the sixteenth century and the end of the seventeenth, Russia conquered territory the size of the modern Netherlands *every year* for *150 years* running. Not surprisingly, it has been the one imperial power after World War II not only to refuse to give up the colonial acquisitions made by its "feudal" and "bourgeois" predecessors, but to increase them by the addition of new dependencies acquired during the war in Eastern Europe and the Far East. Nothing can be further from the truth than the often heard argument that Russia's expansion is due to its sense of insecurity and need for buffers. Thanks to its topography (immense depth of defense, low population density, and poor transport) Russia has always been and continues to be the world's most difficult country to conquer, as Charles XII, Napoleon, and Hitler each in turn found out. As for buffers, it is no secret that today's buffers have a way of becoming tomorrow's homeland, which requires new buffers to protect it. Indeed, a great deal of Soviet military activity in Western Europe in recent years has been justified by the alleged need to defend Russia's interests in Eastern Europe, which interests Russia had originally acquired with the tacit acquiescence of the West as a buffer zone. It is far better to seek the causes of Russian expansionism in internal im-

---

4. Much evidence to this effect can be found on the pages of *USSR and Third World* published in London by the Central Asian Research Centre.

pulses springing from primarily economic conditions and the habits that they breed.

In this connection it deserves note that the population movement, which initially took the form of spontaneous colonization and in time became increasingly dependent on conquest, has from the earliest times brought Russians into intimate contact with a great variety of nations and races. It has taught them how to handle "natives" and how to exploit to their advantage "contradictions" present in neighboring countries for the purpose of weakening and subverting them preparatory to annexation. To understand some of the techniques presently employed on a global scale by Soviet diplomacy one can do no better than study the history of Moscow's conquest of Novgorod (fifteenth century), the Golden Horde (sixteenth century), and the Polish-Lithuanian Commonwealth (eighteenth century), as well as the efforts of Imperial Russia in the nineteenth century (largely frustrated by Western countermeasures) to partition the Ottoman Empire and China. No other country has a comparble wealth of accumulated experience in the application of external and internal pressures on neighbors for the purpose of softening them prior to conquest.

The third historical factor to which attention must be called in assessing Soviet attitudes to détente is the personal background of the elite that at the present time happens to govern the Soviet Union. This group rose to positions of power in the 1930s, in the turmoil of Stalin's purges and massacres—that is, under conditions of the most ruthless political infighting known in modern history. No ruling elite in the world has had to learn survival under more difficult and brutal circumstances. This elite is the product of a process of natural selection under which the fittest proved to be those who knew best how to suppress within themselves everything normally regarded as human—where indeed the "dictator of genius" treated any expression of human qualities as personal disloyalty and usually punished it with deportation or death. No one dealing with Brezhnev and his colleagues ought to forget this fact.[5]

The fourth historical fact bearing on détente is that the elite currently ruling the Soviet Union is for all practical purposes directly descended from a peasantry. This holds true also of those of its members whose parents were industrial workers or urban petty bourgeois *(meshchane)* because a large part of Russian industry was traditionally located in the countryside, and much of the so-called urban population consisted of peasants temporarily licensed to reside in cities. Now the Russian *muzhik* is a very complicated being: The mysteries of his character form a puzzle that has engrossed some of Russia's finest literary minds. Certainly no quick

5. Nor should it be forgotten that the officers who command Soviet Russia's military establishment are veterans of the most brutal war of modern history in which defeat would have spelled enslavement and eventual mass annihilation of their people.

characterization can hope to succeed where some of the greatest writers have tried their talents. However, as far as his social and political attitudes are concerned (and these alone matter where détente is concerned) it must be borne in mind that during the past four centuries (the brief interlude 1861-1928 apart) the majority of Russian peasants have been serfs—that is, they had few if any legally recognized rights, were tied to the soil, and did not own the land they cultivated. They managed to survive under these conditions not by entrusting themselves to the protection of laws and customs, but by exercising extreme cunning and single-mindedly pursuing their private interests. This experience has left deep marks on the psyche of ordinary Russians. The world view of such people, including those running the Communist party apparatus, is better studied from Russian proverbs (for example, Dal's *Poslovitsy russkogo naroda*) than from the collected works of the "coryphaei" of Marxism-Leninism. The basic thrust of these proverbs is that life is hard and that to survive one must learn to take care of oneself and one's own, without wasting much thought on others ("the tears of others are water"). Force is one of the surest means of getting one's way (*"bei Russkogo, chasy sdelaet"*—"beat a Russian and he will make you a watch"). In personal relations, the Russian peasant always was and probably still remains one of the kindest creatures on earth, and nowhere can a stranger in need feel more certain of finding sympathy and help than in a Russian village. But these qualities of decency and empathy (unfortunately, much corrupted by the trauma of Stalinism) have never been successfully institutionalized: They tend to vanish the instant the Russian peasant leaves the familiar environment of personal contacts and becomes· a stranger among strangers. When this happens, he is likely to view the world as a ruthless fighting ground, where one either eats others or is eaten by them, where one plays either the pike or the carp.

These various elements of historical experience blend to create a very special kind of mentality, which stresses slyness, self-interest, reliance on force, skill in exploiting others, and, by inference, contempt for those unable to fend for themselves. Marxism-Leninism, which in its theoretical aspects exerts minor influence on Soviet conduct, through its ideology of "class warfare" reinforces these existing predispositions.

Admittedly, history does not stand still. There are examples on hand to indicate that deep national experiences or vastly changed conditions can indeed alter a people's psychology. The consciousness of a people and the mentality of its elite are constantly affected by life around them. But in the case of Russia, all the great national experiences, especially since 1917, happened to reinforce the illiberal and antidemocratic impulses. It is surely unreasonable to expect that the increase of U.S.-USSR trade from $1 billion to, say, $5 billion a year, or agreements on joint medical research, or broadened (but fully controlled) cultural exchanges will wipe the slate clean of centuries of accumulated and dearly bought experience. Nothing short of a major cataclysm that would demonstrate beyond doubt that impulses rooted in its history have lost their validity is likely to affect the collective outlook of the Russian nation and change it, as defeat has caused the Germans or Japanese to turn away from dictatorships, and the Nazi massacres have caused the Jews to abandon their traditional pacifism. Unless and until that happens, one can ignore Russia's tradition only at great risk.

Détente and Soviet Policy

In order to understand how, in view of what has just been said of its outlook on life, the Soviet government initiated a policy of détente with the West, one must consider the situation in which the Soviet Union found itself after the death of Stalin.

Genealogically, détente is an offset from the "peaceful coexistence" inaugurated by the Khrushchev administration nearly twenty years ago. But "peaceful coexistence" itself was much less of an innovation in Soviet foreign policy than world opinion, anxious to have the burden of the cold war lifted from its shoulders, liked to believe. It had been an essential ingredient of Lenin's political strategy both before and after 1917 that when operating from a position of weakness one had to exploit "contradictions" in the enemy camp, and this entailed a readiness to make compacts with any government or political grouping, whatever its ideology. "Direct action" ran very much against Lenin's grain. In 1920, when he expelled the Anarchists from the Third International, the charge that he leveled against them (and that his successors of the 1950s and 1960s revived against the Chinese communists) was a dogmatic rejection of the *divide et impera* principle. Both he and Stalin made no secret of the fact that in their foreign policy dealings expediency was always the principal consideration. Hitler was barely one year in power (into which he had been carried by a viciously anti-communist campaign) when Stalin approached him in a public overture. At the XVIIth Party Congress, held in 1934, he announced his willingness to establish with Nazi Germany a relationship that today would be characterized as one of détente. Stalin declared on this occasion:

> Of course, we are far from being enthusiastic about [Hitler's] fascist regime in Germany. But it is not a question of fascism here, if only for the reason that fascism in Italy, for example, has not prevented the U.S.S.R. from establishing the best relations with that country.[6]

Inaugurating détentes (as well as calling them off) is for the USSR a relatively easy matter: There exist for such action ample historic precedent and more than adequate theoretical justification. A "soft" foreign line must, therefore, under no conditions be interpreted as prima facie evidence

6. J.V. Stalin, *Works*, vol. 13 (Moscow, 1955) pp. 308-309.

of a change in the basic political orientation of the Soviet Union.

Behind the "peaceful coexistence" drive inaugurated in the mid-1950s and reinforced by decisions made in the early 1970s lay several considerations. Some of these had to do with the need to overcome the disastrous consequences of Stalin's rule; others, with changes in the world situation.

The most immediate task facing Stalin's successors was the need to give the country a chance to lick its wounds after twenty years of privations, terror, and bloodletting of unprecedented dimensions. Stalin had assured himself that no opposition could endanger his dictatorship, but he did so at the cost of draining the citizenry of all vitality. In the mid-1950s the population of the Soviet Union was spiritually exhausted, as can be confirmed by those who had a chance then to visit the country.

Looking beyond these most pressing exigencies, it was thought imperative to extricate the USSR from the diplomatic-military predicament in which Stalin's postwar policies had placed it. Every attempt by Stalin to bully the West had caused the West to close ranks and build up its military potential. The net effect of Stalin's intransigent aggressiveness had been to enhance the role of the United States as leader of the noncommunist majority of humanity and, correspondingly, to isolate the Soviet Union. A different, more pliable and indirect strategy seemed to promise much better results. One had to initiate friendly relations with the freshly liberated colonies of the West, which Stalin had rudely alienated on the grounds that they were dominated by a "national bourgeoisie" allegedly tied to the apron strings of its departed colonial masters. Further, one had to establish contacts with all kinds of political groupings and movements of public opinion in the United States and Western Europe that, without being friendly to the Soviet cause, could nevertheless serve its purposes. In short, instead of following Stalin's (and Lenin's) dictum "who is not with us is against us," it was thought preferable to adopt for an indeterminate time the principle "who is not against us is with us"—a more sophisticated political strategy first devised by the Russian Social Democrats in the 1880s in their struggle against the imperial regime.

The, third problem confronting Stalin's successors derived from the development of strategic nuclear weapons. Stalin had ordered his military to provide him with a nuclear arsenal, but it is doubtful whether he fully appreciated the implications and uses of nuclear weapons. His successors seem to have realized that after Hiroshima nothing would ever be the same again. War with such weapons was suicidal, and this meant that one could no longer count on mere quantitative and qualitative superiority in weapons to assure hegemony. This realization must have strengthened the resolve of the new leadership to depart from the strategy of confrontations with the West, pursued by Stalin in emulation of Hitler.

Such appear to have been the principal considerations behind the decision, taken in 1954-1955, to reverse the "hard" line pursued by Stalin since the end of the war and adopt in its place a "soft" strategy. The plan was simple and attractive: By means of a reasonably long period of relaxation of internal and international tensions to energize the Soviet population and reinfuse it with the enthusiasm of the early years of communism; to break the ring of alliances forged by the United States around the Soviet Union; to gain support of the Third World and public opinion in the West; and in this manner to initiate a gradual shift of the international balance of power in favor of the USSR. One of the implicit assumptions of this strategy was that during the era of "peaceful coexistence" the Soviet Union would greatly improve its economic potential and, by devoting a goodly share of the growing national product to defense, would expand its military power so as to attain parity or even superiority vis-à-vis the United States. The end goal of this policy was to turn the tables on the United States and, by containing the would-be container, drive him into the corner into which he had driven the USSR during the cold war.

The Khrushchev policy succeeded up to a point. The Third World responded enthusiastically to Soviet diplomatic overtures and offers of economic and military aid. Western opinion appeared more than ready to put Stalin out of mind and accept at face value professions of the Soviet government that it had no wish to export revolutions. America's leadership remained suspicious, the more so that every now and then détente was tested by means of strong-arm methods reminiscent of the coldest cold war.[7] But by persuading President Eisenhower to acknowledge in principle the necessity of renouncing war between their two countries, Khrushchev scored a major success. He planted an idea that, once adopted, would have caused the West to give up its strongest weapon against the Soviet Union—superiority in strategic weapons—without the Soviet Union being compelled in return to forfeit political and ideological warfare, at which it excelled.

This policy's principal failure was economic. In his exuberance, a kind of throwback to the early 1930s and First Five-Year Plan when his own political career got underway, Khrushchev seems to have believed that, given a fair chance, the Soviet economy, thanks to the advantages inherent in planning, would catch up and overtake the U.S. economy. He also thought that this economic progress would accelerate the shift in the international balance of power on which he counted to achieve an ultimate isolation of the United States. But being a rather primitive, commonsensical man (judging by his memoirs), Khrushchev had little idea how much the world economy had changed since the days when he had helped Stalin with his Five-Year Plans. While he kept his eyes riveted on statistics of steel production, a technological revolution was reshaping the economies of the

---

7. Malcolm Mackintosh, in E.L. Dulles and R.D. Crane, *Détente: Cold War Strategies in Transition* (New York: Praeger, 1965), pp. 103-120.

capitalist countries. After Khrushchev's removal, it became apparent to the new Soviet leadership that, notwithstanding the upward movement of their productive indices, Russia and its bloc were steadily falling behind the United States, Western Europe, and Japan.[8] One symptom of this fact was the decline in the Eastern bloc's participation in world trade. Between 1966 and 1973 the share of world exports of the USSR and the six "People's Democracies" declined from 11.4 to 9.0 percent; the Soviet Union's share dropped from 4.3 to 3.4 percent.[9] These figures suggested that owing to some basic flaws—technological backwardness, poor management, bad planning—the communist countries not only were not catching up with the capitalist countries but were failing to keep pace with them; and this, in turn, meant that the automatic shift in the balance of power postulated by "peaceful coexistence" would not take place either.

Tackling this matter presented formidable difficulties; and it is testimony to the courage and capacity at objective analysis of the post-Khrushchev Soviet leadership that its members acknowledged the problem and boldly set themselves to deal with it. They had two basic alternatives open to them. One was to carry out major economic reforms of the kind that had been discussed and even halfheartedly attempted in the late 1950s. This course, however, posed certain political dangers. All proposals of economic reform current in the communist bloc called for a certain degree of decentralization of economic decision making. But decentralization of the communist economy always threatens to end up in decentralization of the political process, for where the state owns the economy there can be no firm line separating economics from politics, and no effective way of ensuring that reform stays within safe limits. If there was any chance of the Politburo adopting the path of internal reform it was eliminated by the experience of Czechoslovakia in 1968, which showed how quickly and irreversibly economic reform led to a breakdown of communist controls.

So there was the other alternative left—instead of economic reform, economic aid from abroad. It was easier to swallow the idea that all the Soviet economy needed to put it right was Western technical know-how than to concede that the fault lay with bureaucratic centralism, easier because to concede the latter point meant to put in question the Soviet system as a whole. The decision, formally ratified at the XXIVth Party

8. See Brezhnev's views: "A scientific and technical revolution unprecedented in its rate and scope is now taking place in the world. And it is the communists, [those] who carried out the greatest social revolution, that should be in the front rank of the revolutionary transformations in science and technology. The CPSU believes that one of our most important tasks now is to accelerate scientific and technical progress, to equip the working people with modern scientific and technical knowledge, and to introduce as quickly as possible the results of scientific discoveries." L.I. Brezhnev, *Pravda*, 13 November 1968, cited in Foy D. Kohler et al., *Soviet Strategy for the Seventies: From Cold War to Peaceful Coexistence* (Coral Gables, Florida: Center for Advanced International Studies, University of Miami, 1973), p. 168.

9. *Frankfurter Allgemeine Zeitung*, 24 May 1974.

Congress in 1971, must have been accompanied by anxious soul-searching. It marked one of the major turning points in the history of the Soviet Union, and only the widespread contempt for, and ignorance of, history among people who occupy themselves with Soviet affairs explains why Western opinion has not been made aware of this fact. It had been one of the principal claims of the Bolsheviks before coming to power that Russia was an economic colony of the imperialist West, and one of their proudest boasts upon assuming power was that they had freed Russia from this degrading dependence. The fact that fifty-odd years after the Revolution, the Soviet Union, in the words of Chou En-lai, has to go "begging for loans" and put "its resources for sale"[10] is a tacit admission of stupendous failure. It signifies that notwithstanding all the human sacrifices and privations of the past half century, the Soviet system has not been able to generate the resources, skills, and enterprise necessary to keep the pace set by the allegedly wasteful, crisis-ridden free economies. The humiliation is extreme. To convey what it would mean in terms of American history one would have to imagine the United States in the 1850s, threatened by Civil War, concluding that it was, after all, incapable of governing itself and requesting Britain temporarily to assume charge of its administration. The point needs emphasis because only if one realizes how agonizing the decision to seek Western economic assistance must have been for Soviet leaders can one appreciate how desperate was the need that drove them to it and gain an idea of the price the West could demand for its help. It makes one much less anxious than the present U.S. administration seems to be lest too hard bargaining on our part should cause the USSR to abandon détente.

Major Soviet Strategic Objectives of Detente

The national policy of the Soviet Union is distinguished by a high degree of strategic and tactical coordination. Because it is the same group of people—the Politburo—who bear ultimate responsibility for the totality of domestic and foreign decisions, they have no choice but to package their policies, as it were, into neat bundles, without loose ends. The kind of situation that exists in the United States where authority over people and objects is widely distributed—with the administration pulling one way and Congress another, with industry looking out for its own interest and the media for theirs—such a situation is, of course, unthinkable in the Soviet Union. Even the most sanguine believer in the "interest group" approach to Soviet politics would not go so far as to see in them an arena of untrammeled competition.

10. Speech of 18 February 1974 welcoming the President of Zambia, *USSR and Third World*, vol. 4, no. 2, p. 108.

Lest the use of the terms "strategy" and "tactics" in the Soviet context arouse in the reader the suspicion that we are employing cold war terminology, it must be said at the outset that Soviet theoreticians insist that they are, in fact, thinking in strategic and tactical terms when making political decisions. The following passage, taken from a standard Soviet party manual, makes this point without equivocation:

> The measures which make up the activity of the Marxist-Leninist Party are not the result of improvisations of the party leadership. They represent the concrete expression of the *political line*, which is worked out by the party on the basis of scientific analysis of a given phase of the struggle and a given situation. In the political language to describe this line one also uses the concepts of *tactics* and *strategy*...

> At the present time, Communists talk of strategy or the strategic line when referring to the party's general line, which aims at the fulfillment of the principal tasks of the given historical phase, proceeding from the existing correlation of forces among the classes. In this respect strategy differs from tactics, which defines the *current policy* and which is worked out on the basis of the party's general line for a briefer period (e.g., tactics in an electoral campaign, the attitude toward the maneuvers of right-wing socialist leaders, the approach to left socialists, etc.).[11]

One can, of course, dismiss such claims as meaningless pretense on the grounds that in the end all politics must be improvisation and that no country, the Soviet Union least of all, operates in accord with preconceived "scientific analysis." This argument is correct, but only up to a point. After all, in military affairs, where no one would deny the applicability of the concepts of strategy and tactics, it is improvisation, too, and not "science" that wins battles. Yet who would argue that one can wage war successfully without some strategic concept and tactical skill? In the end, the terms "strategy" and "tactics" always mean economy of force, whether we speak of warfare, of politics, of investment, or of athletic contests; he who seeks to attain any objective with insufficient means must employ some kind of strategic and tactical concept lest he hopelessly scatter his resources. In this sense, any strategy and any improvisation carried out within some strategic design are better than no strategy at all.

The Soviet effort at coordination of policy facilitates the task of the observer. Here we shall attempt to delineate in their broad outlines the principal tasks of the strategy and tactics of détente as they may be perceived by Moscow.

---

11. Gosudarstvennoe Izdatel'stvo Politicheskoi Literatury, *Osnovy Marksizma-Leninizma: Uchebnoe Posobie,* 2nd ed. (Moscow: 1962), pp. 359-360. Emphasis in the original.

Inside the Soviet Union

Internally in the USSR the highest priority is attached to political security—that is, to preventing the idea of relaxation of tensions with the "capitalist" world from leading Soviet citizens to question the necessity of preserving the dictatorial regime. To this end, the Party's leadership has emphatically committed itself to the line that détente does not mean an end to the conflict between capitalism and socialism or any convergence between the two systems.[12]

One of the major tasks of the whole vast agitprop machinery in the USSR is to keep up the "ideological struggle" against hostile or alien ideologies and to forestall any blurring of the lines separating the two systems. Increased internal controls, symbolized by the recent promotion of the head of the KGB to the Politburo and, even more so, by the dismissal of P.N. Demichev as Secretary for Agitation and Propaganda (see below, p. 383) are manifestations of that effort.

Related is the drive to enhance Soviet Russia's military posture. We shall revert to this subject later on. Here we must merely point out that the military effort is no small measure inspired by the fear that détente could lead to internal relaxation and thus to a dissolution of the system. It is as if Soviet leaders felt that by keeping up a steady tempo of armaments they were helping to maintain that state of tension that is required to keep the system intact.

The failure, promises notwithstanding, to give the population more consumer goods probably stems from the same motive. Consumerism, as Russian leaders had the opportunity to observe in the West, leads to a decline in public spirit and an addiction to comfort that significantly diminishes the state's ability to mobilize the citizenry.

Toward the United States

One of the highest priorities of the Soviet Union in dealing with the United States has been to gain recognition as an equal, that is, as one of two world "superpowers," and hence a country with a legitimate claim to have its say in the solution of all international problems, even those without immediate bearing on its national interests. Recognition of this status is essential because only by establishing itself in the eyes of the world as an alternate pole to that represented by the United States can the Soviet Union hope to set in motion the shift in the world balance of power that is the long-term aim of its foreign policy. To achieve and maintain this status, the USSR re-

---

12. Numerous citations to this effect can be found in Kohler et al., *Soviet Strategy for the Seventies.*

quires an immense up-to-date military establishment with a devastating destructive capability, for in Moscow's eyes to be a "superpower" means nothing more or less than to have the capacity to face the United States down in a nuclear confrontation.

It is very much in the interest of the USSR to induce the United States to renounce or at least limit (regulate) the use of those instruments of power politics at which it enjoys a pronounced advantage, and to do so without offering reciprocal concessions. This means, in the first place, reducing to the maximum extent possible the threat posed by the American strategic nuclear arsenal. The various agreements into which the United States has entered with the USSR for the purpose of controlling and limiting the use of nuclear weapons certainly have not been accompanied by concessions on the part of the Soviet Union to restrain those instruments of power politics at which it is superior, namely, subversion and ideological warfare—and in this sense, such agreements are inherently inequitable.

Because of its planned and coordinated character, and because of its unwillingness to relegate authority farther down its bureaucratic hierarchy, the Soviet system is intrinsically offensive-minded: It always prefers to take the initiative, inasmuch as he who initiates an action has better control of his forces than he who responds to the actions of others. Time and again, when it has been forced to respond to firm initiatives (for example, the U.S. blockade of Cuba in 1962 or Israel's preemptive strike against the Arabs in 1967) the Soviet government has reacted in a manner that suggested a mental state bordering on panic. For this reason it is very valuable for the Soviet Union to be aware at all times of its rivals' intentions. The practice of regular U.S.-USSR consultations, instituted in the past decade, works greatly to the advantage of the Soviet leadership. The fact that the Soviet ambassador in Washington has virtually free access to the president, and indeed has been known to travel to Moscow on the same plane with the American secretary of state, assures the Politburo that it is reasonably well informed of major American initiatives before they occur. By terms of the U.S.-USSR agreement of 1973, each party is required to inform the other of any actions endangering the other's security or that of its allies. It is far from clear that the Soviet Union kept its part of the bargain in early October 1973 having learned at least a few days ahead of time of the impending Egyptian-Syrian attack on Israel. At any rate, it was neither commended nor criticized publicly by the U.S. administration for its behavior on this occasion. Yet it is reasonably certain that the Soviet Union would secure from the United States the relevant information should the roles be reversed.

Although it sometimes threatens to seek the capital and technology it requires in Western Europe and Japan, the Soviet Union has no viable alternative to the United States because it is only here that the capital and productivity it needs are available in sufficient quantities. Furthermore, U.S.

corporations control worldwide rights to the most advanced technology. Part of the strategy of détente is to exploit the need of the U.S. economy for raw materials and markets so as to induce it to help with a fundamental modernization of the economy of the Soviet Union. Last but not least, because the United States is the only country able to deal with the USSR as an equal in any contest of wills, other potential investors (most notably Japan) have been reluctant to commit large sums in the USSR without U.S. participation for fear of ultimate expropriation—a fact which makes American economic cooperation doubly valuable to the Russians.

Toward Western Europe

It seems probable that the long-term objective of Soviet foreign policy is to detach Western Europe from its dependence on the United States, especially where defense is concerned, and to make it dependent on the USSR. It is difficult to conceive of any event that would more dramatically enhance Soviet power and tilt the "correlation of forces," so dear to its theorists, to its advantage. Russian military power resting on a Western European economic base would give the USSR indisputable world hegemony—the sort of thing that Hitler was dreaming of when, having conquered continental Europe, he attempted to annex to it Soviet Russia's natural resources and manpower. However, the separation of Western Europe from the United States must not be hurried. The Soviet leadership has taken a measure of U.S. politics and knows (whatever its propagandists may say) that it faces no danger from that side. After all, if the United States had any aggressive intentions toward the USSR it would have made its moves in the late 1940s or early 1950s when its monopoly on nuclear weapons allowed it to do so with impunity. The U.S. forces in Western Europe present no offensive threat to the Soviet Union. Their ultimate removal is essential if the USSR is to control Western Europe, but their purely defensive character does not seriously inhibit Russia's freedom to maneuver. What the Soviet Union fears more is a German-French-English military alliance that might spring into existence should U.S. troops withdraw precipitately from Western Europe. The Russians are well aware that close to the surface of what appears to be a "neutralist" Western Europe there lurk powerful nationalist sentiments that could easily assume militant forms. Nor do they forget that England and France have nuclear deterrents that they could place at West Germany's disposal. Hasty action on their part, therefore, could cause the emergence on their western flank of a nuclear threat probably much greater than that which they face in the east, from China, let alone from the United States. As long as the United States is in control of European defenses, this development is not likely to occur. Hence Soviet strategy is to hurry slowly.

If realized, the European security system for which the Russians have been pressing with moderate success for many years would give them a kind of veto power over West European politics, military affairs included. It would make them arbiters of West European defense and thus preclude the emergence of an effective West European military force equipped with nuclear weapons.

The Soviet Union is seeking to make the West European countries maximally dependent on the Eastern bloc, without, however, losing its own freedom of action. It tries to achieve this end by the following means: promoting heavy indebtedness of the Comecon countries; gaining maximum control of West European energy supplies (oil, natural gas, fuel for nuclear reactors); and promoting "cooperative" arrangements with West European business firms. For its part, the USSR (the other Comecon countries to a lesser extent) seeks to confine Western economic aid to "turnkey operations" and similar devices that minimize dependence on foreign sources. In their dealings with Western Europe, the Russians like to insist on very long-term arrangements, which would have the effect of tying Western economies to the Soviet economic plans. In some cases they even propose deals that would run for up to fifty years.[13] The effect of such economic relations would be increasingly to link the economies of Western Europe with those of Eastern Europe.

Toward the Third World

The Third World that interests the Soviet Union the most is that which adjoins its long and strategically vulnerable southern frontier. This perimeter is an area of primary importance and the theater of its most determined political, economic, and military activity. Suffice it to say that two-thirds of all foreign military and economic aid extended by the USSR between 1954 and 1972 went to six countries located in this region (India, Egypt, Iran, Afghanistan, Iraq, and Turkey). Africa and Latin America are of much smaller concern, and the same holds true of Southeast Asia.

On no political subject have Soviet theoreticians spilled more ink than on what strategy and tactics to adopt toward the underdeveloped countries. Analyzing Soviet behavior in this vast region, one can discern three consecutive strategic lines:

1. In the late 1950s, in the first flush of enthusiasm, the Soviet Union scattered its limited resources far and wide, helping any and all regimes that seemed ready to collaborate with it against the United States and the rest of the "imperialist camp." Much of this "water can" aid strategy ended badly, and a great deal of the investment went down the drain, in large part

---

13. D. Lascelles, *The Financial Times* (London), 6 February 1974.

because the Russians were unfamiliar with the infinite variety of local situations, each calling for fine political and economic nuances.

2. To overcome this squandering of resources, in the early 1960s the theory of "national democracy" was pushed to the fore. This theory viewed the underdeveloped countries as in varying degrees of transition from feudal to socialist society and maintained that it was possible as well as desirable for them to bypass the capitalist phase. Soviet aid went to those countries which were prepared to expand the "public sector" at the expense of the "private," thereby eliminating Western influence, undermining the native bourgeoisie, and creating cadres of socialist functionaries hostile to capitalism. A prerequisite was political "democracy," by which was meant allowing Communist parties in these countries to surface and gradually to assume leadership of the "progressive" forces moving toward socialism. This policy too proved unsuccessful, in part because of the chronic instability of the governments of the "national democracies," and in part because most of these countries remained adamantly hostile toward their native Communist parties. By the late 1960s it became apparent that the Chinese, who had criticized this strategy from the beginning on the grounds that its net effect would be to promote in the Third World sturdy state capitalisms, may well have been correct.

3. Around 1970 the Soviet government began to adopt another strategy toward underdeveloped countries, one based less on political or military and more on economic considerations. Aid at present is extended as part of a broadly conceived Soviet "complex" plan intended gradually to mesh the economics of the underdeveloped countries with those of the Comecon. Its hoped for result is a double effect of complementing Comecon economies (for example, with raw materials) and creating deep ties of economic (and ultimately, political) interdependence.

The common aim of the three consecutive Soviet strategies toward the Third World has been to cut off the capitalist countries from sources of raw materials and cheap labor, to deprive them of military bases, and ultimately to isolate them. The undertaking, however, is complicated and exacerbated by Russia's conflict with China. The Chinese are threatening the USSR from a flank which they had been always accustomed to regard as secure— namely, the political Left. They are trying to wean away the radical and nationalist constituency in the underdeveloped countries that since 1917 had been viewed from Moscow as a safe preserve. The Soviet Union cannot allow China to do this, least of all in regions adjacent to its own territory, and this fact compels it to take vigorous counteraction. From East Africa to Southeast Asia a bitter fight is being waged between Russia and China for hegemony over the local governments. Though little discussed in the press, it may well be the most significant political struggle in the world at large today. By means of military and economic aid programs, the cost of which must represent a heavy burden to their economies, the two powers contend for allies as each seeks to expel the influence of its rival.

Toward Communist China

Having tried every means at its disposal from appeals to sentiment to officially leaked rumors of a preemptive nuclear strike to bring China back into the fold, the Soviet Union appears to have settled on a patient strategy of containment. The immense military force concentrated on China's border (apparently defensive in posture) assures that China will not light-heartedly encroach on Soviet territory. The Soviet effort in the rest of Asia, and among the left-wing, nationalist movements elsewhere, alluded to earlier has so far been successful in preventing the Chinese from seizing control of major territorial or political bases of potential use against the USSR. One of the greatest benefits of détente for the Soviet Union has been the unwillingness of the United States to exploit the Sino-Soviet conflict to its own advantage by pursuing more vigorously a "détente" with China. If détente with the United States had no other justification, this alone would suffice to keep it alive, as far as the Soviet Union is concerned.

The Soviet Union appears to have decided not to exacerbate further its relations with China, but to await opportunities for intervention in internal Chinese affairs, which are likely to open up after Mao's death. In the long run the USSR will probably strive for a breakup of China into several independent territorial entities. After the experience with Mao, even the emergence of a pro-Moscow successor government in Peking would not still Russia's long-term fears of China. A China separated by spacious buffer states (Sinkiang, Inner Mongolia, Manchuria) would be a far more comfortable neighbor to live with.

* * *

The political strategy we have outlined suffers from obvious contradictions. It seems odd, for instance, to urge multinational corporations to invest in the USSR while seeking to expel them from the Third World. Or to ask for economic assistance from the United States while building up a military machine directed against the same United States. Or to intervene in the internal affairs of other countries while denying anyone the right to interfere in its own. But each of the adversaries of this global policy tends to see only one of its facets at a time and to remain unaware of the whole picture, which facilitates the execution of what otherwise might have become an impractical line of conduct.

Soviet Tactics for Implementing Détente

At the very beginning of any discussion of Soviet methods of implementing détente, attention must be called to prudence as a feature common to all Soviet tactics. A certain paradox inheres in the Soviet Union: It is at the same time immensely strong and fatally weak. Its strength derives from the ability to marshall all its national resources in the service of any chosen cause; its weakness, from the necessity always to succeed or at least to appear to do so. The Soviet government lacks a legitimate mandate to rule and can never risk putting its credentials (that is, force) in question. Failure effectively to apply power abroad would at once raise doubts in the minds of Soviet citizens about the regime's ability to cope with internal opposition; and any loss of public faith in the omnipotence of the regime (and hence in the futility of resistance to it) might prove the beginning of the end. Thus the Soviet regime finds itself in the extremely difficult situation of having to create the impression of a relentless advance forward as it in fact moves very cautiously and slowly. It can act decisively only when it has a near 100 percent assurance of success, which, of course, occurs rarely.

Related is the habit of overinsuring by keeping open all options. The Soviet leadership by ingrained habit never places its eggs in one basket. It maintains some form of contact with all foreign political parties, from extreme Right to extreme Left; it builds up conventional forces as well as nuclear ones and simultaneously expands its naval arm—in all the service branches it accumulates masses of weapons, old and new, just to be on the safe side; in its economic drive, once the decision to seek help abroad has been taken, it sought to deal with everybody—the United States, Western Europe, Japan, and even such powers of second rank as Brazil. The lack of selectivity indicates insecurity lurking very close behind the airs of supreme self-confidence that Soviet leaders like to exude in public.

In our discussion of tactics we shall deal, successively, with political, military, and economic measures, concentrating on Soviet operations vis-à-vis Western Europe.

Some Political Tactics

The basic political tactic employed by the USSR on a global scale since its acquisition of nuclear weapons has been to try to reduce all politics to the issue of preserving the peace. The line it advocates holds that the principal danger facing humanity today is the threat of a nuclear holocaust, for which reason anything that in any way risks exacerbating relations between the powers, and above all between the United States and the Soviet Union, is evil. This line (which happens to have been adopted by President Nixon and

Secretary of State Kissinger) has two advantages from the Soviet point of view:

1. It offers it an opportunity to silence external criticism of the Soviet Union, for no matter what the Soviet Union may do or fail to do, good relations with it must never be jeopardized. A crass example of this tactic is to be found in arguments advanced by the USSR and echoed by certain Western politicians and commentators that the West should not support dissident movements inside the USSR, lest this exacerbate relations between the superpowers and thereby heighten the risk of war.

2. It allows the Soviet Union to avoid questions touching on the nature of the peace that is to result from détente. Peace becomes an end in itself. The issue of freedom is relegated to the margin, for once survival is at stake, who is going to haggle over the conditions?

As has been suggested earlier, the Soviet strategy for Europe is gradually to detach the Western half from the United States and bring it within the Soviet orbit. To achieve this end, the Soviet government works intensively to promote and make dependent on its goodwill parties and movements in the West that, whatever their motivation and attitude toward communism, happen at a particular time to further this end. Soviet support of de Gaulle represents a clear example of this tactic. Once the French leader had set himself earnestly to reduce American influence on the Continent, the USSR extended to him the hand of friendship, even though behind him stood the anticommunist Right. Very instructive, too, has been Soviet behavior in the 1974 French presidential election. Although Mitterand ran on a common ticket with the Communist party and in the event of victory was committed to put ministerial posts at its disposal, the Soviet government treated him with reserve. The reason behind this coolness seems to have been, not the fear of embarrassing the left-wing ticket and thus handing useful campaign ammunition to his opponent, but uncertainty about Mitterand's foreign policy views.[14] The same holds true of Moscow's behavior in the U.S. presidential election of 1972. On the face of it, Russia could have been expected to support Senator McGovern, because he advocated drastic cuts in the defense budget and reductions in American military commitments abroad, Europe included. But the Democratic candidate seemed to appeal to isolationist sentiments that at this juncture are not in Soviet Russia's interest. The policy of détente postulates a U.S. administration willing to assume certain global responsibilities (at any rate, in the immediate future); any other administration would be unlikely to favor the huge loans, investments, and sharing of technical knowledge that the Soviet Union seeks from the United States. Further, as noted, Moscow fears a precipitate

---

14. H. Hamm, *Frankfurter Allgemeine Zeitung,* 4 May 1974.

withdrawal of U.S. troops from Europe, as advocated by McGovern, preferring such a withdrawal to proceed piecemeal and in the context of a European "security pact." For all these reasons Moscow preferred to back President Nixon.

Such tactics require Moscow to have friendly access to all kinds of political groupings, no matter what their ideology. It could well happen that a European party commited to anticommunism should also turn out to be very anti-American, in which case its attitudes toward the USSR could be temporarily overlooked. On the other hand, a Communist party in power might choose to pursue an independent foreign policy that was harmful to Soviet interests. It is not inconceivable, for instance, that in view of its advocacy of a "European" policy line, the Italian Communist party may appear in Moscow's eyes a less palatable alternative to the present Christian Democratic government than a fascist one. In general, Moscow does not seem all that anxious to promote at this time Communist parties in Europe, apparently preferring to deal with parties of the center and to the right of it. Direct cooperation with the West European "establishment" has proved very profitable. It is undoubtedly safer to exploit the "bourgeois" desire for profits and peace than to incite the Left and risk a backlash and possibly even open the door to Chinese penetration.

A persistent feature of Soviet policy toward Western Europe has been the effort to break up all political, economic, and military alliances, the very existence of which obstructs Soviet objectives. Originally, the Soviet Union did whatever it could to frustrate the creation of the Common Market (EEC). Later, it reconciled itself to the EEC's existence, although it continues to refuse to treat it as a juridical entity and by various means tries to bypass it. (For example, anticipating the establishment of EEC control over all foreign trade of its member states as of 1 January 1973, the Soviet Union has promoted bilateral "cooperative" arrangements with West European countries, which so far have remained exempt from central EEC management.) The difficulties that the EEC has experienced in recent years, including the breakdown of its unity during the October 1973 war, has certainly not been lost on Moscow.[15] There is also some reason to expect that the Soviet Union may ultimately succeed, as a result of the European "security pact" that it has avidly sponsored, in emasculating NATO.

The pursuit of Soviet strategy in the West entails a steady increase of Soviet intervention in the West's internal life. This effort, so far, has had very limited success, but it represents a development deserving greater attention than it ordinarily receives. In the United States, the Soviet Union has established a lobby that can reveal on occasion an astonishing degree of activity. Represented by diplomats, journalists, and occasional delegates from

15. See Brezhnev's speech of 26 October 1973, in which, in evident reaction to the EEC's gasoline shortages, he urged integrating its economy with that of the USSR.

Eastern Europe, it operates on Capitol Hill, in business organizations, at universities, and in learned societies, and its purpose is the promotion of legislation favorable to the Soviet Union. Perhaps the lobby's most ambitious effort has been mounted against the amendment introduced by Senator Jackson to the Trade Bill which would deny the USSR and other nonmarket economies Most Favored Nation status until they accord their citizens the right of unrestricted emigration. Great pressures have been brought to bear upon Senator Jackson and the co-sponsors of his amendment to have it withdrawn in which, at various stages, the National Association of Manufacturers and some leaders of the Jewish community in the United States, acting in what they considered their constituents' best interests, were involved.

In the United States, these pressures to interfere with domestic politics have so far had little success. In Western Europe the Russians have been more fortunate. The idea is gaining acceptance in Western Europe that nothing must be done that could be interpreted in the USSR as endangering its security or challenging its prestige. An outstanding example of this is the willingness of Norway to prohibit international companies from exploring oil deposits under the waters along its northern seacoast, where the Soviet Union is anxious to keep NATO away from the sea-lanes used by its naval units stationed at Murmansk. Negotiations in progress between the two governments seem to point to the recognition by Norway that oil exploration in this area will be carried out either by itself alone or in cooperation with the Soviet government.[16]

Pressures are being exerted on European governments and private enterprises to prevent the spread of literary works unfavorable to the Soviet Union and to isolate individuals and groups whom the Soviet government dislikes. (A telling instance is the report that the Czech Chess Master Ludek Pachman, who had been a political prisoner in Czechoslovakia following the Soviet invasion, has been unable after his recent emigration to Western Europe to gain admission to internal tournaments; the Icelandic government has rejected a German offer to have him play as a member of the West German team on the grounds that this might annoy the Russians and prevent their participation.)[17]

In all, the results of these internal pressures leave much to be desired from the Soviet point of view, and one wonders whether they are worth the effort (and bad publicity) that they cost. The unexpectedly firm behavior of cer-

16. C. Genrich, *Frankfurter Allgemeine Zeitung*, 21 March 1974, and H. Kamer, *Neue Zurcher Zeitung*, 9 June 1974. The USSR sees nothing wrong, however, in asking the very same international oil companies to help it conduct drilling off the coast of Soviet Sakhalin—*New York Times*, 22 February 1975.

17. *Frankfurter Allgemeine Zeitung*, 31 January 1974. There also exist reports that the movie *One Day in the Life of Ivan Denisovich* will not be shown in Japan, because the film distributor, Toho, fears Soviet objections.

tain European delegations at the Geneva Security Conference in discussions connected with "Basket Three" and involving human cultural exchanges between East and West indicates that powerful sectors of Western opinion not only will not tolerate Soviet repression but insist on the right to bypass the Soviet government and establish contact with its citizenry. Still, the matter deserves close watch; certain forces in the West prefer conciliation at all costs and, willingly or not, help the Soviet government gain acceptance of the principle—from which it alone can benefit—that because of its awesome military arsenal it must always be placated.[18]

Military Policies

It is fair to say that the West has consistently underestimated the Soviet willingness and ability to pay for a large and up-to-date military establishment.[19] Western policymakers have always hoped that sooner or later their Soviet counterparts would conclude that they have enough weapons and decide to devote a growing share of their "national product" to peaceful purposes. This has not happened. The mistaken expectation rests in part on a misunderstanding of Soviet attitudes to military instrumentalities (the belief that they are primarily inspired by a sense of fear and insecurity) and partly from a stubborn faith in Soviet promises to raise Russia's living standards.

The most likely explanation for the relentless Soviet military drive is that nearly all communist expectations—except the reliance on the mailed fist—have been disappointed. The worldwide revolution that the Bolsheviks had expected to follow their seizure of power in Russia did not take place and, as early as the 1920s, had to be given up as a realistic objective. The economic crisis of the West on which they had counted did occur a decade later, but it failed to bring capitalism down. Communist ideology, having attained the apogee of its influence in the 1930s, has since lost much of its appeal and today attracts youth less than it had done before, the more so because it has to compete with anarchism and the Chinese variety of revolutionary doctrine. After its giant achievements in the 1930s, the Soviet economy has not been able to keep up with the pace set by the free economies; the Soviet economic model can hardly attract emulators after the USSR itself has had to seek help outside. In other words, had the Soviet government chosen to rely on the appeal of its ideology or the accomplishments of its economy, it would have consistently found itself on the losing side. Military might alone has never disappointed it. It won the Bolsheviks—in 1917, a tiny party—the Civil War that ensconced them in

18. An important subject in its own right is Soviet subversion in Western Europe (and elsewhere), the breadth and sophistication of which is depicted in *The Peacetime Strategy of the Soviet Union* (London: Institute for the Study of Conflict, 1973).

19. See Albert Wohlstetter, "Is There a Strategic Arms Race?" Foreign Policy, no. 15 (Summer 1974), especially p. 5.

power. It saved the country from the Nazi invaders. It made it possible for Russia to occupy and retain Eastern Europe. Reinforced with a strategic nuclear arsenal, it has enabled the Soviet government to stand up to the United States and exact recognition as an equal. In short, military power has been the instrument by which a party once composed of a small band of émigré radicals gathered around Lenin had managed first to capture power in Russia, then to defeat the greatest war machine of modern times, and finally to rise from the status of a pariah nation to become one of the world's two superpowers. Merely to list these achievements is to gain an insight into the reason behind the single-minded obsession of Soviet leadership with military power. Anyone who counts on a deceleration of the Soviet military effort must be able to come up with some alternate instruments of international policy on which the Soviet leadership could rely with equal assurance of success.

The buildup of Soviet military forces in the 1960s and early 1970s has been phenomenal and, notwithstanding certain international agreements on arms limitations, shows no signs of abating. There is some disagreement among experts whether this buildup bears a measurable relationship to legitimate Soviet defense interests or has become an end in itself, a search for power for power's sake.[20] There is no dispute, however, about the intensity of this effort, of the willingness of the government to allocate talent and money, of the dedication with which the armed forces maintain the martial spirit among the people. The Soviet leadership seems to strive to obtain a marked superiority in all branches of the military, in order to secure powerful forward-moving shields behind which the politicians could do their work. To reach this objective, the Soviet Union must have open to it all the options—to be able to fight general and limited conventional wars near its borders and away from them, as well as nuclear wars employing tactical and/or strategic weapons. The probability of this aim being given up is very low. Only effective pressure from below by a population fed up with seeing so much of the national wealth disappearing in the military budget could do so, but for this to happen, something very close to a revolution would have to occur in Russia. So far, the Soviet government has shown itself willing to limit the production or employment mainly of those weapons in respect to which it was bound to remain inferior to the United States or the further spread of which seemed counterproductive. A good test of its intentions would be to attempt negotiating limitations in the field of naval construction where the USSR is trying to attain parity with the United States. It is a safe prediction that should the U.S. government try to initiate such negotiations at this time it would run into a stone wall.

20. See Thomas W. Wolfe, "Soviet Military Capabilities and Intentions in Europe," in Richard Pipes (Editor), *Soviet Strategy in Europe* (New York: Crane, Russak & Co., 1976), pp. 129-167, and John Erikson, "Soviet Military Posture and Policy in Europe," in Pipes, op. cit., pp. 169-209.

An interesting feature of Soviet military activity in recent years has been the practice of quietly establishing a presence in areas where, should hostilities break out, Soviet forces would already be in place and able to deploy for action. A case in point are Soviet incursions by air and naval units of NATO territories in the North Sea. Potentially even more dangerous are large Warsaw Pact maneuvers held in areas near major NATO troop concentrations.[21] As is known, prior to the invasion of Czechoslovakia, Warsaw Pact troops had been put into a state of readiness in this manner. Something of the same tactic seems also to have been followed, possibly under Soviet guidance, by the Egyptians and Syrians in 1973 preparatory to their combined assault on Israel. The unwillingness of the USSR to agree to an exchange of warnings of such exercises more than a short time in advance indicates that its military leaders contemplate the possibility of using maneuvers as cover for preparing offensive operations against NATO.

Finally, mention must be made of the tactic of "war by proxy." Détente cramps Soviet freedom to engage in military action, for it is a sine qua non of this policy that there must be no direct military confrontations between the United States and the USSR. To get around this limitation, the Soviet leadership seems to be systemically developing a technique of indirect military involvement. In regions where it has a strong need to expel hostile foreign influence (Western or Chinese), and yet fears direct involvement, it seeks to achieve its purpose by employing third parties. It provides its allies with arms and with diplomatic protection; in the event of disaster it undertakes an all-out effort on their behalf, but it does not commit to any appreciable extent its own forces. The use of this technique is especially evident in the Middle East, where the Soviet Union seems to have decided that the explusion of Western political, economic, and military influence and the reduction of Israel to the status of an impotent minor power transcend its day-to-day relations with the Arab states. In an article written upon his return from an extended tour of the Middle East, the editor-in-chief of *Izvestiia*, Lev Tolkunov, has hinted that the Soviet Union had given the Arab countries in their conflict with Israel a blank check. The Arabs could be certain of Soviet backing regardless of the state of their relations with the USSR or the outcome of their initiatives:

> The last war [October 1973] showed that the Soviet stand in the Arab-Israeli conflict is not connected with the current state of affairs in relations between the USSR and certain Arab countries. It was not possible for this principled position to be affected by the artificially created negative factors which manifested themselves in respect to Soviet military experts in some Arab countries. To put it more directly, they know in the Arab capitals that when the threat of war hung

---

21. See John Erikson op. cit., pp. 169-209.

over the Arab world, the Soviet Union proved in deed the constancy of its policy
of active support of the Arab states, by sending arms both to Syria and Egypt.[22]

Those acquainted with the diplomatic history of Europe will find in this
policy a striking echo of the *carte blanche* given by Imperial Germany to
Austria-Hungary in July 1914, promising unconditional support in its quarrel with Serbia, and assurance generally regarded as a prime immediate
cause of World War I.

The first major "war by proxy" was the Indian-Pakistani war; the sec-
ond, the October War, alluded to above. It seems entirely possible that the
USSR may attempt similar action in the future (for example, Iraq and
Afghanistan versus Iran, or India and Afghanistan versus Pakistan).

Economic Policies

The main objective of Soviet economic policy abroad during the era of
détente is to modernize the Soviet industrial establishment. But, as noted,
under the communist system economics is never considered in isolation
from politics, and every economic policy is measured in terms of its likely
political consequences. Indeed, in recent years the economic weapon has
been increasingly used to secure political benefits.

The principal political result desired is increased dependence of the
Western and Third World economies—and therefore, as a corollary, of
Western and Third World governments—on the Soviet Union. We may
single out three means by which this dependence can be accomplished: control of energy supplies, indebtedness, and manipulation of West European
labor.

The Soviet government seems to have realized earlier than its Western
counterparts how great had become the dependence of modern economies
on energy, especially oil, and to have initiated steps to obtain control of this
resource. The single-minded persistence with which the USSR, its failures
notwithstanding, has advanced its influence in the Middle East has had (and
continues to have) as one of its prime motives the desire to establish control
over the oil supplies of that region. Should the Soviet Union succeed in fill-
ing the military vacuum created by the British withdrawal from the Persian
Gulf and sustained by American reluctance to commit forces there, it would
be in a superb position to exercise a stranglehold on European and Japanese
fuel supplies. The October 1973 war unmistakably demonstrated how low

---

22. *Izvestiia*, 25 July 1974. Lest these words be misread to apply only to defensive actions,
Mr. Tolkunov insists in the same article that the October war had discredited the story that the
USSR was supplying the Arabs only with "defensive" weapons, and preventing the Arabs
from attacking Israel, arguing that the distinction between defensive and offensive weapons
was quite arbitrary.

Europe would stoop to ensure the flow of its oil.

The Soviet Union has also been very active in seeking to establish itself as a major fuel supplier to the West. It already furnishes respectable amounts of oil and natural gas to Germany and Italy, and everything points to the further expansion of these deliveries. The recently concluded deal involving supplies of natural gas from Iran to the USSR to be matched by Soviet deliveries to Germany will further enhance Soviet control over West European energy requirements. The same applies to bids (consistently below those made by U.S. firms) to furnish enriched uranium to West European nuclear reactors. All this creates conditions of dependence that the USSR could exploit, should the need arise, much in the manner the Arab oil producers had done in the fall of 1973. It goes without saying that the ambitious plans for U.S.-USSR cooperation in developing Siberian oil and gas fields would give the USSR similar leverage vis-à-vis the United States.

In momentary matters, the Soviet Union has traditionally pursued a very conservative policy. Its patient accumulation of gold reserves, at the time when the world offered more remunerative forms of investment, was part and parcel of the "bourgeois" approach to fiscal matters characteristic of Communists. In recent years, however, the Soviet government appears to have thrown its traditional caution overboard and gone all out for foreign borrowing. The same applies to the "People's Democracies." The obligations assumed are onerous, because before long the Soviet Union will have to set aside a good part (perhaps one-half) of its precious hard currency earnings for debt servicing.[23] In part, this untypically risky policy may be influenced by the belief that inflation will cause a disastrous depreciation of Western currencies while enhancing the value of the raw materials that the Soviet Union is in a position to supply. (If this is indeed the case, this calculation leaves out of account the possibility that inflation could lead to a depression that would, in turn, severely curtail the demand for primary materials; but then, perhaps, the Soviet leaders assume that this time a worldwide depression would be followed by a collapse of the capitalist system, an event that would wipe out their debts altogether.) Another consideration may have to do with the psychology of the debtor-creditor relationship. Heavy Soviet indebtedness to Western governments and banks produces among the latter a vested interest in the preservation and well-being of the Soviet Union and improves the chances of the flow of credits continuing unimpeded.

Studies carried out by specialists in the field of East-West relations[24] indicate that the degree of economic interdependence so far achieved is not

---

23. M. Kaser estimates (quoted in *Sowjetunion 1973*, Munich, 1973, p. 126, from *International Currency Review*, July-August 1973) Soviet foreign indebtedness for goods and services alone (that is, exclusive of capital borrowings) at $8.5 billion in late 1973. In his estimation, should Russia continue to accumulate obligations abroad at the same rate as recently, its external debt in 1980 would rise to $31 billion.

significant. But the danger is there; and should Moscow succeed in realizing its more ambitious plans for economic "cooperation" involving capitalist economies, the interdependence would attain a level at which political consequences of the most serious nature would be bound to ensue.

The steady growth of advanced modern economies and the difficulties of rationalizing production beyond a certain maximal point have resulted in a growing labor shortage; and that, in turn, has enhanced the power of organized labor. In some advanced industrial countries the trade unions have acquired a virtual veto power over government policies. It may be expected that (barring a depression) this power will continue to grow. This development induces the Soviet Union to try to heal the breach between those foreign trade unions that are Communist-controlled, and therefore in some measure manipulable by it, and the free trade unions that either are directed by socialists, Catholics, or some other group or lack political affiliation entirely. One of the by-products of the American-Soviet détente has been to make communism respectable in labor circles and to weaken the resistance of democratic trade unionists to pressures for closer contacts and joint action with communist and communist-dominated trade union organizations. In the past two years, the Soviet Union has succeeded in partly healing the breach created in 1949 when the Communist World Federation of Trade Unions broke up due to the secession from it of democratic labor organizations. The quarantine on communist trade unionism, in effect during the past quarter of a century, seems to have broken down. With the active support of the British Trade Union Congress and the West German Federation of Labor, the recent head of the Central Soviet Trade Union Organization, A.N. Shelepin (a one-time KGB head!) has persuaded European labor leaders to agree to a joint conference. That meeting could well presage an era of collaboration and end up with free trade unionism falling under the sway of the better financed and centrally directed communist movements.[25] Further penetration of European labor, of course, would give Soviet leadership a superb weapon for influencing or even blackmailing West European industry.

Current Soviet Assessment of Détente

What, from Moscow's vantage point, has been the balance sheet of "peaceful coexistence" and détente to date?

On the *debit* side of the ledger two results deserve emphasis:

1. The dispute with China. The foreign policy pursued by the post-Stalinist leadership has served primarily the national interests of the Soviet

---

24. P. Hanson and M. Kaser, "Soviet Economic Relations with Western Europe," in Pipes, op. cit., pp. 213-267, and J. and P. Pinder, "Western European Economic Relations with the Soviet Union, " in Pipes, op. cit., pp. 269-303.

25. A. Beichman, *International Herald-Tribune*, 26-27 January 1974.

Union, not those of the communist community at large. This had been the case even before 1953. As Stalin's words, cited above, assert, and as the historical record demonstrates, the guiding principle of Soviet foreign policy has always been national self-interest. But before Stalin's death, Soviet Russia had been the only major power with a communist regime, and until then one could argue with a certain logic that what was good for the USSR was good for communism. After all, the small East European regimes, put in power by the Red Army, hardly counted (except for Yugoslavia, which quickly fell out with Moscow). China, however, was a great power in its own right, and it would not tolerate a policy among whose primary objectives was an arrangement with the United Statees intended to elevate the USSR to the status of a superpower. Neither references to Lenin's lessons on strategy and tactics, nor arguments based on expediency, nor threats achieved their desired result. The Chinese remained stubbornly convinced that the ultimate winner from détente would be either the Soviet Union or the United States, or both, but never China, and they reacted with the fury of the betrayed.

2. A certain degree of loss of internal control. For this, détente is only partly responsible. The abolition of indiscriminate terror and the intellectual "thaw" of the mid-1950s were principally inspired by the wish to reinvigorate the country and reinfuse it with enthusiasm for the communist cause. Détente, however, undoubtedly accelerated the process by which society in the USSR began to resist totalitarian controls. An authoritarian-demotic regime must have a threat with which to frighten the population into granting it unlimited powers: Napoleon had his "Jacobins," Lenin and Stalin their "counterrevolutionaries" and "interventionists," Hitler his "Jews" and "Communists." Détente in some measure de-Satanizes the external threat and thereby undermines the Soviet regime's claim to unquestioned obedience. To proclaim the cold war over—even while repeating *ad nauseam* that the struggle between the two systems must go on to the bitter end—is to put in question the need in Russia for a repressive regime. It makes it that much more difficult to justify tight controls over foreign travel and over access to information. Implicit in détente is also a certain respect for foreign opinion. To project the image of a country worthy of being a partner of the Western democracies, the Soviet regime cannot simply shoot people for holding seditious ideas. The presence of Western correspondents in the USSR has given Soviet dissenters a powerful weapon with which to neutralize the KGB—at any rate, where better-known public figures are concerned. All this is not without long-term dangers for the regime.[26]

---

26. It is in this light that one may interpret the dismissal of P.N. Demichev from the post of Secretary of the Central Committee for Agitation and Propaganda in November 1974. Demichev, who had held his post since 1965, was responsible for the relatively "liberal" han-

On the *credit* side of the ledger there are the following achievements:

1. The USSR has indubitably achieved the status of an equal partner of the United States. As Gromyko publicly boasts in the passage cited at the beginning of this paper, all major international decisions are now acknowledged to require Soviet participation and acquiescence; no actions that seriously threaten Soviet interests are likely to be taken. The Soviet Union has at long last become a world power. Russia's international prestige is greater than it has ever been in the country's history.

2. The USSR has succeeded in smashing the ring of alliances forged around it by the United States during the late Stalin era. NATO is in disarray; the other alliance systems lead only a paper existence. For its own part, the USSR has succeeded in establishing a strong political and military presence in the Middle East, where its good relations with the Arab countries and India have helped her in considerable measure to eject Western influence and establish the position of a regional patron. Countries that at one time had been solidly wedded to the United States—Germany, Japan, and the states of Southeast Asia, for example—find it increasingly necessary to conduct an "even-handed" foreign policy.[27]

3. On the terms of détente, as laid down by the Brezhnev administration and tacitly accepted by President Nixon, the Soviet Union has not been seriously inhibited in carrying on its assault on the capitalist system. It has remained free to support national liberation movements (without risking similar actions against territories lying within its own orbit); it has been able to encourage "wars by proxy"; and it has been able to lobby and exert pressure abroad, without being obliged to grant the West corresponding rights in the communist bloc.

4. Détente has helped secure for the Soviet Union recognition, by West Germany, of its conquests in East Germany: It has legitimized the existence of two Germanys. The recently held Security Conference legitimized Russia's conquests of the rest of Eastern Europe. Such recognition is of great importance to Russia because it helps undermine whatever hope the people of Eastern Europe may still entertain of some day being freed of Soviet occupation armies and the regimes that these armies keep in power.

---

dling of dissidents. His dismissal has been immediately followed by repressive actions. See A. Solzhenitsyn in *Neue Zurcher Zeitung*, 15 January 1975.

27. In this connection it is interesting to note that polls conducted in recent years in West Germany and Japan have revealed a significant shift in the public's attitude toward the USSR. While Russia's popularity remains very low, a large part of the inhabitants of both countries have come to regard "good relations" with the USSR as essential to their security. In Germany some 19 percent of the persons polled thought good relations with the USSR to be more important than good relations with any other country, the United States included.

It also makes it possible to begin to think of some day incorporating Eastern Europe into the Soviet Union.

5. Détente has already led to a considerable growth of Western investments in the Soviet economy and, if continued, should help the Russians overcome some of the most glaring deficiencies plaguing it. Especially attractive are long-term "cooperation" plans that tie the Western economies to the Soviet, without creating undue Soviet dependence on the West.

It is thus fair to say that, on balance, détente has proved a profitable political strategy for the Soviet Union. It has vastly enhanced the international position of the Soviet Union and enlarged its room for maneuver, while, at the same time, legitimizing its conquests and strengthening its economy. The cost—alienation of China and internal restlessness—has been high, but apparently the Soviet leadership feels that it can prevent both dangers from getting out of hand. This explains why the Soviet leadership is vigorously pressing for détente to continue. There is every reason to expect that it will persist in so doing, no matter what the obstacles and frustrations, because as now defined and practiced, détente primarily benefits the Soviet Union.

TWENTY-ONE

ROBBIN F. LAIRD
ERIK P. HOFFMANN

"The Scientific-Technological Revolution,"

"Developed Socialism,"

and Soviet International Behavior*

Soviet political leaders and social theorists clearly recognize that significant scientific and technical changes have taken place since World War II and are continuing rapidly worldwide. Foremost among these developments are the remarkable scientific discoveries of new sources of energy and materials, and the technological innovations in transportation, telecommunications, weaponry, and countless other fields. Also, Soviet analysts contend that the social structure of an industrializing nation undergoes transformations. For example, urbanization and the emergence of highly educated technical and managerial specialists have multifaceted consequences in all types of societies. Today, many people's beliefs, aspirations, capabilities, knowledge, work, and leisure-time pursuits differ considerably from those of their forebears. But Soviet writers maintain that the nature of these changes depends heavily on the contemporary "scientific-technological revolution" (STR), and on the political and social system in which it unfolds. As Soviet academician P.N. Fedoseev declares:

> The dialectic of the present era is manifested in the fact that in a number of countries the socialist revolution has come before the STR, thereby providing the necessary social conditions for its completion. In these countries the STR serves

*Written especially to appear in Erik P. Hoffmann and Frederic J. Fleron, Jr. (eds.), *The Conduct of Soviet Foreign Policy* (Aldine: Hawthorne, N.Y., 2nd edition, 1980). This research was supported by a grant from the National Science Foundation.

to develop and multiply the achievements of social revolution. In other countries the STR has preceded social revolution, thereby preparing its material prerequisites and deepening the fundamental contradictions of capitalism. The sequence of the scientific-technological and social revolutions is a concrete expression of the basic contradiction of our era (i.e., between capitalism and socialism), and is a manifestation of the many forms of historical development in the contemporary era.[1]

In short, Soviet theorists argue that the STR is having a profound effect on the outlook and activities of human beings and on the relationships among social "classes" and nations.

I. The Nature of the STR[2]

Soviet officials and scholars offer a wide range of views about the nature or essence of the STR. Virtually all Soviet writers agree that the STR is a worldwide phenomenon, that it began in the USSR in the mid 1950's (and a decade or so earlier in the West), and that it has momentous and overwhelmingly favorable implications for the future of mankind, allegedly hastening the development of socialism and the fall of capitalism. But some Soviet authors emphasize that the essence of the STR lies in specific scientific or technical breakthroughs such as logical and control operations, and the automation of the processes of production and management. Other theorists stress the changing nature of work, the greatly enhanced problem-solving capacities of socialist leaders, and the growing capability of socialist societies to shape their physical and economic environments (for instance, to improve the productivity of labor). Still other theorists direct attention to the broader social implications of advances in scientific and technical knowledge—their impact on human needs and aspirations, job satisfaction, leisure, interpersonal relations, education, the professions, demographic patterns, and on evolving attitudes toward nature and ecological questions. And still others insist that the STR consists of three interrelated elements: the natural-scientific and technical, the socioeconomic, and the philosophical-ideological.

An authoritative Soviet definition of the STR—and one that carefully distinguishes between its content and consequences—is offered by Fedoseev:

The scientific and technological revolution is basically the radical qualitative reorganization of the productive forces as a result of the transformation of

1. P.N. Fedoseev, *Dialektika sovremennoi epokhi* (Moscow: Nauka, 3rd ed., 1978), p. 459; also, Fedoseev, "Social Science and Social Progress," *Social Sciences* (Moscow) (hereinafter *SS*), 3 (1979), 21.

2. Parts of this section and the next appeared in somewhat different form in Erik P. Hoffmann, "Contemporary Soviet Theories of Scientific, Technological, and Social Change," *Social Studies of Science*, 9 (February, 1979), 101-113.

science into a key factor in the development of social production. Increasingly eliminating manual labor by utilizing the forces of nature in technology, and replacing man's direct participation in the production process by the functioning of his materialized knowledge, the scientific and technological revolution radically changes the entire structure and components of the productive forces, the conditions, nature, and content of labor. While embodying the growing integration of science, technology, and production, the scientific and technological revolution at the same time influences all aspects of life in present-day society, including industrial management, education, everyday life, culture, the psychology of people, the relationship between nature and society.[3]

Note that this definition emphasizes that the STR is essentially a fundamental transformation of the scientific-technical and human "productive forces" of society. This conceptualization leaves open for theoretical development the likely and desirable effects of the new productive forces on "the social relations of production" (e.g., authority, property, or class relations) and on the "superstructure" (e.g., the political culture, laws, and institutions) of different societies (socialist, capitalist, and Third World). Also, there is room for much more analysis of the reciprocal influences of a nation's superstructure and production relations on its changing productive forces.

In general, Soviet theorists view the STR as a crucially important means of achieving higher forms of "developed socialism"—and eventually "communism." The STR is to be "mastered," and to do so the nature of the opportunities and obstacles it presents must be better understood. Soviet authors have made concerted efforts to clarify their thinking about key concepts such as "science," "technology," and "revolution," and about the interrelationships among these and other elements of the STR.

A recent Soviet study identifies six central components of the STR and offers a lengthy categorization of phenomena that express or reflect these elements. The six fundamental characteristics are:

1) The merging of the scientific revolution with the technical revolution;

2) The transformation of science into "a direct productive force";

3) The organic unification of the elements of the production process into a single automated system whose actions are subordinated to general principles of management and self-management;

4) A qualitative change in the technological basis of industrial and agricultural production, signifying major changes in man-machine relations

3. P.N. Fedoseev, "Social Significance of the Scientific and Technological Revolution," in *Scientific-Technological Revolution: Social Aspects*, in R. Dahrendorf, et al. (London: Sage Publications, 1977), p. 88.

and greatly enhanced human capabilities to manage and control production processes;

5) The formation of a new type of worker, who has mastered scientific principles of production and can ensure that the functioning of production and its future development will be based on the achievements of science and technique;

6) A major shift from "extensive" to "intensive" development of production, utilizing scientific and technical advances to produce dramatic increases in labor productivity.[4]

II. Socio-Political Consequences of the STR

Soviet authors have begun to elaborate on the political and social consequences of the STR and on its policy implications. One of the most significant assessments is General Secretary Brezhnev's injunction in 1971 *"to combine organically the achievements of the scientific-technological revolution with the advantages of the socialist economic system,* and to develop more broadly our own, inherently socialist, forms for combining science with production."*[5] This major policy pronouncement is chiefly an appeal to generate and implement ideas about the modernization of the Soviet political and economic systems under conditions of the STR. Most Politburo and Secretariat members apparently believe that attitudinal and administrative changes are necessary in order to create and take advantage of new opportunities for economic and social progress. Such changes could also forestall new problems associated with the complexities and interdependencies of the STR, and with the possibility of an increasingly unfavorable competitive position vis-à-vis the industrialized nations of the West. The idea is to modify and update traditional Soviet practices and precepts, in the hopes of contributing to and benefiting from the worldwide STR.

Soviet leaders and theorists have offered a variety of ideas about how best to "combine" the achievements of the STR with the advantages of socialism. Despite some differences in the views of Brezhnev, Kosygin, and other top leaders, these analyses have been characterized by an increasing attentiveness to the interconnections between ends and means and between domestic and international politics. In contrast to the utopian theorizing of the Khrushchev years, contemporary Soviet authors focus on the processes, not on the end results, of social change. That is, descriptions of a developed socialist society are now consistently linked to the analysis of the *transition*

4. S.V. Shukhardin and V.I. Gukov, eds., *Nauchno-tekhnicheskaia revoliutsiia* (Moscow: Nauka, 1976), pp. 59-168.

5. From Brezhnev's address to the 24th Party Congress in 1971, in *Materialy XXIV s'ezda KPSS* (Moscow: Politizdat, 1971), p. 57 (italics in original).

to developed socialism and communism. As a consequence, the prescription and evaluation of goals and methods are more closely intertwined with the continuous reassessment of domestic and international conditions.

Soviet analysts begin with a fundamental theoretical or ideological premise. This is the contention that, despite inevitable "nonantagonistic contradictions" between the productive forces and production relations of socialist countries, only in such societies can scientific-technical and social progress proceed simultaneously and further mutual development. G.N. Volkov states:

> The use of the positive results of the STR and the neutralization of its negative consequences are possible only in a society that is not divided into antagonistic classes—a society in which the products of human endeavor do not resist their creators by taking the form of an alienating and ruling force above them, but are subject to centralized social control, under which the fundamental interests of society as a whole and of the individual person do not diverge but coincide.[6]

Soviet theorists also strongly affirm that it is the social and organizational context in which the achievements of the STR are *used*, not those in which they are *generated*, which will decisively shape the purposes served, and hence determine the effects on people's values and human relations. On this basis Soviet writers explain their political leaders' traditional indifference to the cultural consequences of imported Western technology. They found their position on numerous conceptual distinctions between the purportedly value-free and value-laden components of systems of labor, production, and management. For instance, capitalist "forms" of production can allegedly be imbued with socialist "content." Or again, "technique" is considered value-free; "technology" has some values inherent in or associated with it; and socioeconomic production relations are the dominant sources and bearers of values.

It is then assumed or argued (with varying degrees of disdain for Maoist ideas on the subject) that techniques—and even systems of technology—can be imported from Western nations at little or no sociopolitical risk or "cost." Soviet writers confidently expect that selected foreign technology will help to implement *national* Party leaders' conceptions of "scientific," "rational," and "efficient" management of industrial, organizational, and social processes. Information and expertise embodied in techniques and technologies are not viewed as "capitalist" or "socialist," although they are occasionally thought to transmit elements of "technocratic consciousness." Most frequently, scientific discoveries and technological innovations generated in the West are seen as valuable means of serving

---

6. G.N. Volkov, *Istoki i gorizonty progress: Sotsiologicheskie problemy razvitiia nauki i tekhniki* (Moscow: Politizdat, 1976), p. 245.

socialist ends—and sometimes even as a welcome form of cultural diffusion (e.g., labor productivity).

III. The STR and the Historical Competition between Advanced Capitalism and Developed Socialism

Soviet leaders and theorists view the STR as a universal process characteristic of mature productive forces. As V.I. Gromeka states: "The development of productive forces has its own logic, its own internal laws, which to a certain extent are independent from production relations. Thus, the main lines of development in the STR...are identical in both socialist and capitalist countries."[7]

Under capitalist conditions, the STR is an objective force creating "state-monopoly capitalism." State-monopoly capitalism is an advanced form of capitalism which has emerged in response to two basic pressures. First, the monopolization of production has been established to provide the economic base for the development of modern technology, as well as the large marketing efforts needed to sell modern technology. Second, the growing role of the capitalist state has developed in response to the mounting production and consumption needs which have to be met by the capitalist system, such as the funding of large-scale research and development (R & D) projects. As Gromeka notes, "The STR leads to a situation in which the capitalist state takes on the function of leadership and organization of scientific, industrial, and technical construction work...."[8]

The state has become the central actor in state-monopoly capitalism, according to Soviet analysts. In the era of the STR the long-range interests of capitalism cannot be served by market competition among the corporations. The state adjudicates conflicts among the corporations. In order to protect the long-range interests of capitalism, the state occasionally comes into conflict with individual monopolies which operate exclusively from the perspective of the short-term interest of profit. In a word, the state begins to plan. "[State] programming aims primarily not at the satisfaction of the interests of individual monopoly groupings, but at the solution of the difficult problems of monopoly capital as a whole."[9]

Nonetheless, the basic character of capitalism blocks the capacity of the state to exercise genuine comprehensive planning, the only kind of planning adequate to meet the needs of the STR. In fact, the STR accelerates the inherent contradictions within capitalism, such as the contradiction between the private ownership of the means of production and the public needs to be

7. V.I. Gromeka, *NTR i sovremennyi kapitalizm* (Moscow: Politizdat, 1976), p. 15.
8. *Ibid.,* p. 90.
9. *The Political Economy of Capitalism* (Moscow: Progress, 1974), p. 212.

met by the STR. As N.N. Inozemtsev put it, *"The STR does not help to perpetuate capitalism but tends to reproduce its inherent social antagonisms on an ever greater scale and with increasing bitterness...."* [10]

An advanced society possesses a highly developed productive base and sophisticated organizational forms to manage the productive base. Both advanced capitalism and developed socialism confront the realities of such a productive base and the challenges of managing it. Material progress, especially in the advanced stage, is universal in nature. Progress in the material sphere creates the common problems of nurturing, directing, and coping with modern productive forces. The goal of material prosperity also generates pressures for creating internal and international structures and relations appropriate for dealing with the universal forms of science and technology.

Indeed, the universal character of the advanced productive forces places a competitive pressure upon the Soviet leadership, spurring an effort to develop further the effectiveness of the Soviet economic system. A team of Soviet researchers concludes: "Today, in the competition between the two systems under the conditions of the STR, it is necessary to use more fully the advantages of socialism through a more rational or efficient application of material and human resources and by improving the systems of planning and management, etc. Increasing the effectiveness of social production has become a basic problem whose resolution is critical for further social progress." [11]

Soviet analysts view the STR as an objective force that makes possible the construction of "a developed socialist society." Developed socialism is defined as the conjunction of the STR with the advantages of socialism. Briefly stated, a developed socialist society maintains the basic social and political institutions of socialism and adapts them to the challenges of the STR. The maintenance and adaptation functions are to be directed and balanced by national policymaking bodies and elites. Soviet writers contend that centralized planning and guidance are necessary to ensure that socialist ideas are implemented, and that Soviet institutions fulfill their potentials by responding to the challenges, opportunities, and problems presented by the STR. V.I. Kas'ianenko declares: "The achievement of a mature level of development of the productive forces and production relations allows society to use more fully the advantages, objective laws, and potentials of socialism in all spheres of social life." [12]

10. N.N. Inozemtsev, *Contemporary Capitalism: New Developments and Contradictions* (Moscow: Progress, 1974), p. 61 (emphasis in original).

11. *Razvitoe sotsialisticheskoe obshchestvo: Sushchnost', kriterii zrelosti, kritika revizionistskikh kontseptsii* (Moscow: Mysl', 1979), 3rd edition, p. 31.

12. V.I. Kas'ianenko, *Razvitoi sotsializm: Istoriografiia i metodologiia problemy* (Moscow: Mysl', 1976), p. 8.

The Soviet orientation to social change is very much a stage-oriented one. In an advanced society heavy industry has been built; the work force has become largely skilled; mass education has been established; and urbanization has become the dominant mode of life which influences the entire population. The industrialized stage must be completed prior to the possibility of an advanced stage of development. The STR can result in a higher stage of industrialization only when it is merged with the productive forces of a highly industrialized society. Societies in a lower stage of development (e.g., the Third World) can use components of modern science and technology but cannot forge an STR. In contrast to the position of Maoist voluntarism, Soviet theorists argue that a stage of development cannot be transcended but must be passed through. It is possible, however, to shorten the period of change by means of a socialist revolution.

Soviet theorists have identified four stages in the social development of the USSR.[13] The first stage, from 1917 to the Stalin constitution in 1936, was the period of the formation of the basic institutions and values of socialism. The second stage from 1936 to 1967 was the period of the consolidation of these basic structures. The third stage, "developed socialism," began in 1967 and is to continue indefinitely. In this stage the further broadening and deepening of socialism in response to the STR is the central task. The fourth and final stage, "communism," is a classless and stateless society of material abundance.

Thus, developed socialism is a transitional period between the consolidation of socialist structures and the stage of socioeconomic and political communism at home and throughout the world. Developed socialism thereby embodies the ideas of continuity in the basic characteristics of socialism and change in terms of the policy initiatives and responses necessary to reach communism. As Fedoseev has summarized the process: "The developed socialist society is a law-governed stage in the formative period of the communist system, signifying that socialism has finally triumphed and been fully established in every sphere of social life, and that the premises have been created for the full and all-round manifestation of the potentialities and advantages of the socialist system and for the realization of practical steps in the gradual transition to the higher phase of communism."[14]

A major distinction between capitalist and socialist modes of production focuses on the *needs* to be met by scientific, technical, and economic achievements. Soviet writers stress the importance of increasing economic growth and the technological level of the economy on the one hand, and im-

13. See, for example, "Razvitoe sotsialisticheskoe obshchestvo," in A.M. Rumiantsev, ed., *Nauchnyi kommunizm: Slovar'* (Moscow: Politizdat, 1975), pp. 285-289.
14. P.N. Fedoseev, "Developed Socialism: Theoretical Problems," *SS*, 3 (1977), 10.

proving the social and economic well-being of the entire population on the other hand.[15] This is not just a question of meeting already existing needs with economic goods. Rather, needs are to be reconceptualized in conformity with the new opportunities created by economic progress.[16] Both advanced capitalism and developed socialism provide for increasing material prosperity, but in capitalist societies production relations direct the creation and the use of material wealth to consumerism. Socialist production relations are defined with reference to the ability to use science and technology to meet public, as opposed to private, needs, and to distribute material, sociopsychological, and cultural benefits more equitably among the population.

Even under socialism, however, there are conflicts between evolving opportunities to define new needs to be met by the STR and past definitions of the uses of economic power. That is, there are differences between the needs to be served by technology in industrial society and the needs that are generated and can be fulfilled by the growing economic power of *advanced* industrial society. The resolution of such "nonantagonistic contradictions" between different stages of development is central to progress in industrialized socialist states. As Kas'ianenko asserts, "Social progress under socialism occurs dialectically through the overcoming of contradictions and difficulties."[17]

One central contradiction which affects the essential character of developed socialism is that between the universality of the productive forces of advanced society and the antagonistic quality of capitalist and socialist production relations. On the one hand, the shared level of development between advanced capitalism and developed socialism creates a common interest. Hence, "peaceful coexistence" or "detente" are both possible and necessary for the exchange of material goods and for the continued development of the entire industrialized world. On the other hand, the antagonisms between advanced capitalism and developed socialism limit the levels of exchange and exacerbate conflict. As Inozemtsev noted, "The STR opens up unprecedented opportunities to mankind for the most efficient use of natural resources in the interests of mankind and of progress."[18] Cooperation is essential to solve "a series of global problems whose resolution demands collective effort."[19] But cooperation cannot obliterate the competition between capitalism and socialism. The fact that the STR has been

15. *Razvitoe sotsialisticheskoe obshchestvo*, pp. 83-89.

16. *Sotsialisticheskoe obshchestvo: Sotsial'no-filosofskie problemy sovremennogo sovetskogo obshchestva* (Moscow: Politizdat, 1975), pp. 112-127.

17. Kas'ianenko, *Razvitoi sotsializm*, p. 129.

18. Inozemtsev, *Contemporary Capitalism*, p. 55.

19. N.N. Inozemtsev, "Problemy sovremennogo mirovogo razvitiia," in *XXV s'ezd KPSS i razvitie marksistsko-leninskoi teorii* (Moscow: Politizdat, 1977), p. 93.

led by a group of highly developed imperialist powers "is latent with real danger that these [new] opportunities may be used against the vital interests of society...."[20]

The historical competition between socialism and capitalism in the context of advanced modernization focuses upon the ability of socialism to use its inherent advantages to master the new productive forces more effectively and efficiently than capitalism. These advantages inhere in the basic values, property relationships, and institutions of socialism, which must shape and respond to the rapidly evolving productive forces. In other words, the advantages of socialism cannot be realized "automatically" but only by creative political-administrative efforts and accomplishments. Hence, the superiority of socialism in the historical struggle with capitalism must be demonstrated through the ability of developed socialism to carry out a more successful strategy of advanced modernization than is possible through the socioeconomic and political structures of advanced capitalism.

However, "a shift in the correlation of forces in favor of socialism" is taking place, and this shift is profoundly affected by East-West competition in the areas of science, technology, and production. Competitive advantage rests in large part upon the respective dynamism of the socialist and capitalist systems. A. Vakhrameev asserts:

> Marxists have never sought to reduce the balance-of-forces problem to its military-strategic aspects, but have always believed that it has various other ramifications: economic, scientific and technical, political and ideological. [These ramifications] cover not only the whole aggregate of present-day international relations, but also the state of affairs in the various individual countries, mutual relations between classes and parties in these countries, and social processes going forward in the modern world.[21]

Hence, the "correlation of forces" can continue to shift in the favor of socialism only if a developed socialist society strengthens its ability to accelerate and to manage the universal productive forces of the STR. For the STR is an open-ended and somewhat malleable process which is unfolding under both advanced capitalist and developed socialist conditions.

Paradoxically, East-West competition is taking place in an increasingly interdependent setting. The STR is an objective force for the internationalization of problems and opportunities. In his major work on peaceful coexistence, A.O. Chubar'ian commented that "The STR significantly influences the development of international relations, broadening and deepening economic, scientific, and technological ties between countries,

---

20. Inozemtsev, *Contemporary Capitalism,* p. 55.

21. A. Vakhrameev, "Detente and the World Balance of Forces," *International Affairs* (hereinafter *IA*), 1 (1979), 80.

especially those with different social systems."[22] But interdependence does not necessarily reduce conflict and competition. Rather, a developed socialist society must be capable of competing in new ways in a dynamic international division of labor. Also, a developed socialist society must be competitive in an international setting to be able to incorporate advanced technology within a state socialist framework, to enter into mutually beneficial trade and industrial cooperation agreements with other nations, and to serve as a model for less developed countries.

In short, developed socialism in the USSR is evolving in the context of "a new stage of international relations." Advanced modernization under both capitalist and socialist conditions creates the need for greater cooperation between the two types of societies. But technological advances produce more intense and qualitatively different forms of competition as well.[23]

IV. The STR and the New Stage in International Relations

Soviet leaders recognize that the STR is profoundly influencing international politics in the contemporary era. As N.I. Lebedev put it: "Scientific and technological progress makes the world smaller and brings it closer together. This process makes the problems of war and peace even more decisive. Wars, especially of a worldwide nature, were always tragic for humanity. But previous wars did not raise the question of the physical survival of whole countries and peoples. Under contemporary conditions, when a huge quantity of thermonuclear weapons has been stockpiled in the world, the life of every person on the earth depends on the rational solution of foreign policy problems."[24]

Soviet analysts identify at least twelve major changes which the STR has introduced into international life. Here, briefly stated, are these important Soviet perspectives on the STR as a force in present-day international politics.[25]

First: the STR has produced a "revolution in military affairs." The linking of scientific and technological developments to the conduct of war in the modern period has resulted in an extraordinary acceleration of the destructive capacity of weaponry. Modern weapons and all of the basic equipment of the armed services cannot be created and controlled without the application of the most recent scientific achievements. In addition, modern warfare

22. A.O. Chubar'ian, *Mirnoe sosushchestvovanie: Teoriia i praktika* (Moscow: Politizdat, 1976), p. 177.

23. G. Shakhnazarov, "New Factors in Politics at the Present Stage," *SS*, 1 (1977), 48.

24. N.I. Lebedev, *Novyi etap mezhdunarodnykh otnoshenii* (Moscow: Mezhdunarodnye otnosheniia, 1976), p. 68.

25. The purpose of this chapter is to identify basic parameters of consensus among Soviet analysts. For a discussion of the different emphases and disagreements among Soviet writers, see Erik P. Hoffmann and Robbin F. Laird, *The Modernization of the Soviet Union and East-West Relations* (forthcoming).

is becoming more and more automated. The capacity of the contemporary state to engage in warfare increasingly rests upon its scientific and technical potential. "The ever growing role of science in strengthening the military might of a state is now a clearly expressed pattern. Without considering this pattern, it is impossible to examine with sufficient profundity and completeness the present military capability and prospects for strengthening the military might of a state...."[26] Hence, the STR operates as a force for the continual modernization of armaments and of the modes and strategies for conducting war.

Second: the development of thermonuclear weaponry coupled with intercontinental delivery systems has created the possibility for mutual assured destruction of both superpowers. Security is not guaranteed by the continual modernization of warfare. The "revolution" in military technology has thus introduced a need for rational control over its development and use. Arms limitation measures are necessary to exercise such control. As Lebedev wrote, "The STR in military affairs has led to the creation of extremely dangerous means for conducting war...."[27] Significantly, he concludes that thermonuclear warfare "cannot be a means for achieving political goals in international relations. As a result of the new situation, the capitalist states have become interested in avoiding nuclear war and [in] nuclear disarmament."[28] Under such conditions, arms control talks are possible and desirable.

Arms control is necessary to solve another problem as well. The militarization of the STR, which Soviet writers consider to be caused by capitalism, blocks the potential for constructive use of science and technology in the broader human interest. Given successful arms negotiations, the knowledge generated by the STR might be used to deal with the global problems created by the STR itself (e.g., environmental pollution) and by other socioeconomic forces (e.g., population growth). "The STR places before mankind a series of qualitatively new global problems, the solution of which is possible only on the basis of the continual development of mankind's scientific-technical potential."[29] Successful arms control could make it possible for this potential to be realized.

Third: the STR is an objective force for the internationalization of economic life. As M.M. Maksimova affirmed: "In the conditions of the current STR, all countries are equally interested in making use of its

26. N.A. Lomov, ed., *Scientific-Technical Progress and the Revolution in Military Affairs;* translated and published under the auspices of the U.S. Air Force (Washington: GPO, 1974), p. 31.

27. Lebedev, *Novyi etap,* p. 108.

28. *Ibid.*

29. G. Khozin, "Razoruzhenie i nekotorye global'nye problemy sovremennosti," *Mirovaia ekonomika i mezhdunarodnye otnosheniia* (hereinafter *Memo*), 6 (1978), 34. On many themes discussed in this chapter, see especially *Memo*, 6-8 (1979).

achievements and in implementing the advantages of the international division of labor, which is providing ever new opportunities for the enhancement of social production, the acceleration of technological progress, and the establishment of higher living standards for the population."[30] The basic law of economic development in the advanced stage is for increased specialization of production and the deepening of the division of labor both domestically and internationally. Economic autarky is inefficient, leading to wasteful duplication of efforts by competing nations. In Lebedev's view, "Scientific-technological autarky is an impermissible luxury, for in the last analysis it slows down scientific progress and, consequently, the development of the productive forces of each isolated country."[31]

A nascent world economy is emerging which is neither predominantly capitalist nor solely socialist. The movement toward a rational division of economic labor between East and West rests upon the emergence of such a world economy, which Soviet analysts project will eventually become equivalent to a global socialist economy.[32]

The deepening of the international division of labor in the era of the STR will be reflected in the changing forms of economic interaction among nation-states. Historically, the exchange of end products and raw materials has been the basic form of economic intercourse among nations. But under advanced conditions, much greater international cooperation is needed at all stages of the scientific-technological-production process, in order to promote economic growth and efficiency.

One Soviet writer identifies four levels of economic interaction, ranging from the lowest degree of cooperation to the highest. They are: a) trade; b) scientific-technical and industrial collaboration, including specialization in production based on long-term trade and economic agreements; c) joint ventures, including scientific and technical cooperation up to the manufacturing stage; and d) coordination of economic policies, including the establishment of international economic organizations.[33] The attainment of the fourth level is a task for the Soviet bloc, and integration of the socialist economies is indeed the central goal of the comprehensive program of Comecon promulgated in 1972.[34] Soviet authors project that "The international socialist division of labor tends to intensify the interdependence of

30. M.M. Maksimova, "The Soviet Union and the World Economy," *SS*, 4 (1978), 130.

31. Lebedev, *Novyi etap,* p. 145.

32. See, for example, D.I. Kostiukhin, *Sovremennyi mirovoi rynok* (Moscow: Mezhdunarodnye otnosheniia, 1977).

33. E. Shershnev, *On the Principle of Mutual Advantage: Soviet-American Economic Relations* (Moscow: Progress, 1978), pp. 138-148.

34. *Kompleksnaia programma dal'neishego uglubleniia i sovershenstvovaniia sotrudnichestva i razvitiia sotsialisticheskoi ekonomicheskoi integratsii stran-chlenov SEV* (Moscow: Politizdat, 1972).

economic development in the individual socialist countries."[35]

Complete interdependence between East and West is not possible given the competition between them, but the developing world economy is rooted in the "objective" possibility that economic cooperation between the major socialist and capitalist powers can be strengthened at least up to the level of joint ventures. Thus, Soviet writers conclude: "The internationalization of economic life is an objective process in which ever deeper and broader economic interrelations are established between various countries and regions of the world, a process running through the whole of the modern economy. Indeed, it is inherent in both world systems and is worldwide. This objective historical process of internationalization of economic life is based on the growing concentration and specialization of production, which springs from the development of the productive forces...."[36]

Fourth: the ability of a state to participate in the advanced division of labor rests upon the capacity of its domestic economy to compete. The legacy of the autarkic economy has obviously limited the capacity of the Soviet system to succeed in this task. But, increasingly, Soviet writers recognize the necessity of dealing with the problem of modifying some of the processes and characteristics of the Soviet economy, so that the USSR may become more competitive in the international division of labor. Hence, Maksimova's important study of the Soviet Union and the world economy discusses the changes that must be made in the Soviet economy, in order to make it more effective in international competition. She concludes that "In the field of managing foreign economic ties, the further merging of [domestic] production with foreign trade activities is becoming an increasingly pressing objective."[37]

Fifth: the primary goal of the shift from autarky to interdependence is to meet expanding domestic economic needs and consumer expectations. As a major Soviet study on foreign trade concluded: "Foreign economic ties give us great additional opportunities for successfully fulfilling [our] economic plans, for saving time, for increasing the efficiency of production, for accelerating scientific and technological progress, and for attaining the primary objective—the further upgrading of the standard of living of the Soviet people."[38] Hence, foreign policy goals are perceived to be integrally connected with domestic economic challenges and pressures, and the importance of coordinating domestic and international objectives is receiving increasing Soviet attention.

35. P. Alampiev, et al., *A New Approach to Economic Integration* (Moscow: Progress, 1974), p. 26.

36. *Ibid.*

37. M.M. Maksimova, *SSSR i mezhdunarodnoe ekonomicheskoe sotrudnichestvo* (Moscow: Mysl', 1977), p. 185.

38. *Vneshniaia torgovlia SSSR: Itogi deviatoi piatiletki i perspektivy* (Moscow: Mezhdunarodnye otnosheniia, 1977), p. 30.

Sixth: nonmilitary forms of power are thought to be of growing significance in the international arena. Soviet officials have long contended that there are three centers of power in the capitalist world—the United States, Western Europe, and Japan. The power of the Japanese rests almost entirely on a nonmilitary basis, and the growing influence of Western Europe rests upon its economic growth and integration. Soviet analysts take such factors into account more and more when assessing a nation's capabilities and when projecting the future of "interimperialist contradictions."[39]

Seventh: the STR introduces new forms of dependency, especially in terms of technological needs. As G.A. Arbatov has commented, "States which cannot create a sufficiently powerful scientific and technical potential of their own are faced with a difficult dilemma. They have to choose between falling seriously behind...or tying themselves firmly to a country which possesses such a potential...."[40]

Eighth: Soviet leaders recognize that the STR introduces new forms of interdependence as well. The productive forces of advanced society require a vast quantity of raw materials to accelerate development. Highly developed states must secure diverse and stable natural resource bases. Hence, Third World countries which are threatened by the formation of new types of technological dependencies have at their disposal commodities which create reverse dependencies.[41] Oil is a particularly important example of the capitalist world's dependence on certain developing nations. In fact, the STR creates a demand for new raw materials by introducing industries capable of consuming previously unusable material (e.g., only an aluminum industry creates a demand for bauxite).

Ninth: the contemporary international order creates increased objective pressures upon nations to engage in the exchange of information. There has been a worldwide "information explosion." As Y. Kashlev asserts, "The objective social, political, scientific, and technological processes of the modern world are enhancing the role of information and propaganda in society and international relations."[42] This is due in part to a "dramatic and unparalleled expansion of communication technology."[43] It is also due to an "expansion of international economic, commercial, financial, scientific, technical, cultural, and other links...," as Y. Zakharov has argued.[44] The

39. See, for example, L. Maier, et al., "Zapadnoevropeiskii tsentr imperialisticheskogo sopernichestva," *Memo*, 12 (1978), 22-32.
40. G.A. Arbatov, "Nauchno-tekhnicheskaia revoliutsiia i vneshniaia politika SShA," in *SShA: Nauchno-tekhnicheskaia revoliutsiia i tendentsii vneshnei politiki* (Moscow: Mezhdunarodnye otnosheniia, 1974), p. 26.
41. R.M. Avakov, *Razvivaiushchiesia strany: Nauchno-tekhnicheskaia revoliutsiia i problema nezavisimosti* (Moscow: Mysl', 1976).
42. Y. Kashlev, "International Relations and Information," *IA*, 8 (1978), 82.
43. *Ibid.*
44. Y. Zakharov, "International Cooperation and the Battle of Ideas," *IA*, 1 (1976), 86.

exchange of information and contacts among nations must be accelerated, albeit within a controlled context. Zakharov concludes: "This is an objective process which stems from the general laws of the development of the productive forces and the requirements of the international division of labor. The STR is speeding up this process."[45]

Tenth: "The international division of labor in scientific activity acquires ever greater importance," Soviet analysts have noted.[46] Scientific research transcends borders, so that a Soviet researcher may have more in common with, say, a French specialist in the same field than with Soviet colleagues in his own institute. To prevent duplication of research efforts, international communication among scientists and technical specialists is necessary. This is particularly important in areas where the cost of research is extremely high. Moreover, certain types of scientific-technical projects (e.g., space and energy research) are so costly and complex that international financing is often required, or, minimally, a careful international division of labor is feasible to utilize existing knowledge and to reduce expenses.

Eleventh: a number of global problems have emerged whose resolution is in the joint interest of both competing systems. Inozemtsev has stressed the existence of common problems which arise from the contradictions in the development of the human race as a whole.[47] The archetypal "global problem" which requires scientific, technical, and managerial cooperation on an international basis is the control of ecological imbalances and decay. The very emergence of an environmental crisis within the structures of advanced capitalism *and* developed socialism poses the question of the superiority of socialist planning and management. But developed socialist societies, by drawing advanced capitalist nations into global environmental efforts, can demonstrate the inherent advantages of socialism. As R.A. Novikov asserts: "In this new epoch, the further progress of human civilization requires more than ever before the direction of social energy to deal with the preservation of nature, the utilization of natural resources, the rational and comprehensive management of the entire system of 'man-society-nature' from the standpoint not only of the present but of the long run, not only from a national but from a global ecological perspective."[48] Such international cooperation would extend developed socialism's capabilities on a broader global scale, and would promote change within the structures of state monopoly capitalism.

45. *Ibid.*
46. Y. Sheinin, *Science Policy: Problems and Trends* (Moscow: Progress, 1978), p. 122.
47. N.N. Inozemtsev, "The Nature of Contradictions Today," *World Marxist Review,* 9 (September, 1973), 18-19 ff.
48. R.A. Novikov, "Obshchaia kharakteristika osnovnykh mezhdunarodnykh aspektov problemy okruzhaiushchei sredy i prirodnykh resursov na sovremennom etape," in *Problema okruzhaiushchei sredy v mirovoi ekonomike i mezhdunarodnykh otnosheniiakh* (Moscow: Mysl', 1976), p. 31.

Twelfth: Soviet analysts recognize that the complexity and diversity of international interdependence transform the foreign policy machinery of advanced states. Traditional diplomacy is supplemented by the participation of growing numbers of politician-administrators and production executives. These officials work in ostensibly "domestic" functional areas, but have an increasing stake in defining the nature of the foreign policy interests of the state. Internal policymaking and organizational coordination emerge as important foreign policy problems. In addition, traditional diplomatic policymaking is transformed by the participation of experts who must analyze the international environment. This expertise is now considered essential to the formulation and implementation of feasible and effective national policies.[49]

V. Conclusions

Stalin's conception of "socialism in one country" combined a domestic strategy of rapid industrialization with isolation from the outside world. Brezhnev's interpretation of "developed socialism" links internal goals with a different international orientation. Current Soviet perspectives on advanced modernization are predicated on the broadening and deepening of interaction with the outside world. The Soviet occupation of Afghanistan and the USSR's cool relations with the United States and Japan in the beginning of the 1980's may seem to contradict this contention. However, the USSR's active pursuit of detente with the industrialized nations of Western Europe, and the USSR's persistent efforts to increase long-term trade relations with diverse Third World countries, suggest that economic interdependence is still a key part of the Brezhnev administration's integrated domestic and foreign policy objectives.

Present-day Soviet writers perceive the possibilities for peaceful coexistence and detente to rest upon the armed strength of the Soviet Union. In contrast to earlier periods, the military might of the USSR allows it to interact with the capitalist states from a position of strength, rather than from weakness.[50] Hence, one of the critical meanings of the "shift in the correlation of forces in favor of socialism" is the growing significance of Soviet military power in the world at large.

However, the Soviet Union's efforts to cooperate with the West in selected areas is based on confidence not only in the military capacity of the

49. N.M. Nikol'skii, *Nauchno-tekhnicheskaia revoliutsiia: Mirovaia ekonomika, politika, naselenie* (Moscow: Mezhdunarodnye otnosheniia, 1970). In particular, Nikol'skii analyzes the effects of the STR upon the structure of diplomatic machinery on pp. 163-188.
50. See, for example, Marshal A.A. Grechko, "Rukovodiashchaia rol' KPSS v stroitelstve armii razvitogo sotsialisticheskogo obshchestva" in *Problems of the History of the Communist Party* (May, 1974); abridged translation in *Strategic Review* (Winter, 1975).

USSR, but in its economic and scientific capabilities and potential as well.[51] Many Soviet officials recognize that the effective development and utilization of economic and scientific resources require a worldwide division of labor. Autarky has been wasteful, Maksimova and others argue. Correspondingly, economic growth and productivity and the further development of science and technology rest upon a process of interaction with other members of the developed world. This quest for greater effectiveness and efficiency in the science-technology-production cycle goes to the heart of the objective basis of peaceful coexistence—namely, the growing internationalization of scientific, technological, and economic life.

Soviet writers contend that the USSR, primarily because of its vast untapped natural resources in Siberia and elsewhere, is much less dependent on the Third World than the industrialized West, and thus has greater freedom to maneuver in the international arena. The need for Western technology to extract and develop Soviet energy, mineral, and other resources is a form of interdependence, not of dependence in the sense of vulnerability. Soviet leaders and social theorists argue that it will be to the mutual advantage of other socialist and capitalist countries to provide the technology and know-how to promote economic growth and efficiency in the USSR. If certain Western nations choose not to do so, adequate assistance will almost certainly be available from other capitalist nations. And, if not, Soviet scientists and engineers surely have the capabilities to develop their own new technologies—eventually and at greater cost.

Most Soviet writers do not prefer this second alternative, but it is perceived to be a viable one.[52] Some argue that the possibility of different types and degrees of interdependence *and* of autarkic development gives the USSR's leaders a greater range of choice in international economic and political activities than that of their counterparts in the industrialized West. Unlike Western dependence on foreign sources of energy, which will allegedly undermine the entire capitalist way of life, the Soviet Union's increasing participation in the world economy is an important step toward advanced modernization and the eventual establishment of a Communist society.

The historical competition between socialism and capitalism signifies that the Soviet Union's international activities must be turned to competitive advantage in order to demonstrate the economic, social, and ideological, as well as the military, superiority of socialism. The "shift in the correlation of forces in favor of socialism" means that forms of competition other than nuclear war must be relied upon to create a more fully developed socialist society and to demonstrate to the Soviet people and to the peoples of the

51. See Zhores Medvedev's perceptive comments on the Soviet approach to detente in *Soviet Science* (New York: Norton, 1978), pp. 137-203.

52. See footnote 25.

world its advantages over capitalism. Military superiority or parity with advanced capitalism in the context of the thermonuclear age is a necessary but not a sufficient means to guarantee the continued shifting of the balance of power in favor of socialism. Scientific, technological, economic, social, and cultural capabilities must be expanded for the Soviet Union to compete effectively with the West, as the STR runs its course throughout the advanced world.

In summary, the pressures of advanced modernization on the USSR make necessary greater interdependence with other industrialized and developing nations—communist, capitalist, and nonaligned. For example, close Soviet economic ties with the major countries of Western Europe are especially important when relations with the United States and Japan go sour. Soviet analysts are aware of the dangers of the new forms of dependency, as well as of some of the advantages of reverse dependency. But they also understand that without interdependent relationships, the USSR's productive forces will be reduced in efficiency and effectiveness, and their capacity to meet economic and social needs retarded or diminished in comparative or even absolute terms. In the long run, the isolation of the Soviet Union will impact negatively on the material well-being of society and on the development of the scientific and technological base for military power.

The STR has become at once a critical factor in the conduct of modern warfare and in the promotion of domestic economic and social progress. These paradoxical pressures for and constraints on interdependence decisively influence the cooperative and competitive dimensions of East-West relations. As Soviet analysts frequently note, the STR is a compelling "objective" pressure for detente, and detente in the contemporary era is "an historical process wherein competition and cooperation develop simultaneously."[53]

Detente is both a powerful "objective" and "subjective" force in the Soviet view. Shortly after the significant worsening of U.S.-USSR relations in the late 1970's, which was greatly exacerbated by the Red Army's occupation of Afghanistan, a ranking Soviet analyst affirmed:

> Detente has proved *so viable, stable and entrenched in the system of international relations, social life and the psychology of peoples, in the internal and external policies of countries belonging to different systems* that it could not be slowed down, weakened, still less, undermined, by the forces opposing the main trend in international development of the 1970's. Detente possesses major reserves, a considerable development potential. It has already become an objective factor itself, a motive force in the present system of international relations.[54]

---

53. Shakhnazarov, "New Factors," 48.
54. V. Gantman, "Detente and the System of International Relations," *SS*, 2 (1980), 180 (emphases in original).

Thus, leading Soviet officials in the early 1980's continue to insist that the *USSR's* conception of detente is the only feasible mode of conducting East-West relations in the current and emerging international systems.[55]

Above all, Soviet leaders seek to promote those forms of interaction between capitalism and socialism which enable the USSR to realize its allegedly superior potential to fulfill material and spiritual needs. Hence, Soviet foreign policy still consists of selective cooperation and conflict with the West—for example, the avoidance of direct military confrontation, on the one hand, and unceasing "ideological struggle," on the other. This current Soviet policy is surely intended to influence the thinking and behavior of Western leaders, especially those in the United States. Also, praise of the decade-old Brezhnev view of detente may be intended for *Soviet* ears,[56] because some Party and state leaders might be inclined toward all-out confrontation with the United States and a militant challenge to the Western alliance. But the preponderant majority of Soviet officials—especially those with a vested interest in economic interdependence—still seems to favor the ever-changing blend of competition and cooperation that the Brezhnev administration has termed "detente."

55. *Ibid.*, 177. See the additional quotes from Gantman's article in the introductory essay to this section.

56. E.g., *ibid.*, 177, 180 ff.; and G.A. Arbatov, "Vneshniaia politika SShA na poroge 80-kh godov," *SShA,* 4 (1980), 43-54.

Concluding Reflections on the SALT Experience *

In offering these closing reflections on SALT, it may be useful to recall that the SALT experience has been more than a lengthy set of arms control negotiations aimed at agreements on the limitation of strategic arms. Now in its tenth year, SALT also has become a pivotal aspect of great-power relations between the United States and the Soviet Union, a medium through which some accommodation of both the disparate political interests and the perceived strategic necessities of the two sides has been sought.

SALT's Dual Political-Strategic Character

As a political phenomenon, SALT in the early seventies helped to facilitate the passage from cold war to detente. In the process, what might be called a symbiotic relationship developed between SALT and detente, each in a sense seeming to be a necessary condition for the other. While some semblance of progress in SALT has been useful periodically to give detente a boost, it also appears probable that SALT would become increasingly dif-

*Reprinted from Thomas W. Wolfe, *The SALT Experience* (Cambridge, Mass.: Ballinger Publishing Co., 1979), pp. 243-263, by permission of the author, the publisher, and The Rand Corporation. Copyright 1979, Ballinger Publishing Company.

ficult to pursue in the absence of a detente climate. At least, the reaching of agreements would seem likely to become a still more protracted and difficult process, as suggested perhaps by the strung-out history of SALT II, which paralleled a perceptible cooling of detente relations between the United States and the Soviet Union after the high point of the 1972 SALT I accords.

The intimate link between SALT and detente in the political dimension, however, should not obscure the fact that the negotiations in SALT must also address the strategic concerns of each side. Here one finds that the political and strategic functions of SALT have sometimes been out of phase, so to speak. The two answer to somewhat different imperatives and time scales, so that agreements that may have helped to lubricate Soviet-American political relations at a given temporal juncture may not have served to satisfy perceived strategic needs.

SALT I, for example, was politically successful as a benchmark in the warming of Soviet-U.S. relations. But it left important strategic concerns on both sides unassuaged. The U.S. side came away bothered by failure of the accords to relieve the potential Soviet missile threat to the survivability of Minuteman, and by differential quantitative force levels intended to compensate the Soviet Union for a notable, but not necessarily permanent, U.S. technological lead. For its part, the Soviet side's concern to close the qualitative gap in certain strategic technologies, especially MIRV, had not been met, nor had its attempt to defuse the threat of U.S. forward-based systems in Europe been satisfied. SALT I did, of course, bring the two sides into strategic agreement on the ABM issue, although their differences on other issues, such as MIRV, missile throwweight, and FBS, persisted into SALT II.

What was probably the basic strategic deadlock in the pre-Vladivostok phase of SALT II found the Soviet Union determined not to allow significant constraints upon its new fourth-generation missile programs and, above all, its hard-won, but as yet undeployed, MIRV systems. The U.S. side, responsive in part to domestic political pressures, felt that it must rectify the numerical imbalances of the Interim Agreement and, at the same time, maintain some margin of MIRV advantage as insurance against the future linking of superior Soviet throwweight with MIRV technology.

In SALT II, the Vladivostok transaction of November 1974, which came after a two-year negotiating stalemate, probably answered primarily to a need felt on both sides to give detente a political shot in the arm, though it also dealt with the unequal-numbers legacy of SALT I. In its strategic dimension, the Vladivostok tentative accord probably was possible because it set quantitative levels high enough to suit the Soviet side and left enough room to accommodate most of the planned R & D and force modernization programs on both sides. However, though the range of strategic differences was somewhat narrowed, this seeming convergence was in part illusory, as became abundantly clear after Vladivostok when the attempt to draft a follow-up SALT II agreement encountered not only a number of obdurate strategic-technical issues such as those centering on the Soviet Backfire bomber and American cruise missiles, but also a deterioration in Soviet-American political relations.

In the post-Vladivostok SALT II negotiations, stretching out for more than four years, both reductions of strategic offensive arms and qualitative limitations were introduced in SALT as serious propositions for the first time, posing more complex problems than the task of establishing force-level ceilings, upon which in essence the negotiations on strategic offensive arms had previously been concentrated. However, the tolerance of domestic political constituencies in both the United States and the Soviet Union for radical moves in the direction of reductions and qualitative limitations was such that only relatively modest measures dealing with these matters found their way into the "three-tier" SALT II accord—in effect, postponing most of the hardcore problems posed by steep reductions and qualitative restrictions until SALT III.

Throughout SALT I and II, the political-strategic duality of the SALT process has operated to create what might be called a "SALT imperative" —a stake in avoiding actions, strategic or political, that might seriously threaten to derail further negotiations. This imperative certainly has been strained at times, and its durability could become more questionable should the utility of SALT as perceived in the West decline greatly and thus weaken pressure on political leaders to produce SALT "results." How SALT is perceived after about a decade of operation is therefore a matter of some interest.

Several Ways of Looking at SALT

One way of looking at SALT is to see it as an institutional process that has taken on an important role in the historical readjustment of the global-power and political relationship between the United States and the Soviet Union. In this view of SALT, which is essentially the one underlying the opening remarks of this chapter, its process may contribute something to "solving" strategic and political problems, but it is unlikely to culminate in some climactic end product, such as a permanent agreement that will define and govern the Soviet-American strategic relationship indefinitely. Rather, SALT is seen more as a process for establishing rules of the game pro tempore for strategic competition—rules requiring redrafting from time to time, if only because they are reflective of what is essentially a changing and dynamic political-power relationship.

Obviously, there are also other ways of looking at SALT that merit comment. At the risk of some oversimplification, one can identify at least three other distinct schools of thought in the West about the nature of SALT and what it can be expected to accomplish.

At one end of the spectrum, there is a school that regards SALT as the only realistic alternative to an unbridled nuclear arms race that neither side could win, and which both therefore must be equally interested in avoiding.[1] Given the maintenance of some "reasonable" level of strategic retaliatory forces for nuclear deterrence, mutual limitation agreements negotiated in SALT are seen to be greatly preferable to unilateral strategic programs as a means to preserve deterrent stability and enhance national security. Failure to achieve a major new SALT agreement or series of agreements to replace the SALT I Interim Agreement on strategic offensive arms would, in this view, have a number of very undesirable consequences, including higher defense expenditures, sharp deterioration of Soviet-American relations, and increased danger of nuclear war. Hence, the tendency of this school is to argue that even an agreement with many imperfections is better than no agreement at all.

At the opposite end of the spectrum is a school of thought that sees SALT as an essentially unsatisfactory alternative to unilateral strategic planning, even though ongoing negotiations may be politically necessary.[2] Unilateral planning and programs are seen to be more important foundations of deterrence and national security than the kinds of arms control agreements the Soviets have been, or are likely to be, willing to sign, and therefore SALT bargaining needs should not be allowed to dictate the U.S. strategic posture. Should SALT begin to drive strategic policy and become an end in itself, it could damage rather than enhance U.S. national security and political interests, especially those related to the Western alliance system. Failure to achieve a major new SALT agreement would not fundamentally alter U.S.-Soviet relations, in this view, because the basic adversary relationship between the two has never been affected much one way or the other by arms control agreements. Nor would the absence of a SALT II accord necessarily precipitate a new arms race, since SALT undertakings have been essentially tailored to accommodate unilaterally planned strategic programs in any event.

Somewhere about midway between these opposite ends of the spectrum is another perspective that gives SALT good marks as a kind of continuous diplomatic institution useful for "registering" changes in the strategic

1. For a representative statement reflecting this school of thought, see Senator Frank Church *Strategic Arms Limitation Talks and Comprehensive Test Ban Negotiations,* Report to the Committee on Foreign Relations, Senate, August 11, 1978, sanitized and made public, September 1978.

2. For articulate expressions of this school of thought, see Edward N. Luttwak, "Why Arms Control Has Failed," *Commentary,* January 1978, pp. 19-28; Colin S. Gray, "The End of SALT? Purpose and Strategy in US-USSR Negotiations," *Policy Review,* Fall 1977, pp. 31-46.

balance brought about primarily by unilateral efforts, and for trying to establish broad parameters within which future U.S.-Soviet strategic competition may operate.[3] SALT, in this view, is only marginally relevant, if at all, to "solving" U.S. strategic problems like the survivability of land-based missile forces, but at the same time, it is not to be blamed for past failure to resolve problems that were either essentially unsolvable or clearly in the province of unilateral remedial measures. From this standpoint, perhaps the principal recommendation for SALT agreements has lain in their symbolic-political value as a manifest of superpower ability to both compete and cooperate, but even this attribute could decline in value if the negative effects of a new SALT agreement were to constrain unilateral efforts to remedy U.S. strategic and related political problems.

Which of these several viewpoints most aptly conveys the "real" nature of SALT is certainly moot, but the last no doubt comes closest to capturing what Richard Burt, one of SALT's more astute observers, has described as a mood of diminishing optimism and lowered expectations about SALT in the West.[4] In the past few years this mood has crept over many in the West who had initially greeted the negotiations with enthusiasm, and who believed that the SALT I accords meant that the Soviet leadership had come to share prevailing Western notions of deterrent stability—based essentially on not trying to defend hostage populations, and on avoiding unilateral measures that would threaten the survivability of nuclear retaliatory forces.

The erosion of earlier expectations can be attributed to many factors, among which perhaps two of the more important ones have been discussed at some length in this study of the SALT experience. One—the long and often frustrating track record of negotiations in SALT II itself, testifying to the difficulty and complexity of trying to bring the disparate strategic forces of the two sides under a common SALT regime. The other—the uninterrupted momentum of Soviet strategic force modernization, involving large investment in successive generations of new and improved strategic systems and posing serious questions about what Soviet SALT policy and objectives might be.

Comparing Soviet and U.S. SALT Aims

Assumptions widely held during the SALT I period credited the Soviet Union and the United States with much the same set of aims in SALT, which might be summarized as follows: (1) to freeze the strategic balance at the level of parity; (2) to stabilize mutual deterrence; (3) to regulate the

---

3. An able expositor of this school of thought is Richard Burt. See his "The Risks of Asking SALT to Do Too Much," *The Washington Review,* January 1978, pp. 19-33, and "The Scope and Limits of SALT," *Foreign Affairs,* July 1978, pp. 751-70.
4. Burt, in *The Washington Review,* January 1978, p. 19.

strategic competition so as to reduce its resource costs, lower the risks of accidental nuclear war outbreak, and discourage the need for new cycles of improved strategic weapons systems.

It is unlikely, of course, that these ostensible aims ever enjoyed unanimous assent on either side, but the relevant point here is that despite the Soviet Union's continuing public commitment to the success of SALT, there has been growing doubt whether Soviet criteria for "success" in SALT have ever necessarily matched the aims the USSR was once thought to share with the United States. If not, what then can usefully be said about the nature of Soviet SALT policy and objectives, including how and why they may differ from those of the United States?

Soviet SALT policy has had several distinctive characteristics. First, it has been pursued as an integral element of a broader "detente diplomacy," intended among other things to buttress Soviet military power by helping to limit the military-industrial and political response of the United States to the growth of Soviet strategic power. In essence, whereas the primary U.S. SALT aim was to try to stabilize the strategic relationship on the basis of common value assumptions, the Soviet Union's basic strategic aims were to use SALT to protect Soviet strategic gains of the recent past and to improve its future competitive position. In this process, a subsidiary Soviet objective has been to try to contain particular U.S. strategic programs that Moscow has found most disturbing—Safeguard, Trident, the B-1, MX, cruise missiles, among others.

Second, in the service of Soviet aims, the SALT negotiations have had several important political functions, the foremost perhaps having been to "validate" Soviet claims to be a superpower. Another, based on recognition of "strategic equality" between the superpowers, has been to weaken European confidence in the U.S. commitment to the defense of Europe. Helping to ensure against playing of the "Chinese card" at Soviet expense also has been a useful political function from the Soviet viewpoint of the bilateral Soviet-American SALT connection.

Third, Soviet policy probably has not counted upon being consistently able to exercise direct constraints upon U.S. technological and economic capabilities through SALT, but using SALT for indirect influence upon what Vernon Aspaturian has termed the U.S. technological-economic "mobilization potential" appears to have been a considered Soviet aim.[5] Probably the best example was the ABM Treaty, calculated to prevent this potential from being mobilized by the United States deploying an ABM system that the Soviet Union was not in a position to match. Accepting constraints upon their own ABM effort was a price the Soviets proved willing to

---

5. Remarks by Professor Vernon Aspaturian, during arms control seminar at the annual convention of the American Association for the Advancement of Slavic Studies, Washington, D.C., October 14, 1977. From the author's notes.

pay in order to block the deployment of U.S. technology and resources in this field.[6]

Apart from the major exception of the ABM case, and acceptance of a number of less consequential constraints upon Soviet strategic forces as a necessary sacrifice to keep the SALT process alive, a fourth salient characteristic of Soviet SALT policy has been its stout resistance to SALT proposals involving alterations of Soviet military-industrial practices or force plans and doctrine. It has been this latter aspect of Soviet SALT policy that has contributed most to the impression that the SALT process has in no significant way diverted Soviet strategic thinking from its focus upon war-fighting and survival capabilities as inseparable from effective deterrence.

The salient prescription of deterrence in Soviet strategic thinking has been that the better the armed forces are prepared to fight and win a nuclear war, and the society to survive its effects, the more effectively a potential adversary will be deterred.[7] The fact that most of the Soviet political and military leaders have tended to equate effective deterrence with superior warfighting capability does not mean that they have been planning to start a nuclear war, as sometimes claimed or inferred, but this outlook has left them unreceptive to such doctrines as mutual assured destruction—the basic strategic rationale that has tended to inform American SALT policy.[8]

The strategic, political, and conceptual differences between the two sides that in the last analysis probably underlie their differing aims in SALT grow essentially out of the continuing rivalry of the two global powers as exemplars of opposing sociopolitical systems. Without trying to elaborate here on all these differences, one may note a few crucial asymmetries that appear to lie at the heart of the matter.

Apart from disparate strategic conceptions such as those mentioned above regarding what it takes to create effective nuclear deterrence, the most troublesome asymmetries are to be found in the underlying political premises upon which the two parties in SALT have been operating. Throughout most of SALT I and II, the American attitude toward SALT has been mainly informed by the general belief that mutual agreement to regulate strategic competition would promote better U.S.-Soviet relations and contribute to a more stable world environment within which the two global powers could mediate their conflicting interests with less strain upon

6. See Thomas W. Wolfe, *The SALT Experience*, The Rand Corporation, Santa Monica, 1979, Chapter 6, p. 130f.

7. Thomas W. Wolfe, *The SALT Experience*, Chapter 5, pp. 108-09.

8. See Thomas W. Wolfe, *The SALT Experience*, Chapter 1, p. 7.

the existing international order and its established institutions.

Although the Soviet Union also undoubtedly has had an interest in improving U.S.-Soviet relations for a variety of reasons, including the avoidance of dangerous confrontations that might lead to nuclear war and gains to be had from such detente dividends as technology transfer, Soviet interest has stopped well short of cherishing SALT as a means of shoring up the established international order. Rather, the Soviet Union has sought to persuade the United States to accede gracefully to a "fundamental restructuring" of the old international order, or failing this, at least to discourage its "imperialist" adversary from blatantly obstructing the process. In short, SALT and detente, as well as Soviet military power itself, are all seen as instruments of policy useful in one way or another to keep the United States from trying to arrest what, from the Soviet viewpoint, constitutes an inevitable, though admittedly uneven, process of transition to a new "correlation of forces" in the world favorable to the Soviet Union and other "fraternal" countries.

The pragmatic U.S. conception of SALT as part of an ongoing, interactive process involving both competition and accommodation, but essentially aimed at optimizing mutual gains and implying observance by both parties of the same basic set of political ground rules, thus stands in sharp contrast to the teleological Soviet view of history in which SALT is seen as one element in a broad strategy for helping to bring about a preordained shift in the structure of world politics to the advantage of the Soviet Union.

Can SALT Produce Useful Agreements?

Whether such fundamentally dissimilar conceptions can ever be bridged by agreements in SALT seems unlikely. But the relevant question is whether useful SALT agreements can be reached despite such divergent views of its purpose.

For those persuaded that agreements already reached in SALT have indeed been useful on balance for one reason or another, such as curbing the ABM dimension of the arms race, strengthening strategic stability, establishing a precedent for offensive arms restraints, or helping to improve Soviet-U.S. relations, the question tends to answer itself in the affirmative. For those believing that SALT has helped to undermine rather than strengthen strategic stability, to mask the momentum of Soviet weapons programs, and to dampen U.S. unilateral responses needed to repair a deteriorating strategic balance, the answer may well appear negative.

In either case, the point seems to be that judgments as to whether SALT can produce useful agreements depend more on how particular SALT outcomes are perceived in terms of benefits outweighing defects or vice versa, than upon underlying differences of purpose.

Again, the ABM Treaty serves as a relevant illustration. The two sides had different motives for the treaty—those of the Soviet Union probably being dominated, as noted above, by a desire to foreclose competition in an area where the USSR was technologically lagging. The treaty did prove compatible, however, with U.S. aims of shoring up functional strategic stability, and in that context therefore could be regarded as a useful agreement.[9]

For that matter, it might even be argued that the most antithetical political-ideological motivations could conceivably contribute, under some circumstances, to desirable SALT outcomes. For example, should the Soviet leadership come to feel strongly that detente must be preserved in order to keep the United States sedated, so to speak, during a delicate transitional period of history and that new SALT agreements acceptable to the United States were, in turn, necessary to keep detente alive, this interest might override any preferences on the Soviet side for a strategic planning approach bent on maximizing relative advantages for the Soviet Union. If so, one might find a certain irony in a situation where detente politics aimed at constraining the United States could turn out to have a double edge, acting also to circumscribe the avenues available to the Soviet Union for enhancing its own proper position.

SALT Constraints Versus Unilateral Elbowroom

Perhaps the essence of the SALT experience that emerges from this study is the inherent strain—internal contradiction might be a more apt term—between the professed SALT goal of seeing mutually acceptable limits upon strategic forces and the deep-seated impulse to preserve as much unilateral strategic elbowroom as possible.

This inner contradiction has shown up at each major juncture in the history of SALT. It was, of course, present at the very beginning, when the United States entered SALT hoping to slow down the momentum of the Soviet strategic buildup and perhaps to freeze the strategic status quo at a then-favorable level, but unwilling to forgo the unilateral insurance of pressing on with a MIRV deployment program. The Soviet Union, for its part, while prepared to entertain selective constraints that might impede the full realization of U.S. technological advantages in ABM and MIRV, could not bring itself to surrender its own unilateral opportunity to acquire MIRV technology, and in general, treated SALT I as a holding device to permit improvement of the Soviet realtive strategic position.

9. See Burt, in *The Washington Review,* January 1978, p. 32; Stanley Sienkiewicz, "SALT and Soviet Nuclear Doctrine," *International Security,* Spring 1978, p. 100.

Again in the May 1972 Interim Agreement there was mutual acceptance of some constraint—mainly the five-year "stop-in-place" on numbers of strategic missile launchers (which at least the United States and quite possibly the Soviet Union did not intend to exceed anyway)—along with provisions leaving ample room for unilateral programs of strategic modernization and replacement.

In SALT II, a conspicuous example of the tendency to resist long-term constraints that could compromise unilateral freedom of action was the abandonment in mid-1974 of the once-declared goal of a permanent and comprehensive agreement on the limitation of strategic offensive arms. Such an agreement, even though mutual, would have amounted to a strategic freeze, leaving no room for unilateral adjustment to the dynamics of an evolving power-political relationship.

The Vladivostok transition of November 1974 itself owed a good deal to the fact that at bottom it left both parties largely free to carry on most of their then-contemplated R&D and force modernization programs, and its freedom-to-mix provision was certainly a concession to unilateral choice in the planning of force structures. And as SALT II finally was drawing to an apparent close four years later, a similar tendency to leave a generous amount of unilateral breathing space again manifested itself in the three-tier SALT II arrangement, a central feature of which was its formula for constraints of limited duration during the Protocol period upon various strategic systems still under development.

Let it be said at this point that contrary to the unilaterally oriented tendencies stressed above, the proposition also can be made that SALT is gradually creating a new imperative to design strategic forces increasingly responsive to SALT-sanctioned criteria, rather than to unilateral preferences. With each new agreement, or even in anticipation of forthcoming agreements, the independent scope of each side to plan forces and weapons systems in accordance with its traditional practices and concepts may tend to shrink somewhat. (Witness the progressive extension of constraints from the stop-in-place measures of 1972 to the reductions and qualitative limitations introduced into the SALT II accords six years later.) Over time, the argument runs, the cumulative effect of this process of narrowing the scope for autonomous planning and of substituting for it a degree of "joint" Soviet-American strategic planning within the SALT framework could be to greatly reduce asymmetries in the force characteristics on each side, making it easier, in turn, to find further common ground for equitable strategic constraints.

While the long-term effects of SALT may bear out this proposition, which is not without merit, the SALT experience to date seems to yield little evidence that unilateral preferences and programs are becoming readily expendable under the impact of such a SALT imperative. Many of the most stubborn issues in the negotiations have involved resistance to adoption of common strategic criteria, the throwweight parameter being one example, and most of the agreements concluded or seriously discussed seem to have been aimed as much at minimizing encroachments on unilateral freedom of action as at conformity to mutually agreed restrictions.

It has been observed, incidentally, that the two sides in SALT sometimes have not even been able to agree on what constitutes a problem,[10] so that working out a "mutually agreed solution" can founder at the start on this awkward reality—leaving recourse to its own unilateral solution the only real choice available within a particular time span to either side.

Why the urge to preserve unilateral elbowroom has remained resistant to SALT-legislated constraints can be explained in a perfectly logical fashion —as a hedge against future contingencies, because neither side has been too keen about entrusting its ultimate security to agreements with a powerful adversary, or out of awareness on both sides that today's arms control contract could be tomorrow's regret in an uncertain world.

The effects of this phenomenon, however, seem not to have borne uniformly upon the SALT and related strategic policies of the two parties, who—as this study has indicated—entered SALT from disparate strategic positions and with differing strategic philosophies, styles of negotiation, and institutional processes.

Implications of Different U.S. and Soviet SALT Approaches

If a prime asymmetry in the SALT negotiating approaches of the two sides can be identified, it would appear to be that the Soviet Union has displayed less inclination to alter its own basic positions and to accommodate itself to the concerns and preferences of the other party for the sake of achieving agreements than has the United States. It may be argued that deriving some strategic advantage one way or the other from the negotiations makes little difference so long as the essential interests of each side are safeguarded in the actual agreements made. But the deleterious effects of a process in which the United States has more consistently assumed the burden of accommodation could be to fortify the apparent Soviet conviction that the correlation of forces is shifting in their favor and that "realistic" appreciation of this factor will eventually bring about further U.S. acceptance of the substance of Soviet SALT proposals.

In part the more tenacious approach of the Soviet Union in SALT can be attributed to well-known differences in political culture and negotiating tactics. But in larger measure it probably reflects the fact that the Soviet Union entered SALT as the strategically inferior party and came to regard the negotiations as a means by which it might be compensated for technological

---

10. Burt, in *The Washington Review,* January 1978, p. 32.

and other advantages historically enjoyed by the United States, in lieu of narrowing such advantages by unilateral effort alone.

For its part, the United States tended to concede to the Soviet Union its "right," as the world's other superpower, to shorten through SALT negotiations the time required to do what it otherwise intended doing unilaterally—that is, to catch up with the United States in the strategic fields where it was behind and thus achieve "strategic equality." Hence, U.S. acquiescence to agreements that were structured toward this end. In effect, the United States recognized as "legitimate" the Soviet view that SALT should serve to redress asymmetries favoring the United States—technological, geographic, alliance assets, and so on. At bottom, this meant that the United States was "discounting" its advantages in the strategic power arena at below market value for the sake of finding grounds for agreement.

In the course of time, SALT I receded into the past and the SALT II period grew longer without the big dividend expected by the United States having been realized—namely, an unmistakable decision in Moscow to rest the Soviet strategic catch-up effort at parity. This brought to the fore a question long implicit in the SALT experience, but seldom acknowledged in the formal channels of SALT negotiation: Where should the line be drawn at which meeting Soviet claims and preferences would cease to represent proper redress for past inequities and become pressure to tip the balance of strategic advantage to the Soviet side? Obviously the two sides have had different views about where this line should be drawn, but these differences have represented one of the core issues in SALT, which is "legislating" not today's but *tomorrow's*, strategic relationship and the boundaries of constraints that will apply to the differing military-technical-strategic systems of each side.

The purely military significance of how such boundaries may be drawn in SALT is probably of less moment than the political impact. What a gradual accession of strategic advantage to the Soviet Union could mean thus needs to be measured more in political than in narrowly military terms. Although not quantifiable, the political effect of SALT outcome suggesting to other countries that U.S. strategic power could be expected to decline relative to that of the Soviet Union in the years ahead would certainly not be to inspire confidence in America's standing in the world, but might well be to damage it badly. In some sense, a phenomenon akin to the 1978 decline of the dollar abroad could set in—an inexplicable flight of confidence despite a basically strong U.S. economy.

Influencing the Soviets in SALT

What kinds of approaches by the U.S. side may offer the best prospect of bringing the Soviet Union to subscribe to meaningful SALT agreements?

Opinions on this salient question tend to divide along essentially two lines. The first holds that the United States can best persuade the Soviet Union to move in the right direction by the setting of a good example, by the practice of "restraint" in its own strategic programs and by advancing serious SALT proposals that do not "threaten" legitimate Soviet strategic interests. The second view holds that real incentives to bring the Soviets to enter meaningful SALT agreements must pose unpalatable consequences for failure to do so. These would include giving unequivocal evidence of U.S. resolve to carry out whatever unilateral measures might be needed to ensure its security and that of its allies, including programs that could threaten Soviet strategic assets. Or, as expressed by Colin Gray in more picturesque language: "the coin of the SALT negotiations realm is money committed to weapons that speak to Soviet anxieties."[11]

After ten years of the SALT experience, it remains difficult to demonstrate which of these approaches—or any other combination of statecraft, countervailing military power, "bargaining chips," or economic and political "linkages"—may be best calculated to move the Soviet leadership in the direction desired by the United States.[12] One thing that many observers do agree on is that the United States must have a clear conception of how its own strategic policy and its SALT negotiatory positions mesh—which has not always been the case—[13]before it can hope to influence the Soviets effectively.

Several aspects of the SALT record may afford some instruction as to what kinds of U.S. activity have or have not helped to shape Soviet SALT policy decisions. First, to take the formal negotiating process itself, although the bargaining skill and diligence of the U.S. negotiating personnel at the SALT delegation level have been important in working out the substantive details of agreements, it appears doubtful that debate at the delegation level has ever had a real impact on major Soviet policy decisions. Decisions on significant issues seem to have been influenced, when at all, through high-level intervention from outside SALT—the back channel and periodic meetings at the summit or foreign minister level.

The bargaining chip approach affords an obvious means of attempting to influence Soviet decisions, but its efficacy is a contentious matter. Critics assert that it is a devious device upon which military planners have seized as the entering wedge for new programs that otherwise might not receive approval, but which once started usually acquire their own momentum and

    11. Gray, in *Policy Review,* Fall 1977, p. 39.
    12. See Thomas W. Wolfe, *The Military Dimension in the Making of Soviet Foreign and Defense Policy,* The Rand Corporation, Santa Monica, P-6024, October 1977, p. 44.
    13. See comments by Raymond L. Garthoff, cited in Thomas W. Wolfe, *The SALT Experience,* Chapter 4, p. 88.

thus tend to fuel the arms race and jeopardize progress in SALT.[14] Many strategic planners, on the other hand, are themselves less than enthusiastic about the bargaining chip approach on the grounds that it may distort sound planning, and that programs that should receive support on their own merits are subject to being cut back when negotiating exigencies no longer require them. Defenders of the bargaining chip approach, however, see the situation in a different light, asserting, for example, that the bargaining chip function of the U.S. Safeguard ABM system was an important factor in persuading the Soviet side in SALT I to reverse its traditional ABM position and to opt for the ABM Treaty.

In SALT II, the most conspicuous example of a U.S. weapons system that started out as a bargaining chip but became a nonexpendable program was the new class of "reborn" cruise missiles. Although the cruise missile unquestionably had an impact on the Soviet side, which made it a central issue in the post-Vladivostok negotiations, the Soviets have strongly resisted giving up any strategic systems of their own in order to get rid of the cruise missile "threat," thus leaving its efficacy as a means of exerting leverage on Soviet SALT decisions in some doubt.

Another situation with some relevance to how Soviet strategic and SALT policy decisions might be affected by a U.S. "threat" approach is to be seen in the case of the large Soviet land-based ICBM force. It has frequently been remarked that the Soviets have neither displayed much concern about the growing vulnerability of fixed, land-based missiles nor shown a particular interest in moving a larger share of their own strategic arsenal to sea, despite the fact that a preponderance of Soviet delivery forces and throw-weight potential is concentrated in targetable, silo-based ICBMs.

Since it is this same land-based Soviet ICBM force whose growing counterforce potential has been the principal source of U.S. concern about the survivability of the Minuteman leg of the U.S. TRIAD, U.S. SALT policy has sought to secure significant reductions in the size of the Soviet ICBM force and to encourage its restructuring so as to put more of the Soviet delivery vehicle quota in sea-based missiles of lesser yield and accuracy. The Soviet Union, however, apparently has had no incentive compelling enough to lead it to consider major alterations of the ICBM force in which it has such a heavy and ongoing investment. Such an incentive might exist if the vulnerability of the force were to begin bothering the Soviets, but the vulnerability problem will only become serious for the Soviet Union if the United States develops a commensurate counterforce threat.

In this connection, one of the complaints lodged against the three-tier SALT II accord was that its limits on heavy and MIRVed ICBMs were too

---

14. For an analysis covering various bargaining chip examples in SALT, with generally critical findings, see Robert J. Bresler and Robert C. Gray, "The Bargaining Chip and SALT," *Political Science Quarterly*, Spring 1977, pp. 65-88.

high to do much to reduce the Soviet counterforce threat against Minuteman, while its Protocol restrictions could impede U.S. unilateral operations to deal with the Minuteman survivability problem through such systems as MX—which would not only provide a less vulnerable basing mode, but could also pose a more severe counterforce threat to the Soviet ICBM force.[15]

The question posed by all this, therefore, is whether American, and for that matter, Soviet strategic interests might not be best served by a stepped-up U.S. counterforce program. Such a move, however, is strongly opposed by most of the arms control community, even though its effects might be to provide the missing incentive for the Soviets to move in the direction of more stable strategic forces, long a desideratum of the arms control community. The history of SALT abounds with ironies, and this may well be one of the more poignant ones.

At another juncture in the SALT record, a test of alternative U.S. approaches to dealing with the Soviet Union can be found in the case of the November 1974 Vladivostok transaction. In the several months before that meeting, James Schlesinger and Henry Kissinger had advocated somewhat divergent U.S. SALT proposals.[16] The secretary of defense apparently favored proposals with strict constraints and low ceilings as openers, to be backed up, should the Soviets respond negatively, with a hard-line warning that U.S. strategic programs would be put in high gear to match any unilateral effort the Soviet Union might choose to pursue. Kissinger's alternative would seem to have favored adjusting to Soviet preferences for the sake of consummating an agreement, leaving to subsequent negotiations the business of reducing ceilings and finding constraints to deal with possible future threats to strategic stability.

Which of the two alternatives may have been "best" in terms of helping to bring the Soviet leadership around to the agreement reached at Vladivostok is one of those elusive questions that defy categorical answers. But since the second alternative appears to have been closer to the policy track actually followed, it might be argued that Kissinger's strategy was more responsible for the outcome achieved at Vladivostok. At the same time it is also possible that the harder implications of the Schlesinger alternative—such as the strategic R&D retooling for which he had begun to call in early 1974 as preparation, if need be, for a matching competition—had been borne in on the Russians and served as a persuasive factor in the Soviet

15. See Thomas W. Wolfe, *The SALT Experience,* Chapter 11, p. 237f. See also Paul H. Nitze, *Consequences of an Agreement,* Arlington, Va., October 30, 1978, pp. 2-6. (Mimeograph.)

16. See Thomas W. Wolfe, *The SALT Experience,* Chapter 8, pp., 159-166.

decision to sign at Vladivostok. Thus, in a sense, the Vladivostok transaction might be said to have a least partly vindicated both the Kissinger and Schlesinger approaches.

Another potential source of U.S. leverage upon the Soviet Union in SALT has lain in the structural division between the executive and legislative branches of the U.S. government. The fact that there is no guarantee that SALT positions taken by the executive will necessarily be endorsed by Congress has probably given U.S. negotiators at times a good excuse to turn down what might appear to be unreasonable Soviet demands, although it is reported that Brezhnev also has played a similar game by hinting that he could not settle points at issue without ad referendum appraisal by his Politburo colleagues or the military.

With the general increase in U.S. congressional influence upon the SALT process in the course of SALT II, [17] and especially upon the chances of approval of agreements negotiated by the administration, a situation of some delicacy began to confront the Soviet Union. On the one hand, the Soviet leaders presumably considered that failure to conclude a SALT II agreement would aid circles in the United States hostile to the USSR. But at the same time they could not help being aware that an agreement on their preferred terms would face a rough reception in the U.S. Congress. Thus, despite their declarations that they would not let themselves be intimidated by a potential "congressional veto,"[18] the Soviet leaders were placed in a position where they may have felt obliged to adopt a less intractable SALT stance than their preferences otherwise would have dictated.

What Lies Ahead?

Perhaps the best way to conclude these reflections on the SALT I and II experience of the last ten years may be to venture a brief glance ahead at SALT III prospects and at some of the changes that could occur during the next ten years in the SALT process and the kinds of problems with which it will have to deal. Needless to say, the speculative element in these remarks far outweighs their predictive value.

A first presumption is that the SALT process will continue on into a SALT III period and beyond, although there was an outside possibility toward the end of 1978 that a failure to attain congressional approval of the three-part SALT II accords, after the intensive negotiating effort expended upon them might bring about an indefinite suspension or even collapse of

---

17. See Thomas W. Wolfe, *The SALT Experience*, Chapter 2, p. 47.
18. See Thomas W. Wolfe, *The SALT Experience*, Chapter 11, p. 229ff.

the strategic arms negotiations.[19]   Should that be the case, the voluntary extension of the 1972 Interim Agreement probably would become a collateral casualty, especially in light of the pressure of cumulative Soviet strategic weapons acquisitions, mainly SLBMs, upon the IA ceilings.

But assuming survival of the SALT II agreement, the follow-on SALT III negotiations would probably face the general problem (likely to be a never-ending one in the SALT process) of redressing asymmetries left by preceding agreements. In a more specific sense, SALT III might be expected to address, among other things:

* Further reductions and modernization constraints
* The unresolved problems of the "gray-area" systems—SS-20, Backfire, cruise missiles, FBS—as seen from the differing perspectives of the two sides
* Concerns about ICBM vulnerability and the crisis instability of strategic offensive forces, probably brought to the agenda by the U.S. side
* Various issues related to strategic defense, including civil defense and air defense, and possibly reopening of the ABM Treaty
* New questions arising around military activities in space[20]

With respect to further reductions, several kinds of difficulties might be anticipated. On the Soviet side, resistance to substantial reductions, as in the reaction to the Carter March 1977 proposals,[21] would probably be fed not only by Soviet military conservatism and the China factor, but also by the fact that the Soviet Union's international power and prestige rest largely on its massive military machine. To cut deeply into the Strategic Rocket Forces, the "leading" element of their military power, would thus be especially painful for the Soviet leaders, the more so because their technical-economic assets to compensate for any drastic cutback of Soviet military power do not compare with those at the disposal of the United States. For its part, the U.S. side, though less dedicated to high force levels, would have

19. Should failure to resolve the last two or three sticking points have prevented final agreement on a SALT II accord, this too could be a source of doubt about the continuation of SALT. At the time of writing in December 1978, it was not clear whether chances of a last-minute compromise or a hopeless deadlock then existed.

20. U.S.-Soviet talks separate from SALT, on banning antisatellite systems, had begun in Helsinki in June 1978. It was possible that any wider consideration of military activities in space might be kept in that forum also.

21. See Thomas W. Wolfe, *The SALT Experience*, Chapter 11, pp. 223-24.

to take into account the possibility that large reductions would breed the very strategic instability that its arms control policy has traditionally sought to avoid.[22]

Gray-area problems promise to intrude increasingly into the SALT process, making it very difficult for the Soviet Union and the United States to maintain the bilateral character of past strategic negotiations—even if both should wish to keep it that way in SALT III. The core issue could come down to insistence by America's West European allies on cruise missile deployments in Europe to offset a Soviet SS-20/Backfire threat against Europe. To deal with this issue, along with the perennial FBS question, which the Soviets have placed high on their SALT III agenda, will probably make it necessary for the two superpowers to "decompartmentalize" their strategic relationship and find a prescription—possibly a third negotiating forum—that will bring European (NATO and Warsaw Pact) interests into the picture.[23]

The ICBM vulnerability problem and strategic defense considerations could become closely joined in SALT III if what Deborah Shapley has called "technology creep" should begin to make ABM defense look much more practical,[24] thus inviting strategic planners to turn to relatively cheap missile site defense as an alternative to more expensive solutions to the Minuteman vulnerability problem,[25] such as the new MX mobile-based ICBM system. A unilateral planning move in this direction, of course, would run afoul of the ABM Treaty if hard-site defense of more than a single ICBM complex were contemplated, so that the question of changes to the treaty could become a major SALT issue. Whether an attempt to reopen the ABM Treaty would, as one observer has put it, "rattle the foundations of arms control itself,"[26] may perhaps depend to a considerable extent upon the general state of Soviet-American relations at the time—strained or mellow.

Several other factors that might in SALT III or beyond begin to shake the whole previously constructed edifice of SALT agreements can also be discerned upon the horizon. One of these is the dynamism of technology,

22. On the point that one of the paradoxes of arms control is its very success in reducing numbers of weapons could create a situation of dangerous instability, see Luttwak, in *Commentary*, January 1978, p. 22.

23. Harry Gelber, "SALT and the Strategic Future," *Orbis*, Summer 1978, p. 289; Jack H. Harris and William D. Bajusz, "Arms Control And Grey-Area Systems," *Air Force Magazine*, February 1978, p. 36. See also Burt, in *Foreign Affairs*, July 1978, p. 770.

24. Deborah Shapley, "Technology Creep and the Arms Race: Two Future Arms Control Problems," *Science*, October 20, 1978, pp. 289, 291. This is the third of a three-part series on "technology creep"—defined as incremental, often cheap, and usually inconspicuous advances in technology that can sometimes radically transform the capabilities of weapons systems before top policy leaders have become aware of the change.

25. It should be noted that there is considerable question whether missile site defense would in fact turn out to be a substantially cheaper "solution" to the vulnerability problem.

26. Deborah Shapley, "Technology Creep and the Arms Race: A World of Absolute Accuracy," *Science*, September 29, 1978, p. 1196.

leading to greatly improved accuracies of both ICBM and SLBM warheads, and the increasing development of space-based sensor and control systems.[27] Somewhere further down the line, there may be still more esoteric developments such as high-energy laser and particle beam systems, although their feasibility for strategic purposes remains at present a contentious matter.[28]

These trends in strategic technologies promise to make the tasks of arms control far more complex and difficult than ever before, especially with respect to verification. Essentially, the monitoring of SALT compliance in the past has amounted to identifying and counting rather large items of hardware: missiles, missile silos, submarines, bombers, ABM radars, and the like. But the relatively simple procedures required to verify these readily observable objects by unilateral NTM reconnaissance satellites—which helped to make SALT feasible in the first place[29]—may no longer suffice when the items to be verified include not only the existence of small, mobile, and poorly observable delivery vehicles, but also the qualitative attributes of constrained systems.

Taken together with agreements of increasing scope and complexity like the three-part, fifty-page SALT II accords, the problems of implementation and verification could overburden the SALT process to the point that either a return to simpler and less ambitious limitation agreements not relying on close counting and scrupulous verification,[30] or else increased tolerance of intrusive inspection, would be needed in order to keep the SALT process viable.

Another alternative, of course, which some observers have considered not unlikely, would be increasingly to seek solutions to some strategic problems, like Minuteman vulnerability and others in the "technical stability" category, outside the formal framework of SALT itself.[31]

27. The rapid transition to a new technological era, it has been pointed out, poses the problem that new classes of weapons "may very well not fit into traditional categories of strategic or tactical, nuclear or conventional, Earth-based or space-based." Such categories, however, have formed "the conceptual framework of current arms-limitation negotiating strategies." See Kosta Tsipis, "Science And The Military," *Bulletin of the Atomic Scientists,* January 1977, p. 10.

28. For a survey of particle beam weapons development in the United States and the Soviet Union, see the series by Clarence A. Robinson, Jr., "The Beam Weapons Race," "U.S. Pushes Development of Beam Weapons," "Key Beam Weapons Tests Slated," in *Aviation Week & Space Technology,* October 2, 1978, pp. 1-48, October 9, pp. 42-46. See also Richard Burt, "Debate on Missile-Destroyer Arms Picks Up Heat Over Soviet Moves," *New York Times,* December 5, 1978.

29. See Thomas W. Wolfe, *The SALT Experience,* Chapter 1, p. 4ff.

30. See Gelber in *Orbis,* Summer 1978, p. 295.

31. Burt, in *The Washington Review,* January 1978, pp. 32-33.

But if, for political or whatever other reasons, both sides continue to operate under some kind of imperative to maintain the SALT process and its institutions, and to seek further agreements dedicated to progressively extended limitations and controls over strategic forces, then a pertinent question that arises is whether the Soviet Union would consider the breaching of its traditional secrecy safeguards a fair price to pay for keeping SALT workable.

Some small chinks in the Soviet secrecy tradition have been opened in the course of SALT—such as agreement on exchange of a common data base, which may have appeared to the Russians a more momentous concession than to others from a different political culture.[32] Anecdotally, for example, a Soviet official is said to have remarked after the agreement to a common data base had been reached: "There goes 500 years of Russian history." However, the SALT record on the whole hardly encourages one to expect any significant relaxation of Soviet secrecy attitudes.

By and large, the period ahead can be expected to produce more strains and stresses growing out of SALT implementation and compliance issues than before, not only because of the more complicated verification situation mentioned above, but also because the stakes increase as limitations on strategic forces become more restrictive.

With respect to both internal arrangements on each side of ensuring compliance with obligations entered into and the institutional interface between the U.S. and Soviet sides in such joint bodies as the Standing Consultative Commission (SCC), the whole mechanism for supervising treaty observance and making adjustment to new or unforeseen circumstances will certainly be put to a more severe test in carrying out its functions than has been the case to date.[33] In view of the larger burden likely to fall upon the SCC in the future, it is rather curious that virtually no analytical attention at all has been paid it in the literature of SALT. Indeed, at some point in SALT's future, assuming that a series of basic agreements then exists, the negotiating delegations presumably would fade away—leaving the SALT process, institutionally, largely in the care of the SCC.

Without attempting here to anticipate the specifics of future compliance problems that may arise, one may foresee at least two general problems very much related to institutional asymmetries between the two sides. The first of these concerns what some thoughtful observers have considered to be a requirement for a degree of mutual trust—over and above verification machinery as such—in order to make agreements hold up. A statement

32. See Thomas W. Wolfe, *The SALT Experience*, Chapter 11, p. 227f, and note 51, on the limited character of the data base exchange.
33. See Thomas W. Wolfe, *The SALT Experience*, Chapters 2, pp. 34-35, 39; and 3, pp. 70-71.

made by former Senator James W. Fulbright in connection with the ABM Treaty and the Interim Agreement illustrates this viewpoint: "They depend upon the good faith of the parties to them. If we do anything to arouse suspicion on the part of the other party that may raise the question of deceiving or of not wanting to live up to the terms, of course the distrust will be mutual and destroy respect for the agreements."[34]

Given the asymmetrical nature in the two societies of what might be termed self-policing instiutions and practices—involving such phenomena as investigative reporting, fact-finding commissions, and other kinds of private and official inquiry into how the government conducts its business and lives up to its agreements—it would appear that a far more rigorous burden will fall upon the U.S. side to avoid self-policing accusations that might arouse Soviet distrust than vice versa. Indeed, should Senator Fulbright's injunction be widely heeded, one can imagine that in order to demonstrate its own continued good faith and trust, the United States might be prone to lean over backward not to raise embarrassing questions about possible Soviet violations in cases where only ambiguous evidence was available.

The second problem relates to the burden placed upon the national intelligence resources of each side to help monitor the observance of agreements and to detect violations. Here again, the United States would appear to shoulder the greater handicap, if only because its intelligence operations must cope with the problems of peering into a closed society, whereas the Soviet intelligence apparatus operates against a relatively more open one. What effect these particular asymmetries may ultimately have on the durability of SALT agreements is a moot question, though it would seem that they may contribute to a situation making it easier for the Soviet Union to stretch the spirit and the letter of SALT agreements, if it should so choose, than vice versa.

The future of the SALT process, as one sees it being shaped by the various forces and trends posited above, does not appear all that bright. In a nutshell, more complicated SALT agreements become more difficult to implement and verify; "technology creep" not only slips through the cracks in SALT agreements, but threatens to break into a trot or even a gallop that could produce a dynamic, ever-changing strategic situation with which SALT would be hard-pressed to deal effectively; and the institutions, habits, and practices underlying the competitive relationship between the two superpowers over the past decade will change little during the next one.

---

34. *Congressional Record*, 92d Cong., 2d session, August 3, 1972, p. S26692. It may be noted that most U.S. arms control officials have not stressed a requirement for mutual trust. The emphasis has usually been that SALT agreements rely on verification measures, not "on trust of the Soviet Union." See Paul C. Warnke, "Strengthening United States Security Through SALT," address in Racine, Wisconsin, June 29, 1978, U.S. Arms Control and Disarmament Agency release, p. 6.

But, if SALT cannot be expected to usher in the millenium, neither can it be considered a fruitless endeavor. Politically, so long as a kind of imperative exists to keep SALT alive, the spillover effect will also help to keep Soviet-American relations from breaking down, which could—in turbulent times—prove to be one of SALT's more important contributions. Even in a strategic sense, and with a bit of luck, SALT might do better than the SALT experience to date would suggest in helping to bring about a state of affairs approximating what one might call the arms control vision of the strategic future.

In this conception, the numerical growth phase of modern strategic forces has been brought to a close, roughly at a level of parity, by some combination of unilateral calculation and mutual agreement in SALT. The next major phase, to be marked by reductions and qualitative limitations on strategic forces, has now begun. Thanks to the Protocol period of the SALT II accords, a breathing spell has also been provided in which measures can be worked out to tame the more dangerous and dynamic technologies before their deployment can threaten strategic stability. Despite the difficulties ahead, self-interest can be expected to impel both parties to persevere in SALT, in order to enhance their own security.

TWENTY-THREE

FRANKLYN D. HOLZMAN
ROBERT LEGVOLD

The Economics and Politics of
East-West Relations *

Conceived modestly, the idea of East-West interdependence offers a convenient framework for exploring the intersection of politics with economics, of national economic goals with international economic relations, and, ultimately, of East-West efforts to increase economic cooperation with Western efforts to restructure international economic institutions. By *interdependence* we do not mean to imply a decisive set of arrangements, capable of impinging on the most fundamental economic and political choices of the other party. Rather, we have in mind a lesser level of mutual dependence in which both or all parties view cooperation as a useful but not a decisive means for pursuing some or all of their essential economic goals. More simply, we use the term because, better than any other, it underscores the difference between an economic relationship imposed by political confrontation, and reflected in economic warfare and autarky, and an economic relationship benefiting from the easing of political tension, evident in a common recognition of gains, political as well as economic, to be had from cooperation.

*From Franklyn Holzman and Robert Legvold, "The Economics and Politics of East-West Relations," *International Organization* 29, 1 (Winter, 1975) (Madison: The University of Wisconsin Press; ©1975 by the Board of Regents of the University of Wisconsin System), pp. 275-320. Reprinted by permission of the authors and the publisher.

Our primary focus is on the interaction of forces favoring and those obstructing a significant level of East-West economic cooperation—on the "dialectics" of interdependence. The first part of this essay introduces Soviet and East European reasons for wishing to increase their economic involvement with the West. Their eagerness to improve efficiency and growth by importing Western technology, capital, and technique constitutes a major, perhaps the major, *economic* impetus to interdependence. And it provides a justification, beyond the limitations of our individual expertise, for writing this article largely from the perspective of Soviet and East European interests.

In contrast, the second part weighs the fundamental impediments placed on the process of promoting interdependence by the organization and operation of the centrally planned economies. Again, our emphasis is on the Soviet Union and Eastern Europe, because we think that the techniques of central planning in these economies ultimately raise the most significant *economic* obstacles to an extensive interdependence.

In the third and fourth parts of this essay, we turn our attention to the parallel political impulse to and limits on growing interdependence. Part three examines the effect of a changing international order on East-West economic cooperation; part four examines the obstacles still posed by East-West competition and expressed in terms of national security. In both, we have made an attempt to assess the way that these environmental forces and constraints are refracted through each side's foreign policymaking process. Although the approach is comparative in these two sections, the comparison features the Soviet-American relationship.

In the fifth part we broaden our approach somewhat. In order to deal with the politics or dynamics of interdependence, several questions need to be raised. The issues become: (1) the calculations and strategies by which each side draws the most advantage from interdependence, (2) the shape this is likely to give to interdependence, and (3) the impact of East-West interdependence on other dimensions, including the process of institutionalizing a more coherent and stable international economic system. This yields in part six to a discussion of the consequences of increased economic cooperation between East and West for general monetary and trade-supporting institutions and, conversely, the significance of new international economic institutions for a growing East-West economic cooperation.

Interdependence and Communist Domestic Economic Goals

One key to understanding the present Eastern interest in expanding trade and investment with the West is the potential relationship between this trade and investment and the domestic goals of these nations. The major domestic economic goals of the Eastern nations are much the same as those of the Western nations, although they differ in the relative weights attached to them and in the intensity with which they are pursued. The greater intensity with which the Eastern nations pursue most of their goals is partly a function of the fact that in centrally planned economies, the responsibility for national economic goals clearly lies with the governments (since there are no significant private enterprise sectors), which in turn usually employ more direct means of implementing these goals than do Western governments. In what follows, we distinguish six domestic economic goals, viz., rapid growth, efficiency, full employment, price stability, a fairly equitable income distribution, and quality of life. We argue that economic interdependence with the West is desired as a means of achieving the first two of these goals but that it is either irrelevant or secondary to the achievement of the last four.

The major goal of the USSR in the prewar period was rapid growth. After World War II, following the Soviets, the Eastern European nations all adopted rapid growth as their major goal. Typically, rapid growth has been equated with industrialization. When, in the Council of Mutual Economic Cooperation (COMECON), an attempt was made by the USSR around 1960 to substitute international division of labor for universal industrialization, Rumania rejected the proposal because it meant sacrificing rapid industrialization for the privilege of remaining an exporter of agricultural and other raw material products. Undoubtedly, Eastern Europe would have looked to the West in the postwar period for much of the machinery, equipment, and technology it needed had this been possible. It was, of course, largely precluded by the cold war and the virtual semiembargo by the West on trade with the East, especially trade in products that might contain advanced technology or have strategic significance.[1] A new division of labor developed among the COMECON nations in which East Germany and Czechoslovakia became the major suppliers of machinery and equipment. Rapid growth through industrialization appeared to have been a successful strategy in the 1950s, for, as a group, the COMECON nations achieved an average annual growth of GNP of almost 6 percent.[2] The 1960s, however, were a different story. Even by official figures, the rate of growth of GNP declined relative to the 1950s by more than two percentage points on the average.[3]

Why have Eastern growth rates declined? The answers to this question may help us to understand Eastern motives in seeking greater East-West

1. Under Soviet pressure, the Eastern bloc was also consciously redirecting its trade inward. In our opinion, the pace of trade redirection in strategic products was dictated more by the West than by the East.

2. Maurice Ernst, "Postwar Economic Growth in Eastern Europe," in US Congress, Joint Economic Committee, *New Directions in the Soviet Economy, Part IV,* 89th Cong., 2nd sess., 1966, p. 880.

3. The average hides a wide variance, however, which ranges from a 6 percent point drop in the case of East Germany (10.4 to 4.4) to a ½ percent drop in the case of Hungary. Cited in Robert Campbell, *The Soviet-Type Economies: Performance and Evolution,* 3rd ed. (Boston: Houghton Mifflin Co., 1974), p. 120.

economic interdependence in the past decade. Economic growth in the 1950s was *extensive* rather than *intensive*. That is to say, it was due more to a rapid increase in employment and reallocation of factors of production than to an increase in the productivity of factors of production in the existing economic structure. Central planning authorities equipped with enormous powers put unemployed workers to work, moved underemployed peasants out of agriculture and into higher productivity industry, and generated very high rates of investment by reducing the share in GNP of consumption. (The less developed COMECON countries also gained by importing technology from the more advanced nations of the bloc.) However, the gains from reducing unemployment and from restructuring the economy are, of course, one-time gains; and, as Abram Bergson has demonstrated, it takes continually higher rates of investment, in the absence of changes in technology and the like, to achieve a given rate of growth as an economy develops.[4] Apparently, the exhaustion of possible large-scale gains from extensive growth was a major factor in the slowdown of the 1960s.

Evidence that intensive growth had not yet substituted for extensive growth is provided by data on changes in factor productivity. Labor productivity grew much more slowly in Eastern than in Western Europe and Japan, and capital productivity actually *declined* in Eastern Europe from 1961 to 1967, a fact recognized and discussed by Eastern as well as Western economists.[5] Bergson estimates that Soviet increases in GNP per unit of labor and capital (total factor productivity) declined from 1.7 percent per year during 1950-58 to 0.7 percent during 1958-67.[6] In short, the Eastern nations have been unsuccessful at intensive growth—at raising productivity levels—because they are inefficient. Central planning with direct controls and without the use of effective prices and markets can achieve extensive growth but is relatively inefficient in promoting intensive growth.

To achieve intensive growth, the goals of growth and efficiency must be joined. In earlier years, efficiency was largely ignored as a goal.[7] Now that continued rapid growth appears to depend on increasing economic efficiency, particularly in the more advanced socialist nations, efficiency has come to the fore. Greater efficiency is what the reforms in Eastern Europe and the USSR of the past five to ten years have been all about. Greater efficiency encompasses many facets of the Eastern economies, such as ensuring

4. Abram Bergson, "Toward a New Growth Model," *Problems of Communism* 22 (March-April 1973): 1-9.

5. Thad Alton, "Economic Structure and Growth in Eastern Europe," US Congress, Joint Economic Committee, *Economic Developments in Eastern Europe* 91st Cong., 2nd sess., 1970, pp. 63 and 42.

6. See Bergson, "Toward a New Growth Model," p. 3.

7. In fact, efficiency was sacrificed to the goal of growth in the USSR in the thirties and in Eastern Europe in the fifties. At one time or another, all of the socialist goals but full employment have been sacrificed to growth.

that supplies get delivered on time to the enterprises to which they have been allocated, reducing the number of unfinished investment projects, providing consumers not only with enough shoes but also with the right mix of styles and sizes, reducing the output of products no longer being purchased, improving the quality of products, obtaining reasonable gains from foreign trade, and so forth. More directly relevant to growth, greater efficiency also encompasses properly selecting investment projects, developing new technology, and, once having new technology available, getting enterprises to adopt it. We cannot stop at this point to explain all these problems in detail; some are discussed more fully in the next sections. We will say a few words about the question of technology, however, since it is important to our inquiry.

The major reason that plant managers did not introduce new technology in the prereform system was that they had no monetary incentive to do so. Their bonuses were tied to the achievement of output targets. If new technology increased the level of possible output, targets would be raised, leaving the manager no better off than before. Further, changes in technology were often risky—a learning period might be required during which bonuses would be sacrificed, and changes in supply channels might be involved (and these have often been difficult to arrange in a rigid supply system). As for the development of new technology in the first place, the problem has also been organizational. In the communist countries, there is a separation between research and development units and producing enterprises. Thus, there has been no constant feedback between the two as there is in most large Western enterprises. In fact, the research and development people in an industry may be quite divorced from the problems of the industry and may be working on projects that are of little or no interest to the relevant enterprises.[8]

The reforms that have been partially directed at increasing innovation and encouraging adoption of new technology do not appear to be very successful. As we show later, with the exception of Hungary, the reforms are conservative in the sense that they have been mostly designed to improve the existing system of planning with direct controls rather than to change the system radically by introducing markets, prices, and decentralized decision making. They are conservative because a radical reform that substituted market for controls would, in effect, be substituting the market for many of the people who implement the controls, namely, the Party hierarchy.

---

8. This portrayal of the difficulties that the socialist nations have in generating and absorbing new technology does not apply to high priority industries such as military and aerospace. In these industries, people in research and development and producers work closely together. Enterprises have no choice but to adopt whatever new technology is developed. Differences between technologies are often qualitatively important, and old technology is not acceptable. Plant managers in these industries do not have to worry about disruption of supplies with changed methods, since the industries have first priority on whatever materials are needed.

Moreover, allowing greater freedom of managerial decision making with reliance on market forces would undoubtedly threaten to spread to other sectors (e.g., If managers had more decision-making power, would not the unions attempt to increase their powers commensurately?) with an eventual possible impact on the nature of government control, the structure of power, and political freedom.

One other objective of the reforms needs to be mentioned here, namely, the desire to increase the static gains from trade. This has several facets, one of which is relevant to this section. One consequence of central planning with direct controls is that enterprises have little incentive to put out high quality products. This applies to intrabloc as well as to domestic trade. Thus, enterprises prefer to import from the West where possible rather than from Eastern partners, particularly those products whose quality can vary substantially and where the requirements of the importer can only be satisfied if the exporter takes special pains.

Interest in trade with the West, then has increased partly because of dissatisfaction with intrabloc trade, but more importantly because of its potential contribution to growth and effcency goals. This is particularly the case since the internal economic reforms for the most part are too conservative to remove deficiencies in the development and adoption of new technology. Even if they could be more successful, the socialist countries are sufficiently far behind the West in most sectors that importing technology makes good sense anyway. (A congressional study published in 1966 concluded that the USSR lagged behind the US by some 25 years in overall level of technology.[9]) Perhaps the import of technology is also, as we explore later, a means of avoiding more radical reform, at least for those entrenched elements that feel threatened by far-reaching reform. Finally, the Eastern nations are hopeful of financing imports of technology through credits in order to bridge both their "foreign exchange" and "savings" gaps. The foreign exchange gap is discussed in the next section; the savings gap stems in part from the fact that the output goals of the socialist nations are usually excessive, as well as from the declining marginal productivity of capital.

How much do the Eastern nations stand to gain from greater trade and investment with the West? The gains can come in four forms: increased efficiency of domestic industry stimulated by foreign competition, including further international division of labor; gains from the better quality and variety of products imported from the West; gains from the import of capital (i.e., borrowing); and gains from the import of technology. Unfortunately, none of these can be estimated very accurately. In order to suggest

9. Michael Boretsky, "Comparative Progress in Technology, Productivity, and Economic Efficiency: USSR versus USA," in US Congress, Joint Economic Committee, *New Directions in the Soviet Economy, Part II-A*, 89th Cong., 2nd sess., 1966, p. 149.

rough orders of magnitude, we present some mechanical calculations for the USSR. Before proceeding to these, it should be noted that it is not possible to measure the very important kinds of gains in domestic efficiency stimulated by foreign competition. However, it is hardly necessary to do so here, since, with the possible exception of Hungary, the central planners effectively protect domestic industries against competition from abroad and thereby exclude the possibilities of such gains. Only radical domestic reforms can change this situation. We turn now to some simple estimates.

Total Soviet trade is in the neighborhood of $15 billion each way, of which a little more than 20 percent, or $3 billion, is with the industrial West. Suppose that trade with the industrial West were to double (increase by $3 billion each way) at the expense of trade with Eastern Europe. Suppose that the gains from trade with Eastern Europe are 33.3 percent and that this were to double (or triple) by diverting trade to the industrial West. The total gain to the Soviets, under these favorable assumptions would be $1 billion (or $2 billion) a year. These figures must be put in the perspective of an annual GNP of $600 billion.

Suppose now that the Soviet Union were able to obtain credits amounting to some $20 billion over a five-year period, or $4 billion a year. Since gross investment at present is roughly a little below $200 billion, these credits would increase investment by a little more than 2 percent. With GNP increasing by about $30 billion a year, a 2 percent increase in gross investment each year could be responsible for a maximum increase in output of $0.6 billion a year for each of five years and thereafter until depreciated (assuming no difference in the technology embodied in the investment financed by credit as compared to other investment). We say *maximum* because this calculation ignores the contribution to output of labor and other factors. Further, credit repayments would eventually have to be made out of the increments to output.

Suppose now that the credits involved, additionally, the introduction of new technology. Since the technology would have to be paid for out of the credits, the increment to investment would be reduced but the increase in output from each $1 million worth of investment would be greater. How much greater is anyone's guess. We can say no more than to point out that the prospective annual increase in output, taking account of all benefits and costs, would be somewhat greater than in the previous example. And an increase in output of, say, $1 billion a year implies an increase in growth rate from 5 percent ($30 billion/$600 billion) to 5.16 percent; an increase in output of $2 billion implies an increase in growth rate to 5.33 percent;[10] and so forth.

10. We have not considered the case of an import of technology without credits. In this case, the gains would come only from the increase in capital productivity; there would be no increase in the rate of investment. Note: examples in the preceding three paragraphs are based approximately on 1972.

Under the assumed (favorable) conditions, it is clear that the projected gains to the USSR from more trade and investment with the West are substantial and very much worth striving for. A nation whose economy is always stretched taut and overcommitted will appreciate any additional resources that become available. On the other hand, a few billion dollars here or there is not going to make or break the USSR, nor will it substantially affect its declining rates of growth of output and of factor productivity.[11] As noted earlier, growth rates cannot be affected substantially by a small increase in the rate of investment. And while improvements in technology can affect growth rates, to do so on a significant scale requires more than just selected imports in particular industries; rather, what seems to be required, in our opinion, is a radical reform that not only would encourage indigenous development of all kinds of new technology but would also encourage the adoption of this technology by enterprises throughout the economy.

The smaller nations of Eastern Europe stand to gain somewhat more from increased economic interdependence with the West. This is because, being small nations, they all trade a much larger percentage of their GNPs than does the USSR. Further, being small nations, loans and technology from the West could conceivably be available on a more significant scale than is likely to be the case for the giant USSR. On the other hand, Western enterprises and governments may be more wary of making credit and technology available on a large scale to the smaller Eastern nations because, not having attractive exportables like oil and gas, they are not so good a long-run credit risk as the USSR.

What about the other goals? Full employment of labor and stable prices have always been very high priority goals of the socialist nations. These goals are much easier to achieve under socialism than under capitalism because of the greater power of the state to exercise direct controls—to employ the unemployed and to set wages and prices. Further, the socialist nations' achievement of these two goals is quite unrelated to the international sector. There is no temptation or need ever to resort to "beggar-thy-neighbor" devices to achieve full employment; nor is domestic employment ever threatened by imports, since domestic industries are thoroughly protected from competition. And, with the exception of Hungary, internal prices are not organically related to world prices, nor are they affected by trade in general as is the case under capitalism. However, it is important to note that the protection of domestic employment and internal prices from disturbance by external forces impedes radical reforms from opening the socialist economies to foreign competition and increased international interdependence.

---

11. Soviet planners may, of course, have unrealistic perceptions (from our viewpoint) of the possible gains from East-West trade and investment.

A just distribution of income within and between nations is a more explicit goal of socialist than of capitalist nations. The distribution of income
within the nation is a purely internal matter, and it is neither affected by nor
does it affect economic relations with other nations. Within COMECON,
the explicit goal is ultimate equalization of living standards between nations. While some equalization has taken place over the past twenty years,
this appears to have resulted from the simple fact that developing countries
tend to grow faster than more advanced nations, rather than from positive
policies.

Some positive policies have been pursued, however. For many years,
technology, blueprints, and the like were disseminated freely in
COMECON, which means that they moved from the more advanced to the
less advanced nations. There have also been capital flows between
COMECON nations, but on a relatively small scale and not always from
richer to poorer. These capital flows usually do contain an element of sub-
sidy or aid, however, because of the very low interest rates charged—from 2
to 4 percent. It has been estimated that total loans granted among all
socialist nations for 1945 to 1969 amounted to only $10 billion, or less than
$500 million a year. This amounts to a very small fraction of 1 percent of
donors' GNPs in comparison with official loans and grants by major
Western nations of perhaps two-thirds of 1 percent. Further, the capital
flows in COMECON appear to have been dictated as much by economic
factors as by "justice." China, perhaps the poorest socialist nation, was the
second largest lender.[12] To sum up, distributional equity appears to rank
low as a motive for trade and investment by socialist nations.

Quality of life is certainly a socialist goal. It is difficult, however, to pin
down its dimensions and the intensity with which it is pursued. If we look at
crude proxies, it might be argued that the more equal distribution of income
in socialist countries as well as their greater emphasis, at given levels of per
capita GNP, on expenditures on health and education and on subsidization
of the arts are indicators of greater concern with quality. On the other hand,
the relatively high rates of investment, low ratios of consumption to GNP,
and crowded urban living conditions are indicators in the opposite direction.

As far as specific quality factors, such as pollution, congestion, environmental destruction, and the like, are concerned, the socialist nations
are in much better shape than the Western industrialized nations for at least
two reasons. First, they are much less industrialized and also have not
allowed mass ownership of private automobiles. Second, they believe in

---

12. All Soviet bloc figures in this paragraph were estimated from Janos Horvath, "Grant
Elements in Intra-Bloc Aid Programs," *The ASTE Bulletin* 13 (Fall 1971): 1-18. The Western
estimates cited were for the 1962-65 period and were taken from Raymond Mikesell, *The
Economics of Foreign Aid* (Chicago: Aldine Publishing Co., 1968), p. 241.

"keeping their streets clean" and have enough unemployed marginal workers to do this at almost no cost to society. On the other hand, socialism provides no automatic solutions to the environmental and pollution problems that industrialization generates, and every horror story in the West has its counterpart in the East. It turns out that the structure of incentives in socialist enterprises is such that socialist plant managers are no more motivated to stop polluting than are private entrepreneurs. And socialist governments have been no more effective than those in the West in applying corrective measures.[13]

Quality of life goals provide little or no Eastern incentive to greater East-West trade or investment. It is leading to East-West cooperation, however. In 1972, a US-USSR Joint Committee on Cooperation in the Field of Environmental Protection was formed with 30 joint projects; and a twelve-nation East-West International Institute of Applied Systems Analysis was established, which will investigate, among other things, pollution control.

Thus, the incentive for increased trade with the West is explained primarily by the desire of the Eastern nations to maintain growth rates and enhance efficiency through import of capital and technology, as well as to improve the quality of products they import in everyday commodity trade. The gains from trade that would be forthcoming from radical economic reforms, which would open the Eastern economies to foreign competition, are voluntarily forgone. In this regard, the goals of full employment and stable prices can be regarded as impediments to greater interdependence, although they are probably of less importance than factors relating to internal power politics.

Economic Impediments To Interdependence

In this section we explore the limits to interdependence posed by the economic mechanisms employed by the Eastern nations to run their economies. Some of these factors were alluded to above; here we consider them more systematically.

STALINIST MODEL

The major difference between capitalist and communist economic mechanisms is the much greater reliance by communist states on direct controls rather than on market mechanisms in the allocation of resources. Before the economic reform movement of the late 1960s, output goals for major commodities of all the Eastern nations were established by the central authorities, individual output targets were set for enterprises or groups of enterprises, and supply plans specified to whom enterprises were to ship

---

13. See, for example, Marshall Goldman, "The Convergence of Environmental Disruption," *Science,* 2 October 1970, pp. 37-42.

their outputs and from whom they were to procure their material (nonlabor) inputs. The difficulties in planning and coordinating flows of many hundreds, even thousands, of commodities between hundreds of thousands of enterprises cannot be exaggerated. Nor can we exaggerate the problems raised by errors in the plan or unforeseen events. For example, suppose it appears that the steel target will be underfulfilled by one million tons. To increase steel output, it is necessary to increase inputs (hence outputs) of coal, limestone, machinery, labor, and so forth. But more coal, limestone, and machinery require more steel, labor, etc.—and, again, more coal, limestone, and machinery, and so forth. Any error or shortfall in any single output or flow in the interrelated matrix of transactions affects many other sectors or flows and constitutes a nightmare for the planners.

Second, output and supply-planning problems have been exacerbated by the fact that, in practice, planning has chronically amounted to overfull employment planning. That is to say, the plans are drawn too taut, with insufficient allowance for reserves, errors, shortfalls in productivity, and so forth. The result is that output targets never can all be achieved with projected supplies of inputs and productivity changes; in effect, demand is greater than supply, as with inflation in a free-market economy. This condition, of and by itself, is serious. And, as noted, it complicates still further the coordination problems (described above) that are faced by the central planners.[14]

Third, commodity prices in the Eastern bloc nations are usually described as irrational. They are set by the planners, remain fixed for long periods of time, and are not usually market-clearing prices. Not only is demand largely ignored, but the cost or supply side is rendered a poor guide to price setting because of improper accounting for rent, interest, and profits (reflecting a lack of markets for nonlabor factors of production), extensive use of subsidies and sales taxes, and adherence to average rather than to marginal cost pricing. With prices so irrational, planners must, of course, use direct controls to allocate resources; conversely, prices are irrational partly because direct controls rather than decentralized markets are used in allocation.

FOREIGN TRADE BEHAVIOR

From these three features of what might be called Stalinist central planning with direct controls, one can explain several major observable characteristics of the international trade and monetary relations of the communist nations. Later, we consider how the recent internal reforms might modify the picture.

Consider first the related problems of inconvertibility and bilateralism. A

14. Some possible reasons why overfull employment planning is still practiced despite its obvious drawbacks are presented in Franklyn D. Holzman, "Overfull Employment Planning, Input-Output, and the Soviet Economic Reforms," *Soviet Studies* 22 (October 1970): 255-61.

capitalist nation is forced into currency inconvertibility when its exchange rate is overvalued, causing its residents to want to buy more from other countries than the residents of other countries want to buy from it at the existing rate of exchange. As foreign exchange reserves become exhausted, import controls may be applied and/or residents may be prevented from converting domestic currency into foreign exchange for the purpose of spending abroad; that is to say, currency inconvertibility is introduced. One solution to this problem, of course, is to devalue the currency, thereby bringing the nation's prices into line with the prices of other nations, and encouraging exports and discouraging imports. The communist nations undoubtedly suffer from this kind of inconvertibility because of overfull employment planning. This is obvious and we need not dwell on the point. They also suffer from another kind of inconvertibility, one that is quite specific to central planning with direct controls, and that yields less easily, if at all, to therapy. This is called *commodity inconvertibility.*

Commodity inconvertibility means not allowing foreigners to spend freely either their own currencies or your currency on commodities in your country. This does not refer, of course, to the consumer products and services purchased by tourists, embassies, foreign press, etc. It refers to the large mass of intermediate products (coal, oil, machinery) and investment goods directly allocated through the central plan. Commodity inconvertibility does not exist under capitalism. Almost everything that is produced and is movable is usually available for export. Central planners, on the other hand, cannot allow foreigners to import freely for two reasons. First, such imports would destroy the carefully drawn fabric of the central supply plan and would bring production to a halt in all enterprises and industries that found themselves deprived thereby of essential inputs. Second, since prices are irrational, allowing foreigners to shop around freely may lead to large national economic losses in the case of products that are, for one reason or another, priced too low. As a result, with the exception of products imported to meet emergency needs, exports and imports are confined largely to those planned in advance for foreign trade.

One consequence of this kind of inconvertibility is bilateralism. No socialist nation is willing to run a surplus with any other socialist nation because of the difficulties in spending the currency earned in either the country of issue or in any other socialist nation. As a result, each socialist nation plans for a bilateral balance in its trade with every other socialist nation. Rigid bilateralism in intrabloc trade substantially reduces the potential volume and efficiency of this trade. Attempts to introduce some multilateralism, such as the establishment of the International Bank for Economic Cooperation (IBEC) and its "transferable ruble," have all been unsuccessful.

The socialist nations are not, of course, bound to bilateralism in the East-West relations. In effect, they can and do spend the hard currencies earned through surpluses with some Western countries in other Western nations. In this respect, they are not significantly different from most smaller Western nations whose currencies are not used in trade. No socialist nation, however, is willing to use its hard currency earnings in intrabloc imports (which, in theory, could serve as a mechanism for multilateralism) because hard currency is usually worth so much more in terms of commodities imported from the West.

Related to inconvertibility and bilateralism are the twin facts that (1) the socialist nations conduct all of their trade, including intrabloc trade, at world prices rather than at their own prices, and (2) their exchange rates are not real prices but simply accounting units. These characteristics stem specifically from the irrationality of internal prices. With the internal prices of each bloc nation irrational, and irrational in differing ways, there exists within the bloc no consistent set of prices upon which the nations can agree for trading purposes. World trading prices are used to fill the gap. Since Western (rather than Eastern) currencies and prices are used in trade, exchange rates are clearly unnecessary: socialist currencies are never exchanged, and internal prices are not reflected through exchange rates in international trade. It is, in any event, impossible to have a meaningful exchange rate between the currencies of two countries where the prices in one or both nations are irrational.

Stemming directly from commodity inconvertibility, and perhaps just another way of looking at it, is what might be termed a *trade aversion* on the part of the socialist nations. There is a tendency on the part of the planners to avoid trade because they fear the disruptions to the plan that might result from possible disruptions to trade. One way of minimizing such disruptions is through the mechanism of annual and long-term trade agreements, and such agreements are part and parcel of the socialist technique of doing international business. This technique largely quiets planners' fears in intrabloc trade, because each party to a trade agreement programs the foreign trade into its annual plan and guarantees exports and imports. However, it does introduce a rigidity in trade which must be considered a drawback. On the other hand, while trade agreements are also made between the two governments in much of East-West trade, the agreements do not provide the planners with the same kind of security as in intrabloc trade. This is because while the Eastern nation stands ready to buy or sell per agreement, the Western government cannot commit its exporters or importers. The most it can do is to bring the parties together and guarantee that it will not place undue obstacles in the way of trade in the form of licenses, quotas, tariffs, etc.

Another consequence (for our purpose) of central planning with direct controls is the redundancy of tariffs. Since decisions regarding the size and composition of imports are part of the central planning process, and since prices are fixed and not necessarily at market-clearing levels, tariffs can affect the outcome no more than exchange rates can. Decisions to import are controlled, in effect, by what might be termed implicit quotas. The tariffs introduced by the socialist nations and used for most-favored-nation (MFN) purposes do not affect what is to be imported, but they may affect from whom the product is imported by discouraging imports from those nations that do not have MFN status.

Finally, an important consequence of Stalinist type central planning is that socialist nations are faced with persistent hard currency deficits and are deprived of the usual means of coming to grips with the problem in the absence of radical reforms. A major factor behind the deficits is the fact that the existing system of planning protects enterprises from the necessity of having to compete. In the first instance, this is due to overfull employment planning, which produces sellers markets. However, the competitive outlook would be blunted anyway in all intermediate product markets (interenterprise transactions) by the fact that products in these markets are not really sold; it is more accurate to say that they are distributed according to plan. Salesmanship is hardly necessary. The same is true of intrabloc foreign trade. As noted earlier, exports and imports conform to intergovernmental trade agreements, and enterprises find themselves delivering goods into predetermined and protected foreign markets. Further, there is rarely any contact between the exporter and the user of the product (hence little or no feedback) since most trade is conducted not by producers of exports and users of imports but by large foreign trade organizations, each representing hundreds of producers and users.

The end result of some twenty years of this collection of arrangements is a reduced ability to sell or compete on world markets, with the exception of relatively homogeneous raw materials. This inability expresses itself in difficulties in adapting to special requirements of Western buyers, and in low quality, poor packaging, poor servicing, poor marketing, inadequate advertising, and so forth. To have a comparative disadvantage in selling is much more of a problem than just having, as every nation does, a comparative disadvantage in a particular range of products, since selling affects virtually all manufactured products. The USSR has, of course, a wide range of raw materials that it can and does export to the West; the other socialist nations are raw material poor and suffer more intensely from the common socialist difficulty in exporting manufactured products.

A Western nation that found itself with balance-of-payments problems for the reason noted above or for any other reason could almost always improve its position by devaluing its currency. Devaluation would lower the prices of its products to foreign buyers and thereby encourage exports. It would also raise the prices of foreign products and would discourage imports. Unfortunately, this very important adjustment mechanism is not available to the socialist nations. As noted above, they trade with each other and with the rest of the world at world prices; their currencies are never exchanged for other currencies; and their exchange rates are not real prices but simply units of account. The obvious result is that a devaluation has absolutely no effect on either exports or imports.

The following question comes to mind: Can the socialist nations simulate a devaluation or its effects? Imports can, of course, always be reduced, but this is a negative solution and not in consonance with the goal of importing more from the West. The effect of a devaluation on exports can be simulated by simply lowering export prices, which would be equivalent to subsidizing the exports. This solution may work when the exports are not in competition with domestic industry in the importing nation. Where there is domestic competition, however, the Eastern nation may find that it has run afoul of Western antidumping regulations. Given their irrational prices and disequilibrium exchange rates, socialist nations cannot refute dumping charges even when subsidies are not being granted. In fact, partly because of the impossibility of refuting dumping charges, it is becoming common in East-West trade agreements, including the October 1972 Soviet-American arrangements, for the Eastern nations simply to agree to withdraw any export causing distress to local Western producers. This type of agreement legislates away the possibility of Eastern price competition in a large range of markets.

ECONOMIC REFORM

From the above, it is clear that Stalinist type central planning has a considerable impact on foreign trade behavior. The question arises as to how the recent planning reforms in Eastern Europe change this picture. Although inspired by similar problems, the nature of reform has varied from country to country as well as over time. The conservative reforms, which include those in all of the Eastern nations except for Hungary and pre-August 1968 Czechoslovakia, have not changed the essential nature of central planning. Prices have been reformed and rationalized somewhat, but they are still set by central planners, are fixed for long periods of time, and are not adjusted for shifts in supply and, especially, demand. Central planning of output and allocation of supplies still exist, even though management bonuses are based on sales rather than on output.[15] Managers have somewhat more flexibility in hiring workers than they had before and somewhat, though not much, more authority in investing retained profits; and part of the burden of central planning and allocation has been decentralized from the central planning boards and ministries to large associations or subministries (but not to enterprises). In effect, the purpose of these reforms has been not to change fundamentally the nature of central planning but rather to prop up the existing system and to make it work more ef-

15. This was designed to prevent enterprises from producing goods that no one wants and to encourage better quality of output.

fectively. The irrational prices, direct allocation of resources, and taut planning remain; so also, therefore, do commodity inconvertibility, bilateralism, functionless exchange rates, and convertible currency shortages.

The Hungarian reform (like the earlier Czech reform) is much more radical. Central planning of outputs and allocation of supplies have been eliminated and market forces have been assigned to take over these tasks. In principle, most prices are freely determined by these market forces, and enterprises are free to buy from or sell to other enterprises either in Hungary, in other socialist markets, or in the West—wherever profits are greatest. Profits from sales (purchases) in foreign markets are calculated by using the Hungarian exchange rates. We say exchange rates because, in view of the fact that Hungary must trade in two foreign markets, each with its own price system, it must necessarily convert the prices from each system into Hungarian forints at a different exchange rate.[16] Tariffs in this system presumably function in the same way as tariffs in a market economy. Not only do most-favored-nation rates give a favored nation a competitive advantage over one not so favored, but they also enable that nation's exporters to compete more favorably against Hungary's domestic producers.

Under these circumstances, one would expect the Hungarian economy to have broken the bonds of inconvertibility and bilateralism, and also to have shifted a substantial part of its trade from Eastern to Western partners as enterprise decisions based on market criteria were substituted for planners decisions. Why have these events not materialized? While a definitive explanation cannot be ventured, several possibilities come to mind.

The Hungarian economy operates under a number of serious constraints. Overfull employment still exists, although the method of its implementation is somewhat different. Continued existence of overfull employment probably reflects, at least in part, the importance of the socialist goal of guaranteed employment to all persons able to work. Each person views his job as *his* unless he voluntarily leaves for another job. This makes it very difficult for the Hungarians to free their trade to imports that are competitive with domestic products or, in general, to adapt their economy to foreign trade.

A second constraint, particularly serious in light of the full employment goal, is the apparent fear that no Hungarian government could survive inflation of more than a few percent a year. This view probably reflects the terrible experiences with inflation that Hungary suffered after both world wars, as well as the almost ideological predilection of communist countries for maintaining stable prices over long periods of time. One result of the need to preserve price stability, under what may be called inflationary conditions, has been the need for the government to control most prices despite

16. This may seem to be in contradiction to our earlier statement that the socialist nations use world prices. In fact, while world prices provide the base for socialist market prices, they are adjusted by the socialist nations and, in general, are somewhat higher.

the intent of the reform, or the New Economic Mechanism (NEM), which was eventually to free all or most prices. This mixture of free and controlled prices over several years of inflationary pressures, however, is likely to reduce the rationality of internal prices and, therefore, their utility in import and export decisions. At some point, a degree of commodity inconvertibility exists and exchange rates are not as "real" prices as they might be. It should also be noted that given overfull employment, Hungary should have the normal balance-of-payments and currency convertibility problems of the sort that beset capitalist nations suffering from inflationary pressures.

A third major constraint facing Hungary is the fact that, for one reason or another, most of its trade is with the other communist nations, all of which introduced very conservative economic reforms and, therefore, have no mechanisms for conducting trade any differently than before. This means that roughly 20 percent of what Hungary produces and consumes is committed to foreign trade by central planners rather than by plant managers. Enterprises, under NEM, cannot be forced or ordered to export or import from another socialist nation just because the government contracted to do so. The government, however, can induce cooperaton by subsidies, tax rebates, and taxes—and this it does.[17] This constitutes a very substantial deviation from the principles of market operation.

Two possible explanations are offered for the continued dominance of socialist nations among Hungary's trading partners. First, it may be politically difficult for Hungary to break away more abruptly. Second, it may be very costly in economic terms for Hungary to shift the structure of its trade. Hungary depends very heavily on the USSR for energy and other raw material requirements. Under present COMECON pricing arrangements, these needs are met at very favorable prices. Given these favorable terms of trade, it may pay Hungary to continue to trade with socialist nations even though this involves a substantial compromise with the principles of NEM.

AD HOC SOLUTIONS

We have now sketched the negative consequences of both Stalinist central planning and the inadequate economic reforms for greater East-West economic interdependence. A full-blown economic reform that would eliminate central planning by direct controls, free prices to be determined in the market, make profits the goal of plant managers, and eliminate inflationary pressures would lead to the elimination of many, if not all, of the characteristics that impede East-West (not to mention intrabloc) trade. It would also, of course, eventually lead to a partial dissolution of

---

17. Subsidies to exporters, particularly to the West, are also required by the fact that the hard-currency exchange rate (or *multiplier*, as it is called) was set at the average export rate rather than at the marginal export rate (which would have been equal to the marginal import rate in equilibrium).

COMECON as a tightly knit trading bloc, since many enterprises, free to seek the most advantageous market, would take their business to the West. This may not be possible at the moment for political reasons. Should it become possible at a later date because, say, the USSR wishes to sell its raw materials to the West, and should the other (internal) political obstacles to reform be reduced, then commodity convertibility, unreal exchange rates, and all the rest may die a natural death. This is not going to happen immediately, however, and attempts are being made to cope with these problems with what may be called second-best solutions.

Attempts to solve a number of these problems are embodied in the many different kinds of cooperative agreements that have been entered into by large capitalist enterprises, on the one hand, and by socialist state enterprises, on the other. Perhaps the simplest agreements are those in which the Western firm sells the Eastern firm a license to use its technology or a so-called turnkey plant. In the former, a package of technology is sold to the Eastern enterprise, along with whatever training of labor, etc., is required to use it. In the latter, not only the technology but the entire plant and equipment is put together in ready-to-operate form by the seller; all the purchaser has to do is "turn the key." Sales of franchises are similar, but here it is not so much the know-how that is desired as it is the name, e.g., Hilton or Pepsi-Cola. These three kinds of agreements are relatively simple because they automatically terminate with the completion of the plant or the successful transfer of technology.

More complicated are those agreements in which the participants collaborate in production, marketing, research, or any other industrial activity. At one end of the spectrum, the participants strictly maintain their separate identities and all interrelationships are specified by contract and in dollars and cents. At the other end of the spectrum are the true joint ventures in which Eastern and Western participants form a single new organization that encompasses their activities.[18] The new organization reflects joint ownership or pooling of assets, joint management, and a sharing of profits and losses. This kind of organization represents the most radical break with the past since it allows Western individuals an equity (always less than 50 percent) in an Eastern enterprise, in effect, private ownership of the means of production. So far, legislation permitting such arrangements has been passed only in Rumania, Hungary, and Yugoslavia. A major difference, it should be noted, between the cooperative agreements and joint ventures, on the one hand, and other forms of cooperation, on the other, is that the former are temporarily open-ended whereas the latter end with the completion of the single project.

Socialist countries enter into these agreements in order to get better access to Western technology and related production and to management know-

18. It has been common to refer loosely to ordinary coproduction and comarketing arrangements as joint ventures.

how, in effect, to improve their hard-currency earning capacities and to obtain capital (credits), particularly hard-currency capital. Clearly, these
various forms of collaboration do serve the purposes for which they have
been intended by the East. And the coproduction arrangements and joint
ventures have the special advantage of giving the Western partner a continuing interest in the efficiency, profitability, and success of the operation.[19]
(Western motives can all be subsumed under expansion of profits. This is
achieved by expansion of markets [either Eastern or Western], sale of
technology already paid for, access to cheap labor supplies, and so forth).

One other feature of these arrangements deserves special mention,
namely, the payments arrangements. Payments are always made either in
hard currency or in commodities, ususally the commodities produced by the
venture.[20] Because of commodity inconvertibility, it seems highly unlikely
that repayment could ever be in the local Eastern currency.

How successful are or can these arrangements be in meeting the economic
needs of the socialist nations? This question cannot be answered with any
precision, but it does appear at this juncture that the arrangements are very
imperfect substitutes for real economic reforms. Ventures involving import
of technology are likely to be the most successful in achieving the desired
goals of socialist planners, particularly in the case of the smaller East
European nations. Nations of this size must import a lot of technology, in
any case, so that reform or no, they probably would not be able to do much
better. On the other hand, problems relating to the adoption and spread of
technology cannot be solved through international mechanisms but depend
on domestic reform for solution. For the USSR, and perhaps for the larger
Eastern European nations, import of sufficient technology to compensate
for domestic shortcomings could be very expensive in terms of foreign exchange. Further, import of technology may not be feasible in foreign exchange terms in purely domestic industries that are likely to produce neither
exportables nor import substitutes in terms of Western markets.

The use of Western partners to assist in the preparation and marketing of
products in hard-currency markets makes a lot of sense. However, it has its
limitations. First of all, to the extent that Western marketing techniques and
production advice must compensate for domestic deficiencies, the Eastern
nations are, in effect, paying a high cost for these deficiencies. They lose
both part of their profit and part of their potential hard-currency earnings.
Second, because of the pervasiveness in the Eastern nations of an inability
to produce and sell manufactured products to the West, it seems highly
unlikely that cooperative marketing ventures could ever be on a large

19. Thus, for example, while a Western enterprise might sell a license for outdated technology to an Eastern country, it would not likely do so if the arrangement was in the form of a
joint venture.

20. An exception is the Pepsi Cola agreement in which payment to the West is, at least in
part, in the form of vodka to be resold in the West.

enough scale to fill the gap.

Finally, the coproduction and joint ventures do provide the Eastern nations with some Western capital. This is as it should be, since the Eastern nations are poorer than the most advanced Western nations and in the normal course of things would have experienced some capital inflow from the latter. "Things" have been abnormal, however, because of the cold war and inconvertibility, and the normal capital flow mechanism ceased functioning after World War II. It is too early to tell how much capital will flow under joint ventures. At the very least, capital flow will be inhibited, except perhaps into those industries that produce potential exportables to the West, such as oil. Moreover, the socialist nations presumably recognize that repayment in a commodity like oil is essentially repayment in hard currency, and, therefore, that the repayment of the capital is, in effect, competing with (or reducing) future hard-currency imports. Second, even the most radical Eastern joint ventures do not give the Western partner the kind of control that is possible for Western multinationals in many countries. This fact may also inhibit the flow of capital.

The great size of the USSR and its special needs for technology and capital raise questions regarding orders of magnitude. The large Siberian oil and gas projects envisage, as a starter, American investments of around $15 billion. The unprecedented size of these projected investments raises some economic issues, but more important it raises the political issue of whether the United States can afford to put so much "hostage" capital into a potential enemy nation. With this in mind, the question that immediately arises is whether it may not be as, or almost as, economical to devote the funds to developing alternative energy sources in the United States.

To sum up, the various ad hoc cooperative arrangements developed over the past decade to overcome the handicaps, both domestic and international, that the Eastern nations suffer as a result of their planning systems are clearly only second-best solutions and are not good substitutes for thoroughgoing reforms. The Eastern nations will continue to lag technologically, to have difficulties in selling manufactured products in the West, to be unable to devalue their currencies effectively, to find it difficult to trade up to the optimum with Western nations because of the planning rigidities, and so forth. On the other hand, so long as they cannot see their way clear to radical reforms, their problems are certainly ameliorated by the new arrangements.

The Political Impulse To Interdependence

In the second part of this essay, we have argued that significant economic obstacles stand in the way of a profound East-West economic interdependence—that, for the moment, the limits to East-West economic interdependence are ultimately economic. If so, however, the reason these limits have never been remotely approached remains political. Politics—not the structure or the economic goals of centrally planned economies—have dictated the pattern and level of economic cooperation. And politics, as much as the economic advantages of increased cooperation, now dictate their change.

The next two sections try to explore the particular way that the economics of East-West relations yield to political considerations: first, by considering the realignment of circumstances retarding or promoting interdependence; second, by weighing against the movement toward interdependence the parallel political obstacles. In the first instance, the *political impulse* to interdependence, we are primarily concerned with the effect of the international environment on each side's stake in increased economic cooperation. In turn, the impact of the environment is to be judged both in macro terms (how the change in the environment has altered national preoccupations) and in micro terms (how it has altered the interplay of domestic forces influencing these preoccupations). In the second instance, the *political limits* to interdependence, our concern again has a macro dimension, that is, those sides to East-West relations working against cooperation, and a micro dimension, that is, those impediments added by the configuration of competing interests within each state.

Having pieced together the political context of interdependence, we can then turn to its political dynamics. How does the East or the West go about securing the advantages of interdependence and reducing its inconveniences or risks? How do the political and economic imperatives, interests, and expectations of any nation interact? What impact does East-West interdependence have on intra-East or intra-West relations? With rudimentary answers to these questions, something can then be said of the kinds and degree of interdependence likely to emerge. Ultimately, our interest is in the effect that interdependence could (or should) have on the next generation of international economic institutions and, in turn, the potential effect of these on it.

Few things are more striking about the stakes that the East and the West have in economic cooperation than their asymmetry. The West stresses the political advantages of economic cooperation, the East the economic advantages. At the moment, the West, particularly the United States, is inclined to view expanded trade and investment as a valuable part of the broader process by which the East and the West are to sort out their political relationship and put their signature on whatever international order replaces the bipolar world. The East, on the other hand, sees expanded trade and investment as a convenient way to augment its capital and technological resources.

The contrast, of course, oversimplifies. Neither side draws sharp distinctions between the political and economic advantages of cooperation, and certainly neither emphasizes one to the exclusion of the other. Moreover, the contrast grows more blurred the more dependent a country is on trade. Countries in the West that most rely on trade have usually most resisted subordinating economics to politics. (By this standard, it was natural for Khrushchev, the leader of a country whose imports were approximately 3 percent of national income, to say: "We value trade least for economic reasons and most for political purposes."[21] His successors have not changed their minds because this percentage has changed or will soon, but because they have developed a qualitatively different trade dependency.) Thus the West Europeans never enforced the postwar embargo on strategic goods with the same enthusiasm as the United States, and they were noticeably less thorough in composing their lists of strategic items. Today, while the political significance of East-West economic cooperation counts heavily with them, they are again less inclined than the United States to build a formal strategy around the connection between politics and economics.

Still, the difference exists. The so-called strategy of linkages associated with former President Nixon and Secretary Kissinger merely represents the clearest and most explicit attempt to exploit the East's (especially the Soviet Union's) desire for greater trade for political ends. Until menaced by Senator Jackson's own strategy of linkages, economic interdependence had served as an element—a most serviceable element—in a political strategy designed to induce the Soviet Union to deal comprehensively and systematically with issues capable of seriously disrupting the stability of great-power relations, notably the Middle East, Indochina, and the strategic arms race. For the Nixon administration, the Soviet interest in American technology and capital was the rough equivalent of the original Soviet interest in an antiballistic missile (ABM) agreement—that is, a negotiable item prized for the leverage it offered in the pursuit of a range of (artificially) interconnected political objectives. As Kissinger explained when introducing the Strategic Arms Limitation Talk (SALT) accords in June 1972: "We have ... sought to move forward across a broad range of issues so that progress in one area would add momentum to the progress of other areas."[22] Although its point is different, this approach represents the logical extension of economic warfare (and note how easily senators and congressmen turned it into economic warfare); both Secretary Kissinger and Senator Jackson feature the political instrumentalism of the East-West economic relationship, and both protect the subordination of economics to politics.[23]

The Soviet Union, in contrast, has a certain incentive for keeping the two spheres apart. Obviously, Soviet leaders understand the interrelationship

21. *New York Times*, 18 September 1955, quoted in J. Wilczynski, *The Economics and Politics of East-West Trade* (London: Macmillan, 1969), p. 237.

22. Henry A. Kissinger, Congressional Briefing, White House, 15 June 1972, p. 3. (Mimeographed.)

23. Indeed, the simplest version of the linkage principle, that is, using the prospect of MFN and Export-Import Bank credits as a more or less explicit bargaining chip in negotiations with the Soviet Union, is virtually identical with the hortatory side of economic warfare, that is, using aid and trade concessions as rewards for independent East European states, such as Yugoslavia, Rumania, and, once, Poland.

between political environment and economic cooperation. They continually emphasize the importance that increasing trade and technical cooperation has for reducing international tension and, in turn, the importance that reducing tension has for fostering increased trade and technical cooperation. But they have major benefits to secure from economic cooperation as such, and these may not necessarily be served by taxing efforts to promote interdependence with political objectives. They, therefore, seem more inclined to seek separately the considerable political advantages that they expect from East-West détente. Rather than conceive their ambitions (or at least, the way to them) as a whole, Soviet leaders appear to prefer to break détente into its component parts: to pursue their European dream (a stable but divided Europe built around a divided Germany and a *Europe [Occidentale] des Patries*) by means of rather narrowly defined bilateral accords and an expeditious Conference on Security and Cooperation in Europe (CSCE); to regulate the strategic military balance, including many of its multilateral aspects, with the United States alone in SALT; to cope with the challenge of China by manipulating bilateral relations with Japan and the United States as well as by sponsoring an autonomous Asian security system; to facilitate East-West trade and the importation of Western capital, technology, and technique by clearing away the specific institutional and legal obstacles to increased cooperation and by negotiating a network of formal bilateral trade agreements; and to minimize the natural links that exist between virtually all of these concerns.

The difference between the two approaches carries significant implications for the interaction of détente and economic cooperation. That each side desires both tells but a portion of the story. It also matters that the United States chooses still to subordinate one to the other, treating economic interdependence basically as a means to an end; the Soviet Union, in this instance, has not established a similar hierarchy and is, therefore, bound to resist. Like Western Europe, the Soviet Union is opposed to American linkages—whether between the negotiations of mutual force reductions in Europe and CSCE, or between MFN and an interim agreement to limit offensive missile deployments.

Linkages are the natural preference of states whose advantages are in some but not all the areas contested by others. By tying those areas in which the other side is clearly the *demandeur* with those in which the advantage is less clear, gains can be maximized and losses minimized. Tying the Soviet interest in East-West trade to progress in SALT, therefore, has much in common with tying Western Europe's security anxieties to the reordering of Atlantic commercial and monetary relationships. The United States hopes, thus, to squeeze the most from a favorably tilted triangle with Peking and Moscow, from the Soviet Union's greater intrinsic interest in East-West trade, and from the impatience of the East to have the West's formal blessing for what the East calls the "postwar European reality."

Failing a basic shift in the perspectives that the two dominant powers bring to the problem of East-West economic interdependence, the commitment of either to trade and to other forms of economic cooperation will be partially compromised by the different things that each wants from the *process* of promoting cooperation. The difference is fundamental: the United States wants the Soviet Union to get what it wants *conditionally*; the Soviet Union does not want the United States to get what it wants tactically. In turn, the things that each gets from (and yields to) the *process* will depend on: (1) the Soviet capacity for breaking linkages (which country turns out to have a greater stake in the process), (2) the reinforcement the environment provides in breaking linkages (a crisis-ridden environment tends to favor ad hoc solutions), and (3) the extent to which American leaders retain control over the rewards (MFN, export credits, the sacrifice of present or future weapons systems, etc.) around which linkages are built. It is the last variable that makes the American strategy the most vulnerable. It constitutes the chief hazard of a relatively pluralistic policymaking process. (If they could afford to, Soviet leaders should have an easier time putting politics ahead of economics.)

The asymmetry of stakes, however, does not diminish the critical fact that each side has come to have a stake in the economic cooperation. Asymmetry influences each side's approach to economic cooperation, but obviously these differences depend first on both sides' interest in cooperating. That interest is the outcome or, more precisely, the beneficiary of significant change in the international political setting. On a number of past occasions—in 1952 at the Moscow Economic Conference, in 1959 at the time of Camp David, after 1966 with the Japanese—the Soviets have sought to enlarge their trade with the West. But not until Brandt's post-1969 *Ostpolitik* transformed the political character of East-West relations did they permit themselves to contemplate this trade as a significant part of the solution to their economic difficulties. Without the political hopes aroused by progress on the German problem, Soviet leaders would probably not have dared place so much emphasis on the utility of East-West economic cooperation. Without, however, the "normalization" of Soviet-American relations (as the Soviet press has described events since the May 1972 summit) this cooperation would have remained merely feasible, not lucrative. For the Soviet-American relationship is decisive in two respects: first, Soviet leaders know that American sanction is essential to any basic restructuring of East-West relations; second, only the Americans can provide capital and goods on the scale for which the Soviets are hoping. Thus, a modification in the premises of Soviet-American relations has very broad significance.

The mutual accommodation Soviet and American leaders seek to fashion rests, not on a failure to perceive the Soviet-American relationship as still fundamentally competitive nor on any real reconciliation with the nature of the opposing system, but, rather, on the prospect that each may be willing to cease striving for preemptive roles in areas other than those regarded as essential spheres of influence. For the Soviet Union, the United States has not and cannot outgrow its imperialist essence. But when Soviet leaders contend that circumstances have forced American policymakers to abandon their "aggressive globalism," they are acknowledging to themselves that the frustrations of recent American policy have produced a genuine revision in American conduct. For the United States, the Soviet Union remains its most ambitious rival, a rival motivated by an alien ideology. But American leaders, too, have been reassured by the problems posed for Soviet policy by an often intractable and sometimes downright unfriendly world. The American faith in the Sino-Soviet conflict, the imperatives of change in Eastern Europe, and Soviet setbacks in the Third World roughly equal the impact of Vietnam, disenchanted allies, and the domestic distractions on which Soviet leaders count to make the United States a sobered and safer adversary-partner.

Thus, in the first place, it is the limits of power together with an incipient faith in the other side's sensitivity to the limits of power that permits increased cooperation, whether in arms control, scientific research, or trade. The second element of change favoring cooperation is the Soviet Union's belated attainment of effective strategic parity. And the mixed character of Soviet success gives this factor even greater force. For while parity provides the confidence to promote interdependence, the Soviet Union's marked inferiority in other realms, some military and almost all economic, provides the reason for doing so. Third, economic cooperation simply extends a gradual movement toward interdependence occurring in other areas, where the transnational problems of pollution, environmental decay, and resource exploitation leave little choice.

The discussion to this point not only has simplified a number of nations that count in shaping East-West economic relations, but has also simplified the nature of those nations as they come to count; that is, it has ignored the interplay of forces determining the Soviet and American approaches to cooperation. Ultimately, however, the practical way that changes in the international environment work their effect on either's approach is in influencing the political setting and the politics of policymaking. There is, of course, an interplay between the two, since the domestic political process also affects the evolution of the international environment, but not so much as the environment conditions this process. Our argument is the superiority, not the irresponsiveness, of macropolitics to micropolitics.

Two somewhat simplifying shortcuts now need to be abandoned. First is the implicit notion that a nation's foreign policy represents the starting point of international politics. The second is that a nation's policy or, more generally, a nation's behavior can be equated with the preferences of the national leadership—in the United States, the president and his key advisers; in the Soviet Union, the general secretary and his principal political allies. It helps, in making order of basic international trends, to be able to work with "black boxes," and, when it comes time to give this abstraction life, to render the black box as Nixon (now Ford) and Kissinger or as Brezhnev and his lieutenants. Yet without rejecting the validity and the importance of the abstraction or the decisive role of the national leadership, an important part of reality remains concealed until a look is taken at what is happening within the black box. It has to be done, at a minimum, to understand the constraints that the local political context places on the policy of national leaderships.

Much progress has been made lately in developing a systematic theory of the politics of foreign policymaking, though less has been done on the interaction of politics with domestic settings.[24] To be shown the way, however, does not automatically make it possible to follow. Very considerable obstacles stand in the way of rigorous and comprehensive exploration of the micropolitics of East-West economic interdependence. These boil down essentially to the two interrelated problems of access and scale. First, there is no conceivable way to penetrate adequately the politics of Soviet foreign policymaking. Soviet specialists (and even more so, Chinese specialists) simply do not have access to provide anything other than the most rudimentary speculative portrait of the interplay of political forces disgorging policy. Second, even if we had a better idea of what was going on within the black boxes, the task of dealing with the Soviet and American processes, plus the processes under way in all the other countries that matter to East-West economic cooperation, and in a context that is both dynamic and indeterminate, would require superhuman talents of integration.

Thus, the reader is warned that we offer a rather humble version of the way that domestic politics and setting relate to the course of East-West economic relations. Let us begin with our only conceptual device: a way of differentiating the participants in the foreign policymaking process. In the advanced systems of both the East and West, there are what may be termed direct, collateral, and indirect participants. The first are usually those distinctive structures whose functions are naturally associated with foreign policy, and that are often specialized in this area, that tend to initiate policy and sometimes to assume operating responsibility for policy, and that, however biased, tend to see policy integrally rather than particularistically. To use the United States as our Western example, in addition to the president, the direct participants are the State Department, the National Security Council, the Department of Defense, and various subagencies of each, the

24. For the first, see Graham T. Allison, *The Essence of Decision* (Boston: Little, Brown & Co., 1970); and Graham T. Allison and Morton H. Halperin, "Bureaucratic Politics: A Paradigm and Some Policy Implications," in Raymond Tanter and Richard H. Ullman, eds., *Theory and Policy in International Relations* (Princeton, N.J.: Princeton University Press, 1972), pp. 40-79. For significant contributions in the second, more disappointing area, see Henry A. Kissinger, "Domestic Structure and Foreign Policy," *Daedalus* 95 (Spring 1966): 503-29; and Gabriel A. Almond, *The American People and Foreign Policy* (New York: Harcourt, Brace & Co., 1950).

Central Intelligence Agency (CIA), representatives of each in ad hoc group-ings, and, to a much lesser extent, the congressional armed services and foreign relations committees. To use the Soviet Union as our Eastern exam-ple, the equivalents would be the general secretary and his personal secretariat, the international affairs departments of the central committee, the Foreign Ministry, the Ministry of Defense, the Committee on State Security (KGB), and other members of the Politburo regularly consulted on foreign affairs.

By collateral participants we have in mind the other institutions and elements that impinge critically on policymaking, that may deal with foreign policy only as an extension of other concerns, that may not gen-erally initiate or implement policy but that are capable of significantly alter-ing its content, and that command the deference, wariness, or respect of the first group. This category is far more diffuse than the first, varying tremen-dously in the nature of its access to the policymaking process, its effec-tiveness, and particularly, its place in the general political process. In the United States, examples may be as bureaucratic as the Department of Com-merce or Agriculture or as personal as a single prominent university specialist, as shapeless as a congressional bloc or as explicit as the Rand Corporation, as political as the American Federation of Labor–Congress of Industrial Organizations (AFL-CIO) or the International Longshore-man's Union or as aloof as the Council on Foreign Relations, as institu-tionalized as the House Ways and Means Committee or as informal as the anti-ABM lobby. In the Soviet Union, the range is also broad: from the Ministry of Trade and its trading organizations to such adjuncts of the Academy of Sciences as the Institute of World Economy and International Affairs and the Institute for the Study of the USA, from the State Commit-tee on Science and Technology to the complex of military-industrial enter-prises given direct representation in the Politburo.

Participants in the third category do not have direct access to foreign policymaking but may influence its course nonetheless. They do so either because those in the other two categories respond to their interests (or their importuning) or because they, the American media, in particular, play an important role in establishing the political setting. They are usually more difficult to identify in institutional terms, such as the Jewish voter in the United States or the economic reformer in the Soviet Union, more self-interested, such as the American business community or the middle-level *apparatchik*, and sometimes more remote from the system's center of grav-ity, such as the extreme right wing in the United States or dissident intellec-tuals in the Soviet Union.

Because our present theme is the impact of the environment on micro-politics, and because we will soon argue that this impact has been similar in the East (the Soviet Union) and in the West (the United States), we want to be careful to avoid leaving the impression that few differences exist in these participant categories between the United States and the Soviet Union. On the contrary, the fundamental structural differences in political and economic systems produce important distinctions. Most of these stem from the sharp contrast between levels of centralization (concentration of decision-making power), differentiation of political function (role specialization), and participation (access to the decision-making process). Thus, Soviet participants tend to be more consolidated, though not necessarily more monolithic, than American participants. The KGB, for example, has many more concerns than the CIA, since it also incorporates the work of the Federal Bureau of Investigation (FBI), the Customs Service, and, in the judicial system, even some of the work of the district attorney. As a participant in foreign policymaking, it brings all of these concerns, not merely those of the CIA, to bear. Second, the number of collateral participants in the Soviet Union is far smaller than in the United States, and the importance of indirect participants is much less striking. The first results, in general, from the monopolistic position of the Party, and the second, from its authoritarianism. Third, in contrast with the direct participants, the contribution of collateral participants in the Soviet Union appears to be far more compartmentalized than in the United States. International relations specialists in the Soviet Union interpret United States behavior. They do not offer approaches to arms control. That is the sphere of the military. The Committee on Science and Technology explains how much it means for improved planning to enlist the services of Control Data, but it does not worry about the political implications of getting involved with the major capitalist powers. That is the province of Agitprop and others in the Party hierarchy. Compare this circumstance with the broad expertise and influence to which the AFL-CIO pretends or the breadth of inquiry undertaken by Senator Jackson's subcommittees of the Government Operations Committee.

Later we will consider the potential effect of economic interdependence on these differences—whether interdependence is likely to generate pressures for system reform, say, economic decentralization, and whether interdependence can be used to encourage such reform. For the moment, however, we are more concerned with the effect of the environment on the way that the interplay of domestic political forces bears on economic interdependence.

The balance among these forces has shifted toward and perhaps is now in favor of interdependence. Without arguing the untenable—that all elements involved are committed to an unconditional economic partnership—it seems safe to say that a decisive portion of the spectrum has swung away from viewing Soviet-American relations as irretrievably hostile and economic cooperation as an unthinkable danger or betrayal. In both the United States and the Soviet Union, this change is reflected in two fundamental developments.

First, opinion favoring interdependence or, at least, opinion willing to tout the idea appears to prevail in all three categories of participants. But, more important, among the direct participants, those that we have been calling the national leadership now regularly declare their dedication to promoting interdependence. In the Soviet case, this seems to us more significant and, simultaneously, more perilous: more significant because first-category participants in the Soviet Union have a far stronger position vis-à-vis the other two categories than their American counterparts; more perilous because (1) the national leadership (Brezhnev and his allies) is less ascendent over other *first*-category participants than is the American president, and because (2) the issue of interdependence well may be one of the stakes of its uncertain ascendence.

Second, the spectrum has been extended in both countries. As the predominant view inches toward the possibility of interdependence, estimations more sanguine, more hopeful, than anything heard for a long time are now being expressed. Thus, Henry Kissinger may think of interdependence as merely a component of a grand political strategy, but others, some of them relatively frontline participants, place higher value on economic cooperation. The object, former Secretary of Commerce Peter Peterson has noted, is "to build in both countries a vested economic interest in the maintenance of a harmonious and enduring relationship."[25] Leonid Brezhnev may consider it a calculated risk that he turn to the industrial nations of the West and, first among them, to the United States for help in addressing the shortcomings of the Soviet economy, but there is Georgi Arbatov, director of the Institute for the Study of the USA, telling him not to be anxious because the scales have shifted in the United States. Indeed, Arbatov has written in *Kommunist* that "the ruling American bourgeoisie" has come to recognize the arms race and military "adventures" as being a waste, as squandering a huge part of national resources and "only undermining its position in the competitive struggle with other capitalist powers, dooming itself to monetary-financial shocks, and eroding the bases of its economic and political influence in the world."[26] Moreover, this is, according to him, a long-term, not an "episodic," trend, dictated by "objective conditions." Thus cooperation with the United States as an "acceptable partner" (he uses this term) can be something profound and relatively permanent.

Compared with the former secretary of commerce, Arbatov is merely a collateral participant in the policymaking process. But his role is no less interesting or illustrative. As a second-level participant, in one sense, his in-

25. See US Department of Commerce, *U.S.-Soviet Commercial Relations in a New Era*, by Peter G. Peterson (Washington, D.C.: Department of Commerce, 1972), p. 3.

26. G. Arbatov, "O sovetsko-amerikanskikh otnosheniyakh," *Kommunist*, no. 3 (February 1973): 106. Here Arbatov is not merely the equivalent of a prominent American academic. Speaking through *Kommunist*, the chief theoretical organ of the Central Committee of the Communist Party of the Soviet Union, is not the same as speaking in *Foreign Affairs*.

fluence on decision makers at the top is much weaker than the most potent second-level participants in the United States. That is, he clearly participates at their deference and he clearly understands the range of ideas that will be tolerated. (Admittedly, someone like Peterson, too, must stay within the boundaries of good political taste; but the difference is that in the United States, the president determines those boundaries, whereas in the Soviet Union, the *relative strength* of the Soviet leader determines them.) It is difficult to imagine George Meany or Senator Jackson responding to the same constraints. Also, Arbatov tends to be a more effective participant the more he is the client of some part of the highest leadership. This is both a weakness and a strength: a weakness because it deprives him of autonomy, a strength because with the right kind of patronage his ideas acquire considerable currency. Arbatov has been the most fortunate of people in this sense because he has had the ear of the general secretary. His entree is reportedly with Brezhnev's own personal secretariat, two of whom, Y. Alexandrov-Agentov and George Tsukanov, are emerging as prominent figures in the general secretary's foreign policy activities. He was also conspicuously part of the entourage accompanying Brezhnev to the United States in June 1973.[27] But presumably any group or individual in the second category seeks to have an input by the grace of one or two major participants.

Do not misunderstand. We are not suggesting that the evolution of the international environment now ensures the permanent triumph of elements favoring economic interdependence. Nor do we mean to slight the complicated butting and grinding of interest by which each side comes to act. On the contrary, we devote the next section to the problems that the environment still poses and, more important, to the intricate and sometimes inauspicious struggle among viewpoints, interests, and institutions that the shadow of interdependence provokes.

But clearly the ground rules by which that struggle is being waged have changed. Most fundamentally, they have been changed by establishing East-West economic interdependence as a legitimate alternative. Senator Jackson's opposition to trade-facilitating measures is not based on principle, but is an expedient for compelling the Soviet leadership to alter objectionable domestic practices. And those who do oppose economic cooperation in principle, such as Ohio's Representative Charles Vanik, must today fashion their strategy around alliances with liberal congressmen, such as Ogden Reid, who, but for the plight of Soviet Jews, conceive Soviet-American relations quite differently.

Circumstances today resemble very little those of a decade ago. In 1962,

---

27. It is not likely that his influence is diminished by the presence at his institute of relatives of highly placed Soviet officials, such as Ludmila Gvishiani, Kosygin's daughter, or, until his recent posting to the Washington embassy, Gromyko's son, Anatoly.

George Kennan was abandoned by his administration at the first sign of a tussle, and he was left to wonder at Congress's decision to deprive Yugoslavia and Poland of most-favored-nation status. In the same year, Senator William Proxmire introduced an amendment to the foreign aid bill denying all forms of aid to Yugoslavia, an exclusion that was later amended to allow the shipment of surplus wheat, provided that the president determined that it was in the interest of national security and that the recipient was "not participating directly or indirectly in any policy or programs for the Communist conquest of the world."[28] So was the major East-West trade bill of 1966 a victim of Congress's deep-seated inability to imagine the Soviet Union and China as suitable trading partners. Whatever other burdens oppress efforts to advance trade with the East, a widely shared aversion to having truck with the enemy is no longer one of them.[29]

The Political Limits To Interdependence

Relations between adversaries have mellowed over the last several years. Those between friends have in some ways hardened. The character of the international system, as a consequence (or as a tribute), has lost its precision. Foes, internally troubled and no more gifted than we at molding the outside world, are no longer always foes. Friends sometimes are. The ambiguity makes economic interdependence between East and West plausible. But it does not mean that no one any longer has the ability or the reason to distinguish friend from foe. Rivalry between East and West, particularly between the Soviet Union and the United States, may be softened, but it remains a central feature of contemporary international politics. Thus, while the transformation of this rivalry permits growing economic cooperation, the persistence of this rivalry places limits on its growth. (One of the basic questions that events must answer is how long these [political] limits will continue to intervene before the economic limits discussed in part two of this essay.)

Security is never very far removed from the problems of economic policy. In no dimension has security figured more explicitly or more integrally than in East-West relations. And, therefore, none provides a better illustration of their point about the three levels at which economic policy has been assumed to serve national security: (1) for the nation (by risk aversion),

---

28. See George F. Kennan, *Memoirs: 1950-1963* (Boston: Little, Brown & Co., 1972), pp. 293-305. He did not wonder long. On precisely this score he left the diplomatic service once and for all.

29. These burdens are obviously great, but, as the history of the Jackson-Vanik amendment indicates, their effect is not ultimately to preclude a steady growth in Soviet-American trade. In part, of course, this growth may require that the Soviet Union buy without the credit facilities for which it had hoped, but the basic idea of a growth in Soviet-American trade is no longer in question.

(2) for allies and potential victims or dupes of the other side (by economic assistance), and (3) against the other side (by economic denial). The illustration, of course, applies to a period when security had a narrower, more rigorous, and largely military connotation—when, as we have been saying, there was no political impulse to economic interdependence, only political limits. What happens when the limits no longer overwhelm the impulse to interdependence?

Concern for security still seems to us the best way to understand the political impediments to interdependence. Security now has a more diffuse and general sense, to suit a world in which not all challenges to national security are military. Yet, however redefined, it still lurks behind each side's apprehensions over economic cooperation with the other, over accepting an interdependence that one morning may turn out to be too much. *Too much*, reduced to its common essence, means an interdependent relationship in which the other side's net leverage is considerably greater than your own, an interdependent relationship that turns out to have spawned, or perhaps merely to have masked, a dependent relationship. The fear is everyone's. But the way each personalizes it varies significantly, not only between the United States and the Soviet Union, but within the West, and, to a lesser extent, within the East. Add to an asymmetry in the stakes of interdependence the asymmetry in the fears of interdependence.

For the Soviet Union, the concern is essentially that the integrity of its system may be prejudiced, that too much involvement with the advanced capitalist nations will lead to a serious erosion of empire together with a consistent and possibly noisome interference in Soviet domestic affairs. Soviet policymakers evidently spend a good deal of time worrying about the effect on their socialist allies of an economic opening to the West. Hence, the Soviets have made efforts to heighten the impression of COMECON integration since the summer of 1971, to come to terms with the European Economic Community (EEC) on a bloc-to-bloc basis, and to set something of an example of what they regard as an appropriate arrangement with Western traders and, particularly, investors (with Rumania, as always, the unruly pupil). The other care is even easier to see. In Sofia in September 1973, Brezhnev complained of those "naive" enough to believe that "since the Soviet Union and other socialist countries are expressing great interest in...developing political and economic cooperation," they can "bargain for various concessions."

The American concern strikes one as less imaginative. In basic respects it prolongs the preoccupations of the earlier period. Thus, the worry that by trading with or investing in the Soviet Union the United States is "helping the enemy"—that is, permitting Soviet leaders to respond to consumer hopes and a lagging technology without diminishing military spending—recalls the considerations behind the strategic embargo and the other measures of economic denial.[30] Other fears resemble those that once prompted risk-averting policies. For example, some worry that substantial investment in Soviet industrial development may provide the Soviet Union with "hostage capital." Or, as Gregory Grossman has argued in a more subtle variant of the same theme, the Soviet Union will develop through American investors their own lobbyists in the American political process.[31] Conceivably, Grossman has added, the Soviet Union will use the exposed position of American investors to pressure the Americans into, say, restraining the growth of China trade (a proposition not unlike Senator Richard Schweiker's efforts in 1973 to pass a bill interrupting Soviet-American trade until the Arabs lifted their oil embargo, nor unlike Representative Clarence Long's efforts to block expanded trade until a host of foreign policy concessions had been secured). Finally, there is the apprehension that too heavy an involvement in the development of Soviet natural gas may leave the United States dangerously dependent on the Soviet Union for this strategic good.

The Japanese have different concerns. What is for the United States a risk to be averted is for them a way to avert a risk. For more than half a decade, the Japanese have been attracted to the idea of helping the Soviet Union to develop its petroleum and natural gas resources as a way to reduce their own dramatic dependence on Middle Eastern oil.[32] In the short term, therefore, the Japanese have a different, that is, a multilateral rather than bilateral, perspective on risk aversion, though perhaps in the long term the differences are less. The Japanese also have a different perspective on the problem of "helping the enemy," in this case a historic as well as a contemporary adversary. They object not so much to the Soviet Union drawing its fair share of advantages from a far more ambitious trade but rather to it doing so before they have returned a part of the Kurile Islands.

The West Europeans fall somewhere in between. As the parties most sensitive to the implications for security of recent changes in East-West relations, they presumably share American concerns. But, as for the Japanese, it is not so easy for them to frame the problem in simple risk-averting terms. Trade with the East means a great deal more to them—as much as ten times more as a percentage of GNP—and the challenge of maintaining energy supply is more like that of the Japanese than of the Americans. Second, in a

---

30. The point is made by many people in many places. For one clear statement, see Walter Laqueur's remarks in US Congress, Senate, Committee on Government Operations, *Hearings before the Permanent Subcommittee on Investigations of the Committee on Government Operations,* 93rd Cong., 1st sess., 17 April 1973, pp. 1-39.

31. See US Congress, Joint Economic Committee, *Hearings before the Joint Economic Committee,* 93rd Cong., 1st sess., 17, 18, 19 July 1973, p. 143.

32. Kiichi Saeki, "Toward Japanese Cooperation in Siberian Development," *Problems of Communism* 21 (May-June 1972): 1-11. True, the Japanese do seem eager to involve the Americans in their proposed Siberian natural gas projects for reasons that go beyond merely mounting adequate economic resources.

practical sense, they have made a great deal over economic interdependence, perhaps in order to keep minds and hands off the central issue of European security—the military balance. That is, in order to prevent the Soviet Union and the United States, in particular, from turning too early and too casually to European security as arms control, there may be a natural tendency to busy East and West with other forms of détente. It is difficult, therefore, to hedge the prospect of increased economic cooperation with all kinds of doubts and reservations. On the other hand, as the Soviets, they also react to the possibilities that interdependence gives to the other side of interfering in their internal affairs, in this case, in the process of Western European integration. The concern would be less troublesome were the economic and political integration of the Common Market further along or were all members equally bent on promoting integration.

In a phrase, one of the primary political limits to economic interdependence remains the powerful aftertaste of the postwar bipolar contest. But there is potentially another kind of political limit arising from the passing of this international circumstance: in a less neatly divided world, national leaderships can (and often feel compelled to) apply themselves to regulating the economic contact of former foes with former friends and even of foes with foes, where once their only option was to regulate the contact of friends with foes. No longer does China confine itself to fussing over the Soviet-American economic relationship Khrushchev evidently sought to launch in 1959; it now concentrates as well on influencing Japanese trade with the Soviet Union or with Taiwan.[33] And the United States goes about the more direct pursuit of its economic interests able to ignore the political implications of Great Britain selling buses to Cuba or of the Federal Republic of Germany underwriting a consortium's part in China's steel industry.

There is a third political limit to interdependence that, while partially a function of these broader environmental constraints, has a certain force of its own. The process by which any country, even the most autocratic, sets, or happens upon, its foreign policy course constitutes a lumbering, quasi-bureaucratic confusion on which no leader or school of thought can completely impose its will. Thus, while it may be that the changing quality of international politics has given the upper hand to people willing to contemplate a much grander trade between East and West, the domestic political process depreciates the meaning of that upper hand.

Take the Soviet Union, for example. At the center of the picture is Brezhnev, the architect of a *Westpolitik* predicated in part on a considerable increase in the Soviet Union's economic involvement with the industrial

---

33. Peking has more than once made it plain to the Japanese that their participation in the development of the Tyumen oil fields or the Druzhba pipeline will not help to expand Sino-Japanese trade. The Chinese have also refused to do business with Japanese trading firms that trade with Taiwan.

states of the West. Arrayed at other points in the picture are supposedly colleagues and underlings who have little of Brezhnev's enthusiasm for mixing with Western investors and traders. Still elsewhere are presumably miscellaneous elements that, for their own reasons, would like to see this cooperation advance as far as possible, perhaps a good deal further than Brezhnev envisages. Brezhnev's policy emerges from this rather simple confrontation of interests as a moderate middle course whose very success owes to the avoidance of either extreme.

Reality is more complicated. It would be surprising if the lines were so simply and neatly drawn. In actuality, there is an extraordinary range of interests involved, often only obliquely or partially in conflict, and perhaps divided within themselves. In short, the ambiguities of policy correspond to the ambiguities of the process by which policy is formed and even at times to the ambiguities of key participants in the process.

Ambiguity is another way of expressing the third kind of limit to interdependence, i.e., the nature of the policymaking process. Mikhail Suslov, leader of the palace coup in 1964 and primary Party ideologue for more than a decade, is often identified as an opponent of détente and, by the same token, of the *Westpolitik*. To see him as such, however, doubtless distorts his contribution to policy. He is a traditionalist, a guardian of the Soviet Union's essential political values, and, therefore, probably not so much an opponent of détente and cooperation with the West as a cautioning voice. He does not reject economic involvement with the West but rather the tendency to rely too much on the outside in solving Soviet problems and too little on the traditional norms of self-reliance and socialist competition. He does not condemn the *Westpolitik*, not publicly, at least, but he does remind his peers of the need to counteract the infiltration of bourgeois ideas (and tastes) accompanying interdependence.[34] From most indicators, Brezhnev shares the same concerns. But Brezhnev appears to believe that enlisting the West in Soviet development is the surest way to protect the system from the pressures for reform, and, perhaps, this is how he sells the *Westpolitik* to his old colleague. Western technology, capital, and technique are intended as relief to, not from, central planning, a way to keep the planning system intact while the economy is finally shifted over from extensive to intensive growth.

Viewed in this light, the *Westpolitik*'s more natural opponent is Premier Kosygin, the Soviet leader most closely associated with economic reform. But Kosygin's position illustrates perfectly the multiple and sometimes competing concerns that motivate many of the major (direct) participants in policymaking. Thus, while Kosygin has defended much of what the reformers have urged since 1965, and while many of these people no doubt

---

34. See *Pravda*, 15 July 1973, p. 2, for his comprehensive statement on the seventieth anniversary of the Second Congress of the Russian Social Democratic Party.

disapprove of the *Westpolitik* to the extent that it postpones critical choices, he also represents other interests with a different point of view. The influential State Committee for Science and Technology, for example, has a heavy stake in acquiring the assistance of International Business Machines (IBM), Control Data, and others in developing the All-Union Automated System for Planning and Management, a giant computer network that is to serve as the backbone for automated central planning.[35] To complicate the issue further, Kosygin must also respond to the biases of Gosplan and, within Gosplan, to those who resent the rush to bring the computer to planning, the attack on comfortably familiar methods of planning, and the preoccupation with the quality of production and with catering to Soviet consumers. They have no particular interest in promoting vast levels of trade with the West. Presumably they make it easier for Kosygin to understand and communicate with Suslov. Thus, Kosygin brings to the question of East-West economic cooperation a complex and not always easily reconciled set of considerations. But so do most of the critical direct participants, and, for the same reason: they, as Kosygin, both lead and act on behalf of a variety of partially competing collateral participants.

In turn, a good many second-level participants are probably further divided within themselves over this issue. Say, for example, that Soviet Minister of Defense Andrei Grechko, a man bound by profession to be skeptical of East-West economic interdependence, listens to two voices: one maintains that détente is not only risky but a necessity only because the regime has given in to the consumer, that by chasing after Western goods and know-how the leadership is allowing itself to be pushed into an untimely arms control process; the other responds that without Western capital and technology, resources will surely be shifted from the military to other sectors, that, if carefully controlled, the process of arms control can help the Soviet Union to catch up in several of the areas where it lags. It is likely that these voices are each something less than a perfectly matched chorus. For example, those who must mistrust détente may differ in their assessment of East-West economic cooperation. The most reluctant, the navy perhaps, may resist any significant collaboration with the West. Some of its spokesmen have scarcely troubled themselves to conceal their impatience with the formulas of détente worked out by Brezhnev and Nixon.[36] Their fear is evidently that détente will complicate the task of keeping the leadership's attention on the gap between the navies of the two countries, and they know, whatever the current enthusiasm for expanding the Soviet navy, how great the gap is. Others, possibly close to the Strategic Rocket Forces, may have trouble identifying with people who see East-West

35. See Henry R. Lieberman in *New York Times,* 13 December 1973.
36. See, for example, G. Svyatov and A. Kokoshin, *International Affairs* (Moscow), no. 4 (April 1973): 56-62.

cooperation as an essential way to acquire technology and other scarce goods. They have always been favored in both respects. But perhaps they perceive a more relaxed atmosphere, so long as nothing is sacrificed to it, as one means of restraining American defense efforts. Still others, perhaps some within the General Staff, may appreciate the benefits of eliminating the embargo on strategic items but worry about the influence of people too taken with the possibilities of Soviet-American cooperation. There is not the space here to imagine the equivalent divisions within the other defense establishment viewpoint or within a third or a fourth, but we can be sure that they exist.

Thus, back through the process, differentiated interests, many of them far more intricate than our simple model, transform the issue of East-West economic interdependence into a subtly shaded maze of calculations. Rather than making policy formulation a clear-cut resolution of interests for and against increased economic cooperation, these encumbered calculations tend to complicate the process, to confuse its message, and, as a consequence, to modify the impulse to interdependence generated by changes in the international environment.

The same is true, with minor variations, in every country. Other nations may substitute relative chaos for the restricted and rather stylized interest articulation of the Soviet Union, but the effect is largely the same. American behavior (broader and more formidable than merely the administration's policy) is every bit as involved, internally inconsistent, and ambiguous. Indeed, more so.

This partially accounts for the remarkable symmetry in the configuration of Soviet and American attitudes toward economic interdependence. It may be true that the prevailing sentiment in both governments (in effect, the direct participants) favors increased economic cooperation. There may also be considerable support for the idea among collateral and indirect participants. But the relative strength of the idea, by definition, depends on the complete spectrum of opinion.

It seems to us that the symmetry in the present Soviet and American spectrums of opinion places a further restraint on the evolution toward greater East-West economic interdependence. It is not merely that the objective has its skeptics in both countries,[37] not to mention its opponents, public in the United States, less easily identified in the Soviet Union but no fewer, one assumes. Equally important, the balance of force *among* the proponents of economic interdependence appears to be less than ideal. Essentially, the role of vested interests with a purely economic stake in interdependence is too small. True, the number and, in some cases, the names of American firms

---

37. For the moment, we will disregard our categories of participants. It does not matter in this context whether the only Soviet skeptics with enough importance to impede the evolution toward interdependence are in the first category or whether American skeptics with the same clout can be and are in the second category. It only matters that there are such skeptics.

interested in doing business with the Soviet Union are rather impressive, but even the most optimistic estimates do not suggest that American investments in the Soviet Union can in the next two decades amount to more than a small fraction of total American foreign investment. And the political impact of this comparatively small part of the American business community has been and will continue to be easily offset by other vested interests. In the Soviet Union, such elements are even weaker—an odd firm here and there, and 40 politically inconsequential organizations.

Second, functional interests with fundamental economic stake in East-West cooperation that might compensate for the weaknesses of vested interests also wield little influence. These are generally collateral participants. Thus, while the Soviet State Committee on Science and Technology is an important collateral participant, collateral participants occupy an inferior place in the Soviet policymaking process. In the United States, collateral participants have a greater impact on the policymaking process but those most interested in the economic benefits of East-West cooperation are among the least influential. When the director of the Office of East-West Trade urges expanded Soviet-American trade as one of the ways to build up substantial favorable trade balances by which some hope to rectify the American balance of payments, the input is coming from a lesser player.

This means that the momentum behind East-West economic interdependence depends even more than usual on participants whose calculations are primarily political. Classical economic liberalism, with its illusion of self-contained economic and political domains, has never had much to do with economic relations between East and West, and it is unlikely to come to have much more. Even the most enthusiastic advocates of East-West economic cooperation think in political terms: they supply the political reasons to explain why cooperation is safe, and they evaluate economic cooperation according to what are basically political advantages and disadvantages. The Americans ask: Is increased trade likely to create a vested interest in mutual restraint? Promote a liberalization of the Soviet system? Or give the Soviet Union leverage over the United States? The Soviets ask: Is increased trade likely to restore the Soviet Union's competitive position? Strengthen the political base of the regime? Or lead to a high level of external interference in Soviet domestic affairs? And, being realists, these advocates set the limits to economic cooperation in political terms: the West must not convince itself that the Soviet Union so wants Western technology and capital that it will be dictated to in its treatment of dissident intellectuals or Soviet Jews or whatever next comes to mind; the East must not be construed as something less than a powerful competitor or welcomed into the international economic community as one of us.

In both countries, the most important spokesman for increased East-West economic interdependence present mirror-image arguments, and this, when it comes to these last matters, limits the level of economic interdependence they are willing to recommend. Nowhere is that more evident than among the key participants, the national leadership. In the third part of this essay we dealt with the heavy political stake that President Ford and Secretary Kissinger have in economic interdependence. Then we argued that the Soviet leadership has a more intrinsically economic stake in economic interdependence. But that stake is parochial. Brezhnev is not campaigning for expanded trade with the United States and its powerful capitalist friends because he wants to increase wealth all around. The thought that either country views East-West economic interdependence as the path to greater global efficiency and growth borders on the ridiculous—the claim of each notwithstanding.

Briefly then, a significant constraint on the political impulse to East-West economic interdependence derives from two related circumstances. The first is the error of Calvin Coolidge, of a good many contemporary conservatives fearful of continued American fascination with Moscow and Peking, and of a host of Soviet optimists in assuming that "the business of America is business." This is clearly not so, not, at least, in the East-West context. The second derives from the Soviet Union's failure ever to produce its own Calvin Coolidge.

The Politics of Interdependence

Broadly sketched, these seem to us to be the basic circumstances advancing and restraining East-West economic interdependence. The political impulse toward cooperation is, in terms of the postwar confrontation, a revolutionary development. But it is a nascent impulse and still far from self-sustaining or irresistible.

So far we have concentrated on the political context of economic interdependence without discussing the character of interdependence itself as it is likely to emerge over the remainder of the decade. We turn now to this other dimension—the political dynamics of interdependence, its impact on the behavior of the major East-West nations, its potential for stabilizing (or destabilizing) East-West relations, and, ultimately, its place in a reordered international economic system.

The two most fundamental trends in contemporary international politics, as common knowledge has it, are polycentrism—the fragmentation of (imperial) political power—and increasing interdependence—the loss of (national) political power. To what extent the two trends are related, however, is less well known. If they have a cause-and-effect relationship, it may be, with one exception, an essentially negative one. It is difficult to see what the collapse of two hegemonically ordered blocs has contributed to the exponential increase in American investments in Europe and, more recently, to the increase of Japanese and West European investments in the United States, or, secondarily, to environmental pollution, or now to some nations' desire to join forces in coping with long-term energy problems. But it is much less implausible to sense a connection between the frustrations of interdependence and the every-man-for-himself attitude increasingly displayed among the major Western nations. We return to this point in a moment.

The one exception is East-West relations, where cause and effect stand out more clearly. Polycentrism, by both demonstrating and reinforcing a more diffuse East-West rivalry, constitutes an obvious part of the environmental change encouraging the movement toward economic interdependence. In the process, it has significantly enlarged the role of transnationalism, a primary "carrier" of interdependence. Transnationalism, in turn, introduces a strange new dimension into East-West relations whose effects are already proving to be unpredictable. Not merely is there a new set, new at least since 1946, of transnational actors, such as Occidental Petroleum and the Texas Eastern Transmission Company, participating in East-West relations. Another, less conventional type of transnational actor, ironically more powerful in some ways than the businessman from whom he derives his influence, has also appeared: he is the prominent intellectual dissident, like Andre Sakharov (or the president of the American Academy of Sciences), who has sought to use the Soviet leadership's stake in East-West economic cooperation to internationalize the issue of Soviet human rights. One of the accomplishments of the cold war, Raymond Aron pointed out some years ago, was to interrupt transnational contact between nations in the two opposing camps.[38] The growth of interdependence will partially depend on the way the two sides come to terms with its restoration.

The growth of East-West economic interdependence will also partially depend on the shape interdependence takes in other contexts, notably, where it is the most highly developed, between Japan, Western Europe, and the United States. The disintegration of the primitively interdependent (capitalist) world economy created and sustained by American power and interests and the rise of, what Robert Gilpin called in his essay, the mercantilist model must exercise a critical influence on the level and nature of East-West interdependence.

Ironically, the character of West-West interdependence both spurs and sets the limits to East-West interdependence. On the one hand, Soviet and other communist leaderships are heartened by the antagonisms stimulated among the major capitalist powers by the economic burdens of their interdependence. The sudden increase in what communist leaderships perceive as "interimperialist contradictions" (or, in Gilpin's terms, a more "intense international economic competition for markets, investment outlets, and sources of raw materials") makes the West a less formidable economic entity, indeed, no entity at all, and East-West economic cooperation a less

38. Raymond Aron, *Peace and War* (New York: Praeger, 1967), p. 105.

wrenching adventure.

On the other hand, the tensions of West-West interdependence remind both sides that extensive interinvolvement accentuates contending as well as common interests. The point has a double dimension. At one level, the socialist states would be the first to agree with Western economists who argue that a harmonious interdependent world economy must be "an imperial hierarchical system."[39] That is not the degree to which they care to see interdependence perfected nor, considering their general view of economic relations between and with capitalist states, is it a condition in which they would place much confidence. At a second, more practical level, neither East nor West can ignore the lessons of an economic interdependence that has been so easily politicized. The feature of interdependence among Western nations that gives pause, as Edward Morse has suggested, is not only the eruption of frequent international economic crises but also the conscious (political) manipulation of these crises by parties to the relationship.[40]

Therefore, if either or both sides learn from trends in the international economic relations of the West, trends fearfully duplicated in the oil diplomacy of the Arab states, East-West economic interdependence is bound to remain a rather stunted specimen. To the extent that either retains control over the process, prudence is bound to impose qualifications on interdependence. No country, at least none that directs its own destiny, will blithely sanction, let alone aid, a pattern of trade or investment leaving it vulnerable to significant pressure from the *government* of a major opponent. This, it seems to us, means that economic interdependence will likely remain subnational, i.e., that it will not be permitted to impinge on national interests. Thus, while individual American petroleum companies may become deeply involved with the Soviet Union, it would be surprising if any American government would allow the United States to become heavily dependent on the Soviet Union for its oil. Now that an American president has committed the United States to basic self-sufficiency in this area, it seems more probable that the government will be increasingly torn between the economic and political elements of interdependence—between the pressures to underwrite large private deals, such as the $6.5 billion North Star natural gas project, for their salutary political effects and the pressures to spend the money off the California coast, in Alaska, or for coal research as a means of protecting other economic options.[41]

39. Robert Gilpin, "Three Models of the Future," in *International Organization* 29, 1 (Winter 1975) (Madison: The University of Wisconsin Press).

40. Edward L. Morse, "Crisis Diplomacy, Interdependence, and the Politics of International Economic Relations," in Tanter and Ullman, *Theory and Policy in International Relations*, pp. 123-50.

41. North Star will supply at the most only 2 percent of the gas needs of the eastern United States.

Similarly, the Soviet Union and most of the East European countries have made it plain that they are not going to give the multinational corpora-tion the kind of authority it enjoys elsewhere. They have no intention of granting alien institutions the slightest influence over their administered economies. Nor are Soviet leaders prepared to leave their country depend-ent on trade, either by volume or by content. It is virtually inconceivable that trade with the West could exceed 1.5 percent of Soviet GNP over the next decade, or that foreign investments could exceed 3 percent of total in-vestment. More important, the Soviet Union is not looking to the West for the long-term supply of basic goods or resources. The disruption of in-dividual projects or the interruption of technological transfer would be in-convenient but scarcely fatal.

So, too, is the case in the United States. The Soviet Union already possesses the power to make life miserable for half a dozen major American chemical trading firms, and the number and variety of companies depend-ent on Soviet trade will surely double or triple. But that will still give the Soviet Union leverage over less than 3 percent of American trade, and, hence, over less than 0.15 percent of total GNP. Should American invest-ments in the Soviet Union come close to the levels for which Soviet leaders are hoping ($15 to $20 billion over the next decade), the Soviet Union would acquire sizable "hostage capital." But even if one ignores the fact that it is not the Soviet style to renege on such agreements, it takes some imagination to see how Soviet leaders might bring this influence to bear, or, even more so, why they would employ what could be only marginal influence with con-siderable costs to themselves.

If, however, East-West economic interdependence is to be qualified, then the political uses to which it can be put are likely to be qualified as well. The notion that the United States may be able to "use" the Soviet stake in American capital and technology to induce system change does not make sense. This is not to say that the effect of a growing economic interdepend-ence may not lead to internal adjustments, that, for example, the Soviet leadership will not gradually feel obliged to change in order to make the Soviet Union more competitive. But it does mean that the conscious manipulation of economic interdependence to secure political objectives that the other side judges dangerous is not likely to succeed. This expresses both the outer limits of the American strategy of linkages and, ironically, the reason why the United States has been successful in compromising Soviet policy on an issue like Jewish immigration. It is precisely the ap-pearance that the administration is *not* trying to use economic cooperation against the Soviet Union but finds its hands tied by other elements that creates the pressure to which Brezhnev and his friends may have been will-ing to yield. (On how many other occasions Brezhnev will yield or tolerate the impression that he has yielded is a fair question.) In short, the Soviet leadership is at a certain disadvantage in the politics of economic interdependence because it cannot communicate the same lack of control over policy as the American administration can. Neither leadership, however, should expect to have the kind of leverage permitting it to dictate the other's behavior.

This is not to argue that economic relations will or should be less and less contaminated by political considerations. Nations on both sides or on all sides, if that is the way that international relations ought now to be viewed, will make political demands where they have a strong economic hand. But most often these are likely to be random quid pro quos, of fairly marginal political importance (such as the release of Japanese fishermen held by the Soviet Union, a place for France among the superpowers in a future Middle Eastern settlement, or formal recognition of the Common Market by the Chinese), and short of a systematic strategy for altering another country's foreign and domestic policies. Even here, the nation having something of an economic upper hand may find itself using it most of the time simply to protect its own economic interests. The Federal Republic of Germany, for example, may have trouble trading off future credits or technical cooperation against the exit of Volga Germans when these are essential to ensure prompt and full Soviet compliance with promised petroleum deliveries. In short, while both East and West will surely mix narrow political and economic initiatives, the scale of East-West interdependence is unlikely to tolerate linkages that, in broader concerns, do more than prod mutually acceptable political instruments.

Finally, the peculiar asymmetries of polycentrism will give a special character to East-West economic interdependence. Because polycentrism will not soon produce genuine multipolarity—the discrepancies are too great in the power of Japan, Western Europe, China, and the two superpowers—interdependence will also have its discontinuities. For one, China, a prominent player in a polycentric world but no economic match for either superpower or for Japan, may play a much less significant role in the rapid expansion of East-West economic interdependence.

Second, to the extent that China figures in the growth of East-West economic interdependence, its importance is likely to be confined to Asia. Thus, while it is true that Sino-Japanese trade is nearly twice as large as Soviet-American trade and is likely to remain larger than Soviet-American trade for the rest of the decade, the political impact of the first is regional and of the second, global. Trade with the Soviet Union is at the intersection of East with West in the triple sense of geography, comparative politics, and the reach of power. Trade with China is essentially an Asian affair. Japan seeks a larger trade with China (beyond its economic benefits) in order to reduce the political risks of the enlarged trade that it seeks with the Soviet Union. Both in general and in particular, the Japanese view cooperation with China as a critical means of preserving the Asian balance. Thus, their aggregate trade has not only caught up with Soviet-Japanese trade, but

Japanese leaders no doubt hope to lessen the political liability of the importance they attach to obtaining Soviet natural gas and oil by joining the Chinese in the development of their mainland and offshore petroleum. Similarly, China appears to value its trade with the United States and with Western Europe as a counterbalance to its trade with Japan. Unlike the Soviet Union, China does the greatest share (indeed, 80 percent) of its trading with noncommunist countries, but, more significantly, 23 or 24 percent of this is with its economically powerful neighbor. Thus, trade with the United States and with West European countries serves the function of permitting China to expand its trade without forcing the Japanese figure over 25 percent.

Third, the enormous power of the Soviet Union over Eastern Europe means that the level and nature of this region's contribution to East-West economic interdependence will be largely determined in Moscow. Fourth, the level and nature of economic interdependence sanctioned by the Soviet Union for itself and its allies will depend, in part, on its ability to contain other forms of interdependence, such as a freer interchange of ideas and tourists. And, fifth, because the scale of Soviet expectations is so much greater than those of other socialist countries, and because American resources for meeting Soviet expectations are so much greater than (or at least perceived as such by Soviet leaders) those of other capitalist countries, the shape of their economic relationship should fundamentally determine the course of East-West economic interdependence.

East-West Interdependence and International Economic Institutions

In this essay, we have deliberately stressed the basic limits to East-West economic interdependence. We have done so not because we doubt the prospect of a marked increase in trade between East and West, particularly between the United States and the Soviet Union, and not because we dismiss the progress already achieved in reducing the economic and legal barriers to trade and investment. We have done so because our concern is with the potential relevance that increased East-West economic interdependence may have for the restructuring of international economic institutions. Should East-West trade double by 1980, as is perfectly conceivable, should United States-Soviet trade grow fifteenfold (from $200 million in 1971 to $3 billion by 1980), should Western investors sink billions of dollars, yen and deutschemarks into a wide array of joint ventures, should home governments provide additional billions in guarantees and credits, and should the Soviet Union begin selling Ladas in New York and the United States begin constructing Holiday Inns in Moscow, the impact on East-West relations will be considerable. Economic cooperation can, indeed, become an important element in efforts to build a more stable and productive East-

West relationship. But, for reasons to which we now turn, it need not be more than incidental to the process of fashioning new international economic institutions.[42]

Poland, Rumania, and Hungary have each recently become full members of the General Agreement on Tariffs and Trade (GATT). What does this do for East-West trade? Presumably membership in the GATT should increase the East-West trade of the three nations by putting trade on a most-favored-nation basis; that is, the Western members reduce their tariffs and presumably also their quotas on the products of the three nations to the low MFN levels, thus enabling an increase in Eastern exports. Poland and Rumania, not having really meaningful tariffs, must reciprocate in other ways. Poland has agreed to increase its imports from the GATT nations by 7 percent a year, thereby stimulating a tariff or quota reduction. Rumania has agreed to increase its imports from the GATT nations as fast as total Rumanian imports increase. Hungary has insisted that its tariffs, under the New Economic Mechanism, are really tariffs and presumably grants MFN treatment via market mechanisms (i.e., through lowering tariffs) to other GATT nations.

The increase in East-West trade that is likely to result through the GATT, however, will probably be small. Some trade creation will undoubtedly occur as Eastern and Western exports replace domestic production in Western and Eastern nations, respectively. But sizable increments to East-West trade are unlikely to occur unless there is trade diversion, particularly on the Eastern side—trade diversion that reverses, at least in part, the trade diversion of the immediate postwar years. Before World War II, the COMECON nations conducted about 15 percent of their trade with each other; the present figure averages over 60 percent. A substantial shift back toward the undistorted previous levels is undoubtedly justified on commercial grounds and would go a long way toward restoring East-West trade to more normal levels.

It seems highly dubious that this will happen. The main reason is that despite GATT membership the members of COMECON continue to trade with each other as before. Representatives of the ministry of foreign trade of each socialist nation sit down with representatives of the ministry of every other socialist nation each year and together work out the trading pattern for the year to come as well as longer-run patterns. It is almost impossible, when large barter deals of this sort are negotiated, to view individual transactions strictly in terms of commercial considerations. Further, the

42. We have not meant to slight the significance of China's role in a broader East-West economic cooperation. On the contrary, we are merely assuming that the growth of the West's, including Japan's, trade with China will ultimately be constrained by the same structural limitations as Western trade with the Soviet bloc. In one respect, however, we are assuming a more limited role for China—that is, in promoting East-West investment. Its role is likely to be more, though not exclusively, concentrated in trade.

commitments made under these deals are commitments that must be observed, since each nation's overall economic plan is geared to the foreign trade plan; failure to fulfill the latter, particularly imports, could have a serious impact on the former. This suggests that unless the Eastern GATT nations make a conscious decision to cut back their trade with other socialist nations, their East-West trade cannot increase any faster than before. This statement applies to Hungary as well as to Poland and Rumania, despite the fact that Hungarian enterprises, under the New Economic Mechanism, presumably are free—indeed, required—to buy and sell where the profits are highest. For the fact is that the Hungarian government is compelled to fulfill its obligations under trade agreements with other COMECON members, and, though in theory it cannot order an enterprise to ship to or buy from, say, the USSR rather than to or from the West, it can and does induce appropriate behavior by various combinations of taxes and subsidies.

There are several factors that would appear to militate against any really substantial reduction in intrabloc trade and, hence, against an increase in East-West trade, at least in the medium run. First, it seems unlikely that radical economic reforms, of the kind projected but not quite achieved by Hungary, will be implemented. Reforms of this sort, which truly decentralize economic activity, including foreign trade, will undoubtedly lead to a sharp increase in trade with the West. In fact, however, over the last four years, Soviet leaders have been moving in the opposite direction. Far from building on the 1965 reform, they have successfully undone virtually everything promised in that timid venture, for two reasons. First, half-hearted reform does not make sense economically. Marginally improved material incentives and token decentralization within essentially the old setting, as Soviet leaders discovered, only compound problems. Second, and on the other hand, more than half-hearted reform has political risks that Soviet leaders refuse to run. Even before Czechoslovakia, they had sensed a link between economic and political decentralization. To sacrifice control in this one critical sector of political life endangers the Party's preeminence in all others. Soviet leaders believe too deeply in the monopolistic party as a guardian of the nation's purpose to allow any such erosion.[43]

It is a question not merely of keeping things together within the Soviet Union but also within the empire. Economic reform in the Soviet Union would be quickly and eagerly imitated in many of the East European countries. And economic reform in Eastern Europe, Soviet leaders justifiably fear, would create counterpressures against the economic interdependence of their alliance system.

---

43. Because trade forms such a small part of Soviet economic activity, at 2½ to 3 percent of GNP (a much smaller part than the trade of, say, Hungary, which may run as high as 25 percent), the importance of improving its efficiency is easily outweighed by political considerations.

Second, so long as substantial economic reforms are not undertaken by the bloc nations, they will be plagued by the "salesmanship" problems described earlier. The only Eastern nation not so severely restricted is the USSR with its large potential for raw material and energy resource exports that require almost no salesmanship ability. Therefore, with the possible exception of the USSR, increased East-West trade faces a salesmanship barrier.

While the USSR does have easily saleable exports, its appetite for hard-currency imports clearly exceeds its present hard-currency export potential. One factor handicapping the USSR in its attempt to achieve some kind of equilibrium in East-West trade is the fact that it stands as a supplier of oil, other raw materials, and grains to the nations of East Europe. The cost to the USSR in hard currency of this role in intrabloc trade is large indeed. Over the next decade, there will undoubtedly be a conflict between those who, for economic reasons, would like to divert Soviet exports from East Europe to the West and those who, for political reasons, will oppose such a diversion in order to preserve economic interdependence among the bloc nations. In the short run, the smaller bloc nations will suffer if they have to seek energy and raw material resources elsewhere, since Soviet prices have been very reasonable. Over the long run, they may gain if they take the opportunity provided to decentralize their economies and adjust themselves to Western markets.

To return to the GATT, until now Western nations have been willing to accept Eastern nations into the GATT so long as these nations reciprocate MFN in the ways indicated above. In so doing, however, they are overlooking the fact that the Eastern nations discriminate in favor of each other on an unprecedented scale. The 60 percent or so of trade that they conduct with each other is certainly excessive, as we have already noted. Can this be justified on economic grounds? Perhaps it can, in two ways.

First, it could be argued that the COMECON nations are a customs union and therefore are entitled under the GATT to grant each other preferential treatment. They do not consider themselves a customs union, however, nor do they feel that they grant each other preferential treatment; and they resent the fact that the members of the EEC are allowed, under the GATT, to grant each other preferential treatment. Nevertheless, this is one way the GATT can rationalize present COMECON practice, and has explicitly done so in the case of Hungary, whose COMECON trade is exempted from MFN treatment.

Second, and related to the first point, the current practice of Eastern European countries may be justified in order to redefine nondiscrimination for centrally planned economies. An important advantage that trade among centrally planned economies has is that they plan this trade in advance on a national scale and guarantee each other deliveries of large aggregations of goods. Given central planning, this feature of intrabloc trade can be viewed as a large positive value. When the Eastern nations argue that they do not grant each other preferential treatment, they may well have in mind the fact that only other Eastern nations are willing to deal with them on their preferred institutional terms, and that this is worth a lot of "price."

If this be the case, then we will have to face a future in which non-discrimination is defined differently in East and West. This makes something of a mess of the rules of the game, but perhaps the West should not worry too much about it. For one thing, the rules have been breached many times over the years, and, with the recent international monetary crisis, the trend is increasing. Further, East-West trade is still very marginal.[44] Nevertheless, it is extremely important to recognize that so long as radical economic reforms are not undertaken by the Eastern nations, the GATT will not make a substantial contribution toward the increase of East-West trade unless it insists on nondiscrimination in the Western sense; that is to say, unless the GATT forces the Eastern nations to redirect more of their trade to the West. This may of course be impossible without decentralization, for reasons noted earlier, such as bloc export problems. If such reforms are implemented, the reforms themselves would be the important force in increasing East-West trade. The GATT would play a significant but a distinctly subsidiary role.[45]

We turn now to international financial matters—investment, balance-of-payments problems, exchange rates, and the role of the International Monetary Fund (IMF). Rumania has joined the IMF. Undoubtedly other Eastern nations will soon become members. There are advantages to IMF membership that cannot be overlooked. Membership in the IMF can lead to IMF credits, eligibility for World Bank loans, and the right to a share of new issues of special drawing rights—all very desirable, particularly to nations with serious hard-currency balance-of-payments problems. Aside from receiving "manna from heaven," however, it is not clear that membership confers further benefits on the centrally planned economies. Certainly, they do not appear to have much of a stake in the kind of rules of the game that the IMF was set up to insure some 30 years ago. Nor do they appear to have a stake in the future rules presently evolving.[46]

It is somewhat more difficult to understand why the IMF is interested, at this juncture, in encouraging the membership of centrally planned economies. The future framework of Western financial relations remains uncertain. To admit nations into the IMF with such different monetary

44. Raymond Vernon, "Apparatchiks and Entrepreneurs," *Foreign Affairs* 52 (January 1974): 249-62, worries that a significant increase in East-West trade could have a very subversive impact on the rules of the game.

45. COMECON devotes its efforts to promoting socialist integration. In this sense it serves an anti-interdependence role—like the EEC.

46. We are referring here, of course, to commitments to achieve convertibility, to avoidance of trade controls for current balance-of-payments reasons, and to adjustable pegged exchange rates (now something between fixed and floating).

systems and problems can complicate working out the new framework. To give such nations a vote, and the USSR would perforce have a significant vote were it admitted to the IMF, might encumber the future decision-making process without, in our opinion, adding a useful viewpoint. The fact of the matter is that, with the possible exception of Hungary, the COMECON nations are not in a position to aspire to any of the goals of the Western financial community. They are, in effect, nations without real international monetary systems. They trade with each other on a bilateral balance basis, their currencies are completely inconvertible into other currencies as well as into commodities, their exchange rates are not real prices and serve no real function, and the prices at which they trade with each other are borrowed from the capitalist world. When they trade with the West, they are like visitors from another planet: they use the currencies, prices, and exchange rates of the West, but none of the financial magnitudes involved are organically related to their domestic economies. And when they trade with the West, they invariably want to buy more than they can sell, which is a problem that cannot be ameliorated by currency devaluation, the ultimate Western solution.

Before concluding this section, a brief comment is in order on the two COMECON banks, the International Bank for Economic Cooperation (IBEC) and the International Investment Bank (IIB). IBEC was established about a decade ago as a sort of European Payments Union for the socialist nations. Its primary purpose was to multilateralize intrabloc trade. (It also had short-term credit extension powers similar to those of the IMF, but these were secondary.) It was to accomplish this task by creating a "transferable ruble" for all intrabloc payments. Presumably, a surplus of transferable rubles earned with one country could be spent in another, thereby multilateralizing trade. In fact, however, given commodity inconvertibility, transferable rubles were no more capable of being spent on an ad hoc basis than zlotys or forints. No nation was willing to have an export surplus with another because it could not be sure that the rubles earned could be satisfactorily spent. As a result, no multilateralization took place. IBEC failed because it attempted to solve by an administrative device a profoundly economic problem. The International Investment Bank, established in 1971, is an institution designed to multilateralize and expand bloc investment. In principle it is similar to the World Bank, but it is actually more analogous to the investment funds established by the EEC.

IBEC seems to offer little in promoting greater East-West interdependence. Just as membership in the IMF by centrally planned economies, save possibly for Hungary, can only be token at this point, so is this also true of formal ties between the IMF and IBEC. On a small scale, IIB offers possibilities. At this point, however, if there were a formal tie between IIB and, say, the World Bank, it would primarily serve the function of funneling Western investment into the Eastern nations. This is already being accomplished by private business on an increasing scale, and IIB has borrowed money for this purpose in Western capital markets. At the moment, these seem to be more powerful forces for integration than IIB could ever be, just as in the West private capital flows dwarf those originating in intergovernmental institutions. Further, the major problems that serve to impede Western investment in the bloc—politics and currency inconvertibility—would be brought no closer to solution by linking IIB with Western financial organizations.

Greater economic interdependence between East and West has been fostered over the past decade by various kinds of ad hoc developments between private enterprises and socialist governments, rather than by international organizations. Joint ventures, coproduction agreements, comarketing agreements, repayments in kind, and the like have facilitated transfer of management know-how and technology, have made up for lack of marketing skills, have evaded problems of inconvertibility, and so forth. As noted earlier, all of these devices must be viewed as second-best strategies, designed to compensate for systemic deficiencies. As such, they are all suboptimal. Thus, paying a Western enterprise to market your products in the West earns hard currency but not so much as would have been earned if marketing skills were endemic. Or repaying long-term investments in gas and petroleum appears to get around the hard-currency problem, but only by repaying in commodities that are, in effect, the equivalent of hard currency.

Were the Soviet Union to institute major economic reforms and, hence, open the way to radical economic reform in Eastern Europe, then market-facilitating organizations like the GATT and the IMF would become more central to East-West economic cooperation. With radical reforms in all of the COMECON nations, internal markets would be decentralized and internal prices and exchange rates would have an organic relationship to world prices. They would become functional. In these circumstances, the Eastern nations could join the GATT on present Western terms. Eastern enterprises, basing their foreign trade decisions on market criteria and no longer constrained by governmental bilateral agreements, would begin to trade much more with the West. In less than a decade, the relative importance of East-West trade in total world trade could double or increase even more while intrabloc trade could decline, relatively, by a comparable percentage.

It is unlikely that East-West trade would reach prewar proportions, however, since the introduction of market socialism in COMECON would not necessarily mean the dissolution of COMECON nor the end of COMECON as a preferential trading area. In the absence of a drastic change in the political picture, it seems probable that the COMECON nations will continue to grant each other more preferential terms than they grant to the West, even as the nations of the EEC and the European Free Trade Association do. Certainly, however, the degree of preference would be less extreme than it is under the present state-trading system. Radical reforms would also end commodity inconvertibility, and membership in the IMF would become meaningful. Trade, and particularly credits and investment, would be facilitated and "normalized." No longer, for example, would there be an incentive on the part of Western investors to seek repayment in kind. In fact, many of the ad hoc arrangements discussed in the second part of this essay might well wither away.

It is, however, unlikely that political considerations will, in the near term, permit such far-reaching changes. Thus, East-West economic relations should remain essentially a political matter, produced and limited by politics. Their contribution—perhaps gradually a very meaningful contribution—will likely be primarily to the politics of East-West relations.

Soviet Perspectives on North-South Relations

in the Era of

"The Scientific-Technological Revolution" *

According to the leading Soviet officials and foreign policy analysts, the worldwide "scientific-technological revolution" (STR) has influenced the relationship between the industrialized capitalist nations and the countries of the Third World in three major ways.[1]

First, advanced capitalism has devised a strategy of "neoimperialism." This strategy is founded on the West's organizational superiority in the form of the multinational corporation (MNC); its economic superiority in terms of capital resources, marketing skills, and fiscal controls; and its scientific and technological superiority, which makes possible a "one-way" transfer of products and licenses from the developed to the developing world. Industrialized countries are the center of science-based production. The Third World is a raw materials and labor intensive reserve for the United States, Western Europe, and Japan. This division of labor between advanced capitalist and developing nations promotes the transfer of natural resources and semimanufactured products from the Third World to the in-

*Written especially to appear in Erik P. Hoffmann and Frederic J. Fleron, Jr. (eds.), *The Conduct of Soviet Foreign Policy* (Aldine: Hawthorne, N.Y., 2nd edition, 1980). This research was supported by a grant from the National Science Foundation.

1. For a discussion of Soviet views of "the scientific-technological revolution," see the earlier chapter by Laird and Hoffmann in this section. As in that chapter, the purpose here is to identify basic parameters of consensus among Soviet analysts, rather than to highlight or to evaluate contending interpretations.

dustrialized capitalist states. In the process, capital flows from the Western nations to the developing countries. The centrality of foreign capital to economic growth in the Third World, with the concomitant emphasis upon economic development oriented toward the foreign market, is underscored by this division of labor.[2] Hence, Western neoimperialism strives to create asymmetric dependencies in the developing states and to forestall the very real possibility of reverse dependencies (e.g., excessive reliance on Third World oil).

Second, the STR creates particular demands unique to the late twentieth century. For countries that began to modernize in the nineteenth or early twentieth centuries, scientific advances and the use of science-based technology for development were not central. But this is no longer the case. Given the dynamism of the STR in advanced capitalism, the Third World dooms itself to a position of even greater economic inferiority if it does not attempt to gain from and actively contribute to the worldwide STR. In other words, development in the advanced capitalist world is cumulative and exponential, and the ability of the Third World to "catch up" requires the capacity to borrow and effectively utilize the technological accomplishments of the STR. The establishment of an adequate indigenous scientific base, in order to participate in the STR, is a critical component of a strategy for modernization in the Third World. Formulating and implementing a domestic strategy for development is vital to a Third World country's ability to benefit from the STR, and to engage in a mutually advantageous division of labor with the advanced capitalist world.[3]

Third, the possibilities of a shift from an exploitative to an advantageous division of labor are created by the STR and by the internationalization of production. These factors will increasingly enable Third World countries (some states more than others) to exert pressure upon the advanced capitalist world. The concentration of science-based and technology-intensive industries in the West increases the industrialized Western nations' dependency upon the raw materials and the energy resources of developing countries. Because raw material commodities chiefly flow from the Third World to the prosperous capitalist states, the potential for the exercise of

2. See the following: A. Kodachenko, "Neocolonialist Strategy of the West," *Social Sciences* (Moscow) (hereinafter *SS*), 1 (1978), 158-169; N.M. Khriashcheva, *Novaia strategiia neokolonializma* (Moscow: Mezhdunarodnye otnosheniia, 1976); R.M. Avakov, *Razvivaiushchiesiia strany: NTR i problemy nezavisimosti* (Moscow: Mysl', 1976); Vasilii Vakhrushev, *Neocolonialism: Methods and Manoeuvers* (Moscow: Progress, 1973).

3. See the following: G. Skorov, "Scientific and Technological Progress and Social Orientation," *SS*, 1 (1976), 191-204; V.L. Tiagunenko, ed., *The Third World and Scientific and Technical Progress* (Moscow: Nauka, 1976), chapter one; I. Andreev, *The Noncapitalist Way* (Moscow: Progress, 1977), chapter six.

economic leverage is created and heightened by the internationalization of economic life.[4]

The struggle to replace asymmetric dependence with mutually advantageous interdependence is at the core of the "general crisis" of relations between the Third World and advanced capitalism.[5] We shall first examine Soviet perspectives on the nature of the asymmetrical dependence between the West and the Third World, and, in our second and third sections, assess Soviet views of the prospects for "genuine" interdependence and for the creation of a "new international economic order."

I. The Dependence of the Third World on Industrialized Capitalist Nations

Soviet writers contend that the Third World is most dependent on the advanced capitalist world in the areas of science and technology. The vast "technological gap" between the developing and advanced capitalist countries is rooted in vast differences in the scope and depth of capital investment in research and development (R & D), as well as in significant differences in the quantity and quality of personnel trained in the natural, social, engineering, and managerial sciences.

The neoimperialist policy utilizes these gaps to strategic advantage. As two Soviet authors have argued, "Imperialism attempts to use the technological weakness of young states in order to tie them more closely to the scientific and technological potential of the world capitalist economy."[6] The Third World represents a new market for technologically advanced goods, and Western nations compete to penetrate these markets.

Nevertheless, neoimperialism is "dialectically contradictory." In order to expand the scientific and technological potential of the industrialized capitalist states, the Third World must be able to buy new goods and to assimilate them within their own production processes.[7] The contradictory essence of neoimperialism is the attempt to help the Third World become a consumer of scientific and technological production, while preventing the Third World from becoming a producer of scientific and technological knowledge and thereby a competitor to advanced capitalism. As V.G. Solodovnikov asserts: "Life taught the neocolonialists that economic stagnation cannot be a real alternative to neocapitalist development. They learned that steps must be taken to develop capitalism in the former col-

---

4. See G. Skorov, "Developing Nations in the Struggle for Economic Equality," *SS,* 3 (1978), 187-198; and V. Rymalov, "The Agrarian and Raw-Material Basis of Capitalist Economy," *SS,* 3 (1977), 51-66.

5. On the concept of asymmetric dependency, see E. Primakov, "The Developing Countries: Some Problems," *SS,* 3 (1979), 72-82.

6. M.M. Koptev and M.S. Ochkov, *Tekhnicheskaia 'pomoshch' v strategii imperializma* (Moscow: Mysl', 1977), p. 12.

7. *Ibid.,* chapter one.

onies and semicolonies, to form the mechanism of expanded capitalist reproduction, to develop new spheres of monopoly capital investment, and to create an infrastructure meeting the requirements of the STR."[8]

But the development of the Third World through an asymmetric division of labor with advanced capitalism creates a situation in which the STR is having largely negative results in Third World countries. On one level, the STR has stimulated the production of synthetic materials which are increasingly undercutting the competitive position of the Third World's natural resources. A team of senior researchers from several institutes of the USSR Academy of Sciences concludes: "Thus, the developing countries' specialization in raw materials and foodstuffs has resulted in [the fact] that, under the conditions of the revolution in science and technology, their position in the world economy began to worsen."[9]

On a second level, the better wages and professional opportunities in the advanced capitalist states have siphoned off the domestically and foreign-trained specialists from the Third World who are absolutely essential to the creation of a scientific and technological potential in their own countries. This "brain drain" has a demoralizing impact upon the Third World intelligentsia, and, by fostering condescension or indifference toward Third World cultures, further blocks indigenous scientific and technological development. The Academy of Sciences research team elaborates: "The native scientists are brought up as cosmopolitans, indifferent to the destinies of their own countries, skeptical of the possibility of building real modern centers of science and education, and imbued with the idea of the superiority of all things foreign and of 'Western civilization.'"[10]

In short, the STR has resulted in the creation of more sophisticated forms of dependence. Economic growth in the Third World is rooted in the capacity of a given state to become closely linked with the advanced Western scientific and technological communities, in order to accelerate its own development. But Third World leaders and businessmen too often equate the expansion of foreign trade with scientific and technological dependency, which in turn is viewed as a precondition for rapid economic growth. K.N. Brutents, Deputy Chief of the International Department of the CPSU Central Committee, concludes: "Thus, neocolonialism's strategy remains essentially the same: the only alteration is with an eye to the opportunities opened up by the STR. It is now setting its sights on a higher level of economic [read: capitalist] development of the liberated countries and more sophisticated forms of dependence."[11]

---

8. V.G. Solodovnikov, "Neocolonialism in the 1970s," in E.A. Tarabrin, ed., *Neocolonialism and Africa in the 1970s* (Moscow: Progress, 1978), p. 50.

9. Tiagunenko, ed., *op. cit.*, p. 17.

10. *Ibid.*, 95.

11. K. N. Brutents, "Imperialism and the Liberated Countries," *SS*, 1 (1979), 172.

A second dimension of asymmetrical dependence is associated with the activities of the multinational corporation. The MNCs are the critical "commercial-political organizations" through which capitalism is changing the global division of labor and creating innovative forms of dominance vis-à-vis the Third World. N. Sergeev asserts: "In their strategy of keeping the developing nations in the orbit of capitalism, the state-monopoly apparatus of the West is using the international systems of the super monopolies on a growing scale to spread and reinforce their political influence in the new nations."[12]

Soviet analysts recognize that the MNCs nurture economic development, but contend this development is based on exploitation and dependency. First, the Third World economy depends heavily for its technological innovation upon the patent and licensing operations of the MNC.[13] Second, the MNC creates an incomplete production cycle in the Third World economy, in order to take advantage of the cheaper labor resources and to avoid the dangers of nationalization. A group of Soviet researchers asserts:

> By building enterprises to produce certain types of equipment, units, and components in the developing countries, the monopolies seem to be helping these countries toward industrialization and diversification of their economy. The construction of such projects does, indeed, increase employment somewhat, expand exports of finished products, and promote industrial development in general. However, such enterprises do not, as a rule, become an integral part of the industrial-economic complex of the countries concerned, as they are bound by many strings to the head enterprise...outside the country, often being its technological extension....[14]

Briefly stated, Soviet officials and theorists maintain that the MNC blocks the equitable *inter*dependent development of the Third World economy. As Sergeev put it: "By establishing subsidiaries, the transnational corporations wrest key sectors from the economy of the new nations...and include them in their international complexes. The development of these sectors is subordinated to the interests of the monopolies and in many cases comes into conflict with the interests of the countries where these subsidiaries operate."[15] Under such conditions, it becomes difficult for the Third World nations to plan for economic development. The MNC impedes the ability of the developing states to achieve the economic independence necessary to become involved in a "mutually advantageous" division of labor.

12. N. Sergeev, "Developing Nations and the Transnational Corporations," *SS*, 2 (1979), 176.
13. Koptev and Ochkov, *op. cit.*, chapter three.
14. Tiagunenko, ed., *op. cit.*, p. 21.
15. Sergeev, *op. cit.*, 175.

A third dimension of asymmetry lies in the unequal and unfair trade relations between the advanced capitalist and Third World countries. Soviet writers stress several aspects of this relationship:

a) World prices for raw materials have not kept pace with the prices for industrial manufactured goods. The lower level of growth in raw material prices compared to the rise in prices of industrial goods signifies that the STR is having an important negative effect on the trade relations of the developing world. As A. Elianov characterizes the dilemma: "The developing countries are compelled to import most, if not all, of the new equipment and production technologies. At the same time, on the world market their exports, which are practically the only source of paying for their imports, encounter obstacles difficult to surmount, obstacles which are also largely the result of the revolution in science and technology. Among them are, first and foremost, the relative drop in demand and a downward trend in prices of raw materials which are predominant in local exports."[16]

b) The lower level of labor productivity in the Third World means that developing states must sell their industrial production at world prices which are lower than the national cost for production.

c) Third World states tend to be producers and exporters of a single commodity or industrial product, which makes them extremely vulnerable to foreign market fluctuations and limits their ability to respond flexibly to changing world market conditions.

d) The advanced capitalist nations virtually monopolize the transportation system used by the Third World in international trade.

e) The imperialist states have maintained quasicolonial influences over trade relations with their former colonies and with "their" representatives in these Third World countries. In the colonial period, each imperialist state created monopoly control over economic dealings with its colony. Even after political independence, the former colonial powers have to a large extent retained their role as the primary suppliers of industrial and other goods to their liberated colonies. Various methods are used to perpetuate dependence, such as the establishment of mutually complementary markets and the cultivation of certain tastes, attitudes, and consumption habits among Third World elites. Soviet analysts conclude that "dependence is maintained on the basis of carefully preserved economic and other conditions carried [over] from the past...."[17]

A fourth asymmetry consists of the fiscal relationships between the advanced capitalist and Third World countries. The credit and currency systems prior to the oil crisis in 1973 were completely dominated by ad-

---

16. A. Elianov, "The STR and Socio-Economic Problems of the Developing Countries," *SS*, 2 (1973), 133.

17. E. Kamenov and E. Malkhasian, "African Countries' Unequal Position in Trade with Capitalist States," in Tarabrin, ed., *op. cit.,* p. 210.

vanced capitalism. Even with the emergence of petro-dollars as an important influence in the world currency system, the advanced capitalist world uses its fiscal tools to maintain and extend its dominance over the Third World.[18] For example, the debts of Third World nations provide a major opportunity for the exercise of economic leverage against them. As V.S. Baskin avers: "Capitalist creditors seek to take advantage of the difficult financial situation of a debtor country and use the concessions they have...as an instrument by which they can impose upon the latter the kind of domestic financial policy they want and strengthen their own economic positions."[19]

In addition, the flow of foreign "aid" is designed to draw the Third World more closely into the international capitalist division of labor. There has been a steady decline in the use of uncommitted grants-in-aid, which provide maximal flexibility for a Third World state to use this aid in its own interests. Increasingly, aid is given for specific purposes and is "tied" to concrete economic demands of the donor country. The recipient of such aid must use it to buy goods in the donor country. As Baskin notes, "For capitalist states, the tying of credits serves as a powerful means of accelerating the export of goods and services."[20]

Finally, the asymmetrical international dependencies are reflected in the nature of domestic development in the Third World.

a) There is an incomplete production cycle in the industrial sector and foreign management of "local" manufacturing. The integration of production is under the aegis of the MNC, not of the Third World government or one of its corporations.

b) Third World strategies for development rely on foreign involvement, which nurtures domestic economic growth through integration in the international capitalist division of labor.

c) Attention is thereby shifted away from the primacy of domestic developmental needs to foreign market demands, which often do not stimulate those sectors of the domestic economy most important to industrial growth and productivity.

d) Two economies emerge within the Third World state. One economy is "modern, fully or heavily dependent on foreign capital, and producing for export, and the other traditional, the two being not inherently interconnected (or hardly so). The creation of a single economic organism requires enormous effort and radical redistribution of resources, changes in the economic mechanism and, above all, time."[21]

18. G..K. Shirokov, ed., *Neftedollary i sotsial'no-ekonomicheskoe razvitie stran blizhnego i srednego vostoka* (Moscow: Nauka, 1979).

19. V.S. Baskin, "A New Course in the Policy of 'Aid'," in Tarabrin, ed., *op. cit.*, p. 189.

20. *Ibid.*, p. 185.

21. Tiagunenko, ed., *op. cit.*, p. 15.

e) The growth of domestic scientific and technological potential is stunted in favor of foreign technology trade. The emergence of a domestic market for advanced technology and for the products of science-based industries is blocked. This, in turn, lowers the opportunities for overall economic development in the Third World.

In brief, the current international division of labor provides a critical strategic advantage to the advanced capitalist world. The Academy of Sciences researchers conclude:

> The production and technological subjugation of developing countries to the monopolies, based on the 'new international division of labor,' allows them to influence both the general economic and sociopolitical development. In these circumstances the developing countries' efforts to organize on their own the manufacture of industrial goods for export to advanced capitalist countries come up against the resistance of the monopolies....[22]

II. The Struggle for "Genuine" Interdependence

The Third World's struggle for "genuine" interdependence requires the reversal of all basic asymmetries with the industrialized capitalist states. To eliminate the exploitative nature of this relationship, a developing nation must above all build up its own scientific and technological capabilities and launch a domestic "national liberation movement."

A. SCIENTIFIC AND TECHNICAL PROGRESS

Soviet analysts contend that a Third World country can achieve genuine interdependence through the enhancement of its scientific and technological capacities, through control over the activities of the MNC, through the creation of more advantageous terms of trade and credit, and through the realization of a strategy for development which maximizes the benefits to be drawn from foreign economic involvement and which minimizes dependence.

First, Soviet writers stress that a Third World country's ability to formulate and implement a domestic scientific and technological policy is critical to the processes of genuine interdependence. National autarky in scientific development is viewed as neither possible nor desirable under contemporary conditions. To benefit from the worldwide scientific revolution, a country must create its own effective scientific base.

The authoritative collective work of the Academy of Sciences devotes considerable attention to the developing nations' formulations of science policies adequate to the opportunities and pitfalls of interdependence. The

22. *Ibid.*, p. 22.

problem is one of striking a correct balance between "the national effort in setting up an effective research sector and the use of foreign science and technology."[23] Ties with international science must be forged and deepened. But "one should recognize the need to establish a national research base capable of meeting national development demands."[24]

Among the main dimensions of an adequate national research base are: a) the training of research personnel and the provision of material and political support for scientific development, b) the creation of an effective state institution to plan scientific research, c) the establishment of policy guidelines for scientific planning, d) the careful integration of the scientific research plan with the national economic development plan, and e) an appropriate balance between pure and applied science.

Above all, the national research effort of a Third World country must select "priority research fields strictly in keeping with the short- and long-term socioeconomic targets set by short- and long-range development plans."[25] Given the scarcity of resources which a developing state has to commit to a national R & D effort, the productive utilization of scientific and technical knowledge and of material and human capabilities is a critical task. "Vital areas of concern for the developing countries are concentrating resources in spearhead efforts, making rational use of the limited resources available, avoiding duplication of research domestically...[and] carefully selecting imported technology...."[26]

It is also necessary for the Third World state to develop a comprehensive technology policy. The chief priorities for economic growth and productivity must be identified, and the native and foreign technology appropriate to meet these priorities must be generated or selected and then applied to existing or newly created institutions and relationships. The purchase of advanced technologies can serve domestic economic needs only through careful planning and the meshing of technical choices with economic priorities. The development and use of new technologies must be "geared to serve the internal needs of the developing countries and, at the same time, contribute to a changed international division of labor."[27]

Second, control over the activities of the MNC has become a central problem for Third World states. One form of control is the establishment of mixed ownership or joint decisionmaking between the MNC and the Third World nation. Another form is the creation of "a full production cycle on an up-to-date scientific and technological basis,"[28] A. Kodachenko contends. By so doing, Third World leaders can tap the resources of the MNC

23. *Ibid.,* p. 53.
24. *Ibid.,* p. 54.
25. *Ibid.,* p. 66.
26. *Ibid.*
27. *Ibid.,* p. 137.
28. A. Kodachenko, "Neocolonialist Strategy," *SS,* 1 (1978), 169.

in ways conducive to national development. Solodovnikov notes that Third World states, "while not rejecting the services of the international corporations, [must] at the same time seek to eliminate discrimination and institute controls on their activities."[29]

Third, more advantageous terms of trade involve the need to receive higher prices for raw materials and to establish a more stable relationship between raw material prices and the prices of industrial goods. The oil crisis has vividly demonstrated the power of a single commodity group or cartel.[30] Securing better prices for raw materials is highly correlated with coalition building among the producers of the same and different commodities. In fact, collective action and regional cooperation in the Third World are needed to establish a free-trade area among the developing nations. Most important, a united front must be created against the advanced capitalist world, in order to obtain higher prices for raw materials and to avoid numerous kinds of dependencies. The problem of ensuring stable price relationships has been underscored by the developing countries' demand for administrative regulation ("indexing") of the prices of raw material commodities produced in the Third World, and for greater influence over the prices of industrial goods manufactured in the advanced capitalist world.

Fourth, the creation of more favorable terms of finance rests upon the ability of a Third World country to obtain aid through international agencies, rather than through bilateral institutions and relationships. But Soviet writers acknowledge that this goal is extremely difficult to achieve, given the asymmetries in levels of development and the exploitative quality of neoimperialism.

Fifth, the need to formulate a domestic strategy for development is enhanced by the increasing impact of the STR and of the internationalization of production upon the Third World. The Academy of Sciences researchers maintain: "In the current situation, the developing countries seeking to overcome economic backwardness and dependence, and [striving] to bring about an improvement in the conditions of the masses, must stand committed to widescale use of modern scientific and technical achievements in the economy. That, in turn, is only possible if a long-term policy of deepgoing social transformations and cultural upsurge of the masses is mapped out."[31]

B. "NATIONAL LIBERATION MOVEMENTS"

Leading Soviet officials and social theorists view the development of Third World countries as primarily a political challenge to indigenous leaders who

---

29. Solodovnikov, in Tarabrin, ed., *op. cit.,* p. 57.
30. R.N. Andreasian and A.D. Kaziukov, *Opek v mire nefti* (Moscow: Nauka, 1978).
31. Tiagunenko, ed., *op. cit.,* pp. 72-73.

have gained or are capable of gaining the support of the masses. In order to achieve genuine interdependence and socioeconomic progress, a contemporary "national liberation movement" must emerge and be completed. Soviet writers often refer to national liberation movements as *the* national liberation movement. The Soviet purpose is probably to suggest that the efforts of Third World countries to free themselves from their colonial legacies are part of a cohesive or unified global movement.

According to Soviet analysts, national liberation movements have gone through two phases since 1945. The first phase was the political liberation of colonies from imperialist rule. Consequently, the newly independent nations of the Third World are no longer the political reserve for imperialism. The second phase is the struggle for economic independence and socioeconomic development. This current phase is antiimperialist in essence and involves an intense struggle against continuing neoimperialist dependencies, penetration, and constraints on socioeconomic progress. Brutents asserts that the economic basis of present-day national liberation movements "consists of the conflict between the requirements of independent economic development and the sway of the imperialist monopolies, a conflict involving the *whole system of the international capitalist division of labor*. What is more, this conflict is a part of the overall contradiction between the requirements of development of the productive forces in the capitalist world and the narrow framework of the socioeconomic relations of imperialism."[32]

New states oriented either toward capitalist or socialist development must now struggle with the problem of economic independence. For capitalist states, the local bourgeoisie comes into conflict with the MNC over the question of the scope of the benefits to be obtained from their mutual relationship. Much of the impetus for control over the MNC in the Third World comes from the local capitalist elite, which hopes to conduct business with the MNC in order to benefit its class. More and more, this indigenous elite's orientation is antiimperialist and objectively promotes some degree of economic restructuring of the international capitalist division of labor.

For new states inclined toward socialism, however, the struggle is to combine involvement in the international division of labor with control over the central levers of economic development, in order to guide the process of social transformation. The objective is to augment economic wealth while at the same time redistributing it more equitably among the population. That is, the task is to combine involvement in the world economy with the forging of a socialist breakthrough in development. This, as Soviet officials fully recognize, is an extremely difficult challenge.[33]

32. K.N. Brutents, *National Liberation Revolutions Today* (Moscow: Progress, vol. 1, 1977), p. 42 (emphasis in original).
33. *Ibid.*, p. 301.

Hence, the restructuring of international economic relations is founded on the growing antiimperialist sentiment of Third World capitalists. As Brutents affirms: "Despite the efforts of the neocolonialists, who are looking to the class solidarity of the local bourgeoisie in the former colonies and semicolonies, no solid or extensive compromise has yet been reached between that bourgeoisie and imperialism. Such an arrangement has been hampered above all by the objective antiimperialist tendencies in the development of independent national capitalism in the countries of Asia and Africa at the present phase."[34]

But, as a social class, the local capitalists are oriented only toward those reformist measures that promote domestic economic independence. The antiimperialist orientation must be deepened by the development of a revolutionary democratic movement which, by peaceful or coercive means, assumes power in the Third World state. Such a movement must establish a revolutionary polity and society in which there is "a concentration in the state sector of the commanding heights of the national economy, in order successfully to combat foreign capital and create a national economy [based on] the practice of drawing up development plans."[35] Such a state would use its economic leverage to carry out a "marked enhancement of the living standards of the people in order to expand the domestic market for developing industry and agriculture...."[36] The new state would also carry out the transformation of the cultural infrastructure, thereby helping to "muster the 'social energy of the masses for national construction."[37]

In short, a Third World country's commitment to the restructuring of its international economic relations will depend heavily upon the scope and depth of its commitment to domestic socioeconomic transformation. As Skorov succinctly states, "the deeper and the more radical the anticapitalist transformation of the domestic life of liberated countries, the more rapid will be the restructuring of the system of the international capitalist division of labor...."[38]

III. The Creation of a New International Economic Order

Even though the commitment to social change varies considerably in the Third World, the current phase of national liberation movements has impelled developing countries to call for the creation of a "new international economic order."[39] The demand for such an order is antiimperialist in

---

34. *Ibid.*, pp. 10-11.
35. *Ibid.*, p. 173.
36. *Ibid.*
37. *Ibid.*
38. Skorov, "Scientific and Technological Progress," 198.
39. Major Soviet works on this theme are Khriashcheva, *op cit.;* and E.E. Obminskii, *Kontseptsii mezhdunarodnogo ekonomicheskogo poriadka* (Moscow: Mysl', 1977).

essence, and thus it creates an important pressure for genuine interdependence in the world economy. As O.T. Bogomolov, director of the Institute of the Economics of the World Socialist System, writes: "The program of reforms advanced by the developing countries to create the new international economic order is aimed at making the capitalist system of international economic relations more democratic...and establishing equitable participation by all states in solving world economic problems. The implementation of this program, which objectively has antiimperialist overtones, would be a step forward in restructuring the present system of worldwide economic ties."[40]

In the Soviet view, there are eight basic elements of Third World demands for a new international economic order: (1) to establish complete national sovereignty over natural resources, (2) to improve radically the terms of international trade, (3) to receive very considerable financial assistance and to alleviate the problem of Third World debt, (4) to control more effectively the activities of the MNC, (5) to gain better terms for the purchase of new machinery and know-how and to end the "brain drain," (6) to reform the international monetary system, (7) to obtain special concessions for the poorest countries, and (8) to strengthen ties among the developing nations as a means of increasing their economic leverage in world economic policy.[41]

These basic components of the "new international economic order" would, if implemented, go a long way toward establishing an equitable form of interdependence. According to Skorov, the progressive changes in the global economy depend on

> the creation of a new mechanism for the redistribution of the world social product in favor of the liberated nations, through financial compensation for economic losses caused by the fluctuation of prices of raw materials and the growing inflation in the capitalist countries, and also through a substantial expansion of economic assistance [and] the granting of unilateral preferences and other concessions, giving the developing nations better terms in foreign economic relations. It is thus a matter of [making] a major correction in the operation of the uncontrolled market forces of the capitalist world economy.[42]

From the Soviet perspective, the present-day "general crisis of capitalism" is deepened by the pressure for genuine interdependence and by the emergence of economic levers which the Third World can use against the industrialized capitalist world as the internationalization of economic life progresses. The demise of capitalism is also promoted by mounting com-

40. O.T. Bogmolov, "CMEA and the Developing World," *International Affairs,* 7 (1979), 25.

41. See "A New International Economic Order," *SS,* 1 (1978), 170-191.

42. Skorov, "Developing Nations," 191.

petition ("interimperialist contradictions") among the United States, Western Europe, and Japan in their struggle for raw material and manufacturing markets in the Third World. For example, even in the context of a common energy crisis, the West has been unable to develop a coordinated energy policy. Rather, intense competition for available natural resources has emerged.[43] In fact, the deepening of interimperialist contradictions has greatly increased the Third World's economic and political leverage vis-à-vis the industrialized countries of the West. As Brutents concludes:

> The coordination of action by the imperialist powers in the national liberation zone has, perhaps, tended to decline, owing to the general aggravation of the interimperialist contradictions. But this has also been caused to some extent by the fact that against the now obvious prospect of a *protracted* struggle to determine the orientation of the young states' development and the difficulties facing the progressive forces in some of these countries, each imperialist power has tended increasingly to look to its own interests. Meanwhile, the forces of national liberation have greater opportunities than ever before to make use of these contradictions...."[44]

IV. Conclusion: Soviet Policy in the Third World

Soviet analysts consider the USSR's policy of detente to be a major factor exacerbating conflict between advanced capitalist and Third World nations.

First, the recently achieved military parity between developed socialism and advanced capitalism underscores the futility of armed intervention to resolve conflicts in the imperialists' favor. As Brutents affirms, "[Capitalism's] opportunities for resorting to sheer violence and armed suppression against the national liberation movement have been sharply curtailed."[45]

Second, the atmosphere of detente allows the Third World states to solicit aid, trade, and credits from either or both the developed socialist and advanced capitalist powers. For example, Soviet officials and theorists maintain that, under the conditions of detente, the Third World can trade on more advantageous terms with both the advanced capitalist and developed socialist states and can obtain aid more easily.[46]

Third, the common interests of the Third World and the USSR in establishing better trade relations with the West increase pressures for the

---

43. "Energy Crisis: An Assessment by Soviet Scientists," *Problems of the Contemporary World,* 6 (1974).

44. Brutents, *National Liberation Revolutions Today,* pp. 293-294 (emphasis in original).

45. *Ibid.,* p. 292.

46. See *The Soviet Union and the World Economy* (New York: Council on Foreign Relations, 1979), especially the essays by Toby Gati, Robert Legvold, and Elizabeth Valkenier.

creation of the genuine interdependence which detente requires. Soviet writers have noted that, in a developing country's struggle with the West, "The task of utilizing the possibilities of the contemporary international division of labor in the national interest is one of the most important tasks of economic policy."[47] Of course, this is the same goal that the Soviet Union has established for itself in pursuing economic detente with the West. Like a Third World country, the USSR depends upon advanced technology imports and raw material exports. Like Third World states, the USSR wishes to enforce "indexing" in the relationship between raw materials and industrial goods, and Soviet officials attempt to do so through compensation agreements with Western trading partners. And, like Third World nations, the USSR wants to control the selection and use of foreign technologies and products. Two Soviet writers affirm: "The developing countries, being simultaneously components of the world capitalist economy and of the worldwide economy, have been active allies of the socialist countries in the struggle to shape a new system of international economic relations, based on equality and mutual advantage for all those involved."[48] In other words, Soviet analysts perceive the economic interests of both the Third World and of developed socialism to lie in the restructuring of the international division of labor to their mutual advantage.

One important example of congruent interests between the USSR and the Third World concerns relations with the MNCs. A "leftist" critic of Soviet detente policy might ask why a developed socialist state has any dealings at all with a capitalist MNC, which is exploitative in its very essence. The Soviet response to such a challenge is two-fold. For one thing, the MNC is a manifestation of the organizational requirements of the STR, and not just of capitalist production relations. For another, the Soviet Union, by establishing mutually advantageous ties with the MNC, sets an important example for Third World nations. Accordingly, R.S. Ovinnikov has argued that "agreements between MNCs and the Soviet Union and other socialist states have already 'created problems' for these companies in their relationships with developing countries"; closer East-West economic relations thereby "help developing states to deal with MNCs on an equitable basis...."[49]

Fourth, Soviet officials contend that detente accelerates social transformation in the Third World. By demonstrating developed socialism's economic complementarity and competitiveness with advanced capitalism,

47. G.I. Mirskii and A.S. Solonitskii, "Novyi pod'em natsional'no-osvoboditel'nogo dvizheniia," in N.N. Inozemtsev, et al., eds., *Uglublenie obshchego krizisa kapitalizma* (Moscow: Mysl', 1976), p. 57.

48. R.N. Andreasian and A.S. Solonitskii, "New Trends in World Economic Relations under Capitalism," *SS*, 3 (1977), 49-50.

49. R.S. Ovinnikov, *Sverkhmonopolii—novoe orudie imperializma* (Moscow: Mezhdunarodnye otnosheniia, 1978), p. 206.

together with the more equal distribution of material goods among the classes and strata of socialist societies, detente increases the prestige of socialism throughout the Third World. The historical alternative of non-capitalist paths of socioeconomic development is strengthened by the force of this example.

Fifth, to the extent to which detente increases the economic capacity of the Soviet Union, and to the extent to which the internationalization of economic life enhances Soviet scientific and technical potential, the USSR is in a better position to provide material aid to the Third World nations pursuing noncapitalist strategies of development. According to Brutents, "Direct and indirect support from world socialism has an immediate effect on the development of the national liberation movement."[50]

Thus, Soviet analysts conclude that detente promotes the internationalization of scientific, technological, and economic life, which, in turn, improves the chances of achieving genuine interdependence. North-South interdependence need not retard social transformation in the Third World. Rather, interdependence can become one of the critical accelerators of socioeconomic progress in both the Third World and in the socialist states.

50. Brutents, *National Liberation Revolutions Today,* p. 53.

Into the Breach:
New Soviet Alliances in the Third World*

Since 1975, seven pro-Soviet communist parties have seized power or territory in Africa and Asia with armed force. In the spring of 1975, after a North Vietnamese invasion of South Vietnam, North Vietnam's Communist Party took control of the South and its puppet Pathet Lao seized power in a demoralized Laos. After a short civil war in Angola in 1975-76, following the departure of the Portuguese, Agostinho Neto's Marxist-Leninist Popular Movement for the Liberation of Angola (MPLA) defeated two other Angolan parties contending for power. In February 1977, in a "red terror" directed against other military leaders who had previously shared power with him after the fall of Emperor Haile Selassie in 1974, Colonel Mengistu Halie Mariam and his group of communist officers seized power in Ethiopia. In April 1978, Nur Mohammad Taraki's People's Party launched a successful armed coup in Afghanistan against the military government led by President Mohammad Daoud. In June 1978, in South Yemen, the communist group in a ruling coalition of leftists carried out a successful armed coup against President Salim Robaye Ali, the leader of the non-communist leftists, and his army supporters. Finally, in January 1979, after a North Vietnamese invasion of Cambodia, Hanoi replaced the pro-

*Reprinted from *Foreign Affairs* (Spring, 1979) by permission of the author and the publisher. Copyright 1979 by Council on Foreign Relations, Inc.

Chinese communist government of Pol Pot with a pro-Soviet regime.[1]

Although the events leading up to communist victories in each of these cases was complex, involved a variety of indigenous forces, and certainly cannot be attributed only to Soviet manipulation, the Russians were active players in each instance. They were not innocent bystanders.

In Vietnam, Russian arms certainly contributed to the final surge that brought Hanoi's armies to Saigon and the Pathet Lao's to Vientiane in the spring of 1975. In the Angolan case, the Russians launched a massive airlift of sophisticated arms and 10,000 Cuban troops that was decisive in defeating the UNITA (National Union for the Total Independence of Angola), and FNLA (National Front for the Liberation of Angola), which were supported by Zaire and by South African forces. In Ethiopia, after Mengistu's Marxist group seized power, another massive airlift by the Russians of two billion dollars worth of arms, 20,000 Cuban troops, 300 tanks and 3,000 Soviet military technicians was decisive in helping Mengistu rout Somali-led insurgents in the Ogaden and Eritrean secessionists in the north. Three Soviet generals worked out the Ethiopian strategy on the ground in the Ogaden. In Afghanistan, before the Taraki coup, Soviet advisers were well entrenched in the Afghan armed forces; the Soviets were the leading arms suppliers. And in South Yemen, before the communist coup, the Soviets were training the South Yemen army, the Cubans were training the "people's militia"—which played a critical role in neutralizing the army that was loyal to President Ali—and the East Germans were training the security services. Thus, it is difficult to believe, at a minimum, that the Russians were caught by surprise in either case. Finally, by signing a friendship treaty with Vietnam in November 1978, a treaty that was supposed to have neutralized China, the

---

1. Writing in *Problems of Communism* in January-February 1978, the distinguished authority on Africa, Colin Legum, describes both Neto and Mengistu as in that category of "pro-Moscow Marxist-Leninists who, apart from needing Soviet assistance anyway, feel friendship for the communist world...[and] invariably react favorably to Soviet intervention and with hostility to any type of Western intervention." See p. 11 of his article "The USSR and Africa." Taraki is a veteran pro-Soviet Marxist. His biographic sketch appeared in *Literaturnaya Gazeta,* Moscow, on May 17, 1978. *The Washington Post,* May 1, 1978, described Taraki as chairman of "the new, united communist party formed in 1977." See also the London *Times,* October 2 and 3, 1978. Abdel Fattah Ismail, General Secretary of the Yemeni Socialist Party, wrote in the pro-Soviet organ, *World Marxist Review,* January 1979, that his party was guided by "the theory of scientific socialism and that it was determined to deepen its friendship and cooperation with "the socialist community countries headed by the Soviet Union...." The models for socialist development in Afghanistan held out by Ismail as "the most striking" were "the Soviet Republics of Central Asia, socialist Mongolia and Vietnam." Details on recent developments in South Yemen can be found in *The Manchester Guardian Weekly,* July 2, 1978, August 27, 1978, and September 10, 1978. Also see an article by Congressman Paul Findley, Republican from Illinois, in *The Washington Post,* July 7, 1978. For reporting on developments in Afghanistan, see *The Washington Post,* November 7, 1978, November 23, 1978, December 6, 1978; *The New York Times,* November 18, 1978; *The Christian Science Monitor,* November 14, 1978; and *The Manchester Guardian Weekly,* November 12, 1978. For reports on Ethiopia, see *The New York Times,* November 21, 1978, December 6, 1978, December 17, 1978, and *The Washington Post,* January 18, 1978.

Russians in effect gave a green light to the North Vietnamese invasion of Cambodia in December 1978.

Since these seven pro-Soviet communist parties have come to power, Moscow has served notice that it considers all of them to be new allies, and that it intends to help them consolidate power against their internal and external enemies. It has stepped up supplies of arms to most of them. Cuban troops remain in both Angola and in Ethiopia. There are now 6,000 to 7,000 Cuban troops in South Yemen as a result of recent transfers from Ethiopia. In addition to Vietnam, Moscow has signed friendship treaties with Angola (October 1976), Ethiopia (November 1978), and Afghanistan (December 1978), most of which contain clauses calling for consultation in the event of a threat to their security. Although Moscow has not yet signed such a treaty with the new communist government in South Yemen, it has warned that "progressive forces will not abandon it at a time of trial," and Brezhnev has personally pledged aid and support to the new government.

At the same time, the Russians have given extraordinary attention and publicity to all the new communist leaders. Taraki was given a state dinner at the Kremlin at which Brezhnev announced that Soviet-Afghan relations had assumed a "qualitatively new character." And Moscow dispatched Politburo member and Central Committee Secretary Andrei P. Kirilenko to attend the December 1977 congress of the MPLA where the Soviet leader strongly endorsed the congress's avowed purpose of transforming the MPLA into a "vanguard party" based on "scientific socialism"—thus setting an example for other African states.

Meanwhile, the comforting assumption—widespread in certain Western political circles, including sections of the American government—that the Soviets will not be able to consolidate their influence in these countries, an assumption based on earlier Soviet evictions from Egypt, the Sudan and Somalia, may prove to be wrong, at least in the short run. In all seven of these new cases, the need of local communist leaders for Soviet support against their internal and external enemies could lead to growing dependence on Moscow.

Particularly after China's recent armed incursion, Vietnam will clearly require continuing security ties to Moscow. In Angola, Neto requires Cuban troops to help him consolidate power against Jonas Savimbi's UNITA, which still controls most of the food-producing areas in the southern part of Angola and could yet mount a drive to overthrow the MPLA. In Ethiopia, Mengistu needs the Cuban troops because he has not yet completely routed either the Somali-led insurgents in the Ogaden or the popular Islamic-Marxist rebels in Eritrea, both of whom may pose long-term threats to his regime's stability. South Yemen's new communist government sorely needs Soviet protection because it is feared and despised as the potential Cuba of the Arab world by its three violently anti-communist neighbors, Saudi Arabia, North Yemen and Oman. The recent outbreak of border fighting

498 From Cold War to Competitive Coexistence

with North Yemen will make South Yemen even more anxious for Soviet support. Finally, because Afghanistan is Russia's small and vulnerable neighbor, it felt the need for close ties to Moscow even before the communist coup. The need will continue. In sum, all of the new communist states will require Soviet or Cuban arms and protection against continuing threats to their own security which could last for some time. Over time, there is even the possibility that these regimes—particularly if they believe they have no other alternatives—may become increasingly dependent upon the Russians.

II

In addition to the seven instances cited above, in which pro-Soviet communists, with Soviet assistance, have seized power by armed force, there have been several other cases in which armed coups which may have been assisted by the Russians have only narrowly failed. Two such abortive armed coups have recently taken place in Somalia and the Sudan, countries whose leaders must have ranked high on Moscow's "hit list." Somalia's President Siad Barre broke off his Treaty of Friendship with Moscow and expelled Soviet advisers in October 1977. The Sudanese President Ja'far Muhammad Nimeiry, after crushing the Sudanese Communist Party in 1971 and executing its leader, has increasingly become one of the most vehement anti-Soviet spokesmen in the Third World.

On April 9, 1978, President Barre of Somalia announced that his government had put down an attempted military coup undertaken in the interests of the "new imperialists," Barre's code word for Cuba and the Soviet Union. In September 1978, Somali courts sentenced 17 army officers to death and jailed 36 others for their alleged complicity in the coup attempt. What makes Barre's charges plausible is the fact that even before the abortive coup there were reports of groups within the Somali army and government who wanted to reassess Somalia's relations with the Soviet Union. These groups evidently did not approve of Barre's break with Moscow in October 1977.

In July 1976, and again in February 1977, there were attempted coups against President Nimeiry in the Sudan. The Sudanese leadership subsequently charged that these coup attempts were "manipulated by foreign hands." As if to indicate whose foreign hands they suspected, in May 1977, the Sudanese government expelled all 90 Soviet technicians serving with the army and closed the Soviet Embassy's military department. Sudan also requested a reduction of the Soviet Union's diplomatic representation, claiming that the representation included excessive "non-diplomatic" personnel.[2] In June 1977, Nimeiry replaced the expelled Soviet military experts

2. The *Toronto Globe and Mail,* May 19, 1977.

with Egyptians, Chinese and Yugoslavs and during a visit to China he launched a fierce attack on Soviet strategy in Africa.

The assassination in June 1978 of the leader of North Yemen, Col. Ahmed Hussein al-Ghashmi, may also have been related to Soviet-Cuban activities. This assassination was also carried out by a special envoy of South Yemen who carried a booby-trapped parcel to al-Ghashmi's office. It took place four days before the South Yemen communists launched their own coup in South Yemen against President Salim Robaye Ali, whom they subsequently executed. The Soviets, the Cubans and the South Yemen communists had good reasons for wanting to get rid of both Yemeni leaders. The former president of North Yemen, al-Ghashmi, said publicly in June 1976, that North Yemen was planning to ask the Soviet Union to withdraw its military experts from the country. In December 1976, North Yemen signed an economic and technical cooperation agreement with China. Finally, in August 1977, less than a year before he was assassinated, al-Ghashmi ousted the TASS correspondent from North Yemen.

Unfortunately, these events do no exhaust the record of irresponsible Soviet conduct in the Third World. Libya, one of Moscow's most enthusiastic supporters in the Third World, has been implicated in attempted coups against its neighbors in Chad and in the Sudan, and is well known for its support of the most extreme terrorist movements in the Third World. Yet within the past year, Moscow has doubled to more than 2,200 the number of Soviet military advisers stationed in the country.

III

Although it would obviously be absurd to attribute all of these developments to some kind of Soviet "master plan" for the Third World—complex indigenous forces which cannot be manipulated by outsiders are, of course, at work in each case—it is just as obviously naive to believe that there is no pattern in these developments. The Russians evidently have a new strategy for expanding their power and influence in the Third World—a strategy which supplements the less successful one they employed in earlier years.

The first surge of postwar Soviet interest in the Third World took place in the mid-1950s under Soviet Premier Nikita Khrushchev. Khrushchev broke with Stalinist orthodoxy about the unreliability of the "national bourgeoisie," and embraced India's Nehru, Egypt's Nasser, Indonesia's Sukarno, Guinea's Sekou Touré, Algeria's Ben Bella and other Third World leaders as "national democrats" who were laying the groundwork for "socialist revolutions." Under Khrushchev, the Russians told local Communist leaders in the Third World to cooperate with the "national democrats" and even to merge their party organizations with those of the nationalists so as to avoid mutual suspicions and mistrust.

But the fruits of this strategy of alliance with the "national democrats" were often bitter. Nasser's successor, Sadat, ousted the Russians in the mid-1970s and Sudan's President Nimeiry quickly followed suit. Sukarno, Ben Bella and Ghana's President Kwame Nkrumah were overthrown by military coups. In other countries, the nationalists jailed, purged or even executed communist leaders. And even where the Russians managed to maintain some influence over leaders such as Touré in Guinea, Mrs. Gandhi in India, and the Ba'ath socialists in Iraq and Syria, these leaders used the Russians as much for their own purposes as the Russians used them for theirs. None of them faithfully followed the Soviet line on foreign policy.

Having realized the error of excessive cooperation with unreliable "bourgeois nationalist" leaders in the 1950s and 1960s, the Soviets have come up with a new strategy for the 1970s and 1980s. They continue, in some cases, such as Iraq, Syria and Algeria, for example, to support noncommunist "socialists" of one kind or another. But now that more orthodox Marxist-Leninist groups and parties have proliferated in many parts of Asia and Africa, the new element in the Soviet strategy is to help communist parties gain state power. Then, via friendship treaties, arms aid, and Soviet, Cuban or East European advisers, the Soviets will help the local communists hold onto and consolidate power. Ultimately, the aim of this strategy is to establish a new alliance system for the Russians in Africa and Asia, a looser eastern version of the Warsaw Pact.

The evidence of some Soviet success in implementing this strategy can be gleaned from the events following the Vietnamese invasion of Cambodia. Most of the nonaligned countries, even many of the radical ones, opposed that invasion and refused to recognize the new Cambodian communist state imposed by Hanoi. Even Moscow's Warsaw Pact ally, Romania, spoke out publicly against the Vietnamese invasion of Cambodia and refused to recognize the new government. So did Yugoslavia. But in the eight days after the fall of Phnom Penh, 14 nations did declare formal recognition of the new Cambodian government. Those governments were, in the order in which they acted, Vietnam, the Soviet Union, East Germany, Bulgaria, Laos, Hungary, Afghanistan, Czechoslovakia, Poland, Mongolia, Cuba, Angola, Ethiopia, and South Yemen. Thus Moscow's new communist allies in Asia and Africa joined with Moscow's faithful regimes in Eastern Europe, Mongolia and Cuba in a critical test of allegiance to the Soviet Union that most of the Third World and even communist Romania could not pass.

IV

The new pro-Soviet communist regimes in Africa and Asia, imposed by force and backed as they are by Soviet power, pose serious new threats to many of the regional powers which are friendly to the United States. The South Yemen Marxists have already made known their intention to renew their support of the Marxist-Leninist rebel movement of the Dhofar region of neighboring Oman, one of the conservative pro-Western states in the Arabian Peninsula. The Dhofar rebellion, supported by South Yemen Marxists and Cuban advisers, smouldered for more than a decade before it was dealt a crushing blow by Iranian troops several years ago. The Iranians sealed off the border between South Yemen and Oman. Now, with Iran in revolution, South Yemen may be in a better position to rekindle the revolt.

The Omanis are clearly worried. Recent American visitors to Oman were told by the Sultan's advisers that "from Afghanistan to the Horn of Africa, the situation looks very bleak to us." The Omanis fear an attack by South Yemen with its MiG-21 fighters and its Ilyushin bombers, which are currently being flown—so the Omanis say—by Cuban pilots.

Over the longer run, the South Yemen Marxists and their Soviet, Cuban, and East German advisers are undoubtedly aiming to bring down the conservative, pro-Western governments in Saudi Arabia and North Yemen as well.

The events in South Yemen are only one of a number of recent developments that have badly shaken the Saudis. The Saudis were already seriously alarmed over the extension of Soviet and Cuban power to Ethiopia just across the Red Sea, and by the revolution in Iran, just across the Persian Gulf. If the Saudis were to interpret all of these developments as an indication of a declining American power which can no longer guarantee their security, they might be tempted to make their own independent accommodation with Moscow. Such a development, combined with events in Iran, would radically alter the present balance of power in the Middle East.

Pakistan is also increasingly alarmed at the spread of Soviet power. It is now encircled by its old enemy, India, and by communist Afghanistan, both of which have friendship treaties with Moscow. Afghanistan also has long-standing territorial claims to the Pushtunistan region of Pakistan and might revive such claims at an appropriate moment. Iran, a neighbor on which Pakistan was counting to maintain regional stability, is now in the throes of revolution. And Pakistan's faith in China must have been dealt a serious blow by China's inability to stop the Vietnamese invasion of Cambodia. In such circumstances, it would not be surprising if Pakistan sought insurance through improved ties to Moscow.

In Southeast Asia, the spread of Soviet power and Vietnamese influence has greatly alarmed China and all of the ASEAN powers, particularly Thailand. The new pro-Hanoi communist regime in Cambodia brings Vietnam to Thailand's doorstep, and has increased Thai fears about the communist insurgencies in the northeast and the south that have been active for many years. China, on the other hand, now feels encircled by Russia on the north and Russia's ally, Vietnam, on China's southern border. As we have already seen with the Chinese incursion into Vietnam, regional tensions will almost certainly grow in intensity.

In southern Africa, Angola does not pose a larger regional threat for the moment because Neto has sought to improve relations with neighboring Zaire. But Angola is one of the "front line" states close to Rhodesia, Namibia and South Africa, and if events in this region lead to a racial war, Angola could become even a larger staging area for Cuban and black nationalist forces preparing to fight the white minority regimes. That is why the South Africans and Rhodesians keep a wary eye on the Cubans in Angola, and probably continue to nourish hopes of overthrowing Neto.

In sum, the forcible extension of pro-Soviet communism backed by Soviet power to several new areas of the world poses serious new strategic problems for a variety of middle powers, many of whom look to the United States for leadership and support. The danger is not so much that Moscow will achieve hegemony in the Third World. This is unlikely for a great many reasons. The danger is rather that the spread of communism and Soviet power will upset tenuous regional balances of power, lead to intensified regional instabilities, and make even more difficult the settlement of a variety of regional clashes that could lead to war.

V

One shudders to think of what might have been the American response to seven communist takeovers in Asia and Africa at the height of the cold war. Clearly we have been sobered by our experience in Vietnam. But the lack of response today—indeed the lack of comprehension—is just as frightening. Analysts both in and out of government who call attention to these developments are accused of being "cold warriors" with "globalist" points of view that ignore "complex local realities." High-ranking officials in the State Department warn against "abstract geopolitical thinking," and allege that the Soviets have a "loser's mentality." And the Secretary of State himself recently said that the Soviet involvement in the Vietnamese invasion of Cambodia was "unclear," and that we must not accept "oversimplified generalities as applying to different situations."

Certainly the proper American reaction to the communist surge in Africa and Asia is not to send half a million troops to these regions. Certainly the victory of communist forces in the Third World represents the outcome of complex indigenous situations which are not all manipulated by Moscow. Certainly Moscow will have some trouble consolidating its hold on these communist parties in the Third World. Certainly it is true that there is a qualitative difference between the victory of indigenous communist parties in Asia and Africa and the imposition of communism on Eastern Europe by Soviet occupation forces in the immediate aftermath of World War II.

But, in the meantime, are there no general problems for American foreign policy resulting from these developments? Many of our allies and friends are worried by the appearance of pro-Soviet communist parties supported by Soviet arms and Cuban gendarmes on their doorsteps. How do we reassure them? Regional stability is now threatened in many areas. How do we restore it? The credibility of American power has been shaken by these developments and by our apparent lack of response to them. How do we restore it? What is the significance of these developments for U.S.-Soviet relations? Are they compatible with our understanding of détente?

Most important of all, what kind of international order are we likely to build if one of the superpowers believes in the continued, uninhibited use of force to spread "liberation movements," and the other believes either that force is immoral or that is has lost its political utility? These are some of the questions that need to be discussed, and not in a sterile debate between "globalists" and people who profess to understand "local realities"—a debate which drives both sides into extreme positions.

VI

Evidently there are three levels at which these problems have to be addressed. First, there are broad questions that go to the very heart of our relationship with Moscow. Second, there is the need for consultation with our friends and allies in the regions affected, in order to develop strategies for dealing with the new communist regimes. Finally, there is the question of how we should relate to those new communist states.

President Carter's National Security Adviser, Zbigniew Brzezinski, has said on numerous occasions that détente with the Soviet Union is desirable, but that if it is to be enduring, and is to be accepted by the American people, it must be both reciprocal and progressively more comprehensive. "Reciprocal" means that one party cannot feel free to engage in the direct promotion of revolutionary violence while at the same time considering it an act of intervention if the other side affirms its own beliefs. To be comprehensive, détente cannot be conducted selectively. That is, it cannot mean accommodation in one part of the world and uninhibited exploitation of unavoidable turbulence in another. There must be some agreed-upon "rules of the game."

These are sound principles on which to base Soviet-American relations. But there has been little progress so far in getting the Soviets to adhere to them. Partly this is because the Carter Administration itself is divided on how best to pursue détente with the Russians. Partly it is because there is no national consensus, in either the Administration or the Congress, on our relations with Moscow. Partly it is because the President himself has sent inconsistent messages to the Russians. And partly it is because we have not given the Russians enough cause either for hope of better relations through a true détente or for fear of the results of promoting violence in the Third World. Whatever the reasons, Brzezinski's concept of a reciprocal and comprehensive détente, however sound, is not being implemented.

To achieve such a détente, the Administration must make two things clear to Moscow: first, that it will be to the Soviet advantage if they exercise greater self-restraint in the Third World; second, that it will be risky if they don't. In the past we have failed to provide the Russians with sufficient positive or negative incentives for self-restraint. By foolishly imposing congressional restrictions on trade with the Russians, and by linking those restrictions to Soviet emigration policies—rather than to Soviet foreign policy—we have deprived ourselves of positive leverage on Soviet behavior in the Third World. At the same time, we have not been able to demonstrate any kind of military or political response to Soviet activity in the Third World that might be a negative incentive for further Soviet advances. So far, these advances have been virtually cost-free.

There are three steps in particular that we need to take in providing Moscow with positive incentives for restraint. First, Congress should make the kinds of amendments in trade legislation that Senator Adlai Stevenson is now proposing. Stevenson's proposed amendments to the Trade Act would waive the Jackson-Vanik Amendment that ties most-favored-nation trading status to Soviet internal policies. The effect of Stevenson's amendment would be to increase the President's flexibility to trade with Moscow and to use such trade for "linkage." The Russians are still very anxious to obtain American technology and credits. By offering them such a possibility in exchange for real restraint in the Third World, we will at least present them with a difficult choice.

Second, we should engage the Russians in preliminary discussions about regional security problems in various parts of the Third World. We cannot exclude the Russians from all negotiations on regional matters and then ask them for restraints in the regions. Ultimately, Moscow will have to be brought into a Middle East peace settlement. The Russians suspect that it is our intention to freeze them out of a variety of areas of the world in which they have legitimate interest. We should try to make clear to them that this is not our intention. Indeed, much as we dislike it, we will be forced to face up to the fact that Russia is now a global power capable of influencing regional developments almost everywhere. It is time that we engage the Russians in a broad dialogue on regional security issues and offer them a role in helping to maintain regional security.

We also need to sign and to ratify the SALT II agreement as a symbol both of our desire to slow down the nuclear arms race and of our desire to pursue an evenhanded policy between Moscow and Peking. A congressional refusal to ratify SALT at a time when our relations with China are moving forward in high gear might well convince the suspicious Russians that we intend to form a new Chinese-Japanese-European-American axis against them, even though that is not our policy. Such one-sided diplomacy on our part would only increase Soviet paranoia. It could lead the Russians to take even more aggressive actions in the Third World, and against China itself, in a desperate effort to strengthen their position before the imagined anti-Soviet axis materializes.

In sum, there are a variety of overtures we need to make to Moscow in order to assure the Russians that, for our part, we are anxious for a more comprehensive détente.

But along with the "carrots" there should also be some "sticks." The Senate, when it ratifies SALT II, as I expect it will, should warn Moscow in a "sense of the Senate" resolution that the United States will no longer accept a narrow and unreciprocal détente, and that future Soviet conduct in the Third World will influence the future development of détente, including the prospects for SALT III. And Moscow should understand that if it continues to conduct violent interventions in the Third World wherever the opportunity beckons, we will eventually be forced into consolidating our new relationship with China.

We must be clear—and sufficiently modest—about the nature of the demands that we make upon Soviet behavior in the Third World. We cannot realistically expect Moscow to stop selling arms to its client states; but we can expect it to reduce the flow of arms, rather than to increase it, as it has recently been doing. We cannot realistically expect Moscow to stop trying to expand its influence in the Third World; but we can expect Moscow to stop transporting Cuban troops to various trouble spots. And we can expect the Russians to increase pressure on their Cuban allies to withdraw from Angola, Ethiopia, South Yemen and other areas of the world where those troops and "advisers" constitute daggers pointed at important Western interests.[3]

It is true, as the Soviets contend, that the United States intervened in the Third World during the 1950s and 1960s and that, in the sense, Moscow is now giving us back a little of our own medicine. But apart from the case of Vietnam, the United States, even at the heyday of its interventionism, did not employ combat troops to influence the course of events in the Third World. In small countries, a few hundred combat troops on one side or another can make a decisive difference in the outcome of a local war. Thus, we must make it clear to the Russians that in our continuing competition for influence in the Third World, the use of foreign combat troops cannot be allowed. In a word, the Russians should be put on notice that they cannot have both a stable détente with the United States, including expanded economic relations, and a cost-free license to stir the boiling pot of the Third world.

3. There are reportedly a total of between 20 and 40,000 Cubans in 16 African states.

VII

There are also a variety of steps the United States will have to take to reassure pro-Western states—particularly in the Persian Gulf and Red Sea regions—that we will not abandon them. During Secretary of Defense Harold Brown's recent trip to Saudi Arabia, the Pentagon announced that it intended to increase sharply its arms supplies to North Yemen and to the Sudan. Secretary Brown was reported to have told the Saudis that the United States is ready to discuss the creation of a Persian Gulf command led by Americans. Brown also reportedly discussed with the Saudis the possibility of expanding port facilities for American ships in the Indian Ocean naval base of Diego Garcia. Finally, Brown is reported to have assured the Saudis that the United States is creating a "quick strike force" of American paratroopers and marines to be used in case of a request for help by Saudi Arabia or other Gulf nations threatened by a Soviet-supported coup. These are all worthwhile countermeasures. But they may not be enough.

We should also consider security pacts with critical countries such as Saudi Arabia, to assure them of American support in the case of an external threat. And the United States needs to adopt a much higher profile in the entire region from Afghanistan to the Horn of Africa. Oman would welcome a much larger U.S. diplomatic presence. As of February, the American Embassy in Oman had only a staff of five. Oman also wants a stronger CIA station, to assess what is needed in the country and in the region as a whole. Steps such as these are needed as a short-term stopgap to convince the Gulf countries that the United States remains committed to their security.

Over the longer run, of course, the United States will have to guard against overidentifying itself with reactionary regimes standing on feet of clay. Such regimes will prove to be unstable no matter how many U.S. arms and how much U.S. support they receive. Iran dramatically illustrates the danger. At the same time, the United States will have to guard against the opposite danger—of assuming that all authoritarian regimes are equally unstable and unworthy of U.S. support.

It is time, too, for the United States to play a stronger and more creative role in fostering regional organizations which could play an important role in minimizing the kinds of interstate conflicts on which the Russians feed. ASEAN, the organization of non-communist states in Southeast Asia that includes Malaysia, the Philippines, Thailand, Indonesia and Singapore, could provide a useful model. The ASEAN states are increasingly aware that internal weaknesses in the region invite exploitation from outside. They say that the best way to promote regional security is by developing economic well-being and social justice on the one hand, and by forging regional unity on the other. The ASEAN states have adopted a common front in such international agencies as the United Nations Conference on Trade and Development (UNCTAD) and the General Agreement on Trade and Tariffs (GATT); they have intensified their efforts at regional cooperation; they have put forth joint proposals to the United States, the European Community and Japan for a commodity price stabilization scheme; and they have signed a treaty of amity and cooperation, the first binding agreement among Southeast Asian countries in the history of the region. More recently, in an effort to remove territorial frictions with its neighbor Malaysia, the Philippines has dropped its territorial claims to Sabah. Thus, without overemphasizing military activity, the ASEAN countries have gone a long way toward achieving the kind of regional cooperation that is necessary to keep predatory external powers out.

But achieving stability in Southeast Asia, as elsewhere, will in the long run require the participation of the great powers. Now is the time for us to take the lead in convening a new international conference on the future of Indochina, a conference modelled on the 1954 Geneva Conference, which recognized the division of Vietnam and the political neutrality of Laos and Cambodia. Such a conference should include Russia, China, the United States, India, the ASEAN countries, and Vietnam, Laos, and Cambodia. If such a conference were to be successful, it would serve a number of purposes. It would reassure the ASEAN countries. It would set an important example for the peaceful resolution of regional conflicts. And, not least of all, such a conference could be used to demonstrate to both Moscow and Peking that our interest is in regional stability, not in siding with one communist power against another in an effort to gain one-sided advantages that can only raise tensions between the great powers.

Finally, in Northeast Asia, it is time to reverse the Administration's earlier decision to withdraw American combat troops from South Korea. No more troops should be withdrawn until there is an accommodation between the two Koreas. The Administration has wisely modified its earlier decision; it has left open the possibility that the withdrawal would be halted "if conditions so warrant." Conditions do now warrant such a change. The recent rise of regional tension in Southeast and Western Asia make it imperative that Northeast Asia should remain stable. The apparent revival of the North-South Korean dialogue is an encouraging sign, but it may be no more than a North Korean ploy designed to encourage the Carter Administration to continue its planned withdrawal. The only way to test North Korea's sincerity is to insist that American troops remain in South Korea until North and South Korea reach a peaceful settlement that is ratified by the great powers.

VIII

The United States will also have to devise policies designed to deal directly with the new communist governments in Africa and Asia. The place to begin in formulating such policies is with a recognition of the nature of conditions in much of the Third World that breed radicalism, and with a certain degree of empathy for those forces in the Third World that insist on radical change. As contemporary events in Iran demonstrate, radical change in the Third World is inevitable; and, in many places, it is desirable. Such change will come under a variety of auspices, some of them Islamic, as in Iran, some of them Marxist, as in Angola. If the United States places itself in opposition to all such changes, the result will be an isolated, besieged and increasingly nationalistic America that becomes irrelevant to the Third World. In fact, the United States, because of its commitment to pluralism, diversity and social justice, should be in a better position than the Soviet Union, with its monolithic notions of social change, to relate to legitimate Third World aspirations.

A second point of departure for American policy should be a clearer recognition of the nature of the Marxist movements in the Third World and their relationship to the Soviet Union. The potential weak link of the new Soviet alliance system in Asia and Africa is the same weak link that disrupted Soviet alliances with communist Yugoslavia and communist China—national communism. The history of the modern world demonstrates that in the radical mixture we call national communism, the nationalistic ingredient is far more powerful than the Marxist. The best current indications of this can be found in East Asia, where the most intense conflicts are between communist states—between Russia and China, between China and Vietnam, and until recently, between Vietnam and Cambodia. Indeed, in East Asia, the East-East conflict, that is, conflict between communist states, has replaced the East-West conflict as the source of greatest tension. Thus, we can assume that there are already conflicts of interest between the Russians and their new national communist clients in Asia and Africa, and that such conflicts will continue to develop.

Such tensions can already be detected in the relationship between Moscow and Neto's MPLA in Angola. Neto himself fought Portuguese colonial rule for two decades and is as much an Angolan nationalist as he is a communist. Moreover, he has had many differences with the Russians in the past. At times, Moscow even encouraged several of Neto's rivals to overthrow the MPLA leader because he was insufficiently subordinate. There are many recent signs of Neto's concern about excess Soviet and Cuban influence in Angola. Last December, Neto warned publicly about the need to "defend the independence of the Party"; in the same month he fired a Cabinet minister who had signed an agreement with Cuba calling for 6,000 additional Cuban technicians to be sent to Angola. The agreement, Neto said, had been signed without his permission. Neto has also made a marked effort during the past several months to improve relations with the United States. He entertained Senator McGovern and a number of American journalists who accompanied McGovern. Neto has also sought to improve his troubled relations with neighboring Zaire. And recently he has sought to improve relations with Portugal in an effort to get Portuguese technicians to return to Angola. This would make Angola less dependent on Cuban and East European technicians.

In the light of these developments, the United States should reconsider its policy of nonrecognition of Angola. American recognition would encourage those less doctrinaire forces within the MPLA, led by Neto himself, who do not want to become excessively dependent on Russia or Cuba.

By recognizing the new Angolan government, we would not be deserting the noncommunist forces that continue to oppose Neto's government. The conflict between Neto's MPLA and Savimbi's UNITA is likely to go on indefinitely. Savimbi's forces already control much of the south, especially at night. Eventually, a real peace in Angola will require negotiations between these two parties. But the United States will be in a better position to help mediate such efforts if it is directly involved in Angola.

The same principle of encouraging independence from Moscow should be applied in Vietnam. The Vietnamese communists fought a 30-year war against the French, the Japanese and the Americans to gain their independence from external powers. As a result of this experience, they cannot be anxious to become dependent on Moscow. To some extent, Hanoi and Moscow have parallel interests. But it would be a serious error to conclude that Hanoi has overnight become one of Moscow's vassals, even in the wake of China's armed incursion.

There are in fact many signs that Vietnam, like Angola, does not want to become excessively dependent on the Russians. Vietnam wants Japanese and American economic aid in order to rebuild its war-torn economy and to reduce its dependence on the Soviets. The United States should make it clear that if Hanoi demonstrates its independence from Moscow, we shall show more interest both in recognition and in providing assistance. But if Vietnam aligns itself even further with the Russians—and particularly if Vietnam provides Moscow with a base in Cam-ranh Bay and other military facilities—there will be no possibility of such aid.

In sum, the United States should recognize that Marxist parties which come to power in Africa and Asia are not simple agents of Soviet power. If we treat them as if they were, we will force them to become even more dependent on the Russians. This is the mistake we made in dealing with the Chinese communists in the 1950s, and it is the mistake we made in dealing with Ho Chi Minh. We should not repeat it in the 1980s.

The extent to which the new communist states of Africa and Asia follow foreign policy lines independent of Moscow is one basic criterion we should use to judge their behavior. A second is the extent to which they contribute to regional stability and order. Angola is seeking to improve its relations with Zaire. It is also contributing to a peaceful solution in neighboring Namibia. We should watch carefully to see whether Vietnam and the new Cambodian communist government also seek to improve their relations with Thailand and the other ASEAN countries. Where the new communist states demonstrate good will in reaching accommodation with their neighbors, the United States should encourage them.

On the other hand, the new communist regime in South Yemen has declared publicly its intention to rekindle the Dhofar rebellion in neighboring Oman, and it has made its territory available to Soviet airplanes supplying Ethiopia in the war against neighboring Somalia. And the new Ethiopian communist regime itself has shown little restraint in its relations with two of its neighbors, Somalia and the Sudan. Ethiopian units have recently set up fortified camps inside Sudan's territory and Ethiopian MiG fighters, probably piloted by Cubans, have been bombing Sudanese armored units. Under such circumstances, the United States, in conjunction with its regional allies, should seek appropriate policies designed to restrain and to isolate both South Yemen and Ethiopia.

Thus, American policies toward the new communist states of Asia and Africa should be differentiated according to the behavior of these new states. Where they demonstrate independence from Moscow and willingness to contribute to overall regional stability, we should encourage them. Where they do not, we should isolate them.

IX

The challenge of dealing with communism in the Third World is as much a challenge to our understanding as it is to our policy. We need a much more sophisticated national understanding of radical movements and states than we presently have. Compared to the huge amounts of money and effort the government spends on collecting and evaluating military intelligence and "hardware," the amounts which it spends on political analysis are trivial. The problem is not merely a failure of gathering information or even a failure of proper evaluation. Even more serious, it is a failure to ask the right questions.

Many of the "right" questions to ask about the Third World today concern the nature of radical movements—their ideological origins, leadership, foreign policy orientation, social base, and so on. Yet there are very few specialists in the National Security Council, the State Department, the Pentagon, or even the CIA, who possess extensive and detailed knowledge about radical political movements of one kind or another in the Third World. There are even fewer who can relate these movements to the broader political competition between Russia and the United States. To the extent that the United States has such expertise, it can be found in the universities. That university expertise needs to be brought to bear on American policy in a more effective way than has been the case in the past. And the government's own capacity to analyze radicalism in the Third World must be greatly strengthened both qualitatively and quantitatively.

One widely noted recent analytical deficiency was the failure of the American intelligence community to understand and to evaluate the widespread opposition to the Shah in Iran. Unfortunately, this is not an isolated case. Another recent example of such a lack of analysis was the government's abject neglect of developments in South Yemen. Congressman Paul Findley of Illinois, who visted South Yemen frequently in recent years, wrote in *The Washington Post* of July 7, 1978, that he was the only U.S. official, elected or appointed, to visit South Yemen since 1969, when the United States broke off relations with the country. When Findley returned from a recent visit to South Yemen and pleaded for more U.S. involvement in the country before the June 1978 communist coup, the State Department delayed. Even after the coup, according to David Binder, writing in *The New York Times* of August 5, 1978, the State Department concluded that "South Yemen, because it is small and has only 1.5 million people, does not pose a real threat to anyone and hence is not worth larger concern." This remarkable statement came at the very time that 15 Arab League states were organizing an economic, political and cultural boycott directed against South Yemen!

This appalling lack of understanding of developments within the Third World and their relation to U.S. security is a national scandal. We can no longer afford to be ignorant of what is going on in Iran or South Yemen or in the many other Third World countries which have the potential for becoming future "Irans" and future "South Yemens." This lack of understanding extends to our political parties as well. An important part of our difficulties in responding effectively to the Soviet challenge in the Third World is that neither our extreme liberals nor our extreme conservatives properly understand it. The Soviet offensive employs military power in behalf of "just" causes—or at least causes that are often perceived as just by many in the Third World. The extreme liberals in the United States are usually sympathetic to the causes, but they overlook or minimize the Soviet use of force to assist them. The extreme conservatives are primarily concerned with the Soviet use of force, but they generally ignore the political causes on behalf of which that force is employed.

Both stand on abstract principles. The liberals make a fetish of non-interventionism. The conservatives talk in equally abstract ways about "backbone" and "strength," by which they usually mean military power. Both are equally unrealistic—the liberals because non-interventionism is not a policy; the conservatives because more guns and missiles are not a sufficient answer to problems that are essentially political.

X

Over the longer run, there is room for optimism. Soviet expansion in the Third World has already run into a variety of forces that will work against it. The so-called "nonaligned" movement, which incorporates many of the

Third World countries, is deeply split; the Yugoslavs, the Somalis and others have taken the lead in criticizing Cuba as a proxy for Soviet imperialism. This view has considerable support among a broad range of African and Asian countries. China still commands considerable respect in much of Asia and Africa, and Peking's activities will counter those of Moscow. The rigid Soviet stance is incapable of relating effectively to the national, ethnic and religious diversity that is characteristic of much of the Third World. The Russians find it difficult to deal with their friends as equals; yet the proud nationalists of Asia and Africa, having thrown off the shackles of Western colonialism, are not likely to tolerate a new Soviet colonialism. Once radical movements consolidate their power and turn their attention to economic development, the West will become increasingly relevant and the Russians increasingly irrelevant to them.

In many parts of the Third World, such as Northeast Asia and non-communist Southeast Asia, the Russians have not been able to expand their influence very much.[4] Recent events in Afghanistan and South Yemen have alarmed other Third World countries which are generally friendly to Moscow. In Iraq, there has been a new purge of suspected communists in the armed forces. Syria has restricted the writings of pro-Soviet journalists. The Iraqi and Syrian fears of communist infiltration point up the inherent contradiction in the new Soviet strategy. Moscow cannot expect both to woo Arab socialists and to try to replace them with local communists. Finally, the new U.S. ties with China, which have completely altered the global strategic chessboard, may in time more than compensate for Soviet gains elsewhere in Asia and Africa. Thus, while there is room for concern about Soviet expansion, there is no need to adopt Chicken Little's view of the world—that the sky is always falling down.

In fact, the great majority of the nonaligned countries spoke out against the Vietnamese invasion of Cambodia earlier this year, and most of them did not extend recognition to the new Cambodian government. This reflects growing suspicions within the Third World about Soviet policies.

But although there is reason to be cautiously optimistic over the longer run, there is no reason to be complacent. Three very serious dangers now lie on the horizon. The first is that the Soviet expansionist drive in the Third World will make certain regional tensions even more acute. China has already attempted to give Vietnam a "bloody nose" in response to Vietnam's invasion of Cambodia. Will Russia now attempt to bloody China's nose in return? Developments in South Yemen and the Horn of Africa have heightened tensions all over the Indian Ocean, and could even contribute to undermining our efforts to reach a Middle East peace accord.

The second danger is that the Soviets, inspired by a conviction that the United States is still paralyzed by a post-Vietnam trauma, and angered by

4. See my article "The Soviet Quandary in Asia," *Foreign Affairs,* January 1978.

the new American ties to China, will continue or even increase their expansionist policies in the Third World on the assumption that the risks are minimal and the potential gains considerable. From the Soviets' perspective, moreover, what they are doing in the Third World is "just" and legitimate. They are helping to undermine "reactionary," "feudal," or white minority regimes. And the United States is being cast as the defender of the unpopular status quo. To expect the Soviets to give up such a promising field of endeavor, where they can hope to expand their influence while supporting "just" causes, is unrealistic.

The third danger is that this Soviet drive to expand its influence in the Third World will help stimulate a new cold war mentality in the United States which will relate all American difficulties abroad to the "Soviet menace"—a vast oversimplification of the problems we face. Such a mood in the United States could make it impossible to ratify SALT II; it could lead to a resurgence of the chauvinistic elements on the American political scene, and, eventually, to a serious deterioration in Soviet-American relations. Already some leaders of the right-wing of the Republican Party are charging President Carter with "appeasement" and calling him another Neville Chamberlain. This is irresponsible politics, and one can only hope that it does not represent a preview of the electoral campaign in 1980. We certainly need a more thorough public debate about the Soviet challenge and its implications for American foreign policy, but a debate in which the opposition party leaders appeal to the most primitive instincts of the American people is bound to be counterproductive and even dangerous. There is a vast middle ground for American opposition politicians between raising the spectre of "appeasement" on the one hand and accepting the Administration's present policies on the other.

In the past, the United States has displayed an unhealthy tendency to vacillate between unrealistic hopes and unreasonable fears about the Russians. It was the overselling of détente by Nixon and Kissinger that led us to have unrealistic expectations about Soviet behavior in the first place. Let us not now go to the opposite extreme and treat every crisis in the Third World as if it was the last showdown at the O.K. Corral with Moscow. That would make the situation in the Third World even more unstable and much more dangerous. As Adam Ulam has recently reminded us, it is a sobering thought that "no Soviet move or ruse has undercut the effectiveness of U.S. foreign policy as much as what the Americans have done to themselves in the wake of Vietnam and Watergate."[5]

We have the resources, the strength, the technology and the allies to stand up to the Soviet challenge in the Third World without overreacting to it. But

---

5. Adam Ulam, "U.S.-Soviet Relations: Unhappy Coexistence," *Foreign Affairs, America and the World 1978,* p. 567.

we cannot deal with this challenge either by returning to simplistic cold war formulas or by advancing equally simplistic anti-cold war formulas against "globalism." We will have to do better than that.

A New Scramble For Africa? *

I

The most serious element confusing any clear analysis of African problems arises from the role Africa has assumed in the domestic politics of East and West, and the consequent interpenetration of domestic political factionalism, ideological stereotypes, and foreign policy decisions. All of which now makes any separation of Africa from the complex web of East-West relations virtually impossible. "Linkages," to use one of Henry Kissinger's favorite words, were never something that could be evoked only at the convenience of political leaders. Actions produce reactions in politics as in physics. Mr. Brezhnev, for example, played for high stakes in Africa and in the short term the gains of the Soviet Union have been considerable. But the payoff for the Soviet Union in Africa (or the burden from the western point of view) has been as much psychological as strategic.

The military advantages for the Soviets which so concern Western specialists undoubtedly exist, but no less important has been the success Mr. Brezhnev has achieved in refurbishing the image of the Soviet Union as an effective power willing and able to aid revolutionary causes. Indeed, it is only necessary to look back a few years to see how remarkable this change in perceptions has been. Until comparatively recently, few in the Third World found the Soviet Union an attractive model to imitate,[1] partly as a result of the Soviet Union's cautious foreign policy in the period after the Cuban missile crisis of 1962, partly as a result of the apparent viability under Mao of a Chinese communist alternative more attuned to and appropriate to post-colonial Third World countries, and partly in consequence of the harsh bureaucratic and statist policies of the Soviets themselves. Yet today, Soviet action in Africa has done much to reestablish the credibility of the Soviet Union as an effective leader of the world communist movement and to dispel criticism of the lack of revolutionary verity.

The point is not so much that the Left in the Third World loves the Soviet Union any more today than before 1975; but the Left has certainly become obliged to respect Soviet capacity to influence events decisively in their favor in situations when "the revolution" might otherwise have failed. The United States in contrast has in the same period suffered military defeat in Vietnam, bungled its half-hearted intervention in Southern Africa, failed to come up with an effective response to Soviet and Cuban expansionism, seen the collapse of its Iranian proxy and the consequent shattering of its strategic position in the Persian Gulf and northern Indian Ocean. The issue here is not whether the U.S. was wise or unwise in any of these actions, or could have avoided them. The point is that the Soviets have appeared decisive and successful, the United States indecisive and weak, and that these perceptions have aided those in the Soviet Union who urge expansion and weakened those in the United States who urge restraint.

The intrinsic merits of the African struggles in which the great powers have felt obliged to meddle are, therefore, already less significant than the domestic political repercussions of that meddling within the great powers themselves, which has had profoundly negative impact on much more vital bilateral relationships. Thus, whatever Mr. Brezhnev's short-term gains in Angola and Ethiopia during the 1970's, he gravely miscalculated the consequences of Soviet actions in Africa if, for instance, the U.S. Congress rejects SALT II, and does so in part because of anger at what the Soviets and Cubans did in Ethiopia and Angola. If Soviet analysts of the United States thought they were clever in 1975-1976 in reading the mood of Congress better than did that old Congressional hand, Mr. Gerald Ford, thus accurately predicting Congressional rejection of administration pleas for increased aid to anti-Soviet forces in Angola, they overlooked the volatile nature of American politics. Post-Watergate flagellation was bound to end sooner or later. The Soviets cannot expect to preen over the shift of "world historical

---

1. See especially David E. Albright, "The Soviet Model: A Developed Alternative for the Third World?" in Henry W. Morton and Rudolf L. Tokes, eds., *Soviet Politics and Society in the 1970's* (New York, 1974).

forces" in their favor, and at the same time assume their adversaries will not take them at their word.

It is, therefore, not enough for American neo-isolationists to say Africa is far away and insignificant. Africa is very much what we make of it. Perceptions, even myths and obsessions, can at times be more important than events in provoking action. Yet, neither is it always the case that perceptions of threats and strategic challenges reflect real interests or grow from clearly understood roots. Looking back at the rationalizations for great power involvement in Africa in the 1880's, the British historians Robinson and Gallagher concluded that far from reflecting the interests they purported to defend, their strategies were "even more a register of the hopes, the memories, and the neuroses which informed the strategists' picture of the world."[2] Less has changed than might have been expected. Much of the debate on Africa today, both East and West, and on Left and Right, is no less phantasmagorical than it was a hundred years ago.

II

But do the causes as well as the motives for a new scramble exist today? This is the key question. Will current crises in Africa trap the great powers into competition and confrontation as they did a hundred years ago?

The two crises which created the present conjunction of great power intervention and regional upheavals came to a head comparatively recently and almost simultaneously. In April 1974 the armed-forces movement overthrew the decrepit dictatorship in Lisbon and within nine months liquidated Portugal's empire in Africa. In May 1974 the long reign of Emperor Haile Selassie of Ethiopia was brought to an abrupt end, again by young army officers. Both groups acted for reasons which were not dissimilar: exhaustion by frontier wars, the pressure of economic problems at home, and irritation with an unbending autocracy. The young and to begin with largely anonymous officers in Lisbon and in Addis Ababa justified their coups with an eclectic grab-bag of revolutionary rhetoric. Yet each army uprising ended regimes so ancient—the dictatorship in Lisbon had been established in 1926, and Haile Selassie had made the throne his own in 1916—that the repercussions of their actions were almost bound to be startling.

It is perhaps unfair to blame anyone for failing to predict either of these events, though there is less excuse for the failure to have anticipated them as contingencies or to have planned for the aftermath. Ethiopia was one of the United States' principal African clients in terms of military and civilian aid. Portugal was a NATO ally, anachronistic and at times embarrassingly stub-

2. Ronald Robinson and John Gallagher, *Africa and the Victorians, the Official Mind of Imperialism* (London, 1964), p. 470.

born, but nevertheless an ally which had no doubt whatsoever on which side it stood in a bipolar world. The U.S., because of the intimacy of relationships with both these nations, was vulnerable to change, and especially unprepared for the sometimes bewildering reversals and turmoil which was the immediate consequence of each of these revolutions.

The Soviet Union was also caught at some disadvantage by the fast-moving chain of events set in motion in the horn of Africa and in Angola. In the horn, the Soviets had developed a very close relationship with Somalia. In 1974 the two nations signed a treaty of friendship and cooperation, the Soviet Union's first with a sub-Saharan African state.

But Somalia was also one of Ethiopia's traditional enemies and more than casually interested in Somalia tribesmen's revolt in Ethiopia's Ogadan province. In Angola, despite a relationship with the MPLA which went back to the early 1960's, the Soviets had become so disenchanted with the leadership of Agostinho Neto that by 1974 they had ceased any meaningful aid and were rumored to have thrown their support to one of his rivals, Daniel Chipenda, then one of the MPLA's only successful commanders in the field. This was a curious choice for the Soviets, in view of Chipenda's later role as the intermediary between the Zairians and BOSS, the South African security outfit. In any event, partly because of this withdrawal of Soviet support, Neto had been seeking Western assistance, and was so engaged when the coup in Lisbon took place.

There is some irony to the coincidence of the crises in Ethiopia and Portuguese Africa. Ethiopia alone of the African kingdoms had remained free of European colonialism; Portugal first acquired its African outposts in an attempt to circumnavigate Africa, outflank Islam, and link up with the Christian prince in Abyssinia they called "Prester John." Both Ethiopia and the Portuguese territories in Southern Africa, however, were profoundly affected by the nineteenth century division of Africa. The Ethiopians, taking a leaf from the Europeans' book, had expanded their own imperial control, especially into the Ogadan and Eritrea. In the 1970's both of these provinces became the location of major national revolts, the attempted suppression of which helped bring the venerable Haile Selassie down. The frontiers of Angola and Mozambique represented more what other European powers could not decide to divide among themselves as anything else. Consequently, they remained frontiers, like almost all the lines Europeans drew across the map of Africa, bearing little relationship to ethnic concentrations.

In both these regions the United States and the U.S.S.R. were relative newcomers, as indeed they are in Africa as a whole. Their active involvement is almost entirely a post-colonial phenomenon, each power taking advantage of the political vacuum left when the European powers wound up their colonial rule. Each can count some successes and some failures in their relationships with the newly independent states, although until 1975 it was usually the Soviet Union that experienced the reversals and the United States which enjoyed the successes. Dr. Kissinger's claim in 1975 that only the Soviets were acting beyond their "historical" sphere is, therefore, a grossly unhistorical observation.

In fact, the U.S. and the U.S.S.R. began their African interloping virtually at the same time in the late 1950's and early 1960's.[3] Indeed, the Russians were probably first, as they have been casting envious eyes in the direction of the Eastern Mediterranean and the routes to the Indian Ocean via Suez and the Red Sea since well before the U.S. consolidated its own national territory, let alone become much concerned with consolidating anyone else's, so any "historical" U.S. interest in Africa is better forgotten in the contemporary context, as it revolved almost exclusively around the slave trade.

The "historical" importance of the arrival of the U.S. and the U.S.S.R. on the African scene was that it marked a broader shift in international power in which the decaying influence of Europe was being replaced by the emergence of the Third World and the preeminence of the two superpowers themselves. For a critical period Africa had already become a focus of intense rivalry between them that reached a climax in the early 1960's in the former Belgian Congo.

In Ethiopia and the Portuguese territories, however, during the decade between 1963 and 1973 neither great power pushed hard for major changes in the status quo. In Somalia the Soviets matched western arms supplies to Ethiopia (they provided 181 million dollars worth of arms to Somalia between 1967 and 1976, as opposed to the 190 million dollars worth of total arms transfers to Ethiopia from Western countries in this period, 135 million of which was from the U.S.). Soviet aid for the liberation movements in the Portuguese territories was modest in scale—much less than either the Portuguese claimed or the liberation movements wanted,

---

3. Secretary Kissinger in a speech on February 3, 1976, stated that "for the first time in history the Soviet Union could threaten distant places beyond the Eurasian land mass—including the United States....Angola represents the first time that the Soviets have moved militarily at long distances to impose a regime of their choice. It is the first time that the United States has failed to respond to Soviet military moves outside the immediate Soviet orbit. And it is the first time that Congress has halted national action in the middle of a crisis." (*The Washington Post*, February 26, 1976) He repeated this view more starkly in an interview with a group of editors of *Der Speigel* published in *Encounter* (November 1978). "Had we succeeded in Angola there would have been no Ethiopia. The situation in Southern Africa would today be entirely different, and I think this was one of the decisive watersheds." (p. 12) Also see "Statement by Hon. Henry A. Kissinger," *Hearings Before the Subcommittee on African Affairs, U.S. Senate, 94th Congress, 2nd Session, January 3, 4, 6, 1976* (G.P.O., Washington, D.C., 1976). For the contrary "regionalist" argument see Gerald J. Bender, "Angola, The Cubans, and American Anxieties," *Foreign Policy*, no. 31 (Summer 1978), pp. 3-33, and John A. Marcum, "The Lessons of Angola," *Foreign Affairs*, vol. 54, no. 3 (April, 1976), pp. 407-425. The violence of the debate can be seen in Kenneth Adelman and Gerald J. Bender, "Conflict in Southern Africa: A Debate," *International Security*, vol. 3, no. 2 (Fall, 1978).

and the same can be said for what Western support the Portuguese managed to squeeze out of their NATO allies. (Portugal received 280 million dollars worth of arms transfers between 1967 and 1976, most of it, 121 million dollars worth, from France. Fifty million dollars worth came from West Germany, and only 30 million dollars worth from the U.S.). General Spinola concluded in this famous book, *Portugal and the Future* (1974), that neither the West nor the East seemed to have any real interest in bringing the conflict to a resolution one way or the other.[4]

This situation began to change marginally during the early 1970's. The Nixon administration was strongly, if surreptitiously committed to the Portuguese cause. In 1973 the Soviets began providing sophisticated ground-to-air missiles to the PAIGC in Guinea Bissau, something which made the already precarious situation of the Portuguese in that territory almost untenable. The U.S. also in 1973 decided to allow the export of red eye missiles to the Portuguese forces in Africa, a decision aborted by the Lisbon coup of 1974.

Further special circumstances made radical change in Ethiopia and Angola especially dangerous to the great powers. First, extremely complicated internal situations. In Angola, three nationalist groups, all battle-hardened, each with strong ethnic roots, competed with each other as much as they did with the Portuguese. Partly as a consequence of the factionalism within and among the liberation movements in Angola, the Portuguese had been much more successful there from a military point of view than they had been in either Guinea Bissau or Mozambique. With the exception of Unita, which in 1974 was a very poorly armed and small organization, each of the other nationalist movements, the FNLA and MPLA, were as much coalitions of exiles as they were effective insurgency forces.

This was, of course, in striking contrast to both PAIGC in Guinea Bissau or Frelimo in Mozambique, movements which had formidable offensive capacity, controlled large areas of territory and had developed rudimentary administrative structures. Angola had, in 1974, the largest white population in Africa outside South Africa, and whites almost totally dominated Angola's agricultural, transportation and administrative infra-structures.

And it was partly as a result of these differences from the other territories that Angola took on the importance it did when Lisbon's ability to continue the colonial wars ended so abruptly. The speed with which the transfers of power to PAIGC and Frelimo took place during 1974 proved to be deceptive precedents when it came to the complexities of the Angolan situation.

---

4. *World Military Expenditures and Arms Transfers 1967-1976* (U.S. Arms Control and Disarmament Agency, Publication 98, G.P.O., Washington, D.C., July 1978), pp. 158-195. For General Spinola's view see Antonio de Spinola, *Portugal e o Futuro* (Arcadia, Lisbon, 1974), p. 92.

Mr. Kissinger has claimed repeatedly that the U.S. did not oppose the accession to power by "radical movements" in these countries. This is only partly true: the U.S., in fact, was extremely disturbed about the consequences of the independence of the Cape Verde Islands under the auspices of the PAIGC, and there is evidence that the U.S. did contemplate support for anti-Frelimo movements in Mozambique. It was not the lack of desire, but lack of capacity, that prevented the U.S. or anyone else from interfering with the decolonization process in Guinea Bissau and Mozambique. In both countries, the rapidity of the process, the recognition by the Portuguese Armed Forces Movement of the necessity to deal exclusively with PAIGC and Frelimo, and the firm action of the Portuguese in suppressing diversionary attempts, meant that in each situation, because the liberation movements and the Portuguese Army worked in close collaboration, the opportunity for any effective interference never arose.

In Angola no single movement had the capacity to act with the effectiveness of either PAIGC or Frelimo, and by the time Angolan decolonization became the prime order of business, the Portuguese were so divided among themselves that they, too, were unable to provide any consistent or effective opposition to the rapid internationalization of Angola's crisis. Angola, moreover, with a population of about five and a half million, was different in other important ways from all the other Portuguese territories. It was immeasurably rich in natural resources (oil, diamonds, iron) and agricultural production (cotton, coffee, sisal, maize, sugar, tobacco). Unlike all the other territories, Angola had a favorable trade balance with the rest of the world and a firm basis for real independence. These resources (especially since 1964) had been developed in collaboration with large Western enterprises. The sort of leverage which South Africa, for example, could always exercise in Mozambique was not possible in Angola. The options for discrete pressure in Angola were thus much less while the stakes were much higher, and in consequence the temptation by outsiders to use force that much greater.

The second set of special circumstances arose directly from the complex internal situation. The whole structure of Angola was so dominated by and dependent upon whites that the rapid deterioration of the security situation, the burgeoning and at time bloody confrontations between the three nationalist movements, soon created panic among them. After March, 1975 the Angolan whites began to stream out of Angola taking with them almost everything that made the system of government and economy work, throwing an already confused situation into chaos. Angola, by the summer of 1975, in fact, had the misfortune to recreate some of the worst characteristics of two previous African crises, the Congo and the Algerian War, combining militarized battle-hardened nationalists with an environment where the mechanics which made society function had almost totally collapsed. The centralized and autocratic nature of the imperial Ethiopian regime, and the violence, regional revolts and internecine blood-letting which the coup in Addis Ababa let loose, created a similar situation in Ethiopia.

The importance of stressing this chaos in Ethiopia and Angola is to point out the contrast it represents from the situations which had transpired in much of the rest of Africa in the period of decolonization. Almost everywhere else, except perhaps the Congo, Algeria, and Guinea, the transfer of power occurred with the acquiescence (albeit the reluctant acquiescence at times) of the colonial powers, and in consequence, disruption in administration and in the economy had been surprisingly small. The experience of outside powers in their relationship with the new African states were therefore not appropriate to the situations which had developed in either Ethiopia or Angola. Each was, in effect, a new circumstance which required new policies, new policies which would be formulated within an international environment which had itself changed dramatically since 1962— particularly with respect to the relative capacity of the two superpowers to influence events in their favor in Africa. In fact, when the conditions for peaceful transfer had not existed in the early 1960's, the independence of African states had tended to provoke international crises. It should perhaps have been anticipated that they would do so again.

The third set of special factors involved the regional context within which Ethiopia and Angola found themselves. The problems of Ethiopia inevitably intersect with the whole situation in the Middle East and the outcome of the crisis there caused by the overthrow of Haile Selassie was of intimate concern to Egypt, the Sudan, Saudi Arabia, Iran and Israel.

Likewise, developments in Angola or Mozambique could not be isolated from the general crisis in Southern Africa. In South Africa no one doubted that the Portuguese colonies represented a buffer and defense against the tide of majority rule. The de facto alliance of South Africa, Rhodesia and Portugal against insurgency in Southern Africa merely confirmed the obvious. The burden the Portuguese bore on South Africa's behalf had been very considerable indeed: an army of 160,000 in Africa in 1974 (60,000 in Angola alone), defense expenditures of $425 million in the early seventies while South Africa with a GNP three times that of Portugal spent about the same amount ($448 million). With the Portuguese gone, the South African defense budget tripled, standing at $1,332 million for 1975-6. On March 31, 1976 military spending was raised by another 40 percent "to meet increased threats on the borders." South African military expenditures which had been a mere 2.4 percent of the GNP in 1972, were 5.4 percent in 1976. In Rhodesia, military expenditures were only 1.5 percent of the GNP in 1972, but rose to 4.5 percent in 1976.[5]

5. *World Military Expenditures, op cit.,* pp. 59, 61. Also, *The Military Balance, 1974, 1975-76, 1976-77, 1977-78* (International Institute for Strategic Studies, London).

Even more immediate was the manner in which developments within Ethiopia and Angola were linked in each case with nations where both the U.S. and the U.S.S.R. had developed their closest relationship in the continent: Zaire and Somalia. And this circumstance is the key to why these particular African crises triggered super-power intervention, much as had happened a hundred years before.

III

Why did developments in Zaire and Somalia entrap the great powers in the Angolan and Ethiopian crises?

In Zaire the special sensitivity to President Mobutu's desires and his effectiveness in promoting them had five causes. First, through late 1974 and 1975 Zaire was facing a major economic crisis. Copper prices had collapsed and with them Zaire's capacity to finance its balance of payments and service its enormous debts. The chronic incapacity and corruption of Mobutu's regime helped aggravate the problem. International bankers were extremely concerned at this time not so much at the scale of the Zairian problem (though this was in itself quite considerable, three-quarters of a billion dollars in U.S. investment, loans and contracts), as they were at the precedent set should Zaire default. One outcome of this situation was to give the viewpoints of the international financial community, especially in the U.S., France and Belgium, unusual weight where Zairian affairs were concerned.[6] Second, Mobutu possessed some very influential private lines of communication with Washington, and by using them succeeded in circumventing and neutralizing the realistic assessments of the situation in Zaire and Angola being made by many experienced African specialists within the intelligence community and the State Department.[7]

Third, by the end of the summer of 1974, Mobutu had already preempted the strategy to be followed by the West, providing the FNLA with a privileged access to sources of Western support. This was an inevitable consequence of acting in Angola through Zaire. The FNLA had become over the years little more than an extension of Mobutu's own armed forces, and Holden Roberto, the leader of the FNLA, was a man linked to Mobutu by marriage and beholden to him for many past favors.

On September 15, 1974 Mobutu and General Spinola, then the provisional President of Portugal, meeting on the island of Sal in the Cape Verdes, concocted a transitional plan for Angolan decolonization which aimed at placing Roberto at the helm with Savimbi of UNITA and Daniel Chipenda at his side. The objective was to exclude the Neto faction and

---

6. Excellent accounts of the tense negotiations over Zaire's debt and Zaire's economic problems can be found in Nancy Belliveau, *Institutional Invester* (March 1977), pp. 23-28, and Crawford Young, "Zaire: The Unending Crisis," *Foreign Affairs* (Fall 1978), pp. 169-185.

7. The best accounts on this aspect of Zairian-U.S.-Angolan relations can be found in Bruce Oudes' reports in *Africa Contemporary Record* (ed. Colin Legum, Africana Publishing Company, New York), especially vol. 7 (1974-75), pp. A87-A101, and vol. 8 (1975-76), pp. A118-A126.

bring the MPLA (in appearance at least) into the arrangement under the auspices of Chipenda whom they intended to recognize as the MPLA's head.[8]

Chipenda had the great attraction over Neto from the Zairian point of view in that he was agreeable to dealing with the Cabinda issue as one of "local autonomy," something much to Zaire's advantage since Mobutu was supporting an "independence" movement there. Zaire, because of its payments problem, faced a critical shortfall in imported petroleum products, and Cabinda, a small territory to the north of the Congo river separated from Angola proper, had petroleum reserves estimated to be in the region of 300 million tons. Moreover, Gulf Oil of Cabinda paid $400 million in taxes and royalties to the Portuguese in 1974.

Fourth, Zaire played a key role in the overall structures within which the Nixon administration had sought to organize its international relationships. Recognition of limits to U.S. power and ability to engage herself world wide was the original rationale underlying the Nixon doctrine, in effect a policy of selective involvement in building up friendly states in important regions. Paradoxically this doctrine led to greater not lesser involvement, overidentification with the ruling regimes, and a devolution of security responsibilities which the political foundations of many of these states were too narrow to support. As Leslie Gelb reported in the *New York Times,* "the major reason for American involvement in Angola was to maintain good relations with President Mobutu Sese Seko, the man on whom Secretary of State Henry A. Kissinger is banking to oppose Moscow in Africa and to further Washington's interests in various international forums."[9] The then Assistant Secretary of State for African Affairs, Edward W. Mulcahy put it more graphically in testimony before a Senate subcommittee: "We do have...a warm spot in our hearts for President Mobutu."[10]

Of course, this "special relationship" had deeper roots than the Nixon administration, as indeed did those between the United States and the other "regional influentials" such as Brazil and Iran, whose rulers had been helped to power with U.S. assistance. In the case of Zaire the connection dated back to the turmoil of the early 1960's, when U.S. intervention helped dispose of Lumumba, and assisted Mobutu's seizure of power and his consolidation of control.

8. For Spinola's own account of this episode, see Antonio Spinola, *Pais sem Rumo: Contributo para a Historia de uma Revolucao* (Scire, Lisbon, 1978).

9. Cited in "U.S. Policy on Angola," *Hearing Before the Committee on International Relations, House of Representatives, 94th Congress, 2nd Session, January 26, 1976* (G.P.O., Washington, D.C., 1976), p. 13.

10. From "Security Supporting Assistance for Zaire," *Hearing Before the Subcommittee on African Affairs and the Subcommittee on Foreign Assistance of the Committee on Foreign Relations, U.S. Senate, 94th Congress, 1st Session, October 24th, 1975* (G.P.O., Washington, D.C., 1975), p. 32.

Many of the preconceptions about what was feasible in Angola arose from the experience of these operations and many of the key individuals involved in them remained influential behind the scenes in U.S.-Zairian relations as U.S.-Angolan policy was taking shape.[11] It was typical that a young Zaire-raised veteran of the CIA's Zaire operations should have been drafted in to head the CIA's Angola task force when it was established in July 1975. Ironically, John Stockwell's experience in the job after a traumatic stint in Vietnam was to turn him into one of the more spectacular of the CIA's whistle-blowers.[12]

The fifth reason for the deference accorded to Mobutu schemes lay closer to home. Despite the fact that Zaire had been accorded a prime place in U.S. relationships with Africa during the 1970's, top policy makers in Washington remained largely ignorant about what was happening there, largely because of the personal style of the most influential U.S. policy maker of the period, Henry Kissinger. The problem, well into the summer of 1975, was not that Kissinger gave Zaire and Angola too much attention but that he gave them too little. He held Africa, Africans and African specialists in low esteem, and they had been frequent butts for his jokes and humiliations. Moreover, between 1974 and 1976, there were four different assistant secretaries of state for African affairs, and two of them were forced out within less than a year for warning Kissinger that he was creating a debacle in Africa. Portuguese Africa, moreover, had been something of a Nixon speciality. The Spinola-Mobutu decolonization plan in fact had its roots in the Nixon-Spinola summit on June 19, 1974 in the Azores, when Spinola had painted an extraordinary picture for Nixon of communist subversion in Europe and Africa.[13] But Nixon was out of office within two months, and Spinola only survived in his until the end of September.

One major result of these circumstances was that when eventually top U.S. policy makers began taking a serious direct interest in what was happening in Central Africa, it was largely as a result of the direct and serious measures the Soviet Union was taking to counteract the all too obvious attempts by Zaire to exclude the MPLA and Neto from the fruits of the victory which they, with Soviet encouragement, had fought twenty years to achieve. But by then the U.S. was already trapped within a framework of alliances, assumptions, and barely comprehended past failures from which it was difficult to escape. And the salience given in Washington to the fact

11. See especially, Stephen R. Weissman's testimony before the Committee on International Relations, January 26, 1976, *op cit.*, and his book, *American Foreign Policy in the Congo 1960-1964* (Cornell University Press, Ithaca, New York, 1974).

12. John Stockwell, *In Search of Enemies: A CIA Story* (W.W. Norton and Co., New York, 1978).

13. There has been much speculation as to what was discussed between Spinola and Nixon at their June 19, 1974 Azores meeting. The two men met alone with only an interpreter present, and officials on both sides were left in the dark as to the topics covered. Spinola has now given his version of the conversation in *Pais sem Rumo, op cit.*, pp. 158-168.

of Communist support for the MPLA served to cover up the fact that the roots of escalation lay in actions in which the U.S. had been indirectly involved (directly after January 1975) through her Zairian client. The African dimension became almost irrelevant in the process. As Helmut Sonnenfeldt, Counselor in the State Department and Kissinger's closest advisor on Soviet affairs, explained it, the United States "had no intrinsic interest in Angola as such." But "once a locale, no matter how remote and unimportant for us, becomes a focal point for Soviet, and in this instance, Soviet supported Cuban military action, the United States acquires a derivative interest which we simply cannot avoid."

Preoccupation with Soviet intentions, therefore, overwhelmed the warnings that were pouring in from, among others, the U.S. Consul in Luanda, an interagency task force and two assistant secretaries of state for African Affairs on the inside, from such respected African specialists as John Marcum and Gerald Bender on the outside, and from Senator Dick Clark in the Congress, all of whom argued that unless a broad based political strategy aimed at conciliating the factions in Angola was substituted for the attempt to favor some at the expense of the others, the U.S. was doomed to face escalating demands with no certainty of success, doomed indeed to help create a situation where the resolution of the conflict would come through military means, with the U.S. unprepared and incapable of acting to aid the very forces it had encouraged into the conflict.

At no time, until too late, did the U.S. give any serious thought to what a purely military solution to the Angolan crisis would involve, so great was the belief that the old and trusted formula of clandestinity, mercenaries and cash would still work as they had worked so well in the past. By the time it became obvious that this was not enough, the only alternative power with the capacity and desire to intervene was South Africa, which was the last thing the West or the anti-MPLA nationalists should have permitted to become obvious.

At a stroke South African intervention undermined the western groups' credibility in African opinion, overwhelmed the doubts many African states (Nigeria in particular) had about the MPLA and its friends, and made large scale Soviet and Cuban assistance to Neto respectable.

The Soviets, with their long memories, had their own special reasons for being sensitive to the role of Zaire in the Angolan crises. Zaire had been, after all, the scene of Soviet humiliation during the early sixties. It had been precisely because of the unhappy Soviet experiences in places like the former Belgium Congo that the Soviet Union embarked on a major build-

---

14. Helmut Sonnenfeldt, "American-Soviet Relations: Informal Remarks," *Parameters. Journal of the U.S. Army War College.* vol. 6, no. 1, pp. 15-16 (an article adapted from an address before the 22nd Annual National Security Seminar at the U.S. Army War College, June 3, 1976).

up in long-distance support capacity to prevent such a humiliation occuring a second time around. The Soviets, which had only been able to provide Lumumba with 16 transport planes and a few trucks in 1960, were able in 1975 to provide Agostinho Neto with $200 million dollars in military assistance by sea and air, to establish an air bridge with some 46 flights of Soviet medium and heavy air transports, and to airlift in Soviet IL-62's a sizable part of the 11,000 Cuban combat troops sent into Angola during this period.[15]

IV

The Zairian connection, however, while it goes a long way in helping to explain how the U.S. came to be involved in the manner it did in Angola, is not sufficient to explain why the MPLA, with Soviet and Cuban support, won.

The mechanics of the Angolan conflict are by now well known.[16] But the outcome of the Angolan war was more equivocal than either of the great powers seems to have concluded. It is important to any judgement about the consequences of the Angolan imbroglio for great power conflict in Africa and elsewhere in the Third World to understand why. The equivocal outcome derives from three interrelated elements. First, Soviet gains in Angola rested as much on western failures as on the scale of Soviet and Cuban intervention. Second, the Soviet and Cuban intervention, while large, was not disproportionate when contrasted to the total quantity of Western (as opposed to U.S.) aid to FNLA and UNITA. Third, the MPLA itself was much less powerful than the Soviets and particularly the Cubans thought it to be, yet much more so than the West had assumed when embarking on a cut price effort to exclude it from an Angolan settlement.

The West, throughout the Angolan civil war, found itself at cross purposes. French objectives were not the same as American. The Portuguese the Americans supported in Angola were the same groups they opposed in Portugal. South Africa, while useful as a source of intelligence, was a disaster as an ally in conflict. The coincidence of crises in Angola and Portugal, together with the U.S. overestimation of the Communist threat in Portugal, gave the Soviets the opportunity of both appearing conciliatory where they posed no threat, while disguising the central focus of their atten-

---

15. *Strategic Survey 1978* (International Institute for Strategic Studies, London), p. 13.

16. See, for example, the excellent accounts by Tony Hodges, "How the MPLA Won," and Colin Legum, "The Role of the Big Powers," in *After Angola: The War over Southern Africa* (Rex Collins, London, 1976); Charles K. Ebinger, "External Intervention in Internal War: The Politics and Diplomacy of the Angolan Civil War," *Orbis* (Fall, 1976), pp. 669-699; as well as the first-hand report by John Stockwell, *In Search of Enemies, op cit.*, and Nathaniel Davis, "The Angola Decision of 1975: A Personal Memoir," *Foreign Affairs* (Fall 1978), pp. 109-124.

tion. The West's position was fundamentally flawed by the failure to provide any clear objectives for their actions other than the negative objective
of denying the MPLA victory. What sort of Angola, for example, did they
think a UNITA/FNLA victory would look like? The South Africans
seemed to have been thinking of creating some sort of buffer state in the
center south of the country.[17] Zaire seems to have coveted Cabinda. The
MPLA, in contrast, stood firm to the concept of a unitary state; they held
the capital and their main source of ethnic support lay in a broad belt at the
heart of the country. So conscious, in fact, was Neto of the risks of
Balkanization implicit in the FNLA/UNITA offensive that on the day of
Angola's independence he refused to cut the celebratory cake for fear that it
would be a bad omen for the division of Angola. Furthermore, several
likely allies were noticeably missing from the Western line-up. Brazil, for
example, which had been among the first to recognize the Neto regime, and
Israel, despite Kissinger's entreaties, had the good sense for once to keep
clear of the conflict.

It is very difficult to find accurate figures as to the scale of aid. Kissinger
has repeatedly used the $200 million figure as representing the value of arms
transfers from the Soviets to the MPLA in 1975. Other sources place the
figure at $300 million; the U.S. arms control agency says $190 million. U.S.
aid prior to the prohibition by Congress, was in the region of $32 million
but investigators from the House Select Committee on Intelligence
discovered this figure was based on bookkeeping devices that grossly
underestimated the value of the arms provided. But arms imports to Zaire,
over the period of the civil war, rose to $126 million in 1976 as compared
with a mere $27 million the year before. The Chinese also provided support
directly to FNLA and permitted Chinese arms held by the Zairian army to
be released to them also. France and Belgium are estimated to have committed $30-50 million each to Angolan operations, and the South African
defense expenditures rose to nearly 19 percent of all public expenditures
(1,711.7 million rands 1977-78) to accommodate the costs of intervention in
Angola, their actual expenditures exceeding the budget estimates by some
228.7 million rands. There was also considerable support from government
and private sources for Portuguese right-wing forces that were active with
UNITA and the South Africans in the south of Angola in 1975-76 and in the
north with the FNLA during the same period. Later, further funds were
also available in Europe to recruit mercenaries. And some part of the
monies various NATO governments poured surreptitiously into Portugal in

---

17. For some interesting and well-informed comment on this aspect, see "The Battle for
Angola" by Robert Moss, the Editor of the *Economists'* confidential *Foreign Report*,
November 12, 1975, pp. 1-6. Moss was in Southern Angola with the South Africans and was
one of the observers best placed to know their thinking on this question.

1975 went to protect Western objectives in Africa.[18] It seems likely, therefore, that *in toto* these diverse subventions from Western sources matched and may even have surpassed the $200 million figure the Soviets spent. The problem, in any case, was not how much was spent on armaments but the quality of soldiers who used them.

On the other hand, the MPLA, was not the "vanguard of the revolutionary masses" Soviet propaganda and Cuban wishful thinking held them to be. Like their competitors, the MPLA had a restricted ethnic base. Like the others, it had not achieved any startling military victories during the colonial wars. It, too, was a movement whose leadership had been forced to spend most of its time in exile. UNITA and FNLA in fact had more authentic rural African roots, the MPLA in contrast being more a movement of urban intellectuals, assimilated and educated middle-class Africans, mulattoes and whites whose culture was European and Portuguese. The strengths of the MPLA arose in part from these same characteristics. They had skills that the other movements did not possess. Neto, in particular, a Portuguese trained medical doctor, had close personal connections with many of the leading figures of the Portuguese Left which dated back to the 1940's. After the coup in Lisbon, many of these friends were to hold key positions under the new regime and their support enabled Neto first to consolidate his own control over the MPLA, and then provided him with military support that was essential to the MPLA's seizure of ascendency in Luanda and much of Angola by the early summer of 1975. Neto was himself one of the three founding fathers of the independence movements in the Portuguese African colonies, and by 1975 the only survivor. Both his colleagues, Almicar Cabral in Guinea-Bissau, and Eduardo Mondalane in Mozambique, had already been assassinated. The MPLA had been linked for many years with both Frelimo and the PAIGC, and through them to the tri-continental movement, sponsored by Havana. Cuban links with the MPLA were longstanding, and Brazzaville, where the MPLA's headquarters in exile was located, had been since 1965 the headquarters of Cuba's African operations, a location chosen at least in part because the CIA was using Cuban exile pilots in its clandestine operations across the

---

18. These figures are pieced together from Mark M. Lowenthal, "Foreign Assistance in the Angolan Civil War," in Appendix 3 to "Mercenaries in Africa," *Hearing Before the Special Subcommittee on International Relations, House of Representatives, 94th Congress, 2nd Session, August 9, 1976* (G.P.O., Washington, D.C., 1976), from *World Military Expenditures 1967-1976, op cit.,* and *Strategic Survey 1977* (International Institute for Strategic Studies, London), p. 27.

river in Zaire where covert U.S. aid was helping General Mobutu consolidate his hold on the country.[19]

Though Soviet and Cuban connections could guarantee the MPLA the support needed for victory, its own narrowness of base, and the chaos in which the Civil War left the country, did not augur well for its ability to provide stability. The Cubans, once in, were to find as the British found in Egypt in 1882, that if they arrived as soldiers they would be obliged to stay as administrators.

Moreover, the strategic importance of Angola was incidental compared with that of the Horn of Africa. Located on the Strait Bal el Mandab, it has always controlled access to the Indian Ocean by states bordering on the Red Sea, thereby dominating one of the world's leading East-West maritime routes via Suez, while being close to the Middle East oil fields and Indian Ocean oil routes.

The U.S. had had close relationships with Ethiopia dating back to the 1940's, becoming Ethiopia's principal arms supplier after 1953. Somalia, granted its independence in 1960, composed of former Italian and British Somaliland, had turned increasingly to the Soviet Union for support. By 1974, with Soviet assistance, Somalia had built up a formidable 22,000 man, heavily equipped army and granted the Soviets deep-water port facilities at Berbera.

Concern by the great powers about the presence of their enemies in this sensitive region had provided the motive for many past intrigues, punitive expeditions, and wars. But the cause of the massive interventions in the Horn of Africa by the Soviet Union in 1977-78 had more prosaic roots.

Somalis and Ethiopians had old scores to settle. Newly independent Somalia had risked a military confrontation over the Ogaden in 1964, but found itself no match for the U.S.-equipped Ethiopian army. Somalia thereafter turned to the Soviets, sending its military officers to Eastern Europe for training. These officers seized power in 1969.

The Muslim Somali tribes have been traditionally expansionist. By the end of the last century, they ranged over the Ogaden, into what is now Northeastern Kenya, into the coastal cities and the territory of Afars and Issas, in the process laying the foundation for the territorial claims espoused after 1960 by the new Somali state, three-fourths of whose population are nomads.

---

19. Stephen R. Weisman, "CIA Covert Action in Zaire and Angola: Patterns and Consequences," *Political Science Quarterly*, vol. 94, no. 2 (Summer 1979). For background on Cuba's role in Africa see: Nelson P. Valdes, "Revolutionary Solidarity in Angola," *Cuba and the World* edited by Cole Blasier and Carmelo Mesa-Lago (Pittsburgh, 1979), pp. 87-117; William M. Leo Grande, "Cuba-Soviet Relations and Cuban Policy in Africa," *Cuban Studies* (Pittsburgh, January 1980), pp. 1-48; Carla Anne Robinns, "Looking for Another Angola: Cuban Policy Dilemmas in Africa," *Working Papers Number 38* (Latin American Program, Wilson Center, Smithsonian Institution, Washington, D.C.).

The Somali nomads of the Ogaden paid more attention to the rains and the preservation of their herds than to frontiers, and, anyway, the geography of the region binds the high land to the coastal regions. The Ethiopian high plateau provides the water reserve of all Northeastern Africa, as its watering holes and pastures are essential to the nomadic population of the coastal lowlands. The great drought—one of the natural catastrophes which contributed to Haile Selassie's downfall—had also exacerbated the latent conflict between nomads and settled groups in the Ogaden where Ethiopian rule had always been harsh and resented. Lack of rain led the nomads to impose their herds on the cultivated land.

The new regime in Addis Ababa, by showing preference for the settled communities, stimulated the growth of opposition. Religious leaders and small businessmen organized the herdsmen and prepared the basis for the strength of the WSLF (West Somalia Liberation Front). It was in support of the WSLF that Somalia, taking advantage of the chaos in Ethiopia, intervened in the Ogaden in July 1977 with its efficient Soviet-equipped army, rapidly seizing Jijiga and threatening Harar.[20]

This age-old conflict confronted the Soviets with a formidable dilemma: either continuing to support their Somali client or dropping the Somalis and responding to the entreaties of the revolutionaries in Addis Ababa for Soviet support. Support for Ethiopia would not be cheap, as the Soviets themselves had most reason to know since Somali strength had been entirely of their own making.

The U.S., despite its long relationship with Ethiopia, was, for several reasons, incidental to the crisis as it developed. The Pentagon estimated it would take the Ethiopians a decade to re-equip their armed forces. In the event it took less than six months. Nor could the U.S. make up its mind how to react to the social revolution that was going on in Ethiopia. Under the Ford Administration, attempts were made to keep lines of communication open, and U.S. military assistance continued if on a reduced scale, but the revolutionary rhetoric of the new regime worried Washington. The Carter Administration first appeared to encourage Somalia when strains developed between Somalia and the Soviet Union, but then backed off while simultaneously cutting off aid to Addis Ababa on the grounds that "human rights" had been violated. This bungling provided the excuse for Col. Mengistu Haile Mariam to turn wholeheartedly to Moscow and Havana. The Soviets responded with a dramatic reversal of alliances and a massive infusion of material to the tune of over $1 billion, an astounding sum when

20. Good background accounts of Ethiopian-Somali conflict in Serge Thion, "The New Africa: War and Revolution," *Dissent* (Spring 1979), pp. 213-225; and Ethiopia and the Horn, *Hearings Before the Subcommittee on African Affairs of the Committee on Foreign Relations of the U.S. Senate, 94th Congress, 2nd Session, August 4, 5, 6, 1976* (G.P.O., Washington, D.C., 1976); Marine and David Ottaway, *Ethiopia in Revolution;* Tom J. Farar, *War Clouds on the Horn of Africa* (Carnegie Endowment for International Peace, 1979).

it is placed against the Ethiopian GNP, which was estimated to be no more than \$2.5 billion in 1974. Havana sent some 15,000 Cuban combat troops who turned the Somalis back, destroying in the process over three quarters of Somalia's 300 tanks, half her 55-strong combat air force and many of her best trained troops.[21]

But the key fact about the scale of Soviet aid to Ethiopia is not that is was determined by any competition with the Americans. It was not. The massive airlift of Soviet weapons and Cuban troops to Ethiopia was determined by the need to defeat an erstwhile client fighting old battles about cattle, land and water. Geopolitics might have been the rationale. History was the cause.

V

Some years ago Ronald Robinson and Jack Gallagher criticized the theory of imperialism formulated by the English Liberal J.A. Hobson and the Russian Marxist V.I. Lenin. Hobson and Lenin both emphasized the economic or capitalist origins of the scramble for Africa. In contrast, Robinson and Gallagher found that strategic considerations were the preeminent concern in the minds of the leaders of the great powers as they carved up Africa between them and established spheres of influence, throughout most of what is now called the Third World. According to Robinson and Gallagher's interpretation, it was perceived geopolitical threats, concern over strategic routes between Europe and the Indian Ocean, and a combination of nationalistic Islamic revolt in North Africa and expanding conflict within Southern Africa which created the coincidence of external and internal pressures that dragged the great powers into deeper involvement and greater competition than they had either intended or desired.

Today with the increasing internationalization of Third World conflicts, these arguments are surprisingly familiar. Strategists are already in hot debate over Soviet expansionism and, once again, talk is of the Cape route and naval balances or the lack of them. Even the chronology is strikingly similar, since most historians agree that the process which led to the intensification of imperial rivalries between the great powers was set in motion during the early 1880's. Then, as now, it was the very stability of power balances at the points of direct confrontation in Central Europe which shifted the sphere of competition to those peripheral zones where chronic instability, the decay of old imperial administrations, settler intransigence or Islamic revolt offered much scope for self-interested mischief by ambitious outsiders.

21. On the Ogaden war, *Strategic Survey 1977*, pp. 16-26, and *Strategic Survey 1978*, pp. 94-99 (International Institute for Strategic Studies, London). David Steven, "Realignment in the Horn: The Soviet Advantage," *International Security*, vol. 4, no. 2 (Fall 1979), pp. 69-90; Henry Bienen, "Perspectives on Soviet Intervention in Africa," *Political Science Quarterly*, vol. 95, no. 1 (Spring 1980), pp. 29-42.

The conundrum about the role of the great powers in Africa today is that the methods each has chosen to achieve its objectives there, while sufficient to gain temporary success, are not sufficient to guarantee permanent successes. The West, in the final analysis, especially the United States, seems to place faith in economic factors that would gladden the hearts of Lenin and Hobson. But by doing so in practice, as in Zaire, this means relinquishing control of policy-making to the narrow visions of the international financial community.[22] It might be convenient to place the onus of hard decisions on the IMF, but as the French bankers found with the Khedive in Egypt in the 1870's, there was only so much blood that could be squeezed out of a stone. Inter-state relations demand broader vision. Panic that produces temporary bail-outs or quick para-military fixes will not solve basic problems. On the other hand, the Soviet Union's growing faith in military leverage and the belief of many African radicals that "superior force" is the means to resolve their dilemmas, will not work either.[23] The danger for both great powers emerges precisely from the fact that the Soviets attempt military solutions to problems that they lack the economic capacity to resolve, while the West seeks to exercise economic influence while lacking a counter-balancing military force.

The second conundrum today is that each of the African crises which have stimulated super-power rivalry in Africa are peripheral to the fundamental conflicts within the continent. What will really determine the future of Africa will be what happens in South Africa, and the dangers that lie under the surface between Egypt and its neighbors are more threatening to international peace than any conflict in the Horn of Africa. Yet peripheral crises can narrow the room for maneuver as they have in Angola, Zaire and Ethiopia; these can recur at any moment, and undoubtedly, they will.

The third conundrum lies in the realm of perceptions and realities. In the final analysis, perhaps, it matters less what happened than, for example, what Henry Kissinger or Fidel Castro, or Mr. Brezhnev, said happened. Myths are not easily deflated and can, at times, be no less powerful in creating events than events themselves. And no less important, a misinterpretation of the causes of success or failures in specific circumstances can lead to dangerous adventurism.

22. For a persuasive critique of Western policy in Zaire, see Peter Mangold, "Shaba I and Shaba II," *Survival*, vol. XXI, no. 3 (May-June 1979), pp. 107-114.

23. On Soviet policy, William E. Griffith, "Soviet Power and Policies in the Third World: The Case of Africa," 152; *Adelphi Papers*, 152, "Prospects on Soviet Power in the 1980's" (International Institute for Strategic Studies, London, 1979), pp. 39-46; "The Soviet Union and the Third World: A Watershed of Great Power Rivalry," *Report to the Committee on International Relations, House of Representatives, by the Senior Specialists Division, Congressional Research Service, Library of Congress*, May 8, 1977 (G.P.O., Washington, D.C., 1977). Also Colin Legum, "The African Crisis," in *America and the World 1978 (Foreign Affairs* Special Edition, 1979), pp. 633-651.

The experience of Angola and Ethiopia shows that outsiders who transform conflicts beyond the sphere of their own direct relationships into struggles for advantage are obliged to work through clients who cannot be successfully manipulated and, acting on the basis of faulty and biased intelligence, will constantly face the temptation to escalate commitments to a degree that threatens their bilateral relations and narrows their options for response. It is a trap into which Moscow fell as easily as the Americans which is why the situation that has emerged from the Angolan and Ethiopian episodes is so dangerous. This itself would be serious enough in a nuclear age, but in the context of Southern Africa and the Middle East, it is especially volatile.

The irony of all this is that the end of Europe's oldest empire in Africa and the overthrow of Africa's own most venerable dynasty has recreated the type of situation that dragged the great powers into the partition of Africa, first into spheres of influence and then into colonies during the nineteenth century. But if the steeplechase is to begin again, let the participants consider the consequences. Russians would do well to remember why Lenin wrote his pamphlet on imperialism. It was to explain the origins of world war. Geostrategists in the West ponder the words of that great British practitioner of realpolitik, Lord Salisbury, who wondered towards the end of his life what Britain was doing fighting a war "for people whom we despise, and for territory which will bring us no profit and no power."[24] Africans who invite outsiders in to fight old battles remember that when this happened before, Africa lost its freedom for a hundred years.

24. Lord Salisbury's comment cited by Wm. Roger Louis in *Imperialism, The Robinson and Gallagher Controversy* (New York, 1976), p. 19.

Communist Strategies in the Mediterranean*

In looking at Communist strategies in the Mediterranean, one is first and foremost dealing with the policies of the Soviet Union in the region. Yet, use of the plural form "strategies" is more appropriate than it might initially appear. "Strategies" reflects the pluralism that has befallen the international Communist movement. Or perhaps there never was a Communist strategy, but only a Soviet strategy which Communist leaders, parties, and front organizations supported in greater or less degree, or which, to describe today's situation more accurately, they have in greater or less degree opposed. "Strategies" also reflects the diversity of approaches required to deal with the complex politics of the Mediterranean region. Thus, when examining Soviet policies, we should always keep in mind two questions. First, how far are those policies affected, positively or negatively, by the views and actions of other Communist states and parties? And second, how far can the Soviet Union itself follow a single and consistent strategy in an area of many currents and crosscurrents, most, if not all, of which are outside its control?

*Reprinted from *Problems of Communism*, XXVIII, 3 (May-June, 1979), pp. 1-17, by permission of the author and the publisher.

The Mediterranean as Object

The facts of geography and of power have made the Mediterranean many
things: it is an inland sea, the natural arena for the interests and aspirations
of those nations located on its shores; it is a route of empire for powers
which need to go through it in order to achieve their purposes somewhere
else; it is, to mix a few metaphors, the link between two oceans and among
three continents, the fulcrum for any power wishing to expand its influence
into Europe, Western Asia, Africa, and the Atlantic and Indian oceans. No
power since the Roman Empire has been able to dominate it without
challenge. Neither the British in the heyday of their imperial naval power
when they controlled the entrances and the exits at Gibraltar and Suez, nor
the Americans in the years following World War II when the US 6th Fleet
ruled Mediterranean waters, could indefinitely maintain dominance in the
face of competition from rival powers and political changes on the local
scene.

The two world wars of the 20th century marked the triumph of nationalism in the Balkans and on the eastern and southern shores of the
Mediterranean. Many new states, each determined to decide its own
destiny, joined the international community. Thus, politically, the area in
the postwar period has comprised many different pieces: the states of
southern Europe, some associated with the United States for defense and
some not; the Balkan states north of Greece, falling under Communist
regimes after World War II but soon split among themselves on the issue of
relations with Moscow; Greece and Turkey, taken under the American wing
in 1947 when threatened from the north; the newly independent or soon-to-
be-independent Arab nations, absorbed by the question of Palestine and by
lingering quarrels with the former colonial powers; and the new state of
Israel, unaccepted by its neighbors but with powerful support from outside.

No one of these groups of countries had harmony or stability within its
own ranks, and each lived in varying conditions of hostility or indifference
to the others. The unresolved problems found all around the shores of the
Mediterranean created enormous difficulties for the United States and its
Western allies in their attempts to organize the area for purposes of
security. They could, and did, deploy naval power in Mediterranean waters,
and for a time there was no military challenge to that power. But the
Western strategy of deterrence and defense required more than warships
sailing the sea. It required, for example, air power and air bases, shore-
based naval facilities, the ability to bring ground forces and supplies to
Greece and Turkey, and the continued use of the Suez Canal. Thus the West
was involved—for these strategic reasons, as well as others—in all the
political complications and conflicts of the region.

Soviet Policy: Consistency in Variety

The troubles of the West have constituted, in nearly direct ratio, opportunities for the USSR. Yosif Stalin did not successfully exploit them; his attempts to push into the Mediterranean (in Greece, Turkey, Libya, and the Red Sea) came too early and were too crude. N.S. Khrushchev, discovering the technique of playing upon the area's conflicts and tensions, scored some spectacular gains but could not build on them a solid position of strength. Under L.I. Brezhnev, the USSR found the strength, in naval power, but lost the key to political success and compiled a record that was, to put it charitably, a mixed one. The story, of course, is not over. The Soviet Union may be on the verge of new triumphs, especially if the American strategy for settlement of the Arab-Israeli conflict should run aground. Yet in no way will the USSR, any more than the United States, be able to avoid the problem of dealing with countries of the region in the context of the fundamental differences between their local interests and the global concerns of an outside great power.

Analysts of Soviet policy in the Mediterranean have been wrestling for years with a familiar set of questions. Is this policy primarily offensive, aimed at establishing dominance over the Mediterranean and thus sealing the fate of Western Europe militarily by turning its southern flank, or economically by cutting off its lifeblood, the oil of the Middle East? Or is it defensive, aiming to reduce the American threat to Soviet security and to establish the Soviet Union's right to equal status with the United States as a Mediterranean power? Is Moscow following a grand design, or merely responding to opportunities too good to miss? Are the Soviet leaders driven by their ideology—dedicated to the enthronement of Communist parties and the spread of communism—or by a pragmatic pursuit of the national security and other secular interests of the Soviet state?[1] It does not now seem to me useful to try to measure and weigh the evidence in a vain attempt to produce clear answers to those questions. The answer to each of them is "yes and no," and one cannot be more precise than that.

It may be more fruitful to look at the matter from another angle. Despite the different types of leadership in what we can roughly designate as the Stalin, Khrushchev, and Brezhnev periods, Soviet policy toward the Mediterranean has shown remarkable consistency. The determinants have

---

1. On this general topic, see Malcolm Mackintosh, "Soviet Mediterranean Policy," in *Military Forces and Political Conflicts in the Mediterranean,* Paris, The Atlantic Institute, 1970, pp. 25-30; Wolfgang Berner, "The Soviet Alliance Policy in the Mediterranean and Détente," in Stefano Silvestri, Ed., *L'Uso politico della forza militare nel Mediterraneo* (The Political Use of Military Force in the Mediterranean), Bologna, Instituto affari internazionali, Società editrice il Mulino, 1977, pp. 83-99; C.B. Joynt and O.M. Smolansky, *Soviet Naval Policy in the Mediterranean,* Bethlehem, PA, Lehigh University, Department of International Relations, 1972.

been, to use Soviet terminology, both subjective and objective, although it is not always possible to distinguish which is which. Together they set lines of policy that have endured through a series of continuing and often unpredictable changes both in Moscow and on the Mediterranean scene.

The first factor is the historic Russian tradition of southward expansion inherited from the tsars. Imperial Russia devoted over a century of effort—never really successful—to breaking out of the Black Sea and becoming a Mediterranean power. However, the impulse remains and continues to move the leaders of the imperial Soviet Union, who have had greater success.

The second factor, geography, both limits Soviet expansionism and spurs it. What profit is it to break the lock at the Bosporus and Dardanelles—which is not really broken, as the Turks still control that gateway even though the arrangements under the Montreux Convention of 1936 permit Soviet warships to pass through in peacetime—if it is but an entrance to another enclosure? For the Mediterranean is virtually an enclosed sea, with only two openings—at Gibraltar and Suez. Can the Soviets really hope for control of the Mediterranean, or even for a major role there, without the assurance of being able to pass at will through those two openings? They may for a time, at the high point of the Soviet-Egyptian relationship, have had some hopes of attaining this goal at Suez, but can hardly retain them now.

A third factor consistently constraining Soviet actions in the region has been the unfavorable correlation of great-power forces on the scene. As matters have stood throughout the entire period since World War II, the Soviets cannot have looked forward with equanimity to the prospect of war, limited or general, in the confined waters of the Mediterranean. Although it would not be a comfortable place for either side and the Soviet *Eskadra* (squadron) is not a negligible force by any means, the USSR does not have the ships and the aircraft in the area to match the US 6th Fleet in combat.[2]

---

2. It is difficult to assess just what the balance is between the two forces. The Soviet force since the late 1960's has averaged about 60 ships, increasing to as many as 90 in times of crisis (as in October 1973) and decreasing at other times (the late 1970's, for example) to about 50. In number of naval vessels and of "ship-days" it has in recent years been ahead of the 6th Fleet. The latter's advantages lie in the presence of two carrier task forces, the availability of Mediterranean bases, and capability to project power ashore. The Soviet force is strong in missile ships and has recently added, at certain times, two helicopter carriers and, on occasion, two new carriers (the Kiev and the Minsk) capable of launching VSTOL aircraft; but it suffers from lack of bases and of air support. Whatever they might be able to do in war, the more the Soviet forces have a presumed capability against US forces, the more effectively they will serve as a deterrent to US actions. On the subject, see Stefano Silvestri, "Military Power and Stability in the Mediterranean," *Lo Spettatore internazionale* (Bologna), January-March 1978, pp. 5-28; Barry M. Blechman and Stephen S. Kaplan, "The Political Use of Military Power in the Mediterranean by the United States and the Soviet Union," ibid., pp. 29-66; Stansfield Turner and George Thibault, "Countering the Soviet Threat in the Mediterranean," *U.S. Naval Institute Proceedings* (Annapolis, MD), July 1977, pp. 25-32; and Curt Gasteyger, "The Super-Powers in the Mediterranean," *Survival* (London), November-December 1975.

While Soviet forces could inflict a great deal of damage, their mission in the case of hostilities would probably be a suicidal one. With the balance of forces what it has been, the Soviet leaders have had every reason to avoid war with the United States in the Mediterranean, and their conduct over the years clearly reflects such considerations. From the perspective of regional policy, then, the *Eskadra* has primarily been a force for peacetime use and largely for political rather than military effect within the Mediterranean area itself.

(Of course, from a broader perspective, that of Soviet grand strategy, military strength in the Mediterranean cannot be understood except in terms of its global purpose. Militarily as politically, the Mediterranean is not a separate and self-contained area either for the Soviet Union or for the United States. The fact that both keep naval forces there permanently tends to distort the reality that each of these forces is part of a total aggregation of naval power operating all over the world. Both navies have global missions directed, among other things, at reducing the threat from the other and in the last analysis at fighting a general war. The Soviet *Eskadra* in the Mediterranean is drawn from the Northern, Baltic, and Black Sea fleets; it engages in ocean-scale exercises with them[3]; and it has a role in the projection of naval power to the Atlantic and the Indian oceans, and of Soviet influence to the Middle East and Africa. These matters take us beyond our present subject. But they should be mentioned as a corrective to unduly narrow thinking about the specifically Mediterranean military role of naval and other forces of the two superpowers.)

The fourth factor making for consistency, albeit with wide swings, has been the limited effectiveness of Communist ideology, or indeed any ideology, as an instrument for the expansion of Soviet power. Stalin was accustomed to use foreign Communist parties to Soviet ends, and he did not cease to do so after he liquidated the Comintern in 1943. It became apparent in the early postwar years, however, that outside of Eastern Europe, Soviet attempts to manipulate events faced formidable obstacles and heavy risks. The Communist Party of Greece had a strong military force and considerable popular support, but once the British and then the United States took the decision that they would not permit a Communist victory in Greece, Stalin cut his losses and drew back. In France and Italy, the Communist parties were large and well organized, but once dropped by their

---

3. The first worldwide exercises were OKEAN-I, held in 1970 ("Soviet Maneuvers Summarized," *U.S. Naval Institute Proceedings,* November 1970, p. 101). On later exercises, see Robert G. Weinland, "The State and Future of the Soviet Navy in the North Atlantic," in Michael MccGwire and John McDonnell, Eds., *Soviet Naval Influence: Domestic and Foreign Dimensions,* New York, NY, Praeger Publishers, 1977, pp. 412-13. The Commander of the Soviet Navy, Admiral S.G. Gorshkov, gives his concepts of global naval strategy in his *Morskaya moshch' gosudarstva* (The Naval Power of the State), Moscow, Voyennoye Izdatel'stvo Ministerstva Oborony SSSR, 1976.

non-Communist partners in coalition governments, they could not get to power either by elections or by revolution. As the Soviet Communist Party's Central Committee pointed out to Josip Broz Tito and the Communist Party of Yugoslavia in the exchange of correspondence preceding the Soviet-Yugoslav break, the French and Italian comrades were not so fortunate as those of Eastern Europe, who had the Red Army at hand.[4] The Italian election of 1948 was the last clear chance at that time for Soviet power to gain access to the central Mediterranean through the free choice of European voters, but it was the anti-Communist votes that carried the day.

Later in that same year Tito's decision to lead Yugoslavia on an independent Communist course shut off the Kremlin's opportunity to base naval power on Yugoslavia's Adriatic coast. Although Albania's few harbors remained available for another decade, Tirana, too, eventually broke its Moscow connection and closed the Soviet submarine base at Saseno. And so, on the European shores of the Mediterranean the Soviets ended up without a foothold. Turkey, Greece, Albania, Yugoslavia, Italy, France—all had been subjected to military threat, political pressure, the appeal of Soviet ideology, or all three, and every one of them escaped becoming the Soviet Union's corridor to the Mediterranean or its forward base there.

One point deserves further mention: the relationship that developed between Yugoslavia's League of Communists and the Italian Communist Party (PCI), or more pointedly between Marshal Tito and Palmiro Togliatti. While the latter never defied Moscow in the all-or-nothing way that Tito did, he laid out his party's path to socialism as a specifically Italian one and propagated the theory of polycentrism. Moreover, there was no doubt of the importance he and his successors attached to the continued independence of Yugoslavia as a buffer between the Soviet bloc and Italy. If the Kremlin could use Communist ideology to serve state interests, so could Tito, and so also could the leaders of the PCI (even though their state at the time remained in the hands of the class enemy).

On the eastern and southern shores of the Mediterranean, the situation was quite different. There the Communist parties in the Arab states were minuscule, often fractured, and without political importance. Only Syria's could lay claim to some weight, mainly because of the stature of its leader, Khaled Bagdash. Because they were weak, they needed Moscow's aid. But for that same reason, Moscow was not interested in showering aid upon them. Stalin was content to leave the guidance of some of them in the hands of the major Communist parties of Europe. Thus the PCI could serve as mentor of the Egyptian party, and it was natural to expect the French Communist Party (PCF) to set party strategy for the comrades in Algeria as for

---

4. Royal Institute of International Affairs, *The Soviet-Yugoslav Dispute: Text of the Published Correspondence,* London and New York, NY, 1948, p. 51.

those in France. Not until Khrushchev came along with a different approach and, for Arab consumption, a different ideology, did Soviet strategy make some headway in these parts of the Mediterranean.

Khrushchev's Success and Failure

It was Khruschev's immense contribution that he found a formula for implanting Soviet influence in a number of Mediterranean states. This formula had simple elements: first, the delivery of arms to Arab states, to break their dependence on the West and create a new dependence; second, the building of a political and economic relationship with those states based on the calculated self-interest of each party and the willingness of each to pay something in the coin of the interest of the other; and third, a rather vague ideological solidarity grounded in anticolonialism, anti-imperialism, anti-Zionism, national liberation, revolutionary change, and "socialism" in a sense broad enough to evade definition, for precision in that respect could undermine and destroy the cooperation.

The third of these elements—ideology—was an elusive quantity. Looked at coldly, it was no more than verbiage. For the Soviets, the proclaimed solidarity was part of a popular-front strategy, which they were applying across the board in the Third World. Moreover, in the Arab context, the local Communists were the least important participants. In classic Soviet theory they might be the vanguard of the revolution, but the fact was that the target Arab states were being run by radical-nationalist political leaders, most of them military officers, and these were the only possible effective partners for the USSR. These Arab leaders paid little attention to the theories of the "national democratic state" and of the "national coalition of progressive forces" which Soviet scholars and party functionaries elaborated to explain why it was all right for the Soviet Union to be working with leaders and parties that were not Communist at all (indeed, some were anti-Communist). Local Communists might be brought into Arab governments, as they were at times in Syria, or they might be told to dissolve their organizations and join those of the national regime, as they were in Egypt and in Algeria.[5] The real basis for cooperation was not, after all, a common ideology but, from the Arab standpoint, Soviet provision of arms, loans, and political support against Israel; and from Moscow's standpoint, anti-Western action by the Arab states, a chance to expand the USSR's political influence, and Soviet access to local military facilities.

Ideology, nonetheless, has played a significant role in the Soviet-Arab relationship, both in building it up and, where the process has reversed, in

---

5. John K. Cooley, "The Shifting Sands of Arab Communism," *Problems of Communism* (Washington, DC), March-April 1975, pp. 22-42.

breaking it down. The reasons for this interaction are not easy to explain. It may be because both Soviet Communists and Arab nationalists are people who live by appeals to the masses, to the logic of history, to the truth of their respective credos, and to the glory of their destiny. If their relationship was in fact a practical arrangement, even a cynical bargain, between a group of calculating old men and a number of ambitious young men, they did not easily admit it to each other or to themselves. The vague sense of a common socialist cause was a part of the relationship in the early years and in some instances still is. But when differing interests inevitably caused fissure, ideological factors on both sides magnified them, sometimes beyond repair.

Tension began to appear during the Khrushchev era, with Gamal Abdel Nasser, Moscow's first and favorite Arab partner. Soviet policy in the Eastern Mediterranean was centered on Egypt, because of its size, location, and role in the Arab world, and on Nasser, because of what he was. He had a constituency in every Arab country. If he swore by the Soviet Union as the friend and patron of the Arab cause, fraternal Arab governments would follow, or if not, might be replaced by others which would. Yet as the open polemics that broke out between Khrushchev and Nasser in the late 1950's attested, the common cause had not overcome the deep-seated differences. Near the end of Khrushchev's career in 1964, in remarks he chose to make, or was provoked into making, on a formal visit to the high dam at Aswan and in Nasser's presence, he was telling his Arab friends that they should think less about Arab solidarity and more about class solidarity with the USSR.[6] He could not have been more impolitic, but he was only being himself.

The Brezhnev regime in its Mediterranean policy has not escaped the dilemmas posed when ideological "solidarity" confronts real interests. As the Soviet Union and the Arab nationalists have learned more about each other through experience, the earlier illusions and postures have tended to disappear. When concrete interests clash, as those of Egypt and the USSR have since 1972 over arms, military facilities, and Anwar al-Sadat's dealing with the US, the ideological veil is removed. Thus, Egypt's Sadat has become in Soviet eyes not only an ingrate but a traitor to socialism, and he now proclaims communism to be a mortal threat to the security of the Middle East. If Soviet arms are still needed by Syria and Algeria, and may be requested by Jordan as a sign of displeasure with the United States, each undertakes such collaboration on its own terms. In recent years, the Soviet

6. *Pravda* (Moscow), May 18, 1964. For comment on this and other Khrushchev speeches on this theme during his visit to Egypt, see Oles M. Smolansky, *The Soviet Union and the Arab East under Khrushchev,* Lewisburg, PA, Bucknell University Press, 1974, pp. 270-79.

Union's principal arms client in the Mediterranean has been Libya,[7] a country on the extremist fringe of the Arab world with a leader, Muammar Qadhafi, who is a vocal anti-Communist. It is a pure gamble, for any resemblance between Soviet aims and the consequences of Qadhafi's foreign policies is coincidental.

Now that Sadat has taken a course that is not just anti-Soviet but in the eyes of most of the Arab world anti-Arab and pro-Israel, the Soviets may be poised to recover some of the ground they have lost among the Arabs since the October war of 1973. But Soviet efforts to capitalize on this opportunity will lack a firm foundation, and serve more to advance the specific Arab purposes of the moment.

The Yugoslav Ingredient

A factor that should not be underestimated among the causes of the general skepticism about the Soviet Union now prevalent in Mediterranean countries is Tito's Yugoslavia—both its policies and its very existence. Yugoslavia's independent Communist system was already firmly established by the time the Soviets began their thrust into the Mediterranean in the mid-1950's. When Egypt, Syria, Algeria, and other Arab states were using the Soviet Union to free themselves from dependence on the West and to build strength against Israel, they were also cultivating the best of relations with Yugoslavia. Nasser and Tito had a close personal relationship with an ideological base in the evolving theory and practice of positive neutralism or nonalignment. Nasser learned something about the Yugoslav political and economic system and also about Tito's experience with the Russians.[8] Similar conditions pertained with respect to Algeria. Yugoslavia helped the Algerian national liberation movement and recognized its "provisional government" well before it won formal recognition and independence from France; Moscow, meanwhile, was more interested in relations with the French government and with the PCF. After independence, Algeria's new leaders found in Yugoslavia's institutions of "socialist self-management" a body of theory and practice that seemed suited to the Algerian economy.[9] The existence of Yugoslavia, at a time when nationalist Arab leaders attracted to the ideas of socialism were embarking on a new and not closely defined relationship with the Soviet Union, offered a socialist solidarity that was both useful and safe, and at the same time one that counseled caution

---

• 7. The main arms agreement with Libya, concluded in 1974, provided for delivery of about US$1 billion in Soviet weapons. See US Department of State, *Communist Aid to the Less Developed World,* Washington, DC, August 1977, pp. 3-4; and David E. Albright, "The USSR and Africa: Soviet Policy," *Problems of Communism,* January-February 1978, p. 33.

8. Alvin Z. Rubinstein, *Yugoslavia and the Nonaligned World,* Princeton University Press, 1970, pp. 233-83.

9. Ibid., pp. 85-89, 204-07.

against socialist solidarity with a superpower which allowed for only one true socialism.

The Yugoslavs, never modest in their aspirations, tried on several occasions to promote conferences and collaboration on a Mediterranean-wide basis, of Communist, socialist, and other "progressive" parties and political organizations. The principal meeting, with the PCI as cohost, was held in Italy in 1968. [10] These efforts were directed primarily against American imperialism and had as a goal ridding the Mediterranean of US armed forces; and if that goal were to be attained, there would be no need for Soviet forces to balance them, and the socialist and progressive forces in the area would then be able to take in hand their own destiny. Predictably, this bit of Yugoslav logic ran into opposition from orthodox Communist parties taking their line from Moscow and had no concrete results. Nevertheless, Yugoslavia's persistent missionary work in favor of nonalignment and of a nondoctrinaire view of socialism brought a message home throughout the Mediterranean—to Arab countries, to nationalist leaders in Cyprus and in Malta, to socialists of varying hues, and to the Communist parties of Italy, France, and Spain. With all of them, it helped to strengthen the image of the Soviet Union as an outsider, with its own great-power interests, to be dealt with not timidly, not provocatively, but circumspectly and, if necessary, firmly.

This was Tito's own way of dealing with the Russians. When Brezhnev stuck to normal and correct relations, Tito was correct too. When Brezhnev tried pressure, Tito resisted, and the world knew about it. Yugoslavia permitted Soviet warships to use its ports for rest and repair, but on the basis of a law that allowed the same privileges to other navies. [11] The only instances in which Belgrade seemed to bend its nonalignment in Moscow's favor were connected with the Arab-Israeli war of 1967, when Tito went to Moscow to declare solidarity with the Soviet bloc, and that of 1973, when the Soviets were allowed to use Yugoslav facilities and airspace for supply operations to Egypt. [12] But Yugoslavia never pretended to be neutral in the Arab-Israeli conflict. It was on Egypt's side and willing to join the states of the Warsaw Pact in announcing and supporting that position. These decisions displeased the United States, but they pleased the Arabs and most of the peoples of the Mediterranean, as they were calculated to do.

---

10. Milorad Mijovic, "Denuclearization of the Mediterranean," *Review of International Affairs* (Belgrade), No. 344-5, Aug. 5-20, 1964, p. 7; Jospi Djerdja, "Missed Opportunities," ibid., No. 434, May 5, 1968, pp. 6-8; and V. Vladisavljevic, "Mediterranean Confrontation," ibid., No. 449, Dec. 20, 1968, pp. 2-4.

11. *The Washington Post,* Dec. 2, 1976.

12. John C. Campbell, "Yugoslavia," in Adam Bromke and Teresa Rakowska-Harmstone, Eds., *The Communist States in Disarray, 1965-1971,* Minneapolis, MN, University of Minnesota Press, 1972, pp. 182-83; idem, "Soviet Strategy in the Balkans," *Problems of Communism,* July-August 1974, p. 9; and *The New York Times,* Nov. 13, 1973, and Jan. 9, 1977.

It was the Yugoslavs, also, who led the lengthy and successful campaign during the negotiations on European security leading to the Final Act of Helsinki in 1975 to get the Mediterranean recognized as an area urgently requiring international exchanges of views and negotiations on security and cooperation.[13] Those exchanges are now moving forward, at an unhurried pace and with no great display of interest on the part of the superpowers.

If, in a period of uncertainty and possible weakness surrounding Yugoslavia's transition to the post-Tito era, the Soviets should embark on a campaign of pressure or intervention, the reaction throughout the Mediterranean would be one of anger and of fear. Those countries might not be able to do anything effective for Yugoslavia, but whatever the Soviets might gain there, in influence or in access to the Adriatic, would be not only at high risk of war with the West but at high cost in political losses elsewhere.

The Ultimate Constraint

The most compelling constraint on Soviet Mediterranean strategy, and therefore also a factor in its relative consistency, has been the countervailing power of the United States and its allies, which we have mentioned in connection with the naval competition. Perhaps it should be put in broader terms. Whether the context is one of cold war or of detente, what the Soviets do in the Mediterranean or in any other area is conditioned by the requirements of the superpower relationship. In simplest form, it is a calculation of the risk of war. In other aspects, it is a complex weighing of priorities, of how much a political or military gain in the Mediterranean is worth in comparison to the damage it causes to prospects for SALT, relaxed East-West relations in Europe, imports of technology, American good will, and other things the Soviets hope to gain as the fruits of détente.

Soviet policy in the Mediterranean is, of course, simultaneously active both in military measures such as the placement of weapons and the movement of ships and in political and diplomatic activity in two dozen countries. We have said enough about the purposes and practices of this policy to indicate its general thrust: to assert the Soviet Union's right to be there, as a world power and, by virtue of its Black Sea coast, as a Mediterranean state (which the United States is not); to neutralize and, in time, to eliminate the US naval presence represented by the 6th Fleet and by submarines with nuclear missiles; to reduce American political influence and enhance its own; to use the Mediterranean to expand its power beyond, into the Middle

13. "Final Act, Conference on Security and Cooperation in Europe," *Department of State Bulletin* (Washington, DC), No. 1888, Sept. 1, 1975, pp. 323-50 especially, pp. 338-39. See also Radovan Vukadinovic, "The Mediterranean and European Security and Cooperation," *Review of International Affairs,* No. 639, Nov. 20, 1976, pp. 26-29; and the series of articles in ibid., No. 692, Feb. 5, 1979, pp. 8-15.

East, Africa, and Western Europe; and to help along the shift in global correlation of forces in favor of "socialism."

Merely to list these purposes is to call attention to how far they are from
realization, as the Soviet leaders themselves are doubtless well aware. The
record, not the grand purpose, defines the strategy in action. We cannot in
one article look into how the Soviets have pursued their policies in all the
different Mediterranean countries and situations: how they have exploited
instability in Turkey and in Greece and the disputes between the two; how
they have built positions of strength in certain Arab states and cultivated the
Palestine Liberation Organization; how they have preached nonalignment
for Cyprus, Malta, Tunisia, and Morocco in order to draw these states away
from the West, while trying to undermine nonalignment in Belgrade and
pull Yugoslavia back into the Soviet camp; how they have encouraged
tendencies in Western Europe opposed to the North Atlantic Treaty
Organization (NATO). In all these instances, the record is a mixture of advances and retreats, of brilliance and of blunders.

The best tests of strategy are situations of crisis when hard decisions must
be made. Let us therefore take as examples two series of crises in which the
Soviet Union involved itself, both in its regional policy and in its global interests. These are the crises, actually wars, that arose in the Arab-Israeli
conflict, and two critical episodes in the dispute over Cyprus. Both series of
crises were in the Eastern Mediterranean, the most sensitive area for the
USSR.

Moscow and the Arab-Israeli Wars

Let us compare, first, the Soviet course of conduct in the three Arab-Israeli
wars (1956, 1967, and 1973) and the semi-war that took place in 1969-70.
The following summary of the principal declarations and moves may seem
like canned history, but it demonstrates a pattern.[14]

14. Instead of documenting the specific individual points made in describ-
ing these wars, I shall list here a number of general works covering them, with special emphasis
on the role of the Soviet Union: Nadav Safran, *From War to War: The Arab-Israeli Confrontation 1948-1967*, New York, NY, Pegasus, 1969; Kenneth Love, *Suez: The Twice-Fought
War*, New York, NY, and Toronto, McGraw-Hill, 1969; Oles M. Smolansky, *The Soviet
Union and the Arab East Under Khrushchev;* Lawrence L. Whetten, *The Canal War: Four-
Power Conflict in the Middle East*, Cambridge, MA, MIT Press, 1974; Jon D. Glassman,
Arms for the Arabs: The Soviet Union and War in the Middle East, Baltimore, MD, and Lon-
don, Johns Hopkins Press, 1975; Alvin Z. Rubinstein, *Red Star on the Nile: The Soviet-
Egyptian Influence Relationship since the June War*, Princeton, NJ, Princeton University
Press, 1977; Robert O. Freedman, *Soviet Policy Toward the Middle East Since 1970*, New
York, NY, Praeger Publishers, 1975; Yaacov Ro'i, Ed., *From Encroachment to Involvement:
A Documentary Study of Soviet Policy in the Middle East, 1945-1973*, New York, NY, and
Toronto, John Wiley & Sons, Jerusalem, Israel Universities Press, 1974; Galia Golan, Ed.,
Yom Kippur and After: The Soviet Union and the Middle East Crisis, London, Cambridge
University Press, 1977; William B. Quandt, *Decade of Decisions: American Policy Toward the*

THE WAR OF 1956

In 1955, the Soviets made the famous arms deal with Egypt. In February 1956, they warned the Western powers against military intervention in the area. In April, they asserted the right of the USSR, as an interested great power and member of the United Nations Security Council, to take part with the Western powers in dealing with the impending crisis. In July, they supported Nasser's takeover of the Suez Canal Company, insisting that the dispute be resolved by peaceful means. In August, they warned the Western powers against using force, implying that the Soviet Union would be involved if they did. In September, they declared that an aggression against Egypt would touch upon the security of the USSR. In October, they denounced Israel's attack in the Sinai and called for a cease-fire and withdrawal. In November, they announced that volunteers were enrolling in the Soviet Union to fight for Egypt; sent messages to Britain and France saying the USSR was fully resolved to use force to crush their aggression, with veiled threats to hit London and Paris with nuclear weapons; sent a similar note to Israel with the threat of nuclear annihilation; and proposed to the United States a joint US-Soviet military intervention to enforce peace.

All this can be described as bombast and bluff, since the Soviet Union was not in a position to intervene in the fighting and had no intention of doing so. The "volunteers" were never assembled as a force. The Soviets could hardly have intended a nuclear attack on France and Britain. They made their threats after it was clear that the United States had taken a strong stand against its own allies and against Israel and would carry through. Thus, Soviet policy was basically a propaganda operation intended to give the impression that Moscow's warnings had forced the aggressors to stop, and that Egypt was saved by the Soviet Union rather than by the United States, which was pictured as a participant in the aggression. In sum, the Soviet Union made no military moves, took no risks, and maximized its political advantages.

THE WAR OF 1967

A decade later, the Soviet Union was in a stronger position, more active, and less successful. In the intervening years, the Soviets had armed Egypt and Syria and had begun to create a naval force in the Mediterranean. In April 1967, they gave demonstrative political support to Syria after it had engaged Israel in serious air battles. In May, they gave false information to Egypt that Israel was about to attack Syria; encouraged Nasser to mobilize

Arab-Israeli Conflict, 1967-76, Berkeley and Los Angeles, CA, and London, University of California Press, 1977; and Yaacov Ro'i, Ed., *The Limits of Power: Soviet Policy in the Middle East,* New York, NY, St. Martin's Press, 1979.

against Israel; vocally supported his declaration of a blocade of the Strait of Tiran (though it is not clear they knew in advance of his decision); warned that an aggressor (Israel) would receive an energetic Arab and Soviet riposte; and reiterated the vital interest of the USSR in the Middle East because of the danger to Soviet security. In June, they denounced Israel's attack and declared the USSR to be at the Arabs' side (but did not promise actual intervention); sent a threatening note to Israel; proposed in the United Nations a cease-fire and return to prewar lines (a proposal which was defeated); turned aside new Arab appeals for military help; accepted a UN resolution for a cease-fire without conditions; and warned Israel, after its conquest of the Golan Heights, not to push on to Damascus. After failing in an attempt to work out a compromise directly with the United States, the USSR in November accepted UN Security Council 242, which fell short of demanding total and immediate Israeli withdrawal from territory seized in the six-day conflict.

The war of 1967 was a bad experience for the Soviets. There was not much time for them to weigh decisions, so devastating was the initial Israeli attack and so rapid the campaign on the three fronts. Moscow had a role in starting the war, and as in 1956, it made a series of threats. But, again as in 1956, the Soviets did not send substantial military supplies or bring military power to bear on the outcome, despite the growth in their naval strength in the intervening period. Unlike 1956, this war ended in a political as well as military defeat for the Arab side. As a saving gesture, the Soviet "ultimatum" to Israel to halt on the Syrian front was an attempt to show real support, though it is not clear that the Israelis intended to march to Damascus, or that the Soviet Union was prepared to move its own forces into Syria if they had. All in all, the Soviets lost politically among the Arabs and were not compensated by being able, as one of the superpowers, to participate in a postwar settlement (other than to go along with Resolution 242). There was no settlement other than the continuance of the status quo resulting from Israel's victory.

It is likely that the Soviet leadership had to face questions from its own ranks as to whether the pro-Arab policy had been worth the price. But they found no satisfactory alternative, since they were not ready to take the consequences of abandoning the Arab connection. They decided to give more arms than ever, in order to restore a balance with Israel, and to accompany the aid with training programs, a substantial military presence, and moves to gain access to naval and air facilities and to seek a greater degree of control over Arab decisions affecting Soviet interest. Despite these measures, however, Moscow still had no real control over Arab or Israeli decisions for war, no policy for dealing with another round of war that Soviet policy made likely, and no understanding with the United States on limiting the risks in such a development.

THE WAR OF 1973

For Moscow, there was no avoiding the war of 1973. Although the Soviets did not want war, they created a situation which made it possible (as in 1967) and were resigned to its outbreak, or at least did nothing effective to stop it. In April 1973, they made a joint statement with Egypt that if occupied Arab territory was not recovered peacefully, it could be recovered by force. In June, Brezhnev stressed to US President Richard M. Nixon the danger of the situation in the Middle East but did not warn him of the Arab decision for war, despite the agreement the two were at the moment of signing on joint consultation to prevent just such an eventuality. In October, when the Arabs attacked, the Soviets declared their support, but privately recommended a cease-fire to Egypt (which was rejected). However, Moscow did undertake a massive resupply of the Arab military effort. Then, as the tide on the Suez front turned in Israel's favor, the USSR urged Sadat to accept a truce; negotiated with Kissinger a formula for a cease-fire and a UN resolution on settlement; told Sadat the USSR would send troops to Egypt if necessary to maintain the cease-fire; proposed a joint US-Soviet force to maintain it (which the United States refused); sent the famous letter to Nixon saying that if America would not act jointly, the USSR might find it necessary to act alone; made military moves which could indicate an intention to do so; and reacted to the US nuclear alert by stressing the spirit of détente and expressing a willingness to agree on a UN force including great-power contingents.

This bare outline of events tells the story of a situation out of control. The Soviet leaders had tried to restrict Sadat's choices by limiting the weapons they provided, but, not wishing to lose their political investment in the Arab cause, gave him enough to start the war anyway. They kept the Arab armies in action with Soviet supplies, but then had to insist these armies stop fighting in order to prevent a repetition of the disaster of 1967. The affair of the supposed planned unilateral Soviet intervention and the American nuclear alert seems like an aberration on both sides, a horrifying look into the abyss of the moment when the two powers were congratulating themselves on having found a solution to the crisis. Did the Soviets really intend to intervene, or did they make a bluff to get the Americans to bring Israel to heel (which the US did)? What did Washington intend by the alert, and what would it have done if the Soviets had sent troops to Egypt? Fortunately, these questions did not have to be answered in action, but the episode in instructive.

What can be concluded from this brief review of Soviet policy in the three wars? It shows, to repeat a theme, consistency. However, consistency in ineffective policy over a period in which the Soviet Union was steadily growing in military capability and in international prestige is nothing for the Kremlin to cheer about. One sees two conflicting strands of policy and a consequent dilemma of how far to go with one without too much risk of damage to the other. The first is support for the Arab cause as the broad avenue for the Soviet advance into the Mediterranean and Middle East; the second, the need to avoid armed conflict with the United States and the desire to play a superpower role on the basis of equality with the Americans. The great difficulty has been that whether the idea of equality and partnership is accepted—and, if so, on what terms—depends on the United States. These concepts comprise part of the mythology of détente, but just as Moscow interprets détente in its own way in areas where it has the power to do so, it has had to come to terms with the American advantage in the Mediterranean.

In 1956, American power determined the outcome, and the power of the Soviet Union, though it favored the same outcome, was generally irrelevant. In 1967, as the Soviets saw it, America won a war through the military prowess of its proxy, Israel, and nothing could be done about it. Moscow could only begin all over again the game of arming the Arab states. So long as those states, after each lost war, turned again to the Soviet Union, there was always a prospect for the entrenchment of Soviet influence and control. But after the 1973 war, the formula did not work as before. Egypt, the centerpiece of Soviet policy in the region, broke the pattern, and Syria did so in a partial way. The USSR was left in its nominal position of cochairman of the Middle East peace talks in Geneva, but it is only the United States that has been active and influential in the process of negotiating a settlement.

AN EXPERIMENT IN RISK: THE 1969-70 "WAR OF ATTRITION"

Soviet actions in the "war of attrition" on the Suez front in 1969-70 provide something of a contrast to those in the other three Arab-Israeli clashes just discussed. It was a less cataclysmic, more controlled situation, and it could be more favorably exploited by the Kremlin. This conflict, started by Nasser, turned into something of a proxy war between the USSR and the US, with each pouring in the latest-model weapons and keenly observing the performance and the results but avoiding public commitment. When Israel made its superior power felt and Nasser desperately appealed for Soviet help early in 1970, Moscow's decision was no easy one. Since the survival of Nasser's regime hung in the balance, Brezhnev and his colleagues took the plunge and sent not only advanced aircraft and missiles but crews to operate them in combat. In the following months, Soviet military personnel in Egypt reached a total of about 20,000.[15]

---

15. Mohamed Heikal, *The Road to Ramadan*, Glasgow, Fontana/Collins, 1976, pp. 81-88. On the war of attrition, see A.S. Becker, "The Superpowers in the Arab-Israeli Conflict," A.S. Becker et al., *The Economics and Politics of the Middle East*, New York, NY, American Elsevier, 1975, pp. 77-120.

Sending combat forces into action in a Mediterranean country well beyond the Soviet empire was something new. It carried considerable risks: that there would be encounters with Israeli forces on such a scale that the USSR would be at war with Israel, or that the United States would match the Soviet intervention with its own or take military action against the Soviet Union somewhere else. Actually, the Soviets did not calculate so badly. They were able to avoid large-scale fighting with Israeli forces. Their presence caused Israel to cease its deep raids into Egypt, which had shaken the Nasser regime. The United States, despite rumblings from Washington and San Clemente about the need to expel the Russians from Egypt, did not resort to military action. Nevertheless, the situation was a ticklish one for the Soviets, and they do not seem to have wished the proxy war, with its attendant risks, to continue indefinitely. Consequently, in June 1970, when US Secretary of State William P. Rogers proposed a cease-fire, both they and Nasser were ready to accept it. Soviet forces stayed on in Egypt for two more years, but in an atmosphere not always comfortable, for they were a hostage to both Egypt and Israel. Sadat solved the problem for Moscow by demanding their withdrawal. Whether the Soviet leadership was just as glad to see it happen we do not know.

The episode is significant in that it showed Soviet willingness, in a situation involving active fighting, to send combat forces to join the fray. The question is why they chose in this instance to act in a way they had not acted in the full-scale war of 1967, nor would act in the war of 1973. The answer appears to lie in the fact that it could be done unobtrusively, gradually, and still effectively. It could be done in a way that made it possible to gauge the American reaction as the steps were taken, and thus to control the risks. But one need not conclude from this instance that the Soviet leadership would do the same thing again in a comparable situation, or, for that matter, that a similar request for help would be forthcoming from a Mediterranean country.

The USSR and the Cyprus Situation

The pattern of strong declaratory policy and cautious action or inaction evident in Soviet behavior during the various Arab-Israeli clashes, is also observable in Moscow's posture in the Cyprus crises of 1964 and 1974.[16]

16. The series of crises over Cyprus in the years following the establishment of independence in 1960 has been covered in a number of general works, none focused specifically on the role of the Soviet Union. The evidence here on Soviet policy and attitudes comes from the Soviet press and academic articles. For Western writing, most of it emphasizing American policy, see Philip Windsor, *NATO and the Cyprus Crisis*, Adelphi Paper No. 14, London, Institute of Strategic Studies, 1964; Laurence Stern, "Bitter Lessons: How We Failed in Cyprus," *Foreign Policy* (Washington, DC), Summer 1975, pp. 34-78; Van Coufoudakis, "United States Foreign Policy and the Cyprus Question: A Case Study in Cold War

The first of those episodes started with squabbling between Greek and Turkish Cypriots and Cyprus President Makarios's suspension of the constitution late in 1963. The UN Security Council voted for a cease-fire and sent a peacekeeping force, but Turkey continued to threaten intervention to protect the Turkish Cypriots. In July 1964, Khrushchev declared that foreign interference must be stopped; called for the withdrawal of British forces (from bases established by treaty); and warned the Turks against invading the island, which could cause "a dangerous chain reaction." In August, after the Turkish air force bombed Cyprus, US President Lyndon B. Johnson's famous and ill-considered letter to Prime Minister Ismet Inonu—saying that Turkey could not count on American support if it moved against Cyprus and the USSR in turn attacked Turkey—opened the door to further Soviet pressure. Khrushchev told the Turks their use of force would intensify the threat of war; warned that the Soviet Union could not remain indifferent to the threat of armed conflict near to its southern border because the security of the country was at stake; condemned the Turkish bombing of Cyprus; and asked what the Turkish government would think if other countries used the same or more serious means against its territory and people. In September, the Soviets promised arms to Makarios at his request. But in November, after Khrushchev was out of power, the wind shifted. The USSR and Turkey agreed on a joint statement recognizing that there were two national communities in Cyprus. Then in January 1965, Soviet Foreign Minister Andrey Gromyko called for a settlement in which the two communities might choose federation. That statement evoked protests from Makarios and from Athens and was welcomed by the Turks as support for their position. However, Moscow was not taking sides, but trying to engineer an independent and nonaligned Cyprus.

By this time, the crisis was over. There was no Cyprus settlement. Makarios remained president of a nominally independent state, but there was de facto partition as a result of the fighting, and no solution of the constitutional problem. The Soviet Union has played a political and propaganda game only, and remained an outsider. It had not dared much, nor had it accomplished much. The arms support to Makarios was a gesture, not a decisive move. The Soviet Union had tried to assert a role for itself through the United Nations and as a great power, but the United States and Britain were not listening. The latter wanted to keep the affair within the framework of existing treaties and of the Western alliance, and by and large they succeeded, in spite of Makarios. Both Greece and Turkey, however—

Diplomacy,'' in Theodore A. Couloumbis and Sallie M. Hicks, Eds., *Foreign Policy Toward Greece and Cyprus: The Clash of Pinciple and Pragmatism,* Washington, DC, Center for Mediterranean Studies, 1975, pp. 106-38; and John C. Campbell, "The United States and the Cyprus Question, 1974-1975," in Van Coufoudakis, Ed., *Essays on the Cyprus Conflict,* New York, NY, Pella, 1976, pp. 13-25.

to say nothing of Makarios—began to take greater account of the ways in which ties with Moscow might serve their respective interests.

What happened 10 years later in the new Cyprus crisis, when the Soviet Union, with its Mediterranean fleet in place, was much stronger, and NATO, owing to persistent Greek-Turkish differences, was weaker? Nothing very different. In July 1974, when a coup blessed by the colonels' junta in Athens unseated Makarios, Moscow condemned it and blamed it on "NATO circles." This time the Turks invaded Cyprus in force, and the Soviet Union kept on blaming NATO, defended the right of Cyprus to integrity and independence, and called for the withdrawal of foreign troops (without specifying the Turks by name). Moscow insisted on projecting itself into the negotiations for a settlement by sending an observer to the British-Greek-Turkish talks in Geneva (where the United States was an invited observer), and it made the now familiar argument in notes to Greece and Turkey that the presence of large NATO forces in the area constituted a threat to the southern borders of the USSR. In August, the Soviets proposed sending to Cyprus a UN commission (of which the USSR would be a member), and later called for an international conference to resolve the crisis. No such commission or conference came into being.

In 1974, as in 1964, Moscow's declared policy was at times loud, but its conduct was cautious. The USSR said little about Turkish aggression and made no move to supply arms to the Republic of Cyprus. Soviet leaders knew that they could not really affect what was done about Cyprus, but that was not so important to them. The Western powers could not settle the problem, and the result was to keep Greece and Turkey at loggerheads. It was those two nations, not the status of Cyprus, that were the larger objects of Soviet policy, and thanks to American mismanagement of the crisis rather than to Soviet cleverness, both became further alienated from NATO and the United States. When each sees the other as the principal enemy and cannot get satisfactory support from America, both are inclined to regard closer relations with the USSR as useful rather than dangerous. The desire to promote Greek-Turkish discord and the ultimate disintegration of NATO in the Eastern Mediterranean is one reason why the Soviet Union did not throw its weight around militarily in the crises over Cyprus, for such action would have revived Greek and Turkish fears of the menace from the north and breathed new life into the Western alliance.

The Relative Stability of Unequal Balance

As our case studies confirm, Soviet caution in the Mediterranean is induced by America's military presence and commitments. The Greece-Turkey-Cyprus area, despite all the wrangling and consequent weakness, is "NATO country" and not the place to mount a Soviet military challenge. The same considerations apply to the entire Eastern Mediterranean. The USSR has lost its bases in Egypt, which are not fully compensated for by use of facilities made available by Syria and Libya.[17] Although America and Western Europe may not see eye to eye on Israel, the strong American commitment to that country and the new American involvement with Egypt, against the background of the 6th Fleet, make it highly unlikely that the Kremlin will seek change in this part of the region through the use of its own military power.

Could the USSR somehow get rid of the American military presence? Khrushchev used to fill the air with proposals for atom-free zones in the Balkans and the Mediterranean,[18] but the West did not take them seriously. Brezhnev, in 1971, in 1974, and again in 1976, publicly floated the idea of extending détente to the Mediterranean, particularly through the reduction or withdrawal of American and Soviet naval forces with nuclear weapons,[19] but it is not clear what, if anything, he really wanted to negotiate. Agreed limitations might be conceivable; however, the two superpowers cannot be expected to withdraw, although a goodly number of Mediterranean countries might like to see them both do so. It has yet to be proved that turning over the security of the Mediterranean to the Mediterranean countries, logical as it sounds, would in fact provide security. The present military balance may serve much better.

It is an unequal balance, not just in the sense that the 6th Fleet and the allied navies outweigh the Soviet naval force, but because the military dispositions reflect the fact that the entire sea is part of the North Atlantic Treaty area and is vital to the security of Europe. The Soviet Union might use similar logic to say that the region is vital to its security and that this justifies Soviet military superiority there, yet we are dealing here not with symmetry of argument but with historical fact and national conviction and international commitments.[20] That is why the establishment of naval superiority on the Soviet side or the introduction of Soviet ground and air forces in the area—whether they were sent on invitation to Syria, Libya, or Cyprus, or were moved from Hungary into Yugoslavia or from Bulgaria into Greece—would be a dangerous shifting of the balance. If we judge from the past, Soviet leaders have known that very well. They have been

17. Amnon Sella, "Changes in Soviet Political-Military Policy in the Middle East after 1973," in Yaacov Ro'i, *The Limits to Power...*, pp. 32-64.

18. John C. Campbell, "Soviet Strategy in the Balkans," pp. 14-16.

19. Ye. M. Primakov, "The Mainsprings of US Middle East Policy," *SShA: ekonomika, politika, ideologiya* (Moscow), November 1976, p. 5; and Anne M. Kelly and Charles Petersen, *Recent Changes in Soviet Naval Policy: Prospects for Arms Limitations in the Mediterranean and Indian Ocean,* Professional Paper No. 150, Arlington, VA, Center for Naval Analyses, April 1976, pp. 1-11.

20. Soviet writers often point out that Americans deny the right of the USSR to make precisely the same kinds of military deployments and take the same kinds of actions in the Mediterranean—in an area much closer to Russia than to America—that the US does. See, for example, the article by Primakov cited in fn. 19.

liberal with warnings that they would take military action in the Mediterranean on behalf of their security or their friends, but they have not done so, except in the limited Egyptian venture of 1970. And, for its part, the United States has not had occasion to use its forces in a Mediterranean crisis since the landings in Lebanon in 1958.

The Uncertain Future

Is there any permanence in this balance? Does the Soviet Union accept it? From the continuing buildup of overall Soviet strategic and conventional power, one is led to think not. How far the USSR has gained on or surpassed the United States can be endlessly argued, but that the Soviet Union has greatly increased its power, absolutely and relatively, is beyond question. There are two possibilities of a shift in Soviet policy and in the Mediterranean balance as a result of this stronger global position: (1) that the United States will be inhibited from standing up to Soviet pressures against local Mediterranean states, which will then give way; or (2) that the USSR will push toward military superiority in the Mediterranean theater, with consequent readiness to risk conflict there.

There is little doubt their now massive strategic nuclear power has given the Soviet leaders greater confidence to make military moves on the fringes of the Middle East and Africa, though still without committing Soviet combat forces. Is there a momentum in these events, combined with an American passivity as some critics charge, that will carry Moscow into the heart of the Middle East and to the Mediterranean, areas vital to the West? It is not possible to say what Soviet plans may be. We do not have evidence that either of the strategies mentioned above has been adopted. It is still within the power of decision of the West to safeguard its own security. If the West has the will to maintain the balance in the Mediterranean, it can do so.

A new generation of Soviet leaders is in the wings, although not yet identifiable. Whether new leaders will be as circumspect as Brezhnev we do not know. They will have major problems at home, but they will also have the confidence of possessing great military power and may find many situations beckoning them to make use of it or at least to take risks in the knowledge of its availability. A few of these situations would be: Turkey shaken by a deep economic crisis and political unrest; the Greek-Turkish disputes, including Cyprus, still unresolved; the American-sponsored peace settlement process in the Middle East stalled, and Egypt under seige by other Arab states bound to be looking for Soviet support; Yugoslavia facing a plunge into the unknown of life without Tito; Albania, alone after breaking the China tie, perhaps waiting to return to the Soviet fold; Italy beset by economic and social crisis and the apparent inability of its traditional leadership to govern either with the Communists or without them; Portugal and Spain finding the road from dictatorship to democracy a rocky one; Morocco and Algeria close to war over the Western Sahara; Libya still stirring up trouble with its oil money, its Soviet arms, and its penchant for revolution; Lebanon, buffeted by civil war and outside intervention, unable to put itself together again as a functioning state; last but not least, the PLO with its unrequited quest for a Palestinian homeland.

As we have seen, an uncertain or chaotic situation may make a given country a Soviet target, and the foregoing list indicates that the new Soviet leaders will have a variety of choices. It can be safely predicted that Soviet influence will increase in a number of states. The most vulnerable, at first glance, might seem to be those where Communist movements have taken root: Yugoslavia and Albania, where the established Communist parties may confront crises of political succession; and the southern tier of West European states, where Communists will share in the politics and possibly in the governance of these societies.

While there may be a struggle for power in Yugoslavia, no pro-Moscow "Cominformist" groups seem likely to take over, but if there are factions based on nationality differences or policy disputes, some may turn to Moscow for support. Not unless there is a real breakdown of the structure of Communist rule, however, is there likely to be a chance for the Soviets to establish their own chosen group in control, and then only by gross intervention. Everything in the Yugoslav experience goes against the acceptance of Soviet domination, whatever Yugoslavia's internal feuds and weaknesses. Hence, Moscow will continue to face the same choice: either respect Yugoslav independence or take all the risks that open use of force would entail.

Albania is, if anything, more difficult to fathom. A successor to Enver Hoxha might well make up with Moscow in order to get needed aid and to reopen the claim to Yugoslavia's Kosovo region, which is largely inhabited by persons of Albanian descent. That would offer the Kremlin a chance both to put some pressure on the Yugoslavs and to regain access to Albania's Adriatic ports. It would be a nasty situation for Yugoslavia and for the West, but they survived a similar situation in the 1950's.

More important in the Mediterranean's future are the Communist parties of Portugal, Spain, France, and Italy. Of these, the Portuguese CP is the only one fully loyal to Moscow. It had its chance to engineer a seizure of power in 1974-75 but failed, and the Kremlin's discreet help did not change the outcome. The other three parties are usually termed "Eurocommunist" —with its connotation of distance from Moscow's communism—although the PCF may not deserve the label. On the issue of independence of national Communist parties from Moscow's control, an informal Mediterranean grouping of the Spanish, Italian, Yugoslav, and Romanian parties came into being and worked effectively to defend that principle in the negotiations that led up to the meeting and joint declaration of European Communist parties at Berlin in June 1976, and in the subsequent polemics.[21]

At the same time there are ways in which the Eurocommunists, intentionally or not, effectively support Soviet international strategy. This function is perhaps most evident in the case of the PCF, which takes a nationalist French line similar to that of the Gaullists and tries to weaken France's connection with the US and NATO. Matters are less favorable to Soviet designs in Spain, where the Spanish Communist Party (PCE) asserts its acceptance of democracy for Spain and the party's independence from Moscow, which it openly criticizes. Yet, in advocating the abolition of both military blocs (NATO and the Warsaw Treaty Organization) and in downgrading military cooperation with the United States, the PCE on balance can be said to serve Soviet interests.

The situation is perhaps most ambiguous in the case of the Italian party. While the PCI accepts the existence of NATO, it opposes those in Italy who really support the alliance and attacks American policies which would keep the alliance strong—a neutralist stance that some argue serves Soviet purposes now and would serve them even more if the PCI joined the government. The argument has elements of truth. The PCI, in its concentration on domestic matters concerns itself hardly at all with a future Soviet threat in the Mediterranean, although it is very conscious of the importance to Italy and to itself of Yugoslavia's continued independence. Despite open differences with the USSR on the Soviet invasion of Czechoslovakia in 1968, on human rights, and on other issues, the PCI has not broken with Moscow, nor has Moscow broken with the PCI.[22]

Nevertheless, it would be a misunderstanding of the nature of Eurocommunism (Italian style), and a misreading of the whole history of the international Communist movement since 1948 and before, to expect the PCI to serve the strategic aims of the Soviet Union at the expense of Italy's security and independence. If the PCI should come to power, with real responsibility for national interests, it is a safe prediction that the break with the Soviet party thus far avoided would become inevitable. PCI strategy might be Communist—whatever that would mean beyond solidarity with Yugoslavia—and it might envisage a new role for Italy in the Mediterranean, but it would not be Soviet.

21. William E. Griffith, *The Communist and Socialist Parties in Italy, Spain and France: "Eurocommunism," "Eurosocialism," and Soviet Policy,* Cambridge, MA, MIT Press, 1977, pp. 9-11.
22. On the international views of the PCI, see Giuseppe Are, *L'Italia e i mutamenti internazionali 1971-1976* (Italy and International Changes, 1971-1976), Florence, Vallecchi, 1977, pp. 85-105, 132-51; Rudolf L. Tökes, Ed, *Eurocommunism and Détente,* New York, NY, New York University Press for the Council on Foreign Relations, 1978, especially Chapter 2 by Norman Kogan.

The list of opportunities for the Soviet Union will remain a long one, and by pursuing an active strategy, Moscow can doubtless cause the West enormous difficulties. However, the West, by maintaining the military balance, and the peoples of the Mediterranean, by persisting in their resolve to maintain their independence, will serve as major obstacles to Soviet exploitation of such opportunities. If both lose out, the responsibility will be their own.

Soviet Hegemony in Eastern Europe:
The Dynamics of Political Autonomy
and Military Intervention*

The Soviets have dealt in different ways with the East European Communist regimes that have come into conflict with the Soviet Union. Moscow carried out full-scale military interventions against Hungary in 1956 and against Czechoslovakia in 1968. In Yugoslavia, Tito faced both verbal assaults and overt threats of military intervention between 1948 and 1953, as did Gomulka in Poland in October 1956. Khrushchev mounted a ferocious polemical attack on the leaders of the Albanian party in 1961, but did not threaten to use military force. When the Rumanians broke out of the Soviet orbit in the early 1960's, the Soviets refrained from taking even verbal reprisals.**

Most Western observers have concluded that, in these conflicts with East European Communist regimes, the Soviets resorted to military intervention only when certain ideological or strategic issues were at stake. In their view, East European Communists who avoided challenging the Soviets in these particular areas were able to break free of Soviet control and were subjected

*Reprinted from *World Politics* 29, no. 2 (January 1977), by permission of the author and Princeton University Press. Copyright ©1977 by Princeton University Press.

**The author wishes to acknowledge the financial assistance of the American Council of Learned Societies and Marquette University in the preparation of this manuscript.

only to a greater or lesser degree of verbal abuse.[1]

In this study, I will present a different view—that in the conflicts between the Soviet leaders and the leaders of the Communist parties of Yugoslavia, Poland, Albania, Rumania, and Czechoslovakia there was only one real issue at stake: control over the local Communist party. The adversaries in these struggles have been Muscovite factions dependent on Soviet support, and domestic factions seeking to base their rule on genuine popular support. In the struggles between the Muscovite and domestic factions of the Communist parties of Yugoslavia, Poland, Albania, Rumania, and Czechoslovakia, it was not the ideological or strategic issue publicly raised by Moscow that determined whether the Soviets intervened militarily. What really determined whether the Soviets would resort to military intervention against a domestic faction was whether that domestic faction demonstrated to Moscow the capacity and will to mobilize its country for armed resistance. In Hungary, Khrushchev's intervention was not aimed at a domestic faction of the Hungarian party that was trying to take over from the Muscovites. He sent his troops to put down a popular anti-Communist uprising directed against all elements of the Hungarian party committed to preserving a one-party dictatorship.

Policy and Personnel in the Communist Parties of Eastern Europe

After the Bolshevik revolution, Communist parties were formed in every country of Eastern Europe. Each of these parties accepted Lenin's 21 conditions for membership in the Comintern. These conditions called for strict subordination of party members to the party's leadership. During the 1920's, the East European parties accepted an additional condition for membership in the Comintern: their first duty was the defense of the U.S.S.R. In accepting this obligation, the parties of Eastern Europe came under the complete control of Moscow. In the 1930's, Stalin appointed and purged the leaders of these parties, dictated their policies, and even dissolved the Polish Communist Party in order to improve Soviet relations with Hitler. Their ties to Moscow reduced the potential followings of most East European parties, because they appeared to be agencies of a foreign power, and because the policies dictated by Stalin were often inappropriate for the political conditions of Eastern Europe.

At the end of World War II, Soviet armies installed Communist parties in power in East Germany, Poland, Czechoslovakia, Hungary, Rumania, and

---

1. Zbiginiew Brzezinski, *The Soviet Bloc* (Cambridge: Harvard University Press 1974), passim; Robin A. Remington, *The Warsaw Pact* (Cambridge: M.I.T. Press 1971), 165-74; Philip Windsor, *Czechoslovakia 1968* (New York: Columbia University Press 1969), 62-94; Jacques Levesque, "Modèles de conflit entre l'URSS et les autres états socialistes," *Canadian Journal of Political Science*, VII (March 1974).

Bulgaria. In Yugoslavia and Albania, the Communists came to power on their own, as leaders of wartime resistance movements. Despite their different routes to power, all the leaders of the East European parties had originally been appointed by Stalin. From 1945 to 1948, the parties installed by the Red Army enjoyed considerable leeway in their domestic policies; some of them won a substantial degree of popular support by their policies of land reform and nationalization of industry. But, because of their ideological recognition of Stalin as the leader of the Communist movement and because of the unavoidable fact that they could not stay in power without the support of the Soviet army, these parties were still subordinate to the Soviet Union.

The Yugoslav Communists had never been dependent on the Soviet army. After coming to power, they no longer saw their primary duty to be the defense of the U.S.S.R., but the construction of a socialist society in Yugoslavia. As a ruling party, the Yugoslav Communists had to decide whether or not they would let Moscow retain control over matters of policy and personnel. Tito resolved the question in favor of Yugoslav control of the Yugoslav party. Tito's decision led Stalin to the discovery that in a ruling Communist party, the Leninist principle of centralism and the Stalinist model of industrial development both tended to concentrate power over the party in the hands of the local party leader. This discovery prompted him to make strenuous but unsuccessful efforts in 1947 and 1948 to wrest control of the Yugoslav party back from Tito. As a practicing Leninist, Stalin would not voluntarily part with control over a body that had been in his power. He probably also feared that if he permitted Tito to acquire control over the Yugoslav party, the leaders of the other East European parties might try to follow Tito's example.

After failing to overthrow Tito, Stalin launched a campaign to prevent the East European parties still dependent on the Soviet army from consolidating sufficient power to achieve autonomy. He dramatically reasserted the traditional Soviet right to appoint the leaders of the East European parties and to lay down their policies by ordering a massive purge, especially of the "home" Communists who had spent the war years in their own countries. Stalin reserved the leading positions in the East European parties for the "Muscovites"—the Communists who had spent the war in Moscow and were totally dependent on Stalin. He justified these purges by asserting that Titoist agents had infiltrated the East European parties as part of an imperialist plot to begin a new world war.

Stalin demanded that the East European leaders blindly imitate Soviet domestic policies: collectivization, rapid industrialization, and police terror. He also exploited the economies of Eastern Europe for the benefit of the Soviet Union. By insisting that his policies be adopted throughout the Soviet bloc, Stalin established clear criteria by which to evaluate the submissiveness of the East European leaders. Such policies had the effect of so alienating the peoples of Eastern Europe that the party leader in each country and the party itself became even more dependent on Soviet support to stay in power.

Stalin succeeded in pre-empting the autonomy of the East European parties that had been installed by the Soviet army, but he succeeded at the cost of making these parties face the prospect of popular anti-Communist uprisings. Following Stalin's death in 1953, violent demonstrations by workers broke out in East Germany and Czechoslovakia. Polish workers staged similar demonstrations in 1956. Later that year, a student protest in Hungary erupted into a full-scale anti-Communist uprising. After the violence in East Germany and Czechoslovakia, Malenkov and Khrushchev tried to stabilize the explosive situation in Eastern Europe that Stalin had bequeathed to them. To lessen the likelihood of popular revolts and to invest the East European regimes with a modicum of legitimacy, they ordered the leaders of the fraternal parties to adopt a "New Course." The New Course required the East European Communists to adapt their domestic policies to fit local conditions and to satisfy demands for consumer goods.

The purpose of the New Course was not to eliminate Soviet hegemony over Eastern Europe, but to camouflage it. Stalin's successors were no less willing to part with control over the East European parties than Stalin had been. Soviet party leaders probably feared that they would come under sharp attack from their colleagues if they voluntarily gave up one of the "gains of World War II"—a phrase the Soviets still use to refer to the creation of socialist states in Eastern Europe.

In 1955, Khrushchev resumed relations with Yugoslavia in the hope that rapprochement with Tito would aid the East European parties in their quest for legitimacy. If the independent Yugoslav party voluntarily cooperated with the CPSU, then the other parties in the region might claim that by cooperating with the Soviets, they too were demonstrating their independence. In 1955 and 1956, Khrushchev and Tito signed statements that endorsed the right of every socialist country to determine its own method of socialist construction. At the Twentieth Party Congress in 1956, Khrushchev made it part of the Soviet canon that each socialist country would follow its own road to socialism.

To the extent that Khrushchev succeeded in removing the danger of popular anti-Communist uprisings in Eastern Europe, he succeeded in bringing back the specter that had haunted Stalin: the possibility that an East European Leninist party would win enough domestic support to make itself master in its own domain, even though it had not come to power on its own. In ordering the fraternal parties of Eastern Europe to adjust their domestic policies to local conditions, Khrushchev was ordering them to tread a fine line between dependence and autonomy. The Soviets defined dependence as loyalty to Marxism-Leninism, to proletarian internationalism, and to the unity of the socialist camp. They defined autonomy as an exaggeration of national peculiarities, nationalism, and ideological deviation either to the right or the left. The excuses the Soviets were later to give for their intervention against attempts by East European Communists to achieve autonomy was that the leading role of the party was being threatened, a counterrevolution was in the offing, the unity of the socialist camp was in jeopardy, and the imperialists were scheming to restore capitalism in the country.

After the Twentieth Congress of the CPSU, internal power struggles developed in the Polish and Hungarian parties between the Muscovite factions associated with Stalin and loose coalitions of reformers who took Khrushchev at his word and began to seek popular support for extensive domestic reforms. Not surprisingly, the Soviets came out in support of the Muscovites in both countries. In July 1956, a *Pravda* editorial addressed to the intraparty power struggles in Hungary and Poland qualified Khrushchev's proclamation of separate roads to socialism by asserting that though the roads be separate, the goal was the same. In theory, *Pravda*'s goal was one universal form of socialism. In practice, it was preservation of Soviet control over the East European parties. The CPSU daily declared that "the necessary consideration of national peculiarities" would not lead to the "estrangement" of socialist countries, but would contribute to their "solidarity." No one, said *Pravda*, would succeed in destroying the unity of the socialist camp.[2]

The events in Poland and Hungary during October of 1956 revealed to Khrushchev the high price of reconciliation with Tito. In November 1957, the leaders of the East European parties and of the ruling Asian parties met in Moscow to sign a declaration that named the U.S.S.R. as the leader of the socialist camp, and condemned Yugoslavia for its ideological revisionism. It no longer served Soviet purposes to endorse the concept of a truly autonomous East European Communist Party that was capable of winning popular support for its variant of socialism. The Soviets wanted the East European parties to have the appearance of autonomy, but not the reality. The 1957 Moscow declaration duly warned of the dangers inherent in both the Stalin and Khrushchev formulas for maintaining Soviet hegemony over East Europe: "Disregard of national peculiarities by a proletarian party inevitably leads to its divorce from reality, from the masses, and is bound to prejudice the cause of socialism;...and, conversely, exag-

2. *Pravda* editorial, July 16, 1956: "The International Forces of Peace, Democracy and Socialism Are Growing and Gaining in Strength," reprinted in Paul E. Zinner, ed., *National Communism and Popular Revolt in East Europe* (New York: Columbia University Press 1956), 63.

geration of the role of these peculiarities...is just as harmful to the socialist cause."[3]

The only solution that the 1956 declaration could offer for this dilemma was to urge the fraternal parties to combat both tendencies "simultaneously."[4] The meetings of world Communist parties which the Soviets organized in 1960 and 1969 endorsed Khrushchev's inherently unstable formula for maintaining control over the East European parties,[5] as did the party congresses of 1959, 1961, 1966, and 1971. In 1971, Brezhnev told the delegates to the Twenty-Fourth Party Congress that success in the construction of socialism in the countries of the socialist commonwealth depended on the "correct combination of the general and the national-particular."[6] He restated this view at the Twenty-Fifth Party Congress in 1976.[7]

To prevent the fraternal parties of Eastern Europe from exaggerating the role of their national peculiarities, Soviet leaders after Stalin appear to have developed more subtle control devices. Like him, they have tried to exercise the right of *nomenklatura*, the prerogative of the Soviets to appoint officials to high-ranking party and state positions in Eastern Europe. But they have exercised the right of *nomenklatura* in a non-Stalinist manner. Instead of ordering periodic purges, Stalin's successors have tried to make loyalty to Moscow a necessary qualification for promotion in the party and state hierarchies. The Soviets have tried to implant this loyalty by encouraging rising bureaucrats to attend Soviet party and technical schools for advanced training. At these schools, they can establish personal contacts with the Eastern Europeans. The Soviets apparently try to maintain these contacts through "pen-pal" relationships between Soviet and East European officials in comparable positions. The existence of party cells in all important areas of East European life makes it possible for the Soviets to penetrate the

---

3. "Declaration of the Conference of the Representatives of Communist and Workers' Parties of the Socialist Countries," November 14-16, 1957, reprinted in Vaclav Benes, Robert F. Byrnes, and Nicolas Spulber, *The Second Soviet-Yugoslav Dispute* (Bloomington: Indiana University Publications, no date), 19.

4. *Ibid.*

5. "Zaiavlenie soveshchaniia predstavitelei kommunisticheskikh i rabochikh partii" [Declaration of the Conference of the Representatives of Communist and Workers' Parties], *Pravda*, December 6, 1960, p. 2. The same formula appears in the resolutions of the 1969 meeting, "Zadachi bor'by protiv imperializma..." [Tasks in the Struggle Against Imperialism...] in *Mezhdunarodnoe soveshchanie kommunisticheskikh i rabochikh partii: dokumenty i materialy* [International Meeting of the Communist and Workers' Parties: Documents and Materials] (Moscow: Izdatel'stvo politicheskoi literatury 1969), 327.

6. "Report of the CPSU Central Committee...delivered by L.I. Brezhnev" [hereafter referred to as "Report to the Twenty-Fourth Congress"] in The Twenty-Fourth Congress of the Communist Party of the Soviet Union, I (Arlington, Va.: U.S. Government Joint Publications Research Service 1971), 26.

7. Report of the CPSU Central Committee...delivered by Comrade L.I. Brezhnev to the Twenty-Fifth Congress of the CPSU, February 24, 1976" [hereafter referred to as "Report to the Twenty-Fifty Congress"] in Supplement to *Moscow News*, No. 9, 1976, p. 2.

entire political, economic, social, and cultural fabric of an East European country.[8]

It is likely that the Soviet diplomatic and intelligence services alternately flatter, bribe, and cajole these and other officials in the East European parties into placing themselves under obligations to Moscow. The Soviets repay the loyalty of the Muscovites by protecting them from their rivals in the party. In the post-Stalin period, the Muscovite leaders of the East European fraternal parties have usually enjoyed very long tenure in office. During times of economic crisis, the Soviets have been willing to offer economic assistance to ruling Muscovites rather than let them confront excessive criticism from within the party.

Khrushchev and Brezhnev have also tried to close off avenues of departure from the Soviet bloc by making the leaders of the East European parties commit themselves to long-term economic agreements that preclude political autonomy. Since the late 1950's, the countries of the socialist commonwealth have abandoned Stalinist programs of all-round industrialization and have adopted programs of economic specialization within the framework of the Council for Mutual Economic Assistance. Long-range trade and investment projects tie these countries to each other and to the Soviet Union in a net of interdependence. One Western economist has reached the conclusion that since the mid-1960's, the East European countries have economically exploited the U.S.S.R., which has sold them large quantities of raw materials at prices below those of the world markets.[9] The political effect of the economic "exploitation" of the U.S.S.R. was to make the East European leaders dependent on the Soviet Union for subsidies.

The Soviets have also tried to deny the East European parties control over their own military organizations by integrating them into the command structure of the Warsaw Pact, which is dominated by Soviet officers. As Brezhnev told the delegates to the last two party congresses, the Warsaw Pact "has served and continues to serve as the main center for coordinating the foreign-policy activity of the fraternal countries."[10]

Like Stalin, Khrushchev and Brezhnev have tried to exercise control over the foreign and domestic policies of the East European parties. Unlike Stalin, his successors have not evaluated East European policies on the basis of how closely they resemble Soviet policies, but on the basis of whether or not they win enough popular support for the local party to free itself of dependence of the Soviet Union. A commentator in *Izvestiia* explained after the 1968 invasion of Czechoslovakia that, in making a Leninist analysis of a given policy, "It is not *who* champions the immediate given policy that is

---

8. Brezhnev, "Report to the Twenty-Fifth Congress" (fn. 7), 2.

9. Paul Marer, "Soviet Economic Relations with Eastern Europe and Their Impact on East-West and US-USSR Trade," paper delivered January 16, 1975, Harvard University Russian Research Center.

10. Brezhnev, "Report to the Twenty-Fourth Congress" (fn. 6), 27; "Report to the Twenty-Fifth Congress" (fn. 7), 2.

important. It is *whom* these proposals, these measures, benefit that is important."[11]

The Leninist approach of Soviet analysts is demonstrated by the vociferous Soviet objections in 1968 to the very suggestion that Czechoslovakia establish diplomatic relations with Bonn, and the warm Soviet endorsement of Prague's recognition of West Germany in December 1973.[12] Husak's recognition of Bonn strengthened a regime entirely dependent on the Soviets, and complemented the U.S.S.R.'s pursuit of détente. Had Dubcek established relations with West Germany in 1968, he clearly would have moved closer toward autonomy. In Hungary, the Soviets have endorsed Janos Kadar's relatively liberal policies probably because they and Kadar recognize that the Hungarian regime has to atone for its bloody origins in 1956. They seem to be confident that Kadar will remain conscious of his dependence on Moscow no matter how content the Hungarians become with "goulash Communism."

The Soviets and their East European allies do not admit to the existence of the Soviet right of *nomenklatura* in East Europe, nor do they acknowledge Soviet interference in the making of domestic and foreign policies in the region. Evidence of Soviet control over the policies and personnel of the East European parties surfaces only when the East European parties challenge the Soviets for control over these areas—as the Yugoslavs did in 1948, the Poles in 1956, the Albanians and Rumanians in the early 1960's, and the Czechs and Slovaks in 1968.

Immediately after being expelled from the Cominform, the Central Committee of the Yugoslav Communist Party issued a resolution which claimed that Soviet intelligence services had tried to recruit members of the YCP. The Yugoslav resolution condemned the Soviets for their support "of factionalist activity, of traitors" in the YCP.[13] Tito told his compatriots that for all its ideological protestations, the Cominform declaration of June 28, 1948, was "a notorious appeal to forcibly remove the present leadership of Yugoslavia...."[14] In an essay on relations among socialist states, Milovan Djilas, a leading Yugoslav theoretician, asserted that Stalin's policy toward the East European Communist parties was one of "formation of

11. V. Sevruk, "Rosovye slova i chernye dela" [Rosy Words and Black Deeds], *Izvestiia*, August 27, 1968, p. 3. Unless otherwise indicated, all translations in this article are by the author.

12. For Soviet endorsement of Husak's recognition of Bonn as a contribution to detente, see V. Lapskii, "V interesakh sotrudnichestva" [In the Interests of Cooperation], *Izvestiia*, December 14, 1973, p. 4.

13. "Statement of the Central Committee of the Communist Party of Yugoslavia...," June 29, 1948, in Royal Institute of International Affairs: *The Soviet-Yugoslav Dispute* (London: Oxford University Press 1948), 73, 77.

14. "Extract from the Political Report made by Marshal Tito to the Third Congress of the People's Front," April 9, 1949, in Royal Institute of International Affairs, *Documents on International Affairs, 1949-50* (New York: Oxford University Press 1953), 449.

clandestine factions within the various parties for the purpose of exercising control over their line and over individual forums and individual leaders."[15]

Khrushchev later corroborated what Djilas had said. In his secret speech to the Twentieth Congress of the CPSU, Khrushchev declared that Stalin had demonstrated what Khrushchev described as "suspicion and haughtiness" not only to Soviet party members but to "whole parties and nations."[16] Wladyslaw Gomulka also complained that Stalin had tyrannized over the leaders of the East European Communist parties.[17]

In an essay written in December 1955, shortly after his expulsion from the Hungarian Communist Party, Imre Nagy declared that Stalin and his Hungarian lieutenant, Matyas Rakosi, had "exterminated" party members who had opposed the establishment of a Stalinist dictatorship in Hungary and the subordination of Hungarian interests to Stalin's hegemony.[18] When Nagy became premier of the Hungarian Government as a result of the revolution that broke out on October 23, 1956, the Soviet Government obliquely acknowledged the truth of what he had written. In an effort to quell anti-Soviet sentiment in Hungary, the U.S.S.R. issued a declaration on October 30, 1956, in which the Soviet Government admitted that in the history of relations among socialist states there had been "violations and errors which demeaned the principle of equality in relations among socialist states."[19] The Government of the People's Republic of China immediately expressed full agreement with the Soviet declaration. According to the Chinese, there had indeed been "mistakes...misunderstandings and estrangements between certain socialist countries." The Chinese Government specifically mentioned Soviet relations with Yugoslavia, Poland, and Hungary.[20] After the open break between Peking and Moscow, the Chinese made thinly veiled accusations that the Soviets had attempted to interfere in the internal affairs of the Chinese Communist Party.[21]

15. Milovan Djilas, *Lenin on Relations Between Socialist States* (New York: Yugoslav Information Center 1949), 32.

16. "Secret Speech of Khrushchev..." in Russian Institute of Columbia University, *The Anti-Stalin Campaign and International Communism* (New York: Columbia University Press 1956), 63.

17. "Address by Wladyslaw Gomulka Before the Central Committee of the Polish United Workers' Party, October 20, 1956," in Zinner (fn. 2), 228-29.

18. "Ethics and Morals in Hungarian Public Life," in Imre Nagy, *On Communism* (New York: Praeger 1957), 51.

19. "Declaration by the Government of the USSR...," October 30, 1956, in Zinner (fn. 2), 486.

20. "Statement by the Government of the People's Republic of China...," November 1, 1956, *ibid.*, 493.

21. In a statement issued June 14, 1963, the Central Committee of the CCP implied that the Soviets had tried several tactics to obtain control over the Chinese party. See William E. Griffith, *The Sino-Soviet Rift* (Cambridge: M.I.T. Press 1964), esp. pp. 280-81.

The Chinese later added Albania to the list of socialist countries that had endured Soviet attempts to interfere in their internal affairs.[22] The Chinese were referring to Khrushchev's public call, at the Twenty-Second Congress of the CPSU, for the removal of Enver Hoxha and Mehmet Shehu from the leadership of the Albanian party.[23] In April 1964, after the Rumanian Communists had emerged victorious from their struggle with Khrushchev over whether Rumania would subordinate its economic planning to the dictates of the Council for Mutual Economic Assistance, they issued a general statement on the world Communist movement. The Rumanian leaders declared that during the existence of the Comintern, "wrong methods" had been practiced in relations between Communist parties.

According to the Rumanians, these methods "went as far as the removal and replacement of leading party cadres and even entire central committees." The 1964 statement said that the Rumanian party had experienced such methods, which were practiced until the dissolution of the Cominform (1955). In looking at the Communist movement in 1964, the Rumanians concluded that the "danger of reoccurence of the methods and practices generated by the cult of the individual seems possible."[24] They added, "No party is allowed to go over the heads of the party leaders of one country or another, and even less to launch appeals for the removal or the change of the leadership of a party."[25]

Rumanian misgivings about Soviet interference in the internal affairs of the fraternal parties were confirmed by the intensive Soviet efforts during 1968 to deny control of the Czechoslovak Communist Party to the "progressives,"[26] Shortly after the invasion of Czechoslovakia, the Soviet leaders made Dubcek sign the "Moscow Protocol," which demanded that the CSCP "discharge from their posts those individuals whose further activities would not conform to the needs of consolidating the leading role of the working class and the Communist Party."[27]

In examining these conflicts between the Soviets and various East European parties, Western observers have often regarded as genuine the Soviet expressions of dismay over the ideological, economic, or diplomatic politics

22. "The Origin and Development of the Differences Between the Leadership of the CPSU and Ourselves," *Red Flag* and *People's Daily,* September 6, 1963, *ibid.,* 407.

23. "Khrushchev's Speech on Albania...," October 27, 1961, in William E. Griffith, *Albania and the Sino-Soviet Rift* (Cambridge: M.I.T. Press 1963), 235.

24. "Statement of the Stand of the Rumanian Workers' Party...," April 1964, in William E. Griffith, *Sino-Soviet Relations, 1964-65* (Cambridge: M.I.T. Press, 1967), 292-93.

25. *Ibid.,* 294.

26. I have agrued that the reason for the Soviet intervention in Czechoslovakia was to prevent a domestic faction from taking over the party. See "Autonomy and Intervention: The CPSU and the Struggle for the Czechoslovak Communist Party, 1968," *Orbis,* XIX (Summer 1975).

27. "The Moscow Protocol," in Robin A. Remington, ed., *Winter in Prague* (Cambridge: M.I.T. Press 1969), 379.

of a Communist deviant, and have not seen in these protests Soviet attempts to assert control over personnel appointments in the East European parties.[28] They argue that the Soviets are more concerned with keeping the policies of the East European parties within certain limits than with controlling their personnel.

But this is like arguing that the chicken came before the egg. Stalin and his successors have understood that what is at stake in these disputes is not whether the chicken or the egg came first, but who is to control the poultry in whatever form it appears. Even if Soviet leaders have been primarily concerned about the content of a policy pursued by an East European deviant, they have recognized that the best way to secure the adoption of the "correct" policy under constantly changing circumstances is to secure control of cadre appointments in the East European party. Every Soviet leader since Stalin has come to power by acquiring control over both policy and personnel within the CPSU. In dealing with Eastern Europe, the Soviet First Secretary has found that control over the policies and personnel of the fraternal parties is precisely what control over policies and personnel is in Soviet politics: the means and ends of all his endeavors. To cede control of either policy or personnel is to cede control of the other; and to cede control of both to an East European Communist party is to grant autonomy.

The Pursuit of Autonomy by East European Communists

An East European leader may seek autonomy for his party for several reasons. A Leninist party carrying out a program of industrial development has a tendency to concentrate increasingly greater power in the hands of the party leader, to the point at which the leader becomes autonomous of his Soviet patrons. The leader of an East European party may consciously foster this tendency for the sake of sheer personal aggrandizement, a motive not unknown among politicians in any society. An East European First Secretary may also seek autonomy because he feels that it is the best insurance against the possibility that the Soviets may one day decide to replace him. Whatever his reasons for pursuing autonomy, he must seek it by acquiring control over policy and personnel in his party. There are two ways in which East European Communist parties have wrested control of policy and personnel from the Soviets.

One way is for a party leader originally installed by Moscow to travel so far down his own road to socialism that he leaves the Soviet bloc. He can make this journey by gradually extending his control over the lower, then the middle, and finally the upper echelons of the party *apparat*; by gradually winning popular support for his domestic policies; and by gradually

28. Brzezinski (fn. 1), passim; see also Levesque (fn. 1).

acquiring foreign allies. When he is ready to make an open challenge to Moscow's authority, he puts the local Muscovites in the position of being traitors to the East European party, making it very difficult for them to oppose him.

This process is so gradual that it is very difficult for Moscow to halt it before it has passed the point of no return. The party leader appointed by the Soviets who subsequently decides to seek autonomy can make a public show of solidarity with Moscow, and make it awkward for the Soviets to intervene. If they decide to force the issue, they will be reduced to denouncing "hypocritical" protestations of loyalty from a Tito or a Hoxha. The Soviets will find it difficult to reconstitute a Muscovite faction: the rebel leader of the East European party will be able to strike at this faction as soon as it begins to organize.

Tito unintentionally took this road to autonomy during the course of leading the Communist resistance to the German occupation of Yugoslavia. In Rumania, Gheorghiu-Dej quite consciously pursued this route to autonomy, which has been followed by his hand-picked successor, Nicolae Ceausescu. Hoxha pursued a similar course in Albania. He had obtained a considerable degree of control over his party in organizing Albanian resistance to the Italian occupation, but became quasi-dependent on the Soviet Union after 1948 because he feared that Yugoslavia would annex Albania, and because he needed economic aid for his small and backward country. But when the Soviets insisted on the rights of hegemony in the early 1960's and demanded that he break off relations with Peking, Hoxha resisted and demonstrated just who really controlled Tirana. Despite prodigious efforts, Khrushchev was not able to topple him.

According to a well-placed member of the Czechoslovak party, Novotny may have tried to establish his autonomy of Moscow in the mid-1960's. This official asserts that Novotny feared that Khrushchev's overthrow in 1964 would result in Moscow's shift of its support from the Novotny faction of the CSCP to a faction led by Siroky, Kohler, and Bacilek. Novotny took measures to prevent this faction from contacting Moscow. He also began to court the Czechoslovak intelligentsia, to make overtures to the Chinese, Yugoslavs, and Rumanians, to prepare to resist Soviet economic pressure, and to revise Czechoslovak military doctrine.[29] If Novotny did indeed try to embark on the road to autonomy, he quickly found that he had unleased forces in the Czechoslovak party that he could not control.

Another way in which Moscow can lose control over an East European party is through an intraparty battle between Muscovites and reformers in which the reformers triumph. The battle is joined when the ruling Muscovite faction, confident in its support from Moscow, becomes indif-

29. 'Moravus,' "Shawcross' *Dubcek*" in *Survey* XVII (Autumn 1971).

ferent to the internal problems of its society. By neglect and incompetence, the Muscovites drive their country into a general economic, social, and political crisis. A reform faction begins to coalesce within the party around a program of correcting abuses, heading off popular discontent, and perhaps even returning to the democratic socialist ideal that attracted many members to the party. The reformers seek support from the general public, from economic technocrats and especially from the members of the humanist professions.

During the early 1950's in Hungary and Poland, and during the early 1960's in Czechoslovakia, the extreme centralization of the economy practiced by the ruling Muscovites led to general economic stagnation. The reformers in these countries called for decentralization of management and replacement of party *apparatchiki* by technical specialists. To carry out economic decentralization in these countries, the reformers advocated a corresponding decentralization in these countries, the reformers advocated a corresponding decentralization of the state bureaucracy, The Communist reformers in Hungary and Czechoslovakia also wanted to give greater freedom to scientists and creative intellectuals in the hope of revitalizing their societies.

The reformers did not intend to have the party surrender power. They sought to make the party more worthy of its power. Many of the reformers came to realize that the Soviets provided a kind of insurance for whatever risks they ran in carrying out a program of decentralization. The threat of Soviet intervention against anti-Communist movements enabled them to appear as the lesser of evils before domestic critics who might have been tempted to raise the demand for an end to the Communist political monopoly.

The reformers found that the Muscovites and the *apparatchiki* in the party, state, and economic bureaucracies resisted extensive reform because they viewed such measures as a prelude to their dismissal. The Muscovites and the *apparatchiki* would agree with the assessment of reform made by Joe Cannon, the Speaker of the United States House of Representatives, who had to surrender much of his power to the Congressional progressives led by Robert La Follette. Cannon said that the real meaning of reform was, "Get out so I can get in!"

To remove the Muscovites, the Communist reformers had to do battle with the Soviets for control of the party. They also had to emphasize those reforms that had the political effect of reducing the power of the Muscovites. The most effective weapon of the reformers was "truth"— public revelations of the incompetence, illegalities, and hypocrises of the Muscovites, and public revelations of past instances of Soviet interference in the internal affairs of their country. These revelations gave the intraparty feud the quality of a moral struggle between truth and falsehood. In this battle over "truth," control of the information media became crucial.

There have been three different types of outcomes in the battles between reformers and Muscovites for control of the Communist parties in Czechoslovakia, Poland, and Hungary. In Czechoslovakia in 1968, the Muscovites, supported by half a million Soviet soldiers, managed to defeat the reformers in the eighth month of the Soviet occupation. In Poland in 1956, the reformers defeated the Muscovites, but their leader failed to retain enough popular support to maintain the autonomy he had won, and eventually reverted to dependence on the Soviets. In Hungary, the Communist Party disintegrated during the course of the intraparty battle. As the two factions struggled for power, a popular insurrection broke out and almost swept away both factions of the Communist Party. Khrushchev sent the Soviet army into Hungary to put down the popular insurrection and to reorganize the shattered fragments of the party.

Pursuit of autonomy either by a reformer or by a First Secretary originally installed by Moscow has clearly been a risky venture: the Communist seeking autonomy has to give up one source of support for his party while simultaneously acquiring others. Midway through this process, an East European Communist aspiring to autonomy may find that he does not have sufficient support to retain control of his party, and that his party does not have sufficient support to stay in power. If an East European Communist wants to challenge Soviet control over his party, he must carry out three tasks, whether he is a First Secretary originally appointed by Moscow or a reformer who aims to wrest control of the party away from the Muscovites.

1. He must purge the party of Muscovites and potential Muscovites. In order to preclude the appearance of any fifth column within the party, he has to establish personal control over his politburo, central committee, party secretariat, and the lower party organs. Sooner or later he must convene a party congress that will recognize him as the incarnation of the Communist movement in his country—as Tito, Hoxha, and Ceausescu have done. Such public acclaim will make it difficult to remove him.

A Communist leader seeking autonomy from the U.S.S.R. should make the other prominent figures in the party link their fates with his. He has to make it clear that in the event of Soviet intervention, they will all stand or fall together. He has to insist on the "unity" of the party ranks behind him. He would do well to repeat Mehmet Shehu's warning to prospective Muscovites in the Albanian party. Shehu told the delegates to the Albanian party congress in 1961, "For those who stand in the way of party unity, a spit in the face, a sock in the jaw, and if necessary, a bullet in the head...."[30] Once the party is firmly under his control, the East European Communist leader has to establish personal control of his nation's army, security organizations, and state and economic bureaucracies.

2. He has to find diplomatic allies in the Communist camp, in the West, and the Third World. China might offer very real economic and military aid

---

30. Quoted in Griffith (fn. 23), 71.

to help him resist Soviet pressure; Yugoslavia and Rumania would enthusiastically join in exercises devoted to the praise of sovereignty, noninterference in internal affairs, and respect for territorial integrity. The West, particularly the United States, could offer economic and military aid. The Third-World countries courted by the U.S.S.R. might be able to exercise some restraint on Soviet actions.

3. He has to win broad popular support for his regime. There are two sources of this support. One in a domestic program for the development of a socialist society. If the party is to preserve its cohesion, its members will have to believe—or pretend to believe—that the party leader has a genuine and realistic commitment to socialist ideals. If the party leader is to win the cooperation of those segments of the population whose talents are necessary for the construction of socialism, he must evoke genuine popular enthusiasm for "the socialist transformation of Yugoslavia," "the Polish road to socialism," or Dubeck's "democratic socialism." Not only party members but large numbers of ordinary citizens will have to believe that it is worth supporting their domestic order—or at least the future domestic order promised by the party leader.

The second source of potential popular support is nationalism, a sentiment that usually takes an anti-Russian form in Eastern Europe. Handling this issue is an extremely delicate matter. Many party leaders, particularly those who joined the party before 1945, may find nationalism repugnant. They may be reluctant to take up the cause of "national Communism" because they sincerely believe in the ideals of fraternal cooperation with the U.S.S.R. and of unity within the world Communist movement. In 1948, many of the Yugoslav leaders under attack by Stalin found it psychologically very difficult to break with the Communist Party of the Soviet Union. In 1968, most of the leading reformers in the Czechoslovak party could not accept the idea of opposing Czechoslovak nationalism to Soviet claims of hegemony.

Cultivation of nationalism is a risky enterprise for an East European Communist for another reason. Anti-Russian nationalism may take an anti-Communist form directed not only at the Soviet leaders, but at the local leader as well. Nagy faced this problem during the first stages of the Hungarian revolution of 1956. But seeking support as a nationalist is often a necessary risk, for nationalism will usually provide an East European First Secretary with broader and deeper popular support than will his socialist program. All of the East European Communists who have achieved autonomy from the U.S.S.R. have taken stands both as socialists and nationalists. Dubcek's most critical mistake in 1968 was his failure to take up the cause of Czechoslovak nationalism.

Soviet Military Intervention Against East European Communist Parties

Moscow has never willingly acquiesced in the triumph of a domestic faction over the Muscovites. According to Jiri Pelikan, the director of Czechoslovak television before the 1968 intervention, "Whenever the Soviet leaders lose complete control of the upper echelons of any Communist party they will seek to replace them by a takeover inside the party with the help of elements loyal to them within the central committee— elements often under some obligation to the Soviets and corrupted by them.... If they fail, they will not hesitate to embark on a military policing action."[31]

General S.M. Shtemenko, former Chief of Staff on the Warsaw Treaty Organization, made the same point in a recent discussion of the functions of the Pact. According to the late general, one of the missions of the WTO is "suppression of counterrevolutionary and aggressive action against socialist countries." General Shtemenko specifically cited the 1968 intervention in Czechoslovakia as an example of such a mission.[32]

But military intervention is by no means an automatic Soviet response to the takeover of an East European Communist party by a domestic faction. Although the Czech and Slovak reformers seeking control of their own party failed to deter Soviet military action, the domestic factions of four other East European Communist parties succeeded: the Yugoslavs in 1948, the Poles in 1956, the Albanians in 1961, and the Rumanians in the early and mid-1960's. It may be true, as most Western analysts have concluded, that the Soviets did not consider the ideological deviations committed by the Yugoslavs, Poles, Albanians, and Rumanians sufficiently heretical to require military intervention. Such restraint befits a government that describes itself as peace-loving. But perhaps the reason Brezhnev chose to send half a million soldiers to remove Dubcek and his colleagues from power was that, unlike the other East European heretics, the Czech and Slovak reformers did not summon their armies and peoples to the defense of Czechoslovakia's sovereignty.

If the political objective of Soviet military intervention is to deprive a group of intractable East European Communists of control over their own party, the Soviets must justify their military expedition both to their own citizens and to the citizens of the East European state under attack. The justifications the Soviets offered for overthrowing the leaders of the Czechoslovak party in 1968 by armed force were the same justifications the leaders of the Yugoslav party in 1948, of the Polish party in 1956, and of the

31. Jiri Pelikan, *The Secret Vysocany Congress* (London: Penguin Press 1971), 282.
32. Gen Shtemenko's remarks appeared in the early May 1956 edition of *Za Rubezhom*. See David K. Shipler, "Soviet Stresses View Warsaw Pact's Role Is to Quell Revolts," *New York Times*, May 8, 1976.

Albanian party in 1961. Should Moscow again use military force against East European Communists seeking autonomy, it would probably use the same justifications.

1. The local East European party has come under the control of an anti-party clique guilty of a right or left ideological deviation, nationalism, and anti-Sovietism. The clique is threatening the foundations of socialism in its country and, according to the Soviet press, is "objectively" conspiring with the imperialists to wrest the country from the socialist camp. At the same time, the anti-Soviet clique is hypocritically professing its devotion to socialism, the U.S.S.R., the world Communist movement, the Warsaw Pact, and the Council for Mutual Economic Assistance.

2. The "healthy forces" in the local Communist party—that is to say, the "true Marxist-Leninists, loyal to proletarian internationalism"—have rallied the working class to oust the revisionist, chauvinist, anti-Soviet clique. The healthy forces consist of party members who have sided with the Soviets out of opportunism, genuine devotion to the U.S.S.R., or a combination of these motives. In any case, they are dependent on Moscow. But Moscow is also dependent on them. The Soviet leaders require a fifth column in the East European party to legitimize the use of Soviet troops and to form a new government.

In seeking to retain control over an East European party pursuing autonomy, the Soviets would stress the importance of "unity" within the socialist camp. In order to avoid raising the issue of Soviet violation of another country's sovereignty, the Soviets would accuse the rebels of ideological deviations. If the East European Communists complained that Moscow was violating their sovereignty, the Soviets would accuse them of nationalism and chauvinism. Moscow's spokesmen would argue that there are no conflicts between the interests of the socialist commonwealth and the interests of a sovereign East European socialist state, provided these interests are "correctly understood."[33]

---

33. Soviet discussions of relations among socialist states frequently cite Lenin's observation that a "correct understanding" of national interests will lead to the unity of nations. See the argument of F.T. Konstantinov and A.P. Sertsova in Akademia Nauk, SSSR, Institut filosofii and Vysshaia shkola Ts. K., K. P. Ch., *Sovremennyi pravyi revizionizm* [Modern Rightist Revisionism] (Moscow: Izdatel'stvo mysl' 1973, and Prague: Izdatel'stvo svoboda 1973), 396-97:

"The rightist revisionists generally attempt to put national interests in opposition to international interests while slipping to a position of bourgeois nationalism. The betrayal of internationalism is also inherent in Maoism. Nationalists consider patriotism and internationalism as mutually exclusive concepts. They try to speculate on the fact that patriotism and internationalism outwardly appear as forces which seem to go in different directions....However, life shows that in a socialist society there is not only no antagonism between patriotism and

If an East European Communist leader wants to parry Moscow's attempts to depose him and to deter Soviet military intervention, he must refuse to argue with the Soviets over ideological issues and personnel matters. He must take his stand on the issue of national sovereignty. A dispute over ideology and personnel keeps the struggle a private conflict between two Communist parties. A dispute over the right to national sovereignty makes the conflict a struggle between two nations. The East European leader would be able to find a much broader and deeper popular support on the issue of resistance to Russian imperialism than he could on the obtuse ideological issues raised by the Soviets. By raising the issue of sovereignty, a leader would oblige the Soviets to make war on his nation in order to obtain control of his party. In such a conflict, even East European Communists who are deeply devoted to the U.S.S.R. might find themselves echoing the protest of Tito and Kardelj to Stalin in 1948: "No matter how much each of us loves the land of socialism, the U.S.S.R., he can, in no case, love his own country less, which is also developing socialism...."[34] Every Communist party that has achieved autonomy of the Soviet Union has emphatically endorsed the right of each Communist party and each socialist state to sovereignty.

Soviet sources indicate that Moscow has a keen appreciation of the strong desire for national sovereignty among Eastern Europeans and an equally keen appreciation of the fact that East European nationalism is often tied to anti-Russian sentiments. *Nationalism and Internationalism*, a Soviet handbook for political lecturers in the U.S.S.R., notes that "contradictions" sometimes arise in relations between socialist states because of nationalistic and anti-Russian sentiments. The author explains that tsarist interference in the internal affairs of Poland and Hungary implanted anti-Russian feeling in these countries. He cautions that "remnants of reactionary classes" in these countries are still using these emotions to create antagonism toward the U.S.S.R. He also notes that there is a legacy of anti-Soviet sentiment in East Germany as a result of the struggle between German and Soviet armies during World War II.[35]

Other Soviet sources indicate that Moscow has concluded that not only reactionary classes can play on these sentiments, but also leaders of East European Communist parties. In 1969, an article in *Communist of the Armed Forces* declared that nationalism "is ideological preparation

---

socialist internationalism but, on the contrary, there is deep dialectical unity. Under the conditions of socialism, fundamental national interests, correctly understood, objectively combine with the international interests of the entire socialist commonwealth."

34. "Letter from J.B. Tito and E. Kardelj to J.V. Stalin and V.M. Molotov, April 13, 1948," in Royal Institute (fn. 13), 19.

35. Mikhail Osipovich Karamanov, *Internatsionalizm i natsionalizm* [Internationalism and Nationalism] (Moscow: Moskovskii rabochii 1971), 134-35.

for...the instigation of one nation against another and for setting one socialist country against another, especially against the Soviet Union."[36] On the fifth anniversary of the invasion of Czechoslovakia, *Communist of the Armed Forces* quoted Gustav Husak, the internationalist who replaced Dubcek as head of the Czechoslovak party, as saying, "The slogan of sovereignty, emptied of its class content, is a specific and active weapon of the rightist-opportunist, revisionist and anti-socialist forces."[37]

A Soviet political commentator had earlier reached the same conclusion when he surveyed the situation in Czechoslovakia two months after the invasion. He complained that certain Czechs and Slovaks, "who are Communists in word but liberals in deed, are today repeating only one thing: autonomy, noninterference, independence and sovereignty."[38] In 1973, a joint study by Soviet and Czechoslovak political analysts noted that revisionists often employ the slogan of "defense of national sovereignty."[39]

> Using the words about socialism and democracy as a cover, words about defense of national interests and the sovereignty of their countries, for all practical purposes they [the rightist-revisionists] are carrying out wrecking activity specifically aimed against socialism and democracy.

> They are betraying the national interests and true aspirations of their peoples and they are faithfully serving the reactionary elements within the country and the forces of external imperialist aggression.

> Nationalism and anti-Sovietism are the most poisonous weapons in the hands of the bourgeoise for the struggle against world socialism.[40]

An East European Communist who has obtained control of his party and his country by taking a stand as both a nationalist and a socialist can deter a Soviet military intervention if he makes three things clear to Moscow: (1) his army and people will go to war in defense of their national sovereignty; (2) the party members who collaborate with the Soviets will be charged with treason; (3) the East European Communists under attack will continue their resistance underground or in exile. Tito wrote these political deterrents to Soviet intervention into the Yugoslav constitution soon after the 1968 Soviet invasion of Czechoslovakia. Article 252 of the Yugoslav constitution reads, "No one shall have the right to sign or acknowledge capitulation or

36. N. Cherniak, "Burzhuaznyi natsionalizm—otravlennoe oruzhie imperializma" [Bourgeois Nationalism—The Poisonous Weapon of Imperialism], *Kommunist vooruzhennik sil,* No. 12 (June 1969), 16.

37. N. Tarasenko, "Leninskii printsip edinstva sotsialisticheskogo internatsionalizma i patriotizma" [The Leninist Principle of the Unity of Socialist Internationalism and Patriotism], *Kommunist vooruzhennikh sil,* No. 16 (August 1973), 11.

38. K. Ivanov, "Lessons for the Future," *International Affairs* (Moscow) No. 10 (October 1968), 8.

39. Akademia Nauk, SSSR (fn. 33), 408.

40. *Ibid.*, 414.

the occupation of the country on behalf of the Socialist Federal Republic of Yugoslavia. Any such act is unconstitutional and punishable."[41] This article promises that the Yugoslav Government will not surrender even if driven from the country, and that anyone who collaborates with an occupation force will be charged with treason.

Tito first demonstrated his resolve to put up military resistance to a Soviet invasion after 1948, when he faced down a military build-up on his frontiers, as well as thousands of border provocations.[42] In Poland, Gomulka responded in October 1956 in similar fashion to a Soviet threat of military intervention. Khrushchev had ordered Soviet troops to seize strategic locations in Poland and to advance toward Warsaw in order to prevent Gomulka and the reformist faction from taking over the party from the Muscovite "Natolin" faction. Gomulka countered Khrushchev's moves by mobilizing the Polish internal security forces, arming factory workers in Warsaw, and winning the allegiance of many units of the Polish army, which was nominally under the control of Marshal Rokossovsky, a Soviet general with Polish citizenship. According to several Western observers, Gomulka's threat to offer military resistance deterred Khrushchev from carrying out his contemplated intervention. These observers differ, however, on the reasons why Gomulka's action stayed Khrushchev's hand.[43]

A few days after Khrushchev had called for the overthrow of Enver Hoxha in October 1961, the Albanian leader, already in firm control of his party and state, warned the Soviets, "our glorious armed forces are fully in form and prepared to defend the Albanian People's Republic successfully and give a worthy rebuff to any enemy rash enough to violate the sacred frontiers of our beloved socialist fatherland."[44]

In Rumania, the leaders of the Communist Party pre-empted the possibility of Soviet military intervention on behalf of the Muscovite faction by liquidating this faction before the Soviets could develop pretexts for military action. In the process of achieving autonomy, the Rumanian

41. *The Constitution of the Socialist Federal Republic of Yugoslavia* (Novi Sad: Prosveta 1969), 163.

42. Federal People's Republic of Yugoslavia, *White Book* (Belgrade 1951), 472ff.; Vladimir Dedijer, *The Battle Stalin Lost: Memoirs of Yugoslavia, 1948-1953* (New York: Viking Press 1971), 208, 278.

43. Konrad Syrop, *Spring in October: The Polish Revolution of 1956* (London: Weidenfeld and Nicolson 1957), 97; Flora Lewis, *A Case History of Hope* (New York: Doubleday 1958), 205; Richard Hiscocks, *Poland: Bridge for the Abyss?* (New York: Oxford University Press 1963), 214; Adam Bromke, *Poland's Politics: Idealism vs. Realism* (Cambridge: Harvard University Press 1967), 91-94; Adam B. Ulam, *Expansion and Coexistence* (New York: Praeger 1968), 591-94.

44. Hoxha, "Speech Delivered at the Celebration of the 20th Anniversary of the Founding of the Albanian Party of Labor" in Griffith (fn. 23), 224.

leaders established firm control over their own armed forces.[45] When the Soviets invaded Czechoslovakia in 1968, Ceausescu quickly undertook military preparations to prevent a similar attack against Rumania. The Rumanian Government immediately issued a vehement condemnation of the Soviet action.[46] Ceausescu then convened a mass meeting in Bucharest and told the crowd, "It has been said that in Czechoslovakia there was a danger of a counterrevolution; perhaps tomorrow they will say that our meeting has mirrored counterrevolutionary tendencies.... If so, we answer to all that the Rumanian people will not permit anyone to violate the territory of our fatherland....be ready comrades, at any moment to defend our socialist fatherland, Rumania."[47] Ceausescu backed upon his promise to fight by mobilizing the Rumanian army and distributing weapons to militia forces.[48]

By drawing the battlelines, East European Communist leaders have made the political risks of military intervention too high for the Soviets. To offset Soviet military superiority, it is not necessary to have geographical terrain suitable for denying the Soviets their political objectives. By threatening to put up military resistance, a rebel Communist leader confronts the Soviets with the necessity of killing East European soldiers, civilians, and party members. Soviet soldiers could very well find themselves facing the same dilemma that baffled American troops in Vietnam: to make a fine political distinction between friend and foe when there are no visible differences between the two. The soldiers would have to search out and destroy the rebel Communists while simultaneously winning the hearts and minds of the onlookers. While this campaign was under way, the independent Communist regimes in Eastern Europe would issue vociferous condemnations of the U.S.S.R. The Communists under attack might appeal for aid from the Communist parties of Western Europe and China. They might even appeal to the West for military supplies and raise the threat of widening the war.

Tito, Hoxha, Mao, and Ho, in their struggles with militarily stronger opponents during and after World War II, judiciously made their battles primarily political rather than military ones. They conceded territorial objectives to their enemies, but preserved their political organizations. As resisters, they constantly widened their political base by appearing as the defenders of national sovereignty against a foreign invader. Robert G. Wesson has argued that the task at which Communist regimes are most successful is waging wars of national liberation. According to his analysis, the

45. Mary Ellen Fisher, "Ceausescu and the Rumanian Political Leadership, " Ph.D. diss. (Harvard 1974), 195-196.

46. "Official Rumanian Communique on the Military Occupation of Czechoslovakia," August 21, 1968, in Remington (fn. 27), 358.

47. "Balcony Speech by Nicolae Ceausescu on Czechoslovakia," August 21, 1968, *ibid.*, 360-61.

48. Fisher (fn. 45), 315.

psychology and structure of a Leninist party are superbly suited to concentrating the energies of the party and nation on resistance to a foreign invader.[49] Soviet military writers make the same point when they declare that a war in defense of the socialist fatherland inspires a people to give unprecedented support to a Communist regime.[50]

Soviet military theorists are extremely sensitive to the question of whether a war appears to Soviet soldiers as a just one in defense of their socialist homeland or an "unjust" war of imperialist expansion. They warn that the war aim determines the "moral-political factor"—the extent to which the soldiers and civilians on both sides support the war efforts of their governments. They emphasize that the strongest military effort comes from an army that believes it is fighting in defense of its country's sovereignty. Soviet military doctrine declares that a multinational army (such as the Soviet army), is potentially unreliable when committed to offensive wars. According to the Soviets, multinational armies are most likely to be reliable in defensive wars. Soviet military theorists also caution that war has a "reverse effect" on politics: if an army fighting an "unjust" war encounters difficulties on the battlefield, army morale may plummet and domestic opposition to the war may develop. In addition, domestic tensions that existed before the war broke out may become severely exacerbated. As a result of the "reverse effect," a government may face threats to the morale of its troops, the stability of its homefront, and possibly even to the legitimacy of the regime itself.[51]

In spite of the risk of provoking a domestic crisis in the U.S.S.R., the Soviet leaders might still be tempted to order their troops into battle against an East European country. If the Soviet Army was victorious, Moscow would have the enormously difficult task of presenting the conquered population with its new First Secretary, an "honest Communist" drenched in the blood of his compatriots. There is no question that the new leader would be entirely dependent on Moscow and quite loyal. But the question remains whether he and his fellow internationalists would be able to establish a Communist regime with the legitimacy necessary to govern. A loyal but illegitimate regime can be a political liability for the Soviets if it is perpetually on the verge of popular insurrections like those in Berlin in

---

49. Wesson, "War and Communism," *Survey*, XX (Winter 1974).

50. Col. Ia. S. Dziuba writes, "The most important feature of wars in defence of the socialist fatherland is that they are genuinely people's wars in all respects. Owing to the just aims and tasks of such a war, which fully correspond to the working people's interests, the masses take an active part in it, support and implement the policy of the Marxist-Leninist party and government and rally even more closely around them." S.A. Tiushkevich, ed., *Marksizm-Leninizm o voine i armii* [Marxism-Leninism on War and The Military] (Moscow: Voenizdat 1968), 139.

51. For an examination of Soviet military doctrine on these points, see Christopher D. Jones, "Just Wars and Limited Wars: Restraints on the Use of the Soviet Armed Forces," *World Politics*, XXVIII (October 1975).

1953, and Poznan in 1956, and in Budapest in 1956. The prospect of the internal collapse of an East European Communist government threatens contagion within the bloc and acute embarrassment before the non-Communist world. A regime despised by its own people can also be a liability in a less visible way—if it is in constant need of economic subsidies, as the Kadar and Husak governments were in the years following Soviet intervention in their countries.

Rather than run the risks of a difficult military campaign, a political crisis in the U.S.S.R., and the destruction of the domestic political base for an East European Communist regime, Moscow will refrain from military intervention against an East European Communist leader who promises to lead his nation to war in defense of its sovereignty. For the Soviet Union to use the indiscriminate destructive power of its army against a rebellious domestic faction of an East European party is to apply a scorched-earth policy to the ground on which East European Muscovites must stand and on which Soviet rule rests. After ruling out military intervention against a dissident East European Communist regime, the Soviets may resume their attempts to overthrow the rebel leaders by means of an internal coup, as they did against Tito after 1948 and against Hoxha after 1961. Moscow may break off diplomatic relations, call upon other socialist countries to impose an economic blockade, and permit Soviet journalists to give full vent to their ideological indignation at the transgressions of the heretics. Such devices, however, amount to little more than demonstrations of pique.

Like Tito, Hoxha, and Ceausescu, an independent Communist leader will turn to the West or to China or both for trade, economic assistance, and military equipment. His foreign policy will move toward a position of nonalignment. In adjusting Communist ideology to local conditions, he will assert that his version of Marxism has as much theoretical value as Moscow's. If the Soviets persist in accusing him of ideological betrayal, he will, like Tito and Hoxha, proclaim the bankruptcy of Soviet Marxism and declare his capital the center of genuine Marxism. He will do this to provide greater legitimacy for his own regime and to make it more difficult for Soviet sympathizers in his party to espouse Moscow's cause. Provided that the Soviets refrain from polemics, he can, like Ceausescu, confine himself to stressing how important it is for each socialist country to make its own contribution to socialism.

The Soviets have no wish to drive the independent East European Communists into permanent alliances with the West or with Peking. Sooner or later, they will establish a working relationship with an East European party that has achieved independence. Moscow can wait patiently in the hope that an autonomous East European party may some day fall back into dependence on the Soviets, as the Polish party did. The Soviets can also resume their efforts to infiltrate the ranks of the heretic East European party, as the Yugoslavs and Albanians have charged them with doing during the 1970's.

For their part, the autonomous Communists have been willing to seek rapprochement with Moscow because they never wanted to sever relations with the U.S.S.R., but simply wanted the prerogatives of independence. Like the Yugoslavs and Rumanians, independent East European Communists want mutually beneficial economic ties with the Soviet Union, the economic colossus of the region and the principal broker in the Council for Mutual Economic Assistance. An independent Communist state in Eastern Europe may have a genuine fear of revanchism on the part of Germany or some other state, and may want to turn to the Soviet Union as *one* of its protectors. The need of autonomous East European Communists for domestic legitimacy as socialists will recommend demonstrations of ideological solidarity with the world Communist movement—including its most powerful member. Maintaining a working relationship with the U.S.S.R. will also help the autonomous Communist regime to persuade domestic dissidents that the home Communists are preferable to the "healthy forces" that Moscow would install in the event of an anti-Communist uprising.

To sum up: Tito, Gomulka, Ceausescu, and Hoxha have shown that the Soviets will not use force to remove the leadership of a rebellious East European Communist party if the leaders of the party are willing to go to war in defense of their national sovereignty. What the leaders of the Czechoslovak party failed to do in 1968 was to mobilize their army and nation against the threat of Soviet military intervention. In 1956, the Soviet intervention in Hungary was not against a ruling Communist party: Soviet soldiers went into action to save the Hungarian Communists from a popular uprising. To restore the Hungarian party to power, the Soviet army had to crush an impotent coalition government headed by Imre Nagy, a Communist who had taken it upon himself to lead an anti-Communist and anti-Soviet uprising.[52]

52. After the Hungarian rebellion broke out on October 23, 1956, Khrushchev authorized what had previously been anathema: an autonomous Communist government under Imre Nagy, the leader of the reformist faction of the party. Earlier in the year, the Soviets had refused to let Nagy back into power. Now Khrushchev hoped that the rebels would accept the Nagy government and spare the Soviet leader the necessity of suppressing the Hungarian rebellion with Soviet soldiers. By October 30, 1956, when the Soviets issued a formal declaration of their willingness to accept an autonomous Communist regime under Nagy, Nagy had concluded that his compatriots would not support *any* Communist government, even an autonomous one. He saw two choices before him: to align himself with the Soviets against the rebels, or to join the rebels. He chose the second course and formed a multiparty coalition government dominated by non-Communists. Before Nagy could prepare for armed defense of his new government or find diplomatic support from the West, the Soviet army crushed the rebels and installed a new group of Muscovites in control of the shattered fragments of the Communist party. Khrushchev did not ask his soldiers to fight against a unified Communist party supported by an armed nation; he asked them to fight a bitter but very brief campaign against uncoordinated and isolated groups of anti-Communists. The Soviet army did not attack the Hungarian Communists, it rescued them.

Soviet Policy in Asia*

The Soviet Union, geographically part of Asia since its formation (and before, considering the Soviet Union spatially continuous with Tsarist Russia), has been an Asian power of consequence since the 1920s, when it seized Outer Mongolia from China, and particularly since the late 1930s, when it forcibly turned back Japanese probing of the Siberian border. Recent Soviet concern with Asia dates, however, only from the end of World War II, the Communist rise to power in China, and Khrushchev's "forward" strategy in Asia. Since 1950 Asia has become an arena for Moscow's global competition with the United States and, later, for regional competition with China. Therefore, Soviet Asian policy is influenced by more than Russian history or anti-American cold war policies. It is in fact, the product of three sets of factors: historical determinants, domestic priorities, and global and regional political-economic relationships.

History continues to shape Soviet policy toward Asia. Until very recently, circumstances allowed the Russian-Soviet nation-state to give little emphasis to Asia, which made it possible to concentrate attention on Europe

*Reprinted by permission of the author and the publisher, from Volume IX of a major project of the Commission on Critical Choices for Americans. The fourteen volumes of this project were published in 1976 by Lexington Books, D.C. Heath and Company. Volume IX is entitled *The Soviet Empire: Expansion and Détente* edited by William E. Griffith. All rights reserved. © 1976 The Third Century Corporation.

geographically and the United States strategically. These two areas posed the most serious threats to Russian security (the only exception, aside from China very recently, being Japan in the early part of the twentieth century) and it was in Europe, not the United States, that Soviet leaders saw anti-capitalist revolutionary potential. The Soviet Union, therefore, like Russia before it, faced West out of necessity and opportunity. When the West was preoccupied at home or in colonial areas, the Soviet Union, like its Russian predecessor, could live in relative peace. This was the situation during most of the nineteenth century and between the two world wars. When Western expansion was not possible in colonial regions, or when the European balance of power broke down, Russia (or the Soviet Union) became involved in European affairs. Twice during each of the last two centuries Russia became involved in Western wars—Napoleonic expansion and the Crimean War in the nineteenth century and the two world wars during the twentieth century. When the West was weak, Russia attempted to expand geographically or to recoup losses suffered from previous Western incursions, as at the ends of the Napoleonic era and of the two world wars. Throughout, a weak and divided Asia was not a factor in Russian policy.

Several times before 1950, however, Asia did play a major role in Moscow's calculations, all because of the rising power of Japan. In 1905 a weak Russia was defeated by a strong Japan—the first time that Russia had to fight in Asia. At the end of World War I, Japan temporarily occupied portions of Siberia. In 1937 a militaristic Japan probed the Soviet-Chinese border to test Soviet strength and resolve. And in 1945 a strong Soviet army, fresh from victory over the Nazis, pushed out the Japanese forces occupying Manchuria, thus paving the way for Chinese Communist occupation of important regions of northeast China. All four instances gave rise to the operational rule in the Soviet mind, to be cautious, indeed, suspicious, of any strong Asian power and to neutralize that power in order to concentrate on more important European problems.

After 1950, however, the Asian situation changed fundamentally. Japan, the only historical threat to Russia, was critically weakened by the war and temporarily withdrew from conducting an active foreign policy. Its place was taken by the United States, who, allied with and occupying Japan, posed an even greater threat by virtue of its global posture and nuclear weaponry. China, historically weak, quickly recovered its strength through reunification under a Communist government. It was therefore natural for the Soviet Union to ally with Peking to balance the American-Japanese combination, thus preserving the Asian status quo and permitting Moscow to maintain its predominant interest in Europe. Later, however, Japan recovered its economic strength and China, disillusioned with the overly close Soviet tie, broke away from it. This presented Soviet decisionmakers with the unprecedented danger, made worse after 1969 by the emerging

Sino-American proto-coalition, of facing simultaneously three powerful and unfriendly states in Asia. For the first time, therefore, the condition of a relatively quiescent Asia as a requisite for an active policy elsewhere was not met and Moscow therefore had to divide its attention between Europe and Asia.

For Moscow other factors have also changed, some partially compensating for but others aggravating these unprecedented developments. Positively, Soviet power has grown so enormously that by the 1970s it could begin to challenge the United States in distant parts of the globe. This meant that despite Chinese unfriendliness and continued Japanese alliance with America, the Soviet Union could play an active role, particularly in South and Northeast Asia, where access was not blocked overland by China or by sea by the United States. From the mid-1950s, therefore, Moscow could afford to conduct its Asian policy without total reliance on European events. But this newly developed ability was balanced by the necessity to confront the United States strategically everywhere and regionally in Europe and the Middle East, thus preempting energies and attention that might have made for greater Soviet involvement in Asia. Since the beginning of the cold war the Soviet Union has had to give priority to competing with the United States and maintaining its newly won empire in East Europe. Even so, the Vietnam War, Soviet support of India, and the anti-Chinese Soviet military build-up in Siberia demonstrated that Moscow now could act in Asia as well when she so chose.

In evaluating the contribution of historical factors to current and future Soviet Asian policy, equal weight should be given to relative Soviet noninvolvement in the area, and to the fact that the current unprecedented situation undermines the determinative character of the past. The Soviet Union today must play a balance of power game in Asia, given Chinese, Japanese, and American power there. Moscow also finds that she can do so, albeit not as effectively as in Europe and the Middle East. Soviet decisionmakers nonetheless still remember past "lessons," however inapplicable they are today. One such "lesson" is that strong indigenous states (principally Japan, but now China as well) are a danger to Soviet security and cannot be trusted, even in alliance. Another is not to enter a Far East war with an opponent fighting at or near his home base, unless a deliberate build-up of Soviet force has previously occurred. A third is to avoid conflict when more important—e.g., European or global—matters demand attention. A fourth is to promote security through expanding Soviet-controlled territory (or, more likely, controlled by a malleable local government) whenever the principal opponent(s) in Asia are temporarily weak, usually as the result of war. Finally, history shows a Russian propensity to compromise with or neutralize a strong opponent by settling outstanding disputes or by pointing to common extra-regional dangers.

While history thus continues to affect Soviet policy, domestic limitations shape Soviet Asian involvement even more. Several basic characteristics of the Soviet Union limit or channel its involvement in Asia. Most Soviet populations, agriculturally productive land, and industry are in European Russia. The Soviet Far East is quite distant from Moscow and connected to it only by a thin and easily interruptable line of communication. Siberia is still largely empty space, populated by a hardy few mostly located south of the Trans-Siberian railroad and quite close to the Chinese or Mongolian borders. The area is rich in natural resources and has an increasingly large industrial base, but the center of gravity of the Soviet Union will remain west of the Urals for the foreseeable future. So long as Siberian weather patterns, locations of transportation routes, population levels, and industrial trends continue along their present course, it is doubtful whether Soviet policy toward China or even Japan can be much more than defensive in character. Environmental limitations in Soviet Central Asia are less severe, but even there much of the land is marginal, lines of communication to South and Southwest Asia are thin and difficult, the population is largely minority peoples whose loyalty to Moscow is not total, and local industry is not so concentrated or so highly developed as in European Russia. The multinational character of the Soviet Union, half of whose population are non-Great Russian minorities often divided from their national brethren in South and East Asia, gives a defensive tone to Soviet policies toward states bordering on Soviet Central Asia.

Other domestic factors concern political and economic development and the status of the Soviet Communist party in the eyes of the people. Since the Bolshevik Revolution, the overriding tasks of the Soviet Communist party have been to forward the socio-political integration of the Soviet peoples; to develop the national economy in the most expeditious but still Socialist manner (even at the expense of consumer desires and the most rational mode of economic organization and productivity); to convince the population that the Party deserves to continue its overall leadership role and to retain its monopoly on ideology. The Party has succeeded, more or less, in all these respects, but the passage of time, the more advanced nature of the economy, and the increasing sophistication of some sectors of the population are precipitating major social changes. These threaten to undermine the Leninist character of the Party and to convert its leadership into a group more interested in preserving its own power and privileges and in enhancing bureaucratic socialism than in reinvigorating Marxist ideology and carrying out idealistic notions of social, if not political, democracy.

Many realize that the Party must reassert its control over negative trends and turn them in directions more compatible with its interests and goals. The resulting preoccupation with domestic affairs affects the attention which Party leaders give to foreign relations and dictates that as far as possible they be so managed as to give the Kremlin the greatest possible domestic freedom of maneuver. For this reason, as well as for others more strictly concerned with foreign policy, the Party pursues detente with the West; caution in the Middle East, where local conflicts could quickly lead to superpower confrontation; and balance of power politics as the best safeguard from military attack and for access to the "Third World," where today's important radical movements are found. In Asia this gives more impetus to Soviet policies of detente toward Japan; "correctness" combined with strength toward China; engagement with South Asia through support for India; and in Southeast Asia encouragement—to the extent possible consistent with its own military noninvolvement—of violent communist-led revolutionary movements.

Global security relationships, especially with the United States and China, are a third factor influencing Soviet Asian policy. Since the dawn of the nuclear age in 1945, Soviet decisionmakers have had to calculate every policy change from the viewpoint of the danger of nuclear war with the United States. Since Moscow's overriding interest from that time on has been to prevent nuclear destruction of the Soviet homeland, all other aspects of policy have become secondary, sometimes negotiable issues, despite their intrinsic importance under other circumstances. It is true that the fear of nuclear attack has gradually lessened and that other aspects of Soviet policy have correspondingly (although never totally) freed themselves from this constraint. This includes portions of Soviet Asian policy, especially after Moscow and Washington signed the nuclear test ban treaty in 1963 and the two superpowers subsequently negotiated a series of arms control measures.

Nonetheless, the freedom of maneuver for Soviet policy in nonnuclear matters is very limited: any issue, if it touches vital American, Soviet, or Chinese interests can be infused almost instantly with a nuclear content, however remote initially from strategic nuclear matters. The Soviet Union therefore must exercise caution in Asia even when dealing with nonnuclear states or nonmilitary issues. The best recent examples of this are Soviet policy toward Southeast Asia when America was intensely involved in the Vietnam conflict and Soviet policy toward China during and subsequent to the 1969 border crisis. As nuclear weapons spread to other Asian states—at present to India, but potentially also to Japan, South Korea, Taiwan, Pakistan, and Iran—Soviet policy must become increasingly circumspect. On the other hand, to the extent that arms control measures make the use of nuclear weapons less likely, Soviet Asian policy will have relatively greater freedom to pursue its goals. But given the increasing probability of nuclear proliferation and the ever greater difficulty, therefore, of achieving meaningful arms limitation agreements, it seems likely that the nuclear weapons question will continue to limit Soviet behavior in Asia.

Global competition with the United States and China has nonnuclear dimensions that would continue even were nuclear weapons somehow to vanish. The very existence of that competition would bring the Soviet Union into direct conflict with the United States or China, if they did not also possess nuclear weapons. But the presence of nuclear weapons raises the stakes so high that an upper limit, albeit undefined and varying with the issue, is imposed on conflict, limiting its slowing down Soviet reaction time to other states' policy initiatives, and making minor issues more urgent. Nuclear weapons, therefore, limit nonnuclear conflict, but also infuse a military dimension into questions that initially have no such component. Like strongly held ideologies, nuclear weapons penetrate other spheres at will and substitute their own standards of judgment for more traditional modes of conflict management.

The ideological factor is the last, although far from the least important, domestic element in forming Soviet Asian policy. It influences policy in three ways. First, Marxism-Leninism in its current Soviet version is a filter through which definition of all state interests must pass. Secondly, among other means, the Soviet Communist party seeks through ideological appeal to justify its continued monopoly of power over every sphere of domestic life. Categorizing the external world in Marxist-Leninist terms is one means of making good this claim. Third, because the Party wants to avoid domestic challenges to its supreme position, it portrays its foreign policy as the continuation of its domestic program and conducts its foreign relations, even with regard to seemingly nonideological matters, with an eye to their effect upon the Party's domestic status. It is true that in any concrete foreign policy situation ideology takes second place to practical goals and methods, and conflicts between ideology and "power" are usually resolved in favor of the latter. Nonetheless, the Party seems increasingly concerned about the declining degree to which the Soviet population supports Party initiatives for ideological as opposed to material or national interest reasons, and about the domestic effects of external criticism—especially from America and China—of the quality of its rule at home. Because it seeks to insulate domestic developments from the changes sweeping the external world, the Party is hypersensitive to attempts by foreign powers to involve themselves, even if only as critics, in Soviet domestic life.

The international component of Soviet ideology influences Soviet Asian policy directly. Stemming from the Leninist theory of imperialism, it categorizes major Asian trends in optimistic terms and, through addenda to the original formulation, explains why non-Communist Asian states achieved independence from Western colonialism and today pursue nationalistic policies that seem not to make them candidates for early communization. True, latter-day Leninist theory seems merely to rationalize these developments and not to influence policy determination greatly. Thus, such concepts as the "two-stage revolution," the "non-capitalist (but also non-Socialist) path," countries non-Socialist but "oriented toward socialism," "state capitalism," and "national democratic states" have been promulgated to explain why mixed socialist-capitalist neutralism, not communism, is the main current in the Third World. Soviet ideology also tries to show that the trend of events, despite appearances, is toward eventual socialization of the means of production under a bona fide (i.e., Soviet-oriented) Communist party. Despite these problems, theory does supply much of the vocabulary of intra-elite communication in Moscow concerning policy toward neutralist Asian states and it does influence the range of choices which Soviet decisionmakers feel are open and the probability they assign to alternative future developments. Hence ideology should not be discounted even when calculating probable Soviet short-term policies, while in the medium and long terms it exerts an important influence.

With regard to the seven Asian Communist states (six, if one counts North and South Vietnam as one state), Moscow adopts a different ideological position, since these states are within the "movement." It therefore assesses their policies in terms of their adherence to or deviation from the "true" Marxist-Leninist course. But in contrast to the Soviet ideological stance towards non-Communist states, intra-movement ideological pronouncements tend to be very closely connected with "national interest" policies. The clearest example is the mutual reinforcement of these two aspects of Sino-Soviet relations since 1956. Soviet policymakers formulate policies toward other Asian Communist states and nonruling parties in terms of "proletarian internationalism"; approve the foreign policies of the other partners in the same terms when those policies accord with Soviet interests; categorize, by reference to the storehouse of ideological sins, policies not favorable to Soviet national or ideological interests; evaluate in similar terms the domestic policies of ruling and non-ruling Asian Communist parties; and declare, if the occasion arises (as it might well with China), when and why a given Party has departed so far from the Soviet-established norm that it must be excommunicated from the "movement." Soviet ideological policy toward Asian Communist parties is not mere verbal window-dressing: a large percentage of the space in Soviet Asian policy journals and books is devoted to ideological matters, while Soviet policymakers talk as if ideological questions are important policy determinants and in many instances bend their policy decisions to accord with ideological norms. To be sure, nonideological matters are also important in Soviet relations with Asian Communist parties. But in contrast with Moscow's posture toward non-communist states, the ideological factor within the "movement" is much more keenly felt and thus exerts more weight on Soviet policy toward Asian Communist parties.

A third set of factors influencing Soviet Asian policy is the regional international political setting in East, Southeast, and South Asia and its relationship to the two central global relationships: the strategic Sino-Soviet-American triangle and the economic triangle between the developed West—including Japan—, the non-Asian Socialist "commonwealth" headed by the Soviet Union, and the developing Third World, particularly the oil-exporting nations of the Middle East. Important intraregional political relations are bilateral: Sino-Soviet, Soviet-Japanese, and Soviet-Indian, as concerns Moscow; American relations with China, Vietnam, and India; and Sino-Japanese matters. But since the 1960s Moscow's Asian regional policies have greatly depended upon the global strategic triangle. Thus the changing status of Sino-Soviet, Soviet-American and Sino-American competition has influenced the degree of Moscow's interest in and accessibility to Asia. During the early and mid-1950s, when China and Russia were friendly, the Soviet Union had access to the East Asian heartland. Because this also meant Soviet-American and Sino-American estrangement, Moscow had difficulty establishing intensive contacts with Japan, Southeast Asia, and India. After 1963 Soviet-American relations turned reasonably good, Sino-American ties remained poor, and Moscow's relations with China deteriorated, leading to Soviet exclusion from China itself and also from non-Communist Southeast Asia and, as a consequence, precipitating Soviet interest in improving relations with South Asia. When Sino-American relations improved after, and as a result of, Sino-Soviet military clashes in 1969, Russian interest in Japan and India increased, and it found access to Southeast Asia somewhat easier. While many other specific factors helped to determine Soviet policy, changing relations among the three major world powers are an important influence on Moscow's willingness and ability to involve itself in Asia.

The global strategic triangle is also important because it siphons off energies and attention that Moscow could otherwise invest directly in Asia. The Soviet Union must allocate a substantial portion of its available power to global competition with America and China. While the forms, kinds, and totality of Soviet power have risen vastly in the quarter-century since World War II, American power has increased as well and the residue of Moscow's own energies left over to pursue Asian goals has varied widely. The interrelated factors of global tripolar competition and relative Soviet and American power have dictated much of the level and kind of Soviet involvement in Asia. Thus, even though the Soviet Union showed great interest in South Asia from 1954 on, it was unable to make major investments in the area: the disparity between its power and that of the United States left little over for improving relations with "developing" countries, and the gross level of Soviet power was still far below the level where it could afford major involvement in those areas. Later, after the mid-1960s, the absolute level of Soviet power increased and Soviet-American competition became less critical as detente gathered momentum. Moscow's ability to involve itself in Asian matters correspondingly rose, and although the Vietnam conflict took up much of this, once direct great power participation in the war was past, the Soviet Union could increase its involvement greatly in Northeast, Southeast, and South Asia. The new security relationship with India, based on the Friendship Treaty of 1971, and the slowly emerging economic ties with Japan, keyed to a raw materials-industrial products exchange, show the Kremlin's unprecedented ability to back its political goals with the full panoply of policy instruments.

The growth in power of the other two members of the strategic triangle has powerfully influenced Moscow's participation in Asian affairs, particularly as concerns China after the late 1960s. The outbreak of border violence triggered major Soviet troop transfers to the Chinese frontier which, in conjunction with the end of the Vietnam conflict, led to wholesale changes in the Far Eastern military balance of power and to the political earthquakes of Sino-American detente, the Nixon "shocks" administered to Japan, and Soviet-sponsored Indian hegemony on the subcontinent. These developments might have occurred in any case, but their rapidity came in part from Chinese recovery from the Cultural Revolution and from the removal of the Vietnam albatross from around the American neck. The Soviet Union henceforth was "locked in" to intensive contact with Asia.

International economic relations historically have been of little concern to Moscow, given its generally autarchic economy, relatively low level of international trade, and nonparticipation in capitalist international institutions. Recently, however, major world economic changes have materially affected Soviet economic policy toward Asia. One change is the increasing interpenetration of the economies of the capitalist West, including Japan, through multinational corporations and international monetary arrangements. The resultant increased rate and sophistication of technological progress in the West puts pressure on Soviet industry to modernize itself faster. Higher levels of Soviet trade with the West ensue as Moscow seeks to avail itself of the new technology. Because Japan is an important exporter of technology and finished industrial goods and because she desperately needs convenient and plentiful sources of raw materials, a natural (if still potential) confluence of interests exists with the Soviet Union, which needs Japanese goods and technology and which has in Siberia the resources the Japanese desire. And because of the competition with China for Japan's favor, Moscow has a political reason for improving its economic ties with Japan. Similar interests exist between the Soviet Union and the United States, although distance, geography, and politics have brought fewer results.

In Soviet economic relations with "developing" Asian states, such as India, the opposite tends to emerge: the Soviet Union can supply them with needed industrial goods (and to some extent agricultural products) in exchange for primary products and consumer goods. Here also, however, political criteria tend to govern the level of trade. The Soviet government has shied away from close economic ties with non-Socialist Asian states or with economies linked with the United States. This has reduced Soviet trade in Asia to an artificially low level, since most states in the region fall in one of these two categories. Since China is also a political opponent, trade with

Peking has also fallen to low levels. One result of detente with the United States, however, is a rise in Soviet trade with Asian states associated with the West, while estrangement from China has led to more trade with China's Asian opponents.

The second economic triangle, between the developed West as a whole, the Soviet-led "Socialist commonwealth" (but not including China), and the resource-exporting Third World (particularly the Middle East), closely reflects the present political division of the world and hence appeals to Soviet policymakers as a way of categorizing international economic relations. Moscow can claim, with justification, membership along with the United States in both the strategic and economic triangles, can assert a natural economic and political harmony of interests with the Third World against the West, and can claim that the other economic triangle—comprising the United States, Europe, and Japan—is only one element in the larger whole. Soviet policy has not yet gone to these lengths—Moscow is still reacting cautiously to the precipitous economic and political changes resulting from the 1973 Organization of Petroleum Exporting Countries (OPEC) escalation of oil prices—but it seems likely that it will do so. The implications for Soviet Asian economic policy vary with the region under consideration and with Moscow's political relations with the United States and China, which are discussed below. Suffice it to say here that there are many contradictions between Soviet economic and political policies, that they are usually resolved in favor of political primacy, and that, given the importance to Soviet policy of relations with the United States, China, and the Middle East, Moscow's Asian economic policy is more likely to depend on global strategic and economic developments rather than on trends within Asia.

All of these factors—historical, domestic, and global—produce the general character of Soviet Asian policy. In addition, however, there are certain structural characteristics of Asian politics as a whole that, because they have not existed heretofore in their present combination, give a unique cast to the current situation. Because the rapidly increasing power of China has made global strategic politics triangular and because all three members of the strategic triangle are physically present in Asia (even the United States, which through Hawaii, Alaska, and its ties with Japan, Taiwan, and the Philippines, is an Asian territorial state), Asia is the geographic core of the triangle. Only in Asia, principally Northeast Asia, do all three have vital territorial interests. Asia is not the center of world politics; the European-Middle Eastern arena is, and only the Soviet Union and the United States are critically involved there. But given the territorial propinquity of the three major powers in Asia—and given the presence of the world's third economic power, Japan, adjacent to all three strategic nuclear states—Asia occupies an unprecedented place in world politics.

Three other factors add to the situation. First, the United States has committed itself to playing a major role in Asia. This contrasts with the past, when the United States, while never adopting the current European-style isolationist policy toward Asia, did vary the degree of its involvement and sometimes did not protect its Asian interests with the requisite means. There seems little likelihood that America will again voluntarily withdraw from Asia to the point where it need not be considered a major element in regional politics. As a global power, in competition with Russia and China, America must remain involved. Second, for the first time all the major Asian states are strong and active. Not only are America, China, and Russia all at or near the peak of their historic power, but Japan (despite its lack of a strong military and a nuclear capacity) and India (despite its domestic problems) are actively involved, simply because of their domestic strength (economic in Japan's case, military in India's). With the exception of Burma and Bangladesh, Asia is today composed of relatively strong states pursuing active foreign policies. Many of the suggestive parallels with the past thus no longer hold, although it remains true that to the extent that political relationships are determined by *relative* power status, past patterns may persist. Barring civil war, nuclear war, or major economic disaster, each of the major states of the area will continue to pursue activist policies. As a result, Soviet Asian policy will face conditions different from the past.

Third, the range of substantive issues at stake in Asia is also unique. There is the question of how to fit the enormous growth of Chinese economic and military power since 1950 into the overall framework. There is the issue of how to adjust to the newly active and permanent presence of the Soviet Union itself, which in the past was overcome by the combination of distance, the blocking effect of Chinese and South Asia geography, and the lack of available Russian resources. There is the problem of how to accommodate a now-nuclear India within the Asian strategic framework and, more importantly, how to prevent (if that is called for) or arrange for (if it seems wise) a nuclear Japan. There is the persistent problem of the divided states: Korea, and (to some extent) China itself. Can they be reunified without renewed war, and if not, can the continuation of the unnatural division be mitigated on the personal if not the political and economic levels? Finally, there is the increasingly important problem of how to industrialize and modernize Asian states while at the same time solving problems of energy and resource allocation, increasing food production and limiting population growth, and constructing a new and viable framework of international economic institutions.

The growth of Soviet power in the last thirty years has been so great that hardly a problem of international concern in Asia can now be settled without Soviet participation or without taking Soviet interests into account. But the concomitant growth of Japanese, Chinese, and American power has limited the effect of Soviet influence, and the quadrilateral nature of regional Asian politics (Japan is the fourth power in Northeast Asia, India

in South Asia) has produced local balances of power that have so far se-
verely limited Moscow's successful pursuit of its goals. In Northeast Asia,
China has linked itself, albeit tentatively and in no formal manner, with
Japan and the United States to render nearly stillborn Moscow's efforts to
increase its influence in that region. In South Asia, China and the United
States (and also Iran) have found a common interest in opposing expansion
of Soviet involvement in the subcontinent, even though Moscow's ties with
New Delhi are formalized by the new Friendship Treaty and neither Peking
nor Washington possesses great influence in the Indian capital. But the
Chinese military threat, the necessity for India (and Bangladesh) to accept
continual emergency shipments of grain from the United States, and
American-Chinese-Iranian protection of Pakistan balance the new Soviet
involvement.

In Southeast Asia, the situation remains complicated despite the end of
the Vietnam War and the associated conflicts in Cambodia and Laos. Here
too, increasing Chinese and residual U.S. power greatly limited the degree
of Russian penetration. The Soviet Union does have two ways of influencing Southeast Asia: the strong desire of the Vietnamese Communist regime
not to become a Chinese satellite and the advantages of maritime-based
trade, through which Moscow can increasingly appeal to indigenous
regimes. Ultimately, however, the Soviet role in Southeast Asia depends on
the sufferance of Peking and Washington as well as on events and attitudes
within the region itself. As Peking's power grows, Hanoi will increasingly
be less able to maintain its autonomy, whenever Peking chooses to exert
pressure. Presuming the continuation of Sino-Soviet discord, Moscow will
thus be ever less able to intervene in favor of any pro-Soviet forces in the
Vietnamese capital. And although some perceive that the Soviet Union now
possesses a navy nearly the equivalent of the American navy itself, insecure
lines of communication and the lack of attack carriers limit Soviet ability to
protect its merchant marine in any major crisis. Thus, Soviet economic ties
with Southeast Asia depend on the strength of Sino-American détente.

In all three regions of Asia, therefore, increasing Soviet involvement is
being met with American and Chinese countermoves (even if indirect and
often for quite different reasons), while Japan, which would otherwise have
much to gain economically from closer Soviet ties, remains suspicious of
Soviet intentions and is deterred by anticipation of negative Chinese and
American reaction. Since the smaller Asian states tend to follow the
American or the Chinese lead, the current situation is not favorable for a
startlingly larger Soviet role in Asia.

Sino-Soviet Relations: The Key to Soviet Asian Policy

While many factors contribute to Soviet attitudes and policy toward Asia, Moscow's relations with the other global power, the United States, and its relations with the other major regional power, China, form the core of Soviet Asian policy. At present, however, Sino-Soviet relations form the most important of the three bipolar sides of the global strategic triangle, since détente, the term best descriptive of contemporary Soviet-American and Sino-American relations, depends primarily upon continued ideological and organizational disagreement, personal enmity, political hostility, and military confrontation between Moscow and Peking. Were either power to modify its bilateral relations and hence its policy toward the United States, the entire structure of international politics, as well as of Soviet Asian policy, would change as well. Given the dependency of international politics and the Soviet Asian policy on the nature of the strategic triangle, and the unstable nature of Sino-Soviet relations, extremely important modifications in either could result even from relatively small changes in Soviet or Chinese policies toward each other.

The present situation is made up of several elements, of which the most important is the military confrontation along or near the Sino-Soviet border. With over fifty divisions, a huge store of conventional and nuclear weapons, and a well developed logistic infrastructure, the Soviet military can wreak tremendous damage upon almost any series of Chinese targets, occupy important parts of China if not all centers of power, and inflict very high casualties on any Chinese force confronting it. The Chinese have equivalent numbers of troops, an increasing quantity of modern arms and supporting equipment, a nuclear strike potential that will soon be able to reach the entire Soviet Union and can already destroy several Soviet Siberian and Far Eastern population centers, and an army and a populace that would make long-term Soviet occupation of large areas possible only at very high cost. The military situation is thus a stand-off and should continue so for the foreseeable future, barring unforeseen technological breakthroughs, massive new deployments, or conscious, erroneous, or irrational decisions to initiate military action.

A second element is the ideological differences between the two Communist capitals. These gestated for a long time (even before the Chinese Communists came to power in 1949), developed and came into the open in the late 1950s and early 1960s, and have been a major factor every since. While details need not detain us, each Party spends much time and energy discrediting the ideological and organizational claims of the other and pointing to the purity of its own policy. Soviet and Chinese policies and interests are thereby skewed away from a wholly "rational" direction. These questions also affect Soviet and Chinese willingness (or reluctance, as the case may be) to provide material aid to, or support the domestic programs and foreign policies of, third countries. Further, they may modify or eschew policies which in the absence of the ideological dispute they would otherwise consider. For instance, the Soviets occasionally seem anxious to call an international Communist conference to read the Chinese out of the movement and appear willing to make concessions to East European and some nonruling parties if they attend the meeting and follow the Soviet lead. For their part, the Chinese use every forum possible to attack the Soviets, and their pronouncements always contain references to points of ideological and organizational differences, a good example being the anti-Soviet emphasis in Chinese speeches at the 1974 international population conference at Bucharest. Thus American policy toward Moscow and Peking must constantly consider how any initiative would be accepted ideologically in the two capitals.

A third element concerns personalities: the fact that some Soviet and Chinese leaders do not like to deal with their counterparts in the other country. This is particularly true of Mao Tse-tung himself, who has long held personally negative views of the Russian leadership, but it is also evident with many Russians. Much of the latter-day difficulties between the two parties and states can be traced to this element in Mao's personality; hence, some change in Chinese policy after the Party chairman dies, is probable. But the longer the present enmity continues, the more Soviet and Chinese decisionmakers will regard the other side as deficient in personal and national character, and the more difficult it will therefore be, to improve their relations in the post-Maoist period. The Soviets have allowed this to affect their official dealings with the Chinese less than have the Chinese, but even in Moscow there is a pronounced anti-Chinese atmosphere that stems as much from personal dislike of the present Chinese leadership as from disagreement with Chinese political and ideological inclinations.

A final element in contemporary Sino-Soviet relations is the historical legacy and the political policies that flow from it. Moscow-Peking ties are poor because past relationships have been poor. Trade, after having been almost totally ended, continues at an artificially low level. Cultural exchanges and movement of persons, having stopped, remain at a near standstill. Suspicions as to motives, having been aroused, find confirmation whether or not facts support them. The longer present circumstances continue, therefore, the more difficult it will be to change.

What are some alternative future developments in Sino-Soviet relations that might affect Soviet-American relations and hence the fundamental character of international politics? In the short run, it seems likely that not much will change and that the relative freedom of action the United States now enjoys will continue. The reason, aside from the four factors outlined above, is that Mao Tse-tung personally determines the Chinese policy of enmity with the Soviets. As long as he is alive, there is little probability of any major change. But Mao is now quite elderly and may pass away at any time or become so enfeebled as to be effectively removed from having a major voice in new policy initiatives. The short run may thus indeed be short, although even three or four years can characterize a political era. But for the time being Sino-Soviet relations, and hence much of Soviet-American and Sino-American relations, depend upon the heartbeat of Mao Tse-tung.

Thereafter, three possibilities seem likely. The first is that the presesnt relationship will endure with little modification. Patterns and habits having been ingrained, policies, to the extent that they accord with basic Soviet and Chinese interests, would continue. Attempts might be made to patch things up, much as after Khrushchev's fall in 1964, but would fail when both sides conclude that differences were too fundamental for post-Maoist decision-makers to solve. Given the absence of Mao's personal imprint on Chinese policy (as well as, for that matter, of Chou En-lai's), however, Sino-Soviet relations would not get progressively worse. A de facto agreement could emerge preventing further deterioration in relations. Although no improvement would thereby come for some years, Moscow and Peking could count on a no-war no-peace scenario. Trade levels would remain low, military confrontation persist, diplomatic relations continue frosty, and the atmosphere of personal dislike and suspicion of motives endure. It is possible, under these assumptions, to imagine a modest slackening of tensions after Mao's passing. Marginal issues, such as the level and severity of mutual criticism or the lack of cultural or tourist connections, could be settled. The atmosphere would thus improve somewhat. But an agreement to disagree on ideological issues or to refrain from competing for the loyalty of foreign Communist parties or developing states would not be possible, nor would there be settlement of the border problem or mutual thinning out of troops along the boundary. Realizing anew the depths of their differences, the Soviets and the Chinese would return to their old habits and gird for a long, although not necessarily violent, struggle.

The second and third possibilities would probably occur, if at all, once the preliminary stages of the above procedure were completed. In the second case, Soviet and Chinese decisionmakers, gathered to sound each other out, would discover to their surprise that Mao's death had cleared the atmosphere and that the Chinese were now willing to talk in substantive terms and desirous of settling fratricidal ideological disputes. The border question, at the heart of the present difficulties, would be quickly solved. (The question can be solved now and only Chinese, i.e., Mao's, intransigence has prevented it.) A new and large trade agreement would be signed, cultural delegations and the flow of information increase, propaganda levels lower, and a commission be convened to discuss outstanding ideological questions. Such an outcome might require changes in the Soviet leadership, for some in the Brezhnev group seem committed to an anti-Chinese line.

The Soviets are trying to set the stage for such a massive improvement in their ties with Peking, so that when the opportune moment comes they will not have burned their bridges to the Chinese and made rapprochement impossible. Despite its occasionally stringent nature, the volume and tone of Moscow's propaganda is much less than it could be; their forebearing attitude in connection with Chinese spy charges and the seizure of a Soviet helicopter crew is calculated to encourage a more moderate Chinese attitude; and their general posture is one of disappointment at Chinese actions coupled with a wait-and-see attitude. Soviet policy, despite the military build-up and calls for an anti-Chinese Asian collective security system, thus hopes to set the stage for a post-Maoist rapprochement.

The third possibility would also occur at the end of a relatively short post-Maoist period of mutual testing. This time, however, Soviet and Chinese leaders would conclude that, because previous attitudes and policies persisted, each must gird for the worst. The military build-up would therefore resume and possibly even accelerate, and the Soviets would attempt to isolate China from possible allies and free themselves for military action. Border incidents and propaganda attacks would become more severe and more frequent, and a general atmosphere of fear and paranoia would grip both capitals. The stage would be set for Sino-Soviet war.

Third party involvement in a Sino-Soviet military conflict, if it did occur, would depend on its geographic extent, level of casualties, and type of weaponry used. Limited to nonnuclear land engagements causing relatively light losses in the border provinces only, such a war probably would not draw in outside parties, either to protect themselves and their interests or to support one of the two contending sides. At the other extreme, a conflict involving all forms of armaments, including nuclear, and inflicting high civilian as well as military casualties, could involve other states, not only East European Communist countries, but—in the (probable) event that China were the losing side or in the (even more probable) situation of lethal nuclear fallout settling upon Far Eastern and North American countries— the Western community as well. In any case, war between China and Russia would change the international political landscape immeasurably and disfigure Soviet and Chinese foreign policies, and hence world politics as a whole, for many decades.

It is useful to assign probabilities of outcome to each of these alternatives, and to evaluate them in terms of American interests and options. Events are influenced by a myriad of factors, not the least important of which is the order in which things happen. But it is possible to assign different likelihoods to the three possibilities (realizing that these are points along a spectrum of futures) based on the current situation, trends likely to move in some regular manner, and "feel" for the manner in which the various factors might fit together at a given moment.

To this writer, it seems probable that the third alternative, Sino-Soviet military conflict, will not occur. The risks for both sides are too great. The military balance is moving toward equality as Chinese nuclear and conventional levels increase. The time for a successful Soviet "surgical" strike on Chinese nuclear and rocket facilities has long passed; the Chinese will always have enough deliverable warheads left to destroy one or more Soviet cities, a risk unacceptable to the Kremlin. The rigidity that even low-level military conflict would give to every other aspect of Soviet and Chinese foreign policies is in itself probably too high a price to pay for winning a few battles. (A war, given the nature of the Soviet and Chinese nations, would never be "won.") On the other hand, military conflict could be initiated in circumstances similar to Soviet-American nuclear confrontation: a wildly irrational decisionmaker; misinterpretation of radar images, malfunction of early warning systems, and other such technical causes; or a political crisis coupled with military threats that might trigger military preemption.

If military conflict is increasingly unlikely, implications follow for the other two alternatives. An increasingly stable Sino-Soviet military balance may permit Soviet and Chinese decisionmakers to devote more attention and military might to other areas and situations. For the Soviet Union, this might mean increased willingness to involve itself in the Middle East, in an oil crisis-induced depression *cum* civil disruption in Italy, or in the coming Yugoslav succession crisis. Another possibility would stem from Soviet-Chinese efforts, once it became clear that the balance of forces between them had become stable, to come to some arms control agreement, thus enhancing the safety of the balance. Force reductions would provide both states with additional military force for use or potential use elsewhere. It might be possible to couple Soviet-Chinese reductions with East-West force reductions in Europe, depending upon the Soviet-American political atmosphere. In any case, a decrease in the probability of a Sino-Soviet military clash would free both parties for more active roles elsewhere and would remove one of the current bases of détente in Soviet-American (and Chinese-American) relations. The trade-off would thus be a reduction in Sino-Soviet tensions, with the resultant gain of having to worry less about Sino-Soviet war, in return for declining Soviet and Chinese propensities to continue the current emphasis upon "peaceful coexistence" with the United States and its allies.

Continuation of the first alternative, the status quo of frozen relationships, near-zero contacts, and mutual antagonism seems likely as long as Mao is alive and not totally retired from political activity. Mao will not live forever, however, and senility or even political pressure may force him to retire before his physical demise. He does appear to have succeeded in "vaccinating" the Chinese polity against the Soviet revisionist virus, and no Chinese leader now will publicly advocate mitigating the conflict with the Russians, must less setting it aside entirely. Nonetheless, all three recently deposed Chinese military leaders (P'eng Teh-huai, Lo Jui-ch'ing, and Lin Piao) were accused of advocating just such a course, as was Mao's first-designated successor, Liu Shao-ch'i. Therefore, pressure for revision in

Sino-Soviet relations will probably arise again. Without Mao to stop it, pressure to prolong current policy will decline, while, as we note below, the forces favoring Sino-Soviet rapprochement will probably increase.

The one "objective" (i.e., nonpersonality dependent) factor that favors current policy on both sides is the increasing relative power of China. Unless a combination of natural disasters and maladministration throws China off its present course of major yearly increases in industrial and military production, with the resultant ability to conduct a more active foreign policy, China is likely to close the gap, albeit slowly, between itself and the Soviet Union. Perceiving this, Soviet decisionmakers may opt not to seize the opportunity of détente or rapprochement with Peking but instead to prolong or even to intensify confrontation. This would be a major policy change for the Soviets, who currently maintain a watchful policy of waiting for Mao's demise, but it is possible that they may give up hope for improvement, especially if the post-Maoist group were disinclined to settle outstanding disputes with the Soviet Union.

The final alternative, détente, seems to be the most probable Sino-Soviet future. The current confrontation is in one sense ideologically "unnatural," for despite major differences of emphasis and priority and a long history of dispute, the conflict is an internecine one. Soviet and Chinese Marxists continue to hold in common important tenets of the faith, while their differences largely concern how to deal with the United States and its allies. Moreover, as Chinese society modernizes and industrializes, social disparities between the two countries (one reason for Chinese criticism of Soviet policies) will be mitigated. Soviet-style revisionism as a method of organizing society is the probable future for China, a fact that Liu Shao-ch'i clearly perceived and attempted to act upon. There will be other Liu's—Chinese modernizers—in the future.

The legal and procedural issues in the border negotiations are soluble at any time. The differences concern ownership of riverine islands, the boundary location at a number of other places including the Ussuri and Amur river dividing line, and the question of Soviet admission of the "unequal" nature of the pre-1971 border treaties. None but the ownership of the major island fronting on Khabarovsk is other than a minor issue, and that is soluble once the Chinese agree to cede their claim in return for Soviet claims to other islands amounting to approximately the same area. Once Chinese negotiators receive the go-ahead from the Chinese Politburo, a new agreement can be signed. The way will then be open to agreement on border military dispositions as well as talks on trade, cultural and intellectual contacts and ideological differences.

Whether, and to what extent, détente thus defined becomes rapprochement will depend upon political imponderables in the Soviet Union and China and upon the policies of other states, especially the United States. This brings into focus American interests and options as concerns Sino-

Soviet relations. First, it would be disastrous for the United States again to have to face a united Sino-Soviet bloc, this time immeasurably stronger than in the 1950s. Second, it follows that the United States has no interest in the solution of outstanding Sino-Soviet differences, unless major war between the two Communist giants would thereby be averted or unless resolution of differences was made part of, or led directly to, compensatory settlement of Soviet-American and Sino-American differences. Such a settlement could well involve Sino-Soviet-American nuclear and conventional arms control and disarmament; and overall Middle Eastern power distribution as it relates to energy and to Soviet, American, and possibly Chinese involvement in that region; and solutions to such "supranational" issues as environmental quality, world food production and distribution, and inflation. With regard to Sino-American relations, agreement would have to be reached on the Taiwan issue and hence the locus of the American embassy in China; some trade-off of American Far Eastern bases versus Chinese involvement in "national liberation movements" in Southeast Asia; a joint pledge to work towards peaceful solution of the Korean question; and possibly some *modus vivendi* in Southeast Asia.

Third, the United States is interested in the evolution of the domestic character of Soviet—and Chinese—societies in a more open, liberal, and democratic direction and would like to see the Sino-Soviet relationship not hinder those developments. Fourth, and most importantly, the United States is interested in a Sino-Soviet relationship that will maximize Washington's freedom of action in regard to the two Communist states and with respect to third states, regions, and issues. This means that America would not favor trends tending to reunite Moscow and Peking on the basis of an anti-American platform; that Washington would approve Sino-Soviet détente only if it measurably increased the probability of solution of "supranational" problems *and* bilateral Soviet-American and Sino-Soviet issues; and that the United States would seek to link Sino-Soviet rapprochement to an overall East-West settlement. In all these instances, the American interest indicates continual and close involvement in changing Sino-Soviet relations, seeks to triangularize bilateral Sino-Soviet developments inimical to its own policy goals, and attempts to adjust bilateral Soviet-American and Sino-American relations to compensate for —or even to preempt—renewed Sino-Soviet closeness.

Since prospects for a general international settlement are not good, it follows that the United States must try to forestall major changes, either meliorative or war-threatening, in Sino-Soviet relations, or to couple support of Sino-Soviet détente with further progress on important bilateral issues between Washington and the two Communist capitals. What options, keyed to the three alternative Sino-Soviet futures, does the United States possess in this regard or what options could it generate? With regard to the first alternative (no basic change in Sino-Soviet relations), perseverance with current policies is probably desirable, with perhaps some minor modifications. American policy has been to "treat the Soviet Union and China equally." This in practice means leaning to the Chinese side, since the United States had no dealings with Peking for so long, since China needed support during the post-March 1969 period of overt Soviet military threat, and since the Soviet Union is the greater military threat to the United States. If it desires to continue the present Sino-Soviet relationship, however, the United States might not wish to lean too far, lest the Soviet Union feel that it was being used in détente by Peking and Washington for their own ends. Thus, for instance, the granting of most favored nation status to China as means to promote rough trade equality might be withheld for a relatively short time until the Soviet Union is accorded the same treatment. Or conversely, Washington might feel that rising Soviet power requires leaning further toward China to counterbalance it.

Another topic is progress on Strategic Arms Limitation Talks (SALT), Mutual and Balanced Force Reductions (MBFR), and related disarmament and arms control issues. Questions concerning any future Chinese participation are now turned aside by both delegations; i.e., the Sino-Soviet arms question and the emerging Chinese nuclear threat to the American homeland are separated, in public, from the Soviet-American talks. It is questionable how long this separation can continue, for at some point the Chinese nuclear force will become large and sophisticated enough to enter more than marginally into Moscow's and Washington's strategic calculations. To assure continual American progress with Moscow in this area, it might be useful to raise the question of bringing the Chinese into the various talks, noting that increasingly little time remains wherein separate Soviet-American agreements can be worked out. The implied alternative is initiation of Sino-American disarmament talks, which is to Moscow's disadvantage under current assumptions, while the gain would be an earlier and perhaps more advantageous Soviet-U.S. agreement. On the other hand, any Soviet-American agreement that frees the Soviets to deal forcibly with the Chinese would destabilize the Sino-Soviet military situation and might contribute to eventual Sino-Soviet military conflict. In any case, fitting the Chinese into the overall strategic equation is an intricate and delicate process that must be initiated soon.

One way to buttress the status quo is to stress the Sino-American side of the triangle. One way to encourage the Soviets to intensify Soviet-American détente is to show steady progress in settling issues separating Peking and Washington. This is very difficult with respect to recognition, since it is tied to the question of the future of Taiwan. The United States may lack motivation to recognize Peking fully since it may consider it has done that for all intents and purposes in the liaison offices agreement and since the "evolution of forces" on Taiwan seems to be pointing toward eventual de jure or de facto political and economic independence from the Mainland.

However, given Peking's dissatisfaction with the present arrangement, Washington might find it advantageous to propose full recognition and place a consulate-general, or even a Japanese-style trade office, in Taipei instead of a full embassy. On the trade question, the Chinese may change their minds as to the desirability of a large volume of exchange of goods if the balance continues to be one-sidedly in favor of the United States. To build the present temporary level of relations into a permanent factor in Sino-American relations and to forestall major improvement in Sino-Soviet trade, it might be useful to consider granting the Chinese most favored nation status. Finally, one factor in Sino-American relations capable of careful modulation is cultural exchanges, transportation routes, and tourism. While it has usually been China who has rejected American proposals, the United States does possess some cards, some of which could be used in a Soviet-American context. For instance, increased American tourism in China would help balance Sino-American trade and might prompt Moscow to increase the quality of their tourist services to Americans. Exchange of technical delegations and technical information with China where no such agreements with the Soviet Union exist might help Soviet-American negotiations in other areas. These examples show that changes in Sino-American relations will influence the Soviet-American relationship and that if American policy is to continue détente with Moscow, utilizing the Chinese connection, i.e., providing examples of American interest in prolonged détente with Peking, might prove quite helpful.

The second alternative Sino-Soviet future, détente leading to rapprochement, is difficult for the United States to deal with because most of the factors in its favor are beyond American control. So long as relaxation of tensions does not set the stage for a wholesale restructuring of relations between Moscow and Peking, Sino-Soviet détente would not necessarily be contrary to American interests in constructing a peaceful world and in solving "supranational" problems. Even with rapprochement, taking certain steps would encourage Moscow and Peking not to change their current, if separately motivated, orientation toward Washington of cooperation and joint solution of bilateral differences. The United States could continue to work with the Soviet Union and China on common problems but could hint that Sino-Soviet rapprochement might end or curtail mutually beneficial Soviet and Sino-American programs. A distinction should be made between generally beneficial marginal adjustments in the Sino-Soviet relationship (such as reducing the probability of major war through arms control measures) and major improvements (such as settling outstanding ideological differences or solving the border question *in toto*) that might prove detrimental to the United States. Having little to fear from the former, Washington could contribute to making Sino-Soviet (indeed, Sino-American) military conflict less probable, for instance, by transferring technology to the Chinese for a modern satellite-based early warning system against possible Soviet missile attack. This would also improve U.S. security vis-à-vis the Soviet Union by making Moscow less likely to launch a nuclear attack. As solution of "supranational" problems emerges as a central American interest, the United States might wish to contribute to working out new international institutions and mechanisms structured to make it easy for the Soviets and the Chinese to support them separately.

Thorough-going rapprochement would be contrary to American interests. Perhaps the only workable long-run policy to avoid it is to set up in the short term so many points of contact, joint ventures, and exchange programs that Moscow and Peking would be increasingly less tempted to cast off the American in favor of renewed 1950s-style ideological militancy, and be more inclined to continue along the current path of separately developed bilateral ties with Washington. This is easier said than done because Chinese and Soviet goals are often at variance with American interests. Nonetheless, the United States does have several advantages. Russia and China desperately desire American technology, trade, and managerial skills. Building Soviet-American and Sino-American trade into a permanent and important factor in the planned economics of the two countries would help to continue good relations, and implied threats of greatly curtailing such programs would help convince Moscow and Peking not to carry rapprochement too far. While tourism, exchanges, and trade can be shut off almost instantly by either communist power, and should therefore not be counted on greatly to forestall major rapprochement, patterns once set up are broken only with difficulty. The same can be said for purchasing Chinese and Soviet raw materials, especially oil, to the extent that such commodities are available and are compatible with American policies of energy self-sufficiency.

In order to forestall rapprochement, the United States ought not to try to interfere overtly in the internal affairs of either Russia or China. There are short-term gains to be obtained from tying liberalization of American trade policy to liberalization of Soviet (and perhaps Chinese) emigration policy, but in the longer run Soviet (and perhaps Chinese) decisionmakers will become more and more resentful. Short-term gains are likely to backfire in the long run. In a post-Maoist situation, when the Soviets and some Chinese will argue strenuously for rapprochement, items such as the emigration issue, a relatively small matter in other situations, might be magnified many times.

Another area where the United States could build safeguards against anti-American rapprochement is strategic arms control. The Chinese factor is an under-the-table element in Soviet-American negotiations, not only because the Chinese refuse to begin such talks but also because the Chinese nuclear force is still too small to enter greatly into the calculations of the two sides. Because the time wherein this latter situation will continue is decreasing, the United States might well advise the Soviets of the necessity to come to a bilateral agreement speedily. Any such agreement would have to take Chinese reactions into account, in that the current atmosphere of lessened Sino-American antagonism would best not be clouded over by a Soviet-American strategic arms limitation agreement obviously disadvantageous to the Chinese. A point may also come when American interest (i.e., the size of the Chinese nuclear force) will dictate opening separate negotiations with the Chinese or pressing the Soviet jointly to invite Peking to participate openly in the negotiations. The results, *if* agreements were signed, would presumably be the same, but the probability of agreements emerging at all would be vitally affected by the manner in which they were arrived at. To prevent major Sino-Soviet rapprochement, Washington should keep the Chinese reasonably well informed as to American thinking while Soviet-American negotiations proceed (thus enhancing Chinese trust and "educating" Peking in the terminology of this field) and use the possibility of parallel Chinese-American negotiations to convince the Soviets to come to an early agreement.

The best of all possible worlds for the United States would be to sign a significant and realistic agreement with the Russians that recognized the Chinese component, tacitly or explicitly, and then to sign a similar agreement with the Chinese (although details would be different). If this were done before the prospect of major Sino-Soviet rapprochement increases greatly, Washington would possess separate binding agreements with both Moscow and Peking, safeguard the general strategic balance, promote all-around arms control, and minimize the desirability of Soviet-Chinese cooperation at its own expense.

A final area for forestalling Sino-Soviet rapprochement aimed at Washington concerns China's attempts to satisfy its national goals in Asia, to the extent they are consistent with American interests. China will be less interested in Moscow's blandishments if the United States continues to show interest in, and ability to aid, Peking in attaining long-sought goals. China's Asian interest is threefold: recovering Taiwan, providing for national security and economic development, and increasing her influence in surrounding regions. It is exceedingly difficult to satisfy Peking with regard to the Taiwan issue. Nonetheless, despite the evolution of the political and economic situation on Taiwan leading it even farther from reunion with the Mainland, one useful option would be to continue perceptible progress in upgrading relations with Peking and, by implication, lessening ties with Taipei, but in no case attempting to freeze the new status quo in some legal manner. Aside from upgrading the liaison office in Peking to embassy status (which implies full recognition) and downgrading the Taipei embassy to the consulate level, Washington could persist in decreasing the number of American military personnel on Taiwan. Both measures assume Peking's continued adherence to those clauses of the Shanghai Communique concerning nonuse of force in the Taiwan straits area.

Washington could sign an agreement with Peking concernng no first use of nuclear weapons, or indeed, give its blessings to proposals that non-Soviet Asian states, including China, sign some form of collective nonaggression agreement. Chinese desires to increase its influence in East, Southeast, and South Asia, so long as Chinese actions are nonviolent, are probably not inimical to American interests and could well be entertained. There is, further, no reason why China should not establish diplomatic ties with all the states of Asia and increase its levels of trade and cultural exchange. Such developments would tend to improve Sino-American trade imbalances, limit the spread to Soviet influence, and open China further to the beneficial influences (in American, if not Maoist eyes) of closer contact with foreign, especially Western, cultures.

We come, finally, to the alternative of deteriorating Sino-Soviet relations leading ultimately to war. While, as noted above, this prospect is increasingly unlikely, the situation could change were the military balance to move increasingly in Soviet favor or were Moscow's efforts to isolate China, diplomatically and militarily, to be more and more successful. The United States has options in each contingency. Active pursuit of strategic and conventional arms control measures contribute to a stable military balance. If Peking appeared to be in acute need of military hardware to stave off imminent Soviet attack, the United States could supply arms to China. Washington could, within legal limits and in accord with American interests, transfer some kinds of military technology to China, just as it could exchange strategic raw materials with Peking. More indirectly the United States could adopt as a guiding diplomatic principle not to enter into agreements with the Soviet Union, or otherwise accede to Soviet efforts, which were obviously intended to isolate China diplomatically. For instance, during negotiations with the Soviets on European security and force reductions, the United States would wish to avoid allowing Moscow to greatly augment its troop strength against China. Following Soviet agreement mutually to withdraw troops from Central Europe, America and China might also jointly oppose Soviet-sponsored "collective security" arrangements in Asia that did not include both Washington and Peking.

As China grows stronger, however, and can increasingly counter the Soviet threat with her own power, the risk of Sino-Soviet war declines and with it American leverage in the Sino-Soviet relationship and in other arenas of world politics. At some juncture, Chinese strength will be great enough to retaliate with nearly equal effectiveness against most Soviet military initiatives. At that point, and probably long before it the risk of a Sino-Soviet war will decline significantly. Sino-Soviet options relevant to the United States will then be reduced to the choice between continued dispute and limitation of the level of differences through détente or rapprochement. Which way China will turn and what freedom the United States will have, in the superpower triangle, in other geographic areas, and with regard to important substantive issues, will depend on the imponderables: the timing and specific situations. But it will also depend on American actions taken ahead of time.

Two things seem clear whatever the details. One is that even a limited Sino-Soviet combination would be disastrous for the United States. This would be especially so in an era, as many presume the world is now entering, of American-led international cooperation and institution-building. The other is that the Soviet Union and China are rapidly increasing their power to project their influence in distant regions, while the United States, beset with internal difficulties and declining relative power abroad, will be increasingly ill-equipped to deal with a massive display of Soviet power or, in Asia, of Chinese power. The United States will therefore all the more need reliable allies in every area of the world. So long as the United States can maneuver between Russia and China to secure its own goals, American interests elsewhere will be safeguarded. But were Soviet and Chinese power to be ranged against the United States, together or separately, American abilities to build that "new world" of which it dreams will be be severely limited. If joint search for new solutions and new institutions is to be the operative principle of American foreign policy, a major share of Washington's efforts must go to assuring, as a safeguard, the continuation and the expansion of the Western alliance, to integrating the Soviet Union and China, on a separate and piecemeal basis, into the new global system, and above all to discouraging Moscow and Peking from reuniting to fight a new cold war against the West.

Outlook for Sino-Soviet Relations *

Three years after the death of Mao Zedong, the Sino-Soviet conflict has
entered a period of transition and a time of testing. Against a background
of profound changes in China and even more dramatic recent transformation of the international environment in which the two leading Communist
powers contend, a symbolic milestone was reached in the spring of 1979,
when the Chinese announced their intention to abrogate the long-dormant
1950 Sino-Soviet Friendship Treaty and simultaneously proposed talks with
the Soviets about the fundamental issues of the Sino-Soviet relationship.
These talks, which began in September 1979, provide a concrete test of the
geopolitical momentum the conflict has acquired after two decades. In the
absence of the dominant personalities who gave the conflict its initial impetus—Mao and Nikita Khrushchev—how far are the competitors constrained by a mutual perception of fundamentally irreconcilable national interests? How far can either side carry an effort to reduce tensions without in
fact injuring what it regards as a vital national interest? How far does each
side now mean to try?

*Reprinted from *Problems of Communism*, XXVIII, 5-6 (September-December, 1979),
pp. 50-66, by permission of the author and the publisher.

The Duality of Soviet Purpose

As the Brezhnev era nears a close, Soviet policy toward China continues to be characterized by a striking dichotomy of purpose, an internal contradiction of aims inherited from the Khrushchev era. On the one hand, the Soviets would like to do everything possible to weaken, subdue, or isolate the Chinese; on the other hand, they would like to reduce Chinese hostility. For the better part of two decades, the Soviets, while maintaining growing pressure against Chinese external interests in an incessant struggle around the world and close to home, have been the *demandeurs* in repeated attempts to get the Chinese to respond to proposals to improve diverse aspects of bilateral relations. In effect, the Soviets have sought to persuade Beijing to agree to divorce the bilateral relationship from all other considerations, including all the adverse effects on China of Soviet behavior elsewhere.

Over the years, the Soviets have regularly professed bewilderment and sadness that the proposals of this sort which they have intermittently sandwiched among their periodic endeavors to intimidate the Chinese leadership have been considered unacceptable. It will be recalled, for example, that in October 1962, as the Cuban missile crisis developed, Khrushchev vainly asked the Chinese ambassador to open a "clean new page," to return to the relationship "that existed up to 1958,"[1] The following year, in November 1963, Khrushchev sent a letter to Mao proposing, among other things, to resume Soviet technical assistance to China—and, in particular, to send back Soviet experts to help in the oil and mining industries.[2] He reminded the Chinese of his desire that they reopen negotiations to buy entire Soviet plants. And he proposed that new Sino-Soviet commercial and other ties be woven into the five-year plans of the two countries. No part of this program, the Soviets complained, was accepted.

In November 1964, soon after Khrushchev had been ousted, his successors held talks with Zhou Enlai in Moscow and among other things made what the Soviets have subsequently termed "concrete proposals" for expansion of trade and technological cooperation. These were coupled, however, with what the Soviets apparently regarded as modest proposals for "coordinating the foreign policy activities of the PRC [People's Republic of China] and the USSR." The Soviets professed to be surprised and grieved that these met with "obstinate resistance from the Chinese leaders."[3]

Finally, eight years later, in 1972, Moscow, according to Soviet claims,

---

1. "Marxism-Leninism, the Basis of the Unity of the Communist Movement," *Kommunist* (Moscow), No. 15, October 1963.
2. See this Soviet letter, the Chinese reply of Feb. 29, 1964, and the Soviet response of Mar. 7, 1964, in *Seven Letters Exchanged Between the Central Committees of the Communist Party of China and the Communist Party of the Soviet Union* (hereafter *Seven Letters...*), Beijing, Foreign Languages Press, 1964, p. 30.
3. *The New York Times*, Mar. 24, 1966.

advanced through a variety of channels a new series of "concrete proposals" including, among others, renewed suggestions for the resumption of complete-plant deliveries, the signing of a long-term trade agreement, and the organization of cooperation between Soviet and Chinese academies of sciences. These proposals, too, were allegedly "frozen or rejected by Beijing on various pretexts."[4]

The dual Soviet approach toward China—the unrelenting competitive pressure and the unabashed effort to improve selected aspects of bilateral dealings—has in fact been characteristic of Soviet policy toward a number of other powers, and in these cases such a policy has met with some success. Consequently, although Soviet tactics toward Beijing may vary considerably from time to time, neither element in the Soviet posture is likely to be abandoned by either Leonid Brezhnev or his heirs. It is therefore worth asking what the specific impediments have been to a positive Chinese response to Soviet overtures in the past, and whether the Chinese attitude is now likely to change as China moves further away from the Maoist era.

The Three Chinese Walls

In broadest terms, Soviet attempts to build an improved relationship with the Chinese leadership have confronted three fundamental barriers in the minds of the Chinese. These three concentric walls around the Forbidden City will be considered in order of increasing importance.

THE VANISHING "IDEOLOGICAL DISPUTE"

The first and by far the *least* important today is the ideological dimension— the line of distinction in principles that Mao had sought to draw between China and the Soviet Union. This area of differences includes, for example, Mao's long-standing charges that the USSR is in the hands of "fascist" renegades who have restored capitalism, that certain Soviet practices such as the use of material incentives are anathema, and that the Khrushchev and Brezhnev leaderships have betrayed an allegedly consistent and ideologically pure set of past Soviet domestic and foreign policies identified with Yosif Stalin.

Today, by far the most important and frequent Chinese charges against the Soviet Union are that the USSR is a power which everywhere practices "hegemonism" and "expansionism"—an assertion that flows from perceptions of concrete national interest rather than ideological dogma. These charges relate directly to China's primary preoccupation, i.e., its foreign policy concerns.

Meanwhile, the bulk of the Maoist rhetoric which seemed so important

4. *Izvestiya* (Moscow), May 16, 1974.

two decades ago has been blown away by the winds of time, by China's changing foreign policy needs, and by shifts in China's leadership personnel. Whatever it may have been expedient to say during Mao's lifetime, it is unlikely that men such as the late Premier Zhou Enlai, Chairman Hua Guofeng, or Vice Premier Den Xiaoping have genuinely believed that the Soviet Union is led by capitalist renegades or have felt pious horror at Soviet reliance on material incentives. This is particularly evident in view of the pragmatic policies that have been implemented in China in connection with the "four modernizations" program. In any case, no Chinese leader can be unaware that over the last decade certain of the gravest Chinese ideological charges leveled at the Soviets in the early 1960's have become discordant with the Chinese foreign policy. Instead of eternal truths, as originally described, these dicta have now been revealed to have been ephemeral reflections of momentary and long-vanished Chinese needs. Thus, the attacks on Yugoslav "revisionism" as a surrogate for Khrushchev in the late 1950's and early 1960's have been followed, in the late 1970's, by restoration of party relations with the league of Communists of Yugoslavia and even by renewed intimations of some Chinese interest in Yugoslav economic practice.[5]

In sum, it is conceivable that some "ultra-leftist" members of the "gang of four" purged immediately after Mao's death—notably, the propaganda specialist Yao Wenyuan—might, had they remained in power, have been confirmed as the Maoist fundamentalists they had often seemed in the past (although even this is by no means a foregone conclusion). It is possible that such men might have sought to orient China's policy along consistently ideological lines. But, it is clear that so pronounced an ideological perspective has been at best highly exceptional among Mao's heirs, and that there will be a broad consensus within the Chinese leadership to weight future policy toward the Soviet Union largely according to perceptions of hard-and-fast Chinese national interests.

MEMORIES OF THE PAST

The second factor is the collective Chinese memory of all the Soviet Union has done with respect to China in the past—not only the benefits Moscow has provided but the injuries it has inflicted. In this regard, the impact of the former is fading, while the latter remain quite vivid. A highly selective list of the injuries would include Soviet demands in 1958 for what the

---

5. The expressions of interest in the Yugoslav workers' councils which appeared in the Chinese press in the fall of 1978 (e.g., the accounts of Ye Jianying's speech to the fourth session of the Standing Committee of the Fifth National People's Congress on Sept. 13, 1978, in *Peking Review* [Beijing], Sept. 22, 1978, and by the New China News Agency [Beijing—hereafter NCNA], Sept. 13, 1978) evoked memories of Chen Yun's heralded visit to the Yugoslav party congress in the summer of 1956.

Chinese regard as Soviet extraterritorial rights;[6] the final Soviet refusal in 1959 to furnish atomic weapons to China; the devastating withdrawal of Soviet economic experts in 1960; the movement of large Soviet forces to the Chinese border to intimidate China in the mid-1960's; and the use of some of these forces to defeat and humiliate China at Damanskiy (Zhenbao) Island in 1969. One could add to this list innumerable smaller instances of what the Chinese view as past Soviet efforts to bully China and what the Chinese remember as specific Soviet betrayals of Chinese national interests in the way in which the USSR dealt with third parties—for example, in the Taiwan Strait crisis of 1958 and in the growing Sino-Indian conflict in 1959-60.

All of these events are likely to be resented by the great majority of Chinese who recall them. Such resentments will tend to merge with older resentments over matters such as the Comintern's mismanagement of the Chinese revolution in the 1920's and 1930's, the Soviet army's despoiling of Manchuria after World War II, and Stalin's extraction of extraterritorial concessions from Mao in 1950. And for some present Chinese leaders, these generally shared grievances will be augmented by many other past Soviet offenses, such as the attempts over the years to interfere in Chinese party affairs.

This combination of resentments will almost certainly have an important impact on Chinese behavior for a long time to come. Nevertheless, it seems unlikely to be enough to keep Chinese antipathy toward the Soviet Union at past intensity unless past grievances are reinforced by fresh ones.

THE ONGOING GEOPOLITICAL STRUGGLE

The third and by far the most important factor promoting continued Chinese hostility toward the Soviets is Beijing's sense that China confronts and must respond to an ongoing, long-term Soviet effort, not only political but to some extent military, to "encircle" it in the world and in Asia. The genesis and evolution of this geopolitical struggle are worth examining in some detail.

Over the last decade, the central reality of Chinese foreign policy has been Beijing's attempts to reach out into the world—particularly the bourgeois world—to build political bulwarks against the Soviet Union and constraints against the expansion of Soviet influence. This focus was imparted to

---

6. *Renmin Ribao-Hong Qi* (Beijing), joint editorial, Sept. 6, 1963. Also, Mainichi News Service (Tokyo), Jan. 26, 1972, quoting statements made by Chinese officials to a visiting Japanese delegation, spoke of Soviet demands for (a) a Sino-Soviet military radio system in China, with majority control vested in the Soviet Union, and (b) a combined naval squadron. An article by China's Minister of National Defense in July 1978 referred explicitly to this "malicious" Khrushchev proposal to "establish a 'joint fleet' and a 'long wave radio station' in China." See Xu Xiangqian, "Heighten Vigilance, Be Ready to Fight," *Hong Qi*, No. 8, 1978, as reported by NCNA, July 30, 1978.

Chinese policy in the first instance by the traumatic cumulative effects of the Soviet invasion of Czechoslovakia in 1968 and the clashes between the USSR and China on their mutual border one year later. By dramatizing the USSR as a concrete threat to China, these events enabled Zhou Enlai to persuade Mao that the isolation that China had enforced upon itself during the Cultural Revolution had become a dangerous liability. As time went on, this impulse to action imparted by the sense of a specific military threat from the Soviet Union was increasingly supplemented—although not supplanted— by a Chinese perception that the USSR posed a broad-gauged geopolitical threat to Chinese interests. Beijing during the course of the 1970's argued with growing frequency that the Soviet Union had become the one aggressively expansive great power, a "social-imperialist" force intent upon incrementally widening its political and military influence and presence everywhere in the world in "hegemonistic" fashion.

As will be recalled, China, under Zhou's guidance, responded by reassuming the role of a vigorous diplomatic competitor of the Soviet Union in the early 1970's—much to the chagrin of the Soviets, who had become accustomed to an absence of such competition during the Cultural Revolution.[7] "Chairman Mao's revolutionary diplomacy" emerged as a standard Chinese code-term for the process of normalization of relations with the United States and Japan, the multiplication of dealings with Western Europe, and the professed identification with Third World interests as well as cultivation of Third World governments. One common feature of all this activity was the effort to remind diverse audiences of their conflicts of interest with the Soviet Union and to persuade them to increase their resistance to what the Chinese portrayed as the advancing Soviet tide. In dealings with the West, this was summed up by the Chinese thesis that the Soviets were "feinting in the East" (i.e., toward China) while preparing to attack in the West.[8]

Since the death of Mao in September 1976, the Soviets have seen his heirs continue and significantly enlarge the scope of Zhou's diplomatic counteroffensive against them. In a number of regards—such as the rapprochement with Tito—the Chinese have displayed an increased tactical flexibility deriving from the removal of the constraints previously imposed by the presence in the Chinese leadership of the more dogmatic and ideologically oriented "gang of four," as well as by Chairman Mao himself.

The most significant fruits to date of this post-Mao effort came in the period between August and December 1978. It was during these five months that the Chinese, in startling succession, secured the signing of a Sino-

7. For a discussion of the Soviet reaction to this change and of the mounting Soviet disillusionment with Zhou, see H. Gelman, "The Sino-Soviet Conflict in Soviet Eyes," *Current History* (Philadephia, PA), October 1972.

8. Zhou Enlai formally launched this theme as authoritative doctrine in his 1973 report to the 10th Chinese Communist Party Congress, as conveyed by NCNA, Aug. 31, 1973.

Japanese Friendship Treaty with anti-Soviet overtones to which the USSR had long objected, asserted their political presence in Eastern Europe with a demonstrative and spectacular visit by Chairman Hua to Romania and Yugoslavia, and announced agreement on normalization of relations with the United States. In each succeeding case, the Soviets registered a cumulative resentment.

However, despite these 1978 achievements—which the Third Plenum of the 11th CCP Central Committee at the end of the year termed "important successes" in developing the "international united front against hegemonism"[9]—the Chinese have continued to convey the impression that overall they regard themselves as on the defensive against an adversary which, though it has suffered important specific setbacks, has succeeded in pressing forward at many points on the world scene. In the first place, the Chinese believe that the USSR has redoubled its efforts to constrain the scope, and even more the nature, of Western ties with China. The central thread of the unending Soviet diplomatic and propaganda campaign has been the contention that the capitalist industrial states have economic and security relations with the USSR which are more important than their existing and prospective relationships with China, and the suggestion that the former should inhibit the latter. Chinese reactions have sometimes implied concern that these efforts may not prove entirely without effect.[10]

Meanwhile, there is little doubt that the Chinese have remained impressed and deeply disturbed by the spectacular growth of the Soviet-Cuban military role and the rise of Soviet political influence in Africa since 1975. One by-product of the USSR's leapfrogging efforts to improve its position in Africa and weaken that of the West through participation in and assistance to selected armed struggles has been a diminution of Chinese influence in many places, because of China's inability to compete on the new scale. While Africa is surely not a vital Chinese interest, Beijing sees alarming signficance in this evidence of expanding Soviet capabilities for military intervention in the Third World.[11] Moscow's demonstration of its discovery of a new formula for more distant intervention—combining large-scale use of the USSR's logistical support capabilities, Soviet combat supervisors, and thousands of Cuban combat soldiers—has done much to reinforce the Chinese perception that the USSR has assumed what Beijing terms "an offensive posture" on the world scene.[12]

---

9. *Peking Review,* Dec. 29, 1978.

10. Thus, *Renmin Ribao,* Apr. 19, 1979, complained that the Soviets were "trying to blackmail the West...to prevent the West from developing economic relations and normal exchanges with China."

11. See, for example, "The Source of Disturbance in Africa," ibid., Mar. 1, 1978.

12. This reference to the Soviet "offensive posture" is a very common Chinese theme. For particularly broad-ranging Chinese assessments of that world "posture," see the Xu Xiangqian article previously cited (NCNA, July 30, 1978) and "Soviet Social-Imperialism—Most

This perception is also fed by what the Chinese view as other symptoms of the incremental growth of the USSR's political and military presence in the Third World. The Chinese point, in particular, to the 1978 coups staged by strongly pro-Soviet forces in South Yemen and Afghanistan as having improved preexisting Soviet footholds in the Arabian peninsula/Red Sea area, on the one hand, and in South Asia, on the other. While it is unclear to what extent the Chinese believe their unsupported assertions that the Soviets were responsible for both coups,[13] they undoubtedly do take it for granted that the Soviets will seek to build on these advances in each area to the degree that admittedly complex local circumstances permit. And while the Chinese have ardently welcomed the difficulties that the Soviets have encountered as a result of the civil war in Afghanistan, Beijing has continued to speak of Soviet intentions "to try to consolidate its acquired position... and to prepare to push further forward" to the south so as to "acquire an exit to the Indian Ocean."[14]

However, Soviet accomplishments in Indochina are without question the most disturbing recent development for Beijing. From the Chinese perspective, the Soviets, in the wake of the US departure from the peninsula in 1975, have successfully sought to exploit for Soviet benefit Vietnamese conflicts of interest with China which had been submerged while the US was present but which surfaced increasingly thereafter. While the roots of this Vietnamese-Chinese friction are many and in part long-standing, the most important proximate causes were the Vietnamese confrontation with a Cambodian regime allied to China and the Vietnamese resolve to bring in the Soviet Union as a countervailing force to neutralize China and thus enable Hanoi to have its way in all of Indochina. The Soviets have in consequence been able to harness to their own interests the Vietnamese ambition to dominate the entire peninsula. In return for indispensable services to an increasingly isolated Vietnam, they have obtained unprecedented local political and military advantages.

Two landmarks stand out in this process. The first was Vietnam's entry into the Council for Mutual Economic Assistance (CMEA) in June 1978, a formal avowal of economic alignment with the Soviet Union which followed three years of increasing tilt toward Soviet political positions and

---

Dangerous Source of World War," *Peking Review,* July 15, 1977. Both stress what they depict as a serious threat to China's security, as well as to the security of others.

13. See, for example, "Social Imperialist Strategy in Asia," *Beijing Review* (Beijing), Jan. 19, 1979.

14. Beijing Radio, May 8, 1979. The Chinese do not generally stress the fact that Afghanistan is a neighbor of China, or that the Sino-Soviet-Afghan trijunction in actuality adjoins the Soviet Pamir tract which has long been one of the areas at issue in the deadlocked Sino-Soviet border dispute. But these are obviously considerations for Beijing.

growing frigidity in Sino-Vietnamese relations.[15] The second was the signing of the Vietnamese-Soviet Treaty of Peace and Friendship in November of the same year. In retrospect, there appears little doubt that the Vietnamese regarded this document as an instrument for deterrence which would prepare the way for Hanoi to settle its Pol Pot problem once and for all. Thus, the treaty set the stage for the Vietnamese blitzkreig into Cambodia that began in late December.

It appears unlikely, under the circumstances, that the Soviets were surprised by this event, although neither Hanoi nor Moscow may have expected the subsequent Cambodian and Chinese responses. The emergence of prolonged Cambodian resistance to Vietnamese occupation, the intransigent Chinese reaction that became manifest in February 1979 with Beijing's effort to "teach Vietnam a lesson," the opening of what seem likely to prove fruitless and endless Sino-Vietnamese negotiations, and the acceleration of Vietnam's efforts to expel its ethnic Chinese minority have cumulatively created a situation of ongoing uncertainty, tension, and risk for all concerned, including the partners of the November 1978 pact.

Nevertheless, a geopolitical shift has occurred for the time being in the Far East which the Chinese seem to see to be largely, if not entirely, to China's detriment.[16] It is true that Beijing is likely to be gratified at the negative reactions of the members of the Association of Southeast Asian Nations (ASEAN) and of many other states to Vietnamese and Soviet behavior. On the other hand, these are likely to be considerably outweighed in Chinese eyes to Beijing's inability to halt Vietnam's endeavor to consolidate its hold on Indochina with Soviet assistance, by the fact that China for the indefinite future must now be concerned with two hostile frontiers,[17] and by the spectacle of Soviet warships at last in Cam Ranh Bay as the Chinese had so long publicly predicted and feared. In sum, there can hardly

15. Among many other things, the Chinese, whatever their misgivings, had felt obliged to render increasingly public support to Pol Pot in his three years of intransigent behavior on the Vietnamese-Cambodian border; Vietnam had compelled Laos to expel China's military road-builders long present in northwest Laos; China had formally renounced the last vestige of economic assistance to Vietnam; and an angry Sino-Vietnamese diplomatic confrontation has taken place over Vietnamese treatment of ethnic Chinese residents of Vietnam, foreshadowing the much broader international repercussions of Vietnamese expulsion of the "boat people" in 1979. It is also clear in retrospect from 1979 Vietnamese and Chinese statements that during the second half of 1978, as Vietnam moved still closer to the USSR and prepared to oust Pol Pot, both China and Vietnam adopted increasingly assertive postures in skirmishing on the border that separated the two countries.

16. NCNA on May 1, 1979, noted that "on March 3, *Pravda* gleefully announced that 'the balance of forces on the Asian continent has undergone a drastic change' and that 'all these countries [Vietnam, Laos, Kampuchea, and Afghanistan] have formed the principal factor for peace.'"

17. In his report to the National People's Congress on June 18, 1979, Premier Hua Guofeng said that "it is no secret to anyone as to who caused the deterioration of Sino-Soviet relations and where the threat along China's borders comes from." NCNA, June 25, 1979. Emphasis added. Use of the plural "borders" clearly was intended to include the southeastern border.

be a doubt that China views Soviet policy in Indochina as a genuine and irreconcilable challenge to Chinese national interests.

The Cuban-Soviet combination in Africa and the Vietnamese-Soviet efforts in Indochina appear to form a continuum in the Chinese mind. Besides reinforcing the image of broad Soviet outward pressure, these phenomena exacerbate Chinese concern about the growth of the influence of what Beijing perceives as Soviet proxies in the nonaligned movement.[18] At the same time, the Chinese profess concern that Vietnamese success, with Soviet help, in building a formal or tacit Indochinese federation may assist the USSR in reviving the notion of an Asian security system—which Beijing continues to regard as a transparent vehicle for legitimizing a Soviet relationship with China's neighbors to the detriment of Chinese influence.[19]

Finally, there is an additional factor that adds substance and endurance to all such Chinese worries about Soviet competitive activities in Asia and the Far East and makes it difficult for any Chinese government to contemplate a degree of "normalization" with Moscow which might imply acceptance of the legitimacy of those activities. This is the simple fact that the Soviet Union has a permanent territorial presence in the area. Whatever Asian setback the USSR might conceivably suffer in the future, China can never look forward to a time, however distant, when its Soviet competitor might depart. On the contrary, the economic and geopolitical weight that eastern Siberia and the Soviet Far East have in Asia can only be expected to grow in the years ahead, as high-priority Soviet investment continues there, as the second trans-Siberian rail line is completed, and as Soviet forces along the Chinese border are strengthened further. The Chinese must also

18. In the same report cited in fn. 17, Hua asserted that "a superpower has been doing its utmost to exert pressure on and split and undermine the non-aligned movement and change its political direction by machinations through one or two of its lackeys." Chinese propaganda in the spring of 1979 evidenced considerable concern about Cuban preparations for the non-aligned summit scheduled for Havana in September, and warned that Cuba would probably "engage in unscrupulous sabotage activities" at the summit on behalf of the Soviet Union (*Renmin Ribao*, May 18, 1979). At a UNESCO session in July 1979, according to NCNA, "the Vietnamese and Cuban observers, at Moscow's beck and call, took the floor one after the other" to attack Western and Chinese positions, and the Chinese representative replied that this was nothing strange, "because the are twin brothers reared by the same superpower to do mischief in the world" (NCNA, July 14, 1979).

19. The Chinese took particular note of the fact that when "on April 20, 1979, the Presidium of the Supreme Soviet...ratified the Soviet-Afghan treaty..., the Soviet leaders jumped at the chance to declare that the 'creation of an effective system of collective security in Asia ...has become of particular importance lately.'" NCNA suggested that the Soviets had become more active in trying "to breathe life into a particularly dead scheme" in part because of recent events in Southeast Asia (NCNA, May 1, 1979). Prior to the Sino-Vietnamese fighting in early 1979, in the view of *Renmin Ribao*, the USSR had "vainly attempted to push Vietnam as a Trojan Horse into ASEAN in an attempt to drag the ASEAN countries into a so-called 'Asian security system'..." (*Renmin Ribao*, June 22, 1979). More recently, according to statements by Vice Premier Li Xiannian to Japanese journalists, Vietnam's military actions have been designed to make the Indochinese federation a reality, and this federation in turn "is part of the Asian security system that the USSR is attempting to establish" (*Yomiuri Shimbun* [Tokyo], Mar. 5, 1979).

expect the deployment of additional Soviet naval units to Vladivostok and the Far East on a permanent basis with the increasing economic importance of the area, the progress of Soviet naval construction programs, and, perhaps most important, the increasing use of the Far East fleet as one of the sources of support for Soviet political ambitions in Asia. The last consideration has been made vivid for the Chinese by the movement of Soviet naval forces to the South China Sea during and since the Sino-Vietnamese fighting of February 1979.[20]

The Two Main Bilateral Issues

Against this background of contention across a broad geographical canvas, two issues stand out as the most serious tests of the effects of the external contest upon the bilateral relationship. One is the border question; the other is the nature of economic interaction between Moscow and Beijing. How far has improvement been inhibited in each of these areas to date, and why?

THE BORDER

The impasse here is at one and the same time the leading symbol, central issue, and prime hostage of the frozen relationship. The border question has evolved above all as an instrument of Chinese political warfare against the Soviet Union, whose increasing use by Mao and his heirs since 1963-64 has reflected the growth of the underlying hostility. At the same time, it has over the years achieved a life of its own as an important additional stimulus and independent guarantor of that mutual hostility.

In the eyes of the Chinese, the border problem involves a set of specific distant and recent inequities perpetrated upon China by Russia and the USSR which could be glossed over in the case of a friend but cannot properly or safely be evaded in dealings with the prime antagonist. These border grievances, surfaced by the Chinese in 1963 and articulated at length since 1969, have by now become inextricably bound up in the Chinese perception

---

20. On May 23, 1979, it should be noted, Radio Beijing reminded its listeners that "when the guns roared on the border between China and Vietnam, Soviet warships became active and caused trouble in the Beibu Gulf to support Vietnam, the small hegemonist." This broadcast demanded that "more attention" be paid "to the fact that the Soviet Union and Vietnam are now preparing public opinion to accept the establishment of permanent Soviet military bases in Vietnam." The ultimate Soviet purpose, said the broadcast, was "to counter the United States, threaten Japan, control Southeast Asia and encircle China." Many Chinese articles in the spring of 1979 similarly rehearsed Western and Japanese press reports about Soviet naval and air use of facilities at Cam Ranh Bay and Danang, as well as accounts of the arrival of the Soviet aircraft carrier Minsk in the Far East at the end of its long, well publicized journey from the Mediterranean.

of the USSR as an implacable adversary with respect to a broad spectrum of Chinese interests.

The Soviets, for their part, have evidently seen the Chinese as insisting on specific prerequisites for a border settlement which, in the Soviet view, the Chinese must know are incompatible with vital Soviet national interests and which no Soviet leadership can ever grant.[21] The Soviet sense of the Chinese attitude has evidently in turn had operational significance for Soviet economic and military choices which impinge on the Chinese. Despite overwhelming Soviet military superiority and the caution the Chinese have seemingly displayed on the borders since 1969, the impasse appears to have fed Soviet concerns about the long-term vulnerability of the USSR's thinly-populated territory in eastern Siberia and the Far East. Such concerns seem to have been at least a factor in Soviet decisions regarding very large economic and strategic investments in the Far East like the second trans-Siberian railroad (BAM), and they have also prompted Moscow to continue to build up the already sizable Soviet land and naval combat forces in areas adjacent to China.

The Chinese, in turn, have long perceived these very large Soviet forces stationed along the borders and in Mongolia as intended, among other things, to influence the Chinese negotiating position through coercion. In February 1978, Hua Guofeng formalized an earlier Chinese demand that as one of the prerequisites to any general improvement in the relationship, the Soviets reduce their forces confronting China in Asia to the level of the early 1960's.[22] From the Soviet standpoint, however, this is apparently out of the question under present circumstances.

The scope of the Soviet dilemma can best be appreciated in a detailed review of the points at issue in the border negotiations. First, the Chinese have long made clear that the demand Hua enunciated in February 1978 for a general withdrawal of Soviet forces from the Chinese border and Mongolia was not part of the Chinese position in the border negotiations, but rather an additional general requirement for improvement of the relationship, superimposed on the requirement that a satisfactory border settlement be achieved. Second, it is equally clear from many Chinese statements that while the Chinese identify huge tracts of Soviet territory in the Far East which, according to the Chinese, were unfairly taken from China by Tsarist Russia in "unequal treaties during the 19th and early 20th centuries," the Chinese make no claim to any of this territory. The Chinese do, however, require that the Soviets formally acknowledge that the treaties in question were in fact "unequal."[23] This may be a major sticking point for the

---

21. *Izvestiya*, May 16, 1974, and *Pravda* (Moscow), Apr. 1, 1978, contain the most elaborate statements of this Soviet viewpoint and the Soviet versions of the facts reviewed below.

22. *Peking Review*, Mar. 10, 1978.

23. Chinese Foreign Ministry statement of Oct. 8, 1969 (NCNA, Oct. 8, 1969). This remains the most elaborate and authoritative statement of the Chinese position.

Soviets, but it is probably not the gravest problem.

The heart of the matter appears to be the Chinese contention that Tsarist Russia and the Soviet Union have at various times occupied and the USSR continues to hold certain additional Chinese territory not granted to Russia even by the "unequal" treaties. In practice, this seems to be primarily two areas: one in the west, a tract of some 20,000 square kilometers in the Pamirs in Soviet Central Asia, near the trijunction with Afghanistan; the other in the east, consisting of several hundred islands in the Ussuri and Amur border rivers. These areas are the territory China describes as "in dispute."[24] The Chinese demand that as a prerequisite to joint demarcation of an agreed border, both sides must first withdraw all forces from all the territory thus identified as in dispute. Since all such territory is in fact in the hands of the Soviet Union, this amounts, as the Soviets repeatedly complain, to a demand for a unilateral, prior Soviet military evacuation of all the areas and places the Chinese claim, before concrete negotiations can begin. Both Soviet and Chinese press accounts indicate that since the day the Sino-Soviet border talks began in Beijing in October 1969, the talks have been stalemated essentially on this preliminary question.[25]

The Soviets have in particular made it clear that they will never abandon, even momentarily, the large pair of islands at the confluence of the Amur and Ussuri which the Chinese call, collectively, Hei Xiazi, and which the Soviets name Tamarov and Bol'shoy Ussuriysk. As Neville Maxwell has observed, the Chinese hold that these islands lie on the Chinese side of the thalweg, the deepest portion of the main river channel, and hence should rightfully belong to China.[26]

Whatever the legal case, the Soviets have possession. As the Soviet press has pointedly noted, these islands lie immediately adjacent to the large city of Khabarovsk, through which passes the Trans-Siberian Railroad. Moreover, the island proved vital to the defense of the city against the Japanese in the 1930's, when "the sacred blood of Soviet people" was "many times shed on the islands." The Soviets therefore describe them publicly as the "suburbs" of Khabarovsk and supply elaborate detail on plans for economic investment there.[27] In sum, the message conveyed is that

24. Ibid.

25. The Chinese have for a decade contended that at the Zhou-Kosygin meeting in Beijing on Sept. 11, 1969, Aleksey Kosygin agreed to the Chinese demand for a preliminary accord on mutual withdrawal from all disputed areas prior to efforts to settle upon an agreed border. The Soviets have with equal vigor denied that Kosygin made any such oral stipulation.

26. Neville Maxwell, "Why the Russians Lifted the Blockade at Bear Island," *Foreign Affairs* (New York, NY), Fall 1978.

27. *Sovetskaya Rossiya* (Moscow), Aug. 2, 1970. Against this background, a further message about the Soviet attitude toward Hei Xiazi was conveyed by General Secretary Brezhnev's visit to Khabarovsk in April 1978, where he saw a military parade and delivered a speech emphasizing the need for strict vigilance (*The New York Times*, Apr. 10, 1978). The Chinese Minister of Defense reacted to these events by writing that Brezhnev had "personally sneaked into Siberia and the Soviet Far East to encourage the Soviet troops and issue war cries" (Xu Xiangqian, loc. cit.).

the inclusion of Hei Xiazi on the list of disputed areas which must all be evacuated prior to demarcation of the border is, as the Soviets see it, evidence of the intransigence of the Chinese position and a guarantee of continued stalemate.[28]

As a substitute for the preliminary pullback that the Chinese have been requesting, and as a response to the Chinese accusation that the Soviets, by refusing to move their troops, are seeking to negotiate behind an implicit threat to use force, the Soviets have repeatedly tried to get the Chinese to settle for a paper pledge of mutual good behavior. Such efforts took the form of an offer of a separate nonuse of force agreement in 1971, and a proposal for a separate nonagression pact in 1973. Both were publicized in 1974 to demonstrate the allegedly pacific nature of Soviet intentions and the opposite character of Chinese intentions.[29]

But, as Zhou Enlai stated publicly somewhat later, the Chinese had no interest in the USSR's "profuse talk about empty treaties on the non-use of force." They wanted concrete agreement on a troop pullback (although they would accept an empty pledge along with the pullback).[30] In private dealings with the USSR, according to the Soviets, the Chinese cited the 1950 Sino-Soviet treaty as rendering the new document proposed by the Soviets superfluous. However, as the Soviets tell it, when the USSR then asked China to reaffirm the continued validity of this treaty, the Chinese declined.[31] This byplay culminated in April 1979, when the Chinese finally announced formal abrogation of the 1950 treaty.

The sparring reconstructed here unfolded in the intermittent negotiations which have taken place since October 1969 at the vice foreign minister level in Beijing—negotiations led on the Soviet side by V.V. Kuznetov initially and by L.F. Il'ichëv since 1970. Ever since the positions of the two parties were staked out late in 1969, the pattern of the talks has remained a repetitious minuet. At intervals lengthening over the years, but averaging about once a year, the chief Soviet representative has returned to Beijing for a few weeks, evidently primarily to reevaluate the possibility that the Chinese might abandon the demand for a total Soviet pullback from all the disputed areas. Thus far, however, the Chinese have not budged.

THE ECONOMIC DIMENSION

The other central bilateral issue between the two powers over the years has been their economic relationship. Here neither the record of recent years nor immediate prospects are nearly as bleak as those pertaining to the

28. The question of navigation around Hei Xiazi is another matter. As we shall see, after years of stalemate there has been a compromise reached on this question without prejudice to the issue of sovereignty.

29. *Izvestiya*, May 16, 1974.

30. "Report to the Fourth National People's Congress," NCNA, Jan. 13, 1975.

31. *Izvestiya*, May 16, 1974.

border question. But despite a fairly steady improvement in trade turnover since the nadir at the opening of the 1970's, Sino-Soviet trade has to date remained a secondary—indeed, a fairly minor—factor in not only the overall foreign trade but also the internal economic life of both countries. The reasons for this state of affairs can be summarized as (a) politically generated constraints deriving from Chinese assessments of the record of past Soviet economic behavior and (b) Moscow's and Beijing's assumptions about their present objective economic interests.

As for the first set of considerations, one burden the Soviets must overcome is the memory of what happened in the summer of 1960, the watershed year in which the central Soviet role in Chinese modernization came to an end and the Sino-Soviet economic relationship began to disintegrate. At that time, it will be recalled, Khrushchev abruptly canceled almost all Soviet technical assistance to China and withdrew some 1,400 Soviet advisers and experts. Whatever the provocation the Chinese—in the Soviet view—may have given Khrushchev for this action, it was a violation of Soviet contractual obligations, and it dealt the Chinese economy a heavy blow whose effects were felt for many years afterward. Even if Chinese leaders do not believe their own suggestions that it was this Soviet action more than bad harvests and the mistakes of the Great Leap Forward that precipitated the depression of the Chinese economy in 1960-62, they are surely convinced that the Soviets greatly intensified China's difficulties in this period and beyond.

From this time onward, the Chinese have been obsessed with the conviction that they must never again allow the Soviet Union to achieve a position whereby it can use its economic relationship with China for political blackmail. In retrospect, the Chinese probably remember as humiliating the fright their dependence on the USSR caused them in 1960, when they were evidently very apprehensive lest the USSR follow up withdrawal of the experts by cutting off exports of petroleum, an item for which China then relied heavily upon the Soviet Union. The precedent of Stalin's economic boycott of Yugoslavia in the late 1940's was undoubtedly much on the Chinese mind at the time. Press reports of the period indicated that rationing and use of substitutes for petroleum immediately began in Chinese cities, and presumably there was crash stockpiling as well. Thereafter, the Chinese seem to have bent their efforts to reduce their petroleum dependence on the USSR as rapidly as possible. By 1965, they had achieved virtual self-sufficiency.

Past experiences have also evidently long colored Chinese attitudes on the question of whether to incur financial debts to the Soviet Union. For example, on a number of occasions Chinese leaders, including Zhou, have complained to visitors rather bitterly about the onerous burden that repaying the large credits for Soviet war matériel used by China during the Korean war had imposed.[32] The Chinese apparently thought of these credits as being in a different category from their other economic and military indebtedness to the Soviet Union and may possibly even have originally understood that they would not have to pay in full for the matériel. Soviet penuriousness over this matter was evidently one of the reasons China was determined to clear all its debts with the USSR as rapidly as possible and for all time. By 1965, the debts had been paid off, but the notion of accepting any new loans or credits from the Soviet Union remained anathema.

Meanwhile, against this background, the Soviets in recent years appear to have felt that a *fait accompli* was occurring in the orientation of the Chinese economy, that time was passing them by. In the years 1972-74, with the first great flourishing of Zhou Enlai's preferences regarding economic policy toward the industrialized capitalist world, the Chinese turned an important corner in a direction opposite to Soviet desires, by to a significant degree tying the Chinese economy to Western and Japanese inputs of technology. This trend, of course, received another strong push after the death of Mao in 1976 and the quick removal of those elements in the Chinese leadership which had been least enthusiastic about the economic engagement with the West. The "four modernizations" program of the late 1970's under Zhou's policy heirs has served to magnify each of the lines of foreign trade policy seen in the early 1970's: the massive purchase of plants and equipment from the capitalist world, the acquiescence to the presence of more Western and Japanese technicians, and the acceptance of longer-term credits.

To be sure, a substantial retrenchment of such external commitments did begin in China in the spring of 1979. This, however, was a natural consequence of the extraordinary overindulgence in foreign purchasing seen in 1977 and 1978, and of belated realization of the limits of China's ability to absorb Western technology rapidly. There is no evidence to date that the pause has in any way altered the central political fact that the "four modernizations" drive continues to move China progressively further away from China's past economic orientation toward the Soviet Union and into a

---

32. The Feb. 27, 1964 letter from the Chinese to the Soviet party said that "for many years we have been paying the principal and interest on these Soviet loans, which account for a considerable part of our yearly exports to the Soviet Union" (*Seven Letters...*). During the Cultural Revolution a Red-Guard-published chronology of the Sino-Soviet dispute apparently drawn from official sources alleged that Khrushchev in the summer of 1960, in addition to withdrawing the experts, had "called on China to repay all loans plus interest incurred during the Korean War." "Chronicle of Events in the Soviet Revisionist Campaign Against China," US Consulate General Hong Kong, *Current Background* (Hong Kong), No. 850, Apr. 3, 1968. If this allegation has any validity, it is possible that some Chinese payments had previously been deferred. In 1975, Zhou Enlai was reported to have told a senior Japanese visitor that Chinese economic progress had been seriously hampered by a Soviet "demand" for payment of 560 million new rubles, of which 62 percent was for Korean war expenses, 26 percent for economic aid, and 12 percent for plants and harbor facilities in Port Arthur. See *Mainchi Shimbun* (Tokyo), Feb. 6, 1975.

closer relationship with the world economic system, in which the USSR is a minor factor.[33]

Over the same period, Soviet bilateral trade with China, while increasing substantially from the nadir reached in 1970, has remained a relatively small factor in the trade turnover and economic calculations of both parties. Total Sino-Soviet exports and imports in recent years have accounted for about 2 percent of total Chinese foreign trade and a smaller portion of total Soviet foreign trade.[34] This state of affairs has been partly the result of the political factors enumerated above—especially China's evident unwillingness to accept any Soviet credits, whether tacit or explicit.[35] As a consequence of this Chinese attitude, the value of annual trade must be kept in rough balance and renegotiated every year. Thus, Soviet annual sales to China must perforce be limited to the negotiated value of those items that the Chinese are willing to sell to the USSR and that the Soviets are willing to accept in each 12-month period.

These political constraints, important as they are, have been reinforced by increasingly significant considerations of Chinese economic self-interest. Even if the Soviets could get around all of China's politically imposed inhibitions, they would still face the essential economic problem of finding Soviet goods which Beijing would judge competitive in quality with what the Chinese can now obtain in the West and Japan. In this regard, the USSR is likely to continue to be handicapped by its inferiority to the capitalist industrial states in most areas of high civilian technology. Furthermore, the Soviet and Chinese economies, although still at vastly different stages of development, have already become somewhat more competitive and less complementary than they once were. For example, whereas in 1963 Khrushchev could offer superior Soviet expertise for the development of the Chinese oil industry, today the Soviets have no such technical superiority over the Chinese in this field. Moreover, while China was formerly dependent upon the USSR for much of its petroleum, today both countries are oil exporters, and hence in a sense competitors. Similarly, China and the Soviet Union have become two of the world's largest importers of both Western grain and Western technology.

33. Vice Premier Yu Qiuli's report to the National People's congress on the 1979 economic plan, for example, called for US$12 billion in Chinese exports and US$15 billion in imports. These figures represented a 20 percent increase in exports and 40 percent increase in imports over 1978. Yu, furthermore, made clear that Western capital equipment would continue to play an important part in Chinese modernization, despite the adjustments in long-term economic plans. This "major policy decision" for the "energetic expansion of foreign trade" was coupled with a resolve to work to expand hard-currency earnings "by every possible means" (NCNA, June 28, 1979).

34. Richard E. Batsavage and John L. Davie, "China's International Trade and Finance," in US Congress, Joint Economic Committee, *Chinese Economy Post-Mao*, Vol. 1, Washington, DC, US Government Printing Office, 1978, pp. 715-16.

35. It should be pointed out that there is no evidence of Soviet renewal in the last few years of earlier proposals concerning credits. Moscow's present willingness to extend such credits for the sake of uncertain political benefits may be doubtful.

The net impression is that the objective import and export needs of both countries make their trading relationship with each other necessarily much less important than their respective relationships with the industrialized capitalist world. Each has appeared to feel that it has less to obtain from the other than it could get elsewhere.

These considerations do not mean that China will not seek a considerable expansion of existing economic relations with the USSR, if it can do so without yielding what Beijing considers unacceptable political concessions to Moscow. Other things being equal, the need, that the current Chinese "readjustment" emphasizes, to conserve hard currency tends to make increased barter trade with the Soviet Union seem more attractive, and the difficulties experienced in assimilating some advanced Western technology could, in principle, persuade the Chinese of the adequacy for their purposes of some cruder but simpler Soviet manufactures, even if these are not up to the world level.[36] Chinese tendencies to think along these lines may be encouraged by the eclecticism and pragmatism visible in Beijing's search for diverse contributions to its revised model of economic development. Some voices have even been heard asking why China should not draw on Soviet experience as well as that of others.[37]

For a variety of reasons, however, there will probably be firm limits on Chinese movement in this direction. As already noted, the Chinese have publicly indicated that the planned expansion of foreign trade under the new "readjustment" will continue to be oriented largely toward the West and Japan, with the aid of new, large, hard-currency credits.[38] On economic as well as political grounds, authoritative spokesmen have attacked the suitability of the Soviet economy as a model for the new, pragmatic China

36. *Renmin Ribao*, May 8, 1979, stated that "even advanced technology is relative; it changes with changing circumstances. We regard as advanced those things which conform to China's specific conditions, can solve problems and achieve economic results. We cannot afford to recklessly import advanced technology while disregarding actual conditions...Some enterprises are producing up-to-date products with machinery made in the 1940's or 1950's. This spirit is worth promoting."

37. A pro-Beijing publication in Hong Kong, possibly reflecting such attitudes in China, urged the Chinese to seek "to absorb some experience helpful to the four modernizations" from the Soviet Union, arguing that "we can draw from and exploit experiences regardless of whether they are those of our friends or our enemies." *Cheng Ming* (Hong Kong), May 1, 1979.

38. At the National People's Congress session in June 1979, Vice Minister of the State Planning Commission Gu Ming, in discussing the difference between the present "readjustment" and what had happened in 1962, observed that "at that time the Soviet Union perfidiously withdrew its experts, seriously damaging our national economy. Now the international situation is extremely favorable to us, because we implemented the line in foreign affairs formulated by Chairman Mao and Premier Zhou." Radio Beijing, June 20, 1979. The line in question, as mentioned earlier, was the multiplication of economic and other ties to the non-Soviet-dominated world.

in view of the Soviet economy's rigidity and overcentralization,[39] and they have emphasized distortions, dislocations, and shortages deriving from what the Chinese term the Soviet "militarization of the national economy."[40] The Chinese continue to excoriate Soviet trading practices vis-à-vis weaker trading partners. They depict the USSR as "desperately peddling its long-term cooperation programs to the developing countries" so as to exploit them by "selling technologically obsolete machinery and equipment...in exchange for major strategic raw materials."[41] They regularly denounce the Soviet economic relationship with Eastern Europe as calculated to strengthen dependence on the Soviet economy,[42] and they depict Soviet efforts to further the integration of CMEA-state economies as designed to promote "hegemony" in all its aspects, including military and ideological "integration" and the unification of foreign policies.[43]

These attitudes are probably genuine, because they are reinforced by long Chinese experience and bespeak a sensitivity about dependence on the Soviet Union which in all likelihood will persist. Accordingly, it is improbable that Beijing will soon change its position on those questions—such as the acceptance of Soviet credits—which in the past have been most closely associated in Chinese thinking with Soviet efforts to use political leverage. For this and other reasons, it also seems unlikely that the Soviets will be able to transcend a merely supplementary role in Chinese foreign trade for many years, even though substantial growth in Sino-Soviet trade turnover may take place over time. Meanwhile, the Chinese in 1979 appear to have begun to explore the practical limits of economic "normalization" with the Soviet Union, seeking to discover how far such normalization can in fact be pursued without the sacrifice of overriding Chinese political interests. This is part of the more general Chinese exploration of the tolerable limits of "normalization" which we will now consider.

39. Sun Yefang, the leading Soviet-trained economist purged during the Cultural Revolution and since rehabilitated, took this position in an article in the June 1979 issue of *Hong Qi*. He blamed the Soviet system for stifling the spread of technological innovation and called for more rapid replacement of the obsolete equipment imported in the past from the USSR. Other Chinese commentaries have cited Hungary, and to a lesser extent Yugoslavia, as more appropriate economic examples for China.

40. NCNA commentary, "Why Is the Soviet Union Short of Steel?" Apr. 21, 1979.

41. NCNA commentary, "Why Does the Soviet Union Want Long Term Cooperation with the Developing Countries?" Radio Beijing, May 24, 1979.

42. An NCNA commentary, May 7, 1979, examined in some detail the negative impact the freeze in the level of Soviet petroleum exports to Eastern Europe had had on the growth rates of five East European states. *Renmin Ribao*, May 27, 1979, discussed what it depicted as the depressing effects on the economies of manpower-short CMEA states of arrangements to send sizable numbers of workers to projects in the Soviet Union.

43. *Renmin Ribao*, Apr. 24, 1979.

Moderating Symbols and Symptom

Along with the other elements in Sino-Soviet interactions discussed so far, a faintly moderating undercurrent has been detectable in Chinese behavior toward the USSR since Mao's death. From the first months after Mao's disappearance, there have been a variety of published hints of a Chinese view that the extraordinary degree of tension in the bilateral relationship inherited from Mao is an anomaly in the total context of Chinese foreign policy and excessive to the tactical requirements of the ongoing struggle against the USSR. This has been reflected in the very selective reappearance, at long intervals, of symbols suggesting a desire to introduce civility into some aspects of the state-to-state relationship. Although the Chinese quickly rejected a Soviet overture after Mao's death for the resumption of the party-to-party contacts, broken since January 1966,[44] they almost simultaneously revived a formula not used in authoritative Chinese comments for two years, one which affirmed China's willingness to establish or develop relations with "all" countries on the basis of the five principles of peaceful coexistence.[45] A year later, in November 1977, it was publicly revealed that the Chinese Foreign Minister had visited the Soviet national day reception at the Soviet embassy in Beijing for the first time since 1966, while on the same day China invited some Soviet sinologists to visit the Chinese embassy in Moscow. In 1978, Beijing's Sino-Soviet Friendship Association was resuscitated, and for the first time in more than a decade it sent greetings to its Soviet counterpart on the November 1978 anniversary of the Bolshevik Revolution.[46]

Prior to 1979, however, there was only one substantive issue—and that a secondary matter—on which the new Chinese leadership diverged from Mao's tactics toward the USSR sufficiently to allow significant new movement. On this question—the matter of the passage of Chinese river traffic between the Amur and the Ussuri—a modest agreeent was reached in 1977 that apparently involved genuine mutual compromise, but without prejudice to the Chinese claim to Hei Xiazi.[47] Since then, as we have noted, the Chinese have continued to maintain their adamant demand in the border talks for a Soviet preliminary evacuation of Hei Xiazi, along with all other disputed areas.

It should again be stressed, moreover, that this one minor agreement and the few scattered symbols of civility appeared against a background of vehement ongoing mutual denunciation across a broad spectrum of issues. A

44. *The New York Times,* Sept. 15, 1976.

45. This formula was used in the address of China's UN representative in October 1976 (NCNA, Oct. 5, 1976) and in a Chinese announcement on foreign affairs a month later (NCNA, Nov. 2, 1976).

46. NCNA, Nov. 6, 1978.

47. See Maxwell, loc. cit.

month after the November 1977 invitation to the Soviet sinologists to visit the Chinese embassy, for example, *Hong Qi* published an article describing the new Soviet constitution as something "long and stinking" and as an instrument to strengthen "the fascist dictatorship" in the USSR.[48] An editorial article shortly thereafter in a Soviet journal apprised Soviet sinologists—some of whom, the article indicated, took a more optimistic view—of the official judgment that nothing had happened in Beijing to justify a change in Moscow's unrelenting hostile assessment of the Chinese scene.[49] This view can only have been strengthened by public Chinese rejection a few months later of the February 1978 Soviet proposals for talks on the principles of Sino-Soviet relations.

Nevertheless, a difference of view among Soviets as to prospects for some conciliation of China is likely to have persisted, fed by such phenomena as the increasing pragmatism of Chinese economic and social policy, the gradual disappearance of ideological rhetoric from the ongoing Chinese criticism of Soviet policy, and the rehabilitation of former Chinese officials —purged during the Cultural Revolution—who had been associated, under the vastly different circumstances that had prevailed 15 or 20 years earlier, with a more moderate view than Mao's of appropriate tactics toward the USSR.[50] The appearance in 1979 of Chinese proposals for an exploration of the possibility of "normalizing" relations with the Soviet Union is thus likely to have encouraged the view of some in Moscow that forces were stirring in the Chinese party that now might be willing to accept compromises with the USSR more far-reaching than the river navigation agreement.[51]

Subsequent Soviet conduct and remarks suggest, however, that many well-placed Soviets remained highly skeptical on the matter, that events have strengthened their skepticism, and that this skepticism has reinforced a Soviet inclination to give no ground. Formal Soviet statements, for example, have implied suspicion that the Chinese overtures are tactical expedients deriving primary from changing Chinese security needs as a result of the new situation in Indochina.[52]

48. *Hong Qi,* Dec. 5, 1977.

49. *Problemy Dal'nego Vostoka* (Moscow), December 1977.

50. One such recently rehabilitated figure, Wang Jiaxiang—now deceased—was in fact a former ambassador to the USSR and is of symbolic importance for having put forward a proposal in 1962 which specifically envisioned, among other things, conciliation of the USSR. The Chinese press article rehabilitating Wang in fact alluded to this proposal and defended Wang's right to have made it (but not the content of the proposal). See Zhu Zhongli, "Firmly Holding Premier Zhou's Concern for Comrade Wang Jiaxiang," *Gongren Ribao* (Beijing), Apr. 5, 1979.

51. Such a view may also have been encouraged by the publication of the previously mentioned article in a Hong Kong newspaper, which explicitly urged a conciliation of Moscow. *Cheng Ming,* May 1, 1979.

52. *Pravda* on July 11, 1979, asked whether the Chinese were seeking merely "talk about talks," and implied that China was attempting to drive a wedge between the USSR and Vietnam.

As noted earlier, the Sino-Vietnamese hostilities in February 1979 did indeed for the first time force the Chinese to weigh the possibility of a two-front military confrontation, even though the USSR took no action on its borders with China; and in the aftermath of these hostilities, the necessity to face a hostile military presence on two sides has become a semipermanent reality for Beijing. Under these circumstances, China might be thought to have acquired a new reason to seek some mechanism to reduce tensions with the USSR without sacrificing major substantive positions at issue with the Soviets, including especially the ongoing struggle over Indochina. Such an inclination might have been strengthened by the sobering experience of the PLA in dealing with Vietnam in February and by the equally sobering realization—as a result of the ongoing reexamination of China's economic tasks and priorities—that military modernization adequate to the new two-front challenge was going to take a very long time.

Accordingly, when the Chinese in April 1979 gave the USSR formal notice of abrogation of the long-dormant Sino-Soviet friendship treaty of 1950, [53] they simultaneously put forth a proposal for talks—outside of and parallel with the border negotiations—to address bilateral issues. In the ensuing weeks, this was gradually followed by some reduction in the volume of mutual polemics and by one peculiar exchange of esoteric and symbolic gestures by the two antagonists. On June 5, 1979, Radio Moscow broadcast in Chinese a recording of a nonpolemical statement prepared for Soviet radio by the Chinese delegate to an international coal-dressing conference being held in the Soviet Union. Three days later, *Pravda*—apparently to reciprocate for the preparation of the recording—published a two-paragraph nonpolemical account of an antipollution conference that had just been held in Beijing.

At the same time, however, as the prospective talks drew closer, the divergent objectives of the two sides began to emerge. The Soviets made it clear that they conceived the primary purpose of the talks as being the drawing up of a document to record the agreement of the sides on the general principles of a "normalized" relationship, as originally proposed by the USSR in early 1978 and rejected by the Chinese at that time. [54] According to the Western press, China, for its part, implied that some document might be possible and indicated a desire to have the talks result in improved economic, cultural, and scientific relations. [55] But the Chinese conveyed that, above all, they wished to use the talks as a vehicle to air all the concrete foreign policy grievances with the USSR which they lump under the heading

53. NCNA, Apr. 3, 1979. Before and after the signing of the Sino-Japanese Friendship Treaty, Deng Xiaoping had indicated to Japanese newsmen that the Sino-Soviet treaty—which singles out Japan as a prospective antagonist—would be abrogated. See, e.g., Kyodo News Service (Tokyo), Sept. 6, 1978.
54. Soviet Foreign Ministry Note, TASS, June 5, 1979.
55. AFP, May 9, 1979.

of "hegemony" and which we have discussed above.[56] Beijing no longer required prior Soviet cessation of specific "hegemonic" practices—e.g., the stationing of Soviet forces in Mongolia—as a prerequisite for holding such talks, as Premier Hua had in effect done in rejecting the original Soviet proposal for talks in 1978.[57] However, the Chinese made it clear that they would reiterate such demands at the talks, and they left it publicly ambiguous whether they would insist in the talks that the USSR commit itself to concessions of this magnitude as a prerequisite for the document the Soviets had in mind.[58]

Soviet suspicions that the Chinese might intend to ultimately take such a position were apparently intensified by a public exchange of statements in June. In a calculated riposte to the Chinese harping on the Soviet practice of "hegemony," the USSR specified, in a published note to Beijing, that the document envisaged should include a mutual pledge not to recognize "anyone's claims to...hegemony."[59] Alluding to this issue in his address to the Chinese National People's Congress two weeks later, Premier Hua asserted that such verbal statement could not change "the essence of the

56. In July, Vice Foreign Minister Han Nianiong was quoted by a Japanese interviewer as saying that "during the talks, there is a strong possibility China will bring up the issue of a Soviet military withdrawal from Mongolia" (*Mainichi Shimbun*, July 15, 1979). In August, Vice Premier Geng Biao was quoted in a similar interview as asserting that so long as the Soviet Union did not change its attitude toward the "hegemony" issue, the results of the talks would be "obvious" (*Yomiuri Shimbun*, Aug. 12, 1979). In late September, after the talks had begun, Vice Premier Gu Mu, when questioned at a press conference about the economic aspects of the negotiations, stated that "trade between the Soviet Union and China has been going on for years, but the main question [in the talks] is not trade....The basic problem is whether the Soviet Government will change its hegemonistic and expansionist activities in the world" (AFP in Hong Kong, Sept. 28, 1979).

57. For the Hua statement, see *Peking Review*, Mar. 10, 1978. In contrast to this statement, the proposal that the Chinese put forward in April 1979, at the same time that they gave notice of their intention to abrogate the 1950 treaty, did not raise the issue of withdrawal from Mongolia. See NCNA, Apr. 3, 1979.

58. The ambiguity in Chinese intentions with regard to this point, did not begin to fade until a month after the talks commenced. Deng Xiaoping was then asked by a Japanese interviewer if he did not think it would be better, "for the sake of the negotiations, first to sign a cultural exchange agreement, a technical agreement, and documents concerning state relations, and then to negotiate patiently on other difficult questions." Deng replied that "the Soviet side appears to think so; the Soviet Union tries to deceive world opinion by making the negotiations look as if they are progressing to a certain extent without resolving basic questions." But, added Deng, unless they resolve basic questions, the negotiations "are of no value at all." He went on to observe that the 1950 Sino-Soviet treaty had not been of much use, and to suggest that any new treaty with the USSR could be useful only after "obstacles between the two countries are truly removed" (*Asahi Shimbun* [Tokyo], Oct. 19, 1979). The implication of Deng's remarks was that all agreements and documents would have to wait upon the resolution of the "basic" issues China was raising in the talks. That those issues centered on Chinese demands regarding specific Soviet "hegemonistic" practices—such as the stationing of troops in Mongolia—was plain in the statements cited in fn. 58 above.

59. Soviet Foreign Ministry note, TASS, June 5, 1979.

matter," for "whether one was genuinely against hegemonism could be judged only by one's deeds." Furthermore, he went on, "no ambiguity could be tolerated" on the matter. The prospects for the Sino-Soviet talks, he said flatly, "depend on whether the Soviet Government makes a substantive change in its position."[60]

A few weeks later, a major *Pravda* article signed with the "Aleksandrov" pseudonym—used especially for authoritative pronouncements on China—wondered if Beijing was putting forward "preliminary condition" once more or attempting "to put pressure on the other side even before the start of the talks." The author also posed the question of whether China was interested primarily in "the fact of the talks" themselves or simply in using the talks to bring pressure upon Vietnam.[61] The Soviets are clearly highly defensive on this point, since the Vietnamese are likely to be deeply suspicious of any hint of a possible moderation of Sino-Soviet tensions while Hanoi-Beijing relations remain exacerbated and Sino-Vietnamese negotiations deadlocked, while Vietnam is fully extended in desperate struggle in Cambodia, and while Hanoi continues to be isolated and thus heavily dependent on the USSR internationally.[62]

Prospects

As of the fall of 1979, in sum, the probability of significant progress soon toward the normalization of Sino-Soviet bilateral relations seems modest at best because of constraining realities. In view of the long distance China and the Soviet Union have traveled since most of the newly rehabilitated Chinese officials last held office, and the thousand fronts on which their national interests have become engaged in the interim, evidence is still lacking to show the existence of strong sentiment in China favoring the major Chinese concessions that would be required to bridge the gap. Few Chinese of any background appear likely to be willing to yield those concrete Chinese interests—especially around China's periphery—that the expansion of Soviet activities and Soviet presence have challenged over the last 15 years.

60. NCNA, June 25, 1979.
61. *Pravda,* June 11, 1979.
62. The Vietnamese have repeatedly complained that China's use of "anti-hegemonism" in its proposals in the Sino-Vietnamese talks was designed "to deceive the world community" (Radio Hanoi, May 19, 1979). One of the Chinese proposals that is unpalatable to the Vietnamese but is likely to be reiterated to the Soviets, called on both sides to abjure granting military bases to outside powers or trying to secure bases on foreign soil (Han Nianlong's speech in Hanoi, NCNA, Apr. 26, 1979).

Therefore, the prospects are for what Vice Premier Li Xiannian warned in advance would be a long and "tough" negotiation.[63] It seems quite possible that the 1979 Sino-Soviet talks on the overall state of bilateral relations will evolve into another indefinitely protracted negotiation, which might proceed sporadically for years in parallel with the stalemated border talks. To be sure, a compromise that papers over basic differences and permits a modest expansion of bilateral dealings remains conceivable. But large and important steps toward rapprochement appear highly improbable for a long time because of the implausibility of Chinese or Soviet concessions involving important national interests. In short, the fundamental causes of antagonism seem unlikely to be modified.

63. Interview in *Newsweek* (New York, NY), July 16, 1979. Li earlier had stated that China had "no intention of changing even slightly its basic stance on international issues" in talking to the Soviets (Kyodo News Service, June 17, 1979). Deng Xiaoping had said he was pessimistic about improving relations with Moscow because the Soviets were "unlikely to give up their hegemonism and social imperialism" (ibid., May 16, 1979). PLA Deputy Chief of Staff Wu Xiquan told Japanese newsmen in July that "China will not appease but will frontally oppose the world hegemonism of the Soviet Union" (*Mainichi Shimbun,* July 15, 1979).

PART VI

Retrospect and Prospect:
Continuity and Change in the Nature and
Uses of Soviet Power

Predicting the future course of Soviet foreign policy has been a concern of statesmen, scholars, and media analysts for many decades. While some pundits have been correct in their prognostications, many more have been wrong. In the preceding sections of this book, various authors have presented arguments emphasizing the importance of one or more sets of factors (e.g., Communist ideology) that may explain events, phases, or trends in Soviet international behavior—for example, the origins of the Cold War, the nature of "peaceful coexistence," and Soviet relations with developing countries and other one-party socialist states.

In this concluding section, we present a series of essays addressing two major sets of issues: (1) the extent of continuity and change between Stalinist and post-Stalinist Soviet foreign policy, and (2) the relative impact of internal and external factors on Soviet international behavior. A careful analysis of these issues will provide the reader with a fuller understanding of what we know and do not know about Soviet activities abroad, and why they may have been undertaken. This analysis may also help scholars and policymakers discern underlying patterns in Soviet thinking and behavior, and thereby anticipate and influence Soviet actions. But we do not claim to possess any secret formula that will enable one to predict Soviet initiatives and responses in the international arena in the months and years ahead. If anything, wisdom lies in a deeper appreciation of what we do not and cannot know.

Following the dictum that those who ignore the errors of the past are doomed to repeat them, many students of Soviet society have attempted to identify elements of continuity and change in the foreign policy of the USSR. Charles Gati, comparing the Stalinist and post-Stalinist periods, concludes that the elements of continuity are much more significant than the elements of change. In Gati's view, Soviet Russia is a pragmatic and cautious power that has, since its inception in 1917, pursued both the competitive and cooperative aspects of peaceful coexistence and detente. Gati affirms: "If there has been a basic pattern in Soviet foreign policy from Lenin to Brezhnev, it is characterized by the persistent, though cautious, pursuit of opportunities abroad—'persistent' because the overall objective of advancing Soviet influence has not changed and 'cautious' because the Soviet leaders have sought to promote Soviet influence so gradually as to make strong and concerted Western countermeasures unjustifiable" (p. 662).

Gati acknowledges that there have been some important changes in the nature and scope of the issues and problems that Stalin's successors have had to deal with, and that the international system itself has changed considerably since World War II. But Gati argues that the opportunistic thrust of Soviet foreign policy has not changed much at all since the time of Lenin and Stalin. That is, Khrushchev and Brezhnev have skillfully adapted the fundamental aims and components of Leninist and Stalinist strategies to new international circumstances and to new Soviet capabilities. Gati concludes that "Stalin's foreign policy was less aggressive and revolutionary than is commonly assumed; that his successors' foreign policy has been more aggressive and revolutionary than is commonly assumed; and therefore that there has been more continuity in the conduct of Soviet foreign policy than is commonly assumed" (p. 646).

William Zimmerman directly challenges this view. He contends that since the death of Stalin there have been important changes in the *substance* of Soviet foreign policy, and in the *processes* by which it has been made and carried out. While Gati affirms that Soviet international behavior is a "mix of assertiveness and accommodation," Zimmerman finds this characterization to be of little use in analyzing continuity and change. Zimmerman maintains that Gati's argument is so general that it fails to recognize the shifts in emphasis between competition and cooperation, and that it obscures some fundamental changes in Soviet motivations, perspectives, and behavior during the Khrushchev and Brezhnev periods. Hence, Zimmerman concludes that change rather than continuity has been the hallmark of post-Stalin foreign policy.

All of the authors in this section identify and assess the importance of various internal and external influences on Soviet foreign policy. For example, Gati examines three *internal* factors that shape Soviet policy and behavior: (1) "the substantially increased relative power of the Soviet

Union since Stalin's time"; (2) "the apparent decline of ideological rigidity"; and (3) "the broadening of the decisionmaking process since Stalin, including the rise of elite factions and competing interests."

Analyzing the first factor, Gati argues that neither domestic weakness nor strength can be correlated with an assertive *or* an accommodative foreign policy. Assessing the second factor, he seriously questions whether a dogmatic ideological environment will necessarily lead to foreign policy assertiveness, and whether a decline in ideological zeal will lead to foreign policy accommodation. As for the third factor, Gati maintains that we simply cannot assume that fewer Soviet decisionmakers with limited knowledge of international life will produce an assertive foreign policy. Nor can we infer that a broadening of the decisionmaking process and its informational base will produce an accommodative policy. Hence, Gati concludes that there is insufficient evidence to support generalizations about the domestic influences on the foreign policy of the USSR.

In contrast, Zimmerman finds at least one major area in which there is a probable linkage between the Soviet policymaking process and Soviet international behavior. Zimmerman emphasizes that there has been a dramatic increase in both the quantity and quality of Soviet research on foreign affairs since 1956. Newly established organizations, the most prominent of which are the Institute of the World Economy and International Relations and the Institute of the United States and Canada, have conducted many policy-relevant studies of international politics and economics. Zimmerman views this increased research capacity as a major "structural adaptation" in the USSR, based on Khrushchev's and Brezhnev's recognition that "Stalin's policies were inadequate partly because they were uninformed," and that "low-information systems are low-performance systems" (p. 668). Indeed, the contemporary Soviet leaders are gathering vastly greater information about the outside world than did Stalin, and this information is being utilized in the formulation and implementation of foreign policy.

But for what *purposes* is this information being used, and what *effects* is it having on the thinking and behavior of the Soviet leadership? These are the key questions. Zimmerman believes that the greater knowledge and sophistication of Soviet officials are reshaping their "psychological environment" (see the diagram on page 8), and that these evolving elite values, attitudes, and images may, in turn, be having a moderating influence on Soviet policy and behavior. For example, Zimmerman would probably maintain that Khrushchev and Brezhnev placed much greater emphasis on East-West cooperation and interdependence than did Stalin, and that Khrushchev's and especially Brezhnev's informed and differentiated perspectives on the Third World helped to produce many diplomatic and economic ties where none existed previously (see chapters 21 and 24).

Gati, Alexander Dallin (see chapter 3), and others would agree that Soviet foreign policy is now based on significantly more and better information about international relations and about the domestic politics, economies, and social life of other nations. Gati would be likely to argue, however, that institutional changes in a political system do not necessarily produce changes in the attitudes and behavior of its leaders, let alone attitudinal and behavioral changes of a conciliatory or cooperative nature in foreign policy. And Gati would conclude that increased information about the external environment enhances the capability of a government to pursue either a more assertive *or* a more accommodative foreign policy. Furthermore, in the case of the Soviet Union, better policy-relevant informàtion has sometimes led to the irresponsible use of this greater power, as in Hungary in 1956, Cuba in 1962, Czechoslovakia in 1968, and various Third World countries in the 1970's.

The role of information in Soviet policymaking is important, because it can shed some light on the current Western debate about the extent to which the foreign policy of the USSR is and can be influenced by *external* factors. The Khrushchev and particularly the Brezhnev administrations have valued more timely and accurate information about the USSR's complex and changing international and domestic environments. But Gati criticizes Zimmerman's hypothesis that more sophisticated Soviet perspectives on world events will help to restrain the USSR's assertiveness, and that moderate Soviet international behavior can be encouraged by the diplomatic activities of Western nations, especially a "strong and reassuring," rather than a "weak and threatening," U.S. posture toward the USSR. Gati argues that, while the West can alter Soviet policies in marginal ways, there is good reason "to be skeptical about the possibility of achieving 'a lasting adaptation' in Soviet foreign policy as a consequence of external influences." In his view, a more knowledgeable and experienced Soviet elite is likely to utilize these capabilities by taking advantage of economic and geopolitical opportunities in the international system.

Helmut Sonnenfeldt, the top Soviet specialist in the Nixon-Kissinger administration, would probably agree with at least part of Gati's conclusion. Sonnenfeldt contends that "experience does not bear out the hope that acts of American self-restraint induce reciprocal acts by the Soviets; on the contrary, they tend to make negotiations more difficult." For example, Sonnenfeldt maintains that "external powers, notably the United States, have had little ability to influence the growth of Soviet military power." Sonnenfeldt concludes that the drive to amass military power is a major element of continuity in the foreign policy of the USSR and "seems pervasive among the Soviet ruling elite regardless of generation."

At the same time, Sonnenfeldt is convinced that the United States can and must try to influence the role the USSR plays in the world. One thing American policies can do is to "maximize the restraints upon the uses of

Soviet power." Sonnenfeldt believes that the "gradual emergence of the USSR from isolation" is an important precondition for the greater impact of external factors on Soviet policy and actions. For example, the SALT negotiations may influence the *uses* of Soviet military power and, to a lesser extent, the nature and development of weapons technology (see chapter 22). Another important example is the formulation and implementation of a U.S. and West European "economic strategy that uses Soviet needs to draw the USSR into the disciplines of international economic life" (p. 729, see also chapter 23). Sonnenfeldt affirms that "it would be both desirable and feasible for Western nations to evolve harmonized concepts in [many] respects, with the goal of reducing the autarkic nature of Soviet economic decisionmaking and complicating Soviet resource choices" (p. 730).

Sonnenfeldt maintains that there are at least seven specific issue areas in which the external environment can have some effect on Soviet policy. All of these areas transcend territorial boundaries and must be reckoned with in Soviet policy calculations: (1) currency fluctuations and inflationary trends beyond Soviet borders, (2) global energy shortages and price rises, (3) the spread of nuclear weapons and nuclear manufacturing capabilities around the world, (4) the industrial and agricultural development of the oceans, (5) the exploration and commercial use of outer space, (6) the need to curb environmental pollution, and (7) international civil aviation.

Since the USSR is a major part of an increasingly interdependent world, all seven of these factors are bound to have an impact on Soviet foreign policy *and* on Soviet domestic development. Indeed, Sonnenfeldt concludes that "In these and other ways, the Soviet Union has slowly and often grudgingly accepted foreign constraints on its freedom of action" (p. 731).

Opportunity as well as adversity, and choice as well as circumstance, are increasingly compelling all industrialized nations to participate more actively in the international community. Robert Keohane and Joseph Nye, two American political scientists, suggest that a nation's *sensitivity* and *vulnerability* to external influences are very important dimensions of power and interdependence. "Sensitivity means liability to costly effects imposed from outside before policies are altered to try to change the situation. Vulnerability can be defined as an actor's liability to suffer costs imposed by external events even after policies have been altered....Sensitivity interdependence can be social or political as well as economic....The vulnerability dimension of interdependence rests on the relative availability and costliness of the alternatives that various actors face."[1] In other words, a nation's openness to external influences may be a strength or a weakness, and permeability does not necessarily produce malleability. Much depends

---

1. Robert Keohane and Joseph Nye, *Power and Interdependence: World Politics in Transition* (Boston: Little, Brown, 1977), pp. 13 ff.

on a country's capacity to respond purposefully and effectively to the constructive opportunities and problems posed by the international environment. Conversely, external forces may penetrate a closed society with great difficulty, but have a considerable impact when they do. In any case, criteria and standards for assessing the sensitivity and vulnerability of a nation are essential to understanding the influence of external factors on its domestic and foreign policies.

Robert Legvold develops these insights and suggests that a nation's power is "increasingly a matter of managing interdependence and, therefore, increasingly a matter of the structure and range of one's dependencies. To be positioned at the intersection of numerous and different forms of interdependence is power—unless too many of them are seriously unequal" (p. 679).

Legvold goes on to argue that the international setting has changed so much in the past three decades that the United States now finds itself in "a world in which fewer and fewer of our problems are caused by the Soviet Union or can be solved by it, save for the ultimate matter of nuclear war" (p. 674). Legvold identifies five major elements of change in the international system: (1) the transformation of alliances, (2) the exponential growth of interdependence, (3) the collapse of the old economic order and the challenges confronting a new one, (4) the regionalization of international politics, and (5) the changing strategic and conventional military balance between the two superpowers (pp. 676-77).

Of particular relevance to our present discussion are the second and third elements of change. Legvold, emphasizing the economic as well as the military dimensions of power, states that the increasingly interdependent world and the changing international economic order "have made the issue of national security far more complex than defending the integrity of one's territory and political values. Increasingly, the stake is also in the security of foreign markets and key resources, in the freedom from economically dislocating external price increases, and even in the success of other governments' domestic programs" (p. 676).

Legvold suggests that in the present international system "the Soviet-American rivalry has now evolved into something less intensive and something more extensive." Because of the USSR's greatly increased military capabilities and its growing economic needs, Party leaders in the 1970's and 1980's are shifting from a "preoccupation [with] the struggle to secure Soviet power against the external world to a quest for a larger place in it" (pp. 690-91). Also, "the elusiveness of opportunity in U.S.-USSR relations and "the distractions of multiple international challenges" have induced the Soviet leadership to focus its hopes and fears less on the United States and more on Western and Eastern Europe, China, and the Third World.

Vernon Aspaturian sees the USSR "increasingly drawn into the intersecting vortex of the various international environments in which it acts," and contends that Soviet policy will be more and more affected by external influences (pp. 697 ff.). But Aspaturian disagrees somewhat with Sonnenfeldt, Legvold, and others about the primary reasons for these developments and about the relative importance of specific external factors that shape Soviet behavior. Aspaturian views the mounting Soviet assertiveness in the Third World (especially in the 1970's) as largely the result of diminishing American power and the will to use that power. While Soviet military capabilities increased greatly in the 1960's and 1970's, the "withering" of American "global reflexes" made it possible for the USSR to *use* those capabilities to support pro-Russian elements in selected Third World countries.

Yet, Aspaturian argues that the currently low "costs" and "risks" of an assertive Soviet foreign policy do not make such a policy inevitable. Indeed he thinks these costs and risks will become much greater in the coming decades, increasing the possibility of moderation in Soviet foreign policy. Aspaturian observes that the changing international environment and internal economic difficulties present the USSR with a very important choice. Should the Party leadership "step up its militancy in foreign policy," or should it "reallocate priorities and pay greater attention to chronic and serious domestic problems, now that such a shift would not be at the expense of either lessened defense or a reduction of diplomatic gains" (p. 704)? On these and other key issues, top Soviet leaders have had differing views and will no doubt continue to have disagreements of varying intensity.

Sonnenfeldt stresses the importance of the domestic and international pressures on the USSR to participate responsibly in mutually advantageous economic, political, and arms limitation ties with the major Western industrialized states, including cooperative efforts to solve the global problems described above. But Sonnenfeldt, contending that American policies and diplomacy can have only marginal effects on Soviet behavior, implicitly affirms that the USSR's sensitivity to external factors is greater than its vulnerability. The diminishing ability of the United States to influence Soviet policies is largely the result of the growing economic and political power of Western Europe and Japan, of the multipolar nature of the present international system, and of the USSR's increasing military might.

In contrast, Aspaturian emphasizes the centrality of the U.S.-USSR relationship and the continuing ability of the two superpowers to influence one another and other nations by action and inaction. Aspaturian places particular stress on the strategic balance between the United States and the Soviet Union, which he views as "The single most important equation in the international community today...." Also, he observes that "One of the unnoticed by-products of Soviet-American global rivalry has been the increasingly interpenetrative character of Soviet-American relations, which can no longer be characterized as simply the intersection of foreign policy outputs. Both powers are intimately concerned and have become progressively implicated in the domestic affairs of one another and seek in diverse if unevenly effective ways to influence domestic events and conditions" (pp. 705-6). Aspaturian concludes: "The American domestic condition emerges as one of the most significant changes in the external environment, and appears to be having a fundamental impact on the perception of the Soviet leaders with respect to future Soviet behavior " (p. 704).

Our final three chapters describe the deterioration of U.S.-USSR relations in the mid- and late 1970's, and assess the interconnections between Soviet and Soviet-supported military activities in the Third World and East-West ties in the 1980's. Hedrick Smith raises a fundamental and long-debated question in Western academic and governmental circles: does the USSR seek to communize the world, using force, if necessary, to do so? As conservative Western analysts frequently remind us, no Soviet leader has ever explicitly renounced this Leninist goal. But Soviet actions, not rhetoric, should guide our judgment about the operative or inoperative nature of this time-honored ideological pronouncement.

Smith, for one, concludes that the new Soviet alliances and military involvement in Afghanistan, Angola, Ethiopia, South Yemen, Vietnam, Laos, and Cambodia (see chapter 25) do "not imply a grand design for world conquest but periodic, cold, hard decisions to seize upon targets of opportunity to push out imperially from the Russian heartland or to extend the Soviet reach as a global power—an increasing trend since the mid-1970's....Although there is no evidence that any Soviet master plan lies behind these events, power has a way of creating its own opportunities" (pp. 738, 740).

In our next to last chapter, Sonnenfeldt views the Soviet occupation of Afghanistan as an exceedingly dangerous and portentous event, because its consequences are not "limited in space and time." Afghanistan demonstrates that "The Soviets are in an expansionist—or imperialist—phase of their evolution," and that "They employ an ever-widening definition of their security interests." Sonnenfeldt stresses that the Party leadership must be made to recognize "the benefits of restraint." Soviet intervention in Afghanistan "tells us not so much that 'detente has failed' as that detente, meaning a relationship of mutual restraint in the pursuit of interests, does not automatically spring from good intentions, or fear of war, or economic necessities, or even intensified human contacts" (p. 753). Rather, the United States—in concert with the other major Western industrialized nations—must create and continuously maintain a flexible but integrated "combination of incentives for restrained international conduct and [of] disincentives, including the risk of military counteraction, for assertive and aggressive conduct.'' Sonnenfeldt argues that coordinated Western policies, especially economic sanctions and the credible threat of military reprisals to future acts of Soviet adventurism, are especially important means—perhaps the only possible means—to constrain the USSR's opportunistic international behavior as the 1980's begin.

Raymond Garthoff concludes our volume by suggesting that some kind of compromise between the different Soviet and American conceptions of detente is vastly preferable to a relationship marked by a high degree of confrontation, tension, and misunderstanding. Without trying to justify the Soviet occupation of Afghanistan, Garthoff rejects Sonnenfeldt's contention that the USSR's foreign policy is now in an expansionist or imperialist stage. Instead, Garthoff maintains that the Soviet leadership viewed the domestic conditions in Afghanistan in the late 1970's as a threat to the "vital interests" of the USSR, and that it chose a military response "with reluctance [and] after long consideration."

Most important, Garthoff argues that the reprehensible Soviet intervention in Afghanistan makes detente "more necessary than ever." "Should not actions which contravene detente be vigorously rebuffed, rather than jettisoning detente itself?" That is, should not a rise in international tensions spur, rather than diminish, Western attempts to reduce these tensions? Garthoff affirms that the United States and the whole world have "a very real and vital interest" in sustaining the principle that nations should not impose their will on others by force. And, in order to increase the likelihood that the USSR will not again violate this important principle, he maintains that positive inducements, as well as sanctions, should be used. Hence, Garthoff stresses that the reduction of international conflict and the control of the spiraling and potentially catastrophic arms race should be the paramount goals of Western foreign policies. Ineffective Western efforts to achieve these goals or the abandonment of such efforts "would serve the interests of no one and could jeopardize the interests of all."

Some Western observers conclude that the Soviet invasion of Afghanistan and the American response to it are ushering in "a new Cold War."[2] The Carter administration has indeed introduced a considerable militarization of thought and rhetoric. But both the substance and tone of this "new Cold War" have been rejected by our European allies, and by a major architect of President Carter's foreign policy, former Secretary of State Cyrus Vance.

We need only to observe the altered geopolitical situation to realize that the East-West confrontation of the late 1940's cannot be repeated in the

---

2. The remaining paragraphs of this introductory essay are drawn from the draft of a speech prepared by Robbin F. Laird and Erik P. Hoffmann for delivery by a Presidential candidate.

1980's. Postwar American foreign policy rested upon one overwhelmingly important factor: the predominance of the United States in the international arena. The Cold War years were dominated by American power and, for the most part, by American restraint. The Vietnam War was a later glaring exception, and it clearly demonstrated the limits of U.S. military influence.

Today, there is a much broader distribution of power among the nations of the world. The nature and uses of this power are also changing, as economic power becomes an increasingly significant means of exercising global influence. The decline of the American economy has been a principal cause of the erosion of U.S. power throughout the world. The economic capabilities of our allies now rival our own. Resource-rich countries of the Third World can increase their influence through collaborative efforts, as OPEC has convincingly shown. In short, we live in a world of interdependent nation-states, the vast majority of which are groping for world order and for orderly change.

The Soviet-American rivalry is increasingly shaped in the context of this interdependent world. While competition between the U.S. and the USSR will remain an inescapable element of the international system of the 1980's, to compete successfully with the Soviet Union, we must understand that we are living in a world that is rapidly changing. Our future relations with the USSR will be significantly influenced by the emergence of China as a global power, and by the mounting assertiveness of the West European countries and Japan, individually and collectively.

The strategic and conventional arms build-ups are particularly important dimensions of East-West competiton. The United States and other Western nations must be prepared to counter Soviet military power. But we must do so with the full realization that military might is not enough to deter adversaries, nor to give confidence to allies and the growing number of countries, North and South, that stand outside the East-West rivalry. The Soviet invasion of Afghanistan resembled the action of a nineteenth century imperialist power, and was recognized as such by virtually all of the nations of the world. By responding in kind—that is, by accepting the Soviet leaders' overly militaristic interpretation of national capabilities and national interests—we will imprison ourselves, as well, within the nineteenth century. The international realities of the past decades of the twentieth century, in particular the American experience in Vietnam, the changing world economy, and the growing economic and political power of Western Europe, Japan, and many Third World countries, dictate otherwise.

Given the increasing global interdependence and the opportunities for new forms of international competition and cooperation, U.S. government officials and citizens must continuously reassess the substance and processes of Soviet-American relations. The Soviet Union presents the United States and all Western nations with economic, military, and diplomatic challenges.

It is important that we better understand these challenges in order to define more clearly the national interests of the U.S., and to develop more appropriate responses to changing Soviet aims and capabilities. The U.S. need not respond to global trends as if every new development works to Soviet advantage. We are a superpower economically and militarily, whereas the USSR is a superpower only militarily. We must make renewed efforts to build upon *all* of our strengths—political, economic, military, and cultural —and thereby enhance our ability to compete and cooperate with the Soviet Union effectively and judiciously in the decades and century ahead.

The Stalinist Legacy in Soviet Foreign Policy *

Since Stalin's death in 1953, many Western students of Soviet foreign policy have tended to emphasize "change" rather than "continuity" in the international orientation of the Soviet Union—change for the better, evolution towards moderation and restraint. Their conclusion, it seems, is that Soviet foreign policy—responding both to a new external environment and to different internal circumstances—has successfully shed its Stalinist past. Having substantially reduced its revolutionary commitments, the Soviet Union is said to have begun to transform itself into an essentially status-quo power—steady and ambitious but not reckless, at times assertive but not adventurist, and invariably pragmatic. Not the aggressive revolutionary power it used to be and hence not unlike other major powers, the Soviet Union is thus seen as primarily, if not exclusively, interested in protecting its own security and achievements in an atmosphere of relative international stability.[1]

* ©1980 by Charles Gati. Also appears in Stephen F. Cohen, Alexander Rabinowitch, and Robert Sharlet (eds.), *The Soviet Union Since Stalin* (Bloomington, Indiana: Indiana University Press, 1980).
    1. As Robert C. Tucker has written, for example, the Soviet "commitment to world Communist revolution, while still intact ideologically, has become very weak as a political motivation and has ceased to be a mainspring of Soviet initiative in world affairs." See his "United States-Soviet Cooperation: Incentives and Obstacles," Chapter 17 above.

Is such a general appraisal of post-Stalin Soviet foreign policy—and the cautious optimism it has produced in the West—really warranted? Did de-Stalinization in foreign policy accompany Soviet domestic de-Stalinization? I think not. The year 1953, it seems, was not a watershed in Soviet foreign policy.[2] When post-Stalin Soviet foreign policy patterns are compared and contrasted with Stalinist behavior from 1928 to 1953, it appears to this writer that there was far more "continuity" than "change." As a basic approach to the outside world, Stalin's conduct of foreign policy was calculating and circumspect, and his historic mix of expansion and accommodation, or revolutionary assertiveness and peaceful coexistence, which served the Soviet state so well for so long, has remained deeply ingrained in the Soviet political mind. On balance, Stalin cannot be said to have placed more emphasis on revolution making than his successors have on upholding or maintaining the status quo. Essentially cautious and opportunistic, the Soviet leaders from Lenin to Brezhnev have displayed revolutionary assertiveness when and where it seemed safe to do so, while favoring the status quo and peaceful coexistence when and where it seemed necessary or useful to do so. All of them, and perhaps especially Stalin, consistently refused to risk the security of the Soviet Union for distant, revolutionary goals; after all, it was Stalin who as early as the mid-1920s had already advocated, and subsequently implemented, a largely inward-looking posture for the emerging Soviet state ("socialism in one country") against Trotsky's more radical, outward-looking alternative of "permanent revolution." Stated another way, Stalin's foreign policy—taken as a whole from 1928 to 1953—must be seen as conservative.

It is true, of course, that the *scope* of Soviet foreign policy has changed; Stalin did not develop a coherent policy towards the colonial areas of Asia and Africa, for example, while his successors have certainly done so towards what is now the Third World. It is also true that some of the *issues* on the Soviet agenda are new—such as the current preoccupation with and the management of nuclear weapon systems so destructive as to make wars more dangerous and the consequences of nuclear wars unthinkable. And it is true that it remained for Stalin's successors to cope with such *problems* as the rise of new communist party-states and to define the meaning of "socialist internationalism" and "international relations of a new type." Yet, important as some of these changes in the scope, issues, and problems of Soviet foreign policy may seem, they do not appear to be so far-reaching as to assume that Stalin himself could not or would not have made them. Indeed, if Stalin could now survey the achievements, strategies, and methods

2. Marshall D. Shulman was the first to call attention to "significant changes in [Soviet foreign policy] outlook and behavior which began to be manifested before the death of Stalin." *Stalin's Foreign Policy Reappraised* (New York: Atheneum, 1965).

of Soviet foreign policy since 1953, would he not endorse its general thrust, offering heartfelt congratulations to his successors for their skillful adaptation of his approach to new international circumstances?

Furthermore, even if one were inclined to dismiss as political rhetoric Khrushchev's own remark—to the effect that, when it comes to foreign policy towards the West, he and his colleagues did regard themselves as Stalinists[3]—the fact remains that Stalin's foreign policy has never been subjected to extensive criticism in the Soviet Union—not even during the height of the domestic de-Stalinization campaign in the mid-1950s. In point of fact, Stalin was criticized for only two foreign policy errors or shortcomings: the country's military unpreparedness on the eve of World War II and his unduly harsh, and ultimately counterproductive, treatment in 1948-49 of Marshal Tito's Yugoslavia (and, by implication, the rest of Eastern Europe). Compared to the charges leveled against him for his "crimes" in domestic affairs, Stalin's foreign policy record was not found wanting. He was not accused of excessive aggressiveness or adventurism, nor did his successors ever promise to de-Stalinize Soviet foreign policy and indeed place it on new foundations.

The reason for the apparent gap between the promise and early pursuit of domestic de-Stalinization on the one hand and the lack of de-Stalinization in foreign policy on the other is self-evident. While his successors believed that Stalin's domestic policies—particularly the intimidation and terror aimed against the Soviet elite—began to threaten the cause of socialism within the Soviet Union, his foreign policy record, by contrast, spoke well of Stalin's skills in promoting Soviet security and hence the cause of socialism abroad. After all, when Stalin became *primus inter pares* in 1928, the Soviet Union was weak and vulnerable, an essentially second-rate power; yet twenty-five years later, by 1953, it could claim to have become one of the two superpowers. His successors, having inherited a tested and successful approach to the outside world, had no reason either to criticize or to change the basic orientation of Stalin's foreign policy.

Thus, the central arguments of this essay are that Stalin's foreign policy was less aggressive and revolutionary than is commonly assumed; that his successors' foreign policy has been more aggressive and revolutionary than is commonly assumed; and therefore that there has been more continuity in the conduct of Soviet foreign policy than is commonly assumed.

---

3. Khrushchev was reported to have said, "The imperialists call us Stalinists. Well, when it comes to fighting imperialism, we are all Stalinists." Thomas Whitney, ed., *Khrushchev Speaks* (Ann Arbor: University of Michigan Press, 1963), p. 2.

Stalin's Foreign Policy Revisited

The emphasis in Western studies on "change" rather than "continuity" in Soviet foreign policy since 1953 stems in part from an undue emphasis on Stalin's foreign policy from the end of World War II to the Korean war. Admittedly, this was an era of expansion and unprecedented aggressiveness in the Soviet conduct of foreign relations, beginning with the imposition of Soviet domination on Eastern Europe, the provocation of the Berlin crisis of 1948-49, the unnecessary and avoidable conflict with Marshal Tito's Yugoslavia, all coupled with intransigent statements and undiplomatic posturing. While some of these policies were indicated by the geopolitical opportunity World War II had created, Stalin—no doubt dizzy with success—probably did push too hard during the early years of the Cold War. His aggressiveness provided glue for Western unity against the Soviet Union—as expressed by the Truman Doctrine, the establishment of NATO in 1949, and the consideration of such radical countermeasures as the use of atomic weapons against Moscow during the Berlin confrontation (recommended by Churchill, but quickly rejected by both the British and U.S. governments). To the extent that Stalin's postwar policies led to the mobilization of the West and the containment of further Soviet advances, therefore, these policies were not only unduly assertive, but—from the perspective of long-term Soviet interests—probably quite counterproductive.

It should be stressed, however, that aggressive Soviet behavior in the early Cold War years was only one aspect of the Stalinist pattern in foreign policy. Stalin was also at the helm when a pragmatic Soviet Union first sought to ally itself with Hitler's Nazi Germany and then ended up forming a grand coalition with such bastions of imperialism as England and the United States. Stalin was at the helm when communists fought shoulder to shoulder with noncommunists in the Spanish Civil War. Stalin was at the helm when, in the early 1930s, the Soviet Union concluded a number of treaties and cooperative agreements with such bourgeois states as France, Poland, Czechoslovakia, Finland, Estonia, and Latvia. Stalin was at the helm in 1935 when the Seventh Congress of the Communist International, reversing the dicta of the Comintern's 1928 Sixth Congress, issued a rather differentiated analysis of complex trends in the capitalist world—an analysis which justified the broad, flexible, coalition-seeking approach—the "Popular Front" strategy—adopted by communist parties everywhere. Stalin was at the helm when, throughout the 1930s, the Soviet Ministry of Foreign Affairs was headed by Maxim Litvinov, a cultivated man who knew how to treat Western diplomats and statesmen, disarming them with the kind of charm and eloquence such modern-day imitators as Foreign Minister Gromyko or Ambassador Dobrynin can only envy. And Stalin was at the helm when certain features of Marxist-Leninist ideology pertaining to international relations were repeatedly modified to accommodate the immediate foreign policy needs of the Soviet Union.

Stalin's thinking in nonideological, power-political terms—meaning that he recognized both the uses to which Soviet power could be put and the limitations of that power—was even demonstrated during the expansionary postwar era. A reluctant supporter of uncertain revolutionary causes abroad, Stalin denied extensive assistance not only to his comrades in the French Communist Party, but to Mao's revolutionary forces in the Chinese civil war as well. A master of *Realpolitik*, he wanted to be on the winning side and hence kept the door open to Mao's enemy, the Kuomintang's Chaing Kai-shek, as long as the outcome of the civil war was in doubt. Even in Eastern Europe, in the fall of 1945, when Stalin thought that he might need Western cooperation for the time being, he dramatically reversed previous decisions and as a gesture of goodwill ordered competitive elections in Bulgaria and then agreed to free elections in Hungary.[4] Moreover, and despite the apparent contradiction, at a time when Stalin was proceeding with the widespread purge of Jews in the Soviet Union, he was also supporting the Zionist cause for the establishment of a Jewish state in Palestine— no doubt calculating that such a state would weaken the British in the Middle East. And, finally, it was Stalin who around 1950 gave new emphasis to the old concept of "peaceful coexistence" and who subsequently initiated

---

4. Stalin's pragmatism in Bulgaria was witnessed by the British representative to the Allied Control Commission in Sofia:

In August, 1945, the Allied Control Commission in Bulgaria was discussing the advisability of the Bulgarians holding a general election on a single list. The British and American delegates on the Commission opposed a single list as being "undemocratic," while the Russians supported it as the only "democratic" method of holding an election. Since Stalin always worked at night, all other Soviet officials also had to work at night, so the sessions of the Commission began at 8:00 P.M. and lasted until 4:00 A.M. On this occasion the discussions started on a Wednesday evening and the elections were due to be held the following Sunday. The discussions on Wednesday, Thursday, and Friday proved fruitless, and we assembled again, much dispirited, on Saturday evening at 8:00 P.M. to listen once more to the Soviet argument in favor of a single list. The Russian side of the negotiations was conducted by the Soviet Commander in Chief in Bulgaria, Colonel-General (later Marshal of the Soviet Union) S.S. Biryuzov. He was obviously trying to drag out the discussions until the polling booths opened at 7:00 A.M. on Sunday morning so that nothing could be done about the matter, because the population would already be voting for or against the single list of candidates. But at 1:30 A.M. the telephone rang in the anteroom of the Russian general's office, and he sent his aide, a major, to answer it. When the major lifted the telephone to his ear, he stood there, as though struck dumb. The general thought his aide had become ill, so he strode over in a masterly fashion to the phone and seized it. Immediately he came smartly to attention, and stood upright for about five minutes while we could hear a voice crackling over the line. Then he said, "Yes, Comrade Stalin," and came back to us to declare: "As is well known, the Soviet government has always opposed the holding of general elections on a single list. The elections will be postponed until a more democratic method can be found." The Bulgarian prime minister was then sent for, told that the elections were to be put off, and the polling booths to be closed.

Malcolm Mackintosh, "Stalin's Policies towards Eastern Europe: The General Picture," in

the coalitionary "peace campaign" of the early 1950s.[5]

Although a brief summary of this kind cannot do justice to the complexities of Stalin's conduct of foreign affairs, it does suggest that Stalin was a rather cautious guardian of Soviet interests in international life. During his last years, as Adam Ulam notes, his policies "created an air of tension which, apart from being a source of danger to Russia, was largely unnecessary."[6] Moreover, the language he used to assess international developments and explain Soviet goals abroad contained more ideological referents than can be found in his successors' pronouncements. But Stalin's actual policies invariably reflected his sensitivity to the international balance of forces; as a result he made all the necessary compromises in order to gain time and hence, he thought, to gain strength.

The Sources of Soviet Conduct

Of all the contemporary explanations of the Stalinist pattern in Soviet foreign policy, George F. Kennan's 1947 "X" article turned out to be the most influential.[7] Dealing with the motivation—the issue that has always fascinated analysts of Soviet behavior—he identified the two main sources of Soviet conduct as Marxist-Leninist ideology and what he called the "circumstances of power" in the Soviet Union. Kennan, it will be recalled, found the Marxist view of capitalism and the Leninist view of imperialism quite germane to understanding and evaluating Soviet behavior abroad; he concluded that insofar as the Soviet leaders thought that capitalism contained the seeds of its own destruction and that imperialism would lead to war and revolution, they had to expect and promote the collapse of the noncommunist world. As to the "circumstances of power"—a struggling economy, succession problems, generational conflicts, and the like—their cumulative effect, Kennan thought, was a sense of insecurity which served to reinforce the leaders' ideological disposition to seek appropriate foreign outlets for their revolutionary zeal, beliefs, commitments, or goals.

While Kennan emphasized the internal sources of Soviet foreign policy, more recent analyses fall into two broad categories. "Microanalytic" studies, like Kennan's, stress the changing domestic environment of Soviet conduct; "macroanalytic" explanations emphasize the changing external environment as the primary factor in determining, and limiting, Soviet

---

Thomas T. Hammond, ed., *The Anatomy of Communist Takeovers* (New Haven: Yale University Press, 1975), pp. 229-43. (The quotation appears on pp. 239-40.)

5. See Shulman, *Stalin's Foreign Policy Reappraised.*

6. Adam B. Ulam, *Expansion and Co-existence* (New York: Praeger, 1968), p. 543.

7. X [George F. Kennan], "The Sources of Soviet Conduct," *Foreign Affairs,* 25, 4 (July 1947), pp. 566-82. For one of many critiques of Kennan's essay, see Charles Gati, "X Plus 25: What Containment Meant," *Foreign Policy,* 7 (Summer 1972), pp. 22-40.

behavior in international life.[8] As we shall see, both schools of thought have successfully identified a number of important changes in the "environments" of Soviet foreign policy. What remains unclear, however, is whether such "environmental changes"—the inputs into Soviet policy— have actually caused changes in the course of Soviet behavior itself. At issue, therefore, is the influence of the internal and external environment on policy.

Internal Influences on Soviet Foreign Policy

The *first*, and by far the most important, change in the internal environment of Soviet foreign policy has been the substantially increased relative power of the Soviet Union since Stalin's reign. Although its economy remains uneven and technologically quite inferior to that of the West, the diverse and steadily growing military capability of post-Stalin Russia testifies to its new status in world politics. If Stalin's foreign policy had in part stemmed from a sense of weakness and insecurity—from what Kennan had called the "circumstance of power"—what policy change would follow enhanced Soviet domestic strength?

To answer this question, one should assume for the moment that the Soviet leaders do feel confident about their achievements and that they therefore believe some or most of the self-congratulatory messages they so often deliver about the momentous successes of the Soviet state. Would it follow that the new Soviet leaders' confidence about internal strength should help them *overcome* their often-noted historic sense of inferiority vis-à-vis the outside world, especially the West? In policy terms, does it follow that their self-confidence about domestic strength would lead them to pursue a more accommodating foreign policy?

Alternatively, one may suppose that, despite their remarkable achievements, the post-Stalin leaders still lack sufficient confidence in the viability of the Soviet domestic order. Perhaps they measure their accomplishments against more ambitious ultimate objectives or against the

8. See Alexander Dallin, "Soviet Foreign Policy and Domestic Politics: A Framework for Analysis," Chapter 3 above; Alexander Dallin, "The Domestic Sources of Soviet Foreign Policy," in Seweryn Bialer, ed., *The Domestic Context of Soviet Foreign Policy* (Boulder: Westview Press, 1980); Morton Schwartz, *The Foreign Policy of the USSR: Domestic Factors* (Encino & Belmont, California: Dickenson Publishing Company, 1975); Marshall D. Shulman, "Toward a Western Philosophy of Coexistence," *Foreign Affairs,* 52, 1 (October 1973), pp. 35-58; William Zimmerman, "Elite Perspectives and the Explanation of Soviet Foreign Policy," Chapter 2 above; William Zimmerman, "Choices in the Postwar World: Containment and the Soviet Union," in Charles Gati, ed., *Caging the Bear: Containment and the Cold War* (Indianapolis: Bobbs-Merrill, 1974), pp. 85-108; Robert Legvold, "The Nature of Soviet Power," Chapter 34 below.

power of the United States, and thus find these accomplishments lacking. In that case, their self-congratulatory messages may be no more than New Year's resolutions—the sort of official optimism and wishful thinking so characteristic of political discourse everywhere. Would it follow then that the Soviet leaders' apparent lack of self-confidence about the internal health of the Soviet Union should *reinforce* their historic sense of inferiority vis-à-vis the outside world, especially the West? In policy terms, does it follow that such lack of self-confidence about domestic strength would prompt them to compensate for perceived weakness at home by pursuing an assertive or even aggressive foreign policy?

Because of the widespread belief that Stalin's putative "intransigence" stemmed from a desire to overcome domestic weakness and insecurity and because his successors' putative "moderation" is said to stem from the country's newly acquired domestic strength, the question goes to the heart of the controversy about "change" and "continuity" in Soviet foreign policy. Alas, the evidence—either about Stalin or his successors—is far from conclusive.

In his analysis of the interwar period—an era of considerable Soviet weakness, of course—Alexander Dallin, for example, at first offered this conclusion, suggesting that Soviet weakness led to accommodation: "More than once the response of the [weak] Soviet regime to potential foreign threats was one of reluctant accommodation, retrenchment, and even appeasement—from the treaties of Brest-Litovsk (1918) and Riga (1920) to the Litvinov Protocol and the effort to propitiate Japan in 1931-31....The reluctant alliance with France and Czechoslovakia in 1934-35 responded to a similar defensiveness born of a quest for time in which to improve the relative power position of the Soviet state." But in a carefully worded footnote, Dallin added this qualification: "It is well to note, however, that perceived weakness need not always produce a conciliatory mood in Moscow; nor does the willingness to seek a détente or compromise need to stem from weakness alone."[9] More recently, Dallin has reiterated his earlier observation ("...historically a good deal of Soviet policy in the early years of the regime can be shown to have been the product of keenly perceived inferiority compared to the 'capitalist' enviroment"), but he has come to reject more emphatically the "domestic-weakness-leads-to-foreign-policy-moderation" hypothesis: "It would be a serious error to equate weakness, as perceived in the Kremlin, with willingness to compromise or yield, and the perception of [domestic] strength with inflexibility or intransigence in Soviet foreign policy."[10] In Stalin's time, then, the relationship between real or perceived domestic weakness, on the one hand, and foreign policy accommodation, on the other, remains essentially unclear.

9. Dallin in Hoffmann and Fleron, pp. 41-42.
10. Dallin, "Domestic Sources."

As for the post-Stalin era, Morton Schwartz has explicitly identified the two contradictory interpretations. On the one hand, noting that Moscow's "greatly enhanced military power and prestige may tend to encourage a policy of increased assertiveness and even aggressiveness toward the outside world," he offers the following observation: "The USSR's recent achievements, therefore, may tend to reinforce Russia's historic sense of hostility toward the outside world, and lead to a more assertive policy, one which will now strive for a decisive shift in the world balance of forces. Convinced of their superiority—a conviction strengthened by their vast military power—the Kremlin leaders may be anxious to flex their new muscles. Thus, in the years ahead they may probe for ways to expand Soviet influence around the world." On the other hand, however, Schwartz seems to find the opposite interpretation somewhat more plausible: "The Kremlin leaders'...increased sense of physical security...will tend to reduce Soviet anxieties about the outside world. It also might, over time, exert a moderating influence on some of the historic traits—suspiciousness, nervous aggressiveness, xenophobia—which have made the USSR so difficult to deal with in the past. A secure Soviet leadership has already become a somewhat more relaxed Soviet leadership....To the extent such judgments can be accurately gauged, Russia seems to have overcome its historic sense of inferiority."[11]

These tentative and carefully worded analyses suggest that no causality can be documented, that none of the four possible hypotheses is necessarily valid:

Domestic weakness---------→ Foreign policy accommodation
Domestic weakness---------→ Foreign policy assertiveness
Domestic strength ---------→ Foreign policy accommodation
Domestic strength ---------→ Foreign policy assertiveness

If we could validate any of these hypotheses, the answer would have considerable implications for Western policy. It would indicate whether the West should try to encourage, or the extent it can, a strong and confident Soviet Union, or whether it should try to keep Moscow, to the extent it can, weak and uncertain of its relative power position. But since we do not have an answer, our advice about "keeping" Russia strong or weak has to be prudent and qualified. Perhaps the situation is analogous to child psychology, where it is assumed that (a) a child's *good* behavior may stem either from his self-confidence ("he is well-behaved because he feels confident about himself") or from his lack of such self-confidence ("he is well-behaved or meek because of his fear of retribution"), but it is also assumed that (b) a child's *bad* behavior may stem either from his self-confidence ("he is arrogant because he is over-confident") or from his lack of self-confidence ("he is arrogant because he is compensating for his insecurity").

11. Schwartz, pp. 89-91.

And so it is with the Soviet Union: we simply do not know the influence of its newly acquired domestic strength on Soviet foreign policy.

The *second* frequently discussed change in the post-Stalin domestic order has been the apparent decline of ideological rigidity. The reason given for a more pragmatic and more flexible Soviet approach to the outside world is that the new leaders did not experience the early, prerevolutionary days and that their "mind-set" was thus formed during the years of socialist construction. Party bureaucrats, managers, soldiers, and engineers, they have devoted their lives to the solution of practical tasks, not to the making of revolution. While they have certainly participated in political intrigues, most of them did not take part in prerevolutionary conspiracies.

Moreover, the new Soviet leaders have repeatedly modified Stalin's ideology of international affairs. Wars were once said to be inevitable; now they are not. Revolutions were also once said to be inevitable; now there is peaceful transition to socialism too. The international class struggle used to be the major dogma of foreign policy; now it receives less public emphasis than peaceful coexistence. Autarky was to exclude devious foreign influences; now it is the international division of labor and even interdependence that pave the road to socialism and communism. Automation used to show capitalist inhumanity; now computers (often imported) are the new signposts of the scientific-technological revolution. At Lenin's grave, Stalin pledged to uphold the sacred and unshakable unity of the international communist movement; now his successors have yet to find an ideologically adequate explanation for Soviet military contingency plans against China. To be an ideologist in Moscow today is like being a White House spokesman for Richard Nixon, with all the pleasure that can be derived from making yesterday's facts inoperative today.

Yet it remains doubtful whether Stalin's successors have actually been less influenced by ideological precepts than Stalin was supposed to have been. After all, ideological innovation and foreign policy flexibility, not doctrinal rigidity, were Stalin's traits, and his successors have only outperformed him in ideological gymnastics. But even if one were to assume otherwise, does the professed decline of ideological rigidity amount to flexibility, and then does more flexibility necessarily translate into an accommodating or moderate foreign policy? It may well be, instead, that neither of the two possible hypotheses is valid:

Rigid ideological environment $-- \longrightarrow$ Foreign policy assertiveness
Decline of ideological zeal $----- \longrightarrow$ Foreign policy accommodation

Without denying the steady erosion of faith since Lenin's days and the far-reaching, though only long-term, implications of this process for the future of Soviet political culture, what should be emphasized, therefore, is that the necessity of legitimizing every twist and turn in foreign policy by ideological incantation is hardly a novel phenomenon in Soviet history. After all, Stalin offered an equally eloquent ideological rationale for the "hard" line adopted in 1928 as for the "soft" line in 1935; his successors presented an ideological explanation for their 1968 military intervention in Czechoslovakia (the "Brezhnev Doctrine") and for their more recent détente policies toward the West ("peaceful coexistence").

Furthermore, consider the difference between Stalin and his successors with regard to the potentially most important ideological issue—the "inevitability of war" controversy. Given the unbridgeable antagonism between the forces of socialism and imperialism, Stalin saw no way to avoid either small or large confrontations between the two sides. In 1953-54, however, Malenkov revised Stalin's assessment, stating that—because of the destructive quality of atomic weapons and because of the increasing might of the Soviet Union—an all-out war with imperialism was no longer inevitable—it could be avoided. This was, and remains, good news, of course, but one must still observe that (1) Stalin's belief in the inevitability of war did not propel him to begin such wars (as he always sought to enhance Soviet power and influence gradually, indeed incrementally), and that (2) his successors have not, of course, denounced "small" or "just" wars: the so-called wars of national liberation (Cuba, Vietnam, Cambodia, etc.) and military intervention in their sphere (Hungary and Czechoslovakia).

In international life—where actions speak louder than words—it does not make much difference that Stalin professed to believe in (but did not start) an all-out confrontation with the West, while his successors neither profess to believe in nor have started such an all-out confrontation. It should also be recalled that the "peace campaign" began in the late 1940s at Stalin's initiative. In the final analysis, Malenkov's revision of Stalin's dogma merely signifies the acceptance of, and the concurrent ideological rationalization for, what Stalin had practiced. Moreover, the same can be said about other changes in the "ideological environment" of Soviet foreign policy since Stalin's time. After all, *Pravda* still holds, for example, that "there are essentially no neutrals in the struggle between the two world systems."[12] And according to the authoritative Soviet *Diplomatic Dictionary*, peaceful coexistence "is a specific form of class struggle between socialism and capitalism." *Plus ça change, plus c'est la même chose.*

The *third* change in the domestic environment of Soviet foreign policy has been identified as the broadening of the decision-making process since Stalin, including the rise of elite factions and competing interests. Vernon V. Aspaturian, for example, has noted that the armed forces, the managers of heavy industries, and party bureaucrats tend to benefit from and hence support a more aggressive Soviet foreign policy stance, while a number of

12. April 30, 1969.

other groups, elite and especially nonelite—such as the state bureaucracy; managers of light industries, consumer goods, and agriculture; cultural, professional, and scientific groups; and much of the population at large—tend to benefit from and hence support the relaxation of international tension.[13] As a minimum, we know enough to say that foreign policy alternatives are debated more openly among a wider circle of advisers and decision makers, and it is also quite likely that resource allocation between military and non-military uses is a particularly lively issue.[14]

Concurrently, the Soviet view of international life has become more differentiated. As William Zimmerman reminds us,[15] the field of international relations could develop only after Stalin's death, with specialists now covering all conceivable aspects of foreign-policy analysis and international-relations theory from the classical balance of power to simulation and beyond. As any recent visitor to the Institute on the USA and Canada or the Institute of World Economy can tell, a new generation of competent international relations specialists has been produced during the last two decades, who are no longer expected merely to supply such "information" as the leadership wants to hear and read. The more prestigious among them are surely heard, even if their influence is probably not much greater than that of Western academics on their governments.

The surfacing of a variety of interests and the apparent competition for resources and influence within the bureaucracy—combined with the availability of more knowledge about the outside world—strongly suggest a decision-making process characterized by compromises and political deals. Such compromises and deals at times may produce a "soft" line on foreign policy in exchange for a "hard" line on some domestic issue, while at other times it could be the other way around. (With respect to foreign policy alone, a "soft" line in one region of the world might necessitate a "hard" line in another.) Thus, speaking of the early 1970s, Marshall D. Shulman observed: "The net result of these conflicting domestic pressures has been that Brezhnev has won a free hand to implement his policy of 'peaceful coexistence' abroad, while the apparatus of orthodoxy and control has been given a free hand to tighten the lines of ideological vigilance at home and to prosecute the 'ideological struggle' between capitalism and Soviet socialism with renewed vigor."[16]

Once again, the controversial issue here is less the existence of such "con-

13. Aspaturian, "Internal Politics and Foreign Policy in the Soviet System," in Aspaturian, *Process and Power,* pp. 491-551.

14. For a dissenting view, see William E. Odom, "Who Controls Whom in Moscow," *Foreign Policy,* 19 (Summer 1975), pp. 109-23.

15. William Zimmerman, *Soviet Perspectives on International Relations, 1956-1967* (Princeton: Princeton University Press, 1969).

16. Marshall D. Shulman, "Trends in Soviet Foreign Policy," in Michael MacGwire, Ken Booth, and John McDonnell, eds., *Soviet Naval Policy* (New York: Praeger, 1975), pp. 8-10.

flicting domestic pressures" and factional political struggle (which had been particularly evident during the two succession crises of 1953-56 and 1964-68) than their consequence for foreign policy. For the apparent necessity of political deals and compromises in the Kremlin need not always lead to an accommodating foreign policy; the deal could also produce the opposite—"relaxation" at home and "vigilance" abroad. In other words, the mere existence of divergent interests, needs, views, perceptions, and approaches cannot be said to ensure any consistent pattern in Soviet foreign policy—conciliatory, centrist, or belligerent; the fact that competing interests have been compromised does not require a foreign policy of restraint.

Nor can one necessarily expect moderation from the post-Stalin foreign policy elite, even if it is better informed and more sophisticated. True, as Triska and Finley have shown, those in the elite who regularly deal with foreign policy use fewer ideological stereotypes when discussing international politics than do their colleagues whose primary preoccupation is party work or economic affairs.[17] But does more expertise mean more caution? Did the Soviet leaders establish large institutes and request more information on foreign policy in order to learn how to cope better with the outside world, or to learn how best to outmaneuver an increasingly complex outside world? Since we do not know how incoming information is processed, what the parameters of the policy debates are, and, in particular, what political benefits or penalties are derived from the transmittal of "bad news" and the offering of new ideas, it seems that we cannot be sure about the validity of any of the following hypotheses:

Narrow (Stalinist) decision making--------→ Foreign policy
                                                                        assertiveness
Broadening of decision-making process----→ Foreign policy
                                                                        accommodation
Limited knowledge of international life----→ Foreign policy
                                                                        assertiveness
Expanding knowledge of international life--→ Foreign policy
                                                                        accommodation

External Influences on Soviet Foreign Policy

The apparent lack of causality between domestic inputs and foreign policy makes it particularly apposite to explore the external environment of Soviet conduct. Is that environment, or could that environment be, a source of

17. Jan F. Triska and David D. Finley, *Soviet Foreign Policy* (New York: Macmillan, 1968), pp. 124-25.

change for the better in Soviet foreign policy?

To begin with a few simple assumptions, we may take it for granted that members of the international community engage in activities which have a bearing, direct or indirect, on the Soviet Union. States engage in generally self-serving activities: they do what is advantageous for their own interests (though not necessarily disadvantageous to the Soviet Union). Under all circumstances, however, given the military might, economic power, political influence, and global reach of the Soviet Union—in short, its preeminent position in the international system—most states have reason to seek to alter some aspect or feature of Soviet foreign policy. In turn, as the Soviet Union does not operate in a political, military, or economic vacuum, it has to respond to at least some of these attempts at influencing its behavior.[18]

The primary external demands on the Soviet Union are (1) for foreign policy "moderation" (i.e., demands on Moscow to help *maintain* the status quo by refraining from war and intervention) and (2) for "assistance" (i.e., demands to help *change* the status quo by extending political support, and economic as well as military aid). Since these two broad categories of demands are mutually exclusive, the Soviet Union—taking into account domestic needs, pressures, and preferences as well—must evaluate and respond to such contradictory external demands, trying to satisfy as many of its more important or more powerful foreign audiences and constituencies as possible. Should it endanger détente by transporting Cuban troops to Africa? Should it support the confrontationists or the moderates in the Middle East? Should it encourage, to the extent it can, the French Communist Party's drive for power, or should it acquiesce in the perpetuation of a French bourgeois government whose independent policies may exacerbate tension within NATO?

Such, we may presume, are Moscow's agonizing choices, with no option offering only benefits, and hence decisions have to be made in each case with due consideration of the likely costs and benefits. Simply stated, the Soviet Union is linked to too many external causes, issues, and audiences whose demands on and expectations of the Soviet Union greatly differ. To the extent that the Soviet Union has become a vital nexus in the international system and to the extent that the international system has become more complex and atomized, Moscow can satisfy some of these demands and expectations some of the time; it cannot satisfy all of them all of the time.

The international environment in which Soviet foreign policy operates has dramatically changed since Stalin's reign. The international communist movement has disintegrated. The communist bloc Stalin built after World

---

18. Like Shulman (note 2 above), William Zimmerman has emphasized the "reactive propensity" of the Soviet Union. For a full and by far the most discriminating treatment, see his chapter in Gati, *Caging the Bear*, pp. 85-108.

War II has all but ceased to act as a more or less united entity. Almost one hundred new, often radical states have been born, of which the resource-rich developing states have come to present a major challenge to the Western industrialized world. Interdependence is a new economic fact of international life. The "leading role" of the United States in the Atlantic alliance has eroded. Such issues as German reunification and the "liberation" of Eastern Europe are no longer on the Western agenda. The extraordinarily rapid modernization of weapon-systems, spearheaded by the United States, has led to fundamental revisions in the concepts and strategies of warfare.

These and many other developments signify the transformation of the international system since Stalin's time. Some of them—such as the development of new weapons—seem to constitute demands on Moscow for caution and accommodation; others—the rise of new states, for example—may mean opportunities for the expansion of Soviet influence. Considering, for the moment, only the more hopeful of these external influences—those which seem to call for Soviet "moderation"—it seems that the Soviet Union can respond to them in one of two ways. First, its responses can be a tactical reaction—an essentially limited adjustment to external demands. It is the well-known "one step backward," the postponement rather than the cancellation of policy implementation, a temporary concession whose primary purpose is to gain time. We need not concern ourselves very much with this type of response. It originated with Lenin, of course, and it has long been recognized as part of the repertoire of Soviet diplomacy.

The other kind of reaction, as Zimmerman suggests, is far more complex —and seldom recognized. It can begin, perhaps, as a tactical adjustment to international reality, but over time—if properly stimulated and reinforced —it would evolve towards and indeed transform itself into a *learned* response. Learning from the benefits of experience and subjected to carefully orchestrated external stimuli, the Soviet "organism" would thus become capable of genuine and presumably lasting, if not permanent, attitude-modification and "structural adaptation."[19] If the Soviet Union does have the capability of producing such a response, as Zimmerman argues, the implications would be far reaching indeed. It would signal a major opportunity—and responsibility—for the outside world to influence the outcome of debates within the Soviet foreign policy elite and to do so with the objective of contributing to durable change. The United States, for example, could act and speak in such a way as to reinforce the position of "moderates" in the Kremlin; we could attempt to show, by words and deeds, the benefits of détente and cooperation for both sides.

Zimmerman's intriguing hypothesis rests on his critique of American foreign policy toward the Soviet Union during the early years of the Cold

19. Ibid.

War. He argues that the United States was quite insensitive to foreign policy debates—the Varga debates—then taking place in the Kremlin, noting that Stalin's objectives were more fluid and tentative than we had assumed—including, until 1947, his plans for the "people's democracies" of Eastern Europe. But since the United States had assumed that Stalin was determined to establish satellite regimes in that region and then reach Western Europe as well, we responded by a policy of *threatening* military and political mobilization, as if the Soviet Union had no alternative but to do what it eventually did.* The inference to be drawn from Zimmerman's analysis is that if the West had only been less "threatening" and more "reassuring," postwar Soviet foreign policy might have been less assertive, more accommodating. Moreover, Stalin and his colleagues would have *learned* at that time that peaceful coexistence with the West was a genuine and rewarding option.

Putting aside the historical illustration, there is reason to be skeptical about the possibility of achieving "lasting adaptation" in Soviet foreign policy as a consequence of external influences. For one thing, there is the practical problem of policy coordination by the outside world. Neither now nor in the future can we expect to know the parameters of internal debates on foreign policy in the Kremlin. (Was the Varga debate, for example, about policy or timing?) But assuming that we could make a good guess at the choices discussed, can the outside world then coordinate its policies in such a way as to bring about the desired result? After all, while the United States is the most closely watched and surely the most important single external input, it is not the only one, and even if we could develop a set of finely tuned policies aimed at properly "educating" and influencing the Kremlin, wouldn't other foreign policies from other sources tend to cancel out or at least mitigate the impact of what we would be trying to accomplish?

Even more fundamental is the problem of conceiving the appropriate mix of external inputs. It is not at all clear whether the outside world should be or should appear to be weak or strong, reassuring or threatening, in order to generate "moderation" in Soviet foreign policy. Could Soviet strategic superiority, for example, help the Soviet leaders *overcome* their historic sense of inferiority vis-à-vis the West—a possibly valid but rather risky assumption—and thus produce a more accommodating Soviet foreign policy? Alternatively, should the United States aim at strategic superiority, following our long-held belief that only from a position of strength can we influence and moderate the Soviet Union? But if that approach only tends to *reinforce* a sense of inferiority in the Soviet leadership, wouldn't the concessions likely be only tactical or short lived?

*My own research essentially confirms Zimmerman's conclusion about the tentativeness of Stalin's goals, except that I find that Moscow's pre-1947 ambivalence applied probably to Hungary and definitely to Czechoslovakia rather than all of Eastern Europe.

Accordingly, unless we have some reasonably accurate assessment of the impact of external "strength" versus external "weakness" on the Soviet foreign policy debates—in other words, unless we know what combination of external incentives and prohibitions may pave the way to a lasting tendency towards foreign policy moderation—we cannot be confident about the international environment producing such moderation in Moscow. This is not to deny the import of what the non-Soviet world does or is, or how it goes about conducting its relations with the Soviet Union; it is only to suggest that external environmental influences entering into the calculations of the Soviet leadership will not by themselves generate enduring change in Soviet conduct. In the final analysis, it is not a set of often conflicting demands, conditions, or policy inputs that make for change; only *the balance of perceived needs* will do so: the Soviet leaders themselves must judge external developments to be such as to necessitate policy reassessment.

The Balance of Perceived Needs: Key to "Change"?

So far, this essay has focused on the *logic* of assigning change to Soviet foreign policy on the basis of analyzing the internal and external environments of Soviet conduct. Yet, fascinating as it is to speculate about changing influences on Soviet behavior, the proof of the pudding is not in the kitchen but in the eating, and hence the ultimate criterion by which a judgment can be rendered has to be the *record*—the output—of Soviet foreign policy itself.

Looking at the record, what "new departures" stand out in the history of Soviet foreign policy and how can we account for them?

(1) The Soviet Union discarded the early ideal of "revolutionary diplomacy" almost immediately after its establishment in 1917. Accepting the practice of what it had once regarded as "bourgeois" diplomatic intercourse with the outside world, the Soviet leaders promptly decided to enter into regular negotiations with other states and generally observe the diplomatic protocol. Mainly because of his desire to make peace with Germany and thus cement his shaky regime at home, Lenin did not hesitate to tell Trotsky that the very survival of the Soviet state required the adoption of "old" diplomatic practices.

(2) The Communist International's "exclusionary" strategy of the 1920s better known as the "United Front from below"—was replaced in the early 1930s by the "inclusionary" or Popular Front strategy. Sanctioned at the Soviet-dominated Seventh Comintern Congress in 1935, the new approach encouraged all Communist parties to cooperate with the noncommunist left in order to form a united front against the rise of fascism. Inherent in this fundamental shift was the danger of reducing the once-sacred

"leading role" and the ideological purity of Communist parties. Yet Stalin accepted the potential danger of ideological erosion by socialists, social democrats, and others because he assumed that only a broader left coalition could ensure the security of the Soviet Union and defeat the greater danger —Nazi Germany and its allies.

(3) Compared to the cautious, quasi-isolationist posture in the interwar period, Stalin initiated an expansionary phase in Soviet foreign policy after World War II. With the establishment of pro-Soviet regimes in Eastern Europe, "socialism in one country" gave way to "socialism in one region," as the prewar revolutionary rhetoric could now be translated into policy. As noted earlier, the change was due to the opportunity created by World War II and the lack of countervailing power in the international system.

(4) Around 1950-51, in the aftermath of the Berlin crisis and the Korean war, the confrontationist strategy of the postwar years was replaced by the peace campaign in Europe and the sudden opening to the Third World. Unable to break the European impasse and unwilling to risk a military showdown with the United States, Stalin—and subsequently his successors —shelved the rigid "two-camp" doctrine of 1946-47, resuscitated the "peaceful coexistence" line, and shifted to a rather low-key, low-tension policy towards the outside world. Clearly, the lesson of Berlin and Korea was that the confrontationist strategy had failed to advance Soviet interests and should therefore be modified. For years to come, the Soviet Union was to look beyond the old world for new gains, relying less on the military than on the economic instrument of foreign policy.

(5) Since the mid-1950s, Stalin's successors have come to accept, however grudgingly, a degree of experimentation in Eastern Europe. Khrushchev's overture to Tito in 1955 marked the beginning of greater Soviet tolerance towards national traditions and characteristics in Eastern Europe. Despite subsequent interventions aimed at curtailing far-reaching liberalization in the region, Stalin's insistence on strict uniformity was altered—no doubt because it had created chronic and dangerous instability.

(6) Having learned during the Cuban missile crisis that its inferior military posture vis-à-vis the United States had been a major political handicap, the Soviet Union initiated a massive program of military investments in the 1960s to catch up with, and possibly surpass, the United States in the arms race. An estimated 12 to 15 percent of the Soviet GNP has since been devoted to military procurements, presumably in order to avoid the kind of humiliation Moscow suffered in 1962.

These are among the more important new departures—some accommodating, some assertive in character—in the history of Soviet foreign policy. They suggest three conclusions.

The *first* is that in each case the Soviet leaders embarked on a new course either when the previous policy had failed to produce the desired end or when a new opportunity for the expansion of Soviet influence had presented itself. Irrespective of whether the new course was initiated under or after Stalin, it was usually the Soviet leaders' perception of policy failure that prompted the adoption of new approaches and solutions. In the case of Tito's rehabilitation in 1955, there was the additional factor of Khrushchev using the issue as part of his political struggle against those who, like Molotov and Malenkov, had been implicated in the early anti-Tito campaign under Stalin. On the whole, however, the perceived needs of the Soviet state rather than political infighting can be said to have produced new departures in Soviet conduct—traditional needs as intangible as security, power, influence, or prestige and as tangible as economic and military progress.

The *second* conclusion is that the record of Soviet foreign policy indicates tactical adjustments rather than lasting adaptations. While it may be premature to make a definitive judgment about the most recent period, it is quite clear that, as Zbigniew Brzezinski and others have noted, Soviet policy toward the outside world has been characterized by a cyclical pattern—"by alternating offensive and defensive phases."[20] On the same point, Henry Kissinger is worth quoting at greater length: "Peace offensives, of course, are not new in Soviet history. Peaceful coexistence has been avowed since the advent of Communism in Russia. It was stressed particularly between 1934-1939; between 1941-1946; at the time of the Geneva Summit Conference of 1955; again on the occasion of Khrushchev's visit to the United States in 1959; and following the Cuban Missile Crisis in 1962....On each occasion the period of relaxation ended when an opportunity for expanding Communism presented itself."[21] Given the cyclical pattern of the past, it would require excessive optimism, if not naiveté, to emphasize aspects of lasting change in Soviet foreign policy since Stalin.

Third, the record both under and after Stalin suggests neither a rigid "master plan" for global conquest nor a conservative policy aimed at the maintenance of the status quo. If there has been a basic pattern in Soviet foreign policy from Lenin to Brezhnev, it is characterized by the persistent, though cautious, pursuit of opportunities abroad—"persistent" because the overall objective of advancing Soviet influence has not changed and "cautious" because the Soviet leaders have sought to promote Soviet influence so gradually as to make strong and concerted Western countermeasures unjustifiable.

In the final analysis, post-Stalin Soviet foreign policy reflects a curious paradox. For while the internal and external environments in which it operates are different now, the Soviet leaders—under conflicting pressures

20. Zbigniew Brzezinski, "The Competitive Relationship," in ibid., pp. 157-99, esp. pp. 186-87.
21. Henry A. Kissinger, *The Troubled Partnership: A Reappraisal of the Atlantic Alliance* (Garden City: Doubleday Anchor Books, 1966), pp. 189-90.

and impulses and facing demands for both change and continuity—have nonetheless continued to rely on the old, historic mix of assertiveness-and-accommodation. Stalin's heirs must assume that this mix has served the Soviet Union well—that it has been a success, not a failure—and hence they perceive no need for the kind of change de-Stalinization has signified in the domestic realm.

The Soviet Union and the West:

A Critique of Gati *

One of the enduring preoccupations of students of Soviet foreign policy has been their emphasis on the theme of continuity and change. Charles Gati has aimed a number of broadsides, largely intended to assert that continuity with Stalin's foreign policy, rather than change, ought to be emphasized in assessing the quarter century since Stalin's death. Like most broadsides, some hit a target (though not necessarily the intended one), some fall short, and some explode in the cannon.

I believe the following is a fair characterization of Gati's position. First, elements about Soviet foreign policy in the 1960s and 1970s sometimes pointed to as distinctive turn out on several occasions to have had their counterpart during Stalin's rule. In other words, Stalin's foreign policy is closer to current Soviet foreign policy than is often assumed. Second, on reflection, Soviet foreign policy in the quarter century since Stalin's death has not been as different from Stalin's foreign policy as is commonly asserted. Current Soviet foreign policy, therefore, is closer to Stalin's foreign policy than is widely assumed. Third, because in fact there has not been as great a change as has sometimes been claimed, it is inappropriate to assume that there has been, or is likely to be, a change for the better in

* Reprinted from Stephen F. Cohen, Alexander Rabinowitch, and Robert Sharlet (eds.), *The Soviet Union Since Stalin* (Bloomington, Indiana: Indiana University Press, 1980), pp. 305-311, by permission of the author and the publisher.

Soviet foreign policy. Those who see a moderation in Soviet foreign policy over the past quarter century are thus in error.

Fourth, those students of Soviet foreign policy—and Gati includes me in this category—who argue that the United States should act to strengthen the hand of the moderates in the Soviet ruling group do not in practice have any substantive advice to give to American decision makers about how best to moderate Soviet behavior. In the brief commentary that follows, I will address each of these propositions.

On Reconsidering Soviet Foreign Policy and the Stalin Period

Some elements of continuity between Stalin's foreign policy and the contemporary foreign policy of the USSR should be emphasized. It is important, for example, to point out that Stalin was capable of remarkable ideological gymnastics and flexibility in foreign policy. It certainly bears stressing that Soviet foreign policy has always been typified by a tendency to minimize risk. It is also appropriate to stress that cavalier attitudes toward leaders of nonruling parties were characteristic of Stalin as well as his successors. "Proletarian internationalism" for Stalin, as for Brezhnev, have been code words for the primacy of the interests of the Soviet Union. Similarly, there is some validity to the argument, first made by Marshall Shulman, that Stalin's peace offensive was a harbinger of the post-Stalinist policy of peaceful coexistence. In this sense "post-Stalinist" foreign policy began while Stalin was living. And, one can argue, as I have elsewhere,[1] that there are many parallels between the perspectives on the West adopted by Khrushchev and his successors and those which were entertained by Eugen Varga and his colleagues in the last years of World War II and immediately afterward.

Even in view of these similarities, however, the distinctive features of Stalin's overall approach to international politics should be emphasized. Stalin viewed politics, especially international politics, almost exclusively in terms of mobilization—mobilization here having both political and military connotations. His world view was bi-polar, and he perceived international politics as a zero-sum game, in the spirit of the formula *kto-kogo*—who does in whom? For Stalin, capitalist encirclement was an attribute of international politics that was not altered by the security afforded by the communist takeovers in Eastern Europe and Asia after World War II. Being surrounded by countries "democratic and friendly to the Soviet Union" was not enough assurance for Stalin; in the last years of his life he considered capitalist encirclement a political, not a geographical, concept. (Capitalist encirclement, it should be remembered, served also to legitimate

---

1. Charles Gati, ed., *Caging the Bear* (New York: Bobbs Merrill, 1974), "Choices in the Post-War World." pp. 85-108.

the practice of "permanent purge," even as the USSR progressed toward communism.) Stalin persisted in believing in the inevitability of war between capitalist states. He placed great stock in economic autarky for the Soviet Union and regarded such a policy as essential to Soviet security. Finally, because of Stalin's absolute monopoly over the interpretation of doctrine, the possession of policy-relevant expertise by individuals was often dangerous.

Stalin's postures stand in stark contrast to the general outlook of his successors. The mobilization rhetoric—the vocabulary of "struggle," "front," "rotten compromise"—has been replaced by the rhetoric of "problems," "complexity," "reasonable compromise." The inevitability-of-war doctrine has been scrapped, as has the doctrine of capitalist encirclement. In light of these and other changes, a discussion of Stalin's ideological gymnastics which fails to note the dogmatisms to which he clung, and which his successors have systematically abandoned, is misleading. Similarly, it bears noting that Stalin's siege mentality, which manifested itself most clearly in his insistence on autarky, has been abandoned, even at a time when the capitalist world has shown, for the first time in a long while, the boom and bust characteristics that Marxists-Leninists have traditionally insisted are essential features of capitalism.

Finally, I am persuaded that the "post-Stalinist" features of Stalin's last years were largely not his doing but were the result of initiatives by others who were in direct challenge to Stalin. In 1952 Stalin was adamantly opposed to those in the Soviet Union who were advocating concessions to the West, and he reiterated the inevitability-of-war doctrine in his last major statement, *Economic Problems of Socialism in the USSR*, just prior to the Nineteenth Party Congress. At the Nineteenth Congress, however, Malenkov was careful to assert merely that the danger persisted that war *might* break out between capitalist states. It may be that the 1952 turn to the right was made in spite of Stalin rather than at his behest; if so, that may explain why, at the time of his death, Stalin was preparing another major purge, one victim of which almost certainly would have been Malenkov.

Post-Stalin Continuity in Soviet Foreign Policy?

With regard to Gati's second point, I am skeptical about the utility of describing the foreign policy of Stalin and his successors toward the West in more or less the same breath. To be told that one can describe Soviet foreign policy under Stalin and under his successors as a "mix of assertiveness and accommodation" is to be told very little. I seek from Gati a more substantive discussion of how the USSR's mix of assertiveness and accommodation under either Stalin or Brezhnev differentiates Soviet behavior from, for instance, American foreign policy under Roosevelt, Truman, Nixon, and

Carter, or German foreign policy under Hitler, Adenauer, Brandt, and Schmidt. At the same time, characterizing Brezhnev's, Khrushchev's, and Stalin's foreign policy as an undifferentiated mix of assertiveness and accommodation obscures differences in, for example, the nature of Soviet-American relations in 1950 and as we begin the 1980s.

"Peaceful coexistence" as practiced under Khrushchev and Brezhnev has been different from the Cold War. Peaceful coexistence entails a blend of cooperation and conflict, to be sure—"assertiveness and accommodation," perhaps—but to remind us of the persistence of U.S.-Soviet conflict is not the same as to assert a basic continuity of Soviet foreign policy under Stalin and his successors. Among the major features of Soviet-American relations twenty-five years after Stalin's death that distinguish them from relations in 1948-53 are the following. (1) While elites on each side regard the other side as expansionist, there is much less disposition to believe that the other side is bent on destroying its opponent. (2) Each side recognizes the importance of creating an environment in which the pursuit of narrow "possessive" interests can be undertaken at less risk. (3) The American-Soviet conflict has become routinized and expressed in ways that were inconceivable while Stalin lived.

By lumping Stalin's foreign policy and the foreign policy of his successors together, Gati has tended to obscure fundamental changes after 1953. Consider, for instance, two major turning points. In 1955 Khrushchev accomplished a major reorientation in Soviet foreign policy. The Soviet Union signed an Austrian State Treaty and pulled out of Austria; the Soviet leadership undertook a major expedition to Asia; relations with Finland were "normalized"; and the Soviet Union advanced a major disarmament proposal. Together, these developments represented a dramatic reversal in Soviet foreign policy. It strains credulity that Stalin would have undertaken this package of moves. Similarly, in the 1970s the USSR has made a commitment to participation in world trade, in sharp contrast to Stalin's autarky.

Measuring Moderation

If Soviet foreign policy has changed more than Gati suggests, then we must examine the nature of the change in Soviet behavior to assess whether it is in the direction of moderation. Two points are in order. First, moderation is a value-laden term; one might define moderation in such a way as to mean a situation, to recall an apt image by Walter Lippmann, in which Soviet children were born singing "God Bless America." Some critics of detente seem to imply this definition when they fault the Soviet Union for pursuing interests opposed to American or Western interests—for engaging in activities of any kind in Africa, for example. Second, moderation needs to be evaluated against capabilities and opportunities foregone as well as against past behavior. Immediately after World War II, the Soviet Union extracted immense resources from Eastern Europe. The Soviet Union took from Eastern Europe about as much as the United States, via the Marshall Plan, put into Western Europe.[2] By that standard, the USSR's behavior in Eastern Europe since the 1950s has certainly been more moderate. Even in the aftermath of the 1973 energy crisis, similarly, the USSR has shown its willingness to restrain its economic demands on the East European states in order to increase the political viability of the Warsaw Pact.

The difference between these standards of moderation should be kept in mind in thinking about U.S.-Soviet relations. The Soviet Union has become a world power in the last twenty-five years; it is no longer merely the continental power it was when Stalin died. As a result, Soviet interests and American interests now clash in places where there was little or no Soviet presence twenty-five years ago. In one sense this implies decreased moderation since Stalin's death. (Moreover, a somewhat more moderate but greatly more powerful Soviet Union might be said to constitute a greater threat to U.S. interests than did a more aggressive but weaker USSR in Stalin's time.) However, the fact that Soviet-American clashes tend to be over peripheral values, to involve conflicts between surrogates, and, often, to be played out in rather stylized ways suggests a considerable moderation in Soviet behavior from the days when "push to the limit" was offset by "know when to stop."

Influencing Soviet Adaptation

Can the West, and the United States in particular, influence Soviet behavior significantly so as to produce "structural adaptation"? On this score, Gati is skeptical. My own view is that there is much evidence that adaptation reflecting changes in values has occurred. There has been a genuine evolution of Soviet elite perspectives on the international system in the past twenty-five years.[3] If nothing else, as Gati has pointed out, the USSR has immensely increased its research capacity with respect to the outside world. This itself is a form of institutional adaptation—a recognition that Stalin's policies were inadequate partly because they were uninformed. The Soviet elite seems to have realized that low-information systems are low-performance systems. In general, much of Soviet behavior in the 1960s and 1970s suggests an analogy with the automobile industry: In a world where

2. Joint Economic Committee, 93rd Congress, 2nd Session, *Reorientation and Commercial Relations of the Economics of Eastern Europe* (Washington: Government Printing Office, 1974).

3. William Zimmerman, *Soviet Perspectives on International Relations, 1956-67* (Princeton: Princeton University Press, 1969).

the United States remains the General Motors of international politics, what is good enough for General Motors is often good enough for the Ford Motor Company of international politics, the USSR. This is not an argument that structural adaptation produces moderation, but merely that competition generates structural adaptation in order better to compete.

The somewhat tougher question, then, is whether in the 1980s the United States can do anything to moderate Soviet behavior. Again Gati is skeptical. He correctly points out there are various external factors which could influence Soviet behavior in different ways. (It is not, however, an assertion which effectively challenges an approach emphasizing macroanalytical variables.) One should bear in mind how difficult it is to induce desired behavior in rivals, allies, or even clients in the recalcitrant realm of world politics.

Nevertheless, something can be said about what kind of behavior by the United States is likely to elicit relatively more moderate Soviet behavior. Inadvertently, Gati provides some guidance on this score when he comments: "It is not at all clear whether the outside world should appear to be weak or strong, reassuring or threatening, to generate 'moderation' in Soviet foreign policy." I read the two pairs—weak-strong, reassuring-threatening—as different continua and not, as Gati seems to imply, more or less similar notions. In my estimations, the best American stance is one that is strong and reassuring; the least preferable American course is to act weak and threatening. In general, the United States should act to reinforce the views of those in the Soviet elite who are prone to emphasize the complexities and difficulties inherent in any effort to foster revolution, and who see that social and political progress is possible within capitalism. The United States should try to strengthen those in the USSR who believe that linkage to the international economic system constitutes an advantage for, not a threat to, Soviet interests. American elites should also be mindful of the role of style and timing in affecting Soviet behavior. There have been instances in recent years when American elites have behaved as if they failed to distinguish between acting forcefully toward the USSR—a course which often has moderated Soviet behavior—and acting provocatively—a course which will never moderate and which will almost always exacerbate Soviet behavior.

Let me illustrate each of the above propositions by citing the United States involvement in Vietnam. Fifteen years after the event it is still stupefying that the United States responded to the Vietcong's attack on Pleiku—itself doubtless a provocation[4]—by bombing North Vietnam while Soviet Premier Alexei Kosygin was in Hanoi in February 1965. How inclined the post-Khrushchev leadership was to aid North Vietnam prior to this episode is subject to dispute. But it is hard to imagine any act which would have

---

4. The United States had decided not to bomb the North while Kosygin was there but did so in response to the attack on Pleiku.

been more calculated to drive the USSR to aid Vietnam. It is equally difficult to imagine an act more likely to undermine the position of the Soviet
commentators who in 1964 and early 1965 had been arguing that the nature
of American imperialism had changed. Hence the United States, by its actions, managed to ensure (the previously shaky) Soviet commitment to
North Vietnam's war of national liberation and at the same time to affect
negatively the internal dialogue in the USSR. Such evidence of the U.S.
capacity to influence Soviet behavior externally and Soviet internal evolution negatively should give us pause before we assume that our actions are
not likely to influence the propensity of Soviet elites to adapt, and indeed to
moderate, Soviet foreign policy behavior.

The Stalinist Legacy:
A Reply to Zimmerman*

In his response to my article "The Stalinist Legacy in Soviet Foreign Policy," William Zimmerman accurately reviews and, in my opinion, mistakenly rejects my skepticism about "lasting change" in Soviet conduct. Our differences, I believe, have to do with Western perceptions of continuity and change in Soviet history and with the extent of Western influence on the long-term evolution of Soviet foreign policy.

With regard to the question of continuity and change in Soviet history, it should be recalled that since the 1920s—and thus well before the post-Stalin era or detente—it has been fashionable in the West to discover a "new" Russia or a "new" Soviet foreign policy. In 1933, for example, Michael T. Florinsky, the historian, noted, "The former crusaders of world revolution at any cost have exchanged their swords for machine tools and now rely more on the results of their labor than on direct action to achieve the ultimate triumph of the proletariat." In 1943, Senator Tom Connally of Texas observed, "Russians for years have been changing their economy and approaching the abandonment of communism and the whole Western world will be gratified at the happy climax of their efforts." In 1956, even Secretary of State John Foster Dulles greeted the post-Stalin "thaw" and the 1955 "spirit of Geneva" by concluding, "The Soviet leaders are scrap-

*©1980 by Charles Gati. Also appears in Stephen F. Cohen, Alexander Rabinowitch, and Robert Sharlet (eds.), *The Soviet Union Since Stalin* (Bloomington, Indiana: Indiana University Press, 1980).

ping thirty years of policy based on violence and intolerance."[1]

Thus, whenever there is a new Soviet emphasis on "peaceful coexistence" or a new Soviet peace offensive, we are told that the Soviet leaders' priorities and attitudes have undergone substantial alterations. As Henry A. Kissinger put it,

> There is a measure of pathos in our continued effort to discover "reasonable" motives for the Soviet leaders to cease being Bolsheviks: the opportunities to develop the resources of their own country, the unlimited possibilities of nuclear energy, or the advantages of expanding international trade. The Kremlin has been able to exploit this attitude by periodically launching policies of "peaceful coexistence," which have inevitably raised the debate whether a "fundamental" shift has occurred in Soviet purposes, thus lulling us before the next onslaught.[2]

I also find George F. Kennan's 1947 comment most appropriate and instructive:

> When there is something the Russians want from us, one or the other of these [negative] features of their policy may be thrust temporarily into the background; and when that happens there will always be Americans who will leap forward with gleeful announcements that "the Russians have changed," and some who will even try to take credit for having brought about such "changes." But we should not be misled by tactical maneuvers. These characteristics of Soviet policy...will be with us, whether in the foreground or the background, until the internal nature of Soviet power changes.[3]

On the question of how much influence the West has had, or can have, on Soviet foreign policy, Zimmerman provides an interesting insight. While he does not demonstrate by specific examples his contention that post-Stalin policy has come to differ significantly from Stalin's conduct, he implies that post-Stalin Soviet behavior *would have* changed for the better if only the United States or the West had acted more wisely (or patiently, or consistently, or in a less threatening way). Hence the new twist: if little or no actual change is manifested in Soviet foreign policy—if, in other words, Moscow has not lived up to our expectations—it must be our fault and thus *we* are responsible for *their* assertive conduct.

This argument, like so many others about the rise of a "new" Russia, stems from an unwillingness to come to terms with the challenge to our liberal values inherent in continuity in Soviet politics and indeed in the permanence of conflict in international life.

---

1. All quotes cited in Henry A. Kissinger, *The Troubled Partnership: A Reappraisal of the Atlantic Alliance* (Garden City: Doubleday Anchor Books, 1966), pp. 190-91.

2. Henry A. Kissinger, *Nuclear Weapons and Foreign Policy* (Garden City: Doubleday Anchor Books, 1958), p. 7.

3. George F. Kennan, "The Ideology of Containment: The X Article," in Charles Gati, ed., *Caging the Bear: Containment and the Cold War* (Indianapolis: Bobbs-Merrill, 1974), p. 15.

The Nature of Soviet Power*

For three decades Soviet power has obsessed American foreign policy. By it we have judged our own; because of it we have committed ourselves far from home and justified our commitment in terms of the menace it represents; around it we have made a world order revolve. For us, Soviet power has been the ultimate measure and the central threat, a seminal idea and a source of orientation.

Should it still be, however, now that international politics are changing so? Or should it still be, because Soviet power is changing so? Is the evolution of the international setting altering the meaning of growing Soviet power? Or is the growth of Soviet power undermining the meaning of an evolving international setting? The ambiguous relationship between the two makes it much harder to know what role the Soviet Union ought to play in our concerns. Judging the significance of larger and more modern Soviet military forces becomes increasingly difficult when traditional frames of reference no longer hold, when the old rules and characteristics of international relations yield to new ones, when the uses to which military power can be put are depreciated, and when the concept of security as such loses its precision, swollen by strange anonymous sources of insecurity, many of

*Reprinted by permission of the author and the publisher from *Foreign Affairs* (October, 1977); Copyright 1977 by Council on Foreign Relations, Inc.

them economic in nature. It is a world in which fewer and fewer of our problems are caused by the Soviet Union or can be solved by it, save for the ultimate matter of nuclear war.

Yet, amidst the loosening of the old order—the deteriorating hierarchies and orthodoxies, the growing number of political actors and political axes, the new imperatives of interdependence—there is also a distracting spectacle of ever-expanding Soviet military power. During these years of passage, the Soviet Union has busied itself with a vast buildup of its armed forces, introducing new technologies, enlarging numbers and most significantly venturing into areas far from its historic spheres of concern. The Soviet Union has spent the decade turning itself into an authentic global superpower able to apply military force in the remotest regions of the world. With the capacity has apparently come the vocation.

"Soviet Russia," Henry Kissinger and his closest counselors used to say, "is only just beginning its truly 'imperial' phase." The prospect does not fit comfortably with our image of the other processes reforming world politics. Hard pressed to reconcile these two perceptions—of an increasingly interdependent (and decentralized) world and of an increasingly "imperial" Soviet Union—we have tended not to try. We have responded rhetorically ("The United States seeks to give the Soviet Union a stake in a more stable and humane international order.") rather than conceptually. And having no clear concept of the relationship between the transformation of Soviet power and the transformation of the global political setting, we have concentrated on familiar apprehensions: Where there is instability, what is the Soviet ability to interfere? How do we keep the Soviet Union from intervening in Angola or in Yugoslavia? Or how do we frustrate Soviet intervention when it occurs? (Phrased by the last Administration, the question was: "How do we create a calculus of risks and benefits that will induce the Soviet Union to behave?") What is the political and psychological impact on our NATO allies of strategic parity or the growth of the Warsaw Pact's conventional forces? What does the Soviet Union hope to accomplish by adding to its military advantage in Central Europe? How well served are Soviet aims by the tensions between Greece and Turkey, the West's economic dislocations, or the possible entry of French or Italian Communists into their governments?

Like our apprehensions, our perception of the Soviet Union as such tends to be narrowly cast. There is a remarkable consensus in most of what is being said about the Soviet Union and the nature of its changing power. People may disagree over details and over what it all adds up to for us all, but on the central characteristics nearly everyone agrees. The common portrait is of a late-arriving military leviathan, in the bloom of military expansion, self-satisfied at last to have matched the power of its great imperialist rival, and fascinated by the potential rewards in the continued accumulation of arms.

But most are also agreed that the Soviet Union is a seriously flawed power: economically disadvantaged, technologically deficient, bureaucratically sclerosed, and threatened by a society that is, in Zbigniew Brzezinski's words, "like a boiling subterranean volcano [straining] against the rigid surface crust of the political system." Something of a deformed giant, Enceladus with 50 withered arms, mighty in military resources and exhilarated by its strength, but backward in other respects and sobered by the need to enlist the West's help in overcoming these problems.

From these two perceptions it is only a short step to another widely shared impression: unable to influence others by the force of its ideology, plagued by an economy that does not measure up, and discredited by its repressive habits at home and among allies, the Soviet Union has but one major trump, its military power. Some argue that this is a historic condition, that all of the regime's expectations have been deceived, save for the accomplishments of force. The failure of the European revolution, capitalism's resilience despite the Great Depression and the constant cycle of lesser economic crises, the collapse of communist unity almost as soon as unity became a practical dream, the unruliness of change in the theoretically revolutionary regions of the Third World, all these are the wreckage of earlier hopes. The Soviet Union's triumphs, they contend—from the conquest of power to the spread of empire, from the early victories in the civil war to the historic defeat of Nazi Germany—have proved to generations of Soviet leaders the trustworthiness of force alone.

Others are simply commenting on what appears to be the Soviet Union's comparative advantage. But either way, because of this perception, our concluding observation takes on greater moment. For, in one form or another, nearly everyone who makes the Soviet Union an interest notes the contrast in what we and they want for the world. Even those who believe the Soviet Union is losing its taste for revolutionary transformations and settling down to traditional power politics nonetheless stress the conflict in the two nations' underlying values. Whether the reasons reach back several centuries, as some insist, or merely back to different political systems, as others suggest, the Soviet Union remains an alienated competitor.

If there is truth in this assessment—and, to a degree, it is utterly true—it is a narrow-minded truth, which does not help us sort out the subtler aspects of the Soviet challenge. I say narrow-minded truth because it bears so little relationship to the Soviet Union's self-image; because it is so thoroughly *our* view of the world. Claiming greater honesty and accuracy on our side is only a partial way out and no service to ourselves, not if the Soviet Union is acting according to its own view. Thus, we have twice handicapped our analyses: first, by not grappling with the interconnection between the evolution of the international order and the evolution of Soviet power and, second, by giving short shrift to the way the Soviet Union views these issues.

We need a broader and richer framework within which to judge the changing nature of Soviet power, one that also incorporates the Soviet understanding of the changing nature of everyone's power. That is what I have tried to sketch here, starting with what seem to me the most conspicuous features of change in the international order, but measured against the lingering and complicating influence of the old order. There follows a brief description of both the new and the faded forms of power and a few comments on Soviet power judged accordingly. My primary concern, however, is the Soviet perspective on these issues. Therefore, I have devoted the second half of the essay to their perceptions of the evolving nature of power within an evolving international setting.

II

Five elements of change strike me as central. The first of these is the transformation of alliances, a specific manifestation of the general erosion of hierarchies. Not that partnerships are ended or that the power to compel loyalty has in all instances dissolved, but the premises of unity are in most cases no longer what they used to be. Among the industrialized countries of the West, the will to subordinate parochial national interests to traditional security concerns and common enterprises thrives less. In the other camp, the core alliance remains intact, but the original socialist alliance long ago disintegrated with Tito's challenge and the Sino-Soviet split. Moreover, the Soviet Union's extended alliance with West European communism is foundering at the moment on the same reluctance to subordinate national concerns.

The second element of change is the exponential growth of interdependence, confronting nations with the peculiar risk of suffering more the more others suffer, and fusing their prospects for prosperity—no longer merely their prospects for tranquility. Gradually and timidly the socialist countries are being drawn into the same process, a process with unfamiliar rules of restraint and mutual concern.

Third, in this increasingly interdependent world, the collapse of the old international economic order and the challenge raised to a new one of, by, and for the industrialized capitalist societies, have rewritten the political agenda, converted economics to a still higher form of politics, and introduced a critical revisionism, sponsored this time not by the East but by the South instead. Together the second and third elements of change have made the issue of national security far more complex than defending the integrity of one's territory and political values. Increasingly the stake is also in the security of foreign markets and key resources, in the freedom from economically dislocating external price increases, and even in the success of other government's domestic economic programs.

Fourth, there is growing regionalization of international politics, the particular form taken by the disintegration of a simplistically bipolar world. Ambitious states like Iran and Nigeria exert greater leadership within their own regions, and in the regions of Africa, Latin America and Southeast Asia many of the local states make it increasingly plain that the stewardship of outside powers is no longer necessary. In Europe and Asia new or restored power centers have emerged, creating a looser and more complicated geometry underpinning the structure of international politics. And cutting across this new structure, the proliferation of nuclear weapons adds to the complexity and hazards of change.

Finally, at the pinnacle where power was once concentrated, a fundamental shift has occured in the military balance between the two superpowers. The Soviet Union is no longer the United States' relative inferior in strategic nuclear power. For nearly a decade it has been our rough equal, and, in the minds of many, a self-confident military competitor eager to do still better.

This last development represents in fact a specter from the old order and is the chief reason we have been slow to think our way through the implications of the Soviet Union's altered power in an altered setting. For two things are at work and both stimulate ancient reflexes: one is the evolution of the whole of Soviet military power and the other is our enduring image of the role military power plays in Soviet conceptions.

Seeing the Soviet Union draw abreast in the strategic arms race has been hard enough. But to face in the same short period the realization that the Soviet Union is turning itself into a first-class naval power capable of challenging our mastery of the seas and meanwhile straining to improve its massive power in Europe has been vastly more disconcerting. All at once the Soviet Union has as many, indeed more and larger missiles than we; it has most of the same (though perhaps somewhat retarded) technologies, MIRV, mobile land-based missiles, and rudimentary high-energy lasers; and still it presses on with new generations of weapons systems. Just as suddenly its navy is out on the high seas, sailing oceans where it has never been before, assuming missions it has never had before, and building ships it has never needed before. But even more disturbing, in Europe, where it already had the advantage, the Soviet Union has not only improved the quality of its arms and the number of its forces on the Central European front, it has radically altered the balance in the Mediterranean and on the northern flank.

Add to this the place that we have long assumed war occupies in Soviet theory, and inevitably our perspective shrinks to a rather traditional set of apprehensions. For the assumption that the Soviet Union accepts the utility of war is deeply ingrained. Because the Soviet leaders have never repudiated Clausewitz's dictum of "war as the extension of policy," we have taken this to mean that they still regard the resort to arms as a legitimate instrument of policy. Hence their apparent conviction that war, even nuclear war, is "winnable," and their unwillingness to accept Western notions of strategic nuclear deterrence. Dedicated to the idea of prevailing in a nuclear conflict, they are, we assume, less intimidated by the prospect of its outbreak and therefore less concerned with doctrines designed to avoid it or, in the event, to limit it. Even granted that they want war no more than we, the way they conceive war and the way they prepare for it prove to us that the Soviet leaders believe in the practical effect of both the threat and the arsenal of war.

For many, the next step in the analysis is obvious: if intellectually the Soviet leaders acknowledge the utility of force and if practically they are dependent on it, then not surprisingly they appear bent on achieving the largest possible margins of military advantage. This is the culminating premise. The Soviet Union is driven—to the limits of its resources and our complacency—to seek superiority over us: to amass still greater forces in Central Europe, that the West Europeans may be properly cowed; to fashion a navy more powerful than ours, that we and our friends may be held hostage to our economic dependencies; to build the capacity for projecting power to the far corners of the globe, that new and volatile nations may be opened to Soviet influence; and, ultimately, to overshadow the American strategic nuclear deterrent, that all these other enterprises may be safely pursued.

Viewed like this, it is no wonder that the Soviet-American relationship is soon largely reduced to its military dimension, our attention fixed on the contingencies and circumstances in which the Soviet Union could exploit its military power, and the solution found in our own military strength. Those who think we find the solution in too much military strength simply reinforce the narrowness of our analysis. Because their arguments usually turn on a more optimistic assessment of the military balance—rather than on any disbelief in our original assumptions about the place of force in Soviet theory, something they are more likely to regard as irrelevant than as wrong —they confine the issue still further to a great debate over comparative military capabilities. Thus, they reduce the Soviet threat but not our preoccupation with it.

III

How ironic that we should be so easily seduced by our traditional apprehensions and so content to build our analysis around the military-political dimension. Interdependence, the other great theme these days, is supposed to depreciate the value of military power. Theoretically the rules are different in an interdependent world, requiring different means. (Theoretically —goes the response—the Soviet Union is not sufficiently a part of this world.)

Though old habits and a lack of imagination prevent us from adjusting, there is also a growing suspicion that conventional means of influence are not what we once thought. The notion that foreign aid, military assistance, cultural diplomacy or any of the other elements of a nation's presence actually translate into leverage over another nation's decisions convinces us less and less, even when it is our adversary's aid, arms, and propaganda effort. Except in rare instances, power is not something usefully approached as a matter of devising, accumulating, and deftly applying mechanisms of influence. Not primarily at least.

For power, we sense, is increasingly unrefinable; increasingly indistinguishable from the setting in which it exists. Power is the capacity to reshape parts of the international order and for the powerful that is a capacity to compromise—to make concessions. Power is allowing monetary regimes or the law of the sea to take another form, allowing the International Monetary Fund, the General Agreement on Tariffs and Trade (GATT), or the Common Market to be changed or supplanted, and allowing other global economic goals, such as income redistribution, to have their day. In this case, there is nothing tangible or portable about it, and by its "application" little chance of imposing change.

Power, however, is also increasingly a matter of managing interdependence and, therefore, increasingly a matter of the structure and range of one's dependencies. To be positioned at the intersection of numerous and different forms of interdependence is power—unless too many of them are seriously unequal. So is opting out of interdependent relationships to the extent that minimizing vulnerabilities enhances power; but by sidelining itself a nation also reduces its power to the extent that the rewards of participation are passed up. That is only the start, however, for power in an interdependent world also depends on how fungible others' dependencies are (that is, how easily their dependencies in one realm can be converted to offset yours in another) and how serviceable your vulnerabilities are (that is, when interdependence is asymmetrical, how much others hurt themselves by hurting you).

IV

If power is to be measured in terms of a country's ability to ferry material support great distances to friends fighting in settings like Angola in 1975, the Soviet Union is immeasurably stronger than it was 15 years earlier when Patrice Lumumba needed help. But if it is to be measured in terms of a country's ability to intervene over the same distances with its own military forces when it does not have friends or when we move to prevent it, the Soviet Union is not strong enough. If it is to be assessed in terms of a country's ability to obtain the material resources that it needs without fear of outside interference, the Soviet Union is less well-off than it was ten years ago but a good deal better off than we. But if it is to be assessed in terms of a country's ability to influence the economic decisions of others impinging on its interests, the Soviet Union is better off now, but not nearly so well off as we.

The trouble is we do not know how to evaluate the power of the Soviet Union. We do not have a sufficiently comprehensive and systematic set of criteria by which to judge. We do not even have sufficient criteria by which to disagree among ourselves. Of course, if we reduce the task to evaluating Soviet military power, we have the grounds for disagreeing, but not for weighing its share of the many other resources by which nations try to shape world politics. To supplement the calculation of Soviet military power with other traditional indices—such as the strength of its economy, the stability of its alliance(s), or the character of its adversaries—accomplishes little. What is more important, that Khrushchev's precise timetable for exceeding our per capita GNP has been long abandoned along with his accompanying fanfare? Or, that the Soviet economy continues to grow more rapidly than those of the vast majority of the world, including our own? Or is the sharp decline in the growth of Soviet total factor productivity more important than either? What is more striking about the large percentage of Soviet resources devoted to national defense, the dedication that it implies or the burden that it represents? And what is more significant about our discovery that this percentage has been even larger than we originally thought, the still greater dedication that it implies or the inefficiency that it betrays? Were we sure of the answers to these questions, we would still have to decide how they balance off against, say, the evolving character of the Chinese threat or the strengths and weaknesses of the Soviet Union's East European alliance.

Neither are we much helped by the tendency to substitute for an analysis of the resources serving Soviet foreign policy a summary of the trends favoring Soviet foreign policy, particularly when the summary is only that. In part, the problem is the same as with undifferentiated and unintegrated categories of power. Not only is it difficult to tell which trends matter most: the American failures in Indochina or the Soviet exclusion from the Middle East; the triumph of the MPLA in Angola or the destruction of Allende in Chile; the disruption on NATO's southern flank or the failed rapprochement after Mao's death. But it is still more treacherous discerning grand patterns among these trends, especially when many trends are quickly reversed. Moreover, the implications of any single trend often defy easy categorization. Take, for example, the case of Eurocommunism. Would the Soviet Union be strengthened by having the Italian Communist Party in government? Who knows? How does a leader in Moscow or one in Washington weigh the damage done to Soviet peace of mind in Eastern Europe by the PCI's heterodoxy, against the reinforcement of the U.S.S.R.'s foreign policy in Western Europe by the Party's lingering orthodoxy? How, when the Soviet leader wants a strong Left to constrain the Italian government but momentarily fears the effect on détente of a government that actually includes the Left?

In part, however, the problem with focusing on trends is in distinguishing their effects. After all, our concern with Soviet power is in what it can accomplish, and this cannot be automatically or easily inferred from what happens.

Given these pitfalls, it makes more sense to put a certain distance between ourselves and the problem of the Soviet Union's evolving (military) power. We need to stand back and contemplate the more basic quesiton of the Soviet Union's ability to shape or alter different parts of its environment. Ultimately this is what determines the importance of the Soviet ability to affect events.

If one starts with interdependence, that complex network of involvements dominating so many of the stakes in international politics, including the structure of the international economic order, the Soviet Union's influence remains marginal. It will not do to dismiss this state of affairs as the Soviet Union's choice, as a game it prefers not to play, and may be the better off thereby. For clearly the Soviet Union *has* chosen to play and would like to play more, were the rules more within its control. Increasingly it has a stake in interdependence but little leverage over the governing institutions and rules. The Soviet Union, as the economist says, is a price-taker.

A third of the animal protein in Soviet diets comes from fish mostly caught off other nations' coasts. To fish there, the Soviet Union is increasingly obliged to enter into joint ventures aiding the development of the poorer countries' fishing industries. Since the early 1960s, the annual increase in Soviet food imports has exceeded that of Japan, the world's largest food importer, and the Soviet Union is now contractually bound to buy at least six million metric tons of American wheat and corn every year. The Soviet Union counts, and has for some years, on buying substantial quantities of foreign technology to reverse productivity lags in Soviet industry and agriculture; to pay for it, it exports a growing portion of its petroleum production—but if it is to maintain these levels of export, it must tap its more inaccessible reserves, and for that it needs more Western technology. Together with its friends in Eastern Europe, it now owes $46 billion to outsiders, including $28 billion to foreign commercial banks.[1]

For all that, however, the Soviet Union has precious little voice in shaping the larger system in which it buys, sells, and borrows. It is a member of none of the major international economic institutions, unless the United Nations Conference on Trade and Development (UNCTAD) be one, and there it is generally disregarded. It has not been much consulted by anyone, including the South, when monetary schemes, balance-of-payment adjustment arrangements, commodity agreements, and regulations of direct foreign investment are discussed. And its own particular pet concerns—such as most-favored-nation agreements, bilateral trade agreements, and a larger role for gold—wait on the goodwill of the capitalist powers and often on their diminished apathy.

---

1. See Richard Portes, "East Europe's Debt to the West: Interdependence Is a Two-way Street," *Foreign Affairs*, July 1977, pp. 751-782.

Our standard explanation misses the point: the point is not that the organization of the Soviet economy makes the Soviet Union an unsuitable participant, but that the international economic order need not accommodate the national organization the U.S.S.R. prefers. Our notion that this is no comment on Soviet power is plainly wrong; in an interdependent world, self-sufficiency is inefficiency, increasingly so in the Soviet Union, and the Soviet leadership knows it. How much of a world power is a nation without much power in the world economy?

On the other hand, not all crucial transactions take place in the economic sphere and not all crucial stakes are material. There is also, for want of a more revealing term, the political order. In theory, the maximum concern is with the Soviet capacity for making the world over in its own image, but few believe any longer in putting the issue so simplistically. Rather, we respond to an incoherent muddle of concerns, beginning with the pace at which the Soviet Union is acquiring footholds or facilities around the world, which jeopardize our power, and finishing with the pace at which change is occurring, which jeopardizes our values. In a place like southern Africa the two become confused—but that is more a matter of our weakness than Soviet strength. Not that we fear for racism, but violent change may give rise to radical regimes and many think there are too many of them already. More immediately, radical regimes may well accord the Soviet Union new facilities for its expanding global military power, which, according to the more pessimistic among us, could be used to shut off the flow of indispensable resources to Western economies. Worried about the fate of our own power and values, we tend to be sloppy about distinguishing between the aggrandizement of Soviet power and the advancement of Soviet values.

Our carelessness arises out of the mistaken apprehension that the growth of Soviet (military) power, and change, like that in Angola, necessarily aid Soviet foreign policy in dealing with its various tasks: that they interact to make it easier for the Soviet Union to sell its Asian collective security scheme or mobilize opposition to Diego Garcia. It also blinds us to the possibility that change may work against the Soviet Union, even in its own camp, quite apart from the growth of Soviet (military) power.

In the military realm, the Soviet Union is unquestionably stronger than it was, but the nature and sweep of its strength is worth exploring. Where arms are an uncontested entrée, the Soviet Union has a growing capacity to influence and, in some rare instances like Angola, to decide events. But sometimes, as in the Horn of Africa, even where order is breaking down and the Soviet access is considerable, confusion and crosscutting interests foil effective Soviet influence. In general, the Soviet Union has a conspicuously greater capacity than it did to constrain our use of military force and, to that extent, to influence events. But where it is the shadow of Soviet power that worries us, as in Europe, if Soviet influence grows, it will largely be influence that *we* have created; when the actual resort to force is so implausible, then dangers like that of "Finlandization" are far more a matter of our state of mind than of actual Soviet capabilities.

Moreover, the capacity to influence, even to control, events guarantees neither control after the event nor control over the larger patterns of change. By and large the Soviet Union is, as we are, the beneficiary or victim of the processes of change, not their source. Nothing in the evolution of Soviet power is altering that. Some have used the images of gardener and architect to identify the nature and limits of our power: the Soviet Union, like us, remains a gardener.

V

None of what has been said so far addresses the constraints a changing international order does or does not impose on Soviet behavior.[2] This, it seems to me, has a great deal to do with the way the Soviet Union judges these issues. For while in some respects it judges these issues as we do, in other important respects, it does not. Thus, Soviet writers and leaders are as sensitive as our own to the rapid transformation of world politics. Like our own, they recognize the fragmentation of power ("the multiplicity of forces each standing up for its own interests"), the transformation of capitalist and proletarian internationalism, the emergence of other axes, North-South and West-West, to compete with the East-West axis, and the growth of interdependence (in its praiseworthy form, the "international division of labor"). But they superimpose on these common perceptions a fundamentally different conception of the underlying forces at work.

For them, the key to the current transformation resides in the shifting "correlation of forces," the balance between history's progressive and retrograde forces—their sense of linear history, predicated on the eternal advance of the Soviet Union and those with whom it identifies and the equally certain retreat of those with whom it does not. At the moment, they contend, the correlation of forces has been radically altered by the dramatic increase in Soviet military power, the continued success of the socialist economies, the growth of the national liberation struggle, an unprecedented convergence of crises in the industrialized capitalist countries, and the

---

2. In urging that we cast our evaluation of Soviet power more broadly, I am aware that I have slighted considerations that many others feature. I have made no effort to appraise the impact of change within the socialist world on Soviet power; no effort to judge whether Soviet power is diminished by the continued erosion of "proletarian internationalism" beyond Eastern Europe but enhanced by its preservation within Eastern Europe; or whether it is enhanced by the rising influence of communists and their allies beyond the Soviet sphere but diminished by the cost of maintaining its own influence within this sphere. Or, whether the combinations are the opposite (because I do not know and because the judgment is history's). I have not attempted to explore the impact on Soviet power of the conflict with China and of our China diplomacy (because the impact is obvious). Nor have I commented on the power that the Soviet Union derives from our growing bilateral economic cooperation—from the so-called "hostage capital" it possesses or the ready-made lobbies that it inherits (because the leverage flows both ways and because this is a marginal consideration in the larger scheme of things.)

strengthening of "democratic" and "peace-loving" forces within the other camp.

Whether they really believe the balance of trends has shifted so swiftly and so unambiguously is difficult to tell. But, in a sense, that is not crucial: first, because the Soviets do not underestimate the residual strength of capitalist societies, least of all the United States, nor overestimate their own military strength. On the contrary, they have the deepest regard for the powers of recovery in Western societies, for their economic dynamism even when decelerated, and for the United States' preeminence among and continued dominance over them; they also seem to understand the limitations of their own military power—in fact, in contrast to many in the West, they still tend to see themselves as militarily inferior to the United States in most respects.

Second, the precise level of Soviet optimism is less important than the conceptual framework sustaining it. It is more important that the Soviet Union, however sensitive to specific trends, still ultimately reduces the evolution of international relations to a single contest. It still imposes (a Soviet speaker would say, understands) the juxtaposition between two historic forces, between two social systems and in these terms judges the ultimate significance of global change.

We make a mistake, therefore, to doubt the force of this idea, to consign it to that category of devices by which the Soviet regime finds self-justification, or to repress it in our haste to transform the Soviet Union into a historically recognizable problem. The mistake has three consequences: it obscures a basic asymmetry in our two conceptions of international change; it conceals the trouble a Soviet observer has with our conception of international change; and it makes it more difficult to understand the role that the Soviet Union assigns itself in promoting international change.

In the first instance, Americans have gradually learned to divide their preoccupations. One of the consequences of a changing environment, we think, is the increasingly diffuse quality of the challenges that it raises. Our problems and the solutions, to the extent that our problems have solutions, exist on different planes and in separate contexts. However much these are interwoven, they cannot any longer be forced into one dimension. On the other hand, the Soviet view of this increasingly intricate environment is still refracted through a single dimension.

Thus, for example, we take the contestation over the new international economic order (NIEO) to be a serious new focus of American foreign policy, and, because the challenge comes from the South, distinct from our competition with the Soviet Union. (Indeed, as an acknowledgement of interdependence and a moderated East-West contest, we now invite the Soviet Union to join us in aiding the developing nations.) But for the Soviet Union the North-South emphasis is misconceived, not merely because this tends to feature a "rich-poor" dichotomy, and the Soviet Union does not like its own ranking, but because a rich-poor dichotomy makes the issue income redistribution, and income redistribution has to do with buying off the oppressed, not revolutionizing the system. Properly conceived, the struggle over a new international economic order is between the two social systems, with the socialist countries in the forefront. As a symptom of imperialism's vulnerabilities, the Soviet Union supports the struggle for a more equitable international economic order; but, recognizing how powerful the industrialized capitalist states remain in this sphere, it prefers to emphasize other areas of change, ones better served by the "shifting correlation of forces," ones that have more to do with restructuring East-West relations, or, as Soviet writers put it, ones more directly concerned with reducing the risks of war, strengthening peaceful coexistence, and advancing "extensive and constructive cooperation."

In the second instance, our insensitivity to Soviet conceptions prevents us from seeing how much we remain the Soviet Union's preoccupation. (Too many people who do take Soviet formulas seriously are no exception, because they confound the "struggle between two social systems" with a struggle between two states or two sets of states.) If there is one great impediment to progressive change, one great benefactor of a reactionary order, in Soviet eyes, it is the United States. China may be a more immediate and noxious threat to the Soviet Union, but its larger meaning is as an objective ally of the anti-progressive forces led by us. Thus, when our theorists and leaders speak of adjusting to a systemic change, creating new equilibriums, fashioning a sounder balance of power, and building on interdependence, these are not treated by the Soviets as concepts for a safer, more stable, and more humane international order, but as a design for saving as much as possible of the old one.

Because of Vietnam and the growing strength of the Soviet Union, Soviet writers say, the American leaders have a more realistic appreciation of the limits of their power and a more constructive approach to relations with the Soviet Union (until the human rights initiatives of the current Administration). No leader more symbolized that change than Henry Kissinger, but Kissinger the theorist, it has often been noted in Soviet analyses, believes in the "balance of power system" and, "however praised or embellished" that concept may be, it is designed to preserve all status quo not only in the international-political but, above all, in the social sphere—"to maintain and strengthen reactionary regimes," to stifle "revolutionary changes in the life of the people."

According to Soviet observers, it is not the imperatives of interdependence, particularly those of reciprocity and mutual restraint, that move American leaders, but rather the opportunities they see in the fragmentation of power. (The concept of interdependence, they say, becomes in our hands a rationalization for Western exploitation of the Third World and an artifice for salvaging imperialist collaboration under

American leadership.) By capitalizing on the conflicts among various "power centers," Soviet analysts maintain, the United States hopes to make itself the arbiter of the system, the regulator of the "equilibrium," and the equilibrium that most bothers them is the so-called "pentagonal world" (the U.S.S.R., the United States, China, Western Europe and Japan). It is not restraint that we are attempting to build into the system, according to them, but flexibility for ourselves, the kind that preserves others' dependencies and frees our hands to control adverse change, to "export counter-revolution."

In turn, Soviet commentators make no bones about their own country's large and active role in the evolution of the international order. As they say, the restructuring of international relations "can never be spontaneous or automatic." Marxist-Leninists cannot rely on "spontaneous development" in international affairs. "Any fundamental restructuring of international relations must be duly planned, controlled, and corrected." Since international politics, in contrast to the imperialists' view, are not a social system, subject to endless, directionless mutations—a "system" whose structure cannot be rectified, only manipulated and exploited—but a process, the progressive forces of the world can and must act to protect and foster this process. The process, of course, is the shifting "correlation of forces," and the Soviet Union, according to its spokesmen, has a growing responsibility for its advance.

Ambitious, militarily strengthened, buoyed by the course of events, persuaded that we are the key obstacle to a more preferable international order, this seemingly is not the kind of Soviet Union that we want to live with. Nor is it one much in step with an encumbered international environment dominated by mutual dependencies. How much worse that is also, according to many of us, invests military power with a high instrumental value.

This, however, misconceives the problem, and no part of it more than the military dimension. For the instrumentalism we see in the Soviet approach to military power is, in the first instance, the instrumentalism they attribute to *us*. The interplay is not easy to sort out, but it starts with our misrepresentation of their theory. Thus, the Soviet concepts that we consult to prove their instrumentalism are in fact those analyzing ours. Their loyalty to Clausewitz, for example, has nothing to do with rationalizing war as an instrument of Soviet foreign policy; it is a way of explaining the phenomenon of war and imperialism's proclivity to war as a means. In twisting their meaning, Soviet commentators complain, we "deliberately lump together the theoretical proposition characterizing the essence of war and the proposition concerning the expedience, or otherwise, of war as a means of achieving political objectives." (This disclaimer we may believe or not, but we have no business using Clausewitz to prove their commitment to war as an instrument of foreign policy).

Seeing military power as an instrument of foreign policy, of course, is much different from proposing was as an instrument of foreign policy. We, they say, have made military power not only an instrument, but *the* instrument, of our postwar foreign policy. And we have not only made it the instrument of our foreign policy—that is, our frequent and ultimate recourse in controlling international change—but we have turned the threat of (nuclear) war into a prop for our frequent military interventions. That is why, according to them, we seek strategic superiority, why we reject parity, why we resort to the subterfuge of "strategic sufficiency" (the formula of the early Nixon years), why we concoct concepts like the "doctrine of limited nuclear options" (deterrence in the late Nixon and Ford years)—why, in short, we struggle to make nuclear war safe, and why we chase so frantically after technological advantage. Our particular approach to deterrence theory, they think, represents our never-ending struggle to salvage political utility for nuclear arms, to make them a shield for the exploitation of other forms of military power. (Our equivalent is the notion that the Soviet commitment to "winning" a nuclear war represents a commitment to an arms buildup that will permit winning without fighting—not, as Soviet theorists claim, a way of fighting a war that others start and hope to win.)

There is no way of knowing whether some or all within the Soviet leadership would be willing to try where we "have failed," whether they can imagine a plausible structure to the strategic balance that would profit Soviet foreign policy. But three lesser conclusions are within our reach: first, to the extent that the Soviet leaders are wrestling with the problem of integrating military power and foreign policy—and they are—it is at the lower end of the spectrum, where we have regularly applied military force to foreign policy ends. To judge from their building programs, they have not yet decided how far they want to go in developing an ability to project force, how far they want to go in preventing or duplicating our practices. Second, the areas where foreign policy and military power are the most likely to mingle are those geographically and naturally isolated from the central balances. And, third, we pay an unnecessary price for our original invidious image of the Soviet Union: in truth, the Soviet Union feels better about itself and the course of events than we assume; trusting events, it is more likely to assign its military power the task—beyond defense—of preventing others from interfering with change than of imposing change.

For in fact the Soviet Union does not see itself as only militarily potent and otherwise as economically disadvantaged, technologically deficient, bureaucratically sclerosed and so on. Its leaders admit to a broad range of problems and limitations but, where we constantly view these in terms of fundamental systemic weaknesses, they regard them as normal and corrigible defects. And where we focus on these defects, treating them as a basic disparagement of the Soviet experience, they tend to downplay them, instead emphasizing their accomplishments, and thus retain a genuine faith in the transcendent significance of that experience. (One could exchange "they" and "we" in these two sentences; that is, the same contrast exists in reverse.)

On the other hand, we tend to analyze the effect of Soviet ideology in narrow, utilitarian terms, that is, by the impact that it has on others, by its power to attract, and by this standard we see the Soviet Union still more weakened. While a Soviet leader is also concerned with the force of ideology, as a practical matter he is more likely to focus on trends that correspond with his values than on the precise number of orthodox disciples that his country inspires (outside the critical sphere of Eastern Europe). Rather than judge the issue only by the number of socialist states in the world or genuine Marxist-Leninists, he will take heart from the number that merely reject the other way; even more will his optimism depend on the basic rhythm of change, say, in Indochina or southern Africa.

There is another side to the story. For the Soviet Union is not only, or even first, the servant of history; it is also a state with mundane interests, like adding Western computers to its economy, securing recognition for the territorial status quo in Eastern Europe, and discouraging the United States from deploying cruise missiles. Its recourse has been the process of détente, which the Soviet leaders say is not only compatible with the process of an evolving correlation of forces, but an essential part of it. Détente is the refinement and restraint that the Soviet Union brings to the basic contest between two social systems. Theoretically, it is the framework within which the Soviet Union bridges the gap between its private needs and the historic vision, but the recriminations of the French Communist Party (against those who would sacrifice social change to detente) and of "some representatives" of national liberation movements indicate that it has not been fully successful.

Were the Soviet participation in détente but a tactical expedient, a kind of winter quartering of the troops, a policy choice to be discarded at the first sign of inconvenience, we might have a right to a more primitive view of the Soviet approach to international change. But it is not. It is a profound and long-term commitment dictated by the Soviet leaders' inability to conceive a better way to pursue their three elemental objectives: (1) nurturing both the processes that restrain the change the Soviet Union fears and those that ease the way to the change it desires; (2) sanctifying the Soviet Union's status as a global power coequal with the United States (that there may be, in Andrei Gromyko's words, "no question of any significance which can be decided without the Soviet Union or in opposition to it") and (3) securing the economic and technological benefits of the "international division of labor." By the last, the Soviet Union engages itself in the interdependent world. This interdependent world, which includes collaboration between socialist and capitalist states, now has the status of a phenomenon determined by "objective realities and laws." And Soviet leaders admit that "no single state is able for long to achieve full development if it cuts itself off from the rest of the world.''

VI

I remember those maps from early television programs on the Soviet Union —or on the communist world as it was then. How the color spread like spilled paint across the areas of Soviet control and ambition. Whatever else it may be, 20 years later, the Soviet global thrust in not that. Indeed it is not even a proper "global thrust," must less an "imperial thrust," if by that we mean the extension of power *and* control, or the attempt to control. The Soviet empire still ends at the Elbe River. And, as far as power is concerned, while the Soviet Union's is clearly enlarged, at least that part of it that is military, we should remember that the portion of military power that is largely redeployed, not additional, power and remains vastly inferior to our own. That is, while the Soviet Navy is modernizing, it is less its transfiguration that should catch our eye, for this has been slow and ambiguous, than the simple decision to send the old navy out to sea. Moreover, of all the naval-related areas, the one in which the Soviet Union lags farthest behind us is in its ability to project force.

It is entirely possible that the Soviet Union intends to improve its capacity for projecting power, that it is ready to try to influence events more actively in various parts of the world and that it believes the timely application of military power may be a primary means. But, if so, the effort will be made with relatively few illusions about the permanence of change or about the limits of influence or about the permanence of influence yielded by change. The closer to home (and to the central military balances), the less utility military power has for Soviet foreign policy, and the more the Soviet Union must rely primarily on processes like détente to influence the trends of concern to it. In the grey area in between, like Yugoslavia, there is no evidence that the Soviet Union regards its military power as an important part of policy, but neither is there any evidence that it disregards the fear that it may be.

In general, the notion of a Soviet global thrust has less to do with the application of power (toward control) than it does with status and access (derived from power). That is, the key proposition is Gromyko's: namely, the Soviet Union as a participant in decisions of concern to it. This indisputably depends, in the Soviet mind and, in part, in reality, on the growing mass of Soviet military power, strategic nuclear power in particular. But it also depends, in larger part, on the nature of local circumstances and, as events in the Middle East have proved since the 1973 war, these are often more powerful.

Phrasing the problem so basically, of course, does not help much in dealing with specific aspects or applications of Soviet power, but this kind of framework (not necessarily this particular one) is essential if we are to have a perspective in which to fit our specific judgments. Too often these days, we focus on particular dimensions of Soviet power without the broader perspective—and end by inventing implications.

VII

Looked at from a distance, what ultimately is the significance of a changing setting in assessing Soviet power? And where do these considerations intersect with the problem of competing Soviet and American perspectives? The answer to the first question, it seems to me, comes out of the fundamental evolution in our perception of the constraints on Soviet power. At the outset, that is 30 years ago when George Kennan wrote his famous essay on the subject, we viewed these constraints as too frail and so we substituted ourselves. Faced with what we deemed to be a messianic expansionist state, which for whatever reasons—the one Kennan stressed was the regime's failure to consolidate its absolute power at home—was struggling to fill "every nook and cranny available to it in the basin of world power," our response was fateful and straightforward: we must, Kennan argued and we agreed, "confront the Russians with unalterable counterforce at every point where they show signs of encroaching upon the interests of a peaceful and stable world."

Since then, however, the international setting has grown constantly more complex, adding powerful new constraints and rendering our own role less obvious. The filled power vacuums in Europe and Asia, the fractured monolith of socialism and most of all the shadow of nuclear war have transformed the context in which we contemplate Soviet ambition. To these commonplaces, we might add the Soviet Union's growing stake in what for it has long been a repugnant international order. The paradox stems not only from the Soviet Union's commitment to economic cooperation with the West and the utility it sees in, say, a stable law of the seas, but also from the disruptions it cannot afford to sponsor if it counts on Western forbearance in the face of its growing global role.[3]

Within this sturdier environment—sturdier because of the obstacles it raises to crude expansionism, not because we have been able to maintain our own mission of checking Soviet power at every point—the Soviet-American rivalry has now evolved into something less intensive and something more extensive. The elusiveness of opportunity and the distractions of multiple international challenges account for the loss of intensity. The broadening of the rivalry reflects the U.S.S.R.'s developing global vocation, or, to extend Kennan's original notion, it reflects the shift in Soviet preoccupation from the struggle to secure Soviet power against the

---

3. If after Angola and the 1973 Middle East War this sounds doubtful, we should not lose sight of the relatively narrow limits within which the Soviet Union acted in both instances, neither case ever being the reckless incursion that many in the West imagined.

external world to a quest for a larger place in it.

Détente has been the process by which we come to terms with both circumstances—with both the changing constraints on Soviet power and the changing nature of the threat it poses. It is also the nearest we have to a replacement for the policy (or process) of containment, now that the extension of Soviet dominion has been essentially contained. The new task is to temper the use of its extended power. (A Soviet speaker would say that détente is the process by which his country capitalizes on its growing power to curb American excesses, or the process by which the United States is led to embrace the principle of peaceful coexistence.)

The contest between us continues—that is the essence of peaceful coexistence—but for us, and presumably for the U.S.S.R., detente introduces the new prospect of managing, not merely maintaining, our rivalry. It is an historic opportunity but one with almost insuperable internal tensions. For, on the one hand, we in our rivalry are challenged to collaborate consciously and explicitly in order to moderate the contest; on the other hand, we in our collaboration must cope with the permanent reality of the contest, a reality constantly underscored by global instabilities and constantly heightened by the evolution of the Soviet Union's military power. The delicate task of designing and perhaps even codifying the "rules of the game," if that is what we set out to do in the Moscow agreements of 1972, is continually interrupted by moments of chaos when in Chile, Angola, Indochina or perhaps Yugoslavia our conflicting interests are reemphasized.

The unhappy consequences of this problem are essentially three, each of which carries its own implicit resolution, though none is within easy reach. The first is the preeminence reserved for the military dimension. It is inevitable and, frankly, desirable that both sides maintain their defenses. Regrettable as it may be, the probable truth is that nuclear weapons, in some rough equilibrium, have kept the peace between us in the past and will be needed to keep it in the future. And the other parts of our military establishment are equally essential, not because the U.S.S.R. is demonstrably eager to sweep across the North German plain at the first opportunity, but because, as the last war in the Middle East demonstrated, events in which the U.S.S.R. has a heavy stake, but over which it has little control, may tempt it to invoke the threat of military intervention.

Still, we both have—or believe we have—an interest in holding these forces to a minimum. Because neither side trusts the other's conviction, however, because the "rules of the game" remain so rudimentary and suspect, and, in these circumstances, because those responsible for national security in both countries demand large margins for error, we move constantly the other way. And the motion becomes our preoccupation: those who see the Soviet side in the arms race in sinister terms judge détente accordingly; those who worry about the dangerous or destabilizing aspects of the arms race base the viability of détente primarily on success in controlling arms. In the process, neither group is coming to grips with the instrumentalism the United States and the Soviet Union each sees in the other's approach to military power.

The first group doubts that the Soviet Union could misunderstand the character and purpose of our military forces, and is thus led to a heightened mistrust of Soviet motives; as a consequence, it places its faith instead in further arming—even as the soundest avenue to arms control. The second group, preoccupied with the enormous demilitarization of the Indian Ocean, tends to repress the dilemma of mutual U.S. and Soviet misperceptions about the role of force in each other's foreign policy. For ultimately the dilemma can only be dealt with by relating our defense preparations to our arms control efforts; it can only be addressed by weighing the secondary costs in the other side's distorted perceptions of the significance of the way we choose to defend ourselves, the arms we build and the doctrines we formulate. Until both countries make that effort, arms control—whether SALT, MBFR, or other negotiations to follow—will remain a fragmented and unsystematic enterprise that may produce agreements but only marginal and ambiguous progress toward a moderated contest.

The second consequence flows from the first. Because of the central place accorded the military dimension, key aspects of the U.S.S.R.-U.S. relationship are broken down and split from their context. I have just commented on how much the processes of arming and of negotiating arms control become divorced from the basic problem of military power in both sides' perceptions. Similarly, because of the prominence granted traditional security concerns, the natural effects of processes like interdependence are distorted and in their place we substitute a preoccupation with their manipulation—by us for gain, against us we fear to our disadvantage. Finally, and in the long run, the process of restructuring U.S.S.R.-U.S. relations tends to lose its coherence and we end, as in Kissinger's last days, by focusing on specific tension areas that threaten to accentuate East-West conflict or be accentuated by it or, as in the current instance, by concentrating on disembodied elements of the relationship such as human rights and arms control.

The third consequence—that is, the interruption in the search for more explicit "rules of the game"—follows from the other two. Though we tend to forget it now, relatively concrete patterns of restraint were discussed at the outset of détente. At the time, the two sides consciously set out to reduce the dangerous, extraneous, or unproductive burdens of competition, actually writing some of these restraints into the Basic Principles of United States-Soviet Relations (the document signed at the May 1972 summit). They included the crucial principle of parity—as stated in the Basic Principles neither side would "either directly or indirectly seek unilateral advantage over the other"—an idea most relevant to the strategic arms race, but in the Soviet mind one sanctioning equality in all forms of power. There were others such as the notion of substituting economic interdependence for (our) earlier economic warfare against the Soviet Union and (their) economic autarky, which was again, in implication, written into the Basic Principles. There was also the important concession, on each side's part, that the other's claimed dedication to peaceful coexistence, that is, to restraint in its foreign policy, might now have real meaning. Indeed, the idea of peaceful coexistence was written into the Basic Principles.

Others might be added, derived more from the observer's imagination, but the point is that the search in general was long ago disrupted: parity as a principle fell victim to the widespread suspicion on both sides' part that it was for the other only a momentary indulgence for want of a choice. Interdependence as a principle has been eroded and partially discredited by the politics of linkages; and peaceful coexistence as a principle suffers from the effects of Angola and the 1973 Middle East war.

The dialectical quality of détente, with its competitive/cooperative essence, makes it hard to revive the search for "rules," for a more explicit *modus vivendi*, for a moderation of means in lieu of agreement over ends. But the search is ultimately the only hope we have of restoring coherence to the quest for a restructured Soviet-American relationship. It includes new and untried standards of behavior like those suggested by Marshall Shulman some years ago—one, the principle of "noninterference by force in processes of internal change," the others, the "right of free access," permitting nations to "compete, not for the control of territory, but for the establishment of mutually beneficial and nonexploitative relations, and thereby for political influence." These are the decisive "rules of the game," for it is they that will tell us how much either side really trusts a moderated contest and wants its advantages.

Vulnerabilities and Strengths of the Soviet Union in a Changing International Environment: The Internal Dimension*

Introduction

During the past five years Soviet perceptions of the international landscape and the role of the Soviet Union within it have undergone serious modifications, which have yet to find their expression in actual behavior, but which may have important policy consequences not only for Soviet foreign policy but for the Soviet domestic scene as well. These important changes have taken place not only in the general interstate system, affecting Soviet-American relations, Sino-Soviet relations and Soviet relations with the Third World, but they have also occurred in the world of communist states and parties, affecting Soviet relations with Eastern Europe, with Western Communist Parties, with "revolutionary-democratic" parties in the Third World, and again with China as well, within the framework of the world communist environment.

Many of these changes, while foreseen and anticipated by the Soviet leadership, have taken place earlier than envisaged, i.e., prematurely in terms of Soviet readiness and ability to cope with them with maximum effect, while others have taken the Soviet leaders by surprise, impelling them to re-examine existing calculations and policies and to search for new approaches, as the perceptions and assumptions upon which current policies are based become outmoded.

These changes have been a mixed bag for the Soviet leadership, with many of the surprising and unexpected changes being of a startlingly

*Reprinted from *Soviet Union*, Vol. 4, No. 1 (1977), pp. 17-39, by permission of the author and the publisher.

favorable character, while still others are creating entirely new and perhaps unforeseen problems. The timing of these changes pose special problems for a Soviet leadership that was primed to confront and deal with different issues or the same issues within an altogether different context. Current Soviet policies, to a substantial degree, had become stabilized on the basis of an internal consensual arrangement across a wide spectrum of issues, involving numerous compromises on the general assessment of the external situation, the balance between internal and external (including defense) priorities, and the re-ordering of a wide range of domestic policies involving the economy, the nationalities, the dissidents, constitutional and political (including succession) problems. The Soviet leadership now appears once again to be engaged in a wide-ranging and fundamental re-examination of the Soviet Union's role and purpose in the international community, stemming from Moscow's status as a global power whose capabilities and reach continue to grow at a time when her prestige and role within the world communist movement appears to be shrinking and under challenge or attack from China, Eastern Europe, Western Europe and the Third World.

This paradox is further compounded by the apparent abandonment of global positions by the United States. Just as the U.S. appears to be repudiating its global conceptions, the existing Soviet communist global design is being progressively undermined by the corrosive impact of idiosyncratic "national" conceptions of Communism, not only in China and Eastern Europe, but also among the non-ruling parties in Western Europe and in the Third World.

The single most important development has been the relatively rapid decline of the U.S. as a global power, as its commitments have been trimmed, its visibility lowered, its willingness to act curtailed and its ability to function debilitated by internal constraining forces involving a wide range of institutional, process, ideological, political, personality and social factors. What makes such a development not entirely pleasant for the Soviet leadership is that these changes confront the Soviet leaders with the necessity to react or respond, which in turn may open up old issues and create entirely new ones.

The continuing transformation of the world communist movement from a voluntaristic universal movement into an objective universal process is itself a consequence of the lessened global commitments of the United States and the erosion of its behavioral credibility, which have opened up new possibilities, choices, and perceptions of interest for other Communist parties that are separate, independent and disassociated from those of Moscow. Thus, the same process—the lowered global visibility of the U.S. —which is prematurely catapulting Moscow towards the apex of the international system is also responsible for eviscerating Moscow's ideological global conceptions of its residual operational relevance, confronting the

Soviet leaders with the serious problem of perhaps becoming the paramount global power in the world, but without an operational global conception to guide its role and behavior.

The decline of the U.S. as a global power and its gradual reassessment of its global conceptions has been apparent to Moscow for some time. To some substantial measure this U.S. decline has not resulted in the automatic accretion of Soviet power, since much of the loss in U.S. power and influence resulted in the improved international position of third powers, China in particular. Not only China, but Japan, Western Europe and the OPEC countries have visibly and measurably enhanced their role and influence in the international community. The continuing dispute with China and the Sino-American rapprochement have been perceived by the Soviet leaders as important factors which have partially compensated for the erosion of the U.S. side in the Soviet-American strategic balance.

The Sino-American rapprochement is viewed in Moscow as having temporarily arrested the decline in America's global position but only postponed its eventual disestablishment as a global power. At the same time, the American connection has served to catapult China into global pretensions somewhat prematurely and incompletely. Chinese power and influence lack an authentic global range although they bear all the earmarks of pre-globalism and serve as a supplemental anti-Soviet presence to the primary American countervailing force against the expansion of Soviet power. What is important, however, is that America's global commitments and range are contracting while those of the Soviet Union are modestly increasing and those of China have apparently reached their immediate limits. It is quite possible that the Soviet leadership may perceive that the variables which up to now have mitigated the loss of American power by diffusing it to third parties have been exhausted and that the continued erosion of American power will in the future automatically reflect itself as a relative gain for the Soviet Union.

If this be the case, then other restraining factors, external and internal, will loom larger in shaping Soviet behavior. It is at this point that important shifts of perception, alignment and power taking place in the international community outside the framework of détente and Soviet-American relations also serve to affect Soviet policy. Détente, so far, is largely although not exclusively an intra-European affair. The détente process was set into motion at a time when the Soviet leaders envisaged that the decline of U.S. power would take place over a relatively protracted period of time and would be neither precipitous nor convulsive. As U.S. power gradually declined, Soviet power would correspondingly grow at a similar pace. The most persuasive indication of this assumption was the reliance which Moscow was placing on the détente in the realm of expanding trade and credits with the capitalist world. This suggested a fairly long period of stability in the relations between the two countries and in the international community generally.

As Soviet capabilities grow, and if the global reflexes of the United States continue to wither, the Soviet Union will be increasingly drawn into the intersecting vortex of the various international environments in which it acts, as they overlap and interlock at various strategic points. The opportunities, options and temptations of the changing international environments will be enormous, but these will be counterbalanced to some degree by the proliferation of responsibilities, increased costs and burdens. Generally speaking, the risk threshold will be lowered, but the costs, burdens and responsibilities involved in taking advantage of new opportunities will increase and this becomes the principal overarching issue of the Soviet leadership as it confronts the changing situation with both apprehension and expectation.

The diminished role of the United States in the international system and the growing isolation of the Soviet Union within the world of communist states and parties comprise two of the three principal general alterations in the international system. Changes within the Third World of an unexpected and startling character have also taken place, as this amorphous collection of states congeals into three distinct categories—developing states, developable states and undevelopable states—to replace the single, somewhat euphemistic appellation of "developing" states. The lowered visibility of the United States on the international horizon and its diminished willingness to intervene in the Third World, has not necessarily exposed them all to the ravages of internal subversion and Soviet expansion, but has released some from dependence upon the United States. In the process, the differential capacity and potential of the states in the Third World to behave as independent actors in the international system have become apparent, as new choices and opportunities—aside from being dependent upon one of the two global powers—have made their appearance. The OPEC states, in particular, have boldly declared their economic and political autonomy, and in the process of challenging the industrial powers of the West, have demarcated for themselves a role and influence in the international system independent of the United States, the Soviet Union, China or the Third World as an aggregate body.

These changes within the Third World, and in particular its differentiation into developing, developable, and undevelopable states, create short-term opportunities but long-range problems for the Soviet Union. Soviet influence in the Third World will probably vary inversely with the individual state's capacity for development. The more capable they are of potential development, the less likely that Soviet influence will be desirable and lasting; the more incapable of development, the more likely the need for dependence upon the Soviet Union and hence the greater the likelihood of Soviet penetration. The Soviet leadership, however, cannot be entirely sanguine about the prospects of creating a new retinue of client states out of international "basket cases." It is precisely the frustrations and resentments of populations in countries whose potential for self-development is low that will be attracted by revolutionary slogans and promises, but they may also become an enormous drain upon the Soviet economy and a strain upon the Soviet political system.

The Impact of Détente *and the Changing Strategic Balance on Soviet Policy and Society*

The single most important equation in the international community today remains the strategic balance between the United States and the Soviet Union, and the increasingly dynamic character of this equation will determine the relationships between the two global powers as well as their individual and joint relationships with the rest of the international community. The nature of the relationship between the U.S. and the U.S.S.R. is characterized as détente in spite of the controversial, ambiguous and uncertain meanings attached to that concept, and this relationship in turn is founded upon a more or less precise military equation called strategic "parity," i.e., rough equality.

The mutual recognition and acceptance of strategic parity as the basis for the existing *détente* arrangement have been achieved only after more than two decades of strategic fluctuation within certain limits, as first the U.S. and then the U.S.S.R. developed a technological, economic or political advantage which threatened to tip the balance in one direction or another. The preservation of the parity formula, either in fact or by mutual ascriptive recognition, constitutes the *sine qua non* for the maintenance of the detente superstructure which it supports. Should the balance falter or should one party no longer accept parity as the basis for political relationships, then the détente superstructure could collapse.

The SALT I treaty represented the formal acceptance by both Moscow and Washington of the parity formula, but both sides were cognizant of the fact that in objective terms the United States enjoyed a measure of real strategic superiority. The parity of SALT I was thus *ascriptive* and also *normative* in the sense that the United States indicated that its policies and behavior would correspond to a condition of parity rather than superiority and that furthermore the United States was willing to allow an ascriptive parity to be transformed into actual equality. The superior qualitative ceilings permitted Moscow in SALT I with respect to size and number of ICBM's and number of SLBM's, without demanding a freeze on qualitative improvements were the *bona fides* that the United States extended to Moscow to demonstrate its sincerity. The Soviet leaders accepted the SALT I formula, but it cannot be ignored that Moscow may have perceived the U.S. position as stemming from neither generosity nor sincerity, but from an awareness of the eroding condition of American power and the self-perception of the U.S. that American power would continue to decline and erode while Soviet power would be free to grow unrestrained by externally imposed ceilings and domestic inhibitions. Thus, the Soviet leaders probably perceived the willingness of the U.S. to ascribe parity to a condition of actual American superiority as a trade-off for Soviet willingness to accept some mutually agreed upon quantitative ceilings on the future growth of Soviet strategic power.

This trade-off was subjected to severe criticism by Senator Jackson, Governor Reagan and to a substantial degree by professional military figures, who contended in effect that the ceilings were much too generous for the Soviet Union, particularly in the absence of qualitative limitations, since it could enable the Soviet side to achieve a substantially measurable quantitative and qualitative advantage over the United States without violating the treaty itself. Although critics of the Nixon-Kissinger policies and later of the Ford-Kissinger policies laced their criticisms with suspicion of Soviet intent and charges of treaty violations, the underlying complaint, which was real but perhaps unpersuasive politically, was that the U.S. strategic position was likely to continue its slide downwards from existing positions while Moscow would press to reach all of the ceilings allowed under SALT I and probably take advantage of every ambiguity in the treaty and to fudge the limits incrementally as well. In large measure, this was more a criticism of Kissinger's diplomatic ineptness or Moscow's anticipated duplicity. After all, given the existing political conditions within the United States, Moscow would need resort to little duplicity at all to achieve strategic superiority if it so chose.

Domestic criticism at home combined with sober second thoughts resulted in the Vladivostok agreement of 1974, which Kissinger with some hyperbole called a "conceptual" breakthrough, which it was indeed, but not necessarily in operational terms. Moscow agreed to accept additional quantitative limitations and to allow more flexible execution of those established by SALT I. For the first time, quantitative limitations were mutually established upon qualitative developments, i.e., the number of multiple independently targeted reentry vehicles was set at 1300 for each side, but at the same time disagreement developed over the precise definition of a strategic weapon, with particular reference to the U.S. cruise missile and the Soviet backfire bomber.

U.S. critics of Kissinger once again complained that the ceilings were too high, meaning, of course, without explicitly stating so, that while it was politically unlikely that the United States could achieve and sustain the allowable ceilings, there were no corresponding domestic restraints upon the Soviet side and that Moscow could still achieve substantial superiority within the revised formulas. What Kissinger's critics were saying, in effect, was that strategic arms agreements should be based upon mutual ceilings which corresponded to the maximum U.S. defense posture which was ob-

be sure, Soviet leaders anticipated that over time, the international situation would develop favorably for Moscow as the domestic situation progressively deteriorated in the United States. Moscow would pursue its foreign policy goals on an extended time-table; in return less risk, but incremental gains would aggregate and be eventually decisive in character.

Current Soviet economic planning and domestic policies are based upon foreign policy perceptions and assumptions that were developed between the Soviet invasion of Czechoslovakia and the signing of SALT I in 1972. These assumptions and perceptions, which may now be outmoded, nevertheless constituted the basis not only for SALT I and related agreements, but for the Helsinki Declaration as well, and while the perceptions and assumptions may no longer be valid from the Soviet perspective, the foreign policy which they support may still continue in force because of the economic plans and expectations which it supports.

Furthermore, there is strong reason to believe that these perceptions and assumptions were developed by Brezhnev and represent the distillation of the best expertise available in the Soviet Union. Thus, not only Brezhnev and his supporters, but the experts and advisers they relied upon, have a powerful vested stake in the success of existing policies. These perceptions and assumptions were as follows:

1) The U.S. still enjoyed strategic superiority and remained as the paramount powr in the international community and this would continue for some time, after which its position would gradually erode down to parity with the U.S.S.R.

2) Strategic parity would be relatively durable and would provide the foundation for a détente and relaxation of international tensions within the overall context of "peaceful co-existence."

3) Since détente was conceived as being relatively long duration, it would provide a basis for expanding Soviet commercial and cultural relations with the United States and the capitalist world and Soviet economic planning and calculations would be based upon this expectation.

4) "Progressive" social forces would continue to operate in the non-capitalist world, particularly in the Third World, which would in general move closer to the Soviet Union on diplomatic, political and eventually ideological issues.

5) It was expected, until just before SALT I, that China would remain isolated and vulnerable to Soviet threats and pressures, and that Moscow would bide its time until the passing of Mao Tse-tung.

6) Over time, Soviet power, prestige and influence would gradually expand while that of the U.S. would correspondingly diminish, but at a rate and tempo insufficient to arouse alarm or to provoke the mobilization of the public to reverse the situation.

It appears, however, that the calculations of the Soviet leadership have been upset. The apparent debilitation of U.S. resolve has manifested itself somewhat prematurely and in advance of the prior deterioration of U.S. society which was expected to precede it. The Soviet leaders are probably aware that the diminished capacity of the United States reflects neither a diminution of material capabilities nor deepseated structural deficiencies, but rather fortuitous volitional and psychological factors expressed in institutional and factional political conflict in a disillusioned post-Vietnam, post-Watergate America. No matter how temporary or transitional American incapacity may be, the immediate effect is to enhance and render more conspicuous the Soviet presence around the globe. It is the absence of American power which emphasizes the presence of Soviet might, rather than greater affirmative action on the part of Moscow. Even a minor and momentary reflex of America's strategic muscle, as in Portugal, for example, was sufficient to deter both Moscow and local Communists from pressing their advantage. Resolve in Moscow at this point is greater than in Washington and the immediate danger is that the Soviet leaders may be tempted into thinking that a superiority in resolve can compensate for inferiority in material capabilities.

It is important to bear in mind that one of the fundamental differences in the Soviet and American conceptions of parity is that the American concept is *normative, ascriptive* and *objective* in design, whereas there is no normative dimension to the Soviet concept of parity. This is a source of considerable confusion and misunderstanding. The American concept of parity, at least since 1967, is that parity is a goal that ought to be *sought* and *maintained* by both parties as a conscious, deliberate, more or less permanent condition. Both parties should strive to maintain parity as the basis for their relationships and each should have a vested stake in assisting the other to sustain it. The Soviet concept of parity is that it is up to each side to hold up its end of the strategic parity formula, and that it is permissible, indeed expected, that one side may falter and be unable to maintain its end of the balance and must accept the political consequences that flow from such a change. Moscow will accept *ascriptive* notions of parity so long as the ascriptive character of the formula benefits the Soviet Union, i.e., it is willing to accept an ascriptive definition of parity temporarily if the U.S. in fact enjoys superiority and will allow the Soviet Union to achieve actual parity, or if the Soviet Union enjoys superiority, calls it parity, but acts on the basis of superiority. Some of the criticism leveled at the Administration's conception of parity reflects the fear that as the strategic balance tips in favor of Moscow either through Soviet cheating or U.S. inability to maintain the posture necessary to sustain parity, the Administration may continue to insist that parity prevails and Moscow will go along because it will expect to benefit from such ascriptive designation.

The Impact of U.S. Politics on Soviet Policy

The American domestic condition emerges as one of the most significant changes in the external environment, and appears to be having a fundamental impact on the perception of the Soviet leaders with respect to future Soviet behavior. This impact is by no means one-sided, for while it creates vistas of new opportunities and options combined with recalculated risk and cost factors, it also introduces a new variable into the Soviet domestic debate as to precisely how to take advantage of this premature, if not exactly unforeseen, windfall. Should Moscow utilize the lowered perception of risks and costs to step up its militancy in foreign policy and increase its gains in that arena? Or should it be satisfied with existing advantages in foreign policy and utilize the lowered risk perceptions and costs calculations to re-allocate priorities and pay greater attention to chronic and serious domestic problems, now that such a shift would not be at the expense of either lessened defense or a reduction of diplomatic gains?

The principal external deterrents to increased militancy in foreign policy in order to take advantage of America's apparent inability or unwillingness to react or respond in marginal or noncritical areas are two in number. (1) The first is the possibility that a renewed Soviet offensive in foreign policy could once again make credible the "Communist threat" and thus galvanize the American public into reversing the American slide and making a determined effort to meet the Soviet challenge. This would mean that the "Cold War" would be resumed with full fury, and given the economic and human resources and capabilities of the United States, the Soviet Union once again might come out second best in such a contest, with incalculable damage to its image of prudence and responsibility which has contributed to its international prestige in recent years. (2) The second external deterrent is economic and could be operative together or independently of the first. Given the inefficient state of the Soviet economy and its manifold deficiencies, particularly in agriculture, increased Soviet militancy in foreign affairs could not only arrest and rupture the extensive international commercial transactions negotiated with the capitalist states, but also seriously interfere with the importation of grain from the United States and other food-exporting countries.

The possible interruption of access to outside technological, financial and economic assistance, at a time when the Soviet economy is in serious difficulty and grain production has been the lowest in a decade, could aggravate the debate over economic priorities, which had been more or less temporarily stabilized. Old wounds would be reopened, painful modifications in the structure of priorities and investments would have to be contemplated, and the various bureaucracies would once again be pitted against one another. The timing for such a renewed battle over priorities comes at a particularly awkward moment, since the aging Soviet leadership is on the brink of passing the torch to the next generation, and the succession problem could become aggravated if it occurs at a time of sharp factional conflict over priorities and changes in the direction of internal and external policies.

Conversely, the changing international environment could overtake events in the Soviet Union and actually provoke a succession problem by creating the opportunity for critics to contest the policies and priorities of a leadership about to pass from the scene, by raising old issues within a new context and challenging the validity of earlier assessments of the international situation.

Thus, whereas the immediate risks of a renewed militancy in foreign policy are currently low, they remain high for the long-run, but even more importantly, the more the Soviet economy is plugged into Western economies and the more its technological development, food consumption, credits and trade depend upon Western good will, then the greater the costs and eventually burdens and strains that the Soviet Union will bear. Hence, although the international situation may appear increasingly tempting to the Soviet leaders, and internal pressures for increased militancy are undoubtedly being exerted, the current leadership is not likely to shift from a policy of détente unless the prospects for success are assured and the gains are immense.

From the Soviet standpoint, the overall strategic balance or "correlation of forces" is shifting in favor of Moscow, not only because of the continuing Soviet military build-up, but also because of the social and political conditions in American society. As early as 1971, on the eve of the SALT I treaty, one Soviet writer focused explicitly on the importance of the link between U.S. domestic political constraints and the impairment of foreign policy:

> "Political reality" also includes the domestic political situation in the U.S. itself, where the popular masses are demanding increasingly, decisively, and loudly the renunciation of military adventures abroad and the administration's turning to face the internal socio-economic problems....Moments arise when the split between the sentiments and feelings of broad public circles and official policy proves so deep that a bourgeois government, wishing to remain in power, either has to correct official policy or resign from power....The present Republican administration must take into account the opinion of the overwhelming majority of voters who support...the reduction of U.S. military commitments abroad.[4]

One of the unnoticed by-products of Soviet-American global rivalry has been the increasing interpenetrative character of Soviet-American relations, which can no longer be characterized as simply the intersection of foreign policy outputs. Both powers are intimately concerned and have become progressively implicated in the domestic affairs of one another and seek in

---

4. A. Trofimenko, "Politicheskii realizm i strategiia 'realisticheskogo sderzhivanii'," *S.Sh.A.: ekonomika, politika, ideologia*, No. 12 (Dec. 1971), pp. 6-7.

diverse if unevenly effective ways to influence domestic events and conditions. As the foreign policies of both countries are mutually perceived as external extensions of domestic policies and interests, each becomes sensitized to the domestic inputs as well as external outputs. The process of interpenetration is far from systematic, and the two powers vary widely in the levers and methods at their disposal as well as the degree to which they permit outside powers access to the political process. The Russians are by no means novices in this connection, but in recent years, they have become more sophisticated in their appreciation and understanding of American institutions and political processes. No longer are they restricted to the crude manipulation of American sympathizers, Communists or Front Organizations, but increasingly they have learned to employ the methods and manners of professional lobbyists and public relations operators, to say nothing of manipulating the press and electronic media to their advantage.

Soviet representatives maintain discrete contacts in both the executive and legislative branches of government, are familiar with the important access and pressure points in the political system, and more importantly are mastering the art of coordinating policies, interests and actions with constituencies in the United States. Thus, the Soviet Union, through adroit behavior, has developed "inadvertent" domestic constituencies, such as farmers, grain dealers, businessmen and others whose interest happen to coincide with those of the Soviet Union and can be expected to exert independent pressure on behalf of their self-interest and in the process advance the interest of the Soviet Union as well.

Soviet policy makers, in the past several years, have witnessed the recrudescence of congressional power in foreign affairs, the mechanics of executive-legislative conflict, and the patterns of factional and polemical politics. Soviet leaders are not unmindful of the fact that many American politicians make pilgrimages to Moscow to advance their political ambitions and this to a degree makes them potentially useful to Soviet policy. Knowledge and access to the American political process becomes an important input into Soviet decision-making and thus affects the Soviet policy-making process. Being aware that a President or Secretary of State is crippled or fettered by Congress or whose position is likely to be repudiated, creates advantages for Moscow. Under certain circumstances, through adroit timing, congressional criticism of Administration policy may coincide inadvertently or fortuitously with Soviet positions and as a result, Congress may by law or inaction provide the Soviet Union with advantages it might not otherwise gain.

Similarly, the Soviet side may use an impending American election or an executive-legislative impasse to delay, postpone or exert pressure on the United States. Thus, the sharp attacks upon Secretary of State Kissinger and the need for additional foreign policy "successes" in the areas of détente and arms control on the part of an incumbent Administration seeking to renew its mandate may create bargaining advantages for Moscow.

The adjustment and accommodation of the Soviet Union to the American political process in order to employ it to advantage in turn feeds back to affect the Soviet decision-making structures, and the two political systems not only interact and intersect but to some degree also become interlocked.

U.S. attempts directly to influence the internal political process and internal events of the USSR is a totally new experience for both sides. Previously restricted largely to the use of short-wave radio broadcasts and other marginal methods, U.S. bargaining over Jewish emigration, the Jackson Amendment and Basket 3 of the Helsinki Agreement are important milestones in this new venture by the United States. The issue of Soviet domestic institutional structures and policy processes is of paramount concern to the United States, not only because they involve questions of civil rights, but also because under existing conditions the Soviet Union enjoys a clear advantage in its ability to influence domestic American politics and policies. In effect, what the United States is pressing for is parity in the realm of mutual access to each other's societies as well as parity in strategic weapons, since in some respects the state of the latter is conditioned and influenced by the former.

In sum, mutual access to each other's policy processes becomes an increasingly important calculation in the overall "correlation of forces" between the two countries. Hence, the interpenetrative character of Soviet and American domestic politics is likely to grow, particularly if executive-legislative conflicts over methods and objectives in foreign policy continue.

The Impact of the Helsinki Agreement on Soviety Society

In this connection the potential impact of the Helsinki Agreement on Soviet society and the Soviet political process invites serious attention. Its capacity for political mischief is immense, insofar as the Soviet regime is concerned, and already the Soviet authorities have been repeatedly placed on the defensive in connection with its implementation. The Helsinki Agreement emerges as an important symbolic expression of détente in Europe, one whose significance was inadvertently enhanced by the eagerness of the Soviet leaders to consummate it. The capacity of the Helsinki Document for political mischief is not restricted to the Soviet Union, but extends to Eastern Europe and its relationship with the U.S.S.R. and even more ominously to Western European Communist Parties and their relationships with the Soviet Union.

The Helsinki Agreement represents basically a compromise between the U.S. and the U.S.S.R. on the basic rules of détente, in which the Soviet Union traded off lip-service to the free flow of ideas and persons in return for a U.S. and Western recognition of the *territorial* status quo, not necessarily the political or ideological status quo.

In return for U.S. agreement on security and boundary questions, the Soviet Union reluctantly accepted the so-called Basket 3 of the Declaration relating to the free flow of ideas, persons, information, communications and other humanitarian and cultural concerns. What the Soviet leaders subscribed to in Basket 3 not only contradicts the Brezhnev Doctrine and certain key principles of Socialist internationalism, but the Soviet constitution itself, and most emphatically Soviet internal practice. To be sure, so far, this represents only lip-service and the implications for the Soviet Union are not immediate but only potential. The danger that the Declaration might unleash forces in Eastern Europe, however, are much more serious. This may account for the defensive Soviet tone concerning Basket 3, its attempt to downgrade it as a secondary aspect of the Helsinki Agreement, and its virtually explicit disavowal of any intention to give most of its provisions any immediate effect inside the Soviet Union.[5] But, if only to deter and arrest their possible implementation in Eastern Europe, the Soviet leaders must refuse to give them effect at home, lest an all too welcome precedent is established for the East Europeans to emulate. Thus, we have the strange spectacle of President Ford explicitly disavowing Soviet interpretations of Basket 1 (security and boundary questions) and Secretary General Brezhnev explicitly repudiating "bourgeois" interpretations of Basket 3 (humanitarian and information questions).[6]

The U.S. and Western Europe have certain expectations concerning détente and these do not always coincide with those of Moscow, but in fact contradict them in many respects. What Moscow considers to be the chief common denominator of détente—i.e., the acceptance of the status quo in Europe, ceilings on strategic weapons and related agreements, and the relaxation of international tensions—the U.S. and Western Europe consider to be essentially Western concessions in return for which Moscow will introduce social and political changes at home that seriously affect East-West relations and serve as confidence inspiring measures.

This trade-off is virtually explicit in the Helsinki Declaration, as Georgii Arbatov has indirectly conceded, while simultaneously attempting to repudiate it:

> After the final act was signed at the Helsinki Conference...the West began making attempts to reduce the significance of the Conference to two propositions: the consolidation of the postwar European frontiers (which the West claims is a great concession to the Soviet Union for which the West expects repayment) and what is termed in diplomatic language the "third basket," covering in the humanitarian and other fields. It is this latter consolidation that is the payment that the Soviet Union

5. Cf. *The New York Times* [hereafter *NYT*], 28 Sept. 1975 and 2 Oct. 1975.
6. See *NYT*, 23 July 1975 for President Ford's statement, and 16 Aug. 1975 for an account of Brezhnev's comments on the Declaration to a visiting U.S. Congressional delegation.

must give to the West for the West's recognition of the existing European Frontiers.[7]

There is little question but that in accepting Basket 3 of the Helsinki Declaration, the Soviet regime committed itself to provisions which are in fundamental conflict with the Brezhnev Doctrine and Soviet social and political policy. Unlike Soviet law or the Soviet Constitution, which are internal documents and which Soviet authorities can contravene without justifying external interference, violating similar provisions in the Helsinki Declaration involves noncompliance with an international agreement and thus external involvement is automatically legitimated. Since the signing of the Helsinki Declaration, the Soviet press, Brezhnev, and other Soviet leaders have been busily attempting to interpret certain provisions of Basket Three out of existence. Thus, Arbatov writes:

> In reference to the item in the Final Act on freedom of information, the Soviet Union intends to earnestly fulfill all provisions recorded. However, if some people regard them as an invitation to fling open the door to subversive and anti-Soviet pro-violence, propaganda, or to fan national and racial strife, then they are laboring in vain. Neither the document signed in Helsinki nor détente will permit such occurrences.[8]

It is clear, even from Soviet accounts, that Moscow committed itself to do something in accordance with Basket Three, but how much remains in considerable dispute. Soviet ideologists must first develop a credible basis for rendering Helsinki compatible with the principle of not extending détente or co-existence into the realm of ideas. This has, of course, been a standard Soviet refrain for some time and reflects essentially a recognized vulnerability that must be protected. The Soviet leaders are painfully aware that Basket Three is incompatible with the nature of their system as it now exists, but they are determined to preserve the essential character of the Soviet social order and will adopt all necessary measures to maximize its maintenance. There are too many glaring weaknesses and obvious malfunctions in Soviet society for the Soviet leaders to risk the importation of competing ideas or to allow the expression of dissident and critical views on the part of its own citizens. For the moment, the West should proceed cautiously, refrain from insisting on the immediate extension of "peaceful co-existence" into the ideological realm, and refrain from demanding that the Soviet leaders "open up" their country to foreign ideals. Demands of this character will serve to reinforce the suspicions of the Soviet leaders who interpret the co-existence of ideologies and the interpenetration of ideas as devices for undermining and weakening the communist system. A prolonged relaxation of international tensions and détente will create manifold internal problems for Soviet society in any event, and will serve to weaken the legitimacy of the Communist Party and hence the Soviet system itself. On the other hand,

7. Georgii Arbatov, "Problemy i suzhdeniia: Manevry protivnikov razriadki," *Izvestiia*, 4 Sept. 1975.
8. *Ibid.*

Western governments, private groups and citizens should engage the Soviet Union in "ideological battle," and should not be inhibited by charges of "psychological warfare," "anti-Soviet slander," or "cold warriorism." If Moscow insists that the "battle of ideas" continues unabated, she must be prepared to accept the consequences.

While the Soviet regime is overtly concerned principally with the risks of Western influences penetrating into Soviet society, the détente and Helsinki pose an even greater threat to Soviet management of Eastern Europe in this regard, to say nothing of the even greater danger of influences which individual countries of Eastern Europe may have upon one another. Influences from the West can always be routinely stigmatized and proscribed as "capitalist," "imperialist," "decadent," etc. while those from China can, with less credibility and effectiveness, be condemned as "heretical." But it would be increasingly difficult to deter mutual contamination within Eastern Europe, as long as the ideas and innovations are derived from a country which has been legitimized as "socialist" by the Soviet regime.

It should be emphasized that the Helsinki Agreement is a European agreement, not a socialist one. The East European states attended and participated in their separate capacities, not as members of a bloc. There exists no unified, authoritative Communist-bloc interpretation of its provisions, although Moscow may attempt to establish such an interpretation at the next meeting of the Warsaw Pact Organization. Each Communist state can interpret the agreement for itself, and indeed East Germany already has on a number of points; and while the Soviet Union may enunciate a "line," it may not be able to enforce it.

Since the Helsinki Agreement contradicts the Brezhnev Doctrine and many internal practices of the East European states, the East European states may erode or abolish certain internal practices relating to humanitarian and informational concerns by justifying their behavior not as defiance of the Soviet Union but as compliance with the Helsinki Agreement. It should not be too surprising to see disputes arise between Moscow and some East European states over whether a certain change in policy is in compliance with Helsinki or in defiance of the principles of socialist internationalism, when in fact it may be both simultaneously. Although many Western critics charged that the Helsinki Agreement might encourage the "Finlandization" of Western Europe, there is the distinct possibility that it may encourage the Finlandization of Eastern Europe, much to the chagrin of Moscow. And should the Soviet Union once again resort to intervention to arrest such developments, it would be in direct contravention of the security and boundary provisions of the Agreement (of which Moscow was the principal author and supporter) and this contributes incrementally to Soviet liabilities as well.

The defensive tone of the Soviet press with respect to the humanitarian and informational provisions of the Helsinki Agreement reflects genuine

Soviet fears and perhaps internal criticism of the concessions made by Moscow. It is noteworthy that American defensiveness about boundaries quickly evaporated once President Ford and Secretary Kissinger explicitly disavowed Soviet interpretations of those provisions. U.S. disavowal of Moscow's interpretations of Basket 1 cannot in any way be construed as non-compliance with Helsinki; they can be construed only as non-compliance with the interpretations which critics like Solzhenitsyn and Brezhnev gave to the American signature. On the other hand, Soviet disavowals of Western interpretations of Basket 3 represent attempts to avoid compliance with Helsinki and this accounts for the defensive and self-conscious tone of the Soviet press. Aside from the possibility that Soviet refusal to implement Basket 3 can always stand as a potential excuse for the U.S. and Western Europe to disavow Basket 1, the Soviet refusal to implement the humanitarian and informational provisions of the Helsinki Agreement exposes Moscow as an open violator of international agreements which she initiated and signed after considerable fanfare and enthusiasm.

Even more critically for Moscow, it would indeed be difficult for Moscow credibly to criticize East European states for taking measures in compliance with the Helsinki Agreement. It is one thing to violate a treaty oneself, still another to force second parties to violate an international agreement, and still yet a third matter to prevent compliance on the part of another state.

Détente is a process as well as an existing condition, and it is as a process that it is likely to influence internal Soviet developments. More pointedly, détente, by creating a less tense international environment cannot but serve as a conditioning factor for future Soviet generations. Just as the current generation was conditioned by the post-Stalinist thaw and Khrushchevian reforms, the same generation will now continue to mature under conditions of international détente, while the succeeding generation will spend its formative years under these conditions. No matter how harsh the ideological rhetoric and propaganda, as long as the détente continues and relaxation of tensions is a fact of existence, it will have increasingly diminished impact since the rhetoric will be out of phase with both Soviet and Western behavior.

And finally, it must be remembered that the future leadership of the country will be recruited from generations not only conditioned by the Khrushchevian reforms and matured in the détente atmosphere, but increasingly their constituencies will be drawn from generations conditioned and matured in an era of détente. The leadership which replaces the current gerontocracy will be under no compulsion to adapt the perceptions or perpetuate the policies and behavioral practices of the existing leadership, but will undoubtedly be animated by different perceptions moved by different issues and problems, and will search for new solutions and approaches.

The Impact of Changes in the Communist World

In this regard, recent developments in the pronouncements and political strategies of West European Communist Parties are of signal significance. It has come as some surprise that the first serious impact of the Helsinki Document has been neither in the Soviet Union nor Eastern Europe but upon the structure and ideology of the Communist Parties of France and Britain. Both, as well as the Spanish Communist Party, have moved closer to the positions of the Italian Communist Party. Both the French and British Parties have become increasingly embarrassed by the primitive political processes in the Soviet Union and they have publicly expressed their displeasure with Soviet treatment of political dissidents in the face of the Soviet signature of the Helsinki Agreement.[9] George Marchais has called upon the French Party to repudiate the concept of the "dictatorship of the proletariat" as an anachronism unsuited to the modern world and all too painfully reminiscent of Hitler, Mussolini and Franco.[10] The joint declaration of the French and Italian Communist Parties, in effect disassociating themselves from Soviet policy, may ultimately have a greater impact upon the Soviet Union and Eastern Europe than the Helsinki Document, but since the Declaration echoes Helsinki in considerable measure, whatever influence the Italian and French developments have upon the Soviet system can indirectly be attributed to Helsinki.[11]

The proliferation of idiosyncratic "national" communist heresies in China, Eastern Europe, and now Western Europe has also been accompanied by the emergence of exotic "Marxist-Leninist" regimes in Africa which Moscow views with considerable ambivalence and apprehension. While the dilution of communism imparts to it greater flexibility and appeal, it simultaneously poses problems of assimilation and cooptation, with the possibility of feedback effects upon Soviet Party structure and ideology. On the other hand, refusal to welcome and accept the "hot-house" and "do-it-yourself" Communist regimes can also serve to isolate the Soviet Union and retrovert its system to simply another form of "national" communism (i.e., Russian), which in turn could arouse the non-Russian nationalities to demand their own form of "national" communism. The appearance and adherence of large numbers of underdeveloped states, particularly in Africa, calling themselves "Marxist-Leninist" could further aggravate the "national problem" in the U.S.S.R. as new states, with the barest credentials of statehood, nationhood, and Marxist-Leninisthood are brought into contact with the more modernized and historically rooted

9. See *NYT*, 5 Feb. 1976.
10. *Ibid.* See also *NYT*, 6 and 7 Feb. 1976.
11. For the first angry reactions to Western communist criticism of Moscow's treatment of dissidents and unwillingness to implement Basket 3, see "O svobodakh podlinnykh i mnimykh," in *P*, 20 Feb. 1976. See also *NYT*, 21 Feb. 1976.

Soviet nations, who remain deprived of authentic statehood.

The Soviet leaders, particularly the ideologues among them, can only view with a mixture of pleasure and dismay the uncontrolled and capricious flowering, first of native "African Socialism" and now African "Marxism-Leninism," which forces Moscow to react and respond to these gestures. Soviet ideologues, charged with maintaining the orthodoxy and purity of Soviet ideology against the ravages of Maoism, Titoism and now West European heresies, will be additionally faced with the burden of maintaining high ideological standards against what may turn out to be pressures of nativist populist parties self-designated as Marxist-Leninist parties.

The response of some African movements to Soviet criticisms of "African socialism" had been to designate themselves almost frivolously into Marxist-Leninist movements, parties and regimes, as if this was all that was called for. This movement from "African socialism" to "African Marxist-Leninism," while welcomed publicly and on the surface by Moscow, is viewed with mixed and ambivalent feelings:

> In countries with a socialist orientation, the revolutionary-democratic parties.... However, premature announcements that revolutionary-democratic parties have become Marxist-Leninist...would not be in the basic interests of the working people. It would be wrong to force this process. [12]

The Outlook: Soviet Expectations and Anxieties

In spite of the vast alterations in the military, political and ideological landscape that have taken place over the past twenty years, the destiny of the world is still shaped and will continue to be conditioned by the strategic

---

12. P.I. Manchkha, "Communists, Revolutionary Democrats and the Noncapitalist Path of Development in African Countries," *Voprosy istorii KPSS*, No. 10 (Oct. 1974), pp. 47-69, as reported in *Current Digest of the Soviet Press*, 21 Jan. 1976, p. 5. The following African countries were described as in a pre-Marxist-Leninist phase of "revolutionary-democracy": Guinea, Mali, Congo, Tanzania, Sierra Leone, and Somalia. While condemning premature proclamations of "Marxism-Leninism," the article concludes by noting that "certain African countries (Congo, for example) are gradually transforming revolutionary-democratic parties into vanguard parties of the working people, and this certainly merits attention." The Congo, of course has declared itself a Marxist-Leninist regime, but it has yet to receive the formal imprimatur from Moscow. While African countries are prematurely marching towards Marxism-Leninism, North Korea seems to be engaged in its own movement in the opposite direction. For some strange reason, Kim Il-Sung has been publishing full-page ads in the *NYT* to display his rhetoric. One such ad on 1 Feb. 1976 revealed that the Korean Democratic Republic had joined "the non-aligned movement as a full member." Kim has also revived the distinctly un-Marxist-Leninist practice of promoting his son Kim Il-Jong to the number two position in the Party and designating him as his successor. See *NYT*, 22 Feb. 1976. Whether Kim's movement into the "non-aligned" camp is designed to disassociate himself from the World communist movement and to shield North Korea from the fallout of the Sino-Soviet conflict, or whether Kim is serving as a communist "Trojan Horse" in the non-aligned group, is not at this point entirely clear.

balance between the U.S.A. and the U.S.S.R. As noted above, the increasing role and power of other states, especially China, is becoming more significant and may in time seriously alter the bipolarization of military power, just as the bipolarization of political and ideological power has already been seriously disrupted. Even more ominous is the possibility that the current transition period may be but a prelude to the military bipolarization of the world along developmental and racial lines. Thus, while it is true that the bi-polar political-ideological international system had been significantly eroded and has given rise to an emergent *political* and *ideological* multipolarity, this has not yet been matched by a corresponding military debipolarization and multi-polarity. The Soviet Union and the U.S.A. together still command virtually 90 percent of the effective and immediately usable stategic and nuclear power in the world today and this fact still conditions and shapes the behavior of other states.

In assessing the motivations of the Soviet Union in entering into a detente arrangement, a multitude of reasons have been advanced, most of them plausible and valid in varying degrees: fear of nuclear war, need for Western trade and technology, to shift economic priorities, lull the West into a false sense of security, gain recognition for Soviet control of Eastern Europe, prepare for possible generational domestic social and political turmoil, and, finally, fear of China. Fear of China must be accounted among the most important immediate reasons for Soviet reasonableness in the West, but "fear of China" is essentially part of a larger, more distant perhaps, but potentially more all-encompassing fear of a unified underdeveloped, demographically congested, non-European world mobilized by China against the developed, European world, of which the Soviet Union geographically and fortuitously becomes an advanced rampart.

Overt Soviet policy, of course, still does not coincide with these latent fears, whose perceptions can be gleaned not only from a close reading of the Soviet literature, and more graphically in conversations with Soviet citizens, and the official Moscow position remains that of an enthusiastic supporter of oppressed peoples everywhere against capitalism, colonialism and imperialism. But it is no secret that Soviet policy makers and citizens have been having second thoughts about the wisdom of encouraging and supporting revolutions in underdeveloped, non-European areas against capitalism, colonialism and imperialism, which has been simultaneously a revolution against the European and developed world, of which the Soviet Union is a part. The self-perception of the Soviet Union as a Eurasian or Asiaoeuropean state, which was once viewed as an asset in Soviet foreign policy, is increasingly assuming the dimensions of a vulnerability, since the Asian populations of the U.S.S.R., particularly those in Central Asia, might under certain circumstances be induced to identify themselves with the broader non-European world rather than with the European part of the U.S.S.R. The disproportionate growth rates of the European and Asian populations of the U.S.S.R. has emerged as a matter of grave concern for

Soviet leaders, as reflected in recent Soviet demographic literature which deplores the low growth rates in the Western parts of the Soviet Union and discusses measures whereby birth rates can be improved at a time when elsewhere in the world, the zero-population growth rate in the Western regions of the U.S.S.R. would be regarded as a boon. It is quite possible, given current demographic trends in the Soviet Union, that the Soviet demographic balance between Asian and European populations may shift in favor of the former at the same time that a shift in the global balance of power takes place between Asia and Europe, which may in turn give way to racial bi-polarization within the U.S.S.R. and possible territorial dismemberment.

The détente thus represents, in the broadest contextual sense, the reentry of the U.S.S.R. into Europe and its primary identification as a European state, as symbolized in the Helsinki Declaration. Soviet adherence to the Helsinki Declaration and the détente thus simultaneously represents a definite movement on the part of the U.S.S.R. in the direction of identifying itself primarily in geographical, racial, developmental, and civilizational terms rather than in ideological terms. From a European *Communist* state, the U.S.S.R. is becoming a *European* Communist state. This transformation, of course, corresponds with an analogous shift in identity by China as well.

Moscow expects numerous advantages to develop as a result of its reidentification with Europe: the expansion of trade and commerce; the importation of Western science and technology; the receipt of long-term financial credits; the establishment of a reliable source of grain; the stabilization of the territorial status quo in Eastern Europe, thus lessening tensions and anxieties in Eastern Europe (particularly East Germany) and the Soviet Union; and most importantly, the demonstration to Western Europe that Moscow is a worthy leader that can deliver peace and create the conditions for economic prosperity. Ultimately, it is hoped that Western Europe, individually and collectively, will progressively become "Chileanized" as communist parties become socially and politically legitimized and enter into West European coalition regimes. This is for the long-term, but for the time being, Moscow is uninterested in moving too fast and seeks instead a cooperative Europe rather than new accretions to the network of European socialist states.

Given the provisions of the joint declaration of the French and Italian Communist Parties, however, the possibility of a Socialist-Communist alliance in Western Europe and the prospect of a "humanized" communism could raise considerably more havoc for the Soviet Union than Maoism. Although China threatens to provide underdeveloped countries with an alternative communist model and thus alienate these countries from Moscow, Maoism has never posed a threat to the character of Soviet or East European Communist societies. A successful coalition regime in France or

Italy, on the other hand, would not only provide an alternative model for Communist parties in developed industrial states (including Japan), but more importantly could infect both East European and Soviet systems. The renunciation of the "Dictatorship of the Proletariat" by Western European parties confronts the Soviet leaders with an ideological crisis of incalculable magnitude. Either Moscow must disavow such a heresy or accept it as an acceptable or tolerable variant of communism, and hence a *legitimate and attractive* model to emulate or borrow from. In spite of these risks and possibilities, Moscow, on balance, would probably still welcome coalition regimes of the Allende type in Western Europe.

Moscow's prudence with respect to domestic events in Portugal as well as the Soviet Union's relative grace when diplomatically humiliated by Sadat and Kissinger in the Middle East, amply demonstrate the importance that the Soviet Union attaches to the preservation of the détente in its present form. In the case of Portugal, it refrained from taking advantage of a situation which could have created a Communist ruled state in Western Europe, whereas in the Middle East, it refrained from overtly attempting to preserve its immense diplomatic, economic and military investment in Egypt in order to preserve the détente. Furthermore, it had earlier taken the unusual step of altering domestic policies and laws concerning emigration in order to meet terms which the U.S. Congress was demanding in return for U.S. credits and "most favored nation" treatment. Only when Congress attempted to convert an informal agreement into an official acknowledgment concerning the precise number of Soviet citizens to be allowed to emigrate and furthermore established a ridiculously low ceiling of $300,000,000 in credits to Moscow, did the Soviet Union balk and repudiate previous arrangements. Nevertheless, the détente progressed along its course and was sealed at Helsinki, again demonstrating the high priority which Moscow attaches to détente with the West.

If the United States appears to have lost considerable prestige, influence, and measurable power in the past five years, and appears to be in danger of losing even more, it should be noted that this has not resulted principally from more aggressive, sinister and duplicitous behavior on the part of the Soviet Union. Rather, it has primarily been the product of the lack of domestic consensus, the turmoil, self-examination, and self-flagellation it has inspired, and the reordering of priorities in accordance with internal pressures. It is not the sinister manipulation of détente by Moscow that may result in Soviet diplomatic gains but the failure of the United States to hold up its end of the strategic balance and exploit its military, economic and technological potential to the limits permitted by the détente arrangement, that is more likely to be responsible. There is little question that the Soviet Union will exploit every ambiguity in the SALT agreements, fudge repeatedly and even cheat, but this is less likely to upset the strategic balance than the erosion of the American end of the strategic balance. When critics of détente charge that the Soviet Union has gained an advantage in the SALT agreements and related entente arrangements, they are really complaining that under conditions of a relaxation of international tensions, the American public and Congress may allow America's military capabilities to erode. This is indeed a serious possibility and the Kremlin will no doubt take advantage of it, but it can hardly be blamed for it. There is no provision in the SALT agreements and the détente relationship that includes a de-escalator clause to the effect that, if U.S. strategic capabilities diminish or fail to reach the limits allowed under the agreements, then the Soviet Union, in fairness, should reduce its capabilities correspondingly. As noted earlier, Soviet decision-makers fully expect this to happen under détente, just as the United States has expectations that détente will condition and influence the Soviet domestic situation. Indeed these are the kinds of mutual expectations that make détente possible.

Détente creates difficult if different problems for both societies; it creates expectations in both societies, although of a different order in each, and the leaderships must contend with these expectations and problems. The Helsinki Agreement, for example, has created manifold problems for the Soviet leadership both inside Eastern Europe and in the propaganda battle with the West. Just as the United States finds it difficult to sustain a domestic consensus and to maintain military readiness under conditions of détente the Soviet leaders find it extraordinarily difficult to handle the blatant contradictions between the provisions of Basket 3 in the Helsinki Agreement and their own practices at home and in Eastern Europe and are betraying remarkable sensitivity to Western charges of non-compliance. Thus Brezhnev, who is probably under attack at home for accepting Basket 3 in the first place, complained in a speech in Warsaw on 9 December 1975, in effect, that unfair advantage was being taken by the West in its constant emphasis on the importance of Basket 3 and Soviet non-compliance. Brezhnev charged that instead of taking the "document as a whole," critics are "succumbing to the temptation to tear separate chunks (i.e., Basket 3) out of it which some regard as tactically more convenient to them." Charging that Western critics were violating the spirit of détente by "using ideological infiltration and economic levers...to weaken our unity... to undermine the mainstays of socialism, now in one fraternal country, now in another," Brezhnev literally pleaded that Moscow intended "to exert efforts to implement" the Helsinki Agreement, but that this was being made difficult by "some influential circles in Western countries" who engage "in campaigns of misinformation or slander against socialist countries...intended to cause a reply reaction and poison the situation."[13]

Just as one can hardly blame Western critics for Brezhnev's inability or unwillingness to implement Basket 3 of the Helsinki Agreement, which is a

13. *NYT,* 10 Dec. 1975.

product of the give-and-take of détente, one can hardly blame Moscow for a large number of developments in the United States that have seriously affected America's international image and effectiveness: the unilateral mothballing of America's only ABM site; the extravagant expenses of an all-volunteer army; the impeachment proceedings and subsequent resignation of President Nixon; the public investigation and excoriation of the CIA, the FBI, and the National Security Agency, along with the exposure of their secrets, misdeeds, plots and conspiracies; congressional cuts in the defense budget; the curtailment of research and development; the periodic calls by legislators and politicians for a unilateral halt to the development and deployment of new weapons systems, and unilateral force reductions in Western Europe; the public discussion before congressional committees of past, current and future U.S. military and diplomatic strategy, etc., etc. Although the United States has long been accustomed to conducting its diplomacy and foreign policy in a fish bowl, discussing intelligence activities and military plans in the same arena is a new departure.

While each of these developments taken separately may be understandable and explainable as justifiable exercises in democratic vitality, commendable and courageous exhibitions in moral self-examination, and admirable reflections of popular control, nevertheless taken as a whole—simultaneously, instantaneously and cumulatively—they project an image of debility, division, confusion and paralysis. Whatever benefits may be yielded in the long run, in the short run, this flood of national public self-exposure cannot but tarnish American prestige, damage its credibility and cripple its diplomacy. Irrespective of what these signals may mean at home, it is quite likely that they send different messages to Moscow and elsewhere.

Russia, America, and Detente*

During the past year, spokesmen in the Carter Administration have on various occasions urged us to be less preoccupied with the Soviet problem. Because of the rise of Soviet military power, it has been said, there was a tendency in recent administrations to see Soviet-American relations as the center of the universe and to pay inadequate attention to other forms of power and trends extant in international affairs, including some of the less than successful ventures of Soviet foreign policy in the past few years. President Carter, in a major address at Notre Dame University last May, suggested that we had been given to an "inordinate fear" of the Soviet Union and that it was time to approach our relations with Moscow with greater confidence.

Nevertheless, the problem of Soviet power remains a central concern for the United States. As Marshall Shulman, formerly of Columbia University and now the principal Soviet affairs advisor to Secretary of State Vance, stated in congressional testimony last October: "there is scarcely an aspect of international life that is not affected by this relationship, and that would not be made more difficult and more dangerous by a high level of Soviet-American tension and unregulated competition."

*Reprinted by permission of the author and the publisher from *Foreign Affairs* (January, 1978); Copyright 1978 by Council on Foreign Relations, Inc.

Some of our debates about Soviet policy have tended to turn more on the definition of the labels that have been attached to it than on substance. "Containment," "cold war," "an era of negotiation," "détente," and a host of other phrases have paraded through the headlines over the years. They all caught elements of the complex realities and challenges confronting American statecraft in dealing with the U.S.S.R., but over time they came to obscure rather than illuminate them. Some of them, like "containment" in its day, and "détente" most recently, have acquired pejorative meanings. It is instructive to go back to the debates over Soviet purposes and American policies 30 years ago to find that invidious definitions of "détente" —like "one-way street" and "giveaway"—had their almost precise antecedents at that time.

President Carter, at Notre Dame, sought to take the curse off "detente" and to return it to respectability by defining it as "progress toward peace," involving cooperation which also implies obligations. This seemed a sensible way to describe the issues in a relationship which, Administration officials have once again wisely reminded us, will long be marked by a mixture of cooperation and competition. Policy, of course, should try to shape this mixture and the contents of each element in ways that protect and advance American interests and values. Put another way, given the weight of the Soviet Union in international affairs as it now exists and evolves, we must be concerned with the role it plays; and our policies must be concerned with how we can help to affect that role. That does not necessarily make the Soviet Union the center of the universe but, for better or worse, a major actor whose future and conduct is of vital importance to us. That broad problem, rather than how to encapsulate the tasks before us in a phrase, is what should engage our concerns.

II

While recognizing the existence of a multiplicity of trends in the international arena—even if we wished it were not so we must begin any consideration of the choices before us with the fact that the Soviet Union is the principal military opponent of the United States in the world and will remain so for the indefinite future. It is not likely that any other single power, or combination of powers, will assume this position for the rest of the century.

America and Russia have been military antagonists since the end of World War II, but the character of this relationship has changed substantially over this period as the U.S.S.R. has become a power of global rather than essentially continental dimensions.

It will remain a matter of speculation whether the Soviet Union or, for that matter, the United States, intended at the end of World War II to become global military competitors. Much argues for the view that the Soviets set out to maintain military forces sufficient, in their estimation, to prevent the recurrence of the near disaster of World War II; in short, their military programs were designed to protect the Soviet periphery on the Eurasian landmass, including territories acquired outright in the course of the war or subjected to Soviet control in its aftermath.

But, as Stalin made clear in early 1946, the commitment to this task was not finite. It involved an open-ended determination to build up the physical strength of the Soviet state. The economic priorities and efforts of the society were single-mindedly geared to this objective, which, moreover, never seemed to be quite within reach. As the outside world reacted by building or rebuilding its own defenses, the Soviets, in turn, saw in them a renewed threat to themselves.

In any case, the advance of military technology and the increasing domination of postwar international politics by Soviet rivalry with the United States, already a strategic power with global concerns, virtually ensured that the U.S.S.R. would gradually acquire forces that could be brought to bear beyond the confines of the Eurasian land mass. It began to do so in earnest in the mid-1950s. This period coincided with accelerated decolonization in the less developed world, and, under Khrushchev's leadership, produced a renewal of the revolutionary optimism that had waned soon after the Bolshevik Revolution. That optimism was almost certainly nourished by a growing sense of power. And Soviet ambitions to support the "national liberation" struggle, in turn, fed the impulse to acquire the instruments of power.

As the process of building large and diverse military forces went forward, a powerful military-industrial interest group evolved within the Soviet political structure. It gradually achieved a major, if not always fully united, voice in Soviet economic decision-making. Soviet political leaders, from the Khrushchev to the Brezhnev eras, never lost the basic propensity to amass power but their ambitions to provide also for a measure of improvement in the lives of the Soviet people and to further the modernization of the Soviet economy involved increasingly complex choices concerning the allocation of resources. It has clearly been the purpose of the military-industrial elite to ensure that in this process the power sector of the economy should always be allotted a large proportion of Soviet economic wealth, skilled manpower and technological resources.

Given the centrality of economic decisions, it was hardly surprising that this broad interest group should seek a significant say in the makeup of the post-Stalin political leadership. It seems fair to say that none of Stalin's successors could consolidate or even attain power against the sustained opposition of the military-industrial elite. In retrospect, it is suggestive that some major Soviet military decisions during the 25 years since Stalin's death seem to have coincided with periods of political maneuver among the top leadership. With the lead times involved, it can thus be noted that the impressive advances in Soviet strategic and naval power in the early and mid-1960s must have stemmed from decisions taken a decade earlier, the period, that is, in which Khrushchev was consolidating his power. Similarly, the wave of Soviet strategic deployments that gathered momentum in the early 1970s, and the impressive modernization of Soviet theater forces in Europe, which began to show its cumulative effects in the same period, must have derived from decisions in the mid-1960s—the period when Brezhnev was consolidating his own authority following the removal of Khrushchev.

Without pressing the suggestion too far, any assessment of the goals of the Soviet military buildup must at least give some weight to such indigenous factors. If there is any validity to this supposition, we may again be entering, if we are not already in, a period in which the bargaining surrounding the emergence of a new leadership will produce military decisions whose effects will become evident probably in the early to mid-1980s.

But apart from speculation concerning the domestic political origins of particular decisions, a steady growth of Soviet military power has been assured by the long-term growth trend of some three to four percent a year in military outlays. The result of this persistent effort has been that in the strategic area the U.S.S.R. has been deploying forced needed, by any reasonable set of criteria, not only to deter attack, but capable of threatening the effectiveness and survival of substantial portions of U.S. strategic strength. Thus, the Soviet land-based missile force now being deployed, though somewhat inhibited by the first SALT agreement, is on the way to placing in jeopardy the fixed land-based ICBM forces of the United States that have long constituted a reliable part of the U.S. deterrent. Further, while under the 1972 ABM treaty both sides agreed to curtail antimissile defenses, major Soviet research-and-development programs continue in this field while a major air defense program is degrading the effectiveness of the present U.S. bomber force.

In addition, the Soviets, after relying for an extended period on a relatively modest and steadily aging heavy bomber force, are now adding to it some of their Backfire bombers and, according to reports, are also developing a new heavy bomber. These forces do not, at present, have to contend with any significant American air defenses.

The Soviets have also steadily increased the size and capabilities of their sea-based strategic forces, whose numbers (over 60 nuclear-powered submarines and over 800 launchers) are substantially larger than those maintained or planned by the United States. In this category, the United States will, however, retain larger numbers of re-entry vehicles for the foreseeable future.

In the roughly quarter of a century since both sides began to deploy strategic nuclear delivery systems, there have been times when the forces of each were vulnerable to disabling attack from the other. In the face of such dangers, various measures could be and were taken by both sides: dispersal of bomber bases, the placing of bombers on airborne alerts, the deployment of missiles in dispersed silos or on mobile launching platforms such as submarines at sea. Moreover, bombers and missiles were equipped with penetration devices to maintain their ability to reach targets despite defensive weapons deployed against them. The purpose of these measures, as far as the United States was concerned, was not only to ensure the effectiveness of its strategic forces if a decision to launch them were to be made; the intent was also to reduce pressures to launch weapons in haste, should there be ambiguous evidence of a possible attack, or, in some other crisis conditions, lest they risk being destroyed before they could be used.

The United States, in this context, developed certain doctrines concerning "stability" in strategic relations and generally deployed forces in numbers and with characteristics consistent with them. The Soviet Union never enunciated such doctrines authoritatively—though there is much evidence that Soviet strategic analysts understand them. The Soviets did, of course, act to protect their own forces by means not unlike some of those used by the United States. But for some time now they have gone beyond this in a manner inconsistent with what Americans regard as compatible with stability. It is this trend, perhaps more than the purely numerical advances in Soviet force levels, that has given rise to concern that the Soviet Union seeks substantial military advantages over the United States.

This American perception is reinforced by the fact that the changes in the strategic relationship have a profound impact on regional military balances, notably in Europe. The Soviets have, of course, long enjoyed regional military advantages on their periphery; that, indeed, has been an outgrowth of the military policies initiated in the Stalinist period. In Europe, where this problem affects American interests most directly and, contrary to our historical tradition, gave rise to treaty commitments, the United States for many years offset Soviet advantages by augmenting NATO's conventional forces with the deployment of nuclear weapons in the theater and the potential use of strategic nuclear forces. Similar conditions prevailed at other points around the Soviet periphery where the United States entered into defense commitments.

But in Europe particularly, the elements in the balance have been steadily shifting as the Soviet Union's own theater nuclear forces and strategic power have grown. And, added to these developments has been the dramatically growing strength of Warsaw Pact conventional forces in recent years, as well as the deployment of large Soviet naval forces on NATO's flanks, to the point where there must now be concern that the U.S.S.R. is acquiring an ability to launch an attack without NATO being able to count on adequate warning and mobilization.

Along with the increase in Soviet strategic and regional power, there has also emerged a substantial and still growing capability for military intervention at large distances from the U.S.S.R. The principal elements in this capability are the large and diversified Soviet navy; a growing merchant fleet that can be used to sustain naval units operating at great distances from home; and a growing number of various types of transport aircraft as well as ships, capable of moving men and equipment to virtually any location in the world (though for more distant places the ability to do so rapidly will be affected by overflight and intermediate landing rights). These forces have never been used for overt military attack. But they have several times been brought into play to supply and support the military preparations, and, in some instances, the military actions of others, usually with the justification that the U.S.S.R. was aiding a "national liberation" struggle. In Angola, for the first time overseas, the Soviets actually transported and equipped a proxy expeditionary force to intervene in a conflict.

The trends briefly reviewed here have convinced many in the West that the Soviet leaders have been pursuing a deliberate policy of achieving military "superiority" over the United States. Soviet spokesmen, including Brezhnev, have vigorously denied any such intent and have solemnly repudiated any notion of a "first strike" against U.S. strategic or other forces. Especially in private meetings with official and private American representatives, Soviet spokesmen, like some Americans, have argued that even if the Soviet Union were to acquire a theoretical ability to destroy a high proportion of American ICBMs and to intercept large numbers of American aircraft, the remaining American strategic capacity would make the risks of any Soviet strategic attack prohibitive. Some Soviet spokesmen, pointing to the American overseas base structure, naval aircraft, and still sizable advantages in numbers of deliverable nuclear warheads, contend that far from seeking superiority the U.S.S.R. is still in the position of catching up. They stress, moreover, that Soviet force planning must also take account of British, French and Chinese nuclear forces, all of which are being, or may be, modernized. One also occasionally encounters claims to a form of "historical justice" according to which the United States, which for so long enjoyed advantages in strategic posture over the Soviet Union, should now get accustomed to having this situation equalized, if not reversed.

The question of whether Soviet military growth has the specific purpose of securing "superiority" in accordance with some systematic schedule and with specified criteria cannot, in fact, be definitively answered. For, as the Soviets undoubtedly realize, the answer does not depend on their desires or plans alone; it depends on American actions as well as those of other military powers.

Despite some hesitations and controversy, the United States has indeed begun to take measures that would, over time, reduce the dangers to the effectiveness of our strategic forces. Thus, the capacity of our bombers to penetrate to their targets can be improved, if not restored to earlier levels, by equipping them with various types of cruise missiles and other devices; our land-based missile force can be reinforced by the projected MX missile, which, in its proposed mobile deployment mode, would be substantially less vulnerable to a highly damaging attack than the Minuteman force; cruise missiles launched from submarines or surface vessels could in time likewise augment our retaliatory capability, something of considerable interest also to our European allies. There are several other technical possibilities open to the United States, which, while not necessarily removing Soviet advantages, in certain areas of strategic power—such as the total payload that can be delivered by the Soviet missile force, the size and payload of individual missiles in that force, or the number of missile launchers—could nevertheless substantially reduce the threat of an effective attack on portions of our strategic force.

Furthermore, some of the technical options open to the United States have the potential of posing increasing threats to the Soviet Union's own land-based strategic forces. For the Soviets, this may be a possibility that is even more troubling than the vulnerability of our Minuteman force is to us, because Soviet land-based missile forces represent a far larger proportion of Soviet strategic power than our land-based forces do for us. This is but one example of the uncertainties the Soviets face in seeking a meaningful advantage over our strategic forces.

There are other vulnerabilities, actual and potential, in the Soviet military position, which, depending on the extent to which the United States and others exploit them, complicate a Soviet quest for superiority. For example, Soviet naval forces of all types, including those carrying strategic missile launchers, must pass through relatively constricted waters on their way to and from home ports. There is little Russia can do about this awkward fact of geography. It may account, in part, for the fact that thus far the Soviets have reportedly maintained on station at sea only a relatively small portion of their 62 nuclear-powered, ballistic missile-carrying submarines with their 800-plus launchers.[1]

More generally, the Soviet Navy, while growing impressively in the number and variety of its vessels and in the skills and experience necessary to operate at great distances from home, does have vulnerable lines of communication. It has few secure ports and anchorages outside the U.S.S.R. in case of war. (The recent expulsion of Soviet military personnel and facilities from Somalia is but the latest instance of the fluctuating success of the Soviet Union in maintaining a far-flung support structure for its long-range military capabilities.) The Soviet navy is also approaching a period when large numbers of ships become obsolescent at about the same time.

The fact that the Soviet Union has not succeeded in surrounding itself with friendly states will continue to impose major military expenditures on it. And the forces that it will find necessary to deploy, particularly vis-à-vis

1. Data on Soviet force levels are in *The Military Balance, 1977-78*, London: IISS, 1977, p. 8.

China, play little direct role in the balance with the United States and the West.

Further afield, while Soviet long-range intervention forces have grown, no one can assume that Soviet military interventions will always go unopposed locally or by possible counterinterventions by the United States or other military forces. The Soviet capacity for sustained or intensive operations overseas remains modest.

In sum, though its military growth has been unremitting and impressive, this has still left the U.S.S.R. with substantial actual and potential limitations on the effectiveness and utility of its armed forces. If the Soviet Union does seek a dominant military position, the United States and other nations retain the ability to impose on the U.S.S.R. continuing heavy requirements for additional and diversified forces. But the United States and others must communicate a readiness to do so not only in words but also through actual defense efforts. Indeed, that is the principal means by which the United States can not only protect its security interests but also stimulate Soviet desires, present in an ambivalent way since the days of Khrushchev, to seek negotiated agreements that limit the growth of international military programs.

Plainly, the Soviets are interested in inhibiting the military programs of potential adversaries, and, equally, they would prefer to do so by cutting down their own programs as little as possible. So far, experience does not bear out the hope that acts of American self-restraint induce reciprocal acts by the Soviets; on the contrary, they tend to make negotiations more difficult. This is not a "bargaining chip" argument, for it is unwise to develop and buy expensive forces simply for the sake of trading them away again on the bargaining table. Forces should be bought to serve requirements, and they should be maintained as long as they are needed. If negotiations or unilateral actions remove or reduce a requirement, then the forces designed to meet it can be adjusted accordingly.

In the current state of negotiations it is rates of changes in forces, upward or downward, that will be the most likely subject of agreement. For example, as has been pointed out by the Administration, no foreseeable SALT agreement is likely to remove or even greatly reduce the vulnerability of our fixed, land-based missile force. If, therefore, the United States wishes to retain an effective and secure land-based component in its strategic force, it will need to take action to proceed with an MX, or similar type of missile. How rapidly it actually does so can be adjusted, by negotiation or otherwise, to the development of the threat to the Minuteman force. If, beyond that, the United States wishes to persuade the U.S.S.R. to consider reducing the counterforce capacity of the Soviet land-based missile force, it may be able to do so by signaling an intention to increase the vulnerabilties of this force by increasing the projected MX force. Whether such an increase actually goes forward can be negotiated or decided in the light of how the

U.S.S.R. disposes of the threatening portions of its own land-based missile force. If a SALT agreement is to have the effect of reducing actual or emerging instabilities in strategic relations, it should not foreclose U.S. programs that safeguard the effectiveness of U.S. forces, though it can also provide an incentive for the Soviets to moderate the most threatening aspects of their strategic dispositions.

In short, the propensity of the Soviet political system to amass power, whether to attain superiority or simply to have it as a tool to implement policy, can probably be affected only marginally by current negotiations. The latter are not likely, in the foreseeable future, to relieve us (and others) of the need to offset some of the gains the Soviet Union has achieved in recent years, particularly in the area of strategic forces and in the European theater. The margin of what may be negotiable will widen as the Soviets become persuaded that negotiation is the most effective way to inhibit the worrisome military programs of their adversaries, in return for inhibitions on their own.

But neither negotiations nor the military programs of the outside world seem likely to divert the Soviet Union from its determination to be the other military superpower in the world. The impulse to amass military power seems pervasive among the Soviet ruling elite regardless of generation. Soviet political dynamics seem to favor it, and the Soviet economic system seems unalterably geared to it.

III

Possession of military power does not necessarily determine how, and how effectively, that power is used. External powers, notably the United States, have had little ability to influence the growth of Soviet military power. Nor are they likely to have anything but a modest direct influence in this respect in the future. But they must and can be concerned with the uses to which that power is put. For the United States, broadly speaking, the purposes of policy toward the Soviet Union must be, on the one hand, to prevent injury to American interests and, on the other, to avoid open warfare. Policy must operate within these limits.

The question with which American statecraft must cope is how to maximize the restraints upon the uses of Soviet power. Part of the answer, as already indicated, is to seek to maintain a military balance, where possible in direct or indirect association with others who share our interest in restraining the uses of Soviet power and the potentially detrimental effects of its existence. This raises complex problems in addition to those alluded to earlier about the size and types of forces we must maintain and acquire over the rest of the century and beyond. Without addressing details here, the general point should be made that military deterrence requires forces that are generally thought to be usable for defined ends should fighting break out with the U.S.S.R. or its clients. To the extent this can be done, it is likely to place restraints on direct and indirect Soviet use of force, because it serves to impose upon Soviet decision-makers substantial uncertainties regarding the outcome.

But the problem does not end or begin with military measures alone. The Soviet Union, both as a polity and as an actor on the world stage, has developed unevenly. The international environment in which its power has developed and can be used is itself in a state of dynamic evolution. Military power does not translate automatically into influence and even less into control. Even in regions where Soviet military power goes essentially unchallenged, such as in Eastern Europe, the Soviet Union has not been able to control or prevent developments which sap Soviet hegemony or, at any rate, undermine the kind of uniformity which Soviet rulers used to consider essential to their own well-being and security.

Elsewhere, in more distant areas, where the projection of Soviet power at one time appeared to confer upon Russia a potentially dominant influence, indigenous and external factors have diluted it or, in some instances, even reduced it to the vanishing point. This is not a law of nature and cannot be relied on to work automatically, especially if the United States itself is uncertain about the Soviet role it prefers to see in these regions. But the history of the last 20 years or so of Soviet "imperial" penetration into distant regions does provide a useful corrective to earlier fears—and Soviet expectations—that Soviet influence once established will become dominant and can only rise.

Among the reasons for the spotty Soviet record is that the Soviet mentality does not adapt easily to the nationalism and peculiarities of other peoples; Soviet ideology and institutions have not proved to be readily applicable or even appealing in other places and societies; Soviet political support is equivocal and frequently self-serving; and Soviet contributions to social and economic development are often inept, inappropriate and irrational, reflecting, as they do, Soviet society itself. For all the Soviet efforts during the last 20 or more years, it is the Western industrialized nations, and the international institutions they have been instrumental in erecting, which have played the greater external role in the development of the new nations around the world. All these factors have limited or even counteracted the effects of Soviet military power in advancing Soviet influence.

One is tempted to conclude from the history of the postwar period, which includes also the increasing diversity within the international communist movement itself, that socialism—Soviet-style—in one country, once a temporary expedient, has in fact become a hallmark of our era. Whether it will remain so will depend, in part, on the evolution of Soviet society itself, on the people who run it after the present generation leaves the scene, and on whether Soviet military power will continue to be balanced so that it cannot become so overwhelming in some place or region as to enable the U.S.S.R. to determine the course of events there for a substantial period of time.

IV

Meanwhile, the steady though uneven expansion of Soviet external influence has been accompanied by, and has indeed contributed to, the gradual emergence of the U.S.S.R. from its isolation. This is most notably the case in the area of economics. Burdened as it is with enormous and constantly rising military expenditures as well as by ponderous and over-centralized bureaucratic controls and a rigid social structure, the Soviet economy has been unable with its own resources to provide for the broad modernization of Soviet life. While impressive by the indices of the 1950s, the Soviet economy lags well behind other industrial countries in technical sophistication and productivity. Trade with the outside world has long been used to fill gaps that the Soviet economy itself could not fill. But the volume and diversity of this trade have steadily increased in recent years; the methods have evolved from barter or straight cash deals to more complex commercial arrangements, including considerable reliance on foreign credits. These latter have now risen to some $40 billion for the Soviet block COMECON countries as a whole; Soviet hard-currency indebtedness is in the neighborhood of ten billion dollars. A substantial volume of economic activity in the U.S.S.R. and other Eastern countries must now be devoted to earning hard currency to finance imports and to service mounting indebtedness.

Brezhnev and other Soviet leaders have affirmed Soviet interest in an international division of labor, though they certainly have not meant by this any total Soviet reliance on certain external sources of supply. Indeed, in their foreign economic policies the Soviets have sought to minimize extended foreign reliance by trying to get foreigners to build up within the U.S.S.R. economic and technical capabilities which the Soviet Union is unable or unwilling to create with its own resources and skills. The Soviets no doubt continue to hanker for some form of autarky even if, for a time, they are prepared to accept something called a division of labor. But there is no reason why the external world needs to accept this Soviet preference. It is true that a systematic long-term policy by the industrialized nations to maximize Soviet economic reliance on the outside world would encounter formidable difficulties. In particular, Western political and economic systems do not readily lend themselves to long-term economic policymaking of any sort, but this is especially so since the long-term management of economic relations with the U.S.S.R. would require large-scale and sustained government involvement. The difficulties in coordinating the policies of several of the principal industrial countries are even greater, despite the fact that these nations should have the incentive to do so since they are linked to each other by security as well as common interests and broad values.

Despite the difficulties, there is scope for an economic strategy that uses Soviet needs to draw the U.S.S.R. into the disciplines of international economic life. The United States, for example, although unable to use periodic Soviet need for grain for specific political purposes, e.g., to affect Soviet conduct in a crisis, did prove able to negotiate an agreement that imposes more orderly practices on Soviet behavior in this field. The 1975 grain agreement requires the Soviets to consult the U.S. government before it can purchase agricultural products above eight million tons a year[2]; it requires the Soviets to purchase a minimum quantity of six million tons of certain specified products from the United States each year even when they would not otherwise do so because of a satisfactory harvest; and it places upon the U.S.S.R. obligations to permit U.S. vessels to ship the products Russia buys.

In the future, it should not be impossible to reinstitute Soviet eligibility for U.S. government export-financing facilities and thereby to influence the flow of credits and the degree to which the Soviet Union balances the reliance on credits with the use of exports to finance its imports. In general, it would be desirable to encourage the U.S.S.R. to pay for more of its imports with exports and to reduce the share of credits in financing imports. If the issue of tariff discrimination were at some point separated by the United States from issues of Soviet emigration policy, to which it is now linked, the Soviet Union might have incentives to devote more high quality resources to exports. Soviet economic planning and priorities could thus become somewhat more susceptible to external demands. Moreover, it would be both desirable and feasible for Western nations to evolve harmonized concepts in these respects, with the goal of reducing the autarkic nature of Soviet economic decision-making and complicating Soviet resource choices.

Soviet economic connections with the outside world seem, in any case, destined to become more extensive and complex. Already, the Soviets are not immune to currency fluctuations and inflationary trends beyond their own borders. Their planners and hard-currency managers must take account of them, and Soviet economic officials have an obvious stake in operating in foreign markets to minimize injury to Soviet financial interests. Western governments should consult and work with one another to ensure that the U.S.S.R. operates responsibly in the international financial community and that individual Western lending institutions do not become excessively exposed vis-à-vis the East.

Over the somewhat longer run, the Soviets may get caught up in international energy shortages and price rises. Russia's own resources, while large, will evidently become increasingly expensive to recover, and international dealings in the energy field on a growing scale may well become part of

---

2. According to press reports, the Soviets may have found a way to circumvent this consulting requirement in signing contracts to buy grain to make up shortfalls in the 1977 harvest. While the purchases involved will apparently be from American sources and thus benefit American farmers in a surplus period, it would be desirable to correct any loophole in the 1975 agreement.

Soviet economic life. Planning should be undertaken sooner rather than later for the time when the Soviets may become large-scale petroleum buyers in international markets. There may be similar needs and opportunities with respect to other commodities. The needs of Moscow's East European allies in these areas may provide useful leverage to help induce Soviet interest in more orderly international arrangements.

Many other fields of actual or potential Soviet involvement in the international system can be cited.

For some years now, the Soviets have sensed the need to participate in international efforts to curb the spread of nuclear weapon manufacturing capacities around the world. Indeed, because most potential nuclear weapons states are not friends of the U.S.S.R., Moscow seems to have sensed the need for restrictive actions even before some Western nations. So far, the Soviets seem to have imposed fewer limitations on their domestic nuclear power development than the United States. The future of the breeder reactor and the "plutonium economy" is uncertain as the United States debates its merits, and other Western nations experience domestic opposition toward these and other kinds of nuclear power facilities which may make the pursuit of coherent nuclear energy policies difficult if not impossible for some years to come. It remains to be seen to what extent these problems, including that of waste disposal, spill over in the U.S.S.R. At any rate, however, Soviet export policies are becoming part of an international regime in this area, and the utility of Soviet nuclear exports for political purposes, by "underselling" Western suppliers, is now probably minimal.

The regime of the world's oceans is another area where the Soviet Union is compelled to participate in international discipline if it does not wish to deny itself the benefits of the available resources. Similarly, the U.S.S.R. should not expect to be able to operate in outer space without submitting to legal and other constraints developed by the international community. Incentives also exist for Soviet participation in international arrangements to curb environmental pollution. The international civil aviation regime is still another example.

V

In these and other ways, the Soviet Union has slowly and often grudgingly accepted foreign constraints on its freedom of action. Will these constraints also affect the way in which the U.S.S.R. pursues its geopolitical interests and ideological ambitions through the use of its military power? The answer depends in part on the extent to which external powers see international politics as composed of interrelated parts. But there can be no definitive answer because the processes whereby the U.S.S.R. is becoming more involved in the international system are frequently only in an early stage and far from fully understood. And even when adequately appreciated, it is not always simple to utilize them for broader political purposes; nor is it obvious how to do so. Moreover, the cost of depriving the Soviet Union of some of the benefits of international interaction may fall not only upon the Soviets. We have, for example, seen how American farmers were opposed to our own government's using possible embargoes on grain exports in order to exert political pressures on the U.S.S.R. Western bankers may well fear the effects of massive defaults by their Eastern clients if econmic relationships become hostage to political vicissitudes.

Yet these are issues that have to be faced. The growing needs of the Soviet Union for access to the assets and products of the West should be satisfied to the extent that Moscow conducts itself with restraint internationally. It is probably not workable to deny a particular benefit or break a specific contract in an effort to affect Soviet conduct in a crisis. But given the interactions that have already evolved, a strategy should be possible whereby these evolving mutual reliances can over time moderate any disposition to let competition drift into crises of such intensity that they will inevitably tear the fabric of interconnections. But, to repeat, such a strategy can work only if the military risks for particular Soviet geopolitical excursions continue to be kept high.

VI

There is a further and perhaps even more controversial and contingent set of factors that needs to be put in the balance. Inflation, environmental pollution and the other issues alluded to above are not the only external forces that fail to respect national or ideological boundaries. Soviet society, in part because of the broadening and intensification of Soviet external relations in the 1970s, is no longer hermetically sealed off from the outside. Blue jeans, rock music, literature and pop art are but a few, and probably the least significant, of the foreign habits and activities that have begun to affect Soviet life. More significant, there probably would never have been major Jewish emigration pressures in 1971-72 if there had been no leap forward in the Soviet Union's relationship with the United States. There probably never would have been any Soviet response—however reluctant and sporadic—to the demands of foreign constituencies of some sections of Soviet society if Soviet leaders had not begun—however hesitatingly—to calculate their interests in terms of their reputation abroad. It is worth noting that even after the Jackson Amendment was enacted and the Soviets angrily rejected their trade agreement with the United States, Jewish emigration continued at over 12,000 a year and individual "hard-core" cases continued to be acted on favorably. As we have learned this past year, Soviet toleration of these kinds of external intrusion is not unlimited, and foreign powers, to be effective in influencing Soviet practices, must calibrate their strategies and tactics with some care. But the principle has been clearly established that the state of human rights within a country is now a matter of legitimate international concern.

The Jewish population is not the only minority in a state composed of minorities. Thus, in the case of ethnic Germans wishing to leave, the Soviets have also been prepared to respond to outside pressures and inducements. Who is to say how foreign constituencies may someday manifest their interest in the condition of the Soviet Union's large and growing Muslim population? And who is to say how the long-suffering Soviet consumer may some day find his frustrations adopted as a cause abroad? Will Soviet youth be forever kept on an intellectual starvation diet compared to their counterparts in other industrial societies?

These lines of speculation should not be pushed too far. The Soviet system is traditionally repressive. Its aristocracy has a vigorous sense of survival in the face of real or imagined threats to its monopolistic hold on power. It possesses a vast panoply of instruments of power to contain unwanted intrusions.

Yet, the Soviet Union can never return to the isolation cell to which Stalin condemned it to make his brand of socialism in one country a reality at home and a virtual impossibility abroad. That isolation is now past history, though there is probably little the Soviets can do for years to come to make themselves "beautiful Russians" around the world. By the same token, the costs and risks of using power for political ends, and the impediments to doing so, are amply present in the world at large. And the world at large, in all its variety, increasingly stretches its influences into domains hitherto controlled by the Soviet rulers.

VII

We have thus entered an era in which the United States and the external world generally can seek increasingly to draw the Soviet Union into the constraints and disciplines but also the advantages of the international system. To do so requires conscious strategies and policies. Passive reliance on historical trends will not suffice. Much progress was made during the 1970s, building on some progress before that, to devise "rules of conduct" for the restrained uses of power. The American-Soviet understandings arrived at during the three summit conferences of the early 1970s, the Helsinki Final Act, and numerous similar understandings between the U.S.S.R. and various Western nations such as France and Germany, have probably gone as far as negotiated documents can go in laying down ground rules for competition. None of these understandings are, however, self-enforcing in the sense that they will be adhered to simply because they have been put on paper. Nor can they be instantly or systematically implemented except where very precise obligations are involved, as in arms control agreements. Many of the understandings, such as the Joint Statement of Principles of 1972, the Agreement on Prevention of Nuclear War of 1973 and the Helsinki Final Act provide standards and goals rather than enforceable commitments to specific, unambiguous modes of behavior.

The Soviets have undoubtedly contravened some of the principles, and they probably consider that we and others have also contravened them. Notions about eschewing efforts at obtaining "unilateral advantage," in particular, are difficult to nail down in the shifting sands of international alignments and in circumstances where the successor states of the old colonial empires continue to be embroiled in territorial and other conflicts and seek external support for their causes. The effects of Soviet, or American, efforts to gain "unilateral advantage" are often unpredictable. The United States has not resisted, and sometimes has sought, opportunities to diminish Soviet influence in places where it had previously flourished—for example, in the Middle East—though this has not always resulted in corresponding American gains.

The Soviets for their part were quite prepared to seek a new role for themselves in southern Africa when the decisions of the U.S. Congress made the risks of doing so seem manageable while the benefits of not doing so were not evident. Their use of Cuban proxy troops—though in fact the Cubans probably pursued objectives of their own as well—opened disturbing vistas of new forms of Soviet expansion. But it also drew the United States and other Western powers more actively into the affairs of southern Africa. The Soviets were not uninvolved in the outbreak of the 1973 October War and the oil embargo, though their role was less active and direct than critics of the policies of the last Administration would have had us believe. But whatever the precise Soviet role, the outcome did nothing to impede, and actually speeded up, the decline of Soviet influence in parts of the Middle East.

Rules of conduct and other formal arrangements to limit the intensity and dangers of competition must thus be buttressed by other policies, furthering the trends discussed above, to reduce over time incentives to adventurism and to strengthen the incentives for restraint and greater interrelatedness.

This necessarily involves arrangements from which the U.S.S.R. can draw benefits, be it in the form of economic relationships or in its ambition to be accepted as a power with global interests. For Americans, this side of the equation has been a difficult one to accept and has given rise to the notion of détente as being a "one-way street." But it is almost certain that disappointments about expected benefits from detente have also led the Soviet Union to question whether or not the costs—in terms of external intrusion, limitations on Soviet freedom of action, reductions in hard-won foreign influence, restiveness in Eastern Europe, diversity among communist parties, continued high levels of American military preparedness, the unpredictability of American conduct and many other equivocal trends from the Soviet standpoint—are worth paying.

Many observers have stressed that U.S.-Soviet relations can no longer be seen as operating independently of other major trends in international politics, even if in military terms the relationship remains largely bipolar.

As noted at the outset, it is often suggested that we should rid ourselves of our fixation with the Soviet Union. The time has come, says one commentator, when "at least for a while, the best way to conduct U.S.-Soviet relations may be to reduce the intensity of the relationship, to cool it."[3] The new Administration, like virtually all its predecessors, entered office with the hope that it could reduce the preoccupation with the Soviet relationship in order to concentrate on "world order politics" and global "architecture."

Yet Soviet military power continues to grow and Soviet involvements in world affairs, whatever the fluctuations, remain on the rise. World order politics which fail to envisage the inclusion of the U.S.S.R. in the disciplines, constraints, and advantages of the international system would hardly be consonant with the facts of the age. Despite its hopes, the new Administration has found itself heavily engaged with the U.S.S.R. and seems to devote as much energy to that relationship as to any other, if not more. It may be that, as President Carter said at Notre Dame, "...the threat of conflict with the U.S.S.R. has become less intensive even though the competition has become more extensive." But the distinctions are not always obvious. And there can be no assurance that an intensification of conflict could not rapidly return.

Thus, given the pervasiveness of U.S.-Soviet interactions, geographically and functionally, our policies toward the U.S.S.R. are likely to remain the most active and far-flung among our external policies. Certainly, because of the military aspect, they will continue to place the largest single external demand upon our resources and the federal budget. And however much we may seek to "de-link" issues in given instances, we will not be able to avoid the essential interrelationship between them. Nor should we. Efforts to regulate military competition by negotiation and agreement will not stand alone as an island in a sea of crises or virulent antagonisms. On the contrary, though it is likely to be limited in impact on military programs, the effectiveness of SALT and other negotiations will depend heavily on the rest of the relationship. Similar points can be made about virtually every major facet of U.S.-Soviet negotiations. Above all, it is unlikely that the incidence and intensity of crises, whatever our diplomatic skill and other restraints, can long be held to moderate levels unless there is in operation a whole range of constraints and incentives that give each side a stake in restraint.

What is involved is, of course, a long-term evolution which requires constant attention and effort and which will see many occasions that will defy clear characterization as to whether they represent progress, retrogression, success, failure or "irreversibility." There is no joy in ambiguity, especially

---

3. Seyom Brown, "A Cooling-Off Period for U.S.-Soviet Relations," *Foreign Policy*, Fall, 1977, p. 21.

for Americans. But that is precisely what will mark our relations with the
Soviet Union for a long time to come. We will probably never stop arguing
over whether we actually have a détente that, in the President's words, constitutes "progress toward peace." That will have to be a judgment of
history.

Russia's Power Strategy:
Reflections on Afghanistan*

World opinion, which was so uplifted only a few days ago by the news that the Soviet Union intended to withdraw its forces from Hungary, has now suffered corresponding shock and dismay at the Soviet attack on the peoples and Government of Hungary.

—President Eisenhower,
after the Soviet suppression of the Hungarian Revolution in 1956.

I tell you that it was with a heavy heart that I have closely followed the events in Czechoslovakia over the past several days.... It is a sad commentary on the Communist mind that a sign of liberty in Czechoslovakia is deemed a fundamental threat to the security of the Soviet system.

—President Johnson,
after the Soviet-led invasion of Czechoslovakia in 1968.

It's only now dawning on the world the magnitude of the action that the Soviets undertook in invading Afghanistan.... This action has made a more dramatic change in my own opinion of what the Soviets' ultimate goals are than anything they've done in the previous time I've been in office.

—President Carter,
after the Soviet invasion of Afghanistan in 1979.

Each time Soviet armies have assaulted a weaker neighbor, American Presidents have reacted with dismay and outrage at the Kremlin's naked use of force. Each time, hope against hope, the Americans have tended to disbelieve the intelligence warnings of political rumblings, urgent missions or ominous troop movements, and have preferred to presume that Moscow would be restrained by other interests or by a concern for the good opinion of the world.

But the narrow circle of the Soviet Politburo, unburdened by a prying press, a contentious Congress or other encumbrances of democracy, has met in secret and decided, according to the cold calculus of power politics, to strike when it felt vital Soviet interests were at stake, no matter what the costs elsewhere. And the Russians have rather shrewdly judged in the past that while the West might react furiously in the short run, Moscow can repair East-West relations when it wants to in the long run.

It is the Soviet style, moreover, to move with sudden stealth and to move massively for the shock effect, throwing adversaries on their heels with little recourse but to protest and accept the *fait accompli*. At home, the Soviet citizenry, fed belated and distorted versions of events by a controlled press, has historically taken patriotic pride in the power of the motherland.

"What must be called imperialism is a vital element of the rationale of the Soviet system," Adam B. Ulam, the Harvard historian of Soviet foreign policy, has written. "Now that the unity of the world Communist movement is irretrievably lost and the doctrine itself has become discredited or irrelevant insofar as the majority of Soviet people is concerned, the regime strives to demonstrate its viability and vitality through foreign expansion."

This does not imply a grand design for world conquest but periodic, cold, hard decisions to seize upon targets of opportunity to push out imperially from the Russian heartland or to extend the Soviet reach as a global power—an increasing trend since the mid-70's.

Surprisingly perhaps, since Afghanistan is such a remote, barren nation locked in the mountain fastness of Central Asia without immediately obvious strategic importance, there is greater alarm here over the Soviet invasion of Afghanistan by 85,000 Soviet troops than over the two earlier invasions of Hungary and Czechoslovakia.

The blood bath in Hungary and the more silent suffocation of Czechoslovakia grew out of the postwar division of Europe. The West vigorously objected to the Brezhnev doctrine of 1968—Moscow's assertion of the right of collective intervention by the Soviet camp in any Soviet satellite where "the cause of socialism" faced the threat of an ideological rollback. Nonetheless, as with Hungary, the Western powers acknowledged Czechoslovakia as part of the Soviet bloc within which Moscow would not permit the boundaries of Communism to recede.

But until Afghanistan, the Kremlin had not applied the Brezhnev doctrine to the third world. It had relied on the proxy armies of Vietnam and Cuba to advance its causes. In June 1978, Soviet Foreign Minister Andrei A. Gromyko seemed to underscore the point that in Africa, Asia and the Middle East, Moscow's policy was to send military aid and advisers but not its own troops. "Not one Soviet soldier with a rifle is in Ethiopia," he declared.

Now, there are Soviet riflemen, paratroopers, tanks and jets all over Afghanistan. For the first time since World War II, the Kremlin has thrust its own armies into a new strategic arena, outside the established Soviet sphere of influence in Eastern Europe. It has immediately and drastically increased the jeopardy of Iran and Pakistan and awakened the fear that Moscow—stronger and more confident than in the 1950's and 1960's—may now be prepared to employ a much bolder strategy of force in the Middle East.

There is a surprising consensus among Government officials and academic thinkers that the invasion of Afghanistan represents what Zbigniew Brzezinski, President Carter's national security adviser, called "a qualitatively new step" with disturbing implications that reach far beyond the Soviet effort to stamp out Islamic tribal rebellion in Afghanistan and to protect its client government in Kabul. President Carter, with some hyperbole, called this, "the gravest risk to world peace since World War II."

"What gives this such a shock effect," said Marshall D. Shulman, the State Department's chief adviser on Soviet policy, "is that it comes after 15 years of Soviet military buildup. What will they decide to do next with all that force?"

If the Afghan rebels seek sanctuary in Pakistan or Iran, policy makers ask, will Soviet forces strike those countries in frustration? If Iran begins to break up under the pressure of minority rebellions, will Moscow be tempted to exploit that chaos or to respond to the summons of some Iranian Marxists to send troops into Iran? Is the Soviet leadership feeling so emboldened by strategic parity and conventional military superiority over the United States as to try to apply the Brezhnev doctrine worldwide—to client states in Southeast Asia or the Horn of Africa? How safe is Yugoslavia after President Tito? Is the Afghanistan invasion merely intended to secure a new Soviet satellite or part of a broader strategy to capitalize on the regional instability gradually to push the West out of the Middle East?

*   *   *

Only since the Arab oil embargo of 1973 has American public attention focused seriously on the strategic arc that lies at the soft underbelly of the

Eurasian landmass. But long before the nuclear age or the discovery of oil in the Arabian Peninsula, geopoliticians postulated a struggle in this area, foreshadowing what may become a Soviet-American contest of power.

In 1904, the British geographer Sir Halford J. Mackinder wrote that whoever ruled Eastern Europe would command the world heartland and in turn the world island (Eurasia and Africa) and "who rules the world island commands the world." Several years later, an American strategist, Nicholas J. Spykman, reformulated the logic of geopolitics this way: "Who controls the rimland (the peripheral areas of the Eurasian continent) rules Eurasia; who rules Eurasia controls the destinies of the world."

By 1968, Mr. Brzezinski, then an academician, wrote in Encounter magazine that once the Soviet Union achieved nuclear parity with the United States, there would be, for the first time in history, "two overlapping global military powers." Once the Russians matched American long-range air- and sea-lift capabilities for projecting force into distant regions, he predicted, there would be growing "probabilities of a new type of confrontation—a direct one between U.S. and Soviet intervention forces."

As Soviet capabilities have indeed increased and as the fabric of détente has frayed, the Ford and Carter Administrations have been troubled by several episodes of Soviet adventurism in the third world.

In the years since Saigon fell and Hanoi conquered Laos, pro-Soviet groups have seized power in Angola, Ethiopia, Southern Yemen and Afghanistan, and Vietnam has marched into Cambodia to oust a pro-Chinese regime under the umbrella of a defense treaty with Moscow.

Although there is no evidence that any Soviet master plan lies behind these events, power has a way of creating its own opportunities. The pattern of change suits Soviet strategic interests and Moscow has been quick to lend a hand. The Kremlin sent arms and transported 20,000 Cuban troops to help pro-Soviet forces in Angola beginning in 1975. Three years later, the Russians dispatched $1 billion in arms plus 20,000 more Cuban troops and 1,500 Soviet military advisers and technicians into Ethiopia, and lesser quantities of arms and advisers to Southern Yemen and to Afghanistan after ardently pro-Soviet Communists seized power in 1978.

Both Government officials and academic analysts believe that Moscow was emboldened to invade Afghanistan, in part, because the West—especially the Americans—mounted no effective counteraction to these Soviet gains.

"We lured them on by reacting so feebly in Angola," contends Adam Ulam of Harvard. "They were exploiting Western impotence and the backwash of Watergate."

"They have been edging toward the kind of power play that we see in Afghanistan," observes Seyom Brown of Brandeis University, a strategy analyst. "In areas of relatively marginal importance to the United States, they could see that the United States was not willing to risk a direct confrontation with them.

"In Afghanistan, they have upped the ante. But given the equalization of strategic power and capabilities, it was only a question of time before the Soviets would move in a more determined way to thrust out and challenge Western dominance in the rimland areas. In areas where the Soviets can pull off a *fait accompli*, they are increasingly tempted to do it. They could calculate that they'd move massively and we'd scream, but that we could do nothing about it."

Rival politicians have made fun of President Carter's assertion that the Soviet invasion drastically altered his perception of the Kremlin. But his aides have been at pains to explain that it was the degree of Soviet deception that so chastened the President.

Although Malcolm Toon, a former American Ambassador to Moscow, said he had regularly warned of the dangers of a Soviet invasion of Afghanistan, the White House contended that they were surprised by the Russians' particularly cynical way of going about it. They had staged an invasion on the pretext of an invitation from a government leader whom they promptly had executed. All this had occurred despite the hopes engendered by détente and in a nominally nonaligned state that had in fact had an ardently pro-Soviet Government for nearly two years.

From all accounts, including some from Moscow, the Kremlin was motivated purely by the cold calculations of *Realpolitik*. As an Islamic border state, backed against the formerly Islamic regions of Soviet Central Asia, Afghanistan has long been a neuralgic point for Russia's rulers. In the 19th century, the czars fenced with the British to insure that Afghanistan would be a friendly buffer state. But what appears new is the Kremlin's current effort to incorporate Afghanistan as an outright satellite of Moscow.

A high-level Soviet military mission to Kabul this past fall apparently concluded that the Soviet-backed military campaign against the Islamic tribal insurrection was on the brink of an embarrassing defeat, barring massive Soviet intervention. According to American specialists, Soviet leaders feared that unless they acted forcibly, they would be faced with a hostile Islamic Government in Kabul.

By Soviet reckoning, the Kremlin had little to lose by invading Afghanistan. Washington was handcuffed by the Iranian crisis and no longer offered the major attractions of détente. Relations with the United States had been souring steadily, and there were only dim prospects for ratification of the strategic-arms treaty. To the east, China was hostile, and in the west, the Europeans had just agreed to deploy more modern nuclear-armed missiles rather than grasp the Soviet carrot of regional arms talks. Better to take a quick gain by converting Afghanistan into a satellite than risk rebellion at the Soviet back door.

Moreover, the Russians have taken their measure of the fickleness of Western opinion. Three years after the Soviet invasion of Hungary, Soviet Prime Minister Nikita S. Khrushchev was warmly received by President Eisenhower for his "spirit of Camp David" summit. A year or so after the invasion of Czechoslovakia, the Russians were on the road toward better relations with the United States.

Then, too, the climate at the pinnacle of Soviet power may have changed a bit this fall. Prime Minister Aleksei Kosygin, the Soviet leader who first advocated the benefits of East-West commerce, has been ill and out of action since mid-October and President Leonid I. Brezhnev, too, has been ailing.

Some American specialists have long believed that in periods of transition to new leadership—and they presume that the transition to the post-Brezhnev era is already under way—the influence of the Soviet military establishment increases. Moreover, the Soviet military and the K.G.B. (the intelligence service) are generally reputed to have more influence in determining Moscow's policy moves in the third world than Soviet diplomats discharging the duties of détente.

In addition, specialists have noted scattered signs that hard-line conservatives and skeptics of détente like Mikhail A. Suslov, the 77-year-old chief Communist Party ideologist, who has long been associated with Soviet military aggression, were somewhat ascendant this fall.

One school of analysts believes that the Kremlin has been deliberately exploiting turmoil in places like the Horn of Africa, Southern Yemen and Afghanistan to feed the turbulence in strategically vital countries like Iran, and to foment insecurity in pro-Western states like Saudi Arabia and Pakistan.

Another school takes a less sinister view: the Russians were sucked unexpectedly into Afghanistan by the original Marxist coup in April 1978, and then, having given support to Kabul, had to protect their stake.

"We'll never know whether the invasion was triggered by internal Afghan reasons or by broader strategic designs," comments Helmut Sonnenfeldt, a ranking Soviet specialist for several American Administrations and a close associate of former Secretary of State Henry A. Kissinger. "But either way, there are broader consequences of having the Soviets in Afghanistan in force.

"You can't ignore that they now also have strong points in the Arabian Peninsula and the Horn of Africa, and they still have influence in places like Syria and Libya. This begins to add up to pretty powerful pressures on that region. And one of the problems is that there's so little power around on our side to balance the Soviet threat."

* * *

Comparisons to Vietnam seem almost inevitable. For Moscow, there is the risk that Soviet forces will become bogged down in a long and inconclusive conflict, proving not Soviet strength but its limitations.

The Kremlin evidently learned from the gradual American escalation in Vietnam, however, and has moved rapidly to amass enough force to overwhelm resistance. Moreover, unlike Washington's policy makers, the Russian's have relatively short supply lines and no significant domestic political dissent to contend with, and they do no face a unified, well-organized insurrection formidably armed by outside powers, like the Vietcong.

One potentially serious cost to Moscow's broader aims in the region is the alarm it has aroused among Islamic nations in the rimland. Some, like Pakistan, Bangladesh and Saudi Arabia, took prominent parts in the United Nations' diplomatic effort to condemn Moscow's power play. Others, like Egypt, Somalia and Oman, are more receptive to Western military links.

Even Iranian propagandists have mocked the Soviet Union as "a bloodthirsty imperialist" power. The Teheran Government condemned the Soviet invasion of Afghanistan as "a hostile act, not only against the people of that country but against all the Moslems of the world." The threat to Iran itself was underscored by the Soviet movement of half their invasion forces into Southwest Afghanistan near the Iranian border.

On the other hand, there are signs that leaders in India, Pakistan, Iran and elsewhere in the rimland are sufficiently intimidated by the raw use of Soviet force that they dare not go too far in offending the Kremlin, especially until they see how vigorously the West will react.

The gravest risk for the Russians is that the Kremlin's gambit in Afghanistan has finally provoked President Carter to play the chess of power politics. They have pushed Washington and Peking into further collaboration and may have galvanized the Western alliance into some new strategy of containment to protect its interests in the rimland.

*   *   *

As the West warmed its relations with the Kremlin in the early 1970's, the theory was that the attractions of détente would tame Soviet adventurism, give them a stake in the status quo and create, as Henry Kissinger used to say, "a calculus of risks and benefits that will induce the Soviet Union to behave."

The bargain President Nixon and Dr. Kissinger thought they had struck in Moscow in 1972 offered the Kremlin strategic parity codified in new arms agreements and far greater access to Western technology, in return for certain limits both on the 10-year Soviet strategic nuclear buildup and on Soviet poaching in the third world at the West's expense.

The Americans considered it a major achievement to get Soviet signatures on a joint declaration of principles in Moscow asserting that "both sides recognize that efforts to obtain unilateral advantage at the expense of the other, directly or indirectly, are inconsistent" with the objectives of détente.

But though there had been a hiatus in global chess moves outside of Indochina, the Soviet leadership never agreed to forswear its support for "wars of national liberation" or the historical "process of socialist construction" around the world. Moscow had in mind two separate tracks—one for strategic accommodation between the superpowers on nuclear and bilateral issues, and the other for its own flexibility in pursuing targets of opportunity to expand Soviet power and influence in the third world.

"Détente does not in the slightest abolish, and cannot abolish or alter, the laws of class struggle," President Brezhnev told the 25th Soviet Communist Party Congress in Moscow in February 1976. Brushing aside American complaints about Soviet involvement in Angola, he declared: "Some bourgeois leaders affect surprise over the solidarity of Soviet Communists, the Soviet people, with the struggle of other peoples for freedom and progress. This is either outright naiveness or, more likely, a deliberate befuddling of minds. We make no secret of the fact that we see détente as the way to create more favorable conditions for peaceful socialist and Communist construction."

By then, not only had President Nixon fallen but the original détente bargain had come apart. The American offer of favorable trade and credit terms had by then been linked with a new issue—Soviet emigration policy for Jews and others—rather than with Soviet behavior in the third world.

By blocking the trade agreement in December 1974, Congress had infuriated the Kremlin and deprived two Administrations of an American carrot to induce Moscow's good behavior in the third world. Meanwhile, the Russians were steadily adding to their military power.

Jimmy Carter sought to continue the basic Republican strategy toward the Russians, though he confused Moscow with policy zigzags—drastic new arms proposals, new coziness with China and attacks on human-rights violations in Moscow, coupled with the assertion that he had put aside the past American obsession with anti-Communism. Some of Mr. Carter's own advisers argued that his ambivalence indirectly encouraged Soviet adventurism in the third world.

After the pro-Soviet coups in Ethiopia, Southern Yemen and Afghanistan, he finally put Moscow on notice. "To the Soviet Union, détente seems to mean a continuing aggressive struggle for political advantage and increased influence in a variety of ways," he said at Annapolis on June 7, 1978. "A competition without restraint and without shared rules will escalate into graver tensions and our relationship as a whole will suffer.

"Our long-term objectives," he declared pointedly, "must be to convince the Soviet Union of the advantages of cooperation and of the cost of disruptive behavior."

Then, last fall, in one of his most costly mistakes with Moscow, President Carter first declared that the presence of a newly discovered Soviet combat brigade in Cuba was "unacceptable," and three weeks later suddenly backed down and accepted the situation, though the Russians refused to budge. At roughly the same time, the Administration was sending diplomatic warnings to Moscow about its concern over the growing Soviet involvement in Afghanistan. Possibly as a result of the Cuba affair, Moscow took these as hollow warnings.

Now, shaken by the Soviet invasion, President Carter has decided to apply the Annapolis strategy by putting a freeze on détente —bowing to political reality by shelving a Senate vote on his cherished arms treaty with Moscow, blocking $2 billion in grain shipments, halting sales of advanced technology, curbing diplomatic and other exchanges, reversing himself and coming out for military aid to Pakistan, and going yet further in courting cooperation with Peking. He and his aides coyly refused to say whether the United States would aid the Afghan rebels.

More broadly, looking back to President Truman's strategy of containment in reaction to Soviet threats to Greece and Turkey in 1947, President Carter has sought to formulate a new Western strategy for the vulnerable rimland region in the 1980's.

Diplomatically, he has been pressing other Western leaders personally to join his campaign of economic sanctions against Moscow on grounds that no nation interested in peace can continue to do business with the superpower that baldly invaded Afghanistan. He would like to hold the Moscow Olympics hostage to Soviet withdrawal.

"If this is a new departure for the Russians and it works, then they're likely to build on it," said Marshall Shulman. "What we have to do is impose as high a price as possible on this action, so they are not tempted to try it again."

Militarily, Washington has now permanently posted an aircraft-carrier task force in the Indian Ocean, persuaded the British to step up use of their joint naval base at Diego Garcia, and begun talks for possible military facilities in Oman, Kenya, Somalia and Egypt. American Air Force electronic surveillance units have been holding joint maneuvers with the Egyptians near Luxor.

Even before the Soviet action, the chaos in Iran had prompted the White House to begin a multi-year, multibillion-dollar effort to create a Rapid Deployment Force—primarily for crises in the rimland region. But it will be a few years in the making and in the meantime, Washington is in a poor position to oppose Soviet armies militarily in Iran or Pakistan.

Some American officials conceive of a new pro-Western alliance in that part of the world, but President Carter prefers to work bilaterally with the countries of the region, letting the non-aligned, the oil producers and the

Islamic powers take their own initiatives and offering them American support.

But in spite of these trends, the Russians have pressed on with their Afghan campaign, undeterred. The Administration thinks they miscalculated the intensity of world reaction, as reflected in the overwhelming 104-18 vote against Moscow at the United Nations. But scornfully, the Kremlin has brushed aside the American-inspired reprisals. President Brezhnev charged that the Americans were poisoning the world atmosphere and predicted the Carter strategy would "boomerang."

The outlook is grim, grimmer than after the invasions of Czechoslovakia and Hungary. The White House now talks of Soviet-American relations as being in a "deep freeze," as entering what some aides call "Cold War II." Now, disenchanted, both East and West have vented the accumulated frustrations of détente, and it will take time to thaw the frigid atmosphere of confrontation and mistrust. There is little hope for any significant upturn in Soviet-American relations before the next American Presidential inauguration, and it may be considerably longer in coming.

For all practical purposes, SALT II is dead for this Congress, and perhaps for good. The arms race is headed for a quickening spiral on both sides. President Carter has vowed to stick to his campaign of economic sanctions, gloomily forecasting that "under even the best of circumstances, normal trade will not soon be resumed with the Soviet Union." And, coming as Moscow prepares its 1981-85 five-year plan, the trade embargo is likely to increase the hard-line impulse in the Kremlin toward economic nationalism and autarchy, just as a new Soviet leadership is reaching for supreme power.

Nuclear prudence seems to preclude a major war. But the superpowers, both feeling challenged, are probing each other on new and untested terrain and that has heightened the risk that they will skid suddenly toward the brink of an unintended clash somewhere in the arc of crisis.

There are no illusions here about the Administration's ability to force a quick Soviet pullout from Afghanistan, but there is an anxious determination to draw the line there. Most American officials seriously doubt that the Kremlin would send troops into Yugoslavia or Rumania. Their real worry is the rimland region, which seems destined for instability, local wars and political upheavals for years to come—an inviting target for Soviet power plays.

If central authority in Iran crumbles, that nation could disintegrate. Pakistan is weak and vulnerable to attack and subversion. South Korea is going through a shaky period. The Southeast Asian conflict could burst beyond Cambodia into Thailand. Practically any of those events could draw in one or both of the superpowers.

For American policy, the Soviet invasion has been a seismic event. It has accelerated the about-face in foreign policy that had already begun under the pressure of events in Iran; it has sealed the end of the post-Vietnam era of hesitant isolationism. With the same born-again abruptness of his Cabinet shakeup last July, Jimmy Carter the diplomatic moralist has become Jimmy Carter the practitioner of power politics, and has carried the sentiments of the country with him.

Unintentionally, the Russians have given him a political boost, providing yet another diversion from the seemingly intractable domestic problems of inflation and energy. By keeping Mr. Carter at his command post in the Oval Office, the Kremlin has enhanced his chances for re-election.

But troubles lie ahead for the President. Countries like Pakistan are still wary of his foreign policy, privately uncertain about the durability of his intentions or his embrace, worried about whether they will be caught by some future reversal of policy. Other Islamic nations hesitate to draw too close to Washington because of objections to its policy toward Israel.

More significantly, as one expert put it, "the Western powers don't have any stomach for a long period of tension with the Russians" and could eventually leave Mr. Carter out on a limb. The Japanese don't want to give up trade, the Germans have special worries about Berlin, and the French are concerned about reviving the opposition alliance of the left. And Mr. Carter has heightened their reluctance to engage in economic warfare by pressing them to invoke sanctions against Iran as well as the Soviet Union. In short, the economic freeze will be hard to sustain and it risks opening political divisions within the alliance.

Fundamentally, the Administration needs to convince both allies and adversaries that it is not engaged in hasty, election-year gimmickry but in a patient, well thought-out strategy to deter the Russians without provoking them, to remove Soviet uncertainty about which specific areas America firmly intends to protect and to alleviate what former Secretary of State Dean Acheson used to call "situations of weakness" around the Soviet Union.

"Every time one of these situations exists," observed Mr. Acheson, "it is an invitation to the Soviet Government to fish in troubled waters. To ask them not to fish, and to say that we will have an agreement that you don't fish, is like trying to deal with a force of nature. Therefore, we go to work to change these situations of weakness so that they won't create the opportunities for fishing."

Implications of the Soviet Invasion of Afghanistan
for East-West Relations *

For many years, the Soviet Union has used its growing military capabilities to assert its influence and establish its presence around the world. But apart from suppressing popular uprisings and pressures for liberalization in Eastern Europe by the actual use of military force, the Soviets have generally avoided injecting their own organized combat units into regional conflicts or domestic upheavals. Instead, they have preferred to ship weapons and equipment, and to send advisers. The fighting has been done by others, notably the Cubans, whose homeland has meanwhile been militarily protected by the Soviets.

The events in Afghanistan in one sense represent the culmination of these trends in that the Soviets are now unabashedly and directly using their own forces. They also represent a new departure because Soviet military power is being used for the first time since the 1940s in an effort to extend Soviet dominance beyond its previous perimeter on the Eurasian landmass by preserving a new addition to the "Socialist camp."

Afghanistan, moreover, although geographically remote in the minds of some, is in fact a strategic position of major significance. For the strongest military power in Eurasia to occupy that country for the first time in history

*Reprinted by permission of the author and the publisher from *NATO Review* (April, 1980); Copyright 1980 by The Atlantic Council of the United States, Washington, D.C.

(even if resistance persists) means that the USSR is now poised along extensive stretches of territory bordering on two countries—Iran and Pakistan—one of which is rich in vital petroleum resources and both of which provide access to sea-lanes of crucial importance to international commerce and to the world's geopolitical balance.

President Carter may not have been far wrong when he said on 8 January, 1980, that "the Soviet invasion of Afghanistan is the greatest threat to peace since the Second World War." It is of course true that the United States fought bloody wars in Korea and Vietnam, in both of which the Soviets provided support for the enemies of those whom we sought to defend. And we have been through a succession of acute confrontations over Berlin, in the Middle East, in parts of Africa and around Cuba. Yet all of these conflicts and crises remained limited in space or time. For much of south-west Asia and the Near East, Soviet occupied Afghanistan may constitute a threat of indefinite duration, radiating outward from the Soviet homeland itself and reinforced by Soviet footholds that have already been established on the Arabian peninsula and in East Africa. It constitutes, as well, a further piece in the encirclement wall which the Soviets have sought to erect against China.

President Carter has solemnly stated in his State of the Union message (23 January, 1980), that "an attempt by an outside force to gain control of the Persian Gulf region will be regarded as an assault on the vital interests of the United States. It will be repelled by use of any means necessary including military force."

Whether the military options opened by the occupation of the territory of Afghanistan will come to be exercised by the Soviet rulers cannot be predicted. If they were, President Carter's ominous comment of 8 January could be confirmed with incalculable consequences. But even if they were not soon exercised, the strategic map of the world would nevertheless have been changed for the worse for all those concerned about the expansion of Soviet influence and power.

Defensive Motivations

This no doubt rather dire assessment of the events in Afghanistan, as they have unfolded thus far, is not to deny that certain "defensive" motivations probably played a significant role in the Soviet decision to march. In the most general sense, the Soviets have for several years observed anxiously how their principal opponents have taken up contact with each other. A hostile coalition stretching from Japan via China to NATO Europe and the United States has almost certainly been a genuine Soviet fear, the more so since in the ebullient 1950s Moscow had proclaimed the end of capitalist encirclement. Counteractions of various kinds—détente with the West; threats as well as siren songs toward Japan; warnings, overtures and counter-encirclement vis-à-vis China—have all been pursued with greater or lesser success.

The 1978 Marxist coup in Afghanistan, at first probably fortuitous but then vigorously sustained by Moscow, may have been seen by the Soviets as an additional, concrete response to what they regard as Western-Chinese hostile manouevrings. When the new pro-Soviet regime began to falter and to come under increasing threat from resistance that was rooted in several of the country's Islamic ethnic groups which also enjoyed external sympathies, the Soviets evidently saw themselves impelled to stop the reversal of the gains of 1978.

Soviet action may have been to some extent motivated by the fear the USSR's own Moslem population might be infected by what was happening in Afghanistan (and Iran). More weighty, however, must have been the judgment that the great and powerful Soviet Union was entitled to enforce order in a country which, by Soviet reckoning, had now come within the scope of the Brezhnev Doctrine. It is worth noting in this regard that just as the Soviets cited the Warsaw Pact as the legal justification for their intervention in Hungary and Czechoslovakia, they have used their treaty of friendship and co-operation with Afghanistan as the legal basis for their latest intervention. Similar treaties exist with such countries as Angola, Mozambique, South Yemen, Ethiopia and Vietnam. The physical distance between these countries and the USSR, and other circumstances, could not easily make them candidates for the massive kind of intervention that took place in Afghanistan should internal turmoil threaten the regimes there. Still, the Soviets do have military access to these countries and have provided themselves with the legal and "moral" justification for intervention.

Whatever the "defensive" rationale for the Soviet action—and acknowledging the importance of attempting to interpret Soviet reasoning as objectively as possible—the practical political-military results are nevertheless as indicated earlier in this article. In the end, a "defensive" set of motives may serve as a more powerful stimulus to action than the desire for pure aggrandizement. And, of course, once having invested blood, military power and prestige to maintain Afghanistan's orientation and to suppress resistance to its regime, it is not so far-fetched a step for the Soviets to push beyond that country's borders in order to secure them against external incursions, real or imagined.

Effect on Détente

What then do these developments mean for détente and, more generally East-West relations?

First of all, I should make clear that I was always uneasy about the use of the term détente as if it encompassed the totality of US-Soviet and East-

West relations. The word seemed to suggest that a condition of relaxation and stability had been reached, that this was the result of mutual fears of war and increasing economic interdependence and that, based on such overriding shared interest, this condition could endure indefinitely even while certain antagonistic elements remained in the relationship.

My own view and, I believe, that of the key political leaders in the US who sought to shape US-Soviet relations ten years ago, was rather different. The basic relationship remained conflictual. The Soviets, with all their internal shortcomings and despite setbacks in third world countries and elsewhere, remained more determined than ever to press their claims to be accepted as a world power. They continued their steadily increasing investments in military capacity. They saw the US as seriously traumatized by Vietnam and in the midst of divisive debates about priorities and the proper role of America in the world. They sensed a mood in Europe, especially in West Germany, that favoured new efforts at reducing the division of the continent. They saw the beginnings of a rapprochement between China and the industrialized West which might or might not be accelerated after the disappearance of the ageing and ill Chinese leaders. However, the 24th CPSU Congress in 1971 signalled Soviet interest in more active economic relations with the West as well as some readiness to practice political restraint and to engage in more intensive negotiations on arms control and other issues.

In these circumstances, the US sought to develop a long-term strategy whose principal components were: (1) improved military strength (including NATO) to repair Vietnam-related slippage and to maintain the increasingly tenuous balance with the USSR; (2) clear indications that the US intended to react vigorously if and when the Soviets sought unilateral international advantages, especially by the use of military instruments, coupled with insistence on the need to act with restraint in crises and to work for reduction of regional tensions; (3) readiness to negotiate equitable agreements on arms limitation; (4) willingness gradually to develop economic relations not only based on mutual commercial interests but geared to the state of political and security relations, and (5) in the context of the foregoing to set down certain rules of conduct to serve as a yardstick for measuring progress. For the US Administration of the day, in short, détente, as those policy approaches regrettably came to be called, was to be a complex process involving a combination of incentives for restrained international conduct and disincentives, including the risk of military counteraction, for assertive and aggressive conduct.

Working in common with the Allies, some results were achieved, e.g. in Berlin and, more broadly, in Central Europe. But it became clear in the mid-seventies that US domestic conditions, especially the aftermath of Vietnam and the Watergate scandal, did not permit these interlocking policy lines to develop as fully as originally conceived. The Soviets, for their part, having always been reluctant to curb their international aspirations, soon discovered that their grandiose expectations of American investments and technology transfers would not materialize. US legislation, linking normalized trade relations to moderations of repressive Soviet emigration practices, led the Soviets themselves to abort the various economic agreements that ensued from the 1972 summit. Along with this, the Soviet hope of using SALT and other arms control negotiations to preclude US and Western defence programmes, intended to maintain an adequate balance with growing and improving Soviet forces, fell short of realization. US defence programmes continued, albeit at a pace slower than that required. At the other end of the spectrum, however, the Soviets found that, especially in Africa but also in the final stages of the Vietnam conflict after the US withdrawal, Americans were not always prepared to ensure that expansionist Soviet conduct incurred a high level of risk.

With the benefits of restraint questionable as far as relations with the US were concerned, and with other industrialized countries unpersuaded of the wisdom of conditioning the growth of economic and other contacts upon broadly practiced political restraint, Soviet leaders proceeded in these circumstances with their policies of actively exploiting third world turbulence. The policies of the Carter administration, combining public pressures on the USSR in the human rights field with numerous arms control initiatives while demonstratively emphasizing closer ties to China and greater concern with the grievances harboured in the less developed countries, did not divert the Soviets from their assertive path.

Thus, after the Angolan intervention, involving mostly Cuban troops and Soviet materiel, there followed additional moves in the Horn of Africa (including a switch of clients from Somalia to Ethiopia), South Yemen, Vietnam and, beginning in 1978, in Afghanistan. Resentful over their exclusion from the diplomacy of the Arab-Israeli conflict after late 1977, the Soviets lent support to those Arabs, especially the more radically inclined ones, rejecting the Egyptian-Israeli peace treaty (Soviet exclusion was, in fact largely due to the extreme positions advocated by Moscow which left virtually no scope for real diplomacy).

In the US meanwhile, increasing doubt arose about the strategic arms limitation negotiations, including about the feasibility and desirability of proceeding to an agreement while the Soviets were so evidently busy trying to shift the international geopolitical balance. More and more, public and Congressional opinion favoured giving priority to more vigorous defence programmes—a mood which the Carter Administration eventually reflected to a degree in its budget proposals and projections.

The overthrow of the Shah of Iran added grave new uncertainties to political trends in the whole region rimming the Indian Ocean, all the way to Turkey. This vast region, adjacent to the southern borders of the USSR and crucial to the health of the world economy, had never been a bastion of strength. Soviet ambitions there had their roots in Czarist times but were further stimulated by indigenous cross-currents and instabilities and by the fluctuating relations among the countries of the region and between them and the Western world. A crucial ingredient of the original détente policies of the 1970s—the maintenance of high risk for Soviet intervention—was even further diminished by the convulsive events in Iran.

Constant Effort Required

Afghanistan thus tells us not so much that " détente has failed" as that détente, meaning a relationship of mutual restraint in the pursuit of interests, does not automatically spring from good intentions, or fear of war, or economic necessities, or even intensified human contacts. Nor is it the product of solemnly signed bilateral and multilateral declarations of principle and intent. The Soviets are in an expansionist—or imperialist—phase of their evolution. They employ an ever-widening definition of their security interests. They may even regard time as working against them in this regard —because of the emergence of China, increasing efforts in the West to correct the military balance, accumulating economic and demographic problems inside the USSR, an almost certain shortfall in energy production in the next few years, and many other factors, including the advanced age of most of the top Soviet leaders. To cope with and restrain these Soviet impulses, and the policies they spawn, requires constant effort—not just by the US but by all who are concerned about a more orderly and less dangerous world.

In the short-run, therefore, the US and its allies, as well as all other countries whose interests are engaged, must concentrate urgently on marshalling the strength, including military strength, that will make the Soviets conscious of the risks of adventure beyond Afghanistan or elsewhere. President Carter's State of the Union address highlights the necessity for this even further. The main burden in the military area must no doubt fall on the US. But NATO allies (as well as Japan) may well have to do more for their own and the common defence, not only while the US is so engaged but also over the longer run. Military and economic assistance to Pakistan and support to other Near Eastern nations should probably also not come exclusively from the US. China, too, may play a part in this respect. Clearly, in the case of military assistance for Pakistan, India's anxieties cannot be overlooked. But perhaps even the Indians are not wholly comfortable with the large new Soviet military forces in their neighbourhood.[1]

---

1. Since this article was completed, the government of Pakistan has declined a proposed US military aid package. The issue of Pakistan's defence against possible Soviet pressures or attack nevertheless remains of great concern.

Normal economic relations with the USSR in the conditions created by Soviet military actions are inappropriate. The US has already curtailed major commerical activities—not without some costs to themselves. Western Europe and Japan have been more reluctant to reduce or sever ties laboriously built up with the East and involving important benefits in both directions. But all Western countries must ask themselves whether such relationships can and should, in fact, be altogether insulated from political circumstances. It cannot be a matter of total indifference in Moscow, as the next Five Year Plan is hammered out, if there were a real possibility that billions of dollars worth of industrial and technological projects as well as agricultural imports, may be jeopardized by further demonstrations of expansionism.

By the same token, there would now seem to be both a new opportunity and a need for the governments of the industrialized democracies to examine ways of pursuing more coherent economic policies as an integral part of the overall effort to deal with the Soviet Union. Above all, difficult as it may be, and reluctant as all Western governments undoubtedly are to intervene excessively in the economic dealings of their business enterprises, the Western world must seek more co-ordinated, or at least mutually reinforcing, approaches. Among the reasons why détente has proved illusive is that Moscow has always had some option of playing allies off against each other. This Soviet scope for manoeuvre ought to be reduced, in economic as well as in other aspects of relations. Moreover, Western nations must reexamine the extent to which their own economies, or individual sectors, should develop dependence on the Soviets.

There has been vigorous discussion in the West and elsewhere concerning the propriety, in current circumstances, of sending national teams to the 1980 summer Olympics in Moscow. I had considerable reservations in 1974 about the award of the games to Moscow (although as a government official at that time, there was nothing that I or others similarly placed could properly do to influence the decisions of the International Olympic Committee). My feeling then was that the games would undoubtedly be exploited by the Soviet authorities as a political demonstration both domestically and internationally. This would be even more strongly the case in the wake of the Soviet military move into south-west Asia and—who knows—elsewhere by summer-time. The Soviet regime, as well as the people of the USSR, should be made aware, by either a shift of venue, or the non-participation of large numbers of national teams, that the international community does not regard Moscow as an appropriate place, under present conditions, for the Olympic games and its associated ceremonies and symbolisms. At the same time, though, I would caution that taking such action with regard to the Olympics is no substitute for urgent, as well as longer-term, measures to raise the concrete risks of further Soviet military ventures.

For the long-run, it is clear that the US must undertake sustained efforts to shape its military forces so that their use is feasible in parts of the world where Soviet power can make itself felt. Europeans may also want and need to address questions of whether and how they can contribute more effectively to the protection of interests outside Europe which are at least as vital to them as to the US. Japan, in turn, may need to consider increasing its efforts for the defence of the water and airspace surrounding it. Increasing contacts on defence matters with China should be carefully pursued by the US and its allies. Such defence programmes should not preclude arms control negotiations, but it is important to recognise that resulting agreements are likely to be marginal in their effects and will not serve as substitutes for added defence efforts.

Dangerous Occurrence

In a nutshell, Afghanistan is not simply a "highway accident," as was once said of Czechoslovakia in 1968. It is a serious and dangerous occurrence, long in the making not as to specific detail but as a type of event. In my view, it has not vitiated the original premises of a tough but flexible policy toward the USSR. What it should remove, once and for all, is the illusion that the agreements of the early seventies assured an irreversible trend toward improved relations. I do not believe it is too late to build the essential structure of relations that was contemplated ten years ago—in *all* its elements.

I would not expect that the Allies, given their differing circumstances—in terms of domestic politics, economic interests, geography, etc.—would want or be able to pursue totally congruent policies. There clearly is and must be scope for policy approaches tailored to the individual perceptions and requirements of the members of a coalition composed of sovereign and democratic states. Yet it would be disastrous if the threat that has now so starkly emerged were to lead to widely divergent definitions of interest and policies. The issue is not whether the Allies "support the US"; the issue is whether the Allies together can act in mutual reinforcement—or at least not at cross-purposes—to pursue their long-standing common goal of security in freedom.

I would be less than candid if I did not express my belief that if urgent actions are not taken now, for the short-run, in areas of immediate danger and, for the long-run, to shape a more consistent overall East-West relationship, we may not soon have the chance again. In any event, the times ahead are extremely perilous. We had better assume that unlike the crises we surmounted during the last 35 years, the present one will not soon permit us to return to "normalcy."

Detente and Afghanistan*

The Soviet military occupation of Afghanistan in the final days of 1979 posed profound questions about the future of East-West "detente" in the 1980's—and, for that matter, as to its nature in the 1970's. Was detente a Western illusion and a Soviet sham? Or did detente mark a significant step forward toward more stable peace, now jeopardized by the Soviet move in Afghanistan—and by Western countermoves? Did the Soviets abandon detente when they moved into Afghanistan, or count on Western acquiescence because of detente? Are we well rid of detente, or are we compelled to sacrifice it to prevent Soviet adventures, or should we seek to salvage it?

First, we must clarify our own and Soviet conceptions of detente and perceptions of world politics. East-West (and Soviet-American) relations have experienced many ups and downs over the past quarter of a century, but during the early 1970's they reached a new level of declared common commitment to resolve differences peaceably, and to reduce arms and tensions. The Declaration of Basic Principles of Mutual Relations signed by

*Printed with permission of the author.

President Nixon and Chairman Brezhnev in Moscow in May 1972 was the central codification of this resolve in American-Soviet relations, and the SALT I agreements on that same occasion marked its most dramatic manifestation. In broader multilateral relations, the signing of the Helsinki Final Act of the Conference on Security and Cooperation in Europe in 1975 was the high-point of a process which also included, even before the Soviet-American Summits, such achievements as the Four Power Berlin Agreement and the agreements between the Federal Republic of Germany and the USSR and GDR. A wide range of agreements, expansion of contacts, and relaxation of tensions developed in the early and mid-1970's. Detente was a reality.

Detente is not, of course, entente—although this distinction was lost on many. Important differences and conflicts of interests remained. Equally important, different *conceptions* of detente were too often unrecognized. The Soviet leaders, for example, made clear that detente in Soviet-Western relations and peaceful coexistence between states with different social-economic political systems did *not* mean an end to ideological competition nor to Soviet support for "progressive" and "national-liberation" struggles. Consequently, later Soviet assistance and support (direct and through Cuban and other "proxies") for radical regimes in Angola in 1975 and Ethiopia in 1978, and radical Marxist seizures of power in South Yemen and Afghanistan in 1978, were regarded by many in the West as inconsistent with East-West detente, while from Moscow's viewpoint they were entirely compatible with it.

Owing in part to developments such as those noted above, detente began in the late 1970's to be questioned by some in the West, especially in the United States.

At the same time, some other aspects of relations were troublesome from the Soviet standpoint. For example, the balanced package of bilateral US-USSR economic and trade agreements negotiated in 1974 was upset by the subsequent addition to it by the American Senate of provisions conditioning trade normalization on assurances of emigration for Soviet Jews. Similarly, the launching of a human rights campaign by the new American Administration in 1977, with particular emphasis on the situation in the Soviet Union, represented—to Moscow—an interference in internal affairs not in keeping with their concept of detente between states with different social systems.

Concerns over growing Soviet military power raised questions of a different kind in the West: were the Soviet leaders pursuing a military build up (in intercontinental strategic forces, European theater forces, and at sea) aimed at military superiority, upsetting the military parity presumed by detente and represented in SALT? Paradoxically, the same questions came to be raised in Moscow as well in the late 1970's—when new American and NATO military programs were seen as threatening to upset the only recently attained strategic parity and to lead again to Western superiority. (One reason for these drastically different evaluations is a difference in focus, with American concerns concentrated on the expected vulnerability of US ICBM's in the early and mid-1980's, and Soviet concerns focused on the late 1980's when the new offsetting U.S. intercontinental and NATO programs, including theater nuclear forces in Europe, would be fully deployed. In addition, each side in the interest of prudence weighs uncertainties about the balance in a conservative way.)

Authoritative Soviet and American spokesmen, including the respective Ministers of Defense, have confirmed a general parity in military power. But the military balance is not static, and both also express concern over the future. There is a natural tendency to hedge against uncertainties in one's own military programs, and such hedging often appears ominous to the other side.

Stemming in part from this reciprocally discrepant perception of strategic trends was growing mutual suspicion and alarm over intentions of the other side. These concerns aggravated evaluations of other political developments. The SALT negotiations eventually culminated in a SALT II Treaty signed in June 1979, but only after each side had decided on compensating military programs which the other perceived as diminishing or circumventing its effectiveness and value, raising dissenting opposition to the treaty at least in the United States.

Some events which impaired confidence in detente were fortuitous. American discovery of a Soviet ground forces brigade in Cuba, for example, provoked a clamorous reaction, particularly before it was realized that the small force had been there for years and did not represent either a new Soviet move or a real threat. But detente was weakened and ratification of SALT delayed, perhaps fatally, by the incident. Even events quite unrelated to East-West relations in their origins, such as the instability generated by the Iranian Revolution and the seizure by Iranian militants of the American Embassy in Tehran, raised the level of general tension. The direct impact of that latter development was, of course, greatest and most significant in the United States, but there was also an impact in the Soviet Union: both the American build up of a large naval armada in the Arabian Sea, and the deteriorating security situation in Afghanistan, occurred in the context of the neighboring Iranian revolution with its attendant instability and unpredictability.

The sudden killing of President Amin and his replacement by Babrak Karmal, and the move into Afghanistan of large Soviet military forces, on December 27, 1979, raised a serious question as to the future of detente. Some would say detente either was shown up to be a cover for aggression, or had now been cast aside by Moscow and outlived its usefulness, but in either case was no longer a valid concept for the West. Some saw it as confirming that the Soviets now believed the correlation of forces in the world had shifted sufficiently to permit them to move openly, even brazenly; more particularly, the move was seen as prompted by American weakness and ir- resolution as shown in response to other challenges, such as the Soviet brigade in Cuba and the Iranian seizure of the American Embassy staff. It was seen as a step in a deliberate design to expand Soviet control into the Middle East toward the oil of the Persian Gulf and the warm waters of the southern oceans. The Soviet move had to be rebuffed and rolled back, and above all future aggrandizement deterred; detente was not in keeping with the need to mobilize Western resolve and strength.

Others in the West have seen the situation, the challenge and the response, and the role of detente quite differently. While condemning the Soviet intervention in Afghanistan, they do not believe that a rise in ten- sions eclipses the value of a continued effort to reduce tensions; on the con- trary, while it may make the task of detente more difficult, it also makes it more necessary. In addition, should not actions which contravene detente be vigorously rebuffed, rather than jettisoning detente itself? Finally, while Soviet motivations for the military occupation of Afghanistan and direct in- terference in its political processes do not justify those actions or mitigate the offense, they may be relevant both to the appropriate response and to the question of whether detente can have a future.

The latter line of evaluation and action is, in this writer's judgment, clearly the correct one.

The Soviet decision to increase substantially their military presence in Afghanistan, and to supplant the unreliable and ineffective Hafizullah Amin with the more disciplined and pro-Soviet Babrak Karmal, was de- cided upon late in 1979, with reluctance after long consideration, when this course was judged the only way to avert a major Soviet defeat and loss of Afghanistan. The overriding Soviet aim was to prevent the collapse or defection of their Afghan satellite and its replacement by an unstable, prob- ably hostile, regime which they feared might be amenable to American and Chinese influence. Afghanistan has a 2400 kilometer border along Moslem Central Asian republics in the Soviet Union, and coupled with Iran com- pletes the link between territories of China and NATO. Such facts do not justify Soviet interference and military intervention. But recognition of them does place it in perspective. The Soviet aim was not an advance toward the oil of the Persian Gulf or open waters of the Indian Ocean. The Soviet Union may have designs on the oil resources of the Gulf, but the occupation of Afghanistan provides neither evidence of such aspiration nor a secure steppingstone to achieve it. Nor was the Soviet decision determined or even influenced by considerations of resoluteness of American policy or the global military balance. In the Soviet view, the United States and the West have no vital interest in Afghanistan and the Soviet Union does. Therefore, they believe their actions there should not preclude detente in bilateral Soviet-American (and East-West) relations.

What are the implications for detente? Outrage, and concern over possible Soviet moves beyond Afghanistan, have led the United States to go beyond the concensus on condemnation reflected in the overwhelming vote of the UN General Assembly on January 14, 1980. It may be prudent to make crystal clear, as President Carter did in his address on January 24, in enunciating the "Carter Doctrine," that the United States has vital interests in the Persian Gulf and would repel an attempt by an outside force to gain control of the Persian Gulf region, by military means, if necessary. Even if such an assault by the Soviet Union is unlikely, it is well to reassure others and to reinforce the deterring elements in any Soviet calculation under conditions tempting them to intervene in this unstable area.

President Carter stressed that we had in the 1970's "sought to establish rules of behavior that would reduce the risk of conflict...for the security and peace of the entire world." With great regret, we see from the Soviet armed intervention in Afghanistan that the Soviet Union does not subscribe to the same rules of behavior which we believe must be incumbent on all states. For this reason above all, even if direct American interests in Afghanistan itself are limited, we—and the whole world—have a very real and vital interest in the *principle* of non-intervention by force. And accordingly, the United States and other members of the Alliance believe that it would not under present conditions be appropriate to conduct "business as usual" with the Soviet Union. The United States believes that a clear demonstration of its strong objections needs to be registered with Moscow—even by some economic measures and a boycott of the Olympic games involving sacrifice by Americans.

The Soviets claim, of course, that their intervention was justified; they view it as assistance to a country to which they are committed by treaty in order to meet a covert intervention from outside. Privately, their most bitter complaint is that the United States reacted disproportionately, applying a double standard; the Soviets regard their action as comparable to the American military and political intervention for security reasons in the neighboring Dominican Republic in 1965.

Revulsion at the Soviet occupation of Afghanistan is widely shared in the non-communist world. There have, however, been some differences in judgment over which specific steps are most appropriate to register objection and concern. Within the Alliance, clearly it would be most effective in impact on Moscow for the solidarity of the Alliance to be evident in the basic positions taken by individual states. Admittedly, there are tendencies to take unilateral action, from which none of us (certainly including the United States) is immune, sometimes inspired by good reasons such as speed of response. But it behooves us all to make every effort to concert our actions to the extent possible. Moreover, consultation may indeed help to identify the best courses of action. Complete unanimity is not to be expected, and perhaps not even appropriate; but common interests can